# BRIEF CONTENTS

Preface: To the Instructor   v
Rhetorical Contents   xxxiii
Selected Visual Contents   xxxvii
Features of *The Bedford Guide* Correlated to the WPA Outcomes Statement   xxxix
Inside LaunchPad for *The Bedford Guide*   xlvi
Pairing *The Bedford Guide* with *LaunchPad Solo for Readers and Writers*   xlviii
How to Use *The Bedford Guide*   l

## A WRITER'S GUIDE

Introduction: Writing in College   3

**PART ONE   A College Writer's Processes**
1. Writing Processes   6
2. Reading Processes   16
3. Critical Thinking Processes   35

**PART TWO   A Writer's Situations**
4. Recalling an Experience   46
5. Observing a Scene   65
6. Interviewing a Subject   84
7. Comparing and Contrasting   105
8. Explaining Causes and Effects   125
9. Taking a Stand   144
10. Proposing a Solution   176
11. Evaluating and Reviewing   196
12. Supporting a Position with Sources   214

**PART THREE   Other Writing Situations**
13. Responding to Literature   250
14. Responding to Visual Representations   281
15. Writing Online   307
16. Writing and Presenting under Pressure   324
17. Writing in the Workplace   338

**PART FOUR   A Writer's Strategies**
18. Strategies: A Case Study   358
19. Strategies for Generating Ideas   369
20. Strategies for Stating a Thesis and Planning   383
21. Strategies for Drafting   404
22. Strategies for Developing   421
23. Strategies for Revising and Editing   442
24. Strategies for Writing in Future Courses   459

## A WRITER'S READER

Introduction: Reading
25. Family   482
26. Gender   501
27. Popular Culture   521
28. Language   546
29. The Good Life   570

## A WRITER'S RESEARCH MANUAL

Introduction: The Nature of Research   601
30. Defining Your Research Project   602
31. Finding Sources   614
32. Evaluating Sources   635
33. Working with Sources   645
34. Integrating Sources   662
35. Writing a Research Paper   674
36. MLA Style for Documenting Sources   680
37. APA Style for Documenting Sources   704

## A WRITER'S HANDBOOK

Introduction: Grammar, or The Way Words Work   729
38. Basic Grammar   730
39. Grammatical Sentences   752
40. Effective Sentences   792
41. Word Choice   814
42. Punctuation   826
43. Mechanics   853
Answers for Lettered Exercises   866

## APPENDICES AND OTHER RESOURCES

Quick Format Guide   Q-1
Quick Research Guide   Q-20
Quick Editing Guide   Q-37

About the Photographs That Open Parts One through Four   A-3
Index   I-1
Correction Symbols
Proofreading Symbols
A Guide to the Handbook

# The Bedford Guide
## *for* College Writers

# The Bedford Guide for College Writers

## with Reader, Research Manual, and Handbook

X. J. Kennedy • Dorothy M. Kennedy • Marcia F. Muth

bedford/st.martin's
Macmillan Learning

Boston | New York

For Bedford/St. Martin's

*Vice President, Editorial, Macmillan Learning Humanities:* Edwin Hill
*Editorial Director, English:* Karen S. Henry
*Senior Publisher for Composition, Business and Technical Writing, Developmental Writing:* Leasa Burton
*Executive Editor:* Molly Parke
*Developmental Editor:* Regina Tavani
*Associate Editor:* Rachel Childs
*Editorial Assistant:* Julia Domenicucci
*Senior Production Editor:* Deborah Baker
*Media Producer:* Melissa Skepko-Masi
*Senior Production Supervisor:* Jennifer Wetzel
*Marketing Manager:* Emily Rowin
*Copyeditor:* Mary Lou Wilshaw-Watts
*Indexer:* Mary White
*Senior Photo Editor:* Martha Friedman
*Photo Researcher:* Krystyna Borgen/Lumina Datamatics
*Permissions Editor:* Elaine Kosta
*Senior Art Director:* Anna Palchik
*Text Design:* Lisa Buckley
*Cover Design:* John Callahan
*Cover and Title Page Photo:* Samuel Borges Photography/Shutterstock
*Composition:* Jouve
*Printing and Binding:* LSC Communications

Manufactured in the United States of America.

1 0 9 8 7 6

f e d c b a

*For information, write:* Bedford/St. Martin's, 75 Arlington Street, Boston, MA 02116
   (617-399-4000)

ISBN 978-1-319-03959-2 (paperback)
ISBN 978-1-319-04211-0 (hardcover)
ISBN 978-1-319-04687-3 (Instructor's Annotated Edition)

### Acknowledgments

*Book cover art, page 1 and throughout:* axyse/iStock/Getty Images.
*Inside cover art, pages 2–3 and throughout:* Tiridifilm/E+/Getty Images.

*Text acknowledgments and copyrights appear at the back of the book on pages A-1–A-2, which constitute an extension of the copyright page. Art acknowledgments and copyrights appear on the same page as the art selections they cover.*

# Preface

## TO THE INSTRUCTOR

The eleventh edition of *The Bedford Guide for College Writers* gives students all the tools they need to succeed as writers, especially in the rapidly changing times in which we now live and write. Whether their writing class meets on campus or online, students benefit from qualities integral to *The Bedford Guide*'s enduring success — clear and succinct instruction, thorough coverage with a flexible organization, and frequent opportunities for active learning, engaging students with what is presented. The eleventh edition extends active learning into the realm of reflection, offering students more opportunities to build deeper awareness of their own writing processes. All aspects of this new edition of *The Bedford Guide* are designed with one overarching goal: to help students to become the confident, resourceful, and *independent* writers they will need to be.

Several key interrelated ideas have shaped this book from the beginning. First, *students learn best by doing.* *The Bedford Guide* therefore includes an exceptional number of opportunities for practice and self-assessment. Throughout the book, we intersperse class-tested Learning by Doing activities and assignments in a helpful rhythm with concise instruction and models of writing. Students have frequent opportunities to apply what they've learned and become comfortable with each step in the process as they go along.

Second, we intend *The Bedford Guide for College Writers* to be an effective, engaging text that gives students *everything they need to write well — all in one flexible book.* Written and developed as four books in one, it offers a process-oriented rhetoric, a provocative thematic reader, an up-to-date research manual, and a comprehensive handbook. *The Bedford Guide* gives students all the tools they need to succeed as writers.

Most importantly, the focus of the book is *building transferable skills.* Recognizing that the college composition course may be one of a student's last classes with in-depth writing instruction, we've made every effort to ensure that *The Bedford Guide* develops writers capable of meeting future challenges. To this end, the book offers supportive, step-by-step guidance; Why Writing Matters features; a full chapter on Strategies for Writing in Future Courses; and varied, end-of-chapter Additional Writing Assignments. These and other features prepare students to apply what they've learned in other courses and in the workplace, meeting whatever rhetorical challenges lie ahead, in college and in life.

Built on these cornerstone concepts, the tremendous success of *The Bedford Guide* has been gratifying. Especially gratifying has been the way that this book has continued to evolve over time. New ideas on teaching and writing and excellent suggestions from users of the book improve and enrich each edition. In addition to incorporating the many new features and topics discussed in detail on pages viii–xi, the eleventh edition expands on popular features, offering many new class-tested Learning by Doing activities and new Take Action charts on focusing a research question, evaluating sources, avoiding plagiarism, and improving word use. These changes and others throughout the book do even more to involve students in their own development as writers.

# Everything You Need

The eleventh edition continues to offer four coordinated composition books integrated into one convenient text — all of them now even better resources for students. *The Bedford Guide* is also available in a brief version, containing the rhetoric and reader, and as a PDF e-book.

The eleventh edition is also available in LaunchPad, Macmillan Learning's online course space. Here, you'll find pre-built units corresponding to the book chapters that you can customize or assign out-of-the box. In addition to a full interactive e-book, the LaunchPad includes multimodal readings, additional Learning by Doing activities, automatically scored reading comprehension quizzes for the readings in Books 1 and 2, and automatically scored chapter review quizzes that are part of the new Reviewing and Reflecting feature in Parts Two and Three in Book 1. The LaunchPad also includes downloadable lecture slides.

## BOOK 1  *A Writer's Guide*

This uniquely accessible — yet thorough — process-oriented rhetoric helps students become better writers, regardless of their skill level. Addressing all the assignments and topics typically covered in a first-year writing course, it is divided into four parts.

Part One, A College Writer's Processes, introduces students to the interconnected processes of writing (Chapter 1), reading (Chapter 2), and critical thinking (Chapter 3). In the eleventh edition, Chapter 3 now introduces students to metacognition and reflection and includes a sample student self-reflection responding to a midterm reflection prompt. This new section prepares students for the many new opportunites for reflection they'll encounter throughout the book.

In Part Two, A Writer's Situations, nine core chapters — each including two sample readings (one by a student) — guide students step-by-step through a full range of common first-year writing assignments. The rhetorical situations in Part Two include recalling an experience (Chapter 4), observing a scene (Chapter 5), interviewing a subject (Chapter 6), comparing and contrasting (Chapter 7), explaining causes and effects (Chapter 8), taking a stand (Chapter 9), proposing a solution (Chapter 10), evaluating and reviewing (Chapter 11), and supporting a position with sources (Chapter 12). If followed sequentially, these chapters lead students through the types of rigorous analytical writing that will comprise most of their college writing. Rearranged and selected chapters readily support a course emphasizing argument, source-based writing, or other rhetorical or thematic approaches.

Part Three, Other Writing Situations, offers helpful strategies and examples to focus students' efforts in five special rhetorical situations: responding to literature (Chapter 13), responding to visual representations (Chapter 14), writing online (Chapter 15), writing and presenting under pressure (Chapter 16), and writing in the workplace (Chapter 17).

Part Four, A Writer's Strategies, is a convenient resource for approaching different writing processes. The first chapter, Strategies: A Case Study (Chapter 18), follows a student as she develops and revises her "recalling an experience" paper through multiple drafts. It also includes her self-reflective portfolio letter. The next five chapters explain and further illustrate stages of common writing processes: generating ideas (Chapter 19), stating a thesis and planning (Chapter 20), drafting (Chapter 21), developing (Chapter 22), and revising and editing (Chapter 23). Marginal annotations in the earlier parts of the book guide students to these chapters, which collectively serve as a writer's toolbox. The part ends with Chapter 24, Strategies for Writing in Future Courses. This revised, more sharply focused chapter includes guidelines for writing in a variety of disciplines including nursing and business and features a new sample psychology assignment and student response.

## BOOK 2  *A Writer's Reader*

*A Writer's Reader* is a thematic reader, unique in a book of this kind. The reader offers 24 selections in all—half of them new—arranged around five themes that provide a meaningful context for students, giving them something to write about. The themes are Family (Chapter 25), Gender (Chapter 26), Popular Culture (Chapter 27), Language (Chapter 28), and the Good Life (Chapter 29). This last distinctive theme considers what different people value as components of a life well lived. Apparatus that encourages critical thinking and writing accompanies each reading. A rhetorical table of contents (p. xxxiii) shows how selections correlate with *A Writer's Guide* and the writing situations assigned there. A biographical headnote and a brief prereading tip or question introduce each reading. Each selection is followed by questions on meaning, writing strategies, critical reading, vocabulary, and connections to other selections; journal prompts; and suggested writing assignments, one personal and the other analytical. These questions lead students from reading carefully for both thematic and rhetorical elements to applying new strategies and insights in their own writing.

BOOK
3

## A Writer's Research Manual

*A Writer's Research Manual* is a remarkably comprehensive guide to source-based writing, detailing all the essential steps for print, electronic, and field research. Updated and reorganized to prepare students who may be completing smaller research segments in place of or in addition to a longer research paper, this manual covers defining the research project (Chapter 30), finding sources (Chapter 31), evaluating sources (Chapter 32), working with sources (Chapter 33), integrating sources (Chapter 34), and writing the research paper (Chapter 35). The eleventh edition includes new assignments on creating research proposals, source evaluations, and an annotated bibliography, as well as a new section on popular versus scholarly sources, expanded coverage of working with Internet sources, and new Source Navigators, Take Action charts, and Learning by Doing activities. Chapters 36 and 37 include extensive coverage of MLA and APA documentation, with ninety-eight MLA-style models reflecting the 2016 MLA update and over seventy APA-style models. In the appendices, a Quick Research Guide conveniently — and briefly — reviews how to find, evaluate, integrate, cite, and document sources. Here also, a Quick Format Guide illustrates academic document design.

BOOK
4

## A Writer's Handbook

A comprehensive handbook clearly explains grammar, style, and usage topics and contains guidelines for multilingual writers. The eleventh edition Handbook features a fresh new design, opens with a Learning by Doing activity that introduces students to error logs, and includes a new chapter covering basic grammar (Chapter 38). It also includes nearly fifty exercise sets for practice in and out of class. Answers to half the questions in most sets are provided at the end of the Handbook so that students can check their understanding. Beyond the coverage in the Handbook, a Quick Editing Guide in the appendices gives special attention to the most troublesome grammar and editing problems.

# New to the Eleventh Edition

The eleventh edition gives students even more opportunities for learning by doing and developing transferable skills. Through innovative activities, assignments, visuals, readings, and examples of students' work, this new edition prepares students for writing challenges in college and beyond. New readings and visuals engage students in contemporary issues, and activities reflect classroom experiences, advances from the always developing field of composition, and the insightful suggestions of many helpful reviewers.

## Focus on Reflection

**Emphasis on Reflection as a Critical Thinking Process.** Throughout the eleventh edition, we've created a framework to help students reflect on their progress as writers and to develop a deeper awareness of their processes that they can carry with them as they move into future courses and the workplace. A new section in Chapter 3, Critical Thinking Processes, sets the stage for this focus, introducing students to the concepts of metacognition and reflection and explaining their value to writers. The chapter also includes a sample student reflection with questions for analysis, as well as a series of reflection prompts to which students can return as they complete assignments in the text.

**Reviewing and Reflecting Activities.** Each chapter in Part Two, A Writer's Situations, and Part Three, Other Writing Situations, now concludes with a new Reviewing and Reflecting feature that lives both in the book and in LaunchPad. The Reviewing portion assesses students' comprehension of key concepts in the chapter through short-answer questions. In LaunchPad, these questions are supplemented by a series of automatically graded questions. The Reflecting portion of the feature prompts students to assess their experience completing assignments in the chapter and to extend that assessment to hypothetical writing situations they may face in the future.

> ### Reviewing and Reflecting
>
> **REVIEW** Working with classmates or independently, respond to the following questions:
>
> 1. What are some strategies for finding an interesting interview subject? Using one or more of these strategies, identify two or three possible interview candidates.
> 2. Once you have conducted an interview, what strategies can you use to evaluate the information that you've gathered and identify the most useful material?
> 3. In interview-based personal profiles, what should the thesis do? Examine the thesis in a personal profile — one written by you or a peer, or by a journalist. Does it accomplish this goal? Why, or why not?
>
> **REFLECT** After completing one of the writing assignments presented in this chapter or supplied by your instructor, turn back to the After Writing questions on page 39 of Chapter 3 and respond to as many of them as you can.
>
> Next, reflect in writing about how you might apply the insights that you drew from this assignment to another situation — in or outside of college — in which you have to conduct an interview. If no specific situations come to mind, imagine that
>
> - in a business course, you have decided to interview an entrepreneur about how he or she achieved success.
> - in a work setting, you have been asked to interview a top executive for a profile in your company's newsletter.

**Many New Class-Tested Learning by Doing Activities, with an Emphasis on Reflection.** Nearly a third of the Learning by Doing activities in the book and LaunchPad are new, and all new activities have been class-tested. One-fifth of the activities focus on reflection — a greater percentage than before. New activities encourage students to reflect on everything from their writing spaces, to grades and feedback in prior courses, to their preparation for writing in various disciplines.

**Error Log Coverage in the Handbook.** The eleventh edition's emphasis on reflection extends to *A Writer's Handbook*, which now opens with a Learning by Doing activity that helps students design an error log to help them better identify and improve upon trouble spots in their writing.

> ### Learning by Doing 🖥 Creating an Error Log
>
> Keeping track of errors will dramatically improve your writing skills. Whether you use a paper notebook or a computer file, maintain a running list of corrections made on your drafts by your instructor or writing tutors. Keep track of the date, the name of the error and its symbol or abbreviation ("pronoun agreement / pn agr"), a sample sentence or word group, and a note about how to fix the mistake. You may also wish to note the type of error: matters of **grammar** are addressed in Chapter 39, **style** is covered in Chapter 40, **word choice** is in Chapter 41, **punctuation** is in Chapter 42, and **mechanics** are in Chapter 43. If you are unsure of the meaning of a grammatical term, check Chapter 38 for a **review of common elements** such as parts of speech or look in the index for specific page numbers.

## Guidance on Writing in Future Courses

Chapter 24 has been refocused on writing for future courses and provides specific guidance on writing in the sciences, nursing, the arts, business, education, history, and psychology. The chapter includes a new sample critical thinking assignment for a developmental psychology course, and a student's response, with questions for analysis.

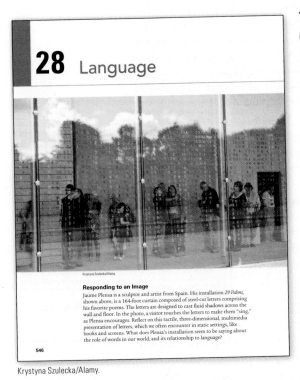

Krystyna Szulecka/Alamy.

## Timely New Readings and a New Chapter on Language in *A Writer's Reader*

Half the readings in *A Writer's Reader* are new in the eleventh edition, including essays by well-known authors such as David Brooks and Judith Ortiz Cofer. The readings reflect a wide range of perspectives, since students come to the composition class varying in age, work background, comfort with technology, life situations, and other factors. The reader also includes a new chapter on language, including old favorites such as Amy Tan and Richard Rodriguez, alongside new selections about today's trending topics. Jenny Jarvie critiques the efficacy of trigger warnings, while Ann Friedman examines the gender inequality in media attention to speech patterns. Throughout *The Bedford Guide*, the readings encourage students to see familiar topics from new angles and to use critical thinking skills to gain insight and understanding.

## A Reframed Research Manual

In the eleventh edition, *A Writer's Research Manual* (Book 3) offers more guidance to students who need to complete smaller research projects in place of or in addition to a traditional long research paper, including assignments on proposals, source evaluations, and annotated bibliographies. It also includes more guidance on working with Internet sources and distinguishing popular and academic sources, as well as new Take Action charts on focusing a research question, evaluating sources, and avoiding plagiarism. The MLA models in Chapter 36 reflect the guidances released in the Modern Language Association's 2016 update.

## Basic Grammar Coverage in *A Writer's Handbook*

Book 4, *A Writer's Handbook*, now helpfully opens with the basics, covering parts of speech; subjects; verbs, objects, and complements; clauses and phrases; and sentence structures. The Handbook has also been redesigned to be more user-friendly than ever.

## More Assessment Opportunities in LaunchPad

The new Reviewing and Reflecting feature found in Parts Two and Three of Book 1 extends to LaunchPad, where students can further test their comprehension of key chapter concepts with automatically scored comprehension questions. Every professional reading selection in the text is now accompanied by an automatically scored reading comprehension quiz to help students deepen their understanding of the material and to help instructors efficiently assess their work. You'll also have access to Exercise Central, a bank of searchable and customizable grammar, punctuation, style, writing, and research exercises. Finally, the LaunchPad for the eleventh edition includes a variety of new LearningCurve adaptive quizzing activities covering everything from argument, to source documentation, to additional grammar and usage topics.

# Get the Most Out of Your Course with *The Bedford Guide for College Writers*

Bedford/St. Martin's offers resources and format choices that help you and your students get even more out of your book and course. To learn more about or to order any of the following products, contact your Bedford/St. Martin's sales representative, e-mail sales support (**sales_support@bfwpub .com**), or visit the Web site at **macmillanlearning.com**.

## Choose from Alternative Formats of *The Bedford Guide for College Writers*

Bedford/St. Martin's offers a range of affordable formats, allowing students to choose the one that works best for them. For details, visit **macmillanlearning.com**.

- Hardcover, *The Bedford Guide for College Writers with Reader, Research Manual, and Handbook*: use ISBN 978-1-319-04211-0.
- Paperback, *The Bedford Guide for College Writers with Reader, Research Manual, and Handbook*: use ISBN 978-1-319-03959-2.
- Paperback, *The Bedford Guide for College Writers with Reader*: use ISBN 978-1-319-04020-8.
- Popular e-book formats: visit **macmillanlearning.com**.

## LaunchPad for *The Bedford Guide for College Writers*: Where Students Learn

LaunchPad provides engaging content and new ways to get the most out of your book. Get an interactive e-book combined with useful, highly relevant materials in a fully customizable course space; then assign and mix our resources with yours. Pre-built units in the LaunchPad combine e-book pages that match the print book page-for-page with autoscored assessment, multimodal reading selections, LearningCurve adaptive quizzing activities, and more. See Inside LaunchPad for *The Bedford Guide for College Writers* (pp. xlvi–xlvii) for a detailed description of available content.

To get the most out of your book, order LaunchPad for *The Bedford Guide for College Writers* packaged with the print book. (LaunchPad for *The Bedford Guide for College Writers* can also be purchased on its own.) An activation code is required. To order LaunchPad with *The Bedford Guide for College Writers with Reader, Research Manual, and Handbook* (hardcover), use ISBN 978-1-319-08120-1. To order LaunchPad with *The Bedford Guide for College Writers with Reader, Research Manual, and Handbook* (paperback), use ISBN 978-1-319-08123-2. To order LaunchPad with *The Bedford Guide for College Writers with Reader*, use ISBN 978-1-319-08116-4.

## LaunchPad Solo for Readers and Writers

*LaunchPad Solo for Readers and Writers* allows students to work on whatever they need help with the most. At home or in class, students learn at their own pace, with instruction tailored to each student's unique needs. For more on using *The Bedford Guide* with *LaunchPad Solo for Readers and Writers*, as well as ordering information, see page xlviii.

## WriterKey

**Draft differently. Comment easily. See revision at work.** Built around best practices for feedback and revision, WriterKey puts student writers at the center of your course. Robust review tools allow you to quickly comment on assignments — using voice or text — and link to a flexible rubric and comment library all from one screen. Students use the same tools to reflect, ask for feedback on specific areas, and review each other's work. Powerful analytics, tied to instructor comments, show writers' strengths and areas for improvement. A side-by-side view of drafts lets students revise their work while they apply teacher and reviewer feedback. After revised drafts are submitted, instructors can compare drafts and view analytic data to see revision in action.

To log in, go to **https://ml.writerkey.com**.

## Instructor Resources

You have a lot to do in your course. Bedford/St. Martin's wants to make it easy for you to find the support you need — and to get it quickly.

*Practical Suggestions for Teaching with The Bedford Guide for College Writers* The instructor's manual, by Dana Waters, Shirley Morahan, and Sylvia A. Holladay, is available as a PDF that can be downloaded from the Bedford/ St. Martin's online catalog at **macmillanlearning.com**. In addition to chapter overviews and teaching tips, it includes sample syllabi, suggested answers to questions, notes on assignments, classroom activities, and more.

**Join Our Community!** The Macmillan English Community is now Bedford/ St. Martin's home for professional resources, featuring *Bedford Bits*, our popular blog site offering new ideas for the composition classroom and composition teachers. Connect and converse with a growing team of Bedford authors and top scholars who blog on *Bits*: Andrea Lunsford, Nancy Sommers, Steve Bernhardt, Traci Gardner, Barclay Barrios, Doug Downs, Susan Bernstein, Elizabeth Wardle, Jack Solomon, Elizabeth Losh, Jonathan Alexander, and Donna Winchell.

In addition, you'll find an expanding collection of additional resources that support your teaching.

- Sign up for webinars.
- Download resources from our professional resource series that support your teaching.
- Start a discussion.
- Ask a question.
- Follow your favorite members.
- Review projects in the pipeline.

Visit **community.macmillan.com** to join the conversation with your fellow teachers.

# Thanks and Appreciation

Many individuals contributed significantly to the eleventh edition of *The Bedford Guide for College Writers*, and we extend our sincerest thanks to all of them.

## Editorial Advisory Board

As we began to prepare the eleventh edition, we assembled an editorial advisory board to respond to the many significant changes we planned and to share ideas about how to make the book more useful to both students and teachers. These dedicated instructors responded thoroughly and insightfully to new features of the text and LaunchPad, answered innumerable questions, and suggested many ideas, activities, and assignments. They also submitted student papers and in ways large and small helped to shape the new and revised sections of the eleventh edition. We are extremely grateful to each one of them:

- Marsha Anderson, Wharton Junior College
- Patricia Boyd, Arizona State University
- Jill Dahlman, University of Nevada–Reno
- Kimberly George, Temple College
- Sandra Grady, Community College of Baltimore County Catonsville
- Jennifer Gray, College of Coastal Georgia
- Stephanie Hyman, Gaston College
- Irma Luna, San Antonio College
- Anna McKennon, Fullerton College
- Terry Novak, Johnson & Wales University

## Other Colleagues

We also extend our gratitude to instructors across the country who took time and care to review this edition, to participate in a focus group, to send us their students' work, and to share excellent suggestions gleaned from their experience. For this we thank

- Jacob Agatucci, Central Oregon Community College
- Sonja Andrus, University of Cincinnati Blue Ash College
- Joe Argent, Gaston College
- Mark Blaauw-Hara, North Central Michigan College
- Mark Brumley, Randolph Community College
- Kimberly Fangman, Southeast Community College
- Stacy Hamilton, Upper Iowa University
- Betty Hart, University of Southern Indiana
- Victoria Hecker, Metropolitan Community College
- Jenn Horn, University of Southern Indiana
- Angela Jacobs, Livingstone College
- Joanne Jacobs, Shenandoah University
- Jeanine Jewell, Southeast Community College
- Douglas King, Gannon University
- Bruce Knauff, Towson University
- Adrienne Kotsko, East Stroudsburg University
- Emelia Kurilla, Lackawanna College
- Jacob Lampell, Community College Baltimore County Catonsville
- Christopher Manuel, South Louisiana Community College
- Phil Martin, Minneapolis Community and Technical College

- Mahdis Marzooghian, Community College Baltimore County Catonsville
- Claudia McIsaac, Santa Clara University
- Melissa Meyers, Garrett College
- Doris Mims, Lone Star College–Montgomery
- Amy Qualls, Harding University
- Eric Sack, Southeast Community College
- Jamie Sadler, Richmond Community College
- Andrew Sippie, Jefferson College
- Jane Splawn, Livingstone College
- Teresa Tande, Lake Region State College
- Joshua Whitney, Southeast Community College
- Donna Wilson, Community College Baltimore County Catonsville
- Sandra Zapp, Paradise Valley Community College

We also want to acknowledge the tremendous and enduring help provided by reviewers of previous editions. Their expert ideas and suggestions live on in the pages of this edition:

Mary Ellen Ackerman, Alice B. Adams, Rosemary R. Adams, Jacob Agatucci, Ted Allder, Patricia Allen, Jennifer Aly, Steve Amidon, David Auchter, Mary Baken, Laura Ballard, Renee Bangerter, Stuart Barbier, Marci Bartolotta, Norman Bates, Barry Batorsky, Shannon Beasley, Randolph A. Beckham, Pamela J. Behrens, Carmine J. Bell, Kay Berg, Sean Bernard, Tanya Boler, Jan Bone, Jeannie Boniecki, Debbie Boyd, Crystal Brothe, Barbara Brown, Karen Davis Brown, Ty Buckman, Rita Buscher-Weeks, Joan Campbell, Sarah Canfield-Fuller, Terri Carine, Tom Casey, Laura Caudill, Sandra L. Cavender, Steve Cirrone, Susan Romayne Clark, Laurie Lopez Coleman, Ted Contreras, Nancy Cook, Connie Corbett-Whittier, Jane Corbly, Monica Cox, Carolyn Craft, Sheilah Craft, Donna Craine, Mary Cullen, P. R. Dansby, Fred D'Astoli, Ed Davis, Andrea Deacon, Patricia Ann Delamar, Sharon Derry, John Dethloff, Marcia Dinneen, Dale Dittmer, Helen Duclos, Irene Duprey-Gutierrez, Corinna Evett, Carol Luers Eyman, Kimberly Fangman, Rosary Fazende-Jones, Patrick Finn, Dwedor Ford, Leora Freedman, Julie Freeman, Lisa J. Friedrich-Harris, LaDonna Friesen, Sandy Fuhr, Jan Fulwiler, Pamela Garvey, Mary Ann Gauthier, Michael Gavin, Caroline Gebhard, Olga Geissler, Barbara Gleason, Robert Gmerlin, Aaron Goldweber, Daniel Gonzales, Sherry F. Gott, Anissa Graham, Daniel V. Gribbin, Robert Grindy, Letizia Guglielmo, Joyce Hall, Russell Hall, Jefferson Hancock, Alyssa Harad, Johnnie Hargrove, Alexis Hart, M. Suzanne Harper, Judy Hatcher, Elaine Hays, Stephen B. Heller, Virginia Scott Hendrickson, Marlene Hess, Diana Hicks, Marita Hinton, Tom Hodges, Susanna Hoeness-Krupsaw, Jane Holwerda, Peter Huk, Patricia Hunt, Sarah Hutton, Karen Keaton Jackson, Diane

Jakacki, Elizabeth Jarok, Barbara Jensen, Greg Jewell, Jean L. Johnson, Ted Johnston, Andrew Jones, Anne D. Jordan, M. L. Kayser, Cynthia Kellogg, Dimitri Keriotis, Saiyeda Khatun, Kate Kiefer, Yoon Sik Kim, Karla Saari Kitalong, Kaye Kolkmann, Fred A. Koslowski III, Brandy Kreisler, Sandra Lakey, Lynn Lampert, Norman Lanquist, Ellen Leonard, Colleen Lloyd, Denise Longsworth, John Lusk, Stephen Ma, Susan Peck MacDonald, Jennifer Madej, Janice Mandile, Phil Martin, Todd McCann, Gerald McCarthy, Miles S. McCrimmon, Jackie McGrath, Linda McHenry, Eileen Medeiros, Jenna Merritt, Elizabeth Metzger, Eric Meyer, Mike Michaud, Heather Michael, Libby Miles, Anthony C. Miller Sr., Lanell Mogab, Sandra Moore, Cleatta Morris, Robert Morse, Julie A. Myatt, Sheryl A. Mylan, Clement Ndulute, Jerry Nelson, Annie Nguyen, Kimme Nuckles, Peggy J. Oliver, Laura Osborne, Brit Osgood-Treston, Roy Kenneth Pace II, Mike Palmquist, Geraldine C. Pelegano, Zachary Perkinson, Susan Perry, Laurel S. Peterson, Mary F. Pflugshaupt, Marianne G. Pindar, John F. Pleimann, Kenneth E. Poitras, Michael Punches, Patrice Quarg, Jeanie Page Randall, Betty Ray, Joan Reteshka, Mark Reynolds, Kira Roark, Peggy Roche, Dawn Rodrigues, Amy Rosenbluth, Samantha Ruckman, Ann Westmoreland Runsick, Karin Russell, Joyce Russo, Sheryl Ruszkiewicz, Laura Saunders, Wendy Schmidt, Nancy J. Schneider, Janis Schulte, Susan Schurman, Patricia C. Schwindt, Sara E. Selby, Herbert Shapiro, Andrea Shaw, Laurie Sherman, Candice Simmons, Suzanne Skipper, Elizabeth Smart, Ognjen Smiljanic, Allison Smith, Patrick Smith, David Sorrells, Ann Spencer-Livingstone, Lori Spillane, Scott R. Stankey, Leroy Sterling, Dean Stover, Ellen Straw, Monnette Sturgill, Ronald Sudol, Tammy Sugarman, Darlene Summers, David Tammer, William G. Thomas, Daphne Thompson, Anthony Vannella, Janice M. Vierk, Dave Waddell, Christopher Walker, Laurie Walker, Lori Weber, Bridgette Weir, Carol Westcamp, Patricia South White, Susan Whitlow, Jim Wilcox, Carmiele Wilkerson, Laura Wind, Mary Zacharias, and Valerie P. Zimbaro.

## Contributors

The eleventh edition could not have been completed without the help of numerous individuals. Special thanks go to Beth Castrodale and Michelle McSweeney, whose thoughtful recommendations and endless diligence played a vital role in shaping the text and *Practical Suggestions*, and to Dana Waters for once again making a key contribution to *Practical Suggestions*. Jill Dahlman (University of Nevada–Reno)and Piper Selden (University of Hawaii at Mānoa) contributed a host of dynamic new Learning by Doing activities and thoroughly reshaped Chapter 24, introducing guidance on writing in various disciplines and other key improvements. Jimidene Murphey (Wharton County Junior College) ably developed the reading comprehension quizzes and the lecture slides available in LaunchPad. Wendy Perkins developed apparatus for new reading selections. Hisayo Tokura-Gallo (Gaston College) contributed the new developmental psychology assignment in Chapter 24 and recommended student Samantha Christopher's response paper for inclusion there. We thank all of them for contributing their time and expertise to this edition.

## Student Writers

We offer sincere thanks to all the students who have challenged us over the years to find better ways to help them learn. In particular, we'd like to thank those who granted us permission to use their essays in the eleventh edition. Focused as this textbook is on student writing, we consider it essential to provide effective sample essays by students. New to the eleventh edition is the writing of Samantha Christopher. Earlier editions, as well as this one, have included the writings of Richard Anson, Cristina Berrios, Linn Bourgeau, Betsy Buffo, Jonathan Burns, Andrew Dillon Bustin, Anne Cahill, Joseph Cauteruccio Jr., Yun Yung Choi, Heather Church, David Ian Cohn, Heather Colbenson, Olof Eriksson, Elizabeth Erion, Alea Eyre, Marjorie Lee Garretson, Jacob Griffin, Sarah E. Goers, Stephanie Hawkins, Alley Julseth, Cindy Keeler, Heidi Kessler, Shannon Kintner, Melissa Lamberth, Emily Lavery, Jenny Lidington, Abigail Marchand, Schyler Martin, Daniel Matthews, Angela Mendy, Jennifer Miller, Susanna Olsen, Shari O'Malley, Candace Rardon, Benjamin Reitz, Lorena A. Ryan-Hines, Lindsey Schendel, Erin Schmitt, Robert G. Schreiner, Rachel Steinhaus, Lacey Taylor, Joshua Tefft, Maria Thompson, Leah Threats, Joel Torres, Lillian Tsu, Donna Waite, Arthur Wasilewski, Christopher Williams, and Carrie Williamson.

## Editorial

We wish to thank Vice President Editorial for the Humanities Edwin Hill; Senior Publisher for Composition Leasa Burton; Editorial Director Karen Henry; and Executive Editor Molly Parke for their continuing support of this title. Development Editor Regina Tavani brought fresh eyes and great insight to this edition, encouraging lively innovation while patiently coordinating text, design, and images. Associate Editor Rachel Childs skilfully developed *A Writer's Reader* and lent her insight to other parts of the book. Senior Editor Adam Whitehurst provided invaluable input on the development of new content for LaunchPad. Editorial Assistant Julia Domenicucci ably and efficiently helped with the many details, large and small, that went into the eleventh edition's development.

Many thanks and heartfelt appreciation also go to Senior Production Editor Deborah Baker, who, with an exacting eye, great patience, and good humor, shepherded the book through production. Under Deb's care, the production process could not have gone more smoothly. Mary Lou Wilshaw-Watts deftly copyedited the text. Melissa Skepko-Masi played a vital role in coordinating the development of the book's LaunchPad. Michael Granger and Michelle Camisa helped immensely with "big picture" issues on the print and digital production fronts, respectively. John Callahan created the lovely redesign of the book's cover. Emily Rowin skillfully coordinated the marketing of the book and offered much good advice based on feedback from the field. We thank Hilary Newman, Kalina Ingham, Martha Friedman, Elaine Kosta, and Krystyna Borgen for coordinating and clearing permissions. Anna Palchik provided expert guidance on the redesign of the Handbook and other text elements, which was adeptly executed by Lisa Buckley.

Marcia Muth is especially grateful to the School of Education and Human Development at the University of Colorado Denver for sponsoring her writing workshops. She also thanks CU Online for its many creative suggestions about online instruction, especially those presented at Web Camp and in *The CU Online Handbook: Teach Differently: Create and Collaborate.* Special appreciation also goes to Mary Finley, University Library at California State University Northridge, and Rodney Muth, University of Colorado Denver, for ongoing expert advice. Finally, we once again thank our friends and families for their unwavering patience, understanding, and encouragement.

# Contents

Preface: To the Instructor   v

Rhetorical Contents   xxxiii

Selected Visual Contents   xxxvii

Features of *The Bedford Guide* Correlated to the WPA Outcomes Statement   xxxix

Inside LaunchPad for *The Bedford Guide*   xlvi

Pairing *The Bedford Guide* with *LaunchPad Solo for Readers and Writers*   xlviii

How to Use *The Bedford Guide*   l

**BOOK 1**

## A WRITER'S GUIDE

Introduction: Writing in College   3

## Part One  A College Writer's Processes   4

### 1.  Writing Processes   6

Writing, Reading, and Critical Thinking   6

A Process of Writing   7

  Getting Started   7

  Generating Ideas   7

  Learning by Doing  Reflecting on Ideas   8

  Planning, Drafting, and Developing   8

  Learning by Doing  Reflecting on Drafts   9

  Revising and Editing   10

  Learning by Doing  Reflecting on Finishing   11

Purpose and Audience   11

  Writing for a Reason   11

  Learning by Doing  Considering Purpose   11

  Writing for Your Audience   13

  Learning by Doing  Considering Audience   13

  Targeting a College Audience   14

  Learning by Doing  Writing for Different Audiences   15

Additional Writing Activities   15

### 2.  Reading Processes   16

A Process of Critical Reading   16

  Learning by Doing  Reflecting on Your Reading Strategies   17

  Getting Started   17

  Preparing to Read   17

  Learning by Doing  Reflecting on Reading Preparation   18

  Responding to Reading   19

  Learning by Doing  Annotating a Passage   21

  Learning by Doing  Reflecting on a Reading Journal   22

Learning from Another Writer: Reading Summary and Response   22

  ■ STUDENT SUMMARY AND RESPONSE: **Olof Eriksson,** The Problems with Masculinity   23

Reading on Literal and Analytical Levels   24

  Learning by Doing  Reading Analytically   26

  Generating Ideas from Reading   26

Learning from Another Writer: Critical
Reading and Response   28

- **STUDENT CRITICAL READING RESPONSE:
Alley Julseth,** Analyzing "The New
Literacy"   28

   Learning by Doing   Reading Critically   30

- **Michael Shermer,** The Science of
Righteousness   30

Reading Online and Multimodal
Texts   31

   Learning by Doing   Reading a Web Site   33

Additional Writing Activities   33

### 3. Critical Thinking Processes   35

A Process of Critical Thinking   35

   Getting Started   36

   Learning by Doing   Thinking Critically to
Explore an Issue   36

   Applying Critical Thinking to Academic
Problems   36

Thinking Critically about Your Own
Writing: Self-Reflection   37

   Details on Self-Reflection   38

   Learning by Doing   Reflecting on Your College
Career   40

   Contexts for Self-Reflection   40

   Learning by Doing   Reflecting on the
Syllabus   41

Learning from Another Writer: Self-
Reflection   41

- **STUDENT SELF-REFLECTION: Khalia
Nadam,** What I Have Learned from My
Research Project   41

Additional Writing Activities   43

### Part Two   A Writer's Situations   44

### 4. Recalling an Experience   46

Learning from Other Writers   47

- **Russell Baker,** The Art of Eating
Spaghetti   48

- **STUDENT ESSAY: Robert G. Schreiner,**
What Is a Hunter?   51

Learning by Writing   54

   The Assignment: Recalling a Personal
Experience   54

   Generating Ideas   55

   Learning by Doing   Reflecting on Your Writing
Space   57

   Planning, Drafting, and Developing   57

   Learning by Doing   Stating the Importance of
Your Experience   58

   Learning by Doing   Selecting and Arranging
Events   58

   Revising and Editing   59

   Learning by Doing   Appealing to the
Senses   60

Reviewing and Reflecting   61

Additional Writing Assignments   62

### 5. Observing a Scene   65

Learning from Other Writers   67

- **Ashley Smith,** Smokejumper
Training   67

- **STUDENT ESSAY: Alea Eyre,**
Stockholm   71

Learning by Writing   73

   The Assignment: Observing a Scene   73

   Generating Ideas   74

   Learning by Doing   Reflecting on Sensory
Details   76

   Planning, Drafting, and Developing   76

   Learning by Doing   Experimenting with
Organization   78

   Revising and Editing   78

   Learning by Doing   Strengthening Your Main
Impression   79

Reviewing and Reflecting   80

Additional Writing Assignments   81

### 6. Interviewing a Subject   84

Learning from Other Writers   86

- **Jon Ronson,** How One Stupid Tweet Blew
Up Justine Sacco's Life   86

- **STUDENT ESSAY: Lorena A. Ryan-Hines,**
Looking Backwards, Moving
Forward   91

Learning by Writing   94
   The Assignment: Interviewing   94
   Generating Ideas   95
   Learning by Doing Analyzing Interview
   Questions   97
   Learning by Doing Interviewing a
   Classmate   98
   Planning, Drafting, and Developing   98
   Learning by Doing Stating a Dominant
   Impression   99
   Revising and Editing   100
   Learning by Doing Detailing with Color   101
Reviewing and Reflecting   102
Additional Writing Assignments   103

## 7. Comparing and Contrasting   105
Learning from Other Writers   107
   ■ César Vargas, How First- and Second-
   Generation Hispanics Can Help Each
   Other   107
   ■ STUDENT ESSAY: Jacob Griffin, Karate
   Kid vs. Kung Fu Panda: A Race to the
   Olympics   110
Learning by Writing   112
   The Assignment: Comparing and
   Contrasting   112
   Generating Ideas   113
   Learning by Doing Making a Comparison-and-
   Contrast Table   115
   Planning, Drafting, and Developing   115
   Learning by Doing Reflecting on Comparison
   and Contrast   116
   Learning by Doing Building Cohesion with
   Transitions   118
   Revising and Editing   118
Reviewing and Reflecting   121
Additional Writing Assignments   122

## 8. Explaining Causes and Effects   125
Learning from Other Writers   126
   ■ Emily Badger, It's Time to Stop Blaming
   Poverty on the Decline in Marriage   127

   ■ STUDENT ESSAY: Yun Yung Choi, Invisible
   Women   130
Learning by Writing   133
   The Assignment: Explaining Causes and
   Effects   133
   Generating Ideas   134
   Learning by Doing Determining Causes and
   Effects   135
   Learning by Doing Making a Cause-and-Effect
   Table   136
   Planning, Drafting, and Developing   137
   Learning by Doing Focusing Your
   Introduction   138
   Revising and Editing   138
Reviewing and Reflecting   141
Additional Writing Assignments   142

## 9. Taking a Stand   144
Learning from Other Writers   146
   ■ Suzan Shown Harjo, Last Rites for Indian
   Dead   146
   ■ STUDENT ESSAY: Marjorie Lee Garretson,
   More Pros Than Cons in a Meat-Free
   Life   149
Learning by Writing   152
   The Assignment: Taking a Stand   152
   Generating Ideas   153
   Learning by Doing Finding a Workable
   Topic   153
   Learning by Doing Reflecting on Evidence for
   Your Argument   158
   Learning by Doing Supporting a Claim   161
   Learning by Doing Examining Your
   Evidence   163
   Learning by Doing Addressing
   Counterarguments   164
   Planning, Drafting, and Developing   164
   Learning by Doing Reflecting on Your
   Thesis   165
   Learning by Doing Identifying Types of
   Appeals   166
   Revising and Editing   166
   Learning by Doing Reflecting on Your
   Draft   169

TAKE ACTION Strengthening Support for a
Stand 170
Recognizing Logical Fallacies 171
Reviewing and Reflecting 172
Additional Writing Assignments 173

## 10. Proposing a Solution 176

Learning from Other Writers 178
- **Wilbert Rideau,** Why Prisons Don't
Work 178
- STUDENT ESSAY: **Lacey Taylor,** It's Not
Just a Bike 181

Learning by Writing 183
The Assignment: Proposing a Solution 183
Generating Ideas 185
Learning by Doing Describing Your
Audience 186
Planning, Drafting, and Developing 187
Learning by Doing Reflecting on a
Problem 188
Learning by Doing Reflecting on Interested
Parties 189
Revising and Editing 189
Learning by Doing Revising for Clear
Organization 191
Reviewing and Reflecting 192
Additional Writing Assignments 193

## 11. Evaluating and Reviewing 196

Learning from Other Writers 198
- **Scott Tobias,** The Hunger Games 198
- STUDENT ESSAY: **Elizabeth Erion,**
Internship Program Falls Short 200

Learning by Writing 202
The Assignment: Writing an
Evaluation 202
Generating Ideas 203
Learning by Doing Developing Criteria 205
Planning, Drafting, and Developing 205
Learning by Doing Stating Your Overall
Judgment 206
Learning by Doing Reflecting on Product
Reviews 207

Revising and Editing 207
Reviewing and Reflecting 209
Additional Writing Assignments 210

## 12. Supporting a Position with Sources 214

Learning from Other Writers 216
- **Charles M. Blow,** Black Dads Are Doing
Best of All 216
- STUDENT ESSAY: **Abigail Marchand,**
The Family Dynamic 219

Learning by Writing 222
The Assignment: Supporting a Position with
Sources 222
Generating Ideas 223
Learning by Doing Identifying Suspect Web
Information 225
Planning, Drafting, and Developing 226
Learning by Doing Questioning Your Thesis
to Aid Your Search for Evidence 227
Learning by Doing Reflecting on
Plagiarism 228
Academic Exchange 230
Revising and Editing 237
Learning by Doing Launching Your
Sources 239
Learning by Doing Checking Your Presentation
of Sources 241
TAKE ACTION Integrating Source
Information Effectively 243
Reviewing and Reflecting 244
Additional Writing Assignments 245

## Part Three Other Writing Situations 248

## 13. Responding to Literature 250

Using Strategies for Literary
Analysis 250
Learning from Other Writers 252

- **Shirley Jackson,** The Lottery   252
  Preparing to Write a Literary Analysis   259

- STUDENT LITERARY ANALYSIS: **Jonathan Burns,** The Hidden Truth: An Analysis of Shirley Jackson's "The Lottery"   260
  A Glossary of Terms for Literary Analysis   262

Learning by Writing: Literary Analysis   264

  The Assignment: Analyzing a Literary Work   264
  Generating Ideas   265
  Learning by Doing Examining Fiction Genres   267
  Planning, Drafting, and Developing   268
  Learning by Doing Developing Your Thesis   269
  TAKE ACTION Strengthening Literary Analysis   271
  Revising and Editing   272

Learning from Another Writer: Synopsis   273

  - STUDENT SYNOPSIS: **Jonathan Burns,** A Synopsis of "The Lottery"   273

Learning by Writing: Synopsis   274

The Assignment: Writing a Synopsis of a Story by Kate Chopin   274

  - **Kate Chopin,** The Story of an Hour   275

Learning from Another Writer: Paraphrase   277

  - STUDENT PARAPHRASE: **Jonathan Burns,** A Paraphrase from "The Lottery"   277
  Learning by Doing Collaborating on a Paraphrase   278

Learning by Writing: Paraphrase   278

  The Assignment: Writing a Paraphrase of a Poem   278

Reviewing and Reflecting   278

Additional Writing Assignments   279

## 14. Responding to Visual Representations   281

Using Strategies for Visual Analysis   282

Level One: Seeing the Big Picture   283

  Source, Purpose, and Audience   283
  Prominent Element   283
  Focal Point   285
  Learning by Doing Seeing the Big Picture   285

Level Two: Observing the Characteristics of an Image   285

  Cast of Characters   286
  Story of the Image   286
  Design and Arrangement   287
  Artistic Choices   288
  Learning by Doing Observing Characteristics   292

Level Three: Interpreting the Meaning of an Image   292

  General Feeling or Mood   292
  Sociological, Political, Economic, or Cultural Attitudes   293
  Language   295
  Signs and Symbols   295
  Themes   296
  Learning by Doing Reflecting on Images   296

Learning from Another Writer: Visual Analysis   297

  - STUDENT ANALYSIS OF AN ADVERTISEMENT: **Logan Sikora,** The Attention Test   297

Learning by Writing   299

  The Assignment: Analyzing a Visual Representation   299
  Generating Ideas   299
  Planning, Drafting, and Developing   300
  Revising and Editing   300

Learning from Another Writer: Visual Essay   301

■ STUDENT VISUAL ESSAY: **Shannon Kintner,** Charlie Living with Autism   301

Reviewing and Reflecting   304

Additional Writing Assignments   305

## 15.  Writing Online   307

Getting Started   308
  Learning by Doing  Reflecting on an Online Writing Course   308
  Class Courtesy   308
  Online Ethics   309
  Learning by Doing  Making Personal Rules   310

Common Online Writing Situations   311
  Messages to Your Instructor   311
  Learning by Doing  Finding a College Voice   312
  Learning from Other Writers: Messages to Your Instructor   312
  Learning by Doing  Contacting Your Instructor   313
  Online Profile   313
  Learning by Doing  Reflecting on Your Social Media Presence   314
  Online Threaded Discussions or Responses   315
  Learning from Other Writers: Threaded Discussion   315
  Learning by Doing  Joining a Threaded Discussion   317

File Management   317
  Learning by Doing  Preparing a Template   318
  Learning by Doing  Organizing Your Files   318

Reviewing and Reflecting   321

Additional Writing Assignments   322

## 16.  Writing and Presenting under Pressure   324

Essay Examinations   325
  Preparing for the Exam   325

Learning from Another Writer: Essay Exam   325
  ■ STUDENT ESSAY ANSWER: **David Ian Cohn,** Response to Psychology Question   325

Generating Ideas   326
  Planning for Typical Exam Questions   327
  Learning by Doing  Asking Questions   329
  Drafting: The Only Version   330
  Revising: Rereading and Proofing   331

Short-Answer Examinations   331

Timed Writings   331
  Learning by Doing  Thinking Fast   333

Online Assessment   333

Oral Presentations   334
  Learning by Doing  Reflecting on Oral Presentations   335

Learning from Other Writers: Visuals for Oral Presentations   335
  ■ FACE-TO-FACE CLASS PRESENTATION: **Andrew Dillon Bustin,** Traditional Urban Design   336

Reviewing and Reflecting   336

Additional Writing Assignments   337

## 17.  Writing in the Workplace   338

Guidelines for Writing in the Workplace   338
  Know Your Purpose   339
  Keep Your Audience in Mind   339
  Use an Appropriate Tone   339
  Present Information Carefully   340

E-mail   341
  Format for E-mail   341

Résumés and Application Letters   341
  Résumés   342
  Learning by Doing  Reflecting on Your Working Life and Goals   344
  Application Letters   345
  Learning by Doing  Planning a Job Application   345
  Learning by Doing  Planning for Your Future Career   346

Business Letters   347
  Format for Business Letters   347

Memoranda   350
   Format for Memoranda   350
Brochures and Presentation Visuals   350
   Format for Brochures   351
   Format for Presentation Visuals   353
Reviewing and Reflecting   354
Additional Writing Assignments   355

## Part Four   A Writer's Strategies   356

## 18. Strategies: A Case Study   358

Generating Ideas   358
Planning, Drafting, and Developing   359
   Rough Draft with Peer and Instructor Responses   360
   Learning by Doing Responding as a Peer   363
Revising and Editing   363
   Revised and Edited Draft   363
   ■ FINAL DRAFT FOR SUBMISSION: Erin Schmitt, Mr. Hertli   365
Reflecting as a Writer   367
   Learning by Doing Writing a Reflective Letter   367
   Reflective Portfolio Letter   368

## 19. Strategies for Generating Ideas   369

Finding Ideas   369
   Building from Your Assignment   370
   Learning by Doing Building from Your Assignment   371
   Brainstorming   371
   Learning by Doing Brainstorming   372
   Freewriting   372
   Learning by Doing Freewriting   373
   Doodling or Sketching   374
   Learning by Doing Doodling or Sketching   375
   Mapping   375

   Learning by Doing Mapping   376
   Imagining   376
   Learning by Doing Imagining   377
   Asking a Reporter's Questions   377
   Learning by Doing Asking a Reporter's Questions   378
   Seeking Motives   378
   Learning by Doing Seeking Motives   380
   Keeping a Journal   380
   Learning by Doing Keeping a Journal   381
Getting Ready   381
   Setting Up Circumstances   381
   Preparing Your Mind   382
   Learning by Doing Reflecting on Generating Ideas   382

## 20. Strategies for Stating a Thesis and Planning   383

Shaping Your Topic for Your Purpose and Your Audience   383
   Learning by Doing Considering Purpose and Audience   384
Stating and Using a Thesis   384
   Learning by Doing Identifying Theses   385
   How to Discover a Working Thesis   385
   Learning by Doing Discovering a Thesis   386
   How to State a Thesis   387
   Learning by Doing Examining Thesis Statements   390
   How to Improve a Thesis   390
   TAKE ACTION Building a Stronger Thesis   391
   How to Use a Thesis to Organize   392
   Learning by Doing Using a Thesis to Preview   392
Organizing Your Ideas   393
   Grouping Your Ideas   393
   Outlining   395
   Learning by Doing Moving from Outline to Thesis   399
   Learning by Doing Outlining   403
   Learning by Doing Reflecting on Planning   403

## 21. Strategies for Drafting  404

Making a Start Enjoyable  404

Restarting  405

Paragraphing  405

Using Topic Sentences  406
Learning by Doing Shaping Topic Sentences  409
Learning by Doing Reflecting on Topic Sentences  409

Writing an Opening  410
Learning by Doing Trying Different Methods of Writing an Opening  412

Writing a Conclusion  413
Learning by Doing Trying Different Methods of Writing a Conclusion  414
Learning by Doing Evaluating Openings and Conclusions  415

Adding Cues and Connections  417
Learning by Doing Reflecting on Transitions  420
Learning by Doing Reflecting on Drafting  420

## 22. Strategies for Developing  421

Giving Examples  422
Learning by Doing Giving Examples  424

Providing Details  424
Learning by Doing Providing Details  426

Defining  426
Learning by Doing Developing an Extended Definition  428

Reasoning Inductively and Deductively  428
Learning by Doing Reasoning Inductively and Deductively  430

Analyzing a Subject  430
Learning by Doing Analyzing a Subject  432

Analyzing a Process  432
Learning by Doing Analyzing a Process  434

Dividing and Classifying  434
Learning by Doing Dividing and Classifying  436

Comparing and Contrasting  436
Learning by Doing Comparing and Contrasting  438

Identifying Causes and Effects  439
Learning by Doing Identifying Causes and Effects  440
Learning by Doing Reflecting on Developing  441

## 23. Strategies for Revising and Editing  442

Re-viewing and Revising  442
Revising for Purpose and Thesis  443
Revising for Audience  444
Learning by Doing Reflecting on Your Audience  445
Revising for Structure and Support  445
Learning by Doing Tackling Macro Revision  446
Working with a Peer Editor  446
Questions for a Peer Editor  447
Meeting with Your Instructor  448
Decoding Your Instructor's Comments  448

Revising for Emphasis, Conciseness, and Clarity  450
Stressing What Counts  450
Cutting and Whittling  451
Keeping It Clear  452

Editing and Proofreading  455
Editing  456
Proofreading  457
Learning by Doing Reflecting on Revising and Editing  458
Learning by Doing Reflecting on Past Grades and Comments  458

## 24. Strategies for Writing in Future Courses  459

Transferring Knowledge  459
Learning by Doing Reflecting on How to Transfer Knowledge  460

What Do They Want?  460
Analyzing Expectations  460
Connecting Expectations and Assessments  461

What Is It?  461
Uncovering Assumptions  462
Learning by Doing Reflecting on the Goals of Other Disciplines  463

How Do I Write It?  463
Learning by Doing Reflecting on New Assignments  464

Writing in the Disciplines  464
Writing in the Sciences  464
Writing in Nursing  466
Writing in the Arts (Art, Drama, Music)  467
Writing in Business  467
Writing in Education  468
Writing in History  469
Writing in Psychology  469
Learning by Doing Examining an Article from a Scholarly Journal  470

Learning from Another Writer: A Developmental Psychology Assignment  471

■ WEEKLY CRITICAL THINKING ASSIGNMENT: Professor Tokura-Gallo  471
■ RESPONSE TO CRITICAL THINKING ASSIGNMENT: Samantha Christopher, Adolescents Are Not Yet Adults  471

Keeping a Portfolio  473
Understanding Portfolio Assessment  474
Tips for Keeping a Portfolio  475
Learning by Doing Reflecting on This Class  477

BOOK 2

# A WRITER'S READER

Introduction: Reading to Write  481

## 25. Family  482

■ **Judith Ortiz Cofer**, More Room  483

The author recounts her Catholic Latina grandmother's ultimate sacrifice: banishing her benevolent husband to his own bedroom in order to gain her freedom and better care for her eight children.

■ **Chris Bentley,** Beyond the Nuclear Family: Can Boomers Make Cohousing Mainstream?  487

A concept of Danish origin, cohousing may gain momentum in the United States as baby boomers look for sustainable, affordable, community-nurturing retirement options.

PAIRED ESSAYS

■ **Michael Cobb,** The Marriage Imperative  491

In the shadow of the Supreme Court decision legalizing same-sex marriage, the author criticizes the hypocrisy of equating human dignity with marriage and determining civil benefits by romantic unions.

■ **Aziz Ansari,** Searching for Your Soul Mate  494

The increased mobility, changing economic structures, and resulting new concept of "emerging adulthood" has fundamentally changed how Americans view marriage and seek life partners, the author argues.

## 26. Gender  501

■ **Brent Staples,** Black Men and Public Space  502

Misperceptions and apprehensions sometimes exist between men and women, the author has found — for example, when he walks at night on a public street.

- **Judy Brady,** I Want a Wife   505

  Everyone's career and personal life could benefit from the support customarily provided by a wife, the author suggests in this classic satire.

- **Cindi May,** The Problem with Female Superheroes   508

  The author claims that oversexualized superheroines, however powerful, reinforce traditional gender roles to the same extent as "helpless maiden" characters.

PAIRED ESSAYS

- **Robert Jensen,** The High Cost of Manliness   512

  The author calls for abandoning the prevailing definition of masculinity, arguing that it is "toxic" to both men and women.

- **Julie Zeilinger,** Guys Suffer from Oppressive Gender Roles Too   516

  The author details the high price paid by men in hiding emotions and shoehorning themselves into society's tough, narrow masculine stereotypes.

## 27. Popular Culture   521

- **Kate Dailey and Abby Ellin,** America's War on the Overweight   522

  The authors analyze the pervasive bias against plus-sized people and the harsh tone of moral condemnation often used in critiques.

- **Adam Sternbergh,** Smile, You're Speaking Emoji   527

  The author historicizes emoji, which, while seemingly frivolous, have emerged as an effective means of conveying sincere emotion in the hostile textual environment in which we live.

- **Stephen King,** Why We Crave Horror Movies   534

  The author examines the appeal of scary movies, watched to reaffirm normalcy and to acknowledge and quell the suppressed, uncivilized "worst in us."

PAIRED ESSAYS

- **Elizabeth Stone,** Grief in the Age of Facebook   537

  Reactions to the tragic death of a talented young woman lead the author to consider the emerging practices of online mourning.

- **Libby Copeland,** Is Facebook Making Us Sad?   541

  Facebook can lead to depression and "presentation anxiety," if we compare ourselves unfavorably with friends who appear to have perfect, fun-filled lives.

## 28. Language   546

- **Clive Thompson,** The New Literacy   547

  The author points to research findings that suggest technology is increasing literacy and improving students' writing.

- **Ann Friedman,** Can We Just, Like, Get Over the Way Women Talk?   549

  Frustrated by recent critiques of women's so-called speech insufficiencies, the author asserts that by speaking naturally women connect to their audience more authentically.

- **Jenny Jarvie,** Trigger Happy   553

  The author argues that trigger warnings, once intended to protect those suffering from PTSD, instead may be overused and reinforce fear and restrict positive discourse, to our collective detriment.

PAIRED ESSAYS

- **Richard Rodriguez,** Public and Private Language   558

  The author, the son of Spanish-speaking Mexican American parents, recounts the origin of his complex views of bilingual education.

- **Amy Tan,** Mother Tongue   564

  A Chinese American writer examines the effects of her mother's imperfect English on her own experience as a daughter and a writer.

## 29. The Good Life 570

- **William Zinsser,** The Right to Fail 571

  As much as many in society do not want to admit it, failure is vitally important, the author argues.

- **William Deresiewicz,** What Is College For? 575

  Current conversations about education focus largely on employability and financial returns and ignore what the author sees as college's true purpose: creating habits of thinking in the ideal gap between childhood and adult responsibilities.

- **Sarah Adams,** Be Cool to the Pizza Dude 580

  The author uses one simple rule to illuminate the principles she follows in everyday life.

PAIRED ESSAYS

- **David Brooks,** The Humility Code 582

  Troubled by society's shift toward valuing "resumé virtues" over "eulogy virtues," the author offers a moral code for restoring balance and building a humble character.

- **Miya Tokumitsu,** In the Name of Love 590

  The author uncovers the narcissistic elitism hidden in today's most popular workplace aphorism: "Do what you love."

## BOOK 3 A WRITER'S RESEARCH MANUAL

Introduction: The Nature of Research 601

## 30. Defining Your Research Project 602
Learning by Doing Reflecting on Research 604
Research Assignments: Working from Sources 604

The Research Proposal 604
The Source Evaluation 604
The Annotated Bibliography 605
The Outline 605
The Research Paper 605
Creating a Schedule 606
Learning by Doing Planning Your Personal Schedule 606
Choosing and Narrowing a Topic 606
Turning a Topic into a Question 608
Learning by Doing Polling Your Peers 608
Moving from Research Question to Working Thesis 608
TAKE ACTION Focusing a Research Question 609
Using Your Working Thesis to Guide Your Research 610
Surveying Your Resources 610
Sample Assignment: Creating a Research Proposal 611

## 31. Finding Sources 614
Searching the Internet 615
Finding Recommended Internet Resources 615
Smart Online Searching 615
Learning by Doing Comparing Web Searches 617
Searching the Library 619
Getting to Know the Library 619
Learning by Doing Reflecting on Your Library Orientation Session 621
Using the Library Catalog 623
Learning by Doing Brainstorming for Search Terms 624
Searching Library Databases 625
Learning by Doing Comparing Databases 628
Using Specialized Library Resources 628
Finding Sources in the Field 629
Interviewing 630
Learning by Doing Interviewing an Instructor 630

Observing   630
Using Questionnaires   631
Corresponding   632
Attending Public and Online Events   634
Reconsidering Your Field Sources   634

## 32. Evaluating Sources   635

TAKE ACTION Evaluating Sources   636

Assessing the Reliability of Sources   637
Learning by Doing Evaluating Your Sources   637
Who Is Responsible for the Source?   637
What Type of Source Is It?   637
Is the Source Scholarly or Popular?   638
What Is the Source's Purpose and Bias?   638
When Was the Source Produced or Published?   639

Using Special Care with Internet Sources   639

Assessing Relevance   641
Considering Your Purpose   641
Learning by Doing Reflecting on Sources in a Dialogic Notebook   642
Reviewing Your Sources   642

Sample Assignment: Preparing a Source Evaluation   643

## 33. Working with Sources   645

Navigating Sources   646

Managing Your Project   646
Starting a Working Bibliography   646
Keeping Track of Sources   646

Capturing Information in Your Notes   647
Reading Actively   656
Quoting   656
Paraphrasing   658
Summarizing   658
Learning by Doing Capturing Information from Sources   659

Sample Assignment: Developing an Annotated Bibliography   660
Learning by Doing Writing an Annotation   661

## 34. Integrating Sources   662

Using Sources Ethically   662

Capturing Evidence without Plagiarizing   663
Quoting and Paraphrasing Accurately   663
TAKE ACTION Avoiding Plagiarism   664
Summarizing Concisely   666
Avoiding Plagiarism   667

Launching and Citing Source Material   669
Launching Evidence from Sources   669
Learning by Doing Talking to the Sources   670
Citing Each Source Clearly   671
Learning by Doing Launching and Citing Your Sources   671

Synthesizing Ideas and Sources   672
Learning by Doing Synthesizing Your Sources   672
TAKE ACTION Integrating and Synthesizing Sources   673

## 35. Writing a Research Paper   674

Planning with a Thesis Statement   674

Drafting   676
Launching and Citing Your Sources as You Draft   676
Beginning and Ending   676
Learning by Doing Focusing with a Reverse Outline   677

Revising and Editing   677
Learning by Doing Meeting Expectations   678

Documenting Sources   679
Learning by Doing Presenting Your Findings   679

## 36. MLA Style for Documenting Sources   680

Citing Sources in MLA Style   682
TAKE ACTION Citing and Listing Sources   683
Listing Sources in MLA Style   687
A Sample MLA Research Paper   695

## 37. APA Style for Documenting Sources 704

Citing Sources in APA Style 704

Listing Sources in APA Style 710

A Sample APA Research Paper 717

**BOOK 4**
## A WRITER'S HANDBOOK

Introduction: Grammar, or The Way Words Work 729

Learning by Doing Creating an Error Log 729

## 38. Basic Grammar 730

1. Parts of Speech 730
2. Subjects 740
3. Verbs, Objects, and Complements 741

Learning by Doing Finding Subjects and Verbs 745

4. Clauses and Phrases 746
5. Sentence Structures 748

## 39. Grammatical Sentences 752

6. Sentence Fragments 752
7. Comma Splices and Fused Sentences 755
8. Verb Form, Tense, and Mood 758
9. Subject-Verb Agreement 771
10. Pronoun Case 775
11. Pronoun Reference 779
12. Pronoun-Antecedent Agreement 782
13. Adjectives and Adverbs 784
14. Shifts 789

Learning by Doing Considering Your Rough Draft 791

## 40. Effective Sentences 792

15. Misplaced and Dangling Modifiers 792
16. Incomplete Sentences 794
17. Mixed Constructions and Faulty Predication 798

18. Parallel Structure 801
19. Coordination and Subordination 804
20. Sentence Variety 810
21. Active and Passive Voice 811

Learning by Doing Considering Language 812

TAKE ACTION Improving Sentence Style 813

## 41. Word Choice 814

22. Appropriateness 814
23. Exact Words 818
24. Bias-Free Language 819
25. Wordiness 822

Learning by Doing Refining Your Wording 823

26. Commonly Confused Words 823

TAKE ACTION Improving Word Use 825

## 42. Punctuation 826

Learning by Doing Tackling Punctuation Patterns 826

27. End Punctuation 826
28. Commas 828
29. Misuses of the Comma 836
30. Semicolons 838
31. Colons 839
32. Apostrophes 841
33. Quotation Marks 844
34. Dashes 848
35. Parentheses, Brackets, and Ellipses 849

## 43. Mechanics 853

Learning by Doing Justifying Conventions 853

36. Abbreviations 853
37. Capital Letters 856
38. Numbers 859
39. Italics 861
40. Hyphens 863
41. Spelling 865

Answers for Lettered Exercises 866

## APPENDICES AND OTHER RESOURCES

### Quick Format Guide  Q-1

A. Following the Format for an Academic Paper  Q-1
B. Integrating and Crediting Visuals  Q-7
C. Preparing a Document Template  Q-12
D. Solving Common Format Problems  Q-13
E. Designing Other Documents for Your Audience  Q-13
F. Organizing a Résumé and an Application Letter  Q-16

### Quick Research Guide  Q-20

A. Defining Your Quest  Q-21
B. Searching for Recommended Sources  Q-24
C. Evaluating Possible Sources  Q-25
D. Capturing, Launching, and Citing Evidence Added from Sources  Q-27
E. Citing and Listing Sources in MLA or APA Style  Q-31

### Quick Editing Guide  Q-37

A. Editing for Common Grammar Problems  Q-38
B. Editing to Ensure Effective Sentences  Q-46
C. Editing for Word Choice  Q-48
D. Editing for Common Punctuation Problems  Q-59
E. Editing for Common Mechanics Problems  Q-62

About the Photographs That Open Parts One through Four  A-3

Index  I-1

Correction Symbols

Proofreading Symbols

A Guide to the Handbook

# RHETORICAL CONTENTS

*(Essays listed in order of appearance; * indicates student essays.)*

## Analyzing a Subject

*Olof Eriksson • The Problems with Masculinity, 23

*Alley Julseth • Analyzing "The New Literacy," 28

Michael Shermer • The Science of Righteousness, 30

Emily Badger • It's Time to Stop Blaming Poverty on the Decline in Marriage, 127

*Marjorie Lee Garretson • More Pros Than Cons in a Meat-Free Life, 149

Charles M. Blow • Black Dads Are Doing Best of All, 216

*Abigail Marchand • The Family Dynamic, 219

Celebrity Culture *[Text, Audio, and Video]*, LaunchPad

*Jonathan Burns • The Hidden Truth: An Analysis of Shirley Jackson's "The Lottery," 260

Frank Deford • Mind Games: Football and Head Injuries *[Audio]*, LaunchPad

*Samantha Christopher • Adolescents Are Not Yet Adults, 471

Chris Bentley • Beyond the Nuclear Family: Can Boomers Make Cohousing Mainstream?, 487

Michael Cobb • The Marriage Imperative, 491

Brent Staples • Black Men and Public Space, 502

Robert Jensen • The High Cost of Manliness, 512

Julie Zeilinger • Guys Suffer from Oppressive Gender Roles Too, 516

Kate Dailey and Abby Ellin • America's War on the Overweight, 522

Stephen King • Why We Crave Horror Movies, 534

Elizabeth Stone • Grief in the Age of Facebook, 537

Libby Copeland • Is Facebook Making Us Sad?, 541

Clive Thompson • The New Literacy, 547

Jenny Jarvie • Trigger Happy, 553

William Zinsser • The Right to Fail, 571

## Analyzing Processes

Michael Shermer • The Science of Righteousness, 30

Wilbert Rideau • Why Prisons Don't Work, 178

Casey Neistat • Texting While Walking *[Video]*, LaunchPad

Aziz Ansari • Searching for Your Soul Mate, 494

Adam Sternbergh • Smile, You're Speaking Emoji, 527

Elizabeth Stone • Grief in the Age of Facebook, 537

Richard Rodriguez • Public and Private Language, 558

## Analyzing Visuals

Multiple Photographers • Observing the *Titanic*: Past and Present *[Visual Essay]*, LaunchPad

Tiana Chavez • ASU Athletes Discuss Superstitions *[Video]*, LaunchPad

*National Geographic* Editors • Hurricane Katrina Pictures: Then & Now, Ruin & Rebirth *[Visual Essay]*, LaunchPad

Brian Hurst • How Your Aggressive Driving Negatively Impacts the Environment *[Infographic]*, LaunchPad

UNICEF Editors • Dirty Water Campaign *[Video]*, LaunchPad

Casey Neistat • Texting While Walking *[Video]*, LaunchPad

Scott Tobias • The Hunger Games, 198

*Consumer Reports* Web Editors • Best Vanilla Ice Cream *[Video]*, LaunchPad

*Shannon Kintner • Charlie Living with Autism *[Student Visual Essay]*, LaunchPad

Adam Sternbergh • Smile, You're Speaking Emoji, 527

Stephen King • Why We Crave Horror Movies, 534

## Arguing

*National Geographic* Editors • Hurricane Katrina Pictures: Then & Now, Ruin & Rebirth *[Visual Essay]*, LaunchPad

Emily Badger • It's Time to Stop Blaming Poverty on the Decline in Marriage, 127

**Brian Hurst** • How Your Aggressive Driving Negatively Impacts the Environment *[Infographic]*, LaunchPad

**Suzan Shown Harjo** • Last Rites for Indian Dead,  146

**\*Marjorie Lee Garretson** • More Pros Than Cons in a Meat-Free Life,  149

**UNICEF Editors** • Dirty Water Campaign *[Video]*, LaunchPad

**Wilbert Rideau** • Why Prisons Don't Work,  178

**\*Lacey Taylor** • It's Not Just a Bike,  181

**Casey Neistat** • Texting While Walking *[Video]*, LaunchPad

**\*Elizabeth Erion** • Internship Program Falls Short,  200

**\*Abigail Marchand** • The Family Dynamic,  219

Celebrity Culture *[Text, Audio, and Video]*, LaunchPad

**Frank Deford** • Mind Games: Football and Head Injuries *[Audio]*, LaunchPad

**\*Samantha Christopher** • Adolescents Are Not Yet Adults,  471

**Judy Brady** • I Want a Wife,  505

**Julie Zeilinger** • Guys Suffer from Oppressive Gender Roles Too,  516

**Kate Dailey and Abby Ellin** • America's War on the Overweight,  522

**Clive Thompson** • The New Literacy,  547

**Ann Friedman** • Can We Just, Like, Get Over the Way Women Talk?,  549

**Jenny Jarvie** • Trigger Happy,  553

**William Deresiewicz** • What Is College For?,  575

**Sarah Adams** • Be Cool to the Pizza Dude,  580

## Comparing and Contrasting

**Michael Shermer** • The Science of Righteousness,  30

**Multiple Photographers** • Observing the *Titanic*: Past and Present *[Visual Essay]*, LaunchPad

**César Vargas** • How First- and Second-Generation Hispanics Can Help Each Other,  107

**\*Jacob Griffin** • Karate Kid vs. Kung Fu Panda: A Race to the Olympics,  110

*National Geographic* Editors • Hurricane Katrina Pictures: Then & Now, Ruin & Rebirth *[Visual Essay]*, LaunchPad

**Scott Tobias** • The Hunger Games,  198

**Charles M. Blow** • Black Dads Are Doing Best of All,  216

**\*Samantha Christopher** • Adolescents Are Not Yet Adults,  471

**Chris Bentley** • Beyond the Nuclear Family: Can Boomers Make Cohousing Mainstream?,  487

**Michael Cobb** • The Marriage Imperative,  491

**Aziz Ansari** • Searching for Your Soul Mate,  494

**Julie Zeilinger** • Guys Suffer from Oppressive Gender Roles Too,  516

**Richard Rodriguez** • Public and Private Language,  558

**David Brooks** • The Humility Code,  582

## Defining

**\*Olof Eriksson** • The Problems with Masculinity,  23

**Michael Shermer** • The Science of Righteousness,  30

**\*Robert G. Schreiner** • What Is a Hunter?,  51

**Brian Hurst** • How Your Aggressive Driving Negatively Impacts the Environment *[Infographic]*, LaunchPad

**Judy Brady** • I Want a Wife,  505

**Robert Jensen** • The High Cost of Manliness,  512

**Clive Thompson** • The New Literacy,  547

**Richard Rodriguez** • Public and Private Language,  558

**William Zinsser** • The Right to Fail,  571

**William Deresiewicz** • What Is College For?,  575

## Describing

**Russell Baker** • The Art of Eating Spaghetti,  48

**\*Robert G. Schreiner** • What Is a Hunter?,  51

**Howie Chackowicz** • The Game Ain't Over 'til the Fatso Man Sings *[Audio]*, LaunchPad

**Ashley Smith** • Smokejumper Training,  67

**\*Alea Eyre** • Stockholm,  71

**\*Jacob Griffin** • Karate Kid vs. Kung Fu Panda: A Race to the Olympics,  110

**\*Erin Schmitt** • Mr. Hertli,  365

**Judith Ortiz Cofer** • More Room,  483

## Dividing and Classifying

**Michael Shermer** • The Science of Righteousness,  30

**Robert Jensen** • The High Cost of Manliness,  512

**Richard Rodriguez** • Public and Private Language,  558

**Miya Tokumitsu** • In the Name of Love,  590

## Evaluating and Reviewing

*Alley Julseth • Analyzing "The New Literacy," 28

Michael Shermer • The Science of Righteousness, 30

Scott Tobias • The Hunger Games, 198

*Elizabeth Erion • Internship Program Falls Short, 200

Consumer Reports Web Editors • Best Vanilla Ice Cream [Video], LaunchPad

*Samantha Christopher • Adolescents Are Not Yet Adults, 471

Cindi May • The Problem with Female Superheroes, 508

Robert Jensen • The High Cost of Manliness, 512

Stephen King • Why We Crave Horror Movies, 534

## Explaining Causes and Effects

Michael Shermer • The Science of Righteousness, 30

César Vargas • How First- and Second-Generation Hispanics Can Help Each Other, 107

Emily Badger • It's Time to Stop Blaming Poverty on the Decline in Marriage, 127

*Yun Yung Choi • Invisible Women, 130

Brian Hurst • How Your Aggressive Driving Negatively Impacts the Environment [Infographic], LaunchPad

Charles M. Blow • Black Dads Are Doing Best of All, 216

Celebrity Culture [Text, Audio, and Video], LaunchPad

Frank Deford • Mind Games: Football and Head Injuries [Audio], LaunchPad

Chris Bentley • Beyond the Nuclear Family: Can Boomers Make Cohousing Mainstream?, 487

Aziz Ansari • Searching for Your Soul Mate, 494

Stephen King • Why We Crave Horror Movies, 534

Libby Copeland • Is Facebook Making Us Sad?, 541

Ann Friedman • Can We Just, Like, Get Over the Way Women Talk?, 549

Amy Tan • Mother Tongue, 564

## Giving Examples

Howie Chackowicz • The Game Ain't Over 'til the Fatso Man Sings [Audio], LaunchPad

Tiana Chavez • ASU Athletes Discuss Superstitions [Video], LaunchPad

César Vargas • How First- and Second-Generation Hispanics Can Help Each Other, 107

*Marjorie Lee Garretson • More Pros Than Cons in a Meat-Free Life, 149

*Elizabeth Erion • Internship Program Falls Short, 200

Consumer Reports Web Editors • Best Vanilla Ice Cream [Video], LaunchPad

*Jonathan Burns • The Hidden Truth: An Analysis of Shirley Jackson's "The Lottery," 260

Frank Deford • Mind Games: Football and Head Injuries [Audio], LaunchPad

Cindi May • The Problem with Female Superheroes, 508

Robert Jensen • The High Cost of Manliness, 512

Kate Dailey and Abby Ellin • America's War on the Overweight, 522

Elizabeth Stone • Grief in the Age of Facebook, 537

Ann Friedman • Can We Just, Like, Get Over the Way Women Talk?, 549

Jenny Jarvie • Trigger Happy, 553

William Zinsser • The Right to Fail, 571

Sarah Adams • Be Cool to the Pizza Dude, 580

## Interviewing a Subject

Jon Ronson • How One Stupid Tweet Blew Up Justine Sacco's Life, 86

*Lorena A. Ryan-Hines • Looking Backwards, Moving Forward, 91

Tiana Chavez • ASU Athletes Discuss Superstitions [Video], LaunchPad

Chris Bentley • Beyond the Nuclear Family: Can Boomers Make Cohousing Mainstream?, 487

Aziz Ansari • Searching for Your Soul Mate, 494

Elizabeth Stone • Grief in the Age of Facebook, 537

Ann Friedman • Can We Just, Like, Get Over the Way Women Talk?, 549

Amy Tan • Mother Tongue, 564

## Observing a Scene

Ashley Smith • Smokejumper Training, 67

*Alea Eyre • Stockholm, 71

Multiple Photographers • Observing the Titanic: Past and Present [Visual Essay], LaunchPad

*Shannon Kintner • Charlie Living with Autism [Student Visual Essay], LaunchPad

Judith Ortiz Cofer • More Room, 483

Miya Tokumitsu • In the Name of Love, 590

## Proposing a Solution

César Vargas • How First- and Second-Generation Hispanics Can Help Each Other, 107

Emily Badger • It's Time to Stop Blaming Poverty on the Decline in Marriage, 127

Wilbert Rideau • Why Prisons Don't Work, 178

*Lacey Taylor • It's Not Just a Bike, 181

Casey Neistat • Texting While Walking [Video], LaunchPad

Frank Deford • Mind Games: Football and Head Injuries [Audio], LaunchPad

David Brooks • The Humility Code, 582

## Recalling an Experience

Russell Baker • The Art of Eating Spaghetti, 48

*Robert G. Schreiner • What Is a Hunter?, 51

Howie Chackowicz • The Game Ain't Over 'til the Fatso Man Sings [Audio], LaunchPad

*Alea Eyre • Stockholm, 71

*Erin Schmitt • Mr. Hertli, 365

Judith Ortiz Cofer • More Room, 483

Chris Bentley • Beyond the Nuclear Family: Can Boomers Make Cohousing Mainstream?, 487

Elizabeth Stone • Grief in the Age of Facebook, 537

Richard Rodriguez • Public and Private Language, 558

Amy Tan • Mother Tongue, 564

## Supporting a Position with Sources

Emily Badger • It's Time to Stop Blaming Poverty on the Decline in Marriage, 127

*Yun Yung Choi • Invisible Women, 130

Brian Hurst • How Your Aggressive Driving Negatively Impacts the Environment [Infographic], LaunchPad

Suzan Shown Harjo • Last Rites for Indian Dead, 146

Charles M. Blow • Black Dads Are Doing Best of All, 216

*Abigail Marchand • The Family Dynamic, 219

Celebrity Culture [Text, Audio, and Video], LaunchPad

*Jonathan Burns • The Hidden Truth: An Analysis of Shirley Jackson's "The Lottery," 260

Frank Deford • Mind Games: Football and Head Injuries [Audio], LaunchPad

*Samantha Christopher • Adolescents Are Not Yet Adults, 471

Chris Bentley • Beyond the Nuclear Family: Can Boomers Make Cohousing Mainstream?, 487

Cindi May • The Problem with Female Superheroes, 508

Kate Dailey and Abby Ellin • America's War on the Overweight, 522

Clive Thompson • The New Literacy, 547

Ann Friedman • Can We Just, Like, Get Over the Way Women Talk?, 549

*Jenny Lidington • Sex Offender Lists: A Never-Ending Punishment, 719

## Taking a Stand

César Vargas • How First- and Second-Generation Hispanics Can Help Each Other, 107

Suzan Shown Harjo • Last Rites for Indian Dead, 146

*Marjorie Lee Garretson • More Pros Than Cons in a Meat-Free Life, 149

UNICEF Editors • Dirty Water Campaign [Video], LaunchPad

Casey Neistat • Texting While Walking [Video], LaunchPad

*Elizabeth Erion • Internship Program Falls Short, 200

Michael Cobb • The Marriage Imperative, 491

Cindi May • The Problem with Female Superheroes, 508

Julie Zeilinger • Guys Suffer from Oppressive Gender Roles Too, 516

Ann Friedman • Can We Just, Like, Get Over the Way Women Talk?, 549

Jenny Jarvie • Trigger Happy, 553

William Deresiewicz • What Is College For?, 575

Sarah Adams • Be Cool to the Pizza Dude, 580

David Brooks • The Humility Code, 582

Miya Tokumitsu • In the Name of Love, 590

*Jenny Lidington • Sex Offender Lists: A Never-Ending Punishment, 719

# SELECTED VISUAL CONTENTS

*(*Asterisk indicates an accompanying Responding to an Image activity.)*

## Advertisements and Public Service Announcements

UNICEF Dirty Water Campaign, LaunchPad
"Don't wait" emergency plan PSA, 176
"Don't Mess with Texas" antilittering sign, 188
No Swearing sign, 246
Parent supervision and toxicity signs on playground, 247
Figure 14.1 Antiviolence PSA, 283
Figure 14.6 Volkswagen advertisement, 288
Figure 14.7 Chevrolet advertisement, 289
Figure 14.11 Hunger PSA, 294
Figure 14.12 Antismoking billboard, 295
Figure 14.13 Anti-drunk driving PSA, 296

## Document Design

Figure 14.8 "Stairway" type design, 290
Figure 17.1 Conventional résumé, 343, Q-18
Figure 17.2 Application letter, 346, Q-19
Figure 17.3 Letter using modified block style, 348, Q-19
Figure 17.4 Business envelope formats, 349
Reflective portfolio letter, 368
Formal outline, 401, 402–3
MLA first page, 697, Q-2
MLA Works Cited, 702–3, Q-3
APA title page, 718, Q-4
APA Abstract, 718, Q-4
APA first page, 719, Q-5
APA References, 725, Q-6
MLA and APA table formats, Q-9
Typefaces, Q-15
List formats, Q-15
Heading levels, Q-16

## Journal Questions and Visual Assignments

Series of four aerial photographs, 4–5, 44–45, 248–49, 356–57. See journal questions about these in the About the Photographs section at the back of the book.

*Man crossing finish line, 46
*Woman sitting by damaged house, 46
*Couple unpacking boxes, 46
*Family at meal, 46
Group of women sharing dinner, 63
Hiker regarding nature, 64
Concert, 64
*Baseball player making catch, 65
View from bicycle, 82
Climbers on Mt. Rushmore, 83
Crowd at store on Black Friday, 83
*Park Geun-hye, 84
*George R. R. Martin, 84
*Sheryl Sandberg, 84
*Elon Musk, 84
Census interview in desert landscape, 104
FEMA worker interviewing flood victim, 104
Job interviews, 104
*Protest following assassination of Martin Luther King Jr., 105
*Vigil for Freddie Gray in Baltimore, 105
Hurricane Katrina Pictures: Then & Now, Ruin & Rebirth, LaunchPad
Classrooms in Nigeria, New York, and Guatemala, 123–24
*Rusted boats; satellite image of Aral Sea, 125
Line graph, Growth in Cell Phone–Only Households, 2004–2014, 142
A lineman repairing infrastructure, 143
Hurricane victims trying to locate cell phone service, 143
*Protest against education cutbacks, 144
Patient watching fundraising walk, 174
Family reading, 175
"Don't wait" emergency plan PSA, 176
Mourners at antidrug march, 194
Cab drivers protesting Uber, 195
Dog at puppy mill, 195
*Judging giant pumpkins, 196
Church at Auvers-sur-Oise (photo), 212
*The Church in Auvers-sur-Oise* by Vincent van Gogh, 212

Office with cubicles, 213
Office with open plan, 213
*Lab workers, 214
*Archaeological dig, 214
*Student in library, 214
*Photographer interview, 214
Contestant in child beauty pageant, 246
No Swearing sign, 246
Parent supervision and toxicity signs on
    playground, 247
*Scene from *The Big Bang Theory*, 482
*Woman proposing to man, 501
*Steve Jobs memorial, 521
*Poem-art installation by sculptor Jaume Plensa, 546
*Collage on the good life, 570

## Other Images

Girl learning to drive, 56
Emergency room, 73
Black Lives Matter rally, 75
David Frost interview with Richard Nixon, 96
Funeral procession for reburial of Native American
    remains, 147
Joan of Arc, 152
Piece of a candy bar, 160
Living wall, 184
Person farming, 190
Set for *The Cabinet of Dr. Caligari* (1920), 204
Mojave Desert, 229
Batman at a donut shop, 284
Future Open sign, 291
Amusement park ride at sunset, 293
Charlie Living with Autism *[Visual Essay]*, 301, and
    LaunchPad
Screenshots from the American Society for the
    Prevention of Cruelty to Animals (ASPCA)
    Web site, 640

## Pairs, Series, and Collages

Series of four aerial photographs, 4–5, 44–45,
    248–49, 356–57
Recalled experiences, 46
Observing the *Titanic*: Past and Present *[Visual Essay]*,
    LaunchPad

Park, Sandberg, Musk, and Martin, 84
Gatherings following the deaths of Martin Luther
    King Jr. and Freddie Gray, 105
Hurricane Katrina *[Visual Essay]*, LaunchPad
Classrooms in Nigeria, New York, and
    Guatemala, 123–24
Rusted boats; satellite image of Aral Sea, 125
Church at Auvers-sur-Oise; *The Church in Auvers-sur-
    Oise* by Vincent van Gogh, 212
Office with cubicles; office with open plan, 213
Students consulting sources, 214
Charlie Living with Autism *[Visual Essay]*, 301, and
    LaunchPad
Collage on the good life, 570

## Representations of Data and Processes

How Your Aggressive Driving Negatively Impacts the
    Environment *[Infographic]*, LaunchPad
Line graph, Growth in Cell Phone–Only Households,
    2004–2014, 142
Line graph, Annual Rise in Cost of Attending
    College, 698
Table samples, Q-9
Figure Q.1 How to Study Model, Q-10
Figure Q.2 Line graph, Number of Automobile
    Accidents Attributed to Driver Distractions in
    Sedgwick County, 2003–2010, Q-11
Figure Q.3 Bar graph, Number of Automobile
    Accidents Attributed to Driver Distractions in the
    State of Kansas and Sedgwick County, 2003–2010,
    Q-11
Figure Q.4 Map, Great Lakes Coastal Flood Study,
    Q-12

## Workplace Documents

Figure 17.1 Conventional résumé, 343, Q-18
Figure 17.2 Application letter, 346, Q-19
Figure 17.3 Letter using modified block style, 348,
    Q-19
Figure 17.4 Business envelope formats, 349
Figure 17.5 Memorandum, 351
Figure 17.6 Brochure, 352
Figure 17.7 PowerPoint slide with too much text, 353
Figure 17.8 PowerPoint slide with brief text, 353

# FEATURES OF *THE BEDFORD GUIDE*, ELEVENTH EDITION, AND ANCILLARIES

Correlated to the Writing Program Administrators (WPA) Outcomes Statement

| WPA Outcomes | Relevant Features of *The Bedford Guide* |
|---|---|
| **Rhetorical Knowledge** | |
| **Learn and use key rhetorical concepts through analyzing and composing a variety of texts** | ■ Ch. 1: Writing Processes, including audience and purpose (pp. 6–15)<br>■ Ch. 2: Reading Processes, including annotation, literal vs. analytical reading, online and multimodal reading (pp. 16–34)<br>■ Ch. 9: Taking a Stand, including finding, testing, and applying evidence; avoiding faulty thinking (pp. 144–75)<br>■ Chs. 2–16: Learning from Other Writers activities guide students through rhetorical analysis of texts in a variety of situations/genres (16–337).<br>■ Chs. 4–17: Learning by Doing activities give students opportunities to apply rhetorical concepts to a variety of situations/genres (46–355).<br>■ Chs. 4–14: Learning by Writing assignments and additional writing assignments require students to use key rhetorical concepts to compose texts in a variety of genres (pp. 46–306).<br>■ Chs. 25–29 (*A Writer's Reader*) offer additional print and multimodal texts, arranged thematically, for students to analyze. Each selection is paired with critical thinking questions, journal prompts, and suggestions for students to compose their own responses (pp. 479–597).<br><br>*For instructors*<br>■ LaunchPad*: Lecture slides |
| **Gain experience reading and composing in several genres to understand how genre conventions shape and are shaped by readers' and writers' practices and purposes** | ■ Chs. 4–17 (Part Two, A Writer's Situations, and Part Three, Other Writing Situations) introduce students to a variety of major and less common situations/genres, to those genres' conventions, and to the relationship between purpose and those conventions via guided analysis of professional and student texts (Learning from Other Writers) and active practice (Learning by Doing activities, Learning by Writing assignments, Additional Writing Assignments) (pp. 44–355).<br>■ Chs. 25–29 (*A Writer's Reader*) are heavily integrated with Parts Two and Three. Teaching Tips in the Instructor's Annotated Edition suggest methods for linking your teaching of the essays to specific situations/genres in Parts Two and Three. Many of the Suggestions for Writing assignments following the texts ask students to respond to the piece in terms of its genre conventions (pp. 479–597).<br>■ A rhetorically organized table of contents covering all readings in the text is available on pages xxxiii–xxxvi. |

*This resource is available packaged with the print book.

| WPA Outcomes | Relevant Features of *The Bedford Guide* |
|---|---|
| **Rhetorical Knowledge** | |
| **Develop facility in responding to a variety of situations and contexts, calling for purposeful shifts in voice, tone, level of formality, design, medium, and/or structure** | ▪ Ch. 1: Purpose and Audience (pp. 11–15)<br>▪ Ch. 9: Learning by Writing (pp. 152–75)<br>▪ Chs. 4–17: Situational consideration of audience and Peer Response questions<br>▪ Attention to specific audiences such as Messages to Your Instructor (pp. 311–13), Online Threaded Discussions (pp. 315–17), workplace audiences (p. 339), and research audiences (pp. 603–5)<br>▪ Ch. 20: Shaping Your Topic for Your Purpose and Your Audience (pp. 383–84)<br>▪ Ch. 23: Revising for Audience (pp. 444–45), Working with a Peer Editor (pp. 446–48), and Meeting with Your Instructor (p. 448)<br>▪ Ch. 24: Strategies for Writing in Future Courses, including writing in different academic disciplines such as the sciences, nursing, the arts, business, education, history, and psychology (pp. 459–77)<br>▪ Ch. 41: Word Choice (pp. 814–25) |
| **Understand and use a variety of technologies to address a range of audiences** | ▪ LaunchPad*: Multimodal readings that integrate audio, video, visuals, and text, representing situations covered in Chs. 4–17 and themes covered in *A Writer's Reader*<br>▪ Visual Activities in Part One, which also includes Reading Online and Multimodal Texts in Ch. 2: Reading Processes<br>▪ Visual Assignment options in Parts Two and Three (Chs. 4–12 and 14–17)<br>▪ Ch. 14: Responding to Visual Representations<br>▪ Ch. 15: Writing Online<br>▪ Ch. 16: Writing and Presenting under Pressure, including oral presentations with visuals<br>▪ *A Writer's Research Manual* with online strategies throughout (Chs. 30–37)<br>▪ Quick Format Guide, including a section on integrating and crediting visuals (pp. Q-1–Q-19)<br>▪ Quick Research Guide, including Searching for Recommended Sources (pp. Q-20–Q-36)<br><br>*For instructors*<br>▪ *Practical Suggestions for Teaching with The Bedford Guide for College Writers*, Ch. 5: Teaching Writing Online: Using Technology in Your Composition Course<br>▪ *Teaching Composition: Background Readings*, Teaching Writing with Computers (pp. 305–37) and Teaching Visual Literacy (pp. 337–76) |
| **Match the capacities of different environments (e.g., print and electronic) to varying rhetorical situations** | ▪ Ch. 15: Writing Online<br>▪ *A Writer's Research Manual* with online strategies throughout (Chs. 30–37)<br>▪ Quick Research Guide, including Searching for Recommended Sources (pp. Q-20–Q-36)<br>▪ LaunchPad*: Multimodal readings that integrate audio, video, visuals, and text, representing situations covered in Chs. 4–17 and themes covered in *A Writer's Reader*<br><br>*For instructors*<br>▪ *Practical Suggestions for Teaching with The Bedford Guide for College Writers*, Ch. 5: Teaching Writing Online: Using Technology in Your Composition Course<br>▪ *Teaching Composition: Background Readings*, Teaching Writing with Computers (pp. 305–37) and Teaching Visual Literacy (pp. 337–76) |

*This resource is available packaged with the print book.

| WPA Outcomes | Relevant Features of *The Bedford Guide* |
|---|---|
| **Critical Thinking, Reading, and Composing** | |
| **Use composing and reading for inquiry, learning, thinking, and communicating in various rhetorical contexts** | ■ Chs. 1–3 (Part One, A College Writer's Processes) includes writing, reading, and critical thinking processes.<br>■ Parts Two, Three, and Four emphasize the connection between reading and writing.<br>■ *A Writer's Reader* with twenty-four readings grouped thematically (pp. 479–597)<br>■ Critical reading apparatus in Part Two, A Writer's Situations (e.g., pp. 48, 50–54), and in *A Writer's Reader* (e.g., pp. 483, 486–87)<br><br>*For instructors*<br>■ *Practical Suggestions for Teaching with The Bedford Guide for College Writers,* Ch. 3: Teaching Critical Thinking and Writing<br>■ *Teaching Composition: Background Readings,* Ch. 1: Teaching Writing: Key Concepts, Philosophies, Frameworks, and Experiences |
| **Read a diverse range of texts, attending especially to relationships between assertion and evidence, to patterns of organization, to interplay between verbal and nonverbal elements, and to how these features function for different audiences and situations** | ■ Each chapter in Parts Two and Three presents multiple text and multimodal selections produced by professional writers and students, organized by situation/genre. Texts are followed by questions that ask students to consider meaning, the effectiveness of the writer's strategies, and *other rhetorical matters.*<br>■ *A Writer's Reader* offers twenty-four additional text and multimodal selections organized around five themes. Texts are followed by questions on critical reading, meaning, writing strategies, and, in the case of multimodal texts, questions on verbal/nonverbal interplay.<br><br>*For instructors*<br>■ LaunchPad*: Reading comprehension quizzes on all professional reading selections (in *A Writer's Guide,* Part Two, and *A Writer's Reader*) |
| **Locate and evaluate primary and secondary research materials, including journal articles, essays, books, databases, and informal Internet sources** | ■ Ch. 12: Supporting a Position with Sources<br>■ Ch. 30: Defining Your Research Project<br>■ Ch. 33: Working with Sources, including capturing information and developing an annotated bibliography<br>■ Chs. 31–34 on finding, evaluating, integrating, and synthesizing sources from the Internet, the library, and the field (pp. 614–73)<br>■ Quick Research Guide (pp. Q-20–Q-36)<br>■ LaunchPad*: Additional Learning by Doing activity on finding and evaluating credible sources (Finding Credible Sources)<br>■ Visual and Source Activity options in Part One and Visual and Source Assignment options in Parts Two and Three |
| **Use strategies — such as interpretation, synthesis, response, critique, and design/redesign — to compose texts that integrate the writer's ideas with those from appropriate sources** | ■ *A Writer's Reader* with journal prompts, writing suggestions, and paired essays (pp. 479–597)<br>■ Ch. 12: Supporting a Position with Sources (pp. 214–47)<br>■ Chs. 31–34 on finding, evaluating, integrating, and synthesizing sources (pp. 614–73)<br>■ Quick Research Guide (pp. Q-20–Q-36) |

*This resource is available packaged with the print book.

| WPA Outcomes | Relevant Features of *The Bedford Guide* |
|---|---|
| **Processes** | |
| **Develop a writing project through multiple drafts** | ▪ Ch. 1: Writing Processes (pp. 6–15) with process overview<br>▪ Chs. 4–14 with situation-specific process guidance<br>▪ Part Four, A Writer's Strategies, shows writing processes in detail, including Ch. 18: Strategies: A Case Study (pp. 358–68), showing one student's stages.<br><br>*For instructors*<br>▪ *Teaching Composition: Background Readings,* Ch. 2: Thinking about the Writing Process |
| **Develop flexible strategies for reading, drafting, reviewing, collaborating, revising, rewriting, rereading, and editing** | ▪ Ch. 1: Writing Processes with an overview of generating ideas, planning, drafting, developing, revising, editing, and proofreading (pp. 6–15)<br>▪ Parts Two and Three with situation-specific process strategies<br>▪ Part Four, A Writer's Strategies, with detailed coverage of writing processes (pp. 356–477)<br><br>*For instructors*<br>▪ *Teaching Composition: Background Readings,* Revising a Draft (pp. 195–246), and Ch. 3: Responding to and Evaluating Student Writing |
| **Use composing processes and tools as a means to discover and reconsider ideas** | ▪ Ch. 19: Strategies for Generating Ideas<br>▪ Ch. 23: Strategies for Revising and Editing<br>▪ Ch. 24: Strategies for Writing in Future Courses<br>▪ Learning by Doing activities throughout the text involve students in hands-on application of relevant composing processes to discover and reconsider ideas.<br>▪ Self-assessment Take Action charts (e.g., p. 170)<br>▪ Checklists help students consider purpose and audience, discover something to write about, get feedback from a peer, revise their draft, and edit for grammatical correctness (e.g., p. 6).<br>▪ Chs. 4–17 (Parts Two and Three): New Reviewing and Reflecting activities help students reconsider ideas learned in each chapter (Reviewing activities expanded in LaunchPad*). |
| **Experience the collaborative and social aspects of writing processes** | ▪ Learning by Doing features including collaborative activities (e.g., pp. 99, 138 161–62) and Peer Response guidelines (Part Two and p. 447)<br>▪ Part Two, A Writer's Situations, Additional Writing Assignments with collaborative options (e.g., p. 122)<br>▪ Ch. 18: Strategies: A Case Study, including Rough Draft with Peer and Instructor Responses (pp. 361–63) and Reflective Portfolio Letter (p. 368)<br>▪ Ch. 30: Defining Your Research Project, including advice on planning collaborative research (p. 602)<br><br>*For instructors*<br>▪ *Practical Suggestions for Teaching with The Bedford Guide for College Writers,* Ch. 2, Creating a Writing Community |

*This resource is available packaged with the print book.

| WPA Outcomes | Relevant Features of *The Bedford Guide* |
|---|---|
| **Processes** | |
| **Learn to give and act on productive feedback to works in progress** | ■ Ch. 23: Strategies for Revising and Editing with peer-editing advice (pp. 452–58)<br>■ Peer Response sections for each chapter in Part Two, A Writer's Situations<br>■ Self-assessment Take Action charts (e.g., p. 170)<br>■ Ch. 18: Strategies: A Case Study, including Rough Draft with Peer and Instructor Responses (pp. 361–63) and Reflective Portfolio Letter (p. 368)<br>■ Ch. 24: Strategies for Writing in Future Courses with Connecting Expectations and Assessments (p. 461)<br><br>*For instructors*<br>■ *Practical Suggestions for Teaching with The Bedford Guide for College Writers,* Ch. 2: Creating a Writing Community |
| **Adapt composing processes for a variety of technologies and modalities** | ■ Visual Activities in Part One, which also includes Reading Online and Multimodal Texts in Ch. 2<br>■ Visual Assignment options in Parts Two and Three (Chs. 4–12 and 14–17)<br>■ Ch. 14: Responding to Visual Representations<br>■ Ch. 15: Writing Online<br>■ Ch. 16: Writing and Presenting under Pressure, including oral presentations with visuals<br>■ Reading Online and Multimodal Texts, pp. 31–33<br>■ LaunchPad\*: Multimodal readings that integrate audio, video, visuals, and text, representing situations covered in Chs. 4–17 and themes covered in *A Writer's Reader*<br>■ Quick Format Guide, including a section on integrating and crediting visuals (pp. Q-1–Q-19)<br><br>*For instructors*<br>■ *Practical Suggestions for Teaching with The Bedford Guide for College Writers,* Ch. 5: Teaching Writing Online: Using Technology in Your Composition Course<br>■ *Teaching Composition: Background Readings,* Teaching Writing with Computers (pp. 305–37) |

*This resource is available packaged with the print book.

| WPA Outcomes | Relevant Features of *The Bedford Guide* |
|---|---|
| **Processes** | |
| **Reflect on the development of composing practices and how those practices influence their work** | ■ Writing Strategies questions following each text and multimodal selection in Parts Two and Three ask students to reflect upon the composing practices of the author and the ways in which they influence the piece at hand.<br>■ Ch. 3: Critical Thinking Processes, including *Thinking Critically about Your Own Writing* (pp. 37–40) and *Learning from Another Writer: Self-Reflection* (pp. 41–42)<br>■ Ch. 18: Strategies: A Case Study, with Reflective Portfolio Letter (p. 368)<br>■ Concluding each chapter in Part Four, A Writer's Strategies, are Learning by Doing activities that ask students to reflect on their practice with the writing strategy covered in the chapter.<br>■ Self-assessment Take Action charts (e.g., p. 391)<br>■ Checklists help students consider purpose and audience, discover something to write about, get feedback from a peer, revise their drafts, and edit for grammatical correctness (e.g., p. 55).<br>■ An Identifying Writing Strategies question following each print and multimodal selection in *A Writer's Reader* asks students to reflect upon the composing practices of the author (p. 486).<br>■ Chs. 4–17 (Parts Two and Three): New Reviewing and Reflecting activities help students reconsider ideas learned in each chapter (Reviewing activities expanded in LaunchPad*). |
| **Knowledge of Conventions** | |
| **Develop knowledge of linguistic structures, including grammar, punctuation, and spelling, through practice in composing and revising** | ■ *A Writer's Handbook* (pp. 727–871) with exercises, including a new chapter on basic grammar (Ch. 38)<br>■ Quick Editing Guide with Editing Checklist (pp. Q-37–Q-64)<br>■ Part Two, A Writer's Situations, revising and editing advice, including cross-references to relevant topics in the Quick Editing Guide<br>■ Ch. 23: Strategies for Revising and Editing<br>■ LearningCurve* exercises on grammar and usage (LaunchPad)<br><br>*For instructors*<br>■ *Practical Suggestions for Teaching with The Bedford Guide for College Writers*, Ch. 4: Providing Support for Underprepared Students |
| **Understand why genre conventions for structure, paragraphing, tone, and mechanics vary** | ■ Part Two, A Writer's Situations, and Part Three, Other Writing Situations<br>■ Ch. 41: Word Choice, Ch. 42: Punctuation, and Ch. 43: Mechanics<br>■ Ch. 20: Shaping Your Topic for Your Purpose and Your Audience (pp. 383–84)<br>■ Ch. 23: Revising for Audience (pp. 444–45) |
| **Gain experience negotiating variations in genre conventions** | ■ Part Two, A Writer's Situations, and Part Three, Other Writing Situations<br>■ Ch. 20: Shaping Your Topic for Your Purpose and Your Audience (pp. 383–84)<br>■ Ch. 23: Revising for Audience (pp. 444–45)<br>■ LaunchPad*: Learning by Doing activity on researching genres (Researching Genre) |

*This resource is available packaged with the print book.

| WPA Outcomes | Relevant Features of *The Bedford Guide* |
|---|---|
| **Knowledge of Conventions** | |
| **Learn common formats and/or design features for different kinds of texts** | ■ Advice on various types of assignments in Parts Two and Three<br>■ Quick Format Guide with MLA and APA paper and table formats<br>■ Examples of varied formats for online course (pp. 311–17) and business communication (pp. 341–50), portfolio letters (pp. 367–68 and 476–77), résumés and application letters (pp. 341–47), presentation visuals (pp. 350–54), and questionnaires (pp. 631–33)<br>■ Ch. 24: Strategies for Writing in Future Courses, including notes on format and citation for writing in the sciences, nursing, the arts, business, education, history, and psychology (pp. 459–77)<br><br>*For instructors*<br>■ *Teaching Composition: Background Readings,* Teaching Visual Literacy (pp. 337–76) |
| **Explore the concepts of intellectual property (such as fair use and copyright) that motivate documentation conventions** | ■ Ch. 34: Integrating Sources, specifically Why Integrating Sources Matters and Using Sources Ethically (pp. 662–63) |
| **Practice applying citation conventions systematically in their own work** | ■ Options for source-based activities (Chs. 1–3) and assignments (Chs. 4–17) concluding each chapter<br>■ Ch. 12: Supporting a Position with Sources (pp. 214–47), including the Academic Exchange (pp. 230–31)<br>■ Take Action self-assessment and revision charts on Integrating Source Information Effectively (p. 243), Integrating and Synthesizing Sources (p. 673), Citing and Listing Sources (p. 683)<br>■ Quick Research Guide (pp. Q-20–Q-36) |

# INSIDE LAUNCHPAD FOR *THE BEDFORD GUIDE FOR COLLEGE WRITERS*

## BOOK 1: *A WRITER'S GUIDE*

### Reviewing and Reflecting

The new Reviewing and Reflecting feature that appears at the end of each chapter in Parts Two and Three includes an additional component in Launch-Pad: an automatically graded quiz that assesses comprehension of the chapter's key concepts.

### Learning by Doing Activities

Most LaunchPad chapters in *A Writer's Guide* include one or two additional Learning by Doing activities designed for an online learning environment.

Ch. 1 · Analyzing Audience
Ch. 2 · Reading Online
Ch. 4 · Recalling from Music
Ch. 5 · Analyzing Advertisements
Ch. 6 · Analyzing Interviews
Ch. 7 · Comparing and Contrasting Experiences of a Major Event
Ch. 8 · Analyzing Causes and Effects
Ch. 9 · Writing Your Representative
Ch. 10 · Proposing a Solution to a Local Problem
Ch. 11 · Evaluating Film
Ch. 12 · Finding Credible Sources
Ch. 13 · Recommending Articles to a Friend
Ch. 14 · Analyzing the Web Site for Your Campus
Ch. 15 · Tracking Your Time Online
Ch. 16 · Using Visuals
Ch. 17 · Considering Job Advertisements
Ch. 19 · Brainstorming from a Video
Ch. 20 · Analyzing a Thesis
Ch. 21 · Identifying Topic Sentences and Identifying Transitions
Ch. 22 · Editing Sentences
Ch. 24 · Researching Genre

### Multimodal Learning from Other Writers Texts

In LaunchPad, the Learning from Other Writers feature in many Part Two and Part Three chapters includes a multimodal text with questions for analysis.

Ch. 4 · Howie Chackowicz, The Game Ain't Over 'til the Fatso Man Sings *[Audio]*
Ch. 5 · Multiple Photographers, Observing the *Titanic*: Past and Present *[Visual Essay]*
Ch. 6 · Tiana Chavez, ASU Athletes Discuss Superstitions *[Video]*
Ch. 7 · *National Geographic* Editors, Hurricane Katrina Pictures: Then & Now, Ruin & Rebirth *[Visual Essay]*
Ch. 8 · Brian Hurst, How Your Aggressive Driving Negatively Impacts the Environment *[Infographic]*
Ch. 9 · UNICEF Editors, Dirty Water Campaign *[Video]*
Ch. 10 · Casey Neistat, Texting While Walking *[Video]*
Ch. 11 · *Consumer Reports* Web Editors, Best Vanilla Ice Cream *[Video]*
Ch. 12 · Celebrity Culture Research Cluster: Cary Tennis, Why Am I Obsessed with Celebrity Gossip?; Karen Sternheimer, Celebrity Relationships: Why Do We Care?; Tom Ashbrook and Ty Burr, The Strange Power of Celebrity; Timothy J. Bertoni and Patrick D. Nolan, Dead Men Do Tell Tales *[Text, Audio, Video]*
Ch. 14 · Shannon Kintner, Charlie Living with Autism *[Student Visual Essay]*
Ch. 16 · Frank Deford, Mind Games: Football and Head Injuries *[Audio]*

### Reading Comprehension Quizzes

In LaunchPad, every reading in Book 1 (with the exception of student essays) is accompanied by an automatically graded reading comprehension quiz.

### LearningCurve

LearningCurve is an adaptive, formative quizzing engine with activities on critical reading, vocabulary, main ideas, supporting details, and organizational patterns.

## BOOK 2: *A WRITER'S READER*

### Reading Comprehension Quizzes

In LaunchPad, every reading in Book 2 is accompanied by an automatically graded reading comprehension quiz.

## BOOK 3: *A WRITER'S RESEARCH MANUAL*

### Learning by Doing

In LaunchPad, most chapters in Book 3 include an additional Learning by Doing activity designed for an online learning environment.

Ch. 30 · Narrowing Online Research
Ch. 31 · Comparing Google and Database Searches
Ch. 32 · Evaluating Online Sources
Ch. 33 · Practicing with Online Sources
Ch. 34 · Quoting and Paraphrasing Accurately
Ch. 35 · Practicing Beginnings

### LearningCurve

LearningCurve activities cover evaluating, integrating, and acknowledging sources in MLA and APA style.

### Exercise Central

Customizable research exercises are available in Exercise Central, a searchable quiz bank.

## BOOK 4: *A WRITER'S HANDBOOK*

### LearningCurve

LearningCurve activities cover grammar, usage, and punctuation.

### Exercise Central

Customizable exercises on grammar, punctuation, and style are available in Exercise Central, a searchable quiz bank.

# PAIRING *THE BEDFORD GUIDE* WITH *LAUNCHPAD SOLO FOR READERS AND WRITERS* HELPS STUDENTS SUCCEED AT THEIR OWN PACE

Use *LaunchPad Solo for Readers and Writers* to integrate skills-based practice into your teaching with *The Bedford Guide for College Writers*. Available free when packaged, it allows you to more efficiently track students' progress with reading, writing, and grammar skills in an active learning arc that complements the book.

To package *LaunchPad Solo for Readers and Writers* with a version of *The Bedford Guide*, use the appropriate ISBN:

- *The Bedford Guide for College Writers with Reader, Research Manual, and Handbook* (hardcover): 978-1-319-08120-1
- *The Bedford Guide for College Writers with Reader, Research Manual, and Handbook* (paperback): 978-1-319-08124-9
- *The Bedford Guide for College Writers with Reader*: 978-1-319-08118-8

For more information about *LaunchPad Solo for Readers and Writers*, visit **macmillanhighered.com/readwrite**.

To sign up for WebEx trainings with pedagogical specialists and access round-the-clock tech support, visit **www.macmillanlearning.com**.

---

**Assigning a Project for Which Students Will Need to Develop a Strong Thesis?**

**Integrate the learning arc in *LaunchPad Solo for Readers and Writers* to provide periodic assessment on core concepts that reinforces the instruction in *The Bedford Guide*.**

Before turning to Chapter 20, Strategies for Stating a Thesis and Planning, in *The Bedford Guide*, you can assign the **pre-test** to determine what knowledge your students already possess about the topic, helping you focus on meeting them where they are.

▼ Thesis Statements

**Thesis Statements**

This unit describes characteristics of an effective thesis statement.

**Add to this Unit**     **Browse Resources for this Unit**

**Pre-Test for Thesis Statements** (Questions with feedback)

**Introduction to Thesis Statements** (Read and Watch)

▶ **Study Pages: Thesis Statements**

**Post-Test for Thesis Statements** (Questions with feedback)

After students have completed the pre-test, have them watch the **introductory video** on thesis statements in *Launch-Pad Solo for Readers and Writers*.

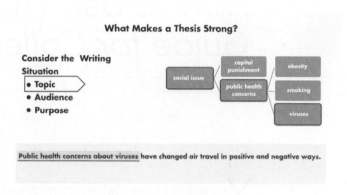

**What Makes a Thesis Strong?**

**Consider the Writing Situation**
- Topic
- Audience
- Purpose

Public health concerns about viruses have changed air travel in positive and negative ways.

---

Then, from *The Bedford Guide,* assign reading and Learning by Doing activities on the results of the pre-test. For example, if many students struggled to identify theses in the pre-test, you might choose to assign and focus considerable class time on the Learning by Doing activity Identifying Theses.

## Learning by Doing Identifying Theses

Working in a small group, select and read five essays from this book (or read those your instructor has chosen). Then, individually, write out the thesis for each essay. Some thesis statements are stated outright (explicit), but others are indirect (implicit). Compare and contrast the thesis statements you identified with those your classmates found. How do you account for differences? Try to agree on a thesis statement for each essay.

---

The **post-test** in *LaunchPad Solo for Readers and Writers* can help you to assess how well students have mastered the topic, and to determine whether some students will require more help before they begin building theses for their projects. Students who require further practice can complete relevant **LearningCurve adaptive quizzing activities**.

2. Frank is writing a reflection about why he decided to become an accountant. He listed several ideas. Which of the following ideas has a topic and a direction that can be developed into an effective thesis statement?

○ I grew up poor.
○ My parents couldn't handle money.
● Being an accountant helps teach financial responsibility, which I learned the hard way.

You are correct! This idea is a promising thesis statement. The topic is the reason why Frank values financial responsibility, and the essay's direction will explain who Frank learned it the hard way. For more help, see Introduction to Thesis Statements.

○ Many people spend without thinking.
Score: 1 of 1

# How to Use *The Bedford Guide for College Writers*

You may be wondering how any textbook can improve your writing. In fact, a book alone can't make you a better writer, but practice can, and *The Bedford Guide for College Writers* is designed to make your writing practice effective and productive. This text offers help — easy to find and easy to use — for writing the essays most commonly assigned in college.

Underlying *The Bedford Guide* is the idea that writing is a necessary and useful skill beyond the writing course. The skills you learn throughout this book are transferable to other areas of your life — future courses, jobs, and community activities — making *The Bedford Guide* both a time-saver and a money-saver. Read on to discover how you can get the most out of this text.

## Finding Information in *The Bedford Guide*

Each of the tools described here directs you to useful information — fast.

**Brief Contents.** In the Brief Contents (see the first book page), you have at a glance the list of topics covered in *The Bedford Guide*. The quickest way to find a specific chapter is by using the Brief Contents.

**LaunchPad Contents.** LaunchPad for *The Bedford Guide* is a customizable online course space with pre-built units corresponding to each chapter. It includes an e-book and a variety of related resources. Facing the inside front cover you will find a guide to content available in LaunchPad, including comprehensive lists of Learning by Doing activities and multimodal readings.

# Contents

Preface: To the Instructor    v

Rhetorical Contents    xxxiii

Selected Visual Contents    xxxvii

Features of *The Bedford Guide* Correlated to the WPA Outcomes Statement    xxxix

Inside LaunchPad for *The Bedford Guide*    xlvi

Pairing *The Bedford Guide* with *LaunchPad Solo for Readers and Writers*    xlviii

How to Use *The Bedford Guide*    l

**BOOK 1**  A WRITER'S GUIDE

Introduction: Writing in College    3

**Part One  A College Writer's Processes**    4

**1. Writing Processes**    6

Writing, Reading, and Critical Thinking    6

A Process of Writing    7
Getting Started    7
Generating Ideas    7
Learning by Doing  Reflecting on Ideas    8
Planning, Drafting, and Developing    8
Learning by Doing  Reflecting on Drafts    9
Revising and Editing    10
Learning by Doing  Reflecting on Finishing    11

Purpose and Audience    11
Writing for a Reason    11
Learning by Doing  Considering Purpose    11
Writing for Your Audience    13
Learning by Doing  Considering Audience    13
Targeting a College Audience    14
Learning by Doing  Writing for Different Audiences    15

Additional Writing Activities    15

**2. Reading Processes**    16

A Process of Critical Reading    16
Learning by Doing  Reflecting on Your Reading Strategies    17
Getting Started    17
Preparing to Read    17
Learning by Doing  Reflecting on Reading Preparation    18
Responding to Reading    19
Learning by Doing  Annotating a Passage    21
Learning by Doing  Reflecting on a Reading Journal    22

Learning from Another Writer: Reading Summary and Response    22
■ STUDENT SUMMARY AND RESPONSE:
  **Olof Eriksson,** The Problems with Masculinity    23

Reading on Literal and Analytical Levels    24
Learning by Doing  Reading Analytically    26
Generating Ideas from Reading    26

xix

**Contents.** Beginning on p. xix, the more detailed list of contents breaks down the topics covered within each chapter. Use this list to find a specific part of a chapter. For example, if you've been asked to read Olof Eriksson's paper "The Problems with Masculinity," a quick scan will show you that it begins on page 23.

**Rhetorical Contents.** This list, beginning on page xxxiii, includes all readings in *The Bedford Guide,* organized by writing strategy or situation, such as Explaining Causes and Effects, or Evaluating and Reviewing. Use this list to locate examples of the kind of writing you're doing and to see how other writers approached their material.

**Selected Visual Contents.** On page xxxvii is a list of many of the photos and other images in *The Bedford Guide,* arranged by type, genre, or purpose. This list can help you locate images, such as an ad or a visual essay, to analyze or compare in your writing. In our visual age, knowing how to read and analyze visuals and then write about them is a valuable skill.

**Locator Guide.** If you find yourself stuck at any stage of the writing process, open the book to the final page. The list there will help you find Learning by Doing activities, self-assessment flowcharts, and other resources. If you're having trouble writing an opening to your paper, for example, use this Locator Guide to turn to the right place at the right time.

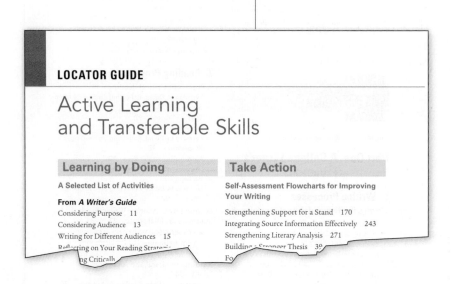

**LOCATOR GUIDE**

## Active Learning and Transferable Skills

### Learning by Doing

A Selected List of Activities

**From *A Writer's Guide***

Considering Purpose   11
Considering Audience   13
Writing for Different Audiences   15
Reflecting on Your Reading Strategi...
...ng Critically

### Take Action

Self-Assessment Flowcharts for Improving Your Writing

Strengthening Support for a Stand   170
Integrating Source Information Effectively   243
Strengthening Literary Analysis   271
Building a Stronger Thesis   39
Fo...

versus *a*, Q-50
Analogy, argument by, 172
Analysis
   of college assignments, 38
   as critical thinking skill, 35–36
   of process. *See* Process analysis
   as reading skill, 24–25, 25 (fig.)
   of subject. *See* Subject analysis
Analytical level of reading, 24–28
"Analyzing 'The New Literacy' "

**Index.** The index is an in-depth list of the book's contents. Turn to page I-1 to find the information available for a particular topic. This example shows you where to look for help with analyzing material, a common assignment in college.

**Guide to the Handbook.** After the index is a guide listing the contents of *A Writer's Handbook.* Turn to this guide for help editing your essays. It gives page numbers for each topic, such as "sentence fragments." If English is not your native language, this guide notes all the Guidelines for Multilingual Writers boxes included in the Handbook, such as What Is the Order for Cumulative Adjectives?

**Marginal Cross-References.** You can find additional information quickly by using the references in the margins — notes on the sides of each page that tell you where to turn in the book.

**Color-Coded Pages.** Several sections of *The Bedford Guide* are color-coded to make them easy to find.

- MLA Style (pp. 680–703). For help using MLA guidelines to document the sources in your paper, turn to the green-edged pages.

- APA Style (pp. 704–25). For help using APA guidelines to document the sources in your paper, turn to the **turquoise**-edged pages.

- Quick Format Guide (pp. Q-1–Q-19). For help formatting your paper, turn to this section at the back of the book, designated with gold-edged pages.

- Quick Research Guide (pp. Q-20–Q-36). For fast help with research processes, sources, or the basics of MLA or APA style, turn to this section at the back of the book, designated with orange-edged pages.

- Quick Editing Guide (pp. Q-37–Q-64). For help as you edit your writing, turn to this section at the back of the book, designated with blue-edged pages.

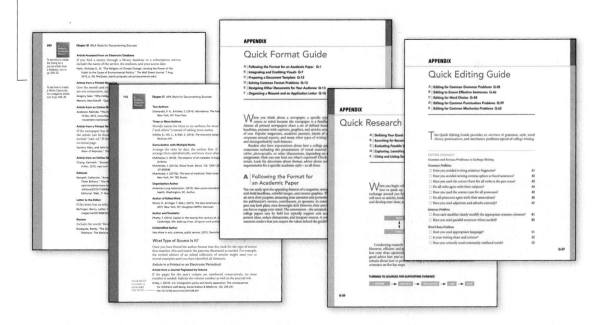

**Navigation Tabs.** Your instructor may use correction symbols, such as *agr* for subject-verb agreement, to indicate areas in your draft that need editing. Tabs at the top of each page in *A Writer's Handbook* link the explanations, examples, and exercises to the particular editing problem.

| Clauses and Phrases | **cl/ph 4b** | 747 |

**Answers to Exercises.** As you complete the Handbook exercises, you'll want to know if you're learning what is expected. Turn to the last section of the Handbook to find the correct answers to the lettered exercises.

# Becoming a Better Writer by Using *The Bedford Guide*

*The Bedford Guide* includes readings, checklists, activities, and other features to help you improve your writing and do well in college and on the job.

**Model Readings.** *The Bedford Guide* is filled with examples of both professional and student essays, located on the beige pages in *A Writer's Guide* and in *A Writer's Reader*. In LaunchPad, multimodal essays are also available. All these essays are accompanied by informative notes about the author, prereading questions, definitions of difficult words, questions for thinking more deeply about the reading, and suggestions for writing.

**Reading Annotations.** Student essays include questions in the margins to spark your imagination and your ideas as you read. Professional essays in *A Writer's Guide* include annotations to point out notable features, such as the thesis and supporting points.

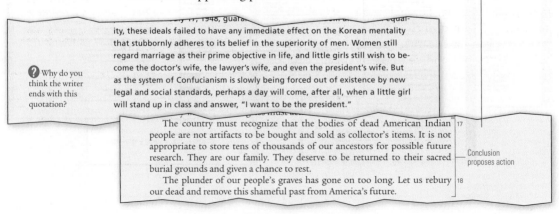

**?** Why do you think the writer ends with this quotation?

...y 17, 1948, guara... ...on a... ...equality, these ideals failed to have any immediate effect on the Korean mentality that stubbornly adheres to its belief in the superiority of men. Women still regard marriage as their prime objective in life, and little girls still wish to become the doctor's wife, the lawyer's wife, and even the president's wife. But as the system of Confucianism is slowly being forced out of existence by new legal and social standards, perhaps a day will come, after all, when a little girl will stand up in class and answer, "I want to be the president."

The country must recognize that the bodies of dead American Indian people are not artifacts to be bought and sold as collector's items. It is not appropriate to store tens of thousands of our ancestors for possible future research. They are our family. They deserve to be returned to their sacred burial grounds and given a chance to rest. — 17

Conclusion proposes action

The plunder of our people's graves has gone on too long. Let us rebury our dead and remove this shameful past from America's future. — 18

**Clear Assignments.** In Chapters 4–14, the Learning by Writing section presents the assignment for the chapter and guides you through the process of writing that type of essay. The Facing the Challenge section in each of these chapters helps you through the most complicated step in the assignment.

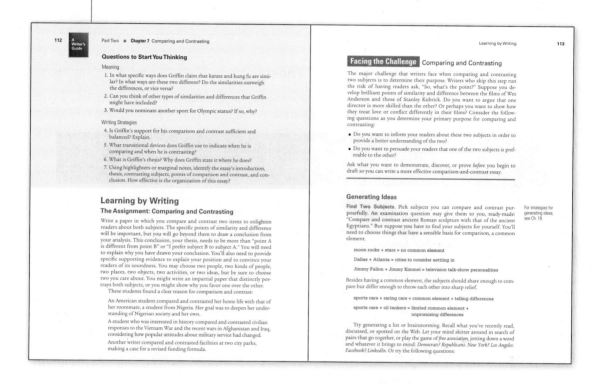

**Questions to Start You Thinking**

Meaning

1. In what specific ways does Griffin claim that karate and kung fu are similar? In what ways are these two different? Do the similarities outweigh the differences, or vice versa?

2. Can you think of other types of similarities and differences that Griffin might have included?

3. Would you nominate another sport for Olympic status? If so, why?

Writing Strategies

4. Is Griffin's support for his comparison and contrast sufficient and balanced? Explain.

5. What transitional devices does Griffin use to indicate when he is comparing and when he is contrasting?

6. What is Griffin's thesis? Why does Griffin state it where he does?

7. Using highlighters or marginal notes, identify the essay's introduction, thesis, contrasting subjects, points of comparison and contrast, and conclusion. How effective is the organization of this essay?

**Learning by Writing**

**The Assignment: Comparing and Contrasting**

Write a paper in which you compare and contrast two items to enlighten readers about both subjects. The specific points of similarity and difference will be important, but you will go beyond them to draw a conclusion from your analysis. This conclusion, your thesis, needs to be more than "point A is different from point B" or "I prefer subject B to subject A." You will need to explain why you have drawn your conclusion. You'll also need to provide specific supporting evidence to explain your position and to convince your readers of its soundness. You may choose two people, two kinds of people, two places, two objects, two activities, or two ideas, but be sure to choose two you care about. You might write an impartial paper that distinctly portrays both subjects, or you might show why you favor one over the other.

These students found a clear reason for comparison and contrast:

An American student compared and contrasted her home life with that of her roommate, a student from Nigeria. Her goal was to deepen her understanding of Nigerian society and her own.

A student who was interested in history compared and contrasted civilian responses to the Vietnam War and the recent wars in Afghanistan and Iraq, considering how popular attitudes about military service had changed.

Another writer compared and contrasted facilities at two city parks, making a case for a revised funding formula.

**Facing the Challenge**   Comparing and Contrasting

The major challenge that writers face when comparing and contrasting two subjects is to determine their purpose. Writers who skip this step run the risk of having readers ask, "So, what's the point?" Suppose you develop brilliant points of similarity and difference between the films of Wes Anderson and those of Stanley Kubrick. Do you want to argue that one director is more skilled than the other? Or perhaps you want to show how they treat love or conflict differently in their films? Consider the following questions as you determine your primary purpose for comparing and contrasting:

■ Do you want to inform your readers about these two subjects in order to provide a better understanding of the two?

■ Do you want to persuade your readers that one of the two subjects is preferable to the other?

Ask what you want to demonstrate, discover, or prove *before* you begin to draft so you can write a more effective comparison-and-contrast essay.

**Generating Ideas**

**Find Two Subjects.** Pick subjects you can compare and contrast purposefully. An examination question may give them to you, ready-made: "Compare and contrast ancient Roman sculpture with that of the ancient Egyptians." But suppose you have to find your subjects for yourself. You'll need to choose things that have a sensible basis for comparison, a common element.

> moon rocks + stars = no common element
>
> Dallas + Atlanta = cities to consider settling in
>
> Jimmy Fallon + Jimmy Kimmel = television talk-show personalities

Besides having a common element, the subjects should share enough to compare but differ enough to throw each other into sharp relief.

> sports cars + racing cars = common element + telling differences
>
> sports cars + oil tankers = limited common element + unpromising differences

Try generating a list or brainstorming. Recall what you've recently read, discussed, or spotted on the Web. Let your mind skitter around in search of pairs that go together, or play the game of *free association*, jotting down a word and whatever it brings to mind: *Democrats? Republicans. New York? Los Angeles. Facebook? LinkedIn.* Or try the following questions:

For strategies for generating ideas, see Ch. 19.

**Learning by Doing.** These activities are designed to let you practice and apply what you are learning to your own writing. They encourage you to make key concepts your own so that you will be able to take what you have learned and apply it in other writing situations and contexts in college and in the workplace.

**Learning by Doing** 🖉 Reflecting on Reading Preparation

How do you approach a college reading assignment? What is your thought process when preparing to read that assignment? Consider your reason or purpose: Why are you reading? Is it to prepare for a test? To write an essay? To perform research? Write a short reflection on the most effective approach for each of these different reading situations.

**Take Action Charts.** These flowcharts focus on common writing challenges. They help you to ask the right questions of your draft and to take active steps to revise effectively. They are a powerful tool in helping you become an independent writer, able to assess what you have written and improve it on your own.

# Take Action Building a Stronger Thesis

Ask each question listed in the left-hand column of the chart to consider whether your draft might need work on that issue. If so, follow the ASK — LOCATE SPECIFICS — TAKE ACTION sequence to revise.

| 1 ASK | 2 LOCATE SPECIFICS | 3 TAKE ACTION |
|---|---|---|
| Could I define or state my **topic** more clearly? | ■ Write out your current working thesis.<br><br>■ Circle the **words** in it that **identify your topic**.<br><br>**WORKING THESIS:** (Adaptability) is essential for World Action volunteers. [What, exactly, does the topic *adaptability* mean?] | ■ Rework the circled topic. State it more **clearly**, and specify what it **means to you**.<br><br>■ Define or identify the topic in terms of your **purpose** and the likely interests of your **audience**.<br><br>**REVISED THESIS:** An ability to adjust to, even thrive under, challenging circumstances is essential for World Action volunteers. |
| Could I define or state my **slant** more clearly? | ■ Write out your current working thesis.<br><br>■ Underline the **words that state your slant**, attitude, or point about your topic.<br><br>**WORKING THESIS:** Volunteering is <u>an invaluable experience</u>. [Why or in what ways is volunteering invaluable?] | ■ Rework your underlined slant. Jot down ideas to **sharpen** it and express an **engaging approach** to your topic.<br><br>■ Refine it to accomplish your **purpose** and appeal to your **audience**.<br><br>**REVISED THESIS:** Volunteering builds practical skills while connecting volunteers more fully to their communities. |
| Could I **limit my thesis** to develop it more successfully? | ■ Write out your current working thesis.<br><br>■ Decide whether it establishes a **task that you could accomplish** given the **available time** and the **expected length**.<br><br>**WORKING THESIS:** Rock and roll has evolved dramatically since the 1950s. [Tracing this history in a few pages would be impossible.] | ■ **Restrict your thesis to a slice of the pie**, not the whole pie.<br><br>■ **Focus on one part or element**, not several. Break it apart, and pick only a chunk.<br><br>■ **Reduce many ideas to one point**, or **convert a negative statement to a positive one**.<br><br>**REVISED THESIS:** The music of the alternative-rock band Wilco continues to evolve as members experiment with vocal moods and instrumentation. |

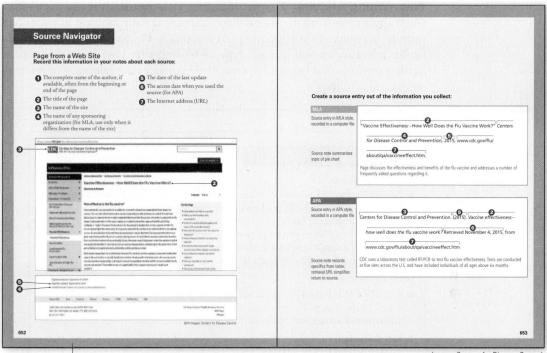

*Images:* Centers for Disease Control.

**Resources for Crediting Sources.** Source Navigators, on pages 648–55, show you where to look in several major types of sources so that you can quickly find the details needed to credit these sources correctly.

**Helpful Checklists.** Easy-to-use checklists help you to consider your purpose and audience, discover something to write about, get feedback from a peer, revise your draft, and edit for grammatical correctness, using references to the Quick Editing Guide (pp. Q-37–Q-64).

---

**VISUAL ANALYSIS CHECKLIST**

**Seeing the Big Picture**

☐ What is the source of the image? What is its purpose and audience?

☐ What prominent element in the image immediately attracts your attention? How and why does it draw you into the image?

☐ What is the focal point of the image? How does the image direct your attention to this point? What path does your eye follow as you observe the image?

**Why Writing Matters.** The writing skills that you learn using *The Bedford Guide* apply to writing in other college courses, at your job, and in your community. Sections at the beginning of Chapters 4–17 consider the current and future relevance to you of each type of writing that you do in this course. Similar sections that begin Chapters 30–35 consider the relevance of research stages and activities.

---

### Why Taking a Stand Matters

**In a College Course**

- You take a stand in an essay or exam when you respond, pro or con, to a statement such as "The Web, like movable type for printing, is an invention that has transformed human communication."
- You take a stand when you write research papers that support your position on juvenile sentencing, state support for higher education, or greater access to affordable housing.

**In the Workplace**

- You take a stand when you persuade others that your case report supports a legal action that will benefit your clients or that your customer-service initiative will attract new business.

**In Your Community**

- You take a stand when you write a letter to the editor appealing to voters to support a local bond issue.

❓ When have you taken a stand in your writing? In what circumstances are you likely to do so again?

# A WRITER'S GUIDE

# A Writer's Guide Contents

## Part One  A College Writer's Processes

1. Writing Processes  6
2. Reading Processes  16
3. Critical Thinking Processes  35

## Part Two  A Writer's Situations

4. Recalling an Experience  46
5. Observing a Scene  65
6. Interviewing a Subject  84
7. Comparing and Contrasting  105
8. Explaining Causes and Effects  125
9. Taking a Stand  144
10. Proposing a Solution  176
11. Evaluating and Reviewing  196
12. Supporting a Position with Sources  214

## Part Three  Other Writing Situations

13. Responding to Literature  250
14. Responding to Visual Representations  281
15. Writing Online  307
16. Writing and Presenting under Pressure  324
17. Writing in the Workplace  338

*All images above:* David L. Ryan/
The Boston Globe/Getty Images.

## Part Four  A Writer's Strategies

18. Strategies: A Case Study  358
19. Strategies for Generating Ideas  369
20. Strategies for Stating a Thesis and Planning  383
21. Strategies for Drafting  404
22. Strategies for Developing  421
23. Strategies for Revising and Editing  442
24. Strategies for Writing in Future Courses  459

Tiridifilm/E+/Getty Images.

# Introduction: Writing in College

As a college writer you probably wrestle with the question, What should I write? You may feel you have nothing to say or nothing worth saying. Maybe your difficulty lies in understanding the requirements of your writing situation, finding a topic, or uncovering information about it. Perhaps you, like many other college writers, have convinced yourself that professional writers have some special way of discovering ideas for writing. But they have no magic. In reality, what they have is experience and confidence, the products of lots of practice writing.

In *The Bedford Guide for College Writers,* we want you to become a better writer by actually writing. To help you do so, we'll give you a lot of practice as well as useful advice to help you build your skills and confidence. Because writing and learning to write are many-faceted tasks, each part of *A Writer's Guide* is devoted to a different aspect of writing. Together, these four parts contribute to a seamless whole, much like the writing process itself.

**Part One, "A College Writer's Processes."** This part introduces writing, reading, and thinking critically—essential processes for meeting college expectations.

**Part Two, "A Writer's Situations."** The nine chapters in Part Two form the core of *The Bedford Guide*. Each presents a writing situation and then guides you as you write a paper in response. You'll develop skills in recalling, observing, interviewing, comparing and contrasting, explaining causes and effects, taking a stand, proposing a solution, evaluating and reviewing, and supporting a position with sources.

**Part Three, "Other Writing Situations."** This part leads you through five special situations that most students encounter at some point—writing about literature or visuals and writing online, under pressure, or at work.

**Part Four, "A Writer's Strategies."** Part Four opens with one student's strategies, showing how a paper evolves from idea to final form. The rest is packed with tips and activities that you can use to generate ideas, plan, draft, develop, revise, edit, and carry to the future what you have learned as a writer.

# A COLLEGE WRITER'S PROCESSES

# 1 Writing Processes

You are already a writer with long experience. In school you have taken notes, written book reports and term papers, answered exam questions, perhaps kept a journal. In the community or on the job you've composed e-mails and perhaps letters. You've sent text messages or tweets to friends, made lists, maybe even written songs or poetry. All this experience is about to pay off as you tackle college writing, learning by doing.

## Writing, Reading, and Critical Thinking

For more on reading critically, see Ch. 2. For more on thinking critically, see Ch. 3.

In college you will expand what you already know about writing. You may be asked not only to recall an experience but also to reflect upon its significance. Or you may go beyond summarizing positions about an issue to present your own position or propose a solution. Above all, you'll read and think critically—not just stacking up facts but analyzing what you discover, deciding what it means, and weighing its value. As you read—and write—actively, you will engage with the ideas of others, analyzing and judging those ideas. You will use criteria—models, conventions, principles, standards—to assess or evaluate what you're doing.

---

WRITER'S CHECKLIST

☐ Have you achieved your purpose?

☐ Have you considered your audience?

☐ Have you clearly stated your point as a thesis or unmistakably implied it?

☐ Have you supported your point with enough reliable evidence to persuade your audience?

☐ Have you arranged your ideas logically so that each follows from, supports, or adds to the one before it?

☐ Have you made the connections among ideas clear to a reader?

☐ Have you established an appropriate tone?

---

In large measure, learning to write well is learning what questions to ask as you write. For that reason, we include questions, suggestions, and activities to help you accomplish your writing tasks and reflect on your own processes as you write, read, and think critically.

# A Process of Writing

Writing can seem at times an overwhelming drudgery, worse than scrubbing floors; at other moments, it's a sport full of thrills—like whizzing downhill on skis, not knowing what you'll meet around a bend. Unpredictable as the process may seem, nearly all writers do similar things:

- They generate ideas.
- They plan, draft, and develop their papers.
- They revise and edit.

These three activities form the basis of most effective writing processes, and they lie at the heart of each writing situation in this book.

## Getting Started

Two considerations—what you want to accomplish as a writer and how you want to appeal to your audience—will shape the direction of your writing. Clarifying your purpose and considering your audience are likely to increase your confidence as a writer. Even so, your writing process may take you in unexpected directions, not necessarily in a straight line. You can skip around, work on several parts at a time, test a fresh approach, circle back over what's already done, or stop to play with a sentence until it clicks.

## Generating Ideas

The first activity in writing—finding a topic and something to say about it—is often the most challenging and least predictable. The chapter section titled "Generating Ideas" is filled with examples, questions, checklists, and visuals designed to trigger ideas that will help you begin the writing assignment.

**Discovering What to Write About.** You may get an idea while texting friends, riding your bike, or staring out the window. Sometimes a topic lies near home, in a conversation or an everyday event. Often, your reading will raise questions that call for investigation. Even if an assignment doesn't appeal to you, your challenge is to find a slant that does. Find it, and words will flow—words to engage readers and accomplish your purpose.

**Discovering Material.** To shape and support your ideas, you'll need facts and figures, reports and opinions, examples and illustrations. How do you find supporting material that makes your slant on a topic clear and convincing? Luckily you have many sources at your fingertips. You can recall your experience and knowledge, observe things around you, talk with others who

For information and journal questions about the Part One photograph, see About the Photographs at the end of the book.

For full chapters on stages of the writing process, see Chs. 18–24.

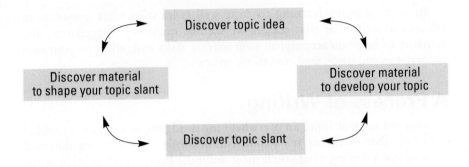

are knowledgeable, read enlightening materials that draw you to new approaches, and think critically about all these sources.

For an online class discussion of writing processes, see pp. 315–17.

### Learning by Doing  Reflecting on Ideas

Think over past writing experiences at school or work. How do you get ideas? Where do they come from? Where do you turn for related material? What are your most reliable sources of inspiration and information? Share your experiences with others in class or online, noting any new approaches you would like to try.

## Planning, Drafting, and Developing

Next you will plan your paper, write a draft, and develop your ideas further. The section titled "Planning, Drafting, and Developing" will help you through these stages for the assignment in that chapter.

**Planning.** Having discovered a burning idea to write about (or at least a smoldering one) and some supporting material (but maybe not enough yet), you'll sort out what matters most. If you see one main point, or thesis, test various ways of stating it, given your purpose and audience:

MAYBE    Parking in the morning before class is annoying.

OR    Campus parking is a big problem.

Next, arrange your ideas and material in a sensible order that will clarify your point. For example, you might group and label your ideas, make an outline, or analyze the main point, breaking it down into parts:

Parking on campus is a problem for students because of the long lines, inefficient entrances, and poorly marked spaces.

But if no clear thesis emerges quickly, don't worry. You may find one while you draft — that is, while you write an early version of your paper.

PLAN

- Identify your purpose and audience
- Decide on one main point
- State a thesis
- Organize ideas by grouping or outlining

DEVELOP

- Explain and support
- Add definitions, examples, and details
- Supply evidence such as facts, statistics, expert testimony, and observations

DRAFT

- Start and restart
- Build paragraphs
- Open and conclude
- Create coherence

**Processes for Planning, Drafting, and Developing**

**Drafting.** As your ideas begin to appear, write them down before they can go back into hiding. When you take risks at this stage, you'll probably be surprised and pleased at what happens, even though your first version will be rough. Writing takes time; a paper usually needs several drafts and maybe a clearer introduction, a stronger conclusion, more convincing evidence, or even a fresh start.

**Developing.** Weave in explanations, definitions, examples, and other evidence to make your ideas clear and persuasive. For example, you may define an at-risk student, illustrate the problems of single parents, or supply statistics about hit-and-run accidents. If you need specific support for your point, use strategies for developing ideas — or return to those for generating ideas. Work in your insights if they fit.

For advice on using a few sources, see the Quick Research Guide, pp. Q-20–Q-36.

## Learning by Doing 🔘 Reflecting on Drafts

Reflect on your past writing experiences. How do you usually plan, draft, and develop your writing? How well do your methods work? How do you adjust them to the situation or type of writing you're doing? Which part of producing a draft do you most dread, enjoy, or wish to change? Why? Write down your reflections, and then share your experiences with others.

## Revising and Editing

You might be tempted to relax once you have a draft, but for most writers, revising begins the work in earnest. Each "Revising and Editing" section provides checklists as well as suggestions for working with a peer.

**Revising.** Revising means both reseeing and rewriting, making major changes so your paper does what you want it to. You might reconsider your purpose and audience, rework your thesis, decide what to put in or leave out, move paragraphs around, and connect ideas better. Perhaps you'll add costs to a paper on parking problems or switch attention from mothers to fathers as you consider single parents.

If you put aside your draft for a few hours or a day, you can reread it with fresh eyes and a clear mind. Other students can also help you by responding to your drafts as engaged readers.

For editing advice, see the Quick Editing Guide, pp. Q-37–Q-64. For format advice, see the Quick Format Guide, pp. Q-1–Q-19.

**Editing.** Editing means refining details, improving wording, and correcting flaws that may stand in the way of your readers' understanding and enjoyment. Don't edit too early, though, because you may waste time on parts that you later revise out. In editing, you usually make these repairs:

- Drop unnecessary words; choose lively and precise words.
- Replace incorrect or inappropriate wording.
- Rearrange words in a clearer, more emphatic order.
- Combine short, choppy sentences, or break up long, confusing ones.
- Refine transitions for continuity of thought.
- Check grammar, usage, punctuation, and mechanics.

**Proofreading.** Finally you'll proofread, taking a last look, checking correctness, and catching doubtful spellings or word-processing errors.

| REVISE | ← PEER → RESPONSE | EDIT | | PROOFREAD |
|---|---|---|---|---|
| • Purpose | | • Grammar | | • Spelling |
| • Thesis | | • Sentences | | • Incorrect words |
| • Audience | | • Word choice | | • Missing words |
| • Structure | | • Punctuation | | • Minor errors |
| • Support | | • Mechanics | | • Minor details |
| • Language | | • Format for paper | | |

## Learning by Doing  Reflecting on Finishing

Think over past high-pressure writing experiences, such as major papers at school or reports at work. What steps do you take to rethink and refine your writing before submitting or posting it? What prompts you to make major changes? How do you try to satisfy concerns of your main reader or a broader audience? Work with others in class or online to collect and share your best ideas about wrapping up writing projects.

# Purpose and Audience

At any moment in the writing process, two questions are worth asking:

WHY AM I WRITING?                    WHO IS MY AUDIENCE?

## Writing for a Reason

Like most college writing assignments, every assignment in this book asks you to write for a definite reason. For example, you'll recall a memorable experience in order to explain its importance for you; you'll take a stand on a controversy in order to convey your position and persuade readers to respect it. Be careful not to confuse the sources and strategies you apply in these assignments with your ultimate purpose for writing. "To compare and contrast two things" is not a very interesting purpose; "to compare and contrast two Web sites *in order to explain which is more reliable*" implies a real reason for writing. In most college writing, your purpose will be to explain something to your readers or to convince them of something.

For more on using your purpose for planning, see pp. 383–84, and for revising, see pp. 443–44.

To sharpen your concentration on your purpose, ask yourself from the start: What do I want to do? And, in revising, Did I do what I meant to do? These practical questions will help you slice out irrelevant information and remove other barriers to getting your paper where you want it to go.

## Learning by Doing  Considering Purpose

Imagine that you are in the following writing situations. For each, write a sentence or two summing up your purpose as a writer.

1. The instructor in your psychology course has assigned a paragraph about the meanings of three essential terms in your readings.
2. You're upset about a change in financial aid procedures and plan to write a letter asking the financial aid director to remedy the problem.

3. You're starting a blog about your first year at college so your extended family can envision the environment and share your experiences.
4. Your supervisor wants you to write an article about the benefits of a new company service for the customer newsletter.
5. Your Facebook profile seemed appropriate last year, but you want to revise it now that you're attending college and have a job with future prospects.

## Audience Characteristics and Expectations

| | General Audience | College Instructor | Work Supervisor | Campus Friend |
|---|---|---|---|---|
| **Relationship to You** | Imagined but not known personally | Known briefly in a class context | Known for some time in a job context | Known in campus and social contexts |
| **Reason for Reading Your Writing** | Curious attitude and interest in your topic assumed | Professional responsibility for your knowledge and skills | Managerial interest in and reliance on your job performance | Personal interest based on shared circumstances |
| **Knowledge about Your Topic** | Level of awareness assumed and gaps addressed with logical presentation | Well informed about college topics but wants to see what you know | Informed about the business and expects reliable information from you | Friendly but may or may not be informed beyond social interests |
| **Forms and Formats Expected** | Essay, article, letter, report, or other format | Essay, report, research paper, or other academic format | Memo, report, Web page, e-mail, or letter using company format | Notes, blog entries, social networking, or other informal messages |
| **Language and Style Expected** | Formal, using clear words and sentences | Formal, following academic conventions | Appropriate for advancing you and the company | Informal, using abbreviations, phrases, and slang |
| **Attitude and Tone Expected** | Interested and thoughtful about the topic | Serious and thoughtful about the topic and course | Respectful, showing reliability and work ethic | Friendly and interested in shared experiences |
| **Amount of Detail Expected** | Enough to inform or persuade general readers | Enough sound or research-based evidence to support your thesis | General or technical information as needed | Much detail or little, depending on the topic |

# Writing for Your Audience

Your audience may or may not be defined in your assignment. Consider the following examples:

For more on planning for your readers, see pp. 383–84. For more on revising for them, see pp. 444–45.

ASSIGNMENT 1          Discuss the advantages and disadvantages of homeschooling.

ASSIGNMENT 2          In a letter to parents of school-aged children, discuss the advantages and disadvantages of homeschooling.

If your assignment defines an audience, as the second example does, you need to think about how to approach those readers and what to assume about their views. For example, what points would you include in a discussion aimed at parents? How would you organize your ideas? Would you discuss advantages or disadvantages first? On the other hand, how might your approach differ if the assignment read this way?

ASSIGNMENT 3          In a newsletter article for teachers, discuss the advantages and disadvantages of homeschooling.

Audiences may be identified by characteristics, such as role (parents) or occupation (teachers), that suggest values to which a writer might appeal. As the chart above suggests, you can analyze preferences, biases, and concerns of readers to engage and influence them more successfully.

## AUDIENCE CHECKLIST

☐ Who are your readers? What is their relationship to you?

☐ What do they know about this topic? What do you want them to learn?

☐ How much detail will they want to read about this topic?

☐ What objections are they likely to raise as they read? How can you anticipate and overcome their objections?

☐ What is likely to convince them? What's likely to offend them?

☐ What tone and style would most effectively influence them?

## Learning by Doing 🎥 Considering Audience

Read the notices on page 14 directed to subscribers of two magazines, *Zapped!* and *works & conversations*. Examine the style, tone, language, sequence of topics, and other features of each appeal. Write a short paragraph about each notice, explaining what you can conclude about the letter's target audience and its appeal to that audience.

## *Zapped!* misses you.

Dear Dan Morrison,

All last year, *Zapped!* magazine made the trek to 5 Snowden Lane and it was always a great experience. You took great care of *Zapped!*, and *Zapped!* gave you hours of entertainment, with news and interviews from the latest indie bands, honest-as-your-momma reviews of musical equipment, and your first glimpse of some of the finest graphic serials being published today.

But, Dan, we haven't heard from you and are starting to wonder what's up. Don't you miss *Zapped!*? One thing's for sure: *Zapped!* misses you.

We'd like to re-establish the relationship: if you renew your subscription by March 1, you'll get 20% off last year's subscription price. That's only $24 for another year of great entertainment. Just fill out the other side of this card and send it back to us; we'll bill you later.

Come on, Dan. Why wait?

Thanks,

**Carly Bevins**

Carly Bevins
Director of Sales

**Figure 1.1** Renewal letter from *Zapped!*

**Figure 1.2** Appeal to readers of *works & conversations*. Richard Whittaker

## Targeting a College Audience

Many of your college assignments may assume that you are addressing general college readers, represented by your instructor and possibly your classmates. Such readers typically expect clear, logical writing with supporting evidence to explain or persuade. Of course, the format, approach, or evidence may differ by field. For example, biologists might expect the findings from your experiment, while literature specialists might look for relevant quotations from the novel you're analyzing.

### COLLEGE AUDIENCE CHECKLIST

☐ How has your instructor advised you to write for readers? What criteria related to audience will be used for grading your papers?

☐ What do the assigned readings in your course assume about an audience? Has your instructor recommended models or sample readings?

☐ What topics intrigue readers in the course area? What problems do they want to solve? How do they want to solve them?

☐ How is writing in the course area commonly organized? For example, do writers tend to follow a persuasive pattern—introducing the issue, stating an assertion or a claim, backing the claim with evidence, acknowledging other views, and concluding? Or do they use conventional headings—perhaps *Abstract, Introduction, Methodology, Findings,* and *Discussion?*

☐ What evidence typically supports ideas or interpretations—facts and statistics, quotations from texts, summaries of research, experimental findings, observations, or interviews?

☐ What style, tone, and level of formality do writers in the field use?

For more strategies for future college writing, see Ch. 24.

## Learning by Doing 🎥 Writing for Different Audiences

Imagine that you've been in a minor car accident. Write out the descriptions of the incident you'd give to the following audiences: a close friend, your parents, a police officer, and the insurance company. How does the language change, if at all? To whom are certain details accentuated or downplayed? Write a paragraph or more to reflect about the differences between the stories.

## Additional Writing Activities

1. Write a few paragraphs or an online posting about your personal goals as a writer during this class. What do you already do well as a writer? What do you need to improve? What do you hope to accomplish? How might you benefit, in college or elsewhere, from improving your writing?

2. **Source Activity.** Select a passage from a textbook or reading assigned in a course. Rewrite the passage for a nonacademic audience (such as readers of a specific magazine or newspaper, visitors to a certain Web site, or interested amateurs).

3. **Source Activity.** Find a nonacademic article, pamphlet, or Web page. Try your hand at rewriting a passage as a college textbook or reading in the field might present the material. Then write an informal paragraph explaining why this task was easy, challenging, or impossible.

4. **Visual Activity.** Working with classmates, examine an academic and a nonacademic resource (such as those for questions 2 and 3 above). Compare and contrast physical features such as page layout, arrangement of text and space, images, color, type size and font, section divisions, and source credits. Write a paragraph about each resource, explaining how its features serve its purpose and appeal to its audience.

# 2 Reading Processes

What's so special about college reading? Don't you just pick up the book, start on the first page, and keep going as you have ever since you met *The Cat in the Hat*? Reading from beginning to end works especially well when you are eager to find out what happens next, as in a thriller, or what to do next, as in a cookbook. On the other hand, the dense, challenging texts typical of college will require closer reading and deeper thinking—in short, a process for reading critically.

## A Process of Critical Reading

For more on critical thinking, see Ch. 3.

Reading critically means approaching whatever you read in an active, questioning manner. This essential college-level skill changes reading from a spectator sport to a contact sport. You no longer sit in the stands, watching graceful skaters glide by. Instead, you charge right into a rough-and-tumble hockey game, gripping your stick and watching out for your teeth.

Critical reading, like critical thinking, is not an activity reserved for college courses. It is a continuum of strategies that thoughtful people use every day to grapple with new information, to integrate it with existing knowledge, and to apply it to problems in daily life:

- They get ready to do their reading.
- They respond as they read.
- They read on literal and analytical levels.

Building your critical reading skills will open the door to information you've never encountered and to ideas unlikely to come up with friends. For this course alone, you will be prepared to evaluate strengths and weaknesses of essays by professionals, students, and classmates. If you research a topic, you will be ready to figure out what your sources say, what they assume and imply, whether they are sound, and how you might use them to help make your point. In addition, you can apply your expanded skills in other courses, your job, and your community.

Many instructors help you develop your skills. Some prepare you by previewing a reading so you learn its background or structure. Others supply reading questions so you know what to look for or give motivational credit for reading responses. Still others may share their own reading processes with you, revealing what they read first (maybe the opening and conclusion) or how they might decide to skip a section (such as Methods in a report whose conclusions they want first).

In the end, however, making the transition to college reading requires your time and energy—and both will be well spent. Once you build your skills as a critical reader, you'll save time by reading more effectively, and you'll save energy by improving both your reading and your writing.

## Learning by Doing 🔟 Reflecting on Your Reading Strategies

Which of the methods discussed in this chapter do you use and find effective when reading textbooks, articles, and other materials for college classes? In what situations do you change your reading methods, and for what purposes? Is each of the methods you use the most effective one for your purpose? If any of the methods covered in this chapter are new to you, can you think of situations in which you might apply them? Based on your responses to these questions and further reflection, how can you improve your reading habits?

## Getting Started

College reading is active reading. Your instructors expect you to do far more than recognize the words on the page. They want you to read their assignments critically and then to think and write critically about what you have read.

Your instructors will want you to learn the strategies that they and other experienced readers apply to complex texts.

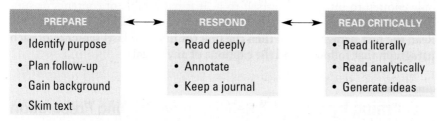

| PREPARE | RESPOND | READ CRITICALLY |
|---|---|---|
| • Identify purpose | • Read deeply | • Read literally |
| • Plan follow-up | • Annotate | • Read analytically |
| • Gain background | • Keep a journal | • Generate ideas |
| • Skim text | | |

## Preparing to Read

Before you read, think ahead about how to make the most of the experience.

**Thinking about Your Purpose.** When you begin to read, ask questions like these about your immediate purpose:

- What are you reading?
- Why are you reading? What do you want to do with the reading?

- What does your instructor expect you to learn from the reading?
- Do you need to memorize details, find main points, or connect ideas?
- How does this reading build on, add to, contrast with, or otherwise relate to other reading assignments in the course?

**Planning Your Follow-Up.** When you are required to read or to select a reading, ask yourself what your instructor expects to follow it:

- Do you need to be ready to discuss the reading during class?
- Will you need to mention it or analyze it during an examination?
- Will you need to write about it or its topic?
- Do you need to find its main points? Sum it up? Compare it? Question it? Spot its strengths and weaknesses? Draw useful details from it?

**Gaining Background.** Knowing a reading's context, approach, or frame of reference can help you predict where the reading is likely to go and how it relates to other readings. Begin with your available resources:

- Do the syllabus and class notes reveal why your instructor assigned the reading? What can you learn from reading questions, tips about what to watch for, or connections with other readings?
- Does your reading have a book jacket or preface, an introduction or abstract that sums it up, or reading pointers or questions?
- Does any enlightening biographical or professional information about the author accompany the reading?
- Can you identify or speculate about the reading's original audience based on its content, style, tone, or publication history?

**Skimming the Text.** Before you actively read a text, skim it—quickly read only enough to introduce yourself to it. If it has a table of contents or subheadings, read those first to figure out what it covers and how it is organized. Read the first paragraph and then the first (or first and last) sentence of each paragraph that follows. Read the captions of any visuals.

## Learning by Doing  Reflecting on Reading Preparation

How do you approach a college reading assignment? What is your thought process when preparing to read that assignment? Consider your reason or purpose: Why are you reading? Is it to prepare for a test? To write an essay? To perform research? Write a short reflection on the most effective approach for each of these different reading situations.

## Responding to Reading

You may be accustomed to reading simply for facts or main ideas. However, critical reading is far more active than fact hunting. It requires responding, questioning, and challenging as you read.

**Reading Deeply.** College assignments often require more concentration than other readings do. Use these questions to dive below the surface:

- How does the writer begin? What does the opening paragraph or section reveal about the writer's purpose and point? How does the writer prepare readers for what follows?

- How might you trace the progression of ideas in the reading? How do headings, previews of what's coming up, summaries of what's gone before, and transitions signal the organization?

- Are difficult or technical terms defined in specific ways? How might you highlight, list, or record such terms so that you master them?

- How might you record or recall the details in the reading? How could you track or diagram interrelated ideas to grasp their connections?

- How do word choice, tone, and style alert you to the complex purpose of a reading that is layered or indirect rather than straightforward?

- Does the reading include figurative or descriptive language, references to other works, or recurring themes? How do these enrich the reading?

- Can you answer any reading questions in your textbook, assignment, or syllabus? Can you restate headings in question form to create your own questions and then supply the answers? For example, change "Major Types of X" to "What are the major types of X?"

For more on figurative language, see p. 262.

For more on evaluating what you read, see Section C in the Quick Research Guide, pp. Q-25–Q-27.

**Annotating the Text.** Writing notes on the page (or on a copy if the material is not your own) is a useful way to trace the author's points, question them, and add your own comments as they pop up. The following passage is the introduction of "Sibling Rivalry, a History," by Peter Toohey. This article was published on the *Atlantic*'s Web site (theatlantic.com) on November 30, 2014. Notice how one writer annotated the passage.

For a Critical Reading Checklist, see p. 27.

At its most benign, <u>family jealousy between siblings reflects a competition for resources—coupled with the bonds of kinship, which are equally strong.</u> St. Augustine, in his *Confessions*, described having "personally watched and studied a jealous baby. He could not yet speak and, pale with jealousy and bitterness, glared at his brother sharing his mother's milk. Who is unaware of this fact of experience?"

*Key point — balance between competition and kinship*

*True! I've seen this look in my own children's faces.*

*Sounds almost like the description of a TV drama*

*Scary stuff. I wonder how extreme things can get with humans.*

*Never heard the term "siblicide" before!*

*Good quote from an authoritative source*

*Maybe sibling cooperation is also beneficial for survival?*

*Will the author explore that angle?*

*Biology helps drive behavior — in multiple species*

This heady mix can lead to all sorts of jealous rivalry and internecine warfare. It's evident in the animal kingdom, where actual family cannibalism also takes place. The animal behaviorist Scott Forbes makes some fascinating links between sibling rivalry in animals and humans. This is not sexual jealousy, but involves real birds and bees. Forbes describes how herpetologists, ornithologists, and mammalogists found that "infanticide—including siblicide—was a routine feature of family life in many species," most commonly seen in birds. Some birds lay two eggs "to insure against failure of the first egg to hatch. If both hatch, the second chick is redundant to the parents, and a potentially lethal competitor to the first-hatched progeny." The healthy older chick often kills the younger to eliminate the competition, and some parents actually encourage siblicide when the death of the nest-mate doesn't naturally occur.

After all, if resources are scarce, it's better that the strongest offspring survive and that their potential efforts go to ensuring that happens. (It's the old story of genetic replication again: Surviving offspring are more likely to have the strongest genes, and they are the ones that have the best chance of reproducing later and passing those genes on.) Forbes thinks that such extreme jealous reactions are not common in the human species, but "the more modest forms of sibling rivalry that are ubiquitous in species with extensive parental care—the scrambles for food and begging competitions—resemble more closely the dynamics that occur in human families."

When you annotate a reading, don't passively highlight big chunks of text. Instead, respond actively using pen or pencil or adding a comment to a file. Next, read slowly and carefully so that you can follow what the reading says and how it supports its point. Record your own reactions, not what you think you are supposed to say:

- Jot down things you already know or have experienced to build your own connection to the reading.
- Circle key words, star or check ideas when you agree or disagree, add arrows to mark connections, or underline key points, ideas, or definitions to learn the reading's vocabulary.
- Add question marks or questions about meaning or implications.
- Separate main points from supporting evidence and detail. Then you can question a conclusion, or challenge the evidence that supports it. (Main points often open a section or paragraph, followed by supporting detail, but sometimes this pattern is reversed.)
- React to quotable sentences or key passages. If they are hard to understand, restate them in your own words.
- Talk to the writer—maybe even talk back. Challenge weak points, respond with your own thoughts, draw in other views, or boost the writer's persuasive ideas.

- Sum up the writer's main point, supporting ideas, and notable evidence or examples.
- Consider how the reading appeals to your head, heart, or conscience.

## Learning by Doing 📷 Annotating a Passage

Annotate the following passage. It opens a report titled *The Evolving Role of News on Twitter and Facebook*, which was published by the Pew Research Center on July 14, 2015.

For a sample annotated passage, see pp. 19–20.

1   The share of Americans for whom Twitter and Facebook serve as a source of news is continuing to rise. This rise comes primarily from more current users encountering news there rather than large increases in the user base overall, according to findings from a new survey. The report also finds that users turn to each of these prominent social networks to fulfill different types of information needs.

2   The new study, conducted by Pew Research Center in association with the John S. and James L. Knight Foundation, finds that clear majorities of Twitter (63%) and Facebook users (63%) now say each platform serves as a source for news about events and issues outside the realm of friends and family. That share has increased substantially from 2013, when about half of users (52% of Twitter users, 47% of Facebook users) said they got news from the social platforms.

3   Although both social networks have the same portion of users getting news on these sites, there are significant differences in their potential news distribution strengths. The proportion of users who say they follow breaking news on Twitter, for example, is nearly twice as high as those who say they do so on Facebook (59% vs. 31%) — lending support, perhaps, to the view that Twitter's great strength is providing as-it-happens coverage and commentary on live events.

4   These findings come at a time when the two social media platforms are increasing their emphasis on news. Twitter is soon set to unveil its long-rumored news feature, "Project Lightning." The feature will allow anyone, whether they are a Twitter user or not, to view a feed of tweets, images and videos about live events as they happen, curated by a bevy of new employees with "newsroom experience." And, in early 2015, Twitter purchased and launched the live video-streaming app Periscope, further highlighting their focus on providing information about live events as they happen. Meanwhile, in May, Facebook launched Instant Articles, a trial project that allows media companies to publish stories directly to the Facebook platform instead of linking to outside sites, and, in late June, Facebook started introducing its "Trending" sidebar to allow users to filter by topic and see only trending news about politics, science and technology, sports or entertainment.

5   As more social networking sites recognize and adapt to their role in the news environment, each will offer unique features for news users, and these features may foster shifts in news use. Those different uses around news features have implications for how Americans learn about the world and their communities, and for how they take part in the democratic process.

For advice on keeping a writer's journal, see Ch. 19.

**Keeping a Reading Journal.** A reading journal is an excellent place to record not just what you read but how you respond to it. As you read actively, you will build a reservoir of ideas for follow-up writing. Address questions like these in a special notebook or digital file:

- What is the subject of the reading? What is the writer's stand?
- What does the writer take for granted? What assumptions does he or she begin with? Where are these stated or suggested?
- What are the writer's main points? What evidence supports them?
- Do you agree with what the writer has said? Do his or her ideas clash with or question your assumptions?
- Has the writer told you more than you wanted to know or failed to tell you something you wish you knew?
- What conclusions can you draw from the reading?
- Has the reading helped you see the subject in new ways?

### Learning by Doing 🖉 Reflecting on a Reading Journal

Consider keeping a reading journal that includes all of your research notes for a specific essay you've been assigned, providing commentary on each entry. Ask questions in the journal. Make observations. All your notes will be kept in one location; think about why this method could be effective for your writing process. What are the advantages of a reading journal? Can you think of any disadvantages? How might you improve your current journal-keeping strategies?

## Learning from Another Writer: Reading Summary and Response

For another reading response on both literal and analytical levels, see pp. 28–29.

Olof Eriksson's instructor asked students to write a one-page reading response, including a summary and a personal response, before writing each assigned essay. Your instructor may also ask you to keep a reading journal or to submit or post online your responses to readings. Your assignment might require brief features such as these:

For more on citing sources, see E1–E2 in the Quick Research Guide, pp. Q-31–Q-36.

- Summary: a short statement in your own words of the reading's main points (without your opinion, evaluation, or judgment)
- Paraphrase: a restatement of a passage using your own words and sentences
- Quotation: a noteworthy expression or statement in the author's exact words, presented in quotation marks and correctly cited

- Personal response: a statement and explanation of your reaction to the reading
- Critique: your evaluation of the strengths or weaknesses of the reading
- Application: a connection between the reading and your experience
- Question: a point that you wish the writer had covered

## Olof Eriksson       Student Summary and Response

## The Problems with Masculinity

Robert Jensen writes in his essay "The High Cost of Manliness" about masculinity and how our culture creates expectations of certain traits from the males in our society. He strongly opposes this view of masculinity and would prefer that sociological constructs like masculinity and femininity were abolished. As examples of expected traits, he mentions strength and competition. Males are supposed to take what they want and avoid showing weaknesses. Then Jensen points out negative consequences of enforcing masculinity, things like rape and men having trouble showing vulnerability. He counters the argument of differences in biology between males and females by pointing out that we do not know how much comes from biology and how much comes from culture, but that both certainly matter and we should do what we can. He is also concerned about giving positive attributes to masculinity, as that effectively tells us they only belong with males. He ends by observing that we are facing challenges now that cannot be met with the current view of masculinity.

1 For Jensen's essay, see pp. 512–14.

I agree with what Jensen says, and I find it a problem today that the definition of masculinity is so closely connected to competition and aggression. Even so, I find that my own definition of masculinity is very close to the general one. I would say it is to be strong and determined, always winning. I'm sure most people have a similar idea of what it is, even as most people would disagree logically. That is why we need to make an effort to change our culture, just as Jensen argues. If we can either abolish masculinity and femininity or simply change them into a lot more neutral and closely related terms, then we will be a lot closer to real equality between the genders. This change will not only help remove most of the negative impacts Jensen brought up but also help pave a better way for future generations, reducing their problems.

2

### Work Cited

Jensen, Robert. "The High Cost of Manliness." *The Bedford Guide for College Writers with Reader, Research Manual, and Handbook*, edited by X. J. Kennedy, Dorothy M. Kennedy, and Marcia F. Muth, 11th ed., Bedford/ St. Martin's, 2017, pp. 512–14.

### Questions to Start You Thinking

Meaning

1. According to Eriksson, what is Jensen's topic and Jensen's position on this topic? Where does Eriksson present this information?

2. What is Eriksson's personal response to the essay? Where does he present his views?

Writing Strategies

3. How does Eriksson consider his audience as he organizes and develops his summary and response?

4. What kinds of material from the essay does Eriksson use to develop his summary?

# Reading on Literal and Analytical Levels

Educational expert Benjamin S. Bloom identified six levels of cognitive activity: knowledge, comprehension, application, analysis, synthesis, and evaluation.[1] (A recent update recasts *synthesis* as *creating* and moves it above evaluation to the highest level.) Each level acts as a foundation for the next. Each also demands higher thinking skills than the previous one. Experienced readers, however, jump among these levels, gathering information and insight as they occur.

The first three levels are literal skills, building blocks of thought. The last three levels—analysis, synthesis, and evaluation—are analytical skills that your instructors especially want you to develop. To read critically, you must engage with a reading on both literal and analytical levels. Suppose you read in your history book a passage about Franklin Delano Roosevelt (FDR), the only American president elected to four consecutive terms.

**Knowing.** Once you read the passage, even if you have little background in American history, you can decode and recall the information it presents about FDR and his four terms in office.

**Comprehending.** To understand the passage, you need to know that a term for a U.S. president is four years and that *consecutive* means "continuous." Thus FDR was elected to serve for sixteen years.

---

[1] Information from Benjamin S. Bloom et al. *Taxonomy of Educational Objectives, Handbook 1: Cognitive Domain*. Longman, 1956. See also the update in David R. Krathwohl, "A Revision of Bloom's Taxonomy: An Overview." *Theory into Practice*, vol. 41, no. 4, Fall 2002, pp. 212–218.

**Applying.**  To connect this knowledge to what you already know, you think of other presidents — George Washington, who served two terms; Grover Cleveland, who served two terms but not consecutively; Jimmy Carter, who served one term; the second George Bush, who served two terms. You realize that four terms are quite unusual. In fact, the Twenty-Second Amendment to the Constitution, ratified in 1951, now limits a president to two terms.

**Analyzing.**  You can scrutinize FDR's election to four terms from various angles, selecting a principle for analysis that suits your purpose. Then you can use this principle to break the information into its components or parts. For example, you might analyze FDR's tenure in relation to that of other presidents. Why has FDR been the only president elected to serve four terms? What circumstances contributed to three reelections?

**Synthesizing.**  To answer your questions, you may read more or review past readings. Then you begin synthesizing — creating a new approach or combination by pulling together facts and opinions, identifying evidence accepted by all or most sources, examining any controversial evidence, and drawing conclusions that reliable evidence seems to support. For example, you might logically conclude that the special circumstances of the Great Depression and World War II contributed to FDR's election to four terms, not that Americans reelected him out of pity because he had polio.

**Evaluating.**  Finally, you evaluate the significance of your new knowledge for understanding Depression-era politics and assessing your history book's approach. You might ask yourself, Why has the book's author chosen to make this point? How does it affect the rest of the discussion? You may also have

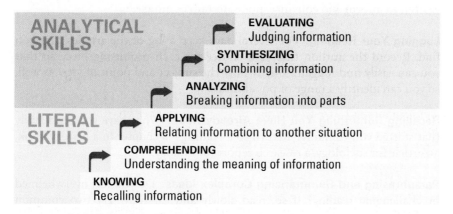

**Literal and Analytical Reading Skills**  Information from Benjamin S. Bloom et al., *Taxonomy of Educational Objectives, Handbook 1: Cognitive Domain,* McKay, 1956.

concluded that FDR's four-term presidency is understandable in light of the events of the 1930s and 1940s, that the author has mentioned this fact to highlight the era's unique political atmosphere, and that it is evidence neither for nor against FDR's excellence as a president.

## Learning by Doing  Reading Analytically

Think back to something you've read recently that helped you make a decision, perhaps a newspaper or magazine article or an electronic posting, How did you analyze what you read, breaking the information into parts? How did you synthesize it, combining it with what you already knew? How did you evaluate it, judging its significance for your decision?

## Generating Ideas from Reading

For more on generating ideas, see Ch. 19.

Like flint that strikes steel and causes sparks, readers and writers provoke one another. For example, when your class discusses an essay, you may be surprised by the range of insights your classmates report. Of course, they may be equally surprised by what you see. Above all, reading is a dynamic process. It may change your ideas instead of support them. Here are suggestions for unlocking the potential of a good text.

**Looking for Meaty Pieces.** Spur your thinking about current topics by browsing through essay collections or magazines in the library or online. Try the *Atlantic, Harper's, New Republic, Commentary,* or special-interest magazines such as *Architectural Digest* or *Scientific American.* Check editorials and op-ed columns in your local newspaper, the *New York Times,* or the *Wall Street Journal.* Search the Internet on intriguing topics (such as silent-film technology) or issues (such as homeless children). Look for meaty, not superficial, articles written to inform and convince, not entertain or amuse.

**Logging Your Reading.** For several days keep a log of the articles that you find. Record the author, title, and source for each promising piece so that you can easily find it again. Briefly note the subject and point of view as well, so you can identify a range of possibilities.

**Recalling Something You Have Already Read.** What have you read lately that started you thinking? Return to a reading—a chapter in a history book, an article for sociology, a research report for biology.

For more on paraphrase and summary, see Ch. 12 and D4–D5 in the Quick Research Guide, pp. Q-29–Q-30.

**Paraphrasing and Summarizing Complex Ideas.** Do you feel overwhelmed by challenging reading? If so, read slowly and carefully. Try two common methods of recording and integrating ideas from sources into papers.

- Paraphrase: restate an author's complicated ideas fully but in your own language, using different wording and different sentence patterns.
- Summarize: reduce an author's main point to essentials, using your own clear, concise, and accurate language.

Accurately recording what a reading says can help you grasp its ideas, especially on literal levels. Once you understand what it says, you can agree, disagree, or question.

**Reading Critically.** Instead of just soaking up what a reading says, try a conversation with the writer. Criticize. Wonder. Argue back. Demand convincing evidence. Use the following checklist to get started.

---

## CRITICAL READING CHECKLIST

☐ What problems and issues does the author raise?

☐ What is the author's purpose? Is it to explain or inform? To persuade? To amuse? In addition to this overall purpose, is the author trying to accomplish some other agenda?

☐ How does the author appeal to you as a reader? Where do you agree and disagree? Where do you want to say "Yeah, right!" or "I don't think so!"? Does the topic or approach engage you?

☐ How does this piece relate to your own experiences or thoughts? Have you encountered anything similar?

☐ Are there important words or ideas that you don't understand? If so, do you need to reread or turn to a dictionary or reference book?

☐ What is the author's point of view? What does the author assume or take for granted? Where does the author reveal these assumptions? Do they make the selection seem weak or biased?

☐ Which statements are facts, verifiable by observation, firsthand testimony, or research? Which are opinions? Does one or the other dominate?

For more on facts and opinions, see Ch. 9.

☐ Is the writer's evidence accurate, relevant, and sufficient? Is it persuasive?

For more on evaluating evidence, see C1–C3 in the Quick Research Guide, pp. Q-25–Q-27.

---

**Analyzing Writing Strategies.** Reading widely and deeply can reveal what others say and how they shape and state it. For some readings in this book, notes in the margin identify key features such as the introduction, thesis statement or main idea, major points, and supporting evidence. Ask questions such as these to help you identify writing strategies:

**WRITING STRATEGIES CHECKLIST**

☐ How does the author introduce the reading and try to engage the audience?

☐ Where does the author state or imply the main idea or thesis?

☐ How is the text organized? What main points develop the thesis?

☐ How does the author supply support — facts, data, expert opinions, explanations, examples, other information?

☐ How does the author connect or emphasize ideas for readers?

☐ How does the author conclude the reading?

☐ What is the author's tone? How do the words and examples reveal the author's attitude, biases, or assumptions?

# Learning from Another Writer: Critical Reading and Response

For Thompson's essay, see pp. 547–48.

Alley Julseth was asked to read an essay on both literal and analytical levels. Her critical reading analysis presents a thoughtful personal response to Clive Thompson's "The New Literacy."

**Alley Julseth**                    **Student Critical Reading Response**

### Analyzing "The New Literacy"

For another reading response, see p. 23.

Being part of a generation that spends an immense amount of time online, I find it rather annoying to hear that youth today are slowly diminishing the art of writing. Because Facebook and Twitter have limited character space, I do use abbreviations such as s.m.h. (shaking my head), "abt" (about), and "u" (you). However, my simplistic way of writing informally for online media has no correlation with my formal writing. In "The New Literacy" essay, Clive Thompson indicates that this lack of correlation seems to be the case with many more students.                    1

Thompson explores the idea that the advancing media is changing the way students write. After citing Professor Sutherland blaming technology for "bleak, bald, sad shorthand" (qtd. in Thompson 547), he goes on to describe the Stanford Study of Writing, conducted by writing professor Andrea Lunsford. She studied over 14,000 examples of student writing from academic essays to e-mails and chats. From these samples, she learned that "young people today write far more than any generation before them" (547). I completely agree with this point based on the large volume I write socializing on the Internet.                    2

I believe that the time I spend online writing one-dimensional phrases does not weaken my formal writing as a student.

Thompson goes on to explain that the new way of writing on the Internet is actually more similar to the Greek tradition of argument than to the essay and letter-writing tradition of the last half century. Lunsford concluded that "the students were remarkably adept at what rhetoricians call *kairos* — assessing their audience and adapting their tone and technique to get their point across" (547). Their Internet writing is like a conversation with another person.

3

I find this conclusion interesting. As I advance in my writing as a student, I remember being taught as a child that there is a distinct line between writing an essay that is due to a teacher and writing a letter to a friend. Although the two are different, there are similarities as well. The nice thing about writing on the Internet is that I can choose what I write about and how I say it. When I'm writing to a friend, sticking to the point isn't exactly the goal, but I do get my main point across. However, I never write a formal essay unless it is assigned. Like the Stanford students, I do not look forward to writing an essay simply for the grade. Writing for a prompt I did not choose does not allow me to put my full-hearted passion into the essay. When I was younger, I wrote essays that were more bland and straight to the point. As I write now, I try to think as though I am reading to a room full of people, keeping my essay as interesting as I can.

4

Thompson ends his piece on the importance of good teaching. This importance is true; teaching is the way students learn how to draw that line between formal and informal writing and how to write depending on audience. I appreciate and completely agree with Thompson's essay. I feel that he describes the younger generation very well. He is pushing away what highbrow critics say, and he is saying we are almost inventing a new way of writing.

5

Work Cited

Thompson, Clive. "The New Literacy." *The Bedford Guide for College Writers with Reader, Research Manual, and Handbook*, edited by X. J. Kennedy, Dorothy M. Kennedy, and Marcia F. Muth, 11th ed., Bedford/St. Martin's, 2017, pp. 547–48.

## Questions to Start You Thinking

Meaning

1. According to Julseth, what is the issue that Thompson raises, and what is his position on this topic? Where does Julseth present this information?

2. What are Julseth's main points in her analysis?

3. How does Julseth apply this reading to her own life?

Writing Strategies

4. How has Julseth demonstrated both literal and critical reading responses?

5. How does Julseth develop her analysis? What kinds of material does she draw from the essay?

---

## Learning by Doing 🔟 Reading Critically

For a sample annotated passage, see pp. 19–20.

Using the advice in this chapter, critically read the following *Scientific American* essay, written by the author of *The Believing Brain* and *The Moral Arc*. First, add your own notes and comments in the margin, responding on both literal and analytical levels. Second, add notes about writing strategies. (Sample annotations are supplied to help you get started.) Finally, write a brief summary of the reading and your own well-reasoned conclusions about it.

---

## Michael Shermer

### The Science of Righteousness

Michael Shermer.

Sounds like Grandpa!

And this sounds like Uncle Bill!

Stories lead to thesis

Which of these two narratives most closely matches your political perspective?

*Once upon a time people lived in societies that were unequal and oppressive, where the rich got richer and the poor got exploited. Chattel slavery, child labor, economic inequality, racism, sexism and discriminations of all types abounded until the liberal tradition of fairness, justice, care and equality brought about a free and fair society. And now conservatives want to turn back the clock in the name of greed and God.*

*Once upon a time people lived in societies that embraced values and tradition, where people took personal responsibility, worked hard, enjoyed the fruits of their labor and through charity helped those in need. Marriage, family, faith, honor, loyalty, sanctity, and respect for authority and the rule of law brought about a free and fair society. But then liberals came along and destroyed everything in the name of "progress" and utopian social engineering.*

Although we may quibble over the details, political science research shows that the great majority of people fall on a left-right spectrum with these two grand narratives as bookends. And the story we tell about ourselves reflects the ancient tradition of "once upon a time things were bad, and now they're good thanks to our party" or "once upon a time things were good, but now they're bad thanks to the other party." So consistent are we in our beliefs that if you hew to the first narrative, I predict you read the *New York Times*, listen to progressive talk radio, watch CNN, are pro-choice and anti-

1

2

3

4

gun, adhere to separation of church and state, are in favor of universal health care, and vote for measures to redistribute wealth and tax the rich. If you lean toward the second narrative, I predict you read the *Wall Street Journal*, listen to conservative talk radio, watch Fox News, are pro-life and anti-gun control, believe America is a Christian nation that should not ban religious expressions in the public sphere, are against universal health care, and vote against measures to redistribute wealth and tax the rich.

Why are we so predictable and tribal in our politics? In his remarkably    5 enlightening book, *The Righteous Mind: Why Good People Are Divided by Politics* —— Writer cites source *and Religion* (Pantheon, 2012), University of Virginia psychologist Jonathan Haidt argues that to both liberals and conservatives, members of the other party are not just wrong; they are righteously wrong—morally suspect and even dangerous. "Our righteous minds made it possible for human beings,"    Quote + summary Haidt argues, "to produce large cooperative groups, tribes, and nations without the glue of kinship. But at the same time, our righteous minds guarantee that our cooperative groups will always be cursed by moralistic strife." Thus, he shows, morality binds us together into cohesive groups but blinds us to the ideas and motives of those in other groups.

The evolutionary Rubicon that our species crossed hundreds of thou-    6  Rubicon?? sands of years ago that led to the moral hive mind was a result of "shared intentionality," which is "the ability to share mental representations of tasks that two or more of [our ancestors] were pursuing together. For example, while foraging, one person pulls down a branch while the other plucks the fruit, and they both share the meal." Chimps tend not to display this behavior, Haidt says, but "when early humans began to share intentions, their ability to hunt, gather, raise children, and raid their neighbors increased exponentially. Everyone on the team now had a mental representation of the task, knew that his or her partners shared the same representation, knew when a partner had acted in a way that impeded success or that hogged the spoils, and reacted negatively to such violations." Examples of modern political violations include Democrat John Kerry being accused of being a "flip-flopper" for changing his mind and Republican Mitt Romney declaring himself "severely conservative" when it was suggested he was wishy-washy in his party affiliation.

Our dual moral nature leads Haidt to conclude that we need both liber-    7 als and conservatives in competition to reach a livable middle ground. As philosopher John Stuart Mill noted a century and a half ago: "A party of order or stability, and a party of progress or reform, are both necessary elements of a healthy state of political life."

# Reading Online and Multimodal Texts

Traditionally, a literate person was someone who could read and write. This    For more on definition remains current, but technologies have vastly increased the com-    responding to images, plexity of reading and writing. Multimodal online texts now combine written    see Ch. 14.

materials with images, sounds, and motions. Such texts can't be confined to the fixed form of a printed page and may be randomly or routinely updated. They also may be accessed flexibly as a reader wanders through sites by following links rather than paging through the defined sequence of a bound book.

Learning to read and write effectively has likewise increased in complexity. Many people simply assume that a reader's eye routinely moves from left to right, from one letter or word to the next. However, eye-movement studies show that readers actually jump back and forth, skip letters and words, and guess at words the eye skips. Online readers also may jump from line to line or chunk to chunk, scanning the page. In addition, multimodal texts may draw the eye to, or from, the typical left-to-right, top-to-bottom path with an image. Analyzing the meaning or impact of an image may require "reading" its placement and arrangement.

What might these changes mean for you as a reader and writer? Your critical reading skills are likely to be increasingly useful, as the essential challenge of deep, thoughtful reading applies to graphic novels, blogs, photo essays, and YouTube videos just as it does to printed books, articles, and essays. In fact, some argue that texts using multiple components and appealing to multiple senses require even more thorough scrutiny to grasp what they are saying and how they are saying it. Here are some suggestions about how you might apply your critical skills in these often media-rich contexts:

- Concentrate on your purpose to stay focused when you read online or multimodal texts, especially if those texts tug you further and further away from your original search or material.
- Create a digital file, reading journal, research journal, or writer's blog so that you have a handy location for responding to new materials.
- Bookmark meaty online readings, sites, or multimodal texts so you can easily return to examine their details. Consider what you see or hear, what the material suggests, and how it appeals to you.
- Read features and effects of visual or multimodal texts as carefully as you read words in print texts. Observe composition, symmetry, sequence, shape, color, texture, brightness, and other visual components.
- Listen for the presence and impact of audio characteristics such as sound effects (accuracy, clarity, volume, timing, emotional power), speech (pitch, tone, dialect, accent, pace), and music (instrumentation, vocals, melody, rhythm, harmony, musical roots, cuts, remix decisions).
- Examine visual or multimodal materials critically—analyzing components, synthesizing varied information, and evaluating effects.
- Evaluate research material that presents evidence to support your points or to challenge other views so that you rely on trustworthy sources.

- Secure any necessary permission to add someone else's visual or other material to your text and to credit your source appropriately.

- Generate even more ideas by rereading this chapter and thinking about how you could apply the skills presented here in new situations.

## Learning by Doing 🔲 Reading a Web Site

Examine this nonprofit organization's Web site: idahorivers.org. Using this chapter as a guide, consider the following questions as you evaluate or "read" the site: Based on the URL address, what kind of information do you expect to find on this Web site? Looking at the pictures on the home page, what do you think this organization does? How is information presented? How easy is it to navigate the page? Is everything understandable? Does the organization use special language or jargon? What might that language tell you about the organization? Does the information seem credible? Why, or why not? Identify specific features on the site that support your position. Write a short reflection to capture your observations. What will you remember the next time you "read" a Web site?

## Additional Writing Activities

1. **Source Activity.** Select an essay from this book. Annotate the reading, marking both its key ideas and your own reactions to it. Review the text and your annotations, and then write two paragraphs, one summarizing the reading and the other explaining your personal response to it.

2. **Source Activity.** Follow up on Activity 1, working with others who have responded to the same essay. Share your summaries, noting the strengths of each. Then develop a collaborative summary that briefly and fairly presents the main points of the reading. (You can merge your existing summaries or make a fresh start.) When you finish the group summary, decide which methods of summarizing work best.

3. **Source Activity.** Follow up on Activity 1 by adding a critical reading analysis and response.

4. **Source Activity.** Select a passage from the textbook or readings for another course you are taking or have taken. Annotate the passage, and make some notes using the Critical Reading Checklist and the Writing Strategies Checklist (pp. 27 and 28) as guides. Pay special attention to the reading's purpose and its assumptions about its audience. Write a paragraph or two about your critical examination of the passage.

For the contents of *A Writer's Reader,* see p. 480.

5. **Visual Activity.** Select a Web page, blog entry, YouTube video, photo from an online gallery, social media post, or another brief online text. "Read" this text critically, adapting reading processes and skills from this chapter. Write a short summary and response, including a link or a print-out of the page or section to which you have responded.

# Critical Thinking Processes

*Critic,* from the Greek word *kritikos,* means "one who can judge and discern"—in short, someone who thinks critically. College will have been worth your time and effort if it leaves you better able to judge and discern—to determine what is more and less important, to make distinctions and recognize differences, to generalize from specifics, to draw conclusions from evidence, to grasp complex concepts, to choose wisely. The effective thinking that you'll need in college, on the job, and in daily life is active and purposeful, not passive and ambling. It is critical thinking.

## A Process of Critical Thinking

Critical thinking, like critical reading, draws on a cluster of intellectual strategies and skills.

For more on critical reading, see Ch. 2.

| Critical Thinking Skill | Definition | Applications for Readers | Applications for Writers |
|---|---|---|---|
| Analysis | Breaking down information into its parts and elements | Analyzing the information in articles, reports, and books to grasp the facts and concepts they contain | Analyzing events, ideas, processes, and structures to understand them and explain them to readers |
| Synthesis | Putting together elements and parts to form new wholes | Synthesizing information from several sources, examining implications, and drawing conclusions supported by reliable evidence | Synthesizing source materials with your own thoughts in order to convey the unique combination to others |
| Evaluation | Judging according to standards or criteria | Evaluating a reading by determining standards for judging, applying them to the reading, and arriving at a conclusion about its value, significance, or credibility | Evaluating something in writing by convincing readers that your standards are reasonable and that the subject either does or does not meet those standards |

These three activities — analysis, synthesis, and evaluation — are the core of critical thinking. They are not new to you, but applying them rigorously in college-level reading and writing may be. When you approach college reading and writing tasks, instructors will expect you (and you should expect yourself) to think, read, write, and think some more.

| THINK → | READ → | WRITE → | THINK |
|---|---|---|---|
| Critically consider a topic or problem | Critically read relevant sources of information | Present information and arguments that will pass the critical scrutiny of readers | Critically reflect on your own thinking, reading, and writing skills |

## Getting Started

You use critical thinking every day to explore problems step by step and reach solutions. Suppose you don't have enough money both to pay your tuition and to buy the car you need. First, you might pin down the causes of your financial problem. Next, you might examine your options to find the best solution, as shown in the graphic on page 37.

You can follow the same steps to examine many types of issues, helping you analyze a situation or dilemma, creatively synthesize to develop alternatives, and evaluate a possible course of action.

## Learning by Doing 🔲 Thinking Critically to Explore an Issue

You've worked hard on a group presentation that will be a major part of your grade — and each member of the group will get the same grade. Two days before the project is due, you discover that one group member has plagiarized heavily from sources well known to your instructor. Working together with classmates, use critical thinking to explore your problem and determine what you might do.

## Applying Critical Thinking to Academic Problems

It is important to support critical thinking with evidence. For advice on selecting and testing evidence, see pp. 162–64.

As you grapple with academic problems and papers, you'll be expected to use your critical thinking skills — analyzing, synthesizing, and evaluating — as you read and write. You may simply dive in, using each skill as needed. However, the very wording of an assignment or examination question may alert you to a skill that your instructor expects you to use, as the first sample assignment in each set illustrates in the chart on page 37.

> **? PROBLEM**
> *You can't afford both your college tuition and the car you need.*

## SOLUTION

**1 IDENTIFY CAUSES**

*Causes in your control:*
Expensive vacation?
Credit-card debt?

*Causes out of your control:*
Medical emergency?
Job loss?
Tuition increase?
Financial aid policy change?

**2 ANALYZE, SYNTHESIZE, AND EVALUATE OPTIONS**

Do without a car          (*how?*)     • Get rides with family or friends?
                                        • Take public transportation?

Decrease your tuition     (*how?*)     • Take fewer courses?

Get more money            (*how?*)     • Get a college loan?
                                        • Get a loan from a family member?
                                        • Get another job?

**3 REACH A LOGICAL CONCLUSION**

Apply for a short-term loan through the college for tuition.

**Critical Thinking in Action**

# Thinking Critically about Your Own Writing: Self-Reflection

The word *reflection* may bring to mind the quiet contemplation of a poet or philosopher, and it may seem to have little to do with the process of learning new academic skills or applying them successfully. However, reflecting on your writing and writing processes — that is, thinking through the difficulties, questions, and successes that arise as you draft and revise papers — can help you become a more active learner, one who is deeply engaged in figuring out your academic strengths and weaknesses and in determining how to turn those weaknesses into strengths. In short, self-reflection and active learning can help you make lasting improvements in your writing skills. Additionally, with time and practice, you'll become more comfortable applying those skills in any writing situation, both in college and beyond.

# Using Critical Thinking for College Assignments

| Critical Thinking Skill | Sample College Writing Assignments |
|---|---|
| *Analysis:* breaking into parts and elements based on a principle | ■ Describe the immediate causes of the 2008 stock market crash. (Analyze by using the principle of immediate causes to identify and explain the reasons for the 2008 crash.)<br>■ Trace the stages through which a bill becomes federal law.<br>■ Explain and illustrate the main provisions of the Affordable Care Act.<br>■ Define *romanticism,* identifying and illustrating its major characteristics. |
| *Synthesis:* combining parts and elements to form new wholes | ■ Discuss the following statement: High-minded opposition to slavery was only one cause, and not a very important one, of the animosity between North and South that in 1861 escalated into civil war. (Synthesize by combining the causes or elements of the North-South animosity, going beyond the opposition to slavery, to form a new whole: your conclusion that accounts for the escalation into civil war.)<br>■ Imagine that you are a trial lawyer in 1921, charged with defending Nicola Sacco and Bartolomeo Vanzetti, two anarchists accused of murder. Argue for their acquittal on whatever grounds you can justify. |
| *Evaluation:* judging according to standards or criteria | ■ Present and evaluate the most widely accepted theories that account for the disappearance of the dinosaurs. (Evaluate, based on standards such as scientific merit, the credibility of each theory.)<br>■ Defend or challenge the idea that houses and public buildings should be constructed to last no longer than twenty years.<br>■ Contrast the models of the solar system advanced by Copernicus and by Kepler, showing how the latter improved on the former. |

## Details on Self-Reflection

Self-reflection involves metacognition, with *meta* meaning "beyond" and *cognition* referring to the process of thinking, learning, or understanding. In the context of writing, *metacognition* means thinking about your own thinking—and about your writing process. In essence, metacognition (and, therefore, self-reflection) is a kind of self-assessment. Throughout the process of producing a piece of writing you ask yourself questions like the following:

BEFORE WRITING

- What do I think is the purpose or reason for this writing assignment? How might this type of writing be relevant beyond this particular assignment or class?
- Am I clear on the requirements of this assignment? If not, what questions might I pose to my instructor?
- Am I having a hard time starting the assignment? What seems to be getting in my way?

DURING WRITING

- Which aspects of completing this assignment are coming fairly easy to me? Which aspects are more challenging, and why?
- Which parts of the writing process am I enjoying most? Which parts are less enjoyable, and why?

AFTER WRITING

- What strategies did I use to draft this paper? Which ones were most successful? Which ones were least successful? Why?
- What was the most valuable thing I learned from this writing assignment? (Think of what you learned not only from your instructor or from this book but also from your own writing process.) What do I wish I had known earlier in the process of completing the assignment?
- Does the feedback that I received from my instructor (or peers) make sense to me? Does this feedback align with any of the concerns I'd expressed in my earlier reflections? Does any of it contradict or complicate those reflections?
- Do I have any remaining questions for my instructor or peers?
- What grade would I give myself on this piece of writing, and why?
- What would I like to do better in the next draft of this paper or in the next writing assignment?

The syllabus for your writing class (or for other classes) might specify desired learning outcomes. And within the syllabus, or in a separate document, a so-called rubric may list (and possibly give examples of) criteria for successful papers. If your instructor has provided learning outcomes or rubrics, you might use these documents for self-reflection.

For example, let's say that in an economics course, the rubric for research papers makes this statement:

> Successful papers will give a new insight into the topic—an insight not provided in lectures, class discussions, or readings.

In the process of generating ideas, then, the writer might repeatedly ask, "Can I draw fresh conclusions from the evidence I've gathered? Would additional research be helpful?" And when it's time to draft a thesis stating the paper's main point, the writer might ask, "Is this truly an original insight? Do I need to spend more time gathering evidence or thinking through the evidence that I've already collected?"

Again, the central aim of self-reflection should be to learn more about what is working well in your writing process and about what needs more effort and attention. Building this kind of self-awareness is an important first step in improving your writing skills and in helping you transfer them more readily to other writing situations, whether in other college courses or in the workplace.

You might record your self-reflections in a designated notebook or journal, or in a digital file. Or you might post your reflections to a blog. Unless your instructor specifies a format for this type of writing, choose the one that is most comfortable and convenient for you.

## Learning by Doing  Reflecting on Your College Career

Consider what Keith Hjortshoj says in his book *The Transition to College Writing*: "Students who get the most out of college usually take the most active responsibility for determining what, how, and why they should learn."[1] Reflect on your own motivation for going to college. Why are you here? How should you adapt your own study habits (or lack thereof) to adjust to college life? How will the work in this course benefit you in later courses and beyond college? How can your classmates help you succeed? What do you think you need to do to become invested in your classwork and your learning?

## Contexts for Self-Reflection

For details on self-reflection and self-assessment in portfolio keeping, see pp. 473–77.

Your instructor might assign self-reflective writing at various points in the course. For example, you might be asked to respond to a "midterm reflection" prompt like the one shown on page 41. Also, if you are required to keep a writing portfolio for your course, you might be asked to complete a series of self-reflections as part of that process. Any ongoing evaluation of your thinking and writing processes will certainly help you write the introduction or cover letter that is usually required at the time you submit a final portfolio. These documents are a form of self-assessment in which you discuss your best or most challenging papers, detail your writing and revision process, and so on.

Whether or not self-reflection is assigned, it is a worthwhile activity, something that you should aim to do at least once a week. Learning by Doing prompts that call for reflection appear throughout this book, and Parts Two and Three include a final Reviewing and Reflecting activity. Even if your instructor does not assign these activities, consider completing at least some of them. The more you practice self-reflection, the more helpful the process will be.

A final word: in addition to building your thinking and writing skills, self-reflection can help you get more out of peer review. In particular, it will allow you to ask peers more specific questions about your writing, encouraging more helpful responses. Consider the differences between the following sets of questions, and the likely benefits of the more specific ones.

| | |
|---|---|
| VAGUE QUESTIONS FOR PEER REVIEWERS | Did you like my paper or not? What did you think of my paper? |
| SPECIFIC QUESTIONS FOR PEER REVIEWERS | I struggled with the organization of the support paragraphs. Does the order of them make sense to you? If not, why not? |
| | I'm not sure that my argument responds adequately to opposing views. Can you think of any counterarguments that I haven't addressed? |

---

[1] Hjortshoj, Keith. *The Transition to College Writing*. Bedford/St. Martin's, 2009.

---

### Learning by Doing 🎬 Reflecting on the Syllabus

Working with a classmate or small group, look over the syllabus for this course, paying special attention to the stated goals, which may be called "outcomes" or "objectives." Write a short reflection about the syllabus. How does it differ from others you may have received in college or high school? Do the goals raise any questions for you? Which ones do you think might be the most challenging and why? Examine your syllabus further. If assignments are listed, do any look particularly difficult? What skills do you currently have that would help you tackle them?

---

# Learning from Another Writer: Self-Reflection

In the following piece of writing, Khalia Nadam responded to this "midterm reflection" prompt for a course on communicating in the biological sciences: "What are the two or three most valuable things that you have learned so far in this course? What do you believe you need to work on more? How might you use what you've learned in other contexts?"

As you read Nadam's writing, notice how she applied critical thinking skills by *analyzing* the challenges of her policy-recommendation assignment and *evaluating* her response to it.

---

**Khalia Nadam**                          **Student Self-Reflection**

#### What I Have Learned from My Research Project

The two or three most valuable things that I have learned so far in this course     1
relate to the policy-recommendation paper that I started the third week of
the semester. This is one of the most challenging assignments that I have ever
worked on. But in spite of that difficulty, or maybe because of it, it has also
been the most rewarding.

As you know from the first draft of my paper, my recommendation is that     2
Kenworth County's land management agencies use social media and other
newer technologies to keep the public and other stakeholders informed about
land management policies, controversies, and other issues. The idea came to
me rather easily, because I interned at one of the agencies last summer, and
I was a personal witness to some of the old-school communication strategies.
(For one thing, the Communications Department was still snail-mailing press
releases to local media and had a weak Internet presence.)

The hard part was researching the full scope of the problem and determin-     3
ing possible solutions. The agency where I interned, and all the other ones that
I contacted for my research, kept mostly paper files, all of them quite outdated.

So I relied mostly on interviewing key personnel and asking questions like these: Why does your agency have no social media presence? Why is there no news feed on the Web site? Other than the press releases being sent to local newspapers and radio stations, what else is being done to get agency news out?

I would say that the most valuable lessons I've learned from this assign-     4
ment are that (1) when researching a current and local issue, interviews can be one of the most valuable ways of gathering evidence, (2) the research process took a lot longer than I thought it would, so I'll try to get an earlier start on future research projects, and (3) I should have created an outline before diving in on my first draft. I ended up doing a ton of reorganizing after that draft, and I have a feeling that even a rough outline would have helped me think through the structure of my writing in advance.

In terms of what I need to work on more, again, I need to get an earlier start     5
on research for future writing projects and do a better job of planning/outlining papers. It is also clear from the feedback I received on my first draft that I need to spend more time on editing and proofreading. Because the final draft is due next Monday, I'm going to devote at least a couple of evenings to both tasks.

I'm confident that I can apply what I've learned in other contexts. In fact,     6
I've already started doing that. While working on the policy-recommendation paper, I was also assigned a research paper for a history course, which I recently completed. Because of what the policy-rec paper taught me about the value of outlining, I prepared a pretty detailed outline for the history paper, and that really helped.

I'm also pretty sure that what I've learned will help me in the workplace.     7
I have been thinking that I would like to work in communications for an environmental organization. So the insights I got from this project should be very helpful. But even if I work in some other field, I can't imagine that I won't benefit from the research and writing skills I've applied to this project.

## Questions to Start You Thinking

### Meaning

1. According to Nadam, what made the policy-recommendation assignment so challenging?

2. How would you summarize the main lessons that she learned from the assignment?

### Writing Strategies

3. Nadam could have responded to the reflection prompt in a single paragraph. What might have been the benefits of going into greater detail about the challenges of her policy-recommendation project?

4. If Nadam had written this reflection just for herself instead of in response to an assignment, might she have used a different approach? For example, can you imagine her using a less formal structure?

# Additional Writing Activities

1. With classmates, identify a common problem for students at your college — juggling a busy schedule, parking on campus, making a class change, joining a social group, or some other issue. Working together, use critical thinking to explore the problem and identify possible solutions. Make notes as you explore the problem and solutions, and put your findings into writing.

2. Working with a classmate or small group, select a sample assignment (not already explained) from the chart on page 37 or from one of your classes. Explain, in writing, how you would approach the assignment to demonstrate your critical thinking. Also, share your strategies for tackling college assignments.

3. Think back over the past month at college, at work (if you hold a job), and in your day-to-day life. Then respond to these two self-reflection prompts: (a) Which experiences have been the most important, because they taught you something valuable, gave you confidence in your abilities, or supported your personal growth in some other way? (b) Which experiences have been the most challenging, and why?

4. **Source Activity.** Using your college's library, or using research tools available on the library's Web site, identify two or three sources that cover (a) a topic you are investigating for a college course or (b) a topic you find personally interesting. Keeping in mind at least three key questions that you have about your topic, read over the sources and try to answer these questions, making notes. (In case you want to revisit these sources later, make sure to record their titles and authors, the publications they came from, and any page numbers.) Afterward, respond to these self-reflection questions: Was it easy to find relevant and helpful sources, or was it more difficult than you expected? Why? To what degree did the sources answer your questions? Do you still feel the need to track down additional information? If so, will you adjust your search strategy in any way? How?

5. **Visual Activity.** Working with a classmate or small group, examine one or more of the photographs that open Parts One through Four of this book (see pages 4–5, 44–45, 248–49, and 356–57). Then, using the critical thinking skills discussed on pages 35–37, share your impressions of the photographs. For example, you might analyze the images by considering their various parts or components and discussing how they work together or set one another apart. Or you might evaluate the images by considering their lighting, their composition, the distance or perspective from which the subjects were photographed, the mood created, and so on.

# A WRITER'S SITUATIONS

# Recalling an Experience

*Images, clockwise from top left:* Frank and Helena/Cultura RM Exclusive/Getty Images; Mario Tama/Getty Images News/Getty Images; Hero Images/Getty Images; Pamela Moore/E+/Getty Images.

## Responding to an Image

Look carefully at a photograph in this grid. In your view, when was this photograph taken? Who might the person or people be? Where are they, and why are they there? What are they doing? What relationships and emotions does the picture suggest with its focal point and arrangement? Write about an experience the image helps you recall or about a possible explanation of events in this picture. Use vivid detail to convey what happened to you or what might have happened to the people in the picture.

Writing from recall is writing from memory, a writer's richest—and handiest—resource. Recall is clearly necessary when you write of a personal experience, a favorite place, a memorable person. Recall also helps you probe your memories of specific events. For example, in a literacy narrative you might examine the significance of your experiences learning to read or write. On the other hand, in a reflection you might begin with an incident that you recall and then explore the ideas that evolve from it.

Even when an instructor hands you a subject that seems to have nothing to do with you, your memory is the first place to look. Suppose you have to write a psychology paper about how advertisers prey on consumers' fears. Begin with what you remember. What ads have sent chills down your back? What ads have suggested that their products could save you from a painful social blunder, a lonely night, or a deadly accident? All by itself, memory may not give you enough to write about, but you will rarely go wrong if you start by jotting down something remembered.

For information and journal questions about the Part Two photograph, see About the Photographs at the end of the book.

## Why Recalling an Experience Matters

**In a College Course**

- You recall your experiences of visiting or living in another region or country to add authority to your sociology paper on cultural differences.
- You recall and record both routine and unusual events in the reflective journal you keep during your internship or clinical experience.

**In the Workplace**

- You recall past successes, failures, or customer comments to provide compelling reasons for adopting your proposals for changing a product or service.

**In Your Community**

- You recall your own experiences taking standardized tests to add impact to your appeal to the local school board to change the testing program at your child's school.

❓ When have you recalled experiences in your writing? What did these recollections add to your writing? In what situations might you rely on recollection again in future writing?

# Learning from Other Writers

Here are two samples of good writing from recall—one by a professional writer, one by a college student. To help you begin to analyze the first reading, look at the notes in the margin. They identify features such as the main idea, or thesis, and the first of the main events that support it in a paper written from recall.

## As You Read These Recollections

Ask yourself the following questions:

1. Is the perspective of the essay primarily that of a child or an adult? Why do you think so?
2. What does the author realize after reflecting on the events recalled? Does the realization come soon after the experience or later, when the writer examines the events from a more mature perspective?
3. How does the realization change the individual?

## Russell Baker

### The Art of Eating Spaghetti

In this essay from his autobiography *Growing Up* (1982), columnist Russell Baker recalls being sixteen in urban Baltimore and wondering what to do with his life.

Yvonne Hemsey/3rd
Party—Misc/Getty Images.

Introduction ——

The only thing that truly interested me was writing, and I knew that 1 sixteen-year-olds did not come out of high school and become writers. I thought of writing as something to be done only by the rich. It was so obviously not real work, not a job at which you could earn a living. Still, I had begun to think of myself as a writer. It was the only thing for which I seemed to have the smallest talent, and, silly though it sounded when I told people I'd like to be a writer, it gave me a way of thinking about myself which satisfied my need to have an identity.

THESIS ——
stating main idea

The notion of becoming a writer had flickered off and on in my head 2 since the Belleville days, but it wasn't until my third year in high school that the possibility took hold. Until then I'd been bored by everything associated with English courses. I found English grammar dull and baffling. I hated the assignments to turn out "compositions," and went at them like heavy labor, turning out leaden, lackluster paragraphs that were agonies for teachers to read and for me to write. The classics thrust on me to read seemed as deadening as chloroform.

Major event 1 ——

When our class was assigned to Mr. Fleagle for third-year English I antici- 3 pated another grim year in that dreariest of subjects. Mr. Fleagle was notorious among City students for dullness and inability to inspire. He was said to be stuffy, dull, and hopelessly out of date. To me he looked to be sixty or seventy and prim to a fault. He wore primly severe eyeglasses, his wavy hair was primly cut and primly combed. He wore prim vested suits with neckties blocked primly against the collar buttons of his primly starched white shirts. He had a primly pointed jaw, a primly straight nose, and a prim manner of speaking that was so correct, so gentlemanly, that he seemed a comic antique.

I anticipated a listless,° unfruitful year with Mr. Fleagle and for a long time was not disappointed. We read *Macbeth*. Mr. Fleagle loved *Macbeth* and wanted us to love it too, but he lacked the gift of infecting others with his own passion. He tried to convey the murderous ferocity of Lady Macbeth one day by reading aloud the passage that concludes

> . . . I have given suck, and know
> How tender 'tis to love the babe that milks me.
> I would, while it was smiling in my face,
> Have plucked my nipple from his boneless gums. . . .

The idea of prim Mr. Fleagle plucking his nipple from boneless gums was too much for the class. We burst into gasps of irrepressible snickering. Mr. Fleagle stopped.

"There is nothing funny, boys, about giving suck to a babe. It is the—the very essence of motherhood, don't you see."

He constantly sprinkled his sentences with "don't you see." It wasn't a question but an exclamation of mild surprise at our ignorance. "Your pronoun needs an antecedent, don't you see," he would say, very primly. "The purpose of the Porter's scene, boys, is to provide comic relief from the horror, don't you see."

*Support for major event 1*

Late in the year we tackled the informal essay. "The essay, don't you see, is the . . ." My mind went numb. Of all forms of writing, none seemed so boring as the essay. Naturally we would have to write informal essays. Mr. Fleagle distributed a homework sheet offering us a choice of topics. None was quite so simpleminded as "What I Did on My Summer Vacation," but most seemed to be almost as dull. I took the list home and dawdled until the night before the essay was due. Sprawled on the sofa, I finally faced up to the grim task, took the list out of my notebook, and scanned it. The topic on which my eye stopped was "The Art of Eating Spaghetti."

This title produced an extraordinary sequence of mental images. Surging up out of the depths of memory came a vivid recollection of a night in Belleville when all of us were seated around the supper table—Uncle Allen, my mother, Uncle Charlie, Doris, Uncle Hal—and Aunt Pat served spaghetti for supper. Spaghetti was an exotic treat in those days. Neither Doris nor I had ever eaten spaghetti, and none of the adults had enough experience to be good at it. All the good humor of Uncle Allen's house reawoke in my mind as I recalled the laughing arguments we had that night about the socially respectable method for moving spaghetti from plate to mouth.

Suddenly I wanted to write about that, about the warmth and good feeling of it, but I wanted to put it down simply for my own joy, not for Mr. Fleagle. It was a moment I wanted to recapture and hold for myself. I wanted to relive the pleasure of an evening at New Street. To write it as

**listless:** Lacking energy or enthusiasm.

I wanted, however, would violate all the rules of formal composition I'd learned in school, and Mr. Fleagle would surely give it a failing grade. Never mind. I would write something else for Mr. Fleagle after I had written this thing for myself.

When I finished it the night was half gone and there was no time left to 10 compose a proper, respectable essay for Mr. Fleagle. There was no choice next morning but to turn in my private reminiscence° of Belleville. Two days passed before Mr. Fleagle returned the graded papers, and he returned everyone's but mine. I was bracing myself for a command to report to Mr. Fleagle immediately after school for discipline when I saw him lift my paper from his desk and rap for the class's attention.

"Now, boys," he said, "I want to read you an essay. This is titled 'The Art 11 of Eating Spaghetti.'"

And he started to read. My words! He was reading *my words* out loud to 12 the entire class. What's more, the entire class was listening. Listening attentively. Then somebody laughed, then the entire class was laughing, and not in contempt and ridicule, but with openhearted enjoyment. Even Mr. Fleagle stopped two or three times to repress a small prim smile.

I did my best to avoid showing pleasure, but what I was feeling was 13 pure ecstasy at this startling demonstration that my words had the power to make people laugh. In the eleventh grade, at the eleventh hour as it were, I had discovered a calling. It was the happiest moment of my entire school career. When Mr. Fleagle finished he put the final seal on my happiness by saying, "Now that, boys, is an essay, don't you see. It's — don't you see — it's of the very essence of the essay, don't you see. Congratulations, Mr. Baker."

Conclusion restating thesis — For the first time, light shone on a possibility. It wasn't a very heartening 14 possibility, to be sure. Writing couldn't lead to a job after high school, and it was hardly honest work, but Mr. Fleagle had opened a door for me. After that I ranked Mr. Fleagle among the finest teachers in the school.

## Questions to Start You Thinking

### Meaning

1. In your own words, state what Baker believes he learned in the eleventh grade about the art of writing. What incidents or statements help identify this lesson for readers? What lesson, if any, did you learn from the essay?

2. Why do you think Baker included this event in his autobiography?

3. Have you ever changed your mind about something you had to do, as Baker did about writing? Or about a person, as he did about Mr. Fleagle?

**reminiscence:** Memory.

Writing Strategies

4. What is the effect, in paragraph 3, of Baker's repetitions of the words *prim* and *primly*? What other devices does he use to characterize Mr. Fleagle vividly? Why do you think Baker uses so much space to portray his teacher?

5. What does the quotation from *Macbeth* add to Baker's account? Had the quotation been omitted, what would have been lost?

6. How does Baker organize the essay? Why does he use this order?

## Robert G. Schreiner                    Student Essay

### What Is a Hunter?

In this college essay, Robert G. Schreiner uses vivid details to bring to life a significant childhood event.

What is a hunter? This is a simple question with a relatively straightforward          1
answer. A hunter is, according to *Webster's New Collegiate Dictionary*, a
person who hunts game (game being various types of animals hunted or
pursued for various reasons). However, a second question is just as simple
but without such a straightforward answer: What characteristics make up a
hunter? As a child, I had always considered the most important aspect of the
hunter's person to be his ability to use a rifle, bow, or whatever weapon was
appropriate to the type of hunting being done. Having many relatives in rural
areas of Virginia and Kansas, I had been exposed to rifles a great deal. I had
done extensive target shooting and considered myself to be quite proficient in
the use of firearms. I had never been hunting, but I had always thought that
since I could fire a rifle accurately I would make a good hunter.

One Christmas holiday, while we were visiting our grandparents in          2
Kansas, my grandfather asked me if I wanted to go jackrabbit hunting
with him. I eagerly accepted, anxious to show off my prowess° with a rifle.
A younger cousin of mine also wanted to come, so we all went out into the
garage, loaded two .22 caliber rifles and a 20-gauge shotgun, hopped into
the pickup truck, and drove out of town. It had snowed the night before, and
to either side of the narrow road swept six-foot-deep powdery drifts. The
wind twirled the fine crystalline snow into whirling vortexes° that bounced
along the icy road and sprayed snow into the open windows of the pickup.
As we drove, my grandfather gave us some pointers about both spotting and
shooting jackrabbits. He told us that when it snows, jackrabbits like to dig
out a hollow in the top of a snowdrift, usually near a fencepost, and lie there

**prowess:** Superior skill.      **vortex:** Rotation around an axis, as in a whirlwind.

soaking up the sunshine. He told us that even though jackrabbits are a grayish brown, this coloration is excellent camouflage in the snow, for the curled-up rabbits resemble rocks. He then pointed out a few rabbits in such positions as we drove along, showing us how to distinguish them from exposed rocks and dirt. He then explained that the only way to be sure that we killed the rabbit was to shoot for the head and, in particular, the eye, for this was on a direct line with the rabbit's brain. Since we were using solid point bullets, which deform into a ball upon impact, a hit anywhere but the head would most likely only wound the rabbit.

 How does the writer convey his grandfather's definition of hunting?

My grandfather then slowed down the pickup and told us to look out for the rabbits hidden in the snowdrifts. We eventually spotted one about thirty feet from the road in a snow-filled gully. My cousin wished to shoot the first one, so he hopped out of the truck, balanced the .22 on the hood, and fired. A spray of snow erupted about a foot to the left of the rabbit's hollow. My cousin fired again, and again, and again, the shots pockmarking the slope of the drift. He fired once more and the rabbit bounced out of its hollow, its head rocking from side to side. He was hit. My cousin eagerly gamboled into the snow to claim his quarry.° He brought it back holding it by the hind legs, proudly displaying it as would a warrior the severed head of his enemy. The bullet had entered the rabbit's right shoulder and exited through the neck. In both places a thin trickle of crimson marred the gray sheen of the rabbit's pelt. It quivered slightly and its rib cage pulsed with its labored breathing. My cousin was about to toss it into the back of the pickup when my grandfather pointed out that it would be cruel to allow the rabbit to bleed slowly to death and instructed my cousin to bang its head against the side of the pickup to kill it. My cousin then proceeded to bang the rabbit's head against the yellow metal. Thump, thump, thump, thump; after a minute or so my cousin loudly proclaimed that it was dead and hopped back into the truck.

3

 Why do you think that the writer reacts as he does?

The whole episode sickened me to some degree, and at the time I did not know why. We continued to hunt throughout the afternoon, and feigning boredom, I allowed my cousin and grandfather to shoot all of the rabbits. Often, the shots didn't kill the rabbits outright so they had to be killed against the pickup. The thump, thump, thump of the rabbits' skulls against the metal began to irritate me, and I was strangely glad when we turned around and headed back toward home. We were a few miles from the city limits when my grandfather slowed the truck to a stop, then backed up a few yards. My grandfather said he spotted two huge "jacks" sitting in the sun in a field just off the road. He pointed them out and handed me the .22, saying that if I didn't shoot something the whole afternoon would have been a wasted trip for me. I hesitated and then reluctantly accepted the rifle. I stepped out onto the road, my feet crunching on the ice. The two rabbits were about seventy feet away, both

4

**quarry:** Prey.

sitting upright in the sun. I cocked and leveled the rifle, my elbow held almost horizontal in the military fashion I had learned to employ. I brought the sights to bear on the right eye of the first rabbit, compensated° for distance, and fired. There was a harsh snap like the crack of a whip and a small jolt to my shoulder. The first rabbit was gone, presumably knocked over the side of the snowdrift. The second rabbit hadn't moved a muscle; it just sat there staring with that black eye. I cocked the rifle once more and sighted a second time, the bead of the rifle just barely above the glassy black orb that regarded me so passively. I squeezed the trigger. Again the crack, again the jolt, and again the rabbit disappeared over the top of the drift. I handed the rifle to my cousin and began making my way toward the rabbits. I sank into powdery snow up to my waist as I clambered to the top of the drift and looked over.

On the other side of the drift was a sight that I doubt I will ever forget.     5 There was a shallow, snow-covered ditch on the leeward side of the drift and it was into this ditch that the rabbits had fallen, at least what was left of the rabbits. The entire ditch, in an area about ten feet wide, was spattered with splashes of crimson blood, pink gobbets of brain, and splintered fragments of bone. The twisted corpses of the rabbits lay in the bottom of the ditch in small pools of streaming blood. Of both the rabbits, only the bodies remained, the heads being completely gone. Stumps of vertebrae protruded obscenely from the mangled bodies, and one rabbit's hind legs twitched spasmodically. I realized that my cousin must have made a mistake and loaded the rifle with hollowpoint explosive bullets instead of solid ones.

I shouted back to the pickup, explaining the situation, and asked if I     6 should bring them back anyway. My grandfather shouted back, "No, don't worry about it, just leave them there. I'm gonna toss these jacks by the side of the road anyway; jackrabbits aren't any good for eatin'."

Looking at the dead, twitching bodies I thought only of the incredible     7 waste of life that the afternoon had been, and I realized that there was much more to being a hunter than knowing how to use a rifle. I turned and walked back to the pickup, riding the rest of the way home in silence.

*❓ Why do you think the writer returns in silence?*

## Questions to Start You Thinking

Meaning

1. Where in the essay do you first begin to suspect the writer's feelings about hunting? What in the essay or in your experience led you to this perception?

2. How would you characterize the writer's grandfather? How would you characterize his cousin?

3. How did the writer's understanding of himself change as a result of this hunting experience?

**compensate:** Counterbalance.

Writing Strategies

4. How might the essay be strengthened or weakened if the opening paragraph were cut out? Without this paragraph, how would your understanding of the author and his change be different?

5. Would Schreiner's essay be more or less effective if he explained in the last paragraph what he means by "much more to being a hunter"?

6. What are some of Schreiner's memorable images?

7. Using highlighters or marginal notes, identify the essay's introduction, thesis, major events, support for each event, and conclusion. How effective is the organization of this essay?

# Learning by Writing

## The Assignment: Recalling a Personal Experience

Write about an experience that changed how you acted, thought, or felt. Use your experience as a springboard for reflection. Your purpose is not merely to tell an interesting story but to show your readers — your instructor and your classmates — the importance of that experience for you.

We suggest you pick an event that is not too personal, too subjective, or too big to convey effectively to others. Something that happened to you or that you observed, an encounter with a person who greatly influenced you, a decision that you made, or a challenge that you faced will be easier to recall (and to make vivid for your readers) than an interior experience like a religious conversion or falling in love.

These students recalled experiences heavy and light:

One writer recalled guitar lessons with a teacher who at first seemed harsh but who turned out to be a true friend.

Another student recalled a childhood trip when everything went wrong and she discovered the complexities of change.

Another recalled competing with a classmate who taught him a deeper understanding of success.

## Facing the Challenge  Writing from Recall

The major challenge writers confront when writing from recall is to focus their essays on a main idea. When writing about a familiar — and often powerful — experience, it is tempting to include every detail that comes to mind and equally easy to overlook familiar details that would make the story's relevance clearer to the reader.

When you are certain of your purpose in writing about a particular event — what you want to show readers about your experience — you can transform a laundry list of details into a narrative that connects events clearly around a main idea. To help you decide what to show your readers, respond to each of these questions in a few sentences:

- What was important to you about the experience?
- What did you learn from it?
- How did it change you?
- How would you reply to a reader who asked "So what?"

Once you have decided on your main point about the experience, you should select the details that best illustrate that point and show readers why the experience was important to you.

## Generating Ideas

You may find that the minute you are asked to write about a significant experience, the very incident will flash to mind. Most writers, though, will need a little time for their memories to surface. Often, when you are busy doing something else — observing the scene around you, talking with someone, reading about someone else's experience — the activity can trigger a recollection. When a promising one emerges, write it down. Perhaps, like Russell Baker, you found success when you ignored what you thought you were supposed to do in favor of what you really wanted to do. Perhaps, like Robert Schreiner, you learned from a painful experience.

For more on each strategy for generating ideas in this section or for additional strategies, see Ch. 19.

**Try Brainstorming.** When you brainstorm, you just jot down as many ideas as you can. You can start with a suggestive idea — *disobedience, painful lesson, childhood, peer pressure* — and list whatever occurs through free association. You can also use the questions in the following checklist:

### DISCOVERY CHECKLIST

- ☐ Did you ever break an important rule or rebel against authority? What did you learn from your actions?
- ☐ Did you ever succumb to peer pressure? What were the results of going along with the crowd? What did you learn?
- ☐ Did you ever regard a person in a certain way and then have to change your opinion of him or her? What produced this change?
- ☐ Did you ever have to choose between two equally attractive alternatives? How might your life have been different if you had chosen differently?
- ☐ Have you ever been appalled by witnessing an act of prejudice or insensitivity? What did you do? Do you wish you had done something different?

A
Writer's
Guide

Gary S Chapman/Photographer's Choice/Getty Images.

**Try Freewriting.** Devote ten minutes to freewriting — simply writing without stopping. If you get stuck, write "I have nothing to say" over and over, until ideas come. After you finish, you can circle or draw lines between related items, considering what main idea connects events.

**Try Doodling or Sketching.** As you recall an experience such as learning to drive, try sketching whatever helps you recollect the event and its significance. Turn doodles into words by adding comments on main events, notable details, and their impact on you.

**Try Mapping Your Recollections.** Identify a specific time period such as your birthday last year, the week when you decided to enroll in college, or a time when you changed in some way. On a blank page, on movable sticky notes, or in a digital file, record all the details you can recall about that time — people, statements, events, locations, and related physical descriptions.

**Try a Reporter's Questions.** Once you recall an experience you want to write about, ask "the five **W**'s and an **H**" that journalists find useful.

- **W**ho was involved?
- **W**hat happened?
- **W**here did it take place?
- **W**hen did it happen?
- **W**hy did it happen?
- **H**ow did the events unfold?

Any question might lead to further questions — and to further discovery.

- **Who** was involved? ⟶ What did the others look like?
  What did they say or do?
  Would their words supply any lively quotations?

- **What** happened? ⟶ What did you think as the event unfolded?
  When did you see its importance?

**Consider Sources of Support.** Because your memory both retains and drops details, you may want to check your recollections of an experience. Did you keep a journal at the time? Do your memories match those of a friend or relative who was there? Was the experience (big game, new home, birth of a child) a turning point that you or your family would have photographed? Was it sufficiently public (such as a community catastrophe) or universal (such as a campus event) to have been in the news? If so, these resources can remind you of forgotten details or angles.

## Learning by Doing 🖋 Reflecting on Your Writing Space

Examine the place you go most frequently to write and study. Begin by creating a sketch or drawing of your writing space. Next, write a short description using details to create a vivid picture in the mind of your reader. Where is your writing space located? Is it a dedicated and private place, like a bedroom, or a shared space, like a study hall or the library? Do you sit at a desk? How are items in your writing space arranged? End your observations with a reflection on how you might improve your writing space to make it better suited to your writing. Can you identify problems with your current space? Is it too noisy? Too confined?

## Planning, Drafting, and Developing

Now, how will you tell your story? If the experience is still fresh in your mind, you may be able simply to write a draft, following the order of events. If you want to plan before you write, here are some suggestions.

For more strategies for planning, drafting, and developing papers, see Chs. 20, 21, and 22.

**Start with a Main Idea, or Thesis.** Jot down a few words that identify the experience and express its importance to you. Next, begin to shape these words into a sentence that states its significance — the main idea that you want to convey to a reader. If you aren't certain yet about what that idea is, just begin writing. You can work on your thesis as you revise.

For more on stating a thesis, see pp. 384–93.

| TOPIC IDEA + SLANT | reunion in Georgia + really liked meeting family |
| WORKING THESIS | When I went to Georgia for a family reunion, I enjoyed meeting many relatives. |

Notice that Russell Baker describes a positive, life-changing experience, while Robert Schreiner focuses on a more disturbing recollection. To help identify the significance or slant of the experience you want to recall, you might state the most positive or troubling aspects of the experience and make a few notes about why you made these choices.

## Learning by Doing Stating the Importance of Your Experience

Work up to stating your thesis by completing these two sentences: The most important thing about my experience is _____. I want to share this so that my readers _____. Exchange sentences with a classmate or a small group, either in person or online. Ask each other questions to sharpen ideas about the experience and express them in a working thesis.

For examples of time markers and other transitions, see pp. 417–20.

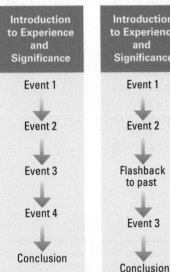

**Establish Your Chronology.** Retelling an experience is called *narration*, and the simplest way to organize is chronologically — relating the essential events in the order in which they occurred. On the other hand, sometimes you can start an account of an experience in the middle and then, through *flashback*, fill in whatever background a reader needs to know.

Richard Rodriguez, for instance, begins *Hunger of Memory*, a memoir of his bilingual childhood, with an arresting sentence:

> I remember, to start with, that day in Sacramento, in a California now nearly thirty years past — when I first entered a classroom, able to understand about fifty stray English words.

The opening hooks our attention. In the rest of his essay, Rodriguez fills us in on his family history, on the gulf he came to perceive between the public language (English) and the language of his home (Spanish).

## Learning by Doing Selecting and Arranging Events

Recall the most important thing that happened to you this month, noting at least three related events in chronological order. Give each event of your story its own short paragraph with details to help your reader understand what happened, how it happened, and what the outcome was. Pay special attention to the order in which events occurred. Print your paragraphs. Now cut the paragraphs apart and arrange them so that, each time, your story starts and ends in a different place. Reflect on how the story changes when the order of events is changed.

**Show Your Audience What Happened.** How can you make your recollections come alive for your readers? Return to Baker's account of Mr. Fleagle teaching *Macbeth* or Schreiner's depiction of his cousin putting the wounded rabbits out of their misery. These writers have not merely told us what happened; they have *shown* us, by creating scenes that we can see in our mind's eye.

For more on providing details, see pp. 424–26.

As you tell your story, zoom in on at least two or three specific scenes. Show your readers exactly what happened, where it occurred, what was said, who said it. Use details and words that appeal to all five senses — sight, sound, touch, taste, smell. Carefully position any images you include to clarify visual details for readers. (Be sure that your instructor approves such additions.)

For more on adding visuals, see the Quick Format Guide, pp. Q-1–Q-19.

## Revising and Editing

After you have written an early draft, put it aside for a few days — or hours if your deadline is looming. Then reread it carefully. Try to see it through the eyes of a reader, noting both pleasing and confusing spots. Revise to express your thoughts and feelings clearly and strongly to your readers.

For more revising and editing strategies, see Ch. 23.

**Focus on a Main Idea, or Thesis.** As you reread the essay, return to your purpose: What was so important about this experience? Why is it so memorable? Will readers see why it was crucial in your life? Will they understand how your life has been different ever since? Be sure to specify a genuine difference, reflecting the incident's real impact on you.

| | |
|---|---|
| WORKING THESIS | When I went to Georgia for a family reunion, I enjoyed meeting many relatives. |
| REVISED THESIS | Meeting my Georgia relatives showed me how powerfully two values — generosity and resilience — unite my family. |

### THESIS CHECKLIST

☐ Does the thesis clearly state why the experience was significant or memorable?

☐ Does the thesis (and the essay) focus on a single main idea, as opposed to various aspects of the experience?

☐ Does it need to be refined in response to any new insights you've gathered while reflecting on, researching, or writing about the experience?

A Writer's Guide

## Peer Response 🔲 Recalling an Experience

For general questions for a peer editor, see p. 447.

Have a classmate or friend read your draft and suggest how you might present the main idea about your experience more clearly and vividly. Ask your peer editor questions such as these about writing from recall:

- What do you think the writer's main idea or thesis is? Where is it stated or clearly implied? Why was this experience significant?
- What emotions do people in the essay feel? How did *you* feel as a reader?
- Where does the essay come alive? Underline images, descriptions, and dialogue that seem especially vivid.
- If this paper were yours, what is the one thing you would be sure to work on before handing it in?

**Add Concrete Detail.** Ask whether you have made events come alive for your audience by recalling them in sufficient concrete detail. Be specific enough that your readers can see, smell, taste, hear, and feel what you experienced. Make sure that all your details support your main idea or thesis. Notice again Robert Schreiner's focus in his second paragraph on the world outside his own skin: his close recall of the snow, of his grandfather's pointers about the habits of jackrabbits and the way to shoot them.

## Learning by Doing 🔲 Appealing to the Senses

Working online or in person with a classmate, exchange short passages from your drafts. As you read each other's paragraphs, highlight the sensory details—sights, sounds, tastes, sensations, and smells that bring a description to life. Then jot down the sense to which each detail appeals in the margin or in a file comment. Return each passage to the writer, review the notes about yours, and decide whether to strengthen your description with more—or more varied—details.

For more on outlining, see pp. 395–403.

For more on transitions, see pp. 417–20.

**Follow a Clear Sequence.** Reconsider the order of events, looking for changes that make your essay easier for readers to follow. For example, if a classmate seems puzzled about the sequence of your draft, make a rough outline or list of main events to check the clarity of your arrangement. Or add more transitions to connect events more clearly. Here are some useful questions about revising your paper:

### REVISION CHECKLIST

- ☐ Where have you shown why this experience was important and how it changed your life?
- ☐ How have you engaged readers so they will keep reading? Will they see and feel your experience?

☐ Why do you begin your narration as you do? Would another place in the draft make a better beginning?

☐ If the events aren't in chronological order, how have you made the organization easy for readers to follow?

☐ In what ways does the ending provide a sense of finality?

☐ Do you stick to a point? Is everything relevant to your main idea or thesis?

☐ If you portray people, how have you made their importance clear? Which details make them seem real, not just shadowy figures?

☐ Does the dialogue sound like real speech? Read it aloud. Try it on a friend.

---

After you have revised your recall essay, edit and proofread it. Carefully check the grammar, word choice, punctuation, and mechanics—and then correct any problems you find. Here are some questions to get you started:

For more editing and proofreading strategies, see pp. 455–58.

### EDITING CHECKLIST

☐ Is your sentence structure correct? Have you avoided writing fragments, comma splices, or fused sentences?  **A1, A2**

☐ Have you used correct verb tenses and forms throughout? When you present a sequence of past events, is it clear what happened first and what happened next?  **A3**

☐ When you use transitions and other introductory elements to connect events, have you placed any needed commas after them?  **D1**

☐ In your dialogue, have you placed commas and periods before (inside) the closing quotation mark?  **D3**

☐ Have you spelled everything correctly, especially the names of people and places? Have you capitalized names correctly?  **E1, E2**

For more help, find the relevant checklist sections in the Quick Editing Guide on p. Q-37, and the Quick Format Guide on p. Q-1.

---

Also check your paper's format using the Quick Format Guide. Follow the style expected by your instructor for features such as the heading, title, running head, page numbers, margins, and paragraph indentation.

## Reviewing and Reflecting

**REVIEW** Working with classmates or independently, respond to the following questions:

To complete more review questions for Ch. 4, go to LaunchPad.

1. What is the major challenge of writing from recall? What is the best way to address this challenge?

2. Asking a reporter's questions is one good strategy for recalling an experience. What are these questions? Try asking them about a significant experience you've had at college, in the workplace, or in your everyday life.

3. Why are concrete details so important in writing that recalls an experience? In an essay that narrates a past event—a paper by you or a peer, or a professional essay—identify concrete details or places where they might be added to strengthen the writing.

**REFLECT** After completing one of the writing assignments presented in this chapter or supplied by your instructor, turn back to the After Writing questions on page 39 of Chapter 3 and respond to as many of them as you can. While addressing these questions, it might be helpful to revisit your response to the Learning by Doing activity on page 57, if you completed it.

Next, reflect in writing about how you might apply the insights that you drew from this assignment to another situation—in or outside of college—in which you have to recall an experience. If no specific situations come to mind, imagine that

- in a psychology course, you are planning to recall a stressful experience in a paper about the short- and long-term effects of stress on physical and mental health.

- in a work setting, you are asked to recall an experience in which you had to show leadership skills or be an effective member of a team.

In your reflection, consider how your purpose might affect decisions about how you will tell your story and about the most relevant and significant details to include.

## Additional Writing Assignments

1. Choose a person outside your immediate family who had a marked effect on your life, either good or bad. Jot down ten details that might show what that person was like: physical appearance, way of talking, habits, or memorable incidents. Then look back at "The Art of Eating Spaghetti" to identify the kinds of detail Baker uses to portray Mr. Fleagle, noting any you might add to your list. Write your paper, including details to help readers experience the person's impact on you.

2. Recall a place you were fond of—your grandma's kitchen, a tree house, a library, a locker room, a vacation retreat. What made it different from other places? Why was it important? What do you feel when you remember it? Write a paper that uses specific, concrete details to explain to your audience why this place was memorable. If you have a photograph of the place, look at it to jog your memory, and consider adding it to your paper.

3. Write a paper or a podcast text to recall a familiar ceremony, ritual, or observation, perhaps a holiday, a rite of passage (confirmation, bar or bat mitzvah, college orientation, graduation), a sporting event, a family custom. How did the tradition originate? Who takes part? How has it changed over the years? What does it add to the lives of those who observe it? Share with your audience the importance of the tradition to you.

4. Recall how you learned to read, write, or see how literacy could shape or change your life. What early experiences with reading or writing do you recall? How did these experiences affect you? Were they turning points for you? Write an essay about the major events in your literacy story—your personal account of your experiences learning to read or write—so that your audience understands the impact of those events on you. If you wish, address a specific audience—such as students or a teacher at your old school, a younger relative, your own children (real or future), or a person involved in your experience.

5. **Source Assignment.** Respond to one of the preceding assignments by supplementing your recollections with information from a source. You might turn to a personal source (family record, photograph, relative's account) or a published account (newspaper story reporting an event, article about a tradition, essay recalling an experience). Jot down relevant details from your source, or write a brief summary of it. Integrate this information in your essay, and be sure to cite your source.

6. **Visual Assignment.** Examine the images on pages 63–64. What do you recall about an experience in a similar social, natural, or urban environment? What events took place there? How did you react to those events? What was their importance to you? How did the experience change you, your ideas, or your decisions? Write an essay that briefly recalls your experience and then reflects on its importance or consequences for you. Add your own photo to your text, if you wish.

Veer/Corbis.

Randall Levensaler/Aurora Photos.

Boone Speed/Aurora Photos.

# Observing a Scene

## 5

Jared Wickerham/Getty Images Sport/Getty Images.

## Responding to an Image

In this 2012 photo, Detroit Tigers outfielder Ryan Raburn reaches up to save a home run. This scene might look and feel quite different to different observers, depending on their vantage points, emotions, and experiences. In this image, what prominent element attracts your attention? Who are the observers? Which details might be important for them? Although visual details are central, what other senses and emotions might come into play?

Most writers begin to write by recalling what they know. Then they look around and add what they observe. Some writing consists almost entirely of observation—a reporter's eyewitness account of a fire, a clinical report by a nurse detailing a patient's condition, a scientist's account of a laboratory experiment, a traveler's blog or photo essay. In fact, observation plays a large role in any writing that describes a person, place, or thing. Observation also provides details to make a point clear or convincing. For example, the abstractions and statistics of a case study can be made more vivid with compelling observations.

If you need more to write about, open your eyes—and your other senses. Take in what you can see, hear, smell, touch, and taste. As you write, report your observations in concrete detail. Of course, you can't record everything your senses bring you. You must be selective based on what's important and relevant for your purpose and audience. To make a football game come alive for readers of your college newspaper, you might mention the overcast cold weather and the spicy smell of bratwurst. But if your purpose is primarily to explain which team won and why, you might stress the most spectacular plays and the players who scored.

## Why Observing a Scene Matters

### In a College Course

- You observe and report compelling information from field trips in sociology, criminal justice, or anthropology as well as impressions of a play, an exhibit, or a historical site for a humanities class.
- You observe clinical practices in health or education, habitats for plants and animals, the changing night sky, or lab experiments to report accurate information and to improve your own future practice.

### In the Workplace

- You observe and analyze to lend credibility to your case study as a nurse, teacher, or social worker or to your site report as an engineer or architect.

### In Your Community

- You observe, photograph, and report on hazards (a dangerous intersection, a poorly lighted park, a run-down building), needs (a soccer arena, a performing arts center), or disasters (an accident, a crime scene, a flood) to motivate action by authorities or fellow citizens.

❓When have you included observations in your writing? How did these observations contribute to your writing? In what situations might you use observation in future writing?

# Learning from Other Writers

Here are two essays by writers who observe their surroundings and reflect on their observations. As you begin to analyze the first reading, look at the notes in the margin. They identify features such as the main impression created in the observation and stated in the thesis, the first of the locations observed, and the supporting details that describe the location.

## As You Read These Observations

Ask yourself the following questions:

1. What does the writer observe? Places? People? Behavior? Things?

2. What senses does each writer rely on? What sensory images does each develop? Find some striking passages in which the writer reports observations. What makes these passages memorable to you?

3. Why does the writer use observation? What conclusion does the writer draw from reflecting on the observations?

## Ashley Smith

### Smokejumper Training

magicvalley.com/The
Times-News.

Ashley Smith, a photojournalist for the *Statesman Journal* in Salem, Oregon, previously served as chief photographer for the *Times-News* in Twin Falls, Idaho. At the *Times-News*, Smith used his skills as a photographer and journalist to vividly capture the training and tasks of smokejumpers, who parachute into remote areas to fight wildfires. Smith's story about smokejumpers, and his accompanying photographs, appeared in the newspaper on September 30, 2013.

Their hands were clean. Months from now, they would be covered in ash, their white fingernails contrasted by burnt earth ground into their fingers. By August, the only memory of today's clean hands would be the lines where sweat cut through the grime of days on the fire line.

*THESIS stating main impression*

But for now, 18 smokejumpers stood around a long, red table doing safety checks on the harnesses that their lives would depend upon in just two days. They spent the winter cast around the country, playing with children, surfing or working odd jobs. Six months is long enough to forget. So, on that first day on April 8, they run their hands along every stitch of the harness, checking it for damage but also using it as an exercise to bring themselves back.

*Vantage point 1*

*Supporting detail*

Fire season has begun.

On April 10, his first jump of the year, Justin Brollier took in the view of snowy mountains around Mountain Home as he fell through the air, his parachute catching. "I really get nervous, keyed up as the jump approaches,

*Vantage point 2*

Supporting detail

thinking of all of the bad scenarios, double checking things," Brollier said. "It's a little claustrophobic° in the airplane. It's choppy, noisy and sweaty, like the roller coaster tick tick to the top. Then you jump and all of the fear goes away. It's quiet. Peaceful for the soul, a sense of calm.

"You have a great love for life. . . . You don't think of bills or other problems." 5

This year's wildfire season saw more than 80 structures burned in Idaho, saw evacuation of some of the most visible pieces of the state, saw hundreds of thousands of acres burning in U.S. Forest Service and U.S. Bureau of Land Management areas. 6

As Idaho and the West burned, national preparedness was declared at Level 5, meaning 80 percent of U.S. wildfire resources were being used, according to the National Interagency Fire Center in Boise. . . . 7

Smokejumpers battle the fires you rarely hear about—fires too remote for TV cameras, and too small to register on the national radar. Without their early intervention, those small fires could explode into devastation. 8

On Aug. 5, after spending the day at the Twin Falls airport, eight smokejumpers were called to fight the Black Warrior Fire. 9

It was a hot summer day with temperatures hanging in the 90s. The firefighters were sweating inside their heavy Kevlar° suits. 10

The Black Warrior Fire was burning at 8,500 feet in a remote corner of the Sawtooth Wilderness.° By the time the smokejumpers arrived, it was still a small fire—10 acres. They were there to stop it before it spread. 11

The flames jumped from island to island of Douglas fir and spruce. The winds were blowing 8–10 mph out of the west, fanning the flames. 12

Though they do it for a living, it's not easy to jump safely out of a plane toward a burning forest. Smokejumpers develop a set of mental calisthenics° to get themselves out the door. 13

Brent Johnson has terrible air sickness, but hates the drowsy feeling he gets from taking Dramamine.° Johnson got so sick on a flight in 1996 that he could not make the jump. After that, he thought about quitting until a friend told him about the Air Force using a spinning chair to combat motion sickness. Johnson found one of the spinning chairs and used it to train his mind. 14

These days, during flights, Johnson concentrates his gaze on one rivet in the Twin Otter to keep himself from getting sick. 15

Johnson still has the chair. He keeps it at the base in Boise. He calls it the "puke chair," and now he pulls it out to help other people with motion sickness in what he calls "puke school." . . . 16

For the hours they are in the plane—a heavy, round-nosed Twin Otter— the smokejumpers trust their lives to the pilot. Diego Calderoni, a BLM 17

---

**claustrophobic:** Pertaining to the fear of being in enclosed or narrow spaces.    **Kevlar:** A strong, fire-resistant material.    **Sawtooth Wilderness:** A federally protected forest area in Idaho.    **calisthenics:** Exercises.    **Dramamine:** An antinausea drug.

smokejumper pilot, grew up hearing stories about flying. His grandfather and great uncle flew during the 1940s, one in World War II and the other in commercial jobs. . . .

The Twin Otter is the John Deere° of planes, Calderoni said, great for carrying a lot of weight and flying slow.  18

The job demands flying through canyons in the Rocky Mountains and dropping smokejumpers at 11,000 feet to battle flames, which he says keeps you on your toes.  19

"Nothing's the same," he said. When flying near mountain ranges or through canyons, where you look out both sides of the plane windows and see rock shooting up, he's always expecting something to go wrong and always has an escape route. What if he loses one of his two engines? He's mentally prepared for that. . . .  20

Smokejumper Justin Reedy stands at the door of the plane looking down at the landing zone for the Black Warrior Fire. In the distance, jagged shadows cast over the Sawtooths in the early morning light. With a firm hit on his left shoulder from the spotter, Reedy plunges out of the plane and begins a five-second count. The count, so ingrained in him from training, is second nature to smokejumpers.  21

Jump, thousand. Look, thousand. Reach, thousand, Wait, thousand. Pull, thousand.  22

The chute catches with a snap. Reedy floats to the ground, surrounded by 125-foot trees. He is still a mile and half southwest of the fire. He begins a hike with more than 80 pounds on his back, across steep terrain to face the fire by hand with his Pulaski — a firefighting tool with an axe on one side, a curved blade on the other.  23

As he gets closer to the fire, he can already hear the echo of chainsaws from firefighters already on scene.  24

Today, approximately 450 smokejumpers are at nine bases across the West and Alaska. The majority of smokejumpers are with the U.S. Forest Service. The Bureau of Land Management has bases in Boise and Fort Wainwright, Alaska. Each fire season, more than 70 members of the BLM Great Basin Smokejumpers fan out from their base in Boise across the West and stage at smaller airports in Idaho, Nevada, Utah, and Colorado, including Twin Falls.  25

Before smokejumpers can join a unit, they have to pass rookie training that starts in the late spring and lasts four weeks.  26

They have to perform grueling marches that include two pack-out tests, one carrying 110 pounds of gear over flat terrain in no more than 90 minutes, and an 85-pound pack carried over 2.5 miles of hilly, broken terrain. . . .  27

Each season, before a smokejumper makes the first fire jump, he or she has to go through a recertification process.  28

**John Deere:** A popular brand of farming equipment, especially tractors.

On April 8, the process began in a weight room with state flags lining the walls. Everything is on the line that day. If they fail any in a series of tests, they don't have a job. [29]

There's nervous laughter as the smokejumpers wait to begin their physical training tests. It's mandatory to complete pushups, situps, and pullups, as well as a timed 1.5-mile run to begin the season. . . . [30]

After the run, 18 firefighters line up around a 20-foot rectangle table with their parachute harnesses. Bright light shines through the windows facing the runway at the Boise airport, as planes pass by in the distance. . . . [31]

The second of the smokejumpers' recertification training takes them to Lucky Peak, outside of Boise. They practice exiting a simulation aircraft, leaping off a 35-foot jump tower and practicing rappelling° out of a tree. [32]

Smokejumpers in their Kevlar suits move like the Michelin Man up the stairs. A jovial° mood fills the small space as smokejumpers cram into the top of the jump tower at Lucky Peak. The mood gets more serious as the spotter briefs the jumpers. [33]

The cable the smokejumpers slide down is about 100 yards from the top of the tower to where the jumpers come to a stop. Smokejumpers such as Matt Matush, of Springfield, Vermont, descend on the cable as an instructor barks out the names of parachute malfunctions they might experience in a real jump. [34]

"Horseshoe, horsehoe," he shouts. [35]

Matush's hands move fast as he solves the issue — 15 seconds in all — then his feet are back on the ground. [36]

## Questions to Start You Thinking

### Meaning

1. What does a smokejumper's job entail? What type of training is required?

2. What are some challenges of the job?

3. What are some ways that smokejumpers have addressed these challenges?

### Writing Strategies

4. In which paragraphs or sections does Smith's use of sensory details capture the experiences of smokejumpers? In general, how successfully has he included various types of observations and details?

5. How does Smith organize his observations? Is this organization effective? Why, or why not?

6. Smith has included some quotations from the smokejumpers. How do these quotations enrich his account?

---

**rappelling:** Descending downward with the aid of ropes.    **jovial:** Cheerful.

# Alea Eyre

## Stockholm

For her first-year composition class, Alea Eyre records her introduction to an unfamiliar location.

The amount of noise and movement bustling around me was almost electrifying. As soon as I stepped off the plane ramp, I was enveloped into a brand new world. I let all my heightened senses work together to take in this new experience. Fear and elation collided in my head as I navigated this new adventure by myself. I was thirteen years old and just taking the final steps of a lonely twenty-six-hour journey across the world from Hawaii to Sweden.

I had never seen so many white folks in one place. Hundreds crowded and rushed to be somewhere. The busy airport felt like a culture shock but not in a bad way. Blonde hair whipped past me, snuggled in caps and scarves. Skin tucked in coats and jeans appeared so shockingly white it almost blinded me. Delicate yet tall and sturdy people zipped around me as if they had to attend to an emergency.

A music-like language danced around my ears, exciting me as I drew closer to the baggage claim. The sound was so familiar yet seemed so distant. I had heard it inconsistently since childhood with the coming and going of my three half sisters. It unfurled off native speakers' tongues, rising and falling in artistic tones. For the past few months, I had studied my Swedish language book diligently, attempting to match my untrained tongue to the rolling Rs and foreign sounds. On paper, the language looked silly, complicated, and unpronounceable. When spoken correctly, it sounded magical and delighted the ears. As I walked swiftly, trying to keep up with the general pace of this international airport, my ears stayed perked up, catching bits and pieces of conversations.

The building was cavernous and had modern wooden architecture that accentuated every corner. Floor to ceiling windows brightened each area, letting in ample light and a view of the dreary early spring surroundings. I felt my eyes widen as I viewed the melting, slushy brown snow and bright green grass peeking up beneath it. Endless birch trees spread before me, and vibrant flowers dotted their roots. Everything inside and out felt so clean and new; even all of the people looked fresh and well dressed. The true Europeans that I had read about for so long were now displayed up close. Pale as they were, none of them looked as if they were sick, overweight, or druggies. I was taken aback, used to the vivid rainbow of shapes, colors, sizes, and overall variety of my Honolulu neighborhood. Every race and social class crammed into the concrete blocks of apartments in my hometown. Everything there felt dirty and unpredictable, but here in Stockholm, everything felt like a lily-white world.

1  ❓ When have you had similar surprises in a new environment?

2

3

4  ❓ What kinds of places does this building bring to mind?

❓ When have you been observed as well as observer?

As I neared the head of the line at customs, sets of eyes from every direction lingered on me. I was still a child, traveling by myself and sticking out against the array of white with my thick dark hair and almond-colored skin. I figured that my features kept them guessing. I was obviously not white, black, or Middle Eastern, but a mix of many different races and cultures that were completely foreign to them. Even back home, people could never guess what my blood combination was. I soon learned that Sweden has extremely strict immigration rules, and hardly anybody can get in. The country took in some Middle Eastern refugees during past wars, but other than that, blonde-haired blue-eyed Swedes turn up around every corner.    5

With my passport stamped and luggage in tow, I descended down a steep escalator, sandwiched in among a family of five. Listening intently to the lilt of their language, I tried to pick up on what they were discussing. Only able to translate a few simple words, I felt discouraged. Exhaustion was creeping up on me both mentally and physically as the initial adrenaline started to wear off. The flights to get here were lengthy and cramped, while the layovers were stressful and rushed. Jet lag settled in and clouded my already foggy head. I needed the luxury of rejuvenating sleep as soon as possible.    6

Finally, the escalator neared the ground floor. I surveyed the crowd anxiously, winding my way through the masses of people. My sister was supposed to be here somewhere, ready to begin a five-month-long period of dealing with my adolescent hormones. I came here to live and learn, go to a Swedish school, and be immersed in a foreign culture. I spotted her, all the way at the end of the floor, near the sets of doors that led to this new world. She stood there, completely still and silent, but smiling and relieved that I actually made it. Her belly filled out the coat she wore, blossoming with her first child. Her hair was long and silky, and her eyes bright and earnest. She glowed with happiness, now looking like a mother. I fell into her arms, feeling ecstatic after not seeing her for years. We left the airport together, beaming as we walked through the crisp, freezing air. As we neared the car, I reached down and touched the melting snow. My virgin hands explored this new texture, and my nerves tingled. Feeling content, I slid into the car and prepared myself for the exciting journey ahead of me.    7

❓ How have you responded to the sights, sounds, and emotions that the writer has described?

## Questions to Start You Thinking

Meaning

1. What is Eyre's response to the scene at the Stockholm airport?

2. What is the point of the overall impression Eyre creates? What does that impression reveal about her?

3. In paragraph 7, what does Eyre mean when she says she prepared herself "for the exciting journey ahead"?

Writing Strategies

4. How does contrasting Honolulu and Stockholm contribute to the vivid impression of the scene Eyre observes?

5. Which sense does Eyre use most effectively? Point to a few examples that support your choice.

6. How does Eyre convey motion and movement? What does this activity contribute to her observation?

7. Using highlighters or marginal notes, identify the essay's introduction, thesis, major vantage points for observation, details supporting each part of the observation, and conclusion. How effective is this organization?

# Learning by Writing
## The Assignment: Observing a Scene

Observe a place near your campus, home, or job and the people who frequent it. Then write a paper that describes the place, the people, and their actions so as to convey the spirit of the place and offer some insight into its impact on the people.

This assignment is meant to start you observing closely enough that you go beyond the obvious. Go somewhere nearby, and station yourself where you can mingle with the people there. Open all your senses so that you see, smell, taste, hear, and feel. Jot down what you immediately notice, especially the atmosphere and its effect on the people there. Take notes describing the location, people, actions, and events you see. Then use your observations to convey the spirit of the scene. What is your main impression of the place? Of the people there? Of the relationship between people and place? Your purpose is not only to describe the scene but also to express thoughts and feelings connected with what you observe.

Three student writers wrote about these observations:

One student, who works nights in the emergency room, observed the scene and the community that abruptly forms when an accident victim arrives: medical staff, patient, friends, and relatives.

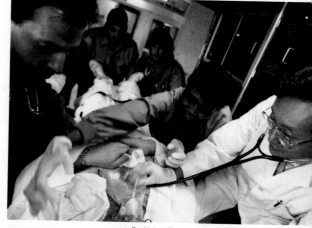

David Joel/The Image Bank/Getty Images.

Another observed a bar mitzvah celebration that reunited a family for the first time in many years.

Another observed the activity in the stands in a stadium before, during, and after a soccer game.

When you select the scene you wish to observe, find out from the person in charge whether you'll need to request permission to observe there, as you might at a school, a business, or another restricted or privately owned site.

## Facing the Challenge   Observing a Scene

The major challenge writers face when writing from observation is to select compelling details that convey an engaging main impression of a scene. As we experience the world, we're bombarded by sensory details, but our task as writers is to choose those that bring a subject alive for readers. For example, describing an oak as "a big tree with green leaves" is too vague to help readers envision the tree or grasp its unique qualities. Consider:

- What colors, shapes, and sizes do you see?
- What tones, pitches, and rhythms do you hear?
- What textures, grains, and physical features do you feel?
- What fragrances and odors do you smell?
- What sweet, spicy, or other flavors do you taste?

After recording the details that define the scene, ask two more questions:

- What overall main impression do these details establish?
- Which specific details will best show the spirit of this scene to a reader?

Your answers will help you decide which details to include in your paper.

## Generating Ideas

Although setting down observations might seem cut-and-dried, to many writers it is true discovery. Here are some ways to generate such observations.

**Brainstorm.** First, choose a scene to observe. What places interest you? Which are memorable? Start brainstorming—listing rapidly any ideas that come to mind. Here are a few questions to help you start your list:

For more on each strategy for generating ideas in this section or for additional strategies, see Ch. 19.

### DISCOVERY CHECKLIST

☐ Where do people gather for some event or performance (a stadium, a place of worship, a theater, an auditorium)?

☐ Where do people meet for some activity (a gym, a classroom)?

☐ Where do crowds form while people are getting things or services (a shopping mall, a dining hall or student union, a dentist's waiting room)?

☐ Where do people pause on their way to yet another destination (a light-rail station, a bus or subway station, an airport, a restaurant on the toll road)?

☐ Where do people go for recreation or relaxation (an arcade, a ballpark)?

☐ Where do people gather (a party, a wedding, a graduation, an audition)?

**Get Out and Look.** If nothing on your list strikes you as compelling, plunge into the world to see what you see. Visit a city street or country hillside, a student event or practice field, a contest, a lively scene—a mall, an airport, a fast-food restaurant, a student hangout—or a scene with only a few people sunbathing, walking dogs, or playing basketball. Observe for a while, and then mix and move to gain different views.

**Record Your Observations.** Alea Eyre's essay "Stockholm" began with some notes about her vivid memories of her trip. She was able to mine those memories for details to bring her subject to life.

Your notes on a subject—or tentative subject—can be taken in any order or methodically. To draw up an "observation sheet," fold a sheet of paper in half lengthwise. Label the left column "Objective," and impartially list what you see,

Protesters take part in a Black Lives Matter rally in St. Paul, Minnesota. AP Images/Richard Tsong-Taatarii.

like a zoologist looking at a new species of moth. Label the right column "Subjective," and list your thoughts and feelings about what you observe. The quality of your paper will depend in large part on the truthfulness and accuracy of your observations. Your objective notes will trigger more subjective ones.

| Objective | Subjective |
|---|---|
| The ticket holders form a line on the weathered sidewalk outside the old brick hall, standing two or three deep all the way down the block. | This place has seen concerts of all kinds — you can feel the history as you wait, as if the hall protects the crowds and the music. |
| Groups of friends talk, a few couples hug, and some guys burst out in staccato laughter as they joke. | The crowd seems relaxed and friendly, all waiting to hear their favorite group. |
| Everyone shuffles forward when the doors open, looking around at the crowd and edging toward the entrance. | The excitement and energy grow with the wait, but it's the concert ritual — the prelude to a perfect night. |

**Include a Range of Images.** Have you captured not just sights but sounds, textures, odors? Have you observed from several vantage points or on several occasions to deepen your impressions? Have you added sketches or doodles to your notes, perhaps drawing the features or shape of the place? Can you begin writing as you continue to observe? Have you noticed how other writers use *images*, evoking sensory experience, to record what they sense? In the memoir *Northern Farm,* naturalist Henry Beston describes a remarkable sound: "the voice of ice," the midwinter sound of a whole frozen pond settling and expanding in its bed.

> Sometimes there was a sort of hollow oboe sound, and sometimes a groan with a delicate undertone of thunder. . . . Just as I turned to go, there came from below one curious and sinister crack which ran off into a sound like the whine of a giant whip of steel lashed through the moonlit air.

## Learning by Doing 🔘 Reflecting on Sensory Details

Step outside with your notebook. Take a deep breath and observe your surroundings. Writing as quickly as you can for five minutes, create a list of sensory details (what you see, hear, smell, feel, and so on). Return to the classroom and write a reflection paragraph that describes your experience using the sensory details you recorded.

## Planning, Drafting, and Developing

For more strategies for planning, drafting, and developing, see Chs. 20, 21, and 22.

After recording your observations, look over your notes, circling whatever looks useful. Maybe you can rewrite your notes into a draft, throwing out details that don't matter, leaving those that do. Maybe you'll need a plan to

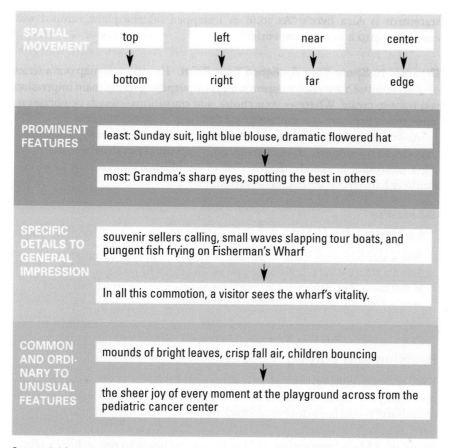

| SPATIAL MOVEMENT | top → bottom | left → right | near → far | center → edge |
|---|---|---|---|---|

| PROMINENT FEATURES | least: Sunday suit, light blue blouse, dramatic flowered hat ↓ most: Grandma's sharp eyes, spotting the best in others |
|---|---|

| SPECIFIC DETAILS TO GENERAL IMPRESSION | souvenir sellers calling, small waves slapping tour boats, and pungent fish frying on Fisherman's Wharf ↓ In all this commotion, a visitor sees the wharf's vitality. |
|---|---|

| COMMON AND ORDINARY TO UNUSUAL FEATURES | mounds of bright leaves, crisp fall air, children bouncing ↓ the sheer joy of every moment at the playground across from the pediatric cancer center |
|---|---|

**Sequential Organization of Details**

help you organize all the observations, laying them out graphically or in a simple scratch outline.

**Start with a Main Impression or Thesis.** What main insight or impression do you want to convey? Answering this question will help you decide which details to include, which to omit, and how to avoid a dry list of facts.

For more on stating a thesis, see pp. 384–93.

| PLACE OBSERVED | Smalley Green after lunch |
|---|---|
| MAIN IMPRESSION | relaxing activity is good after a morning of classes |
| WORKING THESIS | After their morning classes, students have fun relaxing on Smalley Green with their dogs and Frisbees. |

If all the details that you've gathered seem to be overwhelming your ability to arrive at a main impression, take a break (and maybe a walk) and try to think of a statement that sums things up. One good example of a summary statement is Alea Eyre's "As soon as I stepped off the plane ramp, I was enveloped into a brand new world."

For more organization strategies, see pp. 395–403.

For transitions that mark place or direction, see p. 418.

**Organize to Show Your Audience Your Point.** How do you map out a series of observations? Your choice depends on your purpose and the main impression you want to create. Whatever your choice, add transitions—words or phrases to guide the reader from one vantage point, location, or idea to the next.

As you create your "picture," you bring a place to life using the details that capture its spirit. If your instructor approves, consider whether adding a photograph, sketch, diagram, or other illustration—with a caption—would enhance your written observation.

## Learning by Doing 📷 Experimenting with Organization

Take a second look at the arrangement of the details in your observation. Select a different yet promising sequence, and test it by outlining your draft in that order. Ask classmates for reactions as you consider which sequence most effectively conveys your main impression.

## Revising and Editing

For more revising and editing strategies, see Ch. 23.

Your revising, editing, and proofreading will be easier if you have accurate notes on your observations. But what if you don't have enough detail for your draft? If you have doubts, go back to the scene to take more notes.

**Focus on a Main Impression or Thesis.** As you begin to revise, have a friend read your observation, or read it yourself as if you had never seen the place you observed. Note gaps that would puzzle a reader, restate the spirit of the place, or sharpen the description of the main impression you want to convey in your thesis.

| | |
|---|---|
| WORKING THESIS | After morning classes, students have fun relaxing on Smalley Green with their dogs and Frisbees. |
| REVISED THESIS | When students, dogs, and Frisbees accumulate on Smalley Green after lunch, they show how much campus learning takes place outside of class. |

### THESIS CHECKLIST

☐ Does the thesis convey your main impression?

☐ Does the thesis (and the essay) offer an insight into the subject that you are observing?

☐ Could you make the thesis more vivid or specific based on details or insights you've gathered while planning, drafting, and developing your essay?

## Learning by Doing 📷 Strengthening Your Main Impression

Complete these two sentences: The main impression that I want to show my audience is _____. The main insight that I want to share is _____. Exchange sentences with a classmate or small group, and then each read aloud that draft while the others listen for the impression and insight the writer wants to convey. After each reading, discuss with the writer cuts, additions, and other changes to strengthen that impression.

**Add Relevant and Powerful Details.** Next, check your selection of details. Does each detail contribute to your main impression? Should any be dropped or added? Should any be rearranged so that your organization, moving point to point, is clearer? Could some observations be described more vividly, powerfully, or concretely? Could vague words such as *very, really, great,* or *beautiful* be replaced with more specific words? (Use Find to locate repetition, so you can reword for variety.)

## Peer Response 👥 Observing a Scene

Let a classmate or friend respond to your draft, suggesting how to use detail to convey your main impression more powerfully. Ask your peer editor to answer questions such as these about writing from observation:

For general questions for a peer editor, see p. 447.

- What main insight or impression do you carry away from this draft?
- Which sense does the writer use particularly well? Are any senses neglected?
- Can you see and feel what the writer experienced? Would more detail be more compelling? Put check marks wherever you want more details.
- How well has the writer used evidence from the senses to build a main impression? Which sensory impressions contribute most strongly to the overall picture? Which seem superfluous?
- If this paper were yours, what one thing would you work on?

To see where your draft could need work, consider these questions:

### REVISION CHECKLIST

☐ Have you accomplished your purpose—to convey to readers your overall impression of your subject and to share some telling insight about it?

☐ What can you assume your readers know? What do they need to be told?

☐ Have you gathered enough observations to describe your subject? Have you observed with *all* your senses when possible — even smell and taste?

☐ Have you been selective, including details that effectively support your overall impression?

☐ Which observations might need to be checked for accuracy? Which might need to be checked for richness or fullness?

☐ Is your organizational pattern the most effective for your subject? Is it easy for readers to follow? Would another pattern work better?

For more editing and proofreading strategies, see pp. 455–58.

After you revise your essay, edit and proofread it. Carefully check the grammar, word choice, punctuation, and mechanics — and then correct any problems. If you added details, consider whether they're sufficiently blended with the ideas already there. Some questions to get you started:

## EDITING CHECKLIST

For more help, find the relevant checklist sections in the Quick Editing Guide on p. Q-37. Turn also to the Quick Format Guide beginning on p. Q-1.

☐ Is your sentence structure correct? Have you avoided writing fragments, comma splices, and fused sentences?        A1, A2

☐ Have you used an adjective when you describe a noun or pronoun? Have you used an adverb when you describe a verb, adjective, or adverb? Have you used the correct form to compare two or more things?        A7

☐ Is it clear what each modifier in a sentence modifies? Have you created any dangling or misplaced modifiers?        B1

☐ Have you used parallel structure wherever needed, especially in lists or comparisons?        B2

## Reviewing and Reflecting

To complete more review questions for Ch. 5, go to LaunchPad.

**REVIEW** Working with classmates or independently, respond to the following questions:

1. To write a compelling description of a scene, you need to gather a lot of sensory details. How do you decide which ones to include or leave out?

2. What are the benefits of making both objective and subjective observations about a scene that you want to describe? Before answering the

question, you might think of an interesting scene that you have observed on your campus or elsewhere and then make objective and subjective observations about it. How did this process deepen or enrich your perspective?

3. What is the major task of revising the thesis of writing that describes a scene?

**REFLECT** After completing one of the writing assignments presented in this chapter or supplied by your instructor, turn back to the After Writing questions on page 39 of Chapter 3 and respond to as many of them as you can. While addressing these questions, it might be helpful to revisit your response to the Learning by Doing activity on page 76, if you completed it.

Next, reflect in writing about how you might apply the insights that you drew from this assignment to another situation — in or outside of college — in which you have to observe a scene. If no specific situations come to mind, imagine that

- in a human-behavior course, you're asked to observe a busy street or transportation hub, making notes about considerate and inconsiderate behavior and its effects, if any.
- in a business memo, you'd like to describe the clutter and mess in a workplace kitchen so vividly that employees will have an incentive to clean up after themselves.

In your reflection, consider the types of details you might include to get across your main impression.

## Additional Writing Assignments

1. To develop your powers of observation, go for a walk through an unfamiliar scene or a familiar scene worth a closer look (such as a supermarket or an open field). Avoid a familiar subject. Record your observations in two or three detailed paragraphs. Sum up your impression of the place, including any opinion you form through close observation.

2. Select an observation site that relates to your career plans. You might choose a medical facility (for nursing or medical school), a school or playground (for education), or an office complex or work site (for business). Observe carefully, noting details that contribute to your main impression of the place and your insight about work done there. Write an essay to convey these points to an audience interested in the same career path.

3. Observe the details of a specific place on campus as if you were seeing it for the first time. Describe it in an essay for campus readers, a letter to a prospective student (who'll want to know its relevance), or an entry on a travel blog for tourists (who'll want to know why they should stop there).

If you wish, include your own photograph of the scene or a standard campus shot; add a caption that expresses its essence.

4. **Source Assignment.** Locate a community tourist Web site, a town history or architectural survey, a campus guidebook, or a similar resource; select one of its attractions or locations to visit. Put aside the guide while you independently observe and record details about the location. Then present your main impression of the character or significance of the place, supplementing your detailed observations with historical, technical, or other information from your source. Clearly and accurately credit your source so that a reader can easily tell what you observed, what you learned, and where you learned it.

For advice on analyzing an image, refer to Ch. 14, Responding to Visual Representations.

5. **Visual Assignment.** Use one of the following photographs to explore the importance of the observer's point of view. After a preliminary look at the scene, select your vantage point as an observer, and identify the audience your essay will address (for example, readers who would or would not share your perspective). Observe the image carefully, and use its details to support your main impression of the scene from your perspective. Direct your specific insight about it to your audience.

Robert van Waarden/Aurora/Getty Images.

Kevin Steele/Aurora Photos.

Zoran Milich/Moment Mobile/Getty Images.

# 6 Interviewing a Subject

*Images clockwise from top left:* Patsy Lynch/Retna Ltd./Corbis Wire/Corbis; Christian Charisius/Corbis Wire/Corbis; Chris Ratcliffe/Bloomberg via Getty Images; David Paul Morris/Bloomberg via Getty Images.

## Responding to an Image

Suppose that you had an opportunity to interview one of the people shown here. Park Geun-hye (top left) is president of South Korea and the first woman to hold that position. George R. R. Martin (top right) is the author of the series of books on which *Game of Thrones* is based. Sheryl Sandberg (bottom right) is the COO of Facebook. Entrepreneur Elon Musk (bottom left), founder and CEO of Space Exploration Technologies Corporation, also founded Tesla Motors, which builds electric cars. What questions would you most like to ask the interviewee? Based on the person's public image and personality as revealed in these photos, what kind of response would you expect to receive? How do you think the photographer has tried to suggest something about the person?

D on't know what to write about? Go talk with someone. Meet for half an hour with an anthropology professor, and you probably will have plenty of material for a paper. Just as likely, you can get a paper's worth of information from a ten-minute exchange with a mechanic who relines brakes. Both the mechanic and the professor are experts. But even people who aren't usually considered experts may provide you with material.

You can direct a conversation by asking questions to elicit what you want to find out. You do so in an *interview* — a conversation with a purpose — usually to help you understand the other person or to find out what that person knows. You may use what you learn to profile the individual interviewed. However, interviews also provide expert information about a topic, intriguing firsthand accounts of an event or an era, or research samples of selected or representative people.

## Why Interviewing a Subject Matters

### In a College Course

- For your American Studies course, you gather firsthand knowledge about a moment in history by interviewing a veteran, a civil rights activist, a disaster survivor, or a person who experienced a local event.
- You interview a person who mentors students or sponsors internships to gain career advice (perhaps from an early childhood educator, a public safety officer, a health care provider, an artist, or a catering manager).

### In the Workplace

- You interview an "informed source" for a news site, a benefits specialist for a profile in your company newsletter, or your customers or clients for feedback on company products and services.

### In Your Community

- You contact experts to learn about composting food waste through the new city program or about installing a ramp to make your home accessible for your child who uses a wheelchair.

❓ Whom would you like to interview as an intriguing personality? Whom would you like to interview for answers or advice about some of your questions? In what situations might you conduct interviews in the future?

# Learning from Other Writers

Here are two essays whose writers talked to someone and reported the conversations, using direct quotations and telling details to reveal engaging personalities. To help you begin to analyze the first reading, look at the notes in the margin. They identify features such as the main idea, or thesis, and the quotations providing support.

## As You Read These Interview Essays

Ask yourself the following questions:

1. Was the conversation reported from an informal talk or planned as an interview? Does the writer report the conversation directly or indirectly?
2. What does the interview show about the character and personality of the speaker? What does it show about the author who is listening?
3. Why do you think the writer draws on conversation?

## Jon Ronson

### How One Stupid Tweet Blew Up Justine Sacco's Life

Jon Ronson is a journalist, a radio personality, the author of several books, and a documentary filmmaker. The following selections from his February 12, 2015, *New York Times Magazine* article capture his interviews of Justine Sacco, who was widely shamed on social media after posting a tweet that many considered racially offensive. The article was adapted from Ronson's book *So You've Been Publicly Shamed* (2015).

AP Images/Geraint Lewis.

As she made the long journey from New York to South Africa, to visit family during the holidays in 2013, Justine Sacco, thirty years old and the senior director of corporate communications at IAC [InterActiveCorp], began tweeting acerbic° little jokes about the indignities° of travel. There was one about a fellow passenger on the flight from John F. Kennedy International Airport: 1

"'Weird German Dude: You're in First Class. It's 2014. Get some deodorant.'—Inner monologue as I inhale BO. Thank God for pharmaceuticals." 2

Then, during her layover at Heathrow:° 3

"Chilly—cucumber sandwiches—bad teeth. Back in London!" 4

And on December 20, before the final leg of her trip to Cape Town: 5

"Going to Africa. Hope I don't get AIDS. Just kidding. I'm white!" 6

She chuckled to herself as she pressed send on this last one, then wandered around Heathrow's international terminal for half an hour, sporadically° 7

*Vivid story about the interview subject provides context for the interview*

---

**acerbic:** Harsh.　**indignities:** Humiliations.　**Heathrow:** A major airport in west London, England.　**sporadically:** Occasionally.

checking her phone. No one replied, which didn't surprise her. She had only 170 Twitter followers.

Sacco boarded the plane. It was an eleven-hour flight, so she slept. When | 8
the plane landed in Cape Town and was taxiing on the runway, she turned on her phone. Right away, she got a text from someone she hadn't spoken to since high school: "I'm so sorry to see what's happening." Sacco looked at it, baffled.

Then another text: "You need to call me immediately." It was from her | 9
best friend, Hannah. Then her phone exploded with more texts and alerts. And then it rang. It was Hannah. "You're the No. 1 worldwide trend on Twitter right now," she said.

Sacco's Twitter feed had become a horror show. "In light of @Justine | 10
Sacco disgusting racist tweet, I'm donating to @care today" and "How did @JustineSacco get a PR job?! Her level of racist ignorance belongs on Fox News. #AIDS can affect anyone!" and "I'm an IAC employee and I don't want @JustineSacco doing any communications on our behalf ever again. Ever." And then one from her employer, IAC, the corporate owner of The Daily Beast, OKCupid, and Vimeo: "This is an outrageous, offensive comment. Employee in question currently unreachable on an intl flight." The anger soon turned to excitement: "All I want for Christmas is to see @JustineSacco's face when her plane lands and she checks her inbox/voicemail" and "Oh man, @JustineSacco is going to have the most painful phone-turning-on moment ever when her plane lands" and "We are about to watch this @JustineSacco bitch get fired. In REAL time. Before she even KNOWS she's getting fired." . . .

By the time Sacco had touched down, tens of thousands of angry tweets | 11
had been sent in response to her joke. Hannah, meanwhile, frantically deleted her friend's tweet and her account—Sacco didn't want to look—but it was far too late. "Sorry @JustineSacco," wrote one Twitter user, "your tweet lives on forever."

In the early days of Twitter, I was a keen shamer. When newspaper colum- | 12
nists made racist or homophobic statements, I joined the pile-on. Sometimes I led it. . . .

[I]n those early days, the collective fury felt righteous, powerful, and | 13
effective. It felt as if hierarchies° were being dismantled, as if justice were
being democratized. As time passed, though, I watched these shame cam-      Interviewer explains
paigns multiply, to the point that they targeted not just powerful institutions  why he is personally
and public figures but really anyone perceived to have done something offen-  interested in the inter-
sive. I also began to marvel at the disconnect between the severity of the crime  viewee's predicament
and the gleeful savagery of the punishment. It almost felt as if shamings were
now happening for their own sake, as if they were following a script. . . .

Late one afternoon last year, I met Justine Sacco in New York, at a res- | 14
taurant in Chelsea called Cookshop. Dressed in rather chic business attire, Sacco ordered a glass of white wine. Just three weeks had passed since her trip to Africa, and she was still a person of interest to the media. Web sites

**hierarchies:** Systems in which certain people or offices are placed higher than others.

had already ransacked° her Twitter feed for more horrors. (For example, "I had a sex dream about an autistic kid last night," from 2012, was unearthed by BuzzFeed in the article "16 Tweets Justine Sacco Regrets.") A *New York Post* photographer had been following her to the gym.

"Only an insane person would think that white people don't get AIDS," she told me. It was about the first thing she said to me when we sat down.    15

Sacco had been three hours or so into her flight when retweets of her joke began to overwhelm my Twitter feed. I could understand why some people found it offensive. Read literally, she said that white people don't get AIDS, but it seems doubtful many interpreted it that way. More likely it was her apparently gleeful flaunting° of her privilege that angered people. But after thinking about her tweet for a few seconds more, I began to suspect that it wasn't racist but a reflexive° critique of white privilege—on our tendency to naively imagine ourselves immune from life's horrors. Sacco . . . had been yanked violently out of the context of her small social circle. Right?    16

> Quotations show the interviewee's personality and concerns

"To me it was so insane of a comment for anyone to make," she said. "I thought there was no way that anyone could possibly think it was literal."° (She would later write me an e-mail to elaborate on this point. "Unfortunately, I am not a character on *South Park* or a comedian, so I had no business commenting on the epidemic in such a politically incorrect manner on a public platform," she wrote. "To put it simply, I wasn't trying to raise awareness of AIDS or piss off the world or ruin my life. Living in America puts us in a bit of a bubble when it comes to what is going on in the third world. I was making fun of that bubble.")    17

I would be the only person she spoke to on the record about what happened to her, she said. It was just too harrowing°—and "as a publicist," inadvisable—but she felt it was necessary, to show how "crazy" her situation was, how her punishment simply didn't fit the crime.    18

"I cried out my body weight in the first twenty-four hours," she told me. "It was incredibly traumatic. You don't sleep. You wake up in the middle of the night forgetting where you are." She released an apology statement and cut short her vacation. Workers were threatening to strike at the hotels she had booked if she showed up. She was told no one could guarantee her safety.    19

> More quotations from the interviewee convey her emotional state

Her extended family in South Africa were African National Congress supporters—the party of Nelson Mandela.° They were longtime activists for racial equality. When Justine arrived at the family home from the airport, one of the first things her aunt said to her was: "This is not what our family stands for. And now, by association, you've almost tarnished° the family."    20

As she told me this, Sacco started to cry. I sat looking at her for a moment. Then I tried to improve the mood. I told her that "sometimes, things need to reach a brutal nadir° before people see sense."    21

**ransacked:** Raided.    **flaunting:** Displaying.    **reflexive:** Automatic.    **literal:** True; authentic.    **harrowing:** Agonizing.    **Nelson Mandela:** South Africa's first black president and a central figure in overturning the country's system of racial segregation and oppression.    **tarnished:** Spoiled; harmed.    **nadir:** The lowest point.

"Wow," she said. She dried her eyes. "Of all the things I could have been in society's collective consciousness, it never struck me that I'd end up a brutal nadir."    22

She glanced at her watch. It was nearly 6 p.m. The reason she wanted to meet me at this restaurant, and that she was wearing her work clothes, was that it was only a few blocks away from her office. At 6, she was due in there to clean out her desk.    23

"All of a sudden you don't know what you're supposed to do," she said. "If I don't start making steps to reclaim my identity and remind myself of who I am on a daily basis, then I might lose myself."    24

The restaurant's manager approached our table. She sat down next to Sacco, fixed her with a look and said something in such a low volume I couldn't hear it, only Sacco's reply: "Oh, you think I'm going to be grateful for this?"    25

We agreed to meet again, but not for several months. She was determined to prove that she could turn her life around. "I can't just sit at home and watch movies every day and cry and feel sorry for myself," she said. "I'm going to come back."    26

After she left, Sacco later told me, she got only as far as the lobby of her office building before she broke down crying. . . .    27

It's possible that Sacco's fate would have been different had an anonymous tip not led a writer named Sam Biddle to the offending tweet. Biddle was then the editor of Valleywag, Gawker Media's tech-industry blog. He retweeted it to his 15,000 followers and eventually posted it on Valleywag, accompanied by the headline, "And Now, a Funny Holiday Joke from IAC's P.R. Boss."    28

More background on the interviewee's predicament

In January 2014, I received an e-mail from Biddle, explaining his reasoning. "The fact that she was a P.R. chief made it delicious," he wrote. "It's satisfying to be able to say, 'O.K., let's make a racist tweet by a senior IAC employee count this time.' And it did. I'd do it again." Biddle said he was surprised to see how quickly her life was upended, however. "I never wake up and hope I [get someone fired] that day—and certainly never hope to ruin anyone's life." Still, he ended his e-mail by saying that he had a feeling she'd be "fine eventually, if not already."    29

He added: "Everyone's attention span is so short. They'll be mad about something new today."    30

Four months after we first met, Justine Sacco made good on her promise. We met for lunch at a French bistro downtown. I told her what Biddle had said—about how she was probably fine now. I was sure he wasn't being deliberately glib,° but like everyone who participates in mass online destruction, uninterested in learning that it comes with a cost.    31

"Well, I'm not fine yet," Sacco said to me. "I had a great career, and I loved my job, and it was taken away from me, and there was a lot of glory in that. Everybody else was very happy about that."    32

**glib:** Smooth-talking.

Sacco pushed her food around on her plate, and let me in on one of the 33 hidden costs of her experience. "I'm single; so it's not like I can date, because we Google everyone we might date," she said. "That's been taken away from me too." She was down, but I did notice one positive change in her. When I first met her, she talked about the shame she had brought on her family. But she no longer felt that way. Instead, she said, she just felt personally humiliated.

Biddle was almost right about one thing: Sacco did get a job offer right 34 away. But it was an odd one, from the owner of a Florida yachting company. "He said: 'I saw what happened to you. I'm fully on your side,'" she told me. Sacco knew nothing about yachts, and she questioned his motives. ("Was he a crazy person who thinks white people can't get AIDS?") Eventually she turned him down.

After that, she left New York, going as far away as she could, to Addis 35 Ababa, Ethiopia. She flew there alone and got a volunteer job doing P.R. for an NGO° working to reduce maternal-mortality rates. "It was fantastic," she said. She was on her own, and she was working. If she was going to be made to suffer for a joke, she figured she should get something out of it. "I never would have lived in Addis Ababa for a month otherwise," she told me. She was struck by how different life was there. Rural areas had only intermittent° power and no running water or Internet. Even the capital, she said, had few street names or house addresses.

Addis Ababa was great for a month, but she knew going in that she would 36 not be there long. She was a New York City person. Sacco is nervy and sassy and sort of debonair.° And so she returned to work at Hot or Not, which had been a popular site for rating strangers' looks on the pre-social Internet and was reinventing itself as a dating app.

But despite her near invisibility on social media, she was still ridiculed 37 and demonized across the Internet. Biddle wrote a Valleywag post after she returned to the work force: "Sacco, who apparently spent the last month hiding in Ethiopia after infuriating our species with an idiotic AIDS joke, is now a 'marketing and promotion' director at Hot or Not."

"How perfect!" he wrote. "Two lousy has-beens, gunning for a comeback 38 together." . . .

Recently, I wrote to Sacco to tell her I was putting her story in the *Times*, 39 and I asked her to meet me one final time to update me on her life. Her response was speedy. "No way." She explained that she had a new job in communications, though she wouldn't say where. She said, "Anything that puts the spotlight on me is a negative."

THESIS
gives dominant impression of interviewee and makes a larger point

It was a profound° reversal for Sacco. When I first met her, she was des- 40 perate to tell the tens of thousands of people who tore her apart how they had wronged her and to repair what remained of her public persona.° But perhaps she had now come to understand that her shaming wasn't really about her at all. Social media is so perfectly designed to manipulate our

**NGO:** Non-governmental organization. **intermittent:** Occasional. **debonair:** Charming. **profound:** Deep; significant. **persona:** Someone's perceived personality.

desire for approval, and that is what led to her undoing. Her tormentors were instantly congratulated as they took Sacco down, bit by bit, and so they continued to do so. Their motivation was much the same as Sacco's own—a bid for the attention of strangers—as she milled° about Heathrow, hoping to amuse people she couldn't see.

**milled:** Wandered aimlessly.

## Questions to Start You Thinking

### Meaning

1. What faults did Twitter users find in Justine Sacco's tweet about AIDS in Africa? What did Sacco actually mean by the tweet, according to her explanation to Ronson?

2. Why was Ronson personally interested in the public shaming of Sacco? In his view, how have "shame campaigns" changed over the years (paragraph 13)?

3. In the final paragraph, Ronson says, "perhaps [Sacco] had now come to understand that her shaming wasn't really about her at all." What, according to Ronson, might have been the actual purpose of the public ridicule she faced?

### Writing Strategies

4. Ronson provides a good deal of background about Sacco's tweeting fiasco and its consequences before presenting the content of his interviews with her. Do you think this is an effective strategy? Why, or why not?

5. As Ronson indicates, he conducted two separate interviews with Sacco. How, if at all, did the passage of time affect the nature of her responses? What might be the advantages or disadvantages of conducting separate interviews over time?

6. Ronson waits until the end of his essay to make a larger point about Sacco and the motivations behind public shaming. Do you think this is the best place to make this point, or should it have been presented earlier? Explain your reasoning.

## Lorena A. Ryan-Hines          Student Essay

### Looking Backwards, Moving Forward

Lorena Ryan-Hines, a student in a nursing program, wrote this essay after interviewing an experienced professional in her field.

Someone once said, "You cannot truly know where you are going unless you know where you have come from." I don't think I understood this statement until I got the opportunity to sit down with Joan Gilmore, assistant director

1

of nursing at Smithville Health Care Center. With the blur of everyday activities going on during the change of third shift to first shift at the nursing home, I had never recognized what value Joan could bring to the younger nurses. Once we started to talk, I began to realize that, although I am a nurse, I don't know much about how nursing has evolved over the years. During our conversation, I discovered how much history, wisdom, and advice Joan has to share.

❓ Can you identify with Ryan-Hines's work environment and relationship with Joan? In what ways?

Joan tries to stay as active as she can working on the floor so she does not use an office. We decided just to sit down in one of the multi-purpose conference rooms. Joan looks very good for a woman of her age. In fact, no one would ever suspect by looking at her that she is a young sixty-four years old. She is approximately 5'2" tall and dressed in white scrub pants with a flowered scrub top. Although her hair is dyed, the color is a nice natural tone for her. She is not flashy or outspoken, but she knows what she is doing. However, if she has a question, she does not have a problem asking someone else.    2

When we first sat down, we started talking about how she grew up. She was the third child of seven children. Her father worked in a factory and also farmed over one hundred acres. Her mom stayed home to take care of the children. As I watched her talk about her upbringing, a glaze seemed to roll across her face. I could see a slight twinkle in her eyes. She almost appeared to be back in that time and space of childhood. She went on to explain to me that she decided to go to nursing school because it was one of the few jobs, forty-five years ago, that could be productive for a woman.    3

❓ Why do you think that the "dignity cap" was so important for Joan?

She decided to enter the three-year program at St. Elizabeth Hospital's School for Nursing in Dayton, Ohio. Students were not allowed to be married and had to live in the nursing school's brick dormitory. Whenever they were in class and on the floors of the hospital, they were required to wear their uniforms, light blue dresses with white pin stripes. The student nursing cap, the "dignity cap" as Joan called it, was all white. When students graduated, they earned their black stripe which distinguished them as registered nurses. Joan said that she did not think we should continue to wear the all-white uniforms or nursing caps. However, she conveyed a sense of sadness when she said, "I think we have gone too far to the left these days because everyone dresses and looks the same. I think as a nurse you have worked hard and earned the right to stand out somehow."    4

I asked Joan about the pros and cons of being a registered nurse and whether she ever regretted her decision. Her philosophy is that being a nurse is a calling. Although nursing pay is generally considered a decent living wage, sometimes dealing with management, long hours, and the grief of tough cases is hard. Through experience and commitment, a nurse learns to take each day    5 as it comes and grow with it. Even though life-and-death situations can be very stressful and the fast-paced nursing world can be draining, nurses can never forget that patients are people. For Joan, when patients are demanding and short fused, they are not really angry at the nurses but at the situation they are in. She believes that a nurse is always able to help her patients in some way, be it physical or emotional.

The advice Joan gave me about becoming a new registered nurse may be some of the best advice of my life. Each registered nurse specialty has its demands. She recommended working for a while in a medical surgery area. This area is a great place to gain knowledge and experience about multiple acute illnesses and disease processes. From there, nurses can move forward and find the specialty areas that best suit them. This fit is important because nurses need to be knowledgeable and confident, leaders who are not afraid to ask questions when they do not know the answers. To gain the respect of others, nurses also must be willing to help and to let others help them because no one can be a nurse all alone. Joan recommended being courteous, saying "please" and "thank you" when asking someone to do something as well as encouraging others with different talents. Lastly, she urged me always to do my best and be proud of my accomplishments.

6

Afterwards, I thanked her for the advice and her time. She got up smiling and simply walked out of the room and back to the job she has loved for so many years. I found myself sitting back down for a few minutes to reflect on everything she had just told me. Nursing from yesterday to today has changed not only with the technological advances but even the simplest things. Uniforms are nothing like they were forty years ago. The rules back then could never be enforced today. Some things will never change though, like the simple respect a nurse gives another human being. The profound advice Joan gave me is something I will carry with me for the rest of my personal and professional career.

7    ❓ Have you ever received valuable advice from someone like Joan? How has that advice affected you and your decisions?

### Work Cited

Gilmore, Joan. Personal interview, 4 June 2009.

## Questions to Start You Thinking

### Meaning

1. What is the main point of Ryan-Hines's essay?

2. What kind of person is Joan Gilmore? How does Ryan-Hines feel about her?

3. How is Gilmore's history the history of nursing during the last few decades? Is an interview an effective method of relating the history of a profession? Why, or why not?

Writing Strategies

4. Why does Ryan-Hines begin her essay with a quotation and an impression of the nursing home? How does this opening serve as a frame for her conversation with Joan?

5. What details does Ryan-Hines use to describe Joan? What senses does she draw on? Does she provide enough detail for you to form a clear image of Joan?

6. How much of the interview does Ryan-Hines quote directly? Why does she choose to quote directly rather than paraphrase in these places? Would her essay be stronger if she used more of Joan's own words?

7. Using highlighters or marginal notes, identify the essay's introduction, thesis, major emphases, supporting details for each emphasis, and conclusion. How effective is the organization of this essay?

# Learning by Writing

## The Assignment: Interviewing

To interview someone for information, see Additional Writing Assignments on pp. 103–4.

Write a paper about someone who interests you and base the paper primarily on a conversation with that person. Select any acquaintance, relative, or person you have heard about whose traits, interests, activities, background, or outlook on life might intrigue your readers. Your purpose is to show this person's character and personality — to bring your subject to life for your readers.

These students found notable people to interview:

One student wrote about a high school science teacher who had left teaching for a higher-paying job in the educational software industry, only to return three years later to the classroom.

One writer recorded the thoughts and feelings of a discouraged farmer she had known since childhood.

Another learned about adjustment to life in a new country by talking to his neighbor from Somalia.

### Facing the Challenge  Writing from an Interview

The major challenge writers face when writing from an interview is to find a clear focus. They must first sift through the huge amount of information generated in an interview and then decide what dominant impression of the subject to present in an essay.

To identify possible angles, jot down answers to these questions:

■ What did you find most interesting about the interview?

■ What topics did your subject talk about the most?

- What did he or she become most excited or animated about?
- What topics generated the most interesting quotations?

Your answers should help you determine a dominant impression — the aspect of your interviewee's character or personality that you want to emphasize for your readers. Once you have this focus, you can pick the details from the interview that best illustrate the points you want to make. Make sure that all quotations — long or short — are accurate. Use them strategically and sparingly to reveal the character traits that you wish to emphasize. Select colorful quotations that allow readers to "hear" your subject's distinctive voice. To capture the dynamic of conversation, include your own observations as well as actual quotations.

## Generating Ideas

If an image of the perfect subject has flashed into your mind, consider yourself lucky, and set up an appointment with that person at once. If you have drawn a blank, you'll need to cast about for a likely interview subject.

**Brainstorm for Possible Subjects.** Try brainstorming for a few minutes to see what pops into your mind. Your subject need not be spectacular or unusual; ordinary lives can make fascinating reading.

For more on each strategy for generating ideas in this section or for additional strategies, see Ch. 19.

### DISCOVERY CHECKLIST

- ☐ Are you acquainted with anyone whose life has been unusually eventful, stressful, or successful?
- ☐ Are you curious about why someone you know made a certain decision or how that person got to his or her current point in life?
- ☐ Is there an expert or a leader whom you admire or are puzzled by?
- ☐ Do you know someone whose job or hobby interests you?
- ☐ What older person could tell you about life thirty or even fifty years ago?
- ☐ Who has passionate convictions about society, politics, sex, or childrearing?
- ☐ Whose background and life history would you like to know more about?
- ☐ Whose lifestyle, values, or attitudes are utterly different from your own and from those of most people you know?

**Tap Local Interview Resources.** Investigate campus resources such as departmental or faculty Web pages, student activity officers and sponsors, recent yearbook photographs, stories from the newspaper archives, or facilities such as the theater, media, or sports centers. Look on campus, at work,

Former president Richard Nixon, right, is interviewed by David Frost, May 5, 1977. Their exchanges later inspired an award-winning play and the movie *Frost/Nixon*.
AP Images/Ray Stubblebine.

or in your community for people with intriguing backgrounds or experiences. Campuses and libraries often maintain databases of local authorities, researchers, and authors available for press contacts or expert advice. Identify several prospects in case your first choice isn't available.

**Set Up an Interview.** Find out whether your prospect will grant an interview, talk at length—an hour, say—and agree to appear in your paper. If you sense reluctance, find another subject.

Don't be timid about asking for an interview. After all, your request is flattering, acknowledging that person as someone with valuable things to say. Try to schedule the interview on your subject's own ground—his or her home or workplace. The details you observe in those surroundings can make your essay more vivid.

**Prepare Questions.** The interview will go better if you are an informed interviewer with prepared questions. To develop thoughtful questions, find out a bit about your subject's life history, experience, affiliations, and interests.

Ask about the person's background, everyday tasks, favorite activities, and hopes to encourage your subject to open up. Asking for a little imagining may elicit a revealing response. (If your house were on fire, what would you try to save? If you had your life to live over, what would you do differently?) Focus on whatever aspects best reveal your subject's personality. Good questions will help you lead the conversation where you want it to go, get it back on track when it strays, and avoid awkward silences. For example, to interview someone with an unusual job or hobby, try questions like these:

- How long have you been a park ranger?
- How did you get involved in this work?
- How have you learned about the physical features and ecological balance in your park?
- What happens in a typical day? What do you like most or least?
- How has this job changed your life or your concerns?
- What are your plans and hopes for the future?

One good question can get some people talking for hours, and four or five may be enough for any interview, but it's better to prepare too many than too few.

## Learning by Doing 🎧 Analyzing Interview Questions

Listen to several radio interviews on a local station or National Public Radio (which archives many types of interviews, including programs such as *Fresh Air*). As you listen, jot down the names of the interviewer and interviewee, the topic, and any particularly fruitful or useless questions. Working with others in person or online, discuss your conclusions about the success of the interviews you heard. Collaborate on a set of guidelines for preparing good questions and dodging bad ones.

**Be Flexible and Observant.** Sometimes a question won't interest your subject. Or the person may seem reluctant to answer, especially if you're unwittingly trespassing into private territory, such as someone's love life. Don't badger. If you wait silently for a bit, you might be rewarded. If not, just go on to the next question. Should the conversation drift, steer it back: "But to get back to what you were saying about . . ."

Sometimes the most rewarding question simply grows out of what the subject says or an item you note in the environment. Observing your subject's clothing, expressions, mannerisms, or equipment may also suggest unexpected facets of personality. For example, Ryan-Hines describes Joan Gilmore's appearance as she introduces her character.

For more on using observation, see Ch. 5.

## Peer Response 👥 Preparing Questions for an Interview

Ask a classmate to read the questions you plan to use in your interview. Then interview your classmate, asking the following:

- Are the questions appropriate for the person who will be interviewed?
- Will the questions help gather the information I am seeking?
- Are any of the questions unclear? How could I rephrase them?
- Do any of the questions seem redundant? Irrelevant?
- What additional questions would you suggest that I ask?

**Decide How to Record the Interview.** Many interviewers use only paper and pen to take notes unobtrusively. Even though they can't write down everything the person says, they want to look the subject in the eye and keep the conversation lively. As you take notes, be sure to record or sketch details on the scene—names and dates, numbers, addresses, surroundings, physical appearance. Also jot down memorable words exactly as the speaker says them, and put quotation marks around them. When you transcribe your notes, you will know that they are quoted directly.

A telephone or an e-mail interview sounds easy but lacks the interplay you can achieve face-to-face. You'll miss observing possessions that reveal personality or seeing smiles, frowns, or other body language. Meet in person if possible, or set up an online video chat.

Many professionals advise against using a recorder because it may inhibit the subject and make the interviewer lazy about concentrating on the subject's responses. Too often, the objections go, it tempts the interviewer simply to quote rambling conversation without shaping it into good writing. If you do bring a recorder to your interview, be sure that the person you're talking with has no objections. Arm yourself with paper and pen in case the recorder malfunctions. Perhaps the best practice is to combine both methods. Write down the main points, and use your recording to check quotations for accuracy or add more words from the interview.

As soon as the interview ends, write down everything you recall but couldn't record. The questions you prepared for the interview will guide your memory, as will notes you took while talking.

## Learning by Doing 🔘 Interviewing a Classmate

Interview a classmate to learn more about him or her. Record specific details about that person's life, identifying commonalities between the two of you. Perhaps you both attended the same school or share a birthday month. Look for differences, too. For example, your interview partner might have talent in a specific sport or knowledge about a subject that is unfamiliar to you. Does your interview partner have any unique skills or any memories that he or she considers especially significant? Use your notes to write a one-paragraph "spotlight" feature on your classmate.

## Planning, Drafting, and Developing

For more strategies for planning, drafting, and developing, see Chs. 20, 21, and 22.

After your interview, you may have a good notion of what to include in your first draft, what to emphasize, what to quote directly, what to summarize. But if your notes seem a confused jumble, what should you do?

**Evaluate Your Material.** Remember your purpose: to reveal your subject's character and personality through conversation. Start by listing details you're likely to include. Photographs, sketches, or your doodles also may help you find a focus. As you sift your material, try these questions:

> What part of the conversation gave you the most insight into your subject's character and circumstances?
>
> Which direct quotations reveal the most about your subject? Which are the most amusing, pithy, witty, surprising, or outrageous?
>
> Which objects in the subject's environment provide you with valuable clues about his or her interests?

What, if anything, did your subject's body language reveal? Did it suggest discomfort, pride, self-confidence, shyness, pomposity?

What did tone or gestures tell you about the person's state of mind?

How can you summarize your subject's character or personality?

Does one theme run through your material? If so, what is it?

**Focus Your Thesis on a Dominant Impression.** Most successful portraits focus on a single dominant impression of the interview subject.

For more on stating a thesis, see pp. 384–93.

| | |
|---|---|
| DOMINANT IMPRESSION | Del talked a lot about freedom of the press. |
| WORKING THESIS | Del Sampat is a true believer in freedom of the press. |

If you are writing your interview essay in the first person, as Ryan-Hines did, you may personalize the thesis statement by including yourself as the observer:

| | |
|---|---|
| RYAN-HINES'S THESIS | During our conversation, I discovered how much history, wisdom, and advice Joan has to share. |

If you have lots of material and if, as often happens, your conversation rambled, you may want to develop the dominant impression by emphasizing just a few things about your subject — personality traits, views on particular topics, or shaping influences. To find such a focus, try grouping your details in three layers of notes, following the pattern below:

1. Dominant Impression          ☐
2. Main Emphases      ☐     ☐
    points about traits, views, influences
3. Supporting Details    ☐  ☐  ☐  ☐  ☐
    quotations, reported words, description

## Learning by Doing 🔘 Stating a Dominant Impression

How would you characterize in one sentence the person you interviewed? What single main impression do you want to convey? Specify your ideas by completing this sentence: My dominant impression of _____ is _____ . Share your sentence with a classmate or small group, either in person or online. Respond to each other's sentences to help each writer achieve a sentence that is both thoughtful and clear.

For more on selecting and presenting quotations, see D3 (pp. Q-28–Q-29) and D6 (pp. Q-30–Q-31) in the Quick Research Guide. For more on using visuals, see pp. 353–54.

**Bring Your Subject to Life.** A quotation, a physical description, a portrait of your subject at home or at work can bring the person instantly to life in your reader's mind. If your instructor approves adding an image, place it so that it supplements but does not overshadow your essay.

When you quote directly, be as accurate as possible, and don't put into quotation marks anything your subject didn't say. Sometimes you may quote a whole sentence or more, sometimes just a phrase.

**Double-Check Important Information.** Maybe you can't read your hasty handwriting or some crucial information escaped your notes. In such a case, telephone or e-mail the person you interviewed to ask specific questions without taking much time. You might also read back any direct quotations you plan to use so your subject can confirm their accuracy.

## Revising and Editing

For more revising and editing strategies, see Ch. 23.

As you read over your first draft, keep in mind that your purpose was to make the person you interviewed come alive for your reader.

---

### Peer Response 👥 Interviewing a Subject

For general questions for a peer editor, see p. 447.

Have a classmate or friend read your draft and suggest how to make the portrait more vivid, complete, and clear. Ask your peer editor to answer questions such as these about writing from an interview:

- Does the opening make you want to know the person portrayed? If so, how has the writer interested you? If not, what gets in your way?
- What makes the interviewee interesting to the writer?
- What is the writer's dominant impression of the person interviewed?
- Does the writer include any quotations or details that contradict or are unrelated to the dominant impression or insight?
- Do the quoted words or reported speech "sound" real to you? Would you drop any conversation the writer used? If so, mark it.
- Do you have questions about the subject that aren't answered?
- If this paper were yours, what is the one thing you would be sure to work on before handing it in?

---

**Focus on Your Main Idea or Thesis.** Once you have finished a draft, you may still feel swamped by too much information. Will readers find your essay overloaded? Will they understand the dominant impression you want to convey? To be certain that they will, first polish and refine your thesis.

| | |
|---|---|
| WORKING THESIS | Del Sampat is a true believer in freedom of the press. |
| REVISED THESIS | Del Sampat, news editor for the *Campus Times*, sees every story he writes as an opportunity to exercise and defend the freedom of the press. |

## THESIS CHECKLIST

☐ Does the thesis get across a dominant impression of your subject?

☐ Does the thesis convey this dominant impression as specifically as possible?

☐ Could you make the thesis more vivid based on details or insights you gathered from your interview or from planning, drafting, or developing your essay?

## Learning by Doing 🖼 Detailing with Color

Examining an essay you wrote for this class or another, write your thesis on a separate piece of paper. Below this, write one or two key words that describe each of the claims you make in your essay. Assign each claim or piece of support a distinct color. Then, using highlighters or colored pencils — or the highlighting feature of your word-processing program — go through the essay and highlight each claim and the support for it in the assigned color. Afterward, examine your essay. Are any colors misplaced or underrepresented? Also, check for balance. There should be approximately the same amount of discussion for each color. Reflect on the benefits of color coding support or evidence. How might this strategy help with writing a longer essay?

## REVISION CHECKLIST

☐ Are the details focused on a dominant impression you want to emphasize? Are all of them relevant? How do you convey the impression to readers?

☐ How do the parts of the conversation you've reported reveal the subject's unique personality, character, mood, or concerns?

☐ Does your paper need a stronger beginning? Is your ending satisfactory?

☐ Should some quotations be summarized or indirectly quoted? Should some explanation be enlivened by adding specific quotations?

☐ When the direct quotations are read out loud, do they sound as if they're from the mouth of the person you're portraying?

☐ Where might you need to add revealing details about the person's surroundings, personal appearance, or mannerisms?

☐ Have you included your own pertinent observations and insights?

☐ Does any of your material strike you now as irrelevant or dull?

A Writer's Guide

For more editing and proofreading strategies, see pp. 455–58.

After you have revised your essay, edit and proofread it. Carefully check the grammar, word choice, punctuation, and mechanics — and then correct any problems you find.

For more help, find the relevant checklist sections in the Quick Editing Guide on p. Q-37. Turn also to the Quick Format Guide beginning on p. Q-1.

### EDITING CHECKLIST

| | |
|---|---|
| ☐ Is it clear what each *he, she, they,* or other pronoun refers to? Does each pronoun agree with (match) its antecedent? | A6 |
| ☐ Have you used the correct case (*he* or *him*) for all your pronouns? | A5 |
| ☐ Is your sentence structure correct? Have you avoided writing fragments, comma splices, or fused sentences? | A1, A2 |
| ☐ Have you used quotation marks, ellipses (to show the omission of words), and other punctuation correctly in all quotations? | D3 |

## Reviewing and Reflecting

To complete more review questions for Ch. 6, go to LaunchPad.

**REVIEW** Working with classmates or independently, respond to the following questions:

1. What are some strategies for finding an interesting interview subject? Using one or more of these strategies, identify two or three possible interview candidates.

2. Once you have conducted an interview, what strategies can you use to evaluate the information that you've gathered and identify the most useful material?

3. In interview-based personal profiles, what should the thesis do? Examine the thesis in a personal profile — one written by you or a peer, or by a journalist. Does it accomplish this goal? Why, or why not?

**REFLECT** After completing one of the writing assignments presented in this chapter or supplied by your instructor, turn back to the After Writing questions on page 39 of Chapter 3 and respond to as many of them as you can.

Next, reflect in writing about how you might apply the insights that you drew from this assignment to another situation — in or outside of college — in which you have to conduct an interview. If no specific situations come to mind, imagine that

- in a business course, you have decided to interview an entrepreneur about how he or she achieved success.

- in a work setting, you have been asked to interview a top executive for a profile in your company's newsletter.

In your reflection, consider the types of questions that you might ask and how you might bring your interview subject to life.

# Additional Writing Assignments

1. Interview someone from whom you can learn, possibly someone whose profession interests you or whose advice can help you solve a problem or make a decision. Your purpose will be to communicate what you have learned, not to characterize the person you interview.

2. Write a paper based on an interview with at least two members of your extended family about some incident that is part of your family lore. Direct your paper to younger relatives. If accounts of the event don't always agree, combine them into one vivid account, noting that some details may be more trustworthy than others. Give credit to your sources.

3. Briefly talk with fifteen or twenty students on your campus to find out their career goals and their reasons for their choices. Are they feeling uncertain about a career, pursuing the one they've always wanted, or changing careers for better employment options? Are most looking for security, income, or personal satisfaction? Write a short essay summing up what you find out. Provide some quotations to flesh out your survey and perhaps characterize your classmates. Are they materialists? Idealists? Practical people? (Ask your instructor if any campus permission is needed before you begin these interviews.)

4. With the approval of your instructor, plan an individual or collaborative interview project with a possible public outcome — an article for the campus newspaper or alumni magazine, a page for the course Web site, a podcast for the campus radio station, a multimodal presentation for future students (combining written text with audio clips or photographs), or some other option that you or your group have the expertise to prepare. Analyze the purpose of the proposed outlet; select a campus interviewee whose knowledge or experience might assist or intrigue its audience. Develop your questions, conduct your interview, and present it.

5. **Source Assignment.** With your whole class or a small group, collaborate to interview someone from campus or the local community with special knowledge about a matter that concerns the group. Prepare by turning to background sources: your interviewee's Web page, social media presence, or résumé; any campus or local news coverage; public-meeting or presentation records; or relevant statistics. Plan the interview by working together on these questions:

   > What do you want to find out? What lines of questioning will you pursue? What topic will each student ask about? How much time will each have to ask a series of questions? Who will record the interview (if your subject agrees)? Who will take notes (as your record or backup)?

   Preview each other's questions to avoid duplication. Ask open-ended, not yes/no, questions to encourage discussion. Your group's product can be many individual papers or one collaborative effort (such as a paper, an online threaded discussion, or a blog), as your instructor directs. Be sure to credit all of your sources.

For advice on analyzing an image, refer to Ch. 14, Responding to Visual Representations.

6. **Visual Assignment.** Select a photograph of a person from this chapter (p. 84 or below) or elsewhere in the book. Use that image to explore the experience of an interview from the standpoint of what is communicated through expression, body language, clothing, environment, and other nonverbal cues. Use your analysis of the image to support your thesis about the interview relationship it portrays.

Landov.

FEMA/Getty Images.

Joe Raedle/Getty Images News/Getty Images.

# Comparing and Contrasting

*Larger image:* Afro Newspaper/Archive Photos/Gado/Getty Images.
*Inset image:* Drew Angerer/Getty Images News/Getty Images.

## Responding to an Image

Both of these pictures capture protests in Baltimore, Maryland. The top photograph shows university students demonstrating two days after the April 4, 1968, assassination of civil rights leader Martin Luther King Jr. The bottom photograph, taken in April 2015, shows protesters participating in a vigil for Freddie Gray, an African American man who suffered a fatal injury after being taken into police custody. Examine the two photographs carefully, noting similarities and differences. What similar or different qualities are evident in the configuration of the crowds and their leadership, or in the energy or focus of the protesters? What do these and other similarities or differences say about the years the photos were taken or the causes for which the protesters have gathered?

Which city—Dallas or Atlanta—has more advantages or drawbacks for a young single person thinking of settling down to a career? Which of two ads for the same toy appeals more effectively to parents who want to get durability as well as educational value for their money? As singers and songwriters, how are Beyoncé Knowles and Taylor Swift similar and dissimilar? Such questions invite answers that set two subjects side by side.

When you compare, you point out similarities; when you contrast, you discuss differences. When you write about two complicated subjects, usually you need to do both. Considering Mozart and Bach, you might find that each has traits the other has—or lacks. Instead of concluding that one is great and the other inferior, you might conclude that they're two distinct composers, each with an individual style. On the other hand, if your main purpose is to judge between two subjects (such as moving either to Dallas or to Atlanta), you would look especially for positive and negative features, weigh the attractions and faults of each city, and then stick your neck out and make your choice.

## Why Comparing and Contrasting Matter

### In a College Course

- You compare and contrast to "evaluate" the relative merits of Norman Rockwell and N. C. Wyeth in an art history course or the relative accuracy of two Civil War Web sites for a history course.
- You compare and contrast to "describe" a little-known subject, such as medieval funeral customs, by setting it next to a similar yet familiar subject, such as modern funeral traditions.

### In the Workplace

- You compare and contrast your company's products or services with those of competitors.

### In Your Community

- You compare and contrast your options in choosing a financial aid package, cell phone contract, childcare provider, bike helmet, or new mayor.

   ❓ What are some instances when you compare or contrast products, services, opportunities, options, solutions, or other things? When might you use comparison, contrast, or both in your writing? What would you expect them to contribute?

# Learning from Other Writers

In this chapter you will be asked to write a paper setting two subjects side by side, comparing and contrasting them. Let's see how two other writers have used these familiar habits of thought in writing. To help you begin to analyze the first reading, look at the notes in the margin. They identify features such as the thesis, or main idea, the sequence of the broad subjects considered, and the specific points of comparison and contrast.

## As You Read These Comparisons and Contrasts

Ask yourself the following questions:

1. What two (or more) items are compared and contrasted? Does the writer use comparison or contrast only? Does he combine the two? Why?

2. What is the purpose of the comparison and contrast? What idea does the information support or refute?

3. How does the writer organize the essay? Why?

## César Vargas

### How First- and Second-Generation Hispanics Can Help Each Other

César Vargas.

Writer, producer, and marketing strategist César Vargas founded UPLIFTT (United People for Latinos in Film, TV and Theater) and is president of Burning Ones Productions. In this essay, which appeared in both the *Huffington Post* and *Hispanic Trending*, he examines the differing experiences of first- and second-generation Hispanics in the United States.

When scientists recently announced that poor folks experience rapid aging at the cellular level and used both the first generation ("poor" Mexicans) and second generation (and beyond of "non poor" Mexicans) as examples, the differences between those born outside of the States and those born and raised here flashed before my eyes.    1    ⎤
─THESIS

I am very familiar with both. I happen to be both fully bicultural and    2
fully bilingual. I can talk to you about *Chiquilladas,° Carrusel de Niños,° A la cama con Porcel,°* and *The Fresh Prince of Bel-Air, Friends,* and *Seinfeld.* You see, I was born in the Dominican Republic and raised there until I was two months shy of turning thirteen. That is a precarious° age to migrate to another land without knowing a lick of its language and culture besides the exaggerations from Hollywood movies, TV shows, and the occasional compatriota° who

---

*Chiquilladas, Carrusel de Niños:* Popular Spanish-language television shows for children. *A la cama con Porcel:* A comedy show featuring Latin American comedian Jorge Porcel. **precarious:** Risky.    **compatriota:** Person from one's country.

made it seem like money grew on trees and the streets were paved with gold in the States.

Point 1

Subject A

> Most immigrants come from monolithic° cultures. When you are raised in a monolithic culture, there is no "other" to compare yourself to or to make you feel like you're more or lesser than. (I mean culturally, because we do show and experience internal colorism and racism as well as classism.) Once I arrived, the indoctrination° was quick, but not without its usual problems. I couldn't tell people apart based on race, for instance, which was a danger in itself. Not because I was colorblind, but because I had family and friends of

Subject B

> all colors and didn't see the socially constructed separations that are so pronounced here. In the States, race also tends to be linked to culture. Latinos happen to be a special case. We're an ethnicity comprised of many races (and cultures, but lumped into one in the United States).

Point 2

Subject A

> Scientists are saying that those of us born outside do not experience the same stressors those born here experience. Hispanic immigrants also happen to live in Hispanic enclaves—ethnic pockets. They are hardly exposed to the bigotry their kids and nephews experience and they're also most likely to be oblivious about their own racism and colorism, but I digress.° They won't experience the same type of bigotry that bruises the ego and turns a person into a maligned individual. They won't be hypersensitive of how others perceive them and hyperaware of their identity. Both are sort of pummeled

Subject B

> into the heads of those born here—whether they like it or not. Most reactions to that are usually negative: complete denial of a culture to the point of being indignant° about being "boxed" in even if it is benign or beneficial, becoming super Latinos who build unnecessary walls between other people in a multicultural world, mental self-harm, and aggressive behavior towards others. . . .

Point 3

Alternating
Subjects A
and B

> According to research, first-generation Latinos won't suffer the same health problems those born here are afflicted with. So their children might be better off economically, but not physically and mentally because of the stressors aforementioned. (Immigrant children do have an early advantage compared to U.S.-born Hispanics while U.S.-born Hispanic children of immigrants are eventually more successful than both immigrant children and those of the general population.) It's important to note that Spanish-speakers who speak little to no English do get a far worse treatment when it comes to health care: They are constantly dismissed or misdiagnosed by health care providers because of a lack of caring, understanding, and poor training. The dismissal goes beyond health care. So being a Hispanic immigrant is not as gravy as you'd think.

> What I suggest to both first- and subsequent-generation Hispanics is to take care of each other in the areas both need the most help in. Subsequent generations should make sure their parents—as well as those within the community who know little English—are getting proper treatment and they're aware of services available to them. Writing about it in the

3

4

5

6

**monolithic:** Large and uniform.    **indoctrination:** Education in principles or ideology.
**digress:** To stray from one's main point.    **indignant:** Offended.

English-speaking media is a step forward. Also, advocating for better training as well as more thorough services should be part of the grand plan. Those in politics can push for policies to quicken the process. In turn, first-generation Hispanics can show us how to be confident, proud, and to validate ourselves without the negative interference and influence of outside forces.

Another thing: It's one thing to be proud of a culture and another to overcompensate by beating others over the head of how proud you are of being part of it. That tends to push people away and bring numerous problems. That is a main reason why Hispanic immigrants fare better in Hispanic corporate America and Hollywood. (Though this is bringing other problems that we must address.) They are not wrought with the insecurities and self-doubt this nation shoves down the throats of those born and raised here at every turn they take. The negative signals come in the form of overt° and covert° cultural racism—a racism those foreign Hispanics in Hispanic enclaves hardly experience and to such high intensity.    7

I managed to understand second-generation Hispanics because once I arrived I wasn't just pushed into the culture; I willingly submerged myself into it to the point of becoming one. This is the reason why I've made it my business to advocate for those born and raised in the States, but without forgetting that those who brought us here are also experiencing their own difficulties.    8  — Conclusion

Let's take care of each other by healing, emancipating, validating, and uplifting ourselves physically, mentally, and spiritually. *¡Sí, se puede!°*    9

## Questions to Start You Thinking

### Meaning

1. Why, according to Vargas, was it difficult for him to move to the United States just before his thirteenth birthday?

2. According to Vargas, what are some advantages and disadvantages of being a first-generation Hispanic American? A second-generation Hispanic American?

3. What is Vargas's purpose in contrasting the two groups? Is his goal to explain or convince? Or is it something else?

### Writing Strategies

4. Vargas begins by discussing his personal history. Why do you suppose he does this, and how effective is this approach?

5. Which method of organization does Vargas use to arrange his essay? How effectively does he switch between his two subjects?

6. Vargas ends his essay with an appeal. Do you think the earlier parts of the essay set up this appeal adequately? Why, or why not?

---

**overt:** Open; not concealed.     **covert:** Concealed.     ***¡Sí, se puede!:*** "Yes, you can." [in Spanish]

## Jacob Griffin

### Karate Kid vs. Kung Fu Panda: A Race to the Olympics

Student Jacob Griffin compares and contrasts karate and kung fu, asking which of the two deserves to be the first declared an Olympic sport.

About three decades ago, the first Karate Kid waxed on and off, kicking his   1
way into the American sports scene. During the same era, martial arts movies with stars like Jackie Chan began to popularize kung fu with American audiences. Films such as the *Karate Kid* trilogy were instant classics, while kung fu has appeared in *Kill Bill,* the *Matrix* movies, and even the animated *Kung Fu Panda*. Despite the worldwide popularity of both fighting styles, neither has yet been approved for Olympic competition. The International Olympic Committee should consider which of these styles first deserves to be declared an official Olympic sport.

Besides their shared status in movies and popular culture, these two   2
fighting styles are similar because each is an umbrella term for several different variations. The World Karate Federation includes four styles on its official list, while hundreds of kung fu categories are based on types of movement, locations of origin, and specific characteristics. Additionally, both fighting styles promote more than just the physical development of those who practice the art. Neither has combat as its only end. Humility, virtue, and courtesy are all important values in the philosophy of karate, just as the kung fu idea of *qi*, or *ch'i*, expresses the life energy inside practitioners. Each emphasizes spiritual growth as well as physical strength and stamina.

Although both fighting styles have found success in Western pop culture   3
and have encouraged the inner growth of practitioners, karate is the younger of the two. Karate developed on the island chain between China and Japan, where Okinawa, Japan, is today. Given the regional politics, geography, and trade routes, Chinese martial arts probably traveled to Okinawa in the 14th century and then merged with the local fighting system known as *te*. In contrast, kung fu is a popular term for many Chinese martial arts, including hand-to-hand combat and wrestling that date back to the 5th century BC. But, despite this long history, it wasn't until the founding of the People's Republic of China in 1949 that kung fu became a national activity with training manuals, academies, and exams. Given kung fu's ancient roots, karate could be considered an offshoot of Chinese martial arts.

The techniques for each fighting style are also different. Although both use   4
linear and circular movements, karate is usually considered to be more linear than kung fu. This difference means that karate tends to have more straight lines and more direct punches, strikes, and kicks in its sequences. Daniel's crane kick in the first *Karate Kid* film, in which his leg shoots right out in front of him, is the perfect example of karate's directness. This characteristic style might

? Why do you think the writer raises this issue here?

have been developed by the king's bodyguards in Okinawa so that they could take quick control of a contest and fend off multiple attackers. Now the style remains most evident in the short, distinct sets of moves that practitioners must learn and then apply in competition.

In contrast, kung fu is better known for being circular, rather than linear, especially in its hand movements. While just as powerful as karate movements, kung fu's more fluid motions draw their strength from centrifugal° force, as opposed to a direct hit. The movements learned by kung fu practitioners also have more of a flow to them than those in karate, and they tend to be longer, more complicated sets of moves. For these reasons, karate is often considered "hard" and kung fu "soft," although the many kung fu variations have both hard and soft qualities, blurring such distinctions.

Finally, karate and kung fu practitioners wear different uniforms and use different weapons. The traditional karate uniform is white with a white kimono top over which a belt is tied. The color of the belt changes with the practitioner's rank, from white, yellow, and orange in the beginning stages, all the way up to purple, brown, and the famous black belt given to instructors. Karate is also practiced barefoot. When weapons are used in karate, they include the bo staff, a long stick up to six feet, and the *nunchaku*, two shorter sticks connected by a chain.

In contrast, kung fu practitioners may wear a greater variety of uniforms. Their outfits can be black or bold colors (like blue, red, or gold) and made of fabrics such as silk or satin. The tops of kung fu uniforms feature Chinese "frog" buttons, unlike karate's overlapping kimono-style jacket. Colored sashes may be worn as belts are in karate, but this practice of showing rank appears mainly in North American kung fu schools. Kung fu practitioners wear shoes and may use hook swords, butterfly swords, or nine section whips as well as many other weapons.

Because both karate and kung fu are now well established in Western pop culture, which of the two fighting styles deserves to be the first approved as an Olympic sport? Although karate has a rich heritage in Okinawa and Japan, the origins of kung fu stretch back even further and point to the influence of Chinese martial arts on karate as it developed. Furthermore, many more variations gather under the umbrella of kung fu than of karate. Kung fu's movements are usually more connected and complex than karate's shorter, more distinct sequences. Thus, if karate is actually an off-shoot of Chinese martial arts, perhaps kung fu deserves to claim Olympic status before karate does. And yet karate's simplified approach—forever memorialized by Mr. Miyagi's wax on, wax off teachings—might be more fit for an international stage.

**centrifugal:** Moving away from the center.

---

**?** What other differences between martial arts come to mind? Which matter most?

5

6

7

8 **?** How do you think this question should be decided?

### Questions to Start You Thinking

Meaning

1. In what specific ways does Griffin claim that karate and kung fu are similar? In what ways are these two different? Do the similarities outweigh the differences, or vice versa?

2. Can you think of other types of similarities and differences that Griffin might have included?

3. Would you nominate another sport for Olympic status? If so, why?

Writing Strategies

4. Is Griffin's support for his comparison and contrast sufficient and balanced? Explain.

5. What transitional devices does Griffin use to indicate when he is comparing and when he is contrasting?

6. What is Griffin's thesis? Why does Griffin state it where he does?

7. Using highlighters or marginal notes, identify the essay's introduction, thesis, contrasting subjects, points of comparison and contrast, and conclusion. How effective is the organization of this essay?

# Learning by Writing

## The Assignment: Comparing and Contrasting

Write a paper in which you compare and contrast two items to enlighten readers about both subjects. The specific points of similarity and difference will be important, but you will go beyond them to draw a conclusion from your analysis. This conclusion, your thesis, needs to be more than "point A is different from point B" or "I prefer subject B to subject A." You will need to explain why you have drawn your conclusion. You'll also need to provide specific supporting evidence to explain your position and to convince your readers of its soundness. You may choose two people, two kinds of people, two places, two objects, two activities, or two ideas, but be sure to choose two you care about. You might write an impartial paper that distinctly portrays both subjects, or you might show why you favor one over the other.

These students found a clear reason for comparison and contrast:

An American student compared and contrasted her home life with that of her roommate, a student from Nigeria. Her goal was to deepen her understanding of Nigerian society and her own.

A student who was interested in history compared and contrasted civilian responses to the Vietnam War and the recent wars in Afghanistan and Iraq, considering how popular attitudes about military service had changed.

Another writer compared and contrasted facilities at two city parks, making a case for a revised funding formula.

## Facing the Challenge   Comparing and Contrasting

The major challenge that writers face when comparing and contrasting two subjects is to determine their purpose. Writers who skip this step run the risk of having readers ask, "So, what's the point?" Suppose you develop brilliant points of similarity and difference between the films of Wes Anderson and those of Stanley Kubrick. Do you want to argue that one director is more skilled than the other? Or perhaps you want to show how they treat love or conflict differently in their films? Consider the following questions as you determine your primary purpose for comparing and contrasting:

■ Do you want to inform your readers about these two subjects in order to provide a better understanding of the two?

■ Do you want to persuade your readers that one of the two subjects is preferable to the other?

Ask what you want to demonstrate, discover, or prove *before* you begin to draft so you can write a more effective comparison-and-contrast essay.

## Generating Ideas

**Find Two Subjects.** Pick subjects you can compare and contrast purposefully. An examination question may give them to you, ready-made: "Compare and contrast ancient Roman sculpture with that of the ancient Egyptians." But suppose you have to find your subjects for yourself. You'll need to choose things that have a sensible basis for comparison, a common element.

For strategies for generating ideas, see Ch. 19.

> moon rocks + stars = no common element
>
> Dallas + Atlanta = cities to consider settling in
>
> Jimmy Fallon + Jimmy Kimmel = television talk-show personalities

Besides having a common element, the subjects should share enough to compare but differ enough to throw each other into sharp relief.

> sports cars + racing cars = common element + telling differences
>
> sports cars + oil tankers = limited common element + unpromising differences

Try generating a list or brainstorming. Recall what you've recently read, discussed, or spotted on the Web. Let your mind skitter around in search of pairs that go together, or play the game of *free association,* jotting down a word and whatever it brings to mind: *Democrats? Republicans. New York? Los Angeles. Facebook? LinkedIn.* Or try the following questions:

A
Writer's
Guide

## DISCOVERY CHECKLIST

☐ Do you know two people who are strikingly different in attitude or behavior (perhaps your parents or two brothers, two friends, two teachers)?

☐ Can you think of two groups that are both alike and different (perhaps two teams, two clubs, two sets of relatives)?

☐ Have you taken two courses that were quite different but both valuable?

☐ Do you prefer one of two places where you have lived or visited?

☐ Can you recall two events in your life that shared similar aspects but turned out to be quite different (perhaps two sporting events, two romances, two vacations, the births of two children, an event then and now)?

☐ Can you compare and contrast two holidays or two family customs?

☐ Are you familiar with two writers, two artists, or two musicians who seem to have similar goals but quite different accomplishments?

Once you have a list of pairs, put a star by those that seem promising. Ask yourself what similarities immediately come to mind. What differences? Can you jot down several of each? Are these striking, significant similarities and differences? If not, move on until you discover a workable pair.

**Limit Your Scope.** If you want to compare and contrast Japanese literature and American literature in 750 words, your task is probably impossible. But to cut down the size of your subject, you might compare and contrast, say, a haiku of Bashō about a snake with a short poem about a snake by Emily Dickinson. This topic you could cover in 750 words.

**Develop Your Pair to Build Support.** As you examine your two subjects, your goal is twofold. First, analyze each using a similar approach so you have a reasonable basis for comparison and contrast. Then find the details and examples that will support your points. Consider these sources of support:

| | |
|---|---|
| ■ Two events, processes, procedures | Ask a reporter's questions — 5 W's (who, what, where, when, why) and an H (how). |
| ■ Two events from the past | Using the same questions, interview someone present at each event, or read news or other accounts. |
| ■ Two perceptions (public and private) | Interview someone behind the scenes; read or listen to contrasting views. |
| ■ Two approaches or viewpoints | Browse online for Web sites or pages that supply different examples. |
| ■ Two policies or options | Look for articles reporting studies or government statistics. |

For more on interviewing, see Ch. 6.

For advice on finding a few useful sources, turn to B1–B2 in the Quick Research Guide, pp. Q-24–Q-25. For more on using sources for support, see Ch. 12.

## Learning by Doing 🖫 Making a Comparison-and-Contrast Table

After deciding what to compare, write down what you know about subject A and then subject B. Next, divide a page or use your software to create a table with three columns (up and down) and at least half a dozen rows (across). Use the first row to label the columns:

| Categories | Subject A | Subject B |
|---|---|---|
|  |  |  |
|  |  |  |

Now read over your notes on subject A. When you spot related details, identify a logical category for them. Enter that category name in the left column of the second row. Then add related details for subject A in the middle column. Repeat this process, labeling more rows as categories and filling in corresponding details for subject A. (Draw more lines or use the menu to add new rows as needed.)

Next, review your notes on subject B. If some details fall into categories already listed in your table, add those details in the subject B column for each category. If new categories emerge, add them in new rows along with the subject B details. After you finish with your notes, round out the table—adding details to fill in empty cells, combining or adding categories. Select the most promising categories from your table as common features for logical comparison and contrast.

## Planning, Drafting, and Developing

As you start planning your paper, be prepared to cover both subjects in a similar fashion. Return to your table or make a scratch outline so that you can refine your points of comparison or contrast, consolidate supporting details, and spot gaps in your information. Remind yourself of your goal. What is it you want to show, argue, or find out?

For more on planning, drafting, and developing, see Chs. 20, 21, and 22. For more about informal outlines, see pp. 397–400.

**State Your Purpose in a Thesis.** You need a reason to place two subjects side by side—a reason that you and your audience will find compelling and worthwhile. If you prefer one subject over the other, what reasons can you give for your preference? If you don't have a preference, try instead to understand them more clearly, making a point about each or both. Comparing and contrasting need not be a meaningless exercise. Instead, think clearly and pointedly in order to explain an idea you care about.

For more on stating a thesis, see pp. 384–93.

| TWO SUBJECTS | two teaching styles in required biology courses |
|---|---|
| REASON | to show why one style is better |
| WORKING THESIS | Although students learn a lot in both of the required introductory biology courses, one class teaches information and the other teaches how to be a good learner. |

Sometimes comparison and contrast is used in service of a thesis that makes an argument — an argument beyond why, say, subject 1 is better than subject 2. Notice the argument that Jacob Griffin makes in his thesis statement about karate and kung fu:

| GRIFFIN'S THESIS | The International Olympic Committee should consider which of these styles first deserves to be declared an official Olympic sport. |
|---|---|

## Learning by Doing  Reflecting on Comparison and Contrast

Consider the following and write a short reflection. What can be learned by comparing and contrasting? For what writing situations and disciplines would this be a helpful strategy? Can you think of any writing situations for which it would not be beneficial?

**Select a Pattern to Help Your Audience.** Besides understanding your purpose and thesis, readers also need to follow your supporting evidence — the clusters of details that reveal the nature of each subject you consider. They're likely to expect you to follow one of two ways to organize a comparison-and-contrast essay. Both patterns present the same information, but each has its own advantages and disadvantages.

| OPPOSING PATTERN, SUBJECT BY SUBJECT | ALTERNATING PATTERN, POINT BY POINT |
|---|---|
| Subject A | Point 1 |
|    Point 1 |    Subject A |
|    Point 2 |    Subject B |
|    Point 3 | |
| | Point 2 |
| Subject B |    Subject A |
|    Point 1 |    Subject B |
|    Point 2 | |
|    Point 3 | Point 3 |
| |    Subject A |
| |    Subject B |

**Use the Opposing Pattern of Organization.** When you use the opposing pattern of subject by subject, you state all your observations about subject A and then do the same for subject B. In the following paragraph from *Whole-Brain Thinking* (William Morrow, 1984), Jacquelyn Wonder and Priscilla Donovan use the opposing pattern of organization to explain the differences in the brains of females and males.

> At birth there are basic differences between male and female brains. The female cortex is more fully developed. The sound of the human voice elicits more left-brain activity in infant girls than in infant boys, accounting in part for the earlier development in females of language. Baby girls have larger connectors between the brain's hemispheres and thus integrate information more skillfully. This flexibility bestows greater verbal and intuitive skills. Male infants lack this ready communication between the brain's lobes; therefore, messages are routed and rerouted to the right brain, producing larger right hemispheres. The size advantage accounts for males having greater spatial and physical abilities and explains why they may become more highly lateralized and skilled in specific areas.

*Subject A: Female brain*

*Point 1: Development*
*Point 2: Consequences*

*Shift to subject B:*
*Male brain*
*Point 1: Development*
*Point 2: Consequences*

For a single paragraph or a short essay, the opposing pattern can effectively unify all the details about each subject. For a long essay or a complicated subject, it has a drawback: readers might find it difficult to remember all the separate information about subject A while reading about subject B.

**Use the Alternating Pattern of Organization.** There's a better way to organize most long papers: the *alternating pattern* of *point by point*. Using this method you take up one point at a time, applying it first to one subject and then to the other. Jacob Griffin uses this pattern to lead the reader along clearly and carefully, looking at each subject before moving on to the next point.

For Griffin's complete essay, see pp. 110–11. For more on outlines, see pp. 395–403.

THESIS:   The International Olympic Committee should consider which of these styles first deserves to be declared an official Olympic sport.

  I.  Similarities of styles
      A.  American popularity through movies
          1.  Karate
          2.  Kung fu
      B.  Variety within styles
          1.  Karate
          2.  Kung fu
      C.  Emphasis on internal values
          1.  Karate
          2.  Kung fu

II. Differences between styles

    A. Age and origins

        1. Karate

        2. Kung fu

    B. Techniques

        1. Karate's linear movement

        2. Kung fu's circular movement

    C. Uniforms and weapons

        1. Karate

        2. Kung fu

For more on transitions, see pp. 417–20.

**Add Transitions.** Once your essay is organized, you can bring cohesion to it through effective transitional words and phrases — *on the other hand, in contrast, also, both, yet, although, finally, unlike.* Your choice of wording will depend on the content, but keep it varied and smooth. Jarring, choppy transitions distract attention instead of contributing to a unified essay, each part working to support a meaningful thesis.

## Learning by Doing 🖊 Building Cohesion with Transitions

Working on paper or in a file, add color highlights to mark each transitional expression already in your draft. Then check any passages without much highlighting to decide whether your audience will need more cues to see how your ideas connect. Next, check each spot where you switch from one subject or point to another to be sure that readers can easily make the shift. Finally, smooth out the wording of your transitions so that they are clear and helpful, not repetitious or mechanical. Test your changes on a reader by exchanging drafts with a classmate.

## Revising and Editing

For more on revising and editing strategies, see Ch. 23.

**Focus on Your Thesis.** Reconsider your purpose when you review your draft. If your purpose is to illuminate two subjects impartially, ask whether you have given readers a balanced view. Obviously it would be unfair to set forth all the advantages of Oklahoma City and all the disadvantages of Honolulu and then conclude that Oklahoma City is superior on every count.

Of course, if you love Oklahoma City and can't stand Honolulu, or vice versa, go ahead: don't be balanced; take a stand. Even so, you will want to include the same points about each city and to admit, in all honesty, that Oklahoma City has its faults. One useful way to check for balance or thoroughness is to outline your draft and give the outline a critical look.

# Peer Response ✏️ Comparing and Contrasting

You may want a classmate or friend to respond to your draft, suggesting how to present your two subjects more clearly. Ask your peer editor to answer questions like these about comparison and contrast:

For general questions for a peer editor, see p. 447.

- How does the introduction motivate you to read the entire essay?

- What is the point of the comparison and contrast of the two subjects? Is the thesis stated in the essay, or is it implied?

- Is the essay organized by the opposing pattern or by the alternating pattern? Is the pattern appropriate, or would the other one work better?

- Are the same categories discussed for each item? If not, should they be?

- Are there enough details for you to understand the comparison and contrast? Put a check where more details or examples would be useful.

- If this paper were yours, what is the one thing you would be sure to work on before handing it in?

If classmates have made suggestions, perhaps about clearer wording to sharpen distinctions, use their ideas as you rework your thesis.

| WORKING THESIS | Although students learn a lot in both of the required introductory biology courses, one class teaches information and the other teaches how to be a good learner. |
| --- | --- |
| REVISED THESIS | Although students learn the basics of biology in both of the required introductory courses, one class teaches how to memorize information and the other teaches an invaluable lesson: how to be an active learner. |

## THESIS CHECKLIST

☐ Does the thesis make clear the purpose of your comparison and contrast?

☐ Can you see ways to sharpen the distinctions between the subjects that you are comparing or contrasting?

☐ Could you make the thesis more compelling based on details that you gathered while planning, drafting, or developing your essay?

**Vary Your Wording.** Make sure, as you go over your draft, that you have escaped a monotonous drone: A does this, B does that; A has these advantages, B has those. Comparison and contrast needn't result in a paper as symmetrical as a pair of sneakers. Revising and editing give you a chance to add lively details, transitions, dashes of color, and especially variety:

The menu is another major difference between the Cozy Cafe and the Wilton Inn. For lunch, the Cozy Cafe offers sandwiches, hamburgers, and chili. For lunch, the Wilton Inn offers dishes such as fajitas, shrimp salads, and onion soup topped with Swiss cheese. For dinner, the Cozy Cafe continues to serve the lunch menu and adds home-style comfort foods such as meatloaf, stew, macaroni and cheese, and barbecued ribs. By dinner, the Wilton's specialties for the day are posted—perhaps marinated buffalo steak or orange-pecan salmon.

*[Handwritten edits: "L" and "at" above "For lunch"; "features" above "offers"; "For dinner, the Cozy Cafe continues to serve the lunch menu and adds" crossed out; "adding" inserted above; "after five o'clock" inserted above "By dinner"]*

---

## REVISION CHECKLIST

☐ Does your introduction present your topic and main point clearly? Is it interesting enough to make a reader want to read the whole essay?

☐ Is your reason for doing all the comparing and contrasting unmistakably clear? What do you want to demonstrate, argue for, or find out? Do you need to reexamine your goal?

☐ Have you used the same categories for each item so that you treat them fairly? In discussing each feature, do you always look at the same thing?

☐ Have you selected points of comparison and supporting details that will intrigue, enlighten, and persuade your audience?

☐ What have you concluded about the two? Do you prefer one to the other? If so, is this preference (and your rationale for it) clear?

☐ Does your draft look thin at any point for lack of evidence? If so, how might you develop your ideas?

☐ Have you used the best arrangement, given your subjects and your point?

☐ Are there any spots where you need to revise a boringly mechanical, monotonous style ("On one hand, . . . now on the other hand")?

---

For more editing and proofreading strategies, see pp. 455–58.

After you have revised your comparison-and-contrast essay, edit and proofread it. Carefully check the grammar, word choice, punctuation, and mechanics—and then correct any problems you may find.

**EDITING CHECKLIST**

☐ Have you used the correct comparative forms (for two things) and superlative forms (for three or more) for adjectives and adverbs?    A7

☐ Is your sentence structure correct? Have you avoided writing fragments, comma splices, or fused sentences?    A1, A2

☐ Have you used parallel structure in your comparisons and contrasts? Are your sentences as balanced as your ideas?    B2

☐ Have you used commas correctly after introductory phrases and other transitions?    D1

For more help, find the relevant checklist sections in the Quick Editing Guide on p. Q-37. Turn also to the Quick Format Guide beginning on p. Q-1.

# Reviewing and Reflecting

**REVIEW** Working with classmates or independently, respond to the following questions:

To complete more review questions for Ch. 7, go to LaunchPad.

1. What are some characteristics of good subjects for comparison-and-contrast papers? Based on these characteristics, identify some promising subjects.

2. Name a key strategy for developing a strong thesis for a comparison-and-contrast paper. Examine the thesis of a comparison-and-contrast essay — one written by you or a peer, or by a journalist. Did the writer seem to employ this strategy? Why, or why not?

3. Describe the opposing and alternating patterns for organizing a comparison-and-contrast essay. If you have written or are writing a comparison-and-contrast paper, which pattern did you decide to use, and why?

**REFLECT** After completing one of the writing assignments presented in this chapter or supplied by your instructor, turn back to the After Writing questions on page 39 of Chapter 3 and respond to as many of them as you can. While addressing these questions, it might be helpful to revisit your response to the Learning by Doing activity on page 116, if you completed it.

Next, reflect in writing about how you might apply the insights that you drew from this assignment to another situation — in or outside of college — in which you have to compare and contrast two subjects. If no specific situations come to mind, imagine that

- in a finance course, you decide to write about the advantages and disadvantages of renting versus owning a home.

- in a work setting, you must compare and contrast the qualifications of two job candidates to decide whom to hire.

In your reflection, consider the purpose of your comparison and contrast and the details that might be most relevant to that purpose.

# Additional Writing Assignments

1. Listen to two different recordings of the same piece of music as performed by two different groups, orchestras, or singers. What elements of the music does each stress? What contrasting attitudes toward the music do you detect? In an essay, compare and contrast these versions.

2. With a classmate or small group, choose a topic, problem, or campus issue about which your views differ to some extent. Agree on several main points of contrast that you want each writer to consider. Then have each person write a paragraph summing up his or her point of view, concentrating on those main points. After your passages are written, collaboratively develop an introduction that outlines the issue, identifies the main points, and previews the contrasting views. Arrange the paragraphs effectively, add transitions, and write a collaborative conclusion. Revise and edit as needed to produce an orderly, coherent collaborative essay.

3. Compare and contrast yourself with a classmate in a collaborative essay. Decide together what your focus will be: Your backgrounds? Your paths to college? Your career goals? Your lives outside class? Your study habits? Your taste in music or clothes? Your politics? Have each writer use this focus to work on a detailed analysis of himself or herself. Then compare analyses, clarify the purpose and thesis of your comparison, and decide how to shape the essay. If your instructor approves, you might prepare a mixed-media presentation or post your essay to introduce yourselves to the class.

For more on using sources to support a position, see Ch. 12 and the Quick Research Guide beginning on p. Q-20.

4. **Source Assignment.** Write an essay in which you compare and contrast the subjects in any of the following pairs for the purpose of throwing light on both. Turn to readings or essay pairs from this book, a source from the library, an interview with a friendly expert, news coverage, a Web page or image, or another relevant source for details and support. Be sure to credit your sources.

> The coverage of a world event on television and on online news sites
> The experience of watching a film at home and in a theater
> The styles of two athletes playing in the same position (two pitchers, two point guards, two goalies)
> Northern and Southern California (or two other regions)
> Two similar works of architecture (two churches, two skyscrapers, two city halls, two museums, two campus buildings)
> Two articles, essays, or Web sites about the same topic
> Two articles or other types of sources for an upcoming research paper

5. **Visual Assignment.** The following images show classrooms in various parts of the world. Compare and contrast two of the images here in an essay, following the advice in this chapter. Be sure that you identify the purpose of your comparison, organize your subjects and points effectively, and support your points with details that you observe in the images.

Pupils attend class at a Koranic school in Bosso, Nigeria. Issouf Sanogo/AFP/Getty Images.

A student poses a question during a math class in Wellsville, New York. Education Images/Universal Images Group/ Getty Images.

Pupils take part in a lesson at a Christian school in Guazacapán, Guatemala. Education Images/Universal Images Group/ Getty Images.

# Explaining Causes and Effects

*Larger image:* AP Images/Alexander Zemlianichenko. *Inset image:* NASA/Corbis.

## Responding to an Image

Since the 1960s, the size of the Aral Sea in Uzbekistan has greatly decreased, as shown in the inset 2009 satellite image. The decreased area is due largely to short-sighted irrigation projects that diverted the rivers that fed this body of water. The resulting environmental disaster left formerly prosperous fishing villages marooned many miles from any shoreline and brought pollution, hardship, and a more extreme climate to the area. These two images suggest both causes and effects. What causes can you identify? What effects? Also consider artistic choice — the selection of each scene and the vantage point from which it was photographed. What mood does each photograph create? How does each affect you?

When a house burns down, an insurance company assigns a claims adjuster to look into the disaster and ask, Why? He or she investigates to find the answer—the *cause* of the fire, whether lightning, a cooking mishap, or a match that someone deliberately struck—and presents it in a written report. The adjuster also details the *effects* of the fire—what was destroyed or damaged, what replacement or restoration will be necessary, what repairs will be required, how much they will cost, and how long the family may need temporary housing.

Often in college you are asked to investigate and think like the insurance adjuster, tracing causes or identifying effects. To do so, you have to gather information to marshal evidence. Effects are usually easier to identify than causes. Results of a fire are apparent to an onlooker the next day, although its cause may be obscure. For this reason, seeking causes and effects may be an uncertain pursuit, and you are unlikely to set forth definitive explanations with absolute certainty.

## Why Explaining Causes and Effects Matters

### In a College Course

- You explore causes or effects to add depth to your papers whether you are investigating teen parenthood in sociology, romanticism in American fiction, or head traumas in speech pathology.
- You identify causes (such as those for the decline or the revival of the U.S. auto industry) or effects (such as those of widespread unemployment in Detroit) in essay exams.

### In the Workplace

- You consider causes and effects when you recommend changing from one advertising campaign to another to improve sales or from an old procedure to a new one to improve quality, efficiency, or safety.

### In Your Community

- You use causal analysis to help you advocate for more rigorous standards for the fuel efficiency of new vehicles or for stronger school board support for early childhood programs.

  ❓ When have you explained causes, effects, or both in your writing? What situations are likely to require this kind of analysis?

# Learning from Other Writers

The following essays explore causes and effects, each examining a different situation. To help you begin to analyze the first reading, look at the notes in the margin. They identify features such as the thesis, or main idea, and the first of the causes or effects that the paper analyzes.

## As You Read These Cause-and-Effect Essays

Ask yourself the following questions:

1. Does the writer explain causes? Or effects? Or both? Why?

2. Does the writer perceive and explain a chain or series of causal relationships? If so, how are the various causes and effects connected?

3. What evidence does the writer supply? Is the evidence sufficient to clarify the causal relationships and to provide credibility to the essay?

## Emily Badger

### It's Time to Stop Blaming Poverty on the Decline in Marriage

Emily Badger, a staff writer for the *Washington Post*, formerly wrote for *CityLab*, in which the following piece appeared on January 8, 2014. Badger has also contributed to such publications as *Pacific Standard*, *GOOD*, the *Christian Science Monitor*, and the *New York Times*. Here, Badger disputes the widely held belief that fractured family structures cause poverty.

Marlon Correa/The Washington Post via Getty Images.

Nearly half of all children who live in America with a single mother also live in poverty. This is a particularly troubling statistic when paired alongside the demographic° trend that the number of single mothers in America has been rising. This same seismic° population shift also goes by another name: the much-discussed decline in marriage.     1

Taken together, these patterns have yielded a logic that underpins much of how we think about aiding the poor 50 years into America's "war on poverty":° Children are worse off and more likely to be poor when their parents aren't married. Therefore, if we encourage more low-income adults to wed, families will be economically stronger and more emotionally stable. Best of all, poverty will decline.     2

*Introduction to situation*

In fact, this thinking forms the premise in the first five lines of the 1996 welfare reform law:     3

The Congress makes the following findings:

(1) Marriage is the foundation of a successful society.

(2) Marriage is an essential institution of a successful society which promotes the interests of children.

(3) Promotion of responsible fatherhood and motherhood is integral to successful child rearing and the well-being of children.

---

**demographic:** Related to population statistics.     **seismic:** Powerful; greatly significant.     **war on poverty:** A set of policies, initiated by President Lyndon B. Johnson, aimed at reducing poverty in the United States.

That law provides federal funding (still worth $150 million a year 4 today) to programs promoting healthy marriages and responsible father- hood. Over the years, they've taken the form of PSAs° extolling° the virtues of marriage and high-school marriage-ed classes and relationship skills training.

THESIS criticizing common perceptions of the cause of poverty

There are two problems, however, with the basic logic here. It casts pov- 5 erty as the result of a collapse in family values, not as the product of complex structural economic and social factors. And it's wrong.

Expert source cited to back the thesis

"All of these marriage-promotion policies were based on a fundamen- 6 tal misunderstanding of the link between poverty and marriage," says Kristi Williams, an associate professor of sociology at Ohio State Univer- sity and a research associate at the Council on Contemporary Families. "They're assuming people are poor because they don't marry, when I would say there's much more evidence that it's poverty that deters people from marriage."

Fractured family structures don't cause poverty. Poverty causes these fam- 7 ily structures. Reduce poverty through more direct means, and we might ac- tually reverse the retreat of marriage along the way.

"We know marriage has a wide range of benefits, particularly for raising 8 children," Williams says. "And it's not unreasonable to think that it would be nice if all children could enjoy these benefits. The problem is that there's no evidence that the kind of marriages that poor, single parents enter into will have these same benefits."

Study-based evidence

In her own research and elsewhere, studies have overwhelmingly found 9 very few benefits to marriage for single mothers and their children. Williams has looked at more than 30 years worth of national data and found almost no physical or mental health benefits to children of single mothers who later married. Another national study found that nearly two-thirds of single mothers who did later marry were divorced by the time they were 35–44. A study of the marriage-promotion programs funded through welfare reform also found few long-term results.

Why would the institution of marriage be so much less beneficial for 10 these families than for higher-income parents and their children? For one thing, the families of low-income single mothers differ from higher-income, two-parent families in so many ways that have nothing to do with marriage. These families must also contend with everything else that comes from (and contributes to) poverty, from higher unemployment and incarceration° rates, to lower access to good education and quality jobs.

It's clear that married-couple families are better off economically, be- 11 cause there are potentially two workers in the family," says Margaret Simms, a fellow at the Urban Institute and director of its Low-Income Working Families Project. "But you cannot solve poverty by just marrying

**PSAs:** Public service announcements.    **extolling:** Praising.    **incarceration:** Imprisonment.

people if — jointly — they cannot generate sufficient income to raise a family above poverty."

The other problem low-income single mothers face is simply a shortage of men to marry who might bring stability and financial support to a family. Today, the Urban Institute is releasing in-depth research, sponsored by the Department of Health and Human Services, looking at who these men are. 12

The research focuses on men aged 18–44, who have no more than a high school diploma, and who live in families making less than 200 percent of the federal poverty line (that's a mere $23,890 a year). Across the United States, 16.5 million men fit this description, and they are almost entirely located in urban areas. Based on American Community Survey Data from 2008–2010, the marriage rate among these men nationwide was 39 percent, with a low of 25 percent for low-income black men. Among higher-income men in this same age group, the marriage rate is 62 percent. 13

By the same data, more than a quarter of these men have dropped out of high school, decreasing their employment prospects and lifetime earning potential. Their unemployment rates are astronomical° (it's 34.8 percent for the low-income black men). They're significantly more likely to be incarcerated. Half of low-income, working-age men without college degrees also have no health insurance. 14

Each of these disadvantages compounds the others: Unemployed men are more likely to come in contact with law enforcement, and men who've been incarcerated are less likely to be able to get a job. Earlier research also suggests that the average family's income falls by 22 percent in the first year a father is in prison. 15

Marriage-skills training can do little about any of that. 16

If we turned our attention away from such strategies, several other policies would be much more effective in improving the lives of single mothers and their children. Research says that unintended births are particularly detrimental,° suggesting that we'd do better to fund and advocate family planning than marriage values. 17

For single women who do have children (intended or not), policies like paid family leave and high-quality public childcare would enable them to remain in the labor force and increase their earnings. But most of the research on the effectiveness of these strategies doesn't come from model initiatives in the United States. It comes from comparable countries overseas, where poverty rates for single mothers are dramatically lower than in the United States. 18

None of this means that marriage doesn't matter. But it matters in context. 19

"When you ask single mothers what they think about marriage, they overwhelmingly desire it and revere it in some ways," Williams says. "But in a very realistic way, they're always aware of these barriers to having a beneficial union. And they worry that if they do get married, they'll be worse off. And they may be right about that." 20

— Conclusion reinforcing earlier points

**astronomical:** Very high.    **detrimental:** Harmful.

## Questions to Start You Thinking

### Meaning

1. What are Badger's criticisms of the argument that promoting marriage among the poor will make this population more economically successful? What evidence does she use to support her viewpoint?

2. According to Badger, why does marriage seem to be less beneficial to single mothers and their children than to higher-income, two-parent families?

3. In Badger's view, what policies, other than encouraging marriage, might improve the lives of single mothers and their children?

### Writing Strategies

4. In paragraph 3, Badger includes the opening lines of the 1996 welfare reform law. Why might she have chosen to quote the lines instead of summarizing them?

5. Badger backs her thesis with various types of evidence, such as interviews with policy experts and study data. In your opinion, does she provide the right mix of evidence? Why, or why not? Can you think of any other types of sources she might have consulted?

6. Does Badger deal predominantly with causes or effects? Where and to what degree does she examine each of these? How would her essay change if she altered her focus?

---

**Yun Yung Choi**                                    **Student Essay**

### Invisible Women

Yun Yung Choi examines the adoption of a new state religion in her native Korea and the effects of that adoption on Korean women. In 2013, South Korea elected its first woman president, Park Geun-hye (see p. 84). The election of Park, who is the daughter of a previous president of Korea, Park Chung-hee, was considered a major milestone in gender equality for South Korea. Choi wrote this essay prior to Park Geun-hye's election.

For me, growing up in a small suburb on the outskirts of Seoul, the adults'   1
preference for boys seemed quite natural. All the important people that I knew — doctors, lawyers, policemen, and soldiers — were men. On the other hand, most of the women that I knew were either housekeepers or housewives whose duty seemed to be to obey and please the men of the family. When my teachers at school asked me what I wanted to be when I grew up, I would answer, "I want to be the wife of the president." Because all women must become wives and mothers, I thought, becoming the wife of the president would be the highest achievement for a woman. I knew that the birth of a boy was a greatly desired and celebrated event, whereas the birth of a

**?** How would you have answered this question?

girl was a disappointing one, accompanied by the frequent words of consolation for the sad parents: "A daughter is her mother's chief help in keeping house."

These attitudes toward women, widely considered the continuation of an unbroken chain of tradition, are, in fact, only a few hundred years old, a relatively short period considering Korea's long history. During the first half of the Yi dynasty, which lasted from 1392 to 1910, and during the Koryo period, which preceded the Yi dynasty, women were treated almost as equals with many privileges that were denied them during the latter half of the Yi dynasty. This turnabout in women's place in Korean society was brought about by one of the greatest influences that shaped the government, literature, and thoughts of the Korean people—Confucianism.°    2

Throughout the Koryo period, which lasted from 918 to 1392, and throughout the first half of the Yi dynasty, according to Laurel Kendall in her book *View from the Inner Room*, women were important and contributing members of the society and not marginal and dependent as they later became. Women were, to a large extent, in command of their own lives. They were permitted to own property and receive inheritances from their fathers. Wedding ceremonies were held in the bride's house, where the couple lived, and the wife retained her surname. Women were also allowed freedom of movement—that is, they were able to go outside the house without any feelings of shame or embarrassment.    3

With the introduction of Confucianism, however, the rights and privileges that women enjoyed were confiscated. The government of the Yi dynasty made great efforts to incorporate into society the Confucian ideologies, including the principle of *agnation*. This principle, according to Kendall, made men the important members of society and relegated° women to a dependent position. The government succeeded in Confucianizing the country and encouraging the acceptance of Confucian proverbs such as the following: "Men are honored, but women are abased." "A daughter is a 'robber woman' who carries household wealth away when she marries."    4

**?** How do you respond to this historical background?

The unfortunate effects of this Confucianization in the lives of women were numerous. The most noticeable was the virtual confinement of women. They were forced to remain unseen in the *anbang*, the inner room of the house. This room was the women's domain, or, rather, the women's prison. Outside, a woman was carried through the streets in a closed sedan chair. Walking outside, she had to wear a veil that covered her face and could travel abroad only after nightfall. Thus, it is no wonder that Westerners traveling through Korea in the late nineteenth century expressed surprise at the apparent absence of women in the country.    5

**Confucianism:** Ethical system based on the teachings of Chinese philosopher Confucius (551–479 BCE).     **relegated:** Reduced to a less important position.

Women received no formal education. Their only schooling came from government textbooks. By giving instruction on the virtuous° conduct of women, these books attempted to fit women into the Confucian stereotype — meek, quiet, and obedient. Thus, this Confucian society acclaimed particular women not for their talent or achievement but for the degree of perfection with which they were able to mimic the stereotype. 6

A woman even lost her identity in such a society. Once married, she became a stranger to her natal° family, becoming a member of her husband's family. Her name was omitted from the family *chokpo*, or genealogy book, and was entered in the *chokpo* of her in-laws as a mere "wife" next to her husband's name. 7

Even a desirable marriage, the ultimate hope for a woman, failed to provide financial and emotional security for her. Failure to produce a son was legal grounds for sending the wife back to her natal home, thereby subjecting the woman to the greatest humiliation and to a life of continued shame. And because the Confucian ideology stressed a wife's devotion to her husband as the greatest of womanly virtues, widows were forced to avoid social disgrace by remaining faithfully unmarried, no matter how young they were. As women lost their rights to own or inherit property, these widows, with no means to support themselves, suffered great hardships. Thus, as Sandra Martielle says in *Virtues in Conflict*, what the government considered "the ugly custom of remarriage" was slowly eliminated at the expense of women's happiness. 8

This male-dominated system of Confucianism is one of the surviving traditions from the Yi dynasty. Although the Constitution of the Republic of Korea proclaimed on July 17, 1948, guarantees individual freedom and sexual equality, these ideals failed to have any immediate effect on the Korean mentality that stubbornly adheres to its belief in the superiority of men. Women still regard marriage as their prime objective in life, and little girls still wish to become the doctor's wife, the lawyer's wife, and even the president's wife. But as the system of Confucianism is slowly being forced out of existence by new legal and social standards, perhaps a day will come, after all, when a little girl will stand up in class and answer, "I want to be the president." 9

❓ Why do you think the writer ends with this quotation?

## Questions to Start You Thinking

### Meaning

1. What effect does Choi observe? What cause does she attribute it to?
2. What specific changes in Korean culture does Choi attribute to the introduction of Confucianism?

**virtuous:** Moral, honorable.    **natal:** Relating to one's birth.

3. What evidence do you find of the writer's critically rethinking an earlier belief and then revising it? What do you think may have influenced her to change her belief?

Writing Strategies

4. What does Choi gain by beginning and ending with her personal experience?

5. Where does Choi use the strategy of comparing and contrasting?

6. How does Choi consider readers for whom her culture might be foreign?

7. Using highlighters or marginal notes, identify the essay's introduction, thesis, major causes or effects, supporting explanations and details for each of these, and conclusion. How effective is the organization?

# Learning by Writing

## The Assignment: Explaining Causes and Effects

Pick a disturbing fact or situation that you have observed, and seek out its causes and effects to help you and your readers understand the issue better. You may limit your essay to the causes *or* the effects, or you may include both but emphasize one more than the other. Yun Yung Choi uses the last approach when she identifies the cause of the status of Korean women (Confucianism) but spends most of her essay detailing effects of this cause.

The situation you choose may have affected you and people you know well, such as student loan policies, the difficulty of working while going to school, or a challenge facing your family. It might have affected people in your city or region—a small voter turnout in an election, decaying bridge supports, or dog owners not picking up their pets' waste. It may affect society at large—identity theft, immigration laws, or the high cost of health care. It might be gender or racial stereotypes on television, binge drinking, teenage suicide, climate change, or student debt. Don't think you must choose an earthshaking topic to write a good paper. On the contrary, you will do a better job if you are personally familiar with the situation you choose.

These students selected topics of personal concern for causal analysis:

One student cited her observations of the hardships faced by Indians in rural Mexico as one cause of rebellions there.

Another analyzed the negative attitudes of men toward women at her workplace and the resulting tension, inefficiency, and low production.

A third contended that buildings in Miami are not constructed to withstand hurricanes due, in part, to an inadequate inspection system.

## Facing the Challenge   Causes and Effects

The major challenge writers face when exploring causal relationships is how to limit the subject. When you explore a given phenomenon—whether local unemployment or the success of your favorite band—devoting equal space to all possible causes and effects will either overwhelm your readers or put them to sleep. Instead, you need to decide what you want to show your readers—and then emphasize the causal relationships that help achieve this purpose.

Rely on your purpose to help you decide which part of the relationship—cause or effect—to stress and how to limit your ideas to strengthen your overall point. If you are writing about your family's financial stresses, for example, you may be tempted to discuss all the possible *causes* and then analyze all the *effects* the stresses have had on you. Your readers, however, won't want to know about every single complication. Both you and your readers will have a much easier time if you make some decisions about your focus:

- Do you want to concentrate on *causes* or *effects*?
- Which of your explanations are most and least compelling?
- How can you emphasize the points that are most important to you?
- Which relatively insignificant or irrelevant ideas can you omit?

## Generating Ideas

For more strategies for generating ideas, see Ch. 19.

**Find a Topic.** What familiar situation would be informative or instructive to explore? This assignment leaves you the option of writing from what you know, what you can find out, or a combination of the two. Begin by letting your thoughts wander over the results of a particular situation. Has the situation always been this way? Or has it changed in the last few years? Have things gotten better or worse?

When your thoughts begin to percolate, jot down likely topics. Then choose the idea that you care most about and that promises to be neither too large nor too small. A paper confined to the causes of a family's move from New Jersey to Montana might be a single sentence: "My father's company transferred him." But the subsequent effects of the move on the family might become an interesting essay. On the other hand, you might need hundreds of pages to study all the effects of gangs in urban high schools. Instead, you might select just one unusual effect, such as gang members staking out territory in the parking lot of a local school.

### DISCOVERY CHECKLIST

☐ Has a difficult situation resulted from a change in your life (a lost job or a new one; a fluctuation in income; personal or family upheaval following death, divorce, accident, illness, or good fortune; a new school)?

☐ Has the environment changed (due to a drought, a flood or a storm, a fire, a new industry, the collapse of an old industry)?

☐ Has a disturbing situation been caused by an invention (the tablet, the e-reader, social-media platforms, the smartphone)?

☐ Do certain employment trends cause you concern (for women in management, for young people in rural areas, for men in nursing)?

☐ Is a situation on campus or in your neighborhood, city, or state causing problems for you (traffic, housing, access to healthy food, health care)?

## Learning by Doing 🖉 Determining Causes and Effects

Working by yourself, determine the cause and effect of each of these situations:

- Because Taylor studied, she earned an A on her test.
- Due to the lack of rainfall in Texas, water restrictions are in effect.
- Janine was injured in a roller derby bout because she was not wearing all her safety equipment.
- Although Austin had parked for only five minutes in a handicapped parking spot, he received a ticket because he didn't have the required placard.
- Because Denmark's homes and businesses are powered solely by wind, its residents enjoy a lower cost of energy.

**List Causes and Effects.** After noting causes and effects, consider which are immediate (evident and close at hand), which are remote (underlying, more basic, or earlier), and how you might arrange them in a logical sequence or causal chain.

| **Focus on Causal Chain** | | | | | | | | | |
|---|---|---|---|---|---|---|---|---|---|
| **Remote Causes** | → | **Immediate Causes** | → | **Situation** | → | **Immediate Effects** | → | **Remote Effects** |
| Foreign competition | → | Sales, profits drop | → | Clothing factory closing | → | Jobs vanish | → | Town flounders |

Once you figure out the basic causal relationships, focus on complexities or implications. Probe for contributing, related, or even hidden factors. As you draft, these ideas will be a rich resource, allowing you to focus on the most important causes or effects and to skip any that are minor.

For more on thinking critically, see Ch. 3.

| Focus on Immediate Effects | | Focus on Remote Effects |
|---|---|---|
| Factory workers lose jobs | → Households curtail spending | Town economy undermined |
| Grocery and other stores suffer | → Businesses fold | Food pantry, social services overwhelmed |
| Workers lose health coverage | → Health needs ignored | Hospital limits services and doctors leave |
| Retirees fear benefits lost | → Confidence erodes | Unemployed and young people leave |

## Learning by Doing 🔲 Making a Cause-and-Effect Table

Use the Table menu in your word processor or draw on paper a four-column table to help you assess the importance of causes and effects. Divide up your causes and effects, making entries under each heading. Refine your table as you relate, order, or limit your points.

| Major Cause | Minor Cause | Major Effect | Minor Effect |
|---|---|---|---|
| | | | |
| | | | |

For advice on finding a few pertinent sources, turn to the Quick Research Guide, beginning on p. Q-20.

**Consider Sources of Support.** After identifying causes and effects, note your evidence next to each item. You can then see at a glance exactly where you need more material. Star or underline any causes and effects that stand out as major ones. Ask, How significant is this cause? Would the situation not exist without it? (This major cause deserves a big star.) Or would the situation have arisen without it, for some other reason? (This minor cause might still matter but be less important.) Has this effect had a resounding impact? How much detail do you need to give about the results?

As you set priorities — identifying major causes or effects and noting missing information — you may wish to talk with others, use a search engine, or browse the library Web site for sources of supporting ideas, details, and statistics. You might look for illustrations of the problem, accounts of comparable situations, or charts showing current data and projections.

# Planning, Drafting, and Developing

**Start with a Scratch Outline and Thesis.** Yun Yung Choi's "Invisible Women" follows a clear plan based on a brief scratch outline that simply lists the effects of the change:

For Choi's complete essay, see pp. 130–32. For more about informal outlines, see pp. 397–400.

Intro — Personal anecdote
- Tie with Korean history
- Then add working thesis: The turnabout for women resulted from the influence of Confucianism in all aspects of society.

Comparison and contrast of status of women before and after Confucianism

Effects of Confucianism on women
1. Confinement
2. Little education
3. Loss of identity in marriage
4. No property rights

Conclusion: Impact still evident in Korea today but some hints of change

The paper makes its point: it identifies Confucianism as the reason for the status of Korean women and details four specific effects of Confucianism on women in Korean society. And it shows that cause and effect are closely related: Confucianism is the cause of the change in the status of Korean women, and Confucianism has had specific effects on Korean women.

For more about stating your main point in a thesis, see pp. 384–93.

**Organize to Show Causes and Effects to Your Audience.** Your paper's core — showing how the situation came about (the causes), what followed as a result (the effects), or both — likely will follow one of these patterns:

| | | |
|---|---|---|
| I. The situation | I. The situation | I. The situation |
| II. Its causes | II. Its effects | II. Its causes |
| | | III. Its effects |

Try planning by grouping causes and effects, then classifying them as major or minor. If you are writing about why more students accumulate credit-card debt now than a generation ago, you might list the following:

1. available credit for students
2. high credit limits and interest
3. reduced or uncertain income
4. excessive buying

On reflection you might decide that available credit, credit limits, and interest rates are determined by the credit card industry, government regulation, and current economic conditions. These factors certainly affect students, but you are more interested in causes and effects that individual students might be able to influence in order to minimize their debt. You consider whether your own growing debt is due to too little income or too many expenses. You could then organize the causes from least to most important, giving the major one more space and the final place. When your plan seems logical, discuss it or share a draft with a classmate, a friend, or your instructor. Ask whether your organization will make sense to someone else.

**Introduce the Situation.** Begin your draft by describing the situation you want to explain in no more than two or three paragraphs. Tell readers your task — explaining causes, effects, or both. Instead of doing this in a flat, mechanical fashion ("Now I am going to explain the causes"), announce your task casually, as if you were talking to someone: "At first, I didn't realize that keeping six pet cheetahs in our backyard would bother the neighbors." Or tantalize your readers as one writer did in a paper about her father's sudden move to a Trappist monastery: "The real reason for Father's decision didn't become clear to me for a long while."

## Learning by Doing 🖋 Focusing Your Introduction

Read aloud the draft of your introduction for a classmate or small group, or post it for online discussion. Ask your readers first to identify where you state the main point of your essay — why you are explaining causes or effects. Then ask them to share their observations about the clarity of that statement or about any spots where your introduction bogs down in detail or skips over essentials.

For more on using sources for support, see Ch. 12 or the Quick Research Guide beginning on p. Q-20.

**Work in Your Evidence.** Some writers want to rough out a cause-and-effect draft, positioning all the major points first and then circling back to pull in supporting explanations and details. Others want to plunge deeply into each section — stating the main point, elaborating, and working in the evidence all at once. Tables, charts, and graphs can often consolidate information that substantiates or illustrates causes or effects. Place any graphics near the related text discussion, supporting but not duplicating it.

## Revising and Editing

For more revising and editing strategies, see Ch. 23.

Because explaining causes and effects takes hard thought, set aside plenty of time for rewriting. As Yun Yung Choi approached her paper's final version, she wanted to rework her thesis for greater precision with more detail.

WORKING THESIS    The turnabout for women resulted from the influence of Confucianism in all aspects of society.

REVISED THESIS    This turnabout in women's place in Korean society was brought about by one of the greatest influences that shaped the government, literature, and thoughts of the Korean people — Confucianism.

Taking a cue from Choi, ask yourself the following questions about your thesis when you revise any cause-and-effect paper.

## THESIS CHECKLIST

☐ Is the purpose of your cause-and-effect analysis clear from your thesis? Is the thesis (and the rest of the paper) focused on this purpose?

☐ Could the thesis be more specific about the causes or effects you will be discussing?

☐ Could you make the thesis more compelling based on details that you gathered while planning, drafting, or developing your essay?

Choi also faced a problem pointed out by classmates: how to make a smooth transition from recalling her own experience to probing causes.

*(emphasize that everyone thinks that)* ⟶ *widely*

These attitudes toward women, ~~which I once~~ believed to be the

continuation of an unbroken chain of tradition, are, in fact, only a few

hundred years old. During the first half of the Yi dynasty, which lasted    *, a relatively short time, considering Korea's long history*

*[tell when]*

from 1392 to 1910, and during *[the Koryo period,]* women were treated

almost as equals, with many privileges that were denied them during the

latter half of the Yi dynasty. This upheaval in women's place in Korean

society was brought about by one of the greatest influences that shaped the

government, literature, and thoughts of the Korean people: Confucianism.

Because of Confucianism, my birth was not greeted with joy and

celebration but rather with these words of consolation: "A daughter is

her mother's chief help in keeping house."

*(belongs in opening paragraph)*

## Peer Response 👥 Explaining Causes and Effects

Have a classmate or friend read your draft, considering how you've analyzed causes or effects. Ask your peer editor to answer questions such as the following:

For an explanation of causes:

- Does the writer explain, rather than merely list, causes?
- Do the causes seem logical and possible?

For general questions for a peer editor, see p. 447.

- Are there other causes that the writer might consider? If so, list them.

For an explanation of effects:

- Do all the effects seem to be results of the situation the writer describes?

- Are there other effects that the writer might consider? If so, list them.

For all cause-and-effect papers:

- What is the writer's thesis? Does the explanation of causes or effects help the writer accomplish the purpose of the essay?

- Is the order of supporting ideas clear? Can you suggest a better organization?

- Are you convinced by the writer's logic? Do you see any logical fallacies?

- Are any causes or effects hard to accept?

- Do the writer's evidence and detail convince you? Put stars where more or better evidence is needed.

- If this paper were yours, what is the one thing you would be sure to work on before handing it in?

## REVISION CHECKLIST

☐ Have you shown your readers your purpose in presenting causes or effects?

☐ Is your explanation thoughtful, searching, and reasonable?

☐ Where might you need to reorganize or add transitions so your paper is easy for readers to follow?

If you are tracing causes,

☐ Have you made it clear that you are explaining causes?

☐ Do you need to add any significant causes?

For more on evidence, see pp. 157–64. For more on mistakes in thinking called logical fallacies, see pp. 171–72.

☐ At what points might you need to add more evidence to convince readers that the causal relationships are valid, not just guesses?

☐ Do you need to drop any remote causes you can't begin to prove? Or any assertions made without proof?

☐ Have you oversimplified by assuming that only one small cause accounts for a large outcome or that one thing caused another just by preceding it?

If you are determining effects,

☐ Have you made it clear that you are explaining effects?

☐ What possible effects have you left out? Are any of them worth adding?

☐ At what points might you need more evidence that the effects occurred?

☐ Could any effect have resulted not from the cause you describe but from some other cause?

After you have revised your cause-and-effect essay, edit and proofread it. Carefully check the grammar, word choice, punctuation, and mechanics—and then correct any problems you find.

For more editing and proofreading strategies, see pp. 455–58.

## EDITING CHECKLIST

☐ Have you used correct verb tenses and forms throughout? When you describe events in the past, is it clear what happened first and what happened next?          A3

☐ Have you avoided creating fragments when adding causes or effects? (Check revisions carefully, especially those beginning "Because . . ." or "Causing . . .") Have you avoided comma splices or fused sentences when integrating ideas?          A1, A2

☐ Do your transitions and other introductory elements have commas after them, if these are needed?          D1

For more help, find the relevant checklist sections in the Quick Editing Guide on p. Q-37. Turn also to the Quick Format Guide beginning on p. Q-1.

# Reviewing and Reflecting

**REVIEW** Working with classmates or independently, respond to the following questions:

To complete more review questions for Ch. 8, go to LaunchPad.

1. What are some strategies for keeping a cause-and-effect paper focused and not overwhelming for readers?

2. What questions might you ask yourself to identify a topic for a cause-and-effect paper?

3. What are some strategies for organizing a cause-and-effect paper? If you have written or are writing a cause-and-effect paper, which organizational strategies did you find most helpful? Why?

**REFLECT** After completing one of the writing assignments presented in this chapter or supplied by your instructor, turn back to the After Writing questions on page 39 of Chapter 3 and respond to as many of them as you can.

Next, reflect in writing about how you might apply the insights that you drew from this assignment to another situation—in or outside of college—in which you have to explain causes or effects. If no specific situations come to mind, imagine that

- in a biology course, you are writing a paper about the causes and effects of a reduction in the U.S. honeybee population.
- in a work setting, you are writing a report exploring the causes and effects of rapid employee turnover in the customer-service department.

In your reflection, consider how you might keep your examination of causes and effects focused on your purpose.

## Additional Writing Assignments

1. Write an essay about a noticeable, lasting change that has taken place in your lifetime, exploring its causes, effects, or both to help you and your audience understand that change better. The change might have affected only you, such as a move or a decision, or it might have affected your community, region, or society at large (such as new industries or medical breakthroughs).

2. Identify a major event, person, circumstance, habit, or other factor that shaped you as a person. In your journal, write informally about this cause and its effects on you. Use this entry to develop a cause-and-effect essay that will enlighten readers about how you came to be the person that you are now.

3. Write a formal letter addressed to someone who could make a change that you advocate. Support this change by explaining causes, effects, or both. For example, address a college official to support a change in a campus policy, the principal to advocate for a change at your child's school, or your work supervisor to encourage a change in procedures.

4. **Source Assignment.** Read a news or magazine article that probes the causes of a current problem: the shortage of certain types of jobs, for instance, or tuition increases in your state. Write an essay in which you argue that the author has or has not done a good job of explaining the causes of this problem. Be sure to credit the article correctly.

5. **Visual Assignment.** Write an essay explaining the causes, effects, or both captured or implied in the visuals below. Establish the purpose of your explanation, effectively identify and organize the causes or effects, and support your points with details that you observe in the images.

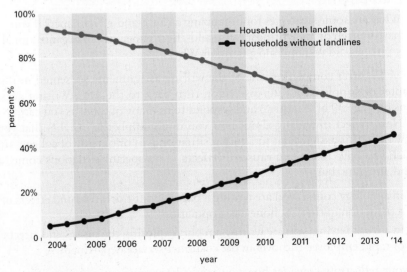

This graph shows a decrease in the percentage of households with landline phones and an increase in the number of households that own only cell phones over a ten-year period. Data from Centers for Disease Control and Prevention.

A lineman repairs storm-damaged telephone lines in McNeill, Mississippi. Landline infrastructure is aging and repairs are expensive, which has led some phone companies to advocate for the relaxation of repair requirements and for the transition of certain areas to wireless-only service. AP Images/Rogelio V. Solis.

In the wake of Hurricane Sandy, some residents in New York City struggled to find cell phone service. Timothy A. Clary/AFP/Getty Images.

# 9  Taking a Stand

Alex Milan Tracy/Corbis News/Corbis.

### Responding to an Image

The signs in this image identify a group and its position. What issue motivates this group? What concerns might have led to this position? Based on the image, what event do you think it portrays? What might the photographer have wanted to convey?

144

Both in and outside of class, you'll hear controversial issues discussed—health care costs, immigration policy, use of alternative energy sources, global outsourcing of jobs, and policing practices. Such controversies may be national, regional, or local. Even in academic fields, experts don't always agree, and issues may remain controversies for years. Taking a stand in response to such issues will help you understand the controversy and clarify what you believe. Such writing is common in editorials, letters to the editor, or columns on the op-ed page in print and online news outlets. It is also the foundation of persuasive brochures, partisan blogs, and Web pages that take a stand.

Writing of this kind has a twofold purpose—to state, and to win your readers' respect for, an opinion. What you say might or might not change a reader's opinion. But if you fulfill your purpose, a reader at least will see good reasons for your views. In taking a stand, you do these things:

- You state your opinion or stand.
- You give reasons with evidence to support your position.
- You enlist your readers' trust.
- You consider and respect what your readers probably think and feel.

## Why Taking a Stand Matters

### In a College Course

- You take a stand in an essay or exam when you respond, pro or con, to a statement such as "The Web, like movable type for printing, is an invention that has transformed human communication."
- You take a stand when you write research papers that support your position on juvenile sentencing, state support for higher education, or greater access to affordable housing.

### In the Workplace

- You take a stand when you persuade others that your case report supports a legal action that will benefit your clients or that your customer-service initiative will attract new business.

### In Your Community

- You take a stand when you write a letter to the editor appealing to voters to support a local bond issue.

  ❓ When have you taken a stand in your writing? In what circumstances are you likely to do so again?

# Learning from Other Writers

In the following two essays, the writers take a stand on issues of importance to them. To help you begin to analyze the first reading, look at the notes in the margin. They identify features such as the thesis, or main idea, and the first of the points that support it in a paper that takes a stand.

## As You Read These Essays That Take a Stand

Ask yourself the following questions:

1. What stand does the writer take? Is it a popular opinion, or does it break from commonly accepted beliefs?

2. How does the writer appeal to readers?

3. How does the writer support his or her position? Is the evidence sufficient to gain your respect? Why, or why not?

## Suzan Shown Harjo

### Last Rites for Indian Dead

AP Images/Manuel Balce Ceneta.

Suzan Shown Harjo is a writer and political activist, advocating for Native American legal rights and cultural protections. As a result of the efforts of Harjo and others like her, the Native American Graves Protection and Repatriation Act was passed in 1990.

*Introduction appeals to readers*

What if museums, universities, and government agencies could put your dead relatives on display or keep them in boxes to be cut up and otherwise studied? What if you believed that the spirits of the dead could not rest until their human remains were placed in a sacred area? 1

*THESIS taking a stand*

The ordinary American would say there ought to be a law—and there is, for ordinary Americans. The problem for American Indians is that there are too many laws of the kind that make us the archaeological property of the United States and too few of the kind that protect us from such insults. 2

*Point 1*

*Supporting evidence*

Some of my own Cheyenne relatives' skulls are in the Smithsonian Institution today, along with those of at least 4,500 other Indian people who were violated in the 1800s by the U.S. Army for an "Indian Crania Study." It wasn't enough that these unarmed Cheyenne people were mowed down by the cavalry at the infamous Sand Creek massacre; many were decapitated and their heads shipped to Washington as freight. (The Army Medical Museum's collection is now in the Smithsonian.) Some had been exhumed° only hours after being buried. Imagine their grieving families' reaction on finding their loved ones disinterred° and headless. 3

**exhumed:** Dug up out of the earth.     **disinterred:** Taken out of a place of burial.

Native Americans march with a truck returning 2,000 skeletal remains of Jemez Pueblo Indian ancestors for reburial in New Mexico. The remains had been in the collections of Harvard University. AP Images/Eddie Moore.

Some targets of the army's study were killed in noncombat situations and beheaded immediately. The officer's account of the decapitation of the Apache chief Mangas Coloradas in 1863 shows the pseudoscientific nature of the exercise. "I weighed the brain and measured the skull," the good doctor wrote, "and found that while the skull was smaller, the brain was larger than that of Daniel Webster."   **4**

*Supporting evidence*

These journal accounts exist in excruciating detail, yet missing are any records of overall comparisons, conclusions, or final reports of the army study. Since it is unlike the army not to leave a paper trail, one must wonder about the motive for its collection.   **5**

The total Indian body count in the Smithsonian collection is more than 19,000, and it is not the largest in the country. It is not inconceivable that the 1.5 million of us living today are outnumbered by our dead stored in museums, educational institutions, federal agencies, state historical societies, and private collections. The Indian people are further dehumanized by being exhibited alongside the mastodons and dinosaurs and other extinct creatures.   **6**

Where we have buried our dead in peace, more often than not the sites have been desecrated. For more than two hundred years, relic-hunting has been a popular pursuit. Lately, the market in Indian artifacts has brought this abhorrent activity to a fever pitch in some areas. And when scavengers   **7** come upon Indian burial sites, everything found becomes fair game, including sacred burial offerings, teeth, and skeletal remains.

One unusually well-publicized example of Indian grave desecration occurred two years ago in a western Kentucky field known as Slack Farm, the site of an Indian village five centuries ago. Ten men—one with a business card stating "Have Shovel, Will Travel"—paid the landowner $10,000 to lease digging rights between planting seasons. They dug extensively on the forty-acre farm, rummaging through an estimated 650 graves, collecting burial goods, tools, and ceremonial items. Skeletons were strewn about like litter.   8

*Question used as transition* ⎯⎯⎯ ⎡ What motivates people to do something like this? Financial gain is the first answer. Indian relic-collecting has become a multimillion-dollar industry. The price tag on a bead necklace can easily top $1,000; rare pieces fetch tens of thousands.   9

And it is not just collectors of the macabre° who pay for skeletal remains. Scientists say that these deceased Indians are needed for research that someday could benefit the health and welfare of living Indians. But just how many dead Indians must they examine? Nineteen thousand?   10

There is doubt as to whether permanent curation of our dead really benefits Indians. Dr. Emery A. Johnson, former assistant Surgeon General, recently observed, "I am not aware of any current medical diagnostic or treatment procedure that has been derived from research on such skeletal remains. Nor am I aware of any during the thirty-four years that I have been involved in American Indian . . . health care."   11

Indian remains are still being collected for racial biological studies. While the intentions may be honorable, the ethics of using human remains this way without the full consent of relatives must be questioned.   12

Some relief for Indian people has come on the state level. Almost half of the states, including California, have passed laws protecting Indian burial sites and restricting the sale of Indian bones, burial offerings, and other sacred items. Representative Charles E. Bennett (D-Fla.) and Senator John McCain (R-Ariz.) have introduced bills that are a good start in invoking the federal government's protection. However, no legislation has attacked the problem head-on by imposing stiff penalties at the marketplace, or by changing laws that make dead Indians the nation's property.   13

Some universities—notably Stanford, Nebraska, Minnesota, and Seattle—have returned, or agreed to return, Indian human remains; it is fitting that institutions of higher education should lead the way.   14

Congress is now deciding what to do with the government's extensive collection of Indian human remains and associated funerary objects. The secretary of the Smithsonian, Robert McC. Adams, has been valiantly° attempting to apply modern ethics to yesterday's excesses. This week, he announced that the Smithsonian would conduct an inventory and return all Indian skeletal remains that could be identified with specific tribes or living kin.   15

**macabre:** Gruesome, ghastly.  **valiantly:** Bravely.

But there remains a reluctance generally among collectors of Indian remains to take action of a scope that would have a quantitative impact and a healing quality. If they will not act on their own — and it is highly unlikely that they will — then Congress must act.

16

Transition to concluding proposal

The country must recognize that the bodies of dead American Indian people are not artifacts to be bought and sold as collector's items. It is not appropriate to store tens of thousands of our ancestors for possible future research. They are our family. They deserve to be returned to their sacred burial grounds and given a chance to rest.

17

Conclusion proposes action

The plunder of our people's graves has gone on too long. Let us rebury our dead and remove this shameful past from America's future.

18

## Questions to Start You Thinking

### Meaning

1. What is the issue Harjo identifies? How extensive does she show it to be?

2. What is Harjo's position on this issue? Where does she first state it?

3. What evidence does Harjo present to refute the claim that housing skeletal remains of Native Americans in museums is necessary for medical research and may benefit living Indians?

### Writing Strategies

4. What assumptions do you think Harjo makes about her audience?

5. What types of evidence does Harjo use to support her argument? How convincing is the evidence to you?

6. How does Harjo use her status as a Native American to enhance her position? Would her argument be as credible if it were written by someone of another background?

7. How does she appeal to the emotions of the readers in the essay? In what ways do these strategies strengthen or detract from her logical reasons?

8. Why does Harjo discuss what legislatures and universities are doing in response to the situation?

## Marjorie Lee Garretson                    Student Essay

## More Pros Than Cons in a Meat-Free Life

Marjorie Lee Garretson's opinion piece originally appeared in the *Daily Mississippian*, the student newspaper of the University of Mississippi, in April 2010.

What would you say if I told you there was a way to improve your overall health, decrease environmental waste, and save animals from inhumane treatment at the same time? You would probably ask how this is possible. The

1

answer is quite simple: go vegetarian. Vegetarians are often labeled as different or odd, but if you take a closer look at their actions, vegetarians reap multiple benefits meat eaters often overlook or choose to ignore for convenience.

The health benefits vegetarians acquire lead us to wonder why more people are not jumping on the meat-free bandwagon. On average, vegetarians have a lower body mass index,° significantly decreased cancer rates, and longer life expectancies. In addition, Alzheimer's disease° and osteoporosis° were linked to diets containing dairy, eggs, and meat.

The environment also encounters benefits from vegetarians. It takes less energy and waste to produce vegetables and grains than the energy required to produce meat. Producing one pound of meat is estimated to require 16 pounds of grain and up to 5,000 gallons of water, which comes from adding the water used to grow the grain crop as well as the animal's personal water consumption. Also, according to the Environmental Protection Agency, the runoff of fecal matter from meat factories is the single most detrimental° pollutant to our water supply. In fact, it is said to be the most significant pollutant in comparison to sources of all other industries combined.

The inhumane treatment of animals is common at most animal factories. The living conditions chickens, cows, pigs, and other livestock are forced into are far removed from their natural habitats. The goal of animal agriculture nowadays seems to be minimizing costs without attention to the sacrifices being made to do so. Animals are crammed into small cages where they often cannot even turn around. Exercise is denied to the animals to increase energy toward the production of meat. Female cows are pumped with hormones to allow their bodies to produce triple the amount of milk they are naturally capable of. Chickens are stuffed tightly into wire cages, and conditions are manipulated to increase egg production cycles. When chickens no longer lay eggs and cows cannot produce milk, they are transported to slaughterhouses where their lives are taken from them—often piece by piece.

Animal factory farms do a great job convincing Americans that their industry is vital to our health because of the protein, calcium, and other nutrients available in chicken, beef, and milk. We are bombarded with "Got Milk?" ads featuring various celebrities with white milk mustaches. We are told the egg is a healthy breakfast choice and lean protein is the basis of many good weight loss diets. What all of the ads and campaigns for animal products leave out are all the hormones injected into the animals to maximize production. Also, the tight living conditions allow for feces to contaminate the animals, their environment, and the potential meat they are growing. It is ironic

**? Do you find** Garretson's discussion of the health benefits of vegetarianism convincing? Why, or why not?

**? Is it possible to** decrease damage to the environment from factory farms without becoming a vegetarian? What other options might there be?

2

3

4

5

**body mass index:** A measurement of body fat, based on height and weight.   **Alzheimer's disease:** An incurable brain disorder causing memory loss and dementia.   **osteoporosis:** A disease that increases risk of bone fractures.   **detrimental:** Harmful.

how irate° Americans react to puppy mills and the inhumane treatment of household pets, but for our meat and dairy products we look the other way. We pretend it is fine to confine cows, pigs, and chickens to tiny spaces and give them hormones and treat them inhumanely in their life and often in the way they are killed. We then cook and consume them at our dinner tables with our families and friends.

Therefore, I encourage you to consider a meat-free lifestyle not only for the sake of the animals and the environment, but most importantly your personal health. All of your daily nutrients can be found in plant-based sources, and oftentimes when you make the switch to being a vegetarian, your food choices expand because you are willing to use vegetables and grains in innovative ways at the dinner table. Going vegetarian is a life-changing decision and one you can be proud of because you know it is for your own health as well as the greater good.

> ❷ Do you agree that Americans are hypocritical about the different treatment of household pets and farm animals? Why, or why not?

6

## Questions to Start You Thinking

Meaning

1. What points does Garretson make to support her position that vegetarianism has multiple benefits?

2. What, according to Garretson, are the environmental consequences of meat-eating?

3. In the author's view, why is it especially troubling that we are willing to "look the other way" (paragraph 5) on the inhumane treatment of farm animals?

Writing Strategies

4. What kind of support does Garretson use to back up her claims about the benefits of vegetarianism? Do you find her argument effective? Why, or why not?

5. To what extent does Garretson account for other points of view? How does the inclusion (or absence) of opposing views affect your opinion on the issue?

6. This article was written as an editorial for a student newspaper. How might Garretson change the article if she were submitting it as an essay or a research paper?

7. Using highlighters or marginal notes, identify the essay's introduction, thesis, major points or reasons, supporting evidence for each point, and conclusion. How effective is the organization of this essay?

**irate:** Angry.

# Learning by Writing

## The Assignment: Taking a Stand

Find a controversy that rouses your interest. It might be a current issue, a long-standing one, or a matter of personal concern: the pros and cons of legalizing medical marijuana, the contribution of sports to a school's educational mission, or the need for menu changes at the cafeteria to accommodate ethnic, religious, and personal preferences. Your purpose isn't to solve a social or moral problem but to make clear exactly where you stand on an issue and to persuade your readers to respect your position, perhaps even to accept it. As you reflect on your topic, you may change your position, but don't shift positions in the middle of your essay.

Assume that your readers are people who may or may not be familiar with the controversy, so provide relevant background or an overview to help them understand the situation. They also may not have taken sides yet or may hold a position different from yours. You'll need to consider their views and choose strategies to enlist their support.

Each of these students took a clear stand:

A writer who pays her own college costs disputed the opinion that working during the school year provides a student with valuable knowledge. Citing her painful experience, she maintained that devoting full time to studies is far better than juggling school and work.

Another writer challenged his history textbook's portrayal of Joan of Arc as "an ignorant farm girl subject to religious hysteria."

A member of the wrestling team argued that the number of weight categories in the sport should be increased because athletes who overtrain to qualify for the existing categories often damage their health.

Joan of Arc (1412–1431), heroine, martyr, saint, and cultural icon who boldly led French forces against the English. DEA/G. DAGLI ORTI/Getty Images.

## Facing the Challenge   Taking a Stand

The major challenge writers face when taking a stand is to gather enough relevant evidence to support their position. Without such evidence, you'll convince only those who agreed with you in the first place. You also won't persuade readers by ranting emotionally about an issue or insulting as ignorant those who hold different opinions. Moreover, few readers respect an evasive writer who avoids taking a stand.

What does work is respect—yours for the views of readers who will, in turn, respect your opinion, even if they don't agree with it. You convey—and gain—respect when you anticipate readers' objections or counterarguments, demonstrate knowledge of these alternate views, and present evidence that addresses others' concerns as it strengthens your argument.

To anticipate and find evidence that acknowledges other views, list groups that might have strong opinions on your topic. Then try putting yourself in the shoes of a member of each group by writing a paragraph on the issue from that point of view.

- What would that person's opinion be?
- On what grounds might he or she object to your argument?
- How can you best address these concerns and overcome objections?

Your paragraph will suggest additional evidence to support your claims.

## Generating Ideas

For this assignment, you will need to select an issue, take a stand, develop a clear position, and assemble evidence that supports your view.

For more strategies for generating ideas, see Ch. 19.

**Find an Issue.** The topic for this paper should be an issue or a controversy that interests both you and your audience. Try brainstorming a list of possible topics. Start with the headlines of a newspaper or newsmagazine, review the letters to the editor, check the political cartoons on the opinion page, or watch for stories on demonstrations or protests. You might also consult the library index to *CQ Researcher*, browse news or opinion Web sites, talk with friends, or consider topics raised in class. If you keep a journal, look over your entries to see what has perplexed or angered you. If you need to understand the issue better or aren't sure you want to take a stand on it, investigate by freewriting, reading, or turning to other sources.

Once you have a list of possible topics, drop those that seem too broad or complex or that you don't know much about. Weed out anything that might not hold your—or your readers'—interest. From your new list, pick the issue or controversy for which you can make the strongest argument.

## Learning by Doing 🌀 Finding a Workable Topic

Make a list of possible topics for an argument essay. Then take a close look at the list, eliminating topics that are too broad, too specific, or not focused. For example, if you are limited to one thousand words, do you have enough space to write about the broad topic of hunger in Africa? You might exchange topic lists with other students and discuss which topics are most or least promising.

**Start with a Question and a Thesis.**  At this stage, many writers try to pose the issue as a question — one that will be answered through the position they take. Skip vague questions that most readers wouldn't debate, or convert them to questions that allow different stands.

| | |
|---|---|
| VAGUE QUESTION | Is stereotyping bad? |
| CLEARLY DEBATABLE | Should we fight gender stereotypes in advertising? |

You can help focus your position by stating it in a sentence — a thesis, or statement of your stand. Your statement can answer your question:

For more on stating a thesis, see pp. 384–93.

| | |
|---|---|
| WORKING THESIS | We should expect advertisers to fight rather than reinforce gender stereotypes. |
| OR | Most people who object to gender stereotypes in advertising need to get a sense of humor. |

Your thesis should invite continued debate by taking a strong position that can be argued rather than stating a fact.

| | |
|---|---|
| FACT | Hispanics constitute 16 percent of the community but only 3 percent of our school population. |
| WORKING THESIS | Our school should increase outreach to the Hispanic community, which is underrepresented on campus. |

Notice that both Suzan Shown Harjo and Marjorie Lee Garretson pose questions in their introductory paragraphs that are then addressed in their thesis statements. If you came up with a debatable question to devise your thesis, you might revisit and revise this question later, to develop a strong introduction.

**Use Formal Reasoning to Refine Your Position.**  As you take a stand on a debatable matter, you are likely to use reasoning as well as specific evidence to support your position. A *syllogism* is a series of statements, or premises, used in traditional formal logic to lead deductively to a logical conclusion.

| | |
|---|---|
| MAJOR STATEMENT | All students must pay tuition. |
| MINOR STATEMENT | You are a student. |
| CONCLUSION | Therefore, you must pay tuition. |

You

All Students: must pay tuition

Nonstudents

For a syllogism to be logical, ensuring that its conclusion always applies, its major and minor statements must be true, its definitions of terms must remain stable, and its classification of specific persons or items must be accurate. In real-life arguments, such tidiness may be hard to achieve.

For example, maybe we all agree with the major statement above that all students must pay tuition. However, some students' tuition is paid for them through a loan or scholarship. Others are admitted under special programs, such as a free-tuition benefit for families of college employees or a back-to-college program for retirees. Further, the word *student* is general; it might apply to students at public high schools who pay no tuition. Next, everyone might agree that you are a student, but maybe you haven't completed registration or the computer has mysteriously dropped you from the class list. Such complications can threaten the success of your conclusion, especially if your audience doesn't accept it. In fact, many civic and social arguments revolve around questions such as these: What—exactly—is the category or group affected? Is its definition or consequence stable—or does it vary? Who falls in or out of the category?

**Use Informal Toulmin Reasoning to Refine Your Position.** A contemporary approach to logic is presented by the philosopher Stephen Toulmin (1922–2009) in *The Uses of Argument* (2nd ed., 2003). He describes an informal way of arguing that acknowledges the power of assumptions in our day-to-day reasoning. This approach starts with a concise statement—the essence of an argument—that makes a claim and supplies a reason to support it.

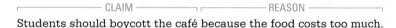

Students should boycott the café because the food costs too much.

You develop a claim by supporting your reasons with evidence—your *data* or grounds. For example, your evidence might include facts about the cost of lunches on campus, especially in contrast to local fast-food options, and statistics about the limited resources of most students at your campus.

However, most practical arguments rely on a *warrant,* your thinking about the connection or relationship between your claim and your supporting data. Because you accept this connection and assume that it applies, you generally assume that others also take it for granted. For instance, nearly all students might accept your assumption that a campus café should serve the needs of its customers. Many might also agree that students should take action rather than allow a campus facility to take advantage of them by charging high prices. Even so, you could state your warrant directly if you thought that your readers would not see the connection that you do. You also could back up your warrant, if necessary, in various ways:

- using facts, perhaps based on quality and cost comparisons with food service operations on other campuses
- using logic, perhaps based on research findings about the relationship between cost and nutrition for institutional food as well as the importance of good nutrition for brain function and learning

- making emotional appeals, perhaps based on happy memories of the café or irritation with its options
- making ethical appeals, perhaps based on the college mission statement or other expressions of the school's commitment to students

As you develop your reasoning, you might adjust your claim or your data to suit your audience, your issue, or your refined thinking. For instance, you might *qualify* your argument (perhaps limiting your objections to most, but not all, of the lunch prices). You might also add a *rebuttal* by identifying an *exception* to it (perhaps excluding the fortunate, but few, students without financial worries due to good jobs or family support). Or you might simply reconsider your claim, concluding that the campus café is, after all, convenient for students and that the manager might be willing to offer more inexpensive options without a student boycott.

———————— REVISED CLAIM ————————  ,  ———— REASON ————
The café should offer less expensive options <u>because</u> most students

can't afford a balanced meal at current prices.

Toulmin reasoning is especially effective for making claims like these:

- Fact — *Loss of polar ice can accelerate ocean warming.*
- Cause — *The software company went bankrupt because of its excessive borrowing and poor management.*
- Value — *Cell phone plan A is a better deal than cell phone plan B.*
- Policy — *Admissions policies at Triborough University should be less restrictive.*

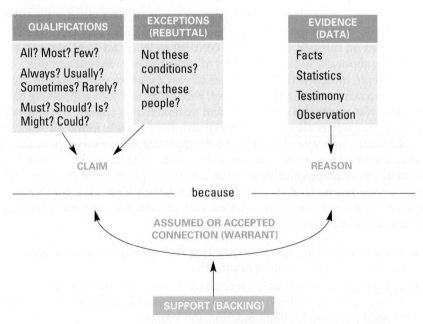

---

☐ What issue or controversy concerns you? What current debate engages you?

☐ What position do you want to take? How can you state your stand? What evidence might you need to support it?

☐ How might you refine your working thesis? How could you make statements more accurate, definitions clearer, or categories more exact?

☐ What assumptions are you making? What clarification of or support for these assumptions might your audience need?

---

**Select Evidence to Support Your Position.** When you state your claim, you state your overall position. You also may state supporting claims as topic sentences that establish your supporting points, introduce supporting evidence, and help your reader follow your reasoning. To decide how to support a claim, try to reduce it to its core question. Then figure out what reliable and persuasive evidence might answer the question.

As you begin to look for supporting evidence, consider the issue in terms of the three general types of claims — claims that require substantiation, provide evaluation, and endorse policy.

1. Claims of Substantiation: What Happened?

   These claims require examining and interpreting information in order to resolve disputes about facts, circumstances, causes or effects, definitions, or the extent of a problem.

   Sample Claims:
   a. Certain types of cigarette ads, such as the once-popular Joe Camel ads, significantly encouraged smoking among teenagers.
   b. Although body cameras worn by police will not always prevent unnecessary use of force, they are showing promise in reducing police brutality.
   c. On the whole, bilingual education programs actually help students learn English more quickly than total immersion programs do.

   Possible Supporting Evidence:
   - Facts and information: parties involved, dates, times, places
   - Clear definitions of terms: *police brutality* or *total immersion*
   - Well-supported comparison and contrast: statistics or examples to contrast suggestions that footage from police cameras sometimes offers inconclusive information with evidence that the footage has significantly reduced the unnecessary use of force
   - Well-supported cause-and-effect analysis: authoritative information to demonstrate how actions of tobacco companies "significantly encouraged smoking" or bilingual programs "help students learn English faster"

2. Claims of Evaluation: What Is Right?

   These claims consider right or wrong, appropriateness or inappropriateness, and worth or lack of worth involved in an issue.

Sample Claims:

a. Research using fetal tissue is unethical in a civilized society.

b. English-only legislation promotes cultural intolerance in our society.

c. Keeping children in foster care for years, instead of releasing them for adoption, is wrong.

Possible Supporting Evidence:

■ Explanations or definitions of appropriate criteria for judging: deciding what's "unethical in a civilized society"

■ Corresponding details and reasons showing how the topic does or does not meet the criteria: details or applications of English-only legislation that meet the criteria for "cultural intolerance" or reasons with supporting details that show why years of foster care meet the criteria for being "wrong"

3. Claims of Policy: What Should Be Done?

These claims challenge or defend approaches for achieving generally accepted goals.

Sample Claims:

a. The federal government should support the distribution of clean needles to reduce the rate of HIV infection among intravenous drug users.

b. Denying children of undocumented workers enrollment in public schools will reduce the problem of illegal immigration.

c. All teenagers accused of murder should be tried as adults.

Possible Supporting Evidence:

■ Explanation and definition of the policy goal: assuming that most in your audience agree that it is desirable to reduce "the rate of HIV infection" or "the problem of illegal immigration" or to try murderers in the same way regardless of age

■ Corresponding details and reasons showing how your policy recommendation would meet the goal: results of "clean needle" trials or examples of crime statistics and cases involving teen murderers

■ Explanations or definitions of the policy's limits or applications, if needed: why some teens should not be tried as adults because of their situations

## Learning by Doing 🎦 Reflecting on Evidence for Your Argument

Reflect on the claim about which you are taking a stand. Think about whether this is a claim of substantiation, evaluation, or policy or some combination. What types of evidence do you think would be most effective for persuading your audience of your claim's validity? Where and how might you find such evidence?

**Consider Your Audience as You Develop Your Claim.** The nature of your audience might influence the type of claim you choose to make. For example, suppose that the nurse or social worker at the high school you attended or that your children now attend proposed distributing free condoms to students. The following table illustrates how the responses of different audiences to this proposal might vary with the claim. As you develop your claims, try to put yourself in the place of your audience. For example, if you are a former student, what claim would most effectively persuade you? If you are the parent of a teenager, what claim would best address both your general views and your specific concerns about your own child?

| Audience | Type of Claim | Possible Effect on Audience |
|---|---|---|
| **Conservative parents who believe that free condoms would promote immoral sexual behavior** | *Evaluation:* In order to save lives and prevent unwanted pregnancies, distributing free condoms in high school is our moral duty. | Counterproductive if the parents feel that they are being accused of immorality for not agreeing with the proposal |
| **Conservative parents who believe that free condoms would promote immoral sexual behavior** | *Substantiation:* Distributing free condoms in high school can effectively reduce pregnancy rates and the spread of STDs, especially AIDS, without substantially increasing the rate of sexual activity among teenagers. | Possibly persuasive, based on effectiveness, if parents feel that their desire to protect their children from harm, no matter what, is recognized and the evidence deflates their main fear (promoting sexual activity) |
| **School administrators who want to do what's right but don't want hordes of angry parents pounding down the school doors** | *Policy:* Distributing free condoms in high school to prevent unwanted pregnancies and the spread of STDs, including AIDS, is best accomplished as part of a voluntary sex education program that strongly emphasizes abstinence as the primary preventative. | Possibly persuasive if administrators see that the proposal addresses health and pregnancy issues without setting off parental outrage (by proposing a voluntary program that would promote abstinence, thus addressing concerns of parents) |

**Assemble Supporting Evidence.** Your claim stated, you'll need evidence to support it. That evidence can be anything that demonstrates the soundness of your position and the points you make—facts, statistics, observations, expert testimony, illustrations, examples, and case studies.

For more about using sources, see Ch. 12 and the Quick Research Guide beginning on p. Q-20.

The four most important sources of evidence are facts, statistics, expert testimony, and firsthand observation.

**Facts.** Facts are statements that can be verified objectively, by observation or by reading a reliable account. They are usually stated dispassionately: "If you pump the air out of a five-gallon varnish can, it will collapse." Of course, we accept many of our facts based on the testimony of others. For example, we believe that the Great Wall of China exists, although we may never have seen it with our own eyes.

Sometimes people say facts are true statements, but truth and sound evidence may be confused. Consider the truth of these statements:

| | |
|---|---|
| The tree in my yard is an oak. | *True* because it can be verified |
| A kilometer is 1,000 meters. | *True* using the metric system |
| The speed limit on the highway is 65 miles per hour. | *True* according to law |
| Fewer fatal highway accidents have occurred since the new exit ramp was built. | *True* according to research studies |
| My favorite food is pizza. | *True* as an opinion |
| More violent criminals should receive the death penalty. | *True* as a belief |
| Murder is wrong. | *True* as a value judgment |

Some would claim that each statement is true, but when you think critically, you should avoid treating opinions, beliefs, judgments, or personal experience as true in the same sense that verifiable facts and events are true.

**Statistics.** Statistics are facts expressed in numbers. What portion of American children are poor? According to statistics from the US Census Bureau, 16.1 million children (or 21.8 percent of all children) lived in poverty in 2012 compared with 14.7 million (or 19.9 percent) in 2013. Clear as such figures seem, they may raise complex questions. For example, how significant is this decrease in the poverty rate? Is it an aberration or part of a longer trend? What percentage of children were poor over longer terms such as fifteen years or twenty?

Most writers, without trying to be dishonest, interpret statistics to help their causes. The statement "Fifty percent of the populace have incomes above the poverty level" might substantiate the fine job done by the government of a developing nation. Putting the statement another way — "Fifty percent of the populace have incomes below the poverty level" — might use the same statistic to show the inadequacy of the government's efforts.

Even though a writer is free to interpret a statistic, statistics should not be used to mislead. On the wrapper of a peanut candy bar, we read that a one-ounce serving contains only 150 calories. The claim is true, but the bar weighs 1.6 ounces. Gobble it all — more likely than eating 62 percent of it — and you'll ingest 240 calories, a heftier snack than the innocent statistic on the wrapper suggests. Because abuses make some readers automatically distrustful, use figures fairly when you write, and make sure they are accurate. If you doubt a statistic, compare it with figures reported by several other sources. Distrust a statistical report that differs from every other report unless it is backed by further evidence.

Few people save some of a candy bar to eat later.

iStockphoto.com/pidjoe.

**Expert Testimony.** By "experts," we mean people with knowledge gained from study and experience in a particular field. The test of an expert is whether his or her expertise stands up to the scrutiny of others who are knowledgeable in that field. The views of Peyton Manning on how to play offense in football carry authority. So do the views of economist and Federal Reserve chairwoman Janet Yellen on what causes inflation. However, Manning's take on the economy or Yellen's thoughts on football might not be authoritative. Also consider whether the expert has any bias or special interest that would affect reliability. Statistics on cases of lung cancer attributed to smoking might be better taken from government sources than from the tobacco industry.

Should you want to contact a campus expert, turn to Ch. 6 for advice about interviews.

**Firsthand Observation.** Firsthand observation is persuasive. It can add concrete reality to abstract or complex points. You might support the claim "The Meadowfield waste recycling plant fails to meet state guidelines" by recalling your own observations: "When I visited the plant last January, I was struck by the number of open waste canisters and by the lack of protective gear for the workers who handle these toxic materials daily."

For more on observation, see Ch. 5.

As readers, most of us tend to trust the writer who declares, "I was there. This is what I saw." Sometimes that trust is misplaced, however, so always be wary of a writer's claim to have seen something that no other evidence supports. Ask yourself, Is this writer biased? Might the writer have (intentionally or unintentionally) misinterpreted what he or she saw? Of course, your readers will scrutinize your firsthand observations, too; take care to reassure them that your observations are unbiased and accurate. Evidence must be used carefully to avoid defending logical fallacies—common mistakes in thinking—and making statements that lead to wrong conclusions. Examples are easy to misuse (claiming proof by example or too few examples). Because two professors you know are dissatisfied with state-mandated testing programs, you can't claim that all—or even most—professors are. Even if you surveyed more professors at your school, you could speak only generally of "many professors." To claim more, you might need to conduct scientific surveys, access reliable statistics from the library or Internet, or solicit the views of a respected expert in the area.

For more on logical fallacies, see pp. 171–72.

## Learning by Doing 🎯 Supporting a Claim

Write out, in one complete sentence, the core claim or position you plan to support. Working in a small group, drop all these "position statements" into a hat, with no names attached. Then draw and read each aloud in turn, inviting the group to suggest useful supporting evidence and possible sources for it. Ask someone in the group to act as a recorder, listing suggestions on a separate page for each claim. Finally, match up writers with claims, and share reactions. (If you are working online, follow your instructor's directions, possibly sending your statement privately to your instructor for anonymous posting for a threaded discussion.) If this activity causes you to alter your stand, be thankful: it will be easier to revise now rather than later.

---

**Record Evidence.** For this assignment, you will need to record your evidence in written form in a notebook or a digital file. Note exactly where each piece of information comes from. Keep the form of your notes flexible so that you can easily rearrange them as you plan your draft.

For more on testing evidence, see B in the Quick Research Guide, pp. Q-24–Q-25.

**Test and Select Evidence to Persuade Your Audience.** Now that you've collected some evidence, sift through it to decide which information to use. Always critically test and question evidence to see whether it is strong enough to carry the weight of your claims.

---

### EVIDENCE CHECKLIST

For advice on evaluating sources of evidence, see C in the Quick Research Guide, pp. Q-25–Q-27.

☐ Is it accurate?
  • Do the facts and figures seem accurate based on what you have found in published sources, reports by others, or reference works?
  • Are figures or quoted facts copied correctly?

☐ Is it reliable?
  • Is the source trustworthy and well regarded?
  • Does the source acknowledge any commercial, political, advocacy, or other bias that might affect the quality of its information?
  • Does the writer supplying the evidence have appropriate credentials or experience? Is the writer respected as an expert in the field?
  • Do other sources agree with the information?

☐ Is it up-to-date?
  • Are facts and statistics — such as population figures — current?
  • Is the information from the latest sources?

☐ Is it to the point?
  • Does the evidence back the exact claim made?
  • Is the evidence all pertinent? Does any of it drift from the point to interesting but irrelevant evidence?

☐ Is it representative?
  • Are examples typical of all the things included in the writer's position?
  • Are examples balanced? Do they present the topic or issue fairly?
  • Are contrary examples acknowledged?

For information on mistakes in thinking, see pp. 171–72.

☐ Is it appropriately complex?
  • Is the evidence sufficient to account for the claim made?
  • Does it avoid treating complex things superficially?
  • Does it avoid needlessly complicating simple things?

☐ Is it sufficient and strong enough to back the claim and persuade readers?
  • Are the amount and quality of the evidence appropriate for the claim and for the readers?
  • Is the evidence aligned with the existing knowledge of readers?
  • Does the evidence answer the questions readers are likely to ask?
  • Is the evidence vivid and significant?

---

## Learning by Doing 🔘 Examining Your Evidence

Examine the evidence that you've gathered to support your thesis, and consider whether or not each piece of evidence directly backs up your thesis. If any evidence does not directly support your thesis, you may want to eliminate it.

You may find that your evidence supports a different stand than you intended to take. Might you find facts, testimony, and observations to support your original position after all? Or should you rethink your position? If so, revise your working thesis. Does your evidence cluster around several points or reasons? If so, use your evidence to plan the sequence of your essay.

In addition, consider whether information presented visually would strengthen your case or make your evidence easier for readers to grasp.

- Graphs can effectively show facts or figures.
- Tables can convey terms or comparisons.
- Photographs or other illustrations can substantiate situations.

Test each visual as you would test other evidence for accuracy, reliability, and relevance. Mention each visual in your text, and place the visual close to that reference. Cite the source of any visual you use and of any data you consolidate in your own graph or table.

Most effective arguments take opposing viewpoints into consideration whenever possible. Doing so demonstrates that the writer respects those viewpoints, thereby encouraging readers to respect the viewpoint the writer presents. Providing evidence that refutes opposing viewpoints can also bolster an argument's strength. Use these questions to help you assess your evidence from this standpoint.

For more on the use of visuals and their placement, see section B in the Quick Format Guide, pp. Q-7–Q-12.

ANALYZE YOUR READERS' POINTS OF VIEW

- What are their attitudes? Interests? Priorities?
- What do they already know about the issue?
- What do they expect you to say?
- Do you have enough appropriate evidence that they'll find convincing?

FOCUS ON THOSE WITH DIFFERENT OR OPPOSING OPINIONS

- What are their opinions or claims?
- What is their evidence?
- Who supports their positions?
- Do you have enough appropriate evidence to show why their claims are weak, only partially true, misguided, or just plain wrong?

ACKNOWLEDGE AND REBUT THE COUNTERARGUMENTS

- What are the strengths of other positions? What might you want to concede or grant to be accurate or relevant?
- What are the limitations of other positions? What might you want to question or challenge?
- What facts, statistics, testimony, observations, or other evidence supports questioning, qualifying, or challenging other views?

## Learning by Doing  Addressing Counterarguments

State your position on a debatable issue (for example, "I think the Snake River dams in Idaho should be demolished"). Then add the word *because* to your statement and list two or three main reasons why you support this position. Think about what a reader would need to understand or consider in order to be persuaded that your position is correct. This will be the nucleus of your argument. Next, consider arguments that might be made in opposition to your views and questions that might be raised. Write some notes on how you would answer or refute these questions and counterarguments. Exchange papers with a partner to see if he or she has anything to contribute.

## Planning, Drafting, and Developing

**Reassess Your Position and Your Thesis.** Now that you have looked into the issue, what is your current position? If necessary, revise the thesis that you formulated earlier. Then summarize your reasons for holding this view, and list your supporting evidence.

WORKING THESIS    We should expect advertisers to fight rather than reinforce gender stereotypes.

REFINED THESIS    Consumers should spend their shopping dollars thoughtfully in order to hold advertisers accountable for reinforcing rather than resisting gender stereotypes.

---

**THESIS CHECKLIST**

☐ Is it clearly debatable — something that you can take a position on? Is it more than just a factual statement?

☐ Does it take a strong position?

☐ Does it need to be refined or qualified in response to evidence that you've gathered or to any rethinking of your original position?

---

■ ■ ■

## Learning by Doing 📷 Reflecting on Your Thesis

Oftentimes, our research shapes our thesis statement, changing the way we once thought. Reflect on your own research to date and the evidence you have collected to support your position, including any counterarguments and possible refutations to those counterarguments. Has your reflection caused you to change your position or your thesis statement? If so, in what ways has your thesis changed? Consider how changes in your thesis statement might make your argument stronger.

■ ■ ■

**Organize Your Material to Persuade Your Audience.** Arrange your notes into the order you think you'll follow, perhaps making an outline. One useful pattern is the classical form of argument:

For more on outlines, see pp. 395–403.

1. Introduce the subject to gain the readers' interest.
2. State your main point or thesis.
3. If useful, supply historical background or an overview of the situation.
4. Present your points or reasons, and provide evidence to support them.
5. Refute the opposition.
6. Reaffirm your main point.

Note that most college papers are organized *deductively* — that is, they begin with a general statement (often a thesis) and then present particular cases to support or apply it. However, when you expect readers to be hostile to your position, stating your position too early might alienate resistant readers or make them defensive. Instead, you may want to refute the opposition first, then replace those views by building a logical chain of evidence that leads to your main point, and finally state your position. Papers that begin with particular details and evidence and then lead up to a larger generalization are organized *inductively*. Of course, you can always try both approaches to see which one works better. Note also that some papers will be mostly based on refutation (countering opposing views) and some mostly on confirmation (directly supporting your position). Others might even alternate refutation and confirmation rather than separate them.

**DEDUCTIVE PATTERN**

**FIRST:** Broad generalization or conclusion. **THEN:** Details, examples, facts, and supporting particulars.

**FIRST:** Particulars, details, examples, facts. **THEN:** Concluding generalization.

**INDUCTIVE PATTERN**

**Define Your Terms.** To prevent misunderstanding, make clear any unfamiliar or questionable terms used in your thesis. If your position is "Humanists are dangerous," you will want to give a short definition of what you mean by *humanists* and by *dangerous* early in the paper.

**Attend to Logical, Emotional, and Ethical Appeals.** The logical appeal engages readers' intellect; the emotional appeal touches their hearts; the ethical appeal draws on their sense of fairness and reasonableness. A persuasive argument usually operates on all three levels. For example, you might use all three appeals to support a thesis about the need to curb accidental gunshot deaths, as the table on page 167 illustrates.

## Learning by Doing 🔲 Identifying Types of Appeals

Bring to class or post links for the editorial or opinion page from a newspaper, newsmagazine, or blog with a strong point of view. Read some of the pieces, and identify the types of appeals used by each author to support his or her point. With classmates, evaluate the effectiveness of these appeals.

For pointers on integrating and documenting sources, see Ch. 12 and D6 (pp. Q-30–Q-31) and E1–E2 (pp. Q-31–Q-36) in the Quick Research Guide.

For more revising and editing strategies, see Ch. 23.

**Credit Your Sources.** As you write, make your sources of evidence clear. One simple way to do so is to incorporate your source into the text: "As analyzed in an article in the May 25, 2015, issue of *Time*" or "According to my history professor, Dr. Harry Cleghorn . . ."

## Revising and Editing

When you're writing a paper that takes a stand, you may fall in love with the evidence you've gone to such trouble to collect. Taking out information is hard to do, but if it is irrelevant, redundant, or weak, the evidence won't help your

| Type of Appeal | Ways of Making the Appeal | Possible Supporting Evidence |
|---|---|---|
| **Logical (logos)** | ■ Rely on clear reasoning and sound evidence to influence a reader's thinking.<br>■ Demonstrate what you claim, and don't claim what you can't demonstrate.<br>■ Test and select your evidence. | ■ Supply current and reliable statistics about gun ownership and accidental shootings.<br>■ Prepare a bar graph that shows the number of incidents each year in Lion Valley during the past ten years, using data from the county records.<br>■ Describe the immediate and long-term consequences of a typical shooting accident. |
| **Emotional (pathos)** | ■ Choose examples and language that will influence a reader's feelings.<br>■ Include effective images, but don't overdo them.<br>■ Complement logical appeals, but don't replace them. | ■ Describe the wrenching scenario of a father whose college-age son unexpectedly returns home at 3 A.M. The father mistakes his son for an intruder and shoots him, throwing the family into turmoil.<br>■ Use quotations and descriptions from newspaper accounts to show reactions of family and friends. |
| **Ethical (ethos)** | ■ Use a tone and approach that appeal to your reader's sense of fairness and reasonableness.<br>■ Spell out your values and beliefs, and acknowledge values and beliefs of others with different opinions.<br>■ Establish your credentials, if any, and the credentials of experts you cite.<br>■ Instill confidence in your readers so that they see you as a caring, trustworthy person with reliable views. | ■ Establish your reasonable approach by acknowledging the views of hunters and others who store guns at home and follow recommended safety procedures.<br>■ Supply the credentials or affiliation of experts ("Ray Fontaine, public safety director for the town of Lion Valley").<br>■ Note ways in which experts have established their authority. ("During my interview with Ms. Dutton, she related recent incidents involving gun accidents in the home, testifying to her extensive knowledge of this issue in our community.") |

case. Play the crusty critic as you reread your paper. Consider outlining what it actually includes so that you can check for missing or unnecessary points or evidence. Pay special attention to the suggestions of friends or classmates who read your draft for you. Apply their advice by ruthlessly cutting unneeded material, as in the following passage:

> The school boundary system requires children who are homeless or whose families move frequently to change schools repeatedly. ~~They often lack clean clothes, winter coats, and required school supplies.~~ As a result, these children struggle to establish strong relationships with teachers, to find caring advocates at school, and even to make friends to join for recess or lunch.

For general questions
for a peer editor, see
p. 447.

## Peer Response  Taking a Stand

Enlist several other students to read your draft critically and tell you whether they accept your arguments. For a paper in which you take a stand, ask your peer editors to answer questions such as these:

- Can you state the writer's claim?

- Do you have any problems following or accepting the reasons for the writer's position? Would you make any changes in the reasoning?

- How persuasive is the writer's evidence? What questions do you have about it? Can you suggest good evidence the writer has overlooked?

- Has the writer provided enough transitions to guide you through the argument?

- Has the writer made a strong case? Are you persuaded to his or her point of view? If not, is there any point or objection that the writer could address to make the argument more compelling?

- If this paper were yours, what is the one thing you would be sure to work on before handing it in?

Use the Take Action chart (p. 170) to help you figure out how to improve your draft. Skim the left-hand column to identify questions you might ask about strengthening support for your stand. When you answer a question with "Yes" or "Maybe," move straight across to Locate Specifics for that question. Use the activities there to pinpoint gaps, problems, or weaknesses. Then move straight across to Take Action. Use the advice that suits your problem as you revise.

### REVISION CHECKLIST

☐ Have you developed your reasoning on a solid foundation? Are your initial assumptions sound? Do you need to identify, explain, or justify them?

☐ Is your main point, or thesis, clear? Do you stick to it rather than drifting into contradictions?

☐ Have you defined all necessary terms and explained your points clearly?

☐ Have you presented your reasons for thinking your thesis is sound? Have you arranged them in a sequence that will make sense to your audience? Have you used transitions to introduce and connect them so readers can't miss them?

☐ Have you used evidence that your audience will respect to support each reason you present? Have you favored objective, research-based evidence (facts, statistics, and expert testimony that others can substantiate) rather than personal experiences or beliefs that others cannot or may not share?

☐ Have you explained your evidence so that your audience can see how it supports your points and applies to your thesis? Have you used transitions to specify relationships for readers?

☐ Have you enhanced your own credibility by acknowledging, rather than ignoring, other points of view or possible objections? Have you integrated or countered these views?

☐ Have you adjusted your tone and style so you come across as reasonable and fair-minded? Have you avoided arrogant claims about proving (rather than showing) points?

☐ Might your points seem stronger if arranged in a different sequence?

☐ In rereading your paper, do you have any excellent, fresh thoughts? If so, where might you make room for them?

☐ Have you credited any sources as expected by academic readers?

## Learning by Doing 📷 Reflecting on Your Draft

Reflect on a draft of a current essay that makes an argument. What have you found most challenging about the process of drafting an argument essay? What have you found most rewarding? How, if at all, has the work of producing multiple drafts caused you to rethink the argument or how you have constructed and supported it?

After you have revised your argument, edit and proofread it. Carefully check the grammar, word choice, punctuation, and mechanics — and then correct any problems you find. Wherever you have given facts and figures as evidence, check for errors in names and numbers.

For more editing and proofreading strategies, see pp. 455–58.

### EDITING CHECKLIST

☐ Is it clear what each pronoun refers to? Does each pronoun agree with (match) its antecedent? Do pronouns used as subjects agree with their verbs? Carefully check sentences that make broad claims about *everyone, no one, some, a few,* or some other group identified by an indefinite pronoun.    A6

☐ Have you used an adjective whenever describing a noun or pronoun? Have you used an adverb whenever describing a verb, adjective, or adverb? Have you used the correct form when comparing two or more things?    A7

☐ Have you set off your transitions, other introductory elements, and interrupters with commas, if these are needed?    D1

For more help, find the relevant checklist sections in the Quick Editing Guide on p. Q-37. Turn also to the Quick Format Guide beginning on p. Q-1.

# Take Action  Strengthening Support for a Stand

Ask each question listed in the left-hand column to consider whether your draft might need work on that issue. If so, follow the ASK—LOCATE SPECIFICS—TAKE ACTION sequence to revise.

| 1<br>ASK | 2<br>LOCATE SPECIFICS | 3<br>TAKE ACTION |
|---|---|---|
| **Did I leave out any main points** that I promised in my thesis or planned to include? | ■ List the main points **your thesis states or suggests**.<br><br>■ List the main points you **meant to include**.<br><br>■ **Highlight each point** from your lists in your draft. | ■ **Add any missing point** from your thesis or plan.<br><br>■ **Express assumptions** (points, main ideas, reasons) that are in your head but not in your draft.<br><br>■ **Revise your thesis**, adding or dropping points until it promises what you can deliver to readers. |
| **Did I leave out evidence** needed to support my points—facts, statistics, expert testimony, firsthand observations, details, or examples? | ■ **Highlight** or **color code** each bit of supporting evidence.<br><br>■ Put a ✓ by passages without any or without enough **specific supporting evidence**. | ■ **Add any missing evidence** you meant to include.<br><br>■ For each ✓, **brainstorm** or **ask questions** (who, what, where, when, why, how) to decide what specific support readers might find convincing.<br><br>■ **Add the evidence, details, or examples** needed to support each main point. |
| **Have I skipped over opposing or alternative perspectives?** Have I treated them unfairly, disrespectfully, or too briefly? | ■ Highlight passages in which you recognize other **points of view** (or copy them into a separate file) so you can look at them on their own.<br><br>■ **Read these passages to see whether they sound fair and respectful.** Jot down notes to yourself about possible revisions. | ■ **Identify or add other points of view** if they're expected and you've left them out.<br><br>■ Acknowledge **credible alternative views**, explaining where you agree and differ.<br><br>■ Reasonably **challenge or counter questionable views**.<br><br>■ Edit your wording so your **tone** is respectful of others. |

☐ Have you correctly punctuated quotations from sources and experts?　　D3

☐ Have you spelled and capitalized everything correctly, especially names of people and organizations?　　E1, E2

## Recognizing Logical Fallacies

Logical fallacies are common mistakes in thinking that may lead to wrong conclusions or distort evidence. Here are a few familiar logical fallacies.

| Term | Explanation | Example |
|---|---|---|
| **Non Sequitur** | Stating a claim that doesn't follow from your first premise or statement; Latin for "it does not follow" | Jenn should marry Mateo. In college he got all A's. |
| **Oversimplification** | Offering easy solutions for complicated problems | If we want to end substance abuse, let's send every drug user to prison for life. (Even aspirin users?) |
| ***Post Hoc, Ergo Propter Hoc*** | Assuming a cause-and-effect relationship where none exists, even though one event preceded another; Latin for "after this, therefore because of this" | After Jenny's black cat crossed my path, everything went wrong, and I failed my midterm. |
| **Allness** | Stating or implying that something is true of an entire class of things, often using *all*, *everyone*, *no one*, *always*, or *never* | Students enjoy studying. (All students? All subjects? All the time?) |
| **Proof by Example or Too Few Examples** | Presenting an example as proof rather than as illustration or clarification; overgeneralizing (the basis of much prejudice) | Armenians are great chefs. My neighbor is Armenian, and can he cook! |
| **Begging the Question** | Proving a statement already taken for granted, often by repeating it in different words or by defining a word in terms of itself | Rapists are dangerous because they are menaces.<br><br>Happiness is the state of being happy. |
| **Circular Reasoning** | Supporting a statement with itself; a form of begging the question | He is a liar because he simply isn't telling the truth. |
| **Either/Or Reasoning** | Oversimplifying by assuming that an issue has only two sides, a statement must be true or false, a question demands a yes or no answer, or a problem has only two possible solutions (and one that's acceptable) | What are we going to do about global warming? Either we stop using all of the energy-consuming vehicles and products that cause it, or we just learn to live with it. |

| Term | Explanation | Example |
|---|---|---|
| **Argument from Dubious Authority** | Using an unidentified authority to shore up a weak argument or an authority whose expertise lies outside the issue, such as a television personality selling insurance | According to some of the most knowing scientists in America, smoking two packs a day is as harmless as eating oatmeal cookies. |
| **Argument *Ad Hominem*** | Attacking an individual's opinion by attacking his or her character, thus deflecting attention from the merit of a proposal; Latin for "against the man" | Diaz may argue that we need to save the polar bears, but he's the type who gets emotional over nothing. |
| **Argument from Ignorance** | Maintaining that a claim has to be accepted because it hasn't been disproved or that it has to be rejected because it has not been proved | Despite years of effort, no one has proved that ghosts don't exist; therefore, we should expect to see them at any time.<br><br>No one has ever shown that life exists on any other planet; clearly the notion of other living things in the universe is absurd. |
| **Argument by Analogy** | Treating an extended comparison between familiar and unfamiliar items, based on similarities and ignoring differences, as evidence rather than as a useful way of explaining | People were born free as the birds; it's cruel to expect them to work. |
| **Bandwagon Argument** | Suggesting that everyone is joining the group and that readers who don't may miss out on happiness, success, or a reward | Purchasing the new Global Glimmer admits you to the nation's most elite group of smartphone users. |

## Reviewing and Reflecting

To complete more review questions for Ch. 9, go to LaunchPad.

**REVIEW**  Working with classmates or independently, respond to the following questions:

1. What characteristics make an issue or a question a good subject for a paper that takes a stand? What characteristics make an issue or a question a weaker subject? With these criteria in mind, think of an issue on campus or in the news that would be a good topic for a taking-a-stand paper.

2. Why is evidence so important in writing that takes a stand?

3. Why is it important to address opposing views in an argument? If you identified a good topic in your answer to question 1, try to state a position on it and list two or three opposing views.

**REFLECT** After completing one of the writing assignments presented in this chapter or supplied by your instructor, turn back to the After Writing questions on page 39 of Chapter 3 and respond to as many of them as you can. While addressing these questions, it might be helpful to revisit your responses to any of the reflective Learning by Doing activities that you completed in Chapter 9 (see pages 158, 165, and 169).

Next, reflect in writing about how you might apply the insights that you drew from this assignment to an argument assignment for another course or to a writing situation outside of college. If no specific assignments or situations come to mind, imagine that

- in a sociology course, you are asked to argue (based on evidence you've gathered) that birth order does, or does not, influence siblings' social or political views.
- in a work setting, you want to make the case that you have the strongest qualifications for an open position. (You will have to imagine a position that would appeal to you, and you may have to invent some of your qualifications.)

In your reflection, consider such factors as your audience's interests, level of knowledge, or possible objections; the types of evidence that you might supply to support your position; the type of reasoning that might be most effective; and so on.

## Additional Writing Assignments

1. Write a letter to the editor of your newspaper or a newsmagazine in which you agree or disagree with the publication's editorial stand on a current question. Make clear your reasons for holding your view.

2. Write one claim each of substantiation, evaluation, and policy for or against a specific policy or proposal. Indicate an audience each claim might address effectively. Then list reasons and types of evidence you might need to support one of these claims. For the same claim, indicate what opposing viewpoints you would need to consider and how you could best do so.

3. Write a short paper, blog entry, or class posting expressing your view on one of these topics or another that comes to mind. Make clear your reasons for thinking as you do.

   | | |
   |---|---|
   | Bilingual education | Raising the minimum wage |
   | Twitter activism | Protecting the gray wolf |
   | Dealing with date rape | Controlling terrorism |
   | Crimes committed by professional athletes | Prayer in public schools |

4. Working with a classmate or a small group online, develop a discussion or collaborative blog to inform your audience about multiple points of view on an issue. Present the most compelling reasons and evidence to support

each view. Counter other views as appropriate with reasons and evidence, but avoid emotional outbursts attacking them. Before you begin posting, decide which view each person will present. Considering your purpose and audience, also decide whether the discussion or blog should cover certain points or be organized in a particular way. Before you post your contribution, write it in a location or file where you can save and return to it. Take some time to revise and edit before you send it or paste it in.

For more on supporting a position with sources, see Ch. 12.

5. **Source Assignment.**  Find a letter to the editor, opinion piece, or blog post that takes a stand that you disagree with. Write a response to that piece, countering its points, presenting your points, and supporting them with evidence. Be sure to cite the other piece, and identify any quotations or summaries from it. Decide which audience to address: The writer? Readers likely to support the other selection? Readers with interest in the issue but without loyalty to the original publication? Some other group?

6. **Visual Assignment.**  Select one of the following images. Analyze its argument, noting its persuasive visual elements. Write an essay that first explains the image's argument, including its topic and its visual appeals to viewers, and then agrees with, disagrees with, or qualifies that argument.

A young person hospitalized with cancer watches a fundraising walkathon. Suzanne Kreiter/The Boston Globe via Getty Images.

A family in Connecticut reads after dinner. Nicole Bengiveno/The New York Times/Redux.

# Don't Wait. Communicate.
## Make your emergency plan today.

## Visit Ready.gov/communicate

The Federal Emergency Management Agency (FEMA) and The Ad Council. Photo by Tony Campbell/Shutterstock.

### Responding to an Image

This advertisement from a public service campaign of the Federal Emergency Management Agency (FEMA) proposes a solution to a problem that affects hundreds of thousands of Americans every year. What is the problem that the image identifies? Why is the problem presented as it is? How might the presentation help viewers understand the problem? What solution does the advertisement suggest? For more of FEMA's proposed solutions, visit fema.gov.

Sometimes when you learn of a problem such as the destruction caused by a natural disaster, homelessness, or famine, you say to yourself, "Something should be done about that." You can do something constructive yourself—through powerful and persuasive writing.

Your purpose in such writing, as political leaders and advertisers well know, is to rouse your audience to action. At college, you might write a letter to your college newspaper or to someone in authority and try to stir your readers to do something. Does some college policy irk you? Would you urge students to attend a rally for a cause or a charity?

The uses of such writing go far beyond these immediate applications. In Chapter 9, you took a stand and backed it up with evidence. Now go a step further, writing a *proposal*—a recommendation for taking action. If, for instance, you have made the claim "Our national parks are in sorry condition," you might urge readers to act—to write to their representatives in Congress or to visit a national park and pick up trash. This paper would be a call to immediate action on the part of your readers. On the other hand, you might suggest that the Department of the Interior be given a budget increase to hire more park rangers, purchase additional park land to accommodate more visitors, and buy more cleanup equipment. This second paper would attempt to forge a consensus about what needs to be done.

## Why Proposing a Solution Matters

### In a College Course

- You identify a problem and propose a solution, tackling issues such as sealed adoption records, rising costs of prescriptions, violence in prisons, and hungry children whose families cannot afford both food and housing.
- You propose a field research study, explaining and justifying your purposes and methods, in order to gain faculty and institutional approval for your capstone project.

### In the Workplace

- You propose developing services for a new market to increase your company's profits.

### In Your Community

- You propose starting a tutoring program at the library for the many adults in your region with limited literacy skills.

❓ What solutions have you proposed? What others might you propose? What situations have encouraged you to write proposals?

# Learning from Other Writers

The writers of the following two essays propose sensible solutions for pressing problems. To help you begin to analyze the first reading, look at the notes in the margin. They identify features such as the introduction of the problem, the thesis, or main idea, and the introduction of the proposed solution.

## As You Read These Proposals

Ask yourself the following questions:

1. What problem does the writer identify? Does the writer rouse you to want to do something about the problem?

2. What solution does the writer propose? What evidence supports the solution? Does the writer convince you to agree with this solution?

3. How is the writer qualified to write on this subject?

Wilbert Rideau.

## Wilbert Rideau

### Why Prisons Don't Work

Wilbert Rideau, editor of the *Angolite*, the Louisiana State Penitentiary news-magazine, and author of his memoir *In the Place of Justice* (2010), offers a voice seldom heard in the debate over crime control — that of the criminal.

*Introduction of the problem*

I was among thirty-one murderers sent to the Louisiana State Penitentiary in 1962 to be executed or imprisoned for life. We weren't much different from those we found here, or those who had preceded us. We were unskilled, impulsive, and uneducated misfits, mostly black, who had done dumb, impulsive things — failures, rejects from the larger society. Now a generation has come of age and gone since I've been here, and everything is much the same as I found it. The faces of the prisoners are different, but behind them are the same impulsive, uneducated, unskilled minds that made dumb, impulsive

*THESIS stating the problem*

choices that got them into more trouble than they ever thought existed. The vast majority of us are consigned to suffer and die here so politicians can sell the illusion that permanently exiling people to prison will make society safe.

Getting tough has always been a "silver bullet," a quick fix for the crime and violence that society fears. Each year in Louisiana — where excess is a way of life — lawmakers have tried to outdo each other in legislating harsher mandatory penalties and in reducing avenues of release. The only thing to do with criminals, they say, is get tougher. They have. In the process, the purpose of prison began to change. The state boasts one of the highest lockup rates in the country, imposes the most severe penalties in the nation, and vies to execute more criminals per capita than anywhere else. This state is so tough that last year, when prison authorities here wanted to punish an

1

2

inmate in solitary confinement for an infraction,° the most they could inflict on him was to deprive him of his underwear. It was all he had left.

If getting tough resulted in public safety, Louisiana citizens would be the safest in the nation. They're not. Louisiana has the highest murder rate among states. Prison, like the police and the courts, has a minimal impact on crime because it is a response after the fact, a mop-up operation. It doesn't work. The idea of punishing the few to deter the many is counterfeit because potential criminals either think they're not going to get caught or they're so emotionally desperate or psychologically distressed that they don't care about the consequences of their actions. The threatened punishment, regardless of its severity, is never a factor in the equation. But society, like the incorrigible° criminal it abhors, is unable to learn from its mistakes.

Prison has a role in public safety, but it is not a cure-all. Its value is limited, and its use should also be limited to what it does best: isolating young criminals long enough to give them a chance to grow up and get a grip on their impulses. It is a traumatic experience, certainly, but it should be only a temporary one, not a way of life. Prisoners kept too long tend to embrace the criminal culture, its distorted values and beliefs; they have little choice — prison is their life. There are some prisoners who cannot be returned to society — serial killers, serial rapists, professional hit men, and the like — but the monsters who need to die in prison are rare exceptions in the criminal landscape.

Crime is a young man's game. Most of the nation's random violence is committed by young urban terrorists. But because of long, mandatory sentences, most prisoners here are much older, having spent fifteen, twenty, thirty, or more years behind bars, long past necessity. Rather than pay for new prisons, society would be well served by releasing some of its older prisoners who pose no threat and using the money to catch young street thugs. Warden John Whitley agrees that many older prisoners here could be freed tomorrow with little or no danger to society. Release, however, is governed by law or by politicians, not by penal professionals. Even murderers, those most feared by society, pose little risk. Historically, for example, the domestic staff at Louisiana's Governor's mansion has been made up of murderers, hand-picked to work among the chief-of-state and his family. Penologists° have long known that murder is almost always a once-in-a-lifetime act. The most dangerous criminal is the one who has not yet killed but has a history of escalating offenses. He's the one to watch.

Rehabilitation can work. Everyone changes in time. The trick is to influence the direction that change takes. The problem with prisons is that they don't do more to rehabilitate those confined in them. The convict who enters prison illiterate will probably leave the same way. Most convicts want to be better than they are, but education is not a priority. This prison houses

*Introduction of the proposed solution*

*Transitions (underlined) for coherence*

---

**infraction:** Violation.    **incorrigible:** Incapable of reform.    **penologists:** Those who study prison management and criminal justice.

4,600 men and offers academic training to 240, vocational training to a like number. Perhaps it doesn't matter. About 90 percent of the men here may never leave this prison alive.

Conclusion summing up solution

The only effective way to curb crime is for society to work to prevent the criminal act in the first place, to come between the perpetrator° and crime. Our youngsters must be taught to respect the humanity of others and to handle disputes without violence. It is essential to educate and equip them with the skills to pursue their life ambitions in a meaningful way. As a community, we must address the adverse life circumstances that spawn criminality. These things are not quick, and they're not easy, but they're effective. Politicians think that's too hard a sell. They want to be on record for doing something now, something they can point to at reelection time. So the drumbeat goes on for more police, more prisons, more of the same failed policies.

Ever see a dog chase its tail?

## Questions to Start You Thinking

### Meaning

1. Does Rideau convince you that the belief that "permanently exiling people to prison will make society safe" is an "illusion" (paragraph 1)?

2. According to Rideau, why don't prisons work?

3. What does he propose as solutions to the problem of escalating crime? What other solutions can you think of?

### Writing Strategies

4. What justifications, if any, for the prison system has Rideau left out of his essay? Do these omissions help or hurt his essay? Why, or why not?

5. What evidence does the author provide to support his assertion that Louisiana's "getting tough" policy has not worked? Does he provide sufficient evidence to convince you? Does he persuade you that action is necessary?

6. What would make Rideau's argument for his proposals more persuasive?

7. Other than himself, what authorities does Rideau cite? Why do you think he does this?

8. Does the fact that the author is a convicted criminal strengthen or weaken his argument? Why do you think he mentions this in his first sentence?

9. How do you interpret the last line, "Ever see a dog chase its tail?" Is this line an effective way for Rideau to end his essay? Explain.

**perpetrator:** One who is responsible for an action or a crime.

**Lacey Taylor**                                      **Student Essay**

## It's Not Just a Bike

Lacey Taylor drew on personal experience in her essay to identify a problem on her campus and to propose solutions for it.

Imagine one day waking up to find that your car had been stolen. To many    1
students, a bicycle is just like a car. They depend on their bicycles for all their
transportation needs, getting to and from classes and work. Too many bicycles
are being stolen on campus, and this situation has become a major problem
for students who depend on them. In the past year, one friend has had two
new bicycles stolen. Just three months ago, I went home for the weekend,
and when I got back, my bicycle was gone. I could not believe that anyone
would do such a horrible thing, but I was wrong, and someone did do it. This
theft was a major blow to me because my bicycle was my only transportation
to work. I am not the only person and will not be the last to have my bicycle
taken, so something should be done and should be done soon. The campus
community should use methods such as posting warning signs, starting an
awareness program, and investing in new technology like cameras, chain
alarms, and tracking devices to help solve this problem.

> ❓ What comparable local problems have you experienced or observed?

Although many solutions are available to help alleviate this problem, some    2
may be as simple as posting signs. Signs are a cheap and easy way to alleviate bike theft. The signs should read that bicycle theft is a crime, punishable
by law, and they should explain the consequences that go along with stealing
bicycles. The signs would need to be posted at all the bicycle racks just like
the signs posted at every parking spot warning about being a tow-away zone.
These signs would not completely solve the problem, but they would discour-
age some potential bicycle thieves.

The school also needs to begin a bicycle-theft awareness program. The pro-    3
gram should inform students about bicycle theft, warning that it happens all
the time and that it could happen to them. The program also would need to tell
students about certain steps that they could take to avoid becoming victims of
bike theft. For example, it could provide information about different methods of
bicycle security such as keeping the serial number in case the bike is stolen and
engraving a name on the bike so that it can be easily identified. The program
also should tell students what to do if a bicycle is actually stolen such as calling
the police and filing a report. This awareness program would prevent many students from ending up with stolen bicycles.

> ❓ What simple informative and preventive methods have been used in your community or on your campus to solve problems?

A more advanced method for solving this problem would be to install secu-    4
rity cameras all around campus. The cameras would keep track of all the activity
going on at the bicycle racks and let the person watching the camera know if
someone is stealing a bicycle. If no one sees the illegal act take place, then the

camera tape could be pulled, watched, and used as evidence against the bike thief. For this solution to succeed, the cameras should be placed a certain way, all facing the bike racks and close enough for a viewer to tell what is going on at the racks. The cameras also need to be in plain sight for everyone to see so that anyone considering stealing a bicycle would think twice before acting. After all, no one wants to be caught doing something illegal on camera. Finally, these cameras should be linked to a TV in the lobby of each dorm. Keeping an eye on the TV, watching for any strange activity, should be part of the job of the resident assistant on duty. The resident assistant then could report a bicycle being stolen to the campus police. These cameras would not only ward off some potential criminals but also help to catch the ones who were not scared off.

A creative solution would be to invest in chain alarms. These chains contain    5
small wires; if the chains are cut, an alarm in the lock goes off just like a car alarm. This alarm would alert people nearby that someone was stealing a bicycle. The sound also might scare the thief into dropping the bike and running off. These chains could be rented out to students by the transportation department. If the rental cost around ten dollars a semester, the chains would pay for themselves over a short period of time and eventually make a profit for the transportation department. If someone never returned the chain at the end of the semester, the student should be fined, and a hold should be placed on his or her account just as the library does with book fines that must be paid before graduation. These chains would help to catch the bike thieves and also, just like the signs and cameras, help to scare off potential thieves.

Finally tracking devices could be placed on all campus bicycles. This would    6
be the most effective solution to the bicycle theft problem because these tracking devices would come into play if all the other solutions failed to do the job. These devices should be small and placed in a hard-to-find spot on the bicycle. If a bike is stolen, then the bike could be traced on a campus police computer and its location identified. Then the police could go through the proper procedure to catch the thief. These tracking devices could be rented out just like the bicycle chains. Even though this method would not stop bicycles from being stolen, it would make it easy to find the bikes and catch the thieves.

Bicycle theft is a major problem that deserves attention. Too many bicycles    7
are being stolen, and bikes are too important to everyday campus life to let this problem go unnoticed. The campus should use simple methods such as posting warning signs or sponsoring an awareness program and also invest in new technology like cameras, chain alarms, and tracking devices to help solve this problem. Bicycle riders should be aware that theft is a problem that could happen to them at any time, but bicycle thieves should not be able to take whatever they like with no action being taken against them. Bicycles, like cars, provide essential transportation, and no one wants to have that necessity stolen.

 Would students on your campus welcome technological solutions to problems like bike theft, or would they worry about privacy, costs, or other issues?

## Questions to Start You Thinking

### Meaning

1. What problem does Taylor identify? Does she convince you that this is an important problem? Why, or why not?

2. What solutions does she propose? Why does she arrange them as she does? Which is her strongest solution? Her least convincing? Can you think of other ideas that she might have included?

3. How effectively would Taylor's proposal persuade various members of a campus audience? Which people would she easily persuade? Which might need more convincing? Can you think of other arguments that would appeal to specific readers?

### Writing Strategies

4. Is Taylor's argument easy to follow? Why, or why not? What kinds of transitions does she use to lead readers through her points? How effective do you find them?

5. Is Taylor's evidence specific and sufficient? Explain.

6. What qualifies Taylor to write about this topic? How do these qualifications contribute to her ability to persuade?

7. Using highlighters or marginal notes, identify the essay's introduction, explanation of the problem, thesis, proposal to solve the problem, and conclusion. How effective is the organization of this essay?

# Learning by Writing

## The Assignment: Proposing a Solution

In this essay you'll first carefully analyze and explain a specific social, economic, political, civic, or environmental problem — a problem you care about and strongly wish to see resolved. The problem may be large or small, but it shouldn't be trivial. It may affect the whole country or mainly people from your city, campus, or classroom. Show your readers that this problem really exists and that it matters to you and to them. After setting it forth, you also may want to explain why it exists. Write for an audience who, once aware of the problem, may be expected to help do something about it.

The second thing you are to accomplish in the essay is to propose one or more ways to solve the problem or at least alleviate it. In making a proposal, you urge action by using words like *should, ought,* and *must*: "This city ought to have a Bureau of Missing Persons"; "Small private aircraft should be banned from flying close to a major commercial airport." Lay out the

A "living wall" or "green wall" is a wall that is completely or partially covered with plants. Nano Calvo/VW Pics/ZUMAPRESS.com.

reasons why your proposal deserves to be implemented; supply evidence that your solution is reasonable and can work. Remember that your purpose is to convince readers that something should be done about the problem.

These students cogently argued for action in their papers:

Based on research studies and statistics, one student argued that using standardized test scores from the SAT or the ACT as criteria for college admissions is a problem because it favors aggressive students from affluent families. His proposal was to abolish this use of the scores.

Another argued that speeders racing past an elementary school might be slowed by a combination of more warning signs, surveillance equipment, police patrols, and fines.

A third argued that cities should consider constructing public buildings with "living walls" in order to reduce energy consumption, improve air quality, and allow for urban agriculture.

## Facing the Challenge  Proposing a Solution

The major challenge writers face when writing a proposal is to develop a detailed and convincing solution. Finding solutions is much harder than finding problems. Convincing readers that you have found a reasonable, workable solution is harder still. For example, suppose you propose the combination of rigorous exercise and a diet low in refined carbohydrates and sugar as a solution for obesity. While these solutions seem reasonable and workable to you, readers who have lost weight and then gained it back might point out that their main problem is not losing weight but maintaining weight loss over time. To account for their concerns and enhance your credibility, you might revise your solution to focus on realistic long-term goals and strategies. For instance, you might recommend that friends walk together two or three times a week to get more exercise. You might also list sources of recipes for easy, tasty, and filling meals that are low in refined carbohydrates.

To develop a realistic solution that fully addresses a problem and satisfies the concerns of readers, consider questions such as these:

- How might the problem affect different groups of people?
- What range of concerns are your readers likely to have?
- What realistic solution addresses the concerns of readers about *all* aspects of the problem?

## Generating Ideas

**Identify a Problem.** Brainstorm by writing down all the topics that come to mind. Observe events around you to identify irritating campus or community problems you would like to solve. Watch for ideas in the news. Browse through issue-oriented Web sites. Look for sites sponsored by large nonprofit foundations that accept grant proposals and fund innovative solutions to societal issues. Be sure to stick to problems that you want to solve, and star the ideas that seem to have the most potential.

### DISCOVERY CHECKLIST

- ☐ Can you recall any problem that needs a solution? What problems do you meet every day or occasionally? What problems concern people near you?
- ☐ What conditions in need of improvement have you observed on television, on the Web, or in your daily activities? What action is called for?
- ☐ What problems have been discussed recently on campus or in class?
- ☐ What problems are discussed in blogs, online or print newspapers, or newsmagazines such as *Time,* the *Week,* or *U.S. News & World Report*?

**Consider Your Audience.** Readers need to believe that your problem is real and your solution is feasible. If you are addressing classmates, maybe they haven't thought about the problem before. Look for ways to make it personal for them, to show that it affects them and deserves their attention.

- Who are your readers? How would you describe them?
- Why should your readers care about this problem? Does it affect their health, welfare, conscience, or pocketbook?
- Have they ever expressed any interest in the problem? If so, what has triggered their interest?
- Do they belong to any organization or segment of society that makes them especially susceptible to — or uninterested in — this problem?
- What attitudes about the problem do you share with your readers? Which of their assumptions or values differ from yours, and how might this difference affect how they view your proposal?

## Learning by Doing  Describing Your Audience

Write a paragraph or so describing the audience you intend to address. Who are they? Which of their circumstances, interests, traits, social circles, attitudes, and values best prepare them to grasp the problem? Which make them most (or least) receptive to your solution? If aspects of the problem or the solution especially appeal (or do not appeal) to them, consider how to present your ideas most persuasively. If you want a second opinion, share your analysis with a classmate.

**Think about Solutions.** Once you've chosen a problem, brainstorm — alone or with classmates — for possible solutions, or use your imagination. Some problems, such as reducing international tensions, present no easy solutions. Still, give some strategic thought to any problem that seriously concerns you, even if it has stumped experts. Sometimes a solution reveals itself to a novice thinker, and even a partial solution is worth offering.

For more on using evidence to support an argument, see pp. 157–64.

**Consider Sources of Support.** To show that the problem really exists, you'll need evidence and examples. If further library research will help you justify the problem, now is the time to do it. Consider whether local history archives, newspaper stories, accounts of public meetings, interviews, or relevant Web sites might identify concerns of readers, practical limits of solutions, or previous efforts that will help you develop your solution.

For more on causes and effects, see Ch. 8 and pp. 439–41. For more on analysis, see pp. 430–32.

For more on comparison and contrast, see Ch. 7. For more on evaluation, see Ch. 11.

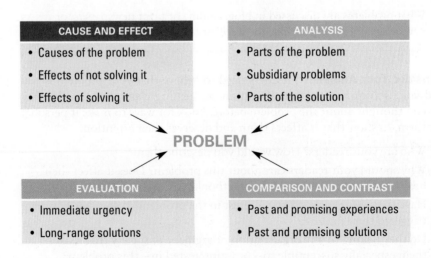

**CAUSE AND EFFECT**
- Causes of the problem
- Effects of not solving it
- Effects of solving it

**ANALYSIS**
- Parts of the problem
- Subsidiary problems
- Parts of the solution

**PROBLEM**

**EVALUATION**
- Immediate urgency
- Long-range solutions

**COMPARISON AND CONTRAST**
- Past and promising experiences
- Past and promising solutions

## Planning, Drafting, and Developing

**Start with Your Proposal and Your Thesis.** A basic approach is to state your proposal in a sentence that can act as your thesis. This is the strategy that Lacey Taylor used for her thesis.

For advice on finding a few sources, see sections A and B in the Quick Research Guide, pp. Q-20–Q-25.

TAYLOR'S THESIS      The campus community should use methods such as posting warning signs, starting an awareness program, and investing in new technology like cameras, chain alarms, and tracking devices to help solve this problem.

Let's look at another example, showing a first draft of a thesis and the proposal it was based on.

For more on stating a thesis, see pp. 384–93.

PROPOSAL         Let people get divorced without having to go to court.

WORKING THESIS   The legislature should pass a law allowing couples to divorce without the problem of going to court.

From such a statement, the rest of the argument may start to unfold, often falling naturally into a simple two-part shape:

1. *A claim that a problem exists.* This part explains the problem and supplies evidence of its significance — for example, the costs, adversarial process, and stress of divorce court for a couple and their family.

2. *A claim that something ought to be done about it.* This part proposes a solution to the problem — for example, legislative action to authorize other options such as mediation.

These two parts can grow naturally into an informal outline.

For more on outlines, see pp. 395–403.

1. Introduction

    Overview of the situation

    Working thesis stating your proposal

2. Problem

    Explanation of its nature

    Evidence of its significance

3. Solution

    Explanation of its nature

    Evidence of its effectiveness and practicality

4. Conclusion

You can then expand your outline and make your proposal more persuasive by including some or all of the following elements:

■ Knowledge or experience that qualifies you to propose a solution (your experience as a player or a coach, for example, that establishes your credibility as an authority on Little League or soccer clubs)

■ Values, beliefs, or assumptions that have caused you to feel strongly about the need for action

A sign from part of a popular and successful antilittering campaign. AP Images/Donna McWilliam.

■ An estimate of the resources — money, people, skills, material — and the time required to implement the solution (perhaps including what is available now and what needs to be obtained)

■ Step-by-step actions needed to achieve your solution

■ Controls or quality checks to monitor implementation

■ Possible obstacles or difficulties that may need to be overcome

■ Reasons your solution is better than others proposed or tried already

■ Any other evidence that shows that your suggestion is practical, reasonable in cost, and likely to be effective

## Learning by Doing 📷 Reflecting on a Problem

Reflect on a problem about which you feel strongly, such as parking availability at school, high tuition, or bad drivers. How could you rectify the problem? Make a brief outline of an essay proposing your solution.

**Imagine Possible Objections of Your Audience.** You can increase the likelihood that readers will accept your proposal in two ways. First, start your proposal by showing that a problem exists. Then, when you turn to your claim that something should be done, begin with a simple and inviting suggestion. For example, a claim that national parks need better care might suggest that readers head for a park and personally size up the situation. Besides drawing readers into the problem and the solution, you may think of objections they might raise — reservations about the high cost, complexity, or workability of your plan, for instance. Persuade readers by anticipating and laying to rest their likely objections.

## Learning by Doing 🔵 Reflecting on Interested Parties

Sketch a picture or diagram that visualizes the problem for which you are offering a solution. Looking at your sketch, determine who might have an interest in either the problem itself or your proposed solution. Could there be individuals who have an interest in a different solution? How much of an interest would each party have in your solution? What objections might each party have to your solution?

**Cite Sources Carefully.** When you collect ideas and evidence from outside sources, you need to document your evidence — that is, tell where you found everything. Follow the documentation method your instructor wants you to use. You may also want to identify sources as you introduce them to assure a reader that they are authoritative.

For pointers on integrating and documenting sources, see Ch. 12 and D6 and E1–E2 (pp. Q-30–Q-36) in the Quick Research Guide.

> According to *Newsweek* correspondent Josie Fair, . . .

> In his biography *FDR: The New Deal Years*, Davis reports . . .

> While working as a Senate page in the summer of 2015, I observed . . .

Introduce visual evidence (table, graph, drawing, map, photo), too.

For more about integrating visuals, see section B (pp. Q-7–Q-12) in the Quick Format Guide.

> As the 2010 census figures in Table 1 indicate, . . .

> The photograph showing the run-down condition of the dog park (see Fig. 2) . . .

## Revising and Editing

For more revising and editing strategies, see Ch. 23.

As you revise, concentrate on a clear explanation of the problem and solid supporting evidence for the solution. Make your essay coherent and its parts clear to help achieve your purpose of convincing your readers.

**Clarify Your Thesis.** Your readers are likely to rely on your thesis to identify the problem and possibly to preview your solution. Look again at your thesis from a reader's point of view.

| | |
|---|---|
| WORKING THESIS | The legislature should pass a law allowing couples to divorce without the problem of going to court. |
| REVISED THESIS | Because divorce court can be expensive, adversarial, and stressful, passing a law that allows couples to divorce without a trip to court would encourage simpler, more harmonious ways to end a marriage. |

Tim MacPherson/Corbis.

## THESIS CHECKLIST

☐ Does your thesis clearly identify the problem?

☐ Does it suggest a solution?

☐ Could the thesis be refined or made more specific based on evidence or insights that you gathered while planning, drafting, or developing your essay?

**Reorganize for Unity and Coherence.** When Heather Colbenson revised her first draft, she wanted to clarify the presentation of her problem.

Why would high schools in farming communities drop

agriculture classes and the FFA program? ~~Small~~ *The main reason that* Small schools are cutting

*is that*

ag programs ~~because~~ the state has not provided significant funding

for the schools to operate. The small schools have to make cuts, and

some small schools are deciding that the agriculture classes are not as

important as other courses. Some small schools are consolidating to

receive more aid. Many of these schools have been able to save their

ag programs.

*One reason is that m*

Many colleges are demanding that students have two years of foreign

language. In small schools, like my own, the students could take either

foreign language or ag classes. Therefore, students choose language

classes to fill the college requirement. When the students leave the ag

classes to take foreign language, the number of students declines, which

makes it easier for school administrators to cut ag classes.

*Move main reason last for emphasis*

*Why did I put a solution here? → Move to end!*

*Rewrite this! Not really college requirements but college-prep courses vs. others when budget is tight*

Her revised paper was more forcefully organized and more coherent, making it easier for readers to follow. The bridges between ideas were now on paper, not just in her mind.

For strategies for achieving coherence, see pp. 417–20.

## Learning by Doing 🔟 Revising for Clear Organization

Check the organization of your draft against your plans and the two-part structure commonly used in proposals (see p. 187). Outline what you've actually done, not what you intended, to see your organization as readers will. Does your draft open with a sufficient overview for your audience? Do you state your actual proposal clearly? Does your draft progress from problem to solution without mixing ideas? Have you included elements appropriate for your audience? Reorganize and revise as needed. Exchange drafts with a classmate if you want a second opinion on organization.

**Be Reasonable.** Exaggerated claims for a solution will not persuade readers. Neither will oversimplifying the problem so the solution seems more workable. Don't be afraid to express reasonable doubts about the completeness of your solution. If necessary, rethink both problem and solution.

## Peer Response 👥 Proposing a Solution

Ask several classmates or friends to review your proposal and solution, answering questions such as these:

- What is your overall reaction to this proposal? Does it make you want to go out and do something about the problem?
- Are you convinced that the problem is of concern to you? If not, why not?
- Are you persuaded that the writer's solution is workable? Why, or why not?
- Has the writer paid enough attention to readers and their concerns?
- Restate what you understand to be the proposal's major points:

   Problem

   Explanation of problem and why it matters

   Proposed solution

   Explanation of proposal and its practicality

   Reasons and procedure to implement proposal

   Proposal's advantages, disadvantages, and responses to other solutions

   Final recommendation
- If this paper were yours, what one thing would you work on?

For general questions for a peer editor, see p. 447.

## REVISION CHECKLIST

☐ Does your introduction invite the reader into the discussion?

☐ Is your problem clear? How have you made it relevant to readers?

☐ Have you clearly outlined the steps necessary to solve the problem?

☐ Where have you demonstrated the benefits of your solution?

☐ Have you considered other solutions before rejecting them for your own?

☐ Have you anticipated the doubts readers may have about your solution?

☐ Do you sound reasonable, willing to admit that you don't know everything? If you sound preachy, have you overused *should* and *must*?

☐ Have you avoided promising that your solution will do more than it can possibly do? Have you made believable predictions for its success?

For more editing and proofreading strategies, see pp. 455–58. For more on documenting sources, see E1–E2 in the Quick Research Guide, pp. Q-31–Q-36.

After you have revised your proposal, edit and proofread it. Carefully check the grammar, word choice, punctuation, and mechanics — and then correct any problems you find. If you have used sources, be sure that you have cited them correctly in your text and added a list of works cited.

Make sure your sentence structure helps you make your points clearly and directly. Using the active voice allows you to emphasize the actor (subject) performing the sentence's action (verb). For example, the sentence "The dean should remedy the problem by spending money on prevention" explicitly identifies and emphasizes the actor (the dean) and does so succinctly. Using the passive voice, by contrast, results in a sentence that doesn't specify the actor: "The problem should be remedied by spending money on prevention." Readers may struggle to determine your intended focus — is it on the dean, or on the problem?

## EDITING CHECKLIST

For more help, find the relevant checklist sections in the Quick Editing Guide on p. Q-37. Turn also to the Quick Format Guide beginning on p. Q-1.

☐ Is it clear what each pronoun refers to? Is any *this* or *that* ambiguous? Does each pronoun agree with its antecedent?  A6

☐ Is your sentence structure correct? Have you avoided writing fragments, comma splices, or fused sentences?  A1, A2

☐ Do your transitions and other introductory elements have commas after them, if these are needed?  D1

☐ Have you spelled and capitalized everything correctly, especially names of people and organizations?  E1, E2

## Reviewing and Reflecting

To complete more review questions for Ch. 10, go to LaunchPad.

**REVIEW** Working with classmates or independently, respond to the following questions:

1. What strategies can you use to identify a problem that interests you—a problem with potential solutions?

2. What questions can you ask to learn more about the audience of a paper that proposes a solution to a problem? Think of a topic for such a paper, and ask these questions about the potential audience. Did going through this process make you think differently about how you might approach the topic? If so, how?

3. What types of information might flesh out an outline for a paper that proposes a solution to a problem, making the proposal more persuasive? If you have written or are writing a proposal paper, ask yourself if you could add any of this type of information to make your paper more effective.

**REFLECT** After completing one of the writing assignments presented in this chapter or supplied by your instructor, turn back to the After Writing questions on page 39 of Chapter 3 and respond to as many of them as you can. It might be helpful to revisit your responses to the Learning by Doing activities on pages 188 and 189, if you completed them.

Next, reflect in writing about how you might apply the insights that you drew from this assignment to another situation—in or outside of college—in which you have to propose a solution to a problem. If no specific situations come to mind, imagine that

- in a civics course, you are writing a paper that proposes strategies for making biking safer along area roadways.
- in a work setting, you want to propose ways to improve employee morale after a recent round of layoffs.

In your reflection, consider the types of solutions that might be most appealing to your potential audience.

## Additional Writing Assignments

1. If you followed the assignment in Chapter 9 and took a stand, now write a few paragraphs extending that paper to propose a solution that argues for action. To gather ideas, brainstorm with classmates first.

2. Brainstorm with classmates to develop a list of campus problems that irritate students or complicate their lives. Write an essay that tackles one of these problems by explaining it and proposing a practical, workable solution. (If you can't identify a workable solution, select a different problem.) Address an audience on your campus or in your college system that could implement a solution. Present your ideas tactfully. After all, they may also be the ones responsible for creating or at least not solving the problem earlier. (If appropriate, investigate any campus history that might help you overcome resistance based on tradition.)

3. Write a memo to your supervisor at work in which you propose an innovation (related to procedures, schedules, policies, or similar matters) that could benefit your department or company.

4. As part of a problem–solution blog or thread for your class, post a concise passage identifying and explaining a problem. (Your instructor may limit the problems to relevant issues.) Then post a second passage identifying and explaining a solution to the problem you identified. Respond to each other's problem–solution statements with questions, comments, or suggestions to develop a focused exchange about the class proposals.

5. **Source Assignment.** Choose from the following list a practice that you find inefficient, unethical or unfair as a solution to a problem. In a few paragraphs, give reasons for your objections. Then narrow the issue as needed to propose a better solution in a persuasive essay. Locate, use, and cite some statistics or other data to help raise readers' awareness.

   Corporate censorship of online reviews      Genetic engineering
   Goods made with child labor                 Outsourcing jobs
   Laboratory experiments on animals           Dumping wastes in the ocean

6. **Visual Assignment.** Select one of the following images. Write an essay that analyzes the problem that it identifies, noting how elements of the image draw the viewer into the problem. Include any solution suggested or implied by the image or your own solution to the problem.

Sid Hastings/Corbis.

Ángel Navarrete/Bloomberg/Getty Images.

AP Images/The Brownsville Herald/Brad Doherty.

# 11 Evaluating and Reviewing

Justin Sullivan/Getty Images News/Getty Images.

## Responding to an Image

In what respects does this photograph of a giant-pumpkin weigh-in capture the essence of such competitions? What overall impression does the image convey? What details contribute to this impression? How does the photograph direct the viewer's eye? In what ways does this image suggest, represent, or comment on a particular set of criteria and process of evaluation?

Evaluating means judging. You do it when you decide what candidate to vote for, pick which television to buy, or recommend a new restaurant to your friends. All of us pass judgments—often snap judgments—as we move through a day's routine. A friend asks, "How was that movie you saw last night?" and you reply, "Terrific—don't miss it" or maybe "Pretty good, but it had too much blood and gore for me."

But to *write* an evaluation calls for you to think more critically. As a writer you first decide on *criteria,* or standards for judging, and then come up with evidence to back up your judgment. Your evaluation zeroes in on a definite subject that you inspect carefully in order to reach a considered opinion. The subject might be a film, a book, or a performance that you review. Or it might be a sports team, a product, or a body of research that you evaluate. The possibilities are endless.

## Why Evaluating and Reviewing Matter

**In a College Course**

- You evaluate theories and methods in the fields you study, including long-standing controversies such as the dispute about teaching methods raging in education for the deaf.
- You evaluate instructors, courses, and sometimes campus facilities and services to help monitor and improve your college.

**In the Workplace**

- You evaluate people, projects, goals, and results, just as your potential was evaluated as a job applicant and your performance is evaluated as an employee.

**In Your Community**

- You evaluate video games for yourself or your children and review films, music, shows, and restaurants as you decide how to spend your money and time.

❓ What have you evaluated within the last few weeks? How have evaluations and reviews been useful for you? How have you incorporated evaluations and reviews into your writing?

# Learning from Other Writers

Here are evaluations by a professional and a student. To help you analyze the first reading, look at the notes in the margin. They identify features such as the thesis, or main idea, and the criteria for evaluation, typical of essays that evaluate.

## As You Read These Evaluations

Ask yourself the following questions:

1. Do you consider the writer qualified to evaluate the subject he or she chose? What biases and prejudices might the writer bring to the task?

2. What criteria for evaluation does the writer establish? Are these reasonable standards for evaluating the subject?

3. What is the writer's assessment of the subject? Does the writer provide sufficient evidence to convince you of his or her evaluation?

## Scott Tobias

### The Hunger Games

Scott Tobias.

Film critic Scott Tobias has reviewed movies for NPR.org, the *Village Voice*, the *Hollywood Reporter*, and the A.V. Club section of the *Onion* (where this review appeared). Here, he evaluates the film version of the popular book *The Hunger Games*.

I f Suzanne Collins's novel *The Hunger Games* turns up on school curricula 50 years from now—and as accessible dystopian° science fiction with allusions° to early-21st-century strife, that isn't out of the question—the lazy students of the future can be assured that they can watch the movie version and still get better than a passing grade. But that's a dubious triumph: A book is a book and a movie is a movie, and whenever the latter merely sets about illustrating the former, it's a failure of adaptation, to say nothing of imagination. When the goal is simply to be as faithful as possible to the material—as if a movie were a marriage, and a rights contract the vow—the best result is a skillful abridgment, one that hits all the important marks without losing anything egregious.° And as abridgments go, they don't get much more skillful than this one. 1

THESIS

Introduction to criterion 1: adaptation of situation

That such a safe adaptation could come of *The Hunger Games* speaks more to the trilogy's commercial ascent than the book's actual content, which is audacious and savvy in its dark calculations. The opening crawl (and a stirring propaganda movie) informs us that "The Hunger Games" 2

---

**dystopian:** Presenting miserable places (as opposed to utopias or perfect places) in fiction. **allusions:** Indirect or casual references. **egregious:** Glaring or outrageous.

are an annual event in Panem, a North American nation divided into 12 different districts, each in service to the Capitol, a wealthy metropolis that owes its creature comforts to an oppressive dictatorship. For the 75 years since a district rebellion was put down, the Games have existed as an assertion of the Capitol's power, a winner-take-all contest that touts heroism and sacrifice—participants are called "tributes"—while pitting the districts against each other. At "The Reaping," a boy and a girl between the ages of 12 and 18 are taken from each district—with odds determined by age and the number of rations they accept throughout the year—and thrown into a controlled arena, where they're forced to kill each other until only one survives.

In District 12, a dirt-poor coal-mining community that looks like a Dorothea Lange° photograph, Katniss Everdeen (Jennifer Lawrence) quietly rebels against the system by hunting game in a forbidden area with her friend Gale (Liam Hemsworth) and trading it on the black market. Katniss prepares her meek younger sister Prim (Willow Shields) for her first Reaping, but the odds of a single entry being selected among teenagers with many entries apiece are long. In the film's most affecting scene, those long odds turn against Prim in a shock that Ross renders in agonizing silence, punctuated only by Katniss screaming that she'll volunteer in her sister's place. She's joined, on the boys' side, by Peeta (Josh Hutcherson), a baker's son whose earnestness masks a gift for strategy that Katniss lacks. Together, with the help of the drunkard Haymitch (Woody Harrelson), the only District 12 citizen ever to win the Games, they challenge tributes that range from sadistic volunteers to crafty kids like the pint-sized Rue (Amandla Stenberg) to the truly helpless and soon-to-be-dead.

Director Gary Ross and his screenwriters do well with the unenviable task of setting the table for the series, but with so many characters and subplots to service, they have to ration as stingily as the Capitol. The Reaping is one of the few sequences that's given time to breathe a little, and it makes all the difference—the hushed crowd, neither roused by propaganda nor open in resistance, says everything about the fear and shimmering resentment that stirs in the districts. Once Katniss volunteers, *The Hunger Games* jets from one plot point to another without emphasizing any to great effect. Ross and company deliver on the franchise more effectively than, say, the first *Harry Potter* movie, but there's little evidence that they had any other agenda in mind.

The primary strength of Collins's book is Katniss herself, a model of steel-spined resourcefulness and power whose internal monologue° roils with daft naiveté and self-doubt, especially when it comes to reading her supposed allies. Absent that monologue, Ross's film mostly has the book's action, and that's enough for a rousing two hours through the surreality of the Capitol—which looks like Dubai meets Nuremberg—and the excitement of the Games themselves, which are sanitized by the PG-13 rating, but nonetheless suspenseful and dread-soaked. And beyond the mayhem are the periodic reminders that the Games are as rigged as any reality show; as with a casino,

3  Introduction to criterion 2: adaptation of characters

4  Introduction to criterion 3: adaptation of plot

5  Limitations of adaptation

---

**Dorothea Lange:** Documentary photographer whose images captured the Depression and the Dust Bowl migration.    **monologue:** One-person speech.

Conclusion, returning
to thesis

it's important that the house always wins, even if that means shaking up the rules as it goes along.

*The Hunger Games* has its share of standalone payoffs, though some are   6
too sketchily developed to have much of an impact, like Katniss's motherly connection to Rue. Nonetheless, it's the first act in a three-act story, and characters who seem thin now may resonate more down the line. With all the dirty work out of the way, perhaps the sequels will come closer to channeling the revolutionary fervor of Collins's books, and perhaps given the current focus on income inequality, find a populist° edge in the process. Whether the films will take on a life of their own is another matter: As of the first installment, it's stenography° in light.

**populist:** Advocating for ordinary people.     **stenography:** Shorthand notes for a copy.

### Questions to Start You Thinking

Meaning

1. How does Tobias categorize *The Hunger Games* film? How does this category influence his review?

2. What does Tobias show in paragraphs 2, 3, and 4? How do the topics of these paragraphs support his overall evaluation?

3. What does Tobias mean when he wonders how well the sequels will convey "the revolutionary fervor of Collins's books" (paragraph 6)? To what extent does he feel that the first film met his expectations?

Writing Strategies

4. What is Tobias's overall judgment of the film? What evidence does he use to support this judgment?

5. In your view, how well does he support his judgment? Point to some specific examples in making your case.

6. Why does Tobias refer to "dystopian science fiction" (paragraph 1) as well as reality shows and casinos (5)? What do such references add to his review?

7. How would you describe Tobias's tone, the quality of his writing that reveals his attitude toward his topic and his readers? Does the tone seem appropriate for his purpose and audience?

## Elizabeth Erion                                    **Student Essay**

### Internship Program Falls Short

Elizabeth Erion drew on two valuable resources for her evaluation: her investigation of the campus internship program and her own experience as an intern. An earlier version of her essay appeared as an editorial in the campus student newspaper.

Since its creation in 1978, the Coram Internship Program has been a mainstay of the Career Development Center. The program matches interested students—usually those entering their junior year—with companies offering paid summer employment. Participating companies vary by year but range from the Guggenheim Museum in New York to the Keck School of Medicine in Los Angeles. In 2011, the program placed thirteen students from the class of 2012 at eleven companies or organizations. While this statistic may at first sound impressive, it accounts for only 2.8% of the class of 2012. Given the popularity of summer internships to lead into one's junior year, it is surprising that a higher percentage of the student body didn't make use of such a seemingly excellent, paid opportunity. But the program's low participation rate may be explained by one of its biggest flaws: its inherently restrictive nature.

By offering funded opportunities at only a certain set of companies, the Coram program limits its utility to a certain set of students—those whose career interests match the industries and whose geographical options match the locations of companies participating during a particular summer. What's more, certain locations and industries are heavily privileged over others. In 2012, nine of the fourteen companies were located in the Boston area. This regionalism is understandable given the college's location in Maine and the high percentage of students and alumni from the Boston area, but it still represents a concerning lack of geographic diversity.

Massachusetts natives probably would find this location far more doable than would students who hail from elsewhere. Local students might have the opportunity to live at home and save significant money (the program stipend does not cover living or travel expenses) or might have an easier time finding roommates or an apartment to sublet due to a strong network of friends and family in the area. They would incur no significant travel costs for a flight, a long train ride, or long-distance gas mileage to arrive and depart from their summer destination. A student from elsewhere who could not afford such expenses or who could not relocate for a personal reason—perhaps a family member who is ill—is at a disadvantage. If students were able to select the locations of their internships, they would be much more likely to participate in the program.

Similarly, students are restricted to opportunities in a certain set of industries. Four of the participating programs in 2012 were in the financial services sector. Five were in science and medicine. Only one opportunity was available for students interested in museum work. The aspiring journalist is out of luck, as the program offers no journalism internships. So too is the student wishing to gain exposure to law firm work. These students are forced to look elsewhere, at both paid and unpaid opportunities. In many sectors—especially the arts—unpaid internships abound, usually located in prohibitively expensive metropolitan areas. Students who cannot afford to take unpaid internships are then left with no options, which jeopardizes their entry into the job market

1 **?** What would you want to gain from an internship program?

2

3

**?** What advice would you give a nonlocal student?

4

after graduating. Had the Coram program offered internships in the desired fields of such students, those students could have spent the summer attaining the experience they needed.

The Coram Internship Program offers an excellent opportunity for the fortunate student who finds a good employment fit with a geographically convenient company. Unfortunately, the percentage of students who are able to find such a fit is prohibitively small, as illustrated by the program's low participation rate. The program's structure denies the chance of obtaining rewarding, paid opportunities to the majority of the college's students, which is problematic given the importance of internships in gaining entry-level employment. Ultimately, the Coram Internship Program proves itself an ineffective career resource for a geographically and professionally diverse student community.

5

> ❓ What kinds of internship opportunities would students on your campus want?

## Questions to Start You Thinking

### Meaning

1. Why does Erion feel that evaluating the internship program is important? Who might belong to the audience that she would like to influence?

2. What does Erion mean when she refers to the internship program's major flaw as "its inherently restrictive nature" (paragraph 1)?

3. Based on her evaluation, what changes do you think Erion would want the Career Development Center or the internship program to make?

### Writing Strategies

4. What criteria does Erion use to judge the internship program? To what extent has the program met these criteria, according to Erion?

5. Does Erion provide enough evidence to support her judgment? Why, or why not?

6. Do you find Erion's use of statistics effective? Why, or why not?

7. Using highlighters or marginal notes, identify the essay's introduction, thesis, criteria for evaluation, supporting evidence, and conclusion. How effective is the organization of the essay?

# Learning by Writing

## The Assignment: Writing an Evaluation

Pick a subject to evaluate—one you have personal experience with and feel competent to evaluate. This subject might be a movie, a TV program, a piece of music, a work of art, a new product, a government agency, a campus facility or policy, an essay or a reading, or anything else you can think of. Then, in a thoughtful essay, analyze your subject and evaluate it. You will need to determine specific criteria for evaluation and make them clear to your readers. In writing your evaluation, you will have a twofold purpose: (1) to set forth your assessment of the quality of your subject and (2) to convince your readers that your judgment is reasonable.

These three students wrote lively evaluations:

A music major evaluated works by American composer Aaron Copland, finding him trivial and imitative, "without a tenth of the talent or inventiveness that George Gershwin or Duke Ellington had in his little finger."

A student planning a career in business management evaluated a software firm in which he had worked one summer. His criteria were efficiency, productivity, appeal to new customers, and employee satisfaction.

A student from Brazil, who had seen firsthand the effects of industrial development in the Amazon rain forest, evaluated the efforts of the U.S. government to protect forests and wetlands, comparing them with efforts in her own country.

## Facing the Challenge   Evaluating and Reviewing

The major challenge writers face when writing evaluations is to make clear to their readers the criteria they have used to arrive at an opinion. When reviewing a movie, you may begin by simply summarizing its story and saying whether you like it or not. However, for readers who wonder whether to see the movie, you need to go further. For example, you might find its special effects, exotic sets, and unpredictable plot effective but wish that the characters had seemed more believable. Based on these criteria, your thesis might maintain that the movie is not realistic but is entertaining and well worth seeing.

Once you've chosen a topic, clarify your standards for evaluating it:

- What features or aspects will you use as criteria for evaluating?
- How could you briefly explain each of the criteria for a reader?
- What judgment or evaluation about your topic do the criteria support?

After identifying your criteria, you can examine each in turn. Explaining your criteria will ensure that you move beyond a summary to an opinion or judgment that you can justify to your readers.

## Generating Ideas

**Find Something to Evaluate.** Try *brainstorming* or *mapping* to identify as many possible topics as you can. Test your understanding of each possible topic by concisely describing or summarizing it.

For more strategies for generating ideas, see Ch. 19.

**Consider Sources of Support.** You'll want to spend time finding material to help you develop a judgment. You might watch a television program on your subject or read an article about it. Perhaps you'll want to review several examples of your subject: watching several films or campus plays, listening to several albums, examining several works of art, testing several products, or interviewing several spectators.

**Establish Your Criteria.** Jot down criteria, standards to apply to your subject based on the features of the subject worth considering. How well, for example, does a popular entertainer score on musicianship, rapport with the audience, selection of material, originality? In evaluating Portland as a home for a young careerist, you might ask: Does it offer ample entry-level positions in growth firms? Any criterion for evaluation has to fit your subject, audience, and purpose. After all, ample entry-level jobs might not matter to an audience of retirees.

For more on comparing and contrasting, see Ch. 7.

**Try Comparing and Contrasting.** Often you can readily size up the worth of a thing by setting it next to another of its kind. (When you *compare*, you point to similarities; when you *contrast*, you note differences.) To be comparable, of course, your two subjects need to have plenty in common. The quality of a Harley-Davidson motorcycle might be judged by contrasting it with a Honda but not with a school bus.

For example, if you are writing a paper for a film history course, you might compare and contrast the classic German horror movie *The Cabinet of Dr. Caligari* with the classic Hollywood movie *Frankenstein*, concluding that *Caligari* is more artistic. Then try listing characteristics of each film, point by point:

Set for *The Cabinet of Dr. Caligari* (1920), in which a man investigates the murder of his friend in a mountain village. Photofest.

|  | *Caligari* | *Frankenstein* |
|---|---|---|
| **Sets** | Dreamlike | Realistic, but with heavy Gothic atmosphere |
|  | Sets deliberately angular and distorted | Gothic sets |
| **Lighting** | Deep shadows that throw figures into relief | Torches highlighting monster's face in night scene |

By jotting down each point and each bit of evidence side by side, you can outline your comparison and contrast with great efficiency. Once you have listed them, decide on a possible order for the points.

**Try Defining Your Subject.** Another technique for evaluating is to define your subject, indicating its nature so clearly that your readers can easily distinguish it from others of its kind. Defining helps readers understand your subject — its structure, habitat, functions. In evaluating a classic television show such as *Roseanne*, you might want to include an *extended* definition of sitcoms over the years, their techniques, views of women, effects on the audience. Unlike a *short definition*, as in a dictionary, an extended definition is intended not simply to explain but to judge: What is the nature of my subject? What qualities make it unique, unlike others of its sort?

For more on defining, see pp. 426–28.

**Develop a Judgment That You Can Explain to Your Audience.** In the end, you will have to come to a decision: Is your subject good, worthwhile, significant, exemplary, preferable — or not? Most writers come to a judgment gradually as they explore their subjects and develop criteria.

---

DISCOVERY CHECKLIST

☐ What criteria do you plan to use in making your evaluation? Are they clear and reasonably easy to apply?

☐ What evidence can back up your judgments?

☐ Would comparing or contrasting help in evaluating your subject? If so, with what might you compare or contrast your subject?

☐ What qualities define your subject, setting it apart from the rest of its class?

---

## Learning by Doing 📷 Developing Criteria

With a small group of classmates, meeting in person or online, discuss the subjects each of you plan to evaluate. Make a detailed report about what you're evaluating. If possible, pass around a product, show a photograph of artwork, play a song, or read aloud a short literary work or an idea expressed in a reading. Ask your classmates to explain the reasons for their own evaluations. Maybe they'll suggest criteria or evidence that hadn't occurred to you.

## Planning, Drafting, and Developing

**Start with a Thesis.** Reflect a moment: What is your purpose? What is your main point? Try writing a paragraph that sums up the purpose of your evaluation or stating a thesis that summarizes your main point.

For more on stating a thesis, see pp. 384–93.

TOPIC + JUDGMENT    Campus revival of *South Pacific*—liked the performers featured in it plus the problems the revival raised

WORKING THESIS    Chosen to showcase the achievements of graduating seniors, the campus revival of *South Pacific* also brings up societal problems.

In reviews of books, movies, and other forms of entertainment, the thesis may grow out of how the subject conforms—or doesn't conform—to certain goals or standards. This is the approach that Scott Tobias used in his review of *The Hunger Games*. (His thesis is underlined.)

> When the goal is simply to be as faithful as possible to the material . . . the best result is a skillful abridgment, one that hits all the important marks without losing anything egregious. <u>And as abridgments go, they don't get much more skillful than this one.</u>

## Learning by Doing 🎯 Stating Your Overall Judgment

Build your criteria into your working thesis statement by filling in this sentence:

This subject is _____ because it _____.
               your judgment               your criteria

With a classmate or small group, compare sentences and share ideas about improving your statement of your judgment and criteria. Use this advice to rework and sharpen your working thesis.

**Consider Your Criteria.**  Many writers find that a list of specific criteria gives them confidence and generates ideas. Consider filling in a chart with three columns—criteria, evidence, judgment—to focus your thinking.

**Develop an Organization.**  You may want to begin with a direct statement of your judgment: Based on durability, cost, and comfort, the Classic 7 is an ideal campus backpack. On the other hand, you may want to reserve judgment by opening with a question about your subject: How good a film is *Mad Max: Fury Road*? Each approach suggests a different organization:

Thesis or main point    →    Supporting evidence    →    Return to thesis

Opening question    →    Supporting evidence    →    Overall judgment

Either way, you'll supply lots of evidence—details, examples, maybe comparisons or contrasts—to make your case compelling. You'll also cluster your evidence around your points or criteria for judgment so that readers know how and why you reach your judgment. You might try both patterns of organization to see which works better for your subject and purpose.

Most writers find that an outline—even a rough list—helps them keep track of points to make. If you compare and contrast your subject with something else, one way to arrange the points is *subject by subject*: discuss subject A, and then discuss subject B. For a longer comparison, a better way to organize is *point by point*, applying each point first to one subject and then the other. If approved by your instructor, you also might include a sketch, photograph, or other illustration of your subject or develop a comparative table summarizing the features of similar items you have compared.

## Learning by Doing 🎥 Reflecting on Product Reviews

Locate and examine three reviews of a specific car model in consumer information sources such as Kelley Blue Book, *Car and Driver*, *Consumer Reports*, J.D. Power, or edmunds.com. Which review appears most reliable and why? Least reliable and why? What evidence did the reviewers use to persuade or dissuade potential car buyers? Reflect on specific content (such as language, pictures, or graphics) that influenced your opinion about whether your chosen car model is worth purchasing.

## Revising and Editing

**Focus on Your Thesis.** Make your thesis as precise and clear as possible.

For more revising and editing strategies, see Ch. 23.

| WORKING THESIS | Chosen to showcase the achievements of graduating seniors, the campus revival of *South Pacific* also brings up societal problems. |
|---|---|
| REVISED THESIS | The senior showcase, the musical *South Pacific*, spotlights outstanding performers and raises timely societal issues such as prejudice. |

### THESIS CHECKLIST

☐ Does the thesis make clear your judgment of your topic?

☐ Can you see ways to make your thesis more precise or detailed?

☐ Could you make the thesis more persuasive or specific based on information that you gathered while planning, drafting, or developing your essay?

**Be Fair.** Make your judgments reasonable, not extreme. A reviewer can find fault with a film and still conclude that it is worth seeing. There's nothing wrong, of course, with a fervent judgment ("This play is the trashiest excuse for a drama I have ever suffered through"), but consider your readers and their likely reactions. Read some reviews in your local newspaper or online, or watch some movie critics on television to see how they balance their judgments. Because readers will have more confidence in your opinions if you seem fair and reasonable, revise your tone where needed. For example, one writer revised his opening after he realized that he was criticizing the audience rather than evaluating the performance.

The most recent performance by a favorite campus group—Rock

Mountain—was an ~~incredibly revolting~~ *disappointing concert* experience. ~~The~~ *Although t*he ~~outlandish~~ crowd

ignored the DJ who introduced the group, and a few ~~nameless members~~ *people*

~~of one social group spent their time~~ tossing *ed* around trash cans in front of

the stage, *, the opening number still announced the group's powerful musical presence.*

---

## Peer Response  Evaluating and Reviewing

For general questions for a peer editor, see p. 447.

Enlist the advice of a classmate or friend as you determine your criteria for evaluation and your judgment. Ask your peer editor to answer questions like these about your evaluation:

- What is your overall reaction to this essay? Does the writer persuade you to agree with his or her evaluation?
- When you finish the essay, can you tell exactly what the writer thinks of the subject? Where does the writer express this opinion?
- How do you know what criteria the writer is using for evaluation?
- Does the writer give you sufficient evidence for his or her judgment? Put stars wherever more or better evidence is needed.
- What audience does the writer seem to have in mind?
- Would you recommend any changes in the essay's organization?
- If this paper were yours, what is the one thing you would be sure to work on before handing it in?

---

### REVISION CHECKLIST

☐ Is the judgment you pass on your subject unmistakably clear?

☐ Have you given your readers evidence to support each point you make?

☐ Have you been fair? If you are championing something, have you deliberately skipped over its disadvantages or faults? If you are condemning your subject, have you omitted its admirable traits?

☐ Have you anticipated and answered readers' possible objections?

☐ If you compare two things, do you look at the same points in both?

For more on comparison and contrast, see Ch. 7.

After you have revised your evaluation, edit and proofread it. Carefully check the grammar, word choice, punctuation, and mechanics—and then correct any problems you find. Make sentences in which you describe the subject of your evaluation as precise and useful as possible. If you have used comparisons or contrasts, make sure these are clear: don't lose your readers in a fog of vague pronouns or confusing references.

For more editing and proofreading strategies, see pp. 455–58.

## EDITING CHECKLIST

☐ Is it clear what each pronoun refers to? Does each pronoun agree with (match) its antecedent?  **A6**

☐ Is it clear what each modifier in a sentence modifies? Have you created any dangling or misplaced modifiers, especially in descriptions of your subject?  **B1**

☐ Have you used parallel structure wherever needed, especially in lists or comparisons?  **B2**

For more help, find the relevant checklist sections in the Quick Editing Guide on p. Q-37. Turn also to the Quick Format Guide beginning on p. Q-1.

# Reviewing and Reflecting

**REVIEW** Working with classmates or independently, respond to the following questions:

To complete more review questions for Ch. 11, go to LaunchPad.

1. How can you establish criteria for evaluating a subject? If you have written or are writing an evaluation or a review, what criteria did you decide upon? Why did you make these particular choices?

2. Why are comparing and contrasting, as well as defining, potentially useful strategies for evaluating and reviewing? If you have used one or both of these strategies, what benefits or challenges did they bring?

3. In writing an evaluation or a review, why is it important to make judgments reasonable, not extreme?

**REFLECT** After completing one of the writing assignments presented in this chapter or supplied by your instructor, turn back to the After Writing questions on page 39 of Chapter 3 and respond to as many of them as you can.

Next, reflect in writing about how you might apply the insights that you drew from this assignment to another situation — in or outside of college — in which you have to evaluate or review something. If no specific situations come to mind, imagine that

- in a media course, you decide to write a comparative review of workplace comedies.
- in a work setting, you must evaluate two cleaning companies to decide which one will best service your company's offices.

In your reflection, consider how you would decide upon criteria for your evaluation or review.

## Additional Writing Assignments

1. Write an evaluation of a college course you have taken or are now taking. Analyze its strengths and weaknesses. Does the instructor present the material clearly, understandably, and engagingly? Are the assignments pointed and purposeful? Is the textbook helpful, readable, and easy to use? Does this course give you your money's worth?

2. Evaluate an unfamiliar magazine, an essay in this textbook, a proposal being considered at work, a source you've read for a college class, an academic Web site about an area that interests you, or a possible source for a research project. Specify your criteria for evaluation, and identify the evidence that supports your judgments.

3. Evaluate a product that you might want to purchase. Establish criteria that matter to you — and to the other prospective purchasers who might turn to you for a recommendation. Consider, for example, the product's features, construction, utility, beauty, color, cost, or other criteria that matter to purchasers. Make a clear recommendation to your audience: buy or not.

4. Visit a restaurant, museum, or tourist attraction, and evaluate it for others who might consider a visit. Present your evaluation as an essay, an article for a travel or lifestyle magazine, or a travel blog that informs about local sites and evaluates what they offer. Specify your criteria, and include plenty of detail to create the local color your audience will expect.

For more on responding to literature, see Ch. 13.

5. **Source Assignment.** Read these two poems on a similar theme, and decide which seems to you the better poem. In a brief essay, set forth your evaluation. Some criteria to apply might be the poet's choice of concrete, specific words that appeal to the senses and his awareness of his audience. Quote, paraphrase, summarize, and accurately credit supporting evidence from the poems.

**Putting in the Seed**
ROBERT FROST (1874–1963)

You come to fetch me from my work tonight
When supper's on the table, and we'll see
If I can leave off burying the white
Soft petals fallen from the apple tree
(Soft petals, yes, but not so barren quite,
Mingled with these, smooth bean and wrinkled pea),
And go along with you ere you lose sight
Of what you came for and become like me,
Slave to a springtime passion for the earth.
How Love burns through the Putting in the Seed
On through the watching for that early birth
When, just as the soil tarnishes with weed,
The sturdy seedling with arched body comes
Shouldering its way and shedding the earth crumbs.

**Between Our Folding Lips**
T. E. BROWN (1830–1897)

Between our folding lips
God slips
An embryon life, and goes;
And this becomes your rose.
We love, God makes: in our sweet mirth
God spies occasion for a birth.
*Then is it His, or is it ours?*
I know not — He is fond of flowers.

6. **Visual Assignment.** Select one of the following pairs of images, and examine their features carefully. Write an essay that evaluates the items portrayed in the images or the images themselves. Specify for your audience your criteria for judging. Observe carefully to identify enough visual detail to support your judgments.

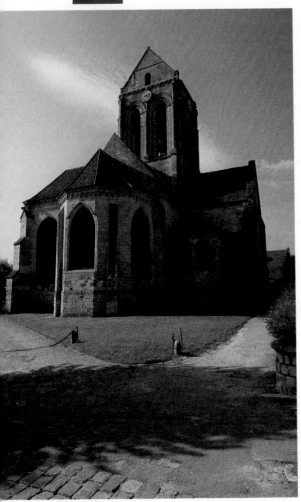

Church at Auvers-sur-Oise, France (2002). Pierre-Franck Colombier/Afp/Getty Images.

*The Church in Auvers-sur-Oise* (1890), painted by Vincent van Gogh (1853–1890). Buyenlarge/Hulton Fine Art Collection/Getty Images.

Designers and software engineers at work in a division of Sony Computer Entertainment, 1999. TWPhoto/Corbis.

People working in an open-plan office. Hannah Mentz/Corbis.

# 12 Supporting a Position with Sources

*Image credits, clockwise from top left:* Romulic-Stojcic/Lumi Images/Corbis; Steve Warmowski/Journal-Courier/The Image Works; Greg Hinsdale/Corbis/Glow Images; Josef Polleross/ASAblanca via Getty Images.

## Responding to an Image

These images show activities that might help a student gather evidence from sources to support a position in a college paper. What does each image suggest about possible sources? What do the images suggest about the process of inquiry? Which activities look most intriguing? What other activities might have appeared in images on this page?

Suppose you surveyed a random group of graduating students about the typical college writing assignment. The odds are good that this assignment might boil down to reading a few texts and writing a paper about them. Simple as this description sounds, it suggests what you probably expect from a college education: an opportunity to absorb and think seriously about provocative ideas. It also suggests the values that lie behind college expectations—a deep respect for the process of inquiry (the academic method of asking and investigating intriguing questions) and for the products of inquiry (the analyses, interpretations, and studies in each academic field).

When you first tackle such assignments, you may wonder "How do I figure out what my instructor really wants?" or "How could I possibly do that?" In response, you may turn to peripheral questions such as "How long does my paper have to be?" or "How many sources do I have to use?" Instead, try to face the central question: "How can I learn the skills I need to use a few sources to develop and support a position in a college paper?"

Unlike a debate or a Super Bowl game, a paper that takes a position generally doesn't have two sides or a single winner. Instead, the writer typically joins the ongoing exchange of ideas about an intriguing topic in the field. Each paper builds on the exchanges of the past—the articles, essays, reports, and books that convey the perspectives, research findings, and conclusions of others. Although reading such sources may seem daunting, you are not expected to know everything yourself but simply to work hard at learning what others know. Your paper, in turn, advances the exchange to convey your well-grounded point of view or to defend your well-reasoned interpretation.

## Why Supporting with Sources Matters

### In a College Course

- You support a position with sources when you write a history paper about an event, synthesizing a first-person account, contemporary newspaper story, and scholarly article.
- You support a position with sources when you write an analysis after reading a short story along with several critical essays about it.

### In the Workplace

- You support a position with sources when you write a report pulling together multiple accounts and records to support your recommendation.

### In Your Community

- You support a position with sources when you write a well-substantiated letter to the editor.

❓ When have you used sources to support a position in your writing? What source-based writing might you do at work or in your community?

# Learning from Other Writers

The selections here illustrate how two different writers draw on evidence from sources to substantiate their points. The notes in the margin of the first reading will help you begin to analyze features such as the thesis, or main idea, and the variety of methods used to introduce and integrate information from sources.

### As You Read These Essays That Support a Position with Sources

Ask yourself the following questions:

1. What thesis, or main idea, expresses the position supported by the essay? How does the writer try to help readers appreciate the importance of this position?

2. How does the writer use information from sources to support a thesis? Do you find this information relevant and persuasive?

3. How does the writer vary the way each source is introduced and the way information is drawn from it?

Damon Winter/
The New York Times/Redux.

## Charles M. Blow

### Black Dads Are Doing Best of All

Since 2008, Charles M. Blow has been a columnist for the *New York Times*, where the following piece appeared on June 8, 2015. Blow joined the *Times* in 1994 as a graphics editor and shortly afterward became the newspaper's graphics director. Later, he served as design director for news. In 2014, Blow published a memoir, *Fire Shut Up in My Bones*. This essay's source references have been adapted to illustrate MLA style.

Background information including statistics

One of the most persistent statistical bludgeons° of people who want to blame black people for any injustice or inequity they encounter is this: According to data from the Centers for Disease Control and Prevention (C.D.C.), in 2013 in nearly 72 percent of births to non-Hispanic black women, the mothers were unmarried. 1

It has always seemed to me that embedded in the "If only black men would marry the women they have babies with . . ." rhetoric was a more insidious° suggestion: that there is something fundamental, and intrinsic° about black men that is flawed, that black fathers are pathologically° prone to 2

---

**bludgeons:** Heavy clubs; tools for bullying or coercion.    **insidious:** Dangerous or deceitful.    **intrinsic:** belonging to a thing by its very nature.    **pathologically:** In a disease-like fashion.

desertion of their offspring and therefore largely responsible for black community "dysfunction."°

There is an astounding amount of mythology loaded into this stereotype, one that echoes a history of efforts to rob black masculinity of honor and fidelity.

**3** THESIS presenting position

Josh Levs points this out in his new book, *All In*, in a chapter titled "How Black Dads Are Doing Best of All (But There's Still a Crisis)." One fact that Levs quickly establishes is that most black fathers in America live with their children: "There are about 2.5 million black fathers living with their children and about 1.7 million living apart from them" (149).

**4**

Direct quotation

"So then," you may ask, "how is it that 72 percent of black children are born to single mothers? How can both be true?" Good question.

**5** Central question, referring back to introductory statistics

Here are two things to consider:

**6**

First, there are a growing number of people who live together but don't marry. Those mothers are still single, even though the child's father may be in the home. And, as the *Washington Post* reported last year:

**7**

"The share of unmarried couples who opted to have 'shotgun cohabitations'—moving in together after a pregnancy—surpassed 'shotgun marriages' for the first time during the last decade, according to a forthcoming paper from the National Center for Health Statistics, part of the Centers for Disease Control and Prevention" (Yen).

**8** One response to the central question, supported by evidence

Furthermore, a 2013 C.D.C. report found that black and Hispanic women are far more likely to experience a pregnancy during the first year of cohabitation than white and Asian women (Copen et al.).

**9**

Second, some of these men have children by more than one woman, but they can only live in one home at a time. This phenomenon° means that a father can live with some but not all of his children. Levs calls these men "serial impregnators," but I think something more than promiscuity° and irresponsibility are at play here.

**10** Paraphrase, and another response to the central question

As *Forbes* reported on Ferguson, Missouri:°

**11**

"An important but unreported indicator of Ferguson's dilemma is that half of young African American men are missing from the community. According to the U.S. Census Bureau, while there are 1,182 African American women between the ages of 25 and 34 living in Ferguson, there are only 577 African American men in this age group. In other words there are more than two young black women for each young black man in Ferguson" (Ozimek).

**12** Supporting evidence

In April, the *New York Times* extended this line of reporting, pointing out that nationally, there are 1.5 million missing black men. As the paper put it: "Incarceration and early deaths are the overwhelming drivers of the gap. Of the 1.5 million missing black men from 25 to 54—which demographers° call the prime-age years—higher imprisonment rates account for almost 600,000.

**13** Additional statistical support

**dysfunction:** A serious breakdown or malfunction.    **phenomenon:** Fact or situation.    **promiscuity:** Having sex with multiple partners.    **Ferguson, Missouri:** Scene of the August 2014 police shooting of an unarmed black teenager; the investigation of the shooting exposed, among other things, deep racial divisions in the city.    **demographers:** Researchers who produce and study population statistics.

Almost one in 12 black men in this age group are behind bars, compared with one in 60 nonblack men in the age group, one in 200 black women and one in 500 nonblack women" (Wolfers et al.). For context, there are about 8 million African American men in that age group overall.

Mass incarceration has disproportionately ensnared° young black men, sucking hundreds of thousands of marriage-age men out of the community.  14

Another thing to consider is something that the *Atlantic*'s Ta-Nehisi Coates pointed out in 2013: "The drop in the birthrate for unmarried black women is mirrored by an even steeper drop among married black women. Indeed, whereas at one point married black women were having more kids than married white women, they are now having less." This means that births to unmarried black women are disproportionately represented in the statistics.  15

Now to the mythology of the black male dereliction° as dads: While it is true that black parents are less likely to marry before a child is born, it is not true that black fathers suffer a pathology of neglect. In fact, a C.D.C. report issued in December 2013 found that black fathers were the most involved with their children daily, on a number of measures, of any other group of fathers — and in many cases, that was among fathers who didn't live with their children, as well as those who did (Jones and Mosher).  16

There is no doubt that the 72 percent statistic is real and may even be worrisome, but it represents more than choice. It exists in a social context, one at odds with the corrosive° mythology about black fathers.  17

*Additional responses to the central question, followed by evidence*

*Conclusion reinforcing the author's position*

## Works Cited

Coates, Ta-Nehisi. "Understanding Out-of-Wedlock Births in Black America." *The Atlantic*, 21 June 2013, www.theatlantic.com/sexes/archive/2013/06/understanding-out-of-wedlock-births-in-black-america/277084/.

Copen, Casey E., et al. "First Premarital Cohabitation in the United States: 2006-2010 National Survey of Family Growth." National Health Statistics Reports, no. 64, National Center for Health Statistics, 4 Apr. 2013, www.cdc.gov/nchs/data/nhsr/nhsr064.pdf.

Jones, Jo, and William D. Mosher. "Fathers' Involvement with Their Children: United States, 2006-2010." *National Health Statistics Reports*, no. 71, National Center for Health Statistics, 20 Dec. 2013, www.cdc.gov/nchs/data/nhsr/nhsr071.pdf.

Levs, Josh. *All In: How Our Work-First Culture Fails Dads, Families, and Businesses—And How We Can Fix It Together.* HarperCollins, 2015.

Ozimek, Adam. "Half of Ferguson's Young African American Men Are Missing." *Forbes*, 18 Mar. 2015, www.forbes.com/sites/modeledbehavior/2015/03/18/half-of-fergusons-young-african-american-men-are-missing/#273f5c58119b.

United States, Centers for Disease Control and Prevention. "About Natality, 2007-2014." *CDC Wonder*, 9 Feb. 2016, wonder.cdc.gov/natality-current.html.

*Each source cited in Blow's essay listed alphabetically by author, with full publication information*

*First line of entry placed at left margin, with subsequent lines indented ½ inch*

**ensnared:** Captured; entrapped.　　**dereliction:** Negligence.　　**corrosive:** Destructive.

Wolfers, Justin, et al. "1.5 Million Missing Black Men." *The New York Times*, 20 Apr. 2015, nyti.ms/1P5Gpa7.

Yen, Hope. "More Couples Who Become Parents Are Living Together But Not Marrying, Data Show." *The Washington Post*, 7 Jan. 2014, www .washingtonpost.com/politics/more-couples-who-become-parents -are-living-together-but-not-marrying-data-show/2014/01/07/2b639a86 -77d5-11e3-b1c5-739e63e9c9a7_story.html.

## Questions to Start You Thinking

### Meaning

1. According to Blow, what are the prevailing stereotypes about black fathers? What position does he take about these stereotypes?

2. What major points does Blow make to counter prevailing views about black fathers?

3. How are demographic changes that pertain to women — in particular, birthrates among married black women — contributing to the "statistical bludgeons" Blow describes in his first paragraph?

### Writing Strategies

4. What types of evidence does Blow use to support his position? How convincing is this evidence to you?

5. Blow alternates between stating some source information in his own words and quoting some directly. What are the advantages and disadvantages of these two approaches?

6. How would you describe Blow's tone, the quality of his writing that reveals his attitude toward his topic and his readers? What specific words, phrases, or sentences contribute to his tone? Does the tone seem appropriate for his purpose and audience? Why, or why not?

## Abigail Marchand                                    **Student Essay**

### The Family Dynamic

Abigail Marchand wrote this essay in response to a reading assigned in her composition class. She used MLA style to cite and list sources.

Children are resilient creatures, and often adults underestimate their vast emotional capabilities, their compassion, and their ability to find the good in everything. When babies are brought home from the hospital, they don't care if their parents are same sex or not. They only want to feel safe, to be held, and most of all to be loved. It is unfortunate that we as a human race allow our own petty ideals to interfere with these simple needs.    1

**❓** What does a "nuclear" family mean to you?

The notion that a child can thrive only in a "nuclear" family has long been dispelled. With the increase in the divorce rate and the number of children born to single mothers, many children are not raised in that traditional family. Thus, the idea of a child being raised by a same-sex couple really shouldn't seem that foreign. According to a 2011 U.S. Census Bureau report, only about 1% of couples are of the same sex (1), but over 115,000 of their households include children (3). Anna Quindlen very directly sums up this situation: "Evan has two moms. This is no big thing." 2

For a variety of reasons, many children today are growing up in a completely different environment than that of their grandparents of the 1950s and 1960s. However, as Quindlen says, "the linchpin of family has commonly been a loving commitment between two adults." Even though a family might have two mothers or two fathers or even one single parent, what should matter is not the quantity of love a child receives but the quality of that love. 3

A child's development will neither be hurt nor helped by a same-sex family. Frankly, the makeup of the family and specifically the absence of an opposite-sex partner have little impact on the day-to-day lives of most children. As two sociologists who reviewed past research studies on parenting concluded, "The gender of parents correlates in novel ways with parent-child relationships but has minor significance for children's psychological adjustment and social success" (Biblarz and Stacey 3). Many same-sex households involve members of the opposite sex in some capacity, whether as friend, aunt, uncle, or cousin. In addition, as children from same-sex families attend schools, they encounter any number of people, both male and female. The argument that the child would interact only with one gender is ludicrous. 4

**❓** How do you view parenting responsibilities—as your parents' child or as your children's parent?

The advantages of a same-sex household would be similar to those of a standard father-and-mother household: Two people are there to help raise the children. Compared to a single mother raising a child alone, the same-sex household would benefit from having another person to shoulder some of the responsibilities. As a parent of four sons, I know the benefits of having a second person to help with transportation to various events, dinner preparation, or homework. Navigating the treacherous landscape of child rearing is far easier with an ally. 5

On a developmental level, a same-sex household would not affect the child's ability to grow and become a productive member of society. Certainly most children can adapt to any situation, and in the case of same-sex relationships, a child usually is brought into the home as a baby, so that environment is all he or she would know. The absence of an opposite-sex parent would never come into question since most children don't concern themselves with the gender of their family members. Instead, they view their caregivers as any other child would—as mommy or daddy. 6

The only disadvantage to same-sex households rests with the concerned    7
citizens bent on "explaining" to the children how their parental unit is somehow doing something wrong. These naysayers pose the greatest risk to the
children because they cannot look beyond the surface of the same-sex partners
to see that most of these households function better than many "normal"
ones. In a recent collection of interviews, seventeen-year-old Chris echoes this
sentiment: "The hardest part about having a gay dad is that no matter how
okay you are with it, there's always going to be someone who will dislike you
because of it" (Snow 3). Garner's interviews with grown-up children of gay
parents also raise the same theme, "the personal impact of a public issue" (15).

In fact, most people are unlikely to recognize a child being raised in a    8
same-sex household unless they specifically know the child's parents. My son
attends daycare with two brothers who have two mothers. I never would have
known this if I hadn't personally met both mothers. Their children are well-
adjusted little boys who are fortunate to have two caring women in their lives.

The real focus should be on whether all of the child's needs are met. It    9    **?** What do you
shouldn't matter if those needs are met by a mother and father, two moth-    think that children
ers, or two fathers. Children should feel loved and cared for above all else.    need from parents
Unfortunately, in the case of same-sex households, external pressures can po-    and from society?
tentially shatter a child's well-being when "well-meaning" people attempt to
interfere with something they know nothing about. It is amazing that people
are more focused on the bedroom activities, activities that never enter a child's
consciousness anyway, than on the run-of-the-mill activities that most same-
sex couples encounter in the rearing of a child. The only real disadvantage to
these households lies solely with the closed minds of intolerance.

## Works Cited

Biblarz, Timothy J., and Judith Stacey. "How Does the Gender of Parents
    Matter?" *Journal of Marriage and Family*, vol. 72, no. 1, Feb. 2010, pp. 3–22.

Garner, Abigail. *Families Like Mine: Children of Gay Parents Tell It Like It Is.*
    Harper Perennial, 2005.

Lofquist, Daphne. "Same-Sex Couple Households." *American Community
    Survey Briefs*, no. 10-03, US Census Bureau, 2011, www.census.gov
    /prod/2011pubs/acsbr10-03.pdf.

Quindlen, Anna. "Evan's Two Moms." *The New York Times*, 5 Feb. 1992,
    www.nytimes.com/1992/02/05/opinion/public-private-evan-s-two-moms.html.

Snow, Judith E. *How It Feels to Have a Gay or Lesbian Parent: A Book by Kids
    for Kids of All Ages.* Routledge, 2004.

For more on MLA cita-
tion style, see E1–E2
in the Quick Research
Guide, pp. Q-20–Q-36.

## Questions to Start You Thinking

### Meaning

1. What position does Marchand support in this essay?
2. What reasons for her view does Marchand supply?
3. How does Marchand see children? What does she expect of families?

### Writing Strategies

4. What types of evidence does Marchand use to support her position? How convincing is this evidence to you?
5. Has Marchand considered alternative views? How does the inclusion (or lack) of these views contribute to or detract from the essay?
6. Marchand uses specific examples in several places. Which of these seem most effective to you? Why?
7. Using highlighters or marginal notes, identify the essay's introduction, thesis, major points, supporting evidence for each point, and conclusion. How effective is the organization of this essay?

# Learning by Writing

## The Assignment: Supporting a Position with Sources

See the contents of *A Writer's Reader* on p. 480.

Identify a cluster of readings about a topic that interests you. For example, choose related readings from this book or from other readings assigned in your class. If your topic is assigned and you don't begin with much interest in it, develop your intellectual curiosity. Look for an angle, an implication, or a vantage point that will engage you. Relate the topic in some way to your experience. Read (or reread) the selections, considering how each supports, challenges, or deepens your understanding of the topic.

Based on the information in your cluster of readings, develop an enlightening position about the topic that you'd like to share with an audience of college readers. Support this position—your working thesis—using quotations, paraphrases, summaries, and syntheses of the information in the readings as evidence. Present your information from sources clearly, and credit your sources appropriately.

Three students investigated topics of great variety:

One student examined local language usage that combined words from English and Spanish, drawing on essays about language diversity to analyze the patterns and implications of such usage.

Another writer used a cluster of readings about technology to evaluate the privacy issues on a popular social media site.

A third, using personal experience with a blended family and several essays on families, challenged misconceptions about today's families.

## Facing the Challenge  Finding Your Voice

The major challenge that writers face when using sources to support a position is finding their own voice. You create your voice as a college writer through your choice of language and angle of vision. You probably want to present yourself as a thoughtful writer with credible insights, someone a reader will want to hear from.

For more on evidence, see pp. 157–64.

Finding your own voice may be difficult in a source-based paper. By the time you have supported your position by quoting, paraphrasing, or summarizing relevant readings, you may worry that your sources have taken over your paper. You may feel there's no room left for your own voice and, even if there were, it's too quiet to jostle past the powerful words of your sources. That, however, is your challenge.

As you develop your voice as a college writer and use it to guide your readers' understanding, you'll restrict sources to their proper role as supporting evidence. Don't let them get pushy or dominate your writing. Use these questions to help you strengthen your voice:

- Can you write a list or passage explaining what you'd like readers to hear from your voice? Where could you add more of this in your draft?

- Have you used your own voice, not quotations or paraphrases from sources, to introduce your topic, state your thesis, and draw conclusions?

- Have you generally relied on your own voice to open and conclude paragraphs and to reinforce your main ideas in every passage?

- Have you alternated between your voice and the voices of sources? Can you strengthen your voice if it gets trampled by a herd of sources?

- Have you used your voice to identify and introduce source material before you present it? Have you used your voice to explain or interpret source material after you include it?

- Have you used your voice to tell readers why your sources are relevant, how they support your points, and what their limits might be?

- Have you carefully created your voice as a college writer, balancing passion and personality with rock-solid reasoning?

Whenever you are uncertain about the answers to these questions, make an electronic copy of your file or print it out. Highlight all of the wording in your own voice in a bright, visible color. Check for the presence and prominence of this highlighting, and then revise the white patches (the material drawn from sources) as needed to strengthen your voice.

## Generating Ideas

**Pin Down Your Working Topic and Your Cluster of Readings.** Specify what you're going to work on. This task is relatively easy if your instructor has assigned the topic and the required set of readings. If not, figure out what limits your instructor has set and which decisions are yours.

For more strategies for generating ideas, see Ch. 19.

- Carefully follow any directions about the number or types of sources that you are expected to use.
- Instead of hunting only for sources that share your initial views about the topic, look for a variety of reliable and relevant sources so that you can broaden, even challenge, your perspective.

For advice about finding and evaluating academic sources, turn to sections B and C in the Quick Research Guide, pp. Q-24–Q-27.

**Consider Your Audience.** You are writing for an academic community that is intrigued by your topic (unless your instructor specifies another group). Your instructor's broad goal probably includes making sure that you are prepared to succeed when you write future assignments, including full research papers. For this reason, you'll be expected to quote, paraphrase, and summarize information from sources. You'll also need to introduce — or launch — such material and credit its source, thus demonstrating that you have mastered the essential skills for source-based writing.

In addition, your instructor will want to see your own position emerge from the swamp of information that you are reading. You may feel that your ideas are like a prehistoric creature, dripping as it struggles out of the bog. If so, encourage your creature to wade toward dry land. Jot down your own ideas whenever they pop into mind. Highlight them in color on the page or on the screen. Store them in your writing notebook or a special file so that you can find them, watch them accumulate, and give them well-deserved prominence in your paper.

ONE STUDENT THINKING THROUGH A TOPIC

*General subject:* Gender

*Assigned topic:* State and support a position about differences in the behavior of men and women.

**Take an Academic Approach.** Your experience and imagination are one deep well from which you can draw ideas whenever you need them. For an academic paper, this deep well may help you identify an intriguing topic, raise a compelling question about it, or pursue an unusual slant. For example, you might recall talking with your cousin about her expensive prescriptions and decide to investigate the controversy about importing low-cost medications from other countries.

For more on reading critically, see Ch. 2.

You'll also be expected to investigate your topic using authoritative sources. These sources — articles, essays, reports, books, Web pages, and other reliable materials — are your second deep well. When one well runs dry for the moment, start pumping the other. As you read critically to tap this second resource, you join the academic exchange. This exchange is the flow of knowledge from one credible source to the next as writers and researchers raise questions, seek answers, evaluate information, and advance knowledge. As you inquire, you'll move from what you already know to deeper knowledge. Welcome sources that shed light on your inquiry from varied perspectives rather than simply agree with a view you already hold.

To see how the academic exchange works, turn to pp. 230–31.

*What do I know about?*          *What do I care about?*

RECALL PERSONAL EXPERIENCES:  Friends at school? Competition for jobs? Pressure on parents to be good role models?

CONSIDER READINGS:  May? Jensen? Zeilinger? Staples? Brady?

⬇

- *Stereotypes of women — emotional and caring*
- *Stereotypes of men — tough and aggressive*
- *What about me? I'm a woman in training to be a police officer — and I'm a mother. I'm emotional, caring, aggressive, and tough.*

*I bet that men and women are more alike than different. What do the readings say? What evidence do they present?*

- RETURN TO THE READINGS.
- TEST AND REFINE YOUR WORKING THESIS.
- LOOK FOR EVIDENCE.

## Learning by Doing 🎥 Identifying Suspect Web Information

Examine one of the following Web sites:

- zapatopi.net/treeoctopus/
- dhmo.org/facts.html

Begin with a short summary of the site's content. Are you persuaded by the arguments presented? Why, or why not? What types of support did you find convincing or weak? Why? Next, look up the tree octopus or dihydrogen monoxide on the hoax-alert Web site snopes.com. What does the Snopes information suggest about the content of the "zapatopi" and "dmho" sites? What do your findings tell you about how to identify and avoid unreliable Web content?

**Skim Your Sources.**  When you work with a cluster of readings, you'll probably need to read them repeatedly. Start out, however, by skimming—quickly reading only enough to find out what direction a selection takes.

- Leaf through the reading; glance at any headings or figure labels.
- Return to the first paragraph; read it in full. Then read only the first sentence of each paragraph. At the end, read the final paragraph in full.
- Stop to consider what you've already learned.

Do the same with your other selections, classifying or comparing them as you begin to think about what they might contribute to your paper.

---

**DISCOVERY CHECKLIST**

☐ What topic is assigned or under consideration? What ideas about it emerge as you brainstorm, freewrite, or use another strategy to generate ideas?

☐ What cluster of readings will you begin with? What do you already know about them? What have you learned about them simply by skimming?

☐ What purpose would you like to achieve in your paper? Who is your primary audience? What will your instructor expect you to accomplish?

☐ What clues about how to proceed can you draw from the two sample essays in this chapter or from other readings identified as useful models?

---

## Planning, Drafting, and Developing

For more on stating a thesis, see pp. 384–93.

**Start with a Working Thesis.** Sometimes you start reading for a source-based paper with a clear position in mind; other times, you begin simply with your initial response to your sources. Either way, try to state your main idea as a working thesis even if you expect to rewrite it — or replace it — later on. Once your thesis takes shape in words, you can assess the richness and relevance of your reading based on a clear main idea.

| FIRST RESPONSE TO SOURCES | Joe Robinson, author of "Four Weeks Vacation," and others say that workers need more vacation time, but I can't see my boss agreeing to this. |
| --- | --- |
| WORKING THESIS | Although most workers would like longer vacations, many employers do not believe that they would benefit, too. |

Sometimes a thesis statement for a position paper will push back against common perceptions or stereotypes. This is the approach that Abigail Marchand and Charles M. Blow used for their thesis statements.

| MARCHAND'S THESIS | It is unfortunate that we as a human race allow our own petty ideals to interfere with these simple needs. |
| --- | --- |
| BLOW'S THESIS | There is an astounding amount of mythology loaded into this stereotype, one that echoes a history of efforts to rob black masculinity of honor and fidelity. |

## Learning by Doing 🖉 Questioning Your Thesis to Aid Your Search for Evidence

Critically evaluating a working thesis can be good first step in planning your search for supporting evidence — or for additional evidence if this thesis is based on some initial reading. A student writer asked the following questions about the working thesis statement on longer vacations. Try asking similar questions about your own working thesis to develop an evidence-gathering strategy. Keep these questions, your answers to them, and your notes about evidence gathering handy as you search for sources.

| Questions | Answers | Implications for Evidence Search |
|---|---|---|
| What parties are involved in the subject or controversy? | Workers and employers | The writer should search for evidence that reflects the concerns of both of these parties. |
| What views might these parties hold on the subject or controversy? | Workers will probably be in favor of longer vacations. Employers will probably be concerned about the costs of increasing vacation days, though it's possible that such a policy could increase workers' morale and productivity. | The writer should look for evidence that tests these assumptions, not just supports them. |
| What other parties or factors do I need to consider? | The larger impact of longer vacations. Would they be good for the economy? Bad? Neutral? | The writer should investigate sources that can answer such questions. |

Bear in mind that often material that questions your initial view of a topic proves more valuable than evidence that supports it, prompting you to rethink your thesis, refine it, or counter more effectively whatever challenges it.

**Read Each Source Thoughtfully.** Before you begin copying quotations, scribbling notes, or highlighting a source, simply read, slowly and carefully. After you have figured out what the source says, you are ready to decide how you might use its information to support your ideas. Read again, this time sifting and selecting what's relevant to your thesis.

- How does the source use its own sources to support its position?
- Does it review major sources chronologically (by date), thematically (by topic), or by some other method?

- Does it use sources to supply background for its own position? Does it compare its position or research findings with those of other studies?
- What audience does the source address? What was its author's purpose?
- How might you want to use the source?

**Join the Academic Exchange.** A well-researched article that follows academic conventions will identify its sources for several reasons. It gives honest credit to the work on which it relies—work done by other researchers and writers. They deserve credit because their information contributes to the article's credibility and substantiates its points. The article also informs you about its sources so you, or any other reader, could find them yourself.

The visual on pages 230–31 illustrates how this exchange of ideas and information works and how you join this exchange from the moment you begin to use sources in your college writing. The middle of the visual shows the opening of a sample article about the health dangers of one type of sugar: fructose. Because this article appears online, it credits its sources by providing a link to each one. A comparable printed article might identify its sources by supplying brief in-text citations (in parentheses in MLA or APA style), footnotes, numbers keyed to its references, or source identifications in the text itself. To the left of and below the source article are two of its sources. The column to the right of the source article illustrates ways that you might capture information from the source.

For more on plagiarism, see D1 in the Quick Research Guide, p. Q-28.

**Capture Information and Record Source Details.** Consider how you might eventually want to capture each significant passage or point from a source in your paper—by quoting the exact words of the source, by paraphrasing its ideas in your own words, or by summarizing its essential point. Keeping accurate notes and records as you work with your sources will help you avoid accidental plagiarism (using someone else's words or ideas without giving the credit due). Accurate notes also help to reduce errors or missing information when you add the source material to your draft.

For more on citing and listing sources, see E1 and E2 in the Quick Research Guide, pp. Q-31–Q-36.

As you capture information, plan ahead so that you can acknowledge each source following academic conventions. Record the details necessary to identify the source in your discussion and to list it with other sources at the end of your paper.

## Learning by Doing 🎯 Reflecting on Plagiarism

You have worked hard on a group presentation that will be a major part of your grade — and each member of the group will get the same grade. Two days before the project is due, you discover that one group member has plagiarized heavily from sources well known to your instructor. First, research your institution's policy on plagiarism. Now check your syllabus. Is there a stated policy on plagiarism for the course? If so, are there differences between the policy of your institution and the policy of your class? Explain the consequences for each. Do you think there are circumstances that would make plagiarism acceptable under either or both policies? If so, describe them. Why do you think students plagiarize? Do you think it has to do with writing ability, or with something else? What about purchasing an essay? Is that a form of plagiarism? Have you ever plagiarized (accidentally or intentionally)? What were the circumstances? What would you do differently today?

The next sections illustrate how to capture and credit your sources, using examples for a paper that connects land use and threats to wildlife. Compare the examples with the original passage from the source.

**Identify Significant Quotations.** When an author expresses an idea so memorably that you want to reproduce those words exactly, quote them word for word. Direct quotations can add life, color, and authority; too many can drown your voice and overshadow your point.

ORIGINAL
The tortoise is a creature that has survived virtually unchanged since it first appeared in the geologic record more than 150 million years ago. The species became threatened, however, when ranchers began driving their herds onto Mojave Desert lands for spring grazing, at the very time that the tortoise awakens from hibernation and emerges from its burrows to graze on the greening desert shrubs and grasses. As livestock trampled the burrows and monopolized the scarce desert vegetation, tortoise populations plummeted. (page 152)

Babbitt, Bruce. *Cities in the Wilderness: A New Vision of Land Use in America.* Island Press-Shearwater, 2005.

TOO MUCH QUOTATION
When "tortoise populations plummeted," a species "that has survived virtually unchanged since it first appeared in the geologic record more than 150 million years ago" (Babbitt 152) had losses that helped to justify setting workable boundaries for the future expansion of Las Vegas.

MEMORABLE QUOTATION
When "tortoise populations plummeted" (Babbitt 152), an unlikely species that has endured for millions of years helped to establish workable boundaries for the future expansion of Las Vegas.

The Mojave Desert. iStockphoto.com/KateLeigh/Getty Images.

**ACADEMIC EXCHANGE** Suppose that you used the article "This Kind of Sugar Triggers Unhealthy Cravings" (excerpted on the right), to support a position. In turn, your source drew on other writings, two of which are excerpted to the left of and below the article. The various ways you might use this source are shown on the right-hand page.

**Direct Source Cited by Your Source:**
*Proceedings of the National Academy of Sciences,* www.pnas.org

> Current Issue > vol. 112 no. 20 > Shan Luo, 6509–6514, doi: 10.1073/pnas.1503358112

**CrossMark**
click for updates

## Differential effects of fructose versus glucose on brain and appetitive responses to food cues and decisions for food rewards

Shan Luo[a,b,c], John R. Monterosso[b,d], Kayan Sarpelleh[a,c], and Kathleen A. Page[a,c,d,1]

Author Affiliations

Edited by Todd F. Heatherton, Dartmouth College, Hanover, NH, and accepted by the Editorial Board April 8, 2015 (received for review February 18, 2015)

| Abstract | Full Text | Authors & Info | Figures | SI | Metrics | Related Content | PDF | PDF + SI |

**Significance**

Fructose compared with glucose may be a weaker suppressor of appetite. Here we sought to determine the effects of fructose versus glucose on brain, hormone, and appetitive responses to food cues and food-approach behavior. We show that the ingestion of fructose compared with glucose resulted in smaller increases in plasma insulin levels and greater brain responses to food cues in the visual cortex and left orbital frontal cortex. Ingestion of fructose versus glucose also led to greater hunger and desire for food and a greater willingness to give up long-term monetary rewards to obtain immediate high-calorie foods. These findings suggest that ingestion of fructose relative to glucose activates brain regions involved in attention and reward processing and may promote feeding behavior.

*Source:* Proceedings of the National Academy of Sciences of the United States, 2015: pnas.org/content/112/20/6509.abstract

**Your Source:**
*Time,* www.time.com

## This Kind of Sugar Triggers Unhealthy Cravings

By Alexandra Sifferlin

May 4, 2015

The findings are still preliminary and the study sample was small, but this isn't the first time that fructose has been linked to possibly unhealthy effects.

So does that mean you should give up eating fruit? No, says study author Dr. Kathleen A. Page, an assistant professor of clinical medicine at the Keck School of Medicine of the University of Southern California told the New York Times. "It has a relatively low amount of sugar compared with processed foods and soft drinks," she said.

---

**Indirect Source Cited by Your Source:** *The New York Times,* www.nytimes.com

## Fructose May Increase Cravings for High-Calorie Foods

By Nicholas Bakalar

May 4, 2015

"No," Dr. Page said. "Don't stop eating fruit. It has a relatively low amount of sugar compared with processed foods and soft drinks — maybe 5 grams in an orange, compared with 25 grams in a 12-ounce can of soda. And it is packed with fiber, which helps slow down the absorption of food, which makes you feel full."

# Information Captured from Your Source

## Sample Working Thesis

A clear thesis statement establishes a framework for selecting source material as useful evidence and for explaining its relevance to readers.

> WORKING THESIS    Given growing evidence of the health dangers of high-fructose food and beverages, it is time to think about taxing these items to help discourage their use.

## Quotation from a Source

A quotation captures the author's exact words directly from the source.

> As Alexandra Sifferlin notes, "this isn't the first time that fructose has been linked to possibly unhealthy effects."

## Quotation from an Indirect Source

A quotation from an indirect source captures the exact words of an author quoted within the source.

> So does that mean you should give up eating fruit? No, says study author Dr. Kathleen A. Page, an assistant professor of clinical medicine at the Keck School of Medicine of the University of Southern California told the *New York Times*. "It has a relatively low amount of sugar compared with processed foods and soft drinks," she said.

If possible, go to the original source to be sure that the quotation is accurate and that you're using it appropriately. (See the bottom of the left-hand page.)

> "Don't stop eating fruit. It has a relatively low amount of sugar compared with processed foods and soft drinks — maybe 5 grams in an orange, compared with 25 grams in a 12-ounce can of soda" (Bakalar).

## Paraphrase of a Source

A paraphrase captures an author's specific ideas fully and accurately, restating them in your own words and sentences.

> Even though they contain fructose, fruits do not pose a health danger because the levels of fructose they contain are so low relative to those in processed foods like soda.

## Summary of a Source

A summary reduces an author's main point to essentials, using your own words and sentences.

> Recent research suggests that fructose consumption may increase cravings for unhealthy food and beverages, and prior studies have suggested the same (Sifferlin). In light of these new findings, we should consider taxing soft drinks and other high-fructose products to promote public health.

## MLA Works Cited Entry

AUTHOR NAME          ARTICLE TITLE                          PUBLICATION    PUBLICATION DATE

Sifferlin, Alexandra. "This Kind of Sugar Triggers Unhealthy Cravings." *Time*, 4 May 2015, time.com/3845210/fructose-sugar-cravings/.

ARTICLE URL

Writers often begin by highlighting or copying too many quotations as they struggle to master the ideas in the source. The better you understand the reading and your own thesis, the more effectively you'll choose quotations. After all, a quotation in itself is not necessarily effective evidence; too many quotations suggest that your writing is padded or lacks originality.

For more on quotations, see D3 in the Quick Research Guide, pp. Q-28–Q-29.

HOW TO QUOTE

- Select a quotation that is both notable and pertinent to your thesis.
- Record it accurately, writing out exactly what it says. Include its punctuation and capitalization. Avoid abbreviations that might later be ambiguous.
- Mark both its beginning and ending with quotation marks.
- Note the page or other location where the quotation appears. If the quotation begins on one page but ends on another, mark where the switch occurs so that the credit in your draft will be accurate no matter how much of the quotation you eventually use.
- Double-check the accuracy of each quotation as you record it.

For more on punctuating quotations and using ellipsis marks, see D3 in the Quick Editing Guide, pp. Q-61–Q-62.

Use an ellipsis mark — three spaced dots ( . . . ) within a sentence or four dots ( . . . . ), a period and three spaced dots, concluding a sentence — to show where you leave out any original wording. You may omit wording that doesn't relate to your point, but don't distort the original meaning. For example, if a reviewer calls a movie "a perfect example of poor directing and inept acting," don't quote this comment as "perfect . . . directing and . . . acting."

**Paraphrase Specific Information.** Paraphrasing involves restating an author's ideas in your own language. A paraphrase is generally about the same length as the original. It conveys the ideas and emphasis of the original in your words and sentences, thus bringing your own voice to the fore. A fresh and creative paraphrase expresses your style without awkwardly jumping between it and your source's style. Be sure to name the source so that your reader knows exactly where you move from one to the other.

Here, again, is the original passage by Bruce Babbitt, followed by a sloppy paraphrase. The paraphrase suffers from a common fault, slipping in too many words from the original. (The borrowed words are underlined in the paraphrase.) Those words need to be expressed in the writer's own language or identified as direct quotations with quotation marks.

ORIGINAL    The tortoise is a creature that has survived virtually unchanged since it first appeared in the geologic record more than 150 million years ago. The species became threatened, however, when ranchers began driving their herds onto Mojave Desert lands for spring grazing, at the very time that the tortoise awakens from hibernation and emerges from its burrows to graze on the greening desert shrubs and grasses. As livestock trampled the burrows and monopolized the scarce desert vegetation, tortoise populations plummeted. (page 152)

Babbitt, Bruce. *Cities in the Wilderness: A New Vision of Land Use in America*. Island Press-Shearwater, 2005.

SLOPPY PARAPHRASE — Babbitt says that the <u>tortoise is a creature</u> in the Mojave that is <u>virtually unchanged</u> over <u>150 million years</u>. Over the millennia, the tortoise would <u>awaken from hibernation</u> just in time <u>for spring grazing</u> on the new growth of the region's <u>shrubs and grasses</u>. In recent years <u>the species became threatened</u>. When cattle started to compete for the same food, the <u>livestock trampled</u> the tortoise <u>burrows and monopolized the desert vegetation</u> while the <u>tortoise populations plummeted</u> (152).

To avoid picking up language from the original as you paraphrase, state each sentence afresh instead of just changing a few words in the original. If possible, take a short break, and then check each sentence against the original. Highlight any identical words or sentence patterns, and rework your paraphrase again. Proper nouns or exact terms for the topic (such as *tortoise*) do not need to be rephrased.

The next example avoids parroting the original by making different word choices while reversing or varying sentence patterns.

PARAPHRASE — As Babbitt explains, a tenacious survivor in the Mojave is the 150-million-year-old desert tortoise. Over the millennia, the hibernating tortoise would rouse itself each spring just in time to enjoy the new growth of the limited regional plants. In recent years, as cattle became rivals for this desert territory, the larger animals destroyed tortoise homes, ate tortoise food, and thus eliminated many of the tortoises themselves (152).

A common option is to blend paraphrase with brief quotation, carefully using quotation marks to identify any exact words drawn from the source.

BLENDED — Babbitt describes a tenacious survivor in the Mojave, the 150-million-year-old desert tortoise. Over the millennia, the hibernating tortoise would rouse itself each spring just in time to munch on the new growth of the sparse regional plants. As cattle became rivals for the desert food supply and destroyed the tortoise homes, the "tortoise populations plummeted" (152).

Even in a brief paraphrase, be careful to avoid slipping in the author's words or closely shadowing the original sentence structure. If a source says, "the president called an emergency meeting of his cabinet to discuss the crisis," and you write, "The president called his cabinet to hold an emergency meeting to discuss the crisis," your words are too close to those of the source. One option is to quote the original, though it doesn't seem worth quoting word for word. Or, better, you could write, "Summoning his cabinet to an immediate session, the president laid out the challenge before them."

For more on paraphrases, see D4 in the Quick Research Guide, p. Q-29.

HOW TO PARAPHRASE

- Select a passage with detailed information relevant to your thesis.
- Reword the passage: represent it accurately but use your own language.
- Change both its words and its sentence patterns. Replace its words with different expressions. Begin and end sentences differently, simplify long sentences, and reorder information.
- Note the page or other location where the original appears in your source. If the passage runs from one page onto the next, record where the page changes so that your credit will be accurate no matter how much of the paraphrase you use.
- After a break, recheck your paraphrase against the original to be certain that it does not repeat the same words or merely replace a few with synonyms. Revise as needed, placing fresh words in fresh arrangements.

For advice on writing a synopsis of a literary work, see pp. 273–75.

**Summarize an Overall Point.** Summarizing is a useful way of incorporating the general point of a whole paragraph, section, or work. You briefly state the main sense of the original in your own words and also identify the source. Like a paraphrase, a summary uses your own language. However, a summary is shorter than the original; it expresses only the most important ideas — the essence — of the original. This example summarizes the section of Babbitt's book containing the passage quoted on pages 229 and 232–33.

SUMMARY    According to Bruce Babbitt, former Secretary of the Interior and governor of Arizona, the isolated federal land in the West traditionally has been open to cattle and sheep ranching. These animals have damaged the arid land by grazing too aggressively, and the ranchers have battled wildlife grazers and predators alike to reduce competition with their stock. Protecting species such as the gray wolf and the desert tortoise has meant limiting grazing, an action supported by the public in order to conserve the character and beauty of the public land.

For more on summaries, see D5 in the Quick Research Guide, pp. Q-28–Q-29.

HOW TO SUMMARIZE

- Select a passage, an article, a chapter, or an entire book whose main idea bears on your thesis.
- Read the selection carefully until you have mastered its overall point.
- Write a sentence or a series of sentences that states its essence in your own words.

# Methods of Capturing Information from Sources

|  | Quotation | Paraphrase | Summary |
|---|---|---|---|
| **Format for Wording** | Use exact words from the source, and identify any additions, deletions, or other changes | Use your words and sentence structures, translating the content of the original passage | Use your words and sentence structures, reducing the original passage to its core |
| **Common Use** | Capture lively and authoritative wording | Capture specific information while conserving its detail | Capture the overall essence of an entire source or a passage in brief form |
| **Advantages** | Catch a reader's attention<br><br>Emphasize the authority of the source | Treat specifics fully without shifting from your voice to the source's | Make a broad but clear point without shifting from your voice to the source's |
| **Common Problems** | Quoting too much<br><br>Quoting inaccurately | Slipping in the original wording<br><br>Following the original sentence patterns too closely | Losing impact by bogging down in too much detail<br><br>Drifting into vague generalities |
| **Markers** | Identify source in launch statement or text citation and in final list of sources<br><br>Add quotation marks to show the source's exact words<br><br>Use ellipses and brackets to mark any changes | Identify source in launch statement or text citation and in final list of sources | Identify source in launch statement or text citation and in final list of sources |

- Revise your summary until it is as concise, clear, and accurate as possible. Replace any vague generalizations with precise words.
- Name your source as you begin your summary, or identify it in parentheses.

**Credit Your Sources Fairly.** As you quote, paraphrase, or summarize, be certain to note which source you are using and exactly where the material appears in the original. Carefully citing and listing your sources will give credit where it's due as it enhances your credibility as a careful writer.

For more on plagiarism, see D1 in the Quick Research Guide, p. Q-28.

Although academic fields prefer specific formats for their papers, MLA style is widely used in composition, English, and other humanities courses. In MLA style, you credit your source twice. First, identify the author's last name (and the page number in the original) in the text as you quote, paraphrase, summarize, or refer to the source. Often you will simply mention the author's name (or a short version of the title if the author is not identified) as you introduce the information from the source. If not, note the name and

For sample source citations and lists, see the readings on pp. 216–21 and the MLA and APA examples in E in the Quick Research Guide, pp. Q-31–Q-36, and in A in the Quick Format Guide, pp. Q-1–Q-7.

page number of the original in parentheses after you present the material: (Walton 88). Next, fully identify the source in an alphabetical list at the end of your paper.

Right now, the methods for capturing information and crediting sources may seem complicated. However, the more you use them, the easier they become. Experienced writers also know some time-tested secrets. For example, how can you save time, improve accuracy, and avoid last-minute stress about sources? The answer is easy. Include in your draft, even your very first one, both the source identification and the location. Add them at the very moment when you first add the material, even if you are just dropping it in so you don't forget it. Later on, you won't have to hunt for the details.

**Let Your Draft Evolve.** No matter how many quotations, paraphrases, and summaries you assemble, chunks of evidence captured from sources do not — on their own — constitute a solid paper. You need to interpret and explain that evidence for your readers, helping them to see exactly why, how, and to what extent it supports your position.

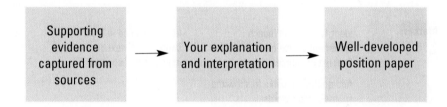

To develop a solid draft, many writers rely on one of two methods, beginning either with the evidence or with the position they wish to support.

**Method 1.** Start with your evidence. Use one of these strategies to arrange quotations, paraphrases, and summaries in a logical, compelling order.

- Cut and paste the chunks of evidence, moving them around in a file until they fall into a logical order.
- Print each chunk on a separate page, and arrange the pages on a flat surface like a table, floor, or bed until you reach a workable sequence.
- Label each chunk with a key word, and use the key words to work out an informal outline.

Once your evidence is organized logically, add commentary to connect the chunks for your readers: introduce, conclude, and link pieces of evidence with your explanations and interpretations. (Ignore any leftovers from sources unless they cover key points that you still need to integrate.) Let your draft expand as you alternate evidence and interpretation.

**Method 2.** Start with your position or your conclusion, selecting a way to focus on how you want your paper to present it.

- You can state your case boldly and directly, explaining your thesis and supporting points in your own words.
- If you feel too uncertain to take that step, you can write out directions, telling yourself what to do in each part of the draft (in preparation for actually doing it).

Either way, use this working structure to identify where to embed the evidence from your sources. Let your draft grow as you pull in your sources and expand your comments.

---

### DEVELOPMENT CHECKLIST

☐ Have you quoted only notable passages that add support and authority?

☐ Have you checked your quotations for accuracy and marked where each begins and ends with quotation marks?

☐ Have you paraphrased accurately, reflecting both the main points and the supporting details in the original?

☐ Does each paraphrase use your own words without repeating or echoing the words or the sentence structure of the original?

☐ Have you briefly stated supporting ideas that you wish to summarize, sticking to the overall point without bogging down in details or examples?

☐ Has each summary remained respectful of the ideas and opinions of others, even if you disagree with them?

☐ Have you identified the source of every quotation, paraphrase, summary, or source reference by noting in parentheses the last name of the writer and the page number (if available) where the passage appears in the source?

☐ Have you ordered your evidence logically and effectively?

☐ Have you interpreted and explained your evidence from sources with your own comments in your own voice?

For more on quotations, paraphrases, and summaries, see D3, D4, and D5 in the Quick Research Guide, pp. Q-28–Q-30.

---

## Revising and Editing

As you read over the draft of your paper, remember what you wanted to accomplish: to develop an enlightening position about your topic and to share this position with a college audience, using sources to support your ideas.

For more on revising and editing strategies, see Ch. 23.

**Strengthen Your Thesis.** As you begin revising, you may decide that your working thesis is ambiguous, poorly worded, hard to support, or simply off the mark. Revise it so that it clearly alerts readers to your main idea.

WORKING THESIS     Although most workers would like longer vacations, many employers do not believe that they would benefit, too.

REVISED THESIS     Despite assumptions to the contrary, employers who increase vacation time for workers also are likely to increase creativity, productivity, and the bottom line.

---

## THESIS CHECKLIST

☐ Is your thesis, or main idea, clear?

☐ Have you made it as specific as possible?

☐ Is it distinguished from the points made by your sources?

☐ Does it take a strong position?

☐ Does it need to be refined or qualified in response to evidence that you've gathered or to any rethinking of your original position?

---

For more about launching sources, see D6 in the Quick Research Guide, pp. Q-30–Q-31.

**Launch Each Source.** Whenever you quote, paraphrase, summarize, or refer to a source, launch it with a suitable introduction. An effective launch sets the scene for your source material, prepares your reader to accept it, and marks the transition from your words and ideas to those of the source. As you revise, confirm that you launch all of your source material well.

In a launch statement, often you will first identify the source — by the author's last name or by a short version of the title when the author isn't named — in your introductory sentence. If not, identify the source in parentheses, typically to end the sentence. Then try to suggest why you've mentioned this source at this point, perhaps noting its contribution, its credibility, its vantage point, or its relationship to other sources. Vary your launch statements to avoid tedium and to add emphasis. Boost your credibility as a writer by establishing the credibility of your sources.

Here are some typical patterns for launch statements:

As Yung demonstrates, . . .

Although Zeffir maintains . . . , Matson suggests . . .

Many schools educated the young but also unified the community (Hill 22). . . .

In *Forward March*, Smith's study of the children of military personnel, . . .

Another common recommendation is . . . ("Safety Manual").

Making good use of her experience as a travel consultant, Lee explains . . .

When you quote or paraphrase from a specific page, include that exact location.

These examples follow MLA style. For more about using either MLA or APA style, see D6 and E in the Quick Research Guide, pp. Q-30–Q-36.

The classic definition of . . . (Bagette 18).

Benton distinguishes four typical steps in this process (248–51).

## Learning by Doing 🔲 Launching Your Sources

Make a duplicate file of your draft or print it. Add highlights in one color to mark all your source identifications; use another color to mark source material:

> The problem of unintended consequences is well illustrated by many environmental changes over recent decades. For instance, if using the Mojave Desert for cattle grazing seemed efficient to ranchers, it also turned out to be destructive for long-time desert residents such as tortoises (Babbitt 152).

Now examine your draft. How do the colors alternate? Do you find color globs where you simply list sources without explaining their contributions? Do you find material without source identification (typically the author's name) or without a location in the original (typically a page number)? Fill in whatever gaps you discover.

**Synthesize Several Sources.** Often you will compare, contrast, or relate two or three sources to deepen your discussion or to illustrate a range of views. When you synthesize, you pull together several sources in the same passage to build a new interpretation or reach a new conclusion. You go beyond the separate contributions of the individual sources to relate the sources to each other and to connect them to your thesis. A synthesis should be easy to follow and use your own wording.

### HOW TO SYNTHESIZE

- Summarize (see pp. 234–35) each of the sources you want to synthesize. Boil down each summary to its essence.
- Write a few sentences that state in your own words how the sources are linked. For example, are they similar, different, or related? Do they share assumptions and conclusions, or do they represent alternatives, opposites, or opponents? Do they speak to chronology, influence, logical progression, or diversity of opinion?
- Write a few more sentences stating what the source relationships mean for your thesis and the position you develop in your paper.
- Refine your synthesis statements until they are clear and illuminating for your audience. Embed them as you move from one source summary to the next and as you reach new interpretations or conclusions that go beyond the separate sources.

**Use Your Own Voice to Interpret and Connect.** By the time your draft is finished, you may feel that you have found relevant evidence in your sources but that they now dominate your draft. As you reread, you may discover passages that simply string together ideas from sources.

DRAFT

    Writers Lisa Jo Rudy and Giulia Rhodes say that video games, television, and other screen-based activities can benefit children on the autism spectrum. Simon Baron Cohen, a professor of developmental psychopathology at the University of Cambridge, says: "We can use computers to teach emotion recognition and to simplify communication by stripping out facial and vocal emotional expressions and slowing it down using e-mail instead of face-to-face real-time modes" (Rhodes). Christopher R. Engelhardt, a researcher at the University of Missouri-Columbia, says, "In-room media access was associated with about 1.5 fewer hours of sleep per night in the group with autism" (Doyle).

*Whole passage repeats "say"/ "says"*

*Jumps from one source to the next without explanations or transitions*

When your sources overshadow your thesis, your explanations, and your writing style, revise to restore balance. Try strategies such as these to regain control of your draft:

- Add your explanation and interpretation of the source information so that your ideas are clear.
- Add transitions, and state the connections that you assume are obvious.
- Arrange information in a logical sequence, not in the order in which you read it or recorded notes about it.
- Clarify definitions, justify a topic's importance, and recognize alternative views to help your audience appreciate your position.
- Reword to vary your sentence openings, and avoid repetitive wording.

Thoughtful revision can help readers grasp what you want to say, why you have included each source, and how you think that it supports your thesis.

REVISION

    As the parent of a child on the autism spectrum, I have long questioned whether I should limit my son's screen time in some way. Based on my recent research, I have concluded that it is probably beneficial to allow him to play video games, one of his favorite activities, but that I should place some restrictions on his access to them.

*Identifies author's experience to add to credibility; draws conclusions based on her research*

    Clearly, playing video games, watching television, and participating in other screen-based activities can provide certain benefits for children on the autism spectrum. For example, these activities can aid these children's learning, help them connect with peers, and give them a greater sense of control over their environment (Rudy, Rhodes). Simon Baron Cohen, a professor of developmental psychopathology at the University of Cambridge, has noted the benefits of computers to people with autism: "We can use computers to teach emotion recognition and to simplify communication by stripping out facial and vocal emotional expressions and slowing it down using e-mail instead of face-to-face real-time modes" (Rhodes).

*Adds a transition and introduces a summary*

*Introduces a quotation*

However, unrestricted screen access is not without drawbacks. Recently, for example, a group of researchers at the University of Missouri-Columbia found that boys on the autism spectrum who had bedtime access to television, computers, and video games slept less each night (Engelhardt, Mazurek, and Sohl).

According to Christopher R. Engelhardt, the researcher who led the study, "In-room media access was associated with about 1.5 fewer hours of sleep per night in the group with autism" (Doyle).

*Adds more transitions and introduces additional source material*

**List Your Sources as College Readers Expect.** When you use sources in a college paper, you'll be expected to identify them twice: briefly when you draw information from them and fully when you list them at the end of your paper, following a conventional system. The list of sources for the draft and revision in the previous section would include these entries.

Doyle, Kathryn. "Bedroom Computers, TV May Add to Autism Sleep Issues." *Reuters*, 18 Nov. 2013, www.reuters.com/article/us-bedroom-sleep-idUSBRE9AH11V20131118.

Engelhardt, Christopher R., et al. "Media Use and Sleep Among Boys with Autism Spectrum Disorder, ADHD, or Typical Development." *Pediatrics*, vol. 132, no. 6, Dec. 2013, pp. 1081-89.

Rhodes, Giulia. "Autism: How Computers Can Help." *TheGuardian.com*, 26 Feb. 2012, www.theguardian.com/lifeandstyle/2012/feb/26/computer-geeks-autism.

Rudy, Lisa Jo. "Top 10 Good Reasons for Allowing Autistic Children to Watch TV and Videos." *About.com*, 13 May 2015, autism.about.com/od/inspirationideas/tp/TVOK.htm.

## Learning by Doing 🎥 Checking Your Presentation of Sources

Use your software to improve the presentation of source materials in your draft. For example, search for all quotation marks in your paper. Make sure that each is one of a pair surrounding every quotation. Also, be sure each quotation's source and location are identified. Try color highlighting in your final list of sources to help you spot and refine details, especially common personal errors. For instance, if you forget periods after names of authors or mix up semicolons and colons, highlight those marks so you slow down and focus on them. Then correct or add marks as needed. After you check your entries, remove the highlighting.

Use the Take Action chart (p. 243) to figure out how to improve your draft. Skim the left-hand column to identify questions you might ask about integrating sources in your draft. When you answer a question with "Yes" or "Maybe," move straight across to Locate Specifics for that question. Use the activities there to pinpoint gaps, problems, or weaknesses. Then move straight across to Take Action. Use the advice that suits your problem as you revise.

## Peer Response  Supporting a Position with Sources

For general questions for a peer editor, see p. 447.

Have several classmates read your draft critically, considering how effectively you have used your sources to support a position. Ask your peer editors to answer questions such as these:

- Can you state the writer's position on the topic?

- Do you have any trouble seeing how the writer's points and the supporting evidence from sources connect? How might the writer make the connections clearer?

- How effectively does the writer capture the information from sources? Would you recommend that any of the quotations, paraphrases, or summaries be presented differently?

- Are any of the source citations unclear? Can you tell where source information came from and where quotations and paraphrases appear in a source?

- Is the writer's voice clear? Do the sources drown it out in any spots?

- If this paper were yours, what is the one thing you would be sure to work on before handing it in?

### REVISION CHECKLIST

☐ Do you speak in your own voice, interpreting and explaining your sources instead of allowing them to dominate your draft?

☐ Have you moved smoothly back and forth between your explanations and your source material?

☐ Have you credited every source in the text and in a list at the end of your paper? Have you added each detail expected in the format for listing sources?

☐ Have you been careful to quote, paraphrase, summarize, and credit sources accurately and ethically? Have you hunted up missing details, double-checked quotations, and rechecked the accuracy of anything prepared hastily?

After you have revised your paper, edit and proofread it. Carefully check the grammar, word choice, punctuation, and mechanics—and then correct any problems you find. Be certain to check the punctuation with your quotations, making sure that each quotation mark is correctly placed and that you have used other punctuation, such as commas, correctly.

# Take Action  Integrating Source Information Effectively

Ask each question listed in the left-hand column to determine whether your draft might need work on that issue. If so, follow the ASK — LOCATE SPECIFICS — TAKE ACTION sequence to revise.

| 1 ASK | 2 LOCATE SPECIFICS | 3 TAKE ACTION |
|---|---|---|
| Have I tossed in **source material** without **preparing my audience** for it? Do **I repeat the same words** in my launch statements? | ■ **Underline each launch statement** (the sentence or its part that introduces source material). Decide if it assures readers that the source is **credible, logical, and relevant** to your thesis.<br><br>■ **Highlight repeated words** (*says, states*) or **transitions** (*also, then*). | ■ **Sharpen underlined launch statements**, perhaps noting (a) author credentials significant to readers, (b) source's historical or current contributions, or (c) source's relationship to other sources.<br><br>■ **Edit the highlighted words** (and other repeated expressions) **for variety and precision.** For *says*, try *emphasizes, suggests, reviews, presents,* or *explains.* For *also*, try *in addition, furthermore,* or *similarly.* |
| **Is my own voice lost?** Have I allowed my sources to take over my draft? Have I strung together too many quotations? | ■ **Highlight** the material from **sources in one color** and **your own commentary in another**.<br><br>■ **Check the color balance in each paragraph.** If the source color dominates, consider how to restore your own voice. | ■ **Restore your voice in each paragraph** by adding a **topic sentence** in your own words that links to your thesis and a conclusion that sums up.<br><br>■ **Add transitions** (*further, in contrast, as a result*) and **explanations** where you move point to point or source to source.<br><br>■ **Reduce what you quote** to focus on striking words. Sum up, or drop the rest.<br><br>■ **Weave in your ideas until they, not your sources, dominate.** |
| **Have I identified a source only once or twice** even though I use it throughout a section? | ■ Select a passage that relies on sources. **Highlight your ideas in one color** and **those from sources in a different color.**<br><br>■ Add a **slash** to mark each **switch between two sources or between your ideas and a source.** | ■ At each slash marking a **source switch**, add a **launch statement** for the second source.<br><br>■ At each slash (or color change) marking a **switch to your ideas**, phrase your comment so that it doesn't sound like more of the source.<br><br>■ At each slash (or color change) marking a switch **from your ideas, identify the source** again.<br><br>■ When you quote and then continue with the same source, **identify it again.** |

## EDITING CHECKLIST

For more help, find the relevant checklist sections in the Quick Editing Guide on p. Q-37. Turn also to the Quick Format Guide beginning on p. Q-1.

☐ Do all the verbs agree with their subjects, especially when you switch from your words to those of a source?  **A4**

☐ Do all the pronouns agree with their antecedents, especially when you use your words with a quotation from a source?  **A6**

☐ Have you used commas correctly, especially where you integrate material from sources?  **D1**

☐ Have you punctuated all your quotations correctly?  **D3**

# Reviewing and Reflecting

To complete more review questions for Ch. 12, go to LaunchPad.

**REVIEW** Working with classmates or independently, respond to the following questions:

1. What are some strategies for making sure that your voice shines through in a source-based position paper?

2. Briefly define each of the following strategies for capturing information from sources: quoting, paraphrasing, and summarizing. If you have written or are writing a source-based paper, pay special attention to your use of quotations, paraphrases, and summaries, perhaps highlighting each in a different color. Have you used each strategy to its best advantage? If not, what revisions might you make?

3. What does it mean to "launch" a source? What do you do to prepare an effective launch statement?

**REFLECT** After completing one of the writing assignments presented in this chapter or supplied by your instructor, turn back to the After Writing questions on page 39 of Chapter 3 and respond to as many of them as you can. While addressing these questions, it might be helpful to revisit your response to the Learning by Doing activity on pages 228–29, if you completed it.

Next, reflect in writing about how you might apply the insights that you drew from this assignment to another situation—in or outside of college—in which you have to support a position with sources. If no specific situations come to mind, imagine that

■ in a political science course, you decide to write a paper that argues against harsh punishments for low-level drug offenders. You plan to incorporate evidence from news articles, political science journals, and government sources of sentencing data.

■ in a work setting, you plan to argue for a raise based on the fact that your performance has exceeded expectations set for you the previous year, on your high customer-service ratings, on positive reviews from supervisors, and on other evidence.

In your reflection, consider how you would draw on various evidence to support your position.

## Additional Writing Assignments

1. **Source Assignment.** Read several sources about the same topic. Instead of using them as evidence to support your ideas on the topic, analyze how well they function as sources. State your thesis about them, and evaluate their strengths and weaknesses, using clear criteria. (See, for example, the criteria in C3 in the Quick Research Guide, pp. Q-26–Q-27.)

2. **Source Assignment.** Locate several different accounts of a notable event in newspapers, magazines, published letters or journals, books, blogs, social media, or other sources, depending on the time when the event occurred. State and support a thesis that explains the differences among the accounts. Use the accounts as evidence to support your position.

3. **Source Assignment.** Browse in your library's new book and periodical areas (on site or online) or in specialty search engines to identify a current topic of interest to you. (Adding the current or previous year's date to a search is one way to find recent publications or acquisitions.) Gather and evaluate a cluster of resources on your topic. Write an essay using those readings to support your position about the new development.

4. **Source Assignment.** Following the directions of your instructor, use several types of sources to support your position in an essay. One option might be to select paired or related readings (from this book), and also to interview someone with the background or experience to act as another valuable source of information. A second option might be to view and evaluate a film, television program, radio show, podcast, blog, Web site, art exhibit, or performance or other event. Then supplement your review by reading several articles that review the same event, evaluate a different or related production, or discuss criteria for similar types of items or events.

For more on interviewing, see Ch. 6. For more on reviewing and evaluating, see Ch. 11.

5. **Source Assignment.** Create a concise Web site that addresses a question of interest to you. Select and read a few reliable sources about that question, and then create several screens or short pages to explain what you have learned. For example, you might want to define or explain aspects of the question, justify the conclusion you have reached, or evaluate alternative answers as well as your own. Credit all of your sources, and supply links when appropriate.

6. **Visual Assignment.** Examine the following images, and analyze one (or more) of them. Use the image to support your position in an essay, perhaps a conclusion about the image or about what it portrays. Point out relevant details to persuade your audience of your view. Cite the images correctly, using the style your instructor specifies.

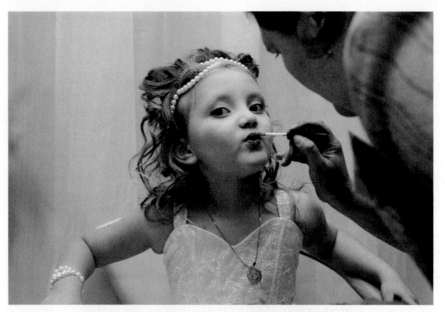

Konstantin Zavrazhin/Getty Images News/Getty Images.

Patrick Strattner/Getty Images.

Barry Lewis/In Pictures/Corbis.

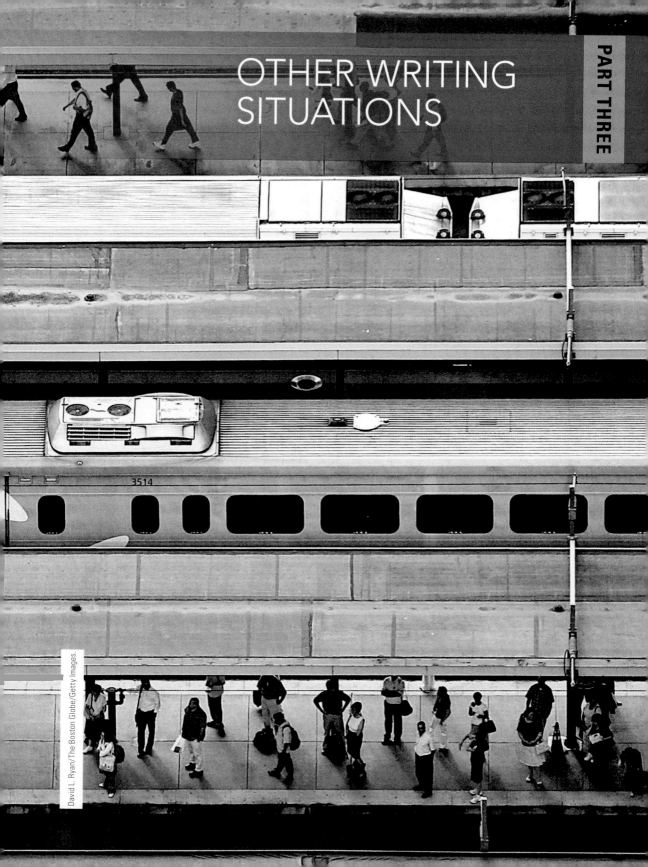

OTHER WRITING SITUATIONS

PART THREE

# 13 Responding to Literature

As countless readers know, reading fiction gives pleasure and delight. Whether you read Stephen King or Stephen Crane, you can be swept up into an imaginative world where you journey to distant lands and meet exotic people. You may also meet characters like yourself with familiar as well as new ways of viewing life. By sharing the experiences of literary characters, you gain insight into your own problems and tolerance of others.

## Why Responding to Literature Matters

### In a College Course
- You apply methods of literary analysis to spot themes, images, symbols, and figures of speech in history speeches, political essays, or business case studies.
- You respond to plays in your theater class, novels in cultural studies, essays in philosophy, or poetry in Literature 2.

### In the Workplace
- You use literary analysis as you critique the characters, plot, setting, point of view, and theme for your company's advertising campaign.

### In Your Community
- You support the library's story hour for your children, the community theater's plays, and the hospital's journal project for wounded veterans.

❓ When have you responded to a short story, novel, poem, or play? In what situations might you respond to literature in future writing?

## Using Strategies for Literary Analysis

More often than not, a writing assignment in a literature or humanities course requires you to read closely a literary work (short story, novel, play, or poem) and then to divide it into elements, explain its meaning, and support your interpretation with evidence from the work. You might also be asked to evaluate a selection or to compare and contrast several readings. Such analysis is not an end in itself; its purpose is to illuminate the meaning of the work, to help you and others understand it better.

This way of writing about literature, called *literary analysis,* requires you to analyze, interpret, and evaluate what you read. Because literary analysis has its own vocabulary—as do fields as diverse as scuba diving, gourmet cooking, and engineering—a handy glossary presents terms used to discuss the elements of fiction, poetry, and drama (see pp. 262-63). The chapter concludes with two writing activities—synopsis (summarizing the events in a narrative) and paraphrase (expressing the content of a work in your own words)—that can help you prepare to write a literary analysis or to integrate essentials about the literary work into your analysis.

For a sample literary analysis, see pp. 260–61. For a sample synopsis, see pp. 273–74; for a sample paraphrase, see p. 277.

To begin your analysis, first read closely and mark key points in the text to comprehend its meaning. Next reread the work, *at least* twice more, each time checking your interpretations and identifying possible evidence to back up your claims as you analyze and evaluate. Use this checklist to structure several close readings, each for a different reason.

---

### READING CHECKLIST

#### Reading to Comprehend

☐ What is the literal meaning? Write a few sentences explaining the overall situation—what happens to whom, where, when, why, and how.

☐ What are the facts of the situation—the events of the plot, the aspects of the setting, and the major attributes, words, and actions of the characters?

☐ What does the vocabulary mean, especially in titles or poems? Look up both unfamiliar words and words whose familiar meanings don't fit the context.

For more on literal and critical reading, see Ch. 2.

#### Reading to Analyze

☐ What are the main parts or elements of the work? Read, read aloud, mark, or make notes on theme, character, language, style, symbol, or form.

☐ What does the literary work mean? What does it imply?

☐ What does it suggest about the human condition? How does it expand your understanding? What insights can you apply to your own life?

For information and journal questions about the Part Three photograph, see About the Photographs at the end of the book.

#### Reading to Evaluate

☐ How do you assess the work's soundness and plausibility?

☐ Are the words and tone appropriate for the purpose and audience?

☐ Does the author achieve his or her purpose? Is it a worthwhile purpose?

# Learning from Other Writers

Jonathan Burns was assigned to write a literary analysis of "The Lottery," a provocative short story by Shirley Jackson. Read this story yourself to understand its meaning. Then read on to see what Burns made of it.

## Shirley Jackson

### The Lottery

AP Images.

The morning of June 27th was clear and sunny, with the fresh warmth of a full-summer day; the flowers were blossoming profusely and the grass was richly green. The people of the village began to gather in the square, between the post office and the bank, around ten o'clock; in some towns there were so many people that the lottery took two days and had to be started on June 26th, but in this village, where there were only about three hundred people, the whole lottery took less than two hours, so it could begin at ten o'clock in the morning and still be through in time to allow the villagers to get home for noon dinner. 1

The children assembled first, of course. School was recently over for the summer, and the feeling of liberty sat uneasily on most of them; they tended to gather together quietly for a while before they broke into boisterous play, and their talk was still of the classroom and the teacher, of books and reprimands. Bobby Martin had already stuffed his pockets full of stones, and the other boys soon followed his example, selecting the smoothest and roundest stones; Bobby and Harry Jones and Dickie Delacroix—the villagers pronounced his name "Dellacroy"—eventually made a great pile of stones in one corner of the square and guarded it against the raids of the other boys. The girls stood aside, talking among themselves, looking over their shoulders at the boys, and the very small children rolled in the dust or clung to the hands of their older brothers or sisters. 2

Soon the men began to gather, surveying their own children, speaking of planting and rain, tractors and taxes. They stood together, away from the pile of stones in the corner, and their jokes were quiet and they smiled rather than laughed. The women, wearing faded house dresses and sweaters, came shortly after their menfolk. They greeted one another and exchanged bits of gossip as they went to join their husbands. Soon the women, standing by their husbands, began to call to their children, and the children came reluctantly, having to be called four or five times. Bobby Martin ducked under his mother's grasping hand and ran, laughing, back to the pile of stones. His father spoke up sharply, and Bobby came quickly and took his place between his father and his oldest brother. 3

The lottery was conducted—as were the square dances, the teenage club, the Halloween program—by Mr. Summers, who had time and energy to devote to civic activities. He was a round-faced, jovial man and he ran the coal 4 business, and people were sorry for him, because he had no children and his wife was a scold. When he arrived in the square, carrying the black wooden box, there was a murmur of conversation among the villagers, and he waved and called, "Little late today, folks." The postmaster, Mr. Graves, followed him, carrying a three-legged stool, and the stool was put in the center of the square and Mr. Summers set the black box down on it. The villagers kept their distance, leaving a space between themselves and the stool, and when Mr. Summers said, "Some of you fellows want to give me a hand?" there was a hesitation before two men, Mr. Martin and his oldest son, Baxter, came forward to hold the box steady on the stool while Mr. Summers stirred up the papers inside it.

The original paraphernalia for the lottery had been lost long ago, and the 5 black box now resting on the stool had been put into use even before Old Man Warner, the oldest man in town, was born. Mr. Summers spoke frequently to the villagers about making a new box, but no one liked to upset even as much tradition as was represented by the black box. There was a story that the present box had been made with some pieces of the box that had preceded it, the one that had been constructed when the first people settled down to make a village here. Every year, after the lottery, Mr. Summers began talking again about a new box, but every year the subject was allowed to fade off without anything's being done. The black box grew shabbier each year; by now it was no longer completely black but splintered badly along one side to show the original wood color, and in some places faded or stained.

Mr. Martin and his oldest son, Baxter, held the black box securely on the 6 stool until Mr. Summers had stirred the papers thoroughly with his hand. Because so much of the ritual had been forgotten or discarded, Mr. Summers had been successful in having slips of paper substituted for the chips of wood that had been used for generations. Chips of wood, Mr. Summers had argued, had been all very well when the village was tiny, but now that the population was more than three hundred and likely to keep on growing, it was necessary to use something that would fit more easily into the black box. The night before the lottery, Mr. Summers and Mr. Graves made up the slips of paper and put them in the box, and it was then taken to the safe of Mr. Summers's coal company and locked up until Mr. Summers was ready to take it to the square the next morning. The rest of the year, the box was put away, sometimes one place, sometimes another; it had spent one year in Mr. Graves's barn and another year underfoot in the post office, and sometimes it was set on a shelf in the Martin grocery and left there.

There was a great deal of fussing to be done before Mr. Summers declared 7 the lottery open. There were the lists to make up — of heads of families, heads of households in each family, members of each household in each family. There was the proper swearing-in of Mr. Summers by the postmaster, as the official of the lottery; at one time, some people remembered, there had been a recital of some sort, performed by the official of the lottery, a perfunctory, tuneless chant that had been rattled off duly each year; some people believed that the official of the lottery used to stand just so when he said or sang it, others believed that he was supposed to walk among the people, but years and years ago this part of the ritual had been allowed to lapse. There had been, also, a ritual salute, which the official of the lottery had had to use in addressing each person who came up to draw from the box, but this also had changed with time, until now it was felt necessary only for the official to speak to each person approaching. Mr. Summers was very good at all this; in his clean white shirt and blue jeans, with one hand resting carelessly on the black box, he seemed very proper and important as he talked interminably to Mr. Graves and the Martins.

Just as Mr. Summers finally left off talking and turned to the assembled 8 villagers, Mrs. Hutchinson came hurriedly along the path to the square, her sweater thrown over her shoulders, and slid into place in the back of the crowd. "Clean forgot what day it was," she said to Mrs. Delacroix, who stood next to her, and they both laughed softly. "Thought my old man was out back stacking wood," Mrs. Hutchinson went on, "and then I looked out the window and the kids was gone, and then I remembered it was the twenty-seventh and came a-running." She dried her hands on her apron, and Mrs. Delacroix said, "You're in time, though. They're still talking away up there."

Mrs. Hutchinson craned her neck to see through the crowd and found her 9 husband and children standing near the front. She tapped Mrs. Delacroix on the arm as a farewell and began to make her way through the crowd. The people separated good-humoredly to let her through; two or three people said, in voices just loud enough to be heard across the crowd, "Here comes your Missus, Hutchinson," and "Bill, she made it after all." Mrs. Hutchinson reached her husband, and Mr. Summers, who had been waiting, said cheerfully, "Thought we were going to have to get on without you, Tessie." Mrs. Hutchinson said, grinning, "Wouldn't have me leave m'dishes in the sink, now, would you, Joe?" and soft laughter ran through the crowd as the people stirred back into position after Mrs. Hutchinson's arrival.

"Well, now," Mr. Summers said soberly, "guess we better get started, get 10 this over with, so's we can go back to work. Anybody ain't here?"

"Dunbar," several people said. "Dunbar, Dunbar." 11

Mr. Summers consulted his list. "Clyde Dunbar," he said. "That's right. 12 He's broke his leg, hasn't he? Who's drawing for him?"

"Me, I guess," a woman said, and Mr. Summers turned to look at her. 13 "Wife draws for her husband," Mr. Summers said. "Don't you have a grown boy to do it for you, Janey?" Although Mr. Summers and everyone else in the village knew the answer perfectly well, it was the business of the official of the lottery to ask such questions formally. Mr. Summers waited with an expression of polite interest while Mrs. Dunbar answered.

"Horace's not but sixteen yet," Mrs. Dunbar said regretfully. "Guess I 14 gotta fill in for the old man this year."

"Right," Mr. Summers said. He made a note on the list he was holding. 15 Then he asked, "Watson boy drawing this year?"

A tall boy in the crowd raised his hand. "Here," he said. "I'm drawing for 16 m'mother and me." He blinked his eyes nervously and ducked his head as several voices in the crowd said things like "Good fellow, Jack," and "Glad to see your mother's got a man to do it."

"Well," Mr. Summers said, "guess that's everyone. Old Man Warner 17 make it?"

"Here," a voice said, and Mr. Summers nodded. 18

A sudden hush fell on the crowd as Mr. Summers cleared his throat and 19 looked at the list. "All ready?" he called. "Now, I'll read the names — heads of families first — and the men come up and take a paper out of the box. Keep the paper folded in your hand without looking at it until everyone has had a turn. Everything clear?"

The people had done it so many times that they only half listened to the 20 directions; most of them were quiet, wetting their lips, not looking around. Then Mr. Summers raised one hand high and said, "Adams." A man disengaged himself from the crowd and came forward. "Hi, Steve," Mr. Summers said, and Mr. Adams said, "Hi, Joe." They grinned at one another humorlessly and nervously. Then Mr. Adams reached into the black box and took out a folded paper. He held it firmly by one corner as he turned and went hastily back to his place in the crowd, where he stood a little apart from his family, not looking down at his hand.

"Allen," Mr. Summers said. "Anderson. . . . Bentham." 21

"Seems like there's no time at all between lotteries anymore," Mrs. Delacroix 22 said to Mrs. Graves in the back row. "Seems like we got through with the last one only last week."

"Time sure goes fast," Mrs. Graves said. 23

"Clark. . . . Delacroix." 24

"There goes my old man," Mrs. Delacroix said. She held her breath while 25 her husband went forward.

"Dunbar," Mr. Summers said, and Mrs. Dunbar went steadily to the box 26 while one of the women said, "Go on, Janey," and another said, "There she goes."

"We're next," Mrs. Graves said. She watched while Mr. Graves came 27 around from the side of the box, greeted Mr. Summers gravely, and selected a slip of paper from the box. By now, all through the crowd there were men holding the small folded papers in their large hands, turning them over and over nervously. Mrs. Dunbar and her two sons stood together, Mrs. Dunbar holding the slip of paper.

"Harburt. . . . Hutchinson." 28

"Get up there, Bill," Mrs. Hutchinson said, and the people near her laughed. 29

"Jones." 30

"They do say," Mr. Adams said to Old Man Warner, who stood next to 31 him, "that over in the north village they're talking of giving up the lottery."

Old Man Warner snorted. "Pack of crazy fools," he said. "Listening to the 32 young folks, nothing's good enough for *them*. Next thing you know, they'll be wanting to go back to living in caves, nobody work anymore, live *that* way for a while. Used to be a saying about 'Lottery in June, corn be heavy soon.' First thing you know, we'd all be eating stewed chickweed and acorns. There's *always* been a lottery," he added petulantly. "Bad enough to see young Joe Summers up there joking with everybody."

"Some places have already quit lotteries," Mrs. Adams said.                                   33

"Nothing but trouble in *that*," Old Man Warner said stoutly. "Pack of   34
young fools."

"Martin." And Bobby Martin watched his father go forward. "Over-   35
dyke. . . . Percy."

"I wish they'd hurry," Mrs. Dunbar said to her older son. "I wish they'd   36
hurry."

"They're almost through," her son said.                                                       37

"You get ready to run tell Dad," Mrs. Dunbar said.                                            38

Mr. Summers called his own name and then stepped forward precisely   39
and selected a slip from the box. Then he called, "Warner."

"Seventy-seventh year I been in the lottery," Old Man Warner said as he   40
went through the crowd. "Seventy-seventh time."

"Watson." The tall boy came awkwardly through the crowd. Someone said,   41
"Don't be nervous, Jack," and Mr. Summers said, "Take your time, son."

"Zanini."                                                                                     42

After that, there was a long pause, a breathless pause, until Mr. Summers,   43
holding his slip of paper in the air, said, "All right, fellows." For a minute, no one moved, and then all the slips of paper were opened. Suddenly, all the women began to speak at once, saying, "Who is it?" "Who's got it?" "Is it the Dunbars?" "Is it the Watsons?" Then the voices began to say, "It's Hutchinson. It's Bill." "Bill Hutchinson's got it."

"Go tell your father," Mrs. Dunbar said to her older son.                                     44

People began to look around to see the Hutchinsons. Bill Hutchinson   45
was standing quiet, staring down at the paper in his hand. Suddenly, Tessie Hutchinson shouted to Mr. Summers, "You didn't give him time enough to take any paper he wanted. I saw you. It wasn't fair!"

"Be a good sport, Tessie," Mrs. Delacroix called, and Mrs. Graves said, "All   46
of us took the same chance."

"Shut up, Tessie," Bill Hutchinson said.                                                      47

"Well, everyone," Mr. Summers said, "that was done pretty fast, and now   48
we've got to be hurrying a little more to get done in time." He consulted his next list. "Bill," he said, "you draw for the Hutchinson family. You got any other households in the Hutchinsons?"

"There's Don and Eva," Mrs. Hutchinson yelled. "Make *them* take their   49
chance!"

"Daughters draw with their husbands' families, Tessie," Mr. Summers   50
said gently. "You know that as well as anyone else."

"It wasn't *fair*," Tessie said.                                                              51

"I guess not, Joe," Bill Hutchinson said regretfully. "My daughter draws 52
with her husband's family, that's only fair. And I've got no other family
except the kids."

"Then, as far as drawing for families is concerned, it's you," Mr. Summers 53
said in explanation, "and as far as drawing for households is concerned,
that's you, too. Right?"

"Right," Bill Hutchinson said.                                          54

"How many kids, Bill?" Mr. Summers asked formally.                      55

"Three," Bill Hutchinson said. "There's Bill, Jr., and Nancy, and little 56
Dave. And Tessie and me."

"All right, then," Mr. Summers said. "Harry, you got their tickets back?" 57

Mr. Graves nodded and held up the slips of paper. "Put them in the box, 58
then," Mr. Summers directed. "Take Bill's and put it in."

"I think we ought to start over," Mrs. Hutchinson said, as quietly as she 59
could. "I tell you it wasn't *fair.* You didn't give him time enough to choose.
*Every*body saw that."

Mr. Graves had selected the five slips and put them in the box, and he 60
dropped all the papers but those onto the ground, where the breeze caught
them and lifted them off.

"Listen, everybody," Mrs. Hutchinson was saying to the people around her. 61

"Ready, Bill?" Mr. Summers asked, and Bill Hutchinson, with one quick 62
glance around at his wife and children, nodded.

"Remember," Mr. Summers said, "take the slips and keep them folded 63
until each person has taken one. Harry, you help little Dave." Mr. Graves
took the hand of the little boy, who came willingly with him up to the box.
"Take a paper out of the box, Davy," Mr. Summers said. Davy put his hand
into the box and laughed. "Take just *one* paper," Mr. Summers said. "Harry,
you hold it for him." Mr. Graves took the child's hand and removed the
folded paper from the tight fist and held it while little Dave stood next to
him and looked up at him wonderingly.

"Nancy next," Mr. Summers said. Nancy was twelve, and her school 64
friends breathed heavily as she went forward, switching her skirt, and took
a slip daintily from the box. "Bill, Jr.," Mr. Summers said, and Billy, his face
red and his feet overlarge, nearly knocked the box over as he got a paper out.
"Tessie," Mr. Summers said. She hesitated for a minute, looking around defi-
antly, and then set her lips and went up to the box. She snatched a paper out
and held it behind her.

"Bill," Mr. Summers said, and Bill Hutchinson reached into the box and 65
felt around, bringing his hand out at last with the slip of paper in it.

The crowd was quiet. A girl whispered, "I hope it's not Nancy," and the 66
sound of the whisper reached the edges of the crowd.

"It's not the way it used to be," Old Man Warner said clearly. "People ain't 67
the way they used to be."

"All right," Mr. Summers said. "Open the papers. Harry, you open little 68
Dave's."

Mr. Graves opened the slip of paper and there was a general sigh through 69
the crowd as he held it up and everyone could see that it was blank. Nancy and
Bill, Jr., opened theirs at the same time, and both beamed and laughed, turning
around to the crowd and holding their slips of paper above their heads.

"Tessie," Mr. Summers said. There was a pause, and then Mr. Summers 70
looked at Bill Hutchinson, and Bill unfolded his paper and showed it. It was
blank.

"It's Tessie," Mr. Summers said, and his voice was hushed. "Show us her 71
paper, Bill."

Bill Hutchinson went over to his wife and forced the slip of paper out of 72
her hand. It had a black spot on it, the black spot Mr. Summers had made
the night before with the heavy pencil in the coal-company office. Bill
Hutchinson held it up, and there was a stir in the crowd.

"All right, folks," Mr. Summers said. "Let's finish quickly." 73

Although the villagers had forgotten the ritual and lost the original black 74
box, they still remembered to use stones. The pile of stones the boys had
made earlier was ready; there were stones on the ground with the blowing
scraps of paper that had come out of the box. Mrs. Delacroix selected a stone
so large she had to pick it up with both hands and turned to Mrs. Dunbar.
"Come on," she said. "Hurry up."

Mrs. Dunbar had small stones in both hands, and she said, gasping for 75
breath, "I can't run at all. You'll have to go ahead and I'll catch up with you."

The children had stones already, and someone gave little Davy Hutchinson 76
a few pebbles.

Tessie Hutchinson was in the center of a cleared space by now, and she 77
held her hands out desperately as the villagers moved in on her. "It isn't fair,"
she said. A stone hit her on the side of the head.

Old Man Warner was saying, "Come on, come on, everyone." Steve Adams 78
was in the front of the crowd of villagers, with Mrs. Graves beside him.

"It isn't fair, it isn't right," Mrs. Hutchinson screamed, and then they were 79
upon her.

For an essay about
*The Hunger Games,*
a novel and film that
also comments on
societal traditions,
see p. 198.

## Questions to Start You Thinking

Meaning

1. Where does this story take place? When?

2. How does this lottery differ from what we usually think of as a lottery?
   Why would people conduct a lottery such as this?

3. What does this story mean to you?

Writing Strategies

4. Can you see and hear the people in the story? Do they seem to be real or
   based on fantasy? Who is the most memorable character to you?

5. Are the events believable? Does the ending shock you? Is it believable?

6. Is the story realistic, or is Jackson using it to represent something else?

## Preparing to Write a Literary Analysis

As Jonathan Burns first read "The Lottery," he was carried along to the startling ending. Then he reread to understand the story well enough to identify and analyze elements such as setting, character, or tone. He began turning understanding into text by writing a synopsis to clarify the literal events in the story. Summing up events immediately suggested writing about the story's undertone of violence, but he decided that it would be hard to write about something so subtle.

For Burns's synopsis, see pp. 273–74; for his paraphrase, see p. 277.

Then he considered the characters in the story, especially Mr. Summers, Tessie Hutchinson, or the memorable Old Man Warner. Burns experimented by paraphrasing Old Man Warner's comments from one paragraph. But he decided not to focus on the characters because he couldn't think of more than the vague statement that they were memorable. He considered other elements — language, symbols, ambiguity, foreshadowing — and dismissed each in turn. All of a sudden, he hit on the surprise ending. How did Jackson manipulate all the details to generate such a shock?

To focus his thinking, he brainstormed for possible essay titles about the ending: Death Comes as a Surprise, The Unsuspected Finish, and his straightforward choice "The Hidden Truth." After reviewing his notes, Burns realized that Jackson uses characterization, symbolism, and ambiguous description to build up to the ending. He listed details under those three headings to plan his paper informally:

For more on seeking motives of characters, see pp. 378–80.

Title: The Hidden Truth

Working Thesis: In "The Lottery" Jackson effectively crafts a shock ending.

For more on stating a thesis, organizing ideas, and outlining, see Ch. 20.

1. Characterization that contributes to the shock ending
   –The children of the village
   –The adults of the village
   –Conversations among the villagers

2. Symbols that contribute to the shock ending
   –The stones
   –The black box

3. Ambiguous description that contributes to the shock ending
   –The word "lottery"
   –Comments: "clean forgot," "wish they'd hurry," "It isn't fair."
   –Actions: relief, suspense

Then he drafted the following introduction:

For more on introductions, see pp. 410–13.

Unsuspecting, the reader follows Shirley Jackson's softly flowing tale of a rural community's timeless ritual, the lottery. Awareness of what is at stake — the savage murder of one random member — comes slowly. No sooner does the realization set in than the story is over. It is a shock ending.

What creates the shock that the reader experiences reading "The Lottery"? Jackson carefully produces this effect, using elements such as language, symbolism, and characterization to lure the reader into not anticipating what is to come.

With his synopsis, his paraphrase, his plan, his copy of the story, and this starting point, Burns revised the introduction and wrote his essay.

**Jonathan Burns**                    Student Literary Analysis

### The Hidden Truth: An Analysis of Shirley Jackson's "The Lottery"

It is as if the first stone thrown strikes the reader as well as Mrs. Hutchinson. And even though there were signs of the stoning to come, somehow the reader is taken by surprise at Tessie's violent death. What factors contribute to the shock ending to "The Lottery"? On closer examination of the story, the reader finds that through all the events leading up to the ending, Shirley Jackson has used unsuspicious characterizations, unobtrusive symbolism, and ambiguous descriptions to achieve so sudden an impact.

By all appearances, the village is a normal place with normal people. Children arrive at the scene first, with school just over for the summer, talking of teachers and books, not of the fact that someone will die today (252). And as the adults show up, their actions are just as stereotypical: the men talk of farming and taxes, while the women gossip (252). The scene conveys no trace of hostility, no sense of dread in anyone: death seems very far away here.

The conversations between the villagers are no more ominous. As the husbands draw slips of paper for their families, the villagers make apparently everyday comments about the seemingly ordinary event of the lottery. Mr. Summers is regarded as a competent and respected figure, despite his wife being "a scold" (253). Old Man Warner criticizes other towns that have given up their lottery tradition and brags about how many lotteries he's seen (255–56). The characters' comments show the crowd to be more a close-knit community than a murderous mob.

The symbols of "The Lottery" seem equally ordinary. The stones collected by the boys (252) are unnoticed by the adults and thus seem a trivial detail. The reader thinks of the "great pile" (252) as children's entertainment, like a stack of imaginary coins, rather than an arsenal. Ironically, no stones are ever thrown during the children's play, and no violence is seen in the pile of stones.

Similarly, Jackson describes the box and its history in great detail, but nothing seems unusual about it. It is just another everyday object, stored away in the post office or on a shelf in the grocery (253). Every other day of the year, the box is in plain view but goes virtually unnoticed. The only indication that the box has lethal consequences is that it is painted black (253), yet this is an ambiguous detail, as a black box can also signify mystery or magic, mystical forces that are sometimes thought to exist in any lottery.

In her ambiguous descriptions, Jackson refers regularly to the village's lottery and emphasizes it as a central ritual for the people. The word *lottery* itself is ironic, as it typically implies a winning of some kind, like a raffle or sweepstakes. It is paralleled to square dances and to the teenage club, all activities people anticipate

The numbers in parentheses are page-number citations following MLA style. For more on citing and listing sources, see D6 and E (pp. Q-30–Q-36) in the Quick Research Guide.

1

2

3

4

5

6

under the direction of Mr. Summers (252). There is no implied difference between the occurrences of this day and the festivities of Halloween: according to Jackson, they are all merely "civic activities" (252). Equally ambiguous are the people's emotions: some of the villagers are casual, such as Mrs. Hutchinson, who arrives late because she " 'clean forgot' " what day it is (254), and some are anxious, such as Mrs. Dunbar, who repeats to her son, " 'I wish they'd hurry,' " without any sign of the cause of her anxiety (256). With these descriptive details, the reader finds no threat or malice in the villagers, only vague expectation and congeniality.

Even when it becomes clear that the lottery is something no one wants to win, Jackson presents only a vague sense of sadness and mild protest. The crowd is relieved that the youngest of the Hutchinsons, Davy, doesn't draw the fatal slip of paper (258). One girl whispers that she hopes it isn't Nancy (257), and when the Hutchinson children discover they aren't the winners, they beam with joy and proudly display their blank slips (258). Suspense and excitement grow only when the victim is close to being identified. And when Tessie is revealed as the winner of the lottery (258), she merely holds her hands out "desperately" and repeats, " 'It isn't fair' " (258).

7

With a blend of character, symbolism, and description, Jackson paints an overall portrait of a gentle-seeming rural community, apparently no different from any other. The tragic end is sudden only because there is no recognition of violence beforehand, despite the fact that Jackson provides the reader with plenty of clues in the ample details about the lottery and the people. It is a haunting discovery that the story ends in death, even though such is the truth in the everyday life of all people.

8

## Questions to Start You Thinking

### Meaning

1. What is Burns's thesis?

2. What main points does he use to support the interpretation in his thesis? What specific elements of the story does he include as evidence?

### Writing Strategies

3. How does this essay differ from a synopsis, a summary of the events of the plot? (For a synopsis of "The Lottery," see pp. 273–74.)

4. Does Burns focus on the technique of the short story or on its theme?

5. Is his introduction effective? Compare and contrast it with his first draft (p. 259). What did he change? Which version do you prefer?

6. Why does he explain characterization first, symbolism second, and description last? How effective is this organization? Would discussing these elements in a different order have made much difference?

7. Is his conclusion effective?

8. How does he tie ideas together as he moves from paragraph to paragraph? How does he keep the focus on ideas and technique instead of plot?

## A Glossary of Terms for Literary Analysis

**Characters** Characters are imagined people. The author shows what they are like through their actions, speech, thoughts, attitudes, and background. Sometimes a writer also includes physical characteristics or names or relationships with other people. For example, in "The Lottery," the description of Mr. Summers introduces the lottery official as someone with civic interests who wants to avoid slip-ups (paragraphs 4, 9, and 10).

**Figures of Speech** Figures of speech are lively or fresh expressions that vary the expected sequence or sense of words. Some common types of figurative language are *simile*, a comparison using *like* or *as*; *metaphor*, an implied comparison; and *personification*, the attribution of human qualities to nonhuman creatures or things. In "The Lottery," three boys *guard* their pile of stones "against the *raids*" of others (paragraph 2).

**Imagery** Images are words or groups of words that refer to any sense experience: seeing, hearing, smelling, tasting, touching, or feeling. The images in "The Lottery" help readers envision the "richly green" grass (paragraph 1), the smooth and round stones the children gather (paragraph 2), the "hush" that comes over the crowd (paragraph 19), and Mrs. Dunbar "gasping for breath" (paragraph 75).

**Irony** Irony results from readers' sense of discrepancy. A simple kind of irony, *sarcasm*, occurs when you say one thing but mean the opposite: "I just love scrubbing the floor." In literature, an *ironic situation* sets up a contrast or incongruity. In "The Lottery," horrifying actions take place on a sunny June day in an ordinary village. *Ironic dialogue* occurs when a character says one thing, but the audience or reader is aware of another meaning. When Old Man Warner reacts to giving up the lottery as "wanting to go back to living in caves" (paragraph 32), he implies that such a change would return the villages to a more primitive life. His comment is ironic because the reader is aware that this lottery is a primitive ritual. A story has an *ironic point of view* when readers sense a difference between the author and the narrator or the character who perceives the story; Jackson, for instance, clearly does not condone the actions of the villagers.

**Plot** Plot is the arrangement of the events of the story—what happens to whom, where, when, and why. If the events follow each other logically and are in keeping with the characters, the plot is *plausible*, or believable. Although the ending of "The Lottery" at first may shock readers, the author uses *foreshadowing*, hints or clues such as the villagers' nervousness about the lottery, to help readers understand future events or twists in the plot.

Most plots place the *protagonist*, or main character, in a *conflict* with the *antagonist*, some other person or group. In "The Lottery," a reader might see Tessie as the protagonist and the villagers as the antagonist. *Conflict* consists of two forces trying to conquer each other or resist being conquered—not merely vaguely defined turmoil. *External conflicts* occur outside an individual—between two people, a person and a group (Tessie versus the villagers), two groups (lottery supporters and opponents), or even a character and the environment. *Internal conflicts* between two opposing forces or desires occur within an individual (such as fear versus hope as the lottery slips are drawn). The *central conflict* is the primary conflict for the protagonist that propels the action of the story. Events of the plot *complicate* the conflict (Tessie arrives late, Bill draws the slip) and lead to the *climax*, the moment when the outcome is inevitable (Tessie draws the black dot). This outcome is the *resolution*, or conclusion (the villagers stone Tessie). Some stories let events unfold without any apparent plot—action and change occur inside the characters.

**Point of View** The point of view, the angle from which a story is told, might be the author's or a character's. The *narrator* is the one who tells the story and perceives the events, perhaps with limited knowledge or a part to play. Two common points of view are those of a *first-person narrator* (*I*), the *speaker* who tells the story, and a *third-person narrator* (*he, she*) who tells the story from an all-knowing perspective, from the perspective of a single character, or from numerous, shifting perspectives. The point of view may be *omniscient* (the speaker knows all and has access to every character's thoughts and feelings); *limited omniscient* (the speaker knows the thoughts and feelings of one or more characters, but not all); or *objective* (the speaker observes the characters but cannot share their thoughts or feelings). In "The Lottery," a third-person objective narrator seemingly looks on and reports what occurs without knowing what the characters think.

**Setting** Setting refers to the time and place of events and may include the season, the weather, and the people in the background. The setting often helps establish a literary work's *mood* or *atmosphere*, the emotional climate that a reader senses. For example, the first sentence of "The Lottery" establishes its setting (paragraph 1).

**Symbols** Symbols are tangible objects, visible actions, or characters that hint at meanings beyond themselves. In "The Lottery," the black box suggests outdated tradition, resistance to change, evil, cruelty, and more.

**Theme** A theme is a work's main idea or insight—the author's observation about life, society, or human nature. Sometimes you can sum up a theme in a sentence ("Human beings cannot live without illusion"); other times, a theme may be implied, hard to discern, or one of several in a work.

To state a theme, go beyond a work's topic or subject by asking, What does the author say about this subject? Details from the story should support your statement of theme, and your theme should account for the details. "The Lottery" treats subjects such as the unexpected, scapegoating, outmoded rituals, and violence; one of its themes might be stated as "People are selfish, always looking out for number one."

# Learning by Writing: Literary Analysis
## The Assignment: Analyzing a Literary Work

For this assignment, you are to be a literary critic—analyzing, interpreting, and evaluating a literary selection for your classmates. Your purpose is to deepen their understanding because you will have devoted time and effort to digging out the work's meaning. Even if they too have studied the work carefully, you will try to convince them that your interpretation is valid.

Choose a literary work that intrigues you or expresses a worthwhile meaning. Your selection might be a short story, a poem, a play, or a novel. (Follow directions if your instructor wants to approve your choice, assign the literary work, or limit your options to several works read by your class.) After careful analysis of the work, write an essay as the expert critic, explaining the meaning you discern, supporting your interpretation with evidence from the work, and evaluating the effectiveness of literary elements used by the author and the significance of the theme.

You cannot include everything about the work in your paper, so you should focus on one element (such as character, setting, or theme) or the interrelationship of two or three elements (such as characterization and symbolism). Although a summary, or *synopsis,* of the plot is a good beginning point, retelling the story is not a satisfactory literary analysis.

These college writers successfully responded to such an assignment:

One showed how the rhythm, rhymes, and images of Adrienne Rich's poem "Aunt Jennifer's Tigers" mesh to convey the poem's theme of tension between a woman's artistic urge and societal constraints.

Another, a drummer, read James Baldwin's "Sonny's Blues" and established Sonny's credibility as a musician—based on attitudes, actions, struggles, and his relationship with his instrument and with other musicians.

A psychology major concluded that the relationship between Hamlet and Claudius in Shakespeare's *Hamlet* represents tension, jealousy, and misunderstanding between stepsons and stepfathers.

## Facing the Challenge   Analyzing Literature

The major challenge that writers face when analyzing a literary work is to state and support a thesis that takes a stand. If you simply explain the literal meaning of the work—retelling the story or summing up the topic of an essay or a poem—your readers will be disappointed. Instead, they expect a clear thesis that presents your specific interpretation. They want to see how you analyze the work and which features of the work you use to support your position about it. For instance, your thesis might identify a theme—an insight, main idea, or observation about life—developed in the work. Then your essay would show how selected features of the work express, develop, or illustrate this theme. On the other hand, your thesis might present your analysis of how a story, poem, or play works. Then your essay might discuss how several elements—such as the mood established by the setting, the figurative language used to describe events, and the arc of the plot—work together to develop its meaning. Whatever the case that you argue, your thesis needs to be clearly focused and your supporting evidence needs to come from the words and expressions of the work itself.

## Generating Ideas

Read several literary works from the course options to find two or three you like. Next, reread those that interest you. Select one that strikes you as especially significant—realistic or universal, moving or disturbing, believable or shocking—with a meaning you wish to share with classmates.

For more on analysis, see pp. 430–32.

Analyzing a literary work is the first step in interpreting meaning and evaluating literary quality. As you read the work, identify its elements and analyze them. Then focus on *one* significant element or a cluster of related elements. As you write, restrict your discussion to that focus.

We provide three checklists to guide you in analyzing different types of literature. Each of these is an aid to understanding, *not* an organizational outline for writing about literature. The first checklist focuses on short stories and novels, but some of its questions can help you analyze setting, character, theme, or your reactions as a reader for almost any kind of literary work.

### DISCOVERY CHECKLIST

**Analyzing a Short Story or a Novel**

☐ What is your reaction to the story? Jot it down.

☐ Who is the *narrator*—not the author, but the one who tells the story?

☐ What is the *point of view*?

☐ What is the *setting* (time and place)? What is the *atmosphere* or *mood*?

☐ How does the *plot* unfold? Write a synopsis, or summary, of the events in time order, including relationships among those events (see pp. 273–74).

For a glossary of literary terms, see pp. 262–63.

☐ What are the *characters* like? Describe their personalities, traits, and motivations based on their actions, speech, habits, and so on. What strategies does the author use to develop the characters? Who is the *protagonist*? The *antagonist*? Do any characters change? Are the changes believable?

☐ How would you describe the story's *style*, or use of language? Is it informal, conversational, or formal? Does the story use dialect or foreign words?

☐ What are the *external conflicts* and the *internal conflicts*? What is the *central conflict*? Express the conflicts using the word *versus,* such as "dreams versus reality" or "the individual versus society."

☐ What is the *climax* of the story? Is there any *resolution*?

☐ Are there important *symbols*? What might they mean?

☐ What does the *title* of the story mean?

☐ What are the *themes* of the story? Are they universal (applicable to all people everywhere at all times)? Write down your interpretation of the main theme. How is this theme related to your own life?

☐ What other literary works or life experiences does the story remind you of?

When looking at a poem, consider the elements specific to poetry and those shared with other genres, as the following checklist suggests.

### DISCOVERY CHECKLIST

### Analyzing a Poem

☐ What is your reaction to the poem? Jot it down.

☐ Who is the *speaker* — not the author, but the one who narrates?

☐ Is there a *setting*? What *mood* or emotional *atmosphere* does it suggest?

☐ Can you put the poem into your own words — paraphrase it?

☐ What is striking about the poem's language? Is it informal or formal? Does it use irony or figurative language: *imagery, metaphor, personification*? Identify repetition or words that are unusual, used in an unusual way, or *archaic* (no longer commonly used). Consider *connotations*, the suggestions conjured by the words: *house* versus *home,* though both refer to the same place.

☐ Is the poem *lyric* (expressing emotion) or *narrative* (telling a story)?

☐ How is the poem structured or divided? Does it use *couplets* (two consecutive rhyming lines), *quatrains* (units of four lines), or other units? How do the beginning and end relate to each other and to the poem as a whole?

☐ Does the poem use *rhyme* (words that sound alike)? If so, how does the rhyme contribute to the meaning?

☐ Does the poem have *rhythm* (regular meter or beat, patterns of accented and unaccented syllables)? How does the rhythm contribute to the meaning?

☐ What does the *title* of the poem mean?

☐ What is the major *theme* of the poem? How does this underlying idea unify the poem? How is it related to your own life?

☐ What other literary works or life experiences does the poem remind you of?

A play is written to be seen and heard, not read. You may analyze what kind it is and how it would appear onstage, as this checklist suggests.

**DISCOVERY CHECKLIST**

**Analyzing a Play**

☐ What is your reaction to the play? Jot it down.

☐ Is the play a serious *tragedy* (which arouses pity and fear in the audience and usually ends unhappily with the death or downfall of the *tragic hero*)? Or is it a *comedy* (which aims to amuse and usually ends happily)?

☐ What is the *setting* of the play? What is its *mood*?

☐ In brief, what happens? Summarize each act of the play.

☐ What are the characters like? Who is the *protagonist*? Who is the *antagonist*? Are there *foil characters* who contrast with the main character and reveal his or her traits? Which characters are in conflict? Which change?

☐ Which speeches seem especially significant?

☐ What is the plot? Identify the *exposition* or background information needed to understand the story. Determine the main *external* and *internal* conflicts. What is the *central conflict*? What events *complicate* the central conflict? How are these elements of the plot spread throughout the play?

☐ What is the *climax* of the play? Is there a *resolution* to the action?

☐ What does the *title* mean?

☐ Can you identify any *dramatic irony,* words or actions of a character that carry meaning unperceived by the character but evident to the audience?

☐ What is the major *theme*? Is it universal? How is it related to your life?

☐ What other literary works or life experiences does the play remind you of?

# Learning by Doing 🎬 Examining Fiction Genres

Compare two stories that you have both read and watched on film (for example, stories from the *Harry Potter, Hunger Games,* or *Divergent* series). Choose a single scene that appears in both the book and the movie. Reflect on the two versions and how they are presented. How do the book and film versions differ? What might account for those differences? In responding to these questions, consider how the genre (book or film) affects the presentation. You may also wish to consider a book that has been converted to a graphic novel. How do those genres differ?

## Planning, Drafting, and Developing

For more on planning, drafting, and developing, see Chs. 20, 21, and 22.

When you write your analysis, your purpose is to explain the work's deeper meaning. Don't try to impress readers with your brilliance. Instead, regard them as friends in whose company you are discussing something familiar to all, though they may not have studied the work as carefully as you have. This assumption will help you decide how much evidence from the work to include and will reduce summarizing.

**Identify Your Support.** After you have determined the major element or cluster of elements that you intend to focus on, go through the work again to find all the passages that relate to your main point. Mark them as you find them, or put them on note cards or in a computer file, along with the page references. If you use any quotations, quote exactly.

For more on stating a thesis, see pp. 384–93.

**Develop Your Main Idea or Thesis.** Begin by trying to express your point in a thesis statement that identifies the literary work and the author.

> WORKING THESIS  In "The Lottery," Shirley Jackson reveals the theme.

But this statement is too vague, so you rewrite it to be more precise:

> IMPROVED  In "The Lottery" by Shirley Jackson, the theme is tradition.

This thesis is better but still doesn't state the theme clearly or precisely. You try other ways of expressing what Jackson implies about tradition:

> IMPROVED  In "The Lottery" by Shirley Jackson, one of the major themes is that outmoded traditions can be harmful.

Adding *one of* shows that this is not the story's only theme, but the rest is vague. What does *outmoded* mean? How are traditions harmful?

> MORE PRECISE  In "The Lottery" by Shirley Jackson, one of the major themes is that traditions that have lost their meaning can still move people to act abnormally without thinking.

This thesis is better but may change as you write. For instance, you might go beyond interpretation of Jackson's ideas by adding *tragic* to convey your evaluation of her observation of the human condition:

EVALUATION
ADDED

In "The Lottery," Jackson reveals the tragic theme that traditions that have lost their meaning can still move people to abnormal and thoughtless action.

Or you might say this, alerting readers to your main points:

PREVIEW
ADDED

In "The Lottery," Jackson effectively uses symbolism and irony to reveal the theme that traditions that have lost their meaning can still move people to abnormal action.

Focus on analyzing ideas, not retelling events. Maintain that focus by analyzing your thesis: divide it into parts, and then develop each part in turn. The thesis just presented could be divided into (1) use of symbolism to reveal theme and (2) use of irony to reveal theme. Similarly, you might divide a thesis about character change into the character's original traits, the events that cause change, and the character's new traits.

## Learning by Doing 🎯 Developing Your Thesis

Follow the preceding pattern for developing a thesis statement. Start with your working thesis. Then improve it, make it more precise, and consider adding an evaluation or preview. Present your thesis drafts to a classmate or small group, perhaps asking questions like these: What wording needs to be clearer? What idea could I narrow down? What point sounds intriguing? What might a reader want me to emphasize? Continue to refine your thesis as you work on your essay.

**Introduce Your Essay.** Tie your beginning to your main idea, or thesis. If you are uncertain how to begin, try one of these openings:

For more on introductions, see pp. 410–13.

- Focus on a character's universality (pointing out that most people might feel as Tessie in "The Lottery" did if their names were drawn).
- Focus on a theme's universality (discussing briefly how traditions seem to be losing their meaning in modern society).
- Quote a striking line from the work ("and then they were upon her" or "'Lottery in June, corn be heavy soon'").
- Make a statement about the work's point, your reaction when you read it, a parallel personal experience, or the writer's technique.
- Ask a "Have you ever?" question to draw readers into your interpretation.

---

## Peer Response 🔲 Responding to Literature

For general questions for a peer editor, see p. 447.

Ask a classmate to read your draft and to consider how effectively you have analyzed the literary work and presented your analysis. Ask your peer editor to answer specific questions such as these:

- What is your first reaction to the literary analysis?
- In what ways does the analysis add to your understanding of the literary work? In what ways does it add to your insights into life?
- Does the introduction make you want to read the rest of the analysis? What changes would you suggest to strengthen the opening?
- Is the main idea clear? Is there sufficient relevant evidence from the work to support that point? Put stars wherever additional evidence is needed. Put a check mark by any irrelevant information.
- Does the essay go beyond plot summary to analyze elements, interpret meaning, and evaluate literary merit? If not, how might the writer revise?
- Is the analysis organized by ideas instead of events? What changes in organization would you suggest?
- Do the transitions guide you smoothly from one point to the next? Do the transitions focus on ideas, not on time or position in the story? Note any places where you would suggest adding transitions.
- If this paper were yours, what is the one thing you would be sure to work on before handing it in?

---

For more on citing and listing literary works, see MLA style in E (pp. Q-31–Q-36) in the Quick Research Guide.

**Support Your Interpretation.** As you develop your analysis, include supporting evidence — descriptions of setting and character, summaries of events, quotations of dialogue, and other specifics. Cite page numbers (for prose) or line numbers (for poetry) where the details can be found in the work. Integrate evidence from the story with your comments and ideas.

For a list of transitions showing logical connections, see p. 418.

Keep the focus on ideas, not events, by using transition markers that refer to character traits and personality change, not to time. Say "Although Mr. Summers was . . ." instead of "At the beginning of the story Mr. Summers was . . ." Write "Tessie became . . ." instead of "After that Tessie was . . ." State "The villagers in 'The Lottery' changed . . . ," not "On the next page . . ."

For more on conclusions, see pp. 413–15.

**Conclude Your Essay.** When you reach the end, don't just stop. Close as you might open — with a personal experience, a comment on technique, a quotation — to provide a sense of finality. Refer to or reaffirm your thesis. Often an effective conclusion ties in directly with the introduction.

Use the Take Action chart (p. 271) to help you figure out how to improve your draft. Skim the left-hand column to identify questions you might ask about your literary analysis. When you answer a question with "Yes" or "Maybe," move straight across to Locate Specifics for that question. Use the

# Take Action  Strengthening Literary Analysis

Ask each question listed in the left-hand column to consider whether your draft might need work on that issue. If so, follow the ASK — LOCATE SPECIFICS — TAKE ACTION sequence to revise.

| 1 ASK | 2 LOCATE SPECIFICS | 3 TAKE ACTION |
|---|---|---|
| Could I state my **overall thesis** or **main idea** more clearly? | ■ Write out your **current thesis**.<br><br>■ **Highlight key words** that pin down your main idea about the literary work.<br><br>■ Circle any **words** that seem **vague** or **general**. | ■ Replace circled words with **clear, concrete, exact** words.<br><br>■ **Narrow down** any broad **terms** or **claims**.<br><br>■ **Reveal your analysis** of significant elements instead of telling what happened.<br><br>■ Decide whether to add an **evaluation** or a **preview** of your main points. |
| Could I present my **main points** more specifically? | ■ **Underline or list the main points** you want to present.<br><br>■ **Confirm the relevance of each point** for your stated thesis (not just your general idea).<br><br>■ Read the passage about each point and use an **X** to **mark any gap in development.** | ■ If any points do not connect to your thesis, **rework the thesis** or **replace the points**.<br><br>■ If any points lack development, **add explanation, examples, or details** to clarify your analysis.<br><br>■ Read your draft aloud, listening for logical jumps or weak connections. **Use specifics to fill in gaps or spell out connections.** |
| Could I add more or better **evidence** from the literary work? | ■ **Color-code each bit of supporting evidence** in your draft.<br><br>■ Put a ✓ by any passages with **little, no, or irrelevant support.**<br><br>■ Jot down ideas about **compelling examples** and **details** to add support. | ■ Return to each ✓ to work in **strong, persuasive support** based on analysis.<br><br>■ Figure out how to **fit in more examples** and **details**.<br><br>■ **Smooth out each paragraph**, making sure each main point is clear for a reader and that **transitions** link your ideas and evidence. |

activities there to pinpoint gaps, problems, or weaknesses. Then move straight across to Take Action. Use the advice that suits your problem as you revise.

## Revising and Editing

For more revising and editing strategies, see Ch. 23.

As you read over your draft, keep in mind your thesis and the evidence that supports it.

### REVISION CHECKLIST

☐ Have you clearly identified the literary work and the author near the beginning of the analysis?

☐ Is your main idea or thesis clear? Does everything else relate to it?

☐ Have you focused on one element or a cluster of related elements in your analysis? Have you organized around these ideas rather than events?

☐ Do your transitions focus on ideas, not on plot or time sequence? Do they guide readers easily from one section or sentence to the next?

☐ Are your interpretations supported by evidence from the literary work? Do you need to add examples of dialogue, action, or description? Have you selected details relevant to the points of analysis, not interesting sidelights?

☐ Have you woven the details from the work smoothly into your text? Have you cited their correct page or line numbers? Have you quoted and cited carefully instead of lifting language without proper attribution?

☐ Do you understand all the words and literary terms you use?

☐ Have you tried to share your insights into the meaning of the work with your readers, or have you slipped into trying to impress them?

For more editing and proofreading strategies, see pp. 455–58.

After you have revised your literary analysis, check the grammar, word choice, punctuation, and mechanics—and then correct any problems you find. Make sure that you smoothly introduce all of your quotations and references to the work and weave them into your own discussion.

### EDITING CHECKLIST

For more help, find the relevant checklist sections in the Quick Editing Guide on p. Q-37. Turn also to the Quick Format Guide beginning on p. Q-1.

☐ Have you used the present tense for events in the literary work and for comments about the author's presentation?                    A3

☐ Have you used quotation marks correctly whenever you give the exact words of the literary work?                    D3

☐ Have you used correct manuscript format for your paper?

# Learning from Another Writer: Synopsis

You may write synopses of literary works to help you prepare to write about them or to sum up information about them for an essay or exam. A synopsis can help you get the chronology straight, pick out significant events and details, and relate parts of a work to each other. Condensing a story to a few hundred words forces you to focus on what's most important, often leading to a statement of theme.

A *synopsis* is a summary of the plot of a narrative—a short story, a novel, a play, or a narrative poem. It describes the literal meaning, condensing the story to the major events and most significant details. Do not include your interpretation, but summarize the work in your own words, taking care not to lift language or sentence structure from the work itself. To prepare for writing his literary analysis of "The Lottery" (pp. 252–58)—making sure he had the sequence of events clear—Jonathan Burns wrote a synopsis of the story.

For more on summarizing and paraphrasing, see Ch. 12 and D (pp. Q-27–Q-31) in the Quick Research Guide.

---

**Jonathan Burns**                                    **Student Synopsis**

## A Synopsis of "The Lottery"

Around ten o'clock on a sunny June 27, the villagers gathered in the square for a lottery, expecting to be home in time for lunch. The children came first, gathering stones and talking as they enjoyed the summer vacation. Then came the men, followed by the women. When parents called, the children joined their families.    1

Mr. Summers, who always conducted the town lottery, arrived with the traditional black wooden box and placed it on the three-legged stool that Mr. Graves had brought out. The villagers remained apart from these men, but Mr. Martin and his son reluctantly helped hold the shabby black box as Mr. Summers mixed the paper slips in it, now substituted for the original wooden chips. To prepare for the drawing, they listed the members of every household and swore in Mr. Summers. Although they had dropped much of the original ritual, the official still greeted each person individually.    2

Tessie Hutchinson rushed into the square, telling her friend Mrs. Delacroix she had almost forgotten the day. Then she joined her husband and children. When Mr. Summers asked if everyone was present, he was told that Clyde Dunbar was absent because of a broken leg but that his wife would draw for the family. Summers noted that the Watson boy was drawing for his mother and checked to see if Old Man Warner was present.    3

The crowd got quiet. Mr. Summers reminded everybody of the procedure and began to call the family names in alphabetical order. People in the group joked and talked nervously until Mr. Summers finished calling the roll. After a    4 pause, the heads of households opened their slips. Everybody wondered who had the special slip of paper, who had won the lottery. They discovered it was Bill Hutchinson. When Tessie complained that the drawing hadn't been done fairly, the others told her to "Be a good sport" (256).

Mr. Graves put five slips into the box, one for each member of the          5
Hutchinson family, although Tessie kept charging unfairness. The children drew first, then Tessie, then Bill. The children opened their slips and held up blank pieces of paper. Bill opened his, also blank. Tessie wouldn't open hers; Bill had to do it for her, revealing its black spot.

Mr. Summers urged everyone to complete the process right away. They          6
picked up stones, even young Davy Hutchinson, and started throwing them at Tessie, as she kept screaming, "It isn't fair, it isn't right" (258). Then the villagers stoned her.

## Questions to Start You Thinking

### Meaning

1. In what ways does this synopsis help you understand the story better?

2. Why isn't a synopsis as interesting as a short story?

3. Can you tell from this synopsis whether Burns understands Jackson's story beyond the literal level? How can you tell?

### Writing Strategies

4. Does Burns retell the story accurately and clearly? Does he get the events in correct time order? How does he show the relationships of the events to each other and to the whole?

5. Does Burns select the details necessary to indicate what happened in "The Lottery"? Why do you think he omits certain details?

6. Are there any details, comments, or events that you would add to his synopsis? Why, or why not?

7. How does this synopsis differ from Burns's literary analysis (pp. 260–61)?

# Learning by Writing: Synopsis

## The Assignment: Writing a Synopsis of a Story by Kate Chopin

Kate Chopin was a nineteenth-century American writer whose female characters search for identity and freedom from oppression. Write a synopsis of two to three hundred words of Chopin's "The Story of an Hour." Keep your synopsis of the plot true to the original, noting accurate details in time order.

DISCOVERY CHECKLIST

☐ What are the major events and details of the story?

☐ In what time order do events take place?

☐ How are the story's parts related (without adding interpretations)?

☐ Which of the author's words might you want to quote?

## Kate Chopin
## The Story of an Hour

The Granger Collection, NYC.

Knowing that Mrs. Mallard was afflicted with a heart trouble, great care 1
was taken to break to her as gently as possible the news of her husband's
death.

It was her sister Josephine who told her, in broken sentences, veiled hints 2
that revealed in half concealing. Her husband's friend Richards was there,
too, near her. It was he who had been in the newspaper office when intelligence of the railroad disaster was received, with Brently Mallard's name leading the list of "killed." He had only taken the time to assure himself of its
truth by a second telegram, and had hastened to forestall any less careful, less
tender friend in bearing the sad message.

She did not hear the story as many women have heard the same, with a 3
paralyzed inability to accept its significance. She wept at once, with sudden,
wild abandonment, in her sister's arms. When the storm of grief had spent
itself she went away to her room alone. She would have no one follow her.

There stood, facing the open window, a comfortable, roomy armchair. 4
Into this she sank, pressed down by a physical exhaustion that haunted her
body and seemed to reach into her soul.

She could see in the open square before her house the tops of trees that 5
were all aquiver with the new spring life. The delicious breath of rain was
in the air. In the street below a peddler was crying his wares. The notes of a
distant song which someone was singing reached her faintly, and countless
sparrows were twittering in the eaves.

There were patches of blue sky showing here and there through the clouds 6
that had met and piled one above the other in the west facing her window.

She sat with her head thrown back upon the cushion of the chair, quite 7
motionless, except when a sob came up into her throat and shook her, as a
child who has cried itself to sleep continues to sob in its dreams.

She was young, with a fair, calm face, whose lines bespoke repression 8
and even a certain strength. But now there was a dull stare in her eyes,
whose gaze was fixed away off yonder on one of those patches of blue sky.

It was not a glance of reflection, but rather indicated a suspension of intelligent thought.

There was something coming to her and she was waiting for it, fearfully. 9
What was it? She did not know; it was too subtle and elusive to name. But
she felt it, creeping out of the sky, reaching toward her through the sounds,
the scents, the color that filled the air.

Now her bosom rose and fell tumultuously. She was beginning to rec- 10
ognize this thing that was approaching to possess her, and she was striving
to beat it back with her will—as powerless as her two white slender hands
would have been.

When she abandoned herself a little whispered word escaped her slightly 11
parted lips. She said it over and over under her breath: "Free, free, free!" The
vacant stare and the look of terror that had followed it went from her eyes.
They stayed keen and bright. Her pulses beat fast, and the coursing blood
warmed and relaxed every inch of her body.

She did not stop to ask if it were not a monstrous joy that held her. 12
A clear and exalted perception enabled her to dismiss the suggestion as
trivial.

She knew that she would weep again when she saw the kind, tender 13
hands folded in death; the face that had never looked save with love upon
her, fixed and gray and dead. But she saw beyond that bitter moment a long
procession of years to come that would belong to her absolutely. And she
opened and spread her arms out to them in welcome.

There would be no one to live for during those coming years; she would 14
live for herself. There would be no powerful will bending her in that blind
persistence with which men and women believe they have a right to impose
a private will upon a fellow creature. A kind intention or a cruel intention
made the act seem no less a crime as she looked upon it in that brief moment
of illumination.

And yet she had loved him—sometimes. Often she had not. What did it 15
matter! What could love, the unsolved mystery, count for in face of this possession of self-assertion which she suddenly recognized as the strongest impulse of her being.

"Free! Body and soul free!" she kept whispering. 16

Josephine was kneeling before the closed door with her lips to the 17
keyhole, imploring for admission. "Louise, open the door! I beg; open the
door—you will make yourself ill. What are you doing, Louise? For heaven's
sake open the door."

"Go away. I am not making myself ill." No; she was drinking in a very 18
elixir of life through that open window.

Her fancy was running riot along those days ahead of her. Spring days, 19
and summer days, and all sorts of days that would be her own. She breathed
a quick prayer that life might be long. It was only yesterday she had thought
with a shudder that life might be long.

She arose at length and opened the door to her sister's importunities. 20
There was a feverish triumph in her eyes, and she carried herself unwittingly

like a goddess of Victory. She clasped her sister's waist, and together they descended the stairs. Richards stood waiting for them at the bottom.

Someone was opening the front door with a latchkey. It was Brently 21 Mallard who entered, a little travel-stained, composedly carrying his gripsack and umbrella. He had been far from the scene of the accident, and did not even know there had been one. He stood amazed at Josephine's piercing cry; at Richards's quick motion to screen him from the view of his wife.

But Richards was too late.                                                  22

When the doctors came they said she had died of heart disease—of joy 23 that kills.

# Learning from Another Writer: Paraphrase

Like a synopsis, a *paraphrase* conveys the meaning of the original piece of literature and the relationships of its parts in your own words. A paraphrase, however, converts the original poetry to your own prose or the original prose to your own words in a passage about as long as the original.

As Jonathan Burns read through "The Lottery" preparing to write his analysis, he paid close attention to several of the characters that he planned to mention. To sharpen his understanding of Old Man Warner, he wrote a paraphrase of that character's comments in paragraph 32.

**Jonathan Burns**                                    **Student Paraphrase**

### A Paraphrase from "The Lottery"

Old Man Warner criticized people who were willing to give up the lottery as stupid idiots or uppity young people who were not satisfied with anything. He claimed that such people would be content to quit work and move to caves. Then he repeated an old folk expression about a good corn crop following the June lottery and claimed that without it the villagers would end up living on weeds and nuts. Finally, he maintained that the lottery had been a tradition forever. He even criticized Mr. Summers as a youngster, faulting him for not being serious enough about the lottery (255–56).

### Questions to Start You Thinking

Meaning

1. In what ways do you think this paraphrase helped Jonathan Burns understand Old Man Warner better?

2. Why isn't a paraphrase as interesting as the original passage in a story?

Writing Strategies

3. To what extent does Burns paraphrase clearly and accurately? Would you add or drop any details or comments from his paraphrase?

4. How does this paraphrase differ from Burns's synopsis (pp. 273-74)?

## Learning by Doing 🎙 Collaborating on a Paraphrase

Working with a classmate or small group, select from "The Lottery" a short paragraph that describes or reveals a character in the story. Either (1) collaboratively compose a paraphrase, line by line, of that paragraph, or (2) separately write a paraphrase, then exchange and comment as peer editors on each of your drafts. Either way, present the meaning of the passage, but stick to your own words and sentence structures.

# Learning by Writing: Paraphrase

## The Assignment: Writing a Paraphrase of a Poem

See p. 211 and the Additional Writing Assignments section below for poems you might paraphrase.

You can benefit from paraphrasing poetry—expressing the content of a poem in your own words without adding opinions or interpretations. A paraphrase forces you to divide the poem into logical sections, then to figure out what the poet says in each section and how the parts relate. It also prepares you to state its theme—its main idea or insight—in a sentence or two.

### DISCOVERY CHECKLIST

☐ What are the poem's major sections? What does the poet say in each one?

☐ How are the sections of the poem related?

☐ Are any words unfamiliar or used in a special sense, different from the usual meanings? What do those words mean in the context of the poem?

☐ Does the poet use images to create sensory pictures or figurative language (see p. 262) to create comparisons? How do these contribute to the meaning?

## Reviewing and Reflecting

To complete more review questions for Ch. 13, go to LaunchPad.

**REVIEW** Working with classmates or independently, respond to the following questions:

1. Describe the major tasks involved in a literary analysis. What is the major challenge of this type of writing?

2. What problems should you look for in a draft of a literary analysis—problems that you can take action on to strengthen the analysis? If you have prepared

a draft of a literary analysis, can you identify any of these issues in your work? If so, what revisions might help? Make notes about these.

3. How does a synopsis differ from a literary analysis? In what contexts are synopses used?

**REFLECT** After completing a literary analysis, turn back to the After Writing questions on page 39 of Chapter 3 and respond to as many of them as you can.

Next, reflect in writing about how you might apply the insights that you drew from the literary analysis to another situation—in or outside of college—in which you have to analyze something. If no specific situations come to mind, imagine that

- in a history course, you examine media portrayals of civil rights demonstrations from both the 1960s and today, analyzing journalists' choices about what to focus on, whom to interview, and how to describe the events. This process enables you to draw fresh conclusions about how such portrayals have changed over time or how they have remained the same.
- in a business report, you analyze responses to a customer survey about a new product and share your interpretation of the feedback.

In your reflection, consider the advantages and challenges of going beyond a straight summary of material.

## Additional Writing Assignments

1. **Source Assignment.** Analyze the themes of "The Story of an Hour" or another literary work from an earlier era and assigned by your instructor. Which themes are relevant now? How do they relate to twenty-first-century readers and their issues?

2. **Source Assignment.** Write an essay comparing and contrasting a literary element in two or three assigned or optional short stories or poems.

For more on writing a comparison-and-contrast essay, see Ch. 7.

3. **Source Assignment.** Write an essay comparing and contrasting a literary element in a short story and another type of narrative such as a novel or film that tells a story. For example, for "The Lottery" (a short story) and *The Hunger Games* (either the novel or the film), you might compare themes (such as the power of traditions like the lottery and the reaping), settings (such as the village and the Seam), or characters (such as Tessie Hutchinson and Katniss Everdeen or Mr. Summers and District 12's escort Effie Trinket). Use specific evidence from each narrative to support your conclusions.

4. **Source Assignment.** Read the poem below by Robert Frost (1874–1963). Write an essay using a paraphrase of the poem as a springboard for your thoughts on a fork in the road of your life—a decision that made a difference for you.

For another poem by Robert Frost, see p. 211.

**The Road Not Taken**
Two roads diverged in a yellow wood,
And sorry I could not travel both

And be one traveler, long I stood
And looked down one as far as I could
To where it bent in the undergrowth;

Then took the other, as just as fair,
And having perhaps the better claim,
Because it was grassy and wanted wear;
Though as for that the passing there
Had worn them really about the same,

And both that morning equally lay
In leaves no step had trodden black.
Oh, I kept the first for another day!
Yet knowing how way leads on to way,
I doubted if I should ever come back.

I shall be telling this with a sigh
Somewhere ages and ages hence:
Two roads diverged in a wood, and I —
I took the one less traveled by,
And that has made all the difference.

For more on writing
a comparison-and-
contrast essay, see
Ch. 7.

5. **Source Assignment.** Read the poem below by Edwin Arlington Robinson (1869–1935). Have you known and envied someone like Richard Cory, a person everyone thought had it all? What happened to him or her? What did you discover about your impression of the person? Analyze the poem and draw on experience as you write a personal response essay to compare and contrast the person you knew with Richard Cory.

### Richard Cory

Whenever Richard Cory went down town,
We people on the pavement looked at him:
He was a gentleman from sole to crown,
Clean favored, and imperially slim.

And he was always quietly arrayed,
And he was always human when he talked;
But still he fluttered pulses when he said,
"Good-morning," and he glittered when he walked.

And he was rich — yes, richer than a king —
And admirably schooled in every grace:
In fine, we thought that he was everything
To make us wish that we were in his place.

So on we worked, and waited for the light,
And went without the meat, and cursed the bread;
And Richard Cory, one calm summer night,
Went home and put a bullet through his head.

For more about
analyzing visuals, see
Ch. 14. For more on
analysis in general,
see pp. 430–32.

6. **Source Assignment.** Write a critical analysis of a song, a movie, or a television show. Play or view it several times to pull out specific evidence to support your interpretation. If your instructor approves, present your analysis in a podcast, a multimedia format, or a series of Web pages.

# Responding to Visual Representations

## 14

Images are a constant and persistent presence in our lives. The sign atop a taxi invites us to try the new ride at a local tourist attraction. The lettering on a pickup truck urges us to call for a free landscaping estimate. During campaign season, politicians beam at us from brochures, billboards, and screens. On television, video, and the Web, advertising images surround us, trying to shape our opinions about everything from personal hygiene products to snack foods to political issues.

Besides ads, all sorts of cartoons, photos, drawings, paintings, logos, graphics, and other two-dimensional media work to evoke responses. The critical skills you develop for analyzing these still images also apply to other visual representations, including television commercials, films, and stage productions. Whether visual images provoke a smile or a frown, one thing is certain: visuals help to structure our views of reality.

## Why Responding to Visuals Matters

### In a College Course

- You respond to images of people and places in class discussions and papers for sociology, foreign language, and international business classes.
- You write reports on digital images during your health-sciences lab or clinical experience.

### In the Workplace

- You evaluate the values conveyed by proposed images for a new Web page.

### In Your Community

- You gather recent newspaper images of local teens to document the need for a community sports program.

❓ When have you responded to visuals in your writing? In what situations might you analyze images in future writing?

# Using Strategies for Visual Analysis

Just as you annotate or respond to a written text, do the same to record your observations and interpretations of images. Include a copy of the image, if available, when you solicit peer review or submit your essay. Begin your visual analysis by conducting a *close reading* of the image. Like a literal and critical reading of a written text, a close reading of an image involves careful, in-depth examination of the advertisement, photograph, cartoon, artwork, or other visual on three levels:

- **What is the big picture?** What is the source of the image? What is its purpose? What audience does it address? What prominent element in the image stands out? What focal point draws the eye?
- **What characteristics of the image can you observe?** What story does the image tell? What people or animals appear in the image? What are the major elements of the image? How are they arranged?
- **How can you interpret what the image suggests?** What feeling or mood does it create? What is its cultural meaning? What are the roles of any signs, symbols, or language that it includes? What is its theme?

For more on literal and critical reading of texts, see Ch. 2. For checklists for analyzing images, see pp. 285, 291, and 296.

As you analyze visuals, you may discover that your classmates respond differently than you do to some images, just as they might to a written text. Your personal cultural background and your experiences may influence how you see the meaning of an image. As a result, your thesis interpreting the meaning of an image or analyzing its effectiveness will be your own—shaped by your responses and supported by your observations.

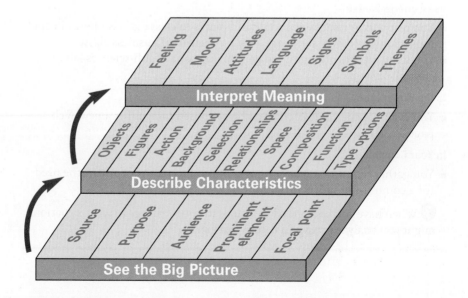

# Level One: Seeing the Big Picture

Begin your close reading of an image by discovering what you can about its origins and overall composition. If you include the image in a paper, you will need to cite the source and its "author" or artist, just as you would if you were including text from a reading, an article, or a literary work.

For more on crediting sources of visuals, see section B in the Quick Format Guide, pp. Q-7–Q-12.

## Source, Purpose, and Audience

Identifying the background of an image is sometimes complicated. For example, an image may appear in its original context or in a different situation, used seriously, humorously, or allusively.

- What is the context for the image? If it is an ad, when and where did it run? If it is a photograph, painting, or other work of art, who is the artist? Where and how has it been published, circulated, or exhibited?
- What is the purpose of the image?
- What audience does it aim to attract? How does it appeal to viewers?

## Prominent Element

Next, examine the overall composition of the image. Ask yourself, "Is there one prominent element—object, person, background, writing—in the image that immediately attracts my attention?"

Answering that question is easy for a visual that showcases a single object or person, as in Figure 14.1. There, the child is the obvious prominent element. Her dark eyes, framed by her dark hair, draw the viewer to her alert, intent expression. That expression suggests her capacity to learn from all she observes. The text above and below her image reinforces this message as it cautions adults to be careful what they teach children through their own conduct.

Identifying the prominent element can be more complicated for a visual showing a whole scene or inviting many interpretations. For example, what draws your eye in Figure 14.2 (p. 284)? Many people would first notice the neon sign on the left. The sign is bright, colorful (in a photo otherwise dominated by black and white tones), and framed neatly by the first window panel. People who read from left to right and top to bottom—including most Americans and Europeans—typically read photographs in the same way. For this reason, artists and photographers often position key elements—those they want viewers to see right away—somewhere in the upper left quadrant, drawing the viewer's eye into the image at the upper left corner. (See Figure 14.3.)

**Figure 14.1** Public service announcement with one prominent element.

EVERY TIME YOU SCREAM AT A DRIVER, SHE LEARNS A LESSON.

You're always teaching. *Teach carefully.*

www.ACTAgainstViolence.org

MetLife Foundation

**Figure 14.2 (top)** Photograph by Ian Pool. *All photos on this page: Ian Pool.*

**Figure 14.3 (above left)** Photograph divided into quarters.

**Figure 14.4 (above right)** Z pattern often used to read images.

**Figure 14.5 (right)** Close-up detail of photograph.

## Focal Point

There is another reason the reader's eye might be drawn first to the neon sign on the left in Figure 14.2. This simple yet bold sign communicates much about the place as a whole, announcing it to be an inexpensive, down-to-earth restaurant, offering simple fare. It probably opens early and stays open late, maybe even all night, serving average people of modest means. As a focal point, therefore, this sign sets up an important point of contrast with the unusual customer seated at the right. Because of the left-to-right and top-to-bottom reading pattern, most of us view photographs in a Z pattern, as shown in Figure 14.4. Thus, the bottom right corner of an image is a second important position that a skilled photographer can use to hold viewers' attention. When you look at the "big picture," you can see an image's overall composition, identify its prominent element, and determine its focal point.

---

**VISUAL ANALYSIS CHECKLIST**

### Seeing the Big Picture

- ☐ What is the source of the image? What is its purpose and audience?

- ☐ What prominent element in the image immediately attracts your attention? How and why does it draw you into the image?

- ☐ What is the focal point of the image? How does the image direct your attention to this point? What path does your eye follow as you observe the image?

---

## Learning by Doing 🔟 Seeing the Big Picture

Working with a classmate or a small group, select another image in this book such as one that opens or closes a chapter. Consider the image's purpose and audience (in its original context or in this book), but concentrate on its prominent element, which draws the viewer's eye, and its focal point, which suggests the center of its action or moment. Share analyses in a class discussion, or report or post yours for another group.

# Level Two: Observing the Characteristics of an Image

As you read a written text literally, you become aware of what it presents, what it means, and how it applies in other situations. Similarly, your close reading of an image includes observing its *denotative* or literal characteristics. At this stage, you focus on exactly what the image depicts — observing it objectively — rather than probing what it means or signifies.

## Cast of Characters

**Objects.** Examine the condition, colors, sizes, functions, and positions of the objects included in the image. In Figure 14.2, for example, the main object outside is a luxurious black car, parked at the far right. Though little of the car is visible, its sleek design, wide tire, and position near the Batman figure mark it as the iconic Batmobile. In contrast, the objects inside the restaurant are mundane and predictable: a trash can, three potted plants, a narrow blue cash machine, tables and chairs, stainless steel food-service machines, a napkin dispenser, and stacks of empty cups.

**Figures.** Look closely at any figures (people, animals) in the image. Consider facial expressions, poses, hairstyles and colors, ages, sexes, ethnicity, possible education or occupation, apparent relationships, and so on.

Figure 14.2 shows a lone, seated man, framed by the window panel and silhouetted against the white floor-to-ceiling blinds. The man wears a black cape, a close-fitting, rubberized suit, a wide gold belt, gloves, and boots, an outfit that accentuates his muscled physique. A mask hides all but the lower part of his face. Like no other detail, the mask's large, pointy ears identify the figure as the comic-book superhero Batman.

## Story of the Image

**Action.** The action shown in an image suggests its "plot" or story, the events surrounding the moment it captures. Figure 14.2 shows Batman eating a quick dinner or late-night snack. It suggests his earlier actions driving to the place, parking outside, ordering his food, and taking a seat at a small corner table.

**Background.** The background in an image shows where and when the action takes place. In Figure 14.2, the background is a bagel and donut shop on a winter night. This eatery—well lit and ordinary—sharply contrasts with its only customer, the figure of Batman, who is dark and mysterious, both in costume and mission. Because he is usually engaged in dangerous and high-minded crime-fighting crusades, the background seems designed to surprise viewers, who might ask, "What is the Dark Knight doing in a place like this?" Beyond the physical details of the photograph's background, fans will know that Batman is the secret disguise of the billionaire industrialist-playboy Bruce Wayne, a man traumatically orphaned who has vowed to devote his life to bringing criminals to justice. For anonymity, he does his crime-fighting and detective work clothed in the mystique and costume of Batman, a creature of the night. Throughout all his comic-book exploits, he is known for his intelligence, athleticism, command of technology, sense of justice—and damaged psyche.

## Design and Arrangement

**Selection of Elements.** When you look at the design of an image, reflect on both the elements included and their organization.

- What are the major colors and shapes? How are they arranged?
- Does the image look balanced? Are light and dark areas symmetrical?
- Does the image appear organized or chaotic?
- Is one area darker (heavier) or brighter (lighter) than other areas?
- What emotion, historical period, or memory does the image evoke?

In Figure 14.2, the shapes and colors are arranged so that the building's interior looks like daytime — bright, safe, warm, and cozy — which accentuates the cold, dark, and dangerous night outside. The bright areas in the middle of the photograph are surrounded by shadowy spaces with Batman sitting on the edge between the two. In this way, the image balances light and dark. Batman has come in for a few moments, but the photo's organization still connects him with the inhospitable world outside.

**Relationship of Elements.** Visual elements may be related to one another or to written text that appears with them. In Figure 14.2, for instance, the sign identifies a familiar, everyday location. However, the four big plate glass window panels, stretching across the front of the shop, suggest the way that drawings in a comic book march across a page, separated into neat rectangular frames. But here, no "thought balloon" emerges from Batman's head, allowing viewers to share his thoughts and learn why he is out of context. The photograph is arranged to raise, not answer, the question of what Batman is doing here. It invites viewers to interpret what is happening, to insert their own thought balloons over Batman's head. At the same time, it makes the point that we rarely know other people's stories, thoughts, and interior lives. When we see strangers in public settings, they are essentially unknowable, as this figure is.

**Use of Space.** An image may be surrounded by "white space" — empty space without text or graphics — or it may be "busy," filled with visual and written elements. Effective white space provides relief from a busy layout or directs the reader's eye to key elements. The image in Figure 14.2 uses the white-tiled wall above the counter and the white blinds to set off the shadowy darkness. Figure 14.6 (p. 288) specifically uses empty white space to call attention to the Volkswagen's small size. When this advertisement was produced back in 1959, many American cars were large and heavy. The VW, a German import, provided consumers with an alternative, and the advertising emphasized this contrast.

**Figure 14.6** Volkswagen advertisement, 1959.

## Artistic Choices

Whatever the form of an image, the person who composes it considers its artistic effect, function, and connection to related text.

**Composition Decisions.** Aesthetic or artistic choices may vary with the designer's preferences and the characteristics of the medium. A photographer might use a close-up, medium, or wide-angle shot—and also determine the angle of the shot, the lighting, and the use of color. Compare Figures 14.2 and 14.5 to

**Figure 14.7** Chevrolet advertisement, 1955. Advertising Archive/Courtesy Everett Collection.

see how a close-up may leave out context but accent detail, such as Batman's white cup. On the other hand, in the Volkswagen ad (Figure 14.6), the white space creates the effect of a long shot taken from below with a telephoto lens. We see the car as it might appear through the wrong end of a pair of binoculars. This vantage point shrinks the car so that the small vehicle looks even smaller.

**Function Decisions.** An image that illustrates a point needs to serve the overall purpose of the document. In other words, form should follow function. Of the many illustrations available—photographs, drawings, charts, graphs,

For sample presentation visuals, see pp. 335–36 and 353. For a sample brochure, see pp. 351–52. For sample tables and figures, see B (pp. Q-7–Q-12) in the Quick Format Guide. For sample photographs, turn to the images opening Chs. 4–12 and 25–29.

tables—certain types are especially suited to certain functions. For example, the 1955 Chevrolet ad, Figure 14.7 (p. 289), shows people having a good time enjoying a summer day near the shore. This illustration suggests that Chevrolet purchasers will enjoy life, a notion that undoubtedly suits the advertiser's goals. Likewise, a pie chart effectively conveys parts of a whole, while a photograph captures the drama and intensity of the moment—a child's rescue, a family's grief, an earthquake's toll. When you look at visuals in publications, consider how they function and why the writer might have chosen them.

**Typeface Options.** Many images, especially advertisements, combine image and text, using the typeface to set a mood and convey an impression. For example, Times New Roman is a common typeface, easy to read and somewhat conservative, whereas *Freestyle Script* is considered informal—almost playful—and looks handwritten. Any printed element in an image may be trendy or conservative, large or small, in relation to the image as a whole. Further, it may inform, evoke emotion, or decorate the page.

Look back at Figure 14.6, the 1959 Volkswagen ad. The words "Think small" are printed in a sans serif typeface, one "without serifs," the small tails at the ends of the letters. This type is spare and unadorned, just like the VW itself. The ad also includes significant text across the bottom of the page. While this text is difficult to read in the reproduction in this book, it humorously points out the benefits of driving a small imported vehicle instead of one of the large, roomy cars common at the time.

In contrast to the VW ad campaign, the 1955 Chevrolet marketing strategy promoted big vehicles, as Figure 14.7 illustrates. Here the cars are shown in medium to close-up view to call attention to their length. Happy human figures in and beside the cars emphasize their size, and the cars are painted in bright colors, unlike the VW's serviceable black. The primary text below the scene is large enough to be read in the reproduction here. It asks which sporty Chevy would be most fun for the reader—the Bel Air Convertible, the Handyman Station Wagon, or the stylish Sport Coupe. Then some "fine print"—difficult to read in the reproduction—notes other features of each car, such as its top, interior, and power.

Other images besides ads use type to set a mood or convey feelings and ideas. Figure 14.8 is a design student's response to an assignment that called for using letters to create an image. The simple typeface and stairlike arrangement help viewers "experience" the word *stairway*. Similarly, the plain, slanted type in Figure 14.9 suggests movement toward the future, reinforcing the message of the words.

**Figure 14.8** Stairway. © Eunjin Kim, Samsung Art and Design Institute.

**Figure 14.9** Type that contributes to meaning. Andrew Dillon Bustin.

---

## VISUAL ANALYSIS CHECKLIST

### Observing the Characteristics of an Image

☐ What objects are included in the image?

☐ What figures (people or animals) appear in the image?

☐ What action takes place in the image? What is its "plot" or story?

☐ What is in the background? In what place does the action take place?

☐ What elements, colors, and shapes contribute to the design? How are they arranged or balanced? What feeling, memory, or association is evoked?

☐ How are the pictorial elements related to one another? How are they related to any written material? What do these relationships tell you as a viewer?

☐ Does the image include white space, fill its space, or seem busy?

☐ What composition decisions has the designer or artist made? What type of shot, shot angle, lighting, or color is used?

☐ What is the function of the image? How does form support function?

☐ What typefaces are used? What impressions do they convey?

---

---

## Learning by Doing  Observing Characteristics

Working with a classmate or a small group, continue analyzing the image you selected for the activity on page 285. Examine a major characteristic—such as characters, story, design, or artistic choices—to determine exactly what it shows. Report or post your conclusions for your class or another group.

---

# Level Three: Interpreting the Meaning of an Image

When you read a written text analytically, you examine its parts from different angles, synthesize the material by combining it with related information, and finally evaluate or judge its significance. When you interpret an image, you do much the same, actively examining what the image *connotes* or suggests, speculating about what it means.

Because interpretation is more personal than observation, this process can reveal deep-seated individual and cultural values. In fact, interpreting an image is sometimes emotional or difficult because it may require you to examine beliefs that you are unaware of holding. You may even feel that too much is being read into the image because the process takes patience.

Like learning to read critically, learning to interpret images is a valuable skill. When you give an image a close, patient, in-depth examination, you can often deepen your understanding of its creator's artistic, political, economic, or other motives. You can also become more aware of the cultural values and personal views you bring to an image and gain a better sense of why you respond to it as you do.

## General Feeling or Mood

To begin interpreting an image, consider what feeling or mood it creates and how it does so. In Figure 14.2 (p. 284), the mood created by the photo of Batman is one of loneliness and isolation without even the companionship of someone working behind the counter. Yet the campy humor in the photo leads one to wonder whether the figure is an actor, a guest from a costume party, or somehow, improbably, the Caped Crusader himself. Is he waiting to meet someone? Has he stopped to relax after battling evildoers all night? Is he a regular or a one-time visitor?

Whatever the story, the image shrinks a superhero down to human size, simply having a snack. From the perspective of the photograph, the Batman figure looks relatively small and vulnerable, despite his imposing costume. He looks like someone who is resting and recharging his energy level but will soon go back out into the night. He suggests a policeman taking a break from his beat, or a worker or student on a coffee break. The image might be suggesting that in the real world, the superheroes are regular people, like us. Indeed, we all might be on heroic missions, just by going about our daily work, getting an education, raising children, and participating in community life.

Another image might capture or represent a different version of this feeling or mood. As Figure 14.10 illustrates, people take many kinds of breaks, finding carefree moments of escape in various ways. Perhaps Batman unwinds at a late-night donut shop while the people in Figure 14.10 enjoy a ride at a boardwalk and are lifted up on a short, circular detour from their normal routine. Here, a lighthearted mood predominates. The seated figures are not alone; some are paired off on the ride's gondola benches, with feet dangling. The soft colors of the sunset, which set off the palm trees in the background, infuse the scene with warmth although the ride's angular shapes might suggest a slightly menacing mechanical contraption. Although the mood of Figure 14.2 is wintery, and the mood of this photo is summery, both invite reflection on what it means to take a break.

## Sociological, Political, Economic, or Cultural Attitudes

On the surface, the Volkswagen ad in Figure 14.6 (p. 288) is simply an attempt to sell a car. But its message might be interpreted to mean "scale down"—lead a less consumer-oriented lifestyle. If Volkswagen had distributed this ad in the 1970s, it would have been unremarkable—faced with

**Figure 14.10** Photograph conveying a mood. Thomas Janisch/Moment Mobile/Getty Images.

the first energy crisis that adversely affected American gasoline prices, many advertisers used ecological consciousness to sell cars. In 1959, however, energy conservation was not really a concern. Contrasted with other automobile ads of its time, the Volkswagen ad seems somewhat eccentric, making the novel suggestion that larger cars are excessively extravagant.

Whereas the Volkswagen ad suggests that "small" refers to both size and affordability, the Chevrolet ad in Figure 14.7 (p. 289) depicts a large vehicle, "stealing the thunder from the high-priced cars." Without a large price tag, the Chevrolet still offers a large lifestyle, cruising in a convertible or vacationing at the shore. Figure 14.11 deliberately contrasts presence and

**Figure 14.11** Public service advertisement using a missing element to convey a message. Feeding America, 360i and the Ad Council.

absence, with a missing spoon suggesting a missing meal for those suffering from hunger. What's missing also may be more subtle, especially for viewers who wear the blinders of their own times, circumstances, or expectations. For example, viewers of today might readily notice the absence of people of color in the 1955 Chevrolet ad. An interesting study might investigate what types of magazines originally carried this ad, whether their readers recognized what was missing, and whether (and how) Chevrolets were also advertised in publications aimed at Asian, African, or Spanish-speaking Americans.

## Language

Just as you examine figures, colors, and shapes in an image, so you need to examine its words, phrases, and sentences to interpret what it suggests. Does its language provide information, generate an emotional response, or do both? Do its words repeat a sound or concept, signal a comparison (such as a "new, improved" product), carry sexual overtones, issue a challenge, or offer a philosophy of life? The words in the center of the Chevolet ad in Figure 14.7 (p. 289) associate the car with a sporty, fun-filled lifestyle. On the other hand, VW's "Think small" ad in Figure 14.6 turns compactness into a goal, a desirable quality in a car and, by extension, in life.

Frequently advertisements employ wordplay—lighthearted or serious—to get their messages across. Consider the public service advertisement in Figure 14.12. The billboard shows a romantic—indeed, a seductive—scene. The sophisticated couple gaze deeply into each other's eyes as the man kisses the woman's hand. However, the verbal exchange undermines that intimate scene and viewers' expectations about what happens next. Instead of a similar compliment in response to "Your scent is intoxicating," the billboard makes plain its antismoking position with the reply: "Yours is carcinogenic." In just seven words, the billboard counters the suave, romantic image of smoking with the reality of smelly, cancer-causing tobacco smoke.

## Signs and Symbols

Signs and symbols, such as product logos, are images or words that communicate key messages. In the Chevrolet ad in Figure 14.7, the product logo concludes the ad, promoting "motoramic" fun and power. Sometimes a product logo alone may be enough, as in the Hershey chocolate company's holiday ads with little more than a single Hershey's Kiss.

**Figure 14.12** Billboard showing wordplay. Bill Aron/PhotoEdit.

The "It's Not Like I'm Drunk" Cocktail

2 oz. tequila
1 oz. triple sec
1/2 ounce lime juice
Salt
1 too many
1 automobile
1 missed red light
1 false sense of security
1 lowered reaction time

Combine ingredients. Shake.
Have another. And another

**Never underestimate
'just a few.' Buzzed driving is
drunk driving.**

Ad
Council.org

U.S. Department of Transportation

**Figure 14.13** Poster conveying a theme.

## Themes

The theme of an image is not the same as its plot. When you identify the plot, you identify the story that is told by the image. When you identify the theme, you explain what the image is about. An ad for a diamond ring may tell the story of a man surprising his wife with a ring on their twenty-fifth wedding anniversary, but the advertisement's theme could be sex, romance, commitment, or another concept. Similarly, the theme of a soft-drink ad might be competition, community, compassion, or individualism.

Through close reading, you can unearth details to support your interpretation of the theme and convince others of its merit. For example, the image in Figure 14.13, appears to illustrate a recipe for a tasty margarita. However, the list of ingredients suggests a tale of too many drinks and a drunk-driving accident after running a red light. Instead of promoting an alcoholic beverage or promising relaxing fun, this public service announcement challenges the assumption that risky behavior won't carry consequences. Its text reminds viewers of its theme: well-being comes not from alcohol-fueled confidence but from responsible choices.

---

### VISUAL ANALYSIS CHECKLIST

#### Interpreting the Meaning of an Image

☐ What general feeling do you get from looking at the image? What mood does it create? How does it do so?

☐ What sociological, political, economic, or cultural attitudes are reflected?

☐ What language is included in the image? How does the language function?

☐ What signs and symbols can you identify? What role do these play?

☐ What theme or themes can you identify in the image?

---

## Learning by Doing 🎥 Reflecting on Images

Further examine the image you selected for the activity on page 285 and consider how the following are expressed: feeling or mood, attitude, language, signs or symbols, and overall theme. Write a reflection about the image. How does the image address these aspects? How is meaning created visually? Give a detailed account that explains how the image conveys meaning.

# Learning from Another Writer: Visual Analysis

Because visual images surround us, you may be asked to respond to them and to analyze them, concentrating on persuasive, cultural, historical, sociological, or other qualities. Logan Sikora analyzed a television commercial to investigate how advertisers influence our perceptions.

---

**Logan Sikora**                    **Student Analysis of an Advertisement**

## The Attention Test

The commercial for the 2015 Škoda Fabia has gotten a lot of media attention, [1] including headlines like this one: "You Won't Be Able to Take Your Eyes Off This Cheap Škoda Hatchback" (Sorokanich). Although this claim certainly is warranted, the attention viewers pay to the Škoda Fabia has little to do with the car and almost everything to do with the design and content of the commercial, an instructive example of how advertisers shape our perceptions to their advantage.

At the start of the commercial, the following words appear on the screen: [2] "The Attention Test" (Škoda). We are then taken to a street scene that features an unimpressive blue hatchback parked between a scooter and a black van, with shops in the background. (The car is the Škoda Fabia, an economy car built by the Czech subsidiary of Volkswagen.) At this point the voiceover begins, and throughout it the camera never veers from the parked Fabia:

> To test just how much attention the attention-stealing design of the new Škoda Fabia actually steals, we left one parked on this ordinary road in West London. We wanted to see if its sharp, crystalline shapes, bold lines, and lower, wider profile would attract the desired level of attention. Will the seventeen-inch black alloy wheels stop passers-by in their tracks? Will the angular headlights attract the attention of other road users? Will a crowd gather to check out its fresh, sporty look? Well, not quite. But did the attention-stealing design distract *you* from noticing that the entire street has been changing right before your very eyes? Don't believe us? Have another look. Did you spot the van changing to a taxi? How about the scooter changing to a pair of bicycles? Or the lady holding a pig? Let alone the fact that the entire street is now completely different. Didn't think so. So there we have it. Proof that the new Škoda Fabia is truly attention-stealing. (Škoda)

The narrator is right: it is likely that most viewers' eyes will stay trained [3] on the blue car, not noticing all the changes that take place in the background until the narrator points them out. The car remains the center of attention because it is the focal point not only of the camera but also of much of the narrator's commentary, which refers to the Fabia's "attention-stealing design," "sharp, crystalline shapes," and so on. The lesson here is that an automobile company doesn't need a sports car to attract this kind of attention; it just needs the right kind of advertising.

Viewers' focus on the car in the Škoda commercial is an example of selective attention, a result of the fact that we can pay attention to only so many things at the same time. As writer and psychology expert Kendra Cherry has noted, "Attention acts somewhat like a spotlight, highlighting the details that we need to focus on and casting irrelevant information to the sidelines of our perception." Effective advertising trains that spotlight carefully, setting our visual priorities to advertisers' advantage. 4

Another appealing aspect of the Škoda commercial is its tongue-in-cheek humor, from references to the "fresh, sporty look" of the plain-looking car to the mention of the "lady holding a pig." The advertiser wants us to feel as if we are in on the joke, while also making a pitch for the Fabia. As noted in a blog post from Lumen, an "attention technology" company, humor is an especially effective approach for reaching Millennials, an important audience for advertisers. 5

Given its design, content, and humor, the Škoda commercial certainly is appealing; more than that, it sheds an interesting light on strategies that advertisers use to attract, and hold, our attention. 6

### Works Cited

Cherry, Kendra. "What Is Selective Attention?" *About Education*, psychology .about.com/od/cognitivepsychology/fl/What-Is-Selective-Attention.htm. Accessed 5 Sept. 2015.

"Marketing to Millennials: Is It a Tougher Task?" *Lumen Research*, 8 Apr. 2015, www.lumenresearch.com/new-blog/marketing-to-millenials.

Škoda. *YouTube*, 26 Feb. 2015, www.youtube.com/watch?v=qpPYdMs97eE. Advertisement.

Sorokanich, Bob. "Video: You Won't Be Able to Take Your Eyes Off This Cheap Škoda Hatchback." *Car and Driver,* 4 Mar. 2015, blog.caranddriver.com/ video-you-wont-be-able-to-take-your-eyes-off-this-cheap-skoda-hatchback/.

## Questions to Start You Thinking

### Meaning

1. How does the commercial keep viewers focused on the blue car?

2. In what way is this focus an example of selective attention?

3. What other strategies does the commercial use to appeal to viewers?

### Writing Strategies

4. Where does Sikora introduce her thesis and her major supporting points?

5. How does Sikora ensure that readers know enough about the commercial to follow her discussion?

6. What different kinds of support does Sikora draw from her sources?

# Learning by Writing

## The Assignment: Analyzing a Visual Representation

Find a print or online advertisement that uses an image to promote a product, service, or nonprofit group. Study the ad carefully, using the three Visual Analysis checklists (pp. 285, 291, 296) to observe the characteristics of the image and interpret meaning. Write an essay analyzing how the ad uses visual elements to persuade viewers to accept its message. Include a copy of the ad with your essay or supply a link to it. If your instructor approves, you may select a brochure, flyer, graphic, photo essay, artwork, sculpture, campus landmark, or other visual option for analysis.

## Facing the Challenge     Analyzing an Image

The major challenge that writers face when analyzing an image is to state a clear thesis about how the image creates its impact and then to support that thesis with relevant detail. Although you may analyze the many details that an image includes, you need to select and group those that support your thesis in order to develop a successful essay. If you try to pack in too many details, you are likely to distract your audience and bury your main point. On the other hand, if you include too few, your case may seem weak. In addition, you need to select and describe your details carefully so that they persuasively, yet fairly, confirm your points about the image.

## Generating Ideas

Browse through print or online publications to gather several possibilities—ads that make clear appeals to viewers. Look for ads that catch your eye and promise rich detail for analysis.

As you consider how an ad tries to attract a viewer's attention, try several approaches. For example, think about the purpose of the ad and the audience likely to view it where it is published or circulated. Consider the same appeals you might identify in written or spoken texts: its logical appeal to the mind, its emotional appeal to the heart, and its ethical appeal, perhaps to trust the product or sponsor. Look also for the specific visual components analyzed in this chapter—elements that guide a viewer's attention, develop the ad's persuasive potential, and convey its meaning.

### DISCOVERY CHECKLIST

☐ What is the overall meaning and impact of the ad?

☐ What main points about the ad seem most important? Which details support each point most clearly and fairly?

☐ How do the ad's visual elements contribute to its persuasiveness? Which elements appeal most strongly to viewers?

## Planning, Drafting, and Developing

Begin working on a thesis that states how the advertisement tries to attract and influence viewers. For example, you might identify a consistent persuasive appeal used in major components of the ad, or you might show how several components work together to persuade particular viewers.

| | |
|---|---|
| WORKING THESIS | The dog food ad has photos of puppies to interest animal lovers. |
| IMPROVED | The Precious Pooch dog food advertisement uses photos of cuddly puppies to appeal to dog owners. |
| MORE PRECISE | The Precious Pooch dog food advertisement shows carefully designed photos of cuddly puppies to soften the hearts and wallets of devoted dog owners. |

**Point Out the Details.** Identify details — and explain their significance — to guide readers through your supporting evidence. Help them see exactly which visual elements create an impression, solidify an appeal, or connect with a viewer as you say that they do. Avoid general description for its own sake, but supply enough relevant description to make your points clear.

**Organize Support for Your Thesis.** As you state your thesis more precisely, break down the position it expresses into main points. Then list the relevant supporting detail from the ad that can clarify and develop each point.

**Open and Conclude Effectively.** Begin by introducing to your audience both the ad and your thesis about it. Describe the ad briefly but clearly so that your readers start off with an overall understanding of its structure and primary features. State your thesis equally clearly so that your readers know how you view the ad's persuasive strategy. Use your conclusion to pull together your main points and confirm your thesis.

## Revising and Editing

Exchange drafts with your peers to learn what is — or isn't — clear to someone else who is not immersed in your ad. Then revise as needed.

REVISION CHECKLIST

☐ Have you briefly described the ad as you open your essay?

☐ Have you stated your thesis about how the ad persuades its audience?

☐ Have you identified visual features and details that support your view?

☐ Do you need more detail about the ad's figures, action, or design?

☐ Do you need more on the feeling, attitude, theme, or meaning conveyed?

☐ Have you moved smoothly between each main point about the effectiveness of the ad and the detail from the ad that demonstrates the point?

After you have revised your visual analysis, check the grammar, word choice, punctuation, and mechanics — then correct any problems you find.

## EDITING CHECKLIST

☐ Have you used adjectives and adverbs correctly to present the ad?          **A7**

☐ Have you placed modifiers correctly so that your descriptions are clear?          **B1**

☐ Have you used correct manuscript format for your paper?

For more help, find the relevant checklist sections in the Quick Editing Guide on p. Q-37. Turn also to the Quick Format Guide beginning on p. Q-1.

# Learning from Another Writer: Visual Essay

Besides responding to visual representations designed by others, you might have opportunities to create your own series of images and text. Visual essays can record an event or a situation, or they can support an observation, an interpretation, or a position, usually through a combination of image and text or a multimedia text incorporating sound or video.

## Shannon Kintner                    **Student Visual Essay**

### Charlie Living with Autism

In this excerpt from a photo essay, we get a glimpse into the life of Charlie, a five-year-old boy diagnosed with non-severe autism. Shannon Kintner took this series while a student at the University of Texas, though not for a class nor as part of her job at the *Daily Texan*. She did the project on her own to learn more about autism, to gain experience, and to develop her portfolio, a collection of work that demonstrates one's interests and abilities. To view the rest of the slideshow, read a brief article about Charlie, and complete more activities, go to LaunchPad.

Mindy Minto, Charlie's mother, wipes pizza sauce off Charlie's shoulder during dinner one night. Charlie has echolalia, which means he repeats certain phrases to apply to all scenarios; he often says "popcorn, please" to indicate that he is hungry. Shannon Kintner.

A behavioral therapist guides Charlie's hand while writing his name. Charlie just wrote his name by himself for the first time in mid-April. Shannon Kintner.

Charlie plays with his dog, Lola, before dinner. Both of Charlie's parents have described the two as best friends. Shannon Kintner.

Kari Hughes, a behavioral therapist, asks Charlie to point out certain objects pictured on flashcards. His at-home therapy balances between a few minutes of playtime for every five achievements he makes, such as identifying flashcards or completing a puzzle. Shannon Kintner.

## Questions to Start You Thinking

Meaning

1. What story does the selection of images tell?

2. The photographer shows Charlie eating with his family, learning with his teacher, and playing with his dog. How does this variety enhance the viewer's experience?

3. Autism is a complex condition that can affect language ability, intellectual functioning, and behavioral patterns. Some symptoms often generally linked to autism include repetitive behavior; restricted interests; trouble having easy-flowing, "back-and-forth"-style communications; and difficulty with social interactions, which depend on the ability to read facial expressions and other cues. However, autism, as expressed in individuals, varies a great deal from person to person and from setting to setting, and it changes as a person with autism grows and develops. How does this photo essay help us to better understand—and to put a human face on—a word one often hears: *autism*?

Writing Strategies

4. How would you describe the nature of Kintner's written text? Why do you think that she uses this approach?

5. What is the effect of Kintner's title for her photo essay?

# Reviewing and Reflecting

To complete more review questions for Ch. 14, go to LaunchPad.

**REVIEW** Working with classmates or independently, respond to the following questions:

1. What are the three main strategies for conducting a close reading of an image? If you haven't done so already, try applying these strategies to an advertisement, to a photograph accompanying a news story, or to some other image. Make notes about what you discover.

2. What do you do when you interpret an image, as opposed to making a straightforward observation of it?

3. What is the major challenge of analyzing an image? How do you see yourself addressing this challenge? Jot down some possible answers.

**REFLECT** After completing one of the writing assignments presented in this chapter or supplied by your instructor, turn back to the After Writing questions on page 39 of Chapter 3 and respond to as many of them as you can. While addressing these questions, it might be helpful to revisit your response to the Learning by Doing activity on page 296, if you completed it.

Next, reflect in writing about how you might apply the insights that you drew from this assignment to another situation — in or outside of college — in which you have to respond to visual representations. If no specific situations come to mind, imagine that

- in an art history course, you decide to write about how emotions are portrayed in the paintings of the Early Renaissance artist Sandro Botticelli (1445–1510).

- you are an executive at a hotel chain that's preparing a new print advertisement for its beachside properties. The draft of the ad shows the exterior of one of these hotels, and there's no suggestion that the hotel is right on the ocean or that it is a vacation destination. You plan to write a memo that points out the problems with the draft ad and suggests better choices for images, use of color, typography, and so on.

In your reflection, consider the visual elements that seem most relevant to your purpose.

## Additional Writing Assignments

1. **Visual Activity.** Select an image such as an advertisement, a visual from a magazine or image database, or a CD or album cover. Make notes on its "literal" characteristics (see pp. 285–92). Then bring your image and notes to class. In small groups of three to five students, share your images and discuss your literal readings.

2. **Visual Activity.** In a small group, pick one or two of the images analyzed for activity 1. Ask each group member, in turn, to suggest possible interpretations of the images. (For guidance, see pp. 292–96.) What different interpretations do group members suggest? How do you account for the differences? Share your findings with the rest of the class.

3. **Visual Assignment.** Find a Web page that draws a strong emotional response. Study the page closely, observing its characteristics and interpreting its meaning. Write an essay in which you explain the techniques by which the page evokes your emotional response. If appropriate, you also may want to define a standard for its type of Web page and evaluate the site in terms of that standard. Include a link to the page with your essay.

4. **Visual Assignment.** Volkswagen continues to produce thought-provoking advertisements like the one shown in Figure 14.6 on page 288. Search online for some of the company's recent ads (try "VW" or "Volkswagen commercials"). View one or two ads, considering such features as their stories or "plots"; the choice of figures, settings, and images; the angles from which subjects are filmed; and any text messages included. Based on your analysis, decide what message you think that the company wants to communicate about its cars. In your essay, describe this message, the audience

For criteria for visual analysis, review this chapter. For more on comparison and contrast (Ch. 7), evaluation (Ch. 11), or other relevant situations, turn to Part Two.

that Volkswagen seems to aim for, and the artistic choices in the ads that appeal to this audience.

5. **Visual Assignment.** Compile a design notebook. Over several weeks, collect ten or twelve images that appeal to you. Your teacher may assign a genre or theme, or you may wish to choose examples of a genre such as snack food ads, portraits, photos of campus landmarks, or landscape paintings. On the other hand, your collection might revolve around a theme, such as friendship, competition, community, or romance. "Read" each image closely, and write short responses explaining your reactions. At the end of the collection period, choose two or three images. Write an essay to compare or contrast them, perhaps analyzing how they illustrate the same genre, convey a theme, or appeal to different audiences.

6. **Visual Assignment.** Prepare your own visual essay on a topic that engages or concerns you. Decide on the purpose and audience for your essay. Take, select, and arrange photographs that will help to achieve this purpose. (Use the guidelines in this chapter to help you evaluate your own photos.) Add concise complementary text to the photos. Ask your classmates to review your essay to help you reach the clearest and most effective final form.

7. **Visual Assignment.** Using the advice in this chapter, analyze an episode in a television series, a film, a multimodal blog, a YouTube or other video, a television or video commercial, or a campus theater, dance, or other production. Analyze the visual elements of your selection, and also evaluate it in terms of criteria that you explain to your audience.

For a sample essay responding to a film, see Ch. 11.

# Writing Online

## 15

Perhaps you are an experienced online writer—texting friends, chatting with family, updating your social-network page, and commenting on YouTube videos. On the other hand, perhaps you need help from coworkers or from younger or more experienced classmates to master new online tasks. Either way, you—like most college students—are increasingly likely to be an online academic writer. Many college classes are now offered in three formats, all likely to expect online writing:

- **face-to-face classes,** meeting in person at a set time and place but possibly with online communication and paper submissions
- **online classes** with synchronous (scheduled at the same time) or asynchronous (unscheduled, but available when convenient) virtual meetings, discussions, activities, paper exchanges, and submissions
- **hybrid (or blended) classes** with both in-person and online meetings, discussions, activities, paper exchanges, and submissions

In addition, any of these three class formats may rely on the campus course or learning management system (CMS or LMS), a Web-accessible environment where class participants can access information, communicate with each other, and post papers or other assignments. This chapter will review likely online activities in your current course, whatever its format.

## Why Writing Online Matters

### In a College Course

- You need to take a course offered only online, so you want to be ready to meet deadlines, manage files, and contribute to online discussions.
- You want to improve your online discussion contributions so that they sound more academic and professional.

### In the Workplace

- You need to help online customers in a friendly yet efficient manner.

**In Your Community**

■ You design an online tenant newsletter to unify your neighbors and help motivate your apartment manager.

❓ When have you done academic or professional writing online? How effective was this writing? In what situations might you need to do such writing in the future?

# Getting Started

Many schools provide an orientation program for new or returning students as well as directions for using online campus resources. Whatever the format of your course, you are expected to have or to gain technical skills sufficient to meet course requirements. Find out how to tap campus resources for immediate crises, self-help tutorials, and technology consultation. In addition, your instructors will supply a syllabus, course policies, assignments, assessment criteria, and other information for each course. Especially for online work, remember these two essential survival skills: read first, and then ask questions.

## Learning by Doing 🔟 Reflecting on an Online Writing Course

If you are enrolled in an online or hybrid writing class, review your syllabus and assignments. How, if at all, does the course seem to differ from a traditional one in terms of the nature and amount of work assigned, the level of participation expected, the type of help available, and so on? Do you anticipate any special problems or challenges? Do any questions about the course come to mind? If you do have questions, make sure to get answers from your instructor.

## Class Courtesy

All of your classes—face-to-face, online, or hybrid—have expectations for conduct and procedures. Some rules, such as keeping food and beverages out of a computer lab or laptop-cart classroom, obviously protect the equipment for everyone's benefit. Although explicit rules may vary by campus or instructor, conduct yourself in ways that demonstrate your attentiveness, courtesy, and consideration for others. During a face-to-face class, avoid texting or taking phone calls. When technology problems inevitably arise, ask about solutions instead of blaming the online environment for snags. Online, consider both your tone and level of formality. Use the relative anonymity of online participation to advance your intellectual growth, not to make negative comments at the expense of others. Think twice before you post each message so you don't regret a hasty attack, a bad joke, a personal

## Common Interactive CMS or LMS Options

| CMS or LMS Options | Typical Functions | Components Your Class Might Use |
|---|---|---|
| **Course Materials** | Handy essential information, available online for reference anytime during the course | Course syllabus and calendar, required and background readings, online reserve readings coordinated with the library, optional sources and links, reading or writing assignments, directions for activities, class and lecture notes, study guides, assessment criteria, online tutorials, podcasts, videos, and Webliographies |
| **Course Communication** | Convenient and varied systems for course messages and discussions, limited to class members | Convenient e-mail (to the whole class, a small group, or an individual), notices about changes or cancellations, text messaging, social networking, chats, threaded discussions, paper exchanges, a comment system, and a whiteboard for graphics or drawings |
| **Class Profiles** | Individual introductions posted for all the class to read, establishing each person's online personality and presence | Descriptions of the individual's background, interests, or expectations of the class, possibly with a photo or other personal representation; possibly CMS or LMS reports on whole-class patterns to allow for timely improvements |
| **Threaded Discussions** | Series of related exchanges focused on a specific course topic, question, or issue (open to all classmates or only to a group) | Questions and comments exploring and thinking critically about a topic along with any subthreads that evolve during discussion |
| **Text Exchanges and Responses** | Drafts and final papers posted for response from other students or for assessment by the instructor | Overall responses to the strengths, weaknesses, and effectiveness of the paper as well as detailed comments noted in the file; possibly options for feedback requests |

revelation, or an emotional rant. If you are uncertain about what is appropriate, ask your instructor for guidelines, and observe the conventions of professional communication. Strive to be a thoughtful learner who treats others respectfully as colleagues in a learning community.

## Online Ethics

Respect class or campus guidelines for online text exchanges with other students. Treat each other courteously and respectfully, address others in an appropriate classroom manner, and follow directions designed to protect each other's privacy and hard work. Your instructor may provide cautions about sharing personal or confessional information, especially because your CMS, LMS, or campus may retain indefinite access to class materials.

In addition, find out whether your papers might be routinely or randomly submitted to a plagiarism-detection site. Be certain that you understand your campus rules about plagiarism and your instructor's directions about online group exchanges so that you do not confuse individual and collaborative work. Further, use sources carefully as you do online research:

# Common Interactive Online Options

| Online Options | Typical Functions | Applications Your Class Might Use |
|---|---|---|
| **Class Blogs** | Individual or collaborative blogs or journals for a sequence of public (whole class) or private (small group or instructor) comments on a topic or theme | Regular comments to encourage writing, reflecting, exploring, analyzing, and sharing ideas that could evolve into more fully developed written pieces |
| **Class Wiki** | An encyclopedia of collaborative entries explaining terms relevant to a course topic or issue | An existing or evolving set of essential key terms, activities, concepts, issues, or events |
| **Class Ning** | Private social network for class members (as a whole or in special-interest groups) to share information and exchange ideas | List of relevant campus or community events, participant profiles, and a forum or blog to comment on key topics |
| **Text Exchanges** | Texts submitted for response from others through messages with attached files (to use software to add comments) or a real-time document-sharing Web site (to use its comment system) | Overall comments on strengths, weaknesses, and effectiveness; suggestions noted in the file (perhaps color-coded by respondent); one-on-one exchanges, such as questions and answers, about a draft |
| **Audio Applications** | Recorded spoken comments, including responses to drafts, in-person group discussions, presentation or podcast practices, podcasts, course lectures, or interviews | Verbal comments to strengthen personal connections, recorded by the instructor or peers for one student or a group; class interviews of content or research experts (authors, librarians, faculty) |
| **Visual Applications** | Organized and archived photos, videos, Web shots, or other images | Visual materials to prompt, inform, illustrate texts, or add to presentation software |
| **Course Resources** | Public social-network page, department Web page, program resources, library Web site, open-source materials, online writing lab (OWL), Web pages | Opportunities for building a supportive online academic group and accessing recommended course resources |

For more about using sources, see the Quick Research Guide beginning on p. Q-20.

- Distinguish your writing and your ideas from those of sources so that you avoid blurring or confusing the two.
- Keep track of sources so that you can credit their words and ideas accurately, following the style expected by your instructor.
- Respect intellectual property rights by asking permission and crediting sources if you integrate someone else's images or media in your paper.

## Learning by Doing 📷 Making Personal Rules

Using brainstorming or mapping, develop the list of rules only you know that you need — rules to bring out your best as an online student or writer. For example, do you need a personal "rule" about checking for your USB drive, card, or portable hard drive after every computer session on campus so you don't lose your work? Or do you need a "rule" about backing up files? List your rules in an e-mail message to yourself. Then sum up the most important points, using your software's word count tool to limit this statement to the 140 characters allowed by Twitter for a tweet. If you wish, also note your "rules" in your cell phone notepad for quick reference along with your online course PIN number, if needed. Return to standard English — correct grammar, punctuation, capitalization, and complete words, not abbreviations — for material submitted to your instructor.

# Common Online Writing Situations

The expectations for your college writing may be the same whether you hand in a printed paper during class, send the file to your instructor, or post your work in a CMS or LMS. Some assignments might specify required, encouraged, or accepted online features such as links for references or multimedia components. For other online writing, consider the conventions — accepted practices readers are likely to expect — and the class directions.

## Messages to Your Instructor

Learning online requires a lot of communication. Because you aren't meeting — and communicating — face-to-face, you need to engage actively in other types of exchanges. First, welcome available communication by reading posted assignments and directions that advise you about how to meet expectations successfully. Next, initiate communication, asking specific questions online about what to do and how to do it.

When you e-mail your instructor with a question, practice respectful professional communication. Think about your audience — a hardworking teacher who probably posts many class materials and responds to many questions from students in different courses. You can guess that a busy instructor appreciates a direct question from a motivated student who wants help. Ask specific questions well before deadlines, and give your instructor plenty of time to reply. Consider your tone so that you sound polite, interested, and clear about what you need to know.

| | |
|---|---|
| VAGUE | I don't know how to start this assignment. |
| SPECIFIC | I've listed my ideas in a scratch outline, but I'm not sure what you mean by . . . |

If your class uses a CMS or LMS, send your message through that system (unless your instructor asks you to use his or her campus e-mail address). Right away your instructor will know which class you're in and, in a small composition class, recognize you by your first name. If you e-mail outside the CMS, send the message from your campus account, and use the subject line to identify the course name or number and your problem: Deadline for Comp 101 Reading, or Question about Math 110 Study Guide.

If you are unsure how to address your instructor, begin with "Hello, Professor Welton" or "Hi, Ms. Welton," following the instructor's preference if known. Avoid too much informality, such as greeting your instructor with "Yo, Prof" or "Hiya, Chief," asking "Whatzup with the paper?" or closing with "Later." Conclude with your name (including your last name and a section number if the class is large).

Proofread and spell-check your message before you send it so that your writing does not look hasty or careless. Consider setting it to return an automatic "read" confirmation when the recipient opens it so that you do not need to e-mail again to check its arrival. Avoid e-mailing from a personal account that might be mistaken for spam and blocked from the campus system. Remember that your instructor's relationship with you is professional, not social; do not send social-networking invitations or forward humorous stories or messages about politics, religion, or other personal topics.

## Learning by Doing 🗓 Finding a College Voice

Working with a small group in person or online, list at least a dozen popular greetings, closings, and other expressions currently part of your (or your friends') informal voice in text messaging, social networking, or other informal electronic communication. Translate each expression into a clear, polite version without abbreviations, shortcuts, or unconventional spelling or grammar — in short, a version appropriate for a message to an instructor in your "college" voice.

## Learning from Other Writers: Messages to Your Instructor

Here are two requests sent to the students' instructor in an online composition class, one asking about how to cite an assigned reading and the other about the instructor's comments on a draft.

STUDENT QUESTION ABOUT AN ASSIGNMENT

From: Heather Church

Subject: Reading Response

Hi, Ms. Beauchene,

I want to make sure I am doing this assignment correctly. Is the source an online newspaper article? Also, I can't find out how to cite part of a sentence included in my response. If I quote "binge drinking," for example, do I have to say the page number next to it? I thought that I would cite this as if it is an article with no author. Is that correct?

Thank you.

Heather

STUDENT QUESTION ABOUT COMMENTS ON A DRAFT

From: Arthur Wasilewski

Subject: Comments on Last Paper

Hello, Professor Beauchene,

I would like to ask you a question about your corrections. You changed the last sentence of the last paragraph. I was wondering if you could explain the change. Is it something structural or grammatical? Or was it changed for the sake of style or flow?

Arthur

## Questions to Start You Thinking

### Meaning

1. Why is Heather Church contacting the instructor? What does she want to know?

2. Why is Arthur Wasilewski contacting the instructor? What does he want to know?

### Writing Strategies

3. What impression on their instructor do you think that the students wanted to make? What features of their messages indicate this?

## Learning by Doing 🔲 Contacting Your Instructor

Write an e-mail to your instructor requesting information. For example, you might have a question about requirements, assessment criteria for your first essay, procedures for activities such as timed quizzes, or policies such as penalties for late work. Clearly and briefly specify what you want to know. As you ask your question, also try to show your instructor that you are a thoughtful, hardworking learner. Exchange drafts with classmates to learn what they would suggest to make your question clearer or your tone more appropriate.

## Online Profile

Because you may never meet your online classmates in person, you may be asked to post a brief online profile introducing yourself to the class. You also might be asked to interview a classmate so that each of you can post an introduction of the other. Such assignments are intended to increase online camaraderie. However, if you feel shy or wish to retain anonymity, cover suggested topics such as academic interests or writing experiences, but stick to general background with limited personal detail. If you prefer not to post a photograph of yourself, consider an image or icon of a pet, possession, or favorite place. If the class already has much in common — for example, all in the same discipline or program — you might include your career plans. Avoid overly personal revelations, gushing enthusiasm, and clipped brevity.

The following profiles, illustrating a personal post and an interview, combine some personal background with academic and career interests.

From: LaTanya Nash

Subject: My Profile as a Future Nurse

After almost a month in the hospital when I was six, I knew that I wanted to be a nurse. That's when I found out how important nurses are to patients and how much they can add to a patient's recovery. I've had after-school and summer jobs in an assisted living center for seniors and a center for children with disabilities. Now that I'm starting college, I'm ready to work on my nursing degree. I'm glad to have this writing class because I've learned from my jobs how important it is for nurses to write clearly.

## Learning by Doing  Reflecting on Your Social Media Presence

Carefully review the content of your Facebook, Twitter, Instagram, or Tumblr account(s), trying to see it from the point of view of a college instructor. Then imagine that your instructor has asked you to create a profile on an online platform for your course. What information seems appropriate for a personal profile for a course, and what information might be irrelevant or off-putting to instructors or fellow students? Write a brief reflection about content you would include in the profile and content you would omit from it, explaining the reasons for your choices.

From: Lainie Costas

Subject: Interview of Tomas

After interviewing Tomas online, I want to introduce a classmate who has just started college this semester. He has been working since high school — doing everything from washing dishes to making pizzas. Now he's planning on getting a business degree to help him start his own restaurant. He already knows what employees need to do, but he wants to learn about things like business plans, finances, and advertising. Like me, he's a little worried about starting with a writing class, but I know from his messages that he has plenty of interesting things to say.

# Online Threaded Discussions or Responses

When you add your response to a topic in a threaded discussion, an interactive forum, or a class reading blog, follow your instructor's directions, and also read responses from classmates to clarify how to meet the assignment. Because everyone participating already understands the writing situation, you don't need to write a full introduction as you would in an essay. Instead, simply dive in as requested—for example, add your thoughtful comments on a reading, identify and explain a key quotation from it, or reflect on your own reading or writing processes. If you comment on a previous post, do so politely; clarify how your ideas differ without any personal criticism. Follow length guidelines, and be sure to proofread and spell-check your post.

# Learning from Other Writers: Threaded Discussion

The following string of messages begins with the instructor's explanation of the assignment—responding to an assigned reading in one of two specific ways—followed by a few responses of students. Notice how each writer responds personally but sticks to the focus by extending the "thread." Directions for other discussions might emphasize different ways to extend the thread—for example, responding specifically to a preceding comment, summarizing several comments and adding to them, synthesizing and then advancing ideas, raising a different but relevant line of consideration, comparing or contrasting possible responses, tracing possible causes and effects, or other paths that apply your critical thinking skills.

STUDENT ONLINE THREADED DISCUSSION

Instructor Kathleen Beauchene and Students Cristina Berrios, Joshua Tefft, Leah Threats, Arthur Wasilewski, and Joel Torres

Discussion of Writing Processes

**Message no. 2706**

**Author:** Kathleen Beauchene (ENGL1010_600_Beauchene)

**Date:** Saturday, October 10, 2:37pm

In the attached file, you will read about one author's writing process. In your post, you may either comment on a point he makes or share your own writing process, what works or doesn't work for you.

**Message no. 2707**

**Author:** Cristina Berrios

**Date:** Saturday, October 10, 4:02pm

I find that the author's writing process is similar in many ways to how most write, but I do not always have time to write and rewrite and organize and write and so on. . . . Of course I can see if you are a professional writer rewriting and making sure that your work can be produced to sell, but in my eyes I only need to make sure that my story is interesting, consecutive and progressive, and grammatically correct to the best of my ability. . . . Luckily I work in an office where I can interact closely with colleagues who are willing to listen to my "draft" (some of them are college students as well) and give me feedback.

**Message no. 2708**

**Author:** Joshua Tefft

**Date:** Saturday, October 10, 4:43pm

My writing process, like most people's, is similar to what the author does, given I have a lot of time anyway. I really have trouble with not erasing initial drafts, that is, incomplete drafts. I always find myself too critical of my work before it is anywhere near the final stages. But I've begun to learn to receive outside criticism before I put my own on it; this usually gives me a more open-minded perspective on my writing. But I've realized it's a long process to get the results one wants.

**Message no. 2709**

**Author:** Leah Threats

**Date:** Saturday, October 10, 11:49pm

My writing process includes a lot of thought process before I go anywhere near writing a first draft. Then I begin to write and reread it a few times while in the first paragraph, change wording, cut and paste all over the paper. Then I will move on to the middle of the paper, make sure my introduction has enough to it, and the mid section is full of "beef." Then in the ending, I try to make sure I don't leave the writer thinking, What else? . . . I do take the time to make sure I am not shortchanging my reader. As a person who LOVES to read, I want to be able to draw the reader into whatever it is I am writing to them.

**Message no. 2711**

**Author:** Arthur Wasilewski

**Date:** Sunday, October 11, 1:41pm

I approach the writing process with a shoot-from-the hip mentality. Whatever comes to my head first is usually the right idea. I'll think about the idea throughout the whole day or week, and transcribe it to paper after I've gone through a few mental iterations of my original idea.

**Message no. 2713**

**Author:** Joel Torres

**Date:** Sunday, October 11, 8:21pm

After reading this attachment I realize there are some things I sort of start to do in my own writing process, but stop halfway or do not go through thoroughly. I have used the outline idea from time to time. I should go into more depth and organize the ideas in my papers better in the future though. The whole concept of sleeping between drafts does not sit well with me. I find that when I sit down and write a paper, it is best when I dedicate a couple of hours and get into the "zone" and let the ideas flow through me. If the paper is a research paper, I usually do best when I type it directly onto a word processor. When the assignment is an essay or something along the lines of a written argument or a literary work, I like to handwrite and then go back and type it after. Distractions for me are a huge issue; TV, other Web sites, and just lack of focus definitely hurt my writing and are obstacles I must overcome every time a written assignment is due.

## Questions to Start You Thinking

Meaning

1. What did the instructor ask the class to do in the discussion?

2. Highlight or jot down a few key words to sum up the approach of each student in the threaded discussion.

Writing Strategies

3. In what ways do the students show that they are focused on the "thread" that connects their contributions to the discussion?

---

**Learning by Doing** 📷 Joining a Threaded Discussion

Read the preceding sample online discussion of writing processes. Write your addition to the string, explaining your process — what works or doesn't work.

---

# File Management

Electronic submission of papers is convenient, saving trees as well as time. Writing online has immediacy—potentially a 24/7 audience, ready to read and respond to your writing. On the other hand, online college writing requires longer-term planning, especially to organize and manage files in classes that encourage revising drafts or developing a portfolio.

**Using File Templates.** No matter how you submit an essay or a research paper, instructors generally expect you to use MLA, APA, or another academic style accepted in the field. These styles specify page layout, font style and size, paragraph indentations, formats for citations, and many other details that determine both the look and the approach of the paper.

For sample pages, see the Quick Format Guide (pp. Q-1–Q-19). For sample source citations in MLA and APA style, see the Quick Research Guide, pp. Q-20–Q-36.

Instead of treating each paper as a separate item, set up a template for any style you are required to use in a specific class or field of study. Check your software menu for Tools, File, or Format, or go to Help for directions on making a template, a basic paper format with built-in design features. Refine the details, using samples and checklists in this book as well as your instructor's directions and comments on the format of your drafts. When you begin a new draft, call up your template, and start writing. The template will automatically format the features you have customized. If you need several templates, keep them clearly labeled in a template folder.

## Learning by Doing 🖰 Preparing a Template

Set up a template for your papers for your composition class or your portfolio. Follow your instructor's directions about the academic style to follow and any special features to add. Turn to the campus computer lab or writing center if you need help preparing the template or figuring out what it should include.

**Naming and Organizing Files.** Check your syllabus or assignments to find out whether you need to follow a certain system or pattern for naming your files. Such systems help an instructor to see at a glance who wrote which assignment for which class: Lopez Recall 101Sec2. If you are expected to save or submit your drafts or build a portfolio, you will want to add a draft number, draft code (noting a first draft or a later revision), or a date: Lopez Recall 3, Lopez Recall Dft, Lopez Recall Rev, or Lopez Recall 9-14-17. Remember that your downloaded essay will be separated from your e-mail message; be certain that the file label alone will be clear.

Even if you are not required to submit your drafts, it's a good idea to save each major stage as you develop the paper instead of always reworking the same file. If you set up a folder for your course, perhaps with subfolders for each assignment, your writing records will be organized in a central location. Then you can easily go back to an earlier draft and restore something you cut or show your development to your instructor if asked to do so. You also have a handy backup if you lose a draft or forget to save it to your flash drive (or forget the flash drive itself).

## Learning by Doing 🖰 Organizing Your Files

Consider how to best organize files for your courses. Review your sylla-bus to see if your professor has a system for naming files. Then sketch a directory structure for your current classes, and compare ideas with a few classmates, helping each other to improve file organization plans. A good file organization strategy is to start by creating the most general folder for a course (for example, "Comp 101") and then to create subfolders with informative titles, such as "Paper drafts," "Responses to readings," and "Other assignments."

**Inserting Comments.** When you need to exchange files with other students for peer responses, use your software menu (Tools, Options, or Inserts), try its Help feature, or find a tutorial on the class comment system—track-and-comment word-processing tools, CMS or LMS posts, or a document-sharing site with comment options. If the directions seem complicated, print the Help page, and refer to it as you learn the system.

A comment system typically allows you to use color to show cross-outs and additions or to add initials or color to identify comments in "balloons" in the margin. Less formal options include adding comments or a note at the end of a paragraph, highlighted in yellow. Be sure to send your peer response file on time with helpful suggestions.

## COMMENT CHECKLIST

☐ How do you post or send a draft for peer or instructor review?

☐ How do you access Help or a tutorial about adding comments?

☐ What do you do to turn the Comment function on and off?

☐ How do you add comments in the text and in balloons or boxes in the margins using the color that identifies you as a reader?

☐ What do you need to do to read, print, save, or delete comments?

☐ How do you access the file-exchange site your class uses?

☐ How do you record and identify your comments on other writers' papers?

☐ How do you retrieve your own draft with the comments of others?

**Polishing Electronically.** As you revise and edit a draft, use all your resources, online and off. Call up the assignment or syllabus. Review what is required and how it will be assessed. Reread any comments from your peers or instructor. Use the Find or Search menu to hunt for repeated errors or too many repetitions of a favorite word or transition. Use the spelling and grammar checkers in your software, CMS, or LMS, even for short messages, so that you always present careful work. If your concentration slips, go offline: print out your draft and read it aloud.

**Submitting Papers Online.** It's usually easy to walk into a face-to-face class and hand in a printed paper. Online, you might hit snags—problems with a transmittal message if your CMS, LMS, or e-mail system is down; problems with a drop box or forum that closes early due to an error or a power outage; problems with a file, attaching or remembering to attach yours or opening someone else's. Try to avoid sending an assignment two minutes before the deadline because a time crunch may increase problems.

Many instructors will see "the computer ate my homework" as a problem you should have solved, not an acceptable excuse for late work. If you have trouble transmitting a file, send a short separate message to your instructor to explain how you are solving the problem, or ask your instructor to confirm the file's safe arrival. (Instructors are likely to prefer that you keep explanations to a minimum, concentrate on solutions, and use an automatic "read" reply to confirm receipt.) If your computer has a problem, you are responsible for going to the lab or using another computer to submit your work on time. If your campus system is temporarily down, you are responsible for submitting your work as soon as access is restored.

No matter what software you use, "translate" your file to the required format — maybe Word (.doc or .docx) but often Rich Text Format (.rtf), a general format most word-processing software can read. Check your File menu for two different commands: Save (to save the file to the location where you routinely store class files) and Save As (to save the file in a different format, to a different location, or with a different name). If you consistently add the date at the end of the file name, you will simplify finding and sending the most current version. If you use the same name or same date for duplicate files in different formats, you also will know that they correspond. Once the correct file is properly formatted, attach it to your message. If your file is returned with comments from your instructor or classmates, give it a new name and date so it does not replace your original.

**Backing Up Your Files.** No matter how tired or rushed you are, always save and back up your work, preferably using several methods. Use a backup card, portable drive, smart stick, file storage site, or whatever is available and efficient for you. Label or identify your equipment with your name so that you could pull your drive out of the lost-and-found basket at the library or someone could arrange to return it to you.

If you are working on a campus computer, carry your drive with you on a neck strap or clipped to your backpack so that your current work is always with you. If you are working on a major project with a tight deadline, attach major drafts to an e-mail to yourself. If you back up your files at home or in your room, do so every day. Then, if a file is damaged or lost, your hard drive fails during finals week, or you leave your drive at the library, you can still finish your writing assignments on time.

---

### FILE CHECKLIST

☐ What academic style and paper format is expected in your class? Have you prepared a template or file format in this style?

☐ Have you saved the files that show your paper's development during several drafts? Have you named or dated them so that the sequence is clear?

☐ Have you named a file you are submitting as directed? Have you used Save As to convert it to the required file format?

☐ Have you developed a file storage system so that you have a folder for each course and a subfolder for all related files for a specific paper?

☐ Do you carry a flash drive or other storage device with you so that you can work on your papers in the computer lab or library whenever you have time?

☐ Do you consistently back up your files every time you write using a flash drive, portable drive, or other device?

☐ If a CMS or LMS is new to you, do you know — exactly — when your assignment is due? Do you know how to submit the file, confirm its arrival, and download your paper when it is returned with comments?

## Reviewing and Reflecting

**REVIEW** Working with classmates or independently, respond to the following questions:

To complete more review questions for Ch. 15, go to LaunchPad.

1. What are three typical formats for courses these days, and what do the formats involve?

2. What three things can you do to use source material ethically while conducting online research?

3. What are some good strategies to follow when sending messages to instructors? Are any of these strategies new to you? If so, consider trying them out in your next message to an instructor. Do you think they made the communication more effective? Why, or why not?

**REFLECT** After completing one of the writing assignments presented in this chapter or supplied by your instructor, turn back to the After Writing questions on page 39 of Chapter 3 and respond to as many of them as you can. While addressing these questions, it might be helpful to revisit your response to the Learning by Doing activities on pages 308 and 314, if you completed them.

Next, reflect in writing about how you might apply the insights that you drew from this assignment to another situation — in or outside of college — in which you have to communicate electronically. If no specific situations come to mind, imagine that

- in an economics course, your instructor has asked you to contribute informed views to a class blog about the benefits and drawbacks of globalization.

- you are a human resources professional, and on your company's intranet site, you must monitor and contribute to a discussion board about how to improve a corporate wellness program.

In your reflection, consider the strategies you would use to communicate as politely and productively as possible.

## Additional Writing Assignments

1. Begin a reflective electronic journal. Add entries daily or several times each week to record ideas, observations, thoughts, and reactions that might enrich your writing. Use your file as a resource as you write assigned essays. Post selections, if you wish, for class or small-group discussion.

2. Write a comparison-and-contrast essay based on your experiences with face-to-face, online, or hybrid courses. Consider starting with a table with columns to help you systematically compare features of the class formats, the learning requirements or priorities they encourage, any changes in your priorities or activities as a student, or other possible points of comparison.

3. Blog about your writing experience. Post regular entries as you work on a specific essay or writing project, commenting on the successes, challenges, and surprises that the college writer meets.

4. Establish a collaborative blog with others in your class about a key course topic or possible sources or ideas for your writing or research projects. Decide on a daily or weekly schedule for blogging.

5. Start a threaded discussion about resources for your course topic, current assignment, research project, or other class project. Ask contributors to identify a resource, explain how to locate or access it, evaluate its strengths, and describe any limitations.

6. Set up a small-group or class Wiki, encouraging everyone to identify terms, concepts, strategies, activities, or events of significance to the course, a common academic program, or a shared writing interest. Write and edit collaboratively to arrive at clear, accurate, and useful explanations of these items to help everyone master the course (or program) material.

7. Set up a class Help Board on your CMS or LMS, a place where a student can post an immediate problem while working on the course reading or writing. Ask participants to respond to at least two or three questions for each that they post. Ask your instructor to add advice as needed.

8. Working with a small group, use a document-sharing system to draft an essay or other project, giving all group members and your instructor access to the process. Work collaboratively through simultaneous or sequential drafting, using chat or other electronic messaging to discuss your work. When your draft is complete, have all participants (including

your instructor, if possible) share reflections about both the process and the outcome.

9. Use an available communication system (for example, for a Web-based telephone call, conference call, or video call; for a real-time online meeting; or for an audio chat) for a conversation with a classmate or small group. Set a specific time for the meeting, and circulate any materials ahead of time. The purpose of the conversation might be discussing a reading, responding to each other's current draft, reviewing material before an exam, or a similar group activity. After the conversation, write an evaluation of the experience, including recommendations for the next time you use the technology.

10. **Source Assignment.** Conduct some research using your college's online catalog. Look up several courses that you must or might take during the next few terms. What formats—face-to-face, online, or hybrid—are available for these courses? In what ways would the courses differ, based on the catalog or a linked description? How might each format appeal to your strengths, learning preferences, and educational circumstances? Write a short report that summarizes what you learn and then uses that information to explain which choices might best suit you.

11. **Visual Assignment.** Prepare graphics, take photographs, or identify images (credited appropriately) that contribute to one of the other assignments for this chapter.

# 16 Writing and Presenting under Pressure

Most college writing is done for assessment — that is, most of the papers you hand in are eventually evaluated and graded. But some college writing tasks exist *only* as methods of assessment, designed to allow you to demonstrate what you have mastered. You often need to do such writing on the spot — a quiz to finish in twenty minutes, a final exam to complete in a few hours, an impromptu essay to dash off in one class period. How do you discover and shape your ideas in a limited time?

This chapter provides tips for three types of in-class writing — the essay exam, the short-answer exam, and the timed writing assignment. It also covers online assessments, the writing portfolio, and the oral presentation, which may include software slides.

## Why Writing and Presenting under Pressure Matters

### In a College Course
- You write under pressure when you take reading quizzes in biology or annotate bibliography entries in history.
- You work under pressure as you prepare an oral presentation about your internship.

### In the Workplace
- You meet frequent deadlines as you justify your productivity and report on customer service problems.

### In Your Community
- You learn that the school board is about to vote on closing your child's school, so you need to alert other parents right away.

❓ When have you most often needed to write or speak under pressure? How might you reduce stress in such situations in the future?

# Essay Examinations

In many courses an essay exam is the most important kind of in-class writing. Instructors believe that such writing shows that you have examined material critically and can clearly communicate your thoughts about it.

## Preparing for the Exam

Some instructors favor an open-book exam in which you bring your books and perhaps your notes to class for reference. For this exam, memory and recall are less important than reasoning and selecting what matters. On the other hand, for a closed-book exam, you need to fix in your memory vital names, dates, and definitions. Either way, prepare by imagining likely questions and then planning answers. If your instructor supplies sample questions, pattern new ones after them. Look for main ideas and questions in relevant textbook chapters. Ask yourself: How do ideas relate? How might they be combined? What can I conclude?

# Learning from Another Writer: Essay Exam

To look at techniques for answering *any* exam question, let's take one example. A final exam in developmental psychology posed this question:

> What evidence indicates innate factors in perceptual organization? You might find it useful to recall any research that shows how infants perceive depth and forms.

David Ian Cohn sat back and thought over the course reading. What perception research had used babies for subjects? He jotted down an informal outline, took a deep breath, and wrote a straightforward answer.

## David Ian Cohn                    Student Essay Answer
### Response to Psychology Question

Research on infants is probably the best way to demonstrate that some factors in perceptual organization are innate. As the cliff box experiment shows, an infant will avoid what looks like a drop-off, even though its mother calls it and even though it can feel glass covering the drop-off area. The same infant will crawl to the other end of the box, which appears (and is) safe. Apparently, infants do not have to be taught what a cliff looks like.

Psychologists have also observed that infants are aware of size constancy. They recognize a difference in size between a 10 cm box at a distance of one meter and a 20 cm box at a distance of two meters. If this phenomenon is not innate, it is at least learned early, for the subjects of the experiment were infants of sixteen to eighteen months.

When shown various patterns, infants tend to respond more noticeably to patterns that resemble the human face than to those that appear random. This seemingly innate recognition helps the infant distinguish people (such as its mother) from less important inanimate objects.

Infants also seem to have an innate ability to match sight with sound. When simultaneously shown two television screens, each depicting a different subject, while being played a tape that sometimes matched one screen and sometimes the other, infants looked at whichever screen matched what they heard—not always, but at least twice as often.

## Questions to Start You Thinking

### Meaning

1. What is the main idea of Cohn's answer?
2. If you were the psychology instructor, how could you immediately see that Cohn had thoroughly dealt with—and only with—the question?

### Writing Strategies

3. In what places is Cohn's answer concrete and specific, not general?
4. Suppose Cohn had tacked on a conclusion: "Thus I have conclusively proved that there are innate factors in perceptual organization, by citing much evidence showing that infants definitely can perceive depth and forms." Would that sentence strengthen his answer? Why, or why not?

## Generating Ideas

When the clock is ticking away, generating ideas right on the exam sheet saves time. First read over all the questions carefully. If you don't understand what a question calls for, ask your instructor right away. If you are offered a choice, cross out questions you are not going to answer so you don't waste time on them by mistake. Annotate questions, underline important points, and scribble short definitions. Write reminders that you will notice while you work: TWO PARTS! or EXAMPLE OF ABORIGINES' RIGHTS.

**Outline a Concrete Answer.** Instructors prefer concrete and specific answers to those that wander in the clouds of generality. David Cohn's informal outline helped him cite evidence—particular experiments with infants—all the way through.

> Thesis: Research on infants is probably the best way to demonstrate that some factors in perceptual organization are innate.
> Cliff box—kid fears drop despite glass, mother; knows shallow side safe

Size constancy—learned early if not intrinsic
Shapes—infants respond more/better to face shape than nonformed
Match sound w/ sight—2 TVs, look twice as much at right one

**Focus on the Question.** Instructors prefer answers that are organized and coherent rather than rambling. Check the question for directive words that define your task: *evaluate, compare, discuss, explain, describe, summarize, trace the development of.* To put yourself on the right track, incorporate a form of such a word in your first sentence.

| | |
|---|---|
| QUESTION | Define socialism, and give examples of its main types. |
| ANSWER | Socialism is defined as . . . |
| ANSWER | Socialism is an economic and political concept, difficult to define because it takes many forms. It . . . |

## Planning for Typical Exam Questions

Most exam questions fall into types. If you can recognize them, you will know how to organize and begin to write.

For examples of many methods of development, see Ch. 22.

**The cause-and-effect question** asks for *causes, effects,* or both.

What were the immediate causes of the Dust Bowl in the 1930s?

Describe the main economic effects of a low prime interest rate.

**The compare or contrast question** asks you to point out similarities (*compare*), differences (*contrast*), or both. Directions to *show similarities* or *identify likenesses* ask for comparisons, while those to *distinguish, differentiate,* or *show differences* ask for contrasts, perhaps to evaluate in what respects one thing is better than the other. You explain not one subject but two, paralleling your points and giving both equal space.

Compare and contrast *iconic memory* and *eidetic imagery,* defining the terms and indicating how they differ and are related or alike.

After supplying a one-sentence definition of each term, a student proceeded first to contrast and then to compare, for full credit.

Iconic memory is a picturelike impression that lasts for only a fraction of a second in short-term memory. Eidetic imagery is the ability to take a mental photograph, exact in detail, as though its subject were still present. But iconic memory soon disappears. Unlike an eidetic image, it does not last long enough to enter long-term memory. IM is common; EI is unusual: very few people have it. Iconic memory and eidetic imagery are similar, however: both record visual images, and every sighted person of normal intelligence has both abilities to some degree.

**The definition question** requests explanation in many forms, short and extended.

> Explain three common approaches to parenting—*permissive, authoritarian-restrictive,* and *authoritative.* [Supply a trio of definitions.]

> Define the Stanislavsky method of acting, citing outstanding actors who followed it. [Explain a single method and give examples.]

**The demonstration question** asks you to back up a statement.

> Demonstrate the truth of Freud's contention that laughter may contain elements of aggression. [Explain Freud's claim and supply evidence to support it, maybe crowd scenes, a joke, or examples from reading.]

**The discussion question** isn't an invitation to ramble.

> Discuss three events that precipitated Lyndon B. Johnson's withdrawal from the 1968 presidential race.

Try rewording the question to help you focus your discussion.

> Why did President Johnson decide not to seek another term? Analyze and briefly explain three causes.

A discussion question may announce itself with *describe, explain,* or *explore.*

> Describe the national experience following passage of the Eighteenth Amendment. What did most Americans learn from it?

Provided you know that this amendment banned the sale, manufacture, and transportation of alcoholic drinks and that it was finally repealed, you can discuss its effects—or perhaps the reasons for its repeal.

**The divide or classify question** asks you to slice a subject into sections, sort things into kinds, or break the idea, person, or process into parts.

> Identify the ways in which each resident of the United States uses, on average, 1,595 gallons of water a day. How and to what degree might a person reduce this amount?

First, divide up water uses—drinking, cooking, bathing, washing cars, and so on. Then give tips for conservation and tell how effective each is.

> What different genres of film did Robert Altman direct? Name at least one outstanding example of each kind.

Sort films into categories—possibly comedy, war, drama, mystery, Western— and give examples.

**The evaluation question** asks you to think critically and present a judgment based on criteria.

> Evaluate this idea, giving reasons for your judgments: cities should stop building highways to the suburbs and instead build public lightrail.

Other argument questions might begin "Defend the idea of..." or "Show weaknesses in the concept of..." or otherwise call on you to take a stand.

**The process analysis question** often begins with *trace*.

> Trace the stages through which a bill becomes a state law.

> Trace the development of the medieval Italian city-state.

Both questions ask you to tell how something occurs or occurred, dividing the process into steps and detailing each step. The next question calls for the other type of process analysis, the "how-to" variety:

> An employee, late for work daily by fifteen to thirty minutes, has been on the job only five months but shows promise of learning skills that your firm needs badly. How would you deal with this situation?

**The response question** might supply a statement, a comment, or a quotation, asking you to test the writer's opinion against what you know. Carefully read the statement, and jot down contrary or supporting evidence.

> Was the following passage written by Gertrude Stein, Kate Chopin, or Tillie Olsen? On what evidence do you base your answer?
>
> > She waited for the material pictures which she thought would gather and blaze before her imagination. She waited in vain. She saw no pictures of solitude, of hope, of longing, or of despair. But the very passions themselves were aroused within her soul, swaying it, lashing it, as the waves daily beat upon her splendid body. She trembled, she was choking, and the tears blinded her.

If you were familiar with the stories of Kate Chopin, who specializes in physical and emotional descriptions of impassioned women, you would point to language (*swaying*, *lashing*) that marks the passage as hers.

## Learning by Doing 🎯 Asking Questions

Working by yourself or with a study group, review your study guide, class notes, textbook, or other material for an exam. Make your own list of likely questions, or review your instructor's list of sample questions. Consider each question, and identify its type, using the preceding list or adding categories. Then underline, circle, or highlight the key words that tell you what your answer needs to do.

## Drafting: The Only Version

When you have two or more essay questions to answer, block out your time roughly based on the points or minutes your instructor allots to each. Give extra minutes to a complicated question with several parts. Then pace yourself as you write. For example, wrap up question 2 at 10:30 and move on.

As you draft, give yourself room for second thoughts by writing on only one side of the page in your exam booklet and skipping every other line. Should you wish to add material later, you can do so with ease.

**Begin with the Easy Questions.** Many students find that it boosts their morale to start with the question they feel best able to answer. Unless your instructor specifies otherwise, why not skip around? Clearly number or label each answer as your instructor does. Then begin in such a way that the instructor will immediately recognize which question you're answering.

QUESTION

Compare and contrast the 1930s depression with the recession
of 2008 on.

ANSWER

Compared to the paralyzing depression that began in 1929, the recession
that began in 2008 seems like . . .

**State Your Thesis at the Start.** Try making your opening sentence a thesis statement that immediately makes clear the main point. Then the rest of your answer can back up that statement. Get started by turning the question into a statement and using it to begin an answer.

QUESTION

What reasons for leasing cars and office equipment, instead of purchasing them, can be cited for a two-person partnership?

ANSWER

I can cite at least four reasons for a two-person partnership to lease cars and office equipment. First, under present tax laws, the entire cost of a regular payment under a leasing agreement may be deducted. . . .

**Stick to the Question.** Throwing into your answer everything you have learned in the course defeats the purpose of the exam—to use your knowledge, not to parade it. Answer by selecting and shaping *what matters*. On the other hand, if a question has two parts, answer both.

Name three styles of contemporary architecture. Evaluate one of them.

**Stay Specific.** Pressed for time, some exam takers think, "I haven't got time to get specific here. I'll just sum this up in general." That's a mistake. Every time you throw in a broad statement ("The Industrial Revolution was beneficial for the peasant"), take time to add specific examples ("In Dusseldorf, as Taine notes, deaths from starvation among displaced Prussian farmworkers dropped from a peak of almost 10 percent a year").

## Revising: Rereading and Proofing

If you pace yourself, you'll have a few minutes left to look over your work. Check that your ideas are clear and hang together. Add sentences where new ones are needed. If you recall a key point, add a paragraph on a blank left-hand page. Just draw an arrow to show where it goes. Naturally, more errors occur when you write under pressure than when you have time to proofread carefully. Simply add words with carets (∧) or neatly strike them out.

When your paper or blue book is returned, consider these questions as you look it over so that you improve your essay exam skills:

### ESSAY EXAM CHECKLIST

- ☐ Did you answer the whole question, not just part of it?
- ☐ Did you stick to the point, not throw in unrequested information?
- ☐ Did you make your general statements clear by citing evidence or examples?
- ☐ Did you proofread for omissions and lack of clarity?
- ☐ On what questions do you feel you did a good job, whatever your grade?
- ☐ If you had to write this exam over again, how would you now go about it?

# Short-Answer Examinations

The *short-answer exam* may call on you to identify names or phrases from your reading, in a sentence or a few words.

> Identify the following: Clemenceau, Treaty of Versailles, Maginot line.

> Georges Clemenceau—This French premier, nicknamed The Tiger, headed a popular coalition cabinet during World War I and at the Paris Peace Conference demanded stronger penalties against Germany.

Writing a short identification is much like writing a short definition. Mention the general class to which a thing belongs to make clear its nature.

For more about defining, see pp. 426–28.

> Treaty of Versailles—pact between Germany and the Allies that . . .
> Maginot line—fortifications that . . .

# Timed Writings

Many instructors give you experience in writing on demand by assigning impromptu in-class essays. Their purpose is to test writing skills, not recall. Although time is limited, the setting controlled, and the subject assigned, your usual methods of writing can still serve you well.

**Budget Your Time.** For an in-class essay with forty-five minutes to write, try to spend ten minutes preparing, thirty minutes writing, and five minutes rereading and making last-minute changes. Plan quickly to leave time to get ideas on paper in an essay — the part you will be graded on.

For common types of exam questions, see pp. 327–29.

**Consider Types of Topics.** Often you can expect the same types of questions for in-class writings as for essay exams. Do what the key words say.

> What were the *causes* of World War I?

> *Compare and contrast* the theories of capitalism and socialism.

> *Define* civil rights.

Add your personal twist to a general subject, but note the key words.

> *Analyze* a problem in education that is *difficult to solve*.

> *Discuss ways to cope* with stress.

Standardized tests often ask you to respond to a short passage, testing not only your writing ability but also your reading comprehension.

> Thomas Jefferson stated, "If a nation expects to be ignorant and free, in a state of civilization, it expects what never was and never will be." *How* is his comment *relevant* to education today?

**Choose Your Topic Wisely.** For on-the-spot writing, the trick is to make the topic your own. If you have a choice, pick the one you know about, not one to impress your readers. They'll be most impressed by logical argument and solid evidence. Bring a broad subject down to something you have experienced. Have you seen traffic jams, power outages, or condos ruining beaches? Then write about increased population, using these examples.

**Think before You Write.** Despite your limited time, read the instructions or questions carefully, restrict your topic to something you know about, focus on a main idea, and jot down main points for development. If a good hook to open or conclude occurs to you, use it, too.

**Don't Try to Be Perfect.** No one expects in-class essays to read as smoothly as reports written over several weeks. You can't polish every sentence or remember the exact word for every spot. And never waste time recopying.

**Save Time to Proofread.** Your best-spent minutes may be the last few when you read over your work. Cross out errors and make neat corrections using asterisks (*), arrows, and carets (^). Watch for the following:

- letters omitted (-*ed* or -*s*), added (develop*e*), or inverted (rec*ie*ve)
- wrong punctuation (a comma instead of a period)
- omitted apostrophes (*dont* instead of *don't*)
- omitted words ("She going" instead of "She *is* going")
- wrong (*except* instead of *accept*) or misspelled words (*mispelled*)

---

## Learning by Doing 🎯 Thinking Fast

Practice planning quickly for timed writing or tests as a class. Brainstorm to explore approaches to sample topics provided in this chapter. Select one class member (or three, in turn) to record ideas on the board. Devote exactly ten minutes of discussion per topic. Focus on these key parts of a successful response:

- possible thesis sentences
- possible patterns of organization
- possible kinds and sources of evidence

Expect a wide range of ideas. Spend the last part of class evaluating them.

---

# Online Assessment

The outcomes or standards for assessing the qualities and effectiveness of a specific essay for a composition class are probably the same whether a course is face-to-face, hybrid, or online. On the other hand, online activities can significantly expand the options for class participation. If your class uses a learning or course management system (LMS or CMS) or has other online components, find out which activities are required and which recommended. Class sites or systems may track and report detailed data on participation such as the following:

For more on writing online, see Ch. 15.

- time spent online and active
- time and activity (even keystrokes) within class units and tools
- completion of tasks by the deadline or within the allotted time
- number of attempts to complete tasks
- quantity and quality of contributions to threaded discussions (sorted alphabetically to group each individual's contributions)
- number of correct multiple-choice or other objective answers

Also consider nonstatistical measures of your performance and your engagement. For example, suppose your instructor asks you to post a question about a challenging reading and also to respond to two questions from other students. You might receive credit simply for making a conscientious effort to do both, whether your answers were correct or not. After all, the purpose of the assignment is to generate discussion. On the other hand, if you are asked to submit your final, revised version of an essay, posting it before the deadline would be only the first step, followed by your instructor's assessment based on the criteria for the assignment.

Once you know the many ways that your online participation can be measured, you are prepared to view time online as a possible limitation or deadline, as well as a measure of effort and attention. You also are prepared to read assignment prompts more critically. For example, suppose you are asked to write a short answer to a question, perhaps with thirty minutes allowed and about 250 words (one double-spaced page) expected. How is your instructor likely to assess your 174 words written in nine minutes? How will your response compare with someone else's 249 words and twenty-nine minutes of attention? Will your instructor think that you felt pressured and rushed, ignored the implications of the directions, didn't care enough to use the time allowed, or simply said what you had to say?

# Oral Presentations

In many courses students make oral presentations. Individuals might summarize final essays, research reports, or capstone projects. Groups or teams might prepare pro-and-con debates, roundtable presentations of viewpoints, organized analyses, problem-solution proposals, or field reports. Such presentations require thoughtful written materials and confident oral delivery, perhaps using visuals prepared with PowerPoint or other software.

Because presentations draw on multiple skills, you may feel anxious or uncertain about how to prepare. You need to write under pressure, preparing a speaking script or notes as well as text for any presentation slides. You need to speak under pressure, making your presentation and possibly fielding questions. You may be assessed on both your prepared content and your actual presentation. Nevertheless, each presentation provides valuable experience, preparing you for future classes, job interviews, workplace reports, professional talks, and community appearances.

**Start Early.** Get organized, don't procrastinate, and draw on your writing strategies when a presentation looms. Review your assignment and any assessment criteria; be sure you understand what is expected. If you are reporting on a paper or project, finish it well ahead of the deadline. If your presentation requires separate reading or research, get it done early. If you are working with a group, establish a timetable with regular face-to-face meetings or online checkpoints so everyone is prepared. This advance work is necessary to leave time to plan the presentation as a separate activity—and avoid just walking in, looking disorganized or ill-prepared.

**Develop Your Oral Presentation.** As you work on the presentation itself, consider your audience and purpose, the time allotted, and the formality expected. Think hard about an engaging start—something surprising, intriguing, or notable to help your audience focus. Map out the main points appropriate for your audience and situation. Preview them so your words tell listeners what's major, what's minor, and what's coming up. Be selective: listeners can absorb only limited detail.

Instead of writing out a speech like an essay, record your main points on cards or on a page using easy-to-read type. Then practice—speaking out loud, timing yourself, revising your notes, testing your talk on a friend, or maybe recording yourself so you can catch rough spots. If you feel nervous, practice taking a deep breath or counting to five before you begin. Also practice looking around the room, making eye contact. Connecting with your audience turns anonymous faces into sympathetic people.

**Align Your Visuals.** As your talk takes shape, work on any slides or images for projection or distribution. Listeners appreciate concise visuals that support — not repeat — your words. If possible, project a few in the room where you will speak. Sit there, as your audience will, to see how large the type needs to be for easy reading. Try to align your slides with your main points so they appear steadily and appropriately. Aim for a simple, professional look without busy designs or dramatic colors. All this preparation will improve your presentation and reduce any fears about public speaking.

---

**PRESENTATION CHECKLIST**

☐ Have you developed your presentation as effectively as possible?

☐ Do you begin and end with an engaging flair?

☐ Have you stated your points clearly in an order easy to follow?

☐ Are your words, tone, and level of formality well chosen for the situation?

☐ Have you practiced enough to look relaxed and avoid getting lost?

☐ Have you taken a deep breath and looked around at your audience before speaking? Have you continued to make eye contact as you present?

☐ Have you projected your voice and spoken slowly so everyone could hear?

☐ Does your appearance — posture, dress — increase your credibility?

☐ Do you stick to the expected time, format, procedure, or other guidelines?

☐ Are your visuals clear, spacious, and easy to read?

☐ Do the design, text, and presentation of your visuals complement your talk?

---

## Learning by Doing 📷 Reflecting on Oral Presentations

Based on what you have read in this chapter, reflect on a previous oral presentation that you made in this or any other class, or for your job. What skills or suggestions from this chapter might have made your presentation better? What new skills might you apply as you prepare your next oral presentation? Write a paragraph reflecting on these strategies and how they might improve your presentation skills.

# Learning from Other Writers: Visuals for Oral Presentations

This series of images on urban design was prepared by a student for a face-to-face presentation in his geography class. As this student reported on urbanization, he showed slides with images of the ten most populous cities in the world as well as summaries of key points from sources on this topic. Traditional Urban Design, the example here, combines text and images.

**Andrew Dillon Bustin**    **Face-to-Face Class Presentation**

**Traditional Urban Design**

## TRADITIONAL URBAN DESIGN

❖ High residential densities
❖ Mixed land uses
❖ Gridded street patterns
❖ Land use plans that maximize social contact, spatial efficiency, and local economy

*Image credits: left,* Arthur Tilley/Stockbyte/Getty Images; *center,* David C Phillips/Garden Photo World/Corbis; *right,* The Granger Collection, NYC.

### Questions to Start You Thinking

Meaning

1. What information does the slide present?

2. How do the images relate to the words?

Writing Strategies

3. How does the slide try to appeal to an audience of classmates?

4. If the presenter were your classmate, what helpful comments would you make about his slide?

## Reviewing and Reflecting

To complete more review questions for Ch. 16, go to LaunchPad.

**REVIEW** Working with classmates or independently, respond to the following questions:

1. What are some good strategies for preparing for an essay exam? Which strategies have worked well for you in the past and why? Has this chapter introduced you to any other strategies that you would like to try?

2. What are some ways to draft strong responses to essay exams, even when there are multiple questions?

3. What are the key steps in developing an oral presentation? If you have made an oral presentation in the past, or if you are currently working on one, what has been the greatest challenge for you? In what ways might you address that challenge in the future?

**REFLECT** After completing one of the writing assignments presented in this chapter or supplied by your instructor, turn back to the After Writing questions on page 39 of Chapter 3 and respond to as many of them as you can. While addressing these questions, it might be helpful to revisit your response to the Learning by Doing activity on page 335, if you completed it.

Next, reflect in writing about how you might apply the insights that you drew from this assignment to another situation—in or outside of college—in which you have to write or present under pressure. If no specific situations come to mind, imagine that

- for a nursing course, you need to prepare for a closed-book essay exam on best practices for treating diabetic patients.

- you are an employee of a food-service company, and you need to give a presentation to a business that is considering your products and services for its cafeteria. You want to make the case that your offerings are superior to those of your competitors in terms of quality and cost-effectiveness.

In your reflection, consider strategies for meeting writing and presentation goals under deadline.

## Additional Writing Assignments

1. Review available information about an upcoming exam as well as advice about such exams in this chapter. Write a set of directions for yourself, explaining the process for preparing for your exam. (Follow your directions.)

2. Prepare for an examination by writing sample questions about major issues in the course. Then outline possible answers to these questions.

3. **Source Assignment.** Prepare an oral presentation on a topic approved by your instructor. Consider expanding on a recent essay, exploring a campus issue, proposing a change for your campus or workplace, or interpreting a distinctive community feature.

4. **Visual Assignment.** Prepare presentation slides or other visuals to project or distribute as part of an oral presentation such as assignment 3.

# 17 Writing in the Workplace

Most of the world's workplace communication takes place in writing. Although a conversation or voice mail may be forgotten or ignored, a written message provides a permanent record of a business exchange, often calling for action. This chapter first outlines some general guidelines for workplace writing and then shows you types likely to prove useful.

## Why Writing in the Workplace Matters

**In a College Course**

- You write job applications, memos, and letters in your business communications course.
- You prepare a compelling application — letter, résumé, and memo of understanding about your goals — for the summer internship program.

**In the Workplace**

- You personalize letters and e-mails to clients every day, providing company services.

**In Your Community**

- You write a letter of support for a grant proposal to open a high school health clinic.

❓ When have you already prepared workplace writing? In what situations might you do so in the future?

EFFECTIVE WORKPLACE WRITING

Respectful tone • Clear purpose

Concise, clear, well-organized presentation • Reader's point of view

## Guidelines for Writing in the Workplace

Good workplace writing succeeds in achieving a clear purpose. When you write to a business, your writing represents you; when you write as part of your job, your writing represents your company as well.

## Know Your Purpose

Your purpose, or reason for writing, helps you select and arrange information; it sets a standard for measuring your final draft. Most likely you will want to create a certain response in your readers.

DISCOVERY CHECKLIST

- ☐ Do you want to inform—announce something, update others, explain some specialized knowledge, or reply to a request?

- ☐ Do you want to motivate some action—get a question answered, a wrong corrected, a decision made, or a personnel director to hire you?

- ☐ When your readers are finished reading what you've written, what do you want them to think? What do you want them to do?

## Keep Your Audience in Mind

Consider all your workplace writing from your audience's point of view. If you don't know the person to whom you are writing, make educated guesses based on what you know about the position or company. Your purpose is not to express your ideas but to have readers act on them, even if the action is simply to notice your grasp of the situation. To motivate, focus on how "you, the reader" will benefit instead of what "I, the writer" would like.

| "I" ATTITUDE | Please send me the form so I can process your order. |
| "YOU" ATTITUDE | To make sure that you receive your shipment promptly, please send me the order form. |

DISCOVERY CHECKLIST

- ☐ What do your readers already know about the subject? Are they experts in the field? Have they been kept up to date on the situation?

- ☐ What do your readers need to know? What information do they expect you to provide? What do they need before they can take action?

- ☐ What can you assume about your readers' priorities and expectations? Will they expect a clear, efficient overview or detailed background?

- ☐ What is most likely to motivate readers to take the action you want?

## Use an Appropriate Tone

Tone is the quality of writing that reveals your attitude toward your topic and your readers. If you show readers that you respect them, they are far more likely to view you and your message favorably. Most workplace writing today ranges from the informal to the slightly formal. Gone are extremely formal phrases such as *enclosed herewith* or *pursuant to the stated request*. At the other extreme, slang, or a casual, overly friendly style, might cast doubts on your credibility. Strive for a relaxed and conversational style, using simple sentences and familiar words.

Observe business etiquette in courteous writing. If you have a complaint, recall that your reader may not have caused the problem—and courtesy is more likely than sarcasm or insults to motivate help. When delivering bad news, remember that your reader may interpret a bureaucratic response as unsympathetic. And if you have made a mistake, acknowledge it.

### REVISION CHECKLIST

- ☐ Have you avoided slang terms and extremely casual language?
- ☐ Have you avoided unnecessarily formal or sophisticated words?
- ☐ Are your sentences of a manageable length?
- ☐ Have you used the active voice ("I am sending it") rather than the passive voice ("It is being sent")?
- ☐ Does anything you've written sound blaming or accusatory?
- ☐ Do you hear a friendly, considerate, competent person behind your words?
- ☐ Have you asked someone else to read your writing to check for tone?

## Present Information Carefully

For sample business documents, see the figures later in this chapter. For more on adding visuals and formatting job applications, see the Quick Format Guide beginning on p. Q-1.

In business, time is money: time wasted reading poorly written material is money wasted. Organize so that readers can move through your writing quickly and easily. Make the topic absolutely clear from the beginning, usually in the first paragraph of a letter or the subject line of a memo or e-mail message. Use the conventional format that readers expect (see Figures 17.3 and 17.5 later in this chapter). Break information into easily processed chunks; order these chunks logically and consistently. Finally, use topic sentences and headings (when appropriate) to label each chunk of information and to give readers an overview of your document.

### REVISION CHECKLIST

For more revising and editing strategies, see Ch. 23.

- ☐ Have you kept your letter, memo, or résumé to a page or two?
- ☐ Have you cut all unnecessary or wordy explanations?
- ☐ Have you scrutinized every word to ensure that it can't be misinterpreted? Have you supplied all the background information readers need?
- ☐ Have you emphasized the most important part of your message? Will readers know what you want them to do?

☐ Have you followed a consistent, logical order and a conventional format?

☐ If appropriate, have you included labels and headings?

# E-mail

Because *e-mail* is so easy, speedy, and convenient, it dominates business communication. Communication advances — such as texting and tweeting — may simplify quick exchanges and arrangements. On the other hand, traditional letters and memos may still be preferred for formal, official correspondence. However, e-mail messages easily meet traditional needs because they can be (1) transmitted within organizations (like memos) or between them and other parties (like letters), (2) printed or stored electronically (like permanent file copies), (3) written with standard components and length (like traditional memos or letters), or (4) used to cover transmittals (with formal reports, memos, or other documents attached).

E-mail's conversational quality also necessitates professional caution. Although regular correspondents may write informally and overlook each other's quirks, your e-mail messages are part of your company's official record and have no guarantee of privacy. Without warning, your confidential exchange can be intercepted, reviewed by others, forwarded to other computers, distributed electronically, or printed.

## Format for E-mail

E-mail headings are predetermined by your system and typically follow memo format: *To:*, *cc:*, *Subject:*, and an automatic *From:* line with your name as sender. Write messages that readers find helpful, efficient, and courteous.

- Use a clear subject line to simplify replying and archiving.
- Move promptly to your purpose: state what you need and when.
- Be concise, adding headings and space between sections if needed.
- Follow company practice as you include or delete a trail of replies.
- Observe company etiquette in copying messages to others.
- Avoid personal statements, humor, or informality that might undermine your professional credibility.

# Résumés and Application Letters

The most important business correspondence you write may be the résumé and letter you use to apply for a job. In any economic climate — but especially in a weak one with reduced job prospects — your materials should be carefully developed and crafted. They need to reflect as many applicable skills and experiences as possible, including your summer, campus, part-time, or full-time employment as you attend college. First, prepare for job prospects by developing opportunities systematically, well before graduation:

- Turn to campus career services as well as local library or community resources to investigate job opportunities and career strategies.
- Consider internships or volunteer posts relevant to your goals.
- Attend preprofessional or career-oriented workshops or gatherings.
- Network with workplace and professional contacts to learn about your future options and prospects.

Remain flexible, too. Instead of looking only for the single job title you want, consider what other experiences might build your skills on your way to that job. For example, if you are in a public health program and want to join a major city health department, by all means gain expertise so you can pursue that job despite the city's recent budget cutbacks. But also consider rural or statewide positions, hospital outreach, companies with employee health programs, or the growing field of senior care. Take advantage of serendipity—the surprise that offers a new or unexpected option.

Finally, as opportunities arise, apply your college writing experience to the workplace in order to draft and revise effectively. Direct, persuasive, correct prose can help you stand out from the crowd.

## Résumés

For more on résumé format and another student sample, see the Quick Format Guide beginning on p. Q-1.

In a résumé, you present yourself as someone qualified to excel at a job and be an asset to the organization. Job seekers often have copies of a single résumé on hand, but you may want to customize yours for each application if you can easily print attractive copies. Either way, keep it to one page unless you have extensive relevant work experience.

A résumé is highly formatted but allows many decisions about style, organization, and appearance. A typical résumé consists of a heading and labeled sections that detail experience and qualifications. Highlight labels with underlining, boldface, or larger type. Within a section, use brief, pointed phrases and clauses, not complete sentences. Use action verbs (*supervised, ordered, maintained*) and active voice whenever possible. Arrange information to please the eye; use the best paper and clearest printer you can. (See Figure 17.1.)

For electronic applications, you may need a résumé in several forms: a text file for attaching to an e-mail, an electronically readable version for a company to scan into its database, or a Web version for posting on your site or a job site. Format these versions carefully so that recipients can easily read what you supply. Turn to your campus career center for résumé samples and advice about alternate formats.

**Heading.** The heading is generally centered (or otherwise pleasingly aligned) on the page with separate lines for your name; street address; city, state, and zip code; phone number; and e-mail address.

**Anne Cahill**
402 Pigeon Hill Road
Windsor, CT 06095
(860) 555-5763
acahill783@yahoo.com

Aligns heading with
contact information

Labels sections

| | |
|---|---|
| **Objective** | Position as Registered Nurse in pediatric hospital setting |
| **Education** | **University of Connecticut**, Storrs, CT. Bachelor of Science, Major in nursing, May 2015. GPA: 3.5; licensed as Registered Nurse by the State of Connecticut in June 2015 |
| | **Manchester Community Technical College**, Manchester, CT. Associate degree in occupational therapy, May 2009. GPA: 3.3. |

Specifies background
and experience

**Work Experience**

| | |
|---|---|
| *9/10–present* | **Certified Occupational Therapy Assistant**, Johnson Memorial Hospital, Stafford Springs, CT<br>• Assist children with delayed motor development and cerebral palsy to develop skills for the activities of daily life |
| *9/08–9/10* | **Nursing Assistant**, Woodlake Healthcare Center, Tolland, CT<br>• Helped geriatric residents with activities of daily living<br>• Assisted nursing staff in treating acute care patients |
| *9/06–9/08* | **Cashier**, Stop and Shop Supermarket, Vernon, CT<br>• Trained newly hired cashiers |

Places current
information first

| | |
|---|---|
| **Clinical Internships** | **St. Francis Hospital**, Hartford, CT<br>• Student Nurse, Maternity and Postpartum, spring 2015 |
| | **Hartford Hospital**, Hartford, CT<br>• Student Nurse, Pediatrics, fall 2014 |
| | **Visiting Nurse and Community Health**, Mansfield, CT<br>• Student Nurse, Community, spring 2014 |
| | **Manchester General Hospital**, Manchester, CT<br>• Student Nurse, Medical-Surgical, fall 2013 |
| **Computer Skills** | • Proficient with Microsoft Office, Database, and Windows applications and electronic records<br>• Experienced with Internet research |
| **Activities** | • Student Union Board of Governors, University of Connecticut, class representative<br>• Intramural soccer |
| **References** | Available upon request |

Adds relevant skills
for health-care record
keeping

**Figure 17.1**
Conventional
résumé.

**Employment Objective.** This optional section allows personnel officers to see at a glance your priorities and goals. Try to sound confident and eager but not pompous or presumptuous.

**Education.** This section is almost always included, often first. Specify each postsecondary school you've attended, your major, your date of graduation (or expected graduation), and your grade point average (if it reflects well on you). You can also add any awards, honors, or relevant course work.

**Experience.** In this key section, list each job, most recent first. You can include full- and part-time jobs. For each, name the organization, your position, your responsibilities, and the dates you held the job. Describe any involvement in unusual projects or responsibility for major developments. Highlight details that show relevant work experience and leadership ability. Minimize information unrelated to the job you're seeking.

**Skills.** List any special skills (data processing, technical drawing, multiple languages) that aren't obvious from your education and work experience.

**Activities.** You can specify either professional interests and activities (*Member of Birmingham Bricklayers Association*) or personal pursuits (*skiing, hiking, needlepoint*) showing that you are dedicated and well-rounded.

**References.** If a job advertisement requests references, provide them. Always contact your references in advance to make sure they are willing to give you a good recommendation. For each person, list the name, his or her organization and position, and the organization's address and phone number. If references have not been requested, you can simply note "Available on request."

As you prepare your résumé, and possibly your professional Web site, also consider your electronic trail and workplace etiquette. A future employer may well assume that anything you write at work is company correspondence, without personal rights to privacy, and that anywhere you go online at work will represent or be subsidized by the company. That same employer is unlikely to be amused by your confessional Facebook page or your party photos. Though you might consider social media materials personal, they may seem very public to an employer who checks your background and your credibility. Your electronic presence should correspond with the reliable-future-employee presence you wish to project.

## Learning by Doing 📷 Reflecting on Your Working Life and Goals

What are the differences between a job, a vocation, and a career? Do you have any of these three now? If so, what does the position entail? What do you like about it, and what are its drawbacks or limitations? If money were no object, what might you do instead? Would you view this as a job, a vocation, or a career? Why? Write a brief reflection in which you respond to these questions.

## Application Letters

When writing a letter applying for a job, follow all the guidelines for other business letters. As you compete against others, your letter and résumé are all the employer has to judge you on. Your immediate objective is to obtain an interview, so read any advertisement critically.

For general guidelines for business letters, see pp. 347–50. For more on letter format and another sample, see the Quick Format Guide beginning on p. Q-1.

- What qualifications are listed? Ideally, you should have them all. If you lack one, try to find something in your background that compensates, some similar experience in a different form.
- What else can you tell about the organization or position from the ad? How does the organization represent itself? (Check its Web site.)
- How does the ad describe the ideal candidate? As a team player? A dynamic individual? If you feel that you are the person this organization is seeking, portray yourself this way in your letter.

Your letter should spark your readers' interest, convince them you're qualified, and motivate them to interview you. If possible, address your letter to the person who screens applicants and sets up interviews; you may need to call the organization to find out this person's name. In the first paragraph, identify the job, indicate how you heard about it, and summarize your qualifications. In the second paragraph, expand on your qualifications, highlighting key information on your résumé. Add details if necessary to show that you're a better candidate than others. In the third paragraph, restate your interest in the job, ask for an interview, and let your prospective employer know how to reach you. (See Figure 17.2.) If you get an interview, follow up with a thank-you note. The note may reemphasize your qualifications and strong interest in the position.

## Learning by Doing 🎯 Planning a Job Application

Look for a job advertisement for a position or in a field that might interest you. Check the newspaper, a professional publication, or an organization's Web site. First, analyze the ad to identify what type of applicant it seeks, noting qualifications, experience, ambitions, or other expectations. Then list the kind of information an applicant might supply in response. Discuss your analysis with a classmate or small group to see whether your interpretations match.

**Figure 17.2**
Application letter.

Follows standard
letter format

Addresses specific
person

Identifies job sought
and describes interest

Explains qualifications

Confirms interest and
supplies contact
information

Encloses résumé and
proof of certification

402 Pigeon Hill Road
Windsor, CT 06095
July 8, 2016

Sheryl Sullivan
Director of Nursing
Center for Children's Health and Development
St. Francis Hospital and Medical Center
114 Woodland Street
Hartford, CT 06105

Dear Ms. Sullivan:

I am writing to apply for the full-time position as a pediatric nurse at the Center for Children's Health and Development at St. Francis Hospital, which was advertised on the Eastern Connecticut Health Network Web site. I feel that my varied clinical experiences and my desire to work with children ideally suit me for the job. In addition, I am highly motivated to grow and succeed in the field of health care.

For the past five years, I have worked as a certified occupational therapy assistant. In this capacity, I help children with delayed motor function acquire the skills necessary to achieve as high a level of independence as possible. While working as a COTA, I attended nursing school with the ultimate goal of becoming a pediatric nurse. My varied clinical experiences as a student nurse and my previous experience as a nurse's aide in a geriatric center have exposed me to many types of care. I feel that these experiences have helped me to become a well-rounded caregiver.

I believe that I would be a strong addition to the medical team at the Children's Center. My clinical experiences have prepared me to deal with a wide range of situations. In addition, I am dedicated to maintaining and enhancing the well-being of children. I am enclosing proof of my recent certification as a Registered Nurse in the state of Connecticut. Please write to me at the address above, e-mail me at acahill783@yahoo.com, or call me at (860) 555-5763. Thank you for your consideration. I look forward to hearing from you.

Sincerely,

*Anne Cahill*

Anne Cahill

Enclosures

---

## Learning by Doing 🎯 Planning for Your Future Career

Make an appointment with your advisor or your school's career counselor, and with his or her assistance, figure out what classes you must take to pursue your future career. (If you are undecided about a career, you might discuss possible options with the advisor or counselor.) What volunteer work, internships, or other activities would help you build skills necessary for the career or help you stand out from other job candidates? If you plan to attend graduate school, what steps do you need to take to ensure the greatest chance of acceptance into a graduate program?

# Business Letters

To correspond with outside individuals or groups, organizations use business letters to request and provide information, motivate action, respond to requests, and sell goods and services. Because letters become part of a permanent record, they can be checked later to determine exactly who said what and when. Keep a copy and back up every letter you write.

A good business letter is brief—limited to one page if possible. It supplies what the reader needs, no more. A letter of inquiry might simply request a booklet, sample, or promotional piece. A special request might add why you are writing, what you need, and when you need it. On the other hand, a letter of complaint focuses on your problem—what product is involved, when and where you purchased it, why you are unhappy, and how you'd like the problem solved. Include specifics such as product numbers and dates, and maintain a courteous tone. Because they are so brief, business letters are often judged on details—format, appearance, openings, closings.

## Format for Business Letters

The format of business letters (see Figure 17.3) is established by convention.

- Use 8½-by-11-inch paper, with matching envelopes. Print on only one side of the page.
- Single-space and use an extra line of space to separate paragraphs and the different elements of the letter. In very short letters, it's acceptable to leave additional space before the inside address.
- Leave margins of at least one inch on both sides; try to make the top and bottom margins fairly even, although you may have a larger bottom margin if your letter is very short.
- Pay attention to grammar, punctuation, spelling, and mechanics. Your readers will.

**Return Address.** This is your address or the address of the company for which you are writing. Abbreviate only the state using its two-letter postal abbreviation. Omit a return address on preprinted letterhead stationery.

**Date.** Supply this on the line right after the return address. Spell out the month; follow it by the day, a comma, and the year.

**Inside Address.** This is the address of the person to whom you are writing. Begin with the person's full name and title (*Mr.*, *Ms.*, *Dr.*, *Professor*); when

**Figure 17.3** Letter using modified block style.

Uses standard format for return address, date, and inside address

Uses name of position for salutation

Introduces situation and explains purpose

Requests action

States expectation of resolution

Ends with conventional closing, signature, typed name, and e-mail address (if unknown to addressee)

---

1453 Illinois Avenue — Return address
Miami, FL 33133
January 26, 2016 —— Date

Customer Service Department
Fidelity Products, Inc.
1192 Plymouth Avenue
Little Rock, AR 72210

Inside address

Dear Customer Service Representative: — Salutation

On January 12 I purchased a Fidelity media cabinet (Model XAR) from my local Tech-Mart. I have been unable to assemble the cabinet because the instructions are unclear. These instructions are incomplete (step 6 is missing) and are accompanied by diagrams so small and dark that it is impossible to distinguish the numbers for the different pieces.

Please send me usable instructions. If I do not receive clear instructions within the next three weeks, I will have to return my media cabinet to the Tech-Mart where I purchased it and request a full refund.

Body

I have used your equipment for more than ten years and have been very satisfied, so I was particularly disappointed to find that the media cabinet did not come with clear directions for assembly. I look forward to a prompt resolution of this problem.

Sincerely, — Closing

*James Winter*

James Winter — Name
jwin12@campus.net

---

addressing a woman without a professional title, use *Ms.* unless you know that she prefers *Miss* or *Mrs.* The second line should identify the position the person holds, and the third line should name the organization. If you don't know your reader, start with the name of the position, department, or organization. Avoid abbreviations except for the state.

**Salutation.** Skip a line. Then type *Dear* followed by the person's title and last name (*Dear Dr. Diaz*). If you don't know who will read your letter, use that person's position (*Dear Editor*) or organization (*Dear Angell's Bakery*) in place of a name. End with a colon.

**Body.** Present your message. Leave one line of space between paragraphs; begin each paragraph even with the left margin (no indentations). Paragraphs should generally be no longer than seven or eight typed lines.

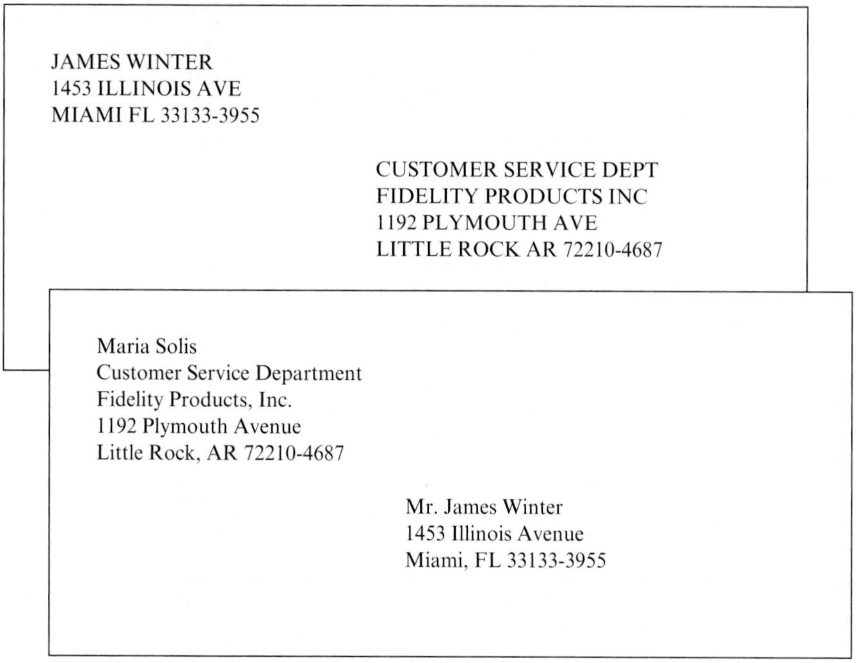

```
JAMES WINTER
1453 ILLINOIS AVE
MIAMI FL 33133-3955


              CUSTOMER SERVICE DEPT
              FIDELITY PRODUCTS INC
              1192 PLYMOUTH AVE
              LITTLE ROCK AR 72210-4687
```

```
   Maria Solis
   Customer Service Department
   Fidelity Products, Inc.
   1192 Plymouth Avenue
   Little Rock, AR 72210-4687


             Mr. James Winter
             1453 Illinois Avenue
             Miami, FL 33133-3955
```

**Figure 17.4** Envelope formats.

U.S. Postal Service format

Conventional format

**Closing.** Leave one line of space after the last paragraph, and then use a conventional closing followed by a comma: *Sincerely, Sincerely yours, Respectfully yours, Yours truly.*

**Typed Name with Position.** Leave four lines of space after the closing, and type your name in full, even if you will sign only your first name. Do not include a title before your name. If you are writing on behalf of an organization, you can include your position on the next line. You may add your e-mail address or telephone number here unless already supplied.

**Signature.** Print the letter, and sign your name in the space above the typed name. Unless you have a personal relationship with the recipient, use both your first and last names. Do not include a title before your name.

**Abbreviations at End.** Leave at least two lines of space between your typed name and any abbreviations used to communicate more about the letter. Put each abbreviation on a separate line. If you send a copy to someone other than the recipient, use *cc:* followed by the name of the person or organization receiving a copy. If the letter is accompanied by another document in the same envelope, use *Enc.* or *Enclosure.* If the letter has been typed by someone else, the writer's initials are capitalized, followed by a slash and the typist's initials in lowercase format: *VW/dbw.*

**Modified and Full Block Style.** To format a letter using *modified block style* (see Figure 17.3), imagine a line running down the center of the page from top to bottom. Align the left side of the return address, date, closing, signature, and your typed name with this center line. Use *full block style* on letterhead stationery with the organization's name and address. Omit typing the return address, and align all elements at the left margin.

**Envelope Formats.** The U.S. Postal Service recommends an easy-to-scan format with all capital letters, standard abbreviations, and no punctuation. However, conventional format (see Figure 17.4) is always safe to use.

# Memoranda

A *memorandum* (*memo* for short) is a form of communication used within a company to request or exchange information, make announcements, and confirm conversations. Memos frequently convey information to large groups — an entire team, department, or organization. Generally, the topic is quite narrow and apparent at a glance. Memos tend to be written in the first person (*I* or *we*) and can range from very informal (if written to a peer) to extremely formal (if written to a high-ranking superior on an important matter). Most are short, but the format can be used to convey proposals and reports; long memos freely use headings, subheadings, lists, and other features that are easy to skim. (See Figure 17.5.)

## Format for Memoranda

Although every organization has its own format for memos, the heading generally consists of a series of lines with clear labels (followed by colons).

| | |
|---|---|
| Date: | (date on which memo is sent) |
| To: | (person or persons to whom it is primarily addressed) |
| cc: | (names of anyone else who receives a copy) |
| From: | (name of the writer) |
| Subject: *or* Re: | (concise, accurate statement of the memo's topic) |

The subject line often determines whether a memo is read. (The old-fashioned abbreviation *Re:* for *regarding* is still used, but we recommend the more common *Subject.*) Accurately sum up the topic in a few words ("Agenda for 12/10 meeting," "Sales estimates for new product line").

# Brochures and Presentation Visuals

For more on understanding visuals, see Ch. 14.

When you design a workplace brochure, presentation slide, or other visual document, you write the text and also direct a reader's attention using tools such as type options, lists, white space, headings, repetition, and color.

INTERLINK SYSTEMS, INC.

To:          All Employees
From:        Erica Xiang *EX*
Subject:     Changes in employee benefits
Date:        October 26, 2015

Each fall the Human Resources group looks closely at the company's health insurance benefits to make certain that we are providing an excellent level of coverage in a way that makes economic sense. To that end, we have made some changes to our plan, effective January 1, 2016. Let me outline the three major changes.

1.  We are pleased to be able to offer employees the opportunity, through a **Flexible Spending Account**, to pay for dependent care and unreimbursed health expenses on a pre-tax basis, a feature that can result in considerable savings. I have attached a summary and will provide more information on this benefit at our staff meeting tomorrow, October 27, at 10:30 A.M. I will be available immediately after the meeting to answer any specific questions.

2.  Those of you who have taken advantage of our **vision care benefit** in the past know that it offers significant help in paying for eye exams, eyeglasses, and contact lenses. The current plan will change slightly on January 1. Employees and covered dependents will be eligible to receive up to $50 each year toward the cost of a routine eye exam and up to $100 every two years toward the cost of eyeglasses or contact lenses. If you see a provider within our health insurance network, you will pay only $10 per office visit.

3.  We at Interlink Systems feel strongly that our health insurance benefits are excellent, but as you know, the cost of such plans continues to rise every year. In the interest of maintaining excellent coverage for our employees, we will raise our **employee contribution**. Starting January 1, we are asking employees with single coverage to contribute $12.50 more per pay period toward the cost of medical insurance, and employees who cover dependents to contribute $40 more per pay period. Even with this increase, the amount the company asks its employees to contribute towards the premiums (about 8%) is significantly less than the nationwide average of 30%.

Please contact me if you have questions or concerns about the changes that I have outlined in this memo. You can reach me at x462 or at exiang@interlink.net.

Enclosure

**Figure 17.5**
Memorandum.

Uses standard format to identify readers, writer, topic, and date

Explains purpose, noting reader's priorities

Previews clear organization in blocks

Uses friendly tone to note new benefit

Offers assistance

Introduces benefit change with positive background

Presents increased cost carefully, noting coverage quality and high employer contribution

Offers more help and supplies contact information

Notes enclosure

## Format for Brochures

Although workplace brochures do not follow a specific format, artists and designers aim to attract readers' attention by making important elements prominent. Consider Figure 17.6, for example, which shows the opening page of a

**Figure 17.6**
Portion of a brochure. Federal Student Aid.

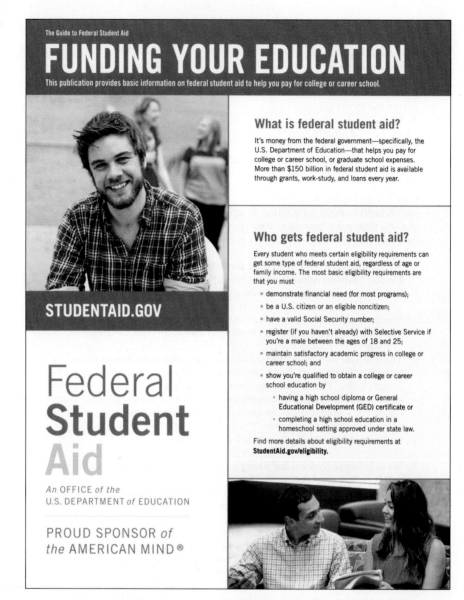

The Guide to Federal Student Aid

# FUNDING YOUR EDUCATION

This publication provides basic information on federal student aid to help you pay for college or career school.

**STUDENTAID.GOV**

## Federal Student Aid

*An* OFFICE *of the*
U.S. DEPARTMENT *of* EDUCATION

PROUD SPONSOR *of*
*the* AMERICAN MIND ®

### What is federal student aid?

It's money from the federal government—specifically, the U.S. Department of Education—that helps you pay for college or career school, or graduate school expenses. More than $150 billion in federal student aid is available through grants, work-study, and loans every year.

### Who gets federal student aid?

Every student who meets certain eligibility requirements can get some type of federal student aid, regardless of age or family income. The most basic eligibility requirements are that you must

- demonstrate financial need (for most programs);
- be a U.S. citizen or an eligible noncitizen;
- have a valid Social Security number;
- register (if you haven't already) with Selective Service if you're a male between the ages of 18 and 25;
- maintain satisfactory academic progress in college or career school; and
- show you're qualified to obtain a college or career school education by
  - having a high school diploma or General Educational Development (GED) certificate or
  - completing a high school education in a homeschool setting approved under state law.

Find more details about eligibility requirements at **StudentAid.gov/eligibility.**

government brochure about federal student aid. The picture of the smiling young man immediately draws the eye, as do the large headlines above and below his picture: "Funding Your Education" and "Federal Student Aid." Additionally, bold, colored type attracts attention to key questions ("What is federal student aid?" and "Who gets federal student aid?"), which are then answered. Overall, these prominent elements make the purpose of the brochure clear.

Also note that the key questions are in parallel form, providing consistency and coherence, and the question/answer pairings are separated by white space so the breaks between topics are clear.

For more on parallel structure, see B2 (pp. Q-47–Q-48) in the Quick Editing Guide.

## Format for Presentation Visuals

Effective use of space is important in visuals—such as PowerPoint or other presentation slides. Providing ample space and limiting the text on each slide helps readers absorb your major points. The slide in Figure 17.7 for recruiting service learning participants has too much text, making it hard to read and potentially distracting. In contrast, Figure 17.8 has less text and more open space, making each point easier to read. Its bullets highlight the main points, meant only to summarize major issues and themes. The type sizes for the slides are large enough to be viewed: 44 points for the heading and 32 points for the body.

The "white space" without text in these slides is actually blue. Some public-speaking experts believe that black type on a white background can be too stark; instead, they recommend a dark blue background with yellow or white type. Others believe that black on white is fine and may be what the audience is used to. Presentation software makes it easy to experiment with these options or to use your employer's templates.

**Figure 17.7** Presentation slide with too much text and too little space.

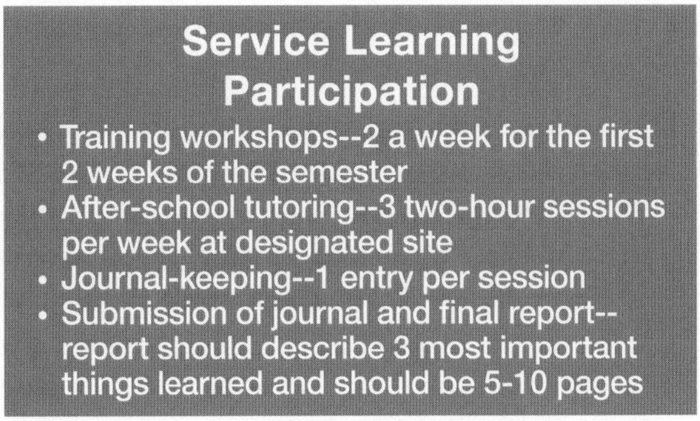

**Figure 17.8** Presentation slide with brief text and effective use of space.

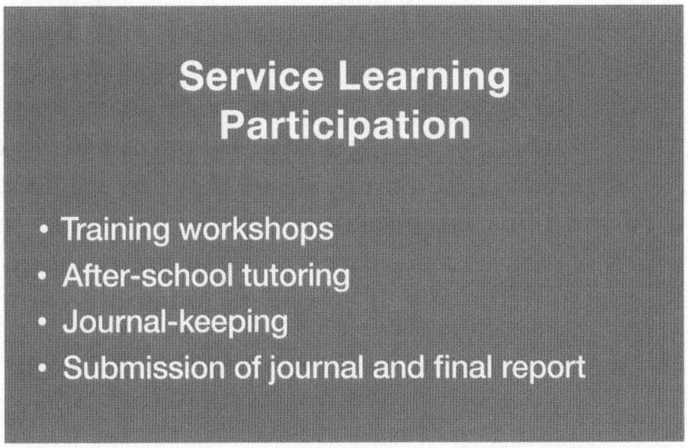

In addition to designing slides effectively, keep the following advice in mind as you prepare and deliver a presentation:

- It is a good idea to save backup copies of your slides in case your original file is lost or corrupted. E-mail the file to yourself or copy it onto a jump drive. If it contains animation or videos, consider copying it onto a disk.
- Slides shouldn't simply repeat the spoken content of a presentation. Instead, they should provide information to support or offer fresh insights into the speaker's points. For example, a speaker discussing a company's sales growth over a five-year period might show a bar chart that makes the extent of this growth instantly clear.
- Similarly, speakers shouldn't read from their slides, an approach that can bore the audience quickly. Again, slides should be seen as engaging support for a presentation, not as a teleprompter for the speaker.

## Reviewing and Reflecting

To complete more review questions for Ch. 17, see the LaunchPad.

**REVIEW** Working with classmates or independently, respond to the following questions:

1. In workplace writing, why is it important to keep your purpose clearly in mind? What are typical purposes of this type of writing?

2. What are some effective ways to present information in business writing so that you don't waste readers' time? If you haven't yet applied some of these strategies, which do you think would be most helpful to you, and why?

3. What are the major sections or components of a résumé? Identify the two sections that you think will be most challenging for you and try to draft them. If you have already written these sections, revise them using the advice from the text. Afterward, consider getting feedback on your work from your instructor or your peers.

**REFLECT** After completing one of the writing assignments presented in this chapter or supplied by your instructor, turn back to the After Writing questions on page 39 of Chapter 3 and respond to as many of them as you can. While addressing these questions, it might be helpful to revisit your response to the Learning by Doing activity on pages 344–45, if you completed it.

Next, reflect in writing about how you might apply the insights that you drew from this assignment to another situation—in or outside of college—in which you have to produce writing or presentation materials that are suitable for a business setting. If no specific situations come to mind, imagine that

- in a business course, you are required to make a presentation about a product or service that you conceived of as part of the course. You want to make sure that your presentation highlights the appeal of your product or service and that your PowerPoints are visually effective.

- you are applying for your dream job in a field that interests you. (This field might be your major if you've selected one.) You want to create a résumé and application letter that highlight your accomplishments and skills and that are tailored to the requirements of the job.

In your reflection, consider how you would address your purpose and audience.

## Additional Writing Assignments

1. Use the job advertisement you located for the activity on page 345, or find one that interests you for immediate or future employment. Write your letter of application for this job, following the advice in this chapter.

For another sample letter, see p. Q-19.

2. Prepare a current résumé, designed as your standard print version or tailored to a specific job. Follow the advice and format explained in this chapter.

For another sample résumé, see p. Q-18.

3. Prepare your own example of a workplace document introduced in this chapter. After you have drafted, revised, and edited it, print a second copy. In its margins add notes to point out features of its format and content. Revise your document and the notes if you wish.

4. **Source Assignment.** Working individually or collaboratively with a small group, investigate the job-hunting or career advice available on campus or in your local community. Identify what you or users might want to learn about these resources (such as how to access or use them). Prepare a brief report on your findings for fellow students interested in using such resources productively.

5. **Source Assignment.** Interview a personnel manager or another person who hires people in your field of interest. Prepare by developing a brief set of questions about issues of interest to you — what kinds of jobs are typically available, how the selection process works, what background is typically required or desired, how students might prepare for employment, what tips the person would give job-seekers, or similar matters. After the interview, write an essay reporting what you have learned to other interested students. Also write a brief business letter thanking the person you interviewed.

For more about conducting an interview, see Ch. 6.

6. **Visual Assignment.** Select two or three workplace Web sites for close examination. Analyze how — and how well — each represents its corporate, small business, professional, or other workplace to visitors. Adapt the guidelines for workplace writing (pp. 338–41), and use them as criteria to evaluate the site's purpose, audience, tone, and presentation.

# A WRITER'S STRATEGIES

# 18 Strategies: A Case Study

For Erin's assignment, see Chapter 4, Recalling an Experience. For more on writing processes, see Chs. 19–23.

W hen Erin Schmitt enrolled in Rhetoric and Composition I, her first major college assignment was to write an essay reflecting on a personal experience. She needed to pick a specific experience that she could convey to her readers. Then she needed to reflect on its significance to show why it mattered to her. In this chapter, you can follow her writing processes as she generates ideas, develops her first draft, gathers responses from readers, revises and edits her draft, and writes a reflective letter to accompany the essay in her writing portfolio.

**?** Use the questions in the margin to help you develop your own essay alongside Erin.

## Generating Ideas

Erin thought back over her experiences before entering college. She had studied hard to get into college, knowing how important her high school record was for both admissions and financial aid. Although lots of students shared the stress of worrying about grades or money or both, she didn't think that she could narrow those issues to a notable experience. Then she thought about her last day at her job assisting an elderly man and the compelling recognition she had had just before she came to campus. She started mapping these recollections in the diagram on page 359.

**?** What significant experience do you recall that might engage your readers?

When Erin finished her diagram, she felt confident that she had remembered a significant event and that she could make a compelling point about it. To fill out her ideas, she also answered the six reporter's questions.

Who: Mr. Hertli; me

What: Increased appreciation of life

When: While reading an atlas the last time I assisted Mr. Hertli

Where: Mr. Hertli's literature-crammed office/study

Why: Mr. Hertli's blindness

**?** How might you generate ideas about your recollections?

How: Asked to read atlas → confusion → saw child in old, blind Mr. Hertli → appreciation of life

358

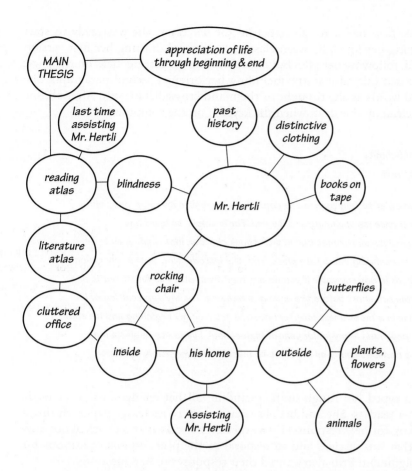

For more information and journal questions about the Part Four photograph, see About the Photographs at the end of the book.

Erin was confident that she had discovered something meaningful to write about. She wanted to share her reflection about life's connections with readers. She thought that she could focus on it as a main idea or thesis to shape her essay. After working for Mr. Hertli for a long time, she could remember plenty of vivid details to bring her experience to life for readers and could see how her whole paper might fall into place.

**?** What do you think is the importance of your experience?

## Planning, Drafting, and Developing

When Erin looked over her notes, she realized that she could easily organize her ideas in a logical sequence: first introduce the experience and its importance, next present events in chronological order as they had happened, and then return to their importance.

Assisting Mr. Hertli  →  Last time assisting Mr. Hertl  →  Reading atlas  →  Young and old  →  Appreciation of life

**?** What organization would suit your needs?

Once Erin had a rough structure for her essay, she was ready to start developing her ideas. Between classes, she started drafting her first version by hand, following her plan but concentrating on getting ideas on the page. She crossed out false starts, including her original second paragraph. She inserted words as she thought of them and crossed some out. After all, she would clean up this draft when she keyed it on the computer.

❓ How are you starting your draft? What process works for you?

*Erin Schmitt*

*1st Draft*

> *often*
> *In order to fully appreciate something, to realize its value, one ∧ must experience its beginning and its end. For example, to learn and appreciate all the material in a textbook chapter, ~~inst~~ reading and understanding must take place from the introduction to the conclusion. A book is not enjoyable if you do not read from start to finish, nor is a movie cut short before the ending is revealed. ~~The~~ My appreciation of life*
> *life's*
> *came in a most unexpected connection between ~~my~~ beginning and its end.*
> *~~Beginning In my junior year of high school, I began to assist a man who had lost nearly all his sight to macular degeneration.~~ Mr. Hertli*

For Peer Response questions for Erin's assignment, see p. 60.

Erin typed her rough draft, including all her changes, to get it ready for other readers. She and her classmates were to exchange papers during a workshop for peer response. Erin expected her classmates to ask about anything that wasn't clear and to respond to the peer response questions for the assignment. Erin also wanted their responses to her questions:

❓ What do you want to ask your readers?

- Is the scene I'm recalling clear? Does it come alive when you read it?
- Do I reflect enough? Should I add more about my insight?

Erin's instructor also required a conference about the draft to discuss revisions. Both sets of comments—handwritten notes and highlighting from a fellow student and electronic "balloons" from her instructor—are shown next to Erin's rough draft.

*Peer: You got the reflection part started right away.*

❓ Would any of the general comments about Erin's draft also apply to your draft?

## Rough Draft with Peer and Instructor Responses

In order to fully appreciate something, to realize its value, one often must experience its beginning and its end. For example, to learn and appreciate all the material in a textbook chapter, reading and understanding must take place from the introduction to the conclusion. A book is not enjoyable if you do not read from start to finish, nor is a movie cut short before the ending is revealed.

1

*Instructor: Good idea to draw readers in with analogies.*

My appreciation of life came in a most unexpected connection between life's beginning and its end.

Peer: I highlighted how you arranged the details to lead us into the house. Good progression. I can really see the scene here.

Mr. Hertli was a brilliant old Swiss man whom I assisted every week for the last two years of my high school career. He lived 25 minutes away from my home, down a winding road surrounded by trees, grazing horses, and the occasional house. Trees arched over his steep driveway, as if bowing to all who enter, welcoming anyone with insight, help, or simply company. Mr. Hertli's house was of a very traditional build, and was surrounded by nature. Goats fed on grasses and horses galloped and played within a fenced-off grazing area. Ducks swam on a pond and dozens of sun-colored butterflies danced around bunches of tall purple flowers between which a few stepping-stones were nestled, as a walkway to the front door.

*Instructor: Effective visual details here.*

2

Inside sat Mr. Hertli, always rocking in a chair and listening to books-on-tape in one of the various languages familiar to him. He was very tall, thin, and elderly, and wore dress slacks and a suit jacket no matter what the occasion. His leather shoes were obviously very old, and showed scuffs and wear which told stories of Switzerland, war, research, and accomplishment. Mr. Hertli also wore very dark sunglasses morning and evening to protect the mere one or two percent of his eyesight that had not yet been stolen from him by macular degeneration.

*Instructor: Try Edit/Find to catch repetition.*

3

Peer: I like how you led up to him. You even got his history in with the shoes!

Mr. Hertli was an accomplished man. He had been through immigration, served the United States in war, earned various degrees, had written a book on evolution and creationism, and was fighting for his life against a terminal lung disease. He was extremely intelligent, and it was my job to read him scientific journals and books, record information and data for his next work-in-progress, manage his correspondence, fill out paperwork, dispense his medications, and do nearly all the things a blind person can not do alone.

4

Peer: The details here end on a big point.

Peer: I could see him in ¶3. Now I feel like I know him, too.

One particular day, I was assisting Mr. Hertli in his office. Crimson carpeting lined the floor of the tiny literature-crammed room. Journals and books lay sprawled on every surface, and there was barely room for a computer on a desk and two chairs somewhere in all the mess. A cord around Mr. Hertli's head fed oxygen through his nose, while the other end trailed out the door, down the steps, and into the living room where an oxygen-dispensing machine always sat, always humming. We sorted through music, storing old German and Swiss instrumental classics on a new device for the blind which stored numerous songs, audio books, and other audio literature for playback. As we waited for the media to download into the device, Mr. Hertli inquired about recent political events concerning the country of Georgia. He desired to know the geographic location of Georgia. "Read the atlas," he said, and although I had grown to understand and love his thick European accent, I sat staring at him in bafflement at his words,

5

*Instructor: Does everything here support your main idea? Could you be more selective to sharpen your focus?*

which he, fortunately, could not see. I reached under a desk and pushed past books about Darwin, God, evolution, and history, and found a large, blue-covered atlas, aged by years of learning, discovery, and research. Brushing the dust off, I opened the book to the index, and searched for "Georgia." I turned to the page to which the index directed me, and unsuccessfully tried to describe Georgia's relation to Turkey, Russia, and Azerbajan. "Show me," he said. Show him! How could I, for he could not see, after all, and now I had to find a way to make him see?!

*Peer: The quotes are good, but the whole ¶ seems long — maybe split it? Or drop some detail?*

I placed the wide atlas across his wobbly knees, in his lap, facing him. Taking his hand, I slowly directed Mr. Hertli's finger around the perimeter of each country, saying, "This is Turkey. To the east, here is Georgia." He pointed and repeated the countries back to me, and I asserted that, yes, that was Azerbajan or Russia.

6

*Peer: Spelled right?*

It was as though I were teaching a small child, who could not read, and who did not know the least about geography. And how strange it was to be feeling such a way. After all, I was helping a well-educated, cultured man, in this most elementary, basic way. In this aged man, nearing the end of his life, I saw the character of a young boy, beginning to learn a concept new to him.

7

*Peer: When I read your draft online, my software said this was a fragment. Is it? Are fragments OK in here?*

This would be the last time I helped Mr. Hertli, as I would be beginning college just a few days later. Mr. Hertli was now completely blind. Like a mother afraid to send her child to school for the first time, I was afraid to cease my assistance of this somewhat helpless man. For when I had seen this connection—the young, new child in the old, I came to realize just how valuable life itself is.

8

*Instructor: More reflection here on the significance?*

*Peer: I get what you're saying, but maybe explain it more? This flat statement seems too abrupt.*

**?** What have your readers noted or suggested for your draft?

Erin also received some overall comments with suggestions for revision.

PEER

I really think you did a good job creating the experience. You're a very descriptive writer, and I liked being able to imagine the experience—the road, the animals, the flowers by the house. I also liked how you used contrasting paragraphs—long paragraph 5 to explain the situation and then short paragraph 6 for the outcome. (But I still think 5 might be too wordy.) You got the reflection part started at the beginning, too, so I knew you were thinking about it. I just wasn't that sure about how you ended with it. My own son traces things with his hands, so I could see what you meant about Mr. Hertli, but I expected you to explain it more. Maybe you could add here to make the conclusion stronger when you revise.

INSTRUCTOR

Erin, you've selected and developed a provocative experience that changed your thinking. However, readers need more explanation and interpretation to share the intensity of your experience.

If you explained its significance more fully, your conclusion would be more compelling. I'm wondering if you're trying to find that significance by synthesizing—the reading and thinking skill we discussed in class last week. You seem to be pulling together your actual experience with Mr. Hertli and your insight about the young child who grew up to be this man in order to develop a new idea that goes beyond them. Besides strengthening your concluding reflections as you revise, look also at your fine selection of details. They enrich your description, but try to make sure that all of them are forceful and relevant.

> ❓ What has your instructor suggested about your draft?

---

## Learning by Doing 🎯 Responding as a Peer

If Erin were in your class, what questions would you want to ask her? What advice for her revision would you supply in your peer response?

---

# Revising and Editing

Erin collected the comments about her draft. To help her focus on the purpose of the essay, she reread the assignment. She decided that reflecting more would strengthen her main idea, or thesis—and her instructor had already pointed out the importance of a strong thesis in college writing.

> ❓ What is your revision plan for your draft?

Erin concentrated first on revising her conclusion because all her readers had suggested strengthening it. Then she went back to the beginning to make other changes, responding to comments and editing details. Erin's changes are marked in the following version of her draft. The comments in the margins point out some of her revision and editing decisions.

> ❓ What changes do you want to mark in your draft?

## Revised and Edited Draft

In order to fully appreciate something, to realize its value, one often must experience its beginning and its end. For example, to learn and appreciate all the material in a textbook chapter, reading and understanding must take place from the introduc*ory paragraph* to the conclusion. A book is not enjoyable *without reading* ~~if you do not~~ from start to finish, nor is a movie cut short before the ending is revealed. My appreciation of life came in a most unexpected connection between life's beginning and its end.

> 1 *Oops! What about a title? Just Mr. Hertli?*
>
> *Focus looks OK here.*

Mr. Hertli was a brilliant ~~old~~ Swiss man whom I assisted every week for the last two years of my high school career. He lived *twenty-five* 25 minutes away from my home, down a winding road, surrounded by trees, grazing horses, *goats and sheep,* and the occasional house. Trees arched over his steep driveway, as if bowing to all who enter, welcoming anyone with insight, help, or simply company. Mr. Hertli's house

> 2 *Need to write out numbers that are a word or two*

was of ~~a very~~ traditional build, and was surrounded by nature. Goats fed on grasses and horses galloped and played within a fenced-off grazing area. Ducks swam on a pond and dozens of sun-colored butterflies danced around bunches of tall purple flowers between which a few *worn* stepping-stones were nestled, as a walkway to the front door.

Inside sat Mr. Hertli, always rocking in a chair and listening to "books-on-tape" in one of the various languages familiar to him. He was ~~very~~ tall, thin, and elderly, and wore dress slacks and a ~~suit~~ jacket no matter what the occasion. His leather shoes were obviously very old, and *they* showed scuffs and wear which told stories of Switzerland, war, research, and accomplishment. Mr. Hertli also wore ~~very~~ dark sunglasses morning and evening to protect the mere one or two percent of his eye sight that had not yet been stolen from him by macular degeneration.

3

Mr. Hertli was an accomplished man. He had been through immigration, served the United States in war, earned various degrees, ~~had~~ written a book on evolution and creationism, and was *now* fighting for his life against a terminal lung disease. He was extremely intelligent, and it was my job to read him scientific journals and books, record information and data for his next work-in-progress, manage his correspondence, fill out paperwork, dispense his medications, and do nearly all the things a blind person (can not) do alone.

4

One particular day, I was assisting Mr. Hertli in his office. Crimson carpeting lined the floor of the tiny literature-crammed room. Journals and books lay sprawled on every surface, ~~and there was~~ *with* barely room for a computer on a desk and two chairs somewhere in all the mess. *One end of a* A cord around Mr. Hertli's head fed oxygen through his nose, while the other end trailed out the door, down the steps, and into the living room where an oxygen-dispensing machine *constantly* *constantly* ~~always~~ sat, ~~always~~ humming. We sorted through music, storing old German and Swiss instrumental classics on a new device for the blind which ~~stored~~ ~~numerous songs, audio books, and other audio literature~~ *saved audio files* for playback. As we waited for the media to download ~~into the device~~, Mr. Hertli inquired about recent political events concerning the country of Georgia. He desired to know the geographic location of Georgia. "Read the atlas," he said, and although I had grown to understand and love his thick European accent, I sat staring ~~at him~~ in bafflement at his words, ~~which he, fortunately, could not see~~. I reached under a desk and pushed past books about Darwin, God, evolution, and

5

*Too much repetition — plus wordy*

*Make this one word*

*My goal — set the scene but drop extra words!*

*Too much detail here?*

history, ~~and found~~ _to find_ a large, blue-covered atlas, aged by years of learning, _and_ discovery, ~~and research~~. Brushing the dust off, I opened the book to the index, and searched for "Georgia." I turned to the page to which the index directed me, and unsuccessfully tried to describe Georgia's relation to Turkey, Russia, and Azerbaijan. "Show me," he said. Show him? How could I, for he could not see, after all, and now I ~~had~~ _was_ to find a way to make him see!

Check commas — end of the textbook

Luckily my reader asked about the spelling.

I placed the wide atlas across his wobbly knees, in his lap, facing him. Taking his _fragile_ hand, I slowly directed Mr. Hertli's finger around the perimeter of each country, saying, "This is Turkey. To the east, here is Georgia." He pointed and repeated the countries ~~back~~ to me, and I asserted that, yes, that was _indeed_ Azerbaijan, _Armenia,_ or Russia.

6

¶ 5 set up situation — this ¶ tells what happened

_This moment_ It ~~was~~ _felt_ as though I were teaching a small child, who could not read, and who did not know the least about geography. And how strange it was to be feeling such a way. After all, I was helping a well-educated, cultured man, in a this most elementary, basic way! In this aged man, nearing the end of his life, I saw the character of a young _small_ boy, beginning to learn a concept new to him.

7

Combine with ¶ 6 — event with meaning?

This would be the last time I helped Mr. Hertli, as I would ~~be beginning~~ _begin_ college just a few days later. Mr. Hertli was now completely, _one hundred percent_ blind. Like a mother afraid to send her child to ~~school for the first time~~ _kindergarten_, I was _now_ afraid to cease my ~~assistance of this somewhat~~ _care for this seemingly_ helpless man. For when I had seen this connection, the young, _new,_ ~~new child in the old~~ _still learning within an_ man, I came to realize just how valuable _and how unified_ life itself is. _Mr. Hertli showed me how our younger selves provide deep roots for us as we get older and how our older selves still preserve our youth. Young and old, we are all somehow connected, one and the same, no one being of greater worth than the other. No matter our age, we will always have this link, through generations, and I have grown to appreciate this of life._

8

My big goal here is adding more reflection.

I want to show how old and young connect.

After Erin finished revising and editing, she spell-checked her final version and proofread it one more time. Then she submitted her final draft.

❓ How might you strengthen your essay as you revise and edit?

## Final Draft for Submission

Erin Schmitt
Professor Hoeness-Krupsaw
ENG 101.004
19 September 2016

For more on the MLA paper format, see A in the Quick Format Guide, p. Q-1.

Mr. Hertli

In order to fully appreciate something, to realize its value, one often must experience its beginning and its end. For example, to learn and appreciate all the material in a textbook chapter, reading and understanding must take

1

place from the introductory paragraph to the conclusion. A book is not enjoyable without reading from start to finish, nor is a movie cut short before the ending is revealed. My appreciation of life came in a most unexpected connection between life's beginning and its end.

2   Mr. Hertli was a brilliant Swiss man whom I assisted every week for the last two years of my high school career. He lived twenty-five minutes away from my home, down a winding road, surrounded by trees, grazing horses, goats and sheep, and the occasional house. Trees arched over his steep driveway, as if bowing to all who enter, welcoming anyone with insight, help, or simply company. Mr. Hertli's house was of traditional build and was surrounded by nature. Goats fed on grasses and horses galloped and played within a fenced-off grazing area. Ducks swam on a pond and dozens of sun-colored butterflies danced around bunches of tall purple flowers between which a few worn stepping-stones were nestled as a walkway to the front door.

3   Inside sat Mr. Hertli, always rocking in a chair and listening to "books-on-tape" in one of the various languages familiar to him. He was tall, thin, and elderly and wore dress slacks and a jacket no matter what the occasion. His leather shoes were obviously very old, and they showed scuffs and wear which told stories of Switzerland, war, research, and accomplishment. Mr. Hertli also wore dark sunglasses morning and evening to protect the mere one or two percent of his sight that had not yet been stolen from him by macular degeneration.

4   Mr. Hertli was an accomplished man. He had been through immigration, served the United States in war, earned various degrees, written a book on evolution and creationism, and was now fighting for his life against a terminal lung disease. He was extremely intelligent, and it was my job to read him scientific journals and books, record information and data for his next work-in-progress, manage his correspondence, fill out paperwork, dispense his medications, and do nearly all the things a blind person cannot do alone.

5   One particular day, I was assisting Mr. Hertli in his office. Crimson carpeting lined the floor of the tiny literature-crammed room. Journals and books lay sprawled on every surface with barely room for a computer on a desk and two chairs somewhere in all the mess. One end of a cord around Mr. Hertli's head fed oxygen through his nose, while the other end trailed out the door, down the steps, and into the living room where an oxygen-dispensing machine constantly sat, constantly humming. We sorted through music, storing old German and Swiss instrumental classics on a new device for the blind which saved audio files for playback. As we waited for the media to download, Mr. Hertli inquired about recent political events concerning the country of Georgia. He desired to know the geographic location of Georgia. "Read the atlas," he said, and although I had grown to understand and love his thick European accent, I sat, staring in bafflement at his words. I reached under a desk and pushed past books about Darwin, God, evolution, and history to find a large, blue-covered atlas, aged by years of learning and discovery. Brushing the dust off, I opened the book to the index and searched for "Georgia." I turned to the page to which the index directed

me and unsuccessfully tried to describe Georgia's relation to Turkey, Russia, and Azerbaijan. "Show me!" he said. Show him? How could I, for he could not see, after all, and now I was to find a way to make him see?

I placed the wide atlas across his wobbly knees, in his lap, facing him.   6
Taking his fragile hand, I slowly directed Mr. Hertli's finger around the perimeter of each country, saying, "This is Turkey. To the east, here is Georgia." He pointed and repeated the countries to me, and I asserted that, yes, that was indeed Azerbaijan, Armenia, or Russia. This moment felt as though I were teaching a small child, one who could not read and who did not know the least about geography. And how strange it was to be feeling such a way. After all, I was helping a well-educated, cultured man in this most elementary, basic way! In this aged man, nearing the end of his life, I saw the character of a small young boy, beginning to learn a concept new to him.

This would be the last time I helped Mr. Hertli, as I would begin college   7
just a few days later. Mr. Hertli was now completely, one hundred percent blind. Like a mother afraid to send her child to kindergarten, I was now afraid to cease my care for this seemingly helpless man. For when I had seen this connection, the new, young child still learning within an old man, I came to realize just how valuable and how unified life itself is. Mr. Hertli showed me how our younger selves provide deep roots for us as we get older and how our older selves still preserve our youth. Young and old, we are all somehow connected, one and the same, no one being of greater worth than the other. No matter our age, we will always have this link, through generations, and I have grown to appreciate this of life.

# Reflecting as a Writer

Erin's assignment asked her to reflect on her experience as she wrote about its significance for her. Her instructor also required a reflective letter, following the time-honored advice of writer and teacher Peter Elbow. Here Erin needed to consider her goals, strengths, remaining challenges, and responses to readers during her writing process. The letter and the essay would become part of her writer's portfolio due at the end of the term.

For more about portfolios, see Ch. 24.

## Learning by Doing Writing a Reflective Letter

Select one of the following options, and write a reflective letter to your instructor.

1. Reflect on your responses to Erin's writing strategies and processes. For example, you might consider how her processes do and do not relate to yours or what you have learned from her that you might like to apply to your writing.
2. Reflect on your own first essay, as Erin did. Consider your goals, strengths, remaining challenges, and responses to readers.

## Reflective Portfolio Letter

For sample business letter formats, see pp. 347–50 and E in the Quick Format Guide, pp. Q-13–Q-16.

Campus Box A-456
September 19, 2016

Dr. Susanna Hoeness-Krupsaw
English Department
State University
1234 University Road
Campustown, OH 23456

Dear Dr. Hoeness-Krupsaw:

❓ What do you want to say in a reflective letter?

The main goal of my essay was to describe accurately and vividly the significant experience of reading to a blind, elderly man during my last two years of high school. When writing the essay I was attempting to give the reader insight to the details and scenery I experienced while visiting this man. By accurately describing the scene of most significance in great detail, I hoped to convey and emphasize that significance to the reader.

The strengths I had in writing this essay were in detailing and flow. I believe my descriptions accurately put images in the mind of the reader. I began my writing process by planning with a diagram. After creating this diagram, the essay easily formed in my mind and on paper. However, if I could revise the essay further, I would focus more on word choice and strength. I would also revise and strengthen my reflections as well as my concluding paragraph. When writing, I had some difficulty in putting into words exactly what my experience made me think and feel.

The feedback I received regarding my essay was mostly positive. However, almost all feedback suggested adding more reflection at the end of my final draft. I believe this strengthened my essay overall. I would like to get a response from the reader asserting that my essay vividly conveyed images and that the importance of this event is easily understood.

I may be contacted regarding this essay at eschmitt@campus.edu or 555-5555.

Sincerely,


Erin E. Schmitt

Enc.

# Strategies for Generating Ideas

**19**

For most writers, the hardest part of writing comes first—confronting a blank page. Fortunately, you can prepare for that moment by finding ideas and getting ready to write. All the tested techniques here have worked for writers—professionals and students—and some may work for you.

## Finding Ideas

When you begin to write, ideas may appear effortlessly on the paper or screen, perhaps triggered by resources around you—something you read, see, hear, discuss, or think about. (See the top half of the graphic below.) But at other times you need idea generators, strategies to try when your ideas dry up. If one strategy doesn't work for your task, try another. (See the lower half of the graphic.)

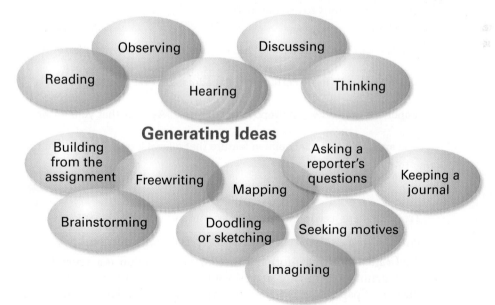

## Building from Your Assignment

For more detail about this assignment, turn to pp. 54–55 in Ch. 4.

Learning to write is learning what questions to ask yourself. Your assignment may trigger this process, raising some questions and answering others. For example, Ben Tran jotted notes in his book as his instructor and classmates discussed his first assignment — recalling a personal experience.

The assignment clarified what audience to address and what purpose to set. Ben's classmates asked about length, format, and due date, but Ben saw three big questions: Which experience should I pick? How did it change me? Why was it so important for me? Ben still didn't know what he'd write about, but he had figured out the questions to tackle first.

*What event? What consequences?*

Write about one specific experience that changed how you acted, thought, or felt. Use your experience as a springboard for reflection. Your purpose

*Tell the story but do more — reflect & show importance.*

is not merely to tell an interesting story but to show your readers—your

*What purpose? 2 parts!*

*What readers? class + prof.*

instructor and your classmates—the importance of that experience for

you.

Sometimes assignments assume that you already know something critical — how to address a particular audience or what to include in some type of writing. When Amalia Blackhawk read her argument assignment, she jotted down questions to ask her instructor.

*Anything OK? Or only newspaper type of issue?*

Select a campus or local issue that matters to you, and write a letter to

*My classmates? The publication's readers?*

the editor about it. Be certain to tell readers what the issue is, why it is

*Editor of what?*

important, and how you propose to address it. Assume that your letter

*What's my purpose? Persuading readers to respect my view or to agree?*

will appear in a special opinion feature that allows letters longer than the

usual word-count limits.

*How long is the usual letter? How long should mine be? Anything else letters like this should do?*

Try these steps as you examine an assignment:

1. *Read through the assignment once* to discover its overall direction.

2. *Read it again*, marking information about your situation as a writer. Does the assignment identify or suggest your audience, your purpose in writing, the type of paper expected, the parts typical of that kind of writing, or the format required?

3. *List the questions that the assignment raises for you.* Exactly what do you need to decide — the type of topic to pick, the focus to develop, the issues or aspects to consider, or other guidelines to follow?

4. *Finally, list any questions that the assignment doesn't answer or ask you to answer.* Ask your instructor about these questions.

## Learning by Doing 🗨 Building from Your Assignment

Select an assignment from this book, another textbook, or another class, and make notes about it. Are there unanswered questions you want to clarify with your instructor? If so, make a list of these questions, and then exchange your list and assignment with a classmate. Make notes for your peer, suggesting possible answers or additional questions that might be posed to the instructor. Then compare responses.

## Brainstorming

A *brainstorm* is a sudden insight or inspiration. As a writing strategy, brainstorming uses free association to stimulate a chain of ideas, often to personalize a topic and break it down into specifics. Start with a word or phrase, and spend a set period of time simply listing ideas as rapidly as possible. Write down whatever comes to mind with no editing or going back.

As a group activity, brainstorming gains from varied perspectives. At work, it can fill a specific need — finding a name for a product or an advertising slogan. In college, you can brainstorm with a few others or your entire class. Sit facing one another. Designate one person to record on paper, screen, or chalkboard whatever the others suggest. After several minutes of calling out ideas, look over the recorder's list for useful results. Online, toss out ideas during a chat or post them for all to consider.

On your own, brainstorm to define a topic, generate an example, or find a title for a finished paper. Angie Ortiz brainstormed after her instructor assigned a paper ("Demonstrate from your experience how electronic technology affects our lives"). She wrote *electronic technology* on the page, set her alarm for fifteen minutes, and began to scribble.

> Electronic technology
> Cell phone, laptop, tablet. Plus smart TV, cable, DVDs. Too much?!
> Always on call — at home, in car, at school. Always something playing.
> Spend so much time in electronic world — phone calls, texting, social
>     media. Cuts into time really hanging with friends — face-to-face time.
> Less aware of my surroundings outside of the electronic world?

When her alarm went off, Angie took a break. After returning to her list, she crossed out ideas that did not interest her and circled her final promising question. A focus began to emerge: the capacity of the electronic world to expand information but reduce awareness.

When you want to brainstorm, try this advice:

1. *Launch your thoughts with a key word or phrase.* If you need a topic, try a general term (*computer*); if you need an example for a paragraph in progress, try specifics (*financial errors computers make*).

2. *Set a time limit.* Ten minutes (or so) is enough for strenuous thinking.

3. *Rapidly list brief items.* Stick to words, phrases, or short sentences that you can quickly scan later.

4. *Don't stop.* Don't worry about spelling, repetition, or relevance. Don't judge, and don't arrange: just produce. Record whatever comes to mind, as fast as you can. If your mind goes blank, keep moving, even if you only repeat what you've just written.

When you finish, circle or check anything intriguing. Scratch out whatever looks useless or dull. Then try some conscious organizing: Are any thoughts related? Can you group them? Does the group suggest a topic?

## Learning by Doing 🖉 Brainstorming

From the following list, choose a subject that interests you, that you know something about, and that you'd like to learn more about—in other words, that you might like to write on.

| | | |
|---|---|---|
| challenges/fears | the environment | health/fitness |
| dreams | family | pets |
| education | food | technology/social media |
| entertainment | friends | work |

For five minutes write as quickly as you can about your subject, listing everything that comes to mind about it, including all pertinent details. If your writing brings up a debatable issue (such as whether or not workplaces should offer flexible schedules), consider pros, cons, and alternative points of view. If it calls to mind an event (such as a memorable family occasion), list the details of the event in chronological order. Exchange your work with a peer, and see if you can add new ideas or insights to each other's brainstorming.

## Freewriting

To tap your unconscious by *freewriting*, simply write sentences without stopping for about fifteen minutes. The sentences don't have to be grammatical, coherent, or stylish; just keep them flowing to unlock an idea's potential.

Generally, freewriting is most productive if it has an aim—for example, finding a topic, a purpose, or a question you want to answer. Angie Ortiz wrote her topic at the top of a page—and then explored her rough ideas.

For Ortiz's brainstorming, see p. 371.

Electronic devices—do they isolate us? I chat all day online and by phone, but that's quick communication, not in-depth conversation. I don't really spend much time hanging with friends and getting to know what's going on with them. I love listening to music on my phone on campus, but maybe I'm not as aware of my surroundings as I could be. I miss seeing things, like the new art gallery that I walk by every day. I didn't even notice the new sculpture park in front! Then, at night, I do assignments on my computer, browse the Web, and watch some cable. I'm in my own little electronic world most of the time. I love technology, but what else am I missing?

Angie's result wasn't polished prose. Still, in a short time she produced a paragraph to serve as a springboard for her essay.

If you want to try freewriting, here's what you do:

1. *Write a sentence or two at the top of your page or file*—the idea you plan to develop by freewriting.

2. *Write without stopping for at least ten minutes.* Express whatever comes to mind, even "My mind is blank," until a new thought floats up.

3. *Explore without censoring yourself.* Don't cross out false starts or grammar errors. Don't worry about connecting ideas or finding perfect words. Use your initial sentences as a rough guide, not a straitjacket. New directions may be valuable.

4. *Prepare yourself*—if you want to. While you wait for your ideas to start racing, you may want to ask yourself some questions:

   What interests you about the topic? What do you know about it that the next person doesn't? What have you read, observed, or heard about it?

   How might you feel about this topic if you were someone else (a parent, an instructor, a person from another country)?

5. *Repeat the process, looping back to expand a good idea if you wish.* Poke at the most interesting parts to see if they will further unfold:

   What does that mean? If that's true, what then? So what?

   What other examples or evidence does this statement call to mind?

   What objections might a reader raise? How might you answer them?

## Learning by Doing 🎯 Freewriting

Select an idea from your current thinking or a brainstorming list. Write it at the top of a page or file, and freewrite for fifteen minutes. Share your freewriting with your classmates. If you wish, loop back to repeat this process.

## Doodling or Sketching

If you fill the margins of your notebooks with doodles, harness this artistic energy to generate ideas for writing. Elena Lopez began to sketch her collision with a teammate during a soccer tournament (Figure 19.1). She added stick figures, notes, symbols, and color as she outlined a series of events.

Try this advice as you develop ideas by doodling or sketching:

1. *Give your ideas room to grow.* Open a new file using a drawing program, doodle in pencil on a blank page, or sketch on a series of pages.

2. *Concentrate on your topic, but welcome new ideas.* Begin with a key visual in the center or at the top of a page. Add sketches or doodles as they occur to you to embellish, expand, define, or redirect your topic.

**Figure 19.1** Doodling or sketching to generate ideas.

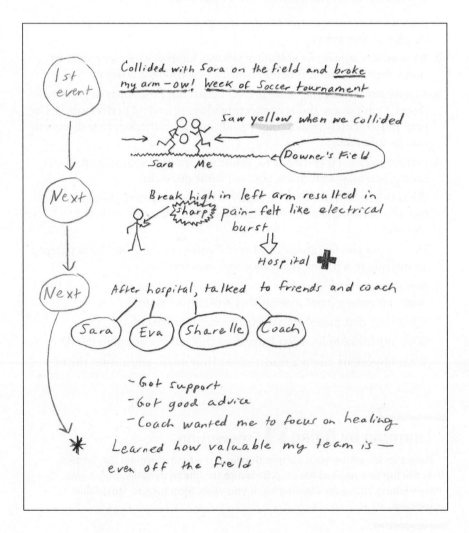

3. *Add icons, symbols, colors, figures, labels, notes, or questions.* Freely mix visuals and text, recording ideas without stopping to refine them.

4. *Follow up on your discoveries.* After a break, add notes to make connections, identify sequences, or convert visuals into descriptive sentences.

## Learning by Doing 🎥 Doodling or Sketching

Start with a doodle or sketch that illustrates your topic. Add related events, ideas, or details to develop your topic visually. Share your material with classmates; use their observations to help you refine your direction as a writer.

## Mapping

Mapping taps your visual and spatial creativity as you position ideas on the page, in a file, or with cloud software to show their relationships or relative importance. Ideas might radiate outward from a key term in the center, drop down from a key word at the top, sprout upward from a root idea, branch out from a trunk, flow across page or screen in a chronological or causal sequence, or follow a circular, spiral, or other form.

Andrew Choi used mapping to gather ideas for his proposal for revitalizing the campus radio station (Figure 19.2). He noted ideas on colored sticky notes—blue for problems, yellow for solutions, and pink for implementation details. Then he moved the sticky notes around on a blank page, arranging them as he connected ideas.

Here are some suggestions for mapping:

1. *Allow space for your map to develop.* Open a new file, try posterboard for arranging sticky notes or cards, or use a large page for notes.

2. *Begin with a topic or key idea.* Using your imagination, memory, class notes, or reading, place a key word at the center or top of a page.

3. *Add related ideas, examples, issues, or questions.* Quickly and spontaneously place these points above, below, or beside your key word.

4. *Refine the connections.* As your map evolves, use lines, arrows, or loops to connect ideas; box or circle them to focus attention; add colors to relate points or to distinguish source materials from your own ideas.

After a break, continue mapping to probe one part more deeply, refine the structure, add detail, or build an alternate map from a different viewpoint. Also try mapping to develop graphics that present ideas in visual form.

**Figure 19.2**
Mapping to
generate ideas.

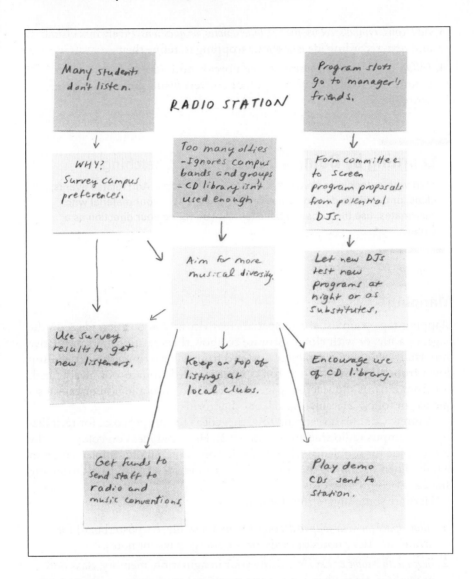

---

## Learning by Doing  Mapping

Start with a key word or idea that you know about. Map related ideas, using
visual elements to show how they connect. Share your map with classmates, and then use their questions or comments to refine your mapping.

---

## Imagining

Your imagination is a valuable resource for exploring possibilities—analyzing
an option, evaluating an alternative, or solving a problem—to discover surprising ideas, original examples, and unexpected relationships.

Suppose you asked, "What if the average North American lived more than a century?" No doubt many more people would be old. How would that shift affect doctors, nurses, and medical facilities? How might city planners respond? What would the change mean for shopping centers? For television programming? For leisure activities? For Social Security?

Use some of the following strategies to unleash your imagination:

1. *Speculate about changes, alternatives, and options.* What common assumption might you question or deny? What deplorable condition would you remedy? What changes in policy, practice, or attitude might avoid problems? What different paths in life might you take?

2. *Shift perspective.* Experiment with a different point of view. How would someone on the opposing side respond? A plant, an animal, a Martian? Shift the debate (whether retirees, not teens, should be allowed to drink) or the time (present to past or future).

3. *Envision what might be.* Join the others who have imagined a utopia (an ideal state) or an anti-utopia by envisioning alternatives — a better way of treating illness, electing a president, or ordering a chaotic jumble.

4. *Synthesize.* Synthesis (generating new ideas by combining previously separate ideas) is the opposite of analysis (breaking ideas down into component parts). Synthesize to make fresh connections, fusing materials — perhaps old or familiar — into something new.

For more about analysis and synthesis, see pp. 24–26.

## Learning by Doing 🖭 Imagining

Begin with a problem that cries out for a solution, a condition that requires a remedy, or a situation that calls for change. Ask "What if?" or start with "Suppose that" to trigger your imagination. Share ideas with your classmates.

## Asking a Reporter's Questions

Journalists, assembling facts to write a news story, ask themselves six simple questions — the five *W*'s and an *H*:

| | | |
|---|---|---|
| Who? | Where? | Why? |
| What? | When? | How? |

In the *lead,* or opening paragraph, of a good news story, the writer tries to condense the whole story into a sentence or two, answering all six questions.

A giant homemade fire balloon [*what*] startled residents of Costa Mesa [*where*] last night [*when*] as Ambrose Barker, 79, [*who*] zigzagged across the sky at nearly 300 miles per hour [*how*] in an attempt to set a new altitude record [*why*].

Later in the news story, the reporter will add details, using the six basic questions to generate more about what happened and why.

For your college writing, use these questions to generate details. They can help you explore the significance of a childhood experience, analyze what happened at a moment in history, or investigate a campus problem. Don't worry if some go nowhere or are repetitive. Later you'll weed out irrelevant points and keep those that look promising.

For a topic that is not based on your personal experience, you may need to do reading or interviewing to answer some of the questions. Take, for example, the topic of the assassination of President John F. Kennedy, and notice how each question can lead to further questions.

- *Who* was John F. Kennedy? What kind of person was he? What kind of president? Who was with him when he was killed? Who was nearby?
- *What* happened to Kennedy? What events led up to the assassination? What happened during it? What did the media do? What did people across the country do? What did someone who remembers this event do?
- *Where* was Kennedy assassinated — city, street, vehicle, seat? Where was he going? Where did the shots likely come from? Where did they hit him? Where did he die?
- *When* was he assassinated — day, month, year, time? When did Kennedy decide to go to this city? When — precisely — were the shots fired? When did he die? When was a suspect arrested?
- *Why* was Kennedy assassinated? What are some of the theories? What solid evidence is available? Why has this event caused controversy?
- *How* was Kennedy assassinated? How many shots were fired? Specifically what caused his death? How can we get at the truth of this event?

## Learning by Doing 🖎 Asking a Reporter's Questions

Choose one of the following topics, or use one of your own:

A memorable event in history or in your life
A concert or other performance that you have attended
An accomplishment on campus or an occurrence in your city
An important speech or a proposal for change
A questionable stand someone has taken

Answer the six reporter's questions about the topic. Then write a sentence or two synthesizing the answers to the six questions. Incorporate that sentence into an introductory paragraph for an essay that you might write later.

## Seeking Motives

In much college writing, you will try to explain motives behind human behavior. In a history paper, you might consider how George Washington's conduct shaped the presidency. In a literature essay, you might analyze the motives of Hester Prynne in *The Scarlet Letter*. Because people, including characters in fiction, are so complex, this task is challenging.

For more on writing about literature, see Ch. 13.

To understand any human act, according to philosopher-critic Kenneth Burke, you can break it down into five components, a *pentad*, and ask questions about each one. Burke's pentad overlaps the reporter's questions but also can show how components of a human act affect one another, taking you deeper into motives. Suppose you are writing a political-science paper on President Lyndon Baines Johnson (LBJ), sworn in as president right after President Kennedy's assassination in 1963. A year later, he was elected to the post by a landslide. By 1968, however, he had decided not to run for a second term. You use Burke's pentad to investigate why.

1. *The act:* What was done?

    Announcing the decision to leave office without standing for reelection.

2. *The actor:* Who did it?

    President Johnson.

3. *The agency:* What means did the person use to make it happen?

    A televised address to the nation.

4. *The scene:* Where, when, and under what circumstances did it happen?

    Washington, DC, March 31, 1968. Protesters against the Vietnam War were gaining influence. The press was increasingly critical of the war. Senator Eugene McCarthy, an antiwar candidate for president, had made a strong showing against LBJ in the New Hampshire primary.

5. *The purpose or motive for acting:* What could have made the person do it?

    LBJ's motives might have included avoiding probable defeat, escaping further personal attacks, sparing his family, making it easier for his successor to pull out of the war, and easing dissent among Americans.

Next, you can pair Burke's five components and ask about the pairs:

| | | |
|---|---|---|
| actor to act | act to scene | scene to agency |
| actor to scene | act to agency | scene to purpose |
| actor to purpose | act to purpose | agency to purpose |

| | |
|---|---|
| PAIR | actor to agency |
| QUESTION | What did LBJ [actor] have to do with his televised address [agency]? |
| ANSWER | Commanding the attention of a vast audience, LBJ must have felt in control—though his ability to control the situation in Vietnam was slipping. |

Not all the paired questions will prove fruitful; some may not even apply. But one or two might reveal valuable connections and start you writing.

----

## Learning by Doing  Seeking Motives

Choose a puzzling action—perhaps something you, a family member, or a friend has done; a decision of a political figure; or something in a movie, on television, or in a book. Apply Burke's pentad to seek motives for the action. If you wish, also pair up components. When you believe you understand the individual's motivation, write a paragraph explaining the action, and share it with classmates.

----

## Keeping a Journal

For ideas about keeping a reading journal, see p. 22.

Journal writing richly rewards anyone who engages in it regularly. You can write anywhere or anytime: all you need is a few minutes to record an entry and the willingness to set down what you think and feel. Your journal will become a mine studded with priceless nuggets—thoughts, observations, reactions, and revelations that are yours for the taking. As you write, you can rifle your well-stocked journal for topics, insights, examples, and other material. The best type of journal is the one that's useful to *you*.

**Reflective Journals.** When you write in your journal, put less emphasis on recording what happened, as you would in a diary, than on *reflecting* about what you do or see, hear or read, learn or believe. An entry can be a list or an outline, a paragraph or an essay, a poem or a letter you don't intend to send. Describe a person or a place, set down a conversation, or record insights into actions. Consider your pet peeves, fears, dreams, treasures, or moral dilemmas. Use your experience as a writer to nourish and inspire your writing, recording what worked, what didn't, and how you reacted to each.

For more on responding to reading, see Ch. 2.

For responsive journal prompts, see the end of each selection in *A Writer's Reader*.

**Responsive Journals.** Sometimes you *respond* to something in particular—your assigned reading, a classroom discussion, a movie, a conversation, or an observation. Faced with a long paper, you might assign *yourself* a focused response journal so you have plenty of material to use.

**Warm-Up Journals.** To prepare for an assignment, you can group ideas, scribble outlines, sketch beginnings, capture stray thoughts, record relevant material. Of course, a quick comment may turn into a draft.

**E-Journals.** Once you create a file and make entries by date or subject, you can record ideas, feelings, images, memories, and quotations. You will find it easy to copy and paste inspiring e-mail, quotations from Web pages, or images and sounds. Always identify the source of copied material so that you won't later confuse it with your original writing.

**Blogs.** Like traditional journals, blogs aim for frank, honest, immediate entries. Unlike journals, they often explore a specific topic and may be available publicly on the Web or privately by invitation. Especially in an online class, you might blog about your writing or research processes.

## Learning by Doing 🔟 Keeping a Journal

Keep a journal for at least a week. Each day record your thoughts, feelings, observations, and reactions. Reflect on what happens, and respond to what you read, including selections from this book. Then bring your journal to class, and read aloud to your classmates the entry you like best.

# Getting Ready

Once you have generated a suitable topic and some ideas related to that topic, you are ready to get down to the job of actually writing.

## Setting Up Circumstances

If you can write only with your shoes off or with a can of soda nearby, set yourself up that way. Some writers need to hear blaring rap music; others need quiet. Create an environment that puts you in the mood for writing.

**Devote One Special Place to Writing.** Your place should have good lighting and space to spread out. It may be a desk in your room, the dining room table, or a quiet library cubicle—someplace where no one will bother you, where your mind and body will settle in, and preferably where you can leave projects and keep handy your computer and materials.

**Establish a Ritual.** Some writers find that a ritual relaxes them and helps them get started. You might open a soda, straighten your desk, turn music on (or off), and create a new file on the computer.

**Relocate.** If you're stuck, try moving from library to home or from kitchen to bedroom. Try an unfamiliar place—a restaurant, an airport, a park.

**Reduce Distractions.** Most of us can't prevent interruptions, but we can reduce them. If you expect your boyfriend to call, call him before you start writing. If you have small children, write when they are asleep or at school. Turn off your phone, and concentrate hard. Let others know you are serious about writing; allow yourself to give it full attention.

**Write at Your Best Time.** Some think best early in the morning; others favor the small hours when their stern self-critic might be asleep, too. Either time can also reduce distractions from others.

**Write on a Schedule.** Writing at a predictable time of day worked marvels for English novelist Anthony Trollope, who would start at 5:30 A.M., write 2,500 words before 8:30 A.M., and then go to his job at the post office. (He wrote more than sixty books.) Even if you can't set aside the same time every day, it may help to decide, "Today from four to five, I'll write."

## Preparing Your Mind

Ideas, images, or powerful urges to write may arrive like sudden miracles. Even if you are taking a shower or heading to a movie, yield to impulse and write. Encourage such moments by opening your mind to inspiration.

**Talk about Your Writing.** Discuss ideas in person, by phone, or online with a classmate or friend, encouraging questions, comments, and suggestions. Or talk to yourself, recording your thoughts on your phone while you walk your dog or wait for your laundry to dry.

**Lay Out Your Plans.** Tell a nearby listener—your next-door neighbor, spouse, parent, friend—why you want to write this paper, what you'll put in it, how you'll lay it out. If you hear "That sounds good," you'll be encouraged. If you see a yawn, you'll still have ideas in motion.

**Keep a Notebook or Journal Handy.** Always keep some paper in your pocket or backpack or on the night table to write down good ideas that pop into your mind. Imagination may strike in the grocery checkout line, in the doctor's waiting room, or during a lull on the job.

**Read.** The step from reading to writing is a short one. Even when you're reading for fun, you're involved with words. You might hit on something for your paper. Or read purposefully: set out to read and take notes.

---

### DISCOVERY CHECKLIST

- ☐ Is your environment organized for writing? What changes might help you reduce distractions and procrastination?

- ☐ Have you scheduled enough time to get ready to write? How might you adjust your schedule or your expectations to encourage productivity?

- ☐ Is your assignment clear? What additional questions might you want to ask about what you are expected to do?

- ☐ Have you generated enough ideas that interest you? What might help you expand, focus, or deepen your ideas?

---

## Learning by Doing 🎬 Reflecting on Generating Ideas

Select one method of generating ideas that you find to be a productive or enjoyable way to begin writing. Reflect on your success using the method itself to generate ideas about why it works for you. In a pair or a team, have each person advocate for his or her preferred method, presenting its benefits, acknowledging its limitations, and trying to persuade others to give it a try.

# Strategies for Stating a Thesis and Planning

# 20

Starting to write often seems a chaotic activity, but the strategies in this chapter can help create order. For most papers, you will want to consider your purpose and audience and then focus on a central point by discovering, stating, and improving a thesis. To help you arrange your material, the chapter also includes advice on grouping ideas and outlining.

## Shaping Your Topic for Your Purpose and Your Audience

As you work on your college papers, you may feel as if you're juggling — selecting weighty points and lively details, tossing them into the air, keeping them all moving in sequence. Busy as you are juggling, however, your performance almost always draws a crowd — your instructor, classmates, or other readers. They'll expect your attention, too, as you try to achieve your purpose — probably informing, explaining, or persuading.

For critical questions about purpose, see p. 384.

Think carefully about your audience and purpose as you plan. If you want to show your classmates and instructor the importance of an event, start by deciding how much detail they need. If most of them have gotten speeding tickets, they'll need less information about that event than city commuters might. However, to achieve your purpose, you'll need to go beyond what happened to why the event mattered to you. No matter how many tickets your readers have gotten, they won't know what that experience means to you unless you share that information. They may incorrectly assume that you worried about being late to class or having to pay higher insurance rates. In fact, you had suddenly realized your narrow escape from an accident like your cousin's, a recognition that motivated you to change.

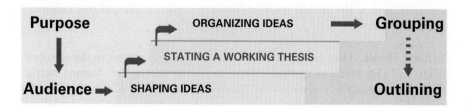

**Purpose** → ORGANIZING IDEAS → **Grouping**

STATING A WORKING THESIS

**Audience** → SHAPING IDEAS → **Outlining**

Similarly, if you want to persuade county officials to change the way absentee ballots are distributed to college students, you'll need to support your idea with reasons and evidence—drawing on state election laws and legal precedents familiar to these readers as well as experiences of student voters. You may need to show how your proposal would solve existing problems and also why it would do so better than other proposals.

Plan for your purpose and audience using questions such as these:

- *What is your general purpose?* What do you want to accomplish? Do you want readers to smile, think, or agree? To learn, accept, respect, care, change, or reply? How might your writing accomplish your aims?

- *Who are your readers?* If they are not clearly identified by your assignment or situation, what do you assume about them? What do they know or want to know? What opinions do they hold? What do they find informative or persuasive? How might you appeal to them?

- *How might you narrow and focus your ideas about the topic,* given what you know or assume about your purpose and audience? Which slant would best achieve your purpose? What points would appeal most strongly to your readers? What details would engage or persuade them?

- *What qualities of good writing have been discussed in your class,* explained in your syllabus, or identified in readings? What criteria have emerged from exchanges of drafts with classmates or comments from your instructor? How might you demonstrate these qualities to readers?

## Learning by Doing 🔯 Considering Purpose and Audience

Think back to a recent writing task—a college essay, a job application, a report or memo at work, a letter to a campus office, or some other piece. Write a brief description of your situation as a writer at that time. What was your purpose? Who—exactly—were your readers? How did you account for both as you planned? How might you have made your writing more effective?

## Stating and Using a Thesis

Most pieces of effective writing are unified around one main point. That is, all the subpoints and supporting details are relevant to that point. Generally, after you have read an essay, you can sum up the writer's main point in a sentence, even if the author has not stated it explicitly. We call this summary statement a *thesis*.

**Explicit Thesis.**  Often a thesis will be explicit, plainly stated, in the selection itself. In "The Myth of the Latin Woman: I Just Met a Girl Named María" from *The Latin Deli* (University of Georgia Press, 1993), Judith Ortiz Cofer states her thesis at the end of the first paragraph: "You can leave the Island, master the English language, and travel as far as you can, but if you are a Latina, especially one like me who so obviously belongs to Rita Moreno's gene pool, the Island travels with you." This clear statement, strategically placed, helps readers see her point.

**Implicit Thesis**. Sometimes a thesis is implicit, indirectly suggested rather than directly stated. In "The Niceness Solution," a selection from Bruce Bawer's *Beyond Queer* (Free Press, 1996), Paul Varnell describes an ordinance "banning rude behavior, including rude speech," passed in Raritan, New Jersey. After discussing a 1580 code of conduct, he identifies four objections to such attempts to limit free speech. He concludes with this sentence: "Sensibly, Raritan Police Chief Joseph Sferro said he would not enforce the new ordinance." Although Varnell does not state his main point in one concise sentence, readers know that he opposes the Raritan law and any other attempts to legislate "niceness."

The purpose of most academic and workplace writing is to inform, to explain, or to convince. To achieve any of these purposes, you must make your main point crystal clear. A thesis sentence helps you clarify your idea and stay on track as you write. It also helps your readers see your point and follow your discussion. Sometimes you may want to imply your thesis, but if you state it explicitly, you ensure that readers cannot miss it.

## Learning by Doing 🄣 Identifying Theses

Working in a small group, select and read five essays from this book (or read those your instructor has chosen). Then, individually, write out the thesis for each essay. Some thesis statements are stated outright (explicit), but others are indirect (implicit). Compare and contrast the thesis statements you identified with those your classmates found. How do you account for differences? Try to agree on a thesis statement for each essay.

*If you select the essays yourself, choose them from Chs. 4–12.*

## How to Discover a Working Thesis

It's rare for a writer to develop a perfect thesis statement early in the writing process and then to write an effective essay that fits it exactly. What you should aim for is a *working thesis* — a statement that can guide you but that you will ultimately refine. Ideas for a working thesis are probably all around you.

Your topic identifies the area you want to explore. To convert a topic to a thesis, you need to add your own slant, attitude, or point. A useful thesis contains not only the key words that identify your *topic* but also the *point* you want to make or the *attitude* you intend to express.

*In Chs. 4–12, look for specific advice under headings that mention a thesis and for the Thesis Checklists. Also, watch for the pink labels that identify thesis examples in the readings.*

Topic   +   Slant or Attitude or Point   =   Working Thesis

Suppose you want to identify and write about a specific societal change.

TOPIC IDEA          **old-fashioned formal courtesy**

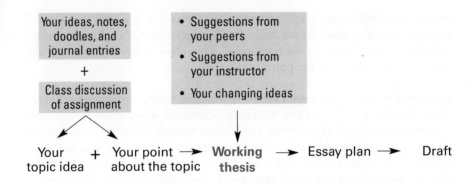

Now you experiment, testing ideas to make the topic your own.

TRIAL          Old-fashioned formal courtesy is a thing of the past.

Although your trial sentence emphasizes change, it's still circular, repeating rather than advancing a workable point. It doesn't say anything new about old-fashioned formal courtesy; it simply defines *old-fashioned*. You still need to state your own slant—maybe why things have changed.

TOPIC IDEA + SLANT     old-fashioned formal courtesy + its decline as gender
                       roles have changed

WORKING THESIS     As the roles of men and women have changed in our
                   society, old-fashioned formal courtesy has declined.

For advice about
revising a thesis,
see pp. 443–44.
With this working thesis, you could focus on how changing societal attitudes toward gender roles have caused changes in courtesy. Later, when you revise, you may refine your thesis further—perhaps restricting it to courtesy toward the elderly, toward women, or, despite stereotypes, toward men. The chart on page 388 suggests ways to develop a working thesis.

Once you have a working thesis, be sure its point accomplishes the purpose of your assignment. Suppose your assignment asks you to compare and contrast two local newspapers' coverage of a Senate election. Ask yourself what the point of that comparison and contrast is. Simply noting a difference won't be enough to satisfy most readers.

NO SPECIFIC POINT     The *Herald*'s coverage of the Senate elections was
                      different from the *Courier*'s.

WORKING THESIS        The *Herald*'s coverage of the Senate elections was
                      more thorough than the *Courier*'s.

## Learning by Doing 🔘 Discovering a Thesis

Write a sentence, a working thesis, that unifies each of the following groups of details. Then compare and contrast your theses with those of your classmates. What other information would you need to write a good paper on each topic? How might the thesis statement change as you write the paper?

1. Recycling reduces waste and saves space in landfills.
   Recycling reduces air and water pollution.
   Recycling reduces our impact on forests, wetlands, and other homes for wildlife.
   Manufacturing with recycled material saves energy.
   Recycling programs create jobs.
2. Voter turnout among 18- to 25-year-olds is relatively low.
   Because of this low turnout, young people's interests may be underrepresented.
   Voting, and other political involvement, can make a difference.
   Young people who vote for civic leaders can help make sure that government truly represents their interests.
   Young people who vote on policy issues can help shape a better future for themselves and others.

## How to State a Thesis

Once you have a notion of a topic and main point, use these pointers to state or improve a thesis to guide your planning and drafting.

- *State the thesis sentence exactly.* Replace vague or general wording with concise, detailed, and down-to-earth language.

  TOO GENERAL          There are a lot of troubles with chemical wastes.

  Are you going to deal with all chemical wastes, throughout all of history, all over the world? Will you list all the troubles they can cause?

  MORE SPECIFIC        Careless dumping of leftover paint is to blame for a recent outbreak of skin rashes in Atlanta.

  For an argument, you need to take a stand on a debatable issue that would allow others to take different positions. State yours exactly.

  SPECIFIC STAND       The recent health consequences of carelessly dumping leftover paint require Atlanta officials both to regulate and to educate.

- *State just one central idea in the thesis sentence.* If your paper is to focus on one point, your thesis should state only one main idea.

  TOO MANY IDEAS       Careless dumping of leftover paint has caused a serious problem in Atlanta, and a new kind of biodegradable paint has been developed, and it offers a promising solution to one chemical waste dilemma.

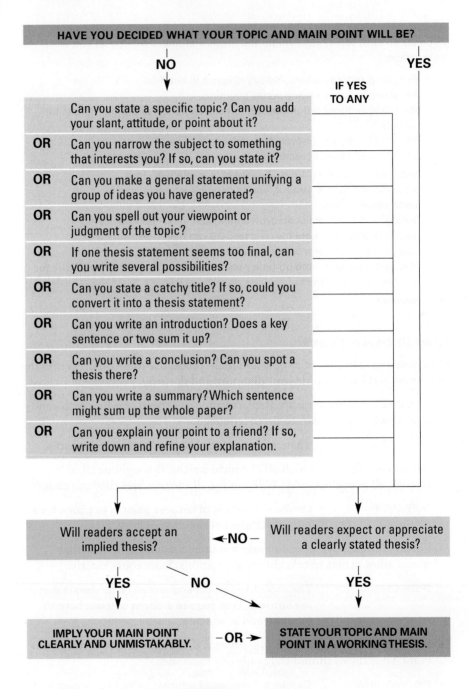

**HAVE YOU DECIDED WHAT YOUR TOPIC AND MAIN POINT WILL BE?**

NO

YES

IF YES
TO ANY

Can you state a specific topic? Can you add your slant, attitude, or point about it?

**OR**  Can you narrow the subject to something that interests you? If so, can you state it?

**OR**  Can you make a general statement unifying a group of ideas you have generated?

**OR**  Can you spell out your viewpoint or judgment of the topic?

**OR**  If one thesis statement seems too final, can you write several possibilities?

**OR**  Can you state a catchy title? If so, could you convert it into a thesis statement?

**OR**  Can you write an introduction? Does a key sentence or two sum it up?

**OR**  Can you write a conclusion? Can you spot a thesis there?

**OR**  Can you write a summary? Which sentence might sum up the whole paper?

**OR**  Can you explain your point to a friend? If so, write down and refine your explanation.

Will readers accept an implied thesis?   ◄—NO—   Will readers expect or appreciate a clearly stated thesis?

YES          NO                                     YES

**IMPLY YOUR MAIN POINT CLEARLY AND UNMISTAKABLY.**   —OR ►   **STATE YOUR TOPIC AND MAIN POINT IN A WORKING THESIS.**

| | |
|---|---|
| ONE CENTRAL IDEA | Careless dumping of leftover paint has caused a serious problem in Atlanta. |
| OR | A new kind of biodegradable paint offers a promising solution to one chemical waste dilemma. |

- *State your thesis positively.* You can usually find evidence to support a positive statement, but you'd have to rule out every possible exception in order to prove a negative one. Negative statements also may sound half-hearted and seem to lead nowhere.

| | |
|---|---|
| NEGATIVE | Researchers do not know what causes breast cancer. |
| POSITIVE | The causes of breast cancer still challenge researchers. |

Presenting the topic positively as a "challenge" might lead to a paper about an exciting quest. Besides, to show that researchers are working on the problem would be relatively easy, given an hour of online research.

- *Limit your thesis to a statement that you can demonstrate.* A workable thesis is limited so that you can support it with sufficient convincing evidence. It should stake out just the territory that you can cover thoroughly within the length assigned and the time available, and no more. The shorter the essay, the less development your thesis should promise or require. Likewise, the longer the essay, the more development and complexity your thesis should suggest.

| | |
|---|---|
| DIFFICULT TO SHOW | For centuries, popular music has announced vital trends in Western society. |
| DIFFICULT TO SHOW | My favorite piece of music is Beethoven's Fifth Symphony. |

The first thesis above could inform a whole encyclopedia of music; the second would require that you explain why that symphony is your favorite, contrasting it with all the other musical compositions you know. The following thesis sounds far more workable for a brief essay.

| | |
|---|---|
| POSSIBLE TO SHOW | In the past two years, a rise in the number of preteenagers has resulted in a comeback for heavy metal on the local concert scene. |

Unlike a vague statement or a broad, unrestricted claim, a limited thesis narrows and refines a topic, restricting your essay to a reasonable scope.

| | |
|---|---|
| TOO VAGUE | Native American blankets are very beautiful. |
| TOO BROAD | Native Americans have adapted to cultural shifts. |
| POSSIBLE TO SHOW | For some members of the Apache tribe, working in high-rise construction has allowed both economic stability and cultural integrity. |

For more on revising a thesis, see pp. 443–44.

If the suggestions in this chapter have helped you draft a working thesis—even an awkward or feeble one—you'll find plenty of advice about improving it in the next few pages and more later about revising it. But what if you're freezing up because your thesis simply won't take shape? First, relax. Your thesis will emerge later on—as your thinking matures and you figure out your paper's true direction, as peer readers spot the idea in your paper you're too close to see, as you talk with your instructor and suddenly grasp how to take your paper where you want it to go. In the meantime, plan and write so that you create a rich environment that will encourage your thesis to emerge.

## Learning by Doing 🔲 Examining Thesis Statements

You have been assigned an essay of one thousand words (approximately four double-spaced pages). Review the following thesis statements:

1. Violence in television shows or movies can be harmful to children.
2. Students have developed a variety of techniques to conceal inadequate study from their instructors.
3. I don't know how to cook.
4. Volunteering at a women's shelter gave me an inside look at the consequences of domestic abuse, and I learned how to incorporate volunteer work into my busy schedule.
5. Trophy hunting of animals should be outlawed.
6. No war is a just war.
7. The government's "war on drugs" is a failure.

With your classmates, discuss each thesis statement and answer the following questions:

- Is the thesis stated clearly?
- Does the thesis state just one idea?
- Is the thesis stated positively?
- Is the thesis sufficiently limited for an essay of this size?
- Is the thesis too broad or too narrow?
- Is the thesis debatable?
- How might the thesis be improved?

## How to Improve a Thesis

Simply knowing what a solid working thesis *should* do may not help you improve your thesis. Whether yours is a first effort or a refined version, turn to the Take Action chart to help you figure out how to improve your thesis.

# Take Action  Building a Stronger Thesis

Ask each question listed in the left-hand column of the chart to consider whether your draft might need work on that issue. If so, follow the ASK — LOCATE SPECIFICS — TAKE ACTION sequence to revise.

| **1** ASK | **2** LOCATE SPECIFICS | **3** TAKE ACTION |
|---|---|---|
| Could I define or state my **topic** more clearly? | ■ Write out your current working thesis. <br><br> ■ Circle the **words** in it that **identify your topic**. <br><br> **WORKING THESIS:** (Adaptability) is essential for World Action volunteers. [What, exactly, does the topic *adaptability* mean?] | ■ Rework the circled topic. State it more **clearly**, and specify what it **means to you**. <br><br> ■ Define or identify the topic in terms of your **purpose** and the likely interests of your **audience**. <br><br> **REVISED THESIS:** An ability to adjust to, even thrive under, challenging circumstances is essential for World Action volunteers. |
| Could I define or state my **slant** more clearly? | ■ Write out your current working thesis. <br><br> ■ Underline the **words that state your slant**, attitude, or point about your topic. <br><br> **WORKING THESIS:** Volunteering is an invaluable experience. [Why or in what ways is volunteering invaluable?] | ■ Rework your underlined slant. Jot down ideas to **sharpen** it and express an **engaging approach** to your topic. <br><br> ■ Refine it to accomplish your **purpose** and appeal to your **audience**. <br><br> **REVISED THESIS:** Volunteering builds practical skills while connecting volunteers more fully to their communities. |
| Could I **limit my thesis** to develop it more successfully? | ■ Write out your current working thesis. <br><br> ■ Decide whether it establishes a **task that you could accomplish** given the **available time** and the **expected length**. <br><br> **WORKING THESIS:** Rock and roll has evolved dramatically since the 1950s. [Tracing this history in a few pages would be impossible.] | ■ **Restrict your thesis to a slice of the pie**, not the whole pie. <br><br> ■ **Focus on one part or element**, not several. Break it apart, and pick only a chunk. <br><br> ■ **Reduce many ideas to one point**, or **convert a negative statement to a positive one**. <br><br> **REVISED THESIS:** The music of the alternative-rock band Wilco continues to evolve as members experiment with vocal moods and instrumentation. |

Skim down the left-hand column to identify questions you might ask about your working thesis. When you answer a question with "Yes" or "Maybe," move straight across to Locate Specifics for that question. Use the activities there to pinpoint gaps, problems, or weaknesses. Then move across to Take Action. Use the advice that suits your problem as you revise.

## How to Use a Thesis to Organize

For more on using a thesis to develop an outline, see pp. 396–97.

Often a good, clear thesis will suggest an organization for your ideas.

| | |
|---|---|
| WORKING THESIS | Despite the disadvantages of living in a downtown business district, I wouldn't live anywhere else. |
| FIRST ¶S | Disadvantages of living in the business district |
| NEXT ¶S | Advantages of living there |
| LAST ¶ | Affirmation of your preference for downtown life |

Just putting your working thesis into words can help organize you and keep you on track. A clear thesis can guide you as you select details and connect sections of the essay.

For more on key terms in college assignments, see p. 332.

In addition, your thesis can prepare your readers for the pattern of development or sequence of ideas that you plan to present. As a writer, you look for key words (such as *compare, propose,* or *evaluate*) when you size up an assignment. Such words alert you to what's expected. When you write or revise your thesis, you can use such terms or their equivalents (such as *benefit* or *consequence* instead of *effect*) to preview for readers the likely direction of your paper. Then they, too, will know what to expect.

| | |
|---|---|
| WORKING THESIS | Expanding the campus program for energy conservation would bring welcome financial and environmental benefits. |
| FIRST ¶S | Explanation of the campus energy situation |
| NEXT ¶S | Justification of the need for the proposed expansion |
| NEXT ¶S | Financial benefits for the college and students |
| NEXT ¶S | Environmental benefits for the region and beyond |
| LAST ¶ | Concluding assertion of the value of the expansion |

As you write, however, you don't have to cling to a thesis for dear life. If further investigation changes your thinking, you can change your thesis.

| | |
|---|---|
| WORKING THESIS | Because wolves are a menace to people and farm animals, they ought to be exterminated. |
| REVISED THESIS | The wolf, a relatively peaceful animal useful in nature's scheme of things, ought to be protected. |

You can restate a thesis any time: as you write, revise, or revise again.

## Learning by Doing 🖾 Using a Thesis to Preview

Each of the following thesis statements is from a student paper in a different field. With your classmates, consider how each one previews the essay to come and how you would expect the essay to be organized into sections.

1. Although the intent of inclusion is to provide the best care for all children by treating both special- and general-education students equally, some people in the field believe that the full inclusion of disabled children in mainstream classrooms may not be in the best interest of either type of student. (From "Is Inclusion the Answer?" by Sarah E. Goers)

2. With ancient Asian roots and contemporary European influences, the Japanese language has continued to change and to reflect cultural change as well. (From "Japanese: Linguistic Diversity" by Stephanie Hawkins)

3. *Manifest destiny* was an expression by leaders and politicians in the 1840s to clarify continental extension and expansion and in a sense revitalize the mission and national destiny for Americans. (From ethnic studies examination answer by Angela Mendy)

4. By comparing the *Aeneid* with *Troilus and Criseyde*, one can easily see the effects of the code of courtly love on literature. (From "The Effect of the Code of Courtly Love: A Comparison of Virgil's *Aeneid* and Chaucer's *Troilus and Criseyde*" by Cindy Keeler)

5. The effects of pollutants on the endangered Least Tern entering the Upper Newport Bay should be quantified so that necessary action can be taken to further protect and encourage the species. (From "Contaminant Residues in Least Tern [*Sterna antillarum*] Eggs Nesting in Upper Newport Bay" by Susanna Olsen)

# Organizing Your Ideas

When you organize an essay, you select an order for the parts that makes sense and shows your readers how the ideas are connected. Often your organization will not only help a reader follow your points but also reinforce your emphases by moving from beginning to end or from least to most significant, as the table on page 394 illustrates.

## Grouping Your Ideas

While exploring a topic, you will usually find a few ideas that seem to belong together—two facts on New York traffic jams, four actions of New York drivers, three problems with New York streets. But similar ideas seldom appear together in your notes because you did not discover them all at the same time. For this reason, you need to sort your ideas into groups and arrange them in sequences. Here are six ways to work:

1. *Rainbow connections.* List the main points you're going to express. Highlight points that go together with the same color. When you write, follow the color code, and integrate related ideas at the same time.

2. *Emphasizing ideas.* Make a copy of your file of ideas or notes. Use your software tools to highlight, categorize, and shape your thinking by grouping or distinguishing ideas. Mark similar or related ideas in the

| Organization | Movement | Typical Use | Example |
|---|---|---|---|
| **Spatial** | Left to right, right to left, bottom to top, top to bottom, front to back, outside to inside | ■ Describing a place, a scene, or an environment<br>■ Describing a person's physical appearance | Describe an ocean vista, moving from the tidepools on the rocky shore to the plastic buoys floating offshore to the sparkling water meeting the sunset sky. |
| **Chronological** | What happens first, second, and next, continuing until the end | ■ Narrating an event<br>■ Explaining steps in a procedure<br>■ Explaining the development of an idea or a trend | Narrate the events that led up to an accident: leaving home late, stopping for an errand, checking messages while rushing along the highway, racing up to the intersection. |
| **Logical** | General to specific (or the reverse), least important to most, cause to effect, problem to solution | ■ Explaining an idea<br>■ Persuading readers to accept a stand, a proposal, or an evaluation | Analyze the effects of last year's storms by selecting four major consequences, placing the most important one last for emphasis. |

same way; call out major points. Then move related materials into groups.

Highlighting

Boxing

Showing color

Using **bold**, *italics*, underlining

- Adding bullets
1. Numbering

Changing **fonts**

Varying print sizes

3. *Linking.* List major points, and then draw lines (in color if you wish) to link related ideas. Figure 20.1 illustrates a linked list for an essay on Manhattan driving. The writer has connected related points, numbered their sequence, and supplied each group with a heading. Each heading will probably inspire a topic sentence to introduce a major division of the essay. Because one point, chauffeured luxury cars, failed to relate to any other, the writer has a choice: drop it or develop it.

4. *Solitaire.* Collect notes and ideas on roomy (5-by-8-inch) file cards, especially to write about literature or research. To organize, spread out the cards; arrange and rearrange them. When each idea seems to lead to the next, gather the cards into a deck in this order. As you write, deal yourself a card at a time, and turn its contents into sentences.

5. *Slide show.* Use presentation software to write your notes and ideas on "slides." When you're done, view your slides one by one or as a collection. Sort your slides into the most promising order.

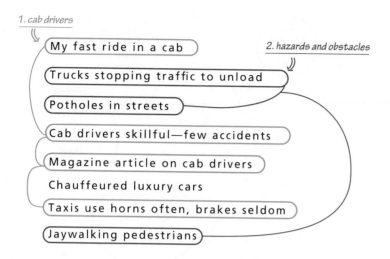

1. *cab drivers*

2. *hazards and obstacles*

**Figure 20.1** The linking method for grouping ideas.

6. *Clustering.* Clustering is a visual method for generating as well as grouping ideas. In the middle of a page, write your topic in a word or a phrase. Then think of the major divisions into which you might break your topic. For an essay on Manhattan drivers, your major divisions might be *types* of drivers: (1) taxi drivers, (2) bus drivers, (3) truck drivers, (4) New York drivers of private cars, and (5) out-of-town drivers of private cars. Arrange these divisions around your topic, circle them, and draw lines out from the major topic. You now have a rough plan for an essay. (See Figure 20.2.)

Around each division, make another cluster of details you might include — examples, illustrations, facts, statistics, opinions. Circle each specific item, connect it to the appropriate type of driver, and then expand the details into a paragraph. This technique lets you know where you have enough specific information to make your paper clear and interesting — and where you don't. If one subtopic has no small circles around it (such as "Bus Drivers" in Figure 20.2), either add specifics to expand it or drop it.

## Outlining

A familiar way to organize is to outline. A written outline, whether brief or detailed, acts as a map that you make before a journey. It shows where to leave from, where to stop along the way, and where to arrive. If you forget where you are going or what you want to say, you can consult your outline to get back on track. When you turn in your essay, your instructor may request an outline as both a map for readers and a skeletal summary.

- Some writers like to begin with a working thesis. If it's clear, it may suggest how to develop or expand an outline, allowing the plan for the paper to grow naturally from the idea behind it.

For more on thesis statements, see pp. 384–93.

**Figure 20.2** The clustering method for grouping ideas.

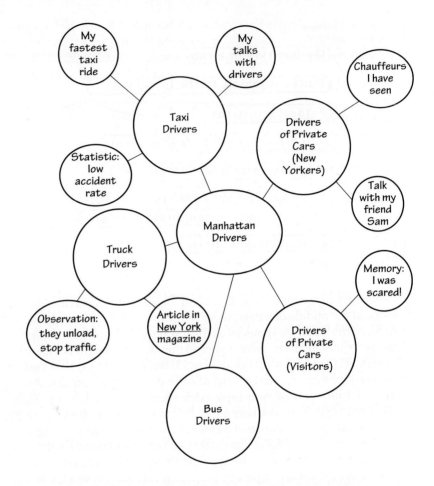

For more on using outlining for revision, see pp. 445–46.

- Others prefer to start with a loose informal outline — perhaps just a list of points to make. If readers find your papers mechanical, such an outline may free up your writing.
- Still others, especially for research papers or complicated arguments, like to lay out a complex job very carefully in a detailed formal outline. If readers find your writing disorganized and hard to follow, this more detailed plan might be especially useful.

**Thesis-Guided Outlines.** Your working thesis may identify ideas you can use to organize your paper. (If it doesn't, you may want to revise your thesis and then return to your outline or vice versa.) Suppose you are assigned an anthropology paper on the people of Melanesia. You focus on this point:

Working Thesis: Although the Melanesian pattern of family life may look strange to Westerners, it fosters a degree of independence that rivals our own.

If you lay out your ideas in the same order that they follow in the two parts of this thesis statement, your simple outline suggests an essay that naturally falls into two parts — features that seem strange and admirable results.

1. Features that appear strange to Westerners
   - A woman supported by her brother, not her husband
   - Trial marriages common
   - Divorce from her children possible for any mother
2. Admirable results of system
   - Wives not dependent on husbands for support
   - Divorce between mates uncommon
   - Greater freedom for parents and children

When you create a thesis-guided outline, look for the key element of your working thesis. This key element can suggest both a useful question to consider and an organization, as the table on page 394 illustrates.

**Informal Outlines.** For in-class writing, brief essays, and familiar topics, a short or informal outline, also called a *scratch outline,* may serve your needs. Jot down a list of points in the order you plan to make them. Use this outline, for your eyes only, to help you get organized, stick to the point, and remember ideas under pressure. The following example outlines a short paper explaining how outdoor enthusiasts can avoid illnesses carried by unsafe drinking water. It simply lists the methods for treating potentially unsafe water that the writer plans to explain.

Working Thesis: Campers and hikers need to ensure the safety of the water that they drink from rivers or streams.

Introduction: Treatments for potentially unsafe drinking water

1. Small commercial filter
   - Remove bacteria and protozoa including salmonella and E. coli
   - Use brands convenient for campers and hikers
2. Chemicals
   - Use bleach, chlorine, or iodine
   - Follow general rule: 12 drops per gallon of water
3. Boiling
   - Boil for 5 minutes (Red Cross) to 15 minutes (National Safety Council)
   - Store in a clean, covered container

Conclusion: Using one of three methods of treating water, campers and hikers can enjoy safe water from natural sources.

This simple outline could easily fall into a five-paragraph essay or grow to eight paragraphs — introduction, conclusion, and three pairs of paragraphs in between. You won't know how many you'll need until you write.

| Sample Thesis Statement | Type of Key Element | Examples of Key Element | Question You Might Ask | Organization of Outline |
|---|---|---|---|---|
| **A varied personal exercise program has four main *advantages*.** | Plural word | Words such as *benefits*, *advantages*, *teenagers*, or *reasons* | What are the types, kinds, or examples of this word? | List outline headings based on the categories or cases you identify. |
| **Wylie's *interpretation* of Van Gogh's last paintings unifies aesthetics and psychology.** | Key word identifying an approach or vantage point | Words such as *claim*, *argument*, *position*, *interpretation*, or *point of view* | What are the parts, aspects, or elements of this approach? | List outline headings based on the components that you identify. |
| ***Preparing* a pasta dinner for surprise guests can be an easy process.** | Key word identifying an activity | Words such as *preparing*, *harming*, or *improving* | How is this activity accomplished, or how does it happen? | Supply a heading for each step, stage, or element that the activity involves. |
| ***Although* the new wetland preserve will protect only some wildlife, it will bring several long-term benefits to the region.** | One part of the sentence subordinate to another | Sentence part beginning with a qualification such as *despite*, *because*, *since*, or *although* | What does the qualification include, and what does the main statement include? | Use a major heading for the qualification and another for the main statement. |
| **When Sandie Burns arrives in her wheelchair at the soccer field, other parents soon see that she is a *typical* soccer mom.** | General evaluation that assigns a quality or value to someone or something | Evaluative words such as *typical*, *unusual*, *valuable*, *notable*, or other specific qualities | What examples, illustrations, or clusters of details will show this quality? | Add a heading for each extended example or each group of examples or details you want to use. |
| **In spite of these tough economic times, the student senate *should* strongly recommend extended hours for the computer lab.** | Claim or argument advocating a certain decision, action, or solution | Words such as *should*, *could*, *might*, *ought to*, *need to*, or *must* | Which reasons and evidence will justify this opinion? Which will counter the opinions of others who disagree with it? | Provide a heading for each major justification or defensive point; add headings for countering reasons. |

An informal outline can be even briefer than the preceding one. To answer an exam question or prepare a very short paper, your outline might be no more than an *outer plan* — three or four phrases jotted in a list:

> Isolation of region
> Tradition of family businesses
> Growth of electronic commuting

The process of making an informal outline can help you figure out how to develop your ideas. Say you plan a "how-to" essay analyzing the process of buying a used car, beginning with this thesis:

> Working Thesis: Despite traps that await the unwary, preparing yourself before you shop can help you find a good used car.

The key word here is *preparing.* Considering *how* the buyer should prepare before shopping for a used car, you're likely to outline several ideas:

> –Read car blogs, car magazines, and *Consumer Reports.*
> –Check craigslist, dealer sites, and classified ads.
> –Make phone calls to several dealers.
> –Talk to friends who have bought used cars.
> –Know what to look and listen for when you test-drive.
> –Have a mechanic check out any car before you buy it.

After some horror stories about people who got taken by car sharks, you can discuss, point by point, your advice. You can always change the sequence, add or drop an idea, or revise your thesis as you go along.

---

## Learning by Doing 🎯 Moving from Outline to Thesis

Based on each of the following informal outlines, write a thesis statement expressing a possible slant, attitude, or point (even if you aren't sure that the position is entirely defensible). Compare thesis statements with classmates. What similarities and differences do you find? How do you account for these?

1. Smartphones
   Get the financial and service plans of various smartphone companies.
   Read the phone contracts as well as the promotional offers.
   Look for the time period, flexibility, and cancellation provisions.
   Check the display, keyboard, camera, apps, and other features.
2. Popular Mystery Novels
   Both Tony Hillerman and Margaret Coel have written mysteries with Native American characters and settings.
   Hillerman's novels feature members of the Navajo Tribal Police.

> Coel's novels feature a female attorney who is an Arapaho and a Jesuit priest at the reservation mission who grew up in Boston.
> Hillerman's stories take place mostly on the extensive Navajo Reservation in Arizona, New Mexico, and Utah.
> Coel's are set mostly on the large Wind River Reservation in Wyoming.
> Hillerman and Coel try to convey tribal culture accurately, although their mysteries involve different tribes.
> Both also explore similarities, differences, and conflicts between Native American cultures and the dominant culture.

> 3. Downtown Playspace
> Downtown Playspace has financial and volunteer support but needs more.
> Statistics show the need for a regional expansion of options for children.
> Downtown Playspace will serve visitors at the Children's Museum and local children in Head Start, preschool, and elementary schools.
> It will combine an outdoor playground with indoor technology space.
> Land and a building are available, but both require renovation.

**Formal Outlines.** A *formal outline* is an elaborate guide, built with time and care, for a long, complex paper. Because major reports, research papers, and senior theses require so much work, some professors and departments ask a writer to submit a formal outline at an early stage and to include one in the final draft. A formal outline shows how ideas relate one to another—which ones are equal and important (*coordinate*) and which are less important (*subordinate*). It clearly and logically spells out where you are going. If you outline again after writing a draft, you can use the revised outline to check your logic then as well, perhaps revealing where to revise.

When you make a full formal outline, follow these steps:

- Place your thesis statement at the beginning.
- List the major points that support and develop your thesis, labeling them with roman numerals (I, II, III).
- Break down the major points into divisions with capital letters (A, B, C), subdivide those using arabic numerals (1, 2, 3), and subdivide those using small letters (a, b, c). Continue until your outline is fully developed. If a very complex project requires further subdivision, use arabic numerals and small letters in parentheses.
- Indent each level of division in turn: the deeper the indentation, the more specific the ideas. Align like-numbered or -lettered headings under one another.
- Cast all headings in parallel grammatical form: phrases or sentences, but not both in the same outline.

For more on parallelism, see B2 (pp. Q-47–Q-48) in the Quick Editing Guide.

For more on analysis and division, see pp. 432–36.

CAUTION: Because an outline divides or analyzes ideas, some readers and instructors disapprove of categories with only one subpoint, reasoning that you can't divide anything into one part. Let's say that your outline on earthquakes lists a 1 without a 2:

> D. Probable results of an earthquake include structural damage.
>     1. House foundations crack.

Logically, if you are going to discuss the *probable results* of an earthquake, you need to include more than one result:

    D. Probable results of an earthquake include structural damage.
       1. House foundations crack.
       2. Road surfaces are damaged.
       3. Water mains break.

Not only have you now come up with more points, but you have also emphasized the one placed last.

A *formal topic outline* for a long paper might include several levels of ideas, as this outline for Linn Bourgeau's research paper illustrates. Such an outline can help you work out both a persuasive sequence for the parts of a paper and a logical order for any information from sources.

Crucial Choices: Who Will Save the Wetlands If Everyone Is at the Mall?
Working Thesis: Federal regulations need to foster state laws and educational requirements that will help protect the few wetlands that are left, restore as many as possible of those that have been destroyed, and take measures to improve the damage from overdevelopment.

    I. Nature's ecosystem
      A. Loss of wetlands nationally
      B. Loss of wetlands in Illinois
        1. More flooding and poorer water quality
        2. Lost ability to prevent floods, clean water, and store water
      C. Need to protect humankind
    II. Dramatic floods
      A. Midwestern floods in 1993 and 2011
        1. Lost wetlands in Illinois and other states
        2. Devastation in some states
      B. Cost in dollars and lives
        1. Deaths during recent flooding
        2. Costs in millions of dollars a year
      C. Flood prevention
        1. Plants and soil
        2. Floodplain overflow
   III. Wetland laws
      A. Inadequately informed legislators
        1. Watersheds
        2. Interconnections in natural water systems
      B. Water purification
        1. Wetlands and water
        2. Pavement and lawns
   IV. Need to save wetlands
      A. New federal laws
      B. Reeducation about interconnectedness
        1. Ecology at every grade level
        2. Education for politicians, developers, and legislators
      C. Choices in schools, legislature, and people's daily lives

A topic outline may help you work out a clear sequence of ideas but may not elaborate or connect them. Although you may not be sure how everything will fit together until you write a draft, you may find that a *formal sentence outline* clarifies what you want to say. It also moves you a step closer to drafting topic sentences and paragraphs even though you would still need to add detailed information. Notice how this sentence outline for Linn Bourgeau's research paper expands her ideas.

Crucial Choices: Who Will Save the Wetlands If Everyone Is at the Mall?
Working Thesis: Federal regulations need to foster state laws and educational requirements that will help protect the few wetlands that are left, restore as many as possible of those that have been destroyed, and take measures to improve the damage from overdevelopment.

I. Each person, as part of nature's ecosystem, chooses how to interact with nature, including wetlands.
   A. The nation has lost over half its wetlands since Columbus arrived.
   B. Illinois has lost even more by legislating and draining them away.
      1. Destroying wetlands creates more flooding and poorer water quality.
      2. The wetlands could prevent floods, clean the water supply, and store water.
   C. The wetlands need to be protected because they protect and serve humankind.

II. Floods are dramatic and visible consequences of not protecting wetlands.
   A. The midwestern floods of 1993 and 2011 were disastrous.
      1. Illinois and other states had lost their wetlands.
      2. Those states also suffered the most devastation.
   B. The cost of flooding can be tallied in dollars spent and in lives lost.
      1. Nearly thirty people died in floods between 1995 and 2011.
      2. Flooding in 2011 cost Illinois about $216 million.
   C. Preventing floods is a valuable role of wetlands.
      1. Plants and soil manage excess water.
      2. The Mississippi River floodplain was reduced from 60 days of water overflow to 12.

III. The laws misinterpret or ignore the basic understanding of wetlands.
   A. Legislators need to know that an "isolated wetland" does not exist.
      1. Water travels within an area called a watershed.
      2. The law needs to consider interconnections in water systems.
   B. Wetlands naturally purify water.
      1. Water filters and flows in wetlands.
      2. Pavement and lawns carry water over, not through, the soil.

IV. Who will save the wetlands if everyone is at the mall?
   A. Federal laws should require implementing what we know.
   B. The vital concept of interconnectedness means reeducating everyone from legislators to fourth graders.
      1. Ecology must be incorporated into the curriculum for every grade.
      2. Educating politicians, developers, and legislators is more difficult.
   C. The choices people make in their schools, legislative systems, and daily lives will determine the future of water quality and flooding.

## Learning by Doing 🎥 Outlining

1. Using one of your groups of ideas from the activities in Chapter 19, construct a formal topic outline that might serve as a guide for an essay.
2. Now turn that topic outline into a formal sentence outline.
3. Discuss both outlines with your classmates and instructor, bringing up any difficulties you met. If you get better notions for organizing, change the outline.

## Learning by Doing 🎥 Reflecting on Planning

Reflect on the purpose and audience for your current paper. Then return to the thesis, outline, or other plans you have prepared. Will your plans accomplish your purpose? Are they directed to your intended audience? Make any needed adjustments. Exchange plans with a classmate or small group, and discuss ways to continue improving them.

# 21 Strategies for Drafting

Learning to write well involves learning what key questions to ask yourself: How can I begin this draft? What should I do if I get stuck? How can I flesh out the bones of my paper? How can I end effectively? How can I keep my readers with me? In this chapter we offer advice to get you going and keep you going, drafting the first paragraph to the last.

## Making a Start Enjoyable

A playful start may get you hard at work before you know it.

- **Time Yourself.** Set your watch, phone alarm, or egg timer, and vow to draft a page before the buzzer sounds. Don't stop for anything. If you're writing nonsense, just push on. You can cross out later.

- **Slow to a Crawl.** If speed quotas don't work, time yourself to write with exaggerated laziness, maybe a sentence every fifteen minutes.

- **Scribble on a Scrap.** If you dread the blank paper or screen, try starting on scrap paper, the back of a list, or a small notebook page.

- **Begin Writing What You Find Most Appetizing.** Start in the middle or at the end, wherever thoughts come easily to mind. As novelist Bill Downey observes, "Writers are allowed to have their dessert first."

- **State Your Purpose.** Set forth what you want to achieve: To tell a story? To explain something? To win a reader over to your ideas?

- **Slip into a Reader's Shoes.** Put yourself in your reader's place. Start writing what you'd like to find out from the paper.

- **Nutshell It.** Summarize the paper you want to write. Condense your ideas into one small, tight paragraph. Later you can expand each sentence until the meaning is clear and all points are adequately supported.

- **Shrink Your Immediate Job.** Break the writing task into small parts, and tackle only the first, perhaps just two paragraphs.

- **Seek a Provocative Title.** Write down a dozen possible titles for your paper. If one sounds strikingly good, don't let it go to waste!

- **Record Yourself.** Talk a first draft into a recorder or your phone. Play it back. Then write. Even if it is hard to transcribe your spoken words, this technique may set your mind in motion.
- **Speak Up.** On your feet, before an imaginary cheering crowd, spontaneously utter a first paragraph. Then—quick!—record it or write it out.
- **Take Short Breaks.** Even if you don't feel tired, take a break every half hour or so. Get up, walk around the room, stretch, or get a drink of water. Two or three minutes should be enough to refresh your mind.

# Restarting

When you have to write a long or demanding essay that you can't finish in one sitting, you may return to it only to find yourself stalled. You crank your starter and nothing happens. Your engine seems reluctant to turn over. Try the following suggestions for getting back on the road.

- **Leave Hints for How to Continue.** If you're ready to quit, jot down what might come next or the first sentence of the next section. When you return, you will face not a blank wall but rich and suggestive graffiti.
- **Pause in Midstream.** Try breaking off in midsentence or midparagraph. Just leave a sentence trailing off into space, even if you know its closing words. When you return, you can start writing again immediately.
- **Repeat.** If the next sentence refuses to appear, simply recopy the last one until that shy creature emerges on the page.
- **Reread.** When you return to work, spend a few minutes rereading what you have already written or what you have planned.
- **Switch Instruments.** Do you compose on a laptop? Try longhand. Or drop your pen to type. Write on note cards or colored paper.
- **Change Activities.** When words won't come, turn to something quite different. Run, cook a meal, or nap. Or reward yourself—after you reach a certain point—with a call to a friend or a game. All the while, your unconscious mind will work on your writing task.

# Paragraphing

An essay is written not in large, indigestible lumps but in *paragraphs*—small units, each more or less self-contained, each contributing some new idea in support of the essay's thesis. Writers dwell on one idea at a time, stating it, developing it, illustrating it with examples or a few facts—*showing* readers, with detailed evidence, exactly what they mean.

For more on developing ideas within paragraphs, see Ch. 22.

Paragraphs can be as short as one sentence or as long as a page. Sometimes length is governed by audience, purpose, or medium. Journalists expect newspaper readers to gobble up facts like popcorn, quickly skimming short one- or two-sentence paragraphs. College writers, in contrast, should assume their readers expect to read well-developed paragraphs.

When readers see a paragraph indentation, they interpret it as a pause, a chance for a deep breath. After that signpost, they expect you to concentrate on a new aspect of your thesis for the rest of that paragraph. This chapter gives you advice on guiding readers through your writing—using opening paragraphs to draw them in, topic sentences to focus and control body paragraphs, and concluding paragraphs to wrap up the discussion.

# Using Topic Sentences

A *topic sentence* spells out the main idea of a paragraph in the body of an essay. It guides you as you write, and it hooks your readers as they discover what to expect and how to interpret the paragraph. As the topic sentence establishes the focus of the paragraph, it also relates the paragraph to the topic and thesis of the essay as a whole. (Much of the advice on topic sentences for paragraphs also extends to thesis statements for essays.) To convert an idea to a topic sentence, add your own slant, attitude, or point.

For more on thesis statements, see pp. 384–93.

Main Idea  +  Slant or Attitude or Point  =  Topic Sentence

How do you write a good topic sentence? Make it interesting, accurate, and limited. The more pointed and lively it is, the more it will interest readers. Even a dull, vague start is enlivened once you zero in on a specific point.

| | |
|---|---|
| MAIN IDEA + SLANT | television + everything that's wrong with it |
| DULL START | There are many things wrong with television. |
| POINTED TOPIC SENTENCE | Of all the disappointing television programming, what I dislike most is melodramatic news. |
| ¶ PLAN | Illustrate the point with two or three melodramatic news stories. |

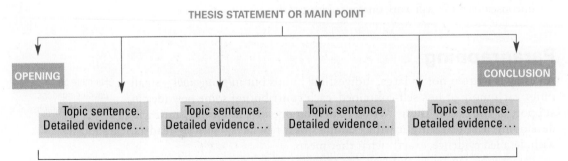

THESIS STATEMENT OR MAIN POINT

OPENING

CONCLUSION

Topic sentence. Detailed evidence...

Topic sentence. Detailed evidence...

Topic sentence. Detailed evidence...

Topic sentence. Detailed evidence...

TRANSITIONS USED THROUGHOUT FOR COHERENCE

A topic sentence also should be an accurate guide to the rest of the paragraph so that readers expect just what the paragraph delivers.

| | |
|---|---|
| INACCURATE GUIDE | **All types of household emergencies can catch people off guard.** [The paragraph covers steps for emergency preparedness — not the variety of emergencies.] |
| ACCURATE TOPIC SENTENCE | **Although an emergency may not be a common event, emergency preparedness should be routine at home.** |
| ¶ PLAN | **Explain how a household can prepare for an emergency with a medical kit, a well-stocked pantry, and a communication plan.** |

Finally, a topic sentence should be limited so you don't mislead or frustrate readers about what the paragraph covers.

| | |
|---|---|
| MISLEADING | **Seven factors have contributed to the increasing obesity of the average American.** [The paragraph discusses only one — portion size.] |
| LIMITED TOPIC SENTENCE | **Portion size is a major factor that contributes to the increasing obesity of average Americans.** |
| ¶ PLAN | **Define healthy portion sizes, contrasting them with the large portions common in restaurants and in packaged foods.** |

**Open with a Topic Sentence.** Usually the topic sentence appears first in the paragraph, followed by sentences that clarify, illustrate, and support what it says. It is typically a statement but can sometimes be a question, alerting the reader to the topic without giving away the punchline. This example from "The Virtues of the Quiet Hero," Senator John McCain's essay about "honor, faith, and service," was presented in 2005 as part of the "This I Believe" series on National Public Radio's *All Things Considered*. Here, as in all the following examples, we have put the topic sentence in *italics*.

> *Years later, I saw an example of honor in the most surprising of places.* As a scared American prisoner of war in Vietnam, I was tied in torture ropes by my tormentors and left alone in an empty room to suffer through the night. Later in the evening, a guard I had never spoken to entered the room and silently loosened the ropes to relieve my suffering. Just before morning, that same guard came back and retightened the ropes before his less humanitarian comrades returned. He never said a word to me. Some months later on a Christmas morning, as I stood alone in the prison courtyard, that same guard walked up to me and stood next to me for a few moments. Then with his sandal, the guard drew a cross in the dirt.

> We stood wordlessly there for a minute or two, venerating the cross, until the guard rubbed it out and walked away.

This paragraph moves from the general to the specific. The topic sentence clearly states at the outset what the paragraph is about. The second sentence introduces the situation McCain recalls. Then the next half-dozen sentences supply two concrete yet concise illustrations of his central point.

**Place a Topic Sentence near the Beginning.** Sometimes the first sentence of a paragraph acts as a transition, linking what is to come with what has gone before. Then the *second* sentence might be the topic sentence, as illustrated in the following paragraph from *Tim Gunn's Fashion Bible: The Fascinating History of Everything in Your Closet* by Tim Gunn with Ada Calhoun (Gallery Books, 2012). The paragraph immediately before this one summarizes how the early history of shoe design often tried to balance competing desires for modesty, alluring beauty, and practicality. This prior paragraph begins, "Modesty got the better of the shoe industry in the seventeenth century," and concludes, "It wasn't until the late 1930s that sling-backs and open-toed heels gave us another glimpse at the toes and heels."

> Heel height has fluctuated ever since, as have platforms. One goal of a high shoe is to elevate the wearer out of the muck. Before there was pavement (asphalt didn't even appear until 1824, in Paris), streets were very muddy. People often wore one kind of shoe indoors, like a satin slipper, and another outside, perhaps with some kind of overshoe. One type of overshoe was called pattens, which were made of leather, wood, or iron, and lifted the wearer up a couple of inches or more from the sidewalk to protect the sole of the shoe from grime. Men and women wore these from the fourteenth to the mid-nineteenth century, when street conditions started to become slightly less disgusting.

**End with a Topic Sentence.** Occasionally a writer, trying to persuade the reader to agree, piles detail on detail. Then, with a dramatic flourish, the writer *concludes* with the topic sentence, as student Heidi Kessler does.

> A fourteen-year-old writes to an advice columnist in my hometown newspaper that she has "done it" lots of times and sex is "no big deal." At the neighborhood clinic where my aunt works, a hardened sixteen-year-old requests her third abortion. A girl-child I know has two children of her own, but no husband. A college student in my dorm now finds herself sterile from a "social disease" picked up during casual sexual encounters. Multiply these examples by thousands. *It seems clear to me that women, who fought so hard for sexual freedom equal to that of men, have emerged from the battle not as joyous free spirits but as the sexual revolution's walking wounded.*

This paragraph moves from particular to general—from four examples about individuals to one large statement about American women. By the time you finish, you might be ready to accept the paragraph's conclusion.

**Imply a Topic Sentence.** It is also possible to find a perfectly unified, well-organized paragraph that has no topic sentence at all, like the following from "New York" (*Esquire,* July 1960) by Gay Talese:

> Each afternoon in New York a rather seedy saxophone player, his cheeks blown out like a spinnaker, stands on the sidewalk playing "Danny Boy" in such a sad, sensitive way that he soon has half the neighborhood peeking out of windows tossing nickels, dimes, and quarters at his feet. Some of the coins roll under parked cars, but most of them are caught in his outstretched hand. The saxophone player is a street musician named Joe Gabler; for the past thirty years he has serenaded every block in New York and has sometimes been tossed as much as $100 a day in coins. He is also hit with buckets of water, empty beer cans and eggs, and chased by wild dogs. He is believed to be the last of New York's ancient street musicians.

No one sentence neatly sums up the writer's idea. Like most effective paragraphs that do not state a topic sentence, this one contains something just as good — a *topic idea*. The author doesn't wander aimlessly. He knows exactly what he wants to achieve — a description of how the famous Joe Gabler plies his trade. Because Talese keeps this purpose firmly in mind, the main point — that Gabler meets both reward and abuse — is clear to the reader as well.

## Learning by Doing 🖸 Shaping Topic Sentences

In a small group, answer these questions about each topic sentence below:

> Will it catch readers' attention? Is it accurate? Is it limited?
> How might you develop the idea in the rest of the paragraph?
> Can you improve it?

1. Television commercials stereotype people.
2. Living away from home for the first time is hard.
3. It's good for a child to have a pet.
4. A flea market is a good place to buy jewelry.
5. Pollution should be controlled.
6. Everybody should recycle wastes.

## Learning by Doing 🖸 Reflecting on Topic Sentences

Review the rough draft of a current essay, highlighting or underlining each of the topic sentences. Then ask the following questions: How well does each topic sentence support the thesis? Based on the topic sentences, do you understand what will be covered in each paragraph? What revisions would strengthen these sentences? After you have answered these questions and made necessary revisions, write a brief reflection. What have you learned about how to write effective topic sentences? What new strategies might you use in the future?

# Writing an Opening

Even writers with something to say may find it hard to begin. Often they are so intent on a brilliant opening that they freeze. They forget even the essentials — set up the topic, stick to what's relevant, and establish a thesis. If you feel like a deer paralyzed by headlights, try these ways of opening:

- Start with your thesis statement, with or without a full opening paragraph. Fill in the rest later.
- Write your thesis statement — the one you planned or one you'd now like to develop — in the middle of a page. Go back to the top, and concisely add the background a reader needs to see where you're going.
- Write a long beginning for your first draft; then cut it down to the most dramatic, exciting, or interesting essentials.
- Simply set down words — any words — on paper, without trying to write an arresting opening. Rewrite later.
- Write the first paragraph last, after you know where your essay goes.
- Move your conclusion to the beginning, and write a new ending.
- Write a summary for yourself and your readers.

Your opening should intrigue readers — engaging their minds and hearts, exciting their curiosity, drawing them into the world set forth in your writing.

## DISCOVERY CHECKLIST

- ☐ What vital background might readers need?
- ☐ What general situation might help you narrow down to your point?
- ☐ What facts or statistics might make your issue compelling?
- ☐ What powerful anecdote or incident might introduce your point?
- ☐ What striking example or comparison would engage a reader?
- ☐ What question will your thesis — and your essay — answer?
- ☐ What lively quotation would set the scene for your essay?

☐ What assertion or claim might be the necessary prelude for your essay?

☐ What points should you preview to prepare a reader for what will come?

☐ What would compel someone to keep on reading?

---

**Begin with a Story.** Often a simple anecdote can capture your readers' interest and thus serve as a good beginning. Here is how Dan Leeth opens his essay "Trails of Treasure" (*Encompass*, November/December 2013):

> It was my first ever hike. I was 9 years old when my father's friend, Scotty, invited us to join him on a trek into the Superstition Mountains, a rugged jumble of bluffs, buttes, crags, cliffs and canyons rising 35 miles east of Phoenix. Naturally, I wore my Roy Rogers cowboy boots. Six blisters later, I realized why Roy rode and seldom walked. Only Scotty's tales of treasure kept me going.

Most of us, after an anecdote, want to read on. What will the writer say next? How does the anecdote launch the essay? Leeth continues, explaining that the hike introduced him to the territory of the long-lost—and long-sought—golden treasure trove known as the Lost Dutchman Mine.

**Comment on a Topic or Position.** Sometimes a writer expands on a topic, bringing in vital details, as Greg Lukianoff and Jonathan Haidt do to open their article "The Coddling of the American Mind" (*The Atlantic*, September 2015):

> Something strange is happening at America's colleges and universities. A movement is arising, undirected and driven largely by students, to scrub campuses clean of words, ideas, and subjects that might cause discomfort or give offense. Last December, Jeannie Suk wrote in an online article for the *New Yorker* about law students asking her fellow professors at Harvard not to teach rape law—or, in one case, even use the word *violate* (as in "that violates the law") lest it cause students distress. In February, Laura Kipnis, a professor at Northwestern University, wrote an essay in the *Chronicle of Higher Education* describing a new campus politics of sexual paranoia—and was then subjected to a long investigation after students who were offended by the article and by a tweet she'd sent filed Title IX complaints against her. In June, a professor protecting himself with a pseudonym wrote an essay for *Vox* describing how gingerly he now has to teach. "I'm a Liberal Professor, and My Liberal Students Terrify Me," the headline said. A number of popular comedians, including Chris Rock, have stopped performing on college campuses. . . . Jerry Seinfeld and Bill Maher have publicly condemned the oversensitivity of college students, saying too many of them can't take a joke.

After announcing their topic and their particular viewpoint regarding it, Lukianoff and Haidt supply a series of anecdotes to support that viewpoint.

**Ask a Question.** An essay can begin with a question and answer, as James H. Austin begins "Four Kinds of Chance," in *Chase, Chance, and Creativity: The Lucky Art of Novelty* (Columbia UP, 1978):

> What is chance? Dictionaries define it as something fortuitous that happens unpredictably without discernible human intention. Chance is unintentional and capricious, but we needn't conclude that chance is immune from human intervention. Indeed, chance plays several distinct roles when humans react creatively with one another and with their environment.

Beginning to answer the question in the first paragraph leads readers to expect the rest of the essay to continue the answer.

For more on thesis statements, see pp. 384–93.

**End with the Thesis Statement.** Opening paragraphs often end by stating the essay's main point. After capturing readers' attention with an anecdote, gripping details, or examples, you lead readers in exactly the direction your essay goes. In response to the question "Should Washington stem the tide of both legal and illegal immigration?" (*Insight on the News*, 11 March 2002), Daniel T. Griswold uses this strategy to begin his answer:

> Immigration always has been controversial in the United States. More than two centuries ago, Benjamin Franklin worried that too many German immigrants would swamp America's predominantly British culture. In the mid-1800s, Irish immigrants were scorned as lazy drunks, not to mention Roman Catholics. At the turn of the century a wave of "new immigrants" — Poles, Italians, Russian Jews — were believed to be too different ever to assimilate into American life. *Today the same fears are raised about immigrants from Latin America and Asia, but current critics of immigration are as wrong as their counterparts were in previous eras.*

## Learning by Doing 🔟 Trying Different Methods of Writing an Opening

Choose three methods of writing an opening, selecting from the previously discussed methods (begin with a story, comment on a topic or position, ask a question, end with the thesis statement) or from the following list:

- Offer a startling statistic or an unusual fact.
- Introduce a quotation or a bit of dialogue.
- Provide historical background.
- Define a key term or concept.
- State a problem, contradiction, or dilemma.
- Use a vivid example or image.
- Develop an analogy.

Write (or rewrite) an introduction to a paper using the three methods you have chosen. Which method do you think is most effective and engaging, and why? Swap introductions with a writing partner and ask your partner which introduction he or she thinks is most effective and why.

# Writing a Conclusion

The final paragraphs of an essay linger longest for readers, as in E. B. White's "Once More to the Lake" from *One Man's Meat* (Tilbury House, 1941). White describes his return with his young son to a vacation spot he had loved as a child. As the essay ends in an unforgettable image, he realizes the inevitable passing of generations.

> When the others went swimming my son said he was going in, too. He pulled his dripping trunks from the line where they had hung all through the shower and wrung them out. Languidly, and with no thought of going in, I watched him, his hard little body, skinny and bare, saw him wince slightly as he pulled up around his vitals the small, soggy, icy garment. As he buckled the swollen belt, suddenly my groin felt the chill of death.

White's classic ending opens with a sentence that points back to the previous paragraph as it also looks ahead. Then White leads us quickly to his final, chilling insight. And then he stops.

It's easy to say what *not* to do at the end of an essay: don't leave your readers half expecting you to go on. Don't restate all you've just said. Don't introduce a brand-new topic that leads away from your point. And don't signal that the end is near with an obvious phrase like "As I have said." For some answers to "How *do* you write an ending, then?" try this checklist.

### DISCOVERY CHECKLIST

☐ What restatement of your thesis would give readers satisfying closure?

☐ What provocative implications of your thesis might answer "What now?" or "What's the significance of what I've said?"

☐ What snappy quotation or statement would wrap up your point?

☐ What closing facts or statistics might confirm the merit of your point?

☐ What final anecdote, incident, or example might round out your ideas?

☐ What question has your essay answered?

☐ What assertion or claim might you want to restate?

☐ What summary might help a reader pull together what you've said?

☐ What would make a reader sorry to finish such a satisfying essay?

For more on punctuating quotations, see D3 (pp. Q-61–Q-62) in the Quick Editing Guide.

**End with a Quotation.** An apt quotation can neatly round out an essay, as literary critic Malcolm Cowley shows in *The View from Eighty* (Viking, 1980), his discussion of the pitfalls and compensations of old age.

> "Eighty years old!" the great Catholic poet Paul Claudel wrote in his journal. "No eyes left, no ears, no teeth, no legs, no wind! And when all is said and done, how astonishingly well one does without them!"

**State or Restate Your Thesis.** In a sharp criticism of American schools, humorist Russell Baker in "School vs. Education" ends by stating his main point, that schools do not educate.

> Afterward, the former student's destiny fulfilled, his life rich with Oriental carpets, rare porcelain, and full bank accounts, he may one day find himself with the leisure and the inclination to open a book with a curious mind, and start to become educated.

**End with a Brief Emphatic Sentence.** For an essay that traces causes or effects, evaluates, or argues, a pointed concluding thought can reinforce your main idea. Stick to academic language, but craft a concise, pointed sentence, maybe with a twist. Nathaniel Rich ends his review of Gary Rivlin's *Katrina: After the Flood* (*New York Times*, 5 August 2015) with a short, solemn sentence that invokes the sentiment of the previous sentence for additional impact:

> New Orleans has always been a place where utopian fantasies and dystopian realities mingle harmoniously. May New Orleans always remain so. Or at least may it always remain.

**Stop When the Story Is Over.** Even a quiet ending can be effective, as long as it signals clearly that the essay is finished. When *Smithsonian* (November 2013) featured articles on "101 Objects That Made America," space-age historian Andrew Chaikin prepared the selection on "Neil Armstrong's Spacesuit." His engaging account of the suit's model number, cost, construction, technical qualities, and wearability describes the essential features that protected Armstrong as he took his famous first step on the moon. Then Chaikin concludes his article with this succinct paragraph:

> "Its true beauty, however," said Armstrong, "was that it worked."

## Learning by Doing 🎥 Trying Different Methods of Writing a Conclusion

Choose three methods of writing a conclusion, selecting from the following list:

- End with a brief, emphatic sentence or mind-blowing quotation.
- State or restate your thesis.

- Briefly summarize your essay's key points.
- Answer the "So what?" or "Who cares?" questions about your topic. Why does this issue matter? Who should care about it? Who is harmed if no one pays attention to it?
- Propose a course of action, or offer a recommendation for future studies or future solutions.
- Discuss the topic's wider significance or implications.
- Redefine a key term or concept discussed in your essay.

Write (or rewrite) the conclusion to a paper using the three methods you have chosen. Which method do you think is most effective and engaging, and why? Swap conclusions with a writing partner and ask your partner which conclusion he or she thinks is most effective and why.

## Learning by Doing 🎯 Evaluating Openings and Conclusions

Openings and conclusions frame an essay, contributing to the unity of the whole. The opening sets up the topic and main idea; the conclusion reaffirms the thesis and rounds off the ideas. Discuss the following with your classmates.

1. Here are two possible opening paragraphs from a student essay on the importance of teaching children how to swim.

   A. Humans inhabit a world made up of over 70 percent water. In addition to these great bodies of water, we have built millions of swimming pools for sports and leisure activities. At one time or another most people will be faced with either the danger of drowning or the challenge of aquatic recreation. For these reasons, it is essential that we learn to swim. Being a competitive swimmer and a swimming instructor, I fully realize the importance of knowing how to swim.

   B. Four-year-old Carl, curious like most children, last spring ventured out onto his pool patio. He fell into the pool and, not knowing how to swim, helplessly sank to the bottom. Minutes later his uncle found the child and brought him to the surface. Because Carl had no pulse, his uncle administered CPR until the paramedics arrived. Eventually the child was revived. During his stay in the hospital, his mother signed him up for beginning swimming classes. Carl was a lucky one. Unlike thousands of other children and adults, he got a second chance.

   - Which introduction is more effective? Why?
   - What would the body of this essay consist of? What kinds of evidence would be included?
   - Write a suitable conclusion for this essay.

2. If you were to read each of the following introductions from professional essays, would you want to read the entire essay? Why?

A. During my ninth hour underground, as I scrambled up a slanting tunnel through the powdered gypsum, Rick Bridges turned to me and said, "You know, this whole area was just discovered Tuesday." (David Roberts, "Caving Comes into Its Golden Age: A New Mexico Marvel," *Smithsonian,* November 1988)

B. From the batting average on the back of a George Brett baseball card to the interest rate fluctuations that determine whether the economy grows or stagnates, Americans are fascinated by statistics. (Stephen E. Nordlinger, "By the Numbers," *St. Petersburg Times,* 6 November 1988)

C. "What does it look like under there?"

It was always this question back then, always the same pattern of hello and what's your name, what happened to your eye and what's under there. (Natalie Kusz, "Waiting for a Glass Eye," *Road Song* [Farrar, 1990], rpt. in *Harper's,* November 1990)

3. How effective are these introductions and conclusions from student essays? Could they be improved? If so, how? If they are satisfactory, explain why. What would be a catchy yet informative title for each essay?

A. Recently a friend down from New York astonished me with stories of several people infected—some with AIDS—by stepping on needles washed up on the New Jersey beaches. This is just one incident of pollution, a devastating problem in our society today. Pollution is increasing in our world because of greed, apathy, and Congress's inability to control this problem. . . .

Wouldn't it be nice to have a pollution-free world without medical wastes floating in the water and washing up on our beaches? Without cars and power plants spewing greenhouse gases? With every corporation abiding by the laws set by Congress? In the future we can have a pollution-free world, but it is going to take the cooperation of everyone, including Congress, to ensure our survival on this Planet Earth.

B. The divorce rate rose 700 percent in the last century and continues to rise. More than one out of every two couples who are married end up divorcing. Over one million children a year are affected by divorce in the family. From these statistics it is clear that one of the greatest problems concerning the family today is divorce and the adverse effects it has on our society. . . .

Divorce causes problems that change people for life. The number of divorces will continue to exceed the 700 percent figure unless married couples learn to communicate, to accept their mates unconditionally, and to sacrificially give of themselves.

4. Using a topic that you generated in Chapter 19, write at least three different introductions with conclusions. Ask classmates which is most effective.

# Adding Cues and Connections

Effective writing proceeds in some sensible order, each sentence following naturally from the one before it. Yet even well-organized prose can be hard to read unless it is *coherent* and smoothly integrates its elements. Readers need cues and connections — devices to tie together words in a sentence, sentences in a paragraph, paragraphs in an essay.

**Add Transitional Words and Sentences.** Many words and phrases specify connections between or within sentences and paragraphs. In fact, you use transitions every day as cues or signals to help others follow your train of thought. For example, you might say to a friend, "Well, *on the one hand*, a second job would help me save money for tuition. *On the other hand*, I'd have less time to study." But some writers rush through, omitting links between thoughts or mistakenly assuming that connections they see will automatically be clear to readers. Often just a word, phrase, or sentence of transition inserted in the right place transforms a disconnected passage into a coherent one. In the chart on page 418, *transitional markers* are grouped by purpose or the kind of relation or connection they establish.

Occasionally a whole sentence serves as a transition. The opening of one paragraph may hark back to the last one while revealing a new or narrower direction. The next excerpt is from "Preservation Basics: Why Preserve Film?" a Web page of the National Film Preservation Foundation (NFPF) at filmpreservation.org. The first paragraph introduces the organization's mission; the next opens with a transitional sentence (italics ours) that introduces major challenges to that mission.

> Movies have documented America for more than one hundred years. Since Thomas Edison introduced the movie camera in 1893, amateur and professional filmmakers have used motion pictures to tell stories, record communities, explain the work of business and government, and illustrate current events. They captured, with the immediacy unique to the moving image, how generations of Americans have lived, worked, and dreamed. By preserving these films, we save a century of history.
>
> *Unfortunately, movies are not made to last.* Created on perishable plastic, film decays within years if not properly stored. Already the losses are high. The Library of Congress has documented that only 20 percent of U.S. feature films from the 1910s and 1920s survive in complete form in American archives; of the American features produced before 1950, about half still exist. For shorts, documentaries, and independently produced works, we have no way of knowing how much has been lost.

The first paragraph establishes the value of *preserving* the American film legacy. The next paragraph uses key words related to preservation and its absence (*perishable, decays, losses, lost*) to clarify that what follows builds on what has gone before. The paragraph opens with a short, dramatic transition to one of the major problems: time and existing loss.

## Common Transitions

| | |
|---|---|
| **TO MARK TIME** | then, soon, first, second, next, recently, the following day, in a little while, meanwhile, after, later, in the past, finally |
| **TO MARK PLACE OR DIRECTION** | in the distance, close by, near, far away, above, below, to the right, on the other side, opposite, to the west, next door |
| **TO SUMMARIZE OR RESTATE** | in other words, to put it another way, in brief, in simpler terms, on the whole, in fact, in a word, to sum up, in short, in conclusion, to conclude, therefore |
| **TO RELATE CAUSE AND EFFECT OR RESULT** | therefore, accordingly, hence, thus, for, so, consequently, as a result, because of, due to, eventually, inevitably |
| **TO ADD OR AMPLIFY OR LIST** | and, also, too, besides, as well, moreover, in addition, furthermore, in effect, second, in the second place, again, next |
| **TO COMPARE** | similarly, likewise, in like manner, in the same way |
| **TO CONCEDE** | whereas, on the other hand, with that in mind, still, and yet, even so, in spite of, despite, at least, of course, no doubt, even though |
| **TO CONTRAST** | on the other hand, but, or, however, unlike, nevertheless, on the contrary, conversely, in contrast, instead, counter to |
| **TO INDICATE PURPOSE** | to this end, for this purpose, with this aim |
| **TO EXPRESS CONDITION** | although, though |
| **TO GIVE EXAMPLES OR SPECIFY** | for example, for instance, in this case, in particular, to illustrate |
| **TO QUALIFY** | for the most part, by and large, with few exceptions, mainly, in most cases, generally, some, sometimes, typically, frequently, rarely |
| **TO EMPHASIZE** | it is true, truly, indeed, of course, to be sure, obviously, without doubt, evidently, clearly, understandably |

**Supply Transition Paragraphs.** Transitions may be even longer than sentences. In a long and complicated essay, moving clearly from one idea to the next will sometimes require a short paragraph of transition.

So far, the physical and psychological effects of driving nonstop for hundreds of miles seem clear. The next consideration is why drivers do this. What causes people to become addicted to their steering wheels?

Use a transition paragraph only when you sense that your readers might get lost if you don't patiently lead them by the hand. If your essay is short, one question or statement beginning a new paragraph will be enough.

A transition paragraph also can help you move between one branch of argument and your main trunk or between a digression and your main direction. In this excerpt from *The Film Preservation Guide: The Basics for Archives, Libraries, and Museums,* the writer introduces the importance of inspecting film and devotes the next paragraph to a digression—referring readers to an inspection sheet in the appendix.

> Inspection is the single most important way to date a film, identify its technical characteristics, and detect damage and decay. Much can be learned by examining your film carefully, from start to finish.
>
> A standardized inspection work sheet (see appendix B) lists things to check and helps organize notes. This type of written report is the foundation for future preservation actions. Collecting the information during inspection will help you make informed decisions and enable you to document any changes in film condition over time.
>
> Signs of decay and damage may vary across the length of the film. . . .

The second paragraph acts as a transition, guiding readers to specialized information in the appendix and then drawing them back to the overall purpose of inspection: assessing the extent of damage to a film.

**Select Repetition.** Another way to clarify the relationship between two sentences, paragraphs, or ideas is to repeat a key word or phrase. Such purposeful repetition almost guarantees that readers will understand how all the parts of a passage fit together. Note the word *anger* in the following paragraph (italics ours) from *Of Woman Born* (Norton, 1976), poet Adrienne Rich's exploration of her relationship with her mother.

> And I know there must be deep reservoirs of *anger* in her; every mother has known overwhelming, unacceptable *anger* at her children. When I think of the conditions under which my mother became a mother, the impossible expectations, my father's distaste for pregnant women, his hatred of all that he could not control, my *anger* at her dissolves into grief and *anger* for her, and then dissolves back again into *anger* at her: the ancient, unpurged *anger* of the child.

**Strengthen Pronouns.** Because they always refer back to nouns or other pronouns, pronouns serve as transitions by making readers refer back as well. Note how certain pronouns (in italics) hold together the following paragraph from "Misunderstood Michelle" by columnist Ellen Goodman in *At Large* (Summit Books, 1981):

> I have two friends who moved in together many years ago. *He* looked upon this step as a trial marriage. *She* looked upon it as, well, moving in together. *He* was sure that in a matter of time, after *they* had built up trust and confidence, *she* would agree that marriage was the next logical step. *She,* on the other hand, was thrilled that here at last was a man *who* would never push *her* back to the altar.

The paragraph uses other transitions, too: time markers (*many years ago, in a matter of time, after*), *on the other hand* to show a contrast, and repetition of words related to marriage (*trial marriage, marriage, the altar*). All serve the main purpose of transitions—keeping readers on track.

## Learning by Doing  Reflecting on Transitions

Select a reading from this book and circle the transitions. Then state the purpose of each transition, according to the chart on page 418. Next, using the same chart, replace each transition with an alternative. Read the paragraph and reflect on the differences you see or "hear" with each new word. Do you think these changes alter the author's meaning? Are your choices better? Worse? Why? After you have completed this process, write a brief reflection: What is the most valuable lesson you have learned about how to use transitions?

## Learning by Doing  Reflecting on Drafting

Think about how you wrote your last successful draft. What did you do? How did you shape your paragraphs? How did you manage transitions to guide readers? What was your secret for success? Write out drafting directions for yourself—ready for your next assignment. Compare directions with a classmate or small group, and exchange any useful advice.

# Strategies for Developing

# Strategies for Developing

**22**

How can you spice up your general ideas with the stuff of real life? How can you tug your readers deeper and deeper into your essays until they say, "I see just what you mean"? Well-developed essays have such power because they back up general points with evidence that comes alive for readers. This chapter covers nine indispensable methods of development—giving examples, providing details, defining, reasoning inductively and deductively, analyzing a subject, analyzing a process, dividing and classifying, comparing and contrasting, and identifying causes and effects. A strong essay almost always requires a combination of strategies.

Whenever you develop or revise a piece of writing, you face a challenge: How do you figure out what to do? Sometimes you may suspect that you've wandered into the buffet line at the Writer's Grill. You watch others load their plates, but still you hesitate. What will taste best? How much will fit on your plate? What will create a memorable experience? For you as a writer, the answers to such questions are individual, depending on your situation, the clarity of your main idea or thesis, and the state of your draft.

For lists of essays using various methods of development, turn to the Rhetorical Contents following the full table of contents.

---

## DISCOVERY CHECKLIST

### Purpose

- [ ] Does your assignment recommend specific methods of development?
- [ ] Which methods might be most useful to explain, inform, or persuade?
- [ ] What type of development might best achieve your specific purpose?

### Audience

- [ ] Which strategies would best clarify your topic for readers?
- [ ] Which would best demonstrate your thesis to your readers?
- [ ] What kinds of evidence will your specific readers prefer? Which strategies might develop this evidence most effectively?

### Thesis

☐ What development does your thesis promise or imply that you will supply?

☐ What sequence of development strategies would best support your thesis?

### Essay Development

☐ Has a reader or peer editor pointed out any ideas in your draft that need fuller, more effective, or more logical development?

☐ Where might your readers have trouble following or understanding without more or better development?

### Paragraph Development

☐ Should any paragraphs with one or two sentences be developed more fully?

☐ Should any long paragraphs with generalizations, repetition, and wordy phrasing be developed differently so that they are richer and deeper?

---

# Giving Examples

An example — the word comes from the Latin *exemplum,* "one thing chosen from among many" — is a typical instance that illustrates a whole type or kind. Giving examples to support a generalization is probably the most often used means of development. This example, from *In Search of Excellence* (Harper and Row, 1982) by Thomas J. Peters and Robert H. Waterman Jr., explains the success of America's top corporations:

> Although he's not a company, our favorite illustration of closeness to the customer is car salesman Joe Girard. He sold more new cars and trucks, each year, for eleven years running, than any other human being. In fact, in a typical year, Joe sold more than twice as many units as whoever was in second place. In explaining his secret of success, Joe said: "I sent out over thirteen thousand cards every month."
>
> Why start with Joe? Because his magic is the magic of IBM and many of the rest of the excellent companies. It is simply service, overpowering service, especially after-sales service. Joe noted, "There's one thing that I do that a lot of salesmen don't, and that's believe the sale really begins *after* the sale — not before. . . . The customer ain't out the door, and my son has made up a thank-you note." Joe would intercede personally, a year later, with the service manager on behalf of his customer. Meanwhile he would keep the communications flowing.

Notice how Peters and Waterman focus on the specific, Joe Girard. They don't write *corporation employees* or even *car salespeople.* Instead, they zero in on one particular man to make the point come alive.

| Joe Girard | Level 4: Specific Example |
|---|---|
| car salespeople | Level 3: Even More Specific Group |
| corporation employees | Level 2: More Specific Group |
| America's top corporations | Level 1: General Group or Category |

This ladder of abstraction moves from the general—America's top corporations—to a specific person—Joe Girard. The specific example of Joe Girard makes closeness to the customer *concrete* to readers: he is someone readers can relate to. To check the level of specificity in a paragraph or an outline, draw a ladder of abstraction for it. Do the same to restrict a broad subject to a topic for a short essay. If you haven't climbed to the fourth or fifth level, you are probably too general and need to add specifics.

An example doesn't have to be a specific individual. Sometimes you can create a picture of something unfamiliar or give an abstraction a personality. In this paragraph from *Beyond Addiction: How Science and Kindness Help People Change* (Scribner, 2014), the authors clarify the effects of drug abuse on the brain, after referring to the fried-egg image from the old "This is your brain on drugs" advertisements:

> Our colleague John Mariani, M.D., an addiction psychiatrist, teacher, clinician, and researcher at Columbia University, suggests we think of a broken leg instead of a fried egg. A bone breaks, and with help—a cast and crutches to prevent reinjury while the person returns to a normal routine, physical therapy to regain strength and flexibility, and family and friends to help and to keep up morale—the bone heals and the person can work, play, run, and jump again. The leg may be more vulnerable to breaking after all that, and the person will need to take care to protect it, but the person can adapt and, for the most part, the body heals. The brain is no exception. Given help and time, therapy and sometimes medication, concerted effort, and measures to safeguard against returning to substance use, brains do heal from the effects of drugs—perhaps not without a trace, but with enough resilience to justify optimism.

An example isn't a trivial doodad you add to a paragraph for decoration; it is what holds your readers' attention and makes an idea concrete and tangible. To give plenty of examples is one of the writer's chief tasks, and you can generate more at any point in the writing process. Begin with your experience, even with an unfamiliar topic, or try conversing with others, reading, digging in the library, or browsing on the Web.

For ways to generate ideas, see Ch. 19.

## DISCOVERY CHECKLIST

☐ Are your examples relevant to your main idea or thesis?

☐ Are your examples the best ones you can think of? Will readers find them strong and appropriate?

☐ Are your examples truly specific? Or do they just repeat generalities?

☐ From each paragraph, can you draw a ladder of abstraction to at least the fourth level?

---

## Learning by Doing  Giving Examples

To help you get in the habit of thinking specifically, fill in a ladder of abstraction for five of the following general subjects. Then share your ladders with classmates, and compare and contrast your specifics with theirs.

Examples:

| iceberg |
| lettuce |
| vegetable |
| food |

| Prius |
| Toyota |
| hybrid cars |
| automobiles |
| land vehicles |
| transportation |

| | | |
|---|---|---|
| art | favorite foods | sports |
| books | movies | television |
| clothes | music | vacations |
| college courses | pets or wild animals | videos |

## Providing Details

A *detail* is any specific, concrete piece of information — a fact, a bit of the historical record, your own observation. Details make scenes and images more realistic and vivid for readers. They also back up generalizations, convincing readers that the writer can make broad assertions with authority.

Mary Harris "Mother" Jones told the story of her life as a labor organizer in *The Autobiography of Mother Jones* (1925). She lends conviction to her generalization about a nineteenth-century coal miner's lot with ample evidence from her own experience and observations.

> Mining at its best is wretched work, and the life and surroundings of the miner are hard and ugly. His work is down in the black depths of the earth. He works alone in a drift. There can be little friendly companionship as there is in the factory; as there is among men who build bridges and houses, working together in groups. The work is dirty. Coal dust grinds itself into the skin, never to be removed. The miner must stoop as he works in the drift. He becomes bent like a gnome.
>
> His work is utterly fatiguing. Muscles and bones ache. His lungs breathe coal dust and the strange, damp air of places that are never filled with sunlight. His house is a poor makeshift and there is little to

encourage him to make it attractive. The company owns the ground it stands on, and the miner feels the precariousness of his hold. Around his house is mud and slush. Great mounds of culm [the refuse left after coal is screened], black and sullen, surround him. His children are perpetually grimy from playing on the culm mounds. The wife struggles with dirt, with inadequate water supply, with small wages, with overcrowded shacks.

Although Mother Jones, not a learned writer, relies on short, simple sentences, her writing is clear and powerful because of the specific details she uses. Her opening states two generalizations: (1) "Mining . . . is wretched work," and (2) the miner's "life and surroundings" are "hard and ugly." She supports these with a barrage of factual evidence and detail, including well-chosen verbs: "Coal dust *grinds* itself into the skin." The result is a moving, convincingly detailed portrait of the miner and his family.

In *Lipstick Jihad: A Memoir of Growing Up Iranian in America and American in Iran* (Public Affairs, 2005), Azadeh Moaveni uses details to evoke the "drama and magic" of a childhood visit to Iran.

To my five-year-old suburban American sensibilities, exposed to nothing more mystical than the Smurfs, Iran was suffused with drama and magic. After Friday lunch at my grandfather's, once the last plates of sliced cantaloupe were cleared away, everyone retired to the bedrooms to nap. Inevitably there was a willing aunt or cousin on hand to scratch my back as I fell asleep. Unused to the siesta ritual, I woke up after half an hour to find the bed I was sharing with my cousin swathed in a tower of creamy gauze that stretched high up to the ceiling. "Wake up," I nudged him, "we're surrounded!" "It's for the mosquitoes, *khareh,* ass, go back to sleep." To me it was like a fairy tale, and I peered through the netting to the living room, to the table heaped with plump dates and the dense, aromatic baklava we would nibble on later with tea. The day before I had helped my grandmother, Razi joon, make *ash-e gooshvareh,* "earring stew"; we made hoops out of the fresh pasta, and dropped them into the vat of simmering herbs and lamb. Here even the ordinary had charm, even the names of stews.

To guide readers through her details, Moaveni uses transitions — chronological (*After Friday lunch, after half an hour, The day before*), spatial (*through the netting to the living room*), and thematic (*To me it was like a fairy tale*).

For more on transitions, see pp. 417–20.

Quite different from Moaveni's personal, descriptive details are the comparative statistics in *Families and Faith: How Religion Is Passed Down across Generations* by Vern L. Bengtson, with Norella M. Putney and Susan Harris (Oxford University Press, 2013). Before reporting his current findings, Bengtson sums up societal changes during his ongoing research project, begun over thirty-five years ago and surveying grandparents, parents, participants, and now their offspring, covering 117 years of birth dates.

Since World War II, there has been unprecedented change at the most intimate level of American society: family life. The rate of divorce increased slowly through the first half of the twentieth century and then rose dramatically over the next few decades. By 1990, one out of every two marriages ended in divorce, and by the end of the century, almost as many children lived in single-parent households—most headed by mothers—as in dual-parent households. Of those children in two-parent households, one-quarter lived in "blended" families with stepparents and stepsiblings.

For more on observing a scene, see Ch. 5.

Providing details is a simple yet effective way to develop ideas. All it takes is close attention and precise wording to communicate details to readers. What would they see, hear, smell, or feel on the scene? Would a bit of reading or research turn up just the right fact or statistic? Effective details must have a specific purpose: to make your images more evocative or your point more convincing as they support—in some way—your main idea.

---

### DISCOVERY CHECKLIST

☐ Do all your details support your point of view, main idea, or thesis?

☐ Do you have details of sights? Sounds? Tastes? Touch? Smells?

☐ Have you added enough details to make your writing clear and interesting?

☐ Have you arranged your details in an order that is easy to follow?

---

## Learning by Doing 🔲 Providing Details

For more on brainstorming, see pp. 371–72.

With classmates or alone, brainstorm specific details on one of the following topics. Include details that appeal to all five senses. Group related details, and write a paragraph or two using them. Begin by stating a main idea that conveys an engaging impression of your topic (not "My grandmother's house was in Topeka, Kansas" but "My grandmother's house was my childhood haven").

| | | |
|---|---|---|
| a childhood memory | a memorable event | a challenging game |
| the things in my room | a TV or movie star | an unforgettable vacation |
| my home | a favorite song or artist | the cafeteria |
| my favorite restaurant | a good friend | a life-changing incident |

# Defining

*Define* means "to set bounds to." You define a thing, word, or concept by describing it to distinguish it from all similar things. If people don't agree on the meaning of a word or an idea, they can't share knowledge about it. Scientists take special care to define their terms precisely. "Climate Engineering," a *State of the Science Fact Sheet* from the National Oceanic and Atmospheric Administration, opens with a definition:

> Climate engineering, also called geoengineering, refers to deliberate, large-scale manipulation of Earth's climate intended to counteract human-caused climate change.

After outlining why this topic needs study, the fact sheet identifies its two main subdivisions:

> Two different climate engineering approaches are commonly considered:
>
> - Removing some $CO_2$ from the atmosphere to reduce its greenhouse gas effect
> - Increasing the reflection of sunlight away from Earth back to space, thus cooling the planet

If you use a word in a special sense or invent a word, you have to explain it or your readers will be lost. In his article "When Past Disasters Are Prologue" (*Nautilus*, Issue 4), David Ropeik examines the utility of past disasters for predicting future ones, improving preparedness and survival rates, and increasing risk awareness. For instance, after a video of a comet colliding with Jupiter and several movies on the same theme, the public became aware of objects that might collide with the earth. Ropeik identifies and defines the term for this behavior.

> What happened with asteroids is an example of what cognitive psychologists call the Availability Heuristic, a phenomenon whereby we tend to pay more attention to, and worry more about, matters that readily come to mind. Here's an example: Does the letter *r* appear more frequently as the first letter in words, or the third? As you search through the words you know to figure this out, the first letter is the first thing that comes to mind. As a result, most people say *r* is more common as a first letter in words, but in fact it is more common as the third. The effect is compounded when strong emotions, like fear, are brought into play. Emotionally powerful experiences burn more deeply into our memories and are more readily summoned, and the speed and power of that recall give those memories disproportionate influence on our perceptions.

You might define an unfamiliar word to save readers a trip to the dictionary or a familiar but often misunderstood concept — such as *guerrilla, liberal,* or *minimum wage* — to clarify the meaning you intend. The more complex or ambiguous the idea, thing, movement, phenomenon, or organization, the longer the definition you will need to clarify the term for your readers.

---

## DISCOVERY CHECKLIST

☐ Have you used definitions to help your readers understand the subject matter, not to show off your knowledge?

☐ Have you tailored your definition to the needs of your audience?

☐ Is your definition specific, clear, and accurate?

☐ Would your definition benefit from an example or from details?

---

## Learning by Doing 🔲 Developing an Extended Definition

Write an extended definition (a paragraph or so) of a word listed below.
Begin with a one-sentence definition of the word. Then, instead of turning to
a dictionary or textbook, expand and clarify your ideas using strategies in
this chapter — examples, details, induction or deduction, analysis, division,
classification, comparison, contrast. You may also use *negation* (explaining
what something is by stating what it is not). Share your definition with
classmates.

| | | | |
|---|---|---|---|
| dieting | intelligence/ignorance | plagiarism | success |
| fear | love | privacy | sustainability |
| gender | peace | racism | war |

---

# Reasoning Inductively and Deductively

For more on reasoning,
see Chs. 3 and 9.

For more on the
statement-support
pattern, see A2
(pp. Q-22–Q-24) in the
Quick Research Guide.

For more on induction
and deduction, see
Ch. 9.

A typical paragraph is likely to rely on both generalizations and particulars.
A *generalization* is a broad statement that establishes a point, viewpoint,
or conclusion. A *particular* is an instance, a detail, or an example — specific
evidence that a general statement is reasonable. Your particulars support your
generalizations; compelling instances, details, and examples back up your
broader point. Likewise, your generalizations pull together your particulars,
identifying patterns or connections that relate individual cases.

To link particulars and generalizations, you can use an inductive or a
deductive process. An *inductive process* begins with the particulars — a convincing number of instances, examples, tests, or experiments. Together,
these particulars substantiate a larger generalization. In this way a number
of long-term studies of weight loss can lead to a consensus about the benefits of walking, eating vegetables, or some other variable. Less formal inductive reasoning is common as people *infer* or conclude that particulars
do or do not support a generalization. If your sister ate strawberries three
times and got a rash each time, she might infer that she is allergic to them.
Induction breaks down when the particulars are too weak or too few to
support a generalization: not enough weight-loss studies have comparable
results or not enough clear instances occur when strawberries — and nothing
else — trigger a reaction.

A *deductive process* begins with a generalization and applies it to another case. When your sister says no to a piece of strawberry pie, she does
so because, based on her assumptions, she *deduces* that it, too, will trigger

a rash. Deduction breaks down when the initial generalization is flawed or when a particular case doesn't fit the generalization. Suppose that each time your sister ate strawberries she drizzled them with lemon juice, the real culprit. Or suppose that the various weight-loss studies defined low-fat food so differently that no one could determine how their findings might be related.

Once you have reached your conclusions — either by using particulars to support generalizations or by applying reliable generalizations to other particulars — you need to decide how to present your reasoning to readers. Do you want them to follow your process, perhaps examining many cases before reaching a conclusion about them? Or do you want them to learn your conclusion first and then review the evidence? Because academic audiences tend to expect conclusions first, many writers begin essays with thesis statements and paragraphs with topic sentences. On the other hand, if your readers are likely to reject an unexpected thesis initially, you may need to show them the evidence first and then lead them gently to your point.

In "Disaster Planning for Libraries: Lessons from California State University, Northridge," librarian Mary M. Finley opened her presentation at the Eighth Annual Federal Depository Library Conference with a broad generalization and then supported it with specifics from her campus:

> In Northridge we learned that a university with facilities for over 25,000 students can be changed in less than thirty seconds into a university with no usable buildings, no electrical power, no water, and no telephone service. California State University, Northridge (CSUN) is about a mile from the epicenter of the Northridge Earthquake of January 17, 1994, and the damage total for the campus stands at over 400 million dollars. The earthquake happened at 4:31 a.m. on a holiday during semester break, so only a few people were in university buildings during the quake. Fortunately, no one was seriously injured on campus. All of the buildings on campus were damaged, some beyond repair.

At the end of her presentation, she reversed her approach. She detailed several extensive action plans, listing specific procedures, issues, and questions that fellow librarians might consider to prepare for disasters on their own campuses. Based on these particulars, she personalized her broad concluding generalization:

> Please understand that a disaster can happen to your library and that the time it chooses to happen could be in the next minute. An earthquake, hurricane, tornado, flood, fire, or explosion will not ask for your permission in advance. But you can choose to be well prepared. Think about what would make your library a safer place to be during a disaster. Think about what you can do to make it easier for your library to recover from a disaster.

☐ Do your generalizations follow logically from your particulars? Can you substantiate what and how much you claim?

☐ Are your particulars typical, numerous, and relevant enough to support your generalizations? Are your particulars substantial enough to warrant the conclusion you have drawn?

☐ Are both your generalizations and your particulars presented clearly? Have you identified your assumptions for your readers?

☐ How do you expect your reasoning patterns to affect readers? What are your reasons for opening with generalizations or reserving them until the end?

☐ Is your reasoning in an explanation clear and logical? Is your reasoning in an argument rigorous enough to withstand scrutiny? Have you avoided generalizing too broadly or illogically connecting generalizations and particulars?

## Learning by Doing 🖋 Reasoning Inductively and Deductively

Skim a recent magazine for an article that explores a health, environmental, or economic issue. Read the article, looking for paragraphs organized inductively and deductively. Why do you think the writer chose one pattern or the other in the various sections of the article? How well do those patterns work from a reader's point of view? Sum up your conclusions.

# Analyzing a Subject

When you *analyze* a subject, you divide it into its parts and then examine one part at a time. If you have taken any chemistry, you probably analyzed water: you separated it into hydrogen and oxygen, its two elements. You've heard many a commentator or blogger analyze the news, telling us what made up an event—who participated, where it occurred, what happened. Analyzing a news event may produce results less certain and clear-cut than analyzing a chemical compound, but the principle is similar—to take something apart for the purpose of understanding it better.

Analysis helps readers grasp something complex: they can more readily take it in as a series of bites than one gulp. For this reason, college textbooks do a lot of analyzing: an economics book divides a labor union into its component parts, an anatomy text divides the hand into its bones, muscles, and ligaments. In your papers, you might analyze and explain to readers anything from a contemporary subculture (What social groups make up the homeless population of Los Angeles?) to an ecosystem (What

For more on division and classification, see pp. 434–36. For more on process analysis, see pp. 432–34. For more on cause and effect, see pp. 439–40.

animals, plants, and minerals coexist in a rain forest?). Analysis is so useful that you can apply it in many situations: breaking down the components of a subject to classify them, separating the stages in a process to see how it works, or identifying the possible results of an event to project consequences.

In *Cultural Anthropology: A Perspective on the Human Condition* (West, 1987), Emily A. Schultz and Robert H. Lavenda briefly but effectively demonstrate by analysis how a metaphor like "the Lord is my shepherd" makes a difficult concept ("the Lord") easy to understand.

> The first part of a metaphor, the metaphorical subject, indicates the domain of experience that needs to be clarified (e.g., "the Lord"). The second part of a metaphor, the metaphorical predicate, suggests a domain of experience which is familiar (e.g., sheep-herding) and which may help us understand what "the Lord" is all about.

When you plan an analysis, you might label slices in a pielike circle or arrange subdivisions in a list running from smallest to largest or least to most important. Make sure your analysis has a purpose — that it will show something about your subject or tell your readers something they didn't know before. For example, to show the ethnic composition of New York City, you might divide the city geographically into neighborhoods — Harlem, Spanish Harlem, Yorkville, Chinatown, Little Italy. To explain New York's social classes, however, you might start with homeless people and work up to the wealthy elite. The way you slice your subject into pieces depends in part on the point you want to make about it — and the point you end up making depends in part on how you've sliced it up. You may also find that you have a stronger point to make — that New York City's social hierarchy is oppressive and unstable, for example.

How can you help readers follow your analysis? Some writers begin by identifying the subdivisions into which they will slice the subject ("The federal government has three branches"). If you name or label each part you mention, define your terms, and clarify with examples, you will also distinguish each part from the others. Finally, transitions, leading readers from one part to the next, help make your essay readable.

For more on transitions, see pp. 417–20.

---

## DISCOVERY CHECKLIST

- ☐ Exactly what will you try to achieve in your analysis?
- ☐ How does your analysis support your main idea or thesis?
- ☐ How will you break your subject into parts?
- ☐ How can you make each part clear to your readers?
- ☐ What definitions, details, and examples would help clarify each part?
- ☐ What transitions would clarify your movement from part to part?

---

---

## Learning by Doing  Analyzing a Subject

Analyze one of the following subjects by making a list of its basic parts or elements. Then use your list as the basis for a paragraph or short essay explaining each part. Be sure to identify the purpose or point of your analysis. Compare your analysis with those of others in your class who chose the same subject.

| | |
|---|---|
| a news source | a song, album, or musical group |
| parking | social media |
| a reality TV show | a computer or other technological device |
| a good teacher or course | a family, tribe, clan, or neighborhood |
| a healthy lifestyle | leadership, heroism, or service |

---

# Analyzing a Process

Analyzing a process means telling step-by-step how something is, was, or could be done. You can analyze an action or a phenomenon — how a skyscraper is built, how a revolution begins, how sunspots form. You can also explain large, long-ago events that you couldn't possibly have witnessed or complex technical processes that you couldn't personally duplicate. In "Can Artificial Meat Save the World?" (*Popular Science*, 18 November 2013), Tom Foster explains the process of producing an innovative meat-free "meat."

> On the other side of Columbia, at a biotech start-up incubator on the edge of the University of Missouri campus, the scientists at Modern Meadow are working on a very different solution to the meat-production crisis. When I visit, a 3-D printer about the size of an HP desktop unit streams a line of yellowish goo onto a petri dish. Back and forth, the machine creates a series of narrow rows a hair's breadth apart. After covering a few inches of the dish, the printer switches direction and lays new rows atop the first ones in a crosshatch pattern. There's no noise but an electric whir, no smell, nothing to suggest that the goo is an embryonic form of meat that will turn into a little sausage. Once the printer finishes its run, the result looks something like a large Band-Aid.
>
> To reach this stage, about 700 million beef cells spent two weeks growing in a cell-growth medium in a wardrobe-size incubator. The cells were then spun free in a centrifuge, and the resulting slurry, which is the consistency of honey, was transferred to a large syringe that acts as the business end of the printer.
>
> The printed cells will now go back into an incubator for a few more days, during which time they will start to develop an extracellular matrix, a naturally occurring scaffold of collagens that gives cells structural support. The result is actual muscle tissue.

In contrast, the *directive*, or "how-to," process analysis tells readers how to do something (how to box, invest for retirement, clean a painting) or how to make something (how to draw a map, blaze a trail, fix chili). Especially on Web sites, directions may consist of simple step-by-step lists with quick advice for browsers. In essays and articles, however, the basics may be supplemented with advice, encouragement, or relevant experience. In "How to Catch More Trout" (*Outdoor Life*, May 2006), Joe Brooks identifies the critical stages in the process in his first paragraph:

> Every move you make in trout fishing counts for or against you. The way you approach a pool, how you retrieve, how you strike, how you play the fish, how you land him—all are important factors. If you plan your tactics according to the demands of each situation, you'll catch a lot more trout over a season.

Then Brooks introduces the first stage:

> The first thing you should do is stand by the pool and study it awhile before you fish. Locate the trout that are rising consistently. Choose one (the lowest in the pool, preferably), and work on him. If you rush right in and start casting, you'll probably put down several fish that you haven't seen. And you can scare still more fish by false-casting all over the place. A dozen fish you might have caught with a more careful approach may see the line and go down before you even drop the fly on the surface.

He continues with stages and advice until he reaches the last step:

> The safest way to land a fish is to beach it. If no low bank is handy, you can fight a fish until he is tired and then pull his head against a bank or an up-jutting rock and pick him up. Hold him gently. The tighter your grip, the more likely he is to spurt from your fingers, break your leader tippet, and escape. Even if you intend to put him back, you want to feel that he is really yours—a trout you have cast and caught and released because you planned it that way.

Brooks skillfully addresses his audience—readers of *Outdoor Life*, people who probably already know how to fish and hunt. As his title indicates, Brooks isn't explaining how to catch trout but how to catch *more* trout. For this reason, he skips topics for beginners (such as how to cast) and instead urges readers to try more sophisticated tactics to increase their catch.

Process analysis can also turn to humor, as in this paragraph from "How to Heal a Broken Heart (in One Day)" by student Lindsey Schendel.

> To begin your first day of mourning, you will wake up at 11 a.m., thus banishing any feelings of fatigue. Forget eating a healthy breakfast; toast two waffles, and plaster them with chocolate syrup instead of maple. Then make sure you have a room of serenity so you may cry in peace. It is important that you go through the necessary phases of denial and depression. Call up a friend or family member while you are still in your

serious, somber mood. Explain to that person the hardships you are facing and how you don't know if you can go on. Immediately afterwards, turn on any empowering music, get up, and dance.

For more on transitions, see pp. 417–20.

Like more serious process directions, this paragraph includes steps or stages (sleeping late, eating breakfast, crying and calling, getting up and dancing). They are arranged in chronological order with transitions marking the movement from one to the other (*To begin, then, while, immediately afterwards*).

Process analyses are wonderful ways to show readers the inside workings of events or systems, but they can be difficult to follow. Divide the process into logical steps or stages, and put the steps in chronological order. Add details or examples wherever your description might be ambiguous; use transitions to mark the end of one step and the beginning of the next.

---

### DISCOVERY CHECKLIST

☐ Do you thoroughly understand the process you are analyzing?

☐ Do you have a good reason to analyze a process at this point in your writing? How does your analysis support your main idea or thesis?

☐ Have you broken the process into logical and useful steps? Have you adjusted your explanation of the steps for your audience?

☐ Is the order in which you present these steps the best one possible?

☐ Have you used transitions to guide readers from one step to the next?

---

## Learning by Doing 🎯 Analyzing a Process

Analyze one of the following processes or procedures in a paragraph or short essay. Then share your process analysis with classmates. Can they follow your analysis easily? Do they spot anything you left out?

| | |
|---|---|
| administering CPR | making a healthy snack |
| bathing a pet | making a meal |
| buying a car | planning a party |
| job hunting | registering for college courses |
| kicking a bad habit | studying for a test |

## Dividing and Classifying

For more on analyzing a subject, see pp. 430–32.

To divide is to break something down, identifying or analyzing its components. It's far easier to take in a subject, especially a complex one, a piece at a time. The thing divided may be as concrete as a medical center (which you might divide into specialty units) or as abstract as a knowledge of art (which you might divide into sculpture, painting, drawing, and other forms). To classify is to make sense of a potentially bewildering array of things — works of literature, this year's movies — by sorting them into categories (*types* or *classes*) that you can deal with one at a time. Literature is customarily arranged by genre — novels, stories, poems, plays. Movies might be sorted by audience (children, teenagers, mature adults). Dividing and classifying are like two sides of the same coin. In theory, any broad subject can be *divided* into components, which can then be *classified* into categories. In practice, it's often difficult to tell where division stops and classification begins.

In the following paragraph from *David and Goliath: Underdogs, Misfits, and the Art of Battling Giants* (Little, Brown, 2013), Malcolm Gladwell uses division to simplify for modern readers what might be an unfamiliar subject: the types of warriors deployed in ancient battles.

> Ancient armies had three kinds of warriors. The first was cavalry — armed men on horseback or in chariots. The second was infantry — foot soldiers wearing armor and carrying swords and shields. The third were projectile warriors, or what today would be called artillery: archers and, most important, slingers. Slingers had a leather pouch attached on two sides by a long strand of rope. They would put a rock or lead ball into the pouch, swing it around in increasingly wider and faster circles, and then release one end of the rope, hurling the rock forward.

Gladwell's intent, however, is less to enlighten readers about historical warfare than, as the book's subtitle suggests, to help them think differently about contemporary contests by considering the advantages of disadvantages. After he classifies Goliath as "heavy infantry" and David as "a slinger, and slingers beat infantry, hands down," readers are equipped to interpret their ancient Biblical contest differently.

Classification also helps to identify patterns and relationships that might otherwise be missed. In "How Wonder Works" (*Aeon*, 21 June 2013), Jessie Prinz explores the nature of wonder, "humanity's most important emotion," fed and unified by science, religion, and art. To do so, he classifies various human reactions to novelty, spectacle, and all sorts of natural and creative works — in short, responses that identify and express wonder.

> These bodily symptoms point to three dimensions that might in fact be essential components of wonder. The first is *sensory*: wondrous things engage our senses — we stare and widen our eyes. The second is *cognitive*: such things are perplexing because we cannot rely on past experience to comprehend them. This leads to a suspension of breath, akin to the freezing response that kicks in when we are startled: we gasp and say "Wow!" Finally, wonder has a dimension that can be described as *spiritual*: we look upwards in veneration; hence Smith's invocation of the swelling heart.

When you divide and classify, your point is to make order out of a complex or overwhelming jumble.

- Make sure the components and categories you identify are sensible, given your purpose, and follow the same principle of classification or analysis for all categories. For example, to discuss campus relations, it makes sense to divide the school population into *instructors, students,* and *support staff*; it would make less sense to divide it into *people from the South, people from other states,* and *people from overseas.*

- Try to group apples with apples, not with oranges, so that all the components or categories are roughly equivalent. For example, if you're classifying television shows and you've come up with *reality shows, dramas, talk shows, children's shows, news,* and *cartoons,* then you've got a problem: the last category is probably part of *children's shows.*

- Check that your final system is easy for readers to understand. Most people can handle only about seven things at once. If you've got more than five or six components or categories, try to combine or eliminate some.

## DISCOVERY CHECKLIST

- ☐ How does your division or classification support your main idea or thesis?
- ☐ Do you use the most logical principle to divide or classify for your purpose?
- ☐ Do you stick to one principle throughout?
- ☐ Have you identified components or categories that are comparable?
- ☐ Have you arranged your components or categories in the best order?
- ☐ Have you given specific examples for each component or category?
- ☐ Have you made a complex subject more accessible to your readers?

For more on brainstorming, see pp. 371–72.

## Learning by Doing 🖉 Dividing and Classifying

Brainstorm on one or two of the following subjects to come up with as many components as you can. With classmates, create one large list by combining items for each subject. Working together, classify the items on the largest list into logical categories. Add or change components or categories as needed.

| students | books | sports | friends |
| teachers | music | movies | drivers |

For sample essays and advice on writing a comparison-and-contrast essay, see Ch. 7.

# Comparing and Contrasting

Set a pair of subjects side by side to compare and contrast them. When you compare, you point out similarities; when you contrast, you discuss differences. You can use two basic methods of organization for comparison and contrast—the opposing pattern and the alternating pattern—as illustrated for a comparison and contrast of two brothers.

| OPPOSING PATTERN, SUBJECT BY SUBJECT | ALTERNATING PATTERN, POINT BY POINT |
|---|---|
| Subject A: Jim | Point 1: Appearance |
|    Point 1: Appearance |    Subject A: Jim |
|    Point 2: Personality |    Subject B: Jack |
|    Point 3: Interests | Point 2: Personality |
| Subject B: Jack |    Subject A: Jim |
|    Point 1: Appearance |    Subject B: Jack |
|    Point 2: Personality | Point 3: Interests |
|    Point 3: Interests |    Subject A: Jim |
| |    Subject B: Jack |

You need a reason to compare and contrast—a final evaluation, perhaps a decision about which thing is better or another purpose. For example, compare Jack and Jim to do more than point out lanky or curly hair. Use their differences to highlight their powerful bond as brothers or their similarities to support a generalization about a family strength.

The next selection comes from "The Epidemic of Childhood Obesity: Learn the Facts" on the *Let's Move* Web site. To answer "How did we get here?" this passage begins with the alternating pattern, first contrasting lifestyles (in alternating paragraphs) for children three decades ago and children today. Next it shifts to snacks, portion sizes, and total caloric intake, each topic alternating within its own paragraph.

> Thirty years ago, most people led lives that kept them at a healthy weight. Kids walked to and from school every day, ran around at recess, participated in gym class, and played for hours after school before dinner. Meals were home-cooked with reasonable portion sizes and there was always a vegetable on the plate. Eating fast food was rare and snacking between meals was an occasional treat.
>
> Today, children experience a very different lifestyle. Walks to and from school have been replaced by car and bus rides. Gym class and after-school sports have been cut; afternoons are now spent with TV, video games, and the Internet. Parents are busier than ever and families eat fewer home-cooked meals. Snacking between meals is now commonplace.
>
> Thirty years ago, kids ate just one snack a day, whereas now they are trending toward three snacks, resulting in an additional 200 calories a day. And one in five school-age children has up to six snacks a day.
>
> Portion sizes have also exploded—they are now two to five times bigger than they were in years past. Beverage portions have grown as well—in the mid-1970s, the average sugar-sweetened beverage was 13.6 ounces compared to today, where kids think nothing of drinking 20 ounces of sugar-sweetened beverages at a time.

> In total, we are now eating 31 percent more calories than we were forty years ago—including 56 percent more fats and oils and 14 percent more sugars and sweeteners. The average American now eats fifteen more pounds of sugar a year than in 1970.

The selection concludes with a final contrast to guide readers to solutions.

> Now that's the bad news. The good news is that by making just a few lifestyle changes, we can help our children lead healthier lives—and we already have the tools we need to do it. We just need the will.

---

### DISCOVERY CHECKLIST

- ☐ Is your reason for comparing and contrasting unmistakably clear? Does it support or develop your main idea or thesis?
- ☐ Have you chosen to write about the *major* similarities and differences?
- ☐ Have you compared or contrasted like things? Have you discussed the same categories or features for each item?
- ☐ Have you selected points of comparison and supporting details that will intrigue, enlighten, and persuade your audience?
- ☐ Have you used the best possible arrangement, given your subject and the point you're trying to make?
- ☐ If you are making a judgment, have you treated both subjects fairly?
- ☐ Have you avoided moving mechanically from "On the one hand" to "On the other hand"?

---

## Learning by Doing 🖋 Comparing and Contrasting

Write a paragraph or two in which you compare and contrast the subjects in one of the following pairs. Exchange drafts with classmates for response, using questions from the Discovery Checklist.

cash versus credit
childhood versus adulthood
dogs versus cats (or other pets)
high school versus college
living in an apartment (or dorm) and living in a house
Nintendo Wii versus Playstation
paper versus plastic at the grocery store
*Star Wars* versus *Star Trek*
two classes you are taking
two familiar cities, communities, or neighborhoods
two musicians, artists, or performers
watching a movie in a theater versus watching at home

# Identifying Causes and Effects

From the time we are children, we ask why. Why can't I go out and play? Why is the sky blue? Why did my goldfish die? Seeking causes and effects continues into adulthood, so it's a common method of development. To explain causal relationships successfully, think about the subject critically, gather evidence, draw judicious conclusions, and clarify relationships.

For sample essays and advice on writing a cause-and-effect essay, see Ch. 8.

In the following passage from "On the Origin of Celebrity" (*Nautilus*, Issue 5), Professor Robert Sapolsky brings his background in biology and neurology to his topic.

> We all feel the magnetic pull of celebrities—we track them, know their net worth, their tastes in furniture, the absurd names of their pets and children. We go under the knives of cosmetic surgeons to look like them. We feel personal connections with them, are let down by their moral failings, care about their tragedies. As I write, my family of musical fanatics is mourning the death of Cory Monteith. We not only feel for the pointless loss of a talented young actor, and for his girlfriend, Lea Michele, but in some confused, inchoate way, also feel heartbroken for Finn and Rachel, the characters they play on *Glee*.
>
> Why the obsession? Because we're primates with vested interests in tracking social hierarchies and patterns of social affiliation. And celebrities provide our primate minds with stimulating gyrations of hierarchy and affiliation (who is sleeping with, feuding with, out-earning whom). Celebrities also reflect the peculiar distance we have traveled culturally since our hominid past, and reveal how distorted our minds can become in our virtual world. We obsess over celebrities because, for better or worse, we feel a deep personal sense of connection with people who aren't real.

Instead of focusing on causes *or* effects, often writers trace a *chain* of cause-and-effect relationships, as Charles C. Mann and Mark L. Plummer do in "The Butterfly Problem" (*The Atlantic*, January 1992).

> More generally, the web of species around us helps generate soil, regulate freshwater supplies, dispose of waste, and maintain the quality of the atmosphere. Pillaging nature to the point where it cannot perform these functions is dangerously foolish. Simple self-protection is thus a second motive for preserving biodiversity. When DDT was sprayed in Borneo, the biologists Paul and Anne Ehrlich relate in their book *Extinction* (1981), it killed all the houseflies. The gecko lizards that preyed on the flies ate their pesticide-filled corpses and died. House cats consumed the dying lizards; they died too. Rats descended on the villages, bringing bubonic plague. Incredibly, the housefly in this case was part of an intricate system that controlled human disease. To make up for its absence, the government was forced to parachute cats into the area.

## DISCOVERY CHECKLIST

☐ Do you clearly tie your use of cause and effect to your main idea or thesis?

☐ Have you identified actual causes? Have you supplied persuasive evidence to support them?

☐ Have you identified actual effects, or are they conjecture? If conjecture, are they logical possibilities? What persuasive evidence supports them?

☐ Have you judiciously drawn conclusions about causes and effects? Have you avoided faulty thinking and logical fallacies?

☐ Have you presented your points clearly and logically so that your readers can follow them easily?

☐ Have you considered other causes or effects, immediate or long-term, that readers might find relevant?

For more on faulty thinking and logical fallacies, see pp. 171–72.

## Learning by Doing  Identifying Causes and Effects

1. Identify some of the *causes* of *five* of the following. Then discuss possible causes with your classmates.

| | | |
|---|---|---|
| failing an exam | ordering take-out | stress |
| moving | losing/winning a game | pollution |
| poor/good health | animal extinction | recycling |

2. Identify some of the *effects* of *five* of the following. Then discuss possible effects with your classmates.

| | | |
|---|---|---|
| a compliment | global warming | passing a test |
| dieting | graduating | spending time outdoors |
| driving under the influence of drugs or alcohol | having a sick family member or friend | suicide |

3. Identify some of the *causes and effects* of *one* of the following, doing a little research as needed. How might you use the chain of causes and effects in an essay? Discuss your findings with your classmates.

| | |
|---|---|
| the online shopping boom | the Supreme Court decision to legalize gay marriage |
| the attacks of September 11, 2001 | |
| the discovery of atomic energy | the uses of solar energy |
| civil rights protest | global climate change |
| recycling | racial tension |

## Learning by Doing 🎞 Reflecting on Developing

Think back to the methods of development that you have used in recent papers. How do you generally develop your papers? What new approaches have you tried or might you try? How do you decide which method to use and where? How do you know when you have developed a section effectively, so that a reader would find it clear and compelling? Working with a classmate or small group, explain your best method, pointing out its advantages and disadvantages.

# 23 Strategies for Revising and Editing

Good writing is rewriting. In this chapter we provide strategies for revising and editing—ways to rethink muddy ideas and emphasize important ones, to rephrase obscure passages and restructure garbled sentences. Our advice applies not only to rewriting whole essays but also to rewriting, editing, and proofreading sentences and paragraphs.

## Re-viewing and Revising

*Revision* means "seeing again"—discovering again, conceiving again, shaping again. It may occur at any and all stages of the writing process, and most writers do a lot of it. *Macro revising* is making large, global, or fundamental changes that affect the overall direction or impact of writing—its purpose,

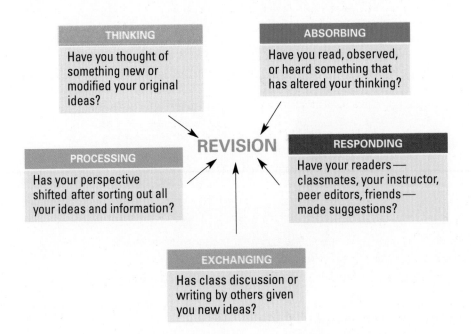

**THINKING**
Have you thought of something new or modified your original ideas?

**ABSORBING**
Have you read, observed, or heard something that has altered your thinking?

**PROCESSING**
Has your perspective shifted after sorting out all your ideas and information?

**REVISION**

**RESPONDING**
Have your readers— classmates, your instructor, peer editors, friends— made suggestions?

**EXCHANGING**
Has class discussion or writing by others given you new ideas?

organization, or audience. Its companion is *micro revising,* paying attention to sentences, words, punctuation, and grammar—including ways to create emphasis and eliminate wordiness.

| MACRO REVISING | MICRO REVISING |
|---|---|
| • **PURPOSE:** Have you refined what you want to accomplish? <br><br> • **THESIS:** Could you state your main point more accurately? <br><br> • **AUDIENCE:** Should you address your readers differently? <br><br> • **STRUCTURE:** Should you reorganize any part of your writing? <br><br> • **SUPPORT:** Do you need to add, drop, or rework your support? | • **EMPHASIS:** Can you position your ideas more effectively? <br><br> • **CONCISENESS:** Can you spot extra words that you might cut? <br><br> • **CLARITY:** Can you make any sentences and words clearer? |

## Revising for Purpose and Thesis

When you revise for purpose, you make sure that your writing accomplishes what you want it to do. If your goal is to create an interesting profile of a person, have you done so? If you want to persuade your readers to take a certain course of action, have you succeeded? When your project has evolved or your assignment grown clearer to you, the purpose of your final essay may differ from your purpose when you began. To revise for purpose, try to step back and see your writing as other readers will.

Concentrate on what's actually in your paper, not what you assume is there. Create a thesis sentence (if you haven't), or revise your working thesis statement (if you've developed one). Reconsider how it is worded:

- Is it stated exactly in concise yet detailed language?
- Is it focused on only one main idea?
- Is it stated positively rather than negatively?
- Is it limited to a demonstrable statement?

Then consider how accurately your thesis now represents your main idea:

- Does each part of your essay directly relate to your thesis?
- Does each part of your essay develop and support your thesis?
- Does your essay deliver everything your thesis promises?

If you find unrelated or contradictory passages, you have several options: revise the thesis, revise the essay, or revise both.

For more on stating and improving a working thesis, see pp. 384–93. For checklists that will help you revise your thesis, see Chs. 4–12.

If your idea has deepened, your topic become more complex, or your essay developed along new lines, refine or expand your thesis accordingly.

WORKING THESIS     The *Herald*'s coverage of the Senate elections was more thorough than the *Courier*'s.

REVISED THESIS     The *Herald*'s coverage of the Senate elections was less timely but more thorough and more impartial than the *Courier*'s.

WORKING THESIS     As the roles of men and women have changed in our society, old-fashioned formal courtesy has declined.

REVISED THESIS     As the roles of men and women have changed in our society, old-fashioned formal courtesy has declined not only toward women but also toward men.

## REVISION CHECKLIST

- ☐ Do you know exactly what you want your essay to accomplish? Can you put it in one sentence: "In this paper I want to . . ."?
- ☐ Is your thesis stated outright in the essay? If not, have you provided clues so that your readers will know precisely what it is?
- ☐ Does every part of the essay work to achieve the same goal?
- ☐ Have you tried to do too much? Does your coverage seem too thin? If so, how might you reduce the scope of your thesis and essay?
- ☐ Does your essay say all that needs to be said? Is everything — ideas, connections, supporting evidence — on paper, not just in your head?
- ☐ In writing the essay, have you changed your mind, rethought your assumptions, made a discovery? Does anything now need to be recast?
- ☐ Have you developed enough evidence? Is it clear and convincing?

## Revising for Audience

What works with one audience can fall flat with another. Your organization, selection of details, word choice, and tone all affect your particular readers. Visualize one of them poring over the essay, reacting to what you have written. What expressions do you see on that reader's face? Where does he or she have trouble understanding? Where have you hit the mark?

## REVISION CHECKLIST

- ☐ Who will read this essay?
- ☐ Will your readers think you have told them something worth knowing?

☐ Are there any places where readers might fall asleep? If so, can you shorten, delete, or liven up such passages?

☐ Does the opening of the essay mislead your readers by promising something that the essay never delivers?

☐ Do you unfold each idea in enough detail to make it clear and interesting?

☐ Have you anticipated questions your audience might ask?

☐ Where might readers raise objections? How might you answer them?

☐ Have you used any specialized or technical language that your readers might not understand? If so, have you worked in brief definitions?

☐ What is your attitude toward your audience? Are you chummy, angry, superior, apologetic, preachy? Should you revise to improve your attitude?

---

## Learning by Doing 🎤 Reflecting on Your Audience

Focus on the audience for a piece of writing that you are working on. (The audience for college writing typically will consist of your instructor and possibly your peers.) Is your word choice appropriate for this audience? Should you add or revise material to address the expectations of your readers or to give them the background they need to understand your subject? If your audience includes peer reviewers, what insights have they provided to help you improve your writing? After answering these questions, write a brief reflection on what you have learned about addressing audience needs and expectations.

## Revising for Structure and Support

When you revise for structure and support, you make sure that the order of your ideas, your selection of supporting material, and its arrangement are as effective as possible. You may have all the ingredients of a successful essay—but they may be a confusing mess.

In a well-structured essay, each paragraph, sentence, and phrase serves a clear function. Are your opening and closing paragraphs relevant, concise, and interesting? Is everything in each paragraph on the same topic? Are all ideas adequately developed? Are the paragraphs arranged in the best possible order? Finally, do you lead readers from one idea to the next with clear and painless transitions?

For more on paragraphs, topic sentences, and transitions, see Ch. 21.

An outline can help you discover what you've succeeded in getting on paper. Find the topic sentence of each paragraph in your draft (or create one, if necessary), and list them in order. Label the sentences *I., II., A., B.,* and so on, to show the logical relationships of ideas. Do the same with the supporting details under each topic sentence, labeling them also with letters and numbers and indenting appropriately. Now look at the outline. Does it make sense on its own, without the essay to explain it? Would a different order or

For more on using outlining for planning, see pp. 395–403.

arrangement be more effective? Do any sections look thin and need more evidence? Are the connections between parts on paper, not just in your head? Maybe too many ideas are jammed into too few paragraphs. Maybe you need more specific details and examples — or stronger ones. Strengthen the outline and then rewrite to follow it.

## REVISION CHECKLIST

☐ Does your introduction set up the whole essay? Does it both grab readers' attention and hint at what is to follow?

☐ Does the essay fulfill all that you promise in your opening?

☐ Would any later passage make a better beginning?

☐ Is your thesis clear early in the essay? If explicit, is it positioned prominently?

☐ Do the paragraph breaks seem logical?

☐ Is the main idea of each paragraph clear? Is it stated in a topic sentence?

☐ Is the main idea of each paragraph fully developed? Where might you need more or better evidence? Should you omit or move any stray bits?

☐ Is each detail or piece of evidence relevant to the topic sentence of the paragraph and the main point of the essay?

☐ Would any paragraphs make more sense in a different order?

☐ Does everything follow clearly? Does one point smoothly lead to the next? Would transitions help make the connections clearer?

☐ Does the conclusion follow logically or seem tacked on?

## Learning by Doing 🖉 Tackling Macro Revision

Select a draft that would benefit from revision. Then, based on your sense of its greatest need, choose one of the revision checklists to guide a first revision. Let the draft sit for a while. Then work with one of the remaining checklists.

## Working with a Peer Editor

There's no substitute for having someone else read your draft. Whether you are writing for an audience of classmates or for a different group (the town council or readers of *Time*), having a classmate go over your essay is a worthwhile revision strategy. To gain all you can as a writer from a peer review, you need to play an active part:

■ Ask your reader questions. (See page 447 for ideas.) Or bring a "Dear Editor" letter or memo, written ahead, to your meeting.

## Questions for a Peer Editor

### First Questions for a Peer Editor

What is your first reaction to this paper?

What is this writer trying to tell you?

What are this paper's greatest strengths?

Does it have any major weaknesses?

What one change would most improve the paper?

### Questions on Meaning

Do you understand everything? Is the draft missing any information that you need to know?

Does this paper tell you anything you didn't know before?

Is the writer trying to cover too much territory? Too little?

Does any point need to be more fully explained or illustrated?

When you come to the end, has the paper delivered what it promised?

Could this paper use a down-to-the-ground revision?

### Questions on Organization

Does the beginning grab your interest and draw you into the main idea? Or can you find a better beginning at a later point?

Does the paper have one main idea, or does it juggle more than one?

Would the main idea stand out better if anything were removed or added?

Might the ideas in the paper be more effectively arranged? Do any ideas belong together that now seem too far apart?

Can you follow the ideas easily? Are transitions needed? If so, where?

Does the writer keep to one point of view — one angle of seeing?

Does the ending seem deliberate, as if the writer meant to conclude, not just run out of gas? How might the writer strengthen the conclusion?

### Questions on Writing Strategies

Do you feel that this paper addresses you personally?

Do you dislike or object to any statement the writer makes or any wording the writer uses? Is the problem word choice, tone, or inadequate support to convince you? Should the writer keep or change this part?

Does the draft contain anything that distracts you or seems unnecessary?

Do you get bored at any point? How might the writer keep you reading?

Is the language of this paper too lofty and abstract? If so, where does the writer need to come down to earth and get specific?

Do you understand all the words used? Do any specialized words need clearer definitions?

- Be open to new ideas — for focus, organization, or details.
- Use what's helpful, but trust yourself as the writer.

Be a helpful peer editor: offer honest, intelligent feedback, not judgment.

See specific checklists in the Revising and Editing sections in Chs. 4–12.

- Look at the big picture: purpose, focus, thesis, clarity, coherence, organization, support.
- When you spot strengths or weaknesses, be specific: note examples.
- Answer the writer's questions, and also use the questions supplied throughout this book to concentrate on essentials, not details.

## Meeting with Your Instructor

Prepare for your conference on a draft as you prepare for a peer review. Reread your paper; then write out your questions, concerns, or current revision plans. Whether you are meeting face-to-face, online, or by audio or video phone, arrive on time. Even if you feel shy or anxious, remember that you are working with an experienced reader who wants to help you improve your writing.

- If you already have received comments from your instructor, ask about anything you can't read, don't understand, or can't figure out how to do.
- If you are unsure about comments from peers, get your instructor's view.
- If you have a revision plan, ask for suggestions or priorities.
- If more questions arise after your conference, especially about comments on a draft returned there, follow up with a call, e-mail message, question after class, or second conference (as your instructor prefers).

## Decoding Your Instructor's Comments

Many instructors favor two kinds of comments:

- Summary comments — sentences on your first or last page — that may compliment strengths, identify recurring issues, acknowledge changes between drafts, make broad suggestions, or end with a grade
- Specific comments — brief notes or questions added in the margins — that typically pinpoint issues in the text

Although brief comments may seem like cryptic code or shorthand, they usually rely on key words to note common, recurring problems that probably are discussed in class and related to course criteria. They also may act as reminders, identifying issues that your instructor expects you to look up in your book and solve. A simple analysis — tallying up the repeated comments in one paper or several — can quickly help you set priorities for revision and editing. Some sample comments follow with translations, but turn to your instructor if you need a specific explanation.

| COMMENTS ON PURPOSE | Thesis? Vague Broad Clarify What's your point? So? So what? |
|---|---|
| POSSIBLE TRANSLATION | You need to state your thesis more clearly and directly so that a reader knows what matters. |

Concentrate on rewording so that your main idea is plain.

COMMENTS ON ORGANIZATION

Hard to follow  Logic?  Sequence? Add transitions? Jumpy

POSSIBLE TRANSLATION

You need to organize more logically so your paper is easy for a reader to follow without jumping from point to point. Add transitions or other cues to guide a reader.

COMMENTS ON SENTENCES AND WORDS

Unclear  Clarify  Awk  Repetition  Too informal

POSSIBLE TRANSLATION

You need to make your sentence or your wording easier to read and clearer. Rework awkward passages, reduce repetition, and stick to academic language.

COMMENTS ON EVIDENCE

Specify  Focus  Narrow down  Develop more Seems thin

POSSIBLE TRANSLATION

You need to provide more concrete evidence or explain the relevance or nature of your evidence more clearly. Check that you support each main point with plenty of pertinent and compelling evidence.

COMMENTS ON SOURCES

Likely opponents?  Source?  Add quotation marks?  Too many quotes  Summarize? Synthesize?  Launch source?

POSSIBLE TRANSLATION

You need to add sources that represent views other than your own. You include wording or ideas that sound like a source, not like you, so your quotation marks or citation might be missing. Instead of tossing in quotations, use your critical thinking skills to sum up ideas, relate them to each other, and introduce them more effectively.

COMMENTS ON CITATIONS

Cite?  Author?  Page?  MLA?  APA?

POSSIBLE TRANSLATION

Add missing source citations in your text and use the expected academic format to present them.

COMMENTS ON FINAL LIST OF SOURCES

MLA?  APA?  Comma?  Period?  Cap?  Space?

POSSIBLE TRANSLATION

Your entries do not follow the expected format. Check the model entries in this book. Look for the presence, absence, or placement of the specific detail noted.

# Revising for Emphasis, Conciseness, and Clarity

After you've revised for the large issues in your draft—purpose, thesis, audience, structure, and support—you're ready to turn your attention to micro revising. Now is the time to look at your language, to emphasize what matters most, and to communicate it concisely and clearly. Your close attention to these aspects of your draft also can strengthen your distinctive voice and style as a writer.

## Stressing What Counts

An effective writer decides what matters most and shines a bright light on it using the most emphatic positions in an essay, a paragraph, or a sentence—the beginning and the end.

**Stating It First.** In an essay, you might start with what matters most. For an economics paper on import quotas (such as the number of foreign cars allowed into a country), student Donna Waite summed up her conclusion.

> Although an import quota has many effects, both for the nation imposing the quota and for the nation whose industries must suffer from it, I believe that the most important effect is generally felt at home. A native industry gains a chance to thrive in a marketplace of lessened competition.

To take a stand or make a proposal, you might open with your position.

> Our state's antiquated system of justices of the peace is inefficient.

> The United States should orbit a human observer around Mars.

In a single sentence, as in an essay, you can stress things at the start. Consider the following unemphatic sentence:

> When Congress debates the Hall-Hayes Act removing existing protections for endangered species, as now seems likely to occur on May 12, it will be a considerable misfortune if this bill should pass, since the extinction of many rare birds and animals would certainly result.

The debate and its probable timing consume the start of the sentence. Here's a better use of this emphatic position:

> The extinction of many rare birds and animals would certainly follow passage of the Hall-Hayes Act.

Now the writer stresses what he most fears—the dire consequences of the act. (A later sentence might add the date and his opinion about passage.)

**Stating It Last.** To place an idea last can throw weight on it. Emphatic order, proceeding from least important to most, is dramatic: it builds up and up. In a paper on import quotas, however, a dramatic buildup might look contrived. Still, in an essay on how city parks lure visitors to the city, the thesis sentence — summing up the point of the essay — might stand at the very end: "For the urban core, improved parks could bring about a new era of prosperity." Giving evidence first and leading up to the thesis at the end is particularly effective in editorials and informal persuasive essays.

A sentence that uses climactic order, suspending its point until the end, is a *periodic* sentence as novelist Julian Green illustrates.

> Amid chaos of illusions into which we are cast headlong, there is one thing that stands out as true, and that is — love.

## Cutting and Whittling

Like pea pickers who throw out dirt and pebbles, good writers remove needless words that clog their prose. One of the chief joys of revising is to watch 200 meandering words shrink to a direct 150. To see how saving words helps, let's look at some strategies for reducing wordiness.

**Cut the Fanfare.** Why bother to announce that you're going to say something? Cut the fanfare. We aren't, by the way, attacking the usefulness of transitions that lead readers along.

For more on transitions, see pp. 417–20.

| WORDY | As far as getting ready for winter is concerned, I put antifreeze in my car. |
|---|---|
| REVISED | To get ready for winter, I put antifreeze in my car. |
| WORDY | The point should be made that . . . |
| | Let me make it perfectly clear that . . . |
| | In this paper I intend to . . . |
| | In conclusion I would like to say that . . . |

**Use Strong Verbs.** Forms of the verb *be* (*am, is, are, was, were*) followed by a noun or an adjective can make a statement wordy, as can *There is* or *There are*. Such weak verbs can almost always be replaced by active verbs.

| WORDY | The Akron game was a disappointment to the fans. |
|---|---|
| REVISED | The Akron game disappointed the fans. |
| WORDY | There are many people who dislike flying. |
| REVISED | Many people dislike flying. |

**Use Relative Pronouns with Caution.** When a clause begins with a relative pronoun (*who, which, that*), you often can whittle it to a phrase.

| WORDY | Venus, which is the second planet of the solar system, is called the evening star. |
|---|---|
| REVISED | Venus, the second planet of the solar system, is called the evening star. |

**Cut Out Deadwood.** The more you revise, the more shortcuts you'll discover. Phrases such as *on the subject of, in regard to, in terms of,* and *as far as . . . is concerned* often simply fill space. Try reading the sentences below without the words in *italics*.

> Howell spoke for the sophomores, and Janet *also spoke* for the seniors.

> He is *something of* a clown but *sort of the* lovable *type*.

> As a major in *the field of* economics, I plan to concentrate on *the area of* international banking.

> *The decision as to* whether *or not* to go is up to you.

**Cut Descriptors.** Adjectives and adverbs are often dispensable.

> WORDY    Johnson's extremely significant research led to highly important major discoveries.

> REVISED    Johnson's research led to major discoveries.

**Be Short, Not Long.** While a long word may convey a shade of meaning that a shorter synonym doesn't, in general favor short words over long ones. Instead of *the remainder,* write *the rest;* instead of *activate, start* or *begin;* instead of *adequate* or *sufficient, enough*. Look for the right word — one that wraps an idea in a smaller package.

> WORDY    Andy has a left fist that has a lot of power in it.

> REVISED    Andy has a potent left.

By the way, it pays to read. From reading, you absorb words like *potent* and set them to work for you.

## Keeping It Clear

Recall what you want to achieve — clear, direct communication with your readers using specific, unambiguous words arranged in logical order.

> WORDY    He is more or less a pretty outstanding person in regard to good looks.

> REVISED    He is strikingly handsome.

Read your draft with fresh eyes. Return, after a break, to passages that have been a struggle; heal any battle scars by focusing on clarity.

> UNCLEAR    Thus, after a lot of thought, it should be approved by the board even though the federal funding for all the cow-tagging may not be approved yet because it has wide support from local cattle ranchers.

> CLEAR    In anticipation of federal funding, the Livestock Board should approve the cow-tagging proposal widely supported by local cattle ranchers.

**MICRO REVISION CHECKLIST**

☐ Have you positioned what counts at the beginning or the end?

☐ Are you direct, straightforward, and clear?

☐ Do you announce an idea before you utter it? If so, consider chopping out the announcement.

☐ Can you substitute an active verb where you use a form of *be* (*is, was, were*)?

☐ Can you recast any sentence that begins *There is* or *There are*?

☐ Can you reduce to a phrase any clause beginning with *which, who,* or *that*?

☐ Have you added deadwood or too many adjectives and adverbs?

☐ Do you see any long words where short words would do?

☐ Have you kept your writing clear, direct, and forceful?

For his composition class, Daniel Matthews was assigned a paper using a few sources. He was to write about an "urban legend," a widely accepted and emotionally appealing — but untrue — tale about events. The following selection from his paper, "The Truth about 'Taps,'" introduces his topic, briefly explaining the legend and the true story about it. The first draft illustrates macro revisions (highlighted in the margin) and micro revisions (marked in the text); the clear and concise final version follows.

**FIRST DRAFT**

*Avoid "you" in case readers have not shared this experience.*

*Anyone who has ever*
~~As you know, whenever you have~~ attended the funeral services for a

*has*
fallen veteran of the United States of America, ~~you have~~ stood fast as a lone

*Rework paragraph to summarize legend when first mentioned.*

bugler filled the air with the mournful ~~and sullenly appropriate~~ last tribute to

*nation*
a defender of the ~~United States of America~~. ~~As most of us know,~~ the name of

INSERT:
*According to this story, Union captain Robert Ellicombe discovered that a Confederate casualty was, in fact, his son, a music student in the South. The father found "Taps" in his son's pocket, and the tune was first played at a military burial as his son was laid to rest (Coulter).*

*legend*              *has*              *ed*
the bugle call is "Taps," and the ~~story~~ behind its origin ~~is one that is gaining~~

*has*
a popularity ~~of its own~~ as it ~~is more and more frequently being~~ circulated in

this time of war and terror. Although ~~it is clear that~~ this tale ~~of the origin~~ of a

beautiful ode to a fallen warrior is heartfelt ~~and full of purposeful intent~~, it is

*As such, i*
an "urban legend." ~~I~~t fails to provide due justice to the memories of the men

responsible for the true origin of "Taps."

General Daniel Butterfield is the *true* originator of the bugle call "Taps," formerly known as "Lights Out." Butterfield served as a general in the Union army during the Civil War and was awarded the Medal of Honor for actions during that time. One of his most endearing claims to fame is the bugle call "Taps," which he composed at Harrison's Landing in 1862 (Warner 167). The bugle call "Taps" originates from another call named "Lights Out"; this call was used by the Army to signal the end of the day. Butterfield, wanting a new and original call unique to his command, summoned bugler Oliver Willcox Norton to his tent one night. and *r*ather than compose an altogether new tune, he instead modified the notes to the call "Lights Out" (US Military District of Washington). *Shortly thereafter* Then this call could be heard being used up and down the Union lines as the other commanders who had heard the call liked it and adapted it for their own use. This call, the modified version of "Lights Out" is also in a way *and itself* a derivative of the British bugle call *"Tattoo," a* "Tattoo" which is very similar in both sound and purpose to "Lights Out," (Villanueva) notes this as well in his paper "24 Notes That Tap Deep Emotion."

*Group all the discussion of the versions in one place.*

*Divide long sentence to keep it clear.*

*Strengthen paragraph conclusion by sticking to its focus.*

REVISED DRAFT

Anyone who has ever attended the funeral services for a fallen veteran of the United States of America has stood fast as a lone bugler filled the air with a mournful last tribute to a defender of the nation. The name of the bugle call is "Taps," and the legend behind its origin has gained popularity as it has circulated in this time of war and terror. According to this story, Union captain Robert Ellicombe discovered that a Confederate casualty was, in fact, his son, a music student in the South. The father found "Taps" in his son's pocket, and the tune was first played at a military burial as his son was laid to rest (Coulter). Although this tale of a beautiful ode to a fallen warrior is heartfelt, it is an "urban legend." As such, it fails to provide due justice to the memories of the men responsible for the true origin of "Taps."

General Daniel Butterfield is the true originator of the bugle call "Taps." Butterfield served in the Union army during the Civil War and was awarded the Medal of Honor for actions during that time. One of his most endearing claims to fame is the bugle call "Taps," which he composed at Harrison's Landing in 1862 (Warner 167). "Taps" originates from another call named "Lights Out," used by the army to signal the end of the day and itself a derivative of "Tattoo," a British bugle call similar in both sound and purpose (Villanueva). Butterfield, wanting a new and original call unique to his command, summoned bugler Oliver Willcox Norton to his tent one night. Rather than compose an altogether new tune, he instead modified the notes to the call "Lights Out" (US Military District of Washington). Shortly thereafter this call could be heard up and down the Union lines as other commanders heard the call and adapted it for their own use.

# Editing and Proofreading

Editing means correcting and refining grammar, punctuation, and mechanics. Proofreading means taking a final look to check correctness and to catch spelling or word-processing errors. Don't edit and proofread too soon. As you draft, don't fret over spelling an unfamiliar word; it may be revised out in a later version. Wait until you have revised to refine and correct. In college, good editing and proofreading can make the difference between a C and an A. On the job, it may help you get promoted. Readers, teachers, and bosses like careful writers who take time to edit and proofread.

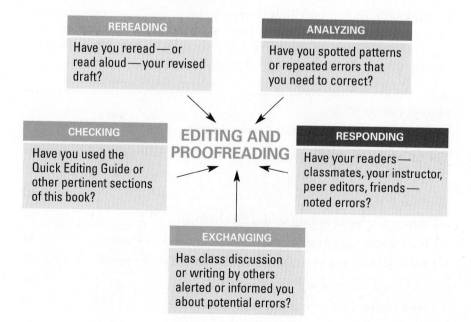

**REREADING**
Have you reread—or read aloud—your revised draft?

**ANALYZING**
Have you spotted patterns or repeated errors that you need to correct?

**CHECKING**
Have you used the Quick Editing Guide or other pertinent sections of this book?

**EDITING AND PROOFREADING**

**RESPONDING**
Have your readers—classmates, your instructor, peer editors, friends—noted errors?

**EXCHANGING**
Has class discussion or writing by others alerted or informed you about potential errors?

## Editing

As you edit, whenever you question whether a word or construction is correct, consult a good reference handbook. Learn the grammar conventions you don't understand so you can spot and eliminate problems in your own writing. Practice until you easily recognize major errors such as fragments and comma splices. Ask for assistance from a peer editor or a tutor in the writing center if your campus has one.

| EDITING | | PROOFREADING |
|---|---|---|
| • **GRAMMAR:** Are your sentences and their parts correct? <br><br> • **SENTENCES:** Are your sentences clear and effective? <br><br> • **WORD CHOICE:** Are your words correct and well selected? <br><br> • **PUNCTUATION:** Do you need to add, correct, or drop any marks? <br><br> • **MECHANICS:** Do you need to correct capitals, italics, or other matters? <br><br> • **FORMAT:** Do you need to adjust margins, spacing, or headings? | → | • **SPELLING:** Have you spell-checked and reread your work attentively? <br><br> • **INCORRECT WORDS:** Have you mistakenly picked any wrong words? <br><br> • **MISSING WORDS:** Have you left out any words? <br><br> • **MINOR ERRORS:** Can you see any small mistakes? <br><br> • **MINOR DETAILS:** Do you need to correct any details? |

Use the Quick Editing Guide (beginning on p. Q-37) to review grammar, style, punctuation, and mechanics problems typically found in college writing. Look for definitions, examples, and a checklist to help you tackle each one. Here is an editing checklist for these problems:

---

### EDITING CHECKLIST

### Common and Serious Problems in College Writing

The following cross-references refer to the Quick Editing Guide section at the back of this book.

| *Grammar Problems* | *Section Number* |
|---|---|
| ☐ Have you avoided writing sentence fragments? | A1 |
| ☐ Have you avoided writing comma splices or fused sentences? | A2 |
| ☐ Have you used the correct form for all verbs in the past tense? | A3 |
| ☐ Do all verbs agree with their subjects? | A4 |
| ☐ Have you used the correct case for all pronouns? | A5 |

☐ Do all pronouns agree with their antecedents? A6

☐ Have you used adjectives and adverbs correctly? A7

*Sentence Problems*

☐ Does each modifier clearly modify the appropriate sentence element? B1

☐ Have you used parallel structure where necessary? B2

*Word Choice Problems*

☐ Have you used appropriate language? C1

☐ Is your writing clean and concise? C2

☐ Have you correctly used commonly confused words? C3

*Punctuation Problems*

☐ Have you used commas correctly? D1

☐ Have you used apostrophes correctly? D2

☐ Have you punctuated quotations correctly? D3

*Mechanics Problems*

☐ Have you used capital letters correctly? E1

☐ Have you spelled all words correctly? E2

For help documenting any sources in your paper, turn to sections D6 and E1–E2 in the Quick Research Guide (pp. Q-30–Q-36).

## Proofreading

*All* writers make mistakes as they put ideas on paper. Because the mind works faster than the pencil (or the computer), a moment's break in concentration — when someone talks or your phone rings — can lead to errors. Making such mistakes isn't bad — you simply need to take the time to find and correct them.

- Let a paper sit several days, overnight, or at least a few hours before proofreading so that you allow time to gain perspective.
- Budget enough time to proofread thoroughly. For a long essay or complex research paper with a list of sources, schedule several sessions.
- Ask someone else to read your paper and tell you if it is free of errors. But take pride in your own work. *Don't* let someone else do it for you.
- Use a dictionary or a spell-checker, but remember that a spell-checker recognizes only correct spelling, not correct choices.
- Keep a list of your habitual errors, especially those your instructor has already pointed out. Double-check for these errors (such as leaving off -*s* or -*ed* endings or putting in unnecessary commas).

Proofreading does take patience but is a skill you can develop. For instance, when you simply glance at the spelling of *environment,* you may miss the second *n.* When you read normally, you usually see only the shells of words — the first and last letters. You fix your eyes on the print only three or four times per line or less. When you proofread, try to look at the letters in each word and the punctuation marks between words. Slow down and concentrate.

## PROOFREADING CHECKLIST

- ☐ Have you read your draft very slowly, looking at every word and letter? Have you tried to see what is actually written, not what you think is there?
- ☐ Have you read your paper aloud so you can see and hear mistakes?
- ☐ Have you read the essay backward so that you look at each word instead of getting caught up in the flow of ideas?
- ☐ Have you read your essay several times, focusing each time on a specific area of difficulty? (For example, read once for spelling, once for punctuation, and once for a problem that recurs in your writing.)

## Learning by Doing Reflecting on Revising and Editing

Think back on your process for finishing your last paper. In what ways did you revise that paper well, working on both macro and micro changes? How might you plan to revise your next paper? In what ways did you edit your last paper well? How might you plan to edit your next paper? Working with a classmate or small group, share your successful approaches face-to-face or online.

## Learning by Doing Reflecting on Past Grades and Comments

Examine at least two graded pieces of writing from this class or another. What types of comments or suggestions did your instructor(s) make on your work? Did you notice that any particular issues or errors were pointed out on more than one occasion? What implications might the comments or suggestions have for how you write or revise future papers? Answer these questions in a brief reflection.

# Strategies for Writing in Future Courses

# 24

## Transferring Knowledge

You may have heard instructors speak of "knowledge transfer," but what does this expression mean? Simply put, knowledge transfer involves taking what you already know and applying it to a new situation. For example, in your composition course you may have gained experience in proposing solutions to problems (a topic covered in Chapter 10 of this book). You might apply this experience to managing patients in a nursing program or to maintaining classroom order in a teaching program.

In other words, when your writing course ends, your days using the writing, reading, and thinking skills you've acquired there are not over. The assumption—and the hope—is that your experience in your writing class will equip you to write successfully in your future courses, workplace, and community. If your writing instructor has asked you to maintain a portfolio or a journal or to complete the reflective activities throughout this book, you'll likely find an encouraging record of the skills you've mastered in the course. Your next task as a college student will be to tackle assignments in a variety of courses. This chapter will help you understand instructors' expectations for writing assignments in those courses, identify the best approaches to meet those expectations, and translate your knowledge into successful papers and projects.

How to transfer learning from one situation to another—and how to do so effectively—often seems a puzzle. To help you solve that puzzle when you need to write different types of papers in different situations, this chapter covers three key questions you might ask:

- What do they want?
- What is it?
- How do I write it?

## Learning by Doing  Reflecting on How to Transfer Knowledge

Reflect for a few minutes about how you have transferred learning in the past. How have you tackled a new task and figured out how to succeed? How have you successfully handled new academic situations — different teaching styles, schools of thought, types of assignments, or levels of expectation? Jot down a few notes about your strategies for success. If possible, share them with classmates.

# What Do They Want?

When you face a challenging or high-stakes writing assignment, your first question is likely to be, What do they want? Your instructor or your work supervisor may — or may not — provide explicit directions about your task. Either way, your first step is to gather information about the assignment.

### ASSIGNMENT CHECKLIST

☐ Do you have a written assignment distributed in class, posted online, provided in your syllabus, or included in your job description?

☐ Have you taken notes on verbal advice or directions? Have you thoughtfully read advice posted online by your instructor?

☐ Does your assignment identify or imply a purpose and an audience?

☐ Does it specify the approach, activity, method, or product?

☐ Does it require a standard format, perhaps based on a style guide, a sample lab report, headings in a journal article, an evaluation form, past annual reports at work, or some other model?

☐ Does it use key words that you recognize from your writing class or other situations? For instance, does it ask you to explain effects, evaluate, or summarize, drawing on skills you have used recently?

☐ What criteria will be used to assess the success of your writing task?

## Analyzing Expectations

When a challenging writing assignment comes from the instructor in a class where you need to succeed, or from the boss you have to satisfy, shift your attention from yourself to your audience. Whether you feel confident, puzzled, or anxious, focus on what is expected. Apply your experience decoding past assignments to analyzing current ones. Do the same with your experience identifying a writing purpose and audience. Try writing notes on or about your assignment to help you tease out all the available clues about how to succeed.

*Starting point = problem + solution*

Once you have defined <u>both a problem and a solution</u> that you wish to propose, write your paper as a <u>grant proposal</u> designed to <u>persuade a funding agency</u> to support your proposal. Be sure to include a <u>statement of the problem</u>, a <u>needs assessment</u>, and a <u>specific proposal</u>.

*Need to check grant format*

*Propose solution — I've done that!*

*Purpose + Audience*

*Good — list of required sections*

## Connecting Expectations and Assessments

Expectations may be most clearly expressed in assessment criteria. What are the standards for performance or outcomes in your course or workplace? How will your paper or project be judged? If you will be graded or assigned points based on the presence, absence, or quality of specific features or components, these are also part of "what they want."

You can be awarded a maximum of 25 points for each of these four features: (1) a <u>clear</u> and <u>compelling</u> <u>introduction</u> to your proposal, (2) a <u>well-researched</u> <u>review of relevant literature</u>, (3) a clear <u>explanation</u> of <u>the theoretical framework</u> for examining the problem, and (4) a <u>clear</u> <u>description</u> and <u>justification</u> of the <u>methods</u> proposed for your study.

Try turning your requirements or assessment criteria into a checklist or self-assessment questions for yourself. For example, you might convert the criteria in the previous example to these four questions:

1. Do I have a clear and compelling introduction to my proposal?
2. Have I included a well-researched review of relevant literature?
3. Do I clearly explain my theoretical framework for examining the problem?
4. Do I clearly describe and justify the methods for my study?

If you worry about forgetting or skipping over the assessment details, try breaking out each expectation as a separate question:

Do I have an introduction? Is it clear? Is it compelling?

# What Is It?

Once you have figured out "what they want," your next challenge is to determine "what it is." As you read and write in a particular field, you may recognize common strategies or approaches. For example, historians frequently use cause-and-effect analysis, natural scientists rely on classification, nurses value accurate description, and specialists in many fields use comparison and contrast to examine cases, techniques, or theories. In addition, many assignments—such as lab reports, proposals, or reviews—require a genre, or type, of writing defined by specific characteristics and assumptions. Identifying assumptions and genre features will help you to tackle each kind of writing more successfully.

## Uncovering Assumptions

In advanced classes, expectations of the field or discipline are likely to underlie those of your instructor. Here, your ingenuity is engaged not in the creation of an analytical approach or a method of investigation but in its application to your particular text, project, or research question. For example, your literature essay will probably rely on a close reading of a novel, poem, or play and take an accepted approach to analyzing the work's characters, images, or other components. Your essay is unlikely to use headings such as Method, Results, or Discussion. However, those divisions are likely essentials for your psychology report on your field study. Such expectations about approach, method, organization, or format reflect the assumptions shared by scholars and researchers in a particular field—their deep agreements, for instance, that a literary study typically relies on textual analysis or that a psychology study typically follows certain research procedures.

When a field or approach is new to you, you won't know if your instructor and others in the field already share established ideas about how a paper should develop. How can you find out what is assumed? First, use your experience as a college writer to check your assignment for clues—such as references, maybe without explanation, to a certain type of paper.

*Maybe quotations? Repeated images? Characters? Setting? Narrator?*

*Relevance for society? Cultural commentary?*

Using textual evidence, write an essay to analyze the novel's attention to

problems of social justice.

*OK Thesis? Evidence?*

*Break into elements? Identify components?*

*What's that? What's in it? Find sources?? Summarize? Or synthesize too?*

*Last ten years? Background OK?*

Prepare a review of the literature on your topic, covering advances

during the last decade.

*New studies? New findings? New theories?*

Also consider the readings assigned in the course or field. For example, many journal articles in psychology, sociology, or education open with an abstract, summing up the reading. Should you add an abstract to your paper? Those same articles may have section headings with identical or similar wording. Should your paper use the same headings? Ask your instructor which features of assigned readings are expected in your paper.

By definition, assumptions and conventions (generally accepted ideas about ways to proceed) are taken for granted within a field. That's why your instructor may assume that once you enroll in a course you already share a certain set of assumptions, even though you may assume those views are what you need to learn. That's also why two researchers—for instance, an art historian and a chemist—could both investigate how to intensify color in a painting but hold different ideas about what's of interest. One might study techniques for applying paint while the other might analyze formulas for mixing paint. Likewise, the engineers at your job probably view products differently than the marketing team does.

Whenever you enter a class, field, or situation that may operate on assumptions new to you, you need to notice what is preferred:

- kinds of studies, analyses, or topics
- research procedures, accepted methods, stages of analysis, or patterns of organization
- methods of argument or explanation
- kinds and quantities of evidence
- use of technical vocabulary, authorial voice, transitions to show shifts, description or explanation, or other features

Then ask what sections, approaches, or features need to be included in your writing. Consider the unstated expectations or criteria that your writing situation—or the situation posed in your assignment—may imply.

## Learning by Doing 🎲 Reflecting on the Goals of Other Disciplines

Examine an assignment from a different class. Drawing on your experience from this class, how can you best decode what the assignment is asking you to do? For example, is the assignment asking you to analyze a problem, compare and contrast two scenarios, or explain a cause and its effect? How might you approach this assignment given the skills you have learned from this class and this chapter?

# How Do I Write It?

You don't need to start from scratch when you face something new. Begin with what you know to prepare for what you don't know. When you face a difficult, unfamiliar, or downright mysterious assignment, apply or adapt your past writing processes and experience to that challenge.

- Underline or annotate your assignment to identify requirements.
- Add notes to yourself, especially to distinguish what you know how to do and what you don't.
- Sort your models to find examples of unfamiliar features or sections.

- Return to the processes used in your writing class so that you generate ideas and plan instead of simply jumping into drafting.

- Turn to the campus writing center, your class study group, or your friends to identify a peer reader who can respond to your draft.

- Get a second opinion from another reader if useful.

- Meet with your instructor, or submit your draft for a preliminary reading (if possible). Use your instructor's advice, especially about the big issues, to help you look critically at your own work.

- Revise first to conform to the unfamiliar assignment. Use your analysis of it to generate your own self-assessment questions.

- Revise again to improve format, organization, clarity, or other matters.

- Edit to improve conventions and genre features as well as to correct errors.

**Learning by Doing** 🗓 Reflecting on New Assignments

Reflect on your writing experience. When you face a new assignment, how do you get started? What are your most reliable strategies? What adjustments have you made or are you making as a college writer? When you face a challenging assignment, how would you apply what you already know and do as a writer?

# Writing in the Disciplines

By flipping quickly through your college course catalog, you'll see how many academic disciplines exist, and each discipline comes with its own type of writing or writing style. For example, scientific reports, like those for chemistry and physics courses, commonly use the passive voice to convey information. Think "the water was poured into the beaker" instead of the more personal and active "I poured water into the beaker." The passive voice removes the individual from the equation and provides a sense of scientific objectivity. Successful writing in the disciplines depends on understanding and following such conventions, which are described in more detail in the following sections.

## Writing in the Sciences

Instructors outside of English may assign logs or journals to familiarize students with a specific subject, such as geology, marine biology, archaeology, or anthropology. These logs or journals will model writing done in the field, the laboratory, school, or another setting by academics or other professionals in the discipline. Your instructors may provide guidance about the type of information that you should record in a log or journal. To give you some examples, you may be asked to take notes on your research findings or to answer questions typically posed in a discipline, supporting your answers with evidence. You might also be asked to reflect on what you've discovered, much as you have done if you have completed any of the Reviewing and Reflecting activities in this textbook. Consider writing in these logs or journals an opportunity to practice using new words, new styles, or anything unfamiliar to you about a discipline. As with any skill, practice makes perfect.

If you are enrolled in a science class involving a lab, you will write lab reports. If you are planning on going into a research field, you will write scientific essays. We'll examine both of these types of writing next.

**Lab Reports.** Typically, lab reports follow a standard format. Your instructor may provide you with a sample lab report to use as a model or merely tell you what is expected. Be certain to follow the instructions carefully and consistently. Successful lab reports typically include the following components:

- **Title page:** This should include the name of the experiment and participants, such as lab partners, as well as the date and place of the experiment.
- **Abstract:** This is a summary of the purpose of the experiment, its findings, and any conclusions you may have drawn.
- **Introduction:** This section includes a statement of objectives and background information.
- **Materials and Methods:** Perhaps the most important section of a lab report, this ensures that others can duplicate the experiment and arrive at the same findings. You should use the past tense for this section, which is generally written in a narrative format.
- **Results:** The Results section presents all findings and any data, including calculations. It should be written in the present tense.
- **Discussion:** The Discussion section presents your interpretation and analysis of the data.
- **References:** This section should include a Works Cited, Bibliography, or References page (follow the appropriate style guide for the discipline) with full citations of all sources referenced, summarized, paraphrased, or directly quoted in the lab report. Scientific papers often use Council of Science Editors (CSE) style to cite and list source material.

**Scientific Essays.** The components of a scientific essay are similar to those of a lab report: **I**ntroduction, **M**aterials and Methods, **R**esults, **A**nalysis, **D**iscussion (these words form the acronym IMRAD). The principal difference between a lab report and a scientific essay is that the scientific essay includes more historical context, placing the experiment in the context of what has come before and inviting further study.

Whether you are writing a lab report or a scientific essay, remember that your audience is other scientists in the field. Therefore, your writing should be factual and objective, not humorous or entertaining.

## Writing in Nursing

In nursing school, you will write about treatments, best practices, medical cases, and patient (sometimes referred to as "client") experiences. As a practicing nurse you might also write memos, assist in the preparation of patient education booklets, and contribute your own research articles to medical journals. In all the writing in this field, it is important to support any claims with observations, data, and evidence.

Following are descriptions of some common types of papers in nursing school.

**A Nursing Philosophy.** A nursing philosophy is a narrative that expresses your reasons for pursuing a career in nursing. It is a place to discuss your values and how past experiences may have shaped your decision to enter the field.

**A Practice Paper.** In practice papers, you apply learned knowledge to client needs. You may be presented with a problem or diagnosis and asked to produce a care plan. This can include a concept map, a visual diagram connecting possible diagnoses and supporting research, the client, and a proposed care plan. Practice papers can also include a process or research essay. Practice papers must include a detailed patient history, a diagnosis of client health issues, recommended interventions and their rationale, expected outcomes, and observed outcomes.

**Case Studies.** Case studies in nursing can include both individuals and groups of people. You may be asked to interpret laboratory results, evaluate data from a previous nurse's notes, prioritize patient medical needs, assess guidelines for health care, and consider the patient's personal history in that care, including language and cultural background. Case studies, like practice papers, also ask you to apply your learned knowledge to the care and treatment of individual clients.

**Research Essays.** Research essays often ask you to look at twenty-five (or more) peer-reviewed journal essays on a particular medical issue in order to determine the best course of treatment or to answer a research question. You may think that twenty-five sources is quite a large number, but in real-world medical practice and research, it is often necessary to gather a lot of information to make effective treatment decisions or to answer challenging questions.

**Literature Reviews.** Literature reviews require you to read and analyze published work. However, unlike a research essay, a literature review summarizes the findings of one or more current journal articles on a topic. The review critically evaluates the information.

**Nursing Narratives.** You may be asked to write two types of nursing narratives: experiential and reflective. An experiential narrative is a record of what happened while caring for a client. A reflective essay asks you to consider your own emotions in a specific scenario.

**Position Papers.** In position papers, you take a stand on a nursing-related issue using the strategies discussed in Chapter 9 of this textbook.

Although writing conventions in nursing vary, all writing in the field should be based on detailed information. The use of first-person voice (the pronoun *I*) is expected in reflective essays; however, when describing a procedure or making clinical observations, it is conventional to use the passive voice, keeping yourself out of the conversation. Direct quotations of sources are rare, with the profession choosing to paraphrase over quote, but you will still need to reference your sources. Typically, writing in the field of nursing uses American Psychological Association (APA) style for citing and listing sources.

For APA guidelines and models, see Ch. 37.

## Writing in the Arts (Art, Drama, Music)

Reviews of books, films, music, and plays are common assignments in many arts-based classes. When writing reviews, include the title; the name of the author/composer, director, or conductor; and any other information that would help to identify the specific artifact that is your subject. Provide an introduction that discusses the criteria used for evaluating the work, and remember to qualify and explain evaluation words, like *good, great*, or *poor*. (What is "good" to one person may be "excellent" to another.)

For more advice on evaluative writing, see Ch. 11.

Reviews of books, films, or plays should include a summary of the work, but the summary should be concise, ideally twenty-five to thirty words. Your task is not to retell the story but rather to review it. As with most essays, you will need strong evidence to convince the reader that your position is accurate. Don't insult, but be honest.

In arts-related writing you do in college, your instructor will probably require you to cite and fully document all sources you refer to, including any work that you review. Often, academic papers in the arts use Modern Language Association (MLA) citation style.

For MLA guidelines and models, see Ch. 36.

## Writing in Business

Many types of writing are produced by business professionals, including business plans; reports; proposals; memos; correspondence; and executive summaries, which briefly outline key points from a larger document, such as a business plan. Reports may compare and contrast one product or plan with another to aid in purchasing and other business decisions.

For more on workplace writing, including advice on brochures and presentation visuals, see Ch. 17.

For more on avoiding biased language, see Ch. 41.

For APA guidelines and models, see Ch. 37.

Businesspeople may also produce marketing materials, such as brochures; Web site content; press releases; and presentations, which can include printed handouts or computer-generated visuals, like PowerPoint slides.

The primary difference between business and academic writing is that business writing generally is less formal. Typically, you may use personal pronouns like *you* or *I*. However, be aware that slang or overly casual language can be off-putting to fellow professionals, especially in formal documents such as business plans and annual reports. Regardless of the type of document you are producing, it is important to avoid words that insult or stereotype individuals or groups by gender, race, ethnic origin, sexual orientation, religion, or physical ability. It is also essential to use concise and clear language. Wordiness wastes readers' time and consequently their money.

If you cite sources in business writing, especially in a college course, you may be required to use a certain citation style. Business writers commonly use APA style or the guidelines presented in the *Chicago Manual of Style*.

## Writing in Education

As in other disciplines, there are common and specialized types of writing in education. These include reflection essays, journals and notes on field work (i.e., student teaching), curriculum designs, lesson plans, "reviews" of instructional materials, case studies, research essays, and self-evaluations.

Reflection-type assignments are similar to the Reviewing and Reflecting exercises that you may have completed in this book. During student teaching, you might be asked to think back on a strategy that you tried in class, considering how well it worked and determining what you might do differently in the future to get better results. If a teaching session goes spectacularly well, you might evaluate your performance to determine whether your success can be duplicated.

Many schools will require that you file lesson plans a week or more in advance. Having distinct lesson plans helps you stay organized in the classroom. In college education classes, you will write lesson plans to practice managing your classroom. To be successful, you will need to review the existing curriculum, discussing how it meets specific objectives.

You may identify trends in the classroom, either as a student or a career teacher. To document these trends, case studies are used. A case study is an observation and analysis of an individual student, teacher, or classroom interaction, and it includes your conclusions and recommendations.

Self-evaluations are another type of writing you may be asked to complete as either a student or a teacher. In these evaluations, you might discuss strengths and weaknesses of lesson plans, how your lesson plan met student learning objectives and outcomes, what you learned about yourself or your students, and how you could improve a teaching method or lesson plan.

You might also be asked to keep a teaching portfolio, a collection of your best work and therefore something of great interest to prospective employers. Generally, a teaching portfolio contains not only sample course materials, like lesson plans or syllabi, but also your teaching philosophy, professional goals, résumé, and evaluations. (Portfolios are used not just in education programs but in a variety of other disciplines.)

For more advice on portfolios, see pp. 473–77.

Like many other fields, writing in education includes a specialized vocabulary that most people in the field will understand. Research essays are formal in nature, similar to writing in the sciences, with few if any personal pronouns. For reflection assignments, it is acceptable to use the first-person *I* voice and viewpoint.

If you cite sources in education writing, you may be required to use a certain citation style. Education writers commonly use APA style or the guidelines presented in the *Chicago Manual of Style*.

For APA guidelines and models, see Ch. 37.

## Writing in History

Historians analyze information about past events to explain how or why something happened. They may also write about important figures in history. Generally speaking, historians write for students, interested readers, or scholars in their field. As a student writer in a history course, your audience typically will consist of your instructor and fellow students.

Forms of writing in history include critical essays, book reviews, and research essays. Generally, critical essays are shorter works that examine one or more primary documents and then formulate a theory about those documents. Book reviews, similar to art reviews, examine and critique a scholarly work. Research essays often pose a question and examine evidence that responds to this question. The focus is *how* or *why* something happened, as opposed to merely reporting an event. When writing a research essay, bear in mind that historians value counterarguments and appreciate writing that considers a variety of viewpoints. Therefore, research different theories or perspectives about the event or historical figure that is the subject of your paper. Also, be aware that the convention in the discipline is to use past tense verbs.

Whenever you cite sources in a history paper, be sure to use the citation style that your instructor specifies. In history, writers commonly follow the guidelines presented in the *Chicago Manual of Style*.

## Writing in Psychology

Writing is an integral part of psychology. Whether it is a journal article for peers, a grant to fund research, or an article for the media, writing in psychology should be clear, logical, concise, and as objective as possible. Writing types for this discipline include literature reviews, research essays, theoretical essays, and poster presentations for conferences.

**Literature Reviews.** Literature reviews require that you evaluate current research on a specific topic. In this type of review, you will not only report on current research but also take a position on it, a position supported by qualitative and quantitative data. In graduate courses, a literature review might be the introduction to your own research. If that is the case, the review discusses past research that supports your work.

**Research Essays.** Research essays in psychology generally report on research done to answer a specific question. In undergraduate psychology courses, your instructor might pose a question that you have to answer by referring to published sources. For an example of this type of assignment, and of a paper written in response to it, see pp. 471–73.

More advanced psychology courses, and professional work in the field, may require original research. Writing that reports on this research generally has the following components: a research question, a literature review, a theory or hypothesis about possible answers to the question, the methodology used to test this hypothesis, results of the research, and an analysis of those results. This writing may also incorporate tables, figures, graphs, or charts.

**Theoretical Essays.** In a theoretical essay, you are asked to examine existing research about a particular topic and to set forth an experiment testing your own theory about the topic. You are expected to support your ideas with evidence from the field, even if it is contradictory.

**Poster Presentations.** Psychologists often attend conferences in which they share innovations and discoveries with peers. In poster presentations, as opposed to formal talks, researchers exhibit data in the form of graphs and tables, making it easier for conference attendees to read information while walking through an exhibit area. If the poster is effective, an attendee might stop to ask questions and learn more about the research. Obviously, the more attractive the poster and the easier it is to read, the more interest the researcher will generate.

APA style is typically used for source citations in psychology papers. For APA guidelines and models, see Ch. 37.

Regardless of the type of writing, psychologists frequently use specialized vocabulary. If you believe that definitions will help readers understand your material, include brief ones. Some other tips: when writing about results, use the present tense, and when writing conclusions, use the past tense. Also, write as objectively as possible, avoiding the use of *you* and *I.*

**Learning by Doing** 🔲 Examining an Article from a Scholarly Journal

Examine an article from a scholarly journal in a field outside of English. (Look at your textbooks for ideas or possible examples.) How is the article set up or designed? What do the headers tell you about its structure and the content? What do the structure and content, as well as other features (such as tables or other graphics), tell you about how information is delivered in this academic field?

# Learning from Another Writer: A Developmental Psychology Assignment

When Samantha Christopher enrolled in the class Developmental Psychology, she analyzed the following critical thinking assignment that Professor Tokura-Gallo distributed to her and her classmates.

## Professor Tokura-Gallo

### Weekly Critical Thinking Assignment

Think about adolescents accused of felony crimes (there are a variety of them, but let's not go into the details). For this assignment, let's focus on the common one for which minors are charged: driving under the influence. Should a sixteen-year-old be tried as an adult if he or she committed the crime of driving while intoxicated? Your job is to take a side: Are you for or against adult prosecution of adolescents under eighteen years of age in North Carolina if the alleged crime was a felony offense? Your argument must be based on what you have learned in Chapter 6 regarding cognitive and peer relationship development.

**Analysis:** This assignment provides students with the ability to apply information they have learned (in this case, Chapter 6 in their psychology textbook) in order to arrive at a position. Completing the assignment successfully will require analysis, synthesis, and evaluation, as well as taking a stand on a legal and societal matter and supporting that position with research-based evidence. Those outside sources will need to be properly referenced using the standard documentation style in psychology—APA. The assignment will require students to apply various writing strategies—cause-and-effect analysis, comparison and contrast, taking a stand, and supporting a position with sources.

## Samantha Christopher

**Response to Critical Thinking Assignment**

### Adolescents Are Not Yet Adults

Recently there have been some debates about whether or not an adolescent under the age of eighteen should be tried as an adult in the state of North Carolina if the alleged crime committed was a felony offense. Evidence shows that several factors differentiate the mental state of an adolescent from that of an adult. In addition, an adolescent lets peers influence him or her to a greater degree than an adult would. For these reasons, teens should not be tried as adults even if the charges they face are felony offenses. 1

Adolescents are able to use dialectical reasoning in solving problems and making decisions. Dialectical reasoning refers to the ability to make a decision 2 based on the positive and negative aspects of that decision (Moshman, 1999). The problem comes with staying with the "reasonable" choice, especially when this choice goes against personal preference (Klaczynski, 2005). While adolescents may know an activity is not condoned, their personal preference may be to do it anyway.

Another huge influence on teenage cognition is egocentrism (Elkind, 1978). Egocentrism consists of four parts that each influence adolescent decision making and the way adolescents act. One part, *pseudostupidity*, is when teens read too much into a situation. This can cause indecisiveness and can lead to a quick decision based on faulty dialectical reasoning. *Imaginary audience* is another aspect of egocentrism. This is an adolescent's tendency to believe that he or she is the continuous center of attention. This same aspect leads teens to think that they can read other people's minds and causes them to jump to conclusions. This can provoke feelings of self-consciousness and cause an individual to make an irrational decision based on what he or she believes others will think of that decision, even if it leads to illegal behavior. *Personal fable* is the most relevant aspect of egocentrism to this debate. This is the belief that one is special, leading to the assumption that while others might get caught doing an illegal activity, he or she would not be. Lastly, there is *apparent hypocrisy*. This is the gap between what people say they believe and what they actually do. Although adolescents might say that drinking and driving is wrong, they might still drink and drive, believing that they are exempt from the rules.

3

The last difference between adults and adolescents is the effect of peer pressure and relationship development between teens. Peer groups serve as a means to experiment with different behaviors, attitudes, and values. Teens look to their peers for guidance as to what they should be like and for validation of their self-worth. This stems from the desire for acceptance, which can provoke teens to do things that may not be acceptable in the larger society but that will help them gain popularity and esteem within their peer group.

4

Most people know a teenager's sense of logic can be skewed. Due to the differences in cognitive processes between teens and adults and the importance of peer relationships to teens, individuals under the age of eighteen can be easily swayed into doing an activity with a slew of negative consequences without truly understanding those consequences. For these reasons, teenagers should not be tried as adults in felony crimes.

5

### References

Elkind, D. (1978). Understanding the young adolescent. *Adolescence, 13*(49), 127-134.

Klaczynski, P. (2005). Metacognition and cognitive variability: Dual process model of decision making and its development. In J. Jacob & P. Klaczynski (Eds.), *The development of decision making in children and adolescents.* Mahwah, NJ: Lawrence Erlbaum Associates.

Moshman, D. (1999). *Adolescent psychological development: Rationality, morality, and identity* (2nd ed.) Mahwah, NJ: Lawrence Erlbaum Associates.

## Questions to Start You Thinking

### Meaning

1. What is the author's position? What pieces of evidence does the author produce to convince readers of that position?

2. How is synthesis demonstrated in this essay? In what spots do you see information and critical thinking come together the most? How does the author's use of synthesis help the reader discern the author's position?

### Writing Strategies

3. Mark up or list notable features in Christopher's paper that you think are typical of its genre, or type, of writing. What features does the paper share with those you've written in this course?

4. How knowledgeable about psychology does Christopher assume her audience to be? How do you know?

# Keeping a Portfolio

In a composition course, and in courses in other disciplines, you may be required to keep a portfolio of your work. Portfolio courses typically emphasize revision and reflection—your ability to identify and discuss your decisions, strengths, or learning processes. To build your portfolio, save all your drafts and notes, keep track of your choices and changes, and eventually select and submit your best writing.

The portfolio, printed or electronic, collects pieces of writing that represent the writer's best work. Compiled over time and across projects, it showcases a writer's talent, hard work, and ability to make thoughtful choices. A course portfolio is usually due as the term ends and includes pieces written and revised for that class. Portfolios may include an introduction (often a self-assessment or rationale) for readers, who might be teachers, supervisors, evaluators, parents, or classmates.

## Understanding Portfolio Assessment

The portfolio method of evaluation and teaching shapes the whole course, beginning to end. Your course will probably emphasize responses to your writing—from your classmates and instructor—but not necessarily grades on separate papers. This method shifts attention to the writing process—to discovery, planning, drafting, peer response, revision, editing—allowing time for your skills to develop before the portfolio is graded. Because this method is flexible, read your assignments carefully, and listen well to determine the kind of portfolio you'll need to keep, such as the following types.

**A Writing Folder.** Students submit all drafts, notes, outlines, doodles, and messy pages—all writing for the course, finished or unfinished. Students may also revise two or three promising pieces for a "presentation portfolio." The folder usually does not have a reflective cover letter.

**A Learning (or Open) Portfolio.** Students submit a variety of materials that have contributed to their learning. They may even determine the contents, organization, and presentation of the portfolio, which might include photos, other images, or nonprint objects that demonstrate learning.

**A Closed Portfolio.** Students must turn in assignments that are specified by the instructor, or their options for what to include may be limited.

**A Midterm Portfolio.** The portfolio is given a trial run at midterm, or the midterm grade is determined by one or two papers that are submitted for evaluation, perhaps with a brief self-assessment.

**A Final or Presentation Portfolio.** The portfolio is evaluated at the end of the course after being revised, edited, and polished for presentation.

**A Modified or Combination Portfolio.** The student has some, but not unlimited, choice in what to include. For example, the instructor may ask for three entries that show certain features or parts of the course.

Find out what your instructor has in mind. For example, your combination portfolio might contain three revised papers (out of five or six required). You decide, late in the term, which three to revise and edit. You also may reflect on how those choices define you as a writer, show your learning, or explain your decisions while writing. Here are some questions your instructor, syllabus, or assignment sheets may answer:

- Is the portfolio paper or electronic?
- How many papers should you include in the portfolio?
- Do all the papers need to be revised? If so, what level of revision is expected? What criteria will be used to assess them?

- How much of the course grade is determined by the portfolio? Are entries graded separately, or does the portfolio receive one grade?
- May you include papers written for other courses or entries other than texts—such as photos, videos, maps, Web pages, or other visuals?
- Do you need an introduction or a cover letter? What approach is expected: Description? Explanation? Exploration? Reflection? Self-assessment?
- Does each entry need its own cover sheet? Should descriptions of your processes or choices appear before or after each entry?

## Tips for Keeping a Portfolio

**Keep Everything, and Stay Organized.** Don't throw anything away! Keep all your notes, lists, drafts, outlines, clusters, responses from readers, copied articles, and source references. On your own computer, *back up everything*. At the computer lab, save your work to a portable drive or card. Organize your files, and invest in a good folder with pockets. Label and store drafts, notes, outlines, and peer-review forms for each assignment.

**Manage Your Time.** The portfolio isn't due until midterm or the end of the course, but plan ahead to save time and frustration. As your instructor returns each assignment with comments, make changes in response while the ideas are fresh. If you don't understand or know how to approach those comments, ask right away. Make notes about what you want to do. Then, even if you want to let a paper simmer, you will have both a plan and fresh insight ready when you work on it again.

**Practice Self-Assessment.** For complex activities, learn to step back and evaluate your own performance. Maybe you have great ideas but find it hard to organize them. Maybe you write powerful thesis statements but run out of ideas to support them. Don't wait until the portfolio cover letter is due to begin assessing your strengths, weaknesses, or preferences.

For more help with self-assessment, see the Peer Response questions, the Revision Checklists, and the Take Action charts throughout *The Bedford Guide.*

Practice self-assessment from the start. After reviewing the syllabus, write a paragraph or two about how you expect to do in this course. What might you do well? Why? What may be hard? Why? For each paper you share with peers or hand in, write a journal entry about what the paper does well and what it still needs. Keep track of your process as you plan, research, or draft each paper—where you get stuck and where things click.

**Choose the Entries Carefully.** If you can select what to include, consider the course emphasis. Of course, you want to select pieces your evaluator will think are "the best," but also consider which show the most promise or potential. Which drafts show creativity, insight, or an unusual approach? Which show variety—different purposes, audiences, or voices? Which show depth—your ability to do thorough research or stay with a topic for several weeks? Also consider the order of the entries—which

piece might work best first or last, and how each placement affects the whole.

For a sample reflective portfolio letter, see p. 368.

**Write a Strong Reflective Introduction or Cover Letter.** Your introduction—usually a self-assessment in the form of a cover letter, a statement, or a description for each of your entries—could be the most important text you write all semester. Besides introducing your collection and portraying you as a writer, it explains your choices in putting the portfolio together. It shows that you can evaluate your work and your writing process. Like a "final exam," your reflective introduction tests what you've learned about good writing, readers' needs, and the details of a careful self-presentation.

### DISCOVERY CHECKLIST

☐ Who will read this reflection?

☐ What qualities of writing will your reader value?

☐ Will the reader suggest changes or evaluate your work?

☐ What will the outcome of the reading be? How much can you influence it?

☐ What do you want to emphasize about your writing? What are you proud of? What have you learned? What did you have trouble with?

☐ How can you present your writing ability in the best light?

If your reader is your instructor, look back over responses on your returned papers. Review the course syllabus and assignment sheets. What patterns do you see in the comments or directions? What could you tell a friend about this reader's expectations—or pet peeves? Use what you've learned to develop a convincing introduction or cover letter.

For more on appeals, see p. 166.

If your readers are unknown, ask your instructor for as much information as possible so you can decide which logical, ethical, or emotional appeals might be most effective. Although you won't know your readers personally, it's safe to assume that they will be trained in portfolio assessment and will share many of your instructor's ideas about good writing. If your college writing program has guidelines, consult them, too.

For more on the format for business letters, see pp. 347–50.

How long should your introduction or cover letter be? Check with your instructor, but regardless of length, develop your ideas or support your claims as in any effective writing. If you are asked to write a letter, follow the format for a business letter: include the date, a salutation, and a closing.

In the reflective introduction, you might try some of the following (but don't try to use all of them):

- Discuss your best entry, and explain why it is your best.
- Detail your revisions—the improvements you want readers to notice.
- Review everything included, touching on the strengths of each.

- Outline your writing and revising process for one or more entries.
- State what the portfolio illustrates about you as a writer, student, researcher, or critical thinker.
- Acknowledge your weaknesses, but show how you've worked to overcome them.
- Acknowledge the influence of your readers on your entries.
- Reflect on what you've learned about writing and reading.
- Lay the groundwork for a positive evaluation of your work.

**Polishing the Final Portfolio.** From the first page to the last, printed or electronic, your portfolio should be ready for public presentation. Take pride in it. Think about creative ways to give it a final distinctive feature, such as adding a colorful cover, illustrations, a table of contents, or a running head. Although a cheerful cover will not make up for weak writing or careless editing, readers will value your extra effort.

## Learning by Doing 🔳 Reflecting on This Class

Write a reflection about your experiences in this class and how they have affected you. As you write the reflection, think about "the five W's and an H" of journalism: Who? What? Where? When? Why? and How? Who were you as a writer and academic at the beginning of the semester? How have you progressed as both an academic and a writer? What have you learned? How have you learned it? Where did you find the most success? The greatest struggles? How did you overcome any difficulties this semester? When do you foresee yourself using the skills you learned this semester? Finally, why does this reflection matter?

# A
# WRITER'S
# READER

# A Writer's Reader Contents

## 25 Family   482

Judith Ortiz Cofer, *More Room*   483

Chris Bentley, *Beyond the Nuclear Family: Can Boomers Make Cohousing Mainstream?*   487

PAIRED | Michael Cobb, *The Marriage Imperative*   491
Aziz Ansari, *Searching for Your Soul Mate*   494

## 26 Gender   501

Brent Staples, *Black Men and Public Space*   502

Judy Brady, *I Want a Wife*   505

Cindi May, *The Problem with Female Superheroes*   508

PAIRED | Robert Jensen, *The High Cost of Manliness*   512
Julie Zeilinger, *Guys Suffer from Oppressive Gender Roles Too*   516

## 27 Popular Culture   521

Kate Dailey and Abby Ellin, *America's War on the Overweight*   522

Adam Sternbergh, *Smile, You're Speaking Emoji*   527

Stephen King, *Why We Crave Horror Movies*   534

PAIRED | Elizabeth Stone, *Grief in the Age of Facebook*   537
Libby Copeland, *Is Facebook Making Us Sad?*   541

## 28 Language   546

Clive Thompson, *The New Literacy*   547

Ann Friedman, *Can We Just, Like, Get Over the Way Women Talk?*   549

Jenny Jarvie, *Trigger Happy*   553

PAIRED | Richard Rodriguez, *Public and Private Language*   558
Amy Tan, *Mother Tongue*   564

## 29 The Good Life   570

William Zinsser, *The Right to Fail*   571

William Deresiewicz, *What Is College For?*   575

Sarah Adams, *Be Cool to the Pizza Dude*   580

PAIRED | David Brooks, *The Humility Code*   582
Miya Tokumitsu, *In the Name of Love*   590

Tiridifilm/E+/Getty Images.

# Introduction: Reading to Write

*A Writer's Reader* is a collection of twenty-four professional essays. We hope, first of all, that you will read these pieces simply for the sake of reading—enjoying and responding to their ideas. Second, we hope that you will actively study these essays as solid examples of the situations and strategies explored in *A Writer's Guide*. The authors represented in this reader have faced the same problems and choices you do when you write. You can learn from studying their decisions, structures, and techniques. Finally, we hope that you will find the content of the essays intriguing—and along with the questions posed after each one, a source of ideas to write about.

Each chapter in *A Writer's Reader* concentrates on a broad theme—family, gender, popular culture, language, and the good life. Some essays focus on the inner world of personal experience and opinion. Others turn to the outer world with information and persuasion. In each chapter, the last two selections explore the same subject, illustrating how different writers use different strategies to address similar issues.

Each chapter in the reader begins with an image and a visual activity to stimulate your thinking and writing. Each selection is preceded by biographical information, placing the author—and the piece itself—in a cultural and informational context. Next a reading note, As You Read, suggests a way to consider the selection. Following each reading are five Questions to Start You Thinking that consistently cover meaning, writing strategies, critical thinking, vocabulary, and connections with other selections in *A Writer's Reader*. Each paired essay is also followed by a question that asks you about a link between the essays. Next come a couple of journal prompts designed to get your writing juices flowing. Finally, two possible assignments make specific suggestions for writing. The first is directed toward your inner world, asking you to draw generally on your personal experience and your understanding of the essay. The second is outer directed, asking you to look outside yourself and write an evaluative or argumentative paper that may require further reading or research.

For more on journal writing, see pp. 380–81.

# 25 Family

Monty Brinton/CBS Photo Archive/Getty Images.

### Responding to an Image

Examine the scene above from the CBS sitcom *The Big Bang Theory*, which depicts former roommates and colleagues Sheldon Cooper and Leonard Hofstadter dining with friends and with Leonard's wife, Penny, in the apartment Sheldon and Leonard shared for nearly a decade. In what ways does the scene reiterate traditional depictions or definitions of families you've encountered? In what ways does it challenge or reinterpret those depictions?

# Judith Ortiz Cofer

## More Room

Born in Puerto Rico and raised in Paterson, New Jersey, Judith Ortiz Cofer is the Regents' and Franklin Professor of English and Creative Writing, Emerita, at the University of Georgia, and she has won numerous awards and honors for her work. Ortiz Cofer's many books include *A Love Story Beginning in Spanish: Poems* (2005); *Call Me Maria* (2006), a young adult novel; *The Meaning of Consuelo* (2003), a novel; *An Island Like You: Stories of the Barrio* (1995), a collection of short stories; and two books of poetry, *Terms of Survival* (1987) and *Reaching for the Mainland* (1987). In the following essay, Ortiz Cofer explores the significance of her grandmother getting her own room in the home she shared with her husband and many children. This piece appeared in *Silent Dancing* (1990), a collection of essays and poetry.

Tanya Cofer.

**AS YOU READ:** What details does Ortiz Cofer provide to show the significance of her grandmother and of her grandmother's room?

My grandmother's house is like a chambered nautilus;° it has many rooms, yet it is not a mansion. Its proportions are small and its design simple. It is a house that has grown organically, according to the needs of its inhabitants. To all of us in the family it is known as *la casa de Mamá.* It is the place of our origin; the stage for our memories and dreams of Island° life.    1

I remember how in my childhood it sat on stilts; this was before it had a downstairs. It rested on its perch like a great blue bird, not a flying sort of bird, more like a nesting hen, but with spread wings. Grandfather had built it soon after their marriage. He was a painter and housebuilder by trade, a poet and meditative° man by nature. As each of their eight children were born, new rooms were added. After a few years, the paint did not exactly match, nor the materials, so that there was a chronology° to it, like the rings of a tree, and Mamá could tell you the history of each room in her *casa,* and thus the genealogy° of the family along with it.    2

Her room is the heart of the house. Though I have seen it recently, and both woman and room have diminished in size, changed by the new perspective of my eyes, now capable of looking over countertops and tall beds, it is not this picture I carry in my memory of Mamá's *casa.* Instead, I see her room as a queen's chamber where a small woman loomed° large, a throne-room with a massive four-poster bed in its center which stood taller than a child's head. It was on this bed where her own children had been born that the smallest grandchildren were allowed to take naps in the afternoons; here too was where Mamá secluded herself to dispense private advice to her daughters, sitting on the edge of the bed, looking down at whoever sat on the rocker where generations of babies had been sung to sleep. To me she looked like a wise empress right out of the fairy tales I was addicted to reading.    3

**chambered nautilus:** A spiral-shaped seashell that has many separate internal compartments. **Island:** A reference to Puerto Rico.  **meditative:** Thoughtful.  **chronology:** Time-based order.  **genealogy:** History; ancestry.  **loomed:** Towered.

Though the room was dominated by the mahogany four-poster, it also 4
contained all of Mamá's symbols of power. On her dresser instead of cosmet-
ics there were jars filled with herbs: *yerba buena, yerba mala,°* the making of
purgatives° and teas to which we were all subjected during childhood crises.
She had a steaming cup for anyone who could not, or would not, get up to
face life on any given day. If the acrid° aftertaste of her cures for malinger-
ing° did not get you out of bed, then it was time to call *el doctor.*

And there was the monstrous chifforobe° she kept locked with a little 5
golden key she did not hide. This was a test of her dominion° over us; though
my cousins and I wanted a look inside that massive wardrobe more than
anything, we never reached for that little key lying on top of her Bible on
the dresser. This was also where she placed her earrings and rosary at night.
God's word was her security system. This chifforobe was the place where I
imagined she kept jewels, satin slippers, and elegant sequined, silk gowns of
heartbreaking fineness. I lusted after those imaginary costumes. I had heard
that Mamá had been a great beauty in her youth, and the belle of many balls.
My cousins had other ideas as to what she kept in that wooden vault: its secret could be money (Mamá did not hand cash to strangers, banks were out
of the question, so there were stories that her mattress was stuffed with dollar bills, and that she buried coins in jars in her garden under rosebushes, or
kept them in her inviolate° chifforobe); there might be that legendary gun
salvaged from the Spanish-American conflict over the Island. We went wild
over suspected treasures that we made up simply because children have to fill
locked trunks with something wonderful.

On the wall above the bed hung a heavy silver crucifix. Christ's agonized 6
head hung directly over Mamá's pillow. I avoided looking at this weapon
suspended over where her head would lay; and on the rare occasions when
I was allowed to sleep on that bed, I scooted down to the safe middle of the
mattress, where her body's impression took me in like a mother's lap. Having
taken care of the obligatory religious decoration with a crucifix, Mamá
covered the other walls with objects sent to her over the years by her children
in the States. *Los Nueva Yores°* were represented by, among other things, a
postcard of Niagara Falls from her son Hernán, postmarked, Buffalo, N.Y.
In a conspicuous gold frame hung a large color photograph of her daughter
Nena, her husband and their five children at the entrance to Disneyland in
California. From us she had gotten a black lace fan. Father had brought it
to her from a tour of duty with the Navy in Europe (on Sundays she would
remove it from its hook on the wall to fan herself at mass). Each year more
items were added as the family grew and dispersed, and every object in the
room had a story attached to it, a *cuento* which Mamá would bestow on
anyone who received the privilege of a day alone with her. It was almost

---

*yerba buena, yerba mala:* Spanish for "good herb" and "bad herb," respectively.  **purgatives:**
Agents, often laxatives, that rid the body of perceived toxins.  **acrid:** Sharp or bitter.
**malingering:** A pretend illness.  **chifforobe:** A piece of furniture that has both drawers
and space for hanging clothes.  **dominion:** Power or control.  **inviolate:** Undisturbed.
*Los Nueva Yores:* The way that Puerto Ricans sometimes refer to the United States.

worth pretending to be sick, though the bitter herb purgatives of the body were a big price to pay for the spirit revivals of her story-telling.

Mama slept alone on her large bed, except for the times when a sick  7
grandchild warranted the privilege, or when a heartbroken daughter came home in need of more than herbal teas. In the family there is a story about how this came to be.

When one of the daughters, my mother or one of her sisters, tells the  8
*cuento* of how Mamá came to own her nights, it is usually preceded by the qualifications that Papá's exile from his wife's room was not a result of animosity between the couple, but that the act had been Mamá's famous bloodless coup° for her personal freedom. Papá was the benevolent° dictator of her body and her life who had had to be banished° from her bed so that Mamá could better serve her family. Before the telling, we had to agree that the old man was not to blame. We all recognized that in the family Papá was as an *alma de Dios,*° a saintly, soft-spoken presence whose main pleasures in life, such as writing poetry and reading the Spanish large-type editions of *Reader's Digest,* always took place outside the vortex° of Mamá's crowded realm. It was not his fault, after all, that every year or so he planted a baby-seed in Mamá's fertile body, keeping her from leading the active life she needed and desired. He loved her and the babies. Papá composed odes° and lyrics to celebrate births and anniversaries and hired musicians to accompany him in singing them to his family and friends at extravagant pig-roasts he threw yearly. Mamá and the oldest girls worked for days preparing the food. Papá sat for hours in his painter's shed, also his study and library, composing the songs. At these celebrations he was also known to give long speeches in praise of God, his fecund wife, and his beloved island. As a middle child, my mother remembers these occasions as a time when the women sat in the kitchen and lamented° their burdens, while the men feasted out in the patio, their rum-thickened voices rising in song and praise for each other, *compañeros*° all.

It was after the birth of her eighth child, after she had lost three at birth  9
or in infancy, that Mamá made her decision. They say that Mamá had had a special way of letting her husband know that they were expecting, one that had begun when, at the beginning of their marriage, he had built her a house too confining for her taste. So, when she discovered her first pregnancy, she supposedly drew plans for another room, which he dutifully executed. Every time a child was due, she would demand, *more space, more space.* Papá acceded° to her wishes, child after child, since he had learned early that Mamá's renowned temper was a thing that grew like a monster along with a new belly. In this way Mamá got the house that she wanted, but with each child she lost in heart and energy. She had knowledge of her body and

---

**coup:** Overthrow of an existing order.    **benevolent:** Kind.    **banished:** Sent away.
*alma de Dios:* Spanish for "a good person."    **vortex:** A powerful force that draws things into it.    **odes:** Poems.    **lamented:** Felt sorry about; regretted.    *compañeros:* Spanish for "companions."    **acceded:** Agreed.

perceived that if she had any more children, her dreams and her plans would have to be permanently forgotten, because she would be a chronically ill woman, like Flora with her twelve children: asthma, no teeth, in bed more than on her feet.

And so, after my youngest uncle was born, she asked Papa to build a large room at the back of the house. He did so in joyful anticipation. Mamá had asked him special things this time: shelves on the walls, a private entrance. He thought that she meant this room to be a nursery where several children could sleep. He thought it was a wonderful idea. He painted it his favorite color, sky blue, and made large windows looking out over a green hill and the church spires beyond. But nothing happened. Mamá's belly did not grow, yet she seemed in a frenzy of activity over the house. Finally, an anxious Papá approached his wife to tell her that the new room was finished and ready to be occupied. And Mamá, they say, replied: "Good, it's for *you*."

And so it was that Mamá discovered the only means of birth control available to a Catholic woman of her time: sacrifice. She gave up the comfort of Papá's sexual love for something she deemed° greater: the right to own and control her own body, so that she might live to meet her grandchildren—me among them—so that she could give more of herself to the ones already there, so that she could be more than a channel for other lives, so that even now that time has robbed her of the elasticity of her body and of her amazing reservoir of energy, she still emanates° the kind of joy that can only be achieved by living according to the dictates° of one's own heart.

**deemed:** Believed to be.    **emanates:** Beams with.    **dictates:** Guiding principles.

## Questions to Start You Thinking

1. **Considering Meaning:** Why did Cofer's grandmother want to have her own room? Why did Cofer's grandfather think she had asked for this room?

2. **Identifying Writing Strategies:** Cofer offers vivid, detailed descriptions throughout her essay. What main impression do these descriptions create of the grandmother and of her room? (For more on how a main impression is conveyed by descriptions, see Chapter 5.)

3. **Reading Critically:** Cofer includes just a brief bit of dialogue in the final paragraph of her essay. Where else might she have added dialogue? What might be the benefit of these additions?

4. **Expanding Vocabulary:** One definition of *secluded* is "withdrawn from or involving little human social activity." How does Cofer's use of the word *secluded* in paragraph 3 broaden and enrich this definition?

5. **Making Connections:** Cofer describes her grandfather as "a benevolent dictator of [her grandmother's] body. . . a saintly-soft-spoken presence" (para. 9). How do you think he conforms or fails to conform to "dominant

conceptions of masculinity" as described in "The High Cost of Manliness" (pp. 512–14). What effect does this have on the relationship between Papa and his family?

## Journal Prompts

1. Write about a room that stands out in your memory. For example, it might be your childhood bedroom or a room in the home of an influential friend or relative. Try to re-create the room by using the types of vivid details that Cofer does.

2. In paragraph 6, Cofer writes of stories being attached to various gifts that her grandmother had received. Tell a story related to a possession that is important to you.

## Suggestions for Writing

1. Cofer suggests that by getting her own room, her grandmother dramatically improved her life: she achieved "the kind of joy that can only be achieved by living according to the dictates of one's own heart" (paragraph 11). Write about something (such as a fulfilled request, an event, a new relationship, or a stroke of luck) that dramatically changed your life for the better. How, specifically, did your life change? Why has this change been so important or meaningful to you?

2. Compare and contrast the attitudes of Cofer's grandmother and grandfather about the benefits versus the burdens of having more children. Do the grandfather's attitudes seem dated to you, or do you think they persist in any way among today's fathers? Support your conclusions with examples.

## Chris Bentley

### Beyond the Nuclear Family: Can Boomers Make Cohousing Mainstream?

Joe Mazza.

Freelance journalist Chris Bentley has written for the *New York Times'* Green blog, the *Chicago Tribune, Next City*, and many other publications. He formerly served as Midwest editor of the *Architect's Newspaper* and as a reporter for *Curious City*, a podcast and weekly radio program based at WBEZ in Chicago. In the following article, which originally appeared in *CityLab*, Bentley examines why baby boomers are taking interest in a form of shared living space known as cohousing.

**AS YOU READ:** What are the benefits of cohousing, according to its supporters?

When architects Kathryn McCamant and Charles Durrett made their first      1
pilgrimage to Denmark in the early 1980s, they were out to learn whatever they could. What they brought back would earn them a reputation as the mother and father of cohousing in the United States.

They visited communities like Copenhagen's Trudeslund (where they would later live), noting the common spaces that linked small clusters of private residences with public life. Kids ran along car-free paths; families gathered around meals in a common house or stayed in their private homes as they pleased.

"I think the thing that really impressed us," says McCamant, "is how normal it is. It seems [there] like the single-family house world is the strange one. That still is what baffles me, that people think it's some radical thing."

Cohousing refers to a kind of shared housing in between that single-family world and the hippie communes° (or hipster co-ops°) it's often confused with. Danish architect Jan Gudmand-Høyer pioneered the model in the late '60s and early '70s, bringing together friends and like-minded utopians° to co-design and develop multi-unit homes that would foster a sense of community among their residents. He talked about reintroducing "play" into daily life or, as he put it, "moving from *Homo productivo* to *Homo ludens*"—from worker drones to more joyful beings.

The idea has caught on in Europe, where somewhere between 1 and 8 percent of Danes live in a form of cohousing. (In the United States, that figure is less than one hundredth of one percent of total housing units.) Gudmand-Høyer's Skråplanet and Trudeslund communities still thrive. But in the United States it has been a slow climb.

About 130 cohousing communities exist in the United States, according to the Cohousing Partners Association, a nonprofit based in Durham, North Carolina. McCamant, whose firm Cohousing Partners has built dozens of communities, predicts the number will double within 10 years. If that happens it will be thanks to one demographic force of nature: baby boomers.°

"A large majority of these communities are being driven by baby boomers looking at downsizing when they retire. For whatever reason, cohousing didn't work for them earlier, but now they're in a transition in life," she says.

McCamant predicts the number will double within ten years.

She could be referring to Alice Alexander, executive director of the Cohousing Association. Alexander, 57, and her husband are residents of one of the nation's newest cohousing communities, or "cohos": Durham Central Park Cohousing.

Mostly empty-nesters,° its members came together several years ago to plan a 24-unit cluster of condominiums with solar water heaters and shared resources, like a media room and performance space for the community's numerous artists and musicians. They successfully petitioned local authorities for a single electric meter, instead of twenty-four.

That communal spirit extends beyond the utility bill. Alexander says daily life among her "true neighbors" is a stark contrast with the suburban subdivisions of her native northern Virginia, where she lived in single-family homes for decades before discovering cohousing.

---

**communes:** Groups of people who share living space, possessions, work, income, and, often, life purposes or values. **co-ops:** Jointly owned and democratically controlled businesses—often, grocers. **utopians:** Idealists. **baby boomers:** Those born between 1946 and 1964. **empty-nesters:** People whose children have grown up and left home.

"I did what everybody did. I was in commuter hell, I didn't know my  12
neighbors, all that. There wasn't a choice, or we didn't know another choice
exists," Alexander says. "Baby boomers are demanding a better way to live.
We want to be sustainable; we want community, happiness."

Currently there is only one resident under age twenty at Durham Cen-  13
tral Park, but other cohos are designed with kids in mind. Early cohousing
began for families with young children, but became something else when
those children grew up—an evolution Alexander predicts could eventually
happen in reverse, as childless cohos for baby boomers are supplanted°
by a new generation of younger people seeking community beyond the
nuclear family.

Last year, Harvard University's Joint Center on Housing Studies looked at  14
the housing needs of America's fifty-and-over population. It called cohousing "an increasingly popular option for those seeking communal settings
and some support outside of institutional living," but noted that the model's
wider adoption faces zoning° challenges. AARP said in 2010 that cohousing
makes sense for seniors, who might use a common room for live-in caregivers, and can otherwise rely on their existing network of community members
for a ride to the doctor or help with a vexing° household task.

Joani Blank, seventy-seven, lives in Swan's Market Cohousing in down-  15
town Oakland, California. She has spent twenty-two years across three
cohos and has visited dozens more. Blank says senior citizens struggle with
the public perception that cohos are like other senior housing or retirement
homes.

"I like living with younger adults. I want to live in a diverse community.  16
That's the way humans used to live—in multigenerational groups," says
Blank, who founded San Francisco's Good Vibrations sex shop in 1977.

The financial structures of cohousing are diverse, too. Blank's Oakland  17
coho is technically a condo association, where every household is a member
of their homeowner association board of directors. Some are structured as
townhouse associations. Most groups acquire a plot of land and enlist a de-
veloper, although Alexander's Durham coho is self-developed.

So far cohousing isn't necessarily less expensive than other market-rate  18
housing options, despite its residents pooling their resources. They have to
hire architects, consultants, and often developers to help custom-design their
communities, typically specifying extra facilities and sustainable features
that may have a long payback period.

It may be difficult for a group to get construction loans or especially  19
mortgages, so they often need a lot of cash upfront. Christopher Leinberger,
a nonresident senior fellow at the Brookings Institution, says although cohos
mesh philosophically with what many aging baby boomers want—dense,
walkable communities—so do a lot of traditional developments that don't
come with so many legal and financial headaches.

---

**supplanted:** Replaced.     **zoning:** Regulations about the number and types of buildings that
can be constructed in particular zones of a town or city.     **vexing:** Difficult or annoying.

"Banks still underwrite° experience every bit as much as they underwrite  20
balance sheets," says Leinberger, who has friends who live in cohousing, but
predicts the trend will stay niche in the United States for the foreseeable future. "There's a lot conspiring against these things."

Supporters, though, point to the intangible° benefits. Alexander says her  21
husband wakes up earlier than he has in years now that they live in cohousing, excited to take on the day in a way he hadn't been before.

The market, too, may be waking up.  22

"I feel like as a movement we are just taking off," says Alexander.  23

**underwrite:** Finance, pay for.   **intangible:** Incapable of being perceived by the sense of
touch.

## Questions to Start You Thinking

1. **Considering Meaning:** Why might cohousing be especially appealing to
   baby boomers, according to Bentley?

2. **Identifying Writing Strategies:** Why do you think Bentley begins the
   essay with the story of Kathryn McCamant and Charles Durrett? Why
   might this be a stronger way to open the essay than, say, beginning with
   predictions about the potential growth of cohousing (the type of information that appears in paragraph 6)?

3. **Reading Critically:** In paragraphs 14, 18, and 19, Bentley points out
   some logistical problems posed by cohousing. However, he doesn't discuss the interpersonal challenges cohousing residents might face. Should
   Bentley have addressed this issue? Why, or why not?

4. **Expanding Vocabulary:** In paragraph 11, Bentley refers to the "communal spirit" of one cohousing development. What does he seem to mean by
   the term *communal* in the context of this essay?

5. **Making Connections:** Compare and contrast the benefits of cohousing
   with the those of a multigenerational family home—specifically, the one
   that belonged to Judith Ortiz Cofer's grandparents (see "More Room,"
   pp. 483–86). Are there any ways in which a multigenerational home can have
   the sort of "communal spirit" noted in paragraph 11 of Bentley's essay?

## Journal Prompts

1. Write about a time when you shared living space with someone to whom
   you are not related. What were some advantages and disadvantages of the
   situation?

2. What places or activities make you feel most connected, in a positive way,
   to a larger community? What qualities of these places or activities foster
   this sense of connection?

## Suggestions for Writing

1. Interview one or two baby boomers about whether cohousing would appeal to them and why. Are they planning any type of postretirement downsizing—perhaps a move to a smaller living space? What factors are driving decisions about what changes, if any, they might make in their living arrangements?

2. Some observers believe that for millennials, cohousing can offer a more affordable and personally rewarding option than renting or buying a traditional apartment or home. (See "Dorms for Grownups: A Solution for Lonely Millennials?" from theatlantic.com, November 6, 2015.) Explore the pros and cons of cohousing for millennials, drawing on at least two sources.

# Michael Cobb

## The Marriage Imperative

Derek Shapton.

Michael Cobb, an English professor at the University of Toronto, is the author of *Single: Arguments for the Uncoupled* (2012) and *God Hates Fags: The Rhetorics of Religious Violence* (2006), both published by the New York University Press. In the following essay, published in the op-ed section of the *New York Times* on June 30, 2015, Cobb offers his interpretation of the Supreme Court's ruling on same-sex marriage.

**AS YOU READ:** What important similarities does Cobb find between married and single people?

N ow all of us single people are pathetic, not just the straight ones. "Marriage responds to the universal fear that a lonely person might call out only to find no one there," writes Justice Anthony M. Kennedy in the majority opinion of the Supreme Court in *Obergefell v. Hodges*. As I read that bit alone in my apartment, I choked on my coffee.   1

Isn't it enough to be denied the "constellation° of benefits that the States   2 have linked to marriage"? A constellation my coupled queer sisters and brethren° now can hold dearly if they just make it official? Once again, being single is the dreary, awful, mournful alternative to marriage. A condition to be pitied, and quickly corrected by a sprint to City Hall.

As I read on, I started to wonder how Justices Sonia Sotomayor and Elena   3 Kagan—two of the most high-profile single women in the federal government—felt as they reviewed and had to join Justice Kennedy's opinion: "No union is more profound than marriage, for it embodies the highest ideals of love, fidelity, devotion, sacrifice, and family."

Senator Lindsey Graham of South Carolina, a Republican presidential   4 hopeful, is also single, and has had to endure some humiliating questions

**constellation:** Collection.     **brethren:** Brothers.

about his marital status, including who would be his "first lady": "Well, I've got a sister, she could play that role if necessary," was his excellent response. I wonder how the senator felt, after last week's decision, when he learned that to be denied marriage is to be "condemned to live in loneliness, excluded from one of civilization's oldest institutions"?

Marriage equality activists could have pursued a different agenda—challenging the need for sexual scrutiny by the state, and the constellation of benefits that belong to marriage—but they didn't. Instead of dreaming up new forms of governance, they asked to be ruled by the ones that already exist.  5

And so old questions remain: Why can't I put a good friend on my health care plan? Why can't my neighbor and I file our taxes together so we could save some money, as my parents do? If I failed to make a will, why is it unlikely a dear friend would inherit my estate?  6

The answers to all these questions are the same: It's because I'm not having sex with those people. (To make matters worse, that also means we probably didn't have children together.) For the only thing that truly distinguishes romance and marriage from other loving intimacies like friendships, other familial relationships and close business partnerships is that sex is (or once was) part of the picture.  7

So yes, marriage equality erases an odious and invidious° distinction among straight and us not-straight citizens for which I'm truly glad and which I celebrate. And it'll make lots of people's lives better. But it also leaves unexamined the reason sex seems to give you benefits and recognition—and why it orders the world and civilization.  8

In granting same-sex couples "equal dignity in the eyes of the law," Justice Kennedy throws everyone under the "just married" limo. Dignity—the state of being worthy of honor or respect—is undeniably appealing. One reading of the majority opinion suggests, however, one isn't dignified unless one can be married. But some of us can't or won't ever find that special someone. We might not have the luck or the timing or the inclination.  9

If dignity is predicated on being lucky in love, then what happens when your luck runs out?  10

*Well*, you join 50.2 percent (or 124.6 million) of America's adults, according to Bureau of Labor Statistics last year. And that means that you'll be misunderstood as living a miserable, lonely life by the other 49.8 percent. They'll deny you adequate language, representation, and consideration—except as the thing to avoid becoming. Even if you're having a happy, rewarding life, they'll assume you're not.  11

But singleness includes *everyone* at some point, even those who are married: love ends; spouses cheat; someone dies first. To be in a marriage, no matter how strong, is always a precarious condition, which means that the dignity you've been given can be taken away at any moment.  12

The grim implication: We're all "condemned" to the ever-present shadow characterization of singleness for at least some time, doomed to "call out  13

**invidious:** Unpleasant.

only to find no one there," which binds us more desperately to the marriage imperative° and rights that aren't ours, no matter how hard we love.

A marriage equality based upon dignity makes pathetic singles of us all.    14

Certainly Justice Kennedy's sense of marital "dignity" is over the top. But    15 it's not just sentimental rhetoric:° It's a kind of legal "term of heart" that can keep you up at night. The words and the value they communicate are impossible to avoid, and often difficult to resist. It's as if the words of Justice Kennedy and my grandmother, who, on her deathbed, begged me to get married, have melded together in my head, declaring my life lacking — emotions meet law and then throw me into a state of emotional insecurity.

I am usually a relatively happy single person who wrote a book advocat-    16 ing for the dignity of single people (a colleague asked if I was writing that book so I could get more dates). But even I hear coupledom's call: I sometimes crave a long-term relationship with that great guy; I watch Ang Lee's take on *Sense and Sensibility* monthly; I've been in a number of relationships that broke my heart — all of which feels very undignified. But none of those longings, hauntings, and hurts should pave the way for my constitutional dignity. I already feel too governed from the inside of my anxious heart, which doesn't make, as my grandmother certainly knew, the best choices.

If you're truly lucky in this life, you might have many relationships that "em-    17 body," in varying degrees, "the highest ideals of love, fidelity, devotion, sacrifice, and family," whether or not those relationships include sex. Better yet, these relationships might give you a general feeling of dignity, well-being, and justice.

Being single doesn't mean that the world is empty and awful. Senator    18 Graham reminded people that his life was not destitute without a wife: "I've got a lot of friends. We'll have a rotating first lady."

What Justice Kennedy, and everyone else too, needs to remember is that    19 simply being yourself — your single self — is already the fundamental form of dignity. Founding your dignity on something as flimsy and volatile as a sexual connection insures dignity's precariousness as it enshrines° your inherent unworthiness as a single individual.

**imperative:** Necessity.    **rhetoric:** Language used to persuade or influence people.    **enshrines:** Encloses.


## Questions to Start You Thinking

1. **Considering Meaning:** Identify the specific language in the Supreme Court's decision on same-sex marriage that makes Cobb choke on his coffee. What disturbs him about this language?

2. **Identifying Writing Strategies:** Why does Cobb refer to Senator Lindsey Graham in his essay? How well do you think his reference to Graham supports his argument?

3. **Reading Critically:** How does Cobb support his contention that the Supreme Court's ruling suggests that "being single is the dreary, awful, mournful alternative to marriage"? Do you agree or disagree with his conclusion?

4. **Expanding Vocabulary:** How does Cobb define *dignity*? Do you agree that the Supreme Court's decision focuses on human dignity? How would you define *dignity*?

5. **Making Connections:** Cobb argues against the notion that marriage is an ideal union. How does Judy Brady in "I Want a Wife" (pp. 505–07) use humor to arrive at the same conclusion? Are there any parts to Cobb's argument that you think she would disagree with?

## Link to the Paired Essay

Both "The Marriage Imperative" and "Searching for Your Soul Mate" (pp. 494–99) discuss the difficulties in finding the perfect mate. How would Cobb respond to Ansari's definition of a soul mate? Would Cobb agree that marriage is the logical next step to finding a soul mate?

## Journal Prompts

1. Do you think all single people are necessarily lonely? Can good friendships and other types of family relationships provide as much companionship as marriage?

2. Think about how marriage is portrayed in the media, and its legal ramifications. In what ways do culture and society try to promote marriage? How?

## Suggestions for Writing

1. Research the controversy surrounding *Obergefell v. Hodges*. Construct an argument that either supports or disagrees with the Supreme Court's ruling on this case.

2. Write an essay responding to Cobb's suggestion that good friends should be able to share a health plan. Defend your position.

## Aziz Ansari

### Searching for Your Soul Mate

John Lamparski/
WireImage/Getty Images.

Aziz Ansari, an American actor and comedian, was born February 23, 1983, in Columbia, South Carolina. After graduating from New York University with a business degree, he decided to pursue his interests in acting and stand-up comedy. He has appeared on stage and on television, most notably as Tom Haverford on NBC's Emmy-nominated comedy *Parks and Recreation*. In 2015, he gained accolades as a writer after Penguin Press published his book *Modern Romance*, which soon became a bestseller. A funny yet thoughtful look at the complexities of modern romance, the following excerpt from the first chapter explores the shift in attitudes toward marriage over the last half century.

**AS YOU READ:** What are men and women looking for today in a spouse? How do they decide when to marry?

Today the average age of first marriage is about twenty-seven for women    1
and twenty-nine for men, and it's around thirty for both men and
women in big cities like New York and Philadelphia.

Why has this age of first marriage increased so dramatically in the past    2
few decades? For the young people who got married in the 1950s, getting
married was the first step in adulthood. After high school or college, you got
married and you left the house. For today's folks, marriage is usually one of
the later stages in adulthood. Now most young people spend their twenties
and thirties in another stage of life, where they go to university, start a career,
and experience being an adult outside of their parents' home before marriage.

This period isn't all about finding a mate and getting married. You have    3
other priorities as well: getting educated, trying out different jobs, having a
few relationships, and, with luck, becoming a more fully developed person. Sociologists even have a name for this new stage of life: emerging adulthood.

During this stage we also wind up greatly expanding our pool of roman-    4
tic options. Instead of staying in the neighborhood or our building, we move
to new cities, spend years meeting people in college and workplaces, and—in
the biggest game changer—have the infinite possibilities provided by online
dating and other similar technologies.

Besides the effects it has on marriage, emerging adulthood also offers    5
young people an exciting, fun period of independence from their parents
when they get to enjoy the pleasures of adulthood—before becoming husbands and wives and starting a family.

If you're like me, you couldn't imagine getting married without going    6
through all this. When I was twenty-three, I knew nothing about what I was
going to be as an adult. I was a business and biology major at NYU. Would
I have married some girl who lived a few blocks from me in Bennettsville,
South Carolina, where I grew up? What was this mysterious "biology business" I planned on setting up, anyway? I have no clue. I was an idiot who definitely wasn't ready for such huge life decisions.[1] . . .

Before the 1960s, in most parts of the United States, single women simply    7
didn't live alone, and many families frowned upon their daughters moving
into shared housing for "working girls." Until they got married, these women
were pretty much stuck at home under fairly strict adult supervision and
lacked basic adult autonomy.° They always had to let their parents know their
whereabouts and plans. Even dating had heavy parental involvement: The
parents would either have to approve the boy or accompany them on the date.

At one point during a focus group with older women, I asked them straight    8
out whether a lot of women their age got married just to get out of the house.
Every single woman there nodded. For women in this era, it seemed that marriage was the easiest way of acquiring the basic freedoms of adulthood.

Things weren't a breeze after that, though. Marriage, most women quickly    9
discovered, liberated them from their parents but made them dependent on a

[1]My Bubba Sparxxx tattoo is a constant reminder.

**autonomy:** Independence.

## Average Age of First Marriage in the United States, 1950–2014

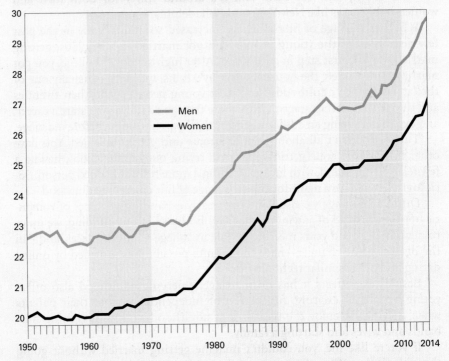

*Data:* U.S. Census Bureau, Decennial Censuses, 1890–1940, and Current Population Survey, Annual Social and Economic Supplements, 1947–2014.

man who might or might not treat them well and then saddled them with the responsibilities of homemaking and child rearing. It gave women of this era what was described at the time by Betty Friedan in her bestselling book *The Feminine Mystique* as "the problem that has no name."[2]

Once women gained access to the labor market and won the right to divorce, the divorce rate skyrocketed. Some of the older women I met in our focus groups had left their husbands during the height of the divorce revolution, and they told me that they'd always resented missing out on something singular and special: the experience of being a young, unencumbered, single woman. 10

They wanted emerging adulthood.... 11

The shift in when we look for love and marriage has been accompanied by a change in what we look for in a marriage partner. When the older folks I interviewed described the reasons that they dated, got engaged to, and then married their eventual spouses, they'd say things like "He seemed like a pretty good guy," "She was a nice girl," "He had a good job," and "She had access to doughnuts and I like doughnuts." 12

[2]In her first draft Friedan named the problem Hampton, but her editors told her it wasn't catchy enough.

When you ask people today why they married someone, the answers are   13
much more dramatic and loving. You hear things along the lines of "She is
my other half," "I can't imagine experiencing the joys of life without him by
my side," or "Every time I touch her hair, I get a huge boner."

On our subreddit we asked people: If you've been married or in a long-   14
term relationship, how did you decide that the person was (or still is) the
right person for you? What made this person different from others? The responses were strikingly unlike the ones we got from the older people we met
at the senior center.

Many were filled with stories that illustrated a very deep connection be-   15
tween the two people that made them feel like they'd found someone unique,
not just someone who was pleasant to start a family with. . . .

From the way they described things, it seemed like their bar for commit-   16
ting to someone was much higher than it had been for the older folks who
settled down just a few generations ago.

To figure out why people today use such exalted° terms when they ex-   17
plain why they committed to their romantic partner, I spoke with Andrew
Cherlin, the eminent° sociologist of the family and author of the book *The
Marriage-Go-Round*. Up until about fifty years ago, Cherlin said, most people
were satisfied with what he calls a "companionate marriage." In this type of
marriage each partner had clearly defined roles. A man was the head of his
household and the chief breadwinner, while a woman stayed home, took care
of the house, and had kids. Most of the satisfaction you gained in the marriage depended on how well you fulfilled this assigned role. As a man, if you
brought home the bacon, you could feel like you were a good husband. As a
woman, if you kept a clean house and popped out 2.5 kids, you were a good
wife. You loved your spouse, maybe, but not in an "every time I see his mustache, my heart flutters like a butterfly" type of way.

You didn't marry each other because you were madly in love; you mar-   18
ried because you could make a family together. While some people said they
were getting married for love, the pressure to get married and start a family
was such that not every match could be a love match, so instead we had the
"good enough marriage."

Waiting for true love was a luxury that many, especially women, could not   19
afford. In the early 1960s, a full *76 percent* of women admitted they would be
willing to marry someone they didn't love. However, only 35 percent of the
men said they would do the same.

If you were a woman, you had far less time to find a man. True love? This   20
guy has a job *and* a decent mustache. Lock it down, girl.

This gets into a fundamental change in how marriage is viewed. Today we   21
see getting married as finding a life partner. Someone we love. But this whole
idea of marrying for happiness and love is relatively new.

---

**exalted:** Exaggerated.     **eminent:** Well-known for achievement in a particular field.

For most of the history of our species, courtship and marriage weren't 22
really about two individuals finding love and fulfillment. According to the
historian Stephanie Coontz, author of *Marriage, a History*, until recently a
marital union was primarily important for establishing a bond between two
families. It was about achieving security—financial, social, and personal. It
was about creating conditions that made it possible to survive and reproduce.

This is not ancient history. Until the Industrial Revolution, most Americans 23
and Europeans lived on farms, and everybody in the household needed to work.
Considerations about whom to marry were primarily practical.

In the past, a guy would be thinking, *Oh, shit, I gotta have kids to work on my* 24
*farm. I need four-year-old kids performing manual labor ASAP. And I need a woman*
*who can make me clothes. I better get on this.* A woman would think, *I better find a*
*dude who's capable on the farm, and good with a plow so I don't starve and die.*

Making sure the person shared your interest in sushi and Wes Anderson 25
movies *and* made you get a boner anytime you touched her hair would seem
far too picky.

Of course, people did get married because they loved each other, but their 26
expectations about what love would bring were different from those we hold
today. For families whose future security depended on their children making
good matches, passion was seen as an extremely risky motivation for getting
hitched. "Marriage was too vital an economic and political institution to be entered into solely on the basis of something as irrational as love," writes Coontz.

Coontz also told us that before the 1960s most middle-class people had 27
pretty rigid, gender-based expectations about what each person would bring
to a marriage. Women wanted financial security. Men wanted virginity and
weren't concerned with deeper qualities like education or intelligence.

"The average couple wed after just six months—a pretty good sign that 28
love was still filtered through strong gender stereotypes rather than being
based on deep knowledge of the other partner as an individual," she said.

Not that people who got married before the 1960s had loveless marriages. 29
On the contrary, back then couples often developed increasingly intense
feelings for each other as they spent time together, growing up and building their families. These marriages may have started with a simmer, but over
time they could build to a boil.

But a lot of things changed in the 1960s and 1970s, including our expec- 30
tations of what we should get out of a marriage. The push for women's equality was a big driver of the transformation. As more women went to college,
got good jobs, and achieved economic independence, they established new-
found control over their bodies and their lives. A growing number of women
refused to marry the guy in their neighborhood or building. They wanted to
experience things too, and they now had the freedom to do it.

According to Cherlin, the generation that came of age during the sixties 31
and seventies rejected companionate marriage and began to pursue something greater. They didn't merely want a spouse—they wanted a soul mate.

By the 1980s, 86 percent of American men and 91 percent of American 32
women said they would not marry someone without the presence of romantic love.

The soul mate marriage is very different from the companionate marriage. 33
It's not about finding someone decent to start a family with. It's about finding the perfect person whom you truly, deeply love. Someone you want to share the rest of your life with. Someone with whom, when you smell a certain T-shirt they own, you are instantly whisked away to a happy memory about the time he or she made you breakfast and you both stayed in and binge-watched all eight seasons of *Perfect Strangers*.

We want something that's very passionate, or boiling, from the get-go. 34
In the past, people weren't looking for something boiling; they just needed some water. Once they found it and committed to a life together, they did their best to heat things up. Now, if things aren't boiling, committing to marriage seems premature.

But searching for a soul mate takes a long time and requires enormous 35
emotional investment. The problem is that this search for the perfect person can generate a lot of stress. Younger generations face immense pressure to find the "perfect person" that simply didn't exist in the past when "good enough" was good enough.

When they're successful, though, the payoff is incredible. According to 36
Cherlin, the soul mate marriage has the highest potential for happiness, and it delivers levels of fulfillment that the generation of older people I interviewed rarely reached.

Cherlin is also well aware of how hard it is to sustain all these good 37
things, and he claims that today's soul mate marriage model has the highest potential for disappointment. Since our expectations are so high, today people are quick to break things off when their relationship doesn't meet them (touch the hair, no boner). Cherlin would also like me to reiterate that this hair/boner analogy is mine and mine alone.

The psychotherapist Esther Perel has counseled hundreds of couples who 38
are having trouble in their marriages, and as she sees things, asking all of this from a marriage puts a lot of pressure on relationships. In her words:

> Marriage was an economic institution in which you were given a
> partnership for life in terms of children and social status and succession
> and companionship. But now we want our partner to still give us all these
> things, but in addition I want you to be my best friend and my trusted
> confidant and my passionate lover to boot, and we live twice as long. So we
> come to one person, and we basically are asking them to give us what once
> an entire village used to provide: Give me belonging, give me identity, give
> me continuity, but give me transcendence° and mystery and awe all in one.
> Give me comfort, give me edge. Give me novelty, give me familiarity. Give
> me predictability, give me surprise. And we think it's a given, and toys and
> lingerie are going to save us with that.

Ideally, though, we're lucky, and we find our soul mate and enjoy that 39
life-changing motherlode of happiness.

But a soul mate is a very hard thing to find. 40

**transcendence:** A state of beyond perception.

## Questions to Start You Thinking

1. **Considering Meaning:** Why do men wait longer to get married today than they did in the 1950s and 1960s? Women? How do their reasons for waiting reflect cultural changes?

2. **Identifying Writing Strategies:** How does Ansari use humor in his essay? What effect does it have on his main points? How does his humor help engage the reader? Refer to specific passages of text in your response.

3. **Reading Critically:** What do you think Betty Friedan meant by her determination that women in the early sixties experienced "the problem that has no name"? How did social expectations contribute to this "problem"?

4. **Expanding Vocabulary:** How do sociologists define the term *emerging adulthood*? What other experiences would you include in this category? Why are these experiences important during the maturation process?

5. **Making Connections:** In the last section of his article, Ansari looks at how modern men and women define a soul mate as the perfect person to marry. After reading "I Want a Wife" (pp. 505–07), do you think that Brady's narrator would be able to find a soul mate today? Do you believe Ansari would argue that male and female roles have changed to the point where Brady's narrator would be able to find a man who could accomplish all that was expected of a wife in 1971?

## Link to the Paired Essay

In "The Marriage Imperative" (pp. 491–93), Michael Cobb argues that "some of us can't or won't ever find that special someone." Why not? What qualities that men and women are looking for today in an ideal mate, as outlined by Ansari, would he find unrealistic and thus unattainable?

## Journal Prompt

Ansari writes that in the past, couples entered into marriage for practical reasons, including the desire to have a family and to enjoy economic stability. Do you think that these needs, along with the yearning for a soul mate, motivate couples to marry today? What expectations do you believe are placed on partners in a modern marriage? How difficult do you think it is to live up to those expectations? What situations could arise that could undermine those expectations?

## Suggestions for Writing

1. Interview a couple who got married before the 1960s and one who recently got married, asking them the following questions: How old were they when they got married? How long had they known each other when they got married? Why did they get married? How do their answers compare with the ones Ansari cites in "Searching for Your Soul Mate"?

2. Write an essay explaining how changes in male and female roles have affected when and why people marry.

# Gender

Cornelia Schauermann/Cultura/Getty Images.

## Responding to an Image

This image portrays an obvious reversal of traditional gender roles — a woman on her knee, proposing marriage to a man. Does it reinforce or conform to traditional ideas about masculinity and femininity, too? Consider each person's posture, facial expression, clothing, physical attributes, and any other elements you notice. Where are they, literally, and in the course of their lives? What do you imagine preceded this moment? What do you imagine will follow for this couple, and how might gender play a role based on the dynamic illustrated here?

# Brent Staples

## Black Men and Public Space

Brent Staples was born in 1951 in Chester, Pennsylvania, and earned a PhD in psychology from the University of Chicago. He wrote for the *Chicago Sun-Times* and *Down Beat* magazine before joining the *New York Times* in 1985, where he moved from metropolitan news to the *New York Times Book Review*. Since 1990, Staples has been a member of the *Times* editorial board, writing regular columns on politics and culture. His work also has appeared in such magazines as *New York Woman, Ms.,* and *Harper's,* and he is the author of the memoir *Parallel Time: Growing Up in Black and White* (1994), winner of the Anisfield-Wolf Book Award. In the following essay, published in a slightly different version in *Ms.* magazine in September 1986, Staples considers how his presence affects other pedestrians at night.

**AS YOU READ:** Identify why other pedestrians respond to Staples with anxiety.

Fred R. Conrad/
The New York Times/Redux.

My first victim was a woman—white, well dressed, probably in her late twenties. I came upon her late one evening on a deserted street in Hyde Park, a relatively affluent neighborhood in an otherwise mean, impoverished section of Chicago. As I swung onto the avenue behind her, there seemed to be a discreet, uninflammatory distance between us. Not so. She cast back a worried glance. To her, the youngish black man—a broad six feet two inches with a beard and billowing hair, both hands shoved into the pockets of a bulky military jacket—seemed menacingly close. After a few more quick glimpses, she picked up her pace and was soon running in earnest. Within seconds, she disappeared into a cross street.

That was more than a decade ago. I was twenty-one years old, a graduate student newly arrived at the University of Chicago. It was in the echo of that terrified woman's footfalls that I first began to know the unwieldy inheritance I'd come into—the ability to alter public space in ugly ways. It was clear that she thought herself the quarry of a mugger, a rapist, or worse. Suffering a bout of insomnia, however, I was stalking sleep, not defenseless wayfarers. As a softy who is scarcely able to take a knife to a raw chicken—let alone hold one to a person's throat—I was surprised, embarrassed, and dismayed all at once. Her flight made me feel like an accomplice in tyranny.° It also made it clear that I was indistinguishable from the muggers who occasionally seeped into the area from the surrounding ghetto. The first encounter, and those that followed, signified that a vast, unnerving gulf lay between nighttime pedestrians—particularly women—and me. And I soon gathered that being perceived as dangerous is a hazard in itself. I only needed to turn a corner into a dicey situation, or crowd some frightened, armed person in a foyer somewhere, or make an errant move after being pulled over by a policeman. Where fear and weapons meet—and they often do in urban America—there is always the possibility of death.

**tyranny:** Injustice or abuse.

In that first year, my first away from my hometown, I was to become thoroughly familiar with the language of fear. At dark, shadowy intersections, I could cross in front of a car stopped at a traffic light and elicit the *thunk, thunk, thunk, thunk* of the driver—black, white, male, or female—hammering down the door locks. On less traveled streets after dark, I grew accustomed to but never comfortable with people crossing to the other side of the street rather than pass me. Then there were the standard unpleasantries with policemen, doormen, bouncers, cabdrivers, and others whose business it is to screen out troublesome individuals *before* there is any nastiness.

I moved to New York nearly two years ago and I have remained an avid night walker. In central Manhattan, the near-constant crowd cover minimizes tense one-on-one street encounters. Elsewhere—in SoHo, for example, where sidewalks are narrow and tightly spaced buildings shut out the sky—things can get very taut indeed.

After dark, on the warrenlike° streets of Brooklyn where I live, I often see women who fear the worst from me. They seem to have set their faces on neutral, and with their purse straps strung across their chests bandolier-style, they forge ahead as though bracing themselves against being tackled. I understand, of course, that the danger they perceive is not a hallucination. Women are particularly vulnerable to street violence, and young black males are drastically overrepresented among the perpetrators of that violence. Yet these truths are no solace against the kind of alienation that comes of being ever the suspect, a fearsome entity with whom pedestrians avoid making eye contact.

It is not altogether clear to me how I reached the ripe old age of twenty-two without being conscious of the lethality nighttime pedestrians attributed to me. Perhaps it was because in Chester, Pennsylvania, the small, angry industrial town where I came of age in the 1960s, I was scarcely noticeable against a backdrop of gang warfare, street knifings, and murders. I grew up one of the good boys, had perhaps a half-dozen fistfights. In retrospect, my shyness of combat has clear sources.

As a boy, I saw countless tough guys locked away; I have since buried several, too. They were babies, really—a teenage cousin, a brother of twenty-two, a childhood friend in his mid-twenties—all gone down in episodes of bravado played out in the streets. I came to doubt the virtues of intimidation early on. I chose, perhaps unconsciously, to remain a shadow—timid, but a survivor.

The fearsomeness mistakenly attributed to me in public places often has a perilous flavor. The most frightening of these confusions occurred in the late 1970s and early 1980s, when I worked as a journalist in Chicago. One day, rushing into the office of a magazine I was writing for with a deadline story in hand, I was mistaken for a burglar. The office manager called security and, with an ad hoc° posse, pursued me through the labyrinthine halls, nearly to my editor's door. I had no way of proving who I was. I could only move briskly toward the company of someone who knew me.

---

**warrenlike:** Like a maze.     **ad hoc:** Spur of the moment.

Another time I was on assignment for a local paper and killing time before an interview. I entered a jewelry store on the city's affluent Near North Side. The proprietor excused herself and returned with an enormous red Doberman pinscher straining at the end of a leash. She stood, the dog extended toward me, silent to my questions, her eyes bulging nearly out of her head. I took a cursory look around, nodded, and bade her good night. 9

Relatively speaking, however, I never fared as badly as another black male journalist. He went to nearby Waukegan, Illinois, a couple of summers ago to work on a story about a murderer who was born there. Mistaking the reporter for the killer, police officers hauled him from his car at gunpoint and but for his press credentials would probably have tried to book him. Such episodes are not uncommon. Black men trade tales like this all the time. 10

Over the years, I learned to smother the rage I felt at so often being taken for a criminal. Not to do so would surely have led to madness. I now take precautions to make myself less threatening. I move about with care, particularly late in the evening. I give a wide berth° to nervous people on subway platforms during the wee hours, particularly when I have exchanged business clothes for jeans. If I happen to be entering a building behind some people who appear skittish, I may walk by, letting them clear the lobby before I return, so as not to seem to be following them. I have been calm and extremely congenial° on those rare occasions when I've been pulled over by the police. 11

And on late-evening constitutionals° I employ what has proved to be an excellent tension-reducing measure: I whistle melodies from Beethoven and Vivaldi and the more popular classical composers. Even steely New Yorkers hunching toward nighttime destinations seem to relax, and occasionally they even join in the tune. Virtually everybody seems to sense that a mugger wouldn't be warbling bright, sunny selections from Vivaldi's *Four Seasons*. It is my equivalent of the cowbell that hikers wear when they know they are in bear country. 12

**berth:** Space. **congenial:** Sociable. **constitutionals:** Walks taken for the purpose of pleasure or health.

## Questions to Start You Thinking

1. **Considering Meaning:** What misconceptions do people have about Staples because he is a young black man? What does he feel causes such misconceptions?

2. **Identifying Writing Strategies:** At the end of the essay, how does Staples use comparison to explain his behavior?

3. **Reading Critically:** What kinds of appeals—emotional, logical, ethical—does Staples use? Are his appeals appropriate for the purpose of his essay? Why, or why not? (For an explanation of kinds of appeals, see pp. 166–67.)

4. **Expanding Vocabulary:** Define *affluent, uninflammatory* (paragraph 1), *unwieldy, quarry, errant* (paragraph 2), *bandolier, solace* (paragraph 5), *lethality*

(paragraph 6), *bravado* (paragraph 7), and *labyrinthine* (paragraph 8). Why do you think Staples uses such formal language in this essay?

5. **Making Connections:** How might Julie Zeilinger's assertions about how society views masculinity in "Guys Suffer from Oppressive Gender Roles Too" (pp. 516–18) help to explain the way Staples is perceived in public?

## Journal Prompts

1. Are stereotypes ever useful? Why, or why not?

2. Have you or someone you know ever been wrongfully stereotyped or prejudged? How did you feel? How did you react?

## Suggestions for Writing

1. Staples describes his feelings about being the object of racial fear. Have you or someone you know ever been the object of that fear or other misconceptions based on prejudice or stereotyping? Write a short personal essay discussing the causes and effects of the experience. What preconceptions were involved? How did you or your acquaintance respond?

2. What do you think causes the stereotype of African American men that Staples is addressing? Write an essay that analyzes this stereotype, drawing on several outside sources to support your analysis.

# Judy Brady

## I Want a Wife

Judy Brady was born in 1937 in San Francisco, where she now makes her home. A graduate of the University of Iowa, Brady has contributed to various publications, including the *Women's Review of Books* and *Greenpeace* magazine, and has traveled to Cuba to study class relationships and education. She edited the book *1 in 3: Women with Cancer Confront an Epidemic* (1991), drawing on her own struggle with the disease, and she continues to write and speak about cancer and its possible environmental causes. In the following piece, reprinted frequently since it appeared in *Ms.* magazine in December 1971, Brady considers the role of the American housewife. While she has said that she is "not a 'writer,'" this essay shows Brady to be a satirist adept at taking a stand and provoking attention.

Judy Brady.

**AS YOU READ:** Ask yourself why Brady says she wants a wife rather than a husband.

belong to that classification of people known as wives. I am A Wife. And,   1
not altogether incidentally,° I am a mother.

**incidentally:** By chance or as an aside.

Not too long ago a male friend of mine appeared on the scene fresh from a recent divorce. He had one child, who is, of course, with his ex-wife. He is looking for another wife. As I thought about him while I was ironing one evening, it suddenly occurred to me that I, too, would like to have a wife. Why do I want a wife?

I would like to go back to school so that I can become economically independent, support myself, and, if need be, support those dependent upon me. I want a wife who will work and send me to school. And while I am going to school I want a wife to take care of my children. I want a wife to keep track of the children's doctor and dentist appointments. And to keep track of mine, too. I want a wife to make sure my children eat properly and are kept clean. I want a wife who will wash the children's clothes and keep them mended. I want a wife who is a good nurturant° attendant to my children, who arranges for their schooling, makes sure that they have an adequate social life with their peers, takes them to the park, the zoo, etc. I want a wife who takes care of the children when they are sick, a wife who arranges to be around when the children need special care, because, of course, I cannot miss classes at school. My wife must arrange to lose time at work and not lose the job. It may mean a small cut in my wife's income from time to time, but I guess I can tolerate that. Needless to say, my wife will arrange and pay for the care of the children while my wife is working.

I want a wife who will take care of *my* physical needs. I want a wife who will keep my house clean. A wife who will pick up after my children, a wife who will pick up after me. I want a wife who will keep my clothes clean, ironed, mended, replaced when need be, and who will see to it that my personal things are kept in their proper place so that I can find what I need the minute I need it. I want a wife who cooks the meals, a wife who is a *good* cook. I want a wife who will plan the menus, do the necessary grocery shopping, prepare the meals, serve them pleasantly, and then do the cleaning up while I do my studying. I want a wife who will care for me when I am sick and sympathize with my pain and loss of time from school. I want a wife to go along when our family takes a vacation so that someone can continue to care for me and my children when I need a rest and change of scene.

I want a wife who will not bother me with rambling complaints about a wife's duties. But I want a wife who will listen to me when I feel the need to explain a rather difficult point I have come across in my course of studies.

I want a wife who will take care of the details of my social life. When my wife and I are invited out by my friends, I want a wife who will take care of the babysitting arrangements. When I meet people at school that I like and want to entertain, I want a wife who will have the house clean, will prepare a special meal, serve it to me and my friends, and not interrupt when I talk about things that interest me and my friends. I want a wife who will have arranged that the children are fed and ready for bed before my guests arrive so that the children do not bother us. I want a wife who takes care of the needs

nurturant: Kind, loving, caring.

of my guests so that they feel comfortable, who makes sure that they have an ashtray, that they are passed the hors d'oeuvres, that they are offered a second helping of the food, that their wine glasses are replenished when necessary, that their coffee is served to them as they like it. And I want a wife who knows that sometimes I need a night out by myself.

I want a wife who is sensitive to my sexual needs, a wife who makes love   7
passionately and eagerly when I feel like it, a wife who makes sure that I am satisfied. And, of course, I want a wife who will not demand sexual attention when I am not in the mood for it. I want a wife who assumes the complete responsibility for birth control, because I do not want more children. I want a wife who will remain sexually faithful to me so that I do not have to clutter up my intellectual life with jealousies. And I want a wife who understands that *my* sexual needs may entail more than strict adherence to monogamy.° I must, after all, be able to relate to people as fully as possible.

If, by chance, I find another person more suitable as a wife than the wife I   8
already have, I want the liberty to replace my present wife with another one. Naturally, I will expect a fresh, new life; my wife will take the children and be solely responsible for them so that I am left free.

When I am through with school and have a job, I want my wife to quit   9
working and remain at home so that my wife can more fully and completely take care of a wife's duties.

My God, who *wouldn't* want a wife?   10

**monogamy:** Sexual relationship with only one partner.

## Questions to Start You Thinking

1. **Considering Meaning:** How does Brady define the traditional role of the wife? Does she think that a wife should perform all of the duties she outlines? How can you tell?

2. **Identifying Writing Strategies:** How does Brady use observation to support her stand? What other approaches does she use?

3. **Reading Critically:** What is the tone or attitude of this essay? How does Brady establish it? Considering that she was writing for a predominantly female—and feminist—audience, do you think Brady's tone is appropriate?

4. **Expanding Vocabulary:** Why does Brady use such simple language in this essay? What is the effect of her use of such phrases as *of course* (paragraph 2), *Needless to say* (paragraph 3), and *Naturally* (paragraph 8)?

5. **Making Connections:** Both Brady and Julie Zeilinger in "Guys Suffer from Oppressive Gender Roles Too" (pp. 516–18) use humor to discuss gender stereotypes. Evaluate their use of humor. Whose is more effective? Why?

## Journal Prompts

1. Exert your wishful thinking—describe your ideal mate.

2. Begin with a stereotype of a husband, wife, boyfriend, girlfriend, father, or mother, and write a satirical description of that stereotype.

## Suggestions for Writing

1. In a short personal essay, explain what you want or expect in a wife, husband, or life partner. Do your hopes and expectations differ from social and cultural norms? If so, in what way(s)? How has your parents' relationship shaped your attitudes and ideals?

2. How has the role of a wife changed since this essay was written? Write an essay comparing and contrasting the twenty-first-century wife with the kind of wife Judy Brady claims she wants.

## Cindi May

### The Problem with Female Superheroes

Cindi May is a professor of psychology at the College of Charleston. Her research focuses on cognitive function in students, the elderly, and those with special needs, and she currently directs a Department of Education TPSID grant studying intellectually disabled students in postsecondary education. May has published several articles in psychology journals including *Aging, Neuropsychology, & Cognition*; *Psychonomic Bulletin and Review Journal of Policy*; and *Practice for Intellectual Disability*, as well as *Scientific American* and *Salon*. In the following article, first published in *Scientific American* on June 23, 2015, May discusses the negative impact of the media's depiction of female superheroes.

Cynthia May.

**AS YOU READ:** How do films depict female superheroes? How has this depiction evolved in the last thirty years?

What do you want to be when you grow up? When pondering this question, most kids have given at least passing consideration to one fantastical if improbable calling: superhero. There is an understandable allure to the superhero position—wearing a special uniform (possibly with powerful accessories), saving the world from evil, and let's not forget possessing a wickedly cool special power like X-ray vision or the ability to fly. 1

But new research by Hillary Pennell and Elizabeth Behm-Morawitz at the University of Missouri suggests that, at least for women, the influence of superheroes is not always positive. Although women play a variety of roles in the superhero genre, including helpless maiden and powerful heroine, the female characters all tend to be hypersexualized, from their perfect, voluptuous° figures to their sexy, revealing attire. Exposure to 2

**voluptuous:** Curvaceous.

this, they show, can impact beliefs about gender roles, body esteem, and self-objectification.°

Consider, for example, superhero movies like *Spider-Man* or *Superman*. 3 These action-packed films typically feature a strong, capable, intelligent man fighting a villainous force. The goal of course is to save humanity, but more often than not there is also an immediate need to rescue a damsel in distress. The female victim is typically delicate, naive, and defenseless, but at the same time sexy and beautiful. What she lacks in strength and cunning she makes up for in kindness and curves. It is not surprising (or insignificant) that she is often the object of the hero's affections.

Pennell and Behm-Morawitz posited that exposure to these stereotypic 4 female victims, whose primary appeal is sexual, may lower women's body esteem, heighten the value they place on body image, and result in less egalitarian° gender role beliefs and expectations. However, female characters have come a long way in the superhero genre, and it's possible that the antidote° to the help-less fair maiden is the competent, commanding superheroine. The *X-Men* films, for example, feature a number of empowering female characters like Storm, Jean Gray, and Dazzler, each of whom wields a unique special ability and displays im-pressive cognitive and physical competence. Perhaps exposure to this new gen-eration of female heroines will result in more egalitarian gender beliefs, higher body esteem, and greater prioritization of physical competence over appearance.

Still, today's superheroines, like their female victim counterparts, are 5 often unrealistic, sexualized representations of female figures, with large chests, curvaceous backsides, and unattainable hourglass dimensions. Their skin-tight outfits accentuate their sexuality with plunging necklines and bare skin, and many of their names (e.g., Risque, Mystique, Ruby Summers) connote, shall we say, a slightly less respectable profession than superheroine.

Pennell and Behm-Morawitz thus speculated that while today's powerful 6 superheroines might elevate egalitarian beliefs about gender roles, their sexu-alized nature might simultaneously have destructive effects on body image and self-objectification.

To explore the effects of watching sexualized female victims and hero- 7 ines, Pennell and Behm-Morawitz asked female college students to watch a thirteen-minute video montage of scenes that either featured female victims from the *Spider-Man* series or female heroines from the *X-Men* series. After watching one of these video montages, participants completed a survey that assessed gender role beliefs, body image, and self-objectification. A num-ber of other measures (e.g., moviegoing habits, enjoyment of different film genres) were included to camouflage the purpose of the study, and in a control condition, participants simply completed the survey but did not watch either film montage.

Gender role beliefs were assessed via the Attitudes toward Women Scale, 8 which evaluated participants' views about men's and women's responsibilities

---

**objectification:** The act of regarding as an object or instrument.    **egalitarian:** Affirming of equal rights.    **antidote:** A counteractive remedy.

at home and in the workplace, appropriate attire and appearance in public, rationality and problem-solving skills, and physical strength. Body image was measured using the Body Esteem Scale, which requires individuals to rate personal satisfaction with general appearance and specific body parts (e.g., face, chest, thighs). Finally, the Self-Objectification Questionnaire required participants to indicate the importance of their body image and body competence to their personal identity.

9    Relative to participants in the control condition, those who viewed the sexualized-victim female character did indeed report less egalitarian gender beliefs. Thus, women who watched the *Spider-Man* montage were less likely to agree with statements such as, "Men and women should share household work equally," and more likely to agree with statements such as, "Men are better at taking on mental challenges than women." They did not, however, experience drops in body esteem or rate the importance of body appearance more highly. It seems that watching the beauty-in-need-of-rescue reinforced traditional gender roles, but did not create the desire to appear more like her physically.

10    What happened when women instead watched the agile and proficient superheroines? Did these characters serve to empower women? Sadly, no. The superheroine montage did nothing to improve egalitarian views about gender roles, though at least it did not lower those views. Pennell and Behm-Morawitz argue that the sexualization of the superheroine characters serves to reinforce rather than challenge stereotypical gender role beliefs, and this effect may overshadow any benefit derived from observing a strong, intelligent, capable female character.

11    Watch out, as these superheroines pack a bigger punch: Relative to control participants, women who watched the *X-Men* montage reported lower body esteem. They also ranked the importance of physical competence more highly. Pennell and Behm-Morawitz suggest that women may admire the power and status of superheroines and consequently desire to emulate° them. Because these sexualized superheroines have unattainable body dimensions and engage in unrealistic physical feats (e.g., saving the world in spiked heels), it's not surprising that female viewers are left feeling dissatisfied with their own physical appearance and prowess.

12    Thus, while the roles for women in superhero movies have evolved from the helpless, easy mark to the commanding, mighty protector, the central appeal of these characters as sexual goddesses is the same. As a consequence, the superheroines, like their victim counterparts, are undermining rather than improving women's perceptions of their own bodies and physical competence. And they are doing nothing to improve beliefs about women's roles in society.

13    These new findings add to a growing literature demonstrating that the gender-related information conveyed in popular media can affect personal perceptions and cultural standards about gender. Expectations and attitudes about gender roles are shaped by a variety of entertainment media, from superhero movies and G-rated children's films to music videos, advertisements,

**emulate:** Successfully imitate.

and video games. One recent study even found that regular viewers of a reality television show featuring pregnant teens had more favorable attitudes about teen pregnancy and believed that the benefits of teen pregnancy outweigh the risks. Clearly the things we watch, even if fantastical or sensationalized, affect our beliefs. Superhero movies and other forms of entertainment, which are often viewed as a temporary escape from reality, may in fact be shaping our realities in ways that are more harmful than heroic.

## Questions to Start You Thinking

1. **Considering Meaning:** According to May, what are the negative effects of female superheroes?

2. **Identifying Writing Strategies:** What kind of evidence does May use to support her conclusion in the last paragraph that "superhero movies and other forms of entertainment . . . may in fact be shaping our realities in ways that are more harmful than heroic"? Does her evidence prove her point? What other types of evidence could she have used?

3. **Reading Critically:** After reading about the results of the study conducted by Hillary Pennell and Elizabeth Behm-Morawitz as outlined in the article, explain how watching female superheroes can impact a woman's self-image as well as her conclusions about gender roles.

4. **Expanding Vocabulary:** What does *egalitarian* mean? What "egalitarian beliefs" is May referring to in paragraph 6?

5. **Making Connections:** Compare and contrast the stereotypical images in May's essay with those in Robert Jensen's "The High Cost of Manliness" (pp. 512–14). Are the negative effects explored in these two essays similar?

## Journal Prompts

1. Do you watch movies with female superheroes? Why, or why not? Why do you think these movies are so popular with American audiences?

2. May admits in paragraph 12 that "the roles for women in superhero movies have evolved from the helpless, easy mark to the commanding, mighty protector." Do you see a similar evolution of women's roles in other forms of media? Do some forms of media present more traditional gender roles than others?

## Suggestions for Writing

1. May notes the impact that media can have on "personal perceptions and cultural standards about gender" (paragraph 13). Write an essay that explores the cultural impact of successful women and media icons such as comedian Amy Schumer and actress Melissa McCarthy.

2. Look at advertisements for clothes and makeup in fashion magazines. How would you describe the women that appear in these ads? Write an essay about the studies that have been conducted on how these ads affect young girls' attitudes about their bodies.

# Robert Jensen

## The High Cost of Manliness

Robert Jensen.

Robert Jensen was born in 1958 and grew up in Fargo, North Dakota. After earning a BA in social studies and secondary education from Moorhead State University and graduate degrees in journalism, Jensen started his career as a newspaper journalist. Now a professor of journalism at the University of Texas at Austin, he teaches courses on media law, ethics, and politics and also regularly contributes to a variety of publications. His recent books include *The Heart of Whiteness: Confronting Race, Racism, and White Privilege* (2005), *Getting Off: Pornography and the End of Masculinity* (2007), and *Plain Radical: Living, Loving, and Learning to Leave the Planet Gracefully* (2015). He also coproduced the documentary film *Abe Osheroff: One Foot in the Grave, the Other Still Dancing* (2008). In the following essay, which first appeared on *Alternet.org* in September 2006, Jensen calls for abandoning the prevailing definition of masculinity, arguing that it is "toxic" to both men and women.

**AS YOU READ:** Identify what Jensen sees as the dominant conception of masculinity in contemporary culture. What does he think of this conception?

It's hard to be a man; hard to live up to the demands that come with the dominant conception of masculinity, of the tough guy. 1

So, guys, I have an idea — maybe it's time we stop trying. Maybe this masculinity thing is a bad deal, not just for women but for us. 2

We need to get rid of the whole idea of masculinity. It's time to abandon the claim that there are certain psychological or social traits that inherently come with being biologically male. If we can get past that, we have a chance to create a better world for men and women. 3

The dominant conception of masculinity in U.S. culture is easily summarized: men are assumed to be naturally competitive and aggressive, and being a real man is therefore marked by the struggle for control, conquest, and domination. A man looks at the world, sees what he wants, and takes it. Men who don't measure up are wimps, sissies, fags, girls. The worst insult one man can hurl at another — whether it's boys on the playground or CEOs in the boardroom — is the accusation that a man is like a woman. Although the culture acknowledges that men can in some situations have traits traditionally associated with women (caring, compassion, tenderness), in the end it is men's strength-expressed-as-toughness that defines us and must trump any femalelike softness. Those aspects of masculinity must prevail° for a man to be a "real man." 4

**prevail:** Dominate.

That's not to suggest, of course, that every man adopts that view of mas-   5
culinity. But it is endorsed in key institutions and activities — most notably
in business, the military, and athletics — and is reinforced through the mass
media. It is particularly expressed in the way men — straight and gay alike —
talk about sexuality and act sexually. And our culture's male heroes reflect
those characteristics: they most often are men who take charge rather than
seek consensus,° seize power rather than look for ways to share it, and are
willing to be violent to achieve their goals.

That view of masculinity is dangerous for women. It leads men to seek to   6
control "their" women and define their own pleasure in that control, which
leads to epidemic levels of rape and battery. But this view of masculinity is
toxic for men as well.

If masculinity is defined as conquest, it means that men will always   7
struggle with each other for dominance. In a system premised on hierarchy°
and power, there can be only one king of the hill. Every other man must in
some way be subordinated° to the king, and the king has to always be nervous about who is coming up that hill to get him. A friend who once worked
on Wall Street — one of the preeminent° sites of masculine competition —
described coming to work as like walking into a knife fight when all the good
spots along the wall were taken. Masculinity like this is life lived as endless
competition and threat.

No one man created this system, and perhaps none of us, if given a choice,   8
would choose it. But we live our lives in that system, and it deforms men, narrowing our emotional range and depth. It keeps us from the rich connections
with others — not just with women and children, but other men — that make life
meaningful but require vulnerability.

This doesn't mean that the negative consequences of this toxic masculin-   9
ity are equally dangerous for men and women. As feminists have long pointed
out, there's a big difference between women dealing with the possibility of being
raped, beaten, and killed by the men in their lives and men not being able to cry.
But we can see that the short-term material gains that men get are not adequate
compensation for what we men give up in the long haul — which is to surrender
part of our humanity to the project of dominance.

Of course there are obvious physical differences between men and   10
women — average body size, hormones, reproductive organs. There may be
other differences rooted in our biology that we don't yet understand. Yet it's
also true that men and women are more similar than we are different, and that
given the pernicious° effects of centuries of patriarchy° and its relentless de-
valuing of things female, we should be skeptical of the perceived differences.

What we know is simple: in any human population, there is wide indi-   11
vidual variation. While there's no doubt that a large part of our behavior is
rooted in our DNA, there's also no doubt that our genetic endowment is

consensus: Agreement.    hierarchy: A grouping based on relative rank.    subordinated:
Lowered in rank.    preeminent: Most important.    pernicious: Destructive.    patriarchy:
Social organization in which the father is supreme; male control of most of the power in a
society.

highly influenced by culture. Beyond that, it's difficult to say much with any certainty. It's true that only women can bear children and breast-feed. That fact likely has some bearing on aspects of men's and women's personalities. But we don't know much about what the effect is, and given the limits of our tools to understand human behavior, it's possible we may never know much.

At the moment, the culture seems obsessed with gender differences, in the context of a recurring intellectual fad (called "evolutionary psychology" this time around, and "sociobiology" in a previous incarnation) that wants to explain all complex behaviors as simple evolutionary adaptations—if a pattern of human behavior exists, it must be because it's adaptive in some ways. In the long run, that's true by definition. But in the short term it's hardly a convincing argument to say, "Look at how men and women behave so differently; it must be because men and women are fundamentally different," when a political system has been creating differences between men and women. 12

From there, the argument that we need to scrap masculinity is fairly simple. To illustrate it, remember back to right after 9/11. A number of commentators argued that criticisms of masculinity should be rethought. Cannot we now see—recognizing that male firefighters raced into burning buildings, risking and sometimes sacrificing their lives to save others—that masculinity can encompass a kind of strength that is rooted in caring and sacrifice? Of course men often exhibit such strength, just as do women. So, the obvious question arises: What makes these distinctly masculine characteristics? Are they not simply human characteristics? 13

We identify masculine tendencies toward competition, domination, and violence because we see patterns of differential behavior; men are more prone to such behavior in our culture. We can go on to observe and analyze the ways in which men are socialized to behave in those ways, toward the goal of changing those destructive behaviors. That analysis is different than saying that admirable human qualities present in both men and women are somehow primarily the domain of one gender. To assign them to a gender is misguided and demeaning° to the gender that is then assumed not to possess them to the same degree. Once we start saying "strength and courage are masculine traits," it leads to the conclusion that woman are not as strong or courageous. 14

Of course, if we are going to jettison° masculinity, we have to scrap femininity along with it. We have to stop trying to define what men and women are going to be in the world based on extrapolations° from physical sex differences. That doesn't mean we ignore those differences when they matter, but we have to stop assuming they matter everywhere. 15

I don't think the planet can long survive if the current conception of masculinity endures. We face political and ecological challenges that can't be met with this old model of what it means to be a man. At the more intimate level, the stakes are just as high. For those of us who are biologically male, we have a simple choice: we men can settle for being men, or we can strive to be human beings. 16

---

**demeaning:** Making less of.   **jettison:** Throw out.   **extrapolations:** Predictions.

## Questions to Start You Thinking

1. **Considering Meaning:** What does Jensen see as the negative consequences of the commonly held idea of masculinity?

2. **Identifying Writing Strategies:** Where in the essay does Jensen use comparison and contrast in writing about men and women? What is his point in doing so?

3. **Reading Critically:** In paragraph 5, Jensen admits that not all men conceive of masculinity in terms of competition and aggression. Do you think he goes on to provide enough evidence to support his claim that this view of masculinity is dominant in U.S. culture? Why, or why not?

4. **Expanding Vocabulary:** In paragraph 12, Jensen refers to the current obsession with gender differences in the United States taking shape as a "recurring intellectual fad." What does he mean by this phrase? What does it add to his argument?

5. **Making Connections:** According to Jensen, "toxic masculinity" (paragraph 9) results from a "political system" that creates "differences between men and women" (paragraph 12). Do you think Brent Staples ("Black Men and Public Space," pp. 502–04) would agree? How are views of black men shaped—or even created—by society? How does the category of race complicate Jensen's analysis?

## Link to the Paired Essay

In paragraph 4, Jensen summarizes the "dominant conception of masculinity in U.S. culture." Would Zeilinger ("Guys Suffer from Oppressive Gender Roles Too," pp. 516–18) agree with his definition of masculinity? Consider where their definitions overlap and whether they differ on any points.

## Journal Prompts

1. Do you agree, as Jensen puts it, that the "worst insult one man can hurl at another . . . is the accusation that a man is like a woman" (paragraph 4)? What do you think about insults that liken a woman to a man?

2. In the essay's final paragraph, Jensen writes that he doesn't think "the planet can long survive if the current conception of masculinity endures." How do you respond to this statement?

## Suggestions for Writing

1. Jensen writes in paragraph 13 about the idea of strength. In an essay, discuss how you define *human strength,* considering the physical, the intellectual, and the emotional.

2. Jensen acknowledges that gender differences are in some part determined by biological factors. However, he is more concerned about the influence

of social conditioning. Write an essay analyzing how a particular social force does or does not contribute to stereotypes of masculinity and femininity. For example, you might consider the influence of some aspect of popular culture, education, sports, or children's toys. Use examples from your experience as well as other evidence to support your point.

Julie Zeilinger.

## Julie Zeilinger

### Guys Suffer from Oppressive Gender Roles Too

Julie Zeilinger founded *The F Bomb*, a critically acclaimed feminist blog that focuses on women's rights, and has published articles in the *Huffington Post*, *Feminist.com*, and *Skirt Magazine*. In 2012, her book *A Little F'd Up: Why Feminism Is Not a Dirty Word* was published. She was named one of the 2016 *Forbes* 30 Under 30 ("the brightest young entrepreneurs, breakout talents, and change agents"). In the following selection, Zeilinger insists that men should be allowed to express their emotions.

**AS YOU READ:** How does Zeilinger contrast internal pressures and external expectations?

Guys are supposed to be rocks, inside and out. They are supposed to be defined more by their muscles and brute force than by any complex or unique personality trait. Ideally, they should physically be so steely and impervious° that they could plausibly be cast in a Transformers film . . . as an actual alien Transformer. If we were to look inside these ideal men, we'd find a tangled mess of barbed wire encapsulating° a ravenous° lion decapitating a tiny bunny. There would probably be a camouflage color scheme thrown in there too. Guys *certainly* aren't allowed to let the world see that they do in fact have emotions. No, they throw those feelings to the feral° beast within. 1

But here's the problem: Guys *do* have emotions. Guys live an external reality that is in complete contradiction with their internal reality. So what can guys do when they experience real honest-to-god feelings? Well, for those who try to adhere° to these masculinity standards to their utmost ability, they have to disconnect. They must detach themselves from their emotions. And it's not just emotions like "sad" or "ecstatic." It's emotions like "empathy" and "sympathy," which, when you think about it, is pretty damn scary. So guys can either detach and live a life numb to a true range of human emotion, or live in a state of contradiction. Not the greatest options. 2

The woes of men don't end there. Oh no. On top of embodying° various types of metals inside and out, guys must also be "successful." But the definition of male success is quite elusive.° It doesn't necessarily mean having a 3

**impervious:** Not vulnerable.   **encapsulating:** Surrounding.   **ravenous:** Very hungry.
**feral:** Wild.   **adhere:** Stick to.   **embodying:** Physically representing.   **elusive:** Hard to pin down.

great, loving family and friends who care about you. It's probably not about becoming an abstract painter, or being the type of passionate, energetic high school teacher who inspires a group of jaded and self-defeating inner-city kids to want more for themselves via the power of the pen and self-expression. No. In order to be successful, guys must be cunning.° They must get ahead of others in order to obtain success, which is usually defined by two things: money and power. In fact, though I kind of hate to use the word "winning" (Charlie Sheen connotations abound), it has become kind of synonymous with "masculinity."

Men feel as much competition and pressure as women do. They have to     4
be strong. They must conceal their emotions. They need to obtain wealth and power. But while we ladies generally deal with this pressure internally, forcing ourselves to get excellent grades and taking out our issues on our bodies, guys are far more external in their expression of the same pressures and competition.

Why do guys like violent video games so much? Why do they feel the     5
need to physically fight (or at least threaten to), even over the stupidest stuff, in a way girls rarely do? Why do they put younger guys through ridiculous hazing, which ranges from gross and uncomfortable (I've heard of senior athletes forcing underclassmen players to eat ten Big Macs in less than ten minutes) to the seriously violent and dangerous (being beaten with two-by-fours)? Better yet, why do they subject themselves to such degrading° abuse at all?

Guys engage in violent activities (whether simulated or real) as a way     6
to release the pressure, but also, circuitously,° as a way to prove their masculinity—as a way to make that competition with other guys an actuality. Guys strictly monitor each other to sniff out and point out "weaknesses" in other guys, which gives them some illusion of feeling stronger and more masculine.

I've always suspected that's why guys love telling jokes about women and     7
gay guys. Even if a guy swears up and down he's not sexist or homophobic, by telling these jokes he is, at the very least, reminding the world he's a straight dude—clearly not the alternatives, which he so disdains.°

And what about guys who dare to take on qualities that could be considered feminine? Like, for instance, guys who care about their appearance, who     8
wear tight clothes, or who are just generally considered "effeminate"? Well, those men are threats. For guys clinging to masculinity standards for dear life, who use those guidelines as a complete roadmap for how to exist in the world, they're terrifying. For some guys, it's a seriously deep terror rooted in the threat of losing their own identity. They see other guys rejecting what has been prescribed of them based on their gender, and they're terrified of the consequences of doing the same. Because if they were to really examine themselves, if they were to reject the masculinity standards that shape their entire

---

**cunning:** Crafty or tricky.   **degrading:** Humiliating or dehumanizing.   **circuitously:** Indirectly.   **disdains:** Regards as inferior.

identity and personality, then they might just find that they never actually had an identity to begin with. And really, what's scarier than that?

But forget the implications for jerks who give any guy who refuses to live up to masculinity standards a hard time. Let's consider how this actually affects the guys who reject traditional masculinity standards. Specifically, let's consider gay men. I asked a young gay friend of mine about his experience, and he had some pretty eloquent things to say. 9

"Being a gay man has instilled a sense of displacement, no matter where I may be, or who I'm with," he said. As a man, he explained, he feels the pressure to meet masculinity standards—which he (and other gay men) may manifest° by engaging in and promoting promiscuity. But he also feels a kinship with women, as he understands what it's like to be marginalized.° "Being a gay man [means] trying to overcome both male and female stigmas," he said. "Gay men and feminists have similar ambitions, but it's hard, because gay men are ultimately men, so they have to strive to promote a sense of masculinity that works for them *and* goes hand-in-hand with the feminist doctrine° of personal pride and worth." 10

And that's how a gay man feels in the context of an overall peaceful and unbothered state. That's not even considering what happens when bullying, violent hate crimes, and homophobia at large get thrown into the mix. 11

In this society, adhering to the standards imposed by masculinity means never developing your true identity, never taking the opportunity to find out who you really are. Expressing feelings and exploring interests—including things that aren't strictly "manly"—are part of being human. But if you want to be the stereotypical man, you have to forget about those things. Just like we girls have to forget about enjoying food and having interests outside of shopping and boys. 12

Sometimes when I look around and see all of my peers, guys and girls alike, desperately trying to live up to their prescribed gender roles, often at the expense of their own well-being, I feel like I'm crazy. I wonder, *Am I the only one who didn't get the memo? Should I be more preoccupied with how many calories are in my food than the fact that it's buttery and delicious and my stomach is so happy it's as if there is a wild conga line proceeding through it? Should I be spending more time trying to get a boyfriend? Is that what life is about?* 13

And I'm sure there are guys who wonder these things too. Who look around and see how they're expected to put as many hours into ESPN and the weight room as they do into basic functions like sleeping and eating, all so that they can talk the talk and walk the walk. *Is this really it?* they must think. *Is this all we're supposed to care about? Things like sex, sports, and food? Of all the things available to us in this world, even if those things are great, are these the only things we're able to come away with?* 14

---

**manifest:** Exhibit.   **marginalized:** Pushed to the edges of society.   **doctrine:** System of beliefs.

## Questions to Start You Thinking

1. **Considering Meaning:** Zeilinger considers many ways in which gender standards can be harmful. What positive effects would men see if they could escape from these expectations? What could men do in a world without rigid gender roles?

2. **Identifying Writing Strategies:** Zeilinger uses humor to point out the excesses of gender roles for men. Where do you think her humor is most effective? What truths about masculinity does she reveal in her exaggerated description of "manly" men?

3. **Reading Critically:** The title of this selection implies a response to another argument or a received opinion. Summarize the assumption about gender roles to which Zeilinger responds. What points in the essay refer to this assumption?

4. **Expanding Vocabulary:** Zeilinger describes her disappointment when she sees her peers struggling with their "prescribed gender roles" (paragraph 13). What does it mean for something to be *prescribed*? How does this word apply to gender norms?

5. **Making Connections:** Both Zeilinger and Cindi May in "The Problem with Female Superheroes" (pp. 508–11) challenge gender roles, insisting that they can be harmful to men as well as women. What rhetorical techniques does each author use to get her point across? Who do you think has the more effective argument? Why?

## Link to the Paired Essay

In the paired essay, Robert Jensen ("The High Cost of Manliness," pp. 512–14) makes an argument similar to Zeilinger's about the harm that comes from rigid notions of masculinity, but he makes his case from a man's point of view. How does the gender of the author affect each essay? How does Zeilinger's perspective differ from Jensen's?

## Journal Prompts

1. Zeilinger suggests that the definition of success that goes along with traditional ideas about masculinity is hollow or even destructive. Do you agree with her? How would you define success? In what ways does the kind of success you want for yourself match or defy what society values?

2. According to Zeilinger, men reinforce gender roles by pointing out "weaknesses" in other men (paragraph 6). This phenomenon may also be true for women who hold each other to feminine roles. Have you ever been on either end (or both ends) of this dynamic — being held by others to gender standards or helping to enforce them on your peers? Why do you think men and women play along with these roles?

## Suggestions for Writing

1. Zeilinger identifies masculinity standards as the cause of many problems for young men. Write an essay analyzing her claims about how rigid masculine roles affect men or how stereotypes change the way men feel and act. Do you agree with her assessment of the effects?

2. The argument of this essay is largely based on the author's personal observations of her peers. To what extent does more formal research about gender support her points? Find an article or a study that examines how gender roles affect young men or women, and write about how it supports (or challenges) Zeilinger's position.

Richard Baker/Corbis News/Corbis.

## Responding to an Image

Following Apple founder Steve Jobs's death in October 2011, mourners created a makeshift shrine outside the Apple Store on London's Regent Street. Examine and comment on the shrine itself. What do the objects included suggest about the mourners' relationships to Apple and their perceptions of Jobs and his place in our culture? Briefly describe your own use of Apple products and your reaction, if any, to Jobs's death. What do you make of the fact that passersby in the photo are capturing the memorial on their Apple iPhones?

## Kate Dailey and Abby Ellin

### America's War on the Overweight

Kate Dailey graduated from Pennsylvania State University and Columbia University's Graduate School of Journalism. She is currently the planning editor for BBC, North America edition. Abby Ellin has graduate degrees in creative writing from Emerson College and in international relations from Johns Hopkins. Her work has appeared in publications such as the *New York Times, Time,* the *Village Voice, Marie Claire, Glamour,* and the *Daily Beast.* She is also the author of *Teenage Waistland: A Former Fat Kid Weighs In on Living Large, Losing Weight, and How Parents Can (and Can't) Help* (2007). In this *Newsweek* essay, Dailey and Ellin grapple with the complicated issues surrounding weight and health in modern America.

**AS YOU READ:** According to the authors, why do so many people have a fat bias?

Practically the minute President Obama announced Regina M. Benjamin, a zaftig° doctor who also has an M.B.A. and is the recipient of a MacArthur "genius grant," as a nominee for the post of Surgeon General, the criticism started. 1

The attacks were vicious — Michael Karolchyk, owner of a Denver "anti-gym," told Fox News's Neil Cavuto, "Obesity is the No. 1 issue facing our country in terms of health and wellness, and she has shown not that she was born this way, not that she woke up one day and was obese. She has shown through being lazy, and making poor food choices, that she's obese." 2

"This is totally disgusting to have someone so big to be advocating health," wrote one YouTube commenter. 3

The anger about Benjamin wasn't the only example of vitriol° hurled at the overweight. Cintra Wilson, style columnist for the *New York Times,* recently wrote a column so disdainful of JCPenney's plus-size mannequins that the *Times*'s ombudsman° later wrote that he could read "a virtual sneer" coming through her prose. A *Newsweek* post about *Glamour*'s recent plus-size model (in fact, a normal-sized woman with a bit of a belly roll) had several commenters lashing out at the positive reaction the model was receiving. "This model issue is being used as a smoke screen to justify [a] self-destructive lifestyle that cost[s] me more money in health care costs," one wrote. Health guru MeMe Roth has made a career out of bashing fat — she called size 12 *American Idol* Jordin Sparks a "bad role model" on national television, and derided size 2 Jennifer Love Hewitt for having cellulite. (That Roth is considered something of an extremist doesn't stop the media attention.) Virtually any news article about weight that is posted online garners a slew of comments from readers expressing disgust that people let their weight get so out of control. The specific target may change, but the words stay the same: Self-destructive. Disgusting. Disgraceful. Shameful. While the debate rages on about obesity and the best ways to deal 4

**zaftig:** Full-bodied.    **vitriol:** Abusive and bitter thought or expression.    **ombudsman:** A person who investigates problems or complaints and attempts to resolve them.

with it, the attitudes Americans have toward those with extra pounds are only getting nastier. Just why do Americans hate fat people so much?

Fat bias is nothing new. "Public outrage at other people's obesity has a lot to do with America from the turn of the 20th century to about World War I," says Deborah Levine, assistant professor of health policy and management at Providence College. The rise of fat hatred is often seen as connected to the changing American workplace; in the early 20th century, companies began to offer snacks to employees, white-collar jobs became more prominent, and fewer people exercised. As thinness became rarer, says Peter N. Stearns, author of *Fat History: Bodies and Beauty in the Modern West* and professor of history at George Mason University, it was more prized, and conversely, fatness was more maligned.

At the same time, people also paid a lot of attention to President Taft's girth; while Taft was large, he wasn't all that much heavier than earlier presidents. Newspapers questioned how his weight would affect diplomacy and solicited the funniest "fat Taft" joke. "This [period] is also when you get ready-to-wear clothing," says Levine. "For the first time, [people were] buying clothes in a certain size, and that encourages a comparison amongst other people." Actuarial tables° began to connect weight and shorter lifespan, and cookbooks published around World War I targeted the overweight. "There was that idea that people who were overweight were hoarding resources needed for the war effort," Levine says. She adds that early concerns were that overweight American men would not be able to compete globally, participate in international business, or win wars.

Fatness has always been seen as a slight on the American character. Ours is a nation that values hard work and discipline, and it's hard for us to accept that weight could be not just a struggle of will, even when the bulk of the research — and often our own personal experience — shows that the factors leading to weight gain are much more than just simple gluttony. "There's this general perception that weight can be controlled if you have enough willpower, that it's just about calories in and calories out," says Dr. Glen Gaesser, professor of exercise and wellness at Arizona State University and author of *Big Fat Lies: The Truth about Your Weight and Your Health,* and that perception leads the nonfat to believe that the overweight are not just unhealthy, but weak and lazy. Even though research suggests that there is a genetic propensity for obesity, and even though some obese people are technically healthier than their skinnier counterparts, the perception remains "[that] it's a failure to control ourselves. It violates everything we have learned about self-control from a very young age," says Gaesser.

In a country that still prides itself on its Puritanical ideals, the fat self is the "bad self," the epitome° of greed, gluttony, and sloth. "There's a widespread belief that fat is controllable," says Linda Bacon, author of *Health at Every Size: The Surprising Truth about Your Weight.* "So then it's unlike a disability where you can have compassion; now you can blame the individual and

---

**actuarial tables:** Calculations and statistics used by insurance companies to determine life expectancy of their policyholders.     **epitome:** Perfect example.

attribute all kinds of mean qualities to them. Then consider the thinner people that are always watching what they eat carefully—fat people are symbols of what they can become if they weren't so virtuous."

But considering that the U.S. has already become a size XL nation— 9 66 percent of adults over 20 are considered overweight or obese, according to the Centers for Disease Control—why does the stigma,° and the anger, remain?

Call it a case of self-loathing. "A lot of people struggle themselves with 10 their weight, and the same people that tend to get very angry at themselves for not being able to manage their weight are more likely to be biased against the obese," says Marlene Schwartz, director of the Rudd Center for Food Policy and Obesity at Yale University. "I think that some of this is that anger is confusion between the anger that we have at ourselves and projecting that out onto other people." Her research indicates that younger women, who are under the most pressure to be thin and who are also the most likely to be self-critical, are the most likely to feel negatively toward fat people.

As many women's magazines' cover lines note, losing the last five pounds 11 can be a challenge. So why don't we have more compassion for people struggling to lose the first 50, 60, or 100? Some of it has to do with the psychological phenomenon known as the fundamental attribution error, a basic belief that whatever problems befall us personally are the result of difficult circumstances, while the same problems in other people are the result of their bad choices. Miss a goal at work? It's because the vendor was unreliable, and because your manager isn't giving you enough support, and because the power outage last week cut into premium sales time. That jerk next to you? He blew his quota because he's a bad planner, and because he spent too much time taking personal calls.

The same can be true of weight: "From working with so many people 12 struggling with their weight, I've seen it many times," says Andrew Geier, a postdoctoral fellow in the psychology department at Yale University. "They believe they're overweight due to a myriad of circumstances: as soon as my son goes to college, I'll have time to cook healthier meals; when my husband's shifts change at work, I can get to the gym sooner. . . ." But other people? They're overweight because they don't have the discipline to do the hard work and take off the weight, and that lack of discipline is an affront to our own hard work. (Never mind that weight loss is incredibly difficult to attain: Geier notes that even the most rigorous behavioral programs result in at most about a 12.5 percent decrease in weight, which would take a 350-pound man to a slimmer, but not svelte,° 306 pounds.)

But why do the rest of us care so much? What is it about fat people that 13 makes us so mad? As it turns out, we kind of like it. "People actually enjoy feeling angry," says Ryan Martin, associate professor of psychology at the

**stigma:** A mark of infamy or disgrace.     **svelte:** Gracefully slender.

University of Wisconsin, Green Bay, who cites studies done on people's emotions. "It makes them feel powerful, it makes them feel greater control, and they appreciate it for that reason." And with fat people designated as acceptable targets of rage — and with the prevalence of fat people in our lives, both in the malls and on the news — it's easy to find a target for some soul-clearing, ego-boosting ranting.

And it may be that, like those World War I–era cookbook writers, we feel 14 that obese people are robbing us of resources, whether it's space in a row of airline seats or our hard-earned tax dollars. Think of health care: when President Obama made reforming health care a priority, it led to an increased focus on obesity as a contributor to health-care costs. A recent article in *Health Affairs,* a public-policy journal, reported that obesity costs $147 billion a year, mainly in insurance premiums and taxes. At the same time, obesity-related diseases such as type 2 diabetes have spiked, and, while diabetes can be treated, treatment is expensive. So the overweight, some people argue, are costing all of us money while refusing to alter the behavior that has put them in their predicament in the first place (i.e., overeating and not exercising).

The reality is much more complicated. It's a fallacy to conflate the 15 unhealthy action — overeating and not exercising — with the unhealthy appearance, says Schwartz: some overweight people run marathons; eat only organic, vegetarian fare; and have clean bills of health. Even so, yelling at the overweight to put down the doughnut is far from productive. "People are less likely to seek out healthy behaviors when they're criticized by friends, family, doctors, and others," says Schwartz. "If people tell you that you're disgusting or a slob enough times, you soon start to believe it." In fact, fat outrage might actually make health-care costs higher. In a study published in the 2005 issue of the *Journal of Health Politics, Policy and Law,* Abigail Saguy and Brian Riley found that many overweight people decide not to get help for medical conditions that are more treatable and more risky than obesity because they don't want to deal with their doctor's harassment about their weight. (For instance, a study from the University of North Carolina found that obese women are less likely to receive cervical exams than their thinner counterparts, in part because they worry about being embarrassed or belittled by the doctor because of their weight.)

The bubbling rage against fat people in America has put researchers like 16 Levine in a difficult position. On the one hand, she says, she wants to ensure that obesity is taken seriously as a medical problem, and pointing out the costs associated with obesity-related illnesses helps illustrate the severity of the situation. On the other hand, she says, doing so could increase the animosity people have toward the overweight, many of whom may already live healthy lives or may be working hard to make healthier choices.

"The idea is to fight obesity and not obese people," she says, and then 17 pauses. "But it's very hard for many people to disentangle the two."

## Questions to Start You Thinking

1. **Considering Meaning:** What is "the fundamental attribution error" (paragraph 11)? Why is it significant for understanding negative attitudes toward overweight people?

2. **Identifying Writing Strategies:** The first four paragraphs of the article provide specific examples of "fat bias." How do they fit into the overall structure of the essay? Why do you think Dailey and Ellin chose these examples?

3. **Reading Critically:** The authors claim that "fat bias is nothing new" (paragraph 5). How effectively do they support this claim? How well do they connect contemporary "fat bias" with a longer historical tradition?

4. **Expanding Vocabulary:** According to one expert, "It's a fallacy to conflate the unhealthy action—overeating and not exercising—with the unhealthy appearance" (paragraph 15). What is a *fallacy*?

5. **Making Connections:** How are attitudes about those who deliver pizzas, explained in Sarah Adams's "Be Cool to the Pizza Dude" (pp. 580–81), similar to those experienced by the overweight in Dailey and Ellin's essay? What solutions does each essay offer to combat these negative attitudes?

## Journal Prompts

1. Do you agree that Americans believe in hard work, self-discipline, and willpower (paragraph 7) and expect such efforts to prevent weight gain? Explore why you agree, do not agree, or want to qualify this assertion.

2. According to the article, younger women are most pressured about weight, but that pressure seems to cross many demographic lines. Have you ever felt pressure to lose weight? Was it difficult or easy to do so? Did your experience give you any insight about weight, weight loss, or fat bias?

## Suggestions for Writing

1. According to one source in the article, people like being angry because that emotion boosts their sense of power (paragraph 13). Do you agree with this? Write a personal essay exploring why or how people experience anger.

2. Dailey and Ellin describe American hostility toward overweight people as a "bubbling rage" (paragraph 16), examining examples of "fat bias," its history in America, and its psychological origins. Investigate American culture through magazines, movies, music, books, television shows, or politics for evidence to support your own thesis in an essay about attitudes toward fatness and thinness.

# Adam Sternbergh

## Smile, You're Speaking Emoji

Adam Sternbergh is a journalist and contributing editor at *New York Magazine* and *Vulture* and the former culture editor of the *New York Times Magazine*. As an author, his *Shovel Ready,* a dystopian novel set in New York City, was a *Newsweek* Favorite Book of 2014 and a *Booklist* Best Crime Novel and Best Crime Debut of 2014. The novel was also nominated for a 2015 Edgar Award for Best First Novel by an American. Sternbergh grew up in Toronto and currently lives with his family in Brooklyn. In the following article, which appeared in the November 17, 2014, issue of *New York Magazine,* Sternbergh examines the reasons why emoji have become such a popular form of communication.

Marvin Orellana.

**AS YOU READ:** Why did emoji become so popular?

1  Consider the tilde. There it is, that little squiggle, hanging out on the far-upper-left-hand side of your computer keyboard. The symbol dates back to ancient Greece, though *tilde* comes from Spanish, and in modern English it's used to indicate "approximately" (e.g., ~30 years) or "equivalence" (x ~ y) in mathematics. And, as of this year, according to a breakdown of the Web site emojitracker by Luminoso, a text-analytics company, the tilde was surpassed in usage on Twitter by the emoji symbol for "joy." Which looks like this: 😂.

2  The Joy emoji — also referred to on the Emojipedia Web site as "Face with Tears of Joy" or "the LOL Emoji" (emoji don't have official names, just nicknames created by their users) — dates back, in North America, to roughly 2011, when Apple put a readily accessible emoji keyboard in iOS 5 for the iPhone. Which means that in three short years, Face with Tears of Joy vanquished the 3,000-year-old tilde.

3  And that's just one emoji. If we count all emoji together — Smiling Face 😃 and Smiling Face with Smiling Eyes 😊 and Grinning Face 😁 and Winking Face 😉 and Smiling Face with Heart-Shaped Eyes 😍 and Kissing Face 😗 and Kissing Face with Closed Eyes 😚 and Face with Stuck-Out Tongue with Tightly Closed Eyes 😝, not to mention House with Garden 🏡 and Convenience Store 🏪 and Tram 🚊 and Love Hotel 🏩 and Ghost 👻 and Money with Wings 💸 and Chart with Upward Trend 📈 and Hamburger 🍔 — then emoji, as a group, are now used more frequently on Twitter than are hyphens or the numeral 5.

4  All of which is to say: The 3,000-year-old tilde might want to consider rebranding itself as Invisible Man with Twirled Mustache.

5  It's easy to dismiss emoji. They are, at first glance, ridiculous. They are a small invasive cartoon army of faces and vehicles and flags and food and symbols trying to topple the millennia-long reign of words. Emoji are intended to illustrate, or in some cases replace altogether, the words we send each other digitally, whether in a text message, e-mail, or tweet. Taken

together, emoji look like the electronic equivalent of those puffy stickers tweens used to ornament their Trapper Keepers.°

And yet, if you have a smartphone, emoji are now available to you as an op-  6
tional written language, just like any global language, such as Arabic and Cat-
alan and Cherokee and Tamil and Tibetan and English. You'll find an emoji
keyboard on your iPhone, nestled right between Dutch and Estonian. . . .

In 2013, in response to the question "Do you use stickers or emoji in mes-  7
sage apps?" 74 percent of people in the United States and 82 percent in
China responded that they have. (Stickers are a kind of *faux* emoji—things
like *Seinfeld* emoji or the *Peanuts* characters you find on Facebook—that you
can send using certain apps but that aren't baked into Unicode.°) Over 470
million Joy emoji are being sent back and forth on Twitter right now—which
makes the Joy emoji the number 1 most popular emoji on Twitter (it tends
to compete for the top spot with the Heart). Lovers have successfully wooed
one another with emoji. Recruiters for ISIS are using emoji in their friendly
sounding, ISIS-promoting tweets. Someone put together a song-length
emoji-translation video of Beyoncé's "Drunk in Love," while someone else
translated R. Kelly's "Trapped in the Closet" into emoji, while someone else
translated all of *Moby-Dick* (titled, inevitably, *Emoji Dick*). There are no fewer
than three emoji-only social networks currently in development: Emojicate,
Emoji.li, and something called Steven. The Web site Emojinalysis will track
your recent emoji use to analyze your emotional well-being. The rapper Drake
recently got an honest-to-God tattoo of an emoji that, depending on whom
you ask, means either "praying hands" or "high five" 🙏. (Drake says praying
hands. "I pity the fool who high-fives in 2014," he clarified via Instagram.)

This elasticity of meaning is a large part of the appeal and, perhaps, the  8
genius of emoji. They have proved to be well suited to the kind of emotional
heavy lifting for which written language is often clumsy or awkward or problematic, especially when it's relayed on tiny screens, tapped out in real time,
using our thumbs. These seemingly infantile cartoons are instantly recogniz-
able, which makes them understandable even across linguistic barriers. Yet
the implications of emoji—their secret meanings—are constantly in flux.

Decoding pictures as part of communication has been at the root of  9
written language since there was such a thing as written language. "What is
virtually certain," writes Andrew Robinson in *Writing and Script: A Very Short
Introduction,* is "that the first written symbols began life as pictures." Pictograms—i.e., pictures of actual things, like a drawing of the sun—were the
very first elements of written communication, found in Mesopotamia, Egypt,
and China. From pictograms, which are literal representations, we moved to
logograms, which are symbols that stand in for a word ($, for example) and
ideograms, which are pictures or symbols that represent an idea or abstract

---

**Trapper Keepers:** The original enclosable three-ring binder, first introduced by Mead in the
1970s.   **Unicode:** An encoding standard for computer transmission and storage of
characters, symbols, and letters.

concept. Modern examples of ideograms include the person-in-a-wheelchair symbol that universally communicates accessibility and the red-hand symbol at a pedestrian crossing that signals not "red hand" but "stop."

Emoji can somewhat magically function as pictograms and ideograms 10 at the same time. The most straightforward example is the Eggplant emoji. On one level, it looks like an eggplant and can be used to communicate "eggplant." On another level, it looks (kind of) like a penis and can be used to communicate all manner of lascivious intent, especially when combined with a peach. 🍆 ✏ As Jenna Wortham, a *New York Times* technology reporter, wrote in an essay about emoji for *Womanzine*'s emoji issue, they "have become an ever-evolving cryptographic° language that changes depending on who we are talking to, and when." In short, emoji are a secret code language made up of symbols that everyone already intuitively understands.

"When it comes to text-based communication, we're babies," explains 11 Tyler Schnoebelen, a linguistics Ph.D. from Stanford who works for Idibon, a text-analytics company. As he says, we've learned to talk, and we've learned to write, but we're only now learning to write at the speed of talking (i.e., text), sending messages over vast expanses, absent any physical contextual clues. If you are talking to someone face-to-face, you don't need an additional word or symbol to express "I'm smiling" because you would, presumably, be smiling. The psychologist Albert Mehrabian, in an oft-cited (and occasionally criticized) study, determined in the 1950s that only 7 percent of communication is verbal (what we say), while 38 percent is vocal (how we say it) and 55 percent is nonverbal (what we do and how we look while we're saying it). This is well and good for face-to-face communication, but when we're texting, 93 percent of our communicative tools are negated.

Enter emoji. 12

Emoji were born in a true eureka moment,° from the mind of a single 13 man: Shigetaka Kurita, an employee at the Japanese telecom company NTT Docomo. Back in the late 1990s, the company was looking for a way to distinguish its pager service from its competitors in a very tight market. Kurita hit on the idea of adding simplistic cartoon images to its messaging functions as a way to appeal to teens. The first round of what came to be called emoji—a Japanese neologism that means, more or less, "picture word"—were designed by Kurita, using a pencil and paper, as drawings on a 12-by-12-pixel grid and were inspired by pictorial Japanese sources, like manga (Japanese comic books) and kanji (Japanese characters borrowed from written Chinese).

Kurita wound up with 176 crude symbols ranging from smiley faces 14 to music notes. This feature proved so popular that the other Japanese telecoms adopted it. In 2007, Apple released the first iPhone—and the global smartphone market boomed. Apple and Google both realized that, in order to crack the Japanese market, they would need to provide emoji functions in

---

**cryptographic:** Secret or encrypted.    **eureka moment:** A sudden insight or epiphany.

their operating systems,° if only for use in Japan. So Apple buried an emoji keyboard in the iPhone where North Americans weren't intended to find it. But eventually tech-savvy users in the United States, who were curious about the Japanese emoji phenomenon, figured out that you could force your phone to open this hidden keyboard by downloading a Japanese-language app, and voilà—suddenly you could bejangle your texts with a smiling Pile of Poo 💩. . . .

The programmers behind each operating system are free to design 15 their emoji as they like. However, the emoji palette—the collection of 722 standardized emoji that are available for you to use—has been encoded by the Unicode Consortium, which was founded in 1990 and consists of a loose network of contributing members. The people who do work for Unicode tend to be computer-programming experts with a side interest in linguistics—a typical biography: "His hobbies include Maltese-language advocacy." They are, in a way, the modern analog to the devout monks who sat and diligently created illuminated manuscripts so that great written works of theology could be widely shared.

Emoji presented a new and unique dilemma to Unicode. "With most 16 text, you don't have things being invented left, right, and center," says Peter Constable, the vice president of Unicode. "The letters of English are the letters of English. We don't have people inventing new letters of English every day." With emoji, however, there are limitless possibilities for new symbols, and it's literally impossible to meet the demand. And so, despite the fact that, as of 2011, you could text a cartoon pile of poo to any person in the world, people in the world were not happy. The world wanted an emoji hot dog! And an emoji avocado! And, understandably, representations of people of color! But in order to add new emoji, Unicode would have to invent them, then design them, then approve them, and then encode them. And Unicode is not in the business of inventing or designing new emoji, any more than it would invent and design new English letters and add them to the alphabet.

Unicode did decide, however, to encode the 250 new emoji to be released 17 this summer, which should show up on your phone as soon as Apple, Google, Microsoft, and other Unicode signatories add them to their operating systems. (Apple's iOS 8, for example, does not have the latest emoji, and the company has declined to comment on when they might go live.) None of these "new" emoji are actually new—instead, the new emoji are all either translations of preexisting font sets known as Wingdings and Webdings, or they are fairly boring new symbols, like the ever-useful Increase Font Size Symbol.

There are, though, a few notable additions, such as th[e] Man in Busi- 18 ness Suit Levitating (also referred to as Jumping emoji or Hovering emoji) 🕴, which is an excellent example of how the technologically convoluted path for new emoji leads to the existence of totally weird and random characters. . . .

Now, at least as far as your Unicode-reading smartphone is concerned, 19 Man in Business Suit Levitating is as legitimate a character as the numeral 5,

**operating systems:** The software required to run programs and applications on a computer.

or the letter *A*, or the tilde, or poo. What that man will mean—well, that's entirely up to you. This is the fun of emoji. The nail-painting emoji 💅, in some circles, has come to mean "I'm not bothered" or "Haters gonna hate." Man in Business Suit Levitating could mean "jumping for joy," or it could mean "mystery." (Online speculators have already nicknamed it "the Man in Black emoji.") As Wortham explains about her favorite emoji, the Tempura Shrimp 🍤, what she loves about it is precisely the fact that it can have many different meanings. Sometimes she uses it to mean a foul or "salty" mood, when she wants to curl up like a shrimp. With some of her friends, the shrimp morphed into a joke that stands in for "Mariah Carey." ("Something about her complexion and the way she's always stuffed into a tube-ish dress," Wortham writes in her shrimp essay.) Others use the shrimp as "quirky filler"—a nod, a wink, an acknowledgment that you're simply thinking of someone. Tempura Shrimp emoji, she writes, has become "a way to be present when there's nothing else to say at all."

Consider the exclamation point. For much of its history, the exclamation 20 point had a fairly simple usage: to straightforwardly and sincerely indicate excitement or, if included in a quotation, vehemence° or volume. ("Get off my lawn!" as opposed to "Get off my lawn.") Yet for a long time, circa the mid-1990s, it seemed linguistically and socially impossible to use an exclamation point unironically. I'll anchor this observation to Peter Bagge's landmark grunge-culture° comic *Hate!*, which debuted in 1990, simply titled *Hate*, but which added the telltale exclamation point to its name at issue No. 16 in 1994. I'll also add, from personal recollection, that if you included an exclamatory phrase such as "I'm so excited!" or "See you tonight!" in any written electronic correspondence up to, say, 1999, you could reliably assume it would be read as the punctuational equivalent of a smirk.

That was how my generation came to use the exclamation point, anyway. 21 More recently, with the advent of new forms such as tweets and text messaging, the exclamation point has reverted to something closer to its original meaning. In fact, it's more or less switched places with the period, so that "I'm excited to see you!" now conveys sincere excitement to see you, while "I'm excited to see you." seems, on a screen at least, to imply the opposite. The exclamation point, once so sprightly and forceful, has come, according to Ben Yagoda in a piece in the *New York Times,* to signify "minimally acceptable enthusiasm." . . .

When I first encountered emoji, I assumed they were used only ironi- 22 cally—perhaps because, as a member of Generation X,° I am accustomed to irony as a default communicative mode. And it's certainly true that emoji have proved popular, unsurprisingly, with early adopters and techno-fetishists and people with trend-sensitive antennae—the kinds of people

---

**vehemence:** Intense conviction.     **grunge-culture:** Youth subculture arising from the Pacific Northwest in the early 1990s characterized by alternative music (Pearl Jam, Nirvana), a nihilistic worldview, and worn clothing.     **Generation X:** Americans born in the early 1960s through the early 1980s.

who might, for example, download a Japanese app to "force" their iPhone to reveal a hidden emoji keyboard. But emoji have also proved to be popular with the least techno-literate and ironic among us, i.e., our parents. Many people I spoke to relayed that their moms were the most enthusiastic adopters of emoji they knew. One woman said that her near-daily text-message-based interaction with her mother consists almost entirely of strings of emoji hearts. Another woman, with a septuagenarian° mother, revealed to me that her mom had recently sent a text relaying regret, followed by a crying-face emoji—and that this was possibly the most straightforwardly emotional sentiment her mother had ever expressed to her.

And now we're getting to the heart of what emoji do well—what perhaps 23 they do better even than language itself, at least in the rough-and-tumble world online. Aside from the widespread difficulty of expressing yourself in real time with your clumsy thumbs, while hunched over a lit screen, and probably distracted by 50 other things, there's the fact that the Internet is mean. The widespread anonymity of the Web has marked its nascent years with a kind of insidious incivility that we all now accept with resignation. Comment sections are a write-off. "Troll" is a new and unwelcome subspecies of person. Twitter's a hashtag-strewn battlefield.

But emoji are not, it turns out, well designed to convey meanness. They 24 are cartoons, first of all. And the emoji that exist—while very useful for conveying excitement, happiness, bemusement, befuddlement, and even love—are not very good at conveying anger, derision, or hate. If we can take as a given that Millennials, as a generation, were raised in a digital environment—navigating, for the first time, digital relationships as an equally legitimate and in some ways dominant form of interpersonal interaction—it stands to reason they might be drawn to a communicative tool that serves as an antidote to ambient incivility. They might be especially receptive to, and even excited about, a tool that counteracts the harshness of life in the online world. They might be taken with emoji.

The word that came up multiple times, in many conversations, with 25 many people about emoji was *soften.*

"The thing it does is soften things," says Tyler Schnoebelen, the linguis- 26 tics expert.

"I use emoji in personal e-mails all the time, because I feel like I'm 27 softening the e-mail," says *Vulture*'s Lindsey Weber, who cocurated the *Emoji* art show.

Alice Robb, who is in her twenties, wrote in the *New Republic* about say- 28 ing goodbye to a friend who was moving across the country via text message. "I texted her an emoji of a crying face. She replied with an image of a chick with its arms outstretched. This exchange might have been heartfelt. It could have been ironic. I'm still not really sure. It's possible that this friend and I are particularly emotionally stunted, but I put at least part of the blame on emoji: They allowed us to communicate without saying anything, saving us

septuagenarian: Someone aged 70–79.

from spelling out any actual sentiments." And yet what's striking is that her whole story is full of actual sentiment—she is no doubt sad that her friend is leaving, and her friend is no doubt sad to be leaving. Adding an emoji to a message doesn't undercut those sentiments (as irony would) but rather says, "I mean this, but it's hard to say it, and I know it's hard, but that makes it no less true." Emoji's default implication isn't irony; its default is sincerity, but sincerity that's self-aware. If the ironic exclamation point was the signature punctuational flourish of Generation X, the emoji—that attempt to bridge the difficult gap between what we feel and what we intend and what we say and what we text—is the signature punctuational flourish of the Millennials.

## Questions to Start You Thinking

1. **Considering Meaning:** How have emoji evolved from pictograms and ideograms?

2. **Identifying Writing Strategies:** Which emoji does Sternbergh use to illustrate his points? Why do you think he chose these? What effect do they have on the reader?

3. **Reading Critically:** In paragraph 24, Sternbergh argues that emoji have become popular as a response to the "meanness" of the Internet. Do you agree with his claim? What kind of evidence does he use to support it? Is his evidence effective?

4. **Expanding Vocabulary:** In paragraph 8, Sternbergh claims that an "elasticity of meaning is a large part of the appeal and, perhaps, the genius of emoji." What does he mean by "elasticity of meaning"? What examples does he give to illustrate this phrase? Can you come up with additional examples?

5. **Making Connections:** Clive Thompson concludes in "The New Literacy" (pp. 547–48) that students today know that "who you're writing for and why you're writing" are crucial components of written communication. How might Thompson respond to the evolution of the emoji as outlined in Sternbergh's article? Do emoji help writers focus on different audiences and how best to communicate with them?

## Journal Prompts

1. In paragraph 24, Sternbergh claims that emoji can be "a tool that counteracts the harshness of life in the online world." Do you agree or disagree with this statement? Do you use emoji in your written communications? Why, or why not? If so, which ones do you use? Why do you use them?

2. Write a few sentences that you would send to a friend, a family member, and a colleague at work that include emoji. Then try to communicate the same thoughts without using them. How difficult was it to communicate without emoji?

## Suggestions for Writing

1. At the end of his essay, Sternbergh claims that emoji are "the signature punctuational flourish of the Millennials," but he earlier notes that mothers are also "enthusiastic adopters of emoji." Write an essay examining how and why different groups of people use emoji.

2. Choose one of the following options: write an essay that celebrates the use of emoji as an effective communication tool, or write an essay that claims that emoji have had a detrimental effect on the art of communication.

Bertrand Langlois/
AFP/Getty Images.

## Stephen King

### Why We Crave Horror Movies

Stephen King was born in 1947 in Portland, Maine, and attended the University of Maine at Orono. He now lives in Bangor, Maine, where he writes his best-selling horror novels, many of which have been made into popular movies. The prolific King is also the author of screenplays, teleplays, short fiction, essays, e-books, novels under the pseudonym Richard Bachman, and *On Writing: A Memoir of the Craft* (2000). His well-known horror novels include *Carrie* (1974), *Firestarter* (1980), *Pet Sematary* (1983), *Misery* (1987), *The Green Mile* (1996), and *Hearts in Atlantis* (1999). His recent books include the final installments of his epic fantasy series *The Dark Tower,* the short story collaboration with his son Joe Hill called *In the Tall Grass* (2012), and the novels *Doctor Sleep* and *Joyland* (2013). In the following essay, first published in *Playboy* in December 1981, King draws on his extensive experience with horror to explain the human craving to be frightened.

**AS YOU READ:** Identify the needs that King says horror movies fulfill for viewers.

think that we're all mentally ill; those of us outside the asylums only hide it    1
a little better—and maybe not all that much better, after all. We've all known people who talk to themselves, people who sometimes squinch their faces into horrible grimaces when they believe no one is watching, people who have some hysterical fear—of snakes, the dark, the tight place, the long drop . . . and, of course, those final worms and grubs that are waiting so patiently underground.

When we pay our four or five bucks and seat ourselves at tenth-row center    2
in a theater showing a horror movie, we are daring the nightmare.

Why? Some of the reasons are simple and obvious. To show that we can,    3
that we are not afraid, that we can ride this roller coaster. Which is not to say that a really good horror movie may not surprise a scream out of us at some point, the way we may scream when the roller coaster twists through a complete 360 or plows through a lake at the bottom of the drop. And horror movies, like roller coasters, have always been the special province° of the

**province:** Sphere; area of interest.

young; by the time one turns forty or fifty, one's appetite for double twists or 360-degree loops may be considerably depleted.

We also go to reestablish our feelings of essential normality; the horror movie is innately conservative, even reactionary.° Freda Jackson as the horrible melting woman in *Die, Monster, Die!* confirms for us that no matter how far we may be removed from the beauty of a Robert Redford or a Diana Ross, we are still light-years from true ugliness.

And we go to have fun.

Ah, but this is where the ground starts to slope away, isn't it? Because this is a very peculiar sort of fun indeed. The fun comes from seeing others menaced—sometimes killed. One critic suggested that if pro football has become the voyeur's° version of combat, then the horror film has become the modern version of the public lynching.

It is true that the mythic, "fairy-tale" horror film intends to take away the shades of gray.... It urges us to put away our more civilized and adult penchant° for analysis and to become children again, seeing things in pure blacks and whites. It may be that horror movies provide psychic relief on this level because this invitation to lapse into simplicity, irrationality, and even outright madness is extended so rarely. We are told we may allow our emotions a free rein ... or no rein at all.

If we are all insane, then sanity becomes a matter of degree. If your insanity leads you to carve up women like Jack the Ripper or the Cleveland Torso Murderer, we clap you away in the funny farm (but neither of those two amateur-night surgeons was ever caught, heh-heh-heh); if, on the other hand, your insanity leads you only to talk to yourself when you're under stress or to pick your nose on your morning bus, then you are left alone to go about your business ... though it is doubtful that you will ever be invited to the best parties.

The potential lyncher is in almost all of us (excluding saints, past and present; but then, most saints have been crazy in their own ways), and every now and then, he has to be let loose to scream and roll around in the grass. Our emotions and our fears form their own body, and we recognize that it demands its own exercise to maintain proper muscle tone. Certain of these emotional muscles are accepted—even exalted—in civilized society; they are, of course, the emotions that tend to maintain the status quo° of civilization itself. Love, friendship, loyalty, kindness—these are all the emotions that we applaud, emotions that have been immortalized in the couplets of Hallmark cards and in the verses (I don't dare call it poetry) of Leonard Nimoy.

When we exhibit these emotions, society showers us with positive reinforcement; we learn this even before we get out of diapers. When, as children, we hug our rotten little puke of a sister and give her a kiss, all the aunts and uncles smile and twit and cry, "Isn't he the sweetest little thing?" Such

---

**reactionary:** Marked by reaction opposed to progress.    **voyeur:** One who takes inordinate pleasure in the act of watching.    **penchant:** Strong inclination.    **status quo:** Existing state of affairs.

coveted treats as chocolate-covered graham crackers often follow. But if we deliberately slam the rotten little puke of a sister's fingers in the door, sanctions follow—angry remonstrance° from parents, aunts, and uncles; instead of a chocolate-covered graham cracker, a spanking.

But anticivilization emotions don't go away, and they demand periodic exercise. We have such "sick" jokes as "What's the difference between a truckload of bowling balls and a truckload of dead babies?" (You can't unload the truckload of bowling balls with a pitchfork . . . a joke, by the way, that I heard originally from a ten-year-old.) Such a joke may surprise a laugh or a grin out of us even as we recoil, a possibility that confirms the thesis: if we share a brotherhood of man, then we also share an insanity of man. None of which is intended as a defense of either the sick joke or insanity but merely as an explanation of [how] the best horror films, like the best fairy tales, manage to be reactionary, anarchistic,° and revolutionary all at the same time. 11

The mythic horror movie, like the sick joke, has a dirty job to do. It deliberately appeals to all that is worst in us. It is morbidity unchained, our most base instincts let free, our nastiest fantasies realized . . . and it all happens, fittingly enough, in the dark. For those reasons, good liberals often shy away from horror films. For myself, I like to see the most aggressive of them—*Dawn of the Dead,* for instance—as lifting a trapdoor in the civilized forebrain and throwing a basket of raw meat to the hungry alligators swimming around in that subterranean river beneath. 12

Why bother? Because it keeps them from getting out, man, it keeps them down there and me up here. It was Lennon and McCartney who said that all you need is love, and I would agree with that. 13

As long as you keep the gators fed. 14

remonstrance: Objection.     anarchistic: Rejecting all forms of control.

## Questions to Start You Thinking

1. **Considering Meaning:** What does King mean when he says that "we're all mentally ill" (paragraph 1)? Is this a serious statement? Why, or why not?

2. **Identifying Writing Strategies:** How does King use analysis, breaking a complex topic into parts, to support his argument?

3. **Reading Critically:** Why do you think King uses the inclusive pronoun *we* so frequently throughout his essay? What effect does the use of this pronoun have on your response to his argument?

4. **Expanding Vocabulary:** Define *innately* (paragraph 4). What does King mean when he says horror movies are "innately conservative"? Does he contradict himself when he says they are also "reactionary, anarchistic, and revolutionary" (paragraph 11)? Why, or why not?

5. **Making Connections:** In "Black Men and Public Space" (pp. 502–04), Brent Staples writes about the reflexive fear and anxiety he arouses in people when walking at night. How might King's view of human nature help explain the reactions to Staples?

## Journal Prompts

1. What is your response to "sick" jokes? Why?
2. Recall a movie that exercised your "anticivilization emotions" (paragraph 11). Describe your state of mind before, during, and after the movie.

## Suggestions for Writing

1. What genre of movie do you prefer to watch, and why? What cravings does this type of movie satisfy?
2. Do you agree that "the horror film has become the modern version of the public lynching" (paragraph 6)? Write an argument in which you defend or refute this suggestion, citing examples from King's essay and from your own moviegoing experience to support your position.

# Elizabeth Stone

## Grief in the Age of Facebook

Elizabeth Stone.

Elizabeth Stone teaches English and media studies at Fordham University. Her critically acclaimed nonfiction work *A Boy I Once Knew: What a Teacher Learned from Her Student* was published in 2002. In 2004 she followed that book with *Black Sheep and Kissing Cousins: How Our Family Stories Shape Us.* In the following article, first published in the *Chronicle Review* on March 5, 2010, Stone recalls the death of one of her students and examines how that death was subsequently mourned on Facebook.

**AS YOU READ:** What questions does the author raise about this form of grieving?

On July 17 last year, one of my most promising students died. Her name       1
was Casey Feldman, and she was crossing a street in a New Jersey resort town on her way to work when a van went barreling through a stop sign. Her death was a terrible loss for everyone who knew her. Smart and dogged,° whimsical and kind, Casey was the news editor of the *Observer*, the campus paper I advise, and she was going places. She was a finalist for a national college reporting award and had just been chosen for a prestigious television internship for the fall, a fact she conveyed to me in a midnight text message,

**dogged:** Hardworking; determined.

entirely consistent with her all-news-all-the-time mind-set. Two days later her life ended.

I found out about Casey's death the old-fashioned way: in a phone conversation with Kelsey, the layout editor and Casey's roommate. She'd left a neutral-sounding voice mail the night before, asking me to call her when I got her message, adding, "It's OK if it's late." I didn't retrieve the message till midnight, so I called the next morning, realizing only later what an extraordinary effort she had made to keep her voice calm. But my students almost never make phone calls if they can help it, so Kelsey's message alone should have raised my antenna. She blogs, she tweets, she texts, and she pings. But voice mail? No.

Paradoxically it was Kelsey's understanding of the viral nature of her generation's communication preferences that sent her rushing to the phone, and not just to call boomers° like me. She didn't want anyone to learn of Casey's death through Facebook. It was summer, and their friends were scattered, but Kelsey knew that if even one of Casey's 801 Facebook friends posted the news, it would immediately spread.

So as Kelsey and her roommates made calls through the night, they monitored Facebook. Within an hour of Casey's death, the first mourner posted her respects on Casey's Facebook wall, a post that any of Casey's friends could have seen. By the next morning, Kelsey, in New Jersey, had reached the *Observer*'s editor in chief in Virginia, and by that evening, the two had reached fellow editors in California, Missouri, Massachusetts, Texas, and elsewhere — and somehow none of them already knew.

In the months that followed, I've seen how markedly technology has influenced the conventions of grieving among my students, offering them solace but also uncertainty. The day after Casey's death, several editorial-board members changed their individual Facebook profile pictures. Where there had been photos of Brent, of Kelsey, of Kate, now there were photos of Casey and Brent, Casey and Kelsey, Casey and Kate.

Now that Casey was gone, she was virtually everywhere. I asked one of my students why she'd changed her profile photo. "It was spontaneous," she said. "Once one person did it, we all joined in." Another student, who had friends at Virginia Tech when, in 2007, a gunman killed 32 people, said that's when she first saw the practice of posting Facebook profile photos of oneself with the person being mourned.

Within several days of Casey's death, a Facebook group was created called "In Loving Memory of Casey Feldman," which ran parallel to the wake and funeral planned by Casey's family. Dozens wrote on that group's wall, but Casey's own wall was the more natural gathering place, where the comments were more colloquial and addressed to her: "casey im speechless for words right now," wrote one friend. "I cant believe that just yest i txted you and now your gone . . . i miss you soo much rest in peace."

Though we all live atomized° lives, memorial services let us know the dead with more dimension than we may have known them during their lifetimes.

**boomers:** Baby boomers, the generation born directly after World War II.    **atomized:** Small; separate.

In the responses of her friends, I was struck by how much I hadn't known about Casey — her equestrian skill, her love of animals, her interest in photography, her acting talent, her penchant° for creating her own slang ("Don't be a cow"), and her curiosity — so intense that her friends affectionately called her a "stalker."

This new, uncharted form of grieving raises new questions. Traditional    9
mourning is governed by conventions. But in the age of Facebook, with self-hood publicly represented via comments and uploaded photos, was it OK for her friends to display joy or exuberance online? Some weren't sure. Six weeks after Casey's death, one student who had posted a shot of herself with Casey wondered aloud when it was all right to post a different photo. Was there a right time? There were no conventions to help her. And would she be judged if she removed her mourning photo before most others did?

As it turns out, Facebook has a "memorializing" policy in regard to the    10
pages of those who have died. That policy came into being in 2005, when a good friend and co-worker of Max Kelly, a Facebook employee, was killed in a bicycle accident. As Kelly wrote in a Facebook blog post last October, "The question soon came up: What do we do about his Facebook profile? We had never really thought about this before in such a personal way. How do you deal with an interaction with someone who is no longer able to log on? When someone leaves us, they don't leave our memories or our social network. To reflect that reality, we created the idea of 'memorialized' profiles as a place where people can save and share their memories of those who've passed."

Casey's Facebook page is now memorialized. Her own postings and lists    11
of interests have been removed, and the page is visible only to her Facebook friends. (I thank Kelsey Butler for making it possible for me to gain access to it.) Eight months after her death, her friends are still posting on her wall, not to "share the memories" but to write to her, acknowledging her absence but maintaining their ties to her — exactly the stance that contemporary grief theorists recommend. To me, that seems preferable to Freud's prescription, in "Mourning and Melancholia," that we should detach from the dead. Quite a few of Casey's friends wished her a merry Christmas, and on the 17th of every month so far, the postings spike. Some share dreams they've had about her, or post a detail of interest. "I had juice box wine recently," wrote one. "I thought of you the whole time :( Miss you girl!" From another: "i miss you. the new lady gaga cd came out, and if i had one wish in the world it would be that you could be singing (more like screaming) along with me in my passenger seat like old times."

It was against the natural order for Casey to die at 21, and her death still    12
reverberates° among her roommates and fellow editors. I was privileged to know Casey, and though I knew her deeply in certain ways, I wonder — I'm not sure, but I wonder — if I should have known her better. I do know, however, that she would have done a terrific trend piece on "Grief in the Age of Facebook."

---

**penchant:** Inclination.    **reverberates:** Echoes or repeats.

## Questions to Start You Thinking

1. **Considering Meaning:** Stone argues that, in the face of grief, technology gives people "solace but also uncertainty" (paragraph 5). How do Casey's friends find consolation in Facebook? What kinds of uncertainty do they face?

2. **Identifying Writing Strategies:** Stone includes in her essay quotes from Casey's Facebook page, written in lowercase with text-messaging abbreviations. How do these quotes convey the feeling of the memorialized Facebook page? What is the effect of the contrast between these casual bits of writing and Stone's more formal essay?

3. **Reading Critically:** How does Stone show that her students and their friends have a different relationship to digital media than she does? How does her relative unfamiliarity with Facebook affect this discussion of how people use technology to mourn a loss?

4. **Expanding Vocabulary:** Stone observes that Casey's friend Kelsey responded *paradoxically* (paragraph 3). What is a *paradox*? How do Kelsey's phone calls to those who knew Casey fit the definition?

5. **Making Connections:** In "The New Literacy" (pp. 547–48), Clive Thompson mentions a study that found that students, in their online communications, "were remarkably adept at what rhetoricians call *kairos*—assessing their audience and adapting their tone and technique to best get their point across" (paragraph 6). In what ways do the online memorials and tributes to Casey reflect this attention to audience? Do you think that Thompson would consider the memorials and tributes part of "the new literacy"? Why, or why not?

## Link to the Paired Essay

Both "Grief in the Age of Facebook" and Libby Copeland's "Is Facebook Making Us Sad?" (pp. 541–44) pay particular attention to college students and the impact of social media on their emotional lives. What do you see as the nature and the extent of the generational divide between people who have grown up with Facebook and those for whom it is a new technology? In what ways does Facebook bridge or boost that divide?

## Journal Prompts

1. As Stone points out, the creators of Facebook only realized after the fact that their site could become a place to mourn people (paragraph 10). Have you used Facebook to acknowledge a loss? If so, how? How else do you or your friends use Facebook in ways that the creators might not have anticipated? What do such uses say about digital media?

2. Stone's essay brings up an old question about how we should deal with death: Should we cultivate an ongoing relationship with the loved

one's memory, as Casey's friends do on Facebook, or should we, as Freud recommends, "detach" from people we have lost (paragraph 11)? Think about someone you have lost—either through death or other circumstances, like a move—and reflect on how you coped.

## Suggestions for Writing

1. At the end of "Grief in the Age of Facebook," Stone imagines Casey writing a "trend piece" of the same title (paragraph 12). Write an essay considering Stone's closing, why she ends on this note, how this conclusion affects you as a reader, or how Casey's approach to this topic might differ from her professor's.

2. Stone says that she learned new things about Casey by looking at her Facebook page (paragraph 8). Do you think that people can gain a deeper understanding of someone from his or her online presence? Write an essay that takes a stand, presenting your own position, supporting Stone's point, or arguing that Facebook is not a good way to get to know someone. Use other technology examples, if you wish, as well as your own experience, observation, or research.

## Libby Copeland

### Is Facebook Making Us Sad?

Libby Copeland, a New York–based freelance journalist, regularly writes on a wide range of topics for *Slate*, an online magazine that features articles on politics, business, technology, and the arts. Before joining *Slate*, Copeland worked for eleven years as a staff writer for the *Washington Post*. Her other publications include articles for *New York Magazine*, the *Wall Street Journal*, and *Cosmopolitan*. In 2009, she won the Feature Specialty Reporting award presented by the American Association of Sunday and Feature Editors. In the following article, published in *Slate*, Copeland reports what researchers have concluded about the effects of social networking.

Libby Copeland.

**AS YOU READ:** Identify how the researchers cited in this article support the claim that a link exists between social networking and loneliness.

There are countless ways to make yourself feel lousy. Here's one more, according to research out of Stanford: Assume you're alone in your unhappiness. "Misery Has More Company Than People Think," a paper in the January [2011] issue of *Personality and Social Psychology Bulletin*, draws on a series of studies examining how college students evaluate moods, both their own and those of their peers. Led by Alex Jordan, who at the time was a Ph.D. student in Stanford's psychology department, the researchers found that

1

their subjects consistently underestimated how dejected° others were—and likely wound up feeling more dejected as a result. Jordan got the idea for the inquiry after observing his friends' reactions to Facebook: He noticed that they seemed to feel particularly crummy about themselves after logging onto the site and scrolling through others' attractive photos, accomplished bios, and chipper status updates. "They were convinced that everyone else was leading a perfect life," he told me.

The human habit of overestimating other people's happiness is nothing 2 new, of course. Jordan points to a quote by Montesquieu:° "If we only wanted to be happy it would be easy; but we want to be happier than other people, which is almost always difficult, since we think them happier than they are." But social networking may be making this tendency worse. Jordan's research doesn't look at Facebook explicitly, but if his conclusions are correct, it follows that the site would have a special power to make us sadder and lonelier. By showcasing the most witty, joyful, bullet-pointed versions of people's lives, and inviting constant comparisons in which we tend to see ourselves as the losers, Facebook appears to exploit an Achilles' heel of human nature. And women—an especially unhappy bunch of late—may be especially vulnerable to keeping up with what they imagine is the happiness of the Joneses.°

In one of the Stanford studies, Jordan and his fellow researchers asked 80 3 freshmen to report whether they or their peers had recently experienced various negative and positive emotional events. Time and again, the subjects underestimated how many negative experiences ("had a distressing fight," "felt sad because they missed people") their peers were having. They also overestimated how much fun ("going out with friends," "attending parties") these same peers were having. In another study, the researchers found a sample of 140 Stanford students unable to accurately gauge others' happiness even when they were evaluating the moods of people they were close to—friends, roommates, and people they were dating. And in a third study, the researchers found that the more students underestimated others' negative emotions, the more they tended to report feeling lonely and brooding over their own miseries. This is correlation,° not causation,° mind you; it could be that those subjects who started out feeling worse imagined that everyone else was getting along just fine, not the other way around. But the notion that feeling alone in your day-to-day suffering might increase that suffering certainly makes intuitive sense.

As does the idea that Facebook might aggravate this tendency. Facebook is, 4 after all, characterized by the very public curation° of one's assets in the form of friends, photos, biographical data, accomplishments, pithy° observations, even the books we say we like. Look, we have baked beautiful cookies. We are playing with a new puppy. We are smiling in pictures (or, if we are moody, we

---

**dejected:** Depressed or downhearted.    **Montesquieu:** (1689–1755); a French philosopher during the Enlightenment era.    **happiness of the Joneses:** A play on the saying "keeping up with the Joneses," which refers to the competitive tendency to attempt the same standard of living as those around you.    **correlation:** A relationship between two or more things.    **causation:** A cause-and-effect relationship.    **curation:** Intentional organization, as for a collection.    **pithy:** Meaningful.

are artfully moody). Blandness will not do, and with some exceptions, sad stuff doesn't make the cut, either. The site's very design—the presence of a "Like" button, without a corresponding "Hate" button—reinforces a kind of upbeat spin doctoring. (No one will "Like" your update that the new puppy died, but they may "Like" your report that the little guy was brave up until the end.)

Any parent who has posted photos and videos of her child on Facebook is    5 keenly aware of the resulting disconnect from reality, the way chronicling parenthood this way creates a story line of delightfully misspoken words, adorably worn hats, dancing, blown kisses. Tearful falls and tantrums are rarely recorded, nor are the stretches of pure, mind-blowing tedium.° We protect ourselves, and our kids, this way; happiness is impersonal in a way that pain is not. But in the process, we wind up contributing to the illusion that kids are all joy, no effort.

Facebook is "like being in a play. You make a character," one teenager tells    6 MIT professor Sherry Turkle in her new book on technology, *Alone Together*. Turkle writes about the exhaustion felt by teenagers as they constantly tweak their Facebook profiles for maximum cool. She calls this "presentation anxiety," and suggests that the site's element of constant performance makes people feel alienated from themselves. (The book's broader theory is that technology, despite its promises of social connectivity, actually makes us lonelier by preventing true intimacy.)

Facebook oneupsmanship may have particular implications for women.    7 As Meghan O'Rourke has noted here in *Slate*, women's happiness has been at an all-time low in recent years. O'Rourke and two University of Pennsylvania economists who have studied the male-female happiness gap argue that women's collective discontent may be due to too much choice and second-guessing—unforeseen fallout, they speculate, of the way our roles have evolved over the last half-century. As the economists put it, "The increased opportunity to succeed in many dimensions may have led to an increased likelihood in believing that one's life is not measuring up."

If you're already inclined to compare your own decisions to those of other    8 women and to find yours wanting, believing that others are happier with their choices than they actually are is likely to increase your own sense of inadequacy. And women may be particularly susceptible to the Facebook illusion. For one thing, the site is inhabited by more women than men, and women users tend to be more active on the site, as *Forbes* has reported. According to a recent study out of the University of Texas at Austin, while men are more likely to use the site to share items related to the news or current events, women tend to use it to engage in personal communication (posting photos, sharing content "related to friends and family"). This may make it especially hard for women to avoid comparisons that make them miserable. (Last fall, for example, the *Washington Post* ran a piece about the difficulties of infertile women in shielding themselves from the Facebook crowings° of pregnant friends.)

---

**tedium:** Boredom.    **crowings:** Joyful noises.

Jordan, who is now a postdoctoral fellow studying social psychology at 9
Dartmouth's Tuck School of Business, suggests we might do well to consider
Facebook profiles as something akin to the airbrushed photos on the covers of
women's magazines. No, you will never have those thighs, because nobody has
those thighs. You will never be as consistently happy as your Facebook friends,
because nobody is that happy. So remember Montesquieu, and, if you're feeling
particularly down, use Facebook for its most exalted purpose: finding fat exes.

## Questions to Start You Thinking

1. **Considering Meaning:** Why is the problem Copeland describes particularly difficult for women? What factors make women especially susceptible to the illusion of perfect happiness that others present on Facebook?

2. **Identifying Writing Strategies:** Copeland turns to a variety of writers
and researchers to support her views about the negative effects of Facebook. What kinds of evidence and expertise does she rely on? What makes
her experts credible?

3. **Reading Critically:** Copeland points out that the relationship between
underestimating negative or overestimating positive experiences of others
and feeling sad about one's own circumstances is "correlation, not causation" (paragraph 3). How does she make the case that Facebook causes
people to feel worse?

4. **Expanding Vocabulary:** Copeland cites the function of the "Like" button as an indication that Facebook encourages *spin doctoring* (paragraph 4).
What does it mean to *spin doctor* one's profile, and why do people do it?

5. **Making Connections:** According to Copeland, "Facebook oneupsmanship may have particular implications for women," leading to a sense of
inadequacy. How do these feelings compare to those generated by images
of female superheroes as outlined by Cindi May in "The Problem with Female Superheroes" (pp. 508–11)?

## Link to the Paired Essay

While Elizabeth Stone ("Grief in the Age of Facebook," pp. 537–39) describes
young people mourning their friend online, Copeland argues that Facebook
actually makes users feel worse about themselves. Can the observations of
both writers be accurate? How can digital media be both a place to express
sadness and also a source of sadness?

## Journal Prompts

1. Do you present a happier version of yourself online than you would face
to face? If so, do you purposefully craft this rosier picture of your life, or
is the rosier picture a product of the way social networks are designed? To
what extent does your online persona represent your emotional life?

2. When she considers why people craft a happier persona online, Copeland suggests that "happiness is impersonal in a way that pain is not" (paragraph 5). Do privacy issues affect these questions of happiness and sadness online? What have you decided is suitable for public view online, and where do you draw the line at what is too personal?

## Suggestions for Writing

1. Write an essay exploring the longstanding human tendency to overestimate others' happiness. Why do you think people are more likely to believe others are happy? How have your own experiences illustrated or defied this tendency?

2. In paragraph 6, Copeland cites an interview conducted by Sherry Turkle in which a student compares Facebook to a play in which users are constantly performing. Recall your experience with social networking, and use it to develop the idea of social networking as playacting — or propose another analogy for this kind of online interaction. If you wish, analyze postings or others' sites to expand your supporting evidence.

Krystyna Szulecka/Alamy.

### Responding to an Image

Jaume Plensa is a sculptor and artist from Spain. His installation *29 Palms*, shown above, is a 164-foot curtain composed of steel-cut letters comprising his favorite poems. The letters are designed to cast fluid shadows across the wall and floor. In the photo, a visitor touches the letters to make them "sing," as Plensa encourages. Reflect on this tactile, three-dimensional, multimedia presentation of letters, which we often encounter in static settings, like books and screens. What does Plensa's installation seem to be saying about the role of words in our world, and its relationship to language?

# Clive Thompson

## The New Literacy

Clive Thompson is a science and technology writer for the *New York Times Magazine, WIRED,* and *New York Magazine*; the video-game columnist for *Slate*; and a finance columnist for *Details*. He has received the National Magazine Award in Canada twice, and in 2002–2003 he was the Knight Science Journalism fellow at MIT. His commentary can be heard on NPR, CNN, and the Canadian Broadcasting Corporation. He also keeps a blog, *Collision Detection*, which "collects bits of offbeat research . . . and musings thereon." Here, Thompson discusses some counterintuitive research by Professor Andrea Lunsford on literacy in the digital age.

Tom Igoe.

**AS YOU READ:** What did the Stanford Study of Writing discover about student writing?

As the school year begins, be ready to hear pundits° fretting once again about how kids today can't write—and technology is to blame. Facebook encourages narcissistic° blabbering, video and PowerPoint have replaced carefully crafted essays, and texting has dehydrated language into "bleak, bald, sad shorthand" (as University College of London English professor John Sutherland has moaned). An age of illiteracy is at hand, right?

Andrea Lunsford isn't so sure. Lunsford is a professor of writing and rhetoric at Stanford University, where she has organized a mammoth project called the Stanford Study of Writing to scrutinize° college students' prose. From 2001 to 2006, she collected 14,672 student writing samples—everything from in-class assignments, formal essays, and journal entries to e-mails, blog posts, and chat sessions. Her conclusions are stirring. 2

"I think we're in the midst of a literacy revolution the likes of which we haven't seen since Greek civilization," she says. For Lunsford, technology isn't killing our ability to write. It's reviving it—and pushing our literacy in bold new directions. 3

The first thing she found is that young people today write far more than any generation before them. That's because so much socializing takes place online, and it almost always involves text. Of all the writing that the Stanford students did, a stunning 38 percent of it took place out of the classroom—life writing, as Lunsford calls it. Those Twitter updates and lists of 25 things about yourself add up. 4

It's almost hard to remember how big a paradigm shift this is. Before the Internet came along, most Americans never wrote anything, ever, that wasn't a school assignment. Unless they got a job that required producing text (like in law, advertising, or media), they'd leave school and virtually never construct a paragraph again. 5

But is this explosion of prose good, on a technical level? Yes. Lunsford's team found that the students were remarkably adept at what rhetoricians call *kairos*—assessing their audience and adapting their tone and technique to best get their point across. The modern world of online writing, particularly 6

---

**pundits:** Critics and commentators.     **narcissistic:** Self-centered.     **scrutinize:** Examine carefully.

in chat and on discussion threads, is conversational and public, which makes it closer to the Greek tradition of argument than the asynchronous° letter and essay writing of 50 years ago.

The fact that students today almost always write for an audience (something virtually no one in my generation did) gives them a different sense of what constitutes good writing. In interviews, they defined good prose as something that had an effect on the world. For them, writing is about persuading and organizing and debating, even if it's over something as quotidian° as what movie to go see. The Stanford students were almost always less enthusiastic about their in-class writing because it had no audience but the professor: It didn't serve any purpose other than to get them a grade. As for those texting short-forms and smileys defiling° *serious* academic writing? Another myth. When Lunsford examined the work of first-year students, she didn't find a single example of texting speak in an academic paper.

Of course, good teaching is always going to be crucial, as is the mastering of formal academic prose. But it's also becoming clear that online media are pushing literacy into cool directions. The brevity of texting and status updating teaches young people to deploy haiku°-like concision.° At the same time, the proliferation° of new forms of online pop-cultural exegesis°—from sprawling TV-show recaps to 15,000-word videogame walkthroughs—has given them a chance to write enormously long and complex pieces of prose, often while working collaboratively with others.

We think of writing as either good or bad. What today's young people know is that knowing who you're writing for and why you're writing might be the most crucial factor of all.

**asynchronous:** Not occurring at the same time. **quotidian:** Ordinary, commonplace. **defiling:** Making dirty; corrupting. **haiku:** Japanese form of poetry having three unrhymed lines of five, seven, and five syllables. **concision:** The quality of being brief; brevity. **proliferation:** Rapid increase. **exegesis:** Explanation or analysis.

## Questions to Start You Thinking

1. **Considering Meaning:** According to the author, what is the effect of the Internet on writing?

2. **Identifying Writing Strategies:** Where does Thompson use comparison and contrast? How does it support his argument?

3. **Reading Critically:** Who seems to be the intended audience for this essay? What is the writer's purpose? How well do you think he achieves it?

4. **Expanding Vocabulary:** In paragraph 5, Thompson writes, "It's almost hard to remember how big a paradigm shift this is." What is a *paradigm shift*? Why is this concept important to Thompson's larger purpose?

5. **Making Connections:** According to Thompson, the Internet and other new forms of media are stimulating literacy. How might Adam Sternbergh ("Smile, You're Speaking Emoji," pp. 527–33) respond to Thompson's article? What would he make of this "paradigm shift"?

## Journal Prompts

1. Thompson claims that people are writing more than ever as they socialize online (paragraph 4). Consider your own time spent writing online, texting, or tweeting. Has this time and involvement made you a better writer? Why, or why not?

2. According to Thompson, students surveyed in the Stanford Study of Writing "defined good prose as something that had an effect on the world" (paragraph 7). Do you agree with this definition? Can you think of a better one? What examples come to mind?

## Suggestions for Writing

1. Drawing on your own experience and observations, write an essay in which you explore the cause-and-effect relationship, positive or negative, between the use of the Internet (or another new media form) and its consequences for writing.

2. In his opening sentence, Thompson anticipates commentary blaming technology for educational gaps or failures, just as video games, television, radio, and even early novels have been criticized over the years as negative influences. Investigate one or several historical examples of people worrying about the bad effects of a new technology. Then write an essay that examines those concerns and their validity, in retrospect.

# Ann Friedman

## Can We Just, Like, Get Over the Way Women Talk?

Stephanie Gonot.

Freelance journalist Ann Friedman writes about gender, media, technology, and culture, and she has contributed to such publications as the *Los Angeles Times*, the *Gentlewoman*, the *New Republic*, the *New York Times Book Review*, *ELLE*, the *Guardian*, and *Los Angeles* magazine. She also cohosts a podcast, *Call Your Girlfriend*, with a good friend, Aminatou Sow. Following is a column that Friedman wrote for nymag.com. In it, she pushes back against criticisms of "the problems inherent in women's speech."

**AS YOU READ:** Which words or vocal characteristics are often criticized when they are part of women's speech?

Like, have you ever noticed that women apologize too much? Sorry, but just humor me for a second here. What if, um, how we're speaking is actually part of what's undermining° us in the workplace, in politics, and anywhere in the public sphere where we want to be taken seriously? I think it could be time for us all to assess how we're talking. Does that make sense to you, too?    1

---

**undermining:** Working against.

It makes sense to tech-industry veteran Ellen Leanse, who explains that
women overuse the word *just,* which sends "a subtle message of subordination."° Essayist Sloane Crosley and comedian Amy Schumer tell us not to say
"sorry" so often. A career coach warns the readers of *Goop*° that women use
too many qualifiers ("I'm no expert, but . . ."), which undermine their
opinions. Radio listeners complain of "vocal fry"° that makes it impossible
to listen to women. And according to a Hofstra University professor, women
who suffer from upspeak — also known as "Valley Girl lift"? — reveal "an un-
explainable lack of confidence" in their opinions when they turn declarative
sentences into questions.

As someone who's never been shy about opening her mouth and telling
you exactly what she thinks, this barrage of information about the problems inherent° in women's speech has me questioning my own voice. Here
I am, thinking that I'm speaking normally and sharing my thoughts on
campaign-finance reform or the Greek debt crisis or the politics of marriage,
when apparently the only thing that other people are hearing is a passive-
aggressive, creaky mash-up of Cher Horowitz,° Romy and Michele,° and the
Plastics.° I'm as much a fan of these fictional heroines as the next woman,
but I want people to hear what I'm saying and take me seriously.

At first blush, all of this speaking advice sounds like empowerment. Stop
sugarcoating everything, ladies! Don't hedge your requests! Refuse to water
down your opinions! But are women the ones who need to change? If I'm
saying something intelligent and all a listener can hear is the *way* I'm saying
it, whose problem is that?

"All the discussion is about what we *think* we hear," the feminist linguist
Robin Lakoff tells me. Lakoff is a professor emerita° at the University of
California, Berkeley, and, forty years ago, pioneered the study of language
and gender. "With men, we listen for what they're saying, their point, their
assertions. Which is what all of us want others to do when we speak," Lakoff
says. "With women, we tend to listen to how they're talking, the words they
use, what they emphasize, whether they smile."

Men also use the word *just.* Men engage in upspeak. Men have vocal fry.
Men pepper their sentences with unnecessary "likes" and "sorrys." I haven't
read any articles encouraging them to change this behavior. The supposed
distinctions between men's and women's ways of talking are, often, not that
distinct. "Forty years after Lakoff's groundbreaking work, we've learned that
all such generalizations are overgeneralizations: none of them are true for
every woman in every context (or even most women in most contexts),"

---

**subordination:** Being in a lower position or rank.     ***Goop:*** An online "lifestyle publication"
overseen by Gwyneth Paltrow.     **vocal fry:** A low vibration, sometimes sounding like a
crackle, that occurs in some people's speech, often at the end of sentences.     **inherent:** Insep-
arable from.     **Cher Horowitz:** The starring character of the 1995 movie *Clueless.*     **Romy
and Michele:** The starring characters of the 1997 movie *Romy and Michele's High School Reunion.*
(Cher Horowitz and Romy and Michele all had "Valley Girl" speaking styles.)     **the Plastics:**
Central characters (all popular high school girls) in the movies *Mean Girls* (2004) and *Mean
Girls 2* (2011).     **emerita:** Retired.

writes feminist linguist and blogger Debbie Cameron. "We've also learned that some of the most enduring beliefs about the way women talk are not just overgeneralizations, they are—to put it bluntly—lies." Maybe we don't sound like a pack of Cher Horowitzes after all.

Still, I care about good diction°—I want to be heard and understood. When I'm writing, it's easy to do a control-F for "I think" and delete all of the wishy-washy words that are diluting my opinions. When I'm speaking, it's much harder to notice which linguistic tics° I exhibit. And until I started cohosting a podcast, I was fairly oblivious to my own vocal patterns. Then the e-mails and tweets started rolling in, advising me and my cohost that we would sound a lot smarter if we could just pay a bit more attention to our speech. The list of complaints mirrors the advice-driven articles I've seen scattered over the internet lately. "Fingernails on a chalkboard," wrote one reviewer on iTunes. "One has up-talk, the other has vocal fry and both use the word *like* every frigging third word. . . . These are the ladies Amy Schumer goofs on."

It quickly became apparent that if we were to take the advice of all of our detractors—carefully enunciating,° limiting our *like*s, moderating our tone to avoid vocal fry—our podcast would sound very different. It would be stripped of its cadence° and its meaning; it would lose the casual, friendly tone we wanted it to have and its special feeling of intimacy. It wouldn't be ours anymore. "This stuff is just one more way of telling powerful women to *shut up you bitch*," says Lakoff. "It makes women self-conscious and makes women feel incompetent and unable to figure out the right way to talk." She adds, "There is no right way." Especially if you want to sound like *yourself*, and not some weird, stilted° robot.

Indeed, as with salary negotiations in which women are damned if they don't ask for a raise and penalized for being overly aggressive if they do, tweaking speech to be more direct and less deferential° comes with its own consequences. "When women talk in ways that are common among women, and are seen as ineffective or underestimated, they're told it's their fault for talking that way," the linguist Deborah Tannen, who's written several best-selling books about gender and language, told me. "But if they talk in ways that are associated with authority, and are seen as too aggressive, then that, too, is their fault when people react negatively." Asking women to modify their speech is just another way we are asked to internalize and compensate for sexist bias in the world. We can't win by eliminating *just* from our e-mails and *like* from our conversations.

Lakoff argues that the very things career coaches advise women to cut out of their speech are actually signs of highly evolved communication. When we use words like *so, I guess, like, actually,* and *I mean*, we are sending signals to the listener to help them figure out what's new, what's

7

8

9

10

---

**diction:** Style of speaking or writing.  **tics:** Recurrent behavioral traits or quirks.  **enunciating:** Pronouncing words clearly.  **cadence:** Rhythm.  **stilted:** Stiffly formal.  **deferential:** Yielding to another.

important, or what's funny. We're connecting with them. "Rather than being weakeners or signs of fuzziness of mind, as is often said, they create cohesion and coherence between what speaker and hearer together need to accomplish—understanding and sharing," Lakoff says. "This is the major job of an articulate social species. If women use these forms more, it is because we are better at being human."

Language is not always about making an argument or conveying infor-   11
mation in the cleanest, simplest way possible. It's often about building relationships. It's about making yourself understood and trying to understand
someone else. As anyone who's ever shared an inside joke knows, it's *fun*. This
can be true even at work or in public—places where women are most likely
to be dismissed because of the way they speak. To assume that our verbal tics
are always negative is to assume that the goal of all speech is the same. Which
of course is patently° ridiculous.

Maybe women *are* undermining themselves a bit when they, like, speak in   12
a way they find more natural. But only in the sense that they are seeking to
articulate their thoughts more authentically and connect more directly with
the people listening to them. Next time I read some advice from a podcast
listener or from some self-styled expert on the internet about how women are
too creaky-voiced, too apologetic, or using a word too much, I know exactly
how I'll respond: As if.

**patently:** Clearly.

## Questions to Start You Thinking

1. **Considering Meaning:** What, according to Friedman, are common criticisms of women's speech? Why does she find these criticisms problematic?

2. **Identifying Writing Strategies:** Notice how Friedman opens her essay,
paying special attention to word choice and punctuation. Why might she
have begun her argument in this way? Do you find this opening effective?
Why, or why not?

3. **Reading Critically:** In paragraph 7, Friedman shares a criticism leveled
at her speaking style, and at that of her cohost, in a podcast. How fair do
you think this criticism is? How does Friedman respond to it?

4. **Expanding Vocabulary:** What does Friedman mean by "upspeak" (paragraphs 2 and 6)? Give an example of a perceived problem with upspeak.

5. **Making Connections:** In "The New Literacy" (pp. 547–48), Clive Thompson
describes as a "myth" the view that texted abbreviations and smileys are
"defiling *serious* academic writing" (paragraph 7). How might Thompson
respond to Friedman's view of language: that it's "often about building
relationships. It's about making yourself understood and trying to understand someone else. As anyone who's ever shared an inside joke knows,
it's *fun*" (paragraph 11)? In general, do Thompson's and Friedman's views
seem aligned or contradictory? Why?

## Journal Prompts

1. Do you find that you frequently use any of the expressions that Friedman refers to (*like, so, I guess, actually, I mean,* and so on) in your speech? When and why do you think you use these expressions?

2. Have you ever been criticized for the way that you speak? Alternatively, have you ever judged others based on their style of speaking? What were the reasons for the criticisms? Has the experience had any lasting effects on you? If so, discuss its impact.

## Suggestions for Writing

1. According to Friedman, feminist linguist Robin Lakoff argues that "the very things career coaches advise women to cut out of their speech are actually signs of highly evolved communication" (paragraph 10). Argue for or against Lakoff's assertion, drawing on your own observations and referring to specific examples.

2. Listen to a podcast or radio program, making notes about the host's use of language and his or her vocal style. For example, does the host use or avoid words and phrases such as *like, I mean, I guess,* or other expressions that sound casual or tentative? Do you notice upspeak, or does the host speak in a more level tone? What adjectives would you use to describe the host's style (e.g., *authoritative, friendly, confident, aggressive, humorous*)? Based on your notes, write about aspects of the host's speaking style that made listening to the podcast a positive or negative experience, or something in between. Also, carefully reflect on your reactions, keeping Friedman's points in mind: Do you think gender bias played any role in your judgment of the host's speaking style? Why, or why not?

# Jenny Jarvie

## Trigger Happy

Born in London in 1975, Jenny Jarvie is a freelance writer currently living in Atlanta, Georgia. She is a former reporter for the *Los Angeles Times,* and her articles have also appeared in the *Atlantic* and the *Sunday Telegraph* in London, as well as the *New Republic* and *Poetry Magazine.* Jarvie holds a master's degree in English literature and philosophy from the University of Glasgow and is the winner of the Catherine Pakenham Award for the most promising young female writer in Britain. In the following article, published on March 3, 2014, in the *New Republic,* Jarvie discusses the negative effects of trigger warnings.

**AS YOU READ:** What is a trigger warning, and how is it being used on college campuses and in American media?

The "trigger warning" has spread from blogs to college classes. Can it be   1
stopped?

The headline above would, if some readers had their way, include a "trigger warning"—a disclaimer to alert you that this article contains potentially traumatic subject matter. Such warnings, which are most commonly applied to discussions about rape, sexual abuse, and mental illness, have appeared on message boards since the early days of the Web. Some consider them an irksome tic of the blogosphere's most hypersensitive fringes, and yet they've spread from feminist forums and social media to sites as large as the *Huffington Post*. Now, the trigger warning is gaining momentum beyond the Internet—at some of the nation's most prestigious universities.

Last week, student leaders at the University of California, Santa Barbara, passed a resolution urging officials to institute mandatory trigger warnings on class syllabi. Professors who present "content that may trigger the onset of symptoms of Post-Traumatic Stress Disorder"° would be required to issue advance alerts and allow students to skip those classes. According to UCSB newspaper the *Daily Nexus*, Bailey Loverin, the student who sponsored the proposal, decided to push the issue after attending a class in which she "felt forced" to sit through a film that featured an "insinuation"° of sexual assault and a graphic depiction of rape. A victim of sexual abuse, she did not want to remain in the room, but she feared she would only draw attention to herself by walking out.

On college campuses across the country, a growing number of students are demanding trigger warnings on class content. Many instructors are obliging with alerts in handouts and before presentations, even e-mailing notes of caution ahead of class. At Scripps College, lecturers give warnings before presenting a core curriculum class, the "Histories of the Present: Violence," although some have questioned the value of such alerts when students are still required to attend class. Oberlin College has published an official document on triggers, advising faculty members to "be aware of racism, classism, sexism, heterosexism, cissexism,° ableism,° and other issues of privilege and oppression," to remove triggering material when it doesn't "directly" contribute to learning goals and "strongly consider" developing a policy to make "triggering material" optional. Chinua Achebe's *Things Fall Apart*, it states, is a novel that may "trigger readers who have experienced racism, colonialism, religious persecution, violence, suicide, and more." Warnings have been proposed even for books long considered suitable material for high-schoolers: Last month, a Rutgers University sophomore suggested that an alert for F. Scott Fitzgerald's *The Great Gatsby* say, "TW: suicide, domestic abuse, and graphic violence."

What began as a way of moderating Internet forums for the vulnerable and mentally ill now threatens to define public discussion both online and off. The trigger warning signals not only the growing precautionary approach to words and ideas in the university, but a wider cultural hypersensitivity to harm and a paranoia about giving offense. And yet, for all the debate about

**Post-Traumatic Stress Disorder:** A mental health disorder triggered by a traumatic event; can lead to flashbacks and severe anxiety.   **insinuation:** Subtle hinting at something derogatory.   **Cissexism:** The privileging and enforcing of gender binaries resulting in prejudice toward those who identify as transgender.   **ableism:** Discrimination favoring able-bodied people.   **ramifications:** Consequences.

the warnings on campuses and on the Internet, few are grappling with the ramifications° for society as a whole.

Not everyone seems to agree on what the trigger warning is, let alone how it should be applied. Initially, trigger warnings were used in self-help and feminist forums to help readers who might have post-traumatic stress disorder to avoid graphic content that might cause painful memories, flashbacks, or panic attacks. Some Web sites, like Bodies Under Siege, a self-injury support message board, developed systems of adding abbreviated topic tags—from SI (self injury) to ED (eating disorders)—to particularly explicit posts. As the Internet grew, warnings became more popular, and critics began to question their use. In 2010, Susannah Breslin wrote in *True/Slant* that feminists were applying the term "like a Southern cook applies Pam cooking spray to an overused nonstick frying pan"—prompting *Feministing* to call her a "certifiable asshole," and *Jezebel* to lament that the debate has "been totally clouded by ridiculous inflammatory rhetoric."

The term only spread with the advent of social media. In 2012, the *Awl*'s Choire Sicha argued that it had "lost all its meaning." Since then, alerts have been applied to topics as diverse as sex, pregnancy, addiction, bullying, suicide, sizeism, ableism, homophobia, transphobia, slut shaming, victim-blaming, alcohol, blood, insects, small holes, and animals in wigs. Certain people, from rapper Chris Brown to sex columnist Dan Savage, have been dubbed "triggering." Some have called for trigger warnings for television shows such as *Scandal* and *Downton Abbey*. Even the *New Republic* has suggested the satirical news site the *Onion* carry trigger warnings.

At the end of last year, *Slate* declared 2013 the "Year of the Trigger Warning," noting that such alerts had become the target of humor. *Jezebel,* which does not issue trigger warnings, raised hackles° in August by using the term as a headline joke: "It's Time To Talk About Bug Infestations [TRIGGER WARNING]." Such usage, one critic argued, amounted to "trivializing" such alerts and "trolling people who believe in them." And in Britain, Suzanne Moore, a feminist columnist for the *Guardian*, was taken to task when she put a trigger warning on her Twitter bioline, mocking those who followed her feeds only to claim offense. Some critics have ridiculed her in turn: "Trigger warning, @Suzanne_moore is talking again." (Moore's Twitter bio now reads, "Media Whore.")

The backlash° has not stopped the growth of the trigger warning, and now that they've entered university classrooms, it's only a matter of time before warnings are demanded for other grade levels. As students introduce them in college newspapers, promotional material for plays, even poetry slams, it's not inconceivable that they'll appear at the beginning of film screenings and at the entrance to art exhibits. Will newspapers start applying warnings to articles about rape, murder, and war? Could they even become a regular feature of speech? "I was walking down Main Street last night when—trigger warning—I saw an elderly woman get mugged."

**raised hackles:** Angered, or bred resentment.    **backlash:** A strong, negative reaction, especially to a social or political movement.

The "Geek Feminism Wiki" states that trigger warnings should be used for   10
"graphic descriptions or extensive discussion" of abuse, torture, self-harm,
suicide, eating disorders, body shaming, and even "psychologically realistic"
depictions of *the mental state* of people suffering from those; it notes that some
have gone further, arguing for warnings before the "depiction or discussion of
any consensual sexual activity [and] of discriminatory attitudes or actions,
such as sexism or racism." The definition on the Queer Dictionary Tumblr is
similar, but expands warnings even to discussion of *statistics* on hate crimes
and self-harming.

As the list of trigger warning–worthy topics continues to grow, there's   11
scant research demonstrating how words "trigger" or how warnings might
help. Most psychological research on PTSD suggests that, for those who have
experienced trauma, "triggers" can be complex and unpredictable, appearing
in many forms, from sounds to smells to weather conditions and times of the
year. In this sense, anything can be a trigger—a musky cologne, a ditsy pop
song, a footprint in the snow.

As a means of navigating the Internet, or setting the tone for academic dis-   12
cussion, the trigger warning is unhelpful. Once we start imposing alerts on
the basis of potential trauma, where do we stop? One of the problems with
the concept of triggering—understanding words as devices that activate a
mechanism or cause a situation—is it promotes a rigid, overly deterministic
approach to language. There is no rational basis for applying warnings because there is no objective measure of words' potential harm. Of course, words
can inspire intense reactions, but they have no intrinsic danger. Two people
who have endured similarly painful experiences, from rape to war, can read
the same material and respond in wholly different ways.

Issuing caution on the basis of potential harm or insult doesn't help us   13
negotiate our reactions; it makes our dealings with others more fraught. As
Breslin pointed out, trigger warnings can have the opposite of their intended
effect, luring in sensitive people (and perhaps connoisseurs of graphic content, too). More importantly, they reinforce the fear of words by depicting an
ever-expanding number of articles and books as dangerous and requiring of
regulation. By framing more public spaces, from the Internet to the college
classroom, as full of infinite yet ill-defined hazards, trigger warnings encourage us to think of ourselves as more weak and fragile than we really are.

What's more, the fear of triggers risks narrowing what we're exposed to.   14
Raechel Tiffe, an assistant professor in Communication Arts and Sciences at
Merrimack College, Massachusetts, described a lesson in which she thought
everything had gone well, until a student approached her about a clip from
the television musical comedy *Glee* in which a student commits suicide. For
Tiffe, who uses trigger warnings for sexual assault and rape, the incident was a
"teaching moment"—not for the students, but for her to be more aware of the
breadth of students' sensitivities.

As academics become more preoccupied with students' feelings of harm,   15
they risk opening the door to a never-ending litany of requests. Last month,
students at Wellesley College protested a sculpture of a man in his underwear

because, according to the Change.org petition, it was a source of "triggering thoughts regarding sexual assault." While the petition acknowledged the sculpture may not disturb everyone on campus, it insisted we share a "responsibility to pay attention to and attempt to answer the needs of all of our community members." Even after the artist explained that the figure was supposed to be sleepwalking, students continued to insist it be moved indoors.

Trigger warnings are presented as a gesture of empathy, but the irony is    16
they lead only to more solipsism, an over-preoccupation with one's own feelings—much to the detriment of society as a whole. Structuring public life around the most fragile personal sensitivities will only restrict all of our horizons. Engaging with ideas involves risk, and slapping warnings on them only undermines the principle of intellectual exploration. We cannot anticipate every potential trigger—the world, like the Internet, is too large and unwieldy.° But even if we could, why would we want to? Bending the world to accommodate our personal frailties does not help us overcome them.

**unwieldy:** Difficult to manage.

## Questions to Start You Thinking

1. **Considering Meaning:** Jarvie states in paragraph 5 that trigger warnings threaten "to define public discussion both online and off." How does she support this argument?

2. **Identifying Writing Strategies:** In paragraph 8, Jarvie notes that trigger warnings have "become the target of humor" in some publications. Why do you think she includes these details? How does this section help support her argument?

3. **Reading Critically:** In paragraph 12, Jarvie writes, "as a means of navigating the Internet, or setting the tone for academic discussion, the trigger warning is unhelpful." What does she mean by "unhelpful"? How does she support this position?

4. **Expanding Vocabulary:** How would you define the word *backlash*, which appears in paragraph 9? What types of backlash has Jarvie identified in her essay?

5. **Making Connections:** After reading William Deresiewicz's article "What Is College For?" (pp. 575–78), how do you think he would respond to the increased use of trigger warnings on college campuses today? Use quotes from the article to support your position.

## Journal Prompts

1. Have you ever been offended by something that you have read or watched on television? How did it make you feel? Do you think there should have been a trigger warning alerting you to the subject matter? Would that

warning have prevented you from reading the article or watching the show?

2. Have you ever participated in a class discussion that grappled with a sensitive topic? How did you, your classmates, and your instructor handle disagreement or any feelings of harm that arose? In retrospect, did you find the discussion to be a productive one? Why or why not?

## Suggestions for Writing

1. Argue in an essay for or against the use of trigger warnings. Make sure you define the term and determine what types of specific trigger warnings you are arguing for or against. Also include where these warnings are or are not appropriate, including on college syllabi, in newspaper articles, on television, and in films.

2. At the end of the essay, Jarvie fears that the use of trigger warnings will lead to restrictions of free speech. Write an argument that either defends or refutes this claim.

## Richard Rodriguez

### Public and Private Language

Christopher Felver/Corbis.

Richard Rodriguez, the son of Spanish-speaking Mexican American parents, was born in 1944 and grew up in San Francisco, where he currently lives. He earned a BA at Stanford University and graduate degrees in English from Columbia University and the University of California at Berkeley. A writer, lecturer, and editor for the Pacific News Service, Rodriguez has served as a contributing editor for *Harper's Magazine, U.S. News & World Report,* and the Sunday Opinion section of the *Los Angeles Times.* He also regularly contributes to PBS's *NewsHour.* His books, which often draw on autobiography to explore race and ethnicity in American society, include *Hunger of Memory* (1982), from which the following selection is drawn; *Days of Obligation: An Argument with My Mexican Father* (1992); and *Brown: The Last Discovery of America* (2002). In "Public and Private Language," he recounts the origin of his complex views of bilingual education.

**AS YOU READ:** Discover the ways in which learning English changed Rodriguez's life and his relationship with his family.

Supporters of bilingual education today imply that students like me miss a great deal by not being taught in their family's language. What they seem not to recognize is that, as a socially disadvantaged child, I considered Spanish to be a private language. What I needed to learn in school was that I had the right—and the obligation—to speak the public language of *los gringos.*° The odd truth is that my first-grade classmates could have become bilingual, in

1

*los gringos:* Spanish for "foreigners," often used as a derogatory term for English-speaking Americans.

the conventional sense of that word, more easily than I. Had they been taught (as upper-middle-class children are often taught early) a second language like Spanish or French, they could have regarded it simply as that: another public language. In my case such bilingualism could not have been so quickly achieved. What I did not believe was that I could speak a single public language.

Without question, it would have pleased me to hear my teachers address me in Spanish when I entered the classroom. I would have felt much less afraid. I would have trusted them and responded with ease. But I would have delayed — for how long postponed? — having to learn the language of public society. I would have evaded — and for how long could I have afforded to delay? — learning the great lesson of school, that I had a public identity.

Fortunately, my teachers were unsentimental about their responsibility. What they understood was that I needed to speak a public language. So their voices would search me out, asking me questions. Each time I'd hear them, I'd look up in surprise to see a nun's face frowning at me. I'd mumble, not really meaning to answer. The nun would persist, "Richard, stand up. Don't look at the floor. Speak up. Speak to the entire class, not just to me!" but I couldn't believe that the English language was mine to use. (In part, I did not want to believe it.) I continued to mumble. I resisted the teacher's demands. (Did I somehow suspect that once I learned public language my pleasing family life would be changed?) Silent, waiting for the bell to sound, I remained dazed, diffident,° afraid.

Because I wrongly imagined that English was intrinsically° a public language and Spanish an intrinsically private one, I easily noticed the difference between classroom language and the language of home. At school, words were directed to a general audience of listeners. ("Boys and girls.") Words were meaningfully ordered. And the point was not self-expression alone but to make oneself understood by many others. The teacher quizzed: "Boys and girls, why do we use that word in this sentence? Could we think of a better word to use there? Would the sentence change its meaning if the words were differently arranged? And wasn't there a better way of saying much the same thing?" (I couldn't say. I wouldn't try to say.)

Three months. Five. Half a year passed. Unsmiling, ever watchful, my teachers noted my silence. They began to connect my behavior with the difficult progress my older sister and brother were making. Until one Saturday morning three nuns arrived at the house to talk to our parents. Stiffly, they sat on the blue living room sofa. From the doorway of another room, spying the visitors, I noted the incongruity° — the clash of two worlds, the faces and voices of school intruding upon the familiar setting of home. I overheard one voice gently wondering, "Do your children speak only Spanish at home, Mrs. Rodriguez?" While another voice added, "That Richard especially seems so timid and shy."

*That Rich-heard!*

With great tact the visitors continued, "Is it possible for you and your husband to encourage your children to practice their English when they are

---

**diffident:** Shy.    **intrinsically:** Essentially; inherently.    **incongruity:** Lack of harmony or appropriateness.

home?" Of course, my parents complied. What would they not do for their children's well-being? And how could they have questioned the Church's authority which those women represented? In an instant, they agreed to give up the language (the sounds) that had revealed and accentuated our family's closeness. The moment after the visitors left, the change was observed. "*Ahora,*° speak to us *en inglés,*"° my father and mother united to tell us.

At first, it seemed a kind of game. After dinner each night, the family gathered to practice "our" English. (It was still then *inglés,* a language foreign to us, so we felt drawn as strangers to it.) Laughing, we would try to define words we could not pronounce. We played with strange English sounds, often overanglicizing our pronunciations. And we filled the smiling gaps of our sentences with familiar Spanish sounds. But that was cheating, somebody shouted. Everyone laughed. In school, meanwhile, like my brother and sister, I was required to attend a daily tutoring session. I needed a full year of special attention. I also needed my teachers to keep my attention from straying in class by calling out, *Rich-heard*—their English voices slowly prying loose my ties to my other name, its three notes, *Ri-car-do.* Most of all I needed to hear my mother and father speak to me in a moment of seriousness in broken—suddenly heartbreaking—English. The scene was inevitable: one Saturday morning I entered the kitchen where my parents were talking in Spanish. I did not realize that they were talking in Spanish however until, at the moment they saw me, I heard their voices change to speak English. Those *gringo* sounds they uttered startled me. Pushed me away. In that moment of trivial misunderstanding and profound insight, I felt my throat twisted by unsounded grief. I turned quickly and left the room. But I had no place to escape to with Spanish. (The spell was broken.) My brother and sisters were speaking English in another part of the house.

Again and again in the days following, increasingly angry, I was obliged to hear my mother and father: "Speak to us *en inglés.*" (*Speak.*) Only then did I determine to learn classroom English. Weeks after, it happened: one day in school I had my hand raised to volunteer an answer. I spoke out in a loud voice. And I did not think it remarkable when the entire class understood. That day, I moved very far from the disadvantaged child I had been only days earlier. The belief, that calming assurance that I belonged in public, had at last taken hold.

Shortly after, I stopped hearing the high and loud sounds of *los gringos.* A more and more confident speaker of English, I didn't trouble to listen to *how* strangers sounded, speaking to me. And there simply were too many English-speaking people in my day for me to hear American accents anymore. Conversations quickened. Listening to persons whose voices sounded eccentrically pitched, I usually noted their sounds for an initial few seconds before I concentrated on *what* they were saying. Conversations became content-full. Transparent. Hearing someone's *tone* of voice—angry or questioning or sarcastic or happy or sad—I didn't distinguish it from the words it

*Ahora:* Spanish for "now."   *en inglés:* Spanish for "in English."

expressed. Sound and word were thus tightly wedded. At the end of a day, I was often bemused, always relieved, to realize how "silent," though crowded with words, my day in public had been. (This public silence measured and quickened the change in my life.)

At last, seven years old, I came to believe what had been technically true since my birth: I was an American citizen.

But the special feeling of closeness at home was diminished by then. Gone was the desperate, urgent, intense feeling of being at home; rare was the experience of feeling myself individualized by family intimates. We remained a loving family, but one greatly changed. No longer so close; no longer bound tight by the pleasing and troubling knowledge of our public separateness. Neither my older brother nor sister rushed home after school anymore. Nor did I. When I arrived home there would often be neighborhood kids in the house. Or the house would be empty of sounds.

Following the dramatic Americanization of their children, even my parents grew more publicly confident. Especially my mother. She learned the names of all the people on our block. And she decided we needed to have a telephone installed in the house. My father continued to use the word *gringo*. But it was no longer charged with the old bitterness or distrust. (Stripped of any emotional content, the word simply became a name for those Americans not of Hispanic descent.) Hearing him, sometimes, I wasn't sure if he was pronouncing the Spanish word *gringo* or saying gringo in English.

Matching the silence I started hearing in public was a new quiet at home. The family's quiet was partly due to the fact that, as we children learned more and more English, we shared fewer and fewer words with our parents. Sentences needed to be spoken slowly when a child addressed his mother or father. (Often the parent wouldn't understand.) The child would need to repeat himself. (Still the parent misunderstood.) The young voice, frustrated, would end up saying, "Never mind"—the subject was closed. Dinners would be noisy with the clinking of knives and forks against dishes. My mother would smile softly between her remarks; my father at the other end of the table would chew and chew at his food, while he stared over the heads of his children.

My *mother!* My *father!* After English became my primary language, I no longer knew what words to use in addressing my parents. The old Spanish words (those tender accents of sound) I had used earlier—*mamá* and *papá*—I couldn't use anymore. They would have been all-too-painful reminders of how much had changed in my life. On the other hand, the words I heard neighborhood kids call *their* parents seemed equally unsatisfactory. *Mother* and *Father; Ma, Papa, Pa, Dad, Pop* (how I hated the all-American sound of that last word especially)—all these terms I felt were unsuitable, not really terms of address for *my* parents. As a result, I never used them at home. Whenever I'd speak to my parents, I would try to get their attention with eye contact alone. In public conversations, I'd refer to "my parents" or "my mother and father."

My mother and father, for their part, responded differently, as their children spoke to them less and less. My mother grew restless, seemed troubled and anxious at the scarcity of words exchanged in the house. It was she who would question me about my day when I came home from school. She smiled at the small talk. She pried at the edges of my sentences to get me to say something more. (What?) She'd join conversations she overheard, but her intrusions often stopped her children's talking. By contrast, my father seemed reconciled to the new quiet. Though his English improved somewhat, he retired into silence. At dinner he spoke very little. One night his children and even his wife helplessly giggled at his garbled English pronunciation of the Catholic Grace before Meals. Thereafter he made his wife recite the prayer at the start of each meal, even on formal occasions, when there were guests in the house. Hers became the public voice of the family. On official business, it was she, not my father, one would usually hear on the phone or in stores, talking to strangers. His children grew so accustomed to his silence that, years later, they would speak routinely of his shyness. (My mother would often try to explain: both his parents died when he was eight. He was raised by an uncle who treated him like little more than a menial servant. He was never encouraged to speak. He grew up alone. A man of few words.) But my father was not shy, I realized, when I'd watch him speaking Spanish with relatives. Using Spanish, he was quickly effusive.° Especially when talking with other men, his voice would spark, flicker, flare alive with sounds. In Spanish, he expressed ideas and feelings he rarely revealed in English. With firm Spanish sounds, he conveyed confidence and authority English would never allow him.

The silence at home, however, was finally more than a literal silence. 17
Fewer words passed between parent and child, but more profound was the silence that resulted from my inattention to sounds. At about the time I no longer bothered to listen with care to the sounds of English in public, I grew careless about listening to the sounds family members made when they spoke. Most of the time I heard someone speaking at home and didn't distinguish his sounds from the words people uttered in public. I didn't even pay much attention to my parents' accented and ungrammatical speech. At least not at home. Only when I was with them in public would I grow alert to their accents. Though, even then, their sounds caused me less and less concern. For I was increasingly confident of my own public identity.

Today I hear bilingual educators say that children lose a degree of "indi- 18
viduality" by becoming assimilated into public society. (Bilingual schooling was popularized in the seventies, that decade when middle-class ethnics began to resist the process of assimilation — the American melting pot.) But the bilingualists simplistically scorn the value and necessity of assimilation. They do not seem to realize that there are *two* ways a person is individualized. So they do not realize that while one suffers a diminished sense of *private* individuality by becoming assimilated into public society, such assimilation makes possible the achievement of *public* individuality.

**effusive:** Talkative; unreserved.

## Questions to Start You Thinking

1. **Considering Meaning:** What created the new "silence" in the Rodriguez household? Explain why.

2. **Identifying Writing Strategies:** How does Rodriguez use comparison and contrast to convey his experience learning English?

3. **Reading Critically:** How does Rodriguez use dialogue to make the experience he recalls more vivid for his readers? Is this strategy effective in helping him achieve his purpose? Why, or why not?

4. **Expanding Vocabulary:** Rodriguez uses the terms *private* and *public*. What do these words mean when used as adjectives to describe "language" and "identity"?

5. **Making Connections:** Rodriguez's parents changed the language spoken at home because they placed a high value on their children's success. Does this sacrifice relate to the decisions described in Judith Ortiz Cofer's "More Room" (pp. 483–86)? Why, or why not?

## Link to the Paired Essay

Both Rodriguez and Amy Tan ("Mother Tongue," pp. 564–68) grew up in homes in which English was spoken as a second language. Compare and contrast how each writer's mastery of English affected his or her parents.

## Journal Prompts

1. Recall a time when your public identity was at odds with your private self.

2. Has an accomplishment that you are proud of ever had a negative effect on another aspect of your life or on other people around you?

## Suggestions for Writing

1. If you speak a second language, write an essay recalling your experience learning it. What were some of your struggles? Can you relate to Rodriguez's experience? How do you use that language today? If you do not know a second language, write an essay in which you analyze possible benefits of learning one. What language would you like to learn? Why?

2. According to Rodriguez, "Supporters of bilingual education today imply that students like me miss a great deal by not being taught in their family's language" (paragraph 1). Rodriguez counters this assumption by showing how his immersion in English allowed him to develop a public identity that ultimately led to his success. At the same time, however, his English-only immersion hurt his family life. Write an essay in which you take a stand on the complex topic of bilingual education, using further reading and research to support your position about how it does or does not benefit students.

# Amy Tan

## Mother Tongue

Amy Tan was born in 1952 in Oakland, California, a few years after her parents immigrated to the United States from China. After receiving a BA and then an MA in linguistics, Tan worked as a specialist in language development before becoming a freelance business writer in 1981. Tan's first short story (1985) became the basis for her first novel, *The Joy Luck Club* (1990), which was a phenomenal bestseller and was made into a movie. Tan's second novel, *The Kitchen God's Wife* (1991), was equally popular. Besides her many novels, she has written a book of autobiographical essays, children's books, and the libretto for an opera based on her novel *The Bonesetter's Daughter* (2001). Her work has been translated into thirty-five languages. Throughout her work run themes of family relationships, loyalty, and ways of reconciling past and present. "Mother Tongue" first appeared in *Threepenny Review* in 1990. In this essay, Tan explores the effect of her mother's "broken" English—the language Tan grew up with—on her life and writing.

**AS YOU READ:** Identify the difficulties Tan says exist for a child growing up in a family that speaks nonstandard English.

I am not a scholar of English or literature. I cannot give you much more than personal opinions on the English language and its variations in this country or others.

I am a writer. And by that definition, I am someone who has always loved language. I am fascinated by language in daily life. I spend a great deal of my time thinking about the power of language — the way it can evoke an emotion, a visual image, a complex idea, or a simple truth. Language is the tool of my trade. And I use them all — all the Englishes I grew up with.

Recently, I was made keenly aware of the different Englishes I do use. I was giving a talk to a large group of people, the same talk I had already given to half a dozen other groups. The nature of the talk was about my writing, my life, and my book, *The Joy Luck Club*. The talk was going along well enough, until I remembered one major difference that made the whole talk sound wrong. My mother was in the room. And it was perhaps the first time she had heard me give a lengthy speech, using the kind of English I have never used with her. I was saying things like, "The intersection of memory upon imagination" and "There is an aspect of my fiction that relates to thus-and-thus"—a speech filled with carefully wrought° grammatical phrases, burdened, it suddenly seemed to me, with nominalized° forms, past perfect tenses, conditional phrases, all the forms of Standard English that I had learned in school and through books, the forms of English I did not use at home with my mother.

Just last week, I was walking down the street with my mother, and I again found myself conscious of the English I was using, and the English I do use

---

**wrought:** Crafted.     **nominalized:** Made into a noun from a verb.

with her. We were talking about the price of new and used furniture and I heard myself saying this: "Not waste money that way." My husband was with us as well, and he didn't notice any switch in my English. And then I realized why. It's because over the twenty years we've been together I've often used that same kind of English with him, and sometimes he even uses it with me. It has become our language of intimacy, a different sort of English that relates to family talk, the language I grew up with.

So you'll have some idea of what this family talk I heard sounds like, I'll   5 quote what my mother said during a recent conversation which I videotaped and then transcribed.° During this conversation, my mother was talking about a political gangster in Shanghai who had the same last name as her family's, Du, and how the gangster in his early years wanted to be adopted by her family, which was rich by comparison. Later, the gangster became more powerful, far richer than my mother's family, and one day showed up at my mother's wedding to pay his respects. Here's what she said in part:

"Du Yusong having business like fruit stand. Like off the street kind. He   6 is like Du Zong—but not Tsung-ming Island people. The local people call putong, the river east side, he belong to that side local people. That man want to ask Du Zong father take him in like become own family. Du Zong father wasn't look down on him, but didn't take seriously, until that man big like become a mafia. Now important person, very hard to inviting him. Chinese way, came only to show respect, don't stay for dinner. Respect for making big celebration, he shows up. Mean gives lots of respect. Chinese custom. Chinese social life that way. If too important won't have to stay too long. He come to my wedding. I didn't see, I heard it. I gone to boy's side, they have YMCA dinner. Chinese age I was nineteen."

You should know that my mother's expressive command of English   7 belies° how much she actually understands. She reads the *Forbes* report, listens to *Wall Street Week*, converses daily with her stockbroker, reads all of Shirley MacLaine's books with ease—all kinds of things I can't begin to understand. Yet some of my friends tell me they understand fifty percent of what my mother says. Some say they understand eighty to ninety percent. Some say they understand none of it, as if she were speaking pure Chinese. But to me, my mother's English is perfectly clear, perfectly natural. It's my mother tongue. Her language, as I hear it, is vivid, direct, full of observation and imagery. That was the language that helped shape the way I saw things, expressed things, made sense of the world.

Lately, I've been giving more thought to the kind of English my mother   8 speaks. Like others, I have described it to people as "broken" or "fractured" English. But I wince when I say that. It has always bothered me that I can think of no way to describe it other than "broken," as if it were damaged and needed to be fixed, as if it lacked a certain wholeness and soundness. I've

---

**transcribed:** Made a written copy of what was said.    **belies:** Contradicts; creates a misleading impression.

heard other terms used, "limited English," for example. But they seem just as bad, as if everything is limited, including people's perceptions of the limited English speaker.

I know this for a fact, because when I was growing up, my mother's "limited" English limited *my* perception of her. I was ashamed of her English. I believed that her English reflected the quality of what she had to say. That is, because she expressed them imperfectly her thoughts were imperfect. And I had plenty of empirical evidence to support me: the fact that people in department stores, at banks, and at restaurants did not take her seriously, did not give her good service, pretended not to understand her, or even acted as if they did not hear her.

My mother has long realized the limitations of her English as well. When I was fifteen, she used to have me call people on the phone to pretend I was she. In this guise, I was forced to ask for information or even to complain and yell at people who had been rude to her. One time it was a call to her stockbroker in New York. She had cashed out her small portfolio and it just so happened we were going to go to New York the next week, our very first trip outside California. I had to get on the phone and say in an adolescent voice that was not very convincing, "This is Mrs. Tan."

And my mother was standing in the back whispering loudly, "Why he don't send me check, already two weeks late. So mad he lie to me, losing me money."

And then I said in perfect English, "Yes, I'm getting rather concerned. You had agreed to send the check two weeks ago, but it hasn't arrived."

Then she began to talk more loudly. "What he want, I come to New York tell him front of his boss, you cheating me?" And I was trying to calm her down, make her be quiet, while telling the stockbroker, "I can't tolerate any more excuses. If I don't receive the check immediately, I am going to have to speak to your manager when I'm in New York next week." And sure enough, the following week there we were in front of this astonished stockbroker, and I was sitting there red-faced and quiet, and my mother, the real Mrs. Tan, was shouting at his boss in her impeccable broken English.

We used a similar routine just five days ago, for a situation that was far less humorous. My mother had gone to the hospital for an appointment, to find out about a benign brain tumor a CAT scan had revealed a month ago. She said she had spoken very good English, her best English, no mistakes. Still, she said, the hospital did not apologize when they said they had lost the CAT scan and she had come for nothing. She said they did not seem to have any sympathy when she told them she was anxious to know the exact diagnosis, since her husband and son had both died of brain tumors. She said they would not give her any more information until the next time and she would have to make another appointment for that. So she said she would not leave until the doctor called her daughter. She wouldn't budge. And when the doctor finally called her daughter, me, who spoke in perfect English—lo and behold—we had assurances the CAT scan would be found, promises that a conference call on Monday would be held, and apologies for any suffering my mother had gone through for a most regrettable mistake.

I think my mother's English almost had an effect on limiting my possibilities in life as well. Sociologists and linguists probably will tell you that a person's developing language skills are more influenced by peers. But I think that the language spoken in the family, especially in immigrant families which are more insular,° plays a large role in shaping the language of the child. And I believe that it affected my results on achievement tests, IQ tests, and the SAT. While my English skills were never judged as poor, compared to math, English could not be considered my strong suit. In grade school I did moderately well, getting perhaps B's, sometimes B-pluses, in English and scoring perhaps in the sixtieth or seventieth percentile on achievement tests. But those scores were not good enough to override the opinion that my true abilities lay in math and science, because in those areas I achieved A's and scored in the ninetieth percentile or higher.

This was understandable. Math is precise; there is only one correct an-　16 swer. Whereas, for me at least, the answers on English tests were always a judgment call, a matter of opinion and personal experience. Those tests were constructed around items like fill-in-the-blank sentence completion, such as, "Even though Tom was _____ , Mary thought he was _____ ." And the correct answer always seemed to be the most bland combinations of thoughts, for example, "Even though Tom was shy, Mary thought he was charming," with the grammatical structure "even though" limiting the correct answer to some sort of semantic° opposites, so you wouldn't get answers like, "Even though Tom was foolish, Mary thought he was ridiculous." Well, according to my mother, there were very few limitations as to what Tom could have been and what Mary might have thought of him. So I never did well on tests like that.

The same was true with word analogies, pairs of words in which you were　17 supposed to find some sort of logical, semantic relationship — for example, "*Sunset* is to *nightfall* as _____ is to _____ ." And here you would be presented with a list of four possible pairs, one of which showed the same kind of relationship: *red* is to *stoplight, bus* is to *arrival, chills* is to *fever, yawn* is to *boring*. Well, I could never think that way. I knew what the tests were asking, but I could not block out of my mind the images already created by the first pair, "*sunset* is to *nightfall*" — and I would see a burst of colors against a darkening sky, the moon rising, the lowering of a curtain of stars. And all the other pairs of words — *red, bus, stoplight, boring* — just threw up a mass of confusing images, making it impossible for me to sort out something as logical as saying: "A sunset precedes nightfall" is the same as "a chill precedes a fever." The only way I would have gotten that answer right would have been to imagine an associative situation, for example, my being disobedient and staying out past sunset, catching a chill at night, which turns into feverish pneumonia as punishment, which indeed did happen to me.

I have been thinking about all this lately, about my mother's English, about　18 achievement tests. Because lately I've been asked, as a writer, why there are not more Asian Americans enrolled in creative writing programs. Why do so many Chinese students go into engineering? Well, these are broad sociological

---

**insular:** Detached or isolated; keeping to oneself.　　**semantic:** Relating to the meaning of language.

questions I can't begin to answer. But I have noticed in surveys—in fact, just last week—that Asian students, as a whole, always do significantly better on math achievement tests than in English. And this makes me think that there are other Asian American students whose English spoken in the home might also be described as "broken" or "limited." And perhaps they also have teachers who are steering them away from writing and into math and science, which is what happened to me.

Fortunately, I happen to be rebellious in nature and enjoy the challenge of disproving assumptions made about me. I became an English major my first year in college, after being enrolled as pre-med. I started writing nonfiction as a freelancer the week after I was told by my former boss that writing was my worst skill and I should hone my talents toward account management. 19

But it wasn't until 1985 that I finally began to write fiction. And at first I wrote using what I thought to be wittily crafted sentences, sentences that would finally prove I had mastery over the English language. Here's an example from the first draft of a story that later made its way into *The Joy Luck Club*, but without this line: "That was my mental quandary in its nascent° state." A terrible line, which I can barely pronounce. 20

Fortunately, for reasons I won't get into today, I later decided I should envision a reader for the stories I would write. And the reader I decided upon was my mother, because these were stories about mothers. So with this reader in mind—and in fact she did read my early drafts—I began to write stories using all the Englishes I grew up with: the English I spoke to my mother, which for lack of a better term might be described as "simple"; the English she used with me, which for lack of a better term might be described as "broken"; my translation of her Chinese, which could certainly be described as "watered down"; and what I imagined to be her translation of her Chinese if she could speak in perfect English, her internal language, and for that I sought to preserve the essence, but neither an English nor a Chinese structure. I wanted to capture what language ability tests can never reveal: her intent, her passion, her imagery, the rhythms of her speech, and the nature of her thoughts. 21

Apart from what any critic had to say about my writing, I knew I had succeeded where it counted when my mother finished reading my book and gave me her verdict: "So easy to read." 22

nascent: Beginning; only partly formed.

## Questions to Start You Thinking

1. **Considering Meaning:** What are the Englishes that Tan grew up with? What other Englishes has she used in her life? What does each English have that gives it an advantage over the other Englishes in certain situations?

2. **Identifying Writing Strategies:** What examples does Tan use to analyze the various Englishes she uses? How has Tan been able to synthesize her Englishes successfully into her present style of writing fiction?

3. **Reading Critically:** Although Tan explains that she writes using "all the Englishes" she has known throughout her life (paragraph 21), she doesn't do that in this essay. What are the differences between the English Tan uses in this essay and the kinds she says she uses in her fiction? How does the language she uses here fit the purpose of her essay?

4. **Expanding Vocabulary:** In paragraph 9, Tan writes that she had "plenty of empirical evidence" that her mother's "limited" English meant that her mother's thoughts were "imperfect" as well. Define *empirical*. What does Tan's use of this word tell us about her present attitude toward the way she judged her mother when she was growing up?

5. **Making Connections:** In paragraph 18, Tan discusses her concern that Asian American students whose language is described as "broken" or "limited" might be steered away from writing and into math and science, just as she was. Based on his observations in "The Right to Fail" (pp. 571–73), how do you think that William Zinsser would respond to such actions by educators? Why?

## Link to the Paired Essay

Tan and Richard Rodriguez ("Public and Private Language," pp. 558–62) recount learning English as they grew up in homes where English was a second language. In what way did they face similar experiences and obstacles? How did learning English affect their self-image and influence their relationship with their family?

## Journal Prompts

1. Describe one of the Englishes you use to communicate. When do you use it, and when do you avoid using it?

2. In what ways are you a "translator," if not of language, then of current trends and fashions, for your parents or other members of your family?

## Suggestions for Writing

1. In a personal essay explain an important event in your family's history, using your family's various Englishes or other languages.

2. Take note of and, if possible, transcribe a conversation you have had with a parent or other family member, with a teacher, and with a close friend. Write an essay comparing and contrasting the "languages" of the three conversations. How do the languages differ? How do you account for these differences? What might happen if someone used "teacher language" to talk to a friend or "friend language" in a class discussion or paper?

# 29  The Good Life

*Image credits, clockwise from top left:* Sally Anscombe/Taxi/Getty Images; Jim West/Alamy; Jose Luis Pelaez Inc/Blend Images/Getty Images; Miha Pavlin/Moment Select/Getty Images.

## Responding to an Image

Look carefully at one of these four photographs. What time of day do you imagine the photograph was taken? Where are the people, and what are they doing? What relationships and emotions does the image suggest? Write about what the photograph seems to be saying about one or more possible elements of a happy life or a life well lived. If the photograph reminds you of your own experiences, either similar or dissimilar, bring those recollections into your written response to the photograph.

# William Zinsser

## The Right to Fail

William Zinsser (1922–2015) was a feature writer for the *New York Herald Tribune* and later the drama and film critic. Although he covered subjects ranging from American landmarks to jazz in his many books and magazine articles, he is probably best known for his classic guides to writing: *On Writing Well* (1976), *Inventing the Truth* (1987), *Writing to Learn* (1988), *Writing about Your Life* (2004), and *Writing Places* (2010). Zinsser taught at Yale University, the New School, and the Columbia University Graduate School of Journalism. In "The Right to Fail," an excerpt from *The Lunacy Boom* (1970), Zinsser makes the case that failure is an important aspect of human experience.

Walter Daran/
The LIFE Picture Collection/
Getty Images.

**AS YOU READ:** Identify the benefits of failure that Zinsser presents.

I like "dropout" as an addition to the American language because it's brief and it's clear. What I don't like is that we use it almost entirely as a dirty word.

We only apply it to people under twenty-one. Yet an adult who spends his days and nights watching mindless TV programs is more of a dropout than an eighteen-year-old who quits college, with its frequently mindless courses, to become, say, a VISTA volunteer. For the young, dropping out is often a way of dropping in.

To hold this opinion, however, is little short of treason in America. A boy or girl who leaves college is branded a failure — and the right to fail is one of the few freedoms that this country does not grant its citizens. The American dream is a dream of "getting ahead," painted in strokes of gold wherever we look. Our advertisements and TV commercials are a hymn to material success, our magazine articles a toast to people who made it to the top. Smoke the right cigarette or drive the right car — so the ads imply — and girls will be swooning into your deodorized arms or caressing your expensive lapels. Happiness goes to the man who has the sweet smell of achievement. He is our national idol, and everybody else is our national fink.°

I want to put in a word for the fink, especially the teen-age fink, because if we give him time to get through his finkdom — if we release him from the pressure of attaining certain goals by a certain age — he has a good chance of becoming our national idol, a Jefferson° or a Thoreau,° a Buckminster Fuller° or an Adlai Stevenson,° a man with a mind of his own. We need mavericks° and dissenters and dreamers far more than we need junior vice presidents, but

**fink:** Tattletale or other contemptible person.    **Jefferson:** Thomas Jefferson (1743–1826), the third president of the United States and the main author of the Declaration of Independence.    **Thoreau:** Henry David Thoreau (1817–1862), an American writer and naturalist.    **Buckminster Fuller:** American inventor, architect, and engineer (1895–1983) who dropped out of Harvard to work on solving global resource and environmental problems.    **Adlai Stevenson:** American politician (1900–1965) who was greatly admired for championing liberal causes but badly lost two presidential elections.    **mavericks:** Nonconformists.

we paralyze them by insisting that every step be a step up to the next rung of the ladder. Yet in the fluid years of youth, the only way for boys and girls to find their proper road is often to take a hundred side trips, poking out in different directions, faltering, drawing back, and starting again.

"But what if we fail?" they ask, whispering the dreadful word across the Generation Gap to their parents, who are back home at the Establishment, nursing their "middle-class values" and cultivating their "goal-oriented society." The parents whisper back: "Don't!"

What they should say is "Don't be afraid to fail!" Failure isn't fatal. Countless people have had a bout with it and come out stronger as a result. Many have even come out famous. History is strewn with eminent dropouts, "loners" who followed their own trail, not worrying about its odd twists and turns because they had faith in their own sense of direction. To read their biographies is always exhilarating, not only because they beat the system, but because their system was better than the one that they beat.

Luckily, such rebels still turn up often enough to prove that individualism, though badly threatened, is not extinct. Much has been written, for instance, about the fitful scholastic career of Thomas P. F. Hoving, New York's former Parks Commissioner and now director of the Metropolitan Museum of Art. Hoving was a dropout's dropout, entering and leaving schools as if they were motels, often at the request of the management. Still, he must have learned something during those unorthodox years, for he dropped in again at the top of his profession.

His case reminds me of another boyhood—that of Holden Caulfield in J. D. Salinger's *The Catcher in the Rye,* the most popular literary hero of the postwar period. There is nothing accidental about the grip that this dropout continues to hold on the affections of an entire American generation. Nobody else, real or invented, has made such an engaging shambles of our "goal-oriented society," so gratified our secret belief that the "phonies" are in power and the good guys up the creek. Whether Holden has also reached the top of his chosen field today is one of those speculations that delight fanciers of good fiction. I speculate that he has. Holden Caulfield, incidentally, is now thirty-six.

I'm not urging everyone to go out and fail just for the sheer therapy of it, or to quit college just to coddle° some vague discontent. Obviously it's better to succeed than to flop, and in general a long education is more helpful than a short one. (Thanks to my own education, for example, I can tell George Eliot from T. S. Eliot, I can handle the pluperfect tense in French, and I know that Caesar beat the Helvetii because he had enough frumentum.°) I only mean that failure isn't bad in itself, or success automatically good.

Fred Zinnemann, who has directed some of Hollywood's most honored movies, was asked by a reporter, when *A Man for All Seasons* won every prize,

---

**coddle:** Indulge; satisfy.     **frumentum:** Latin word for corn or grain.

about his previous film *Behold a Pale Horse,* which was a box-office disaster. "I don't feel any obligation to be successful," Zinnemann replied. "Success can be dangerous—you feel you know it all. I've learned a great deal from my failures." A similar point was made by Richard Brooks about his ambitious money loser, *Lord Jim.* Recalling the three years of his life that went into it, talking almost with elation about the troubles that befell his unit in Cambodia, Brooks told me that he learned more about his craft from this considerable failure than from his many earlier hits.

It's a point, of course, that applies throughout the arts. Writers, play- 11 wrights, painters, and composers work in the expectation of periodic defeat, but they wouldn't keep going back into the arena if they thought it was the end of the world. It isn't the end of the world. For an artist—and perhaps for anybody—it is the only way to grow.

Today's younger generation seems to know that this is true, seems willing 12 to take the risks in life that artists take in art. "Society," needless to say, still has the upper hand—it sets the goals and condemns as a failure everybody who won't play. But the dropouts and the hippies are not as afraid of fail-ure as their parents and grandparents. This could mean, as their elders might say, that they are just plumb lazy, secure in the comforts of an affluent state. It could also mean, however, that they just don't buy the old standards of success and are rapidly writing new ones.

Recently it was announced, for instance, that more than two hundred 13 thousand Americans have inquired about service in VISTA (the domes-tic Peace Corps) and that, according to a Gallup survey, "more than three million American college students would serve VISTA in some capacity if given the opportunity." This is hardly the road to riches or to an executive suite. Yet I have met many of these young volunteers, and they are not pining for traditional success. On the contrary, they appear more fulfilled than the average vice president with a swimming pool.

Who is to say, then, if there is any right path to the top, or even to say 14 what the top consists of? Obviously the colleges don't have more than a partial answer—otherwise the young would not be so disaffected with an education that they consider vapid.° Obviously business does not have the answer—otherwise the young would not be so scornful of its call to be an organization man.

The fact is, nobody has the answer, and the dawning awareness of this 15 fact seems to me one of the best things happening in America today. Suc-cess and failure are again becoming individual visions, as they were when the country was younger, not rigid categories. Maybe we are learning again to cherish this right of every person to succeed on his own terms and to fail as often as necessary along the way.

---

**vapid:** Dull.

## Questions to Start You Thinking

1. **Considering Meaning:** What does Zinsser mean when he says that "dropping out is often a way of dropping in" (paragraph 2)? Why is this especially true for young adults?

2. **Identifying Writing Strategies:** Identify some of the concrete examples that Zinsser uses to illustrate his points. Are his examples extensive and varied enough to be convincing? Why, or why not?

3. **Reading Critically:** Zinsser is savvy enough to admit that his position is "little short of treason in America" (paragraph 3). Where else does he acknowledge that his advice might seem outlandish? How does he counter the opposition?

4. **Expanding Vocabulary:** In paragraph 3, Zinsser writes, "Our advertisements and TV commercials are a hymn to material success." Define *hymn*. What does the word suggest about the American attitude toward material success? How does Zinsser feel about the American dream?

5. **Making Connections:** Zinsser says in paragraph 13 that the volunteers he has met seemed "more fulfilled than the average vice president." How would Miya Tokumitsu ("In the Name of Love," pp. 590–95) view the satisfaction felt by these volunteers? Do you think she would argue that their situation is "masking the . . . exploitative mechanisms of labor" (paragraph 32 of her essay)? Use quotes from her essay to back up your position.

## Journal Prompts

1. What is your definition of the "American dream" (paragraph 3)?

2. Who would you like to share Zinsser's essay with in order to open up that person's mind about failure? Why?

## Suggestions for Writing

1. In paragraph 10, Zinsser offers the following quote from a movie director: "Success can be dangerous—you feel you know it all. I've learned a great deal from my failures." Write an essay in which you recall a personal experience that illustrates this statement.

2. Originally written in 1970, Zinsser's essay includes some examples that may not be familiar to you. Write an essay that supports and updates Zinsser's position by drawing on more current examples from history, literature, sports, current events, or popular culture. Imagine a specific audience for your essay (perhaps a sibling, a friend, or a high school class). Be sure your examples will have an impact on those readers.

# William Deresiewicz

## What Is College For?

Aleeza Nussbaum.

William Deresiewicz is an author, essayist, and literary critic. Born in 1964 in Englewood, New Jersey, Deresiewicz attended Columbia University and taught English at Yale University from 1998 to 2008. He is a contributing writer for the *Nation*, and has had articles published in the *American Scholar*, the *New Republic*, and the *New York Times*. Deresiewicz gained high praise for his book *Excellent Sheep: The Miseducation of the American Elite and the Way to a Meaningful Life* (2014). His essays include "Leadership: The West Point Lecture," "The Death of Friendship," and "What the Ivy League Won't Teach You." In the following excerpt from *Excellent Sheep*, Deresiewicz explores the benefits of a college education.

**AS YOU READ:** What are the real benefits of a college education as outlined by the author?

"Return on investment": that's the phrase you often hear today when 1 people talk about college. How much money will you get out of doing it, in other words, relative to the amount that you have to put in. What no one seems to ask is what the "return" that college is supposed to give you is. Is it just about earning more money? Is the only purpose of an education to enable you to get a job? What, in short, is college for?

We talk, in the overheated conversation we've been having about higher 2 education lately, about soaring tuition, rising student debt, and the daunting labor market for new graduates. We talk about the future of the university: budget squeezes, distance learning,° massive open online courses, and whether college in its present form is even necessary. We talk about national competitiveness, the twenty-first-century labor force, technology and engineering, and the outlook for our future prosperity. But we never talk about the premises that underlie this conversation, as if what makes for a happy life and a good society were simply self-evident, and as if in either case the exclusive answer were more money.

Of course money matters: jobs matter, financial security matters, national 3 prosperity matters. The question is, are they the only things that matter? Life is more than a job; jobs are more than a paycheck; and a country is more than its wealth. Education is more than the acquisition of marketable skills, and you are more than your ability to contribute to your employer's bottom line or the nation's GDP, no matter what the rhetoric of politicians or executives would have you think. To ask what college is for is to ask what life is for, what society is for—what people are for.

Do students ever hear this? What they hear is a constant drumbeat, in 4 the public discourse,° that seeks to march them in the opposite direction.

**distance learning:** Remote education in which instruction and lectures are delivered online.    **discourse:** Discussion.

When policy makers talk about higher education, from the president all the way down, they talk exclusively in terms of math and science. Journalists and pundits — some of whom were humanities majors and none of whom are nurses or engineers — never tire of lecturing the young about the necessity of thinking prudently when choosing a course of study, the naïveté of wanting to learn things just because you're curious about them. "Top Ten Majors" means the most employable, not the most interesting. "Top Ten Fields" means average income, not job satisfaction. "What are you going to do with that?" the inevitable sneering question goes. "Liberal arts" has become a put-down, and "English major" a punch line.

I'm not sure what the practicality police are so concerned about. It's not as if our students were clamoring to get into classes on Milton or Kant. The dreaded English major is now the choice of all of 3 percent. Business, at 21 percent, accounts for more than half again as many majors as all of the arts and humanities combined. In 1971, 73 percent of incoming freshmen said that it is essential or very important to "develop a meaningful philosophy of life," 37 percent to be "very well-off financially" (not well-off, note, but very well-off). By 2011, the numbers were almost reversed, 47 percent and 80 percent, respectively. For well over thirty years, we've been loudly announcing that happiness is money, with a side order of fame. No wonder students have come to believe that college is all about getting a job. . . .

Anyone who tells you that the sole purpose of education is the acquisition of negotiable skills is attempting to reduce you to a productive employee at work, a gullible° consumer in the market, and a docile subject of the state. What's at stake, when we ask what college is for, is nothing less than our ability to remain fully human.

The first thing that college is for is to teach you to think. That's a cliché, but it does actually mean something, and a great deal more than what is usually intended. It doesn't simply mean developing the mental skills particular to individual disciplines — how to solve an equation or construct a study or analyze a text — or even acquiring the ability to work across the disciplines. It means developing the habit of skepticism and the capacity to put it into practice. It means learning not to take things for granted, so you can reach your own conclusions.

Before you can learn, you have to unlearn. You don't arrive in college a blank slate; you arrive having already been inscribed with all the ways of thinking and feeling that the world has been instilling in you from the moment you were born: the myths, the narratives, the pieties,° the assumptions, the values, the sacred words. Your soul, in the words of Allan Bloom,°

**gullible:** Easily convinced.    **pieties:** Uncontested beliefs.    **Allan Bloom:** American philosopher and academic (1930–1992) best known for his controversial bestseller *The Closing of the American Mind: How Higher Education Has Failed Democracy and Impoverished the Souls of Today's Students* (1987).

is a mirror of what is around you. I always noticed, as a teacher of freshmen, that my students could be counted on to produce an opinion about any given subject the moment that I brought it up. It was not that they had necessarily considered the matter before. It was that their minds were like a chemical bath of conventional attitudes that would instantly precipitate out of solution and coat whatever object you introduced. (I've also noticed the phenomenon is not confined to eighteen-year-olds.)

Society is a conspiracy to keep itself from the truth. We pass our lives   9 submerged in propaganda: advertising messages; political rhetoric; the journalistic affirmation of the status quo; the platitudes of popular culture; the axioms of party, sect, and class; the bromides° we exchange every day on Facebook; the comforting lies our parents tell us and the sociable ones our friends do; the steady stream of falsehoods that we each tell ourselves all the time, to stave off the threat of self-knowledge. Plato called this *doxa,* opinion, and it is as powerful a force among progressives as among conservatives, in Massachusetts as in Mississippi, for atheists as for fundamentalists. The first purpose of a real education (a "liberal arts" education) is to liberate us from *doxa* by teaching us to recognize it, to question it, and to think our way around it.

In *Teacher,* Mark Edmundson describes the man who played this role for   10 him when he was seventeen and thereby saved him from the life of thoughtless labor that appeared to be his fate. His teacher's methods were the same as those of Socrates, the teacher of Plato himself: he echoed your opinions back to you or forced you to articulate them for yourself. By dragging them into the light, asking you to defend them or just acknowledge having them, he began to break them down, to expose them to the operations of the critical intelligence—and thus to develop that intelligence in the first place. The point was not to replace his students' opinions with his own. The point was to bring his charges into the unfamiliar, uncomfortable, and endlessly fertile condition of doubt. He was teaching them not what to think but how.

Why college? College, after all, as those who like to denigrate it often say,   11 is "not the real world." But that is precisely its strength. College is an opportunity to stand outside the world for a few years, between the orthodoxy of your family and the exigencies of career, and contemplate things from a distance. It offers students "the precious chance," as Andrew Delbanco has put it, "to think and reflect before life engulfs them." You can start to learn to think in high school, as Edmundson did—you're certainly old enough by then—but your parents are still breathing down your neck, and your teachers are still teaching to the test, in one respect or another. College should be different: an interval of freedom at the start of adulthood, a pause before it all begins. Is this a privilege that most young people in the world can only dream of? Absolutely. But you won't absolve° yourself by throwing it away. Better, at least, to get some good from it.

---

**bromides:** Unoriginal remarks used to calm or placate.     **absolve:** Declare free of responsibility.

College also offers you professors. Yes, it is theoretically possible to learn 12
how to think on your own, but the chances are not good. Professors can let in
some air, show you approaches that wouldn't have occurred to you and put
you on to things you wouldn't have encountered by yourself. Autodidacts°
tend to be cranks, obtuse and self-enclosed. A professor's most important
role is to make you think with rigor: precisely, patiently, responsibly, remorse-
lessly, and not only about your "deepest ingrained presuppositions," as my
own mentor, Karl Kroeber, once wrote, but also about your "most exhilarating new insights, most of which turn out to be fallacious." You want some
people in your life whose job it is to tell you when you're wrong.

College also gives you peers with whom to question and debate the ideas 13
you encounter in the classroom. "Late-night bull sessions"° is another one
of those phrases people like to throw at the college experience, a way of
shaming students out of their intellectual appetites. But the classroom and
the dorm room are two ends of the same stick. The first puts ideas into your
head; the second makes them part of your soul. The first requires stringency;
the second offers freedom. The first is normative; the second is subversive.
"Most of what I learned at Yale," writes Lewis Lapham, "I learned in what I
now remember as one long, wayward conversation in the only all-night restaurant on Chapel Street. The topics under discussion — God, man, existence,
Alfred Prufrock's peach — were borrowed from the same anthology of large
abstraction that supplied the texts for English 10 or Philosophy 116." The
classroom is the grain of sand; it's up to you to make the pearl.

College is not the only chance to learn to think. It is not the first; it is 14
not the last; but it is the best. One thing is certain: if you haven't started by
the time you finish your BA, there's little likelihood you'll do it later. That is
why an undergraduate experience devoted exclusively to career preparation is
four years largely wasted. The purpose of college is to enable you to live more
alertly, more responsibly, more freely: more fully. I was talking with a couple
of seniors during a visit to Bryn Mawr. One of them said, "The question I
leave Bryn Mawr with is how to put my feminist ideals into practice as I go
forward." I liked "ideals," but I loved the first part. A real education sends you
into the world bearing questions, not résumés.

**autodidact:** A self-taught person.    **late-night bull sessions:** Informal, spontaneous conversations about important topics.

## Questions to Start You Thinking

1. **Considering Meaning:** What do most college students today hope to
   get out of the college experience?
2. **Identifying Writing Strategies:** How does Deresiewicz use personal
   experiences to back up his claims? Is this an effective strategy?

3. **Reading Critically:** Deresiewicz argues in paragraph 9 that "society is a conspiracy to keep itself from the truth." What does he mean by this statement? How does he use this in his argument about the importance of a college education?

4. **Expanding Vocabulary:** What does Deresiewicz mean by the phrase "practicality police" in the fifth paragraph? How does he use this term to support his argument?

5. **Making Connections:** How do you think Deresiewicz would respond to David Brooks's "The Humility Code" (pp. 582–89)? Would his call for students to learn how to think generate a struggle "against weakness and sin," which would lead to maturity?

## Journal Prompts

1. Think about why you went to college. What specific things do you want to learn? What do you hope to accomplish with a college degree? Do you think your time at college will enhance your quality of life? How?

2. In the penultimate paragraph, Deresiewicz claims, "the classroom is the grain of sand; it's up to you to make the pearl." What do you think he means by this statement? What kind of pearl would you make?

## Suggestions for Writing

1. One of the benefits of a college education that Deresiewicz points out in paragraph 13 is finding peers "with whom to question and debate the ideas you encounter in the classroom." Many nontraditional college students today who have jobs and families may have little time to debate issues raised in class with their peers. How could these students find another way to experience this important benefit if they cannot participate in "late-night bull sessions"?

2. Interview a classmate about why he or she decided to attend college, and what he or she hopes to gain from the experience. How do these goals compare with yours? With those of the students discussed in the essay?

# Sarah Adams

## Be Cool to the Pizza Dude

Sarah Adams grew up in Wisconsin. She is a professor of English at Olympic Community College in Seattle, Washington. Adams's essay "Be Cool to the Pizza Dude" was one of the first listener-submitted pieces read on National Public Radio for the *This I Believe* series. In this piece, Adams discusses her personal philosophy of life through the lens of pizza delivery.

**AS YOU READ:** What are Adams's four principles?

Nubar Alexanian.

If I have one operating philosophy about life, it is this: "Be cool to the 1 pizza delivery dude; it's good luck." Four principles guide the pizza dude philosophy.

Principle 1: Coolness to the pizza delivery dude is a practice in humility 2 and forgiveness. I let him cut me off in traffic, let him safely hit the exit ramp from the left lane, let him forget to use his blinker without extending any of my digits° out the window or toward my horn because there should be one moment in my harried° life when a car may encroach or cut off or pass and I let it go. Sometimes when I have become so certain of my ownership of my lane, daring anyone to challenge me, the pizza dude speeds by in his rusted Chevette. His pizza light atop his car glowing like a beacon reminds me to check myself as I flow through the world. After all, the dude is delivering pizza to young and old, families and singletons, gays and straights, blacks, whites, and browns, rich and poor, and vegetarians and meat lovers alike. As he journeys, I give safe passage, practice restraint, show courtesy, and contain my anger.

Principle 2: Coolness to the pizza delivery dude is a practice in empathy. 3 Let's face it: We've all taken jobs just to have a job because some money is better than none. I've held an assortment of these jobs and was grateful for the paycheck that meant I didn't have to share my Cheerios with my cats. In the big pizza wheel of life, sometimes you're the hot bubbly cheese and sometimes you're the burnt crust. It's good to remember the fickle spinning of that wheel.

Principle 3: Coolness to the pizza delivery dude is a practice in honor, and 4 it reminds me to honor honest work. Let me tell you something about these dudes: They never took over a company and, as CEO,° artificially inflated the value of the stock and cashed out their own shares, bringing the company to the brink of bankruptcy, resulting in twenty thousand people losing their jobs while the CEO builds a home the size of a luxury hotel. Rather, the dudes sleep the sleep of the just.

Principle 4: Coolness to the pizza delivery dude is a practice in equality. My 5 measurement as a human being, my worth, is the pride I take in performing

**digits:** Fingers.   **harried:** Bothered or distracted by nuisances.   **CEO:** Chief executive officer, the highest-ranking executive at a company.

my job — any job — and the respect with which I treat others. I am the equal of the world not because of the car I drive, the size of the TV I own, the weight I can bench-press, or the calculus equations I can solve. I am the equal to all I meet because of the kindness in my heart. And it all starts here — with the pizza delivery dude.

Tip him well, friends and brethren, for that which you bestow freely and    6
willingly will bring you all the happy luck that a grateful universe knows how to return.


## Questions to Start You Thinking

1. **Considering Meaning:** In your own words, briefly explain the four principles of Adams's philosophy — and how the "pizza dude" helps reveal each of them.

2. **Identifying Writing Strategies:** Why do you think Adams chooses to focus on the "pizza dude," specifically? How would her essay work if her guidelines were more general? How would you describe her writing voice and style — for example, her use of the term *dude*?

3. **Reading Critically:** Adams claims that her philosophy is "good luck" (paragraph 1). In her conclusion, she says that following her advice "will bring you all the happy luck that a grateful universe knows how to return" (paragraph 6). What assumptions on the writer's part do these statements reveal? Do you share them?

4. **Expanding Vocabulary:** Why do you think Adams uses the word *cool* in the way she does here? Is it merely synonymous with *kind* or *nice,* or does it have other important connotations? What are they? What is the history of the term *cool* in slang usage?

5. **Making Connections:** Referring to David Brooks's "The Humility Code" (pp. 582–89), do you think people who are "cool" to the pizza dude would be described as having Adam I or Adam II virtues? Support your answer with evidence from Brooks's essay.


## Journal Prompts

1. Adams writes that the pizza dude reminds her to show restraint, even when her impulses and instincts would have her do otherwise. Write about a time when you have checked yourself in the way Adams describes. What values does such behavior promote?

2. The writer makes a distinction between unscrupulous CEOs and those like the pizza dude who do "honest work" (paragraph 4). What does the term *honest work* mean to you? Do you think Adams's generalizations are fair? Why, or why not?

## Suggestions for Writing

1. Come up with your own four-point "operating philosophy," based on your experiences or observations, and present it in a personal essay. Create guidelines, as Adams does, that can be summarized in one memorable sentence.

2. Read further about various workers and their jobs, or observe and interview someone whose work seems to embody certain values. Write your own essay, based on your reading or your field work, about one job and the value it carries.

## David Brooks

### The Humility Code

Josh Haner/The New York Times/Redux.

David Brooks is a *New York Times* columnist and conservative political commentator. He appears frequently on *PBS News Hour*, NPR's *All Things Considered*, and NBC's *Meet the Press*. Brooks has contributed editorials and film reviews to the *Washington Times* and worked as an editor for the *Wall Street Journal*, the *Weekly Standard*, *Newsweek*, and the *Atlantic Monthly*. His books include *Bobos in Paradise: The New Upper Class and How They Got There* (2000); *On Paradise Drive: How We Live Now (and Always Have) in the Future Tense* (2004); *The Social Animal: The Hidden Sources of Love, Character, and Achievement* (2011); and *The Road to Character* (2015). In the following article, Brooks considers how to live an authentic life.

**AS YOU READ:** What are the main points of Brooks's Humility Code?

Recently I've been thinking about the difference between the résumé virtues and the eulogy virtues. The résumé virtues are the ones you list on your résumé, the skills that you bring to the job market and that contribute to external success. The eulogy virtues are deeper. They're the virtues that get talked about at your funeral, the ones that exist at the core of your being—whether you are kind, brave, honest or faithful; what kind of relationships you formed. 1

Most of us would say that the eulogy virtues are more important than the résumé virtues, but I confess that for long stretches of my life I've spent more time thinking about the latter than the former. Our education system is certainly oriented around the résumé virtues more than the eulogy ones. Public conversation is, too—the self-help tips in magazines, the nonfiction bestsellers. Most of us have clearer strategies for how to achieve career success than we do for how to develop a profound character. 2

One book that has helped me think about these two sets of virtues is *Lonely Man of Faith*, which was written by Rabbi Joseph Soloveitchik in 1965. Soloveitchik noted that there are two accounts of creation in Genesis and argued that these represent the two opposing sides of our nature, which he called Adam I and Adam II. 3

Modernizing Soloveitchik's categories a bit, we could say that Adam I is    4
the career-oriented, ambitious side of our nature. Adam I is the external,
résumé Adam. Adam I wants to build, create, produce, and discover things.
He wants to have high status and win victories.

Adam II is the internal Adam. Adam II wants to embody certain moral    5
qualities. Adam II wants to have a serene inner character, a quiet but solid
sense of right and wrong — not only to do good, but to be good. Adam II
wants to love intimately, to sacrifice self in the service of others, to live in
obedience to some transcendent truth,° to have a cohesive inner soul that
honors creation and one's own possibilities.

While Adam I wants to conquer the world, Adam II wants to obey a calling    6
to serve the world. While Adam I is creative and savors his own accomplishments, Adam II sometimes renounces worldly success and status for the sake
of some sacred purpose. While Adam I asks how things work, Adam II asks
why things exist, and what ultimately we are here for. While Adam I wants to
venture forth, Adam II wants to return to his roots and savor the warmth of a
family meal. While Adam I's motto is "Success," Adam II experiences life as a
moral drama. His motto is "Charity, love, and redemption."

Soloveitchik argued that we live in the contradiction between these two    7
Adams. The outer, majestic Adam and the inner, humble Adam are not fully
reconcilable. We are forever caught in self-confrontation. We are called to
fulfill both personae, and must master the art of living forever within the
tension between these two natures.

The hard part of this confrontation, I'd add, is that Adams I and II    8
live by different logics. Adam I — the creating, building, and discovering
Adam — lives by a straightforward utilitarian logic.° It's the logic of economics. Input leads to output. Effort leads to reward. Practice makes perfect.
Pursue self-interest. Maximize your utility. Impress the world.

Adam II lives by an inverse logic. It's a moral logic, not an economic one.    9
You have to give to receive. You have to surrender to something outside yourself to gain strength within yourself. You have to conquer your desire to get
what you crave. Success leads to the greatest failure, which is pride. Failure
leads to the greatest success, which is humility and learning. In order to
fulfill yourself, you have to forget yourself. In order to find yourself, you have
to lose yourself.

To nurture your Adam I career, it makes sense to cultivate your strengths.    10
To nurture your Adam II moral core, it is necessary to confront your
weaknesses.

We live in a culture that nurtures Adam I, the external Adam, and neglects    11
Adam II. We live in a society that encourages us to think about how to have
a great career but leaves many of us inarticulate about how to cultivate the

---

**transcendent truth:** Absolute truth unaffected by time and space.    **utilitarian logic:**
Based on the ethical view that right and wrong is dependent on whether something has positive or negative consequences.

inner life. The competition to succeed and win admiration is so fierce that it becomes all-consuming. The consumer marketplace° encourages us to live by a utilitarian calculus, to satisfy our desires and lose sight of the moral stakes involved in everyday decisions. The noise of fast and shallow communications makes it harder to hear the quieter sounds that emanate from the depths. We live in a culture that teaches us to promote and advertise ourselves and to master the skills required for success, but that gives little encouragement to humility, sympathy, and honest self-confrontation, which are necessary for building character.

If you are only Adam I, you turn into a shrewd animal, a crafty, self-preserving creature who is adept at playing the game and who turns everything into a game. If that's all you have, you spend a lot of time cultivating professional skills, but you don't have a clear idea of the sources of meaning in life, so you don't know where you should devote your skills, which career path will be highest and best. Years pass and the deepest parts of yourself go unexplored and unstructured. You are busy, but you have a vague anxiety that your life has not achieved its ultimate meaning and significance. You live with an unconscious boredom, not really loving, not really attached to the moral purposes that give life its worth. You lack the internal criteria to make unshakable commitments. You never develop inner constancy, the integrity that can withstand popular disapproval or a serious blow. You find yourself doing things that other people approve of, whether these things are right for you or not. You foolishly judge other people by their abilities, not by their worth. You do not have a strategy to build character, and without that, not only your inner life but also your external life will eventually fall to pieces. 12

Over the past several decades we have built a moral ecology° around the Big Me, around the belief in a golden figure inside. This has led to a rise in narcissism and self-aggrandizement.° This has encouraged us to focus on the external Adam I side of our natures and ignore the inner world of Adam II. . . . 13

To restore the balance, to rediscover Adam II, to cultivate the eulogy virtues, it's probably necessary to revive and follow what we accidentally left behind: the counter-tradition of moral realism, or what I've been calling the crooked-timber school. It's probably necessary to build a moral ecology based on the ideas of this school, to follow its answers to the most important questions: Toward what should I orient my life? Who am I and what is my nature? How do I mold my nature to make it gradually better day by day? What virtues are the most important to cultivate and what weaknesses should I fear the most? How can I raise my children with a true sense of who they are and a practical set of ideas about how to travel the long road to character? 14

I thought it might be useful to draw together the propositions that define the crooked-timber tradition and recapitulate them here in one list, even 15

**consumer marketplace:** A system driven by marketing and advertising that allows consumers to make their own decisions in purchasing goods and services. **moral ecology:** Institutionalized set of norms, values, and assumptions. **self-aggrandizement:** Exaggerating one's power and importance.

if presenting them in numbered-list form does tend to simplify them and make them seem cruder than they are. Together these propositions form a Humility Code, a coherent image of what to live for and how to live. These are the general propositions that form this Humility Code:

1. We don't live for happiness, we live for holiness. Day to day we seek  16
   out pleasure, but deep down, human beings are endowed with moral imagination. All human beings seek to lead lives not just of pleasure, but of purpose, righteousness, and virtue. As John Stuart Mill° put it, people have a responsibility to become more moral over time. The best life is oriented around the increasing excellence of the soul and is nourished by moral joy, the quiet sense of gratitude and tranquillity that comes as a byproduct of successful moral struggle. The meaningful life is the same eternal thing, the combination of some set of ideals and some man or woman's struggle for those ideals. Life is essentially a moral drama, not a hedonistic° one.

2. Proposition one defines the goal of life. The long road to character be-  17
   gins with an accurate understanding of our nature, and the core of that understanding is that we are flawed creatures. We have an innate tendency toward selfishness and overconfidence. We have a tendency to see ourselves as the center of the universe, as if everything revolves around us. We resolve to do one thing but end up doing the opposite. We know what is deep and important in life, but we still pursue the things that are shallow and vain. Furthermore, we overestimate our own strength and rationalize our own failures. We know less than we think we do. We give in to short-term desires even when we know we shouldn't. We imagine that spiritual and moral needs can be solved through status and material things.

3. Although we are flawed creatures, we are also splendidly endowed.° We  18
   are divided within ourselves, both fearfully and wonderfully made. We do sin, but we also have the capacity to recognize sin, to feel ashamed of sin, and to overcome sin. We are both weak and strong, bound and free, blind and far-seeing. We thus have the capacity to struggle with ourselves. There is something heroic about a person in struggle with herself, strained on the rack of conscience, suffering torments, yet staying alive and growing stronger, sacrificing a worldly success for the sake of an inner victory.

4. In the struggle against your own weakness, humility is the greatest virtue.  19
   Humility is having an accurate assessment of your own nature and your own place in the cosmos. Humility is awareness that you are an underdog in the struggle against your own weakness. Humility is an awareness that your individual talents alone are inadequate to the tasks that have been assigned to you. Humility reminds you that you are not the center of the universe, but you serve a larger order.

**John Stuart Mill:** A nineteenth-century philosopher, economist, activist, and proponent of utilitarianism.     **hedonistic:** Committed to seeking pleasure as having utmost importance. **endowed:** Provided with.

5. Pride is the central vice. Pride is a problem in the sensory apparatus. 20
Pride blinds us to the reality of our divided nature. Pride blinds us to our
own weaknesses and misleads us into thinking we are better than we are.
Pride makes us more certain and closed-minded than we should be. Pride
makes it hard for us to be vulnerable before those whose love we need.
Pride makes coldheartedness and cruelty possible. Because of pride we try
to prove we are better than those around us. Pride deludes us into thinking that we are the authors of our own lives.

6. Once the necessities for survival are satisfied, the struggle against sin and 21
for virtue is the central drama of life. No external conflict is as consequential
or as dramatic as the inner campaign against our own deficiencies. This
struggle against, say, selfishness or prejudice or insecurity gives meaning and shape to life. It is more important than the external journey up
the ladder of success. This struggle against sin is the great challenge, so
that life is not futile or absurd. It is possible to fight this battle well or
badly, humorlessly or with cheerful spirit. Contending with weakness
often means choosing what parts of yourself to develop and what parts
not to develop. The purpose of the struggle against sin and weakness is
not to "win," because that is not possible; it is to get better at waging it. It
doesn't matter if you work at a hedge fund or a charity serving the poor.
There are heroes and schmucks in both worlds. The most important
thing is whether you are willing to engage in this struggle.

7. Character is built in the course of your inner confrontation. Character is 22
a set of dispositions, desires, and habits that are slowly engraved during
the struggle against your own weakness. You become more disciplined,
considerate, and loving through a thousand small acts of self-control,
sharing, service, friendship, and refined enjoyment. If you make disciplined, caring choices, you are slowly engraving certain tendencies into
your mind. You are making it more likely that you will desire the right
things and execute the right actions. If you make selfish, cruel, or disorganized choices, then you are slowly turning this core thing inside yourself
into something that is degraded, inconstant, or fragmented. You can do
harm to this core thing with nothing more than ignoble thoughts, even if
you are not harming anyone else. You can elevate this core thing with an
act of restraint nobody sees. If you don't develop a coherent character in
this way, life will fall to pieces sooner or later. You will become a slave to
your passions. But if you do behave with habitual self-discipline, you will
become constant and dependable.

8. The things that lead us astray are short term—lust, fear, vanity, glut- 23
tony. The things we call character endure over the long term—courage,
honesty, humility. People with character are capable of a long obedience
in the same direction, of staying attached to people and causes and
callings consistently through thick and thin. People with character also
have scope. They are not infinitely flexible, free-floating, and solitary.
They are anchored by permanent attachments to important things.

In the realm of the intellect, they have a set of permanent convictions about fundamental truths. In the realm of emotion, they are enmeshed° in a web of unconditional loves. In the realm of action, they have a permanent commitment to tasks that cannot be completed in a single lifetime.

9. No person can achieve self-mastery on his or her own. Individual will, 24 reason, compassion, and character are not strong enough to consistently defeat selfishness, pride, greed, and self-deception. Everybody needs redemptive assistance from outside — from God, family, friends, ancestors, rules, traditions, institutions, and exemplars. If you are to prosper in the confrontation with yourself, you have to put yourself in a state of affection. You have to draw on something outside yourself to cope with the forces inside yourself. You have to draw from a cultural tradition that educates the heart, that encourages certain values, that teaches us what to feel in certain circumstances. We wage our struggles in conjunction with others waging theirs, and the boundaries between us are indistinct.

10. We are all ultimately saved by grace. The struggle against weakness 25 often has a U shape. You are living your life and then you get knocked off course — either by an overwhelming love, or by failure, illness, loss of employment, or twist of fate. The shape is advance-retreat-advance. In retreat, you admit your need and surrender your crown. You open up space that others might fill. And grace floods in. It may come in the form of love from friends and family, in the assistance of an unexpected stranger, or from God. But the message is the same. You are accepted. You don't flail about in desperation, because hands are holding you up. You don't have to struggle for a place, because you are embraced and accepted. You just have to accept the fact that you are accepted. Gratitude fills the soul, and with it the desire to serve and give back.

11. Defeating weakness often means quieting the self. Only by quieting the 26 self, by muting the sound of your own ego, can you see the world clearly. Only by quieting the self can you be open to the external sources of strengths you will need. Only by stilling the sensitive ego can you react with equipoise to the ups and downs of the campaign. The struggle against weakness thus requires the habits of self-effacement — reticence, modesty, obedience to some larger thing — and a capacity for reverence and admiration.

12. Wisdom starts with epistemological modesty.° The world is immea- 27 surably complex and the private stock of reason is small. We are generally not capable of understanding the complex web of causes that drive events. We are not even capable of grasping the unconscious depths

---

**enmeshed:** Entangled.     **epistemological modesty:** Understanding the limits to what we can know.

of our own minds. We should be skeptical of abstract reasoning or of trying to apply universal rules across different contexts. But over the centuries, our ancestors built up a general bank of practical wisdom, traditions, habits, manners, moral sentiments, and practices. The humble person thus has an acute historical consciousness. She is the grateful inheritor of the tacit wisdom of her kind, the grammar of conduct and the store of untaught feelings that are ready for use in case of emergency, that offer practical tips on how to behave in different situations, and that encourage habits that cohere into virtues. The humble person understands that experience is a better teacher than pure reason. He understands that wisdom is not knowledge. Wisdom emerges out of a collection of intellectual virtues. It is knowing how to behave when perfect knowledge is lacking.

13. No good life is possible unless it is organized around a vocation. If you 28 try to use your work to serve yourself, you'll find your ambitions and expectations will forever run ahead and you'll never be satisfied. If you try to serve the community, you'll always wonder if people appreciate you enough. But if you serve work that is intrinsically compelling and focus just on being excellent at that, you will wind up serving yourself and the community obliquely. A vocation is not found by looking within and finding your passion. It is found by looking without and asking what life is asking of us. What problem is addressed by an activity you intrinsically enjoy?

14. The best leader tries to lead along the grain of human nature rather 29 than go against it. He realizes that he, like the people he leads, is likely to be sometimes selfish, narrow-minded, and self-deceiving. Therefore he prefers arrangements that are low and steady to those that are lofty and heroic. As long as the foundations of an institution are sound, he prefers change that is constant, gradual, and incremental to change that is radical and sudden. He understands that public life is a contest between partial truths and legitimate contesting interests. The goal of leadership is to find a just balance between competing values and competing goals. He seeks to be a trimmer, to shift weight one way or another as circumstances change, in order to keep the boat moving steadily forward on an even keel. He understands that in politics and business the lows are lower than the highs are high. The downside risk caused by bad decisions is larger than the upside benefits that accrue from good ones. Therefore the wise leader is a steward for his organization and tries to pass it along in slightly better condition than he found it.

15. The person who successfully struggles against weakness and sin may or 30 may not become rich and famous, but that person will become mature. Maturity is not based on talent or any of the mental or physical gifts that help you ace an IQ test or run fast or move gracefully. It is not comparative. It is earned not by being better than other people at something, but by being better than you used to be. It is earned by being

dependable in times of testing, straight in times of temptation. Maturity does not glitter. It is not built on the traits that make people celebrities. A mature person possesses a settled unity of purpose. The mature person has moved from fragmentation to centeredness, has achieved a state in which the restlessness is over, the confusion about the meaning and purpose of life is calmed. The mature person can make decisions without relying on the negative and positive reactions from admirers or detractors because the mature person has steady criteria to determine what is right. That person has said a multitude of noes for the sake of a few overwhelming yeses.

## Questions to Start You Thinking

1. **Considering Meaning:** How does Brooks describe the Adam II part of our virtues? How does he suggest we nurture this part?

2. **Identifying Writing Strategies:** Why do you think Brooks chose to organize his points into a list? How effective is this method to illustrate his points? What other method could he have used?

3. **Reading Critically:** In paragraph 11, Brooks argues that "we live in a culture that nurtures Adam I, the external Adam, and neglects Adam II." Explain what he means by this statement.

4. **Expanding Vocabulary:** How does Brooks define *humility* in his fourth point in his Humility Code? How does his definition of this word help support his plan for "what to live for and how to live"?

5. **Making Connections:** How do you think Brooks would react to this observation by William Zinsser from "The Right to Fail" (pp. 571–73): "[I]n the fluid years of youth, the only way for boys and girls to find their proper road is often to take a hundred side trips, poking out in different directions, faltering, drawing back, and starting again" (paragraph 4)? Do you think the views of Brooks and Zinsser would align for the most part? Why, or why not?

## Link to the Paired Essay

Would Brooks agree with Miya Tokumitsu's argument in "In the Name of Love" (pp. 590–95) that DWYL leads to "the devaluation of actual work"? Would DWYL fit into any of the propositions of his Humility Code?

## Journal Prompts

1. Which part of your nature do you think is more dominant: the Adam I or the Adam II as Brooks defines them? Give examples to support your conclusion.

2. Brooks spends a lot of time in the article discussing human weakness, insisting that "we are flawed creatures." Do you agree with this judgment?

## Suggestions for Writing

1. Brooks begins his focus on how to live a moral life by referring to images of Adam from the Bible. He uses other religious terms in his argument when he insists that "we live for holiness" in his first point and that "the struggle against sin and for virtue is the central drama of life" in his sixth point. Do you think that his Humility Code is applicable to someone who does not follow the Christian faith? Respond to this question in an essay.

2. To "develop a strategy to build character," Brooks argues that we must follow a code of humility and offers fifteen ways to accomplish this. Do you agree that humility is essential to living an authentic life? What other factors do you think are important in this process? Research what philosophers have said about how to achieve authenticity and compare their conclusions to Brooks's.

## Miya Tokumitsu

### In the Name of Love

Miya Tokumitsu earned a PhD in the history of art from the University of Pennsylvania in 2012. Now a contributing editor at *Jacobin*, she previously worked as an art historian at the University of Melbourne. Her articles have appeared in *Slant Magazine* and *Slate*, and she has gained critical acclaim for her recent book *Do What You Love: And Other Lies about Success and Happiness* (2015). In the following article, Tokumitsu explores the negative effects of doing what you love.

**AS YOU READ:** According to the author, what is the impact of the phrase "do what you love" on American workers?

"Do what you love. Love what you do." 1

The commands are framed and perched in a living room that can 2 only be described as "well-curated." A picture of this room appeared first on a popular design blog, but has been pinned, tumbl'd, and liked° thousands of times by now.

Lovingly lit and photographed, this room is styled to inspire *Sehnsucht*, 3 roughly translatable from German as a pleasurable yearning for some utopian thing or place. Despite the fact that it introduces exhortations to labor into a space of leisure, the "do what you love" living room — where

---

**pinned, tumbl'd, and liked:** In reference to providing positive feedback on, or reposting on, various social network channels (Pinterest, Tumblr, and Facebook).

artful tchotchkes° abound and work is not drudgery but love—is precisely
the place all those pinners and likers long to be. The diptych° arrangement
suggests a secular version of a medieval house altar.

There's little doubt that "do what you love" (DWYL) is now the unofficial   4
work mantra for our time. The problem is that it leads not to salvation, but
to the devaluation of actual work, including the very work it pretends to
elevate—and more importantly, the dehumanization of the vast majority of
laborers.

Superficially, DWYL is an uplifting piece of advice, urging us to ponder what   5
it is we most enjoy doing and then turn that activity into a wage-generating
enterprise. But why should our pleasure be for profit? Who is the audience for
this dictum? Who is not?

By keeping us focused on ourselves and our individual happiness, DWYL   6
distracts us from the working conditions of others while validating our
own choices and relieving us from obligations to all who labor, whether or
not they love it. It is the secret handshake of the privileged and a worldview
that disguises its elitism as noble self-betterment. According to this way of
thinking, labor is not something one does for compensation, but an act of
self-love. If profit doesn't happen to follow, it is because the worker's passion
and determination were insufficient. Its real achievement is making workers
believe their labor serves the self and not the marketplace.

Aphorisms° have numerous origins and reincarnations, but the generic   7
and hackneyed nature of DWYL confounds precise attribution. Oxford
Reference links the phrase and variants of it to Martina Navratilova° and
François Rabelais,° among others. The Internet frequently attributes it to
Confucius,° locating it in a misty, Orientalized past. Oprah Winfrey and
other peddlers of positivity have included it in their repertoires for decades,
but the most important recent evangelist of the DWYL creed is deceased
Apple CEO Steve Jobs.

His graduation speech to the Stanford University class of 2005 provides   8
as good an origin myth as any, especially since Jobs had already been beati-
fied as the patron saint of aestheticized work well before his early death. In
the speech, Jobs recounts the creation of Apple, and inserts this reflection:

> You've got to find what you love. And that is as true for your work as it is for
> your lovers. Your work is going to fill a large part of your life, and the only
> way to be truly satisfied is to do what you believe is great work. And the only
> way to do great work is to love what you do.

In these four sentences, the words *you* and *your* appear eight times.   9
This focus on the individual is hardly surprising coming from Jobs, who

---

**tchotchkes:** Knickknacks, accessories.   **diptych:** Two flat panels attached with a
hinge.   **aphorisms:** Terse sayings stating truths or wise observations.   **Martina Navrati-
lova:** A Czech-American top world tennis player in the 1970s and 1980s known for her political activism.   **François Rabelais:** Priest, physician, and writer (1494–1553) of the French
Renaissance, known for his satire.   **Confucius:** Chinese teacher and philosopher (551–479 BCE)
known for his aphorisms on morality and education.

cultivated a very specific image of himself as a worker: inspired, casual, passionate—all states agreeable with ideal romantic love. Jobs telegraphed the conflation of his besotted worker-self with his company so effectively that his black turtleneck and blue jeans became metonyms° for all of Apple and the labor that maintains it.

But by portraying Apple as a labor of his individual love, Jobs elided the labor of untold thousands in Apple's factories, conveniently hidden from sight on the other side of the planet—the very labor that allowed Jobs to actualize his love.

The violence of this erasure needs to be exposed. While "do what you love" sounds harmless and precious, it is ultimately self-focused to the point of narcissism. Jobs's formulation of "do what you love" is the depressing antithesis to Henry David Thoreau's utopian vision of labor for all. In "Life without Principle," Thoreau wrote,

> . . . it would be good economy for a town to pay its laborers so well that they would not feel that they were working for low ends, as for a livelihood merely, but for scientific, even moral ends. Do not hire a man who does your work for money, but him who does it for the love of it.

Admittedly, Thoreau had little feel for the proletariat° (it's hard to imagine someone washing diapers for "scientific, even moral ends," no matter how well-paid). But he nonetheless maintains that society has a stake in making work well-compensated and meaningful. By contrast, the twenty-first-century Jobsian view demands that we all turn inward. It absolves us of any obligation to or acknowledgment of the wider world, underscoring its fundamental betrayal of all workers, whether they consciously embrace it or not.

One consequence of this isolation is the division that DWYL creates among workers, largely along class lines. Work becomes divided into two opposing classes: that which is lovable (creative, intellectual, socially prestigious) and that which is not (repetitive, unintellectual, undistinguished). Those in the lovable work camp are vastly more privileged in terms of wealth, social status, education, society's racial biases, and political clout, while comprising a small minority of the workforce.

For those forced into unlovable work, it's a different story. Under the DWYL credo, labor that is done out of motives or needs other than love (which is, in fact, most labor) is not only demeaned but erased. As in Jobs's Stanford speech, unlovable but socially necessary work is banished from the spectrum of consciousness altogether.

Think of the great variety of work that allowed Jobs to spend even one day as CEO: his food harvested from fields, then transported across great distances. His company's goods assembled, packaged, shipped. Apple advertisements scripted, cast, filmed. Lawsuits processed. Office wastebaskets emptied and ink cartridges filled. Job creation goes both ways. Yet with the

**metonym:** A word or object used as a stand-in for something with which it is closely associated.    **proletariat:** Working class.

vast majority of workers effectively invisible to elites busy in their lovable occupations, how can it be surprising that the heavy strains faced by today's workers (abysmal wages, massive child care costs, et cetera) barely register as political issues even among the liberal faction of the ruling class?

In ignoring most work and reclassifying the rest as love, DWYL may be 16 the most elegant anti-worker ideology around. Why should workers assemble and assert their class interests if there's no such thing as work?

"Do what you love" disguises the fact that being able to choose a career 17 primarily for personal reward is an unmerited privilege, a sign of that person's socioeconomic class. Even if a self-employed graphic designer had parents who could pay for art school and cosign a lease for a slick Brooklyn apartment, she can self-righteously bestow DWYL as career advice to those covetous of her success.

If we believe that working as a Silicon Valley entrepreneur or a museum 18 publicist or a think-tank acolyte is essential to being true to ourselves—in fact, to loving ourselves—what do we believe about the inner lives and hopes of those who clean hotel rooms and stock shelves at big-box stores? The answer is: nothing.

Yet arduous, low-wage work is what ever more Americans do and will 19 be doing. According to the U.S. Bureau of Labor Statistics, the two fastest-growing occupations projected until 2020 are "Personal Care Aide" and "Home Care Aide," with average salaries of $19,640 per year and $20,560 per year in 2010, respectively. Elevating certain types of professions to something worthy of love necessarily denigrates the labor of those who do unglamorous work that keeps society functioning, especially the crucial work of caregivers.

If DWYL denigrates° or makes dangerously invisible vast swaths of labor 20 that allow many of us to live in comfort and to do what we love, it has also caused great damage to the professions it portends to celebrate, especially those jobs existing within institutional structures. Nowhere has the DWYL mantra been more devastating to its adherents than in academia. The average PhD student of the mid 2000s forwent the easy money of finance and law (now slightly less easy) to live on a meager stipend in order to pursue their passion for Norse mythology° or the history of Afro-Cuban music.

The reward for answering this higher calling is an academic employment 21 marketplace in which around 41 percent of American faculty are adjunct professors—contract instructors who usually receive low pay, no benefits, no office, no job security, and no long-term stake in the schools where they work.

There are many factors that keep PhDs providing such high-skilled labor 22 for such extremely low wages, including path dependency and the sunk costs of earning a PhD, but one of the strongest is how pervasively the

---

**denigrates:** Criticizes.    **Norse mythology:** Northern Germanic/Scandinavian mythology.

DWYL doctrine is embedded in academia. Few other professions fuse the personal identity of their workers so intimately with the work output. This intense identification partly explains why so many proudly left-leaning faculty remain oddly silent about the working conditions of their peers. Because academic research should be done out of pure love, the actual conditions of and compensation for this labor become afterthoughts, if they are considered at all.

In "Academic Labor, the Aesthetics of Management, and the Promise of Autonomous Work," Sarah Brouillette writes of academic faculty, 23

> . . . our faith that our work offers non-material rewards, and is more integral to our identity than a "regular" job would be, makes us ideal employees when the goal of management is to extract our labor's maximum value at minimum cost.

Many academics like to think they have avoided a corporate work environment and its attendant values, but Marc Bousquet notes in his essay "We Work" that academia may actually provide a model for corporate management: 24

> How to emulate the academic workplace and get people to work at a high level of intellectual and emotional intensity for fifty or sixty hours a week for bartenders' wages or less? Is there any way we can get our employees to swoon over their desks, murmuring "I love what I do" in response to greater workloads and smaller paychecks? How can we get our workers to be like faculty and deny that they work at all? How can we adjust our corporate culture to resemble campus culture, so that our workforce will fall in love with their work too?

No one is arguing that enjoyable work should be less so. But emotionally satisfying work is still work, and acknowledging it as such doesn't undermine it in any way. Refusing to acknowledge it, on the other hand, opens the door to the most vicious exploitation and harms all workers. 25

Ironically, DWYL reinforces exploitation even within the so-called lovable professions where off-the-clock, underpaid, or unpaid labor is the new norm: reporters required to do the work of their laid-off photographers, publicists expected to Pin and Tweet on weekends, the 46 percent of the workforce expected to check their work e-mail on sick days. Nothing makes exploitation go down easier than convincing workers that they are doing what they love. 26

Instead of crafting a nation of self-fulfilled, happy workers, our DWYL era has seen the rise of the adjunct professor and the unpaid intern — people persuaded to work for cheap or free, or even for a net loss of wealth. This has certainly been the case for all those interns working for college credit or those who actually purchase ultra-desirable fashion-house internships at auction. (Valentino and Balenciaga are among a handful of houses that auctioned off month-long internships. For charity, of course.) The latter is 27 worker exploitation taken to its most extreme, and as an ongoing Pro Publica investigation reveals, the unpaid intern is an ever larger presence in the American workforce.

It should be no surprise that unpaid interns abound in fields that are 28 highly socially desirable, including fashion, media, and the arts. These industries have long been accustomed to masses of employees willing to work for social currency instead of actual wages, all in the name of love. Excluded from these opportunities, of course, is the overwhelming majority of the population: those who need to work for wages. This exclusion not only calcifies economic and professional immobility, but insulates these industries from the full diversity of voices society has to offer.

And it's no coincidence that the industries that rely heavily on interns— 29 fashion, media, and the arts—just happen to be the feminized ones, as Madeleine Schwartz wrote in *Dissent*. Yet another damaging consequence of DWYL is how ruthlessly it works to extract female labor for little or no compensation. Women comprise the majority of the low-wage or unpaid workforce; as care workers, adjunct faculty, and unpaid interns, they outnumber men. What unites all of this work, whether performed by GEDs or PhDs, is the belief that wages shouldn't be the primary motivation for doing it. Women are supposed to do work because they are natural nurturers and are eager to please; after all they've been doing uncompensated childcare, elder care, and housework since time immemorial. And talking money is unladylike anyway.

The DWYL dream is, true to its American mythology, superficially demo- 30 cratic. PhDs can do what they love, making careers that indulge their love of the Victorian novel and writing thoughtful essays in the *New York Review of Books*. High school grads can also do it, building prepared food empires out of their Aunt Pearl's jam recipe. The hallowed path of the entrepreneur always offers this way out of disadvantaged beginnings, excusing the rest of us for allowing those beginnings to be as miserable as they are. In America, everyone has the opportunity to do what he or she loves and get rich.

*Do what you love and you'll never work a day in your life!* Before succumbing 31 to the intoxicating warmth of that promise, it's critical to ask, "Who, exactly, benefits from making work feel like non-work?" "Why *should* workers feel as if they aren't working when they are?" Historian Mario Liverani reminds us that "ideology has the function of presenting exploitation in a favorable light to the exploited, as advantageous to the disadvantaged."

In masking the very exploitative mechanisms of labor that it fuels, DWYL 32 is, in fact, the most perfect ideological tool of capitalism. It shunts aside the labor of others and disguises our own labor to ourselves. It hides the fact that if we acknowledged all of our work as work, we could set appropriate limits for it, demanding fair compensation and humane schedules that allow for family and leisure time.

And if we did that, more of us could get around to doing what it is we 33 *really* love.

## Questions to Start You Thinking

1. **Considering Meaning:** Tokumitsu argues in paragraph 4 that "'do what you love' (DWYL) . . . leads not to salvation, but to the devaluation of actual work, . . . and more importantly, the dehumanization of the vast majority of laborers." How does she back up this claim?

2. **Identifying Writing Strategies:** Why do you think Tokumitsu uses Steve Jobs as an example of someone who follows the "mantra" of DWYL? How do the details she includes about the late Apple CEO help support her argument?

3. **Reading Critically:** Toward the end of her essay, Tokumitsu claims, "the DWYL dream is, true to its American mythology, superficially democratic" (paragraph 30). Explain what she means by this statement. How does she support it?

4. **Expanding Vocabulary:** In paragraph 7, Tokumitsu argues that "the generic and hackneyed nature of DWYL confounds precise attribution." What does she mean by "hackneyed"? What aspect of DWYL does she consider hackneyed? Is this a fair assessment?

5. **Making Connections:** How would Tokumitsu respond to Sarah Adams's four principles in "Be Cool to the Pizza Dude" (pp. 580–81)? How is the pizza dude a reflection of the workers that she argues are marginalized by DWYL?

## Link to the Paired Essay

David Brooks's second principle in "The Humility Code" (pp. 582–89) declares that "we have an innate tendency toward selfishness and overconfidence." Could these two terms as he defines them be applied to those who follow DWYL?

## Journal Prompts

1. What job would you like to have after you graduate from college? Research the average salary of someone with your career of choice. How much of an impact would salary have on your career choice?

2. Tokumitsu argues that we live in a narcissistic culture, and that the devotion to DWYL is a reflection of that aspect of that culture. How does she defend this argument? Do you think this is a successful defense?

## Suggestions for Writing

1. Tokumitsu argues in her essay that Steve Jobs exploited his workers as he focused on doing the work that he loved. She claims in paragraph 10 that "by portraying Apple as a labor of his individual love, Jobs elided the

labor of untold thousands in Apple's factories, conveniently hidden from sight on the other side of the planet — the very labor that allowed Jobs to actualize his love." Do you think that a successful CEO can DWYL without exploiting the workers who help him/her achieve success? Write an argument defending your answer to this question.

2. In paragraph 21, Tokumitsu focuses on the plight of adjuncts in academia "who usually receive low pay, no benefits, no office, no job security, and no long-term stake in the schools where they work." She claims that colleges exploit adjuncts' devotion to teaching by keeping their salaries so low. Interview two adjuncts at your college. Ask them why they got into the profession, how much they enjoy it, and whether or not they can afford to live on an adjunct's salary.

# A
# WRITER'S
# RESEARCH
# MANUAL

# A Writer's Research Manual Contents

## 30 Defining Your Research Project 602

Research Assignments: Working from Sources   604
Creating a Schedule   606
Choosing and Narrowing a Topic   606
Turning a Topic into a Question   608
Moving from Research Question to Working Thesis   608
Sample Assignment: Creating a Research Proposal   611

## 31 Finding Sources 614

Searching the Internet   615
Searching the Library   619
Finding Sources in the Field   629

## 32 Evaluating Sources 635

Assessing the Reliability of Sources   637
Using Special Care with Internet Sources   639
Assessing Relevance   641
Sample Assignment: Preparing a Source Evaluation   643

## 33 Working with Sources 645

Navigating Sources   646
Managing Your Project   646
Capturing Information in Your Notes   647
Sample Assignment: Developing an Annotated Bibliography   660

## 34 Integrating Sources 662

Using Sources Ethically   662
Capturing Evidence without Plagiarizing   663
Launching and Citing Source Material   669
Synthesizing Ideas and Sources   672

## 35 Writing a Research Paper 674

Planning with a Thesis Statement   674
Drafting   676
Revising and Editing   677
Documenting Sources   679

## 36 MLA Style for Documenting Sources 680

Citing Sources in MLA Style   682
Listing Sources in MLA Style   687
A Sample MLA Research Paper   695

## 37 APA Style for Documenting Sources 704

Citing Sources in APA Style   704
Listing Sources in APA Style   710
A Sample APA Research Paper   717

# Introduction: The Nature of Research

Does cell phone use affect our thinking?

Should law enforcement officers be required to wear body cameras?

Should professional athletes draw legal consequences for hard on-field hits?

Is it true that over a million children in the United States are homeless?

Why is cyberbullying so widespread?

You may ask questions like these, discuss them with friends, or read about them. If so, you're conducting informal research to satisfy your curiosity. In your day-to-day life, you conduct practical research as you solve problems and make decisions. You may want to buy a tablet, consider an innovative medical procedure, or plan a vacation. To become better informed, you may talk with friends, search the Internet, request product information, compare prices, read articles, and check advertising. You pull together and weigh as much information as you can, preparing yourself to make a well-informed decision based on the available evidence. At work you may do the same—conduct research by gathering information, pulling it together, and using it to make decisions about feasibility, marketing, or best practices.

In college, too, you'll conduct research, most likely as part of a class assignment. These projects require information literacy—the capacity to handle information—as well as critical reading and thinking as you join the academic exchange. Rather than merely pasting together information and opinions from others, you'll need to engage actively: inquiring, searching, accessing, evaluating, integrating, and synthesizing information from sources. The goal of college research is to draw original conclusions and arrive at your own fresh view.

# 30 Defining Your Research Project

The chart on page 603 identifies the major stages in a large and complex research process. Understanding your assignment will help you determine which parts of the research process you will need to engage in. For example, smaller projects like proposals or annotated bibliographies will probably not require as much planning and drafting as a full research paper. Whatever stages of the research process your project involves, keep in mind that research is a recursive process, meaning that you'll likely need to move back and forth through at least some of the stages as you progress.

## Why Defining a Research Project Matters

### In a College Course
- You have several small research assignments due, including a research proposal and a source evaluation, in your writing class.
- You apply your planning experience to your capstone research project for your major.

### In the Workplace
- You organize your work group to investigate a potential client base, using available demographic data.

### In Your Community
- You arrange the needs assessment necessary to justify a new recreation center.

  ❓ When have you planned a research project? In what situations do you expect to do so again?

# The Research Process

**ENGAGE Explore a topic** that intrigues you, following your assignment (see pp. 606–07).

**INQUIRE  Narrow your topic** to a workable research question (see p. 608).

**SEARCH  Seek and evaluate reliable sources** that might help you answer your question (see Chs. 31 and 32).

**ORGANIZE  Start your working bibliography** and annotate possible sources when useful (see pp. 646–56).

**INVESTIGATE  Work with your sources** to obtain details; quote, paraphrase, and summarize information from sources (see pp. 656–61).

**SYNTHESIZE  Integrate reliable evidence** to support your answer to your research question (see pp. 672–73).

**PLAN AND DRAFT**  Starting with a thesis statement that answers your research question, **draft a paper** that uses evidence from sources (see pp. 676–77).

**REVISE AND EDIT**  Allow time to **revise and edit** your paper, making sure you have integrated and **documented** sources correctly (see pp. 677–79).

| WEEK 1 | WEEK 2 | WEEK 3 | WEEK 4 | WEEK 5 | WEEK 6 | WEEK 7 | WEEK 8 |

---

## Learning by Doing 🖭 Reflecting on Research

Reflect on your research experience. Have you ever written a research paper? Do you feel confident that you can handle a college research assignment? Or does even the word *research* make you feel anxious? Sum up your past experience. Then list the skills you've already developed in this class that might help you begin your current research project.

---

# Research Assignments: Working from Sources

Research assignments for college courses can take many different forms. The most engaging and complex assignment is usually the research paper, which may be assigned in stages, such as proposal, outline, rough draft, and final paper. Sometimes assignments call for just one stage of a research project, such as an annotated bibliography. All research assignments will require you to work with outside sources. This chapter will help you define and manage your project to help you prepare for the most basic to the most formidable research tasks.

## The Research Proposal

Find a topic that intrigues you, and develop a focused research question about it. Conduct some preliminary research, and adjust your focus if necessary. Once you have a rough picture of how you expect to answer your question, draft a proposal that explains your idea.

Your proposal should include the following:

For a sample research proposal assignment, see pp. 611–13.

- background information explaining your interest in the project and how you arrived at your topic and question
- a summary of your preliminary findings and a likely answer to your research question
- an explanation of possible obstacles you may need to overcome in conducting your research
- a list of two to three sources you find promising, with complete bibliographic information (for MLA style, see pp. 687–88; for APA style, see pp. 710–11)

## The Source Evaluation

Find a topic that intrigues you, and develop a focused research question about it. Conduct some preliminary research, and choose two sources — one print and one online — that are relevant to your topic. For each source, provide the following:

For a sample source evaluation assignment, see pp. 643–44.

- an evaluation of the author's credibility — is the writer a well-known journalist or an expert of some kind?

- an evaluation of the source's (publisher's or sponsor's) reliability
- an evaluation of the author's authority on the topic
- an evaluation of the publication date

## The Annotated Bibliography

Find a topic that intrigues you, and develop a focused research question about it. Conduct some preliminary research, and adjust your focus if necessary. Once you have a rough picture of how you expect to answer your question, narrow your search and choose five to eight sources that are the most relevant and worthwhile for your purposes. For each source, provide the following:

- complete bibliographic information (for MLA style, see pp. 687–88; for APA style, see pp. 710–11)
- a summary of the source's main thesis and supporting evidence
- a description of how the source relates to your research question
- an explanation of how the source relates to other sources you are researching (Is it generally in agreement with, or in opposition to, other sources?)

For a sample annotated bibliography assignment, see pp. 660–61.

## The Outline

Find a topic that intrigues you, and develop a focused research question about it. After conducting whatever research is necessary, synthesize the information you assemble to develop your own reasonable answer to the research question. Then create an outline of how you would present your evidence in a paper. Your outline should include the following main entries:

- thesis statement
- supporting evidence (three or more sections)
- responses to opposing viewpoints
- concluding point

For details on preparing an outline, see pp. 395–403.

## The Research Paper

Write a research paper, following the steps outlined in Chapters 30–35: find and explore a topic that intrigues you, and develop a focused research question about it. Conduct research, evaluating your sources and keeping the information you assemble organized and manageable. Develop your own reasonable answer to your research question and use evidence from sources to support your claim. Then draft, revise, and edit your paper, persuasively using a variety of source material to convey your conclusions. The paper should include the following key features:

- introduction with thesis statement
- supporting evidence for thesis
- clear body paragraphs with transitions

For a sample research paper in MLA style, see pp. 695–703; for a sample research paper in APA style, see pp. 717–26.

- responses to opposing viewpoints
- conclusion that summarizes the main point
- appropriate documentation of five to eight sources

## Creating a Schedule

If your instructor doesn't assign a series of small assignments or deadlines for your research project, create your own. Small assignments may take only a week or two, but a full research paper may take several weeks or an entire semester to complete. Refer to the Research Process chart on page 603 to help you plan.

---

### Learning by Doing  Planning Your Personal Schedule

In accord with your instructor's guidelines and deadlines, plan your research schedule so you'll be motivated and organized. Identify tasks, define specific checkpoints, plan to meet all deadlines, and allow extra time for unexpected problems. Align your schedule with your class, work, family, or other time commitments so that it helps you reserve the many hours that your project will require. Discuss your plans with classmates, making realistic adjustments as needed.

---

Research groups, in class or at work, require cooperative effort but can produce deeper and more creative outcomes than one individual could achieve. If your project is collaborative, you'll need to make agreements with others and meet your commitments. Your team might consolidate all its work or share the research but produce separate papers or presentations. With your instructor's approval, divide the tasks so that all members are responsible for their own portions. Then agree on your due dates and when to assemble for group meetings.

## Choosing and Narrowing a Topic

Many research assignments, no matter the length, require you to begin by choosing a topic that interests you. You may start by considering broad, general topics, but you will need to narrow your topic to keep your project manageable. Narrow a topic by focusing on a particular aspect of it or by considering issues from a local (rather than national or global) perspective.

| Broad Topic | Narrower Topic |
|---|---|
| Military life | Helping members of the military return . . . |
| U.S. education | Measuring learning with standardized tests |
| World hunger | Aiding hungry children in your community |

If you need ideas to help stimulate your curiosity, listen to the academic exchanges around you. Perhaps the reading, writing, or discussion in your geography course alerts you to global environmental threats. Then target your research, maybe narrowing "global threats to forests" to "farming practices that threaten rain forests."

For more about brainstorming writing ideas, see Chs. 1 and 19.

---

## RESEARCH CHECKLIST

### Generating Ideas

☐ What experience can you recall that raises intriguing questions or creates unusual associations in your mind?

☐ What have you observed recently — at school or work, online, or on television today — that you could more thoroughly investigate?

☐ What new perspectives on issues or events have friends, classmates, instructors, commentators, bloggers, or others offered?

☐ What have you read or heard about lately that you would like to pursue?

☐ What problem would you like to solve?

---

Like explorers in new territory, research writers first take a broad look at promising viewpoints, changes, and trends. Then they zero in on a small area.

**Go Online.** You may start by conducting an online search for your topic. You'll likely find many sources but little focus, so your task will be to narrow the list of search results to a more workable collection.

For more on electronic searches, see Ch. 31.

**Browse the Library.** For more focused, academic sources, visit your campus library or its Web site. The library probably subscribes to many general databases (such as Academic Search Premier, Academic OneFile, and Gale Virtual Reference Library), as well as field-specific resources. Ask a reference librarian (electronically or in person) where to start investigating a topic.

**Talk with Experts.** Meet with a professor who specializes in the area you're considering, or talk with friends who are interested in it. Seek out events or virtual groups relevant to your topic and chat with knowledgeable individuals.

For more on interviewing, see Ch. 6 and p. 630.

**Revisit Your Purpose and Audience.** Refine your purpose and your audience analysis in light of your discoveries thus far. Consider what goal you'd like your research to accomplish — whether it's in your personal life, for a college class, or on the job.

For more on purpose and audience, see pp. 11–15 and 383–84.

| | |
|---|---|
| Satisfy curiosity | Analyze a situation |
| Take a new perspective | Substantiate a conclusion |
| Make a decision | Support a position |
| Solve a problem | Advocate for change |

# Turning a Topic into a Question

Once you settle on a topic you're genuinely curious about, formulate questions you think would be worth investigating. As you explore, move from broad to specific by asking more precise questions. Ask exactly what you want to learn, and your task will emerge into focus.

| | |
|---|---|
| BROAD OVERVIEW | Family structures |
| TOPIC | Blended families |
| SPECIFIC QUESTION | How do blended families today differ from those a century ago? |
| | |
| BROAD OVERVIEW | Contemporary architecture |
| TOPIC | Landscape architecture |
| SPECIFIC QUESTION | In what ways have the principles of landscape architecture shaped the city's green design? |

If your question is too broad, you'll be swamped with information. If it has been overdone, you'll struggle to sound fresh. If you haven't settled on a debatable issue, your argument will sound flat. Review the Take Action chart (p. 609) to help focus your research question.

Settling on a research question is a big step in any research project. Keep in mind, however, that until you start your research, you can't know how fruitful your initial question will be. If it doesn't lead you to definite facts or reliable opinions, or if it doesn't encourage you to think critically about those facts or opinions, reword it or throw it out and ask a new question.

## Learning by Doing 🎧 Polling Your Peers

On a blank page, list your three most interesting research ideas with a brief description of each topic's potential. Working with a small group or the whole class, pass your page to the person next to you. On the page you receive, mark a check by the idea that you find most intriguing. Repeat this process until everyone has responded to each page and your page returns to you. Taking into account the group's check marks, turn one topic into a research question, and then outline your tentative approach to it. Decide whether you've found the question you want to explore. Repeat the process if the group wants more response.

# Moving from Research Question to Working Thesis

For more on stating and using a thesis, see pp. 384–93.

Some writers find a project easier to tackle if they have in mind not only a question but also a possible answer, maybe even a working thesis. However, be flexible, ready to change either your possible answer or your question as your research progresses.

# Take Action  Focusing a Research Question

Ask each question listed in the left-hand column to consider whether your research question needs improvement. If so, follow the ASK — LOCATE SPECIFICS — TAKE ACTION sequence to revise.

| 1 ASK | 2 LOCATE SPECIFICS | 3 TAKE ACTION |
|---|---|---|
| Does my question focus on a topic that could be more **interesting** to me or my readers? | ■ A topic has been **overdone** if **average readers are very familiar with it**. <br><br> ■ A topic is **too specific** if **sources are difficult to uncover**. <br><br> ■ A topic is **too bland** or narrow if it **would not engage a broad audience**. | ■ **Read current news and blogs to find new ideas**, or adjust your focus on an older topic to give it a fresh approach. <br><br> ■ **Broaden very narrow topics** so they have more significance to a wider audience and so that sources are readily available to you. <br><br> **TOO NARROW:** How did John F. Kennedy's maternal grandfather influence the decisions JFK made during his first month in office? <br><br> **BROADER:** How did John F. Kennedy's family influence his handling of the Cuban missile crisis? |
| Does my question address a **debatable issue**? Does it allow for a **range of opposing viewpoints**? Will I be able to **support my own view** rather than explain what's generally known and accepted? | ■ Check for **factual questions**. If your question can be answered by a simple *yes* or *no* or with a few statistics, it is not debatable. <br><br> ■ Consider your own view. Rather than simply explaining what's generally known and accepted, you should be prepared to **state an opinion** and **provide support** for that point of view. | ■ As a starting point, **search "pro–con" or "debate" Web sites** to discover current issues that people disagree on. <br><br> ■ **Read about local issues** affecting your community that people may have conflicting views on. <br><br> **TOO FACTUAL:** Are there more African American students or white students in the entering class this year? <br><br> **MORE DEBATABLE:** How does the racial or ethnic diversity of students affect campus relations at our school? |
| Is my question **narrow enough** for a productive investigation in the allotted time frame? | ■ **Consider how you might answer your question.** If the resulting paper would take more time or pages than allotted, it is probably too broad. <br><br> ■ **Conduct a search based on your question.** If a wide range of subtopics appear in your search results, or if many full-length books appear to address your question, the topic is probably too broad for a college research assignment. | ■ **Search for more specific aspects of the topic.** Try to address a smaller component of the issue, such as a shorter time span or a smaller geographical area, to make it more manageable. <br><br> ■ **Ask an instructor, a peer, or a writing center tutor for input.** It may be difficult to assess your own ideas. The input of others can help you find ways to bring your question into focus. <br><br> **TOO BROAD:** How is the climate of the earth changing? <br><br> **NARROWER:** How will El Niño affect the climate in California during the next decade? |

| RESEARCH QUESTION | How does a nutritious lunch benefit students? |
| WORKING THESIS | Nutritious school lunches can improve students' classroom performance. |

## Using Your Working Thesis to Guide Your Research

You probably will revise or replace your working thesis before you finish, but it can guide you now.

- Identify terms to define and subtopics or components to explore.
- List or informally outline points you might develop.
- Note opposing views, alternatives, or solutions likely to emerge.

This early exploration will help you pursue the sources and information you need but avoid any wild-goose chase that might distract you.

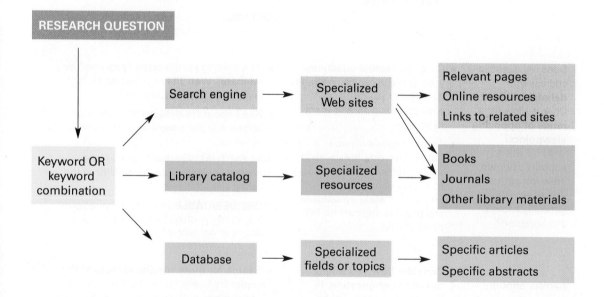

## Surveying Your Resources

For Internet and library search strategies, see Ch. 31.

For advice on creating a working bibliography, see p. 646.

Conduct a quick online search of your library to test whether your question is likely to lead to an ample research paper. You'll need enough ideas, opinions, facts, statistics, and expert testimony to address your question. If you turn up a skimpy list, change search terms. If your search results in hundreds of sources, refine your question. Aim for a question that is the focus of from twelve to twenty available sources. If you need help, talk to a reference librarian.

Also decide which types of sources to target. Some questions require a wide range and others a narrower range restricted by date or discipline. The list below describes a number of source types you can investigate.

- **Opinions on controversies.** Turn to newspaper editorials, opinion columns, issue-oriented sites, and partisan groups for diverse views.
- **News and analysis.** Look for stories from newsmagazines, newspapers, news services, and public broadcasting.
- **Statistics and facts.** Try census or other government data, library databases, annual fact books, and almanacs.
- **Professional or workforce information.** Turn to reports and surveys with academic, government, and corporate sponsors to reduce bias.
- **Research-based analysis.** Try scholarly or well-researched nonfiction, government reports, specialized references, and academic databases.
- **Original records or images.** Check archives, online historical records, and materials held by institutions such as the Library of Congress.

# Sample Assignment: Creating a Research Proposal

A research proposal may be an early part of a larger project or it may be a self-contained assignment. In either case, the basic steps in creating a proposal are the same, and the specific details will depend on your instructor's guidelines. In general, a research proposal makes the case that your topic is interesting, that your research question is worth investigating, and that adequate sources are available. In order to demonstrate the merit of a proposed research project, many instructors require that a proposal include the following:

- background information on the topic
- a focused research question
- a summary of preliminary research findings
- a likely answer to your research question
- a search plan, with a list of possible obstacles to finding sources
- a working bibliography, or short list of promising sources, with complete bibliographic information in a specific style, such as MLA or APA

For his assignment, student Marshall Rivera chose the topic of Head Start, an early childhood intervention program aimed at improving educational outcomes for low-income children. He created the following brief proposal.

Marshall Rivera

English 102: Writing and Research

Professor Willard

24 October 2015

Research Proposal: The Cost-Effectiveness of Head Start

**Background:** Head Start is a federal program created in 1965 as part of President Lyndon B. Johnson's larger initiative of ending poverty in the United States. Operated by the Department of Health and Human Services, Head Start's focus is on preparing young children from low-income families to be ready for school. Head Start claims that children who benefit from early intervention programs are more likely to perform better in school and are therefore more likely to become productive members of society. But critics claim that Head Start is costly and has no lasting effect on the lives of poor children.

**Research Question:** Is Head Start an effective enough program to be worth the federal tax dollars required to run it?

**Summary of Preliminary Findings:** My early research shows mixed reviews of Head Start. Some sources, such as Lindsey Burke at FoxNews.com, strongly criticize the program as a corrupt waste of taxpayer money. Others, such as Amanda Moreno of the *Huffington Post*, insist that Head Start has many worthwhile benefits, even if long-term educational outcomes cannot be clearly demonstrated.

**Likely Answer to Research Question:** My initial thinking is that Head Start is worth the money, although there is probably room for improvement. For example, maybe Head Start should be held accountable for the performance of the children it helps, similar to the way schools are held accountable for student performance as part of the No Child Left Behind Act. On the other hand, critics of Head Start need to understand the many factors that are out of the agency's control, such as child abuse, substance abuse, school violence, and learning disabilities. In some situations, education alone cannot solve all the problems faced by a child. I suspect that Head Start could be part of a successful series of programs that are aimed at improving all aspects of a child's life, from education to nutrition to safety.

**Search Plan:** I plan to uncover sources from both sides of the research question: those in favor of funding Head Start and those opposed to it. My goal is to understand how and why these sources have such different interpretations of the same evidence, which is primarily a large 2010 government study on the effectiveness of Head Start. I also plan to look carefully at the neutral sources that suggest that Head Start is flawed but could be made more effective with some changes. One obstacle I may face in my research is finding unbiased sources. Government sources, which are typically considered reliable, may demonstrate bias in favor of this government-funded program. Many nonprofit and educational sites may also demonstrate this same bias. Likewise, conservative groups that oppose taxes for many federal social programs will probably be automatically biased against Head Start.

### Working Bibliography

Burke, Lindsey M. "Head Start's Sad and Costly Secret—What Washington Doesn't Want You to Know." *FoxNews.com*, 14 Jan. 2013, www.foxnews.com/us/2013/01/14/head-starts -sad-and-costly-secret-what-washington-doesnt-want-you-to -know.html.

Colleluori, Salvatore. "Media Cherry-Pick Facts to Falsely Label Head Start Program a Failure." *Media Matters for America*, 16 Jan. 2013, mediamatters.org/research/2013/01/16 /media-cherry-pick-facts-to-falsely-label-head-s/192284.

Moreno, Amanda. "Why the Head Start Headlines Are Wrong." *The Huffington Post*, 24 Jan. 2013, www.huffingtonpost .com/amanda-moreno-phd/head-start-early-education_b _2533443.html

United States Department of Health and Human Services, Administration for Children and Families. *Office of Head Start*, www.acf.hhs.gov/programs/ohs. Accessed 16 Oct. 2015.

Vinci, Yasmina. "Does Head Start Work?" *Reuters.com*, 27 Dec. 2012, blogs.reuters.com/great-debate/2012/12/27/does-head -start-work/.

# 31 Finding Sources

Although research begins with an intriguing question or issue, it quickly becomes a fast-paced hunt, moving among electronic, print, and human resources. Efficient search strategies will help you find substantial, relevant sources.

Many instructors advocate beginning your research via the campus library, through whose resources you can identify and access reliable information, especially "peer-reviewed" or "refereed" articles—those whose scholarship and research methods have been assessed by experts in the field before publication. Such high-quality sources allow you to draw solid, well-grounded conclusions for your academic audience.

However, instructors also know that for news-oriented topics or opinions on trending social issues you also can find up-to-the-minute, though not necessarily reliable, information on the Internet. Where you begin your research may depend on your experience and the nature of your topic. Even if you start looking for a topic on the Web, turn to your campus library for focus and depth.

## Why Finding Sources Matters

**In a College Course**

- You need to support your paper for the most demanding professor in the entire nursing school, so you know that means more than using Google and Wikipedia.
- Your annotated bibliography is a third of your grade in history, so you need to find books and articles by reliable historians as well as original documents from the time period.

**In the Workplace**

- You organize objectives for the next decade, using available projections for your profession.

**In Your Community**

- You organize focus groups for a community grant proposal, identifying sources to use to help inform participants.

  ❓When have you needed to find specific types of sources? In what situations do you expect to do so again?

# Searching the Internet

The Internet contains resources that vary greatly in quality and purpose. A quick search may turn up intriguing topic ideas or slants, but it may also turn up thousands — maybe millions — of pages of uncertain relevance and timeliness. Some of these pages are motivated by the desire to sell something. Search returns also will not necessarily be designed to meet any academic standards. And a Web search will not include the thousands of private, corporate, or government sites from the "deep" or "hidden" Web that requires passwords, limits access, or simply isn't indexed. The sheer bulk of the information online makes searching for relevant research materials both too easy and too difficult, but a few basic principles can help.

## Finding Recommended Internet Resources

Go first to online resources recommended by your instructor or the department to which the course for which you're conducting research belongs. Their recommendations save search time, help you avoid outdated sites, and take you directly to respected resources prepared by experts (scholars or librarians) for academic researchers (like you). Your college library, on campus or online, will offer many more resources such as those listed in the chart on page 616.

For more on campus library resources, see pp. 619–22.

For more on evaluating sources, see Ch. 32.

## Smart Online Searching

When you look for Internet sources on your own, you'll want to keep your search as focused as possible to save time and retrieve the most appropriate sources.

**Make the Most of Search Engines.** Each online search engine has its own system of locating material, categorizing it, and establishing the sequence for reporting results. One search site, patterned on a library index, might be selective. Another might separate advertising from search results, while a third lists "sponsors" who pay advertising fees first, even though sites listed later might be better matches.

| Resource Type | Description | Examples |
|---|---|---|
| **Research Web Sites** | Sponsored or maintained by libraries, academic institutions, or nonprofit consortiums. Provide reliable links grouped by subject area. | *Internet Public Library* <br> *Michigan eLibrary* <br> *World Wide Web Virtual Library* |
| **Internet Database Locators** | Resources grouped by subject area (e.g., social sciences or business), topic (e.g., literary analysis), or type of information (e.g., statistics). | *Auraria Library Statistics and Facts Guide* |
| **Government Sites** | Allow specialized searches of their own collections. | *Library of Congress* <br> *U.S. Census Bureau* <br> *Catalog of U.S. Government Publications* |
| **E-book Collections** | Digitized texts, including reference books and literary works, now out of copyright. | *Bartleby.com* <br> *Project Gutenberg* |
| **Web Databases** | Various public repositories with no subscription required. | *United Nations* <br> *MedlinePlus* <br> *ProCon.org* |

## RESEARCH CHECKLIST

### Evaluating Search Engines

☐ What does the search engine's home page suggest its typical users want — academic information, business news, sports, shopping, or music?

☐ What does the search engine gather or index — information from and about a Web page (Bing), academic sources (Google Scholar), or a collection of other search engines (Dogpile)?

☐ What can you learn from a search engine's About, Search Tips, or Help?

☐ How does the advanced search work? Does it improve your results?

☐ Does the search engine take questions (Ask), categorize by source type (text, images, news), or group by topic (About)?

☐ How well does the search engine target your query — the words that define your specific search?

☐ Can you distinguish results (popular responses to your query), sponsors (advertisers who pay for priority placement), and other ads by placement, color, or other markers?

## Learning by Doing 🔲 Comparing Web Searches

Working with some classmates, agree on the topic and terms for a test search. (Or agree to test terms each of you selects.) Have everyone conduct the same search using different search engines, and then compare results. Use the checklist above to suggest features for comparison. If possible, sit together, using your laptops or campus computers so that you can easily see, compare, and evaluate the search engine results. Report your conclusions to the class.

**Conduct Advanced Electronic Searches.** Search engines can access millions of records on the Internet, much as a database or library catalog accesses records on the books, periodicals, or other materials found in a library. You can search them by entering keywords into the search bar that appears on the engine's home page.

**Focus the Search Terms.** If the keywords you enter into a search engine are too general, you may be overwhelmed with information. For example, Figure 31.1 illustrates a search for sources on *minimum wage* on Bing that produced 11.8 million entries. For more relevant results, consider the aspects of the topic most necessary to your research and limit your search accordingly. As Figure 31.2 shows, a focused search (*minimum wage + fast food workers*) produced fewer sources on one aspect of minimum wage—fast food workers.

For sample keyword searches, see p. 618 and pp. 624–25.

**Select Limitations for Advanced Searches.** Google, for example, allows you to limit searches to all, exactly, any, or none of the words you enter. Look for directions for limitations such as these:

- a phrase such as *elementary school safety,* requested as a unit (exactly these words) or enclosed in quotation marks to mark it as a unit
- a specific language (human or computer) such as English or Python
- a specific format or type of software such as a PDF file
- a date range (before, after, or between creation, revision, or indexing)
- a domain such as .edu (educational institution), .gov (government), .org (organization), or .com (commercial site or company), which indicates the type of group sponsoring the site
- a part of the world, such as North America or Africa
- the location (such as the title, the URL, or the text) of the search term
- the audio or visual media enhancements
- the file size

A Writer's Research Manual

**Figure 31.1** Results of a keyword search for *minimum wage* using Bing, reporting 11.8 million entries.

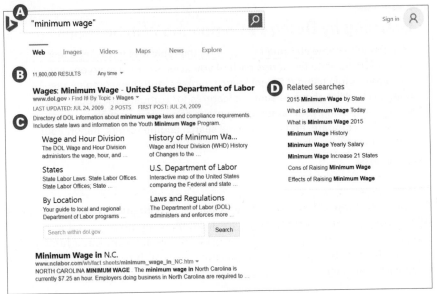

Ⓐ Search terms

Ⓑ Total number of entries located

Ⓒ Highlighted search terms found in entries

Ⓓ Suggested related searches

**Figure 31.2** Advanced search results on *minimum wage + fast food workers* using Bing, reporting 216,000 results.

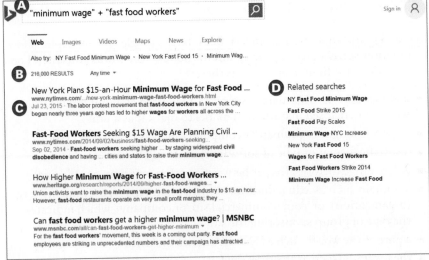

Ⓐ Search terms

Ⓑ Total number of entries located

Ⓒ Highlighted search terms found in entries

Ⓓ Suggested related searches

**Find Specialized Online Materials.** You can locate a variety of material online, ranging from blogs to tweets to video. For the most up-to-date news stories, use a search engine or go to the Web site for a major news outlet (e.g., the BBC, CNN, NBC, the *New York Times*, NPR, Reuters, or the *Wall Street Journal*). Be careful to distinguish expertise from opinion and speculation. Evaluate and use blogs, personal sites, and social media cautiously.

For more on evaluating sources, see Ch. 32.

# Searching the Library

What would you pay for access to a 24/7 Web site designed to make the most of your research time? What if it also screened and organized reliable sources for you—and tossed in free advice from information specialists? Whatever your budget, you've probably already paid—through your tuition—for these services. To get your money's worth, simply use your student ID to access your college library, online or on campus.

## Getting to Know the Library

Visit the library home page for an overview of resources such as these:

- the online catalog for finding the library's own books, journals, newspapers, and materials you can read or check out on campus
- databases (with subscription fees paid) for electronic access to scholarly or specialized citations, abstracts, articles, and other resources
- access to the resources of the state, region, or nation through interlibrary loan (ILL), a regional consortium, or a trip to a nearby library
- links for finding specialized campus libraries, archives, or collections
- pages, tutorials, and tours for advice on using the library productively

To introduce you to the campus library, your instructor may arrange a class orientation. If not, visit the library Web site and campus facility yourself.

---

**RESEARCH CHECKLIST**

**Accessing Library Resources**

☐ What services, materials, and information does the home page present?

☐ How do you gain online access to the library from your own computer? What should you do if you have trouble logging in?

☐ How can you get live help from library staff: by drop-in visit, appointment, phone, e-mail, text message, chat, or other technology?

☐ What resources—such as the library catalog and databases—can you search in the library, on campus, or off campus?

☐ How can you identify databases useful for your project? What tutorials from the library or database provider show how to use them efficiently?

☐ How are print books, journals, magazines, or newspapers organized?

☐ How do you find specialized resources such as government documents, maps, legal records, statistics, videos, images, recordings, or local historical archives? Have you consulted a subject librarian?

☐ Where can you study individually or meet with a group in the library?

☐ What links or no-fee access to reliable Web sites, search engines such as Google Scholar, or academic style guides does the library provide?

☐ What other services — copying, printing, computer access — are available at your library?

**Figure 31.3** Sample home page from the Tuskegee University Libraries.

Ⓐ Overview of libraries and their purpose

Ⓑ Access to library holdings and resources

Ⓒ Information on specific campus libraries

## Learning by Doing 🔄 Reflecting on Your Library Orientation Session

After visiting the library for your class orientation, list the most useful things you have learned — such as directions for access, advice about off-campus use, ways to get search advice, specific resources for your project or major, types of materials new to you, the name of a reference librarian, or helpful tricks for doing faster research. Then list your current questions about your own research project, and figure out where to start looking for the best and fastest answers.

**Target Your Search.** Your campus library may surprise you with its sophisticated technology and easy access to an overwhelming array of resources. Identify and hunt for what you want to find.

- Do you need a mixture of sources? Use the catalog to find specialized books or journals, databases to identify individual articles, reference books to look up definitions or overviews, or government sites or indexes to find reports. If your library offers WorldCat Local or a megasearch system, you can search all types of resources at one time.

- Do you need current or historical information? Look for articles in periodicals (regularly published newspapers, magazines, and journals) for news of the day, week, or year. Turn to scholarly books for well-seasoned discussions.

- Does your instructor require articles from peer-reviewed or refereed journals? Use *Ulrich's Periodicals Directory* or databases to screen for journals that rely on expert reviewers to assess articles considered for publication.

- Do you need opinions about current issues? Search databases for newspapers or magazines that carry opinion pieces, issue-oriented or investigative articles, or contrasting regional, national, or international views.

- Do you need the facts? Check state or federal agencies or nonprofit groups for statistics about people, such as those in your zip code, including information about their education, employment, or health.

**Use the Resources.** Your campus library can help you become a more efficient and productive student. Try its wide variety of resources, advice, and tools: e-books, audio books, podcasts, videos, tutorials, workshops, citation managers, source organizers, and apps for academic tasks (e.g., note takers, time managers, project schedules, group organizers, and file hosting services).

**Sample the Field.** Many libraries supply Library Guides or lists of well-regarded starting points for research within a field. These valuable shortcuts help you quickly find a cluster of useful resources. The chart below supplies only a small sampling of the specialized indexes, dictionaries, encyclopedias, handbooks, yearbooks, and other resources available.

| | Specialized Online Indexes | Print Reference Works | Online Government Resources | Internet Resources |
|---|---|---|---|---|
| **Humanities** | *Essay and General Literature Index; JSTOR* | *The Humanities: A Selective Guide to Information Sources* | EDSITEment (NEH) | Voice of the Shuttle |
| **Film and Theater** | *Film & Television Literature Index; Films on Demand* | *The Oxford Encyclopedia of Theatre and Performance* | Smithsonian Archives Center: Film, Video, and Audio Collections | Cambridge Companions Online |
| **History** | *Historical Abstracts America: History and Life* | *Dictionary of Concepts in History* | The Library of Congress: American Memory | WWW Virtual Library: History Central Catalogue |
| **Literature** | *MLA International Bibliography* | *Encyclopedia of the Novel* | National Endowment for the Humanities | American Studies Journals |
| **Social Sciences** | *Social Sciences Citation Index* | *International Encyclopedia of the Social and Behavioral Sciences* | Fedstats | e-Source from the National Institutes of Health |
| **Education** | *Education Abstracts* | *International Encyclopedia of Education* | National Center for Education Statistics | ERIC: Education Resources Information Center |
| **Political Science** | *Worldwide Political Science Abstracts* | *State Legislative Sourcebook* | FedWorld | Political Resources on the Net; National Security Archive |
| **Women's Studies** | *Women's Studies International* | *Women in World History: A Biographical Encyclopedia* | U.S. Department of Labor Women's Bureau | Institute for Women's Policy Research |
| **Science and Technology** | *General Science Abstracts; Web of Science* | *McGraw-Hill Encyclopedia of Science and Technology* | National Science Foundation | EurekAlert! |
| **Earth Sciences** | *GeoRef* | *Facts on File Dictionary of Earth Science* | USGS (U.S. Geological Survey): Science for a Changing World | Center for International Earth Science Information Network |
| **Environmental Studies** | *Environmental Abstracts* | *Encyclopedia of Environmental Science* | EPA: U.S. Environmental Protection | EnviroLink |
| **Life Sciences** | *Biological Abstracts* | *Encyclopedia of Human Biology* | National Agricultural Library | CAPHIS Top 100 List |

# Using the Library Catalog

A library's catalog is an index of all materials — books, periodicals, digital collections, historical archives, and so on — that the library houses. The catalog may also provide a listing of external materials that may be retrieved through interlibrary loan. The purpose of the catalog is to allow you to find basic information, such as title, author, and date, on materials that you can access through the library.

**Search Creatively.** Electronic catalogs may allow many search options, as the chart below illustrates. Consult a librarian or follow the prompts to find out which searches your catalog allows.

| Type of Search | Explanation | Examples | Search Tips |
|---|---|---|---|
| **Keyword** | Terms that identify topics discussed in source, including works by or about an author, but may generate long lists of relevant and irrelevant sources | ■ workplace mental health<br>■ geriatric home health care<br>■ Creole cookbook<br>■ James Baldwin novels | Use a cluster of keywords to avoid broad terms (*whale, nursing*) or to reduce irrelevant topics using the same terms (*people of color, color graphics*) |
| **Subject** | Terms assigned by library catalogers, often following the Library of Congress Subject Headings (LCSH) | ■ motion pictures (not *films*)<br>■ developing countries (not *Third World*)<br>■ cooking (not *cookbooks*) | Consult the online LCSH or note the linked subject headings with search results to find the exact phrasing used |
| **Author** | Name of individual, organization, or group, leading to list of print (and possibly online) works by author (or editor) | ■ Hawthorne, Nathaniel<br>■ Colorado School of Mines<br>■ North Atlantic Treaty Organization | Begin as directed with an individual's last name first; for a group, first do a keyword search to identify its exact name |
| **Title** | Name of book, pamphlet, journal, magazine, newspaper, video, CD, or other material | ■ *Peace and Conflict Studies*<br>■ *Los Angeles Times*<br>■ *Nursing Outlook* | Look for a separate search option for titles of periodicals (journals, newspapers, magazines) |
| **Identification Numbers** | Library or consortium call numbers, publisher or government publication numbers | ■ MJ BASI, local call number for recordings by Count Basie | Use the call number of a useful source to find related items online or shelved nearby |
| **Dates** | Publication or other dates used to search (or limit searches) for current or historical materials | ■ Vietnam War 1969<br>■ science teaching 2016 | Add dates to keyword or other searches to limit the topics or time of publication |

## Learning by Doing 🎯 Brainstorming for Search Terms

Start with a class topic or your rough ideas for a research question. Working with a classmate or small group, brainstorm in class or online for keywords or synonyms that might be useful search terms for each person's topic. Test your terms by searching several places — the library catalog, a subject-area database, a newspaper database, a reliable consumer Web page, a relevant government agency, or other library resources. Compare search results in terms of type, quantity, quality, and relevance of sources. Note which terms work best in which situations. Then refine your search terms — add limitations, change keywords, narrow the ideas, and so forth. Search again, trying to increase the relevance of what you find.

**Sort Your Search Results.** When your search produces a list of possible sources, click on the most promising items to learn more about them. See Figure 31.4 for a sample keyword search and Figure 31.5 for the online records for one source. Besides the call number or shelf location, the record will identify the author, the title, the place of publication, the date, and often the resource's contents, length, and scope and search terms that may help focus your search. Use these clues to help you select options wisely.

**Browse the Shelves.** A call number, like an address, tells where a book or other resource "resides." College libraries generally use the Library of Congress system, with letters and numbers, rather than the numerical Dewey

**Figure 31.4**
General results of a keyword search on *dyslexia* using an online library catalog.

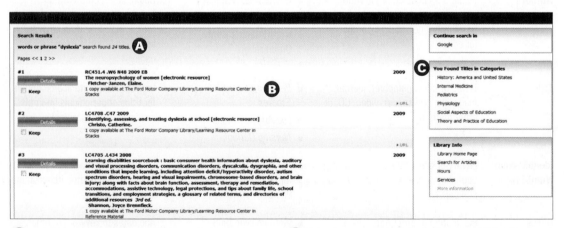

**A** Number of search results

**B** Results screen (linked to full entries) with call numbers, titles, authors, and availability

**C** Topic areas where results were found

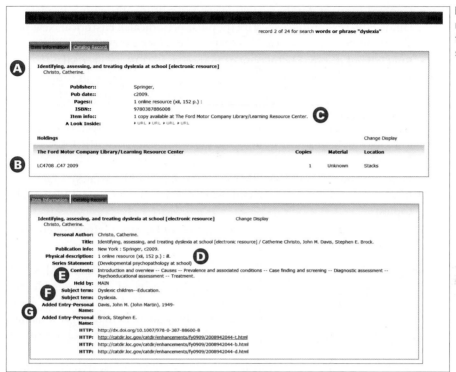

**Figure 31.5** Specific record selected from keyword search results.

Ⓐ Title and author

Ⓑ Call number

Ⓒ Availability and location

Ⓓ Number of pages, illustrations, and type of resource

Ⓔ Contents by part and chapter

Ⓕ Alternate subject headings (often hyperlinked)

Ⓖ Additional authors

decimal system, but both systems group items by subject. With a call number from an online record, follow the library map and section signs to the shelf with a promising book. Once there, browse through its intriguing neighbors, which often treat the same subject.

## Searching Library Databases

Databases gather information. Your library may subscribe to dozens or hundreds to give you easy access to current screened resources, including hard-to-find fee-based Web sources. Check the library site for its database descriptions and lists by topic or field. A librarian can help match your research question to the databases most likely to provide what you need.

- **General databases** with citations, abstracts, or full-text articles from many fields: Academic Search Premier, General OneFile, LexisNexis, OmniFile Full Text

- **General-interest databases** with news and culture of the time: Readers' Guide Full-Text or Retrospective (popular periodicals); Historical New York Times, America's Historical Newspapers, LexisNexis (news)
- **Specialized databases by type of material:** JSTOR, Project MUSE, Sage (scholarly journals); Biological Abstracts (summaries of sources); WorldCat (books); American Periodicals Series Online (digitized magazines from 1741 to 1900)
- **Specialized databases by field:** MedlinePlus, ScienceDirect, GreenFILE (biology, medicine, health); ABI/INFORM (business); AGRICOLA (agriculture)
- **Issue-oriented databases:** PAIS International (public affairs); CQ Researcher (featured issues); Opposing Viewpoints in Context (debatable topics)
- **Reference databases:** Gale Virtual Reference Library, Oxford Reference, Credo Reference

For specific information, select a database that covers the exact field, scholarly level, type of source, or time period that you need. Databases identify sources only in publications they analyze and only for dates they cover. Take tricky research problems to a subject librarian, who may suggest using a different database or older print or CD-ROM indexes for historical research.

**Keywords.** Start your search with the keywords in your research question:

| | | |
|---|---|---|
| college costs | campus budgets | wetlands |

If your first search produces too many sources, narrow your terms:

college tuition increases

state campus budget cuts

Illinois wetlands and Great Midwestern Flood

Or add specifics, such as an author, a title, or a date.

**Advanced Searches.** Fill in the database's advanced search screen to restrict by date or other options, or try common search options. For example, a database might allow wildcard or truncation symbols to find all forms of a term; often * is used for multiple and ? for individual characters (results are limited to the number of characters supplied in the original search).

| child* | children, childcare, childhood |
|---|---|
| wa? | wan, wag, wad |

A database also might allow Boolean searches that combine or rule out terms:

| | |
|---|---|
| AND (narrows: all terms must appear in a result) | Colorado and River |
| OR (expands: any one of the terms must appear) | Colorado or River |
| NOT (rules out: one term must not appear) | Colorado not River |

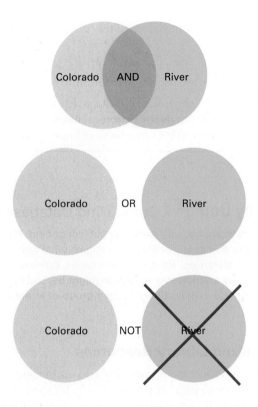

**Search Returns.** Your search calls up a list of records or entries that include your search terms. Click on one of these for specifics about the item (title, author, publication information, date, other details) and possibly a description or summary (often called an *abstract*) or a link to the full text of the item. When you find a useful item, read, take notes, print, save, or e-mail the citation or article to yourself, as your system allows. If the database supplies only an abstract, read it to decide whether you need to track down the full article elsewhere.

---

RESEARCH CHECKLIST

### Selecting Periodical Articles from a Database

☐ What does the periodical title suggest about its audience, interest area, and popular or scholarly orientation? How likely are its articles to supply what you need?

☐ Have the periodical articles been peer-reviewed (evaluated by other scholars prior to acceptance for publication), edited and fact-checked by journalists, or accepted for publication based on popular appeal?

☐ Does the title or description of the article suggest that it will answer your research question? Or does the entry sound intriguing but irrelevant?

☐ Does the date of the article fit your need for current, contemporary, eyewitness, or classic material?

☐ Does the length of the article suggest that it's a short review, a concise overview, or an exhaustive discussion? How much detail will you need?

☐ Does the database offer the full text of the article in direct-scan PDF or reformatted html? If not, is the periodical likely to be available from another database, on its Web site, or on your library's shelves?

## Learning by Doing 🖱 Comparing Databases

Work with others interested in a particular subject or field. Pick at least three databases in that area. For each, investigate what type of response it provides (source references, abstracts, summaries, full-text articles), which dates it covers, how extensive its collection might be, and how you can most successfully use it. Report back to your group or to the entire class.

## Using Specialized Library Resources

Many other library resources are available to you beyond what's accessible from your library's home page. If you need help locating or using materials, consult a librarian. Be sure to request the most current information, as not all reference resources are updated yearly.

**Figure 31.6** Search result from America's Historical Newspapers.
Readex, a Division of NewsBank Inc.

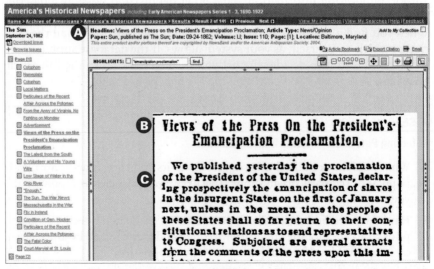

Ⓐ Publication name, date, volume number, page number

Ⓑ Article title (and author, if available)

Ⓒ Text of article

| Types of Specialized Library Resources | Description | Examples |
|---|---|---|
| **Encyclopedias** | Multivolume general references can help you survey a topic; specialized encyclopedias cover a field in much greater depth. | *Encyclopedia of Psychology; Encyclopedia of World Cultures; Gale Encyclopedia of Science* |
| **Dictionaries** | Specialized dictionaries cover foreign languages, abbreviations, and slang as well as the terminology of a particular field. | *Black's Law Dictionary; Stedman's Medical Dictionary; Oxford Dictionary of Natural History* |
| **Handbooks and Companions** | Concise articles survey terms and topics on a specific subject. | *Handbook of Special Education; Bloomsbury Guide to Women's Literature* |
| **Government Documents** | The U.S. government makes a large number of documents available on the Web, plus print and electronic indexes, some available only through libraries. | *Congressional Record Index; Statistical Abstract of the United States* |
| **Atlases** | Maps of countries and regions as well as their history, natural resources, and ethnic groups and other topics. | *Atlas of Structural Geology* |
| **Biographical Sources** | Basic information about prominent people. | *American Men and Women of Science; Who's Who in Politics* |
| **Bibliographies** | List a wide variety of sources on a specific subject and research others have already done. | *The Essential Shakespeare: An Annotated Bibliography of Major Modern Studies* |
| **Specialized Materials** | Other collections, especially those of local or specialized topics. Some collections may be digitized. | Diaries and letters; photographs; pamphlets; unpublished manuscripts |

# Finding Sources in the Field

The goal of field research is the same as that of library and Internet research — to gather the information you need to answer your research question and then to marshal persuasive evidence to support your conclusions. When you interview, observe, or ask questions of people, you generate your own firsthand (or primary) evidence. Before you begin, find out from your instructor whether you need institutional approval for research involving other people ("human subjects approval") from your school's institutional review board (IRB).

## Interviewing

For more on interviewing, see Ch. 6.

Interviews—conversations with a purpose—may be your main source of field material. Whenever possible, interview an expert in the field or, if you are researching a group, someone representative or typical. Prepare carefully.

TIPS FOR INTERVIEWING

- Be sure your prospect is willing to be quoted in writing.
- Make an appointment for a day when the person will have enough time—an hour if possible—for a thorough talk with you.
- Arrive promptly, with carefully thought-out questions to ask.
- Come ready to take notes, including key points, quotations, and descriptive details. If you also want to record, ask permission.
- Really listen. Let the person open up.
- Be flexible; allow the interview to move in unanticipated directions.
- If a question draws no response, don't persist; go on to the next one.
- At the end of the interview, thank the interviewee, and arrange for an opportunity to clarify comments and confirm direct quotations.
- Make additional notes right after the interview to preserve anything you didn't have time to record during the interview.

If you can't talk in person, try a telephone or online interview. Make an appointment for a convenient time, write out questions before you call, and take notes. Federal regulations, by the way, forbid recording a phone interview without notifying the person talking that you are doing so. Always be sure to notify your subject if you are recording them on Skype or another video chat service, too.

## Learning by Doing 📷 Interviewing an Instructor

Interview one of your instructors about his or her current research or field of study. Ask what the particular field requires by way of study or success. Ask if he or she would share tips for students who want to go into that field. Reflect on what it takes for an instructor to be successful and how you might apply this information to your own studies.

## Observing

For more on observing, see Ch. 5.

An observation may provide you with essential information about a setting such as a workplace or a school. Some organizations will insist on your displaying valid identification; in advance, ask your instructor for a statement written on college letterhead declaring that you are a student doing field research. Make an appointment with the organization or individual and, on arrival, identify yourself and your purpose. Before you depart, be sure to thank the necessary parties for arranging the observation.

TIPS FOR OBSERVING

- Establish a clear purpose—decide exactly what you want to observe and why.
- Take notes so that you don't skip important details in your paper.
- Record facts, telling details, and sensory impressions. Notice the features of the place, the actions or relationships of the people there, or whatever relates to the purpose of your observation.
- Consider taking photos or recording video if doing so doesn't distract you from the scene. Photographs can illustrate your paper and help you recall and interpret details while you write. If you are in a private place, get written permission from the owner (or other authority) and any people you photograph.
- Pause, look around, fill in missing details, and check the accuracy of your notes before you leave the observation site.
- Thank the person who arranged your observation so you will be welcome again if you need to return to fill in gaps in your data or test new ideas.

## Using Questionnaires

Questionnaires, or surveys, gather the responses of a number of people to a fixed set of questions. Online services such as SurveyMonkey allow you to quickly develop and deploy questionnaires for free. Professional researchers carefully design sets of questions and then randomly select representative people to respond in order to reach reliable answers. Because your survey will not be that extensive, avoid generalizing about your findings. It's one thing to say that "many students" who filled out a questionnaire hadn't read a newspaper in the past month; it's another to claim that this is true of 72 percent of the students at your school—especially when your questionnaires went only to students in a specific major, and only half of them responded to the e-mail invitation.

A more reliable way to treat questionnaires is as group interviews: assume that you collect typical views, use them to build your overall knowledge, and cull responses for compelling details or quotations. Use a questionnaire to concentrate on what a group thinks as a whole or when an interview to cover all your questions is impractical. (See Figure 31.8 for a sample questionnaire.)

TIPS FOR USING A QUESTIONNAIRE

- Ask yourself what you want to discover with your questionnaire. Then thoughtfully invent questions to fulfill that purpose.
- State questions clearly, and supply simple directions for easy responses. Test your questionnaire on classmates or friends before distributing it to the group you want to study.
- Ask questions that call for checking options, marking *yes* or *no,* circling a number on a five-point scale, or writing a few words so responses are easy to tally. Try to ask for one piece of information per question.

- If you wish to consider differences based on age, gender, or other variables, include some demographic questions.

- Write unbiased questions to elicit factual responses. Don't ask How religious are you? Instead ask What is your religious affiliation? and How often do you attend religious services? Then you could report actual numbers and draw logical inferences about respondents.

- When appropriate, ask open-ended questions that call for short written responses. Although qualitative responses are more difficult to tally than quantitative ones, the answers may supply worthwhile quotations or suggest important issues or factors.

- Try to distribute questionnaires at a set location or event, and collect them as they are completed. If necessary, have them returned to your campus mailbox or another secure location. The more immediate and convenient the return, the higher your return rate is likely to be. If you're conducting the questionnaire online, try to send it out at a time when you know students won't be too busy to respond (such as finals week), and consider sending a reminder as the deadline approaches.

- Use a blank questionnaire or make an answer grid to mark and add up the answers for each question. Total the responses so you can report that a certain percentage selected a specific answer. Many online services will perform this work for you.

- For fill-in or short answers, type up each answer or paste the answers into a new document. (Code each questionnaire with a number in case you want to trace an answer back to its origin.) Try rearranging the answers in the file, looking for logical groupings, categories, or patterns that accurately reflect the responses and enrich your analysis.

## Corresponding

For advice on writing e-mail messages, see p. 341; for business letters, see pp. 347–50.

Does your interview subject live too far away for you to speak to him or her in person? Search online for contact information. If you can't easily locate an e-mail address or phone number, try to locate the individual on social media to introduce yourself, specify your query, and request further information. Do you need information from a group, such as the American Red Cross, or an elected official? The organization's Web site should provide an e-mail address for your request, a physical mailing address, an FAQ page (that answers frequently asked questions), or files of brochures.

### TIPS FOR CORRESPONDING

- Plan ahead, and allow plenty of time for responses to your requests.

- Make your message short and polite. Identify yourself, and explain your request. List any questions. Thank your correspondent.

- Enclose a stamped, self-addressed envelope with the letter. Include your e-mail address in your message.

## QUESTIONNAIRE

Thank you for completing this questionnaire. All information you supply will be kept strictly confidential.

1. What is your age? ____
2. What is your gender? ____
3. What is your class?
   ____ First-year      ____ Sophomore      ____ Junior      ____ Senior
4. Where do you live?
   ____ On campus      ____ Off campus
5. Do you use the on-campus dining facilities?
   ____ Yes      ____ No
6. If you answered "no," please specify why you do not use the on-campus dining facilities.
   ____ The meal plans are too expensive.
   ____ My schedule and commitments preclude me from being on campus for meals.
   ____ The available food options are not suitable to my dietary needs.
   ____ The available food options are of poor nutritional quality.
   ____ Other (please explain) _____
7. Which meals do you routinely obtain from on-campus dining facilities? Check all that apply.
   ____ Breakfast
   ____ Lunch
   ____ Dinner
   ____ Snacks
   ____ Other (please explain) _____
8. Approximately how many meals per week do you eat in the on-campus dining facilities?
   ____ 0
   ____ 1–5
   ____ 6–10
   ____ 10+
9. On a scale of 1 to 5, how satisfied are you with the overall quality of food served in on-campus dining facilities?
   (dissatisfied)  1  2  3  4  5  (extremely satisfied)
10. Would you be interested in receiving information about the nutritional value and purchase history of the food available through on-campus dining services?
    ____ Yes      ____ No      ____ Maybe
11. Would you be more likely to dine on campus, or to dine on campus more frequently, if dining facilities management responded to student demands for more nutritious food options that meet a greater variety of dietary needs?
    ____ Yes      ____ No      ____ Maybe

**Figure 31. 7** Questionnaire asking students about dining preferences.

## Attending Public and Online Events

College organizations bring interesting speakers to campus. Check your campus Facebook page, newspaper, and bulletin boards. In addition, professionals and special-interest groups convene for regional or national conferences. A lecture or conference can be a source of fresh ideas and an excellent introduction to the language of a discipline.

### TIPS FOR ATTENDING EVENTS

- Take notes on lectures, usually given by experts in the field who supply firsthand opinions or research findings.
- Ask questions from the audience or talk informally with a speaker later.
- Record who attended the event, as well as audience reactions and other background details that may be useful in writing your paper.
- Depending on the gathering, a speaker might distribute his or her paper or presentation slides or post a copy online. Conferences often publish their proceedings — usually a set of the lectures delivered — but online publication takes months. Try the library Web site for past proceedings.

If you join an online discussion, you can observe, ask a question, or save or print the transcript for your records.

## Reconsidering Your Field Sources

Each type of field research can raise particular questions. For example, when you observe an event or a setting, are people aware of being observed? If so, have they changed their behavior? Is your random sampling of people truly representative? Have you questioned everyone in a group thoroughly enough?

In addition, consider the credibility and consistency of your field sources. Did your source seem biased or prejudiced? If so, will you need to discount some of the source's information? Did your source provide evidence to support or corroborate claims? Have you compared different people's opinions, accounts, or evidence? Is any evidence hearsay — one person telling you the thoughts of another or recounting actions that he or she hasn't witnessed? If so, can you check the information with another source or a different type of evidence? Did your source seem to respond consistently, seriously, and honestly? Has time possibly distorted memories of past events? Adjust your conclusions based on your field research in accord with your answers to such questions.

# Evaluating Sources

# 32

After you locate and collect information, you need to think critically and evaluate — in other words, judge — your sources.

For more on critical reading and thinking, see Chs. 2–3.

- Which of your sources are reliable?
- What types of sources are you working with?
- What evidence from these sources is most useful for your paper?

Use the Take Action chart on page 636 as you evaluate each of the sources you've found.

## Why Evaluating Sources Matters

### In a College Course

- You found half a dozen sources about your topic, but they wildly disagree; you have to decide what to do next.
- You found a Web site without any author, a testimonial by a TV star you dimly remember, and a boring article by a professor, but you don't know which one to believe.

### In the Workplace

- You have to prepare a recommendation for a client after deciding what data and field reports to provide.

### In Your Community

- You disagree with the mayor's decision to ban urban gardening, so you want to find current, substantial information that will change her mind.

❓ When have you decided which sources to use and which to skip? In what situations do you expect to evaluate sources again?

# Take Action  Evaluating Sources

Ask each question listed in the left-hand column to evaluate your sources. Follow the ASK—LOCATE SPECIFICS—TAKE ACTION sequence to make sure your sources are reliable.

| 1 ASK | 2 LOCATE SPECIFICS | 3 TAKE ACTION |
|---|---|---|
| Is my source **reliable?** | ■ Determine whether the **author has a good reputation as a journalist or scholar** in the field.<br><br>■ Confirm that the **publisher or sponsoring organization** of the source is reputable.<br><br>■ Review the source for any signs of **bias**.<br><br>■ Check the **date** of the source.<br><br>■ Take special care with **Internet sources**. | ■ **Ask a reference librarian or your instructor** if you need help determining an author's or a publisher's reputation.<br><br>■ **Watch out for sources that take extreme positions** on an issue without a fair or logical discussion of opposing viewpoints.<br><br>■ **Check carefully for any author or publisher affiliations (political, religious, corporate, etc.)** that may indicate bias.<br><br>■ In general, **look for the most recent evidence** related to your research question.<br><br>■ **Aim for well-established Internet sites,** such as CNN.com, or sites that are part of **nonprofit** (.org), **educational** (.edu), or **governmental** (.gov) organizations. Review the checklist on pages 639–40 for evaluating Internet sources. |
| What **type of source** am I working with? | ■ Determine whether a source is **primary (firsthand) or secondary (interpreted) evidence.**<br><br>■ Check to see whether a source is **popular or scholarly.** | ■ **Review the description of primary and secondary sources on pages 637–38.** Many research projects benefit from both primary and secondary evidence.<br><br>■ **Review the distinction between popular and scholarly sources on page 638.** Use scholarly sources if you can understand the content; use popular sources if they are well regarded and serious. |
| Is the source **relevant** to my research project? | ■ Review your **research question and purpose**. | ■ **Confirm that the source is appropriate for your purpose.** Including sources that are off topic or irrelevant will dilute your focus and drown out your own voice. |

# Assessing the Reliability of Sources

Not every source you locate will be equally reliable. Print materials and Web sites recommended by your library have been screened by professionals, but each has its own point of view or approach, often a necessary bias to restrict its focus. To determine what evidence is best, do what experienced researchers do—ask key questions about the author, the publisher, and the source itself.

## Learning by Doing 📷 Evaluating Your Sources

Select a source that you expect to be useful for your paper. Using the Take Action chart on page 636, jot down notes as you examine the source for reliability, type, and relevance. Working with a classmate or group, present your evaluations to each other. Then discuss strategies for dealing with the strengths and limitations of the sources you have evaluated. (Use the next sections to help you deepen your evaluation.)

## Who Is Responsible for the Source?

Learn the credentials, affiliation, and reputation of each author and publisher you plan to use. Any source you use to shape or support your ideas should be reliable and trustworthy.

**Credentials.** Check for the author's background in any preface, introduction, or concluding note in an article or a book. For a Web site, look for links leading to other articles by the author or for a link to author information. If necessary, conduct a Web search to learn more about an author's background and expertise.

**Reputation.** Keep in mind that a good measure of someone's credibility is the regard of other experts. Does your instructor or a campus expert recognize or recommend the author? Does a search for the author on Google Scholar produce other sources that cite the author? Is the publisher well established and known for producing quality materials?

**Material with No Author Identified.** If no author is given, try to identify the sponsor, publisher, or editor. On a Web site, check the home page or search for a disclaimer, contact information, or an About page. Avoid any source with no identifiable author or publisher.

## What Type of Source Is It?

Sources can generally be categorized as either primary or secondary, and both types of sources should be carefully examined for authorship and bias. Most research projects benefit from a combination of primary and secondary sources.

**Primary Sources.** A *primary source* is a firsthand account written by an eyewitness or a participant. It contains raw data and immediate impressions. Examples include diaries, letters, news articles written by eyewitnesses to an event, and official reports and data such as census or labor statistics.

**Secondary Sources.** A *secondary source* is an analysis or interpretation of information contained in one or more primary sources. Secondary sources include articles and books based on primary sources (but not articles written by eyewitnesses). A biography of Peter the Great by a modern historian would be a secondary source because it relies on the historian's interpretation of events described in primary sources. An autobiography, on the other hand, is a firsthand source because it is written by the person who experienced the events it covers.

## Is the Source Scholarly or Popular?

Most secondary sources can be considered either scholarly or popular, depending on the publisher or author affiliation.

**Scholarly Sources.** Sources of scholarly information generally include academic journals and Web sites as well as books published by university presses. The material is written by scholars or scientists in the field, and it is usually reviewed by other experts before publication. Scholarly sources generally include extensive in-text citations and bibliographies to document their research. Although scholarly sources are usually quite reputable, they are written for an expert audience; thus, some materials may be too specialized or high level for your use. Examples of scholarly sources include the *Journal of the American Medical Association* and the *Congressional Quarterly*.

**Popular Sources.** Unlike scholarly sources, popular sources are usually written by journalists and other non-scholarly writers and are published for a broader audience. Although they are not typically reviewed by experts in the field, reputable popular sources are edited for clarity and accuracy by a publishing staff. You may find popular publications, such as those by the *New York Times, Scientific American,* CNN.com, and the Smithsonian Institution (si .edu), to be excellent sources of background information; they may even provide important evidence for your research project if the author is well regarded.

## What Is the Source's Purpose and Bias?

Whether primary or secondary, popular or scholarly, reputable or not, authors and publishers often have a purpose in mind when they publish a text. Your job as a researcher is to critically question whether the author or publisher is motivated by a political, a religious, a corporate, or another agenda. To understand the purpose or intention of a source, ask critical questions: Is its purpose to explain or inform? To report new research? To persuade? To add a viewpoint? To sell a product? Does the source acknowledge its purpose in its preface, mission statement, or About Us or FAQ (Frequently Asked Questions) page?

In addition to being aware of a source's purpose, you should watch for an author's or a publisher's point of view, which may shape the source's contents. *Bias* is a preference for a particular side of an issue. Because most authors and publishers have opinions on their topics, there's little point in asking whether they are biased. Instead, ask how that viewpoint affects the presentation of information and opinion. What are the author's or sponsor's allegiances? Does the source treat one side of an issue more favorably than another? Is that bias hidden or stated? Is any important information—especially evidence that might refute this source's argument—notably missing? A strong bias does not invalidate a source. However, if you spot such bias early, you can look for other viewpoints to avoid lopsided analyses.

## When Was the Source Produced or Published?

In most fields, new information and discoveries are reported every year, so a source needs to be up-to-date or at least still timely. New information may appear first in Web postings, media broadcasts, and newspapers and eventually in magazines, though such sources may not have allowed time for experts to consider the information thoughtfully. Later, as material is more fully examined, it may appear in scholarly articles and books. For this reason, older materials can supply a valuable historical, theoretical, or analytical focus.

# Using Special Care with Internet Sources

Like all sources, online postings, blogs, and Web sites reflect the biases, interests, or information gaps of their writers or sponsors. Commercial and organizational sites may supply useful material, but they provide only what supports their goals—selling their products, serving their clients, enlisting new members, or persuading others to accept their activities or views. See Figure 32.1 for a sample evaluation of a Web site that provides both informative and persuasive materials.

More important, keep in mind that many online sources do not go through the traditional editorial, review, and publication processes that generally make printed sources more reliable. Use the checklist that follows to take extra precautions when evaluating Internet sites.

---

**RESEARCH CHECKLIST**

**Evaluating Internet Sources**

☐ Check the URL's domain name (.com, .edu, .gov, etc.) to determine what type of organization is sponsoring the site.

.com: business or commercial site

.edu: educational site

.gov or .us: government site

.mil: military site

.org: nonprofit organization site

☐ Carefully check the part of the URL *before* the domain name to confirm you're on an appropriate site. For example, if you are researching US census data, you want to be on *census*.gov, not *yahoo.about*.com/census_gov.

☐ Review the site's About page for information on the organization's purpose and affiliations. If no About page is available, treat the site with extra caution.

☐ Check the publication date or most recent update. Sites that haven't been updated in more than two years should be treated with caution.

☐ Beware of Web sites with excessive ads or links to commercial sites. Many unreliable sites exist purely as "clickbait," designed solely to earn advertising revenue.

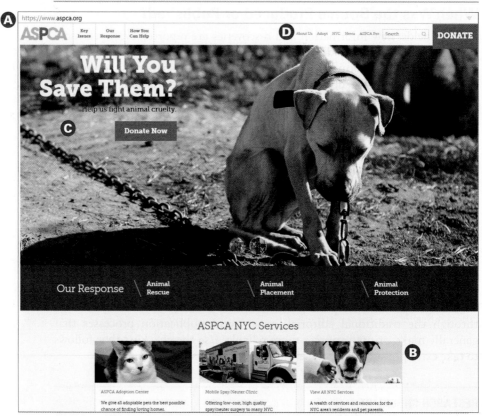

Ⓐ Identifies group as organization (.org), not school (.edu) or company (.com)

Ⓑ Uses engaging animal images

Ⓒ Appeals for support

Ⓓ About Us tab links to page explaining purpose of group

**Figure 32.1A** Evaluating the purpose, audience, and bias of a Web site offering informative and persuasive materials.

**C** Appeals for support

**D** About Us tab links to page explaining purpose of group

**E** Blog section provides searchable collection of articles

**Figure 32.1B** Evaluating the purpose, audience, and bias of a Web site offering informative and persuasive materials.

# Assessing Relevance

Even a highly reliable source needs to be relevant to your research question and your ideas about how to answer that question. An interesting fact or opinion could be just that—interesting. Instead, you need facts, expert opinions, information, and quotations that relate directly to your purpose and audience.

## Considering Your Purpose

As you collect and select sources, consider what makes one source better than another. Think about whether the information it includes is useful for your purposes. Would its strong quotations or hard facts be effective? Does

For a review of selecting sources, see B in the Quick Research Guide, pp. Q-24–Q-25.

For more on testing evidence, see pp. 162–64.

it tackle the topic in a relevant way? For one paper, you might appropriately rely on a popular magazine; for another, you might need the scholarly findings on which the magazine relied. Look for the best sources for your purpose, asking not only Will this do? but also Would something else be better?

## Learning by Doing 🔲 Reflecting on Sources in a Dialogic Notebook

The purpose of keeping a dialogic notebook is to "talk back to" or create a dialogue with your sources, questioning information presented or the source itself, in search of new insight. Create four columns on a piece of paper and label them "Full Citation," "Quote or Summary," "What I Think It Means," and "Information I Still Need." Complete a dialogic notebook entry for at least three of your sources. Next, choose one of the sources and reflect on how you are using that source for your essay. Think about how the source supports (or doesn't support) your thesis, and consider its overall usefulness.

## Reviewing Your Sources

Once you've gathered and evaluated a reasonable collection of sources, it's time to step back and consider them as a group.

- Have you found enough relevant and credible sources to satisfy the requirements of your assignment? Have you found enough to suggest sound answers to your research question?

- Are your sources thought provoking? Can you tell what is generally accepted, controversial, or possibly unreliable? Have your sources enlightened you while substantiating, refining, or changing your ideas?

- Are your sources varied? Have they helped you achieve a reasonably complete view of your topic, including other perspectives, approaches, alternatives, or interpretations? Have they deepened your understanding and helped you reach well-reasoned, balanced conclusions?

- Are your sources appropriate? Do they answer your question with evidence your readers will find persuasive? Do they have the range and depth necessary to achieve your purpose and satisfy your readers?

Use these questions to check in with yourself. Make sure that you have a clear direction for your research — whether it's the same direction you started with or a completely new one. Perhaps you are ready to answer your research question and move ahead with your project. On the other hand, you may want to find other sources to support or challenge your assumptions, to counter strong evidence against your position, or to pursue a tantalizing new direction.

# Sample Assignment: Preparing a Source Evaluation

A source evaluation may be a small part of a larger project or it may be a self-contained assignment. Use the source evaluation to demonstrate your understanding of how to judge the reliability of a source as well as its relevance to your paper.

For her assignment, student Ella Jackson chose to evaluate an online source related to the health benefits of eating organic foods. She used MLA citation style.

---

Ella Jackson

English 101: Composition

Professor Cosby

14 October 2015

Source Evaluation: Internet Source on the Health<br>Benefits of Eating Organic Foods

Watson, Stephanie. "Organic Food No More Nutritious than Conventionally Grown Food." *Harvard Health Blog*, Harvard Medical School, 5 Sept. 2012, www.health .harvard.edu/blog/organic-food-no-more-nutritious -than-conventionally-grown-food-201209055264.

This source is directly related to my research question, "Is organic food healthier than nonorganic food?" It cites a report by Stanford University researchers, who found "very little difference in nutritional content" between organic and conventionally grown food. On the other hand, the same study showed that conventional produce had about one-third more pesticides than organic produce. According to this report, it is unknown whether the pesticide level in conventional foods, which meets current safety standards, may be more damaging to long-term health than the lower amount of pesticides found in organic foods. Perhaps another source can provide some insight into this question.

This source is highly reliable because it was published on a site sponsored by a well-known and highly regarded medical school (Harvard), and it includes evidence from another highly regarded school (Stanford). The author is not a medical expert, but she is an experienced medical journalist who has written and edited more than two dozen books and who served as the executive editor of *Harvard Women's Health Watch* for two years.

The language in the source seems balanced and unbiased. It does not take a strong stand on whether organics are worth the extra cost to consumers, instead stating that whether or not to buy organic food is a personal choice.

One potential problem with the source is its date. I will need to find out if more recent studies have disproven the results of the 2012 Stanford report.

# Working with Sources     33

Working effectively with research sources includes being able to navigate, manage, and take notes on sources.

- Navigating a source means finding your way around it and understanding its crucial information such as author, publisher, and publication date.
- The sources you uncover also need to be managed, that is, kept in order. Managing sources can usually be made more efficient with the help of electronic tools, although traditional paper methods are also effective.
- Taking accurate notes — in the form of quotations, paraphrases, and summaries — is essential for any research project.

## Why Working with Sources Matters

### In a College Course
- You read case studies, theories, industry projections, and much more for your economics class, so you need to capture information efficiently.
- You combine what you learn from clinic observations with information about your own child's diagnosis to direct your paper to an audience of parents.

### In the Workplace
- You use company sales data, but you want to develop an annotated list of industry and government sources to expand available statistics.

### In Your Community
- You agree to write a brief history of your campus social group, presenting the old records accurately but not offending potential contributors on alumni day.

  ❓ When have you quoted, paraphrased, summarized, or credited sources? In what situations do you expect to do so again?

# Navigating Sources

In order to work effectively with the sources you uncover, you need to be able to navigate them — that is, find your way around all the information they contain. The source navigators on pages 648–55 will guide you through articles, books, and online sources.

# Managing Your Project

It is never too early in a research project to begin keeping a record of the sources you uncover. A working bibliography will help you stay organized during the research process and will provide you with essential information when you are ready to complete your assignment. In addition, keeping careful track will help you sort out source material from your own words, an important part of avoiding plagiarism.

## Starting a Working Bibliography

Your working bibliography is a detailed and evolving list of articles, books, Web sites, and other resources that may contribute to your research. It guides your research by recording the sources you plan to consult and adding notes about those you do examine. Each entry in your working bibliography eventually needs to follow the format your instructor expects, generally either MLA or APA style. Start by choosing a recording method you can use most efficiently:

- note cards, recording one source per card
- small notebook, writing on one side of the page
- word-processor file
- citation management software or other database

The table on page 647 lists the types of information to record in your working bibliography.

## Keeping Track of Sources

Rather than relying on memory to track where source information came from, develop efficient techniques that work best for your research purpose.

**Take Advantage of Digital Tools.** When you're researching sources on the Internet or in an online database, become familiar with the tools at your disposal. As a precaution, regularly back up all electronic files you create.

- Download or e-mail search results from library databases to your own computer or storage device, making it easier to find and access these materials again.
- Bookmark useful Web sites or use a curating site such as Scoop.it to manage your most promising online sources.

| Types of Information to Record | The Basics | Common Additions |
|---|---|---|
| **Names** | ■ Complete name of the author, as supplied in the source, unless not identified | ■ Names of coauthors, in the order listed in the source<br>■ Names of any editor, compiler, translator, or contributor |
| **Titles** | ■ Title and any subtitle of an article, Web page, or posting (in quotation marks for MLA)<br>■ Title and any subtitle of a journal, magazine, newspaper, book, or Web site (italicized) | ■ Title of a journal special issue<br>■ Title of a series of books or pamphlets and any item number |
| **Publication Details for Periodicals** | ■ Volume and issue numbers for a journal (and a magazine for APA)<br>■ DOI (digital object identifier) article number<br>■ Section number or letter for a newspaper | ■ Any edition of a newspaper (for MLA) |

- Create a folder to save links, e-mails, online posts, transcripts of chats, and database records. Give each file a descriptive name so that you can retrieve the information quickly later on.
- If a database or Internet search is productive, note where you searched and what keywords you used so you can easily repeat the search if necessary.

**Use Time-Honored Methods for Organizing with Paper.** If you prefer a paper format for keeping track of sources, make use of these helpful techniques.

- Summarize sources on sticky notes or index cards so that you can quickly rearrange them.
- Use a poster board to sketch a "storyboard" for the main "events" that you want to cover in your paper.
- Copy or scan book passages and articles, print electronic sources (noting the site or database and date of access), and keep field material. Be sure the author (or title) and page number appear on each page so you can accurately credit your source.

# Capturing Information in Your Notes

Your goal in capturing source information is to record enough notes and citations that, once they're written, you are independent of the source. Start by reading each source critically and actively; then decide what—and how much—to record so you dig out the useful nuggets without distorting the meaning.

For more examples of capturing information from sources, see pp. 229–35, pp. 663–68, and D in the Quick Research Guide, pp. Q-27–Q-31.

# Source Navigator

## Article in a Print Magazine
### Record this information in your notes about each source:

**1** The complete name of the author

**2** The title of the article

**3** The title of the magazine

**4** The periodical's volume and issue numbers if available, often found on title or contents page

**5** The full date of the issue

**6** The article's page numbers

**SCIENTIFIC AMERICAN**

**4** • July 2015  Volume 313, Number 1

The Science of Health  by Karen Weintraub

Karen Weintraub is a freelance health/science journalist based in Cambridge, Mass., who writes regularly for the Boston Globe, USA Today and the New York Times.

## Can We Stop Aging?

Some researchers believe they will soon be able to slow or even stop the body's clock—at least for a little while

**The majority of older Americans** live out their final years with at least one or two chronic ailments, such as arthritis, diabetes, heart disease or stroke. The longer their body clock ticks, the more disabling conditions they face. Doctors and drug companies traditionally treat each of these aging-related diseases as it arises. But a small group of scientists have begun championing a bold new approach. They think it is possible to stop or even rewind the body's internal chronometer so that all these diseases will arrive later or not at all.

Studies of centenarians suggest the feat is achievable. Most of these individuals live that long because they have somehow avoided most of the diseases that burden other folks in their 70s and 80s, says Nir Barzilai, director of the Institute for Aging Research at the Albert Einstein College of Medicine. Nor does a centenarian's unusual longevity result in an end-of-life decline that lasts longer than anyone else's. In fact, Barzilai notes, research on hundreds of "super agers" suggests exactly the opposite. For them, illness typically starts later and arrives closer to the end. "They live, live, live and then die one day," he says.

Researchers have already developed various techniques to increase the life span of yeast, worms, flies, rats and perhaps monkeys. Adapting these measures to people seems like the next logical step. "There's an emerging consensus that it's time to take what we've learned from aging [research] and begin to translate that into helping humans," says Brian Kennedy, CEO and president of the Buck Institute for Research on Aging, an independent research group in Novato, Calif.

Delaying the aging process by even a few years could offer enormous social benefits as populations around the globe grow increasingly older. The U.S. Census Bureau estimates that one in five Americans will be older than 65 by 2030—up from one in seven in 2014. In 2013 an estimated 44 million people around the world suffered from dementia. That number is expected to jump to nearly 76 million in 2030 and 135 million in 2050—with not nearly enough younger people in a position to be able to take care of them.

Among the handful of approaches that researchers are studying, three stand out. Still unclear: whether the potential benefits outweigh the risks of the treatments.

**EVIDENCE**

OF COURSE, TO CONCLUSIVELY determine whether a treatment works, investigators need a definition of aging and a way to measure the process. They have neither. If a kidney cell divided yesterday, is it one day old or as old as the person in whom it resides? Still, research over the past decade has offered several hints that the damaging aspects of aging—however you define it—can be slowed.

In a 2005 study, Thomas Rando, director of the Paul F. Glenn Center for the Biology of Aging at Stanford University, showed that an elderly mouse whose bloodstream was surgically linked to a young mouse recovered its youthful wound-healing powers. Somehow the older rodent's stem cells, which are responsible for replacing damaged cells, became more effective at giving rise to new tissue. Harvard University biologist Amy Wagers has since found a protein, dubbed GDF11, in the blood that may have contributed to the faster healing. Her experiments, published in *Science* in 2014, found more

*Illustration by Victo Ngai*

**6** • **28** Scientific American, July 2015

## Create a source entry out of the information you collect:

Source entry in MLA style

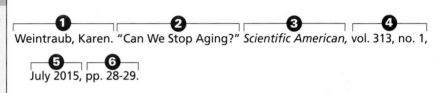

Weintraub, Karen. "Can We Stop Aging?" *Scientific American,* vol. 313, no. 1,

July 2015, pp. 28-29.

Source note with a general
summary of the article

Discusses various strategies research scientists have been investigating to slow the aging
process in humans and the potential risks of such treatments.

Source entry in APA style

Weintraub, K. (2015, July). Can we stop aging? *Scientific American*, *313*(1),

28-29.

Source note with a
technical summary of
the article

Reviews the risks and potential benefits of a number of approaches to delaying the aging
process, including injections of the protein GDF11, administration of existing medications and
nutritional supplements such as the compound everolimus, and the limitation of caloric intake.

### Book
**Record this information in your notes about each source:**

**1** The complete name of the author

**2** The title of the book

**3** The full name of the publisher, as indicated on the title page

**4** The place of publication, using the first city listed, and the state (for APA)

**5** The latest date of publication (from the front or back of the title page)

**6** The call number or library location (for your future use)

**7** Keyword or author (for your filing system)

Front of title page

**2** —

DEAD WAKE

THE LAST CROSSING OF THE

LUSITANIA

**1** —

ERIK LARSON

**3** — CROWN PUBLISHERS

**4** — NEW YORK

Back of
title page

**⑤**

## Create a source entry out of the information you collect:

### MLA

Source entry in MLA style,
recorded on a card

**❼**
D592.L8                                                        Larson

L28

**⑤**
2015

**❶**                         **❷**                        **❹**
Larson, Erik. *Dead Wake: The Last Crossing of the* Lusitania. Crown

**⑤**
Publishers, 2015.

Source note with a
summary and quotation
from the source

Four-day period between Wilson's speech at special session on April 2 and Congress's
approval for war. Pages 342-43 say, "Congress took so long not because there was any
question whether the resolution would pass but because every senator and representative
understood this to be a moment of great significance and wanted to have [Wilson's] remarks
locked forever in the embrace of history."

### APA

Source entry in APA style,
recorded on a card

German involvement

**❶**      **⑤**              **❷**
Larson, E. (2015). *Dead wake: The last crossing of the* Lusitania.

**❸**            **❹**
New York, NY: Crown Publishers.

Source note with a
summary and a lead to
another source

German-Mexican alliance catalyzes America; Wilson subsequently gathers cabinet on
March 20, 1917, to discuss a course of action. Larson quotes historian Barbara Tuchman's
book *The Zimmermann Telegram* (p. 340) in discussion of the press's demand for war.

# Source Navigator

## Page from a Web Site
### Record this information in your notes about each source:

**1** The complete name of the author, if available, often from the beginning or end of the page

**2** The title of the page

**3** The name of the site

**4** The name of any sponsoring organization (for MLA, use only when it differs from the name of the site)

**5** The date of the last update

**6** The access date when you used the source (for APA)

**7** The Internet address (URL)

*Both images:* Centers for Disease Control.

## Create a source entry out of the information you collect:

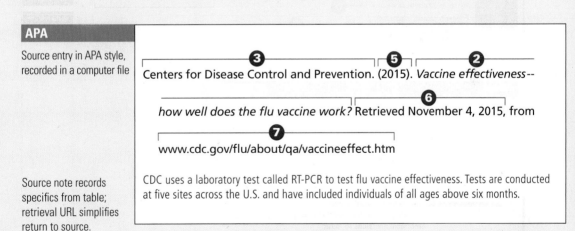

**MLA**

Source entry in MLA style, recorded in a computer file

Source note summarizes topic of pie chart

❷
"Vaccine Effectiveness--How Well Does the Flu Vaccine Work?" *Centers*

❹ ❺
*for Disease Control and Prevention,* 2015, www.cdc.gov/flu/

❼
about/qa/vaccineeffect.htm.

Page discusses the effectiveness and benefits of the flu vaccine and addresses a number of frequently asked questions regarding it.

**APA**

Source entry in APA style, recorded in a computer file

Source note records specifics from table; retrieval URL simplifies return to source.

❸ ❺ ❷
Centers for Disease Control and Prevention. (2015). *Vaccine effectiveness--*

❻
*how well does the flu vaccine work?* Retrieved November 4, 2015, from

❼
www.cdc.gov/flu/about/qa/vaccineeffect.htm

CDC uses a laboratory test called RT-PCR to test flu vaccine effectiveness. Tests are conducted at five sites across the U.S. and have included individuals of all ages above six months.

## Article in a Scholarly Journal from a Database
### Record this information in your notes about each source:

**1** The complete name of the author(s)

**2** The title and any subtitle of the article

**3** The title and any subtitle of the journal

**4** The journal volume and issue numbers

**5** The year of the issue

**6** The printed article's original page numbers if available

**7** The name of the database, subscriber service, or library service (for MLA)

**8** DOI (digital object identifier) if available or URL for journal's home page

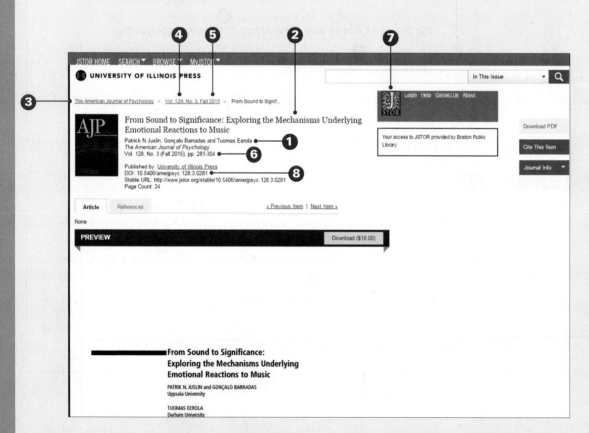

## Create a source entry out of the information you collect:

MLA

Source entry in MLA style, e-mailed from database and recorded in a computer file

**①** **②**

Juslin, Patrick N., et al. "From Sound to Significance: Exploring the

Mechanisms Underlying Emotional Reactions to Music."

**③** **④** **⑤**

*American Journal of Psychology,* vol. 128, no. 3, fall 2015,

**⑥** **⑦** **⑧**

pp. 281–304. *JSTOR,* doi: 10.5406/amerjpsyc.128.3.0281

Source note with a paraphrase of one paragraph in the article

Some researchers are skeptical about whether we can develop a scientific understanding of the relationship between music and human emotions, which is still largely regarded as a mystery.

APA

Source entry in APA style, e-mailed from database and recorded in a computer file

**①** **⑤** **②**

Juslin, P. N., Barradas, G., & Eerola, T. (2015). From sound to significance:

Exploring the mechanisms underlying emotional reactions to music.

**③** **④** **⑥**

*The American Journal of Psychology,* 128(3), 281-304.

**⑧**

doi: 10.5406/amerjpsyc.128.3.0281

Source note with a summary of the article's conclusion and recommendations

In order to properly assess emotional reactions to music, it is necessary to consider how those reactions are mediated by a number of underlying psychological mechanisms, including brain stem reflex, contagion, episodic memory, and musical expectancy.

## Reading Actively

Read the entire article or section of a book before beginning to take notes. On your second reading, take notes by annotating, highlighting, quoting, paraphrasing, and summarizing. Such methods help you absorb, evaluate, and select information from a source. They also help you identify potentially useful materials and, later, integrate them smoothly into your paper.

For more on critical reading and annotating texts, see Ch. 2. For more on evaluating research sources, see Ch. 32.

**Decide What You Need.** Weighing each source carefully and guessing how you might use it—even as you are reading—is part of the dynamic process of research. Distinguish what material is significant for answering your research question and what's only slightly related. If you wish, add your own ratings (*, +, !!, or –, ??) at the top or in the margin.

**Identify What's from Where.** Clearly identify the author of the source, a brief title if needed, and the page number (or other location) where a reader could find the information. These details connect each source note to your corresponding bibliography entry. Adding a keyword at the top of each note will help you cluster related material in your paper.

**Consider the Best Method of Recording Information.** When it comes time to draft your paper, you'll incorporate your source material in three basic ways: quoting, paraphrasing, and summarizing. Notes you take as you read should also use these three forms.

- **Quoting** is transcribing the author's exact words directly from the source. As you read, you can identify a lively or concrete quotation with a highlighter or by highlighting text in a digital document.
- **Paraphrasing** is fully rewording the author's ideas in your own words. You can paraphrase an important passage in the margin of a printout or on a note card, or in a computer file.
- **Summarizing** is reducing the author's main point down to the essentials. To help keep track of your sources, you can attach a summary of a source to the first page of a printout or insert it at the top of a computer file.

The following sections discuss quoting, paraphrasing, and summarizing in greater depth.

## Quoting

If you intend to use a direct quotation, capture it carefully, copying by hand or pasting electronically. Reproduce the words, spelling, order, and punctuation exactly, even if they're unusual. Put quotation marks around the material in your notes so you'll remember that it's a direct quotation.

RECORDING A GOOD QUOTATION

1. Quote sparingly, selecting only strong passages that might add support and authority to your assertions.
2. Mark the beginning and the ending with quotation marks.

## Sample Quotations, Paraphrase, and Summary (MLA Style)

### Passage from Original Source

Obesity is a major issue because (1) vast numbers of people are affected; (2) the prevalence is growing; (3) rates are increasing in children; (4) the medical, psychological, and social effects are severe; (5) the behaviors that cause it (poor diet and inactivity) are themselves major contributors to ill health; and (6) treatment is expensive, rarely effective, and impractical to use on a large scale.

Biology and environment conspire to promote obesity. Biology is an enabling factor, but the obesity epidemic, and the consequent human tragedy, is a function of the worsening food and physical activity environment. Governments and societies have come to this conclusion very late. There is much catching up to do.

— Kelly D. Brownell and Katherine Battle Horgen, *Food Fight: The Inside Story of the Food Industry, America's Obesity Crisis, and What We Can Do about It*, page 51

### Sample Quotations from Second Paragraph

Although human biology has contributed to the pudgy American society, everyone now faces the powerful challenge of a "worsening food and physical activity environment" (Brownell and Horgen 51). As Brownell and Horgen conclude, "There is much catching up to do" (51).

### Sample Paraphrase of First Paragraph

The current concern with increasing American weight has developed for half a dozen reasons, according to Brownell and Horgen. They attribute the shift in awareness to the number of obese people and the increase in this number, especially among youngsters. In addition, excess weight carries harsh consequences for individual physical and mental health and for society's welfare. Lack of exercise and unhealthy food choices worsen the health consequences, especially because there's no cheap and easy cure for the effects of eating too much and exercising too little (51).

### Sample Paraphrase Mixed with Quotation

Lack of exercise and unhealthy food choices worsen the health consequences, especially because they remain "major contributors to ill health" (Brownell and Horgen 51).

### Sample Summary

After outlining six reasons why obesity is a critical issue, Brownell and Horgen urge Americans to eat less and become more active (51).

### Sample Summary Mixed with Quotation

After outlining six reasons why obesity is a critical issue, Brownell and Horgen urge Americans to remedy "the worsening food and physical activity environment" (51).

### Works Cited Entry (MLA Style)

Brownell, Kelly D., and Katherine Battle Horgen. *Food Fight: The Inside Story of the Food Industry, America's Obesity Crisis, and What We Can Do about It*. McGraw/Contemporary, 2004.

3. Carefully write out or copy and paste each quotation. Check your copy — word by word — for accuracy. Check capitalization and punctuation.

4. Record the page number where the quotation appears in the source. If it falls on two pages, note both; mark where the page turns.

5. If you take out one or more irrelevant words, indicate the omission with an ellipsis mark ( . . . ). If you need to add wording, especially so that a selection makes sense, enclose your addition in brackets [like this].

## Paraphrasing

For more on quotations and ellipsis marks, see D3 in the Quick Editing Guide, beginning on p. Q-61, or handbook sections 33 and 35.

When paraphrasing, express an author's ideas, fairly and accurately, in your own words and sentences. Avoid judging, interpreting, or merely echoing the original. A good paraphrase may retain the organization, emphasis, and details of the original, so it may not be much shorter. Even so, paraphrasing is a useful way to walk your readers through the points made in the original.

| | |
|---|---|
| ORIGINAL | "In staging an ancient Greek tragedy today, most directors do not mask the actors." |
| TOO CLOSE TO THE ORIGINAL | Most directors, in staging an ancient Greek play today, do not mask the actors. |
| A GOOD PARAPHRASE | Few contemporary directors of Greek tragedy insist that their actors wear masks. |

### WRITING A GOOD PARAPHRASE

1. Read the entire passage through several times.

2. Divide the passage into its most important ideas or points, either in your mind or by highlighting or annotating the passage.

3. Look away from the original, and restate the first idea in your own words. Sum up the support for this idea. Review the section if necessary.

4. Go on to the next idea, and do the same. Continue in this way.

5. Go back and reread the original passage one more time, making sure you've conveyed its ideas faithfully without repeating its words or sentence structure. Revise your paraphrase if necessary.

## Summarizing

Sometimes a paraphrase uses up too much space or disrupts the flow of your ideas. Instead, you simply want to capture the main ideas of a source "in a nutshell." A summary can save space, distilling detailed text into one or two succinct sentences in your own words. Be careful as you reduce a long passage not to distort the original meaning or emphasis.

### WRITING A GOOD SUMMARY

1. Read the original passage several times.

2. Without looking back, recall and state its central point.

3. Reread the original passage one more time, making sure you've conveyed its ideas faithfully. Revise your summary if necessary.

## Taking Notes with Quotations, Paraphrases, and Summaries

☐ For each source note, have you identified the source (by the author's last name or a keyword from the title) and the exact page? Have you added a keyword heading to each note to help you group ideas?

☐ Have you added a companion entry to your bibliography for each new source?

☐ Have you remained true to the meaning of the original source?

☐ Have you quoted sparingly — selecting striking, short passages?

☐ Have you quoted exactly? Do you use quotation marks around significant words, phrases, and passages from the original sources? Do you use ellipsis marks to show where any words have been omitted and brackets to show where words have been added?

☐ Are most notes in your own words — created by paraphrasing or summarizing?

☐ Have you avoided too closely paraphrasing the source?

## Learning by Doing 🔘 Capturing Information from Sources

Identify a substantial paragraph or passage from a source you might use for your research paper or from a reading in this book (selected by you, your small group, or your instructor). Study the passage until you understand it thoroughly. Then use it as you respond to the following activities.

1. Quoting
   Identify one notable quotation from the passage you selected. Write a brief paragraph justifying your selection, explaining why you find it notable and why you might use it in a paper. Share your paragraph with classmates. In what ways were your reasons for selection similar to or different from those of your classmates?

2. Paraphrasing
   Write a paraphrase of your passage. Use your own language to capture what it says without parroting its words or sentence patterns. Share your paraphrase with classmates. What are its strengths and weaknesses? Where might you freshen the language?

3. Summarizing
   In one or two sentences, summarize the passage you selected. Capture its essence in your own words. Share your summary with classmates. What are its strengths and weaknesses? Where might you simplify or clarify it?

# Sample Assignment: Developing an Annotated Bibliography

An annotated bibliography is a list of sources with a short summary or annotation for each entry. This common assignment quickly informs a reader about the direction of your research. It also shows your mastery of two major research skills: identifying a source and writing a summary.

For a sample source evaluation, see pp. 643–44.

For more on MLA and APA formats, see Chs. 36 and 37.

To develop an annotated bibliography, find out which format you're expected to use to identify sources and what your annotations should do—summarize only, evaluate, or meet a special requirement (such as to interpret). A summary is a brief neutral explanation in your own words of the source's thesis or main points. In contrast, an evaluation is a judgment of the source's accuracy, reliability, or relevance.

Martina Schwartz prepared an annotated bibliography for her research question, How can education be improved in Native American communities? She identified each source as primary (a firsthand or an eyewitness account) or secondary (a secondhand analysis based on primary material), summarized it, and described how she expected it to support her position. The following is a portion of her annotated bibliography.

Brayboy, Bryan McKinley Jones. "Culture, Place, and Power: Engaging the Histories and Possibilities of American Indian Education." *History of Education Quarterly*, vol. 54, no. 3, 2014, pp. 395-402. *Wiley Online Library*, doi: 10.1111/hoeq.12075.

Secondary source. Brayboy, an anthropologist, writes that learning happens not only in the classroom but also in every aspect of life. I plan to use Brayboy's claim to support my argument that education must be reformed to be more cultural and holistic in order to have improved outcomes in Native American communities.

"I will stop 1,800 kids from becoming dropouts." American Indian College Fund, 2012, creativity-online.com/work/american-indian-college-fund-help-a-student-help-a-tribe-3/26344.

Primary source. One of a series of print ads that encourages donations to this fund that assists Native Americans in attending college. According to the text below the photograph, the subject ("Allen") is a student studying early childhood education at a college in Washington. Allen is quoted as saying that children who grow up on reservations don't have positive role models from their own culture, which makes it difficult from them to be successful. I will use this ad as an example of how educational charities aim to help Native American communities.

United States, Executive Office of the President. *2014 Native Youth Report. The White House.* Dec. 2014., www.whitehouse.gov/sites/default/files/docs/20141129nativeyouthreport_final.pdf.

Secondary source. This report interprets numerous statistics and facts (primary evidence). It includes extensive information about education along with data about poverty and nutrition rates. This piece argues in favor of increased tribal control over education and stronger integration of Native American cultures and languages in the classrooms. I will use this report to demonstrate that education needs to be targeted to the needs of the Native American community.

# Learning by Doing 📷 Writing an Annotation

Select one of your sources (or a reading from this book) and write a few sentences to describe what the source covers and why it is relevant to your project. If your instructor has specified a particular approach, tailor your annotation to follow those directions. Exchange annotation drafts with a classmate or small group, and discuss ways to clarify contents or relevance.

# 34 Integrating Sources

For a review of using sources in your writing, see Ch. 12 and D1–D6 in the Quick Research Guide, pp. Q-28–Q-31.

Your researched writing should project your voice and showcase your ideas—your thesis and main points about your research question. It also should marshal compelling support, using the evidence that you have quoted, paraphrased, and summarized from sources. Add this support responsibly, identifying both the sources and the ideas or exact words captured from them.

## Why Integrating Sources Matters

### In a College Course

- You have read many sources for your sociology paper, but now you need to efficiently fit these sources into your paper so you can finish on time.
- You need to integrate your class projects and reading log into your capstone portfolio to complete the final requirement for your credential.

### In the Workplace

- You must synthesize in one collaborative report materials from three rival departments.

### In Your Community

- You know that parents exchange information about autism, but the school board wants academic sources to identify best practices for teachers.

❓ When have you integrated a jumble of sources? In what situations do you expect to do so again?

## Using Sources Ethically

The complex, lively process of research is enriched by the exchange of ideas. However, discussions of research ethics sometimes reduce that topic to one issue: plagiarism. Plagiarists present someone else's work as their own—whether they dishonestly submit as their own a paper purchased from the Web, pretend that passages copied from an article are their own

writing, present the ideas of others without identifying sources, or use someone else's graphics without acknowledgment or permission. Plagiarism is
viewed especially seriously in college because it shows a deep disrespect on
the part of the offender for the work of the academic world—investigating,
evaluating, analyzing, interpreting, and synthesizing ideas. And it may have
serious consequences—a failing grade on a paper, a failing grade for a course,
or dismissal from the institution.

Although individuals often plagiarize on purpose, it's possible to unintentionally plagiarize others' work, too. Most campus policies penalize both
intentional and unintentional plagiarism. Working carefully with sources
and treating ideas and expressions of others respectfully can build the skills
necessary to avoid attribution mistakes. Educating yourself about the standards of your campus, instructor, and profession also can protect you from
ethical errors with heavy consequences. The Take Action chart on page 664
illustrates how to avoid or remedy common situations that can generate
problems.

# Capturing Evidence without Plagiarizing

The ideas, explanations, and details from your sources need to be integrated—
combined and mixed—with your own thoughts and conclusions about the
question you have investigated. Together these components form a unified
whole that conveys your perspective and the evidence that logically supports it.

As explained in Chapter 33, there are three primary ways of taking notes
on a source. **Quoting** reproduces an author's exact words. **Paraphrasing**
restates an author's ideas in your own words and sentences. **Summarizing**
extracts the essence of an author's meaning. As you move from note taking to integrating source material into your own work, you'll want to work
carefully with the evidence you have gathered.

For more about how
to quote, paraphrase,
and summarize, see
pp. 228–35 and
656–59.

## Quoting and Paraphrasing Accurately

To illustrate the art of capturing source material, let's look at a passage from
historian Barbara W. Tuchman. In *A Distant Mirror: The Calamitous Fourteenth
Century* (Knopf, 1978), Tuchman sets forth the effects of the famous plague
known as the Black Death. In her foreword, she admits that any historian
dealing with the Middle Ages faces difficulties. For one, large gaps exist in
the records. Here is her original wording:

ORIGINAL

A greater hazard, built into the very nature of recorded history, is
overload of the negative: the disproportionate survival of the bad side—of
evil, misery, contention, and harm. In history this is exactly the same as in
the daily newspaper. The normal does not make news. History is made by
the documents that survive, and these lean heavily on crisis and calamity,
crime and misbehavior, because such things are the subject matter of the

# Take Action  Avoiding Plagiarism

Ask each question listed in the left-hand column to consider whether you are in danger of plagiarizing. If so, follow the ASK—LOCATE SPECIFICS—TAKE ACTION sequence to correct the situation.

| 1<br>ASK | 2<br>LOCATE SPECIFICS | 3<br>TAKE ACTION |
| --- | --- | --- |
| Am I **prepared** to do research effectively? | ■ **If you've fallen behind, you may be tempted to use shortcuts** such as copying or purchasing work from someone else.<br><br>■ Review your research sources to make sure you have **reliable, relevant sources** that you understand. | ■ **Make a schedule and stick to it.** Review the advice in Ch. 30 to help you stay on track. Be aware that instructors can often detect counterfeit work.<br><br>■ **Ask a reference librarian for guidance if you have trouble finding sources at your reading level.** Consider adjusting your topic if most of the sources you uncover are too advanced.<br><br>■ Check with your instructor or writing center if you are struggling to maintain your schedule. |
| Am I **recording information accurately and fairly**? | ■ Your notes must have **complete and accurate information** in order for you to document your sources properly.<br><br>■ When you quote, paraphrase, or summarize a source, **do so carefully.**<br><br>■ Don't **confuse your own ideas and wording** with the ideas and wording of your sources.<br><br>■ **Different disciplines and instructors prefer different documentation systems.** | ■ **Keep careful records** on what information came from which source. Review Ch. 33 for help navigating sources and managing information.<br><br>■ **Review the types of information to record** from the table Types of Information to Record in Ch. 33.<br><br>■ **Review the sections on quoting, paraphrasing, and summarizing** in Ch. 33.<br><br>■ **Follow the documentation guidelines in the appropriate chapter** (MLA, Ch. 36; APA, Ch. 37). If you are unsure which system to use, ask your instructor. |
| Am I aware of other **ethical issues** that may arise in a research project? | ■ **Group projects** carry their own set of ethical issues.<br><br>■ **Field research** has specific guidelines that should be followed.<br><br>■ **Visuals** may require permission for reprinting.<br><br>■ **Cultural expectations** can vary for research projects. American colleges expect students to acknowledge sources from which they've borrowed words and ideas. American students are also expected to provide an original answer to a researched problem rather than search for the "correct" answer. | ■ Whatever your project, **review your school's plagiarism policy**, and check for any **specific rules about your assignment**.<br><br>■ Check your syllabus or ask your instructor for any **specific guidelines about group projects and field work**. Also see the coverage of field research in Ch. 31.<br><br>■ **Contact the owner of any visuals you plan to reprint** in your project and ask for permission. |

documentary process—of lawsuits, treaties, moralists' denunciations, literary satire, papal Bulls. No Pope ever issued a Bull to approve of something. Negative overload can be seen at work in the religious reformer Nicolas de Clamanges, who, in denouncing unfit and worldly prelates in 1401, said that in his anxiety for reform he would not discuss the good clerics because "they do not count beside the perverse men."

Disaster is rarely as pervasive as it seems from recorded accounts. The fact of being on the record makes it appear continuous and ubiquitous whereas it is more likely to have been sporadic both in time and place. Besides, persistence of the normal is usually greater than the effect of disturbance, as we know from our own times. After absorbing the news of today, one expects to face a world consisting entirely of strikes, crimes, power failures, broken water mains, stalled trains, school shutdowns, muggers, drug addicts, neo-Nazis, and rapists. The fact is that one can come home in the evening—on a lucky day—without having encountered more than one or two of these phenomena.

Although you might highlight this passage as you read it, it is too long to include in your paper. Quoting it directly would let your source overshadow your own voice. Instead, you might quote a striking line or so and paraphrase the rest by restating the details in your own words. Here, the writer puts Tuchman's ideas into other words but retains the source author's major points and credits her ideas.

### PARAPHRASE WITH QUOTATION

Tuchman points out that historians find some distortion of the truth hard to avoid for more documentation exists for crimes, suffering, and calamities than for the events of ordinary life. As a result, history may overemphasize the negative. The author reminds us that we are familiar with this process in our news coverage, which treats bad news as more interesting than good news. If we believed that news stories told all the truth, we would feel threatened at all times by technical failures, crime, and violence—but we are threatened only some of the time, and normal life goes on. The good, dull, ordinary parts of our lives do not make the front page, and the praiseworthy tend to be ignored. "No Pope," says Tuchman, "ever issued a Bull to approve of something." But in truth, social upheaval did not prevail as widely as we might think from the surviving documents of medieval life (xviii).

In this reasonably complete paraphrase, about half as long as the original, most of Tuchman's points are spelled out. The writer doesn't interpret or evaluate Tuchman's ideas—she only passes them on. Paraphrasing helps her emphasize ideas important to her research. It also makes readers more aware of how they support her thesis than a quoted passage would. The writer has directly quoted Tuchman's remark about papal Bulls because it would be hard to improve on that short, memorable statement.

Often you paraphrase to emphasize one point. This passage comes from Evelyn Underhill's classic study *Mysticism* (Doubleday, 1990):

ORIGINAL

In the evidence given during the process for St. Teresa's beatification, Maria de San Francisco of Medina, one of her early nuns, stated that on entering the saint's cell whilst she was writing this same "Interior Castle" she found her [St. Teresa] so absorbed in contemplation as to be unaware of the external world. "If we made a noise close to her," said another, Maria del Nacimiento, "she neither ceased to write nor complained of being disturbed." Both these nuns, and also Ana de la Encarnacion, prioress of Granada, affirmed that she wrote with immense speed, never stopping to erase or to correct: being anxious, as she said, to "write what the Lord had given her, before she forgot it."

Suppose that the names of the witnesses do not matter to a researcher who wishes to emphasize, in fewer words, the renowned mystic's writing habits. That writer might paraphrase the passage (and quote it in part) like this:

PARAPHRASE WITH QUOTATION

Underhill has recalled the testimony of those who saw St. Teresa at work on *The Interior Castle*. Oblivious to noise, the celebrated mystic appeared to write in a state of complete absorption, driving her pen "with immense speed, never stopping to erase or to correct: being anxious, as she said, to 'write what the Lord had given her, before she forgot it'" (242).

## Summarizing Concisely

For Tuchman's original passage, see pp. 663 and 665.

To illustrate how summarizing can serve you, this example sums up the passage from Tuchman:

SUMMARY

Tuchman reminds us that history lays stress on misery and misdeeds because these negative events attracted notice in their time and so were reported in writing; just as in news stories today, bad news predominates. But we should remember that suffering and social upheaval didn't prevail everywhere all the time (xviii).

This summary merely abstracts from the original. Not everything is preserved—not Tuchman's thought about papal Bulls, not examples such as neo-Nazis. But the gist—the summary of the main idea—echoes Tuchman faithfully.

Before you write a summary, an effective way to sense the gist of a passage is to pare away examples, details, modifiers, and nonessentials. Here is the quotation from Tuchman as one student marked it up on a copy, crossing out elements she decided to omit from her summary.

A greater hazard, built into the very nature of recorded history, is overload of the negative: the disproportionate survival of the bad side—of evil, misery, contention, and harm. In history this is exactly the same as in the daily newspaper. The normal does not make news. History is made by the documents that survive, and these lean heavily on crisis and calamity, crime and misbehavior, because such things are the subject matter of the documentary process—of lawsuits, treaties, moralists' denunciations, literary satire, papal Bulls. No Pope ever issued a Bull to approve of something. Negative overload can be seen at work in the religious reformer Nicolas de Clamanges, who, in denouncing unfit and worldly prelates in 1401, said that in his anxiety for reform he would not discuss the good clerics because "they do not count beside the perverse men."

Disaster is rarely as pervasive as it seems from recorded accounts. The fact of being on the record makes it appear continuous and ubiquitous whereas it is more likely to have been sporadic both in time and place. Besides, persistence of the normal is usually greater than the effect of disturbance, as we know from our own times. After absorbing the news of today, one expects to face a world consisting entirely of strikes, crimes, power failures, broken water mains, stalled trains, school shutdowns, muggers, drug addicts, neo Nazis, and rapists. The fact is that one can come home in the evening—on a lucky day—without having encountered more than one or two of these phenomena.

Rewording what was left, she wrote the following condensed version:

SUMMARY

History, like a morning newspaper, reports more bad than good. Why? Because the documents that have come down to us tend to deal with upheavals and disturbances, which are seldom as extensive and long-lasting as history books might lead us to believe (Tuchman xviii).

In writing her summary, the student could not simply omit the words she had deleted. The result would have been less readable and still long. She knew she couldn't use Tuchman's very words: that would be plagiarism. To make a compact, honest summary that would fit smoothly into her paper, she had to condense the passage into her own words.

For more on avoiding plagiarism and using accepted methods of adding source material, see Ch. 12 and D1 in the Quick Research Guide, p. Q-28.

## Avoiding Plagiarism

Never use another writer's words or ideas without giving that writer due credit and transforming them into words of your own. If you do use words or ideas without giving credit, you are plagiarizing. When you honestly summarize and paraphrase, clearly show that the ideas are the originator's; here Tuchman's or Underhill's. In contrast, the next examples are unacceptable paraphrases of Tuchman's passage that use, without acknowledgment, her ideas and even her words. The first example lifts both thoughts and words, underlined and with the lines in the original noted in the margin.

For Tuchman's original passage, see pp. 663 and 665.

### PLAGIARIZED THOUGHTS AND WORDS

Quoted from line 2 ————

Close to lines 5–6 ————

Close to line 19 ————

Lists from lines 19–21 ————

Close to ¶2 opening ————

Sometimes it's difficult for historians to learn the truth about the everyday lives of people from past societies because of <u>the disproportionate survival of the bad side</u> of things. Historical documents, like today's newspapers, tend to lean rather heavily on <u>crisis, crime, and misbehavior.</u> Reading the newspaper could lead <u>one to expect a world consisting entirely of strikes, crimes, power failures, muggers, drug addicts, and rapists.</u> In fact, though, <u>disaster is rarely so pervasive as recorded accounts can make it seem.</u>

For more on planning a research project, see Ch. 30.

This writer didn't understand the passage well enough to put Tuchman's ideas in his or her own words. If you allow yourself enough time to read, think, and write, you're likely to handle sources more effectively than if you procrastinate or rush your research. The next example is a more subtle theft, lifting thoughts but not words.

### PLAGIARIZED THOUGHTS

It's not always easy to determine the truth about the everyday lives of people from past societies because bad news gets recorded a lot more frequently than good news does. Historical documents, like today's news channels, tend to pick up on malice and disaster and ignore flat normality. If I were to base my opinion of the world on what is on the news, I would expect death and destruction around me all the time. Actually, I rarely come up against true disaster.

By using the first-person pronoun *I,* this student suggests that Tuchman's ideas are his own. That is just as dishonest as quoting without using quotation marks, as reprehensible as not citing the source of ideas.

The next example fails to make clear which ideas belong to the writer and which to Tuchman.

### PLAGIARIZED WITH FAULTY CREDIT

Barbara Tuchman explains that it can be difficult for historians to learn about the everyday lives of people who lived long ago because historical documents tend to record only bad news. Today's news is like that, too: disaster, malice, and confusion take up a lot more room than happiness and serenity. Just as the ins and outs of our everyday lives go unreported, we can suspect that upheavals do not play as important a part in the making of history as they seem to.

For more on working with sources, see Chs. 12 and 33 as well as the Quick Research Guide, beginning on p. Q-20. For more on quotation marks, ellipses, and brackets, see section 33 in Ch. 42 and D3 in the Quick Editing Guide, p. Q-61–Q-62.

After rightly attributing ideas in the first sentence to Tuchman, the writer makes a comparison to today's world in sentence 2. In sentence 3, she returns to Tuchman's ideas without giving Tuchman credit. The placement of sentence 3 suggests that this last idea is the student's, not Tuchman's.

As you write, use ideas and words from your sources carefully, and credit those sources. Supply introductory and transitional comments to launch and attribute quotations, paraphrases, and summaries to the original source (for example, "As Tuchman observes . . ."). Rely on quotation marks and other punctuation to show exactly which words come from your sources.

## Avoiding Plagiarism

☐ Have you identified the author of material you quote, paraphrase, or summarize? Have you credited the originator of facts and ideas you use?

☐ Have you clearly shown where another writer's ideas stop and yours begin?

☐ Have you checked each paraphrase or summary against the original for accuracy? Do you use your own words? Do you avoid words and sentences close to those in the original? Do you avoid distorting the original meaning?

☐ Have you checked each quotation against the original for accuracy? Have you used quotation marks for both passages and significant words taken directly from your source? Have you noted the page in the original?

☐ Have you used an ellipsis mark (…) to show your omissions from the original? Have you used brackets ([ ]) to indicate your changes or additions in a quotation? Have you avoided distorting the original meaning?

# Launching and Citing Source Material

In addition to capturing source information effectively, you need to identify and credit all source material clearly.

## Launching Evidence from Sources

Use a launch statement to identify the source of each detail and each idea—whether a quotation, summary, or paraphrase. Whenever possible, help readers see why you have selected particular sources, why you find their evidence pertinent, or how they support your conclusions. Select the verb that conveys to readers each source's contribution. Here is a list of common launch verbs:

For more on the format for source citations in the text, see Ch. 36 for MLA and Ch. 37 for APA.

| | | | |
|---|---|---|---|
| agrees | denies | expresses | reports |
| argues | describes | interprets | says |
| asserts | discusses | notes | states |
| challenges | emphasizes | observes | suggests |
| claims | explains | points out | writes |

Launch statements show not only that you have read your sources but also that you have absorbed and applied what they say about your research question. Try the following strategies to strengthen launch statements.

- Name the author in the sentence that introduces the source:

  As Wood explains, the goal of American education continues to fluctuate between gaining knowledge and applying it (58).

- Add the author's name in the middle of the source material:

  In *Romeo and Juliet*, "That which we call a rose," Shakespeare claims, "By any other name would smell as sweet" (2.2.43–44).

- Note the professional title or affiliation of someone you've interviewed to add authority and increase the credibility of your source:

  According to Jan Lewis, a tax attorney at Sands and Gonzales, . . .
  Briefly noting relevant background or experience can do the same:
  Recalling her tour of duty in Iraq, Sergeant Nelson noted . . .

- Identify information from your own field research:

  When interviewed about the campus disaster plan, Natalie Chan,
  director of Campus Services, confirmed . . .

- Name the author only in the source citation in parentheses if you want to keep your focus on the topic:

  A second march on Washington followed the first (Whitlock 83).

- Explain for the reader why you have selected and included the material:

  As Serrano's three-year investigation of tragic border incidents
  shows, the current policies carry high financial and human costs.

- Interpret what you see as the point or relevance of the material:

  Stein focuses on stem-cell research, but his discussion of potential
  ethical implications (18) also applies to other medical research.

- Relate the source clearly to the thesis or point it supports:

  Although Robinson analyzes workplace interactions, her
  conclusions (289–92) suggest the need to look at the issues in
  schools as well.

- Compare or contrast the point of view or evidence of two sources:

  While Desmond emphasizes the European economic disputes, Lewis
  turns to the social stresses that also set the stage for World War II.

Adding transitional expressions to guide readers can strengthen your launch statements by relating one source to another (*in addition, in contrast, more recently, in a more favorable view*) or particular evidence to your line of reasoning (*next, furthermore, in addition, despite, on the other hand*). However, transitions alone are not enough. Your analysis and your original thought need to introduce and follow from source information.

---

## Learning by Doing  Talking to the Sources

For more on connections and transitions, see pp. 417–20.

Refer back to the dialogic notebook you created (see p. 642). Examine how the sources talk to, support, or question one another. How are they discussing the subject, questioning each other's findings, or supporting one another? How do these sources support your thesis? Write a short reflection about how your sources connect with one another or come together.

---

## Citing Each Source Clearly

Often your launch statement does double duty: naming a source as well as introducing the quotation, paraphrase, or summary from it. Naming, or citing, each source both credits it and helps locate it at the end of your paper in the list of sources, called "Works Cited" (MLA) or "References" (APA). There you provide full publication information so that readers could find your original sources if they wish.

To make this connection clear, identify each source by mentioning the author (or the title if no author is identified) as you add information from the source to your paper. (In APA style, also add the date.) You can emphasize this identification by including it in your launch statement, or you can tuck it into parentheses after the information. Then supply the specific location of any quotation or paraphrase (usually the page number in the original) so that a reader could easily locate the exact material you have used. Check your text citations against your concluding list of sources to be sure that the two correspond.

---

### RESEARCH CHECKLIST

**Capture**

☐ Quote

☐ Paraphrase

☐ Summarize

☐ Synthesize

**Launch**

☐ Identify authority

☐ Provide credentials for credibility

☐ Usher in the source

☐ Connect support to your points

**Cite**

☐ Credit the source in your draft

☐ Link the citation to your final list of sources

☐ Specify the location of the material used

For examples of citations, see Ch. 36 for MLA or Ch. 37 for APA.

---

## Learning by Doing 📷 Launching and Citing Your Sources

Work on a section of your draft that mentions several sources. In your file or on a printout, highlight each launch statement. First, check each highlighted passage to be sure that you have named the author or source and stated the page number for a quotation or paraphrase. (Also add the date in APA style.) Next, check each passage to be sure that you have clearly conveyed to a reader the value or contribution of each source — what it adds to your understanding, how it supports your conclusion, or why you have included it. Exchange drafts with a classmate to benefit from a second opinion.

## Synthesizing Ideas and Sources

Regardless of how you launch sources, you need to figure out how to integrate and synthesize them effectively. When you synthesize sources, you are combining the voices of multiple sources into a coherent voice of your own. Although this voice relies on outside sources, it should present an original point of view.

For more on stating a thesis, see pp. 384–93.

To make sure that your voice isn't drowned out by those of your sources, keep your research question and working thesis — which may still be evolving — in front of you as you integrate information. In addition, use the Take Action chart (p. 673) to review and improve your use of research sources.

For more on synthesizing, see pp. 658–59.

Integrating source notes into your own writing generally requires positioning materials in a sequence, fitting them in place, and then reworking and interpreting them to convert them into effective evidence that advances your case. Synthesizing sources and evidence weaves them into a unified whole.

Build your synthesis on critical reading and thinking: pulling together what you read and think, relating ideas and information, and drawing conclusions that go beyond those of your separate sources. If you have a sure sense of your paper's direction, you may find this synthesis fairly easy. On the other hand, if your research question or working thesis has changed or you have unearthed persuasive information at odds with your original direction, consider these questions:

- Taken as a whole, what does all this information mean?
- What does it actually tell you about the answer to your research question?
- What's the most important thing you've learned?
- What's the most important thing you can tell your readers?

## Learning by Doing 🔧 Synthesizing Your Sources

Working with a classmate or small group, exchange sections of your drafts where you want or need to pull ideas together. Explain what you're trying to say or do in that section. Then ask for ideas about how to synthesize more clearly and forcefully in your draft.

# Take Action  Integrating and Synthesizing Sources

Ask each question listed in the left-hand column to determine whether your draft might need work on that issue. If so, follow the ASK — LOCATE SPECIFICS — TAKE ACTION sequence to revise.

| 1 ASK | 2 LOCATE SPECIFICS | 3 TAKE ACTION |
|---|---|---|
| Do I need to **reexamine the group of sources** that I plan to synthesize? | ■ **List the sources** you're synthesizing. <br><br> ■ **Write out principles** you have used (or could use) to select and group them — chronology to show change over time, theme to show aspects of a topic, comparison to show similarities, or another system. <br><br> ■ **Eliminate any fudging about your sources**: pin down your guesses; summarize or paraphrase quotes; specify rather than generalize. | ■ **Determine how each source develops your principles.** <br><br> ■ **Redefine your principles or your ideas** about what each source shows, as needed. <br><br> ■ Revise your group: **drop or add sources; move some if they don't fit well.** If a source fits into several places, pick the best spot or fill a gap. |
| Do I need to **relate my sources more deeply and clearly to each other?** | ■ For each source, **review your notes so you can sum up its focus.** <br><br> ■ **Highlight connective statements or transitions** already used in your draft to link the sources. <br><br> ■ **Mark any jumps** from source to source without transitions. <br><br> ■ **Read your draft out loud** to yourself, marking any weak or incomplete synthesis of sources. <br><br> ■ **Ask a peer to mark any unclear passages.** | ■ If a connection is missing, review the focus for the source; **add a statement to connect it** to the source before or after it. <br><br> ■ Brainstorm or jot notes to **refine, restate, or expand connections**. <br><br> ■ **Use your notes to deepen connections** as you refine your synthesis. |
| Do I need to **deepen my synthesis** so it goes beyond my sources to my own ideas? | ■ **Schedule several blocks of time** so that you can concentrate on your intellectual task. <br><br> ■ **Mark a check ✓ by any part of your synthesis that reads like a grocery list** (bread, eggs, milk or Smith, Jones, Chu). <br><br> ■ **Star each spot where you repeat the source's point without relating it** to your point or adding your interpretation. | ■ Generate ideas to **build a cache of notes about how you want to relate your sources to your ideas** and what they collectively suggest. Be creative; let your original ideas emerge. <br><br> ■ For each check or star, use your own voice and ideas to **fill gaps, deepen connections, or state relationships.** |

# 35 Writing a Research Paper

Your research project may call for writing a full-length paper, or you may simply want to review steps such as organizing and drafting. Whatever the case, moving from nuggets of information to a smooth, persuasive analysis or argument can be the most challenging part of the research process. Remember that the steps in writing a research paper are similar to the stages in most other writing processes, but in the case of research, you're using outside sources to support your ideas.

## Why Writing a Research Paper Matters

**In a College Course**
- You've read everything for your hardest class, but your grade rides on the final paper you submit.
- You gave an excellent oral presentation about life in your region during the 1940s, but you still have to write up the formal research paper.

**In the Workplace**
- You've gathered all the background information assembled by your team, but now you have to pull it together in a report for your demanding boss.

**In Your Community**
- Your term chairing the citizen committee is ending, so you need to present a final report about types of complaints, criteria for resolution, and recommendations to the board.

❓ When have you written a research paper? In what situations do you expect to do so again?

## Planning with a Thesis Statement

For more on research questions, see pp. 604–10. For advice on stating a thesis, see pp. 384–93.

You began gathering material from library, Internet, and field sources with a question in mind. By now, if your research has been thorough and fruitful, you know your answer. This answer, once it is refined into a clear and direct statement, will most likely serve as your paper's thesis. Working with that thesis in mind, you can organize your ideas and evidence into an outline.

**Refine Your Thesis.** Your thesis clearly, precisely states the point you want to make. It helps you decide what to say and how to say it. When it is clear to your readers, it prepares them for your scope and general message.

If you've used a working thesis to guide your research, sharpen and refine it before drafting, even if you change it later. Explicitly stating it in your opening is only one option. Sometimes you can craft your opening so that readers know exactly what your thesis is even though you only imply it. (Check this option with your instructor if you're unsure about it.) Make your thesis precise and concrete; don't claim more than you can show. If your paper is argumentative — you take a stand, propose a solution, or evaluate something — make your stand, solution, or appraisal clear.

| | |
|---|---|
| TOPIC | Americans' attitudes toward sports |
| RESEARCH QUESTION | Why is America obsessed with sports? |
| THESIS | The national obsession with sports must end. |

**Organize Your Ideas.** It isn't enough for your paper to describe your research steps or to string data together in chronological order. Instead, you need to report the significance of what you found out. If you began with a clear research question, select and organize your evidence to answer it. But don't be afraid to reorganize around a new question.

For more on organizing, drafting, and developing ideas, see Chs. 20–22.

If your material resists taking shape, arrange your source notes or archive in an order that makes sense. This new order then becomes a plan to follow as you write. Or write out an informal or a formal outline, perhaps using your software's outline tool. If you lack source notes for a certain section, reconsider your plan or seek other sources to fill the gap.

**Interpret Your Sources.** On their own, your source notes are only pieces of information. They need your interpretation to transform them into effective evidence. What does each mean in the context of your thesis? Is it strong enough to bear the weight of your claim? Do you need more evidence to shore up an interesting but ambiguous fact? Keep your sources in their supporting role and your voice in the lead. Alternate statements and support to sustain this balance.

**Leave Out Unnecessary Information.** Once you've recorded a source note, you may be tempted to include it in your paper at all costs. Resist. Include only material that answers your research question and supports your thesis. When material does fit, consider how to incorporate it effectively and ethically.

# Drafting

For more on outlining, see pp. 395–403.

An outline is only a skeleton until you flesh it out with details. Use yours as a working plan, but change the subdivisions or sequence if you discover a better way as you draft. Even if everything isn't in perfect order, get something down on paper. Start at the beginning or wherever you feel most comfortable.

## Launching and Citing Your Sources as You Draft

For more on launching source material, see pp. 238–39 and 669–72.

Citing sources as you draft saves time when you put your paper into final form. And it prevents unintentional plagiarism. Right after every idea, fact, quotation, paraphrase, or summary captured from your reading or field research, refer your readers to the exact source of your material. In MLA style, name the author and give the page of the source. (In APA style, add the date.) If you quote a field source, name the speaker, if possible.

When you add a quotation into your draft, copy and paste the passage from your note file, setting it off with quotation marks. Then include the words to launch or introduce the source to show why you've quoted it or what authority it lends to your paper.

If no transition occurs to you as you place a quotation or borrowed idea in your draft, don't sit around waiting for one. A series of slapped-in summaries and quotations makes rough reading, but you can add connective tissue later. Highlight these spots so it's easy to return to them.

## Beginning and Ending

Perhaps you will think of a good beginning and conclusion only after you have written the body of your paper. The head and tail of your paper might simply make clear your answer to your initial question. But that is not the only way to begin and end a research paper.

**Build to Your Finish.** You might start out slowly with a clear account of an event to draw your readers into the paper. You could then build up to a strong finish, saving your strongest argument for the end—after you have presented the evidence to support your thesis. Suppose your paper argues that American children are harmed by the national obsession with sports:

For more strategies for opening and concluding, see pp. 410–16.

- Begin with a real event so you and your reader are on the same footing.
- Explore that event's implications to prepare your reader for your view.
- State your thesis: "The national obsession with sports must end."
- Present each assertion, and support it with evidence captured from well-chosen sources, moving to your strongest argument.
- End with a rousing call to action to stop sports mania.

For more on transitions, see pp. 417–20.

**Sum Up the Findings of Others.** Another way to begin a research paper is to summarize the work of other scholars. One research biologist, Edgar F. Warner, has reduced this time-tested opening to a formula.

First, in one or two paragraphs, you review everything that has been said about your topic, naming the most prominent earlier commentators. Next you declare why all of them are wrong. Then you set forth your own claim, and you spend the rest of your paper supporting it.

That pattern may seem cut-and-dried, but it is useful because it places your research and ideas into a historical and conceptual framework. If you browse in specialized journals, you may be surprised to see how many articles begin this way. Of course, one or two other writers may be enough to argue with. For example, a student writing on the American poet Charles Olson starts her research paper by disputing two views of him.

> To Cid Corman, Charles Olson of Gloucester, Massachusetts, is "the one dynamic and original epic poet twentieth-century America has produced" (116). To Allen Tate, Olson is "a loquacious charlatan" (McFinnery 92). The truth lies between these two extremes, nearer to Corman's view.

Whether or not you fully stated your view at the beginning, you will certainly need to make it clear in your closing paragraph. A suggestion: before writing the last lines of your paper, read over what you have written. Then, without referring to your paper, try to put your view into writing.

## Learning by Doing 🎯 Focusing with a Reverse Outline

We often think of an outline as something writers make before writing a paper. However, a reverse outline can be created using a piece that has already been written. Using the rough or current draft of your research paper, create a reverse outline. Strip away most of the writing to reveal the structure of the essay itself: central points, main ideas, topic sentences, and important pieces of evidence or support. What do you notice about the overall outline form? Do the paragraphs seem balanced? Do you see any gaps in logic or supporting evidence? Can you identify areas that might benefit from a different organization? Would your argument be improved if information was organized from least important to most important or vice versa?

# Revising and Editing

Looking over your draft, you may find your essay changing. Don't be afraid to develop a whole new interpretation, shift the organization, strengthen your evidence, drop a section, or add a new one.

### REVISION CHECKLIST

☐ Have you said something original, not just heaped up statements by others? Does your voice interpret and unify so that your ideas, not those of your sources, dominate?

For advice on integrating sources and avoiding plagiarism, see Ch. 34.

For more revising and editing strategies, see Ch. 23.

For more on using your own voice, see pp. 239–41.

For a sample student essay in MLA style, see pp. 695–703; for a sample APA essay, see pp. 717–26.

☐ Is your thesis (or main idea) clear? Do all your points support your main idea? Does all your evidence support your points?

☐ Does each new idea follow from the one before it? Can you see any stronger arrangement? Have you used transitions to connect the parts?

☐ Do you need more — or better — evidence to back up any point? If so, where might you find it?

☐ Are the words that you quote truly memorable? Are your paraphrases and summaries accurate and clear? Have you launched everything?

☐ Is the source of every quotation, fact, or idea unmistakably clear?

## Learning by Doing 👆 Meeting Expectations

Before you decide that your paper is finished, revisit your instructor's directions. Also take a final look at any comments about earlier drafts. Remedy anything you have overlooked. Follow any specific directions about format, organization, or presentation. Pay attention to what's expected so that you benefit from your hard work.

After you have revised your research paper, edit and proofread it. Carefully check the grammar, word choice, punctuation, and mechanics — and then correct any problems. Check your documentation, too — how you identify sources and how you list the works you cite.

## Peer Response 👥 Writing Your Research Paper

For general questions for a peer editor, see p. 447.

Have a classmate or friend read your draft and suggest how you might make your paper more informative, tightly reasoned, and interesting. Ask your peer editor to answer questions such as these about writing from sources:

- What is your overall reaction to this paper?
- What is the research question? Does the writer answer that question?
- How effective is the opening? Does it draw you into the paper?
- How effective is the conclusion? Does it merely restate the introduction? Is it too abrupt or too hurried?
- Is the organization logical and easy to follow? Are there any places where the essay is hard to follow?
- Do you know which ideas are from the writer and which are from sources?
- Does the writer need all the quotations he or she has used?

- Do you have any questions about the writer's evidence or the conclusions drawn from the evidence? Point out any areas where the writer has not fully backed up his or her conclusions.

- If this paper were yours, what is the one thing you would be sure to work on before handing it in?

---

**EDITING CHECKLIST**

| | |
|---|---|
| ☐ Have you used commas correctly, especially in complicated sentences that quote or refer to sources? | Quick Editing Guide, D1 |
| ☐ Have you punctuated quotations correctly? | Quick Editing Guide, D3 |
| ☐ Have you used capital letters correctly, especially in titles of sources? | Quick Editing Guide, D1 |
| ☐ Have you used correct manuscript form? | Quick Format Guide, A |
| ☐ Have you used correct documentation style? | Chs. 36 and 37 |

---

For quick reviews of other issues, find the relevant checklist sections in the Quick Editing Guide, on p. Q-37. Turn also to the Quick Format Guide, beginning on p. Q-1. For more detailed help with grammatical issues, see Chs. 38–42.

# Documenting Sources

A research paper calls on you to follow special rules for documenting your sources—citing them as you write and listing them at the end of your paper. In humanities courses and the social sciences, most writers follow the style of the Modern Language Association (MLA) or the American Psychological Association (APA). Your instructor will probably suggest which style to follow; if you are not told, use MLA. The first time you prepare a research paper in either style, you'll need extra time to look up exactly what to do in each situation. (See Ch. 36 or 37.)

For more on documentation, see Ch. 36 (MLA), Ch. 37 (APA), or the Quick Research Guide, beginning on p. Q-20.

For more about oral presentations, see pp. 334–36.

## Learning by Doing 🔲 Presenting Your Findings

If you are expected to present your research findings to classmates or at a campus event, you may need to develop an oral presentation, a poster showing the answer to your question, or an online summary. Review your instructor's directions and any relevant advice in this book. View your presentation as a separate project; allow enough time to develop it effectively.

# 36 MLA Style for Documenting Sources

Citing Sources in MLA Style  682

Listing Sources in MLA Style  687

A Sample MLA Research Paper  695

For a brief overview of MLA style, see E1–E2 in the Quick Research Guide, pp. Q-31–Q-36. Turn also to the Quick Format Guide beginning on p. Q-1.

For advice about using APA style, see Ch. 37.

To review how to find details about sources, turn to the Source Navigators on pp. 648–55.

The *MLA Handbook,* Eighth Edition (MLA, 2016), supplies guidance on crediting sources.

MLA style is often used in the humanities, including composition, literature, and foreign languages. Although other disciplines follow other style guides, MLA style can help you get used to scholarly practice. MLA style uses a two-part system to credit sources.

- Briefly cite or identify the source in your text, usually by noting the author's last name in your discussion or in parentheses right after you supply the information from the source. In most cases, complete the in-text citation with the page number in the source.

- Then use the author's name to begin a full description of the source in your concluding alphabetical list, called "Works Cited." For each entry there, look up the sample for that type of source. Follow its pattern for details, format, punctuation, and spacing. Check all similar entries for consistency, too.

Credit your source every time you quote, paraphrase, or sum up someone else's ideas. The only general exception is "common knowledge," uncontested information that readers in a field know and accept. Examples might include dates, facts about events, and popular expressions such as proverbs. Identify your source any time your readers would—or might—wonder about it, especially if you are unsure what they consider controversial.

Use the Take Action chart (p. 683) to figure out how to improve the MLA style in your draft.

# Citing and Listing Sources in MLA Style

Skim the following directory to find sample entries to guide you as you cite and list your sources. Notice that examples are organized according to questions you might ask and that comparable print and electronic sources are grouped together. See pages 696–703 for a sample paper that illustrates MLA style.

## CITING SOURCES IN MLA STYLE

### Who Wrote It?
Individual Author Not Named in Sentence, 682
Individual Author Named in Sentence, 684
Two Authors, 684
Three or More Authors, 684
Organization Author, 684
Author of an Essay from a Reader or Collection, 684
Unidentified Author, 684
Same Author with Multiple Works, 684
Different Authors of Multiple Works, 684

### What Type of Source Is It?
Multivolume Work, 685
Indirect Source, 685
Visual Material, 685

### How Are You Capturing the Source Material?
Overall Summary or Important Idea, 685
Specific Summary or Paraphrase, 685
Blended Paraphrase and Quotation, 686
Brief Quotation with Formal Launch Statement, 686
Brief Quotation Integrated in Sentence, 686
Long Quotation, 686
Quotation from a Sacred Text, 686
Quotation from a Novel or Short Story, 686
Quotation from a Play, 686
Quotation from a Poem, 686

## LISTING SOURCES IN MLA STYLE

### Who Wrote It?
Individual Author, 688
Two Authors, 688
Three or More Authors, 688
Same Author with Multiple Works, 688
Organization Author, 689
Author and Editor, 689
Author and Translator, 689
Unidentified Author, 689

### What Type of Source Is It?
*Article in a Printed or an Electronic Periodical*
Article from a Printed Journal, 689
Article from an Online Journal, 689
Article Accessed from an Electronic Database, 690
Article from a Printed Magazine, 690
Article from an Online Magazine, 690
Article from a Printed Newspaper, 690
Article from an Online Newspaper, 690
Editorial, 690
Letter to the Editor, 690
Review, 690

*Printed or Electronic Book*
Printed Book, 691
Online Book, 691
E-book, 691
Multivolume Work, 691
Revised Edition, 691
Book Published in a Series, 691

*Part of a Book*
Selection from a Book, 691
Two or More Works from the Same Edited Collection, 691
Preface, Introduction, Foreword, or Afterword, 692
Article from a Reference Work, 692

*(continued)*

## Citing and Listing Sources in MLA Style *(continued)*

***Other Printed or Electronic Document***
Government Document, 692
Pamphlet, 692
Doctoral Dissertation, 692

***Online Source***
Entire Web Site, 692
Short Work from a Web Site, 693
Home Page for a Campus Department or
Course, 693
Blog or Blog Entry, 693

***Visual or Audio Source***
Advertisement, 693
Comic or Cartoon, 693

Photograph or Work of Art, 693
Sound Recording, 693
Program on Television or Radio, 694
Film, 694
Live Performance, 694

***Field Source***
Personal Interview, 694
Broadcast Interview, 694
Published Interview, 694
Speech or Lecture, 694
Personal Letter, 694
E-mail, 694
Online Posting, 694

# Citing Sources in MLA Style

The core of an MLA citation is the author of the source. That person's last name links your use of the source in your paper with its full description in your list of works cited. The most common addition to this name is a specific location, usually a page number, identifying where the material appears in the original source, such as (Valero 231). This basic form applies whatever the type of source—article, book, or Web page.

As you check your MLA style, keep in mind these three questions:

- Who wrote it?
- What type of source is it?
- How are you capturing the source material?

## Who Wrote It?

### Individual Author Not Named in Sentence

Place the author's last name in parentheses, right after the source information, to keep readers focused on the sequence and content of your sentences.

One approach to the complex politics of Puerto Rican statehood is to return to the island's colonial history (Negrón-Muntaner 3).

Author with page

# Take Action  Citing and Listing Sources

Ask each question listed in the left-hand column to determine whether your draft might need work on that issue. If so, follow the ASK—LOCATE SPECIFICS—TAKE ACTION sequence to revise.

| 1<br>ASK | 2<br>LOCATE SPECIFICS | 3<br>TAKE ACTION |
|---|---|---|
| Do any of my text citations differ from my Works Cited or References entries—or vice versa? | ■ Circle any material from a source that is not identified.<br><br>■ Add a check mark ✓ by each text citation that matches a Works Cited or References entry.<br><br>■ Add a check mark ✓ by each Works Cited or References entry that matches a text citation.<br><br>■ Circle any source not checked in both places. | ■ Correct each of your circled items by adding what's missing.<br><br>■ Drop from your Works Cited or References any source not cited in your draft. (Or add it to your draft if it belongs there.)<br><br>■ Confirm that authors' names are spelled the same in both places so that the citation and list entry match. |
| Have I inconsistently or incorrectly presented any of the authors in my list of works cited? | ■ Read only the author part of each entry.<br><br>■ Circle any spot where you need to check the arrangement of first and last names.<br><br>■ Circle any spot where you need to check spelling or punctuation.<br><br>■ Mark any entries out of alphabetical order.<br><br>■ Circle any repeated problems. | ■ Look up and correct all circled items.<br><br>■ Correct spelling or punctuation errors, such as a missing comma after the first name of the first of several authors.<br><br>■ Conclude each author section with a period.<br><br>■ Rearrange entries alphabetically as needed.<br><br>■ If you find patterns—repetition of an error—check all entries only for that problem and correct it. |
| Have I inconsistently or incorrectly presented any source titles in my list of works cited? | ■ Read only the title part of each entry, checking the format of each article, journal, book, Web site, or other title.<br><br>■ Circle any entry that you need to correct or look up by type, especially complications (such as an anthology) or tricky details (such as a newspaper section).<br><br>■ Circle any repeated problems. | ■ Look up and correct all circled items.<br><br>■ Use quotation marks for an article or a posting title; use italics for a book, journal, or Web site title.<br><br>■ Correct the capitalization, spelling, or punctuation.<br><br>■ End each title with a period before the final quotation mark or after italics.<br><br>■ If you find patterns—repetition of an error—check all entries only for that problem and correct it. |

### Individual Author Named in Sentence

Name the author in your sentence, perhaps with credentials or experience noted, to capitalize on the persuasive value of the author's "expert" status.

Author ——— The analysis of filmmaker and scholar Frances Negrón-Muntaner connects Puerto Rican

Page ——— history and politics with cultural influences (xvii).

### Two Authors

Include each author's last name either in your sentence or in parentheses.

Ferriter and Toibin note Irish historical objectivity about the famine (5).

Irish historians tend to report the famine dispassionately (Ferriter and Toibin 5).

### Three or More Authors

Name all the authors, or follow the first with "et al." (the Latin abbreviation for "and others"). Identify the source the same way in your list of works cited.

See p. 688 for the
Works Cited entry for
this citation.

Between 1870 and 1900, cities grew at an astonishing rate (Roark et al. 671).

### Organization Author

If a source is sponsored by a corporation, a professional society, or another group, name the sponsor as the author if no one else is specified.

Each year, the Kids Count program (Annie E. Casey Foundation) alerts children's advocates about the status of children in their state.

### Author of an Essay from a Reader or Collection

Suppose you consulted Amy Tan's essay "Mother Tongue" in a collection edited by Wendy Martin. You'd cite Tan as the author, not Martin, and begin your Works Cited entry with Tan's name.

Tan explains the "Englishes" of her childhood and family (32).

### Unidentified Author

For a source with an unknown author, supply the complete title in your sentence or the first main word or two of the title in parentheses.

Use quotation marks
in MLA style for titles
of articles. Use italics
for titles of books,
periodicals, and Web
sites. For more style
conventions,
see pp. 687–88.

Due to download codes and vinyl's beauty, album sales are up ("Back to Black" 1).

### Same Author with Multiple Works

If you are citing several works by the same author, the author's name alone won't identify which work you mean. Add the full title, or identify it with a few key words. For example, you would cite two books by Bill McKibben, *Deep Economy* and *Eaarth: Making a Life on a Tough New Planet,* as follows.

McKibben cites advocates of consistent economic expansion (*Deep Economy* 10) yet calls growth "the one big habit we finally must break" (*Eaarth* 48).

### Different Authors of Multiple Works

Separate more than one source in parentheses with a semicolon. For easy reading, favor shorter, separate references, not long strings of sources.

Ray Charles and Quincy Jones worked together for many years and maintained a strong friendship throughout Charles's life (Jones 58-59; Lydon 386).

## What Type of Source Is It?

Because naming the author is the core of a citation, the basic form applies to any type of source. Even so, a few types of sources may present complications.

### Multivolume Work

Add both volume and page numbers, with a colon between.

Malthus has long been credited with this conservative shift in population theory (Durant and Durant 11: 400-03).

Volume number

### Indirect Source

If possible, find the original source. If you can't access it, add "qtd. in" to show that the material was "quoted in" the source you cite.

Zill says that, psychologically, children in stepfamilies, even those living in a two-parent household, most resemble children in single-parent families (qtd. in Derber 119).

For more on using indirect sources, see pp. 230–31.
Author of original source
Author of source you used

### Visual Material

When you include a visual, help your reader connect it to your text. In your discussion, identify the artist or the artwork, and refer to its figure number.

Johnson's 1870 painting *Life in the South* is a sentimental depiction of African Americans after the Civil War (see fig. 1).

For advice about permission to use visuals, see B1 in the Quick Format Guide, p. Q-8.

Below the visual, supply a figure number and title, including the source.

Fig. 1. Eastman Johnson, *Life in the South,* High Museum of Art, Atlanta.

## How Are You Capturing the Source Material?

How you capture source material—in your words or in a short or long quotation—affects how you credit it. Always set off the source's words using quotation marks or the indented form for a long "block" quotation.

   If material, quoted or not, comes from a specific place in a source, add a page number or other location, such as the section number supplied in an electronic source or the chapter or line in a literary work. No page number is needed for general material (an overall theme or concept) or a source without page numbers (a Web site, film, recording, performance).

For more on capturing and integrating source material, see pp. 228–35, pp. 647–59, and Ch. 34.

For a sample block quotation, see p. 686.

For sample quotations from literature, see pp. 686–87.

### Overall Summary or Important Idea

Terrill's *Malcolm X: Inventing Radical Judgment* takes a fresh look at the rhetorical power and strategies of Malcolm X's speeches.

### Specific Summary or Paraphrase

One analysis of Malcolm X's 1964 speech "The Ballot or the Bullet" concludes that it exhorts listeners to the radical action of changing vantage point (Terrill 129-31).

If you paraphrase or summarize a one-page article, no page number is needed because it will appear in your Works Cited list.

Vacuum-tube audio equipment is making a comeback, with aficionados praising the warmth and glow from the tubes, as well as the sound (Patton).

### Blended Paraphrase and Quotation

When your words are blended with those of your source, clearly distinguish the two. Use quotation marks to set apart the words of your source.

To avoid generalizing about "people-with-dementia" (Pearce xxii), the author simply uses names.

### Brief Quotation with Formal Launch Statement

Vecsey states his claim for baseball: "No other sport has this endurance" (6).

### Brief Quotation Integrated in Sentence

"No other sport" (6), according to Vecsey's *Baseball: A History of America's Favorite Game*, requires players to tolerate double- or tripleheaders.

Double- and tripleheaders require more stamina than any "other sport" (Vecsey 6).

Only baseball, according to Vecsey, "has this endurance" (6).

### Long Quotation

When a quotation is longer than four typed lines, double-space and indent the entire quotation one-half inch instead of using quotation marks. If it is one paragraph or less, begin its first line without extra paragraph indentation. Use ellipsis marks ( . . . ) to show any omission from the middle.

Colon follows complete sentence ——————

Cynthia Griffin Wolff comments on Emily Dickinson's incisive use of language:

No quotation marks ————

Indent ½" ————

> Language, of course, was a far subtler weapon than a hammer. Dickinson's verbal maneuvers would increasingly reveal immense skill in avoiding a frontal attack; she preferred the silent knife of irony to the strident battering of loud complaint. . . . Scarcely submissive, she had acquired the cool calculation of an assassin. (170-71)

No period after page(s) ————

### Quotation from a Sacred Text

Instead of the page, note the version, book, chapter, and verse numbers.

Once again, the author alludes to the same passage: "What He has seen and heard, of that He testifies" (*New American Bible,* John 3.32).

### Quotation from a Novel or Short Story

First note the page number in your own copy. If possible, add the section or chapter where the passage could be found in any edition.

In *A Tale of Two Cities,* Dickens describes Stryver as "shouldering himself (morally and physically) into companies and conversations" (110; bk. 2, ch. 4).

### Quotation from a Play

For a verse play, list the act, scene, and line numbers, divided by periods.

Love, Iago says, "is merely a lust of the blood and a permission of the will" (*Othello* 1.3.326).

### Quotation from a Poem

Add a slash to show where a new line begins. Use "line" or "lines" in the first reference but only numbers in subsequent references, as in these examples from William Wordsworth's "The World Is Too Much with Us." The first reference:

Slash between lines ————

"The world is too much with us; late and soon, / Getting and spending, we lay waste our powers" (lines 1-2).

The next reference:

"Or hear old Triton blow his wreathed horn" (14). ————————————————— Line number

Separate part and line numbers by a period, without the word "line."

In "Ode: Intimations of Immortality," Wordsworth ponders the truths of human existence, "Which we are toiling all our lives to find, / In darkness lost, the darkness of the grave" (8.116-17).

---

**RESEARCH CHECKLIST**

**Citing Sources in MLA Style**

- ☐ Have you double-checked that you acknowledge all material from a source?
- ☐ Have you placed your citation right after your quotation, paraphrase, summary, or other reference to the source?
- ☐ Have you identified the author of each source in your text or in parentheses?
- ☐ Have you used the first few words of the title to cite a work without an identified author?
- ☐ Have you noted a page number or other location when needed and available?
- ☐ Have you added necessary extras, such as volume or poetry line numbers?
- ☐ Have you checked your final draft to be sure that every source cited in your text also appears in your list of works cited?

---

# Listing Sources in MLA Style

At the end of your paper, list the sources from which you have actually cited material. Center the title "Works Cited" at the top of a new, double-spaced page. Alphabetize entries by authors' last names or, for works with no author, by title. When an entry exceeds one line, indent the following lines one-half inch. (In Microsoft Word, use your software menu — Format-Paragraph-Indentation — to set this special "hanging" indentation.)

For a sample Works Cited page, see pp. 702–3 and p. Q-3 in the Quick Format Guide.

In your Works Cited entry for a source, list the author and title (if the source includes those elements), following each one with a period. Next, you'll need to list information for what MLA calls "containers" — the larger work where you found the source. Some sources are self-contained; for example, if you're citing an entire book, the book title is the title of your source, and you won't identify a separate container title. If you are citing a specific story in an anthology, that story title is the title of your source, and you'll identify the container separately, with the book title. If a container is itself part of a larger container (a scholarly journal that you found in an academic database, for example), list the larger container after the smaller one. The elements of a container — including, when applicable, its title; the names of contributors such as editors or translators; the version or edition; the volume and issue numbers; the publisher; the date of publication; and a location such as the page number, DOI, permalink, or URL — are separated by commas. The end of a container is marked by a period.

Here are a few general guidelines to keep in mind as you format your citations:

- Italicize the titles of longer works, such as books, magazines, and Web sites.
- Place the titles of shorter works, such as articles, in quotation marks.
- Look on the title page for the publisher's name; if no name is listed there, look on the copyright page (usually on the back of the title page). Use the complete version of publishers' names, except for terms such as *Inc.* and *Co.*; retain terms such as *Books* and *Press*. For university publishers, use *U* and *P* for *University* and *Press*.
- MLA does not require you to list location information for book publishers.
- You should also look on the copyright and title pages for the latest publication date. (For a Web site, use the copyright date or the date of the most recent update. Check the bottom of a page or the "About" page for the date.)
- If the title of a Web site and the publisher are the same or similar, list only the title of the site.
- Abbreviate all months except May, June, and July.
- If the source has no date, give your date of access at the end: Accessed 24 Feb. 2016.
- Give a permalink or a DOI (digital object identifier) if a source has one. If it doesn't, include a URL (omitting the protocol, such as http://).

## Who Wrote It?

### Individual Author

Buck, Rinker. *The Oregon Trail: A New American Journey.* Simon & Schuster, 2015.

### Two Authors

Name the authors in the order in which they are listed on the title page.

Carmon, Irin, and Shana Knizhnik. *Notorious RBG: The Life and Times of Ruth Bader Ginsburg.* Dey St., 2015.

Last name first to alphabetize
Regular name order

### Three or More Authors

Name all the authors, or follow the name of the first author with the abbreviation "et al." (Latin for "and others"). Identify the source in the same way you cite it in the text.

Roark, James L., et al. *The American Promise.* 6th ed., Bedford/St. Martin's, 2015.

See p. 684 for the citation for this Works Cited entry.

### Same Author with Multiple Works

Arrange the author's works alphabetically by title. Use the author's name for the first entry only; for the rest, replace the name with three hyphens.

Pinker, S. "Now for the Good News: Things Really Are Getting Better." *The Guardian,* 11 Sept. 2015, www.theguardian.com/commentisfree/2015/sep/11/news-isis-syria -headlines-violence-steven-pinker.

---. *The Sense of Style: The Thinking Person's Guide to Writing in the 21st Century.*
Penguin Books, 2014.

### Organization Author

When the author is a corporation, a government agency, or some other organization, begin with the name of the organization.

National Environmental Health Association. *Professional Food Manager.* 5th ed., Wiley, ———— Author
2017.

### Author and Editor

If your paper focuses on the work or its author, cite the author first.

Joyce, James. *A Portrait of the Artist as a Young Man: Centennial Edition.* 1916. Edited
by Seamus Deane, Penguin Books, 2016.

If your paper focuses on the editor or the edition used, cite the editor first.

Deane, Seamus, editor. *A Portrait of the Artist as a Young Man: Centennial Edition.*
By James Joyce, 1916. Penguin Books, 2016.

### Author and Translator

If your paper focuses on the translation, cite the translator first.

Dostoyevsky, Fyodor. *Crime and Punishment.* Translated by Oliver Ready, Penguin
Books, 2015.

Ready, Oliver, translator. *Crime and Punishment.* By Fyodor Dostoyevsky, Penguin
Books, 2015.

### Unidentified Author

"2012 Cars: Safety." *Consumer Reports,* Apr. 2012, pp. 72-76.

## What Type of Source Is It?

Once you find the author format that fits, look for the type of source that best matches. There may be instances in which you have to adapt the models in this section to the source types you encounter in your research.

### Article in a Printed or an Electronic Periodical

#### Article from a Printed Journal

Provide the volume number, issue number, year, and page numbers for all journals.

Pollmann-Schult, Matthias. "Parenthood and Life Satisfaction: Why Don't Children ———— Issue
Make People Happy?" *Journal of Marriage and Family,* vol. 76, no. 2, Apr. 2014, ———— Volume
pp. 319-36. ———— Pages

#### Article from an Online Journal

Supply the information that you would for a print article, and include the URL of the article. If the article is paginated, include page numbers.

Pflugfelder, Ehren Helmut. "Cell Phones, Networks, and Power: Documenting Cell
Phone Literacies." *Kairos,* vol. 19, no. 2, 2015, technorhetoric.net/19.2/topoi/
pflugfelder/.

To see how to create the listing for a journal article from a database, turn to pp. 654–55.

### Article Accessed from an Electronic Database

If you find a source through a library database or a subscription service, include the name of the service, and a permalink or DOI. If the database does not provide a permalink or a DOI, list only the basic URL for the database home page.

Hahn, Nicholas G., III. "The Religion of Climate Change: Lending the Power of the Pulpit to the Cause of Environmental Politics." *The Wall Street Journal*, 7 Aug. 2015, p. A9. *ProQuest*, search.proquest.com.proxy.emerson.edu/.

To see how to create a Works Cited entry for a magazine article, turn to pp. 648–49.

### Article from a Printed Magazine

Give the month and year of the issue or its specific date. If the article's pages are not consecutive, add a + after its initial page.

Gregory, Sean. "Why Colleges Need Helicopter Parents." *Time*, 28 Sept. 2015, pp. 25-26.

Marano, Hara Estroff. "Queen of Consciousness." *Psychology Today*, Feb. 2015, pp. 29+.

### Article from an Online Magazine

Anderson, Melinda. "The Economic Imperative of Bilingual Education." *TheAtlantic.com*, 10 Nov. 2015, www.theatlantic.com/education/archive/2015/11/bilingual-education -movement-mainstream/414912/.

### Article from a Printed Newspaper

If the newspaper has different editions, indicate after the date the one where the article can be found. For example, for the national edition you would include "natl. ed." If the pages for the article are not consecutive, add a + after its initial page.

Santora, Marc, and John Surico. "Angry about Fare Cuts, Uber Drivers in New York Warn of Reprisals." *The New York Times*, 2 Feb. 2016, New York ed., p. A23.

### Article from an Online Newspaper

Chang, Kenneth. "Stonehenge Begins to Yield Its Secrets." *The New York Times*, 9 Nov. 2015, nyti.ms/1HrW7wG.

### Editorial

Rampell, Catherine. "Americans' Loyalty to Employers and Insurance Plans Is Costing Them Billions." *The Washington Post*, 10 Nov. 2015, www.washingtonpost.com/ opinions/americans-loyalty-to-employers-and-insurance-plans-is-costing-them -billions/2015/11/09/8e04a9de-8726-11e5-be39-0034bb576eee_story.html. Editorial.

### Letter to the Editor

If the letter has no title, place "Letter" after the author's name.

Berlinger, Nancy. Letter. *The New Yorker*, 24 Aug. 2015, www.newyorker.com/ magazine/2015/08/24/the-mail-from-the-august-24-2015-issue.

### Review

Include the words "Review of" before the title of the work reviewed.

Boyagoda, Randy. "The Great Calvinist American Novel." Review of *Lila,* by Marilynne Robinson. *The National Review*, 31 Dec. 2014, pp. 47-49.

## Printed or Electronic Book

### Printed Book

Harari, Yuval Noah. *Sapiens: A Brief History of Humankind.* HarperCollins
    Publishers, 2015.

To see how to create
the listing for a book,
turn to pp. 650–51.

### Online Book

After the book publication information, include the title of the site in italics,
the year of online publication, and the URL for the work.

Euripides. *The Trojan Women.* Translated by Gilbert Murray, Oxford UP, 1915. Internet
    Sacred Text Archive, 2011, www.sacred-texts.com/cla/eurip/troj_w.htm.

### E-book

Turkle, Sherry. *Reclaiming Conversation: The Power of Talk in a Digital Age.*
    Penguin Press, 2015. Kindle.

### Multivolume Work

To cite the full work, add the number of volumes ("vols.") after the date or dates.

Bindman, David, and Henry Louis Gates, Jr. *The Image of the Black in Western Art.*
    Belknap Press of Harvard UP, 2010-14. 5 vols.

To cite only one volume, give its number before the publisher. If you wish,
you then can add the total number of volumes after the date or dates.

Bindman, David, and Henry Louis Gates, Jr. *The Image of the Black in Western Art.*
    Vol. 3, Belknap Press of Harvard UP, 2010-14. 5 vols.

### Revised Edition

Comins, Neil F. *Discovering the Essential Universe*, 6th ed., W. H. Freeman, 2015.

### Book Published in a Series

After the publication information, add the series name as it appears on the
title page, followed by any series number.

Whatmore, Richard. *What Is Intellectual History?* Polity Press, 2015. What Is History?

## Part of a Book

Give the author of the part first. Add the editor of the book after its title. For
print books or PDF files with fixed page numbers, include the selection page
numbers after the publication information.

### Selection from a Book

Gans, Herbert. "Deconstructing the Underclass." *Race, Class, and Gender in the United
    States*, edited by Paula S. Rothenberg with Kelly S. Mayhew, 9th ed., Worth
    Publishers, 2014, pp. 104-09.

### Two or More Works from the Same Edited Collection

If you list more than one selection from an anthology, prepare and refer to
an entry for the collection (instead of repeating it for each selection).

Beauchamp, Tom L. "Justifying Physician-Assisted Deaths." LaFollette, pp. 85-91.

LaFollette, Hugh. *Ethics in Practice: An Anthology.* 4th ed., Wiley-Blackwell, 2014.

Velleman, J. David. "Against the Right to Die." LaFollette, pp. 92-100.

**Preface, Introduction, Foreword, or Afterword**

Pustz, Matthew. Introduction. *It Happens at Comic-Con: Ethnographic Essays on a Pop Culture Phenomenon*, edited by Ben Bolling and Matthew J. Smith, McFarland & Company, 2014, pp. vi-viii.

**Article from a Reference Work**

No editor, publisher, or place of publication is needed for online reference works or well-known references such as *Webster's, World Book Encyclopedia,* or *Encyclopaedia Britannica.* No volume and page numbers are needed for online works or reference books that are organized alphabetically. If an article's author is identified by initials, check the list of contributors, which should supply the full name.

Durante, Amy M. "Finn Mac Cumhail." *Encyclopedia Mythica*, 17 Apr. 2011, www.pantheon.org/articles/f/finn_mac_cumhail.html.

## Other Printed or Electronic Document

**Government Document**

Generally, the "author" will be the government, the name of the department, and the agency, if there is one, separated by commas. If the document identifies an author or editor, give that name before the title or after it, if you give the agency as author.

United States, Department of Health and Human Services. *Keep the Beat Recipes: Deliciously Healthy Dinners.* National Institutes of Health, Oct. 2009, healthyeating.nhlbi.nih.gov/pdfs/Dinners_Cookbook_508-compliant.pdf.

**Pamphlet**

U.S. Food and Drug Administration Office of Women's Health. *Your Glucose Meter.* FDA Office of Women's Health, 2014.

**Doctoral Dissertation**

If the study is unpublished, place the title in quotation marks; if published, italicize the title. For a dissertation, follow the title with "Dissertation."

Achord, Rebecca Lynn Kling. "The Effect of Frequent Quizzing on Student Populations with Differing Preparation and Motivation in the High School Biology Classroom." Dissertation, Louisiana State U, 2015.

## Online Source

**Entire Web Site**

If a Web site does not have an update date or publication date, include your date of access at the end. If the site has no author (neither individual nor organizational), begin with the title. If the site has no title, include an identification such as "Home page."

Glazier, Loss Pequeño, director. *Electronic Poetry Center.* State U of New York at Buffalo, 2014, epc.buffalo.edu/.

### Short Work from a Web Site

Place the short work in quotation marks before the name of the site and following the author, if there is one.

Vogel, Pam. "Myths and Facts about the College Debt Crisis." *Media Matters for America*, 2 Oct. 2014, mediamatters.org/research/2015/10/02/myths-and-facts -about-the-college-debt-crisis/205936.

### Home Page for a Campus Department or Course

Department of Communication Studies. *California State University, Northridge, Mike Curb College of Arts, Media, and Communication*, www.csun.edu/mike -curb-arts-media-communication/communication-studies.

### Blog or Blog Entry

Cite a blog as you would an entire Web site. Cite a blog post as you would a short work from a Web site.

Ng, Amy. *Pikaland*. Pikaland Media, 2015, www.pikaland.com/.

Boehm, Mike. "Nonprofit Theaters Are Attracting More Donors, but Audiences Keep Shrinking, Report Says." *Culture Monster*, 5 Nov. 2015, www.latimes.com/ entertainment/arts/culture/la-et-cm-report-nonprofit-theater-audiences-still -dropping-20151103-story.html.

## Visual or Audio Source

### Advertisement

Clarins. *Psychology Today*, Sept. 2015, p. 141. Advertisement.

### Comic or Cartoon

Supply the cartoonist's name and identification as a comic strip or cartoon.

Flake, Emily. *The New Yorker*, 14 Sept. 2015, p. 54. Cartoon.

### Photograph or Work of Art

Supply the place (museum or gallery and city) where the photograph is housed. If you are citing it from a publication, identify that source. For a family or personal photograph, identify who took it and when.

Stieglitz, Alfred. *Self Portrait.* J. Paul Getty Museum, Los Angeles. *Stieglitz: A Beginning Light*, by Katherine Hoffman, Yale UP, 2004, p. 251.

Strand, Paul. *Fifth Avenue, New York*, Museum of Modern Art, New York. Photograph.

Botticelli, Sandro. *The Birth of Venus.* 1482-86, Uffizi Gallery, Florence.

### Sound Recording

Begin with the name of the artist, composer, speaker, writer, or other contributor, based on your interest in the recording.

Bach, Johann Sebastian. *Bach: Violin Concertos.* Performances by Itzhak Perlman and Pinchas Zukerman, English Chamber Orchestra, EMI, 2002.

To see how to create the listing for a Web page, turn to pp. 652–53.

See the directory on pp. 681–82 for entries for other electronic sources, including books and articles.

## Program on Television or Radio

If you are citing a specific episode, place it in quotation marks. Place the name of the program in italics. Include the network. If you viewed the program online, include a URL.

"Hunting the Nightmare Bacteria." *Frontline*, PBS, WGBH, Boston, 7 July 2015.

"At Last, a Fitting Farewell for Richard III." *Weekend Edition*, National Public Radio, KCFR, Denver, 28 Mar. 2015.

## Film

Start with the title, unless you are citing a particular person's work.

*The Martian*. Director Ridley Scott, performances by Matt Damon and Jessica Chastain, Twentieth Century Fox, 2015.

Scott, Ridley, director. *The Martian*. Twentieth Century Fox, 2015.

## Live Performance

*A Confederacy of Dunces*. By Jeffrey Hatcher, directed by David Esbjornson. Huntington Theatre Company, Boston, 18 Dec. 2015.

## Field Source

### Personal Interview

Burzyck, Krista. Personal interview, 5 Feb. 2016.

### Broadcast Interview

Begin with the name of the person who was interviewed, followed by "Interview by" and the interviewer's name, if relevant.

Johnson, Mat. "Mat Johnson on 'Loving Day' and Life as a 'Black Boy' Who Looks White." Interview by Terry Gross. *Fresh Air*, National Public Radio, KCFR, Denver, 29 May 2015.

### Published Interview

Tamblyn, Amber. "Interview with Amber Tamblyn." Interview by Rachel Matlow, *The Believer*, Spring 2015, pp. 123-27.

### Speech or Lecture

Carr, Nicholas. "The World Is Not the Screen: How Computers Shape Our Sense of Place." Radcliffe Institute for Advanced Study, Harvard University, Cambridge, 3 Mar. 2015.

### Personal Letter

Finch, Katherine. Letter to the author, 1 Oct. 2016.

### E-mail

Moore, Jack. "Robinson Lecture." Received by Dan Levine, 11 Aug. 2016.

### Online Posting

Yen, Jessica. "Quotations within Parentheses (Study Measures)." *Copyediting-L*, 18 Mar. 2016, list.indiana.edu/sympa/arc/copyediting-l/2016-03/msg00492.html.

Daniel-Gittens, Kathy-Ann. "Debate: Is There a Role for Badges in Higher Education?" *Humanities and Social Sciences Online*, 9 Oct. 2015, tlcwebinars.wordpress.com/2015/10/08/debate-is-there-a-role-for-badges-in-higher-education/.

---

### RESEARCH CHECKLIST

#### Listing Sources in MLA Style

- ☐ Have you begun each entry with the right pattern for the author's name?
- ☐ Have you figured out what type of source you have used? Have you followed the sample pattern for that type as exactly as possible?
- ☐ Have you used quotation marks and italics correctly for titles?
- ☐ Have you used the conventional punctuation — periods, commas, colons, parentheses — in your entry?
- ☐ Have you accurately recorded the name of the author, title, and publisher?
- ☐ Have you checked the accuracy of numbers for pages, volumes, and dates?
- ☐ Have you checked any entry from a citation management system as carefully as your own entries?
- ☐ Have you arranged your entries in alphabetical order?
- ☐ Have you checked your final list against your text citations so that every source appears in both places?
- ☐ Have you double-spaced your list, just like the rest of your paper? Have you allowed an inch margin on all sides?
- ☐ Have you begun the first line of each entry at the left margin? Have you indented each additional line one-half inch?

---

# A Sample MLA Research Paper

In her paper "Meet Me in the Middle: The Student, the State, and the School," Candace Rardon investigates the rising costs of a college education and how schools have responded to the problem. Besides incorporating many features of effective research papers, this paper also illustrates the conventions for citing and listing sources in MLA style. The marginal annotations explain MLA formatting and citation guidelines, as well as point out effective research writing practices. No cover page is needed for an MLA paper. Because an outline was required by this student's instructor, it precedes the paper shown here. Although this sample paper is presented for easy reading in a textbook, your paper should use the type style and size that MLA suggests: Times New Roman font, 12-point size. Set one-inch margins on all four sides, double-space all lines, and turn off automatic hyphenation. Use your software's Help feature or visit the campus computer lab for assistance setting up this format for your file.

For more on MLA paper format, see the Quick Format Guide, p. Q-20.

Writer's last name, followed by page number in small roman numerals, on upper right corner of all pages of outline

"Outline" centered, one inch from top

Main idea stated in thesis

Double-spacing throughout

Sentence outline providing a skeleton of the research paper

For more on outlines, see pp. 395–403.

½"

1"

Rardon i

Outline

Meet Me in the Middle:

The Student, the State, and the School

Thesis: By taking steps such as practicing cost containment, using technological advancements, and exploring new revenue streams, many schools have been able to keep tuition costs down.

I. Among the various factors to consider when choosing a college, cost is increasingly becoming the most important and, for many, a barrier.

A. Prices for undergraduate tuition at both public and private institutions have steadily increased over the past decades.

B. Students have increasingly taken on more debt in paying for college.

II. State governments have been forced to decrease their funding to public colleges and universities.

A. In the current economic situation, states have been forced to cut budgets and reduce their levels of funding.

B. In 2009 and 2010, thirty-nine states cut the amount budgeted to higher education.

III. With students accepting record debt and states forced to cut their budgets, public colleges and universities have a unique opportunity--even responsibility--to change.

A. Cost containment can decrease a school's budget and reliance on state funds.

B. Operational changes can result in savings through the use of online and technological resources.

C. Schools can explore alternative revenue streams such as grants, patents, and real estate opportunities.

Conclusion: By cutting costs, thinking differently about operations, and looking to new future revenues, schools are ensuring their own vitality and their students' success.

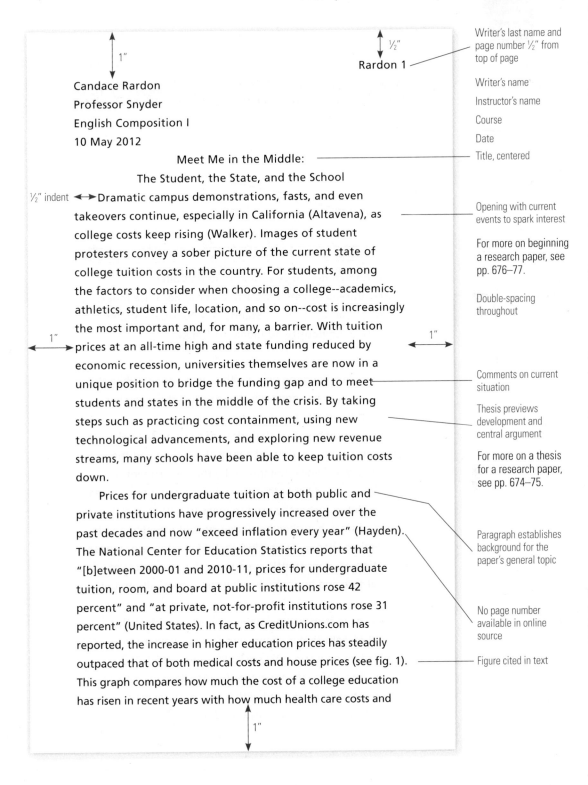

1"

½"

Rardon 1

Writer's last name and page number ½" from top of page

Candace Rardon

Professor Snyder

English Composition I

10 May 2012

Writer's name

Instructor's name

Course

Date

Meet Me in the Middle:

The Student, the State, and the School

Title, centered

½" indent → Dramatic campus demonstrations, fasts, and even takeovers continue, especially in California (Altavena), as college costs keep rising (Walker). Images of student protesters convey a sober picture of the current state of college tuition costs in the country. For students, among the factors to consider when choosing a college--academics, athletics, student life, location, and so on--cost is increasingly the most important and, for many, a barrier. With tuition prices at an all-time high and state funding reduced by economic recession, universities themselves are now in a unique position to bridge the funding gap and to meet students and states in the middle of the crisis. By taking steps such as practicing cost containment, using new technological advancements, and exploring new revenue streams, many schools have been able to keep tuition costs down.

Opening with current events to spark interest

For more on beginning a research paper, see pp. 676–77.

Double-spacing throughout

1"

1"

Comments on current situation

Thesis previews development and central argument

For more on a thesis for a research paper, see pp. 674–75.

Prices for undergraduate tuition at both public and private institutions have progressively increased over the past decades and now "exceed inflation every year" (Hayden). The National Center for Education Statistics reports that "[b]etween 2000-01 and 2010-11, prices for undergraduate tuition, room, and board at public institutions rose 42 percent" and "at private, not-for-profit institutions rose 31 percent" (United States). In fact, as CreditUnions.com has reported, the increase in higher education prices has steadily outpaced that of both medical costs and house prices (see fig. 1). This graph compares how much the cost of a college education has risen in recent years with how much health care costs and

Paragraph establishes background for the paper's general topic

No page number available in online source

Figure cited in text

1"

Rardon 2

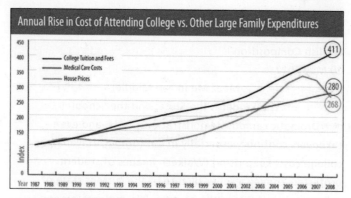

Fig. 1. Annual Rise in Cost of Attending College.
Source: Bureau of Labor Statistics, Consumer Price Index, and All Urban Consumers, Standard & Poor/Case-Shiller Home Price Composite-10 Index (Hoffman).

Figure labeled in caption; source information provided

Source presents and credits findings of another study

house prices have gone up over the same period. While the cost of all three has gone up, the expense of college has increased the most.

As the graph shows, the prices of tuition, medical care, and houses are plotted against both time and the consumer price index. Computed by the Department of Labor's Bureau of Labor Statistics, the consumer price index is a calculation generally used to measure inflation over a period of time, based on how the prices of common goods and services change. From 1989 to 2008, the price of higher education has consistently risen more than the prices of medical care and houses, a burden that often falls on the student.

Key term is defined

Trends in student borrowing point to a crisis in the amount of debt that students and families have to shoulder to afford an education. *Trends in Student Aid 2012*, a College Board report, states that in 2010-11, only 43% of students who graduated with a bachelor's degree from a public four-year institution did so without

Rardon 3

education debt (Baum and Payea). The rest graduated with debt averaging $23,800. Despite a recent 4% drop in borrowing, the first in two decades, these numbers demonstrate the rising financial burden placed on college students. Many continue "making decisions and trade-offs among schools, living arrangements, work, and finances" (Bozick 278). Economist Richard Vedder has summed up the situation: "What we have now is an unsustainable trend" (qtd. in Sandler 199).

Due to the economic recession, states have been forced to cut their budgets and reduce their funding to higher education. The Center on Budget and Policy Priorities reports that in 2009 and 2010, thirty-nine states decreased their budgets for higher education, leading to "reductions in faculty and staff in addition to tuition increases" (Johnson et al. 6). Like California, the state of Florida was forced to raise tuition by 15% in 2009-10. The tuition increases that result from a lack of state funds have become a nationwide threat.

With students accepting record debt and states forced to cut their budgets, public colleges and universities have a unique opportunity--even responsibility--to change. Instead of raising tuition to make up for lost state funds, many schools have begun to cut costs. Through cost containment, schools can decrease their operating budgets and their reliance on state funds. In an article for *Time,* Sophia Yan outlines reductions on more than twenty campuses. For instance, Harvard University saved $900,000 by cutting hot breakfasts during the week in the dining halls. Western Washington University saved $485,000 by cutting its football team, and Whittier College saved $50,000 by cutting first-year orientation by a day. On the theory that "every little bit helps," schools are finding ways to save money.

---

Only one citation needed for material in sequence in a paragraph and clearly from the same source

Facts and statistics support main point

For an explanation of statistics as evidence, see p. 160.

Page numbers provided for quotations

Original quote from another source

Paper continues to lay out background of argument

Transition from background to central argument

First way to avoid raising tuition is explained

Specific examples provide evidence for point

For more on integrating sources, see Ch. 34.

Rardon 4

Going beyond cutbacks in services, schools have also considered operational changes that will result in even more savings. The Delta Project on Postsecondary Education Costs, Productivity, and Accountability, a nonprofit group that analyzes college costs and spending trends, recommends ways to increase productivity:

> Make investments in course redesign and other curricula changes that will make for a more cost-effective curriculum. . . . This includes redesigning large undergraduate courses, creating cost-effective developmental education modules that can be delivered statewide; and redesigning the general education curriculum to enhance community college transfer. (4)

Other suggestions include making buildings more energy efficient and creating work opportunities for jobless students as interns or research assistants (4). Such changes can lead to substantial savings and help schools across the country.

Another alternative to raising tuition is for schools to embrace technological advances. As Kamenetz observes, "Whether hybrid classes, social networks, tutoring programs, games, or open content, technology provides speed skates for students and teachers, not crutches." Specific models have come from the National Center for Academic Transformation, a nonprofit organization that uses information technology to raise student performance and lower costs. Its six course redesign models vary in the amount of in-class instruction replaced by technology (Natl. Center, "Six Models" 1). When the University of Alabama adopted the emporium model for Intermediate Algebra and replaced lectures with an online learning resource center (3), the redesign increased student success, met individual needs, and saved 30% of costs (Natl. Center, "Program"). Of course, such course redesign cannot always be applied across the curriculum, but schools giving

**Annotations (left margin):**
- Point from last paragraph used for transition to new point
- Launch statement refers to organization as author
- Direct quotation longer than four lines set off from text without quotation marks, followed by page number in parentheses
- ½"
- Transition leads to second way to avoid raising tuition
- Quotation source clearly identified but pages are not numbered in source
- Short title added to distinguish two sources by the same author
- Basic models are explained before giving a specific example
- Statistics support claims

Rardon 5

serious thought to current technology can transform the classroom, saving money and helping students.

Finally, schools can supplement income from student tuition by considering additional sources of revenue. *BusinessWeek* writer Francesca Di Meglio reports that many schools already look to grants, patents, real estate, and popular graduate courses to "protect [their] bottom line from fiscal and demographic trends that are making the college business more challenging." As early as the 1950s, three Indiana University researchers patented Crest toothpaste, and its returns went on to fund an on-campus dental research institute. Similarly, in 2004 Emmanuel College in Boston allowed Merck, a large pharmaceuticals company, to build a research facility on an acre of land with a 75-year lease for $50 million. Di Meglio's examples show how schools can tap into these alternative income streams and reduce some of the pressure on tuition.

Rising tuition costs, growing student borrowing, and shrinking government funding have endangered widespread access to a college education. As President Obama himself said in the 2010 State of the Union address, "in the United States of America, no one should go broke because they chose to go to college. . . . It's time for colleges and universities to get serious about cutting their own costs-- because they, too, have a responsibility to help solve this problem." In an era of economic strain, schools can embrace this chance to think creatively about the way they operate. By cutting costs where they spent money in the past, thinking differently about how they operate in the present, and looking to new ways of bringing in revenue in the future, schools can ensure their own vitality and their students' success. When public colleges and universities take such steps to ensure that a college education is available to everyone, meeting students and states in the middle with innovative ideas, students can stop protesting and start welcoming in an era of increased college access.

Third way to avoid raising tuition is introduced

Launch statement names publication and author

Brackets identify words added to original text

Paraphrase of original source

Final sentence in paragraph connects examples from source with overall argument

For more on concluding a research paper, see pp. 676–77.

Ellipses show where words are omitted

Conclusion emphasizes critical points in argument

Conclusion returns to events in opening

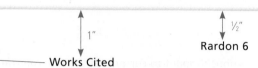

Rardon 6

List of works cited on a
separate page

List alphabetized by
names of authors or by
titles (when no author is
named); names match
source citations in text

First line of entry at left
margin, additional lines
indented ½"

All lines double-spaced,
within and between
entries

## Works Cited

Altavena, Lily. "California State Students Protest by
Fasting." *The New York Times*, 7 May 2012,
nyti.ms/23uNvzJ.

Baum, Sandy, and Kathleen Payea. *Trends in Student Aid
2012.* College Board, 2012, trends.collegeboard.org/
sites/default/files/student-aid-2012-full-report.pdf.

Bozick, Robert. "Making It through the First Year of
College: The Role of Students' Economic Resources,
½" Employment, and Living Arrangements." *Sociology
of Education*, vol. 80, no. 3, 2007, pp. 216-84. *JSTOR*,
www.jstor.org/stable/20452709.

The Delta Project on Postsecondary Education Costs,
Productivity, and Accountability. "Postsecondary
Education Spending Priorities for the American
Recovery and Reinvestment Act of 2009." *The National
Center for Higher Education Management*, Feb. 2009,
nchems.org/news/documents/ARRAStatementFebruary
.2009.pdf.

Di Meglio, Francesca. "Colleges Explore Alternative
Revenue Streams." *BusinessWeek.com*, Bloomberg,
7 Aug. 2008, www.bloomberg.com/news/articles/2008
-08-08/colleges-explore-alternative-revenue
-streamsbusinessweek-business-news-stock-market-and
-financial-advice.

Hayden, Tom. "Rising Cost of College? We Can't Afford
to Be Quiet." *The Chronicle of Higher Education*, 28
Mar. 2010. *Academic OneFile*, go.galegroup.com.proxy
.emerson.edu/ps.

Hoffman, Teri. "Graph of the Week: Annual Rise in Cost
of Attending College vs. Other Large Family
Expenditures." *CreditUnions.com*. Callahan &
Associates, 27 July 2009, www.creditunions.com/articles/
graph-of-the-week-annual-rise-in-cost-of-attending
-college-vs-other-large-family-expenditures/.

Rardon 7

Johnson, Nicholas, et al. "An Update on State Budget Cuts."
*Center on Budget and Policy Priorities.* Center on
Budget and Policy Priorities, 19 Apr. 2010, www.cbpp
.org/research/an-update-on-state-budget-cuts.

Kamenetz, Anya. "The Virtual University." *The American
Prospect*, vol. 21, no. 4, 2010, pp. 22+. *LexisNexis
Academic*, www.lexisnexis.com.proxy.emerson.edu.

The National Center for Academic Transformation. "Program
in Course Redesign: The University of Alabama." *The
National Center for Academic Transformation*, 2005,
www.thencat.org/PCR/R2/UA/UA_Overview.htm.

---. "Six Models for Course Redesign." *The National Center
for Academic Transformation*, 2008, www.thencat.org/
R2R/R2R%20PDFs/
Six%20Models%20for%20Course%20Redesign.pdf.

Obama, Barack. "Remarks by the President in State of the
Union Address." United States Capitol, Washington,
D.C., 27 Jan. 2010.

Sandler, Corey. *Cut College Costs Now! Surefire Ways to
Save Thousands of Dollars.* Adams Media, 2006.

United States, Department of Education, National Center for
Education Statistics. "Fast Facts: Tuition Costs of
Colleges and Universities." *Digest of Education
Statistics,* 2011, nces.ed.gov/fastfacts/display.asp?id=76.

Walker, Brianne. "UC, CSU Tuition Increases: The Causes and
Consequences." *Neon Tommy: Annenberg Digital News*,
USC Annenberg School of Journalism and
Communication, 13 Dec. 2011, www.neontommy.com/
news/2011/12/california-public-colleges-lead-nation
-highest-tuition-and-fees.

Yan, Sophia. "Colleges Find Creative Ways to Cut Back."
*Time*, 21 Sept. 2009, p. 81.

Three hyphens replace repeating exact name from previous entry

# 37 APA Style for Documenting Sources

Citing Sources in APA Style 704
Listing Sources in APA Style 710
A Sample APA Research Paper 717

For a brief overview of APA style, see E2 in the Quick Research Guide, pp. Q-35–Q-36.

Use the Take Action chart on p. 683 to help you figure out how to improve the citation style in your draft. Turn also to the Quick Format Guide beginning on p. Q-1.

To review how to find details about sources, turn to the Source Navigators on pp. 648–55.

The American Psychological Association (APA) details the style most commonly used in the social sciences in its *Publication Manual*, Sixth Edition (APA, 2010). For advice and updates, visit apastyle.org, purchase the manual, or use a library copy.

APA style uses a two-part system to credit sources.

- Briefly cite or identify the author and date of the source in your text, either by mentioning them in your discussion or by noting them in parentheses right after you refer to the information drawn from the source. In many cases, you also supply the page number or other location in the original source.
- Lead from this brief identification, through the author's name, to a full description of the source in your concluding list, called "References."

## Citing Sources in APA Style

The core of an APA citation is the author of the source. That person's last name links your use of the source in your paper with its full description in your list of references. Next comes the source's date, which often tells readers its current or classic status. Include both each time you cite the source in parentheses, but don't repeat the date if you simply refer to the source again unless a reader might mix up sources under discussion.

A common addition is a specific location, such as a page number (using "p." for "page" or "pp." for "pages"), that tells where the material appears in the original source. Unless the source lacks page numbers or other locators, this information is required for quotations and recommended for paraphrases and key concepts. When you supply these elements in parentheses,

# Citing and Listing Sources in APA Style

Skim the following directory to find sample entries to guide you as you cite and list your sources. Notice that the examples are organized according to questions you might ask and that comparable print and electronic sources are grouped together. See pages 718–25 for a sample paper that illustrates APA style.

## CITING SOURCES IN APA STYLE

### Who Wrote It?
Individual Author Not Named in Sentence, 706
Individual Author Named in Sentence, 706
Two Authors, 706
Three or More Authors, 707
Organization Author, 707
Author of an Article from a Reader or Collection, 707
Unidentified Author, 707
Same Author with Multiple Works, 707
Different Authors with Multiple Works, 707

### What Type of Source Is It?
Online Source, 707
Indirect Source, 708
Government or Organization Document, 708
Source without a Date, 708
A Classic, 708
Visual Material, 708
Personal Communication, 709

### How Are You Capturing the Source Material?
Overall Summary or Important Idea, 709
Blended Paraphrase and Quotation, 709
Brief Quotation Integrated in Sentence, 709
Long Quotation, 710

## LISTING SOURCES IN APA STYLE

### Who Wrote It?
Individual Author, 711
Two Authors, 712
Three or More Authors, 712
Same Author with Multiple Works, 712
Organization Author, 712
Author of Edited Work, 712
Author and Translator, 712
Unidentified Author, 712

### What Type of Source Is It?
*Article in a Printed or an Electronic Periodical*
Article from a Journal Paginated by Volume, 712
Article from a Journal Paginated by Issue, 713
Article Accessed through a Library or Subscription Database, 713
Abstract for an Article, 713
Article from a Printed Magazine, 713
Article from an Online Magazine, 713
Article from a Newsletter, 713
Article from a Printed Newspaper, 713
Article from an Online Newspaper, 713
Editorial, 713
Letter to the Editor, 714
Review, 714

*Printed or Electronic Book*
Printed Book, 714
Online Book, 714
E-book, 714
Multivolume Work, 714
Revised Edition, 714
Book without a Date, 714

*Part of a Book*
Selection from a Book, 714
Preface, Introduction, Foreword, or Afterword, 714
Article from a Reference Work, 715

*(continued)*

## Citing and Listing Sources in APA Style *(continued)*

***Other Printed or Electronic Document***
Government Document, 715
Research Report, 715
Report from an Academic Institution, 715
Pamphlet, 715
Doctoral Dissertation, 715

***Internet or Electronic Source***
Document from a Web Site, 715
Section from an Online Document, 716
Document from a Campus Web Site, 716

Blog Post, 716
Computer Software, 716

***Visual or Audio Source***
Sound Recording, 716
Program on Television or
Radio, 716
Film, 716

***Field Source***
Personal Interview, 716
E-mail or Electronic Posting, 716

separate them with commas: (Westin, 2013, p. 48). This basic form applies whatever the type of source — article, book, or Web page.

As you check your APA style, keep in mind these three questions:

- Who wrote it?
- What type of source is it?
- How are you capturing the source material?

## Who Wrote It?

### Individual Author Not Named in Sentence

Climate change is being taught as a fact rather than as a scientific theory (Tice, 2015, p. A15).

### Individual Author Named in Sentence

Tice (2015) voices his concern that climate change is being taught as a fact rather than as a scientific theory (p. A15).

### Two Authors

List the last names of coauthors in the order in which they appear in the source. Join the names with "and" if you mention them in your text and with an ampersand (&) if the citation is in parentheses.

Seifried and de Wilde (2014) have demonstrated the importance of sports marketing in the creation of indoor arenas in the 1920s (p. 453).

Sports marketing played an important role in the creation of indoor arenas in the 1920s (Seifried & de Wilde, 2014, p. 453).

**Three or More Authors**

For three to five authors, include all the last names in your first reference. In any later references, follow only the first author with "et al." (for "and others") in the text or in parentheses. For six authors or more, simply follow the first author with "et al." for all citations.

Compulsive buying behavior has traditionally been described as a type of addiction or pathological disorder (Spinella, Lester, & Yang, 2014, p. 670). New research by Spinella et al., however, suggests that such behavior may be more closely linked to general attitudes about money (p. 671).

Learning disabilities occur with each other, with emotional or attention disorders, or with social deficits (Fletcher, Lyon, Fuchs, & Barnes, 2006, p. 9). Thus Fletcher et al. characterize this likelihood as "co-morbidity" (p. 9).

**Organization Author**

Several factors, including prenatal hormone levels, genetics, and life experiences, can all contribute to a person becoming transgender (American Psychological Association, 2014, p. 2).

**Author of an Article from a Reader or Collection**

Cite the essay author; list the collection editor later with your references.

The body's melatonin production is inhibited by light (Boyle, 2014, p. 49).

**Unidentified Author**

Identify the source with its title in your text or the first few words in parentheses so it is easy to locate in your alphabetical list of references.

Parents need to monitor their child's online activities ("Social Networking," 2012).

**Same Author with Multiple Works**

Three significant trends in parent-school relations evolved (Grimley, 2007) after the original multistate study (Grimley, 1987).

**Different Authors with Multiple Works**

Within a single citation, list the authors of multiple works in alphabetical order (as in your reference list). Separate the works with semicolons.

Several studies have demonstrated a link between celebrity worship and cosmetic surgery among adolescents (Abraham & Zuckerman, 2011; Huh, 2012; Maltby & Day, 2011; Swami et al., 2013).

## What Type of Source Is It?

Naming the author is the core of a citation, regardless of the type of source used. Even so, a few types may present complications.

**Online Source**

Provide an in-text citation for an online source the same way you would for any other source.

Ballor (2015) provides some insight into the shifting of retail from a large and distant experience back to a small, local one.

If you are citing an entire Web site, include the URL in the text, but not in your reference list.

The Common Sense Media Web site (http://www.commonsensemedia.org) provides parents with age-appropriate ratings for movies, books, and television shows.

### Indirect Source

If possible, locate and cite the original source. Otherwise, begin your citation with "as cited in" and name your source.

According to Claude Fischer, the belief in individualism favors "the individual over the group or institution" (as cited in Hansen, 2005, p. 5).

### Government or Organization Document

If no specific author is identified, treat the sponsor as the author. Give its full name in your first citation. If the name is complicated or commonly shortened, you may add an abbreviation in parentheses. In later citations, use just the abbreviation and the date: (APA, 2010).

In *The Impact of Food Advertising on Childhood Obesity* (2010), the American Psychological Association (APA) reports a direct link between number of hours of television watched by and rates of obesity among children.

### Source without a Date

When the date is unknown, use "n.d." ("no date").

Interval training encourages rotation between high-intensity spurts and "active recovery, which is typically a less-intense form of the original activity" (*Interval Training*, n.d., para. 2).

### A Classic

If the original date is unknown, use "n.d." ("no date"). If it is known, include it with your edition's date: (Burton, 1621/1977). For ancient texts, use the year of the translation: (Homer, trans. 1990). For a quotation from a classic, identify lines, sections, or other standard divisions that locate a passage in any edition. For biblical references, specify the version in your initial citation. Classics — ancient or religious — need not be listed as references.

Many cultures affirm the importance of religious covenant in accounts as varied as the biblical "Behold, I make a covenant" in Exodus 34:10 (King James Version) and *The Iliad* (Homer, trans. 1990), which opens with the cause of the Trojan War, "all because Agamemnon spurned Apollo's priest" (Book 1, line 12).

### Visual Material

To refer to your own figure or table, mention its number in your sentence: "As Figure 2 shows, . . ." Clearly cite a visual from a source.

Use of pro-social media among teenagers is likely to result in more empathetic behavior in real life (Prot et al., 2014, Table 2).

To include or adapt a source's table or visual, you may need to request permission from the author or copyright holder. Many sources — from scholarly journals to Web sites—state their permissions policy in the issue or on the site. (Ask your instructor's advice if you are unsure how to proceed.) Credit the material in a "From" or "Adapted from" note below it.

### Personal Communication

Omit personal communications—such as face-to-face, online, or telephone interviews, letters, memos, and e-mail—from your reference list because your readers won't be able to find and use such sources. Simply name your source and the date of the communication in your paper.

J. T. Moore (personal communication, October 10, 2016) has made specific suggestions for stimulating the local economy.

## How Are You Capturing the Source Material?

The way you capture source material—in your own words or in a quotation—affects how you will present and credit it. Always identify words taken directly from a source by using quotation marks or the indented form for a long "block" quotation. Specify the location of quoted words. If you present in your own words material from a specific place in your source, APA also recommends that you add the location. A citation, but no location, is needed for general information, such as your summary of an overall finding.

For more on capturing and integrating source material, see pp. 228–35, 647–59, and Ch. 34.

To identify the location of material in a source, supply the page number. For an unpaginated source, especially online, give the paragraph number it supplies (para. 3). Otherwise, give the section name (or a shortened version), and identify the paragraph within the section (Methods section, para. 2). If appropriate, identify other parts: Chapter 5, Figure 2, Table 3.

The next few examples illustrate how Emily Lavery varied her presentation of sources in her paper "A New Time: Female Education and Teachers in Western Territories," about education during the mid-1800s.

### Overall Summary or Important Idea

Horace Mann and other educational reformers began the Common School Movement, advocating for public primary schools (Nasaw, 1979, p. 30). The movement was revolutionary for education and marked the first attempt to create public school systems, across the United States and all its territories, in order to educate the youth.

### Blended Paraphrase and Quotation

According to Hoffman (2003), Mann's movement sought to develop the "informal rural schools supported by parents" (p. 30) and establish a state-sponsored school system.

### Brief Quotation Integrated in Sentence

Jennifer Madigan (2009) defined a dame school as a "school influenced by the English model of home instruction for small groups of children" (p. 11).

### Long Quotation

If you quote forty words or more, indent the quotation one-half inch and double-space it instead of using quotation marks. After it, add your citation with no additional period, including whatever information you have not already mentioned in your launch statement.

Emma Willard and Catharine Beecher fought for female educational opportunities, such as a more inclusive curriculum and higher educational opportunities. In 1848, Elizabeth Cady Stanton published the "Declaration of Sentiments" at the Seneca Falls Convention to address and rectify the wrongs done to women, including this resolution:

> That the speedy success of our cause depends upon the zealous and untiring efforts of both men and women, for the overthrow of the monopoly of the pulpit, and for securing to woman an equal participation with men in the various trades, professions, and commerce. (p. 73)

### RESEARCH CHECKLIST

### Citing Sources in APA Style

☐ Have you double-checked to be sure that you have acknowledged all material from a source?

☐ Does your citation fall right after a quotation or reference to a source?

☐ Have you identified the author of each source in your text or in parentheses?

☐ Have you used the first few words of the title to cite a work without an identified author?

☐ Have you noted the date (or added "n.d." for "no date") for each source?

☐ Have you added a page number or other location whenever needed?

☐ Have you checked your final draft to be sure that every source cited in your text also appears in your list of references?

# Listing Sources in APA Style

For a sample reference page, see p. 725 or p. Q-6 in the Quick Format Guide.

List your sources at the end of your paper on a new page titled "References," centered at the top. Double-space your list, and organize it alphabetically by authors' last names (or by titles for works without an identified author). Arrange several works by the same author by date, moving from earliest to most recent. If an author has two works published in the same year, arrange these alphabetically, and add a letter after each date (2009a, 2009b) so the date in your text citation leads to the correct entry.

Format each entry with a "hanging indent" so that subsequent lines are indented one-half inch (about five to seven spaces), just as a paragraph is. Include only sources that you actually cite in your paper unless your instructor requests otherwise.

APA style simplifies the following details:

- Supply only initials (with a space between them) for an author's first and middle names.
- Use an ampersand (&, as in a citation in parentheses), not "and" (as you would write in your paper), before the name of the last of several authors.
- Spell out names of months, but abbreviate terms common in academic writing (such as "p.m.," "Vol." for "Volume," or "No." for "Number").
- Capitalize only the first word, proper names, and the first word after a colon in the title of a book, article, or Web site. Capitalize all main words in the title of a journal or other periodical.
- Do not use quotation marks or italics for an article title in your reference list (but use quotation marks if you mention it in your text).
- Italicize a Web site, book, or periodical title (and its volume number).
- List only the first of several cities where a publisher has offices, and add the abbreviated state (unless a university's name identifies it). For locations abroad, spell both city and country.
- Shorten the name of a publisher, but include "Press" and "Books."
- Use "Author" instead of the publisher's name if the two are the same.
- For an article, give volume, issue (if each begins with page 1), and any digital object identifier (DOI), a unique number that identifies it with a permanent Web address. If no DOI is available for an online article, supply the URL for the journal's or publisher's home page, even if you used a database.
- Include an access date only for online sources that might change.
- Omit a final period after the URL.

Keep in mind these two key questions, which are used to organize the sample entries that follow:

Who wrote it?

What type of source is it?

As you prepare your entries, begin with the author. The various author formats apply whatever your source — article, book, Web page, or other material. Then, from the following examples, select the format for the rest of the entry, depending on the type of source you have used. Follow its pattern in your entry, supplying the same information in the same order with the same punctuation and other features.

## Who Wrote It?

### Individual Author

Abeles, V. (2015). *Beyond measure: Rescuing an overscheduled, overtested, underestimated generation.* New York, NY: Simon & Schuster.

### Two Authors

Diamandis, P. H., & Kotler, S. (2014). *Abundance: The future is better than you think*.
New York, NY: Free Press.

### Three or More Authors

Provide names for three to six authors; for more than six, simply use "et al."
("and others") instead of adding more names.

Schiller, B., Hill, C., & Wall, S. (2016). *The economy today* (14th ed.). New York, NY:
McGraw-Hill.

### Same Author with Multiple Works

Arrange the titles by date, the earliest first. If some share the same date,
arrange them alphabetically, and letter them after the date.

Mukherjee, S. (2010). *The emperor of all maladies: A biography of cancer*. New York, NY:
Scribner.

Mukherjee, S. (2015a). Blood feuds. *Blood, 126,* 1264-1265. doi:10.1182/blood-2015
-07-659540

Mukherjee, S. (2015b). *The laws of medicine: Field notes from an uncertain science*.
New York, NY: TED Books.

### Organization Author

American Lung Association. (2015). *New ozone standards will save lives, protect
health*. Washington, DC: Author.

### Author of Edited Work

Skloot, R., & Folger, T. (Eds.). (2015). *The best American science and nature writing
2015*. New York, NY: Houghton Mifflin Harcourt.

### Author and Translator

Piketty, T. (2014). *Capital in the twenty-first century* (A. Goldhammer, Trans.).
Cambridge, MA: Belknap Press. (Original work published 2013)

### Unidentified Author

Vets shine in arts, sciences, public service. (2015, December). *Vietnam, 28*(4), 16.

## What Type of Source Is It?

Once you have found the author format that fits, look for the type of source
that matches. Mix and match the patterns illustrated as needed. For example,
the revised edition of an edited collection of articles might send you to
several examples until you have identified all elements.

### Article in a Printed or an Electronic Periodical

#### Article from a Journal Paginated by Volume

If the pages for the year's volume are numbered consecutively, no issue
number is needed. Italicize the volume number as well as the journal title.

Include the DOI
if provided; no
period added
after the DOI ———

Dreby, J. (2015). U.S. immigration policy and family separation: The consequences
for children's well-being. *Social Science & Medicine, 132,* 245-251.
doi:10.1016/j.socscimed.2014.08.041

### Article from a Journal Paginated by Issue

If each issue begins with page 1, add the issue number in parentheses, without italics, leaving no space after the volume number.

Molano, A., Torrente, C., & Jones, S. (2015). Relative risk in context: Exposure to family and neighborhood violence within schools. *Journal of Latino-Latin American Studies, 7*(1), 9-32.

If you want to list a special issue about a topic, rather than singling out an article, begin with the issue editor or, if none, with the issue title.

Internet memes [Themed issue]. (2015). *Journal of Visual Culture, 13*(3).

### Article Accessed through a Library or Subscription Database

Supply any DOI, or search for and identify the home page for the journal. Name the database only for a source otherwise hard to find.

Powell, A. (2015). Youth "at risk"? Young people, sexual health and consent. *Youth Studies Australia, 26*(4), 21-28. Retrieved from http://www.acys.info/ysa

To see how to create the listing for a journal article from a database, turn to pp. 654–55.

No period added

### Abstract for an Article

If you use only the abstract, cite it, not the full article. Add "Abstract" in brackets after the title, or use it to begin the retrieval line.

Bordun, T. (2015). Onscreen and off-screen flesh and blood: Performance, affect and ethics in Catherine Breillat's films. *Studies in European Cinema, 12*(2), 132-143. Abstract retrieved from EBSCOHost.

### Article from a Printed Magazine

Volk, S. (2015, March). The doctor and the salamander. *Discover, 36*(2), 28-37.

To see how to create the listing for a magazine article, turn to pp. 648–49.

### Article from an Online Magazine

Abrams, L. (2015, April 30). FDA: KIND bars aren't actually healthy. *Salon.com.* Retrieved from http://www.salon.com

### Article from a Newsletter

Grose, J. (2015, October 23). How to negotiate your maternity leave at a small company. *Lenny.* Retrieved from http://www.lennyletter.com/culture/news/a107/how-to-negotiate-your-maternity-leave-at-a-small-company/

### Article from a Printed Newspaper

Weisman, R. (2015, November 12). For Biogen's growth, a new prescription. *The Boston Globe*, p. C1.

### Article from an Online Newspaper

Navarro, M. (2015, November 12). Public housing nationwide may be subject to smoking ban. *The New York Times.* Retrieved from http://www.nytimes.com

### Editorial

Eradicating disease [Editorial]. (2015, October 10). *The Economist, 417*(8959), 13.

### Letter to the Editor

Sims, D. (2014, December 31). A kinder, gentler intelligence [Letter to the editor]. *National Review, 66*(24), 2.

### Review

McCarry, C. (2015, November 6). Science strange and dangerous [Review of the book *End of the cold war*]. *The Wall Street Journal.* Retrieved from http://wsj.com

## Printed or Electronic Book

### Printed Book

To see how to create a listing for a book, turn to pp. 650–51.

Gladwell, M. (2015). *David and Goliath: Underdogs, misfits, and the art of battling giants.* New York, NY: Little, Brown.

### Online Book

Einstein, A. (1920). *Relativity: The special and general theory.* Retrieved from http://www.bartleby.com/173/

### E-book

Varcarolis, E. (2014). *Manual of psychiatric nursing care planning: Assessment guides, diagnoses, psychopharmacology* (5th ed.). Retrieved from http://www.barnesandnoble.com/w/manual-of-psychiatric-nursing-care-planning-elizabeth-m-varcarolis/1100213063?ean=9781437717839

### Multivolume Work

McInness, M., Everad, M., Finlayson, C. M., & Davidson, N. (Eds.). (2016). *Encyclopedia of wetlands* (Vol. 2). New York, NY: Springer.

### Revised Edition

Pierce, B. (2016). *Genetics essentials: Concepts and connections* (11th ed.). New York, NY: Worth.

### Book without a Date

Reade, T. (n.d.). *American Originals.* Wichita, KS: Midtown Press.

## Part of a Book

### Selection from a Book

Stevenson, B. (2015). The high road. In A. Johnson (Ed.), *The best American nonrequired reading 2015* (pp. 387-389). Boston, MA: Houghton Mifflin Harcourt.

### Preface, Introduction, Foreword, or Afterword

Strayed, C. (2015). Introduction. In I. Fitzgerald, *Pen & ink: Tattoos and the stories behind them* (p. 1). New York, NY: Bloomsbury.

### Article from a Reference Work

Norman, C. E. (2003). Religion and food. In *Encyclopedia of food and culture* (Vol. 3, pp. 171-176). New York, NY: Scribner.

## Other Printed or Electronic Document

Many research reports and similar documents are collaborative products, prepared under the auspices of government, academic, or other organizational sponsors. Start with the agency name if no specific author is identified. In parentheses, add any report number assigned by the agency right after the title. Add the publisher (unless it is also the author) before the URL (if there is one).

### Government Document

U.S. Federal Trade Commission. (2015). *House alarms can't stop scammers.* Retrieved from http://www.consumer.ftc.gov/blog/house-alarms-cant-stop-scammers

### Research Report

National Institute on Drug Abuse. (2014). *Principles of adolescent substance use disorder treatment: A research-based guide* (NIH Publication No. 14-7953). Retrieved from https://d14rmgtrwzf5a.cloudfront.net/sites/default/files/podata_1_17_14.pdf

### Report from an Academic Institution

Tavoni, M., & van Vuuren, D. P. (2015). *Regional carbon budgets: Do they matter for climate policy?* Cambridge, MA: Harvard Kennedy School, Belfer Center for Science and International Affairs.

### Pamphlet

Label the source in brackets as a brochure.

U.S. Department of Veterans Affairs. (2012). *Federal benefits for veterans, dependents, and survivors* [Brochure]. Washington, DC: Author.

### Doctoral Dissertation

Scotty, E. (2014). *Sensitivity of atmospheric pollutants to changes in modeled natural and anthropogenic emissions* (Unpublished doctoral dissertation). University of Wisconsin, Madison.

## Internet or Electronic Source

To help a reader find the same material you used, identify a specific document and give its URL.

### Document from a Web Site

Rist, R. C., Martin, F. P., & Fernandez, A. M. (2015). *Poverty, inequality, and evaluation: Changing perspectives.* Retrieved from World Bank Group Web site: http://documents.worldbank.org/curated/en/2015/10/25161477/poverty-inequality-evaluation-changing-perspectives

See the directory on pp. 705–6 for entries for other electronic sources, including books and articles.

For updates to online formats, visit the APA Web site at apastyle .org.

To see how to create the listing for a Web page, turn to pp. 652–53.

### Section from an Online Document

Vitality Institute. (2015). Critical role of prevention in population health improvement. In *Beyond the four walls: Why community is critical to workforce health* (sec. 3). Retrieved from http://thevitalityinstitute.org/site/wp-content/uploads/2015/07 /VitalityInstitute-BeyondTheFourWalls-Report-28July2015.pdf

### Document from a Campus Web Site

Identify the university and sponsoring program or department (if applicable) before giving the URL for the specific page or document.

Allin, C. (2012). *Common sense for college students: How to do better than you thought possible.* Retrieved January 5, 2016, from Cornell College, Department of Politics Web site: http://www.cornellcollege.edu/politics/resources-students /policies/common-sense-cwa.shtml

### Blog Post

Breitenbach, S. (2015, October 19). Many states still grapple with regulating medical marijuana [Blog post]. Retrieved March 28, 2016, from http://www .pewtrusts.org/en/research-and-analysis/blogs/stateline/2015/10/19/many-states -still-grapple-with-regulating-medical-marijuana

### Computer Software

Microsoft Office 2016 [Computer software]. Redmond, WA: Microsoft.

## Visual or Audio Source

### Sound Recording

Atandi Anyona, A., & Koons, R. (Writers). (2012). *Singing against apartheid: An audio essay* [Audio essay]. Retrieved from http://ethnomusicologyreview.ucla.edu /content/singing-against-apartheid-audio-essay

### Program on Television or Radio

Glassman, G., & Klein, L. (Directors/Producers). (2015). "Hagia Sophia: Istanbul's Mystery" [Television series episode]. In V. Abita & M. Catteau (Executive producers), *Nova.* Boston, MA: WGBH.

### Film

Eastwood, C. (Director). (2014). *American sniper* [Motion picture]. United States: Warner Brothers.

## Field Source

### Personal Interview

See the citation on p. 709.

Omit a personal interview from your reference list because it's not accessible to readers. Instead, mention it in your paper as a personal communication.

### E-mail or Electronic Posting

See the citations on p. 709.

Cite inaccessible, nonpublic messages as personal communications. Otherwise, supply author, date, title, a description in brackets such as [Blog post], and a "Retrieved from" line with the URL. If this source is considered unstable, include retrieval date (see blog post citation above).

## Listing Sources in APA Style

☐ Have you started each entry with the appropriate pattern for the author's name? Have you left spaces between the initials for each name?

☐ Have you used "&" (not "and") before the last coauthor's name?

☐ Have you included the date in each entry?

☐ Have you followed the sample pattern for the type of source used?

☐ Have you used capitals and italics correctly for the titles in your entries?

☐ Have you included the conventional punctuation — periods, commas, colons, parentheses — in your entry?

☐ Have you accurately recorded names of the author, title, and publisher?

☐ Have you checked the accuracy of dates, pages, and other numbers?

☐ Have you correctly typed or pasted in the DOI or URL of an electronic source? Have you split a long URL before a punctuation mark? Have you ended without adding a final period after a DOI or URL?

☐ Have you arranged your entries in alphabetical order?

☐ Have you checked your final list of references against your text citations so that every source appears in both places?

☐ Have you double-spaced your reference list, like the rest of your paper? Have you allowed an inch margin on all sides?

☐ Have you begun the first line of each entry at the left margin? Have you used your software to indent each additional line one-half inch (or five to seven spaces)?

☐ Have you checked any entry from a citation management system as carefully as your own entries?

# A Sample APA Research Paper

In "Sex Offender Lists: A Never-Ending Punishment," Jenny Lidington explores the intention of the sex offender registry and its many functional problems. Her scholarly approach is designed to help readers grasp the complexities of a difficult societal issue that often generates strong feelings. Notice how thoughtfully she tackles the topic: defining terms, making distinctions, reviewing history, tracing consequences, distinguishing differences, and establishing the basis for her questions. Her paper illustrates APA paper format and the APA conventions for citing and listing sources. The marginal annotations explain APA formatting and citation guidelines, as well as point out effective research writing practices. Although this sample paper is presented for easy reading in a textbook, your paper should use the type style and size that APA suggests: Times New Roman font, 12-point size. Set one-inch margins on all four sides, double-space all the lines, and turn off automatic hyphenation. Use your software's Help feature or visit the campus computer lab for assistance setting up this format for your file.

For more on APA format, see the Quick Format Guide, p. Q-1.

A
Writer's
Research
Manual

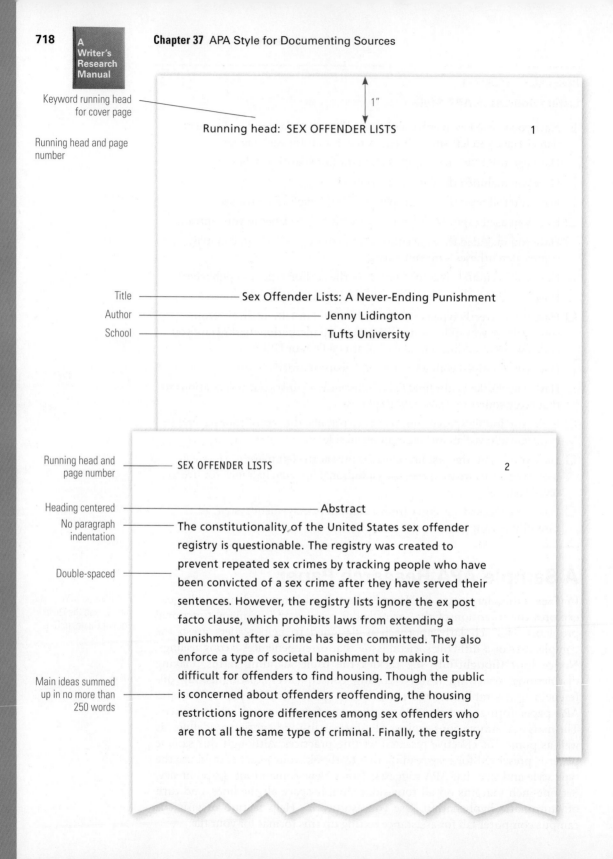

Keyword running head
for cover page

Running head and page
number

↕ 1"

Running head:  SEX OFFENDER LISTS                                      1

Title ——————— Sex Offender Lists: A Never-Ending Punishment
Author ——————————— Jenny Lidington
School ——————————— Tufts University

Running head and
page number
——— SEX OFFENDER LISTS                                      2

Heading centered ——————————— Abstract

No paragraph
indentation

Double-spaced

Main ideas summed
up in no more than
250 words

The constitutionality of the United States sex offender
registry is questionable. The registry was created to
prevent repeated sex crimes by tracking people who have
been convicted of a sex crime after they have served their
sentences. However, the registry lists ignore the ex post
facto clause, which prohibits laws from extending a
punishment after a crime has been committed. They also
enforce a type of societal banishment by making it
difficult for offenders to find housing. Though the public
is concerned about offenders reoffending, the housing
restrictions ignore differences among sex offenders who
are not all the same type of criminal. Finally, the registry

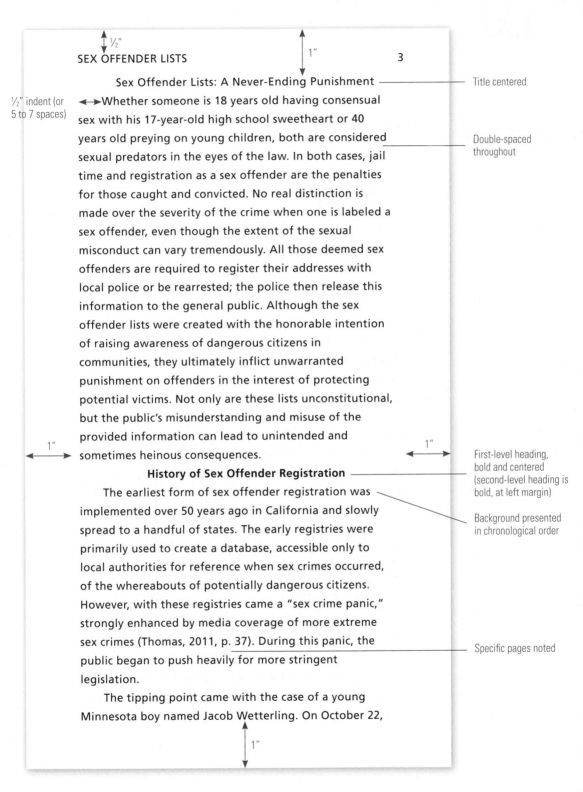

½"

1"

½" indent (or 5 to 7 spaces)

Title centered

Double-spaced throughout

1"

1"

First-level heading, bold and centered (second-level heading is bold, at left margin)

Background presented in chronological order

Specific pages noted

1"

## Sex Offender Lists: A Never-Ending Punishment

Whether someone is 18 years old having consensual sex with his 17-year-old high school sweetheart or 40 years old preying on young children, both are considered sexual predators in the eyes of the law. In both cases, jail time and registration as a sex offender are the penalties for those caught and convicted. No real distinction is made over the severity of the crime when one is labeled a sex offender, even though the extent of the sexual misconduct can vary tremendously. All those deemed sex offenders are required to register their addresses with local police or be rearrested; the police then release this information to the general public. Although the sex offender lists were created with the honorable intention of raising awareness of dangerous citizens in communities, they ultimately inflict unwarranted punishment on offenders in the interest of protecting potential victims. Not only are these lists unconstitutional, but the public's misunderstanding and misuse of the provided information can lead to unintended and sometimes heinous consequences.

### History of Sex Offender Registration

The earliest form of sex offender registration was implemented over 50 years ago in California and slowly spread to a handful of states. The early registries were primarily used to create a database, accessible only to local authorities for reference when sex crimes occurred, of the whereabouts of potentially dangerous citizens. However, with these registries came a "sex crime panic," strongly enhanced by media coverage of more extreme sex crimes (Thomas, 2011, p. 37). During this panic, the public began to push heavily for more stringent legislation.

The tipping point came with the case of a young Minnesota boy named Jacob Wetterling. On October 22,

1989, Jacob was bicycling with his brother and a friend when a masked gunman intercepted them and kidnapped Jacob. It was believed at the time that he had been sexually assaulted and murdered, and in 2016, police were led to Jacob's remains by his attacker, and this longstanding belief was confirmed. In light of this tragedy, the Jacob Wetterling Act was established in 1994, requiring states to create and maintain sex offender registries. Notably, the information on the registries was accessible only to appropriate authorities. While this policy had monumental implications, it did not satisfy the public as communities wanted access to records of sex offenders' residences (Thomas, 2011, p. 42).

On July 29, 1994, another horrific and highly publicized incident occurred that substantiated the argument for public notification and would significantly impact sex offenders' quality of life. Megan Kanka, a 7-year-old girl from New Jersey, was raped and murdered by her neighbor, Jesse Timmenequas. Jesse, unbeknownst to the community, was a repeat sex offender. This event spurred legislators to create the registry reforms the public desired by passing Megan's Law. This legislation amended the Jacob Wetterling Act by requiring community notification of nearby sex offenders' residences. Along with publishing the registration information, other methods of notification were encouraged. Louisiana, for example, required sex offenders "to post signs at their homes declaring their status as sex offenders" (Thomas, 2011, p. 45).

### Constitutional Questions about Sex Offender Registries

Overlooking the rights of perpetrators of abominable crimes can be easy; however, the constitutionality of sex offender registration is entirely questionable. Whatever the crime, the rights of the convicted should be upheld. Because the registration process occurs after an offender is released from incarceration, these lists fail to comply

Figures (not words) used for pages, dates, ages, and numbers with more than one digit

SEX OFFENDER LISTS                                      5

with the ex post facto clause, which prohibits the creation
of laws that add punishments after a crime has been
committed. These lists have been taken to court on
grounds of retrospection, though rulings have not
favored the offenders (Pattis, 2011), and also on grounds
of due process, as offenders have no opportunity to argue
against community notification.

A third constitutional issue is whether the residential
restrictions imposed by the lists constitute banishment, an
illegal form of punishment under the constitution. In
many states, sex offenders are not allowed within a few
blocks of schools, daycare centers, or playgrounds.
Particularly in communities with many facilities,
acceptable livable areas for registered offenders may be
limited or nonexistent. "I never realized how many
schools and parks there were until I had to stay away
from them," a registered sex offender conceded in
Levenson and Cotter's 2005 survey (as cited in Thomas,
2011, p. 129). Essentially, these restrictions, intended to
make given areas safer, create potentially dangerous sex-
offender communities. This was the case in Broward
County, Florida, where 95 registered sex offenders lived
within a five-block tract (Thomas, 2011, p. 129). Those
who cannot find housing or afford available housing are
left homeless though commonly banished from homeless
shelters and hostels, too (Thomas, 2011, p. 129).

### Public Misconceptions

Those who argue that sex offender registries are
constitutional often maintain that the lists are not
punitive and provide the public with vital information
that can prevent future sex crimes. Even those who admit that
the lists may infringe upon offenders' rights argue that any
minor violations are outweighed by the contribution to public
safety. This argument might be the case if the critically flawed
information in sex offender

Multiple authors joined
by *and* in text

Additional source cited
in source where it
was mentioned

SEX OFFENDER LISTS                                    6

lists was not subject to public misinterpretation. One
shortcoming is a lack of specificity: A person who urinated
in public is on the same list as one who repeatedly raped
young children. In California, one of each 375 adults is
registered as a sex offender, a testament to this loose
definition of sex crimes (Leon, 2011, p. 119). Although
offenders are ranked on a scale of one to three (the
worst) in terms of likelihood of reoffending, people tend
to ignore these distinctions. As a police officer stated for
the *Seattle Times*, "People look at them in a bucket. They
say 'Any kind of sex offender is a sex offender, and always
will be a sex offender'" (Farley, 2011, para. 13).

Another flaw lies in the accuracy of the rankings.
Most crimes require a post-incarceration evaluation to
determine whether the criminal is still a threat to society,
but sex offenders have no follow-up. When they are
released from prison, their names go into a sex offender
registry, no matter how much time has passed since the
crime. The "threat level" classification represents the level
at the time of the crime, not the offender's current risk
level. Therapy sessions both during and after prison could
result in the offender no longer posing a threat to the
community. Studies show that within three years of being
released from prison, only 5.3% of sex offenders are
rearrested for another sex crime (Smith, 2003; U.S.
Department of Justice, 2003, p. 1), which further suggests
that the sex offender lists are extremely questionable.

In addition, due to the potentially inaccurate
classifications, offenders may be assigned inappropriate
punishments for their given crime. For example, many sex
offenders whose crimes were not against children (or who
may be children themselves) are given the same living
restrictions as child rapists. The man imprisoned for
having sex with his girlfriend days before she was legally
old enough to give consent does not pose enough risk to

Paragraph number
supplied for online
article without
numbered pages

SEX OFFENDER LISTS 7

restrict him from living near playgrounds and schools. Although some states such as New Jersey and Washington are working to assess risks more accurately, they are the exceptions (Leon, 2011, pp. 141-142).

### Consequences of a Lack of Privacy

These major flaws in the sex offender registry system can have counterproductive and tragic effects. When sex offenders must register, their personal information is not given on a need-to-know basis; it is blazoned across the community where they live. Their names, photographs, license plate numbers, and home and work addresses are posted online for the world to view. They may struggle to find housing, to avoid public disapproval or embarrassing exposure of their pasts, and to pass background checks necessary to find work. Because these offenders are often shunned by the adult world, they may seek companionship with children, which potentially tempts some to offend again. With their faces plastered on local bulletin boards or e-mail alerts, offenders can grow increasingly aggravated, which also may lead them to new crimes (Chen, 2009).

This lack of privacy also makes offenders vulnerable to public vigilantes who can inflict harsh punishments. According to a Los Angeles County study by Gallo et al.,

> A number of judges felt that although the avowed purpose of the registration statute is to facilitate the process of law enforcement by providing a list of suspects . . . the information obtained under section 290 is subject to some abuse—either through police harassment or by indiscriminate revelation to unauthorized persons. (as cited in Leon, 2011, pp. 68-69)

Tragically, public harassment can lead to suicides and murders of registered sex offenders, as was the case for 24-year-old William Elliot. At age 20, Elliot was sentenced

Long quotation (40 words or longer) indented ½" without quotation marks

to four months in jail for having sex with his girlfriend who was two weeks away from turning 16 (the legal age of consent in Maine). Four years later, a young man named Stephen Marshall found Elliot's residential information on an online sex-offender database. Marshall used this information to stalk Elliot and shoot him to death in his own home (Ahuja, 2006). This incident is a horrific example of the unintended effects of public misinterpretation of sex offender lists, but it also calls into question whether these lists can be considered nonpunitive.

### Violations of Rights of Citizens

Perceived as monsters, fiends, and psychopaths, sex offenders are not easily seen as victims; however, as American citizens, they have the same right to life, liberty, and the pursuit of happiness as anyone else. Although the sex registry laws were created with the best of intentions, they violate these constitutional rights and can have gruesome unintended consequences. Most importantly, they are not especially effective.

Many people believe that the typical sex crime is child rape when in reality most sex crimes are much more benign. The dramatic cases encourage regulation that far exceeds what is necessary for most offenders, placing those who have urinated publicly in the same category as pedophiles (Bonnar-Kidd, 2010, p. 416). However, the sex-crime taboos make it difficult for the public to override emotionally charged ideas of the misconduct that the lists represent and then to see the critical flaws in the current registry system. If these lists are to continue to exist, they should no longer serve as dehumanizing blacklists for the public to use at its own discretion.

## References

Ahuja, G. (2006, April 18). Sex offender registries: Putting lives at risk? ABC News. Retrieved from http://abcnews .go.com

Bonnar-Kidd, K. K. (2010). Sexual offender laws and prevention of sexual violence or recidivism. *American Journal of Public Health*, *100*, 412-419. doi:10.2105 /AJPH.2008.153254

Chen, S. (2009, February 19). After prison, few places for sex offenders to live. *The Wall Street Journal*. Retrieved from http://wsj.com

Farley, J. (2011, January 1). Sex-offender rankings: Is there room for gray areas? *The Seattle Times*. Retrieved from http://seattletimes.com

Leon, C. S. (2011). *Sex fiends, perverts, and pedophiles: Understanding sex crime policy in America*. New York, NY: New York University Press.

Pattis, N. (2011, February 7). Time to revisit ex post facto clause for sex offenders [Blog post]. Retrieved from http://www.pattisblog.com/index.php?article =Time_To_Revisit_Ex_Post_Facto_Clause_For_Sex _Offenders_2983

Smith, S. (2003, November 16). Five percent of sex offenders rearrested for another sex crime [Press release]. Retrieved from U.S. Department of Justice, Office of Justice Programs, Bureau of Justice Statistics Web site: http://bjs.ojp.usdoj.gov/content/pub /press/rsorp94pr.cfm

Thomas, T. (2011). *The registration and monitoring of sex offenders: A comparative study*. New York, NY: Routledge.

U.S. Department of Justice, Office of Justice Programs, Bureau of Justice Statistics. (2003). *Recidivism of sex offenders released from prison in 1994* (NCJ 198281). Retrieved from http://bjs.ojp.usdoj.gov/content/pub /pdf/rsorp94.pdf

Page numbering continues

Heading centered

First line of entry at left margin, additional lines indented ½"

List alphabetized by last names of authors, or by titles (when no author is named); names match source citations in text

Supply only initials for authors' first and middle names; leave space between first and middle initials

No period after URL

First word in title and after colon and all proper nouns capitalized

# A
# WRITER'S
# HANDBOOK

# A Writer's Handbook Contents

## 38 Basic Grammar  730

1 | Parts of Speech  730
2 | Subjects  740
3 | Verbs, Objects, and Complements  741
4 | Clauses and Phrases  746
5 | Sentence Structures  748

## 39 Grammatical Sentences  752

6 | Sentence Fragments  752
7 | Comma Splices and Fused Sentences  755
8 | Verb Form, Tense, and Mood  758
9 | Subject-Verb Agreement  771
10 | Pronoun Case  775
11 | Pronoun Reference  779
12 | Pronoun-Antecedent Agreement  782
13 | Adjectives and Adverbs  784
14 | Shifts  789

## 40 Effective Sentences  792

15 | Misplaced and Dangling Modifiers  792
16 | Incomplete Sentences  794
17 | Mixed Constructions and Faulty Predication  798
18 | Parallel Structure  801
19 | Coordination and Subordination  804
20 | Sentence Variety  810
21 | Active and Passive Voice  811

## 41 Word Choice  814

22 | Appropriateness  814
23 | Exact Words  818
24 | Bias-Free Language  819
25 | Wordiness  822
26 | Commonly Confused Words  823

## 42 Punctuation  826

27 | End Punctuation  826
28 | Commas  828
29 | Misuses of the Comma  836
30 | Semicolons  838
31 | Colons  839
32 | Apostrophes  841
33 | Quotation Marks  844
34 | Dashes  848
35 | Parentheses, Brackets, and Ellipses  849

## 43 Mechanics  853

**36** | Abbreviations  853
**37** | Capital Letters  856
**38** | Numbers  859
**39** | Italics  861
**40** | Hyphens  863
**41** | Spelling  865

| Answers for Lettered Exercises  866

# Introduction: Grammar, or The Way Words Work

Hundreds of times a day, with wonderful efficiency, we perform tasks of understanding and constructing complex sentences. Isn't it possible to write well without contemplating grammar at all? Yes. If your innate sense of grammar is reliable, you can write clearly and logically and forcefully without knowing a subjective complement from a handsaw. Most successful writers, though, have practiced for many years to gain this sense. When you doubt a word or a construction, a handbook can clear up your confusion and restore your confidence — just as a dictionary can help your spelling.

This handbook explains the most common grammatical conventions — accepted ways in which skilled writers put words together to convey meaning clearly. The college writer can learn by following these examples, just as an athlete, an artist, or a mechanic can learn by watching professionals.

## Learning by Doing 🔟 Creating an Error Log

Keeping track of errors will dramatically improve your writing skills. Whether you use a paper notebook or a computer file, maintain a running list of corrections made on your drafts by your instructor or writing tutors. Keep track of the date, the name of the error and its symbol or abbreviation ("pronoun agreement / pn agr"), a sample sentence or word group, and a note about how to fix the mistake. You may also wish to note the type of error: matters of **grammar** are addressed in Chapter 39, **style** is covered in Chapter 40, **word choice** is in Chapter 41, **punctuation** is in Chapter 42, and **mechanics** are in Chapter 43. If you are unsure of the meaning of a grammatical term, check Chapter 38 for a **review of common elements** such as parts of speech or look in the index for specific page numbers.

# 38  Basic Grammar

1 | Parts of Speech  730

2 | Subjects  740

3 | Verbs, Objects, and Complements  741

4 | Clauses and Phrases  746

5 | Sentence Structures  748

The English language has rules about how to put words together in order to create clear sentences. These rules are called "grammar," and they are the subject of all the chapters in this handbook. This first chapter, Basic Grammar, gives an overview of the building blocks of language and grammar. Rather than focusing on grammatical correctness, this chapter serves as more of a description of the ingredients—parts of speech, parts of sentences, and types of sentences—you'll need to understand in order to follow the rules explained in more detail in later chapters.

## 1 | Parts of Speech

English has eight basic parts of speech: nouns, pronouns, verbs, adjectives, adverbs, prepositions, conjunctions, and interjections. Each part of speech performs a specific function in a sentence.

### 1a  Nouns

Nouns are words that name people, places, objects, or ideas, and they can be either common or proper. Most nouns are **common**—they refer to people, places, and things in general, and they are usually not capitalized. **Proper nouns** are more specific, unique names, and they are usually capitalized.

## Types of Nouns *at a Glance*

|         | Common (general) | Proper (specific) |
|---------|------------------|-------------------|
| person  | man              | Steve Jobs        |
| place   | country          | Mexico            |
| thing   | book             | *The Bedford Guide for College Writers* |
| idea    | bravery          | Congressional Medal of Honor |

Nouns can perform several different roles in a sentence, primarily as subject (see 2) and object (see 1f and 3a).

*Nelson* gave the *book* to *Miranda.*

## Guidelines for Multilingual Writers
What Are Count and Noncount Nouns and Articles?

**Count Nouns and Articles**

Nouns referring to items that can be counted are called **count** (or **countable**) nouns. Count nouns can be made plural.

> *table, chair, egg*     two *tables*, several *chairs*, a dozen *eggs*

Singular count nouns must be preceded by a **determiner.** The class of words called determiners includes **articles** (*a, an, the*), **possessives** (*John's, your, his, my,* and so on), **demonstratives** (*this, that, these, those*), **numbers** (*three, the third,* and so on), and **indefinite quantity words** (*no, some, many,* and so on).

> *a* dog, *the* football, *one* reason, *the first* page, *no* chance

**Noncount Nouns and Articles**

Nouns referring to items that cannot be counted are called **noncount** (or **uncountable**) nouns. Noncount nouns cannot be made plural.

> I need to learn more grammars.

- Common categories of noncount nouns include types of **food** (*cheese, meat, bread*), **solids** (*dirt, salt, chalk*), **liquids** (*milk, juice, gasoline*), **gases** (*methane, hydrogen, air*), and **abstract ideas,** including emotions (*democracy, gravity, love*).

- Another category of noncount nouns is **mass** nouns, which usually represent a large group of countable nouns (*furniture, mail, clothing*).

- The only way to count noncountable nouns is to use a countable noun with them, usually to indicate a quantity or a container.

> one *piece* of furniture, two *quarts* of water, an *example* of jealousy

*(continued)*

- Noncount nouns, such as *advice,* are never preceded by an indefinite article; they are often preceded by *some.*

  > She gave us ~~a~~ good advice.
  >
  > She gave us ~~a~~ *some* good advice.

- When noncount nouns are *general* in meaning, no article is required, but when the context makes them specific (usually in a phrase or a clause after the noun), the definite article is used.

  | | |
  |---|---|
  | GENERAL | Good continues to fight *evil.* |
  | SPECIFIC | The *evil* that humans do lives after them. |

---

 ## Guidelines for Multilingual Writers
### What Are Definite and Indefinite Articles?

**The Definite Article (*the*)**

- Use *the* with a specific count or noncount noun mentioned before or familiar to both the writer and the reader.

  > She got a huge box in the mail. *The* box contained oranges from Florida. [*The* is used the second time the noun (*box*) is mentioned.]
  >
  > Did you feed *the* baby? [Both reader and writer know which baby.]

- Use *the* before specific count or noncount nouns when the reader is given enough information to identify what is being referred to.

  > *The* furniture in my apartment is old and faded. [Specific furniture]

- Use *the* before a singular count noun to state a generality.

  > *The* dog has been a companion for centuries. [*The dog* refers to all dogs.]

- Use *the* before some geographical names.

  > *Collective Nations:* the United States, the United Kingdom
  >
  > *Groups of Islands:* the Bahamas, the Canary Islands
  >
  > *Large Bodies of Water* (except lakes): the Atlantic Ocean, the Dead Sea, the Monongahela River, the Gulf of Mexico
  >
  > *Mountain Ranges:* the Rockies, the Himalayas

- Use *the* or another determiner when plural count nouns name a definite or specific group; use no article when they name a general group.

  > Hal is feeding *the horses* in the barn, and he has already fed *his cows.*
  >
  > *Horses* don't eat meat, and neither do *cows.*

---

**The Indefinite Article (*a, an*)**

■ Use *a* or *an* with a nonspecific, singular count noun when it is not known to the reader or to the writer.

> Jay has *an* antique car. [The car's identity is unknown to the reader.]
>
> I saw *a* dog in my backyard this morning. [The dog's identity is unknown to the writer.]

■ Use *a* or *an* when the noun is first used; use *the* when it is repeated.

> I saw *a* car that I would love to buy. *The* car was red with tan seats.

■ Use *some* or no article with general noncount or plural nouns.

> I am going to buy a̶ furniture for my apartment.
>
> I am going to buy ⟨some⟩ a̶ furniture for my apartment.

---

## 1b Pronouns

A **pronoun** is a word that takes the place of a noun. The noun that the pronoun is referring to is called the antecedent.

ANTECEDENT
(NOUN)                                                    PRONOUN

> *Nelson* gave the book to Miranda before *he* went to Texas. [*He* takes the place of the antecedent, *Nelson*.]

There are several different types of pronouns, and they perform a variety of different roles in a sentence.

### Personal Pronouns

**Personal pronouns** serve as subjects (see 2), objects (see 3a), or possessives (see 32). The personal pronoun form changes depending on how it's used.

▶ **Personal Pronouns** *at a Glance*

|  | SUBJECTIVE | | OBJECTIVE | | POSSESSIVE | |
|---|---|---|---|---|---|---|
|  | *Singular* | *Plural* | *Singular* | *Plural* | *Singular* | *Plural* |
| *First Person* | I | we | me | us | my/mine | our/ours |
| *Second Person* | you | you | you | you | your/yours | your/yours |
| *Third Person* | he | they | him | them | his | their/theirs |
|  | she |  | her |  | her/hers |  |
|  | it |  | it |  | its |  |

SUBJECTIVE
PRONOUN

*She* will run for president in the next election.

OBJECTIVE
PRONOUN

The catcher tossed the ball to *us*.

POSSESSIVE
PRONOUN

The couple at the bar gave each other *their* phone numbers.

## Indefinite Pronouns

**Indefinite pronouns** do not refer to a specific noun.

INDEFINITE PRONOUNS

| | | |
|---|---|---|
| all | everyone | no one |
| any | everything | nothing |
| anybody | few | one (of) |
| anyone | many | several |
| anything | much | some (of) |
| both | neither (of) | somebody |
| each (of) | nobody | someone |
| either (of) | none | something |
| everybody | | |

*Something* must be done about skyrocketing tuition costs.

## Relative Pronouns

**Relative pronouns** relate a group of descriptive words to a noun in a sentence.

RELATIVE PRONOUNS

| | | |
|---|---|---|
| that | which | whomever |
| what | who | whose |
| whatever | whom | |

DESCRIPTIVE WORD GROUP

*California, which* is experiencing a drought, has imposed tough water restrictions. [*Which* relates the descriptive word group to the noun *California*.]

## Interrogative Pronouns

**Interrogative pronouns** are used to introduce questions.

INTERROGATIVE PRONOUNS

| | |
|---|---|
| what | whom |
| which | whose |
| who | |

*What* is for dinner tonight?

**Demonstrative Pronouns**

**Demonstrative pronouns** are used to specify a particular noun.

DEMONSTRATIVE PRONOUNS

that          this
these         those

*This* building was constructed before *those* roads were paved.

**Reflexive and Intensive Pronouns**

Reflexive and intensive pronouns end with the suffix *-self* or *-selves*.

> **Reflexive and Intensive Pronouns** *at a Glance*
>
> |              | *Singular* | *Plural*    |
> | ------------ | ---------- | ----------- |
> | *First Person*  | myself     | ourselves   |
> | *Second Person* | yourself   | yourselves  |
> | *Third Person*  | himself    |             |
> |              | herself    |             |
> |              | itself     | themselves  |

**Reflexive pronouns** are used as objects when renaming nouns or pronouns that are subjects.

Juanita gave *herself* a raise.

**Intensive pronouns** are used to restate a noun or pronoun for emphasis or clarity.

The *bride* and *groom* made the wedding cake *themselves*. [*Themselves* clarifies the *bride* and *groom* as the makers of the cake.]

For details on using pronouns correctly, see 10, 11, and 12.

## 1c Verbs

**Verbs** are words that usually express action (*swim, eat, sleep*) or being (*is, become, seem, feel*) in a sentence.

**Action Verbs**

**Action verbs** are so named because they show action.

The street performer *sings* a different song each evening.

**Linking Verbs**

**Linking verbs** such as *is, become, seem,* and *feel* show a state of being by linking a noun with a word that renames or describes it.

Although the temperature *is* higher, the air *feels* cooler.

For more details on the way verbs are used in sentences, see 3. For more on using verbs correctly, see 8 and 9.

For details on using adjectives and adverbs correctly, see 13.

**Helping Verbs**

A few verbs accompany a main verb to add information about its action; they are called **helping** or **auxiliary verbs** (*have, must, can*).

I probably *am going* to France this summer. [main verb *going* + helping verb *am*]

## 1d Adjectives

An **adjective**'s job is to provide information about the person, place, object, or idea named by the noun or pronoun. Adjectives answer questions such as *Which one? What kind?* and *How many?* They may appear before or after the noun or pronoun they are describing.

The *small red* car was *expensive*.

## 1e Adverbs

An **adverb** describes a verb, an adjective, or another adverb by answering questions such as *How? When? Where? Why?* and *To what degree?* Adverbs often end in *-ly*, and they may appear before or after the word they are describing.

The *very* tall tree stood *majestically* above the rest. [*Very* describes how *tall* the tree is; *majestically* describes how the tree *stood*.]

## 1f Prepositions

**Prepositions** are small but important words that connect a noun or pronoun to another part of a sentence.

COMMON PREPOSITIONS

| | | | | |
|---|---|---|---|---|
| about | before | except | of | to |
| above | behind | for | off | toward |
| across | below | from | on | under |
| after | beneath | in | out | until |
| against | beside | inside | outside | up |
| along | between | into | over | upon |
| among | by | like | past | with |
| around | down | near | since | within |
| at | during | next to | through | without |

The entire word group that begins with a preposition and ends with a noun is called a **prepositional phrase**. The noun in the prepositional phrase is called the **object** of the preposition.

PREPOSITIONAL PHRASE

The museum allows visitors to sleep *under* the blue *whale*.

## 1g Conjunctions

**Conjunctions** are used to connect related words or word groups in a sentence. The two main types of conjunctions are coordinating and subordinating.

## Guidelines for Multilingual Writers
How Do I Use Prepositions of Location and Time
(*in, on, at*)?

**Location Expressions**

> Elaine lives *in* Manhattan *at* a swanky address *on* Fifth Avenue.

- *In* means "within" or "inside of" a place, including geographical areas, such as cities, states, countries, and continents.

> I packed my books *in* my backpack and left to visit my cousins *in* Canada.

- Where *in* emphasizes *location* only, *at* is often used to refer to a place when a specific *activity* is implied: *at the store* (to shop), *at the office* (to work), *at the theater* (to see a play), and so on.

> Angelo left his bicycle *in* the bike rack while he was *at* school.

- *On* means "on the surface of" or "on top of" something and is used with floors of buildings and planets. It is also used to indicate a location *beside* a lake, river, ocean, or other body of water.

> The service department is *on* the fourth floor.

> We have a cabin *on* Lake Michigan.

- *In, on,* and *at* can all be used in addresses. *In* is used to identify a general location, such as a city or neighborhood. *On* is used to identify a specific street. *At* is used to give an exact address.

> We live *in* Boston *on* Medway Street.

> We live *at* 20 Medway Street.

- *In* and *at* can both be used with the verb *arrive*. *In* indicates a large place, such as a city, state, country, or continent. *At* indicates a smaller place, such as a specific building or address. (*To* is never used with *arrive*.)

> Alanya arrived *in* Alaska yesterday; Sanjei will arrive *at* the airport soon.

**Time Expressions**

- *In* indicates the span of time during which something occurs or a time in the future; it is also used in the expressions *in a minute* (meaning "shortly") and *in time* (meaning "soon enough" or "without a moment to spare"). *In* is also used with seasons, months, and periods of the day.

> He needs to read this book *in* the next three days. [During the next three days]

> I'll meet you *in* the morning *in* two weeks. [Two weeks from now]

*(continued)*

- *On* is used with the days of the week, with the word *weekend*, and in the expression *on time* (meaning "punctually").

  Let's have lunch *on* Friday.

- *At* is used in reference to a specific time on the clock as well as a specific time of the day (*at night, at dawn, at twilight*).

  We'll meet again next Monday *at* 2:15 p.m.

---

 **Guidelines for Multilingual Writers**
What Are Two-Word Verbs?

Many two-word verbs end with a **particle,** a word that can be used as a preposition on its own but becomes part of a **phrasal verb.** Once the particle is added, the verb takes on a new idiomatic meaning that must be learned.

break up: to separate; to end a romantic relationship; to laugh

decide on: to select or to judge a person or thing

eat at: to worry or disturb a person

feel for [a person]: to sympathize with another's unhappiness

see to: to take care of a person or situation

take in [a person]: to house a person; to trick by gaining a person's trust

---

### Coordinating Conjunctions

**Coordinating conjunctions** join elements with equal or near-equal importance. There are seven coordinating conjunctions (shown below), which can be remembered by using the acronym *FANBOYS*.

COORDINATING CONJUNCTIONS

for    and    nor    but    or    yet    so

The suspect has brown hair *and* blue eyes.

Several people saw the crime, *but* only one witness spoke to police.

### Subordinating Conjunctions

**Subordinating conjunctions** join elements that are unequal in importance. A subordinating conjunction can make one clause in a sentence have less emphasis than another.

For more on using coordinating and subordinating conjunctions, see 19.

COMMON SUBORDINATING CONJUNCTIONS

| | | | |
|---|---|---|---|
| after | before | since | until |
| although | even though | so | when |
| as | how | so that | whenever |
| as if | if | than | where |
| as soon as | in order that | that | wherever |
| as though | once | though | while |
| because | rather than | unless | why |

SUBORDINATE CLAUSE      MAIN CLAUSE

*Even though* tickets wouldn't go on sale until Monday, fans started lining

up on Saturday afternoon. [*Even though* is the subordinating conjunction.]

## 1h Interjections

**Interjections** express emotion or surprise and are usually set off from a sentence with a comma or an exclamation point.

*Wow*! These pictures of Pluto are astonishing!

---

## EXERCISE 1–1 Identifying Parts of Speech

Identify the part of speech of each underlined word or word group in the following sentences. Answers for the lettered sentences appear at the end of the Handbook. Example:

         *noun verb*          *adjective*        *preposition*
Bottled water is one of the most popular drinks sold in the United States.

a. Bottled water has been available around the world for centuries.

b. It became very common during the late twentieth century.

c. Americans drink more bottled water than people in other countries do.

d. Interestingly, American tap water is cleaner than water in most parts of the world.

e. Bottled water companies usually label their products spring water, purified water, or mineral water.

1. Liza hopes to stop the school from selling bottled water on campus.

2. She argues that bottled water is expensive and bad for the environment.

3. It wastes tons of plastic every year, and students spend thousands of dollars on a product that should be free.

4. But plenty of students enjoy the convenience of bottled water.

5. They don't want to bring their own reusable bottles from home.

# 2 | Subjects

The **subject** of a sentence or clause identifies the main person, place, object, situation, or idea performing an action or being discussed. Subjects are always nouns or pronouns.

> *Honesty* is the best policy.

> *She* walks to work every day.

## 2a Singular and Plural Subjects

Subjects may be singular, meaning only one, or plural, meaning more than one.

> The tennis *ball* went over the fence.

> Three *dogs* chased the ball.

> SUBJECT
> *Louis* and *Jen* tried to find the ball.

## 2b Simple and Complete Subjects

The **simple subject** consists only of the noun(s) or pronoun(s) that is performing the action or being discussed. The **complete subject** consists of the simple subject and all the modifiers that surround it.

> COMPLETE SUBJECT
> College *students* who balance their work, school, and family are more likely to succeed at all three. [*Students* is the simple subject.]

## 2c Finding the Subject in a Sentence

To find the subject of a sentence, locate the first noun or pronoun in the sentence (see 1a and 1b).

> *Meg* began writing her paper.

However, the first noun or pronoun is not always the subject of a sentence. Sometimes nouns performing other functions come before the subject. Be sure the noun or pronoun is not part of a prepositional phrase (see 1f). It can help to find prepositions and strike out prepositional phrases.

> PREP       NOUN (NOT SUBJ)
> ~~After the holiday~~, when classes resumed, Meg began writing her paper.

Also make sure the noun is not part of a word group beginning with a subordinating conjunction (see 1g). Look for subordinating conjunctions and cross out the word groups that are connected to them.

SUBORD   NOUN
CONJ   (NOT SUBJ)      SUBJECT
~~After the holiday,~~ *~~when classes~~* ~~resumed,~~ *Meg* began writing her paper.

In imperative sentences (sentences that make a request or give a command), the understood subject *you* is often left out.

> **Do not text and drive.** [The subject *you* is understood and is not included in the sentence.]

---

## EXERCISE 2–1  Identifying Subjects

Circle the simple subject and underline the complete subject in each of the following sentences. Answers for the lettered sentences appear at the end of the Handbook. Example:

> The popular children's show (*Sesame Street*) first aired on public television in 1969.

a. Before that time, television shows were made for adults or entire families.

b. Ernie and Bert became familiar characters for all preschoolers.

c. The show inspired countless future programs for children.

d. Although *Sesame Street* was an educational program, it provided entertainment for kids as well.

e. Over 74 million Americans have watched the show since it began.

1. Mika and I spent this morning reviewing our notes for the test.

2. In the bottom drawer, you can find some extra notebooks.

3. Buildings that meet the new flood requirements will not need to have additional insurance.

4. Customers who bring their own bags to the store earn reward points.

5. After watching all the Harry Potter movies in one weekend, Sadie vowed to read all the books again.

---

# 3 | Verbs, Objects, and Complements

**Verbs** provide information about the subject's action or state of being. **Action verbs** show action (*swim, eat, sleep*), and **linking verbs** (*is, become, seem, feel*) link the subject of a sentence with a word that renames or describes it. A few verbs accompany a main verb to add information about time or possibility; they are called **helping** or **auxiliary verbs** (*have, must, can*).

More information about using verbs correctly can be found in 8, 9, and 21.

## 3a　Action Verbs and Objects

Most action verbs (AV) can be followed by one or more objects. A **direct object** (DO) is the target of the verb's action. It usually answers the question *What?* or *Who?*

> AV　　　　　DO
> Kevin *drank* three *sodas* at the movies. [The direct object, *sodas*, answers the question "What did Kevin drink?"]

An **indirect object** (IO) is the recipient of the verb's action. It usually answers the question *For what?* or *For whom?*

> AV　　IO　　　DO
> Kevin *bought me* some *popcorn* at the movies. [The direct object, *popcorn*, answers the question "What did Kevin buy?"; the indirect object, *me*, answers the question "For whom did Kevin buy some popcorn?"]

Some verbs, known as **transitive verbs**, require an object in order to make their meaning clear.

> AV　　　　DO
> Elana *fixed* the flat *tire*. [The direct object, *tire*, answers the question "What did Elana fix?" Without the direct object and its modifiers (*the flat*), the sentence ("Elana fixed.") would not make sense.]

---

###  Guidelines for Multilingual Writers
Do I Use the Preposition *to* or *for* with Indirect Objects?

These sentences mean the same thing:

> I sent the president a letter.
>
> I sent a letter to the president.

In the first sentence, *the president* is the **indirect object**: he or she receives the direct object (*a letter*), which was acted on (*sent*) by the subject of the sentence (*I*). In the second sentence, the same idea is expressed using a **prepositional phrase** beginning with *to*.

- Some verbs can use either an indirect object or the preposition *to*: *give, send, lend, offer, owe, pay, sell, show, teach, tell*. Some verbs can use an indirect object or the preposition *for*: *bake, build, buy, cook, find, get, make*.

> I paid *the travel agent* one hundred dollars.
>
> I paid one hundred dollars *to the travel agent*.
>
> Margarita cooked *her family* some chicken.
>
> Margarita cooked some chicken *for her family*.

- Some verbs cannot have an indirect object; they must use a preposition. The following verbs must use the preposition *to*: *describe, demonstrate, explain, introduce,* and *suggest.*

  Please explain ~~me indirect objects~~ *to me.*

- The following verbs must use the preposition *for*: *answer* and *prepare.*

  He prepared ~~me the punch~~ *for me.*

- Some verbs must have an indirect object; they cannot use a preposition. The following verbs must have an indirect object: *ask* and *cost.*

  Sasha asked *her* a question ~~to her.~~

## 3b  Linking Verbs and Complements

A **linking verb** (LV) shows what the subject of a sentence *is* or *is like.* The linking verb connects the subject with its **subject complement** (SC)—a noun, a pronoun, or an adjective.

> ## Common Linking Verbs *at a Glance*
>
> Some linking verbs tell what a noun is, was, or will be.
>
> > *be, become, remain:* I *remain* optimistic.
> > *grow:* The sky is *growing* dark.
> > *make:* One plus two *makes* three.
> > *prove:* His warning *proved* accurate.
> > *turn:* The weather *turned* cold.
>
> Some linking verbs tell what a noun might be.
>
> > *appear, seem, look:* The child *looks* cold.
>
> Most verbs of the senses can operate as linking verbs.
>
> > *feel, smell, sound, taste:* The smoothie *tastes* sweet.

LV   SC
Julia will *make* a good *doctor.* [The subject complement, *doctor,* is a noun renaming the subject, *Julia.*]

LV   SC
Jorge *is* not the *one.* [The subject complement, *one,* is a pronoun renaming the subject, *Jorge.*]

LV   SC
London weather *seems foggy.* [The subject complement, *foggy,* is an adjective describing the subject, *weather.*]

A verb may be a linking verb in some sentences and a transitive verb in others. If you focus on what the verb means, you can usually tell how it is functioning.

> LV  SC
> I often *grow sleepy* after lunch. [The verb *grow* is a linking verb (meaning "become") because it is followed by a subject complement, *sleepy*.]

> AV  DO
> I often *grow tomatoes* in my garden. [The verb *grow* is a transitive verb (meaning "raise") because it is followed by a direct object, *tomatoes*.]

Object complements are similar to subject complements in that they rename a noun, in this case the object of a verb or preposition. But no linking verb is required with object complements.

> DO  OC
> The judges rated *Hugo* the best *skater*. [The object complement, *skater*, renames the direct object, *Hugo*.]

## 3c  Helping Verbs

Verbs such as *have, must,* and *can* that accompany a main verb to add information about its action are called **helping** or **auxiliary verbs**. Adding a helping or auxiliary verb to a main verb allows you to express a wide variety of tenses and moods. (See 8.) The parts of this combination, called a **verb phrase,** need not appear together and may be separated by other words.

> HELPING  HELPING  MAIN
> VERB  VERB  VERB
> You *should* not *have shot* that pigeon. [*Should* and *have* add information about the main verb *shot*.]

---

> ## Helping Verbs *at a Glance*
>
> Of the twenty-three helping verbs, fourteen can also act as main verbs that identify the central action.
>
> be, is, am, are, was, were, being, been
> do, does, did
> have, has, had
>
> The other nine act only as helping verbs, never as main verbs. As modals, they show actions that are possible, doubtful, necessary, required, and so on.
>
> can, could, should, would, may, might, must, shall, will

## EXERCISE 3–1 Identifying Verbs, Objects, and Complements

Label the underlined word or word group in the following sentences as action verb (AV), linking verb (LV), helping verb (HV), direct object (DO), indirect object (IO), or subject complement (SC). Answers for the lettered sentences appear at the end of the Handbook. Example:

>                                               HV    MV
> Many science and technology inventions are inspired by nature.

a. An entrepreneur named Percy Shaw invented reflectors for road signs after seeing a cat's eyes glowing in his headlights on a foggy night.

b. An inventor named George de Mestral noticed burrs in his dog's fur; he then gave the world Velcro.

c. Many scientists are eager to discover new products.

d. Accidents have also inspired inventions.

e. A machine giving off microwave particles melted a chocolate bar, leading to the invention of the microwave oven.

1. Soda and other sugary beverages are at least partly responsible for increasing obesity rates in children.

2. Some schools sell children soft drinks, which nutritionists say is a bad idea.

3. Milk is more important than sugary drinks for developing bones.

4. Some cities and states have passed laws to tax sodas.

5. Others want extra-large sodas to be completely banned.

## Learning by Doing 🔯 Finding Subjects and Verbs

Being able to identify subjects and verbs in your own writing will make it much easier to find and fix common grammatical problems such as subject-verb agreement errors. Working from a draft of a current or previous assignment, underline all the main subjects you can find, and double underline all the main verbs you can find. Draw a line connecting the subject-verb pairs. Do some subjects have more than one verb? Do some verbs have more than one subject? Do some sentences have multiple subject-verb pairs? All these situations are acceptable if the correct grammar and punctuation are used.

# 4 | Clauses and Phrases

Clauses and phrases are word groups that have a specific function in a sentence. Clauses have both a subject and a verb; phrases do not.

## 4a Clauses

Clauses can be independent or dependent (subordinate). An **independent clause** contains a subject and a verb, expresses a complete thought, and can stand alone as a complete sentence. Independent clauses are often referred to as the **main clause** in a sentence.

MAIN CLAUSE

*Stevie Ray Vaughan was inducted* into the Rock and Roll Hall of Fame in 2015. [*Stevie Ray Vaughan* is the subject of the clause; *was inducted* is the verb.]

A **subordinate clause** looks very similar to an independent clause, with a subject, a verb, and a complete thought, but it cannot stand alone as a sentence because it opens with a **subordinating conjunction**.

SUBORDINATE CLAUSE

*Although* he died in 1995

A subordinate clause may be joined to an independent clause for grammatical correctness.

SUBORDINATE CLAUSE          MAIN CLAUSE

*Although he died* in 1995, *Stevie Ray Vaughan was inducted* into the Rock

and Roll Hall of Fame in 2015. [Note that each clause in this sentence includes a subject and a verb.]

## 4b Phrases

Phrases are groups of related words that do not contain a subject and a verb.

### Prepositional Phrases

A word group that begins with a preposition and ends with a noun is called a **prepositional phrase.** The noun in the prepositional phrase is the object of the preposition. Prepositional phrases can modify nouns or verbs.

PREPOSITIONAL PHRASE

The fox ran *into the woods*. [The prepositional phrase *into the woods* modifies the verb *ran* by describing where the fox ran to.]

PREPOSITIONAL PHRASE

The plants *on the balcony* need water. [The prepositional phrase *on the balcony* describes which plants need water.]

### Verbal Phrases

**Verbals** look like verbs, but they do not function as verbs in a sentence. Verbals include infinitives (*to* + verb), present participles (verb form ending in *-ing*), and past participles (verb form usually ending in *-ed*). (For more on participles, see 8.)

| INFINITIVE | PRESENT PARTICIPLE | PAST PARTICIPLE |
|---|---|---|
| to walk | walking | walked |
| to look | looking | looked |
| to drive | driving | drove |

Verbals can be used on their own or in **verbal phrases,** which consist of the verbal plus any related words. Both verbals and verbal phrases can act as nouns, adjectives, or adverbs.

VERBAL PHRASE AS ADVERB

The team worked nights to avoid the scorching sun. [The verbal phrase *to avoid the scorching sun* modifies the verb *worked*. The verbal is the infinitive *to avoid*.]

VERBAL PHRASE AS NOUN/SUBJECT

Bicycling to work is my favorite way to exercise and help the environment. [The verbal phrase *Bicycling to work* is the subject of the sentence. The verbal is the present participle *bicycling*.]

VERBAL PHRASE AS ADJECTIVE

The letter, signed by Halley's attorney, will be on your desk in the morning. [The verbal phrase *signed by Halley's attorney* modifies the noun *letter*. The verbal is the past participle *signed*.]

### Appositive Phrases

An **appositive** adds information to a noun or pronoun by identifying it in a different way. An appositive can be a single word or a group of words, sometimes called an **appositive phrase**.

APPOSITIVE

My dog, Laika, destroyed the library book.

APPOSITIVE PHRASE

My dog, a Portuguese water dog, is a strong swimmer.

### Absolute Phrases

An **absolute phrase** is an expression, usually a noun followed by a participle, that modifies an entire clause or sentence and can appear anywhere in the sentence.

ABSOLUTE PHRASE

The stallion pawed the ground, chestnut mane and tail swirling in the wind.

## EXERCISE 4–1 Identifying Phrases and Clauses

Label each underlined word group in the following sentences as main clause, subordinate clause, prepositional phrase, verbal phrase, appositive phrase, or absolute phrase. Answers for the lettered sentences appear at the end of the Handbook. Example:

> *subordinate clause*                    *main clause*
> When the winner was announced, everybody cheered.

a. Spending the night in an ice hotel is on my bucket list.
b. I will do well on the test because I studied for three hours.
c. The car, a 1957 Chevy, gleamed like it just came off the assembly line.
d. After searching all morning, we gave up on finding the lost earring.
e. We exited the house hurriedly, dinner still steaming on the table.

1. The Inca site of Machu Picchu is undergoing restoration.
2. The historic city is situated over 7,000 feet above sea level, its terraced fields reaching as high as the clouds.
3. Built by the Incas around 1450, Machu Picchu existed unknown to outsiders for centuries.
4. American Hiram Bingham, who came upon the site in the early twentieth century, embellished the story of his discovery.
5. The city, a UNESCO World Heritage Site, has been open to tourists since 1911.

# 5 | Sentence Structures

Sentences contain familiar patterns of syntax, or word order, that allow us to make sense of them. The main elements of a sentence include subject, verb, object, and complement.

- The **subject** (S) identifies some person, place, object, situation, or idea.
- The **verb** (V) may be an action verb or a linking verb. **Action verbs** (AV) express action; **linking verbs** (LV) express a state of being. **Helping verbs** (HV) accompany the main verb to indicate tense. The verb plus its surrounding objects, complements, and other modifiers is referred to as the **predicate.**
- An **object** may be either direct or indirect. A **direct object** (DO) is the target of the verb's action; an **indirect object** (IO) is the recipient of the verb's action.

■ A **complement** renames or describes a noun. **Subject complements** (SC) rename or describe the subject; **object complements** (OC) rename or describe an object.

## 5a Basic Patterns

All sentences consist of at least one main clause, which includes a subject and a verb.

    S    V
**Alyssa skates.**

Modifiers such as adjectives and adverbs can be added to describe the subject and verb.

    ADJ    S    V    ADV
**The young boy walked slowly.**

Sentences with action verbs often provide more information by including an object.

    S    AV    DO
**Tyler ate a salad.**

    S    AV    IO    DO
**Rosario gave me ten dollars.**

Sentences with linking verbs provide more information by including a complement, which may be either an adjective or a noun.

    S    LV    SC
**Chase is tired.**

    S    LV    SC
**Chase is a golden retriever.**

A sentence with only one clause (a main clause) is called a **simple sentence**. It may contain modifiers, objects, complements, and phrases in addition to the subject and verb.

    S    V    DO
**Even amateur stargazers can locate the Big Dipper in the night sky.**

Like clauses, simple sentences may contain more than one subject, which is called a **compound subject**.

COMPOUND SUBJECT
**Frankie and Bruno played baseball.**

Clauses and simple sentences may also contain more than one verb, called a **compound verb**.

COMPOUND VERB
**Sarah and Tomas sing, act, and dance.**

## 5b Longer Sentences

Clauses may be combined to form longer, more elaborate sentences. A **compound sentence** consists of two or more main clauses joined by a coordinating conjunction such as *and* or *but,* by a semicolon, or by a semicolon followed by a transition word such as *however* or *nevertheless*.

> MAIN CLAUSE     MAIN CLAUSE
> I would like to accompany you, but I can't.

> MAIN CLAUSE     MAIN CLAUSE
> My car broke down; therefore, I missed the first day of class.

A **complex sentence** has one main clause and one or more subordinate clauses.

> MAIN CLAUSE   SUBORD CLAUSE
> I will be at the airport when you arrive.

A **compound-complex sentence** combines a compound sentence (two or more main clauses) and a complex sentence (at least one subordinate clause).

> MAIN CLAUSE   SUBORD CLAUSE   MAIN CLAUSE
> Nobody saw the accident, and when the police arrived, the driver had
>
> already left the scene.

For help with combining clauses correctly, see 19.

## EXERCISE 5–1 Identifying Sentence Types

Identify each sentence below as simple, compound, complex, or compound-complex. Answers for the lettered sentences appear at the end of the Handbook. Example:

> Although Jenna is not superstitious, she will not stay on the thirteenth floor of a hotel. *complex*

a. Manga is a style of Japanese comic book that caught on in the United States in the 1990s.

b. This trunk contains all our old family photos; if it gets destroyed, we would have no way to replace them.

c. Carlo visited Jan's fruit stand at the farmers' market, and he mentioned my name.

d. I walked to the station, rode the train for an hour, and took a bus to the other side of town.

e. Ben and Jerry created a successful ice cream company.

1. After the Soviet Union collapsed in 1989, many eastern European countries gained independence.

2. Russia and the United States have never fought directly against each other in a war.

3. For decades, the two countries have had differing viewpoints and have supported opposing sides in smaller wars.

4. The two countries continue to disagree on many global issues, and they accuse each other of inappropriate actions.

5. Even though they rarely see eye-to-eye, the Russians and the Americans have worked together at important times, and they must strive to find more common ground in the future.

# 39

# Grammatical Sentences

6 | **Sentence Fragments**   752

7 | **Comma Splices and Fused Sentences**   755

8 | **Verb Form, Tense, and Mood**   758

9 | **Subject-Verb Agreement**   771

10 | **Pronoun Case**   775

11 | **Pronoun Reference**   779

12 | **Pronoun-Antecedent Agreement**   782

13 | **Adjectives and Adverbs**   784

14 | **Shifts**   789

## 6 | Sentence Fragments

A **sentence** is a word group that includes both a subject and a verb and can stand alone (see 5a).

A **subject** is the part of a sentence that names something—a person, an object, an idea, a situation—about which the verb in the predicate makes an assertion (see 2).

A **verb** is a word that shows action or a state of being (see 1c and 3).

Unlike a complete sentence, a **fragment** is partial or incomplete. It may lack a subject (naming someone or something), a verb (making an assertion about the subject), or both. A fragment also may otherwise fail to express a complete thought. Unless you add what's missing or reword what's incomplete, a fragment cannot stand alone as a sentence. Even so, we all use fragments in everyday speech, where their context and delivery make them understandable and therefore acceptable.

> That bicycle over there.
>
> Good job.
>
> Not if I can help it.

In writing, fragments like these fail to communicate complete, coherent ideas. Notice how much more effective they are as complete sentences.

> I'd like to buy that bicycle over there.
>
> You did a good job sanding the floor.
>
> Nobody will steal my seat if I can help it.

Some writers use fragments on purpose. Advertisers are fond of short, emphatic fragments that command attention, like quick jabs to the head.

For seafood lovers. Every Tuesday night. All you can eat.

Those who text-message or tweet compress what they write because time and space are limited. They rely on the recipient to fill in the gaps.

Thru with lab. CU @ 8. Pizza?

In college writing, though, it is good practice to express your ideas in complete sentences.

## 6a If a fragment is a phrase, link it to a nearby sentence, or make it a complete sentence.

You have two choices for revising a fragment if it is a phrase: (1) link it to an adjoining sentence, using punctuation such as a comma or a colon, or (2) add a missing subject or verb to make it a complete sentence.

> Malcolm has two goals/ Wealth and power. [The phrase *Wealth and power* has no verb; a colon links it to *goals*.] — *: wealth*

A **phrase** consists of two or more related words that work together but may lack a subject, a verb, or both (see 4b).

> Al ends his stories as he mixes his martinis/ With a twist. [The prepositional phrase *With a twist* has no subject or verb; a comma links it to the main clause.] — *, with*

> To stamp out the union/ That was the bosses' plan. [The infinitive phrase *To stamp out the union* has no main verb or subject; it becomes the sentence subject.]

> The students taking the final exam in the auditorium. [The helping verb *were* completes the verb and makes a sentence.] — *were*

## 6b If a fragment is a subordinate clause, link it to a nearby sentence, or drop the subordinating conjunction.

Some fragments are missing neither subject nor verb. Instead, they are subordinate clauses, unable to express complete thoughts unless linked with main clauses. When you find a subordinating conjunction at the start or in the middle of a word group, that word group may be a subordinate clause. You can (1) combine the fragment with a main clause (a complete sentence) nearby, or (2) make the subordinate clause into a complete sentence by dropping the subordinating conjunction.

A **subordinating conjunction** is a word (such as *because, although, if, when*) used to make one clause dependent on, or subordinate to, another (see 19d–19f.)

> The new law will help create jobs/ If it passes. — *, if*

> Because Jay is an avid skier/ He loves winter in the mountains. — *, he*

## 6c If a fragment has a participle but no other verb, change the participle to a main verb, or link the fragment to a nearby sentence.

A present participle (the *-ing* form of the verb) can serve as the main verb in a sentence only with a form of *be* ("Sally *is working* harder than usual"). A participle alone, used as a main verb, results in a fragment.

> , having
> Jon was used to the pressure of deadlines. ~~Having~~ worked the night shift at the daily newspaper. [The fragment is combined with an adjoining sentence.]

> He had
> Jon was used to the pressure of deadlines. ~~Having~~ worked the night shift at the daily newspaper. [Another form of the verb is used.]

A **compound verb** consists of two or more verbs linked by a conjunction (see 5a).

## 6d If a fragment is part of a compound verb, add it to the sentence with the subject and the rest of the predicate.

> and
> In spite of a pulled muscle, Jeremy ran the race. ~~And~~ won.

### EXERCISE 6–1 Eliminating Fragments

Eliminate any fragments in the following examples. Some sentences may be correct. Possible revisions for the lettered sentences appear at the end of the Handbook. Example:

> and
> Bryan hates parsnips. ~~And~~ loathes squash.

a. Michael had a beautiful Southern accent. Having lived many years in Georgia.

b. Pat and Chris are determined to marry each other. Even if their families do not approve.

c. Jack seemed well qualified for a career in the air force. Except for his tendency to get airsick.

d. Lisa advocated sleeping no more than four hours a night. Until she started nodding off through her classes.

e. They met. They talked. They fought. They reached agreement.

1. Being the first person in his family ever to attend college. Alex is determined to succeed.

2. Does our society rob children of their childhood? By making them aware too soon of adult ills?

3. Richard III supposedly had the young princes murdered. No one has ever found out what really happened to them.

4. For democracy to function, two elements are crucial. An educated populace and a collective belief in people's ability to chart their own course.

5. You must take his stories as others do. With a grain of salt.

---

## EXERCISE 6–2 Eliminating Fragments

Rewrite the following paragraph, eliminating all fragments. Explain why you made each change. Example:

> *and*
> Many people exercise to change their body image/ ~~And~~ may become obsessed with their looks. [The second word group is a fragment because it has no subject. The revised sentence links the fragment to the rest of the sentence.]

Some people assume that only women are overly concerned with body image. However, men often share this concern. While women tend to exercise vigorously to stay slender, men usually lift weights to "bulk up." Because of their desire to look masculine. Both are trying to achieve the "ideal" body form. The muscular male and the slim female. Sometimes working out begins to interfere with other aspects of life. Such as sleeping, eating regularly, or going to school or work. These are warning signs. Of too much emphasis on physical appearance. Preoccupation with body image may turn a healthy lifestyle into an unhealthy obsession. Many people believe that looking attractive will bring them happiness. Unfortunately, when they become compulsive. Beautiful people are not always happy.

---

# 7 | Comma Splices and Fused Sentences

Splice two ropes, and you join them into one. Splice two main clauses by putting only a comma between them, however, and you get a faulty construction called a **comma splice.** Here are two perfectly good main clauses, each separate, each able to stand on its own as a sentence:

> The detective wriggled on his belly toward the campfire. The drunken smugglers didn't notice him.

Splicing those sentences with a comma makes for difficult reading.

> COMMA SPLICE    The detective wriggled on his belly toward the campfire, the drunken smugglers didn't notice him.

Even more confusing than a comma splice is a **fused sentence**: two main clauses joined without any punctuation.

> FUSED SENTENCE    The detective wriggled on his belly toward the campfire the drunken smugglers didn't notice him.

A **main clause** is a group of words that has both a subject and a verb and can stand alone as a complete sentence (see 4a).

Lacking clues from the writer, a reader cannot tell where to pause. To understand the sentence, he or she must halt and reread.

The next two pages show five easy ways to eliminate both comma splices and fused sentences, also called **run-ons.** Your choice depends on the length and complexity of your main clauses and the effect you desire.

## 7a Write separate complete sentences to correct a comma splice or a fused sentence.

Freud has been called an enemy of sexual repression, *the* truth is that he is not a friend of free love.

> .The

## 7b Use a comma and a coordinating conjunction to correct a comma splice or a fused sentence.

If both clauses are of roughly equal weight, you can use a comma to link them — as long as you add a coordinating conjunction after the comma.

> and

Hurricane winds hit ninety miles an hour, they tore the roof from every house on Paradise Drive.

## 7c Use a semicolon or a colon to correct a comma splice or a fused sentence.

A semicolon can connect two closely related thoughts, emphasizing each one.

> ;

Hurricane winds hit ninety miles an hour, they tore the roof from every house on Paradise Drive.

If the second thought illustrates or explains the first, add it with a colon.

> :

The hurricane caused extensive damage, it tore the roof from every house on Paradise Drive.

## 7d Use subordination to correct a comma splice or a fused sentence.

If one main clause is more important than the other or you want to give it more importance, make the less important one subordinate by adding a subordinating conjunction. In effect, you show your reader how one idea relates to another: you decide which matters more.

> When

~~Hurricane~~ winds hit ninety miles an hour, they tore the roof from every house on Paradise Drive.

> , which

Hurricane winds ~~hit ninety miles an hour~~ they tore the roof from every

> ,hit ninety miles an hour.

house on Paradise Drive,

---

*Side notes:*

A **sentence** is a word group that includes both a subject and a predicate and can stand alone (see 5a).

**Coordinating conjunctions** join elements with equal or near-equal importance (see 1g and 19a–19c).

A **main clause** is a group of words that has both a subject and a verb and can stand alone as a complete sentence (see 4a).

For advice on subordination, see 19d–19f. For a list of subordinating conjunctions, see p. 739.

## 7e Use a conjunctive adverb with a semicolon and a comma to correct a comma splice or a fused sentence.

If you want to cram more than one clause into a sentence, you may join two clauses with a **conjunctive adverb.** Conjunctive adverbs show relationships such as addition (*also, besides*), comparison (*likewise, similarly*), contrast (*instead, however*), emphasis (*namely, certainly*), cause and effect (*thus, therefore*), or time (*finally, subsequently*). These transitional words and phrases can be a useful way of linking clauses — but only with the right punctuation.

> Freud has been called an enemy of sexual repression ; however , the truth is that he is not a friend of free love.

A writer might consider a comma plus the conjunctive adverb *however* enough to combine the two main clauses, but that glue won't hold. Stronger binding — the semicolon along with a comma — is required.

For a list of conjunctive adverbs, see p. 809.

---

### EXERCISE 7-1 Revising Comma Splices and Fused Sentences

In the following examples, correct each comma splice or fused sentence in two ways, and decide which way works better. Be creative: don't correct all the same way. Some may be correct as written. Possible revisions for the lettered sentences appear at the end of the Handbook. Example:

> Comic book writer Stan Lee created famous characters such as
> Hulk. He
> Spider-Man and the ~~Hulk, he~~ grew up in New York City.
>
> Lee, who grew up in New York City,
> Comic book writer Stan Lee created famous characters such as
> Hulk.
> Spider-Man and the ~~Hulk, he grew up in New York City.~~

a. Lee's comic book superheroes are ordinary people with flaws they also have extraordinary abilities.

b. Iron Man (Tony Stark) has a superpowered suit and the ability to fly, he is a heavy drinker and suffers from anxiety.

c. Teenaged nerd Peter Parker is another example he has spider-like abilities to spin webs and scale buildings.

d. Thor is a godlike superhero who comes to Earth with super strength and the ability to fly, his weakness is his fondness for humans.

e. Bruce Banner was a brilliant scientist who studied gamma radiation, an accident caused him to turn into a giant destructive hulk when he gets angry.

1. Other well-known superheroes include Superman and Batman, they originated in the 1930s.

2. Superman is the last survivor of the planet Krypton he has x-ray vision and super strength he is weakened by kryptonite.

3. Batman has no superhuman abilities, he fights crime using his ingenuity and his physical prowess.

4. Wonder Woman came along in 1941 she is a warrior princess based on the Amazons of Greek mythology.

5. Many superhero characters are making comebacks in high-budget films, they feature famous actors and impressive special effects.

---

### EXERCISE 7–2  Revising Comma Splices and Fused Sentences

Revise the following passage, using subordination, a conjunctive adverb, a semicolon, or a colon to correct each comma splice or fused sentence. You may also write separate complete sentences. Some sentences may be correct. Example:

> *because*
> English can be difficult to learn, it is full of expressions that don't mean what they literally say.

Have you ever wondered why you drive on parkways and park on driveways, that's about as logical as your nose running while your feet smell! When you think about it, these phrases don't make sense yet we tend to accept them without thinking about what they literally mean we simply take their intended meanings for granted. Think, however, how confusing they are for a person who is just learning the language. If, for example, you have just learned the verb *park,* you would logically assume that a parkway is where you should park your car, of course when most people see a parkway or a driveway they realize that braking on a parkway would be hazardous, while speeding through a driveway will not take them very far. However, our language is full of idiomatic expressions that may be difficult for a person from another language background to understand. Fortunately, there are plenty of questions to keep us *all* confused, such as why Americans commonly refer to going to work as "punching the clock."

---

# 8 | Verb Form, Tense, and Mood

For information on active versus passive voice in verbs, see 21.

A verb's form is the way it appears in order to demonstrate the way it is being used. Verb forms can change in order to show **tense,** which indicates the time that the action took place (last year, next month), and **mood,** which indicates the attitude about the thought being expressed (a command, a wish, a statement).

## 8a  Use the correct form of the verb.

Verbs can take one of five forms and stand alone or with helping verbs to indicate the full range of times when an action or a state of being does, did, might, or will occur.

- The **base** is the simple dictionary form of the verb (*go, sing, laugh*) that is used for the present tense for all but the third-person singular: *I/we/you/*

*they go, sing, laugh.* The base form preceded by *to* (*to go, to sing, to laugh*) is called the **infinitive.**

■ The **-s** form of the verb is the base form with an *-s* or *-es* ending (*goes, sings, laughs*). This form is used for the third-person present tense: *He/she/it goes, sings, laughs.*

■ The **past tense** signals completed action (*went, sang, laughed*). (See 8c.)

■ The **past participle** is combined with helping verbs to indicate action at various past or future times (*have gone, had sung, will have laughed*). (See 8e.) With forms of *be,* it makes the passive voice. (See 21.)

■ The **present participle,** the *-ing* form of the verb (*going, singing, laughing*), is used to make the progressive tenses. (See 8f and 8g.) It also can modify nouns and pronouns ("the *leaking* bottle") or, as a gerund, function as a noun ("*Sleeping all day* pleases me").

## 8b Use the simple present tense for actions that take place once, repeatedly, or continuously in the present.

The simple present tense is the infinitive form of a regular verb plus *-s* or *-es* for the third-person singular (used with *a singular noun* or *he, she,* or *it*).

I like, I watch        we like, we watch

you like, you watch     you like, you watch

he/she/it likes, he/she/it watches     they like, they watch

---

▶ **Verb Tenses** *at a Glance*

Note that these examples show first person only.

SIMPLE TENSES

| *Present* | *Past* | *Future* |
|---|---|---|
| I cook | I cooked | I will cook |
| I see | I saw | I will see |

PERFECT TENSES

| *Present perfect* | *Past perfect* | *Future perfect* |
|---|---|---|
| I have cooked | I had cooked | I will have cooked |
| I have seen | I had seen | I will have seen |

PROGRESSIVE TENSES

| *Present progressive* | *Past progressive* | *Future progressive* |
|---|---|---|
| I am cooking | I was cooking | I will be cooking |
| I am seeing | I was seeing | I will be seeing |
| *Present perfect progressive* | *Past perfect progressive* | *Future perfect progressive* |
| I have been cooking | I had been cooking | I will have been cooking |
| I have been seeing | I had been seeing | I will have been seeing |

The irregular verbs *be* and *have* are special cases for which you should learn the correct forms.

| | |
|---|---|
| I am, I have | we are, we have |
| you are, you have | you are, you have |
| he/she/it is, he/she/it has | they are, they have |

You can use the simple present tense for an action happening right now ("I *welcome* this news"), happening repeatedly in the present ("Judy *goes* to church every Sunday"), or ongoing in the present ("Wesley *likes* ice cream"). In some cases, if you want to ask a question, intensify the action, or form a negative, use the helping verb *do* or *does* before the main verb.

> I *do think* you should take the job. I *don't think* it will be difficult.

> *Does* Christos *want* it? *Do* you *want* it? *Doesn't* anyone *want* it?

You can use the simple present for future action: "Football *starts* Wednesday." With *before, after,* or *when,* use it to express a future meaning: "When the team bus *arrives,* the players will board." Use it also for a general or timeless truth, even if the rest of the sentence is in a different tense.

> Water *freezes* at 32 degrees.

## 8c Use the simple past tense for actions already completed.

Use the past tense for an action at a specific past time, whether stated or implied.

> Nicole *walked* to the theater yesterday.

Though speakers may not pronounce the *-d* or *-ed* ending, standard written English requires that you add it to regular past tense verbs.

>     *used*
> I ~~use~~ to wear weird clothes when I was a child.
>     ^

Most verbs in English are **regular verbs**: they form the past tense in a standard, predictable way. Regular verbs that end in *-e* add *-d* to the base form; those that do not end in *-e* add *-ed*.

> Akira *smiled* all night long.

> Jack *enjoyed* the party.

At least two hundred **irregular verbs** form the past tense in some way other than by adding *-d* or *-ed*.

>     *drove*
> Lauren ~~drived~~ home early.

Because irregular verbs do not follow a standard pattern when they take the past tense, the forms must be memorized.

Most irregular verbs, familiar to native English speakers, pose no problem. For more details on verbs that cause trouble when changing tense, see 8h (*be, have,* and *do*) and 8i (*lie/lay* and *sit/set*).

**Guidelines for Multilingual Writers**
When Do I Use the Past, Present, and Future Tenses of Verbs?

| DURATION OR TIME RELATIONSHIP | PAST TIME: *Yesterday, some time ago, long ago* | PRESENT TIME: *Right now, today, or at this moment* | FUTURE TIME: *Tomorrow, soon, or at some expected or possible moment* |
|---|---|---|---|
| ACTION OR STATE *OCCURS ONCE* | **PAST TENSE:** The team *played* the game last week. | **PRESENT TENSE:** The game *starts* now. | **FUTURE TENSE:** The bus *will arrive* at noon on Friday. **PRESENT TENSE:** The bus *arrives* after lunch. |
| ACTION OR STATE *OCCURS REPEATEDLY* | **PAST TENSE:** The team *played* every Monday of the summer. | **PRESENT TENSE:** The game *starts* on time. | **FUTURE TENSE:** The bus *will arrive* at noon on Fridays. **PRESENT TENSE:** The bus *arrives* at noon on Fridays. |
| ACTION OR STATE *OCCURS CONTINUOUSLY* | **PAST TENSE:** The team *played* their best all season. | **PRESENT TENSE:** The game always *ends* before dark. | **PRESENT TENSE:** The bus *will arrive* at noon from now on. |
| ACTION OR STATE *IS A GENERAL OR TIMELESS FACT* | | **PRESENT TENSE:** A good game *needs* action and suspense. | |
| ACTION OR STATE *IS COMPLETED BEFORE THE TIME OF ANOTHER ACTION* | **PAST PERFECT TENSE:** The team *had practiced* for only two weeks before they played their first game. | | **FUTURE PERFECT TENSE:** The bus *will have arrived* at six other fields before it reaches our stop. |
| ACTION OR STATE *WAS BEGUN IN THE PAST BUT IS STILL GOING ON* | | **PRESENT PERFECT TENSE:** The game *has provided* enjoyment every week. | |

## Past Tense of Common Irregular Verbs
### at a Glance

| BASE | PAST TENSE |
|---|---|
| be, am, is, are | was, were |
| begin | began |
| choose | chose |
| do | did |
| eat | ate |
| go | went |
| have | had |
| speak | spoke |

In the past tense, you can use the helping verb *did* (past tense of *do*) to ask a question or intensify the action. Use *did* (or *didn't*) with the base form of the main verb for both regular and irregular verbs.

| | | |
|---|---|---|
| I walked. | I did walk. | Why did I walk? |
| You watched. | You did watch. | What did you watch? |
| She jogged. | She did jog. | Where did she jog? |

## Guidelines for Multilingual Writers
### How Do I Form Negatives?

You can make a sentence negative by using ***not*** or another negative adverb such as *seldom, rarely, never, hardly, hardly ever,* or *almost never.*

- With ***not***: subject + helping verb + ***not*** + main verb

   Gina did *not* go to the concert.

   They will *not* call again.

- For questions: helping verb + *n't* (contraction for *not*) + subject + main verb

   *Didn't* [for *Did not*] Gina go to the concert?

   *Won't* [for *Will not*] they call again?

- With a negative adverb: subject + negative adverb + main verb *or* subject + helping verb + negative adverb + main verb

   My son *seldom* watches TV.

   Danh may *never* see them again.

- With a negative adverb at the beginning of a clause: negative adverb + helping verb + subject + verb

   *Not only* does Emma struggle with tennis, but she also struggles with golf.

   *Never* before have I been so happy.

*NOTE:* Don't pile up several negatives for intensity or emphasis in a sentence. Readers may consider double negatives (*not never, not hardly, wouldn't not*) sloppy repetition or assume that two negatives cancel each other out.

The students did not ~~never~~ <sup>ever</sup> arrive late.

The students ~~did not~~ never ~~arrive~~ <sup>arrived</sup> late.

**8d**   Use the simple future tense for actions that are expected to happen but have not happened yet.

Although the present tense can indicate future action ("We *go* on vacation next Monday"), most actions that have not yet taken place are expressed in the simple future tense, including promises and predictions.

> George *will arrive* in time for dinner.
>
> *Will* you please *show* him where to park?

To form the simple future tense, add *will* to the base form of the verb.

| | |
|---|---|
| I will climb | we will climb |
| you will climb | you will climb |
| he/she/it will climb | they will climb |

You can also use *shall* to inject a tone of determination ("We *shall overcome!*") or in polite questions ("*Shall* we dance?").

**8e**   Use the perfect tenses for actions completed at the time of another action.

The perfect tenses consist of the verb *have* plus the past participle.

For regular verbs, the past participle is the same as the past tense. For irregular verbs, the past participle follows no set pattern and must be memorized.

See 8h for details on the very irregular verbs *be, have,* and *do;* see 8i for details on the confusing verbs *lie/lay* and *sit/set.*

▶ **Past Tense and Past Participle** *at a Glance*

**REGULAR VERBS**

| *Base* | *Past Tense* | *Past Participle* |
|---|---|---|
| hatch | hatched | hatched |
| look | looked | looked |
| smile | smiled | smiled |

**IRREGULAR VERBS**

| *Base* | *Past Tense* | *Past Participle* |
|---|---|---|
| be, am, is, are | was, were | been |
| begin | began | begun |
| burst | burst | burst |
| choose | chose | chosen |
| do | did | done |
| eat | ate | eaten |
| go | went | gone |
| lay | laid | laid |
| lie | lay | lain |
| set | set | set |
| sit | sat | sat |
| speak | spoke | spoken |

In the perfect tenses, the tense of *have* indicates the tense of the whole verb phrase. The action of a **present perfect** verb was completed before the sentence is uttered. Its helping verb is in the present tense: *have* or *has.*

> I *have* never *visited* Spain, but I *have visited* Mexico.

> *Have* you *called* Mr. Grimaldi? Mr. Grimaldi *has called* for help.

You can use the present perfect tense for an action completed before some other action: "I *have washed* my hands of the whole affair, but I am watching from a distance." With *for* or *since*, it shows an action begun in the past and still going on: "Max *has worked* in this office for years."

The action of a **past perfect** verb was completed before some other action in the past. Its helping verb is in the past tense: *had.*

> The concert *had ended* by the time we found a parking space.

> *Had* you *wanted* to clean the house before your parents arrived?

In informal writing, the simple past may be used when the relationship between actions is made clear by *when, before, after,* or *until.*

> Observers *watched* the plane catch fire before it landed.

The action of a **future perfect** verb will be completed by some point (specified or implied) in the future. Its helping verb is in the future tense: *will have.*

> The builders *will have finished* the house by June.

> When you acquire the new dime, *will* you *have collected* every coin you want?

> The store *will* not *have closed* by the time we arrive.

## 8f Use the simple progressive tenses for actions in progress.

The progressive tenses consist of a form of *be* plus the present participle (the *-ing* form). The tense of *be* determines the tense of the whole verb phrase.

The **present progressive** expresses an action that began in the past and is taking place now. Its helping verb is in the present tense: *am, is,* or *are.*

> I *am thinking* of a country in Africa.

> *Is* Stefan *babysitting* while we *are visiting* her sister?

You can express future action with the present progressive of *go* plus an infinitive phrase.

> I am *going to sign up* for the CPR class.

The **past progressive** expresses an action that took place continuously at some time in the past, whether or not that action is still going on. Its helping verb is in the past tense: *was* or *were.*

> The old men *were sitting* on the porch when we passed.

Lucy *was planning* to take the weekend off.

The **future progressive** expresses an action that will take place continuously at some time in the future. Its helping verb is in the future tense: *will be.*

They *will be answering* the phones while she is gone.

*Will* we *be dining* out every night on our vacation?

## 8g Use the perfect progressive tenses for continuing actions that began earlier.

The **present perfect progressive** indicates an action that started in the past and is continuing in the present. Form it by adding the present perfect of *be* (*has been, have been*) to the present participle (*-ing* form) of the main verb. Often *for* or *since* is used with this tense.

Fred *has been complaining* about his neighbor since the wild parties began.

*Have* you *been reading* Uma's postcards from England?

The **past perfect progressive** expresses a continuing action that was completed before another past action. Form it by adding the past perfect of *be* (*had been*) to the present participle of the main verb.

By the time Khalid finally arrived, I *had been waiting* for half an hour.

The **future perfect progressive** expresses an action that is expected to continue into the future for a specific time and then end before or continue beyond another future action. Form it by adding *will have been* to the present participle of the main verb.

By fall Joanne *will have been attending* school longer than anyone else I know.

---

## EXERCISE 8–1 Identifying Verb Tenses

Underline each verb or verb phrase in the following sentences and identify its tense. Answers for the lettered sentences appear at the end of the Handbook. Example:

    *present progressive*        *simple present*
John <u>is living</u> in Hinsdale, but he <u>prefers</u> Joliet.

a. He has been living like a hunted animal ever since he hacked into the university computer lab in order to change all his grades.

b. I have never appeared on a reality television show, and I will never appear on one unless my family gets selected.

c. James had been at the party for only fifteen minutes when his host suddenly pitched the caterer into the swimming pool.

d. As of next month, I will have been studying karate for six years, and I will be taking the test for my orange belt in July.

e. The dachshund was running at its fastest speed, but the squirrel strolled toward the tree without fear.

1. As of May 1, Ira and Sandy will have been going together for a year.

2. She will be working in her study if you need her.

3. Have you been hoping that Carlos will come to your party?

4. I know that he will not yet have returned from Chicago.

5. His parents had been expecting him home any day until they heard that he was still waiting for the bus.

## 8h Use the correct forms of the very irregular verbs *be*, *have*, and *do*.

The verbs *be*, *have*, and *do* take very irregular forms in the present and past tenses. Refer to the following chart to avoid confusion.

> ### Forms of *Be*, *Have*, and *Do* at a Glance
>
> **be**
>
> | PRESENT TENSE | | PAST TENSE | |
> |---|---|---|---|
> | I am | we are | I was | we were |
> | you are | you are | you were | you were |
> | he/she/it is | they are | he/she/it was | they were |
>
> PAST PARTICIPLE
> been          I have *been* in line for two hours.
>
> PRESENT PARTICIPLE
> being          Kara is *being* extra cautious around her patients.
>
> **have**
>
> | PRESENT TENSE | | PAST TENSE | |
> |---|---|---|---|
> | I have | we have | I had | we had |
> | you have | you have | you had | you had |
> | he/she/it has | they have | he/she/it had | they had |
>
> PAST PARTICIPLE
> had          Ivan has *had* the flu every year since he can remember.
>
> PRESENT PARTICIPLE
> having          Mia is *having* a party on New Year's Eve.

**do**

| PRESENT TENSE | | PAST TENSE | |
|---|---|---|---|
| I do | we do | I did | we did |
| you do | you do | you did | you did |
| he/she/it does | they do | he/she/it did | they did |

PAST PARTICIPLE

done      Gina had *done* all her homework before the class ended.

PRESENT PARTICIPLE

doing      What were you *doing* last night?

**8i**   Use the correct forms of *lie* and *lay* and *sit* and *set*.

Try taking two easy steps to eliminate confusion between *lie* and *lay*.

- Learn the principal parts and present participles of both (see below).
- Remember that *lie* never takes a direct object: "The island *lies* in the ocean." *Lay* always requires an object to answer "Lay what?": "*Lay* that pistol down."

The same distinction exists between *sit* and *set*. The verb *sit* rarely takes a direct object: "He *sits* on the stairs." *Set* almost always takes an object: "He *sets* the bottle on the counter." Note a few easily memorized exceptions: The sun *sets*. A hen *sets*. Gelatin *sets*. You *sit* the canter in a horse show.

> A **direct object** is the target of a verb that completes the action performed by the subject or asserted about the subject (see 3a).

## Forms of *Lie* and *Lay*, *Sit* and *Set* at a Glance

**lie, lay, lain, lying:** recline

| PRESENT TENSE | | PAST TENSE | |
|---|---|---|---|
| I lie | we lie | I lay | we lay |
| you lie | you lie | you lay | you lay |
| he/she/it lies | they lie | he/she/it lay | they lay |

PAST PARTICIPLE

lain      We have *lain* in the sun long enough.

PRESENT PARTICIPLE

lying      At ten o'clock he was still *lying* in bed.

**lay, laid, laid, laying:** put in place, deposit

| PRESENT TENSE | | PAST TENSE | |
|---|---|---|---|
| I lay | we lay | I laid | we laid |
| you lay | you lay | you laid | you laid |
| he/she/it lays | they lay | he/she/it laid | they laid |

*(continued)*

PAST PARTICIPLE

laid          Having *laid* his clothes on the bed, Mark jumped in the shower.

PRESENT PARTICIPLE

laying        *Laying* her cards on the table, Lola cried, "Gin!"

**sit, sat, sat, sitting:** be seated

| PRESENT TENSE | | PAST TENSE | |
|---|---|---|---|
| I sit | we sit | I sat | we sat |
| you sit | you sit | you sat | you sat |
| he/she/it sits | they sit | he/she/it sat | they sat |

PAST PARTICIPLE

sat           I have *sat* here long enough.

PRESENT PARTICIPLE

sitting       Why are you *sitting* on that rickety bench?

**set, set, set, setting:** place

| PRESENT TENSE | | PAST TENSE | |
|---|---|---|---|
| I set | we set | I set | we set |
| you set | you set | you set | you set |
| he/she/it sets | they set | he/she/it set | they set |

PAST PARTICIPLE

set           Paul has *set* the table for eight.

PRESENT PARTICIPLE

setting       Chanh-Duy has been *setting* traps for the mice.

---

**EXERCISE 8–2** Using Irregular Verb Forms

Correct each incorrectly used irregular verb in the following sentences. Some sentences may be correct. Answers for the lettered sentences appear at the end of the Handbook. Example:

> *spoken*
> I have ~~spoke~~ to my professor about my absence last week.

a. Do he need a ride to school tomorrow?

b. I laid down to rest because I felt weak.

c. We will be setting here waiting for you after the show.

d. The class has begun reading Shakespeare this semester.

e. Reese sat the flowers on the table before dinner.

1. As a family rule, the kids all turn off their phones and lie them face down at meal time.

2. Dean has choose to visit London instead of Paris.

3. She have everything: a strong marriage, a stable job, and wonderful kids.

4. We been looking for a new car for a few weeks.

5. We have eaten pasta for dinner every night this week.

---

## 8j Use verbs in the appropriate mood.

Another characteristic of every verb is its **mood.** The indicative mood is most common. The imperative and subjunctive moods add valuable versatility.

The **indicative mood** is used to state a fact, to ask a question, or to express an opinion.

| | |
|---|---|
| FACT | Danika *left* home two months ago. |
| QUESTION | *Will* she *find* happiness as a belly dancer? |
| OPINION | I *think* not. |

The **imperative mood** is used to make a request or to give a command or direction. The understood but usually unstated subject of a verb in the imperative mood is *you.* The verb's form is the base form or infinitive.

| | |
|---|---|
| REQUEST | Please *be* there before noon. [*You* please be there. . . .] |
| COMMAND | *Hurry*! [*You* hurry!] |
| DIRECTION | *Drive* east on State Street. [*You* drive east. . . .] |

The **subjunctive mood** is used in a subordinate clause to express a wish, requirement, suggestion, or condition contrary to fact. The subjunctive mood suggests uncertainty: the action expressed by the verb may or may not actually take place as specified. In any clause opening with *that* and expressing a requirement, the verb is in the subjunctive mood and takes the base or infinitive form.

Professor Vogt requires that every student *complete* the essay promptly.

She asked that we *be* on time for all meetings.

When you use the subjunctive mood to describe a condition that is contrary to fact, use *were* if the verb is *be.* For other verbs, use the simple past tense. Wishes, whether present or past, follow the same rules.

If I *were* rich, I would be happy.

If I *had* a million dollars, I would be happy.

Elissa wishes that Ted *were* more goal oriented.

Elissa wished that Ted *knew* what he wanted to do.

For a condition contrary to fact in the past, use the past perfect tense.

If I *had been* awake, I would have seen the meteor showers.

If Jessie *had known* you were coming, she would have cleaned her room.

**Guidelines for Multilingual Writers**
What Are Conditionals?

**Conditional sentences** usually contain an *if* clause, which states the condition, and a result clause.

- When the condition is true or possibly true in the present or future, use the present tense in the *if* clause and the present or future tense in the result clause. The future tense is not used in the *if* clause.

  If Jane *prepares* her essay early, she usually *writes* very well.

  If Maria *saves* enough money, she *will buy* a car.

- When the condition is not true in the present, for most verbs use the past tense in the *if* clause; for the verb *be,* use *were.* Use *would, could,* or *might* + infinitive form in the result clause.

  If Carlos *had* a computer, he *would need* a monitor, too.

  If Claudia *were* here, she *could do* it herself.

- When the condition was not true in the past, use the past perfect tense in the *if* clause. If the possible result was in the past, use *would have, could have,* or *might have* + past participle (*-ed* or *-en* form) in the result clause. If the possible result is in the present, use *would, could,* or *might* + infinitive form in the result clause.

  If Claudia *had saved* enough money, she *could have bought* a car. [Result in the past]

  If Annie *had finished* law school, she *might be* a successful lawyer now. [Result in the present]

Although use of the subjunctive has grown scarcer over the years, it still sounds crude to write "If I *was* you. . . ." If you ever feel that the subjunctive makes a sentence sound stilted, rewrite it with an infinitive phrase.

> An **infinitive** consists of the base form of a verb plus the word *to* (see 8a).

Professor Vogt requires every student *to complete* the essay promptly.

### EXERCISE 8–3 Using the Correct Mood of Verbs

Find and correct any errors in mood in the following sentences. Identify the mood of the incorrect verb as well as its correct replacement. Some sentences may be correct. Answers for the lettered sentences appear at the end of the Handbook. Example:

The law requires that each person files a tax return by April 15. [Incorrect: *files,* indicative; correct: *file,* subjunctive]

a. Dr. Belanger recommended that Juan flosses his teeth every day.

b. If I was you, I would have done the same thing.

c. Tradition demands that Daegun shows respect for his elders.

d. Please attends the training lesson if you plan to skydive later today.

1. If she was slightly older, she could stay home by herself.

2. If they have waited a little longer, they would have seen some amazing things.

3. Emilia's contract stipulates that she works on Saturdays.

4. If James invested in the company ten years ago, he would have made a lot of money.

# 9 | Subject-Verb Agreement

What does it mean for a subject and a verb to agree? Practically speaking, it means that their forms match: plural subjects take plural verbs, third-person subjects take third-person verbs, and so forth. When your subjects and verbs agree, you prevent a mismatch that could distract readers.

A **subject** is the part of a sentence that names something—a person, an object, an idea, a situation—about which the predicate makes an assertion (see 2).

A **verb** is a word that shows action or a state of being (see 1c and 3).

## 9a A verb agrees with its subject in person and number.

Subject and verb agree in person (first, second, or third):

*I write* my papers on my laptop. [Subject and verb in first person]

*Eamon writes* his papers in the lab. [Subject and verb in third person]

Subject and verb agree in number (singular or plural):

*Grace enjoys* college. [Subject and verb singular]

*She and Jim are* on their vacation. [Subject and verb plural]

The present tense of most verbs is the infinitive form, with no added ending except in the third-person singular. (See 8b–8h.)

| | |
|---|---|
| I enjoy | we enjoy |
| you enjoy | you enjoy |
| he/she/it enjoys | they enjoy |

Forms of the verb *be* vary.

| | |
|---|---|
| I am | we are |
| you are | you are |
| he/she/it is | they are |

## 9b A verb agrees with its subject, not with any words that intervene.

> My *favorite* of O. Henry's short stories *is* "The Gift of the Magi."

A singular subject linked to another noun or pronoun by a prepositional phrase beginning with wording such as *along with, as well as,* or *in addition to* remains a singular subject and takes a singular verb.

> My cousin *James* as well as his wife and son *plans* to vote for Levine.

A **prepositional phrase** includes the preposition and its object (a noun or pronoun), plus any modifiers (see 1f).

## 9c Subjects joined by *and* usually take a plural verb.

In most cases, a compound subject takes a plural verb.

> *Sugar, salt, and fat* adversely *affect* people's health.

However, phrases like *each boy and girl* or *every dog and cat* consider subjects individually, as "each one" or "every one," and use a singular verb.

> *Each man and woman* in the room *has* a different story to tell.

Use a singular verb for two singular subjects that form or are one thing.

> *Lime juice and soda quenches* your thirst.

A **compound subject** is a subject consisting of two or more nouns or pronouns linked by *and* (see 5a).

## 9d With subjects joined by *or* or *nor,* the verb agrees with the part of the subject nearest to it.

> Either they or *Max is* guilty.

Subjects containing *not . . . but* follow this rule also.

> Not we but *George knows* the whole story.

You can remedy awkward constructions by rephrasing.

> Either they are guilty or Max is.

> We do not know the whole story, but George does.

## 9e Most collective nouns take singular verbs.

A **collective noun** is a singular noun that represents a group of people or items. When a collective noun refers to a group of people acting as one, use a singular verb.

> The *jury finds* the defendant guilty.

When the members of the group act individually, use a plural verb.

> The *jury agree* on the verdict.

If you feel that using a plural verb results in an awkward sentence, reword the subject so that it refers to members of the group individually.

The *jurors agree* on the verdict.

## 9f Most indefinite pronouns take a third-person singular verb.

Singular indefinite pronouns take a third-person singular verb.

*Someone is* here for you.

Even when one of these subjects is followed by a phrase containing a noun or pronoun of a different person or number, use a singular verb.

*Each* of you *is* here to stay.

*One* of the elephants *seems* dangerously ill.

---

> ## Indefinite Pronouns *at a Glance*

*Always Singular*

| | | |
|---|---|---|
| anybody | everything | nothing |
| anyone | much | one (of) |
| anything | neither (of) | somebody |
| each (of) | nobody | someone |
| everybody | no one | something |
| everyone | | |

*Always Plural*

| | | | |
|---|---|---|---|
| both | few | many | several |

*May Be Singular or Plural*

| | | | | |
|---|---|---|---|---|
| all | any | either (of) | none | some (of) |

---

## 9g The indefinite pronouns *all, any,* and *some* use a singular or plural verb, depending on their meaning.

I have no explanation. *Is any* needed?

*Any* of the changes considered critical *have* been made already.

*All is* lost.

*All* the bananas *are* gone.

*Some* of the blame *is* mine.

*Some* of us *are* Democrats.

*None*—like *all, any,* and *some*—takes a singular or a plural verb, depending on the sense in which the pronoun is used.

> *None* of you *is* exempt.

> *None* of his wives *were* blond.

## 9h In a subordinate clause with a relative pronoun as the subject, the verb agrees with the antecedent.

A **relative pronoun** is a pronoun that opens a subordinate clause and modifies a noun or pronoun in another clause (see 1b).

To determine the person and number of the verb in a subordinate clause whose subject is *who, which,* or *that,* look back at the word to which the pronoun refers. This word, known as an antecedent, is usually (but not always) the noun closest to the relative pronoun.

> I have a roommate *who studies* day and night. [The antecedent of *who* is the third-person singular noun *roommate*. Therefore, the verb in the subordinate clause is third-person singular, *studies*.]

> Pandas are mammals *that have* trouble reproducing in captivity. [The antecedent of *that* is *mammals,* so the verb is third-person plural, *have*.]

## 9i A verb agrees with its subject even when the subject follows the verb.

Introductory expressions such as *there* or *here* change the ordinary order so that the subject follows the verb. Remember that verbs agree with subjects and that *here* and *there* are never subjects.

> Here *is* a *riddle* for you.

> There *are* forty *people* in my law class.

> Under the bridge *were* a broken-down *boat* and a worn *tire.*

## 9j A linking verb agrees with its subject, not its subject complement.

A **linking verb** is a verb that shows a state of being by linking the sentence subject with a word that renames or describes the subject (see 1c and 3b).

When a form of the verb *be* links two or more nouns, the subject is the noun before the linking verb. Nouns that follow the linking verb are subject complements. Make the verb agree with the subject of the sentence, not the subject complement.

A **subject complement** is a noun, an adjective, or a group of words that follows a linking verb and renames or describes the subject (see 3b).

> *Jim is* a gentleman and a scholar.

> Amy's *parents are* her most enthusiastic audience.

## 9k When the subject is a title, use a singular verb.

> In sixth grade, *Harry Potter and the Chamber of Secrets was* my favorite book.

> "*People*" sung by Barbra Streisand *is* my aunt's favorite song.

**9l** Singular nouns that end in *-s* take singular verbs.

Some nouns look plural even though they refer to a singular subject: *measles, logistics, mathematics, electronics.* Such nouns take singular verbs.

The *news is* that *economics is* now one of the most popular majors.

---

**EXERCISE 9–1** Making Subjects and Verbs Agree

Find and correct any subject-verb agreement errors in the following sentences. Some sentences may be correct. Answers for the lettered sentences appear at the end of the Handbook. Example:

> *are*
> Addressing the audience tonight is the nominees for club president.

a. For many college graduates, the process of looking for jobs are often long and stressful.

b. Not too long ago, searching the classifieds and inquiring in person was the primary methods of job hunting.

c. Today, however, everyone also seem to use the Internet to search for openings or to e-mail their résumés.

d. My classmates and my cousin sends most résumés over the Internet because it costs less than mailing them.

e. All the résumés arrives quickly when they are sent electronically.

1. There are many people who thinks that interviewing is the most stressful part of the job search.

2. Sometimes only one person conducts an interview, while other times a whole committee conduct it.

3. Either the interviewer or the committee usually begin by asking simple questions about your background.

4. Making eye contact, dressing professionally, and appearing confident is some of the qualities an interviewer may consider important.

5. After an interview, most people sends a thank-you letter to the person who conducted it.

---

# 10 | Pronoun Case

Depending on a pronoun's function in a sentence, we say that it is in the **subjective case,** the **objective case,** or the **possessive case.** Some pronouns change form when they change case, and some do not. The personal pronouns *I, he, she, we,* and *they* and the relative pronoun *who* have different forms in the subjective, objective, and possessive cases. Other pronouns, such as *you* and *it,* have only two forms: the plain case (which serves as both subjective and objective) and the possessive case.

> ## Personal Pronouns *at a Glance*
>
> |  | SUBJECTIVE | | OBJECTIVE | | POSSESSIVE | |
> |---|---|---|---|---|---|---|
> |  | Singular | Plural | Singular | Plural | Singular | Plural |
> | *First Person* | I | we | me | us | my/mine | our/ours |
> | *Second Person* | you | you | you | you | your/yours | your/yours |
> | *Third Person* | he | they | him | them | his | their/theirs |
> |  | she | | her | | her/hers | |
> |  | it | | it | | its | |

## 10a Use the subjective case for the subject of a sentence or clause.

**A subject** is the part of a sentence that names something—a person, an object, an idea, a situation—about which the verb makes an assertion (see 2).

Jed and *I* ate the granola.

*Who* cares?

Maya recalled that *she* played baseball.

Election officials are the people *who* count.

A pronoun serving as the subject for a verb is subjective even when the verb isn't written but is only implied:

    *I*
Jed is hungrier than ~~me~~. [The verb *am* is implied: Jed is hungrier than I *am*.]

Don't be fooled by a pronoun that appears immediately after a verb, looking as if it were a direct object but functioning as the subject of a clause. The pronoun's case is determined by its role, not by its position.

    *whoever*
We were happy to interview ~~whomever~~ was running. [The subjective pronoun *whoever* is the subject of the verb *was running*.]

## 10b Use the subjective case for a subject complement.

**A subject complement** is a noun, an adjective, or a group of words that follows a linking verb and renames or describes the subject (see 3b).

When a pronoun functions as a subject complement, it plays essentially the same role as the subject and its case is subjective.

                *he*         *I*
The phantom graffiti artist couldn't have been ~~him~~. It was ~~me~~. [The subject pronouns *he* and *I* are subject complements.]

## 10c Use the subjective case for an appositive to a subject or subject complement.

**An appositive** is a word or group of words that adds information by identifying a subject or object in a different way (see 4b).

A pronoun in apposition to a subject or subject complement is like an identical twin to the noun it stands beside. It has the same meaning and case.

                    *she*
The class officers—Ravi and ~~her~~—announced a senior breakfast. [The subjective pronoun *she* helps rename the subject, *officers*.]

## Objective Case

**10d** Use the objective case for a direct object, an indirect object, the object of a preposition, or the subject of an infinitive.

The custard pies hit *him* and *me*. [The objective pronouns *him* and *me* are direct objects of the verb *hit*.]

Mona threw *us* towels. [The objective pronoun *us* is an indirect object of the verb *threw*.]

Mona threw towels to *him* and *us*. [The objective pronouns *him* and *us* are direct objects of the preposition *to*.]

We always expect *him* to win. [The objective pronoun *him* is the subject of the infinitive *to win*. This is the only case in which an objective pronoun is used as a subject.]

Mona agreed to keep the secret between ~~she~~ *her* and ~~I~~ *me*. [The objective pronouns *her* and *me* are direct objects of the preposition *between*.]

**10e** Use the objective case for an appositive to a direct or indirect object or the object of a preposition.

Mona helped all of us — Mrs. Van Dumont, ~~he~~ *him*, and ~~I~~ *me*. [The objective pronouns *him* and *me* are in apposition to the object *us*.]

Bob gave his favorite students, Tom and ~~she~~ *her*, an approving nod. [The objective pronoun *her* is in apposition to the object *students*.]

## Possessive Case

**10f** Use the possessive case to show ownership.

Possessive pronouns can function as adjectives or as nouns. *My, your, his, her, its, our,* and *their* function as adjectives by modifying nouns or pronouns.

*My* new bike is having *its* first road test today.

The possessive pronoun *its* does not contain an apostrophe. *It's* with an apostrophe is a contraction for *it is*, as in "*It's* a beautiful day for bike riding."

The possessive pronouns *mine, yours, his, hers, ours,* and *theirs* can discharge the whole range of noun duties, serving as subjects, subject complements, direct objects, indirect objects, or objects of prepositions.

| | |
|---|---|
| SUBJECT | *Yours* is the last vote we need. |
| SUBJECT COMPLEMENT | This day is *ours*. |
| DIRECT OBJECT | Don't take your car; take *mine*. |
| INDIRECT OBJECT | If we're honoring requests, give *hers* top priority. |
| OBJECT OF A PREPOSITION | Give Mia's request priority over *theirs*. |

**A direct object** is the target of a verb that completes the action performed by the subject or asserted about the subject (see 3a).

**An indirect object** is a person or thing affected by the subject's action, usually the recipient of the direct object, through the action indicated by a verb (see 3a).

**The object of a preposition** is the noun or pronoun that follows the preposition, connecting it to the rest of the sentence (see 4b).

**An infinitive** consists of the base form of a verb plus the word *to* (see 8a).

A **gerund** is a form of a verb, ending in *-ing*, that functions as a noun (see 8a).

## 10g Use the possessive case to modify a gerund.

A possessive pronoun (or possessive noun) is the appropriate escort for a gerund. As a noun, a gerund requires an adjective for a modifier.

> *his*
> Mary is tired of ~~him~~ griping. [The possessive pronoun *his* modifies the gerund *griping*.]
>
> *their* *his*
> I can stand ~~them~~ being late every day but not ~~him~~ drinking on the job.
> [The possessive pronoun *their* modifies the gerund *being*; the possessive pronoun *his* modifies the gerund *drinking*.]

A **present participle** is a form of a verb ending in *-ing* that cannot function alone as a main verb but can act as an adjective (see 8a).

However, editing possessives can be confusing because two different verb forms both end in *-ing*: gerunds that act as nouns and present participles that act as adjectives. If you are not sure whether to use a possessive for a gerund or an objective pronoun with a word ending in *-ing*, look closely at your sentence. Which word—the pronoun or the *-ing* word—is the object of your main verb? That word functions as a noun; the other word modifies it.

> Mr. Phipps remembered *them* smoking in the boys' room. [Mr. Phipps remembers *them*, those naughty students. *Them* is the object of the verb, so *smoking* is a participle modifying *them*.]

> Mr. Phipps remembered *their* smoking in the boys' room. [Mr. Phipps remembers *smoking*, that nasty habit. The gerund *smoking* is the object of the verb, and the possessive pronoun *their* modifies it.]

## EXERCISE 10–1 Using Pronoun Case Correctly

Replace any pronouns used incorrectly in the following sentences. Explain why each was incorrect. (Consider all these examples as written—not spoken—English, so apply the rules strictly.) Some sentences may be correct. Answers for the lettered sentences appear at the end of the Handbook. Example:

> *she*
> That is ~~her~~, the new university president, at the podium. [*She* is a subject complement.]

a. I didn't appreciate you laughing at her and I.

b. Lee and me would be delighted to serenade whomever will listen.

c. The managers and us servers are highly trustworthy.

d. The neighbors were driven berserk by him singing.

e. Jerry and myself regard you and she as the very people who we wish to meet.

1. Have you guessed the identity of the person of who I am speaking?

2. It was him asking about the clock that started me suspecting him.

3. They—Jerry and her—are the troublemakers.

4. Mrs. Van Dumont awarded the prize to Mona and I.

5. The counterattack was launched by Dusty and myself.

# 11 | Pronoun Reference

The main use of pronouns is to refer in a brief, convenient form to some **antecedent** that has already been named. A pronoun usually has a noun or another pronoun as its antecedent. Often the antecedent is the subject or object of the same clause in which the pronoun appears.

> Josie hit the *ball* after *its* first bounce.

> Smashing into *Greg*, the ball knocked off *his* glasses.

The antecedent also can appear in a different clause or even a different sentence from the pronoun.

> Josie hit the *ball* when *it* bounced back to *her*.

> The *ball* smashed into *Greg*. *It* knocked off *his* glasses.

A pronoun as well as a noun can be an antecedent.

> My *dog* hid in the closet when *she* had *her* puppies. [*Dog* is the antecedent of *she*; *she* is the antecedent of *her*.]

## 11a Name the pronoun's antecedent: don't just imply it.

When editing, be sure you have identified clearly the antecedent of each pronoun. A writer who leaves a key idea unsaid is likely to confuse readers.

> Ted wanted a Norwegian canoe because he'd heard that ~~they~~ <sup>Norwegians</sup> produce the lightest canoes afloat.

An **antecedent** is the word to which a pronoun refers (see 1b).

To clarify what noun or pronoun *they* refers to, the writer must supply an antecedent for *they*.

---

 **Guidelines for Multilingual Writers**
How Do I Use Relative Pronouns Correctly?

Be sure to use relative pronouns (*who, whose, which, that*) correctly in sentences with adjective clauses. Use *who*, not *which*, for a person. Select *that* to introduce necessary information that defines or specifies; reserve *which* for additional, but not defining, information.

- Do not omit the relative pronoun when it is the subject within the adjective clause.

  > The woman <sup>who</sup> *gave us directions to the museum* told us not to miss the Picasso exhibit. [*Who* is the subject of the adjective clause.]

- In speech and informal writing, you can imply (not state) a relative pronoun when it is the object of a verb or preposition within the adjective clause. In formal writing, you should use the relative pronoun.

For more on choosing *that* or *which*, see 28e.

---

*(continued)*

> FORMAL  Jamal forgot to return the book *that I gave him*. [*That* is the object of *gave*.]
>
> INFORMAL  Jamal forgot to return the book *I gave him*. [The relative pronoun *that* is implied.]
>
> FORMAL  This is the box *in which we found the jewelry*. [*Which* is the object of the preposition *in*.]
>
> INFORMAL  This is the box *we found the jewelry in*. [The relative pronoun *which* is implied.]
>
> *NOTE:* When the relative pronoun is omitted, the preposition moves to the end of the sentence but must not be left out.
>
> ■ *Whose* is the only possessive form of a relative pronoun. It is used with persons, animals, and things.
>
> I bought a chair ~~that its~~ *whose* legs were wobbly.
>
> *NOTE:* When in doubt about a pronoun, you can rephrase the sentence: I bought a chair *with wobbly legs*.

Watch out for possessive nouns. They won't work as antecedents.

On ~~William's~~ *William* canoe, he *his* painted a skull and bones.

In ~~Hemingway's~~ *the* story, he *Hemingway* describes the powerful sea.

**An antecedent** is the word to which a pronoun refers (see 1b).

## 11b  Give the pronoun *it, this, that,* or *which* a clear antecedent.

Vagueness arises, thick as fog, whenever *it, this, that,* or *which* points to something a writer assumes is said but indeed isn't. Often the best way out of the fog is to substitute a specific noun or expression for the pronoun.

I was an only child, and it *my solitary life* was hard.

*Because* Judy could not get along with her younger brother, ~~This is the reason~~ she wanted to get her own apartment.

## 11c  Make the pronoun's antecedent clear.

Confusion strikes if a pronoun points in two or more directions. When more than one antecedent is possible, the reader wonders which the writer means.

> CONFUSING  Hanwei shouted to Kenny to take off his burning sweater.

Whose sweater does *his* mean — Kenny's or Hanwei's? Simply changing a pronoun won't clear up the confusion. The writer needs to revise enough to move the two possible antecedents out of each other's way.

| | |
|---|---|
| CLEAR | "Kenny!" shouted Hanwei. "Your sweater's on fire! Take it off!" |
| CLEAR | Flames were shooting from Kenny's sweater. Hanwei shouted to Kenny to take it off. |
| CLEAR | Hanwei realized that his sweater was on fire and shouted to Kenny for help. |

## 11d Place the pronoun close to its antecedent to keep the relationship clear.

Watch out for distractions that slip in between noun and pronoun. If your sentence contains two or more nouns that look like antecedents to a pronoun, your readers may become bewildered.

| | |
|---|---|
| CONFUSING | Harper steered his dinghy alongside the cabin cruiser that the drug smugglers had left anchored under an overhanging willow in the tiny harbor and eased it to a stop. |

What did Harper ease to a stop? By the time readers reach the end of the sentence, they are likely to have forgotten. To avoid confusion, keep the pronoun and its antecedent reasonably close together.

| | |
|---|---|
| CLEAR | Harper steered his dinghy into the tiny harbor and eased it to a stop alongside the cabin cruiser that the drug smugglers had left anchored under an overhanging willow. |

Never force your readers to stop and think, "What does that pronoun stand for?" You, the writer, have to do this thinking for them.

---

### EXERCISE 11–1 Making Pronoun Reference Clear

Revise each sentence or group of sentences so that any pronoun needing an antecedent clearly points to one. Possible revisions for the lettered sentences appear at the end of the Handbook. Example:

I took the money out of the wallet and threw *~~it~~ the wallet* in the trash.

a. I could see the moon and the faint shadow of the tree as it began to rise.

b. Katrina spent the summer in Paris and traveled throughout Europe, which broadened her awareness of cultural differences.

c. Most managers want employees to work as many hours as possible. They never consider the work they need to do at home.

d. I worked twelve hours a day and never got enough sleep, but it was worth it.

e. Kevin asked Mike to meet him for lunch but forgot that he had class at that time.

1. Bill's prank frightened Josh and made him wonder why he had done it.
2. Korean students study up to twenty subjects a year, including algebra, calculus, and engineering. Because they are required, they must study them year after year.
3. Pedro Martinez signed a baseball for Chad.
4. When the bottle hit the windshield, it shattered.
5. My friends believe they are more mature than many of their peers because of the discipline enforced at their school. However, it can also lead to problems.

---

# 12 | Pronoun-Antecedent Agreement

A pronoun's job is to fill in for a noun, much as an actor's double fills in for the actor. Pronouns are a short, convenient way to avoid repeating the noun.

> The sheriff drew a six-shooter; he fired twice.

In this action-packed sentence, first comes a noun (*sheriff*) and then a pronoun (*he*) that refers back to it. *Sheriff* is the antecedent of *he*. Just as verbs need to agree with their subjects, pronouns need to agree with the nouns they stand for without shifting number, person, or gender in midsentence.

## 12a Pronouns agree with their antecedents in person and number.

A pronoun matches its antecedent in person (first, second, or third) and in number (singular or plural), even when intervening words separate the pronoun and its antecedent. Here, noun and pronoun disagree in person (third person *campers*; second person *your*):

> *their*
> All campers should bring ~~your~~ knapsacks.

Here, noun and pronoun disagree in number (singular *camper*; plural *their*):

> *his or her*
> Every camper should bring ~~their~~ knapsack.

## 12b Most antecedents joined by *and* require a plural pronoun.

A **compound subject** is plural; use a plural pronoun to refer to it.

> *George,* who has been here before, *and Jenn,* who hasn't, need *their* maps.

If the nouns in a compound subject refer to the same person or thing, they make up a singular antecedent. Use a singular pronoun too.

> The *owner and founder* of this company carries *his* laptop everywhere.

A **compound subject** is a subject consisting of two or more nouns or pronouns linked by *and* (see 5a).

**12c** A pronoun agrees with the closest part of an antecedent joined by *or* or *nor*.

If your subject is two or more nouns (or a combination of nouns and pronouns) connected by *or* or *nor*, look closely at the subject's parts. Are they all singular? If so, your pronoun should be singular.

> Neither *Joy nor Jean* remembered *her* book last week.

> If *Sam, Arthur, or Dieter* shows up, tell *him* I'm upstairs.

If the part of the subject closest to the pronoun is plural, the pronoun should be plural.

> Neither *Joy nor her sisters* rode *their* bikes today.

> If you see *Sam, Arthur, or their friends*, tell *them* I'm upstairs.

**12d** An antecedent that is a singular indefinite pronoun takes a singular pronoun.

Most indefinite pronouns (such as *everyone* and *anybody*) are singular in meaning, so the pronouns that refer to them are also singular.

For a list of indefinite pronouns, see p. 734.

> *Either* of the boys can do it, as long as *he* tries.

**12e** Most collective nouns used as antecedents require singular pronouns.

When the members of a group (such as a committee, family, jury, or trio) act as a unit, use a singular pronoun to refer to them.

> The *cast* for the play will be posted as soon as the director chooses *it*.

When the group members act individually, use a plural pronoun.

> The *cast* will go *their* separate ways when summer ends.

**12f** A pronoun agrees with its antecedent in gender.

> If your *mother* brings you to camp, invite *her* for lunch.

---

EXERCISE 12–1 **Making Pronouns and Antecedents Agree**

If any nouns and pronouns disagree in number, person, or gender in the following sentences, substitute pronouns that agree with the nouns. If you prefer, strengthen any sentence by rewriting it. Some sentences may be correct. Possible revisions for the lettered sentences appear at the end of the Handbook. Example:

> *it*
> A cat expects people to feed ~~them~~ often.　　*Or*
>
> *Cats expect*
> ~~A cat expects~~ people to feed them often.

a. Many architects find work their greatest pleasure.

b. Neither Melissa nor James has received their application form yet.

c. He is the kind of man who gets their fun out of just sipping one's beer and watching his Saturday games on TV.

d. Many a mother has mourned the loss of their child.

e. When one enjoys one's work, it's easy to spend all your spare time thinking about it.

1. All students are urged to complete your registration on time.

2. When a baby doesn't know their own mother, they may have been born with some kind of vision deficiency.

3. Each member of the sorority has to make her own bed.

4. If you don't like the songs the choir sings, don't join them.

5. Young people should know how to protect oneself against AIDS.

# 13 | Adjectives and Adverbs

Adjectives provide information about the person, place, object, or idea named by the noun or pronoun.

> The *thin, lightweight* laptop fits in my purse.

## Adjectives and Adverbs *at a Glance*

ADJECTIVES
1. Typically answer the question Which? or What kind?
2. Modify nouns or pronouns

ADVERBS
3. Answer the question How? When? Where? or sometimes Why?
4. Modify verbs, adjectives, and other adverbs

An adverb describes a verb, an adjective, or another adverb.

> The phones arrived *yesterday*; we *quickly* restocked the shelves with the *incredibly* popular models.

**13a** Use an adverb, not an adjective, to modify a verb, an adjective, or another adverb.

*awfully*
It's ~~awful~~ hot today.

*Awful* is an adjective, so it can modify only nouns or pronouns. An adverb is needed to modify the adjective *hot*.

**13b** Use an adjective, not an adverb, as a subject complement or an object complement.

Her old car looked *awful*. [The adjective *awful* is a subject complement: it follows a linking verb and modifies the subject, *car*.]

An **object complement** completes the description of a direct object and can be an adjective or a noun, but never an adverb.

> Early to bed and early to rise makes a man *healthy, wealthy,* and *wise*. [The adjectives modify the direct object *man*.]

When you are not sure whether you're dealing with an object complement or an adverb, look closely at the word's role in the sentence. If it modifies a noun, it is an object complement and should be an adjective.

> The coach called the referee *stupid* and *blind*. [*Stupid* and *blind* are adjectives modifying the direct object *referee*.]

If it modifies a verb, you want an adverb instead.

> In fact, the ref had called the play *correctly*. [*Correctly* is an adverb modifying the verb *had called*.]

**13c** Use *good* as an adjective and *well* as an adverb.

> This sandwich tastes *good*. [The adjective *good* is a subject complement following the linking verb *tastes* and modifying the noun *sandwich*.]

> Al's skin healed *well* after surgery. [The adverb *well* modifies the verb *healed*.]

Only if the verb is a linking verb can you safely follow it with *good*. Other kinds of verbs need adverbs, not subject complements.

*well*
After a bad start, the game ended ~~good~~.

Complications arise when we write or speak about health. It is perfectly correct to say *I feel good,* using the adjective *good* as a subject complement after the linking verb *feel*. However, generations of confusion have nudged the adverb *well* into the adjective category, too. A nurse may speak of "a well baby"; greeting cards urge patients to "get well"—meaning, "become healthy." Just as *healthy* is an adjective here, so is *well*.

When someone asks, "How do you feel?" you can duck the issue with "Fine!" Otherwise, in speech *good* or *well* is acceptable; in writing, use *good*.

> An **object complement** is a noun, an adjective, or a group of words that renames or describes a direct object (see 3b).

> A **linking verb** is a verb that shows a state of being by linking the sentence subject with a word that renames or describes the subject (see 1c and 3b).

For advice on using commas with adjectives, see 28d.

 **Guidelines for Multilingual Writers**
What Is the Order for Cumulative Adjectives?

**Cumulative adjectives** are two or more adjectives used directly before a noun and not separated by commas or the word *and*.

> She is an *attractive older French* woman.

> His *expressive large brown* eyes moved me.

Cumulative adjectives usually follow a specific order of placement before a noun. Use this list as a guide, but keep in mind that the order can vary.

1. Articles or determiners

   *a, an, the, some, this, these, his, my, two, several*

2. Evaluative adjectives

   *beautiful, wonderful, hardworking, distasteful*

3. Size or dimension

   *big, small, huge, obese, petite, six-foot*

4. Length or shape

   *long, short, round, square, oblong, oval*

5. Age

   *old, young, new, fresh, ancient*

6. Color

   *red, pink, aquamarine, orange*

7. Nation or place of origin

   *American, Japanese, European, Bostonian, Floridian*

8. Religion

   *Protestant, Muslim, Hindu, Buddhist, Catholic, Jewish*

9. Matter or substance

   *wood, gold, cotton, plastic, pine, metal*

10. Noun used as an adjective

    *car* (as in *car mechanic*), *computer* (as in *computer software*)

**13d** Form comparatives and superlatives of most adjectives and adverbs with *-er* and *-est* or *more* and *most*.

Comparatives and superlatives are forms that describe one thing in relation to another. Put most adjectives into comparative form (for two things) by adding *-er* and into superlative form (for three or more) by adding *-est.*

> The budget deficit is *larger* than the trade deficit.

> This year's trade deficit is the *largest* ever.

We usually form the comparative and superlative of potentially cumbersome long adjectives with *more* and *most* rather than with *-er* and *-est.*

> The lake is ~~beautifuller~~ *more beautiful* than I'd imagined.

For short adverbs that do not end in *-ly,* usually add *-er* and *-est.* With all others, use *more* and *most.*

> The trade deficit grows *fastest* and *most uncontrollably* when exports fall.

> Do not use *more* or *most* in addition to adding *-er* or *-est* to the adjective or adverb.

> Eric thought Hitchcock's *Rear Window* was ~~more~~ scarier than *Psycho.* [To say *more scarier* is redundant; deleting *more* corrects the sentence.]

No matter how wonderful something is, we can call it the *best* only when we compare it with more than one other thing. Any comparison between two things uses the comparative form, not the superlative.

> Chocolate and vanilla are both good, but I like chocolate ~~best~~ *better*. [Changing the superlative *best* to the comparative *better* corrects the sentence.]

**13e** Use the correct comparative and superlative forms of irregular adjectives and adverbs.

Use irregular adjectives and adverbs (such as *bad* and *badly*) with care.

> Tom's golf game is no ~~worser~~ *worse* than George's.

For negative comparisons, use *less* and *least* for adjectives and adverbs.

> Michael's speech was *less dramatic* than Louie's.

> Paulette spoke the *least dramatically* of all.

> ## Irregular Adjectives and Adverbs *at a Glance*

| ADJECTIVES | COMPARATIVE | SUPERLATIVE |
|---|---|---|
| good | better | best |
| bad | worse | worst |
| little | less, littler | least, littlest |
| many, some, much | more | most |

| ADVERBS | COMPARATIVE | SUPERLATIVE |
|---|---|---|
| well | better | best |
| badly | worse | worst |
| little | less | least |

## 13f Omit *most* with an adjective or adverb that is already superlative.

Some words, such as *top*, *favorite*, and *unique*, mark whatever they modify as one of a kind. They need no further assistance to make their point.

> Lisa has a ~~most~~ unique background.

---

## EXERCISE 13–1 Using Adjectives and Adverbs Correctly

Find and correct any incorrect use of adjectives and adverbs in the following sentences. Some sentences may be correct. Answers for the lettered sentences appear at the end of the Handbook. Example:

>            *well*
> The merger worked out ~~good~~ for both companies.

a. The field unit carried out their orders exact.

b. Marin felt badly that her mother could not make it to the ceremony.

c. After living in both the city and the suburbs, Aaron decided he liked the city best.

d. The orphaned dogs appear sadly in the animal shelter's cages.

e. Nico enjoys watching all sports, but his most favorite is basketball.

1. Drones are unpiloted air vehicles that are often remotely controlled by someone on the ground.

2. Opal is one of the rarest gemstones.

3. People sometimes behave strange when they are in a new environment and they are concerned for their safety.

4. The library is a more quieter place to study than the coffee shop.

5. That was the worse dinner I have ever had in my entire life.

# 14 | Shifts

Just as you can change position to view a scene from different vantage points, in your writing you can change the time or perspective. However, shifting tense or point of view unconsciously or unnecessarily within a passage creates ambiguity and confusion for readers.

## 14a Maintain consistency in verb tense.

In a passage or an essay, use the same verb tense unless the time changes.

> The driver yelled at us to get off the bus, so I ~~ask~~ *asked* him why, and he ~~tells~~ *told* me it ~~is~~ *was* none of my business.

A verb's **tense** refers to the time when the action of a verb did, does, might, or will occur (see 8).

## 14b If the time changes, change the verb tense.

To write about events in the past, use past tense verbs. To write about events in the present, use present tense verbs. If the time shifts, change tense.

> I *do* not *like* the new television programs this year. The comedies *are* too realistic to be amusing, the adventure shows *don't have* much action, and the law enforcement dramas *drag* on and on. Last year the programs *were* different. The sitcoms *were* hilarious, the adventure shows *were* action packed, and the dramas *were* fast paced. I *prefer* last year's reruns to this year's shows.

The time and the verb tense change appropriately from present (*do like, are, don't have, drag*) to past (*were, were, were, were*) back to present (*prefer*), contrasting this year's *present* with last year's *past* programming.

NOTE: When writing about literature, the accepted practice is to use present tense verbs to summarize what happens in a story, poem, or play. When discussing other aspects of a work, use present tense for present time, past tense for past, and future tense for future.

> Steinbeck *wrote* "The Chrysanthemums" in 1937. [Past tense for past time]

> In "The Chrysanthemums," Steinbeck *describes* the Salinas Valley as "a closed pot" cut off from the world by fog. [Present tense for story summary]

## 14c Maintain consistency in the voice of verbs.

Shifting unnecessarily from active to passive voice may confuse readers.

> My roommates and I *sit* up late many nights talking about our problems.
> *We discuss grades*
> ~~Grades~~, teachers, jobs, money, and dates ~~are discussed~~ at length.

For more on using active and passive voice, see 21.

## 14d Maintain consistency in person.

Person indicates your perspective as a writer. First person (*I, we*) establishes a personal, informal relationship with readers as does second person (*you*), which brings readers into the writing. Third person (*he, she, it, they*) is more

For more on pronoun forms, see 1b and 10.

formal and objective. In a formal scientific report, second person is seldom appropriate, and first, if used, might be reserved for reporting procedures. In a personal essay, using *he, she,* or *one* to refer to yourself would sound stilted. Choose the person appropriate for your purpose, and stick to it.

> they
> College students need transportation, but ~~you~~ need a job to pay for the insurance and the gasoline.

> he or she has
> Anyone can go skydiving if ~~you have~~ the guts.

## 14e  Maintain consistency in the mood of verbs.

Avoid shifts in mood, usually from indicative to imperative.

For examples of the three moods of verbs, see 8j.

> They also advised them to    their
> Counselors advised students to register early. ~~Also~~ pay tuition on time.
> [Edits make both indicative.]

## 14f  Maintain consistency in level of language.

To impress readers, writers sometimes inflate their language or slip into slang. The level of language should fit your purpose and audience throughout an essay. For a personal essay, use informal language.

INCONSISTENT  I felt like a typical tourist. I carried an expensive digital camera with lots of icons I didn't quite know how to decode. But I was in a quandary because there was such a plethora of picturesque tableaus to record for posterity.

Instead of suddenly shifting to formal language, the writer could end simply: *But with so much beautiful scenery all around, I couldn't decide where to start.*
For an academic essay, use formal language.

INCONSISTENT  Puccini's *Turandot* is set in a China of legends, riddles, and fantasy. Brimming with beautiful melodies, this opera is music drama at its most spectacular. It rules!

Cutting the last sentence avoids an unnecessary shift in formality.

---

### EXERCISE 14–1  Maintaining Grammatical Consistency

Revise the following sentences to eliminate shifts in verb tense, voice, mood, person, and level of language. Possible revisions for the lettered sentences appear at the end of the Handbook. Example:

> I needed the job at the restaurant, so I tried to tolerate the insults of my
> I could
> boss, but ~~a person can~~ take only so much.

a. Dr. Jamison is an erudite professor who cracks jokes in class.

b. The audience listened intently to the lecture, but the message was not understood.

c. Scientists can no longer evade the social, political, and ethical consequences of what they did in the laboratory.

d. To have good government, citizens must become informed on the issues. Also, be sure to vote.

e. Good writing is essential to success in many professions, especially in business, where ideas must be communicated in down-to-earth lingo.

1. Our legal system made it extremely difficult to prove a bribe. If the charges are not proven to the satisfaction of a jury or a judge, then we jump to the conclusion that the absence of a conviction demonstrates the innocence of the subject.

2. Before Morris K. Udall, Democrat from Arizona, resigns his seat in the U.S. House of Representatives, he helped preserve hundreds of acres of wilderness.

3. Anyone can learn another language if you have the time and the patience.

4. The immigration officer asked how long we planned to stay, so I show him my letter of acceptance from Tulane.

5. Archaeologists spent many months studying the site of the African city of Zimbabwe, and many artifacts were uncovered.

---

## Learning by Doing 🔲 Considering Your Rough Draft

One method of finding weak spots in an essay is to read it backward, sentence by sentence. This takes the essay out of the "normal" reading realm, where the brain is prone to insert assumed information that does not exist, and allows you to take each sentence on its own merit. This method also allows reviewers to better identify sentence fragments and run-on sentences, as well as missing words. Try this method to see what weak spots you find in your own essay. Write a reflection about what you discover.

# 40 Effective Sentences

15 | Misplaced and Dangling Modifiers   792

16 | Incomplete Sentences   794

17 | Mixed Constructions and Faulty Predication   798

18 | Parallel Structure   801

19 | Coordination and Subordination   804

20 | Sentence Variety   810

21 | Active and Passive Voice   811

## 15 | Misplaced and Dangling Modifiers

The purpose of a **modifier,** such as an adjective or adverb, is to give readers more information. To do so, the modifier must be linked clearly to whatever it is meant to modify or describe.

### 15a  Keep modifiers close to what they modify.

**Misplaced modifiers** — phrases and clauses that wander away from what they modify — produce results more likely to amuse readers than to inform them. Place your modifiers as close as possible to whatever they modify.

> *in colorful packages.*
> She offered toys to all the children ~~in colorful packages.~~ [The phrase *in colorful packages* modifies *toys*, not *children*.]

> *from the crates*
> We removed the dishes ~~from the crates~~ that got chipped. [The clause *that got chipped* modifies *dishes*, not *crates*.]

### 15b  Place each modifier so that it clearly modifies only one thing.

A **squinting modifier** is one that looks two ways, leaving the reader uncertain whether it modifies the word before or after it. To avoid ambiguity, place your modifier close to the word it modifies and away from another that might cause confusion.

| | |
|---|---|
| SQUINTING | The book that appealed to Amy *tremendously* bored Marcus. |
| CLEAR | The book that *tremendously* appealed to Amy bored Marcus. |
| CLEAR | The book that appealed to Amy bored Marcus *tremendously*. |

---

## EXERCISE 15–1  Placing Modifiers

Revise the following sentences, which contain modifiers that are misplaced or squinting. Possible revisions for the lettered sentences appear at the end of the Handbook. Example:

> *Using a flashlight in the dark,*
> ˌPatti found the cat ˌ~~using a flashlight in the dark~~.

a. The bus got stuck in a ditch full of passengers.

b. He was daydreaming about fishing for trout in the middle of a meeting.

c. The boy threw the paper airplane through an open window with a smirk.

d. I reached for my sunglasses when the glare appeared in the glove compartment.

e. High above them, Sally and Glen watched the kites drift back and forth.

1. In her soup she found a fly at one of the best restaurants in town.

2. Andy learned how to build kites from the pages of an old book.

3. Alex vowed to return to the island sometime soon on the day he left it.

4. The fish was carried in a suitcase wrapped in newspaper.

5. The reporters were informed of the crimes committed by a press release.

---

## 15c  State something in the sentence for each modifier to modify.

Generally readers assume that a modifying phrase at the start of a sentence refers to the subject of the main clause to follow. If readers encounter a modifying phrase midway through a sentence, they assume that it modifies something just before or (less often) after it.

> *Feeling tired after the long hike, Jason* went to bed.

> *Alicia, while sympathetic,* was not inclined to help.

Sometimes a writer slips up, allowing a modifying phrase to dangle. A **dangling modifier** is one that doesn't modify anything in its sentence.

| | |
|---|---|
| DANGLING | *Noticing a pain behind his eyes,* an aspirin seemed a good idea. [The opening doesn't modify *aspirin* or, in fact, anything.] |

> A **main clause** is a group of words that has both a subject and a verb and can stand alone as a complete sentence (see 4a).

To correct a dangling modifier, first figure out what noun, pronoun, or noun phrase the modifier is meant to modify. Then make that word or phrase the subject of the main clause.

CLEAR        *Noticing a pain behind his eyes, he* decided to take an aspirin.

Another way to correct a dangling modifier is to turn the dangler into a clause that includes the missing noun or pronoun.

*Although she is talented, her*
~~Her~~ progress, ~~although talented,~~ has been slowed by poor work habits.

Sometimes rewriting will clarify what the modifier modifies.

*Although*              *she*       *hampered*
~~Her progress, although~~ talented, has been ~~slowed~~ by poor work habits.

---

### EXERCISE 15–2 Revising Dangling Modifiers

Revise any sentences that contain dangling modifiers. Some sentences may be correct. Possible revisions for the lettered sentences appear at the end of the Handbook. Example:

*Joan realized that*        *her*
Angry at her poor showing, geology would never be ~~Joan's~~ favorite class.

a. Unpacking the suitcase, a horrible idea occurred to me.

b. After fixing breakfast that morning, the oven might be left on at home.

c. Trying to reach my neighbor, her phone was busy.

d. Desperate to get information, my solution was to ask my mother to drive over to check the oven.

e. With enormous relief, my mother's call confirmed everything was fine.

1. After working six hours, the job was done.

2. Further information can be obtained by calling the specified number.

3. To compete in the Olympics, talent, training, and dedication are needed.

4. Pressing hard on the brakes, the car spun into a hedge.

5. Showing a lack of design experience, the architect advised the student to take her model back to the drawing board.

---

# 16 | Incomplete Sentences

A fragment fails to qualify as a sentence because it lacks a subject or a predicate (or both) or it fails to express a complete thought. However, a sentence with the essentials can still miss the mark. If it lacks a crucial word or phrase, the sentence may be *incomplete*. When you make comparisons and use elliptical constructions, be certain that you complete the thought you want to express.

## Comparisons

**16a**  Make your comparisons clear by stating fully what you are comparing with what.

INCOMPLETE      Roscoe loves spending time online more than Diane.

Does Roscoe prefer the company of a keyboard to the company of his friend? Or, of these two people, is Roscoe (and not Diane) the online addict? Adding a word would complete the comparison.

CLEAR      Roscoe loves spending time online more than Diane *does.*

CLEAR      Roscoe loves spending time online more than *with* Diane.

**16b**  When you start to draw a comparison, finish it.

The unfinished comparison is a favorite of advertisers — "Our product is better!" — because it dodges the question "Better than what?" A sharp writer knows that any item must be compared *with* something else.

*than any other fabric.*
Scottish tweeds are warmer.

**16c**  Be sure the things you compare are of the same kind.

A sentence that compares should reassure readers on two counts: the items are similar enough to compare, and the terms of comparison are clear.

INCOMPLETE      The engine of a Ford truck is heavier than a Piper Cub airplane.

What is being compared? Truck engine and airplane? Or engine and engine? Because a truck engine is unlikely to outweigh a plane, we can guess the writer meant to compare engines. Readers, however, should not have to make the effort to complete a writer's thought.

CLEAR      The engine of a Ford truck is heavier than *that of* a Piper Cub airplane.

CLEAR      A Ford truck's engine is heavier than a *Piper Cub's.*

In this last example, parallel structure (*Ford truck's* and *Piper Cub's*) helps make the comparison concise as well as clear.

For more on parallel structure, see 18.

**16d**  To compare an item with others of its kind, use *any other.*

A comparison using *any* shows how something relates to a group without belonging to the group.

Alaska is larger than *any* country in Central America.

A comparison using *any other* shows how one member of a group relates to other members of the same group.

Death Valley is drier than *any other* place in the United States.

## EXERCISE 16–1 Completing Comparisons

Revise the following sentences by adding needed words to any comparisons that are incomplete. (There may be more than one way to complete some comparisons.) Some sentences may be correct. Possible revisions for the lettered sentences appear at the end of the Handbook. Example:

> I hate hot weather more than you¸^do.^   *Or*
>
> I hate hot weather more than ^I hate^ you.

a. The movie version of *The Brady Bunch* was much more ironic.

b. Taking care of a dog is often more demanding than a cat.

c. I received more free calendars in the mail for 2016 than any year.

d. The crime rate in the United States is higher than Canada.

e. Liver contains more iron than any meat.

1. Driving a sports car means more to Jake than his professors.

2. People who go to college aren't necessarily smarter, but they will always have an advantage at job interviews.

3. I don't have as much trouble getting along with Michelle as Karen.

4. A hen lays fewer eggs than a turtle.

5. Singing is closer to prayer than a meal of Chicken McNuggets.

## Elliptical Constructions

Robert Frost begins his well-known poem "Fire and Ice" with the following lines:

> Some say the world will end in fire, / Some say in ice.

When Frost wrote that opening, he avoided needless repetition by implying certain words rather than stating them. The result is more concise and more effective than a complete version of the same sentence would be:

> Some say the world will end in fire, some say the world will end in ice.

This common tactic produces an **elliptical construction** — one that leaves out (for conciseness) words that are unnecessary but clearly understood by readers. Elliptical constructions can be confusing, however, if a writer gives readers too little information to fill in those missing words.

**16e** When you eliminate repetition, keep all the words essential for clarity.

An elliptical construction avoids repeating what a reader already knows, but it should omit only words that are stated elsewhere in the sentence, including prepositions. Otherwise, your reader may fill the gap incorrectly.

> *to*
> The train neither goes‸nor returns from Middletown.

**16f** In a compound predicate, leave out only verb forms that have already been stated.

Compound predicates are prone to incomplete constructions, especially if the verbs are in different tenses. Be sure no necessary part is missing.

A **compound predicate** is a predicate consisting of two or more verbs linked by a conjunction (see 5a).

> *voted*
> Lee never has‸and never will vote to raise taxes.

**16g** If you mix comparisons using *as* and *than*, include both words.

To contrast two things, use the comparative form of an adjective followed by *than*: *better than, more than, fewer than*. To show a similarity between two things, sandwich the simple form of an adjective between *as* and *as*: *as good as, as many as, as few as*. Often you can combine two *than* or two *as* comparisons into an elliptical construction.

For more on comparative forms, see 13d–13f.

> The White House is smaller [than] and newer than Buckingham Palace.
>
> Some elegant homes are as large [as] and as grand as the White House.

However, merging a *than* comparison with an *as* comparison won't work.

> *than*
> The White House is smaller‸but just as beautiful as Buckingham Palace.

---

**EXERCISE 16–2** Completing Sentences

Revise the following sentences by adding needed words to any constructions that are incomplete. (There may be more than one way to complete some constructions.) Some sentences may be correct. Possible revisions for the lettered sentences appear at the end of the Handbook. Example:

> *seen*
> The general should have‸but didn't see the perils of invasion.

a. Eighteenth-century China was as civilized and in many respects more sophisticated than the Western world.

b. Pembroke was never contacted, much less involved with, the election committee.

c. I haven't yet but soon will finish my research paper.

d. Ron likes his popcorn with butter, Linda with parmesan cheese.

e. George Washington always has been and will be regarded as the father of this country.

1. You have traveled to exotic Tahiti; Maureen to Asbury Park, New Jersey.

2. The mayor refuses to negotiate or even talk to the civic association.

3. Building a new sewage treatment plant would be no more costly and just as effective as modifying the existing one.

4. You'll be able to tell Jon from the rest of the team: Jon wears white Reeboks, the others black high-tops.

5. Erosion has and always will reshape the shoreline.

# 17 | Mixed Constructions and Faulty Predication

> A **phrase** consists of two or more related words that work together but may lack a subject, a verb, or both (see 4b).

Sometimes a sentence contains all the necessary ingredients but still doesn't make sense.

## 17a Link phrases and clauses logically.

A **mixed construction** results when a writer connects phrases or clauses (or both) that don't work together as a sentence.

> A **clause** is a group of related words that includes both a subject and a verb (see 4a).

MIXED    In her efforts to solve the tax problem only caused the mayor additional difficulties.

The prepositional phrase *In her efforts to solve the tax problem* is a modifier; it can't act as the subject of a sentence. The writer, however, has used this phrase as a noun — the subject of the verb *caused*. To untangle this mixed construction, the writer has two choices: (1) rewrite the phrase so that it works as a noun, or (2) use the phrase as a modifier, not as a subject.

> A **preposition** is a transitional word (such as *in, on, at, of, from*) that leads into a phrase (see 1f).

REVISED    Her efforts to solve the tax problem only caused the mayor additional difficulties. [With *in* gone, *efforts* becomes the subject.]

REVISED    In her efforts to solve the tax problem, the mayor created additional difficulties. [The phrase now modifies the verb *created*.]

To fix a mixed construction, check your links — especially prepositions and conjunctions.

Jack~~,~~ although he was picked up by the police~~,~~ but was not charged.

*Although*
Jack, ~~although~~ he was picked up by the police, ~~but~~ was not charged. *Jack*

**Guidelines for Multilingual Writers**
How Can I Avoid Mixed Constructions, Faulty Predication, and Subject Errors?

**Mixed constructions** result when phrases or clauses are joined even though they do not logically go together. Combine clauses with either a coordinating conjunction or a subordinating conjunction, never both.

> Although baseball is called "the national pastime" of the United States, ~~but~~ football is probably more popular.

> *Baseball*
> ~~Although baseball~~ is called "the national pastime" of the United States, but football is probably more popular.

**Faulty predication** results when a verb and its subject, object, or modifier do not match. Do not use a noun as both the subject of the sentence and the object of a preposition.

> *there are*
> In my neighborhood, has several good restaurants.

> *My*
> ~~In my~~ neighborhood has several good restaurants.

**Subject errors** include leaving out and repeating subjects of clauses.

- Do not omit *it* used as a subject. A subject is required in all English sentences except commands (imperatives).

  > *It is*
  > Is interesting to visit museums.

- Do not repeat the subject of a sentence with a pronoun.

  > My brother-in-law, ~~he~~ is a successful investor.

For more on coordination and subordination, see 19.

**Coordinating conjunctions** join elements with equal or near-equal importance (see 1g and 19a–19c).

A **subordinating conjunction** is a word (such as *because, although, if, when*) used to make one clause dependent on, or subordinate to, another (see 1g and 19d–19f).

## 17b  Relate the parts of a sentence logically.

**Faulty predication** refers to a skewed relationship between a verb and some other part of a sentence.

> FAULTY    *The temperature of water freezes at 32 degrees Fahrenheit.*

At first glance, that sentence looks all right. It contains both subject and verb. It expresses a complete thought. What is wrong with it? The writer has mismatched the subject and verb. The sentence tells us that *temperature freezes*, when science and common sense tell us *water* freezes. The writer needs to select a subject and verb that fit each other.

> REVISED    *Water freezes at 32 degrees Fahrenheit.*

Faulty predication also results from a mismatched verb and direct object.

> *the number of students who can attend college.*
> Rising costs diminish ~~college for many students.~~

A **subject** is the part of a sentence that names something—a person, an object, an idea, a situation—about which the verb makes an assertion (see 2).

A **verb** is a word that shows action or state of being (see 1c and 3).

A **direct object** is the target of a verb that completes the action performed by the subject or asserted about the subject (see 3a).

A **linking verb** is a verb that shows a state of being by linking the sentence subject with a word that renames or describes the subject (see 1c and 3b.)

Costs don't *diminish college.* To correct this error, the writer changed the sentence so that its direct object follows logically from its verb. Subtler predication errors result when a writer uses a linking verb to forge a false connection between the subject and a subject complement.

> FAULTY    *Industrial waste* has become *an important modern priority.*

Is it *waste* that has become a *priority?* Or is it *solving problems caused by careless disposal of industrial waste?* A writer who says all that, though, risks wordiness. Why not just replace *priority* with a closer match for *waste?*

> REVISED    *Industrial waste* has become *a modern menace.*

Mismatches between a verb and another part of the sentence are easier to avoid when the verb is active rather than passive.

The idea of giving thanks for a good harvest ~~was not done first by~~ the Pilgrims.
*(did not originate with)*

## 17c Avoid starting a definition with *is when* or *is where.*

A definition needs to fit grammatically with the rest of the sentence.

> Dyslexia is ~~when you have~~ a reading disorder.

> *To shoot a layup,*
> ~~A layup is where~~ a player dribbles in close to the basket and then makes a one-handed, banked shot.

## 17d Avoid using *the reason is because . . .*

Anytime you start an explanation with *the reason is,* what follows *is* should be a subject complement: an adjective, a noun, or a noun clause. *Because* is a conjunction; it cannot function as a noun or an adjective.

> *that*
> The reason Al hesitates is ~~because~~ no one supported him last year.

> ~~The reason~~ Al hesitates ~~is~~ because no one supported him last year.

---

### EXERCISE 17–1 Correcting Mixed Constructions and Faulty Predication

Correct any mixed constructions and faulty predication you find in the following sentences. Possible revisions for the lettered sentences appear at the end of the Handbook. Example:

> *worsened*
> The storm ~~damaged~~ the beach erosion.    *Or*

> *beach.*
> The storm damaged the ~~beach erosion.~~

a. The cost of health insurance protects people from big medical bills.

b. In his determination to prevail helped him finish the race.

c. The AIDS epidemic destroys the body's immune system.

d. The temperatures are too cold for the orange trees.

e. A recession is when economic growth is small or nonexistent and unemployment increases.

1. The opening of the new shopping mall should draw out-of-town shoppers for years to come.

2. The reason the referendum was defeated was because voters are tired of paying so much in taxes.

3. In the glacier's retreat created the valley.

4. A drop in prices could put farmers out of business.

5. The researchers' main goal is cancer.

# 18 | Parallel Structure

You use **parallel structure,** or parallelism, when you create a series of words, phrases, clauses, or sentences with the same grammatical form. The pattern created by the series — its parallel structure — emphasizes the similarities or differences among the items, whether things, qualities, actions, or ideas.

> My favorite foods are roast beef, apple pie, and linguine with clams.
>
> Louise is charming, witty, intelligent, and talented.
>
> Manuel likes to swim, ride, and run.
>
> Dave likes movies that scare him and books that make him laugh.

Each series is a perfect parallel construction, composed of equivalent words: nouns in the first example, then adjectives, verbs, and adjective clauses.

## 18a In a series linked by a coordinating conjunction, keep all elements in the same grammatical form.

A coordinating conjunction (*and, but, for, or, nor, so, yet*) cues your readers to expect a parallel structure. Whether your series consists of single words, phrases, or clauses, its parts should balance one another.

For more on coordination, see 19a–19c.

> *clumsy*
> The puppies are tiny, ~~clumsily bumping into each other,~~ and cute.

Two elements in this series are parallel one-word adjectives (*tiny, cute*), but the third, the verb phrase *clumsily bumping,* is inconsistent.

A **gerund** is a form of a verb, ending in *-ing*, that functions as a noun (see 8a).

An **infinitive** consists of the base form of a verb plus the word *to* (see 8a).

Don't mix verb forms, such as gerunds and infinitives, in a series.

Plan a winter vacation if you like skiing and ~~to skate~~. *skating.*

Plan a winter vacation if you like skiing *to ski* and to skate.

In a series of phrases or clauses, be sure that all elements in the series are similar in form, even if they are not similar in length.

You can take the key, or ~~don't forget~~ *you can* to leave it under the mat. [The declarative clause starting with *You can* is not parallel to the imperative clause starting with *don't forget*.]

## 18b In a series linked by correlative conjunctions, keep all elements in the same grammatical form.

A **correlative conjunction** is a pair of linking words such as *either/or* or *not only/but also* that appear separately but work together to join elements of a sentence. When you use a correlative conjunction, follow each part with a similarly structured word, phrase, or clause.

I'm looking forward ~~to~~ either *to* attending Saturday's wrestling match or to seeing it on closed-circuit TV. [*To* precedes the first part (*to either*) but follows the second part (*or to*).]

Take my advice: try neither ~~to be~~ *to be* first nor last in the lunch line. [*To be* follows the first part but not the second part.]

### Correlative Conjunctions *at a Glance*

| | | |
|---|---|---|
| as . . . as | just as . . . so | not only . . . but also |
| both . . . and | neither . . . nor | whether . . . or |
| either . . . or | not . . . but | |

For more on comparisons, see 16a–16d and 16g.

## 18c Make the elements in a comparison parallel in form.

A comparative word such as *than* or *as* cues the reader to expect a parallel structure. This makes logical sense: to be compared, two things must resemble each other, and parallel structure emphasizes this resemblance.

Philip likes ~~fishing~~ *to fish* better than to sail.

Maintaining railway lines is as important to the public transportation system as ~~to buy~~ *buying* new trains.

## 18d Reinforce parallel structure by repeating rather than mixing lead-in words.

Parallel structures are especially useful when a sentence contains a series of clauses or phrases. For example, try to precede potentially confusing clauses with *that, who, when, where,* or some other connective, repeating the same connective every time to help readers follow them with ease.

> No one in this country needs a government *that* aids big business at the
> *that*
> expense of farmers and workers, ~ravages the environment in the name of
> *that*
> progress, or ~slashes budgets for health and education.

If the same lead-in word won't work for all elements in a series, try changing the order of the elements to minimize variation.

> *and expensive, but uncomfortable and*
> The new school building is large ~but not very comfortable, and expensive,~ ~but~ unattractive.

---

## EXERCISE 18–1  Making Sentences Parallel

Revise the following sentences by substituting parallel structures for awkward ones. Possible revisions for the lettered sentences appear at the end of the Handbook. Example:

> In the Rio Grande Valley, the interests of conservationists, government
> *immigrants*
> officials, and ~those trying to immigrate~ collide.

a. The border separating Texas and Mexico marks not only the political boundary of two countries, but it also is the last frontier for some endangered wildlife.

b. In the Rio Grande Valley, both local residents and the people who happen to be tourists enjoy visiting the national wildlife refuges.

c. The tall grasses in this valley are the home of many insects, birds, and there are abundant small mammals.

d. Two endangered wildcats, the ocelot and another called the jaguarundi, also make the Rio Grande Valley their home.

e. Many people from Central America are desperate to immigrate to the United States by either legal or by illegal means.

1. Because the land along the Rio Grande has few human inhabitants and the fact that the river is often shallow, many illegal immigrants attempt to cross the border there.

2. To capture illegal immigrants more easily, the U.S. government has cut down tall grasses, put up fences, and the number of immigration patrols has been increased.

3. For illegal immigrants, crossing the border at night makes more sense than to enter the United States in broad daylight, so the U.S. government has recently installed bright lights along the border.

4. The ocelot and the jaguarundi need darkness, hiding places, and to have some solitude if they are to survive.

5. Neither the immigration officials nor have wildlife conservationists been able to find a solution that will protect both the U.S. border and these endangered wildcats.

# 19 | Coordination and Subordination

Coordination and subordination can use conjunctions to specify relationships between ideas. Coordination connects thoughts of equal importance; subordination shows how one thought affects another.

## 19a Use coordination to join clauses or sentences that are related in theme and equal in importance.

The car skidded for a hundred yards. It crashed into a brick wall.

These two clauses make equally significant statements about the same subject, a car accident. Because the writer has not linked the sentences, we can only guess that the crash followed from the skid.

The car skidded for a hundred yards, and it crashed into a brick wall.

Now the sequence is clear: first the car skidded; then it crashed. That's coordination. There are three main ways to join clauses using coordination.

1. Join two main clauses with a comma and a coordinating conjunction (*for, and, nor, but, or, yet, so*).

    Ari does not want to be placed on your mailing list. ~~He does not~~ want a salesperson to call him.      *, nor does he*

2. Join two main clauses with a semicolon and a conjunctive adverb. Conjunctive adverbs show relationships such as addition, comparison, contrast, emphasis, cause and effect, or time.

    The guerrillas did not observe the truce. ~~They~~ never intended to.      *; furthermore, they*

3. Join two main clauses with a semicolon or a colon.

    The army wants to negotiate. ~~The~~ guerrillas prefer to fight.      *; the*

    The guerrillas have two advantages. ~~They~~ know the terrain, and the people support them.      *; they*

A **conjunction** is a linking word that connects words or groups of words through coordination or subordination (see 1g).

A **clause** is a group of related words that includes both a subject and a verb (see 4a).

**Coordinating conjunctions** join elements with equal or near-equal importance.

For a list of common conjunctive adverbs, see p. 809.

For more on semicolons and colons, see 30 and 31.

## 19b Coordinate clauses only if they are clearly and logically related.

Whenever you hitch together two sentences, make sure they get along. Will the relationship between them be evident to your readers?

FAULTY          The sportscasters were surprised by Easy Goer's failure to win the Kentucky Derby, but it rained on derby day.

Readers need enough information to see why two clauses are connected.

COORDINATED          The sportscasters were surprised by Easy Goer's failure to win the Kentucky Derby; *however, he runs poorly on a muddy track,* and it rained on derby day.

Choose a coordinating conjunction, conjunctive adverb, or punctuation mark that accurately reflects this relationship.

The sportscasters all expected Easy Goer to win the Kentucky Derby, ~~and~~ *but* Sunday Silence beat him.

## 19c Coordinate clauses only if they work together to make a coherent point.

When a writer strings together several clauses in a row, often the result is excessive coordination. Packing too much information into a single sentence can make readers dizzy, unable to pick out which points really matter. Each key idea deserves its own sentence so readers see its importance.

> ### Coordinating Words *at a Glance*
>
> **Coordinating Conjunctions**
> and, but, for, nor, or, so, yet
>
> **Common Conjunctive Adverbs**
>
> | | | | |
> |---|---|---|---|
> | accordingly | finally | likewise | otherwise |
> | also | furthermore | meanwhile | similarly |
> | anyway | hence | moreover | still |
> | as | however | nevertheless | then |
> | besides | incidentally | next | therefore |
> | certainly | indeed | nonetheless | thus |
> | consequently | instead | now | undoubtedly |

EXCESSIVE          Easy Goer was the Kentucky Derby favorite, and all the sportscasters expected him to win, but he runs poorly on a muddy track, and it rained on derby day, so Sunday Silence beat him.

REVISED    Easy Goer was the Kentucky Derby favorite, and all the sportscasters expected him to win. However, he runs poorly on a muddy track, and it rained on derby day. Therefore, Sunday Silence beat him.

Excessive coordination may result from repeating the same conjunction.

EXCESSIVE    Phil was out of the house all day, so he didn't know about the rain, so he went ahead and bet on Easy Goer, so he lost twenty bucks, so now he wants to borrow money from me.

REVISED    Phil was out of the house all day, so he didn't know about the rain. He went ahead and bet on Easy Goer, and he lost twenty bucks. Now he wants to borrow money from me.

---

## EXERCISE 19–1 Using Coordination

Revise the following sentences, adding coordination where appropriate and removing faulty or excessive coordination. Possible revisions for the lettered sentences appear at the end of the Handbook. Example:

The wind was rising, ~~and~~ leaves tossed on the trees, and the air seemed to

crackle with electricity, ~~and we~~ **. We** knew that a thunderstorm was on the way.

a. Professional poker players try to win money and prizes in high-stakes tournaments. They may lose thousands of dollars.

b. Poker is not an easy way to make a living. Playing professional poker is not a good way to relax.

c. A good "poker face" reveals no emotions. Communicating too much information puts a player at a disadvantage.

d. Hidden feelings may come out in unconscious movements. An expert poker player watches other players carefully.

e. Poker is different from most other casino gambling games, for it requires skill and it forces players to compete against each other, and other casino gambling pits players against the house, so they may win out of sheer luck, but skill has little to do with winning those games.

1. The rebels may take the capital in a week. They may not be able to hold it.

2. If you want to take Spanish this semester, you have only one choice. You must sign up for the 8 a.m. course.

3. Peterson's Market has raised its prices. Last week tuna fish cost $1.29 a can. Now it's up to $1.59.

4. Joe starts the morning with a cup of coffee, which wakes him up, and then at lunch he eats a chocolate bar, so that the sugar and caffeine will bring up his energy level.

5. The *Hindenburg* drifted peacefully over New York City. It exploded just before landing.

---

## 19d Subordinate less important ideas.

Subordination is extremely useful because it shows your readers the relative importance of ideas, how one follows from another or affects another. You stress what counts, thereby encouraging your readers to share your viewpoint. You can subordinate one sentence to another in either of the following ways.

For a list of subordinating words, see p. 808.

1. Turn the less important idea into a subordinate clause by introducing it with a subordinating conjunction such as *because, if,* or *when.*

   Jason has a keen sense of humor. He has an obnoxious, braying laugh.

From those sentences, readers don't know what to feel about Jason. Is he likable or repellent? The writer needs to show which trait matters more.

A **main clause** is a group of words that has both a subject and a verb and can stand alone as a complete sentence (see 4a).

> *Although Jason has a keen sense of humor,* he has an obnoxious, braying laugh.

This revision makes Jason's sense of humor less important than his annoying hee-haw. The less important idea is stated as a subordinate clause opening with *Although*; the more important idea is stated as the main clause.
    The writer could reverse the meaning by combining the other way:

A **relative pronoun** is a pronoun that opens a subordinate clause and modifies a noun or pronoun in another clause (see 1b).

> *Although Jason has an obnoxious, braying laugh,* he has a keen sense of humor.

That version makes Jason sound fun to be with, despite his mannerism.
    Which of Jason's traits to emphasize is up to the writer. What matters is that, in both combined versions, the writer takes a clear stand by making one sentence a main clause and the other a subordinate clause.

2. Turn the less important idea into a subordinate clause by introducing it with a relative pronoun such as *who, which,* or *that.*

   Jason, *who has an obnoxious, braying laugh,* has a keen sense of humor.

   Jason, *whose sense of humor is keen,* has an obnoxious, braying laugh.

## 19e Express the more important idea in the main clause.

Sometimes a writer accidentally subordinates a more important idea to a less important one and turns the sentence's meaning upside down.

| | |
|---|---|
| FAULTY SUBORDINATION | Although the heroism of the Allied troops on D-Day lives on in spirit, many of the World War II soldiers who invaded Normandy are dead now. |

## Subordinating Words *at a Glance*

### Common Subordinating Conjunctions

| | | | |
|---|---|---|---|
| after | before | since | until |
| although | even though | so | when |
| as | how | so that | whenever |
| as if | if | than | where |
| as soon as | in order that | that | wherever |
| as though | once | though | while |
| because | rather than | unless | why |

### Relative Pronouns

| | | | |
|---|---|---|---|
| that, which | what | who | whom |
| whose | whatever | whoever | whomever |

## Guidelines for Multilingual Writers
### What's the Difference between Prepositions and Conjunctions?

Prepositions and conjunctions may seem similar, but they have different functions in a sentence. To make things even more confusing, some words, such as *but, for, after,* and *until,* can work as either a conjunction or a preposition. Here are some tips to keep in mind:

■ **Coordinating conjunctions** join words, phrases, or clauses.

WORDS: Jacob excels at English, history, *and* French.

PHRASES: Cats enjoy sleeping in the daytime *but* creeping around at night.

CLAUSES: Alicia is taking many science classes, *for* she wants to become a doctor.

■ **Subordinating conjunctions** come at the beginning of a clause, giving that clause less emphasis than the main clause in the sentence. Remember that all clauses have a subject and a verb.

*After* she finished the book, Deanne began writing a summary.

The bus driver stayed with the student *until* the ambulance arrived.

■ **Prepositions** introduce short phrases that consist of the preposition, a noun (the object of the preposition), and any articles or adjectives. Note that prepositional phrases do not contain subjects or verbs.

*After* Thanksgiving dinner, Carla always takes a long walk *around* the neighborhood.

*On* New Year's Eve, everyone *but* Isadora stayed awake *until* midnight.

We waited *for* the package, but it never came.

This sentence is accurate. Does the writer, however, want to stress death over life? This is the effect of putting *are dead now* in the main clause and *lives on* in the subordinate clause. Instead, the writer can reverse the two.

REVISED
Although many of the World War II soldiers who invaded Normandy are dead now, the heroism of the Allied troops on D-Day lives on in spirit.

## 19f Limit the number of subordinate clauses in a sentence.

Excessive subordination strings too many ideas together without helping readers pick out what matters.

Debate over the Strategic Defense Initiative (SDI), ~~which was originally~~ *has to some extent focused on the wrong question. The plan*

proposed as a space-based defensive shield that would protect America

from enemy attack, ~~but which critics~~ *Critics* have suggested amounts to creating *, however, that it*

a first-strike capability in space, ~~has to some extent focused on the wrong~~

~~question.~~

> A **subordinate clause** is a group of words that contains a subject and a verb but cannot stand alone because it depends on a main clause to help it make sense (see 4a and 19d).

---

### EXERCISE 19–2 Using Subordination

Revise the following sentences, adding coordination where appropriate and removing faulty or excessive coordination where appropriate. Possible revisions for the lettered sentences appear at the end of the Handbook. Example:

The tiny house movement is a social ~~movement. It~~ involves people *movement that* downsizing to homes much smaller than traditional houses.

a. The average cost of a single-family home in the United States is over $275,000. It costs less than one-tenth of that to build a tiny house.

b. American homes average about 2,500 square feet. They have three bedrooms, two bathrooms, and a garage for two or more cars.

c. A tiny house is between 100 and 400 square feet. It enables simpler living in a smaller, more efficient space.

d. Tiny houses come in all shapes, sizes, and forms. They are much more customizable than traditional mobile homes.

e. The tiny house movement, which people are joining for many reasons, is popular because people who want to be environmentally conscious can build a tiny house so that they will have fewer financial concerns once they build the house, which will give them more time and freedom.

1. We may not realize it. Dozens of books are banned every year in schools, classrooms, and libraries.

2. Some communities feel that books contain dangerous themes and inappropriate language. They want to prevent children and teens from gaining access to them.

3. Young adult books such as the Twilight and Harry Potter series focus on what some people consider to be satanic or occult themes. These are often targeted by censorship groups.

4. Books could be made available only to the appropriate age group. They would not need to be banned.

5. If people who want to ban classics such as *The Grapes of Wrath* and *To Kill a Mockingbird* had actually read those books, they would realize that, although they may contain strong themes and language, their overall message is positive.

# 20 | Sentence Variety

For a review of sentence types, see 5.

Most writers rely on some patterns more than others to express ideas directly and efficiently, but sometimes they combine sentence elements in unexpected ways to emphasize ideas and to surprise readers.

### 20a  Normal Sentences

In a **normal sentence,** a writer puts the subject before the verb at the beginning of the main clause. This pattern is the most common in English because it expresses ideas in the most straightforward manner.

> Most college *students* today *want* interesting classes.

### 20b  Inverted Sentences

In an **inverted sentence,** a writer inverts or reverses the subject-verb order to emphasize an idea in the predicate.

> NORMAL    *My peers are uninterested* in reading.
>
> INVERTED    How *uninterested* in reading *are my peers*!

### 20c  Cumulative Sentences

In a **cumulative sentence,** a writer piles details at the end of a sentence to help readers visualize a scene or understand an idea.

> They came walking out in heavily brocaded yellow and black costumes, the familiar "toreador" suit, heavy with gold embroidery, cape, jacket, shirt and collar, knee breeches, pink stockings, and low pumps.
>
> —Ernest Hemingway, "Bullfighting Is Not a Sport—It Is a Tragedy"

### 20d  Periodic Sentences

The positions of emphasis in a sentence are the beginning and the end. In a **periodic sentence,** a writer suspends the main clause for a climactic ending, emphasizing an idea by withholding it until the end.

> Leaning back in his chair, shaking his head slowly back and forth, frustrated over his inability to solve the equation, Franklin scowled.

**EXERCISE 20–1** Increasing Sentence Variety

Revise the following passage, adding sentence variety to create interest, emphasize important ideas, and strengthen coherence.

We are terrified of death. We do not think of it, and we don't speak of death. We don't mourn in public. We don't know how to console a grieving friend. In fact, we have eliminated or suppressed all the traditional rituals surrounding death.

The Victorians coped with death differently. Their funerals were elaborate. The yards of black crepe around the hearse, hired professional mourners, and solemn procession leading to an ornate tomb are now only a distant memory. They wore mourning jewelry. They had a complicated dress code for the grieving process. It governed what mourners wore, and it governed how long they wore it. Many of these rituals may seem excessive or even morbid to us today. The rituals served a psychological purpose in helping the living deal with loss.

# 21 | Active and Passive Voice

ACTIVE          Intelligent students read challenging books.

PASSIVE        Challenging books are read by intelligent students.

These two statements convey similar information, but their emphasis is different. The first sentence is active: the subject (*students*) performs the verb's action (*read*). The second sentence is passive: the subject (*books*) receives the verb's action (*are read*). The active sentence states its idea directly; the passive sentence states its idea indirectly.

## 21a In most cases, use the active voice rather than the passive voice.

Verbs in the **active voice** consist of principal parts and helping verbs. Verbs in the **passive voice** consist of the past participle (*-ed* or *-en* form) preceded by a form of *be* ("you *are given*," "I *was given*," "she *will be given*"). Most writers prefer the active to the passive voice because it is clearer and simpler, requires fewer words, and identifies the actor and the action more explicitly.

ACTIVE VOICE    *Sergeants give* orders. *Privates obey* them.

Normally the subject of a sentence is the focus of readers' attention. If that subject does not perform the verb's action but instead receives the action, readers may wonder: What did the writer mean to emphasize?

PASSIVE VOICE   *Orders are given* by sergeants. *They are obeyed* by privates.

Other writers misuse the passive voice to try to lend pomp to a humble truth (or would-be truth). For example, "Slight technical difficulties are being experienced" may replace "The airplane needs repairs." Some even use the passive voice deliberately to obscure the truth.

## 21b Use the passive voice in certain cases.

You do not need to drop the passive voice entirely from your writing. Sometimes the performer of a verb's action is irrelevant, as in a lab report, which emphasizes the research, not the researcher. Sometimes the performer is understood:

> Automobiles are built in Detroit.

Other times the performer is unknown and simply omitted:

> Many fortunes were lost in the stock market crash of 1929.

It's a good idea, though, to substitute the active voice for the passive unless you have a good reason for using the passive:

> *I babysat for five*
> ~~Five~~ children ~~were babysat by me~~ last week.

---

### EXERCISE 21–1 Using Active and Passive Voice Verbs

Revise the following passage, changing the passive voice to the active voice in each sentence, unless you can justify keeping the passive. Example:

> *Many species of animals reached the*
> ~~The~~ Galápagos Islands ~~were reached by many species of animals~~ in ancient times.

The unique creatures of the Galápagos Islands have been studied by many scientists. The islands were explored by Charles Darwin in 1835. His observations led to the theory of evolution, which he explained in *On the Origin of Species*. Thirteen species of finches on the islands were discovered by Darwin, all descended from a common stock; even today this variety of species can be seen by visitors to the islands. Each island species has evolved by adapting to local conditions. A twig is used by the woodpecker finch to probe trees for grubs. Algae on the ocean floor are fed on by the marine iguana. Salt water can be drunk by the Galápagos cormorant, thanks to a salt-extracting gland. Because of the tameness of these animals, they can be studied by visitors at close range.

---

## Learning by Doing 🔟 Considering Language

Examine the sentence style of a written artifact (essay, piece of writing, song, Internet meme, etc.). What problems can you find with its modifiers, parallelism, variety, and other issues discussed in this chapter? Do you think the syle choices were intentional? How might you improve the writing?

# Take Action   Improving Sentence Style

Ask each question listed in the left-hand column to consider whether your draft might need work in that area. If so, follow the ASK—
LOCATE SPECIFICS — TAKE ACTION sequence to revise.

| 1 ASK | 2 LOCATE SPECIFICS | 3 TAKE ACTION |
|---|---|---|
| Have I missed opportunities to **emphasize comparable ideas** by stating them in comparable ways? | ■ Read your sentences, looking for **lists** or **comparable items**.<br><br>■ Underline items in a series to **compare the ways you present them**.<br><br>**DRAFT:** Observing primates can reveal how they cooperate, their tool use, and building secure nests. | ■ Rework so that items in a series all follow the **same grammatical pattern**.<br><br>■ Select the common pattern based on the **clarity** and **emphasis** it adds to your sentence.<br><br>**PARALLEL:** Observing primates can reveal how they cooperate, use tools, and build secure nests. |
| Do my sentences sound alike because they repeat the same opening, pattern, or length? | ■ Add a **line break** at the end of every sentence in a passage so you can easily compare sentence **openings, patterns, or lengths.**<br><br>■ **Count the words** in each sentence with your software (or do it yourself).<br><br>■ Search for **variations** such as colons (:) and semicolons (;) to see how often you use them. | ■ **Rewrite for variety** if you repeat openings (*During, Because, After, Then, And*).<br><br>■ **Rewrite for directness** if you repeat indirect openings (*There are, There is, It is*).<br><br>■ **Rewrite to vary sentence lengths.** Tuck in a few short sentences. Combine choppy sentences. Add a complicated sentence to build up to your point.<br><br>■ Try some **colons** or **semicolons** for variety. |
| Have I relied on sentences in the **passive voice** instead of the active voice? | ■ Reread each sentence. If its **subject also performs the action**, it is in the **active voice**. (Underline the performer; double underline the action.)<br><br>■ If the **sentence subject does not perform the action**, your sentence is in the **passive voice**. You have tucked the performer into a *by* phrase or have not identified the performer. | ■ **Consider changing passive voice to active.** Make the performer of the action the sentence subject (which reduces extra words by dropping the *by* phrase).<br><br>**PASSIVE:** The primate play area was arranged by the zookeeper. (9 words; emphasizes object of the action)<br><br>**ACTIVE:** The zookeeper arranged the primate play area. (7 words; emphasizes zookeeper who performed the action) |

# 41 Word Choice

22 | Appropriateness 814

23 | Exact Words 818

24 | Bias-Free Language 819

25 | Wordiness 822

26 | Commonly Confused Words 823

## 22 | Appropriateness

When you talk to people face-to-face, you can gauge their reactions to what you say. Often their responses guide your tone and your choice of words. When you write, you can't see your readers. Instead, you must imagine yourself in their place, focusing on their responses when you revise.

Besides affecting how well you achieve your purpose as a writer, your language can affect how well you're regarded by others. When you accurately assess the tone, formality, and word choice expected in a situation, you use the power of language to enhance your position. When you misjudge, you risk being misunderstood or judged harshly.

### 22a Choose a tone appropriate for your topic and audience.

Like a speaker, a writer may come across as friendly or aloof, furious or merely annoyed, playful or grimly serious. This attitude is the writer's **tone,** and it strongly influences the audience's response. For instance, readers might reject as inappropriate a humorous approach to terrorist attacks. To convey your tone, use sentence length, level of language, and vocabulary. The key is to be aware of your readers and their expectations.

### 22b Choose a level of formality appropriate for your tone.

Considering the tone you want to convey helps you choose words that are neither too formal nor too informal. **Formal** language is typically impersonal and serious. Usually written, formal language is marked by relatively complex sentences and a large vocabulary. It doesn't use contractions (such as *doesn't*).

In contrast, **informal** language more closely resembles ordinary conversation. It uses relatively short sentences and common words. It may include contractions, slang, and references to everyday objects and activities (cheeseburgers, T-shirts, apps). The writer may use *I* and address the reader as *you*.

The right language for most college essays lies somewhere between formal and informal. If your topic and tone are serious (say, for a research project on homelessness), then your language may lean toward formality. If your topic is not weighty and your tone is light (say, for a humorous personal essay about giving your dog a bath), then your language may be informal.

---

**EXERCISE 22–1 Choosing an Appropriate Tone and Level of Formality**

Revise the following passages to ensure that both the tone and the level of formality are appropriate for the topic and audience. Example:

> I'm sending you this letter because I want you to meet with me and give me some info about the job you do.
>
> *I am writing to inquire about the possibility of an informational interview about your profession.*

1. Dear Senator Crowley:

   I think you've got to vote for the new environmental law, so I'm writing this letter. We're messing up forests and wetlands — maybe for good. Let's do something now for everybody who's born after us.

   Thanks,
   Glenn Turner

2. The United States Holocaust Memorial Museum in Washington, D.C., is a great museum dedicated to a real bad time in history. It's hard not to get bummed out by the stuff on show. Take it from me, it's an experience you won't forget.

3. Dear Elaine,

   I am so pleased that you plan on attending the homecoming dance with me on Friday. It promises to be a gala event, and I am confident that we will enjoy ourselves immensely. I understand a local group by the name of Electric Bunny will provide musical entertainment. Please call me at your earliest convenience to inform me when to pick you up.

   Sincerely,
   Bill

---

## 22c Choose common words instead of jargon.

**Jargon** is the term for the specialized vocabulary used by people in a certain field, such as music, carpentry, law, or sports. Nearly every academic, professional, and recreational field has its own jargon. To a specialist addressing other specialists, jargon is convenient and necessary. Without technical terms, after all, two surgeons could hardly discuss a patient's anatomy. To an outsider, though, such terms may be incomprehensible. To communicate with readers without confusing them, avoid unnecessary jargon.

> *caught* *criminal*
> The police ~~apprehended~~ the alleged ~~perpetrator of the crime~~ in the
> *area* *arrest*
> ~~vicinity~~ of White Hills, and now they will ~~proceed to book~~ him.

For more on wordiness, see 25. For more on euphemisms (indirect wording to avoid unpleasant topics), see 22d.

Jargon often results in unnecessarily wordy language because the writer is attempting to sound intellectual or seeking to avoid speaking directly about an issue.

> *lost over* *some*
> Katrina ~~reduced her weight in excess of~~ 15 pounds by adding ~~a certain~~
> *exercise* *daily routine.*
> ~~amount of mobile activity~~ to her ~~quotidian procedure.~~

Many instances of jargon come from business and technical language. Avoid using technological terms such as *interface* and *input* to refer to nontechnical ideas. Also avoid ending words with the suffix *-ize* (as in *privatize*) and in the hyphenated term *-wise* (as in *time-wise*).

> *sell* *to private buyers.*
> The government intends to ~~privatize~~ federal land/
>
> *electorate to vote and to express its views to elected officials.*
> A democracy needs the ~~electorate's input.~~

---

## EXERCISE 22–2 Avoiding Jargon

Revise the following sentences to eliminate the jargon. If necessary, revise extensively. If you can't tell what a sentence means, decide what it might mean, and rewrite it so that its meaning is clear. Possible revisions for the lettered sentences appear at the end of the Handbook. Example:

> *cut*
> ~~The proximity of~~ Mr. Fitton's knife ~~to~~ Mr. Schering's arm ~~produced a~~
> ~~violation of the integrity of the skin.~~

a. Everyone at Boondoggle and Gall puts in face time at the holiday gatherings to maximize networking opportunities.

b. This year, in excess of fifty employees were negatively impacted by Boondoggle and Gall's decision to downsize effective September 1.

c. The layoffs made Jensen the sole point of responsibility for telephone interface in the customer-service department.

d. The numerical quotient of Jensen's telephonic exchanges increased by a factor of three post-downsizing, yet Jensen received no additional fiscal remuneration.

e. Jensen was not on the same page with management re her compensation, so she exercised the option to terminate her relationship with Boondoggle and Gall.

1. The driver-education course prepares the student for the skills of handling a vehicle on the highway transportation system.
2. In the heart area, Mr. Pitt is a prime candidate-elect for intervention of a multiple bypass nature.
3. The deer hunter's activity of quietizing a predetermined amount of the deer populace balances the ecological infrastructure.

## 22d  Use euphemisms sparingly.

**Euphemisms** are plain truths dressed attractively, sometimes hard facts stated gently. To say that someone *passed away* instead of *died* is a common euphemism—humane, perhaps, in breaking terrible news to an anxious family. In such language, an army that *retreats* makes *a strategic withdrawal*, a person who is *underweight* turns *slim,* and an acne cream treats not *pimples* but *blemishes.*

## 22e  Avoid slang in formal writing.

Slang, when new, can be colorful ("She's not playing with a full deck"), playful ("He's wicked cute!"), and apt (*ice* for diamonds, a *stiff* for a corpse). Most slang, however, quickly seems as old and wrinkled as the Jazz Age's *twenty-three skidoo!* Your best bet is to stick to words that are usual but exact.

### EXERCISE 22-3  Avoiding Euphemisms and Slang

Revise the following sentences to replace euphemisms with plainer words and slang with Standard English. Possible revisions for the lettered sentences appear at the end of the Handbook. Example:

> *Someone stole* ~~Some dude ripped off~~ my wallet, so I am ~~currently experiencing a~~ *now in debt.* ~~negative cash flow.~~

a. At three hundred bucks a month, the apartment is a steal.
b. The soldiers were victims of friendly fire during a strategic withdrawal.
c. Churchill was a wicked good politician.

1. Saturday's weather forecast calls for extended periods of shower activity.
2. The caller to the talk-radio program sounded totally wigged out.
3. We anticipate a downturn in economic vitality.

# 23 | Exact Words

Good writing depends on knowing what words mean and how to use them precisely.

## 23a Choose words for their connotations as well as their denotations.

The **denotation** of a word is its basic meaning—its dictionary definition. *Excited, agitated,* and *exhilarated* all denote a similar state of physical and emotional arousal. The **connotations** of a word are the shades of meaning that set it apart from its synonyms. You might be *agitated* by the prospect of exams next week, but *exhilarated* by your plans for the vacation afterward. When you choose one of several options, you base your choice on connotation.

> Advertisers have given light beer a macho image by showing football
>          *guzzling*                 *gusto.*
> players ~~sipping~~ the product with ~~enthusiasm.~~

## 23b Avoid clichés.

A **cliché** is a trite expression, once vivid or figurative but now worn out from too much use. Clichés abound when writers and speakers try hard to sound lively but don't invent anything vigorous, colorful, and new. If your writing includes clichés such as the following, delete them or rewrite them in your own words.

COMMON CLICHÉS

| | |
|---|---|
| a sneaking suspicion | last but not least |
| above and beyond the call of duty | make a long story short |
| add insult to injury | through thick and thin |
| beyond a shadow of a doubt | tip of the iceberg |
| few and far between | tried and true |

## 23c Use idioms in their correct form.

**Idioms,** or **idiomatic expressions** are phrases that, through long use, have become standard even though their construction may defy logic or grammar. Many idioms require you to choose the right preposition or which article, if any, to use before a noun. When in doubt, use a dictionary.

>                   *with*                                 *to*
> In order to comply ~~to~~ the zoning laws, be sure ~~and~~ check with the building department.

**Common Idiomatic Expressions** *at a Glance*

| | |
|---|---|
| abide by (not *abide with*) | sure to (not *sure and*) |
| according to (not *according with*) | think of, about (not *think on*) |
| capable of (not *capable to*) | try to (not *try and*) |
| comply with (not *comply to*) | type of (not *type of a*) |
| plan to (not *plan on*) | |

---

**EXERCISE 23–1** Selecting Words

Revise the following passage to replace inappropriate connotations, clichés, and faulty idioms. Example:

> *popular*
> The Mayan city of Uxmal is a ~~common~~ tourist attraction. The ruins
> *ancient times*
> have stood alone in the jungle since ~~time immemorial~~.

We spent the first day of our holiday in Mexico arguing around what we wanted to see on our second day. We finally agreed to a day trip out to some Mayan ruins. The next day we arrived on the Mayan city of Uxmal, which is as old as the hills. It really is a sight for sore eyes, smack-dab in a jungle stretching as far as the eye can see, with many buildings still covered in plants and iguanas moving quickly over the decayed buildings. The view from the top of the Soothsayer's Temple was good, although we noticed storm clouds gathering in the distance. The rain held up until we got off of the pyramid, but we drove back to the hotel in a lot of rain. After a day of sightseeing, we were so hungry that we could have eaten a horse, so we had a good meal before we turned in.

---

# 24 | Bias-Free Language

Thoughtful writers try to avoid harmful bias in their language. They respect their readers and don't want to insult them, anger them, or impede communication. Be on the lookout for words that insult or stereotype individuals or groups by gender, age, race, ethnic origin, sexual preference, or religion.

## 24a Avoid terms that include or imply *man.*

Substitute a gender-neutral term for *man* or a word starting with *man.*

> *Human beings study people's cruelty to one another.*
> ~~Mankind studies man's inhumanity to man.~~

Similarly, you need not simply replace the ending *-man* with *-person*. Instead, think about meaning and find a truly neutral synonym.

*letter carrier?*
Did you leave a note for the ~~mailman~~?

*flight attendant*
Ask your ~~stewardess~~ for a pillow.

## 24b Use plural instead of singular forms.

Replace the singular with the plural (*they* and *their* for *he* and *his*).

*students value their*
Today's ~~student values his~~ education.

When a singular indefinite pronoun is an antecedent, its pronoun must also be singular.

For more on pronoun-antecedent agreement, see 12.

*his or her*
Everyone is set in ~~their~~ ways. [The combined pronoun *his or her* is singular, so it correctly refers to the singular indefinite pronoun *Everyone*.]

Alternatively, you could recast the sentence with a plural antecedent.

*People are*
~~Everyone is~~ set in their ways. [Now the plural pronoun *their* agrees with the plural antecedent *People*.]

## 24c Where possible, omit words that denote gender.

You can make your language more bias-free by omitting pronouns and other words that needlessly indicate gender.

There must be rapport between a stockbroker and ~~his~~ client, a teacher and ~~her~~ student, a doctor and ~~his~~ patient.

Also treat men and women equally in terms of description or title.

*husband*
I now pronounce you ~~man~~ and wife.

*Ms.*
Please page Mr. Pease, Mr. Mankodi, and ~~Emily~~ Brillantes.

## 24d Avoid condescending labels.

A responsible writer does not call women *chicks, babes, woman drivers,* or any other names that imply that they are not to be taken seriously. Nor should an employee ever be called a *girl* or *boy*. Avoid terms that put down individuals or groups because of age (*old goat, the grannies*), race or ethnicity (*Indian giver, Chinaman's chance*), or disability (*gimpy, handicapped*).

*administrative assistants*
The ~~girls in the office~~ got Mr. Birt a birthday cake.

*has old-fashioned ideas.*
My neighbor ~~is just an old fogy.~~

When describing a group, try to use the label or term that its members prefer.

> *Asian*
> Alice wants to study ~~Oriental~~ culture.

## 24e  Avoid implied stereotypes.

Sometimes a stereotype is linked to a title. Aside from obvious exceptions, never assume that all the members of a group are of the same gender.

> *families.*
> Pilots have little time to spend with their ~~wives and children.~~

Avoid stereotyping individuals or groups, negatively or positively.

> Roberto isn't very good at paying his rent on time, ~~which doesn't surprise me because he is from Mexico.~~

## 24f  Use *Ms.* for a woman with no other known title.

*Ms.* is the preferred title of polite address for women because, like *Mr.* for men, it does not indicate marital status. Use *Miss* or *Mrs.* only if you know that the woman prefers this form. If a woman holds a doctorate, professional office, or position with a title, use that title rather than *Ms.*

Ms. Jane Doe, Editor                                       Dear Ms. Doe:
Professor Jane Doe, Department of English    Dear Professor Doe:
Senator Jane Doe, Washington, D.C.              Dear Senator Doe:

---

### EXERCISE 24–1  Avoiding Bias

Revise the following sentences to eliminate bias. Possible revisions for the lettered sentences appear at the end of the Handbook. Example:

> *Firefighters need*              *their*
> ~~A fireman needs~~ to check ~~his~~ equipment regularly.

a. Our school's athletic program will be of interest to black applicants.

b. The new physicians include Dr. Scalia, Anna Baniski, and Dr. Morton.

c. The diligent researcher will always find the sources he seeks.

1. Simon drinks like an Irishman.

2. Like most Asian Americans, Soon Li excels at music and mathematics.

3. Dick drives a Porsche because he likes the way she handles on the road, despite the little old ladies who slow down traffic.

# 25 | Wordiness

For strategies for
cutting extra words,
see Ch. 23.

Conciseness takes more effort than wordiness. For clarity, simplify expressions or omit them (*area of, field of, kind of, sort of, type of, very*).

| SAMPLE WORDY PHRASES | CONCISE |
|---|---|
| a large number of | many |
| a period of a week | a week |
| arrive at an agreement, conclude an agreement | agree |
| at an earlier point in time | before, earlier |
| due to the fact that | because |
| lend assistance to | assist, aid, help |
| past experience, past history | experience, history |
| persons of the Methodist faith | Methodists |
| plan ahead for the future | plan |
| resemble in appearance | look like |
| sufficient number (or amount) of | enough |
| true facts | facts, truth |
| utilize, make use of | use |

## EXERCISE 25–1 Eliminating Wordiness

Revise the following passage to eliminate wordiness. Example:

> *A*
> At this point in time, a debate ~~pertaining to~~ *about* freedom of speech is raging *currently*
> across our campuses.

The media in recent times have become obsessed with the conflict on campuses across the nation between freedom of speech and the attempt to protect minorities from verbal abuse. Very innocent remarks or remarks of a humorous nature, sometimes taken out of context, have gotten a large number of students into trouble for the violation of college speech codes. Numerous students have become very vocal in attacking these "politically correct" speech codes and defending the right to free speech. But is the campaign against the politically correct really pertaining to freedom of speech, or is it itself a way in which to silence debate? Due to the fact that the phrase "politically correct" has become associated with liberal social causes and sensitivity to minority feelings, it now carries a very extraordinary stigma in the eyes of conservatives. To accuse someone of being politically correct is to refute their ideas before hearing their argument. The attempt to silence the opposition is a dangerous sign of our times and suggests that we are indeed in a cultural war.

## Learning by Doing 🎥 Refining Your Wording

After you have read or skimmed through Chapter 41, consider which types of words you most often wrestle with. Do you have trouble regulating your tone, your attitude, and your degree of formality? Do you lapse into specialized jargon, slang, or clichés? Do you fall into biased or stereotypical wording rather than sticking to fair, neutral language? Or are you just plain wordy? Identify the problem you want to tackle, review the section about it, and plan a strategy—maybe highlighting words to reconsider, maybe applying your instructor's past suggestions in the current paper, or maybe searching for key words or passages to rephrase. After you have made improvements, exchange papers with a peer, and help each other spot any other word choice issues.

# 26 | Commonly Confused Words

The brief list that follows includes words and phrases that are commonly misspelled or confused. For a more comprehensive list, see the Glossary of Troublemakers on pages Q-50–Q-59 in the Quick Editing Guide. For tips on improving your spelling, see 41.

> ## Commonly Confused Homonyms *at a Glance*
>
> **accept** (v., receive willingly); **except** (prep., other than)
> Mimi could *accept* all of Lefty's gifts *except* his ring.
>
> **affect** (v., influence); **effect** (n., result)
> If the new rules *affect* us, what will be their *effect*?
>
> **capital** (adj., uppercase; n., seat of government); **capitol** (n., government building)
> The *Capitol* building in our nation's *capital* is spelled with a *capital* C.
>
> **cite** (v., refer to); **sight** (n., vision or tourist attraction); **site** (n., place)
> Did you *cite* Aunt Peg as your authority on which *sites* feature the most interesting *sights*?
>
> **complement** (v., complete; n., counterpart); **compliment** (v. or n., praise)
> For Lee to say that Sheila's beauty *complements* her intelligence may or may not be a *compliment*.
>
> **desert** (v., abandon; n., hot, dry region); **dessert** (n., end-of-meal sweet)
> Don't *desert* us by leaving for the *desert* before *dessert*.
>
> **elicit** (v., bring out); **illicit** (adj., illegal)
> By going undercover, Sonny should *elicit* some offers of *illicit* drugs.

*(continued)*

**led** (v., past tense of *lead*); **lead** (n., a metal)

Gil's heart was heavy as *lead* when he *led* the mourners to the grave.

**principal** (n. or adj., chief); **principle** (n., rule or standard)

The *principal* problem is convincing the media that the high school *principal* is a person of high *principles*.

**stationary** (adj., motionless); **stationery** (n., writing paper)

Hubert's *stationery* shop stood *stationary* until a flood swept it away.

**their** (pron., belonging to them); **there** (adv., in that place); **they're** (contraction of *they are*)

Sue said *they're* going over *there* to visit *their* aunt.

**to** (prep., toward); **too** (adv., also or excessively); **two** (n. or adj., numeral: one more than one)

Let's not take *two* cars *to* town—that's *too* many unless Hal comes *too*.

**who's** (contraction of *who is*); **whose** (pron., belonging to whom)

*Who's* going to tell me *whose* dog this is?

**your** (pron., belonging to you); **you're** (contraction of *you are*)

*You're* not getting *your* own way this time!

---

## EXERCISE 26–1 Commonly Confused Words

Edit the following passage to correct any misused words. You may need to refer to the longer list on pages Q-50–Q-59 or to a dictionary. Example:

*There*
~~Their~~ are many different ways to use a degree in psychology.

The principal job is of course psychologist, but a master's degree is required too practice therapy. For graduates just starting out with a psychology degree, a good idea would be to except a job in human resources, working on cite for a major corporation. This work is somewhat unique because it exposes employees to a wide variety of careers in a short period of time. In regards to other fields for psychology majors, job seekers might consider either real estate, law enforcement, or market research. The starting salary range for jobs in these areas is anywheres from $35,000 to $50,000 per year. Alot of psychology majors pursue graduate degrees in law, social work, criminal justice, and education. In most cases, an employee with a master's degree will earn more money then one with only a bachelor's degree. Psychology majors should try and consider all their options early so they can focus there education on the career path that suits them best.

# Take Action  Improving Word Use

Ask each question listed in the left-hand column to consider whether your draft might need work in that area. If so, follow the ASK—LOCATE SPECIFICS—TAKE ACTION sequence to revise.

| 1 ASK | 2 LOCATE SPECIFICS | 3 TAKE ACTION |
|---|---|---|
| Have I used words in an **appropriate and bias-free tone?** | ■ Read your draft out loud. Put a ✔ by words that sound **too formal or too informal** for your audience. Also listen for and mark **jargon, euphemisms, and slang.** <br><br>■ Circle **words that refer to men**, including masculine pronouns *(he, his)* or terms that imply men *(mailman)*. Also circle words that may be **offensive to certain groups** of people, or words that suggest **bias.** | ■ Return to each check mark to reword sections that are not the appropriate tone for your audience, and revise any jargon, euphemisms, and slang to more **straightforward language.** <br><br>■ Review circled words and change sexist or offensive language to be more **inclusive** and **balanced.** |
| Have I used words that **clearly express my meaning?** | ■ Read your draft out loud. Put a ✔ by words that may have an **unwanted connotation** or that sound **trite** or **clichéd.** <br><br>■ Circle (or use your software's grammar checker to highlight) words that are **often mistaken for others,** such as *affect/effect.* | ■ Return to each check mark and revise as needed to improve **connotation** and **clarity.** <br><br>■ Revise any **misused** words. |
| Have I used **more words than needed** to say what I mean? | ■ Read your draft out loud. Put a ✔ by anything that sounds **long-winded, repetitive, or chatty.** <br><br>■ Use past papers to help you list **your favorite wordy expressions** (such as *a large number of* for *many*) or **extra words** (such as *very* or *really*). | ■ At each check, rephrase with **simpler** or **more exact words.** <br><br>■ Search for **wordy expressions;** replace or trim them. <br><br>■ Highlight a passage; use the Tools or Review menu to count the number of words. **See how many extra words you can drop.** |

# 42 Punctuation

27 | End Punctuation 826

28 | Commas 828

29 | Misuses of the Comma 836

30 | Semicolons 838

31 | Colons 839

32 | Apostrophes 841

33 | Quotation Marks 844

34 | Dashes 848

35 | Parentheses, Brackets, and Ellipses 849

## Learning by Doing 🎯 Tackling Punctuation Patterns

Check comments in past drafts or final papers for similar punctuation errors that suggest a pattern. Have readers questioned your use of commas? Do you guess about where to put colons? Look up the Handbook guidelines for that punctuation problem, and write out useful "rules" in your own words. Present your "rules" or your remaining questions to a small group of classmates.

## 27 | End Punctuation

Three marks can signal the end of a sentence: the period, the exclamation point, and the question mark.

**27a** Use a period to end a declarative sentence, a directive, or an indirect question.

Most sentences are **declarative,** meaning that they make a statement.

Many people on earth are malnourished.

A period, not a question mark, ends an **indirect question,** which states
that a question was asked or is being asked.

For examples of direct
questions, see 27c.

> The counselor asked Marcia why she rarely gets to class on time~~?~~.
>
> I wonder why Roland didn't show up~~?~~.

## 27b Use a period after some abbreviations.

A period within a sentence shows that what precedes it has been shortened.

> Dr. Lene V. Hau's speech will be broadcast at 8:00 p.m.

The names of many organizations (YMCA, PTA), countries (USA, UK),
and people (JFK, FDR) are abbreviated using all capitals without periods.
Other abbreviations, such as those for designations of time, use periods.
When an abbreviation ends a sentence, follow it with one period, not two.

For more on
abbreviations, see 36.

## 27c Use a question mark to end a direct question.

> How many angels can dance on the head of a pin?

The question mark comes at the end of the question even if the question is
part of a longer declarative sentence.

For advice on
punctuating indirect
quotations and
questions, see 33. For
examples of indirect
questions, see 27a.

> "What'll I do now?" Marjorie wailed.

## 27d Use an exclamation point to end an interjection or an urgent command.

Rarely used in college writing, an exclamation point signals strong emotion.

An **interjection** is a
word or expression
that inserts an
outburst of feeling
(see 1h).

> We've struck an iceberg! We're sinking! I can't believe it!

It may mark an interjection or emphasize an urgent directive.

> Oh, no! Fire! Hurry up! Help me!

---

### EXERCISE 27–1  Using End Punctuation

If needed, correct end punctuation in the following sentences. Give reasons
for any changes you make. Some sentences may be correct. Answers for the
lettered sentences appear at the end of the Handbook. Example:

> Tom asked Cindy if she would be willing to coach him in tennis~~?~~. [Not a
> direct question]

a. The question that still troubles the community after all these years is why
   federal agents did not act sooner?

b. I wonder what he was thinking at the time?

c. If the suspect is convicted, will lawyers appeal the case?

1. What will Brad and Emilia do if they can't take vacations at the same time.

2. When a tree falls in a forest, but no one hears it, does it make a sound.

3. What will happen next is anyone's guess.

# 28 | Commas

Like a split-second pause in conversation, a well-placed comma helps your readers to catch your train of thought. It keeps them from stumbling over a solid block of words or drawing an inaccurate conclusion.

> Lyman paints, fences, and bowls.

Without the commas, the sentence reads as if Lyman is a painter who works with both a large and a small brush. The commas clarify that Lyman wields a paintbrush, a sword, and a bowling ball.

### 28a Use a comma with a coordinating conjunction to join two main clauses.

*A **main clause** is a group of words that has both a subject and a verb and can stand alone as a complete sentence (see 4a).*

When you join main clauses with a coordinating conjunction (*and, but, for, or, nor, so, yet*), add a comma after the first clause, right before the conjunction.

COORD CONJ

| MAIN CLAUSE | MAIN CLAUSE |

> The pie whooshed through the air, but the agile Hal ducked.

If your clauses are short and parallel in form, you may omit the comma. Or you may keep the comma to throw emphasis on your second clause.

Spring passed and summer came.       Spring passed, and summer came.

They urged but I refused.       They urged, but I refused.

*A **phrase** consists of two or more related words that work together but may lack a subject, a verb, or both (see 4b).*

CAUTION: Don't use a comma with a coordinating conjunction that links two verbs or phrases.

> The mustangs galloped, and cavorted across the plain.

> The lights flickered momentarily, and then went out completely.

### 28b Use a comma after an introductory clause, phrase, or word.

*A **clause** is a group of related words that includes both a subject and a verb (see 4a).*

> *Weeping,* Lydia stumbled down the stairs.
>
> *Before that,* Arthur saw her reading an old love letter.
>
> *If he knew who the writer was,* he didn't tell.

Placed after any such opening word, phrase, or subordinate clause, a comma tells your reader, "Enough preliminaries: now the main clause starts."

EXCEPTION: You need not use a comma after a single introductory word or a short phrase or clause if there is no danger of misreading.

> *Sooner or later* Lydia will tell us the whole story.

---

### EXERCISE 28–1 Using Commas

Add any necessary commas to the following sentences, and remove any commas that do not belong. Some sentences may be correct. Answers for the lettered sentences appear at the end of the Handbook. Example:

> During the guided tour of the Mayan ruins⌄ James had no access to phone service or e-mail.

a. He was so upset about his lack of connection to the outside world that he might as well have not even come on the trip.

b. When we returned to the hotel he couldn't wait to check for any messages.

c. James logged on to the hotel wifi immediately but he was surprised to find that he hadn't gotten any e-mails all morning.

d. His office hadn't called him nor had his friends left him any messages.

e. He pretended to be relieved that nothing urgent had come up at work but I think he was secretly annoyed that everyone was doing fine without him.

1. Some people say that we are overly wired in this age of modern gadgets but others just can't get enough technology.

2. How often do we stop to look around and talk with other people on the train or in a coffee shop?

3. One family instituted a "tech-free Tuesday" in their home so nobody had access to wifi, telephones, or television.

4. They played games together after dinner, and read books before going to sleep.

5. The teenage kids hated it at first but they ended up enjoying their night off from digital connections.

---

## 28c Use a comma between items in a series.

When you list three or more items, whether they are nouns, verbs, adjectives, adverbs, or entire phrases or clauses, separate them with commas.

> Country ham⌄ sweet corn⌄ and potatoes weighted Grandma's table.

> Joel prefers music that shakes⌄ rattles⌄ and rolls.

Notice that no comma *follows* the coordinating conjunction.

> We climbed the Matterhorn, voyaged beneath the sea, and/ flew on a rocket through space.

NOTE: Some writers omit the comma *before* the final item in the series. This custom may throw off the rhythm of a sentence and, in some cases, obscure the writer's meaning. Using the comma in such a case is never wrong and is preferred in academic style; omitting it can create confusion.

> I was met at the station by my cousins, brother and sister.

Are these people a brother-and-sister pair who are the writer's cousins? Or are they a group consisting of the writer's cousins, her brother, and her sister? If they are more than two people, a comma would clear up the confusion.

> I was met at the station by my cousins, brother, and sister.

## 28d Use a comma between coordinate adjectives but not between cumulative adjectives.

Adjectives that function independently of each other, though they modify the same noun, are called **coordinate adjectives.** Set them off with commas.

> Ruth was a clear, vibrant, persuasive speaker.

> Life is nasty, brutish, and short.

CAUTION: Don't use a comma after the final adjective before a noun.

> My professor was a brilliant, caring/ teacher.

To check whether adjectives are coordinate, ask two questions. Can you rearrange the adjectives without distorting the meaning? (*Ruth was a persuasive, vibrant, clear speaker.*) Can you insert *and* between them? (*Life is nasty and brutish and short.*) If the answer to both is yes, the adjectives are coordinate. Removing any one of them would not greatly affect the others. Use commas between them to show that they are separate and equal.

**Coordinating conjunctions** join elements of equal or near-equal importance (see 1g and 19a–19c).

NOTE: If you link coordinate adjectives with *and* or another coordinating conjunction, omit the commas except in a series (see 28c).

> New York City is huge/ and dirty/ and beautiful.

**Cumulative adjectives** work together to create a single unified picture of the noun they modify. No commas separate them.

> Ruth has two small white poodles.

> Who's afraid of the big bad wolf?

For more on cumulative adjectives, see p. 786.

If you remove, rearrange, or insert *and* between cumulative adjectives, the effect is distorted (*two white small poodles; the big and bad wolf*).

## EXERCISE 28-2 Using Commas

In these sentences, add any necessary commas, remove any unneeded ones, and change any incorrect punctuation. Some sentences may be correct. Answers for the lettered sentences appear at the end of the Handbook. Example:

Mel has been a faithful, hardworking, consistent band manager.

a. Mrs. Carver looks like a sweet, little, old lady, but she plays a wicked electric guitar.

b. Her bass player, her drummer and her keyboard player all live in the same retirement community.

c. They practice individually in the afternoon, rehearse together at night and play at the community's Saturday night dances.

d. The Rest Home Rebels have to rehearse quietly, and cautiously, to keep from disturbing the other residents.

e. Mrs. Carver has organized the group, scheduled their rehearsals, and acquired backup instruments.

1. When she breaks a string, she doesn't want her elderly crew to have to grab the guitar change the string and hand it back to her, before the song ends.

2. The Rest Home Rebels' favorite bands are U2, Arcade Fire and Lester Lanin and his orchestra.

3. They watch a lot of MTV because it is fast-paced colorful exciting and informative and it has more variety than soap operas.

4. Just once, Mrs. Carver wants to play in a really, huge, sold-out, arena.

5. She hopes to borrow the community's big, white, van to take herself her band and their equipment to a major, professional, recording studio.

## 28e Use commas to set off a nonrestrictive phrase or clause.

A **nonrestrictive modifier** adds a fact that, while perhaps interesting and valuable, isn't essential. You could leave it out of the sentence and still make sense. Set off the modifier with commas before and after.

Potts Alley, *which runs north from Chestnut Street,* is too narrow for cars.

At the end of the alley, *where the fair was held last May,* a getaway car waited.

A **restrictive modifier** is essential. Omit it and you significantly change the meaning of the modified word and the sentence. Such a modifier is called *restrictive* because it limits what it modifies: it specifies this place, person, or

> A **modifier** is a word, phrase, or clause that provides more information about other parts of a sentence (see 15).

action and no other. Because a restrictive modifier is part of the identity of whatever it modifies, no commas set it off from the rest of the sentence.

> They picked the alley *that runs north from Chestnut Street* because it is close to the highway.

> Anyone *who robs my house* will be disappointed.

Leaving out the modifier in that last sentence changes the meaning from potential robbers to humankind.

NOTE: Use *that* to introduce (or to recognize) a restrictive phrase or clause. Use *which* to introduce (or to recognize) a nonrestrictive phrase or clause.

> The food *that I love best* is chocolate.

> Chocolate, *which I love,* is not on my diet.

## 28f   Use commas to set off nonrestrictive appositives.

An **appositive** is a word or group of words that adds information by identifying a subject or an object in a different way (see 4b).

Like the modifiers discussed in 28e, an **appositive** can be either restrictive or nonrestrictive. If it is nonrestrictive—if the sentence still makes sense when it is omitted or changed—then set it off with commas before and after.

> My third ex-husband, *Hugo,* will be glad to meet you.

> We are bringing dessert, *a blueberry pie,* to follow dinner.

If the appositive is restrictive—if you can't take it out or change it without changing your meaning—then include it without commas.

> Of all the men I've been married to, my ex-husband *Hugo* is the best cook.

### EXERCISE 28–3 Using Commas

Add any necessary commas to the following sentences, and remove any commas that do not belong. Draw your own conclusions about what the writer meant to say, as needed. Some sentences may be correct. Possible revisions for the lettered sentences appear at the end of the Handbook. Example:

> Jay and his wife‸the former Laura McCready‸were college sweethearts.

a. We are bringing a dish vegetable lasagna, to the potluck supper.

b. I like to go to Central Bank, on this side of town, because this branch tends to have short lines.

c. The colony, that the English established at Roanoke disappeared mysteriously.

d. If the base commanders had checked their gun room where powder is stored, they would have found that several hundred pounds of gunpowder were missing.

e. Brazil's tropical rain forests which help produce the air we breathe all over the world, are being cut down at an alarming rate.

1. The aye-aye which is a member of the lemur family is threatened with extinction.
2. The party, a dismal occasion ended earlier than we had expected.
3. The general warned that the concessions, that the military was prepared to make, would be withdrawn if not matched by the rebels.
4. Although both of Don's children are blond, his daughter Sharon has darker hair than his son Jake.
5. Herbal tea which has no caffeine makes a better after-dinner drink than coffee.

## 28g Use commas to set off conjunctive adverbs.

When you drop a conjunctive adverb into the middle of a clause, set it off with commas before and after.

> Using lead paint in homes has been illegal, *however*, since 1973.
>
> Builders, *indeed*, gave it up some twenty years earlier.

For a list of common conjunctive adverbs, see p. 809.

## 28h Use commas to set off parenthetical expressions.

Use a pair of commas around any parenthetical expression or any aside from you to your readers.

> Home inspectors, *for this reason*, sometimes test for lead paint.
>
> Cosmic Construction never used lead paint, *or so their spokesperson says*, even when it was legal.

## 28i Use commas to set off a phrase or clause expressing contrast.

> It was Rudolph, *not Dasher*, who had a red nose.

EXCEPTION: Short contrasting phrases beginning with *but* need no commas.

> It was not Dasher/ but Rudolph/ who had a red nose.

## 28j Use commas to set off an absolute phrase.

The link between an absolute phrase and the rest of the sentence is a comma, or two commas if the phrase falls in midsentence.

> *Our worst fears drawing us together*, we huddled over the letter.
>
> Luke, *his knife being the sharpest*, slit the envelope.

An **absolute phrase** is an expression, usually a noun followed by a participle, that modifies an entire clause or sentence and can appear anywhere in the sentence (see 4b).

## EXERCISE 28–4  Using Commas

Add any necessary commas to the following sentences, and change any punctuation that is incorrect. Answers for the lettered sentences appear at the end of the Handbook. Example:

> The officer͵ a radar gun in his hand͵ gauged the speed of the passing cars.

a. The university insisted however that the students were not accepted merely because of their parents' generous contributions.

b. This dispute in any case is an old one.

c. It was the young man's striking good looks not his acting ability that first attracted the Hollywood agents.

d. Gretchen learned moreover not always to accept as true what she had read in celebrity magazines.

e. The hikers most of them wearing ponchos or rain jackets headed out into the steady drizzle.

1. The lawsuit demanded furthermore that construction already under way be halted immediately.

2. It is the Supreme Court not Congress or the president that ultimately determines the legality of a law.

3. The judge complained that the case was being tried not by the court but by the media.

4. The actor kneeling recited the lines with great emotion.

5. Both sides' patience running thin workers and management carried the strike into its sixth week.

For advice on using
punctuation marks
with quotations, see
33g–33i; for advice on
using quotation marks,
see 33a–33d.

## 28k  Use commas to set off a direct quotation from your own words.

When you briefly quote someone, distinguish the source's words from yours with commas (and, of course, quotation marks). When you insert an explanation into a quotation (such as *he said*), set that off with commas. The comma always comes *before* the quotation marks.

> Shakespeare wrote, "Some are born great, some achieve greatness, and some have greatness thrust upon them."

> "The best thing that can come with success," commented the actress Liv Ullmann, "is the knowledge that it is nothing to long for."

EXCEPTION:  Do not use a comma with a very short quotation or one introduced by *that*.

Don't tell me "yes" if you mean "maybe."

Jules said that "Nothing ventured, nothing gained" is his motto.

Don't use a comma with any quotation run in to your own sentence and read as part of it. Often such quotations are introduced by linking verbs.

Her favorite statement at age three was "I can do it myself."

Shakespeare originated the expression "my salad days, when I was green in judgment."

A **linking verb** is a verb that shows a state of being by linking the sentence subject with a word that renames or describes the subject (see 1c and 3b).

## 28l Use commas around *yes* and *no*, mild interjections, tag questions, and the name or title of someone directly addressed.

| | |
|---|---|
| YES AND NO | *Yes,* I'd like a Rolls-Royce, but, *no,* I didn't order one. |
| INTERJECTION | *Well,* don't blame it on me. |
| TAG QUESTION | It would be fun to ride in a Silver Cloud, *wouldn't it*? |
| DIRECT ADDRESS | Drive us home, *James.* |

An **interjection** is a word or expression that inserts an outburst of feeling (see 1h).

## 28m Use commas to set off dates, states, countries, and addresses.

On June 6, 1995, Ned Shaw was born.

East Rutherford, New Jersey, seemed like Paris, France, to him.

His family moved to 11 Maple Street, Middletown, Ohio.

Do not add a comma between state and zip code: *Bedford, MA 01730.*

---

### EXERCISE 28–5 Using Commas

Add any necessary commas to the following sentences, remove any commas that do not belong, and change any punctuation that is incorrect. Some sentences may be correct. Answers for the lettered sentences appear at the end of the Handbook. Example:

When Alexander Graham Bell said "Mr. Watson come here, I want you" the telephone entered history.

a. César Chávez was born on March 31 1927, on a farm in Yuma, Arizona.

b. Chávez, who spent years as a migrant farmworker, told other farm laborers "If you're outraged at conditions, then you can't possibly be free or happy until you devote all your time to changing them."

c. Chávez founded the United Farm Workers union and did indeed, devote all his time to changing conditions for farmworkers.

d. Robert F. Kennedy called Chávez, "one of the heroic figures of our time."

e. Chávez, who died on April 23, 1993, became the second Mexican American to receive the highest civilian honor in the United States, the Presidential Medal of Freedom.

1. Yes I was born on April 14 1988 in Bombay India.

2. Move downstage Gary, for Pete's sake or you'll run into Mrs. Clackett.

3. Vicki my precious, when you say, "great" or "terrific," look as though you mean it.

4. Perhaps you have forgotten darling that sometimes you make mistakes, too.

5. Well Dotty, it only makes sense that when you say, "Sardines!," you should go off to get the sardines.

# 29 | Misuses of the Comma

Just as important as including the comma where it belongs is omitting the comma in places where it does *not* belong. Be aware of the following common misuses of the comma.

## 29a Do not use a comma to separate a subject from its verb or a verb from its object.

The athlete driving the purple Jaguar/ was Jim Fuld. [The comma separated subject from verb.]

The governor should not have given his campaign manager/ such a prestigious appointment. [The comma separated verb from direct object.]

For lists of coordinating words, see p. 805.

## 29b Do not use a comma with compound subjects or verbs joined by correlative or coordinating conjunctions.

Do not divide a compound subject or verb unnecessarily with a comma.

Neither Peter Pan/ nor the fairy Tinkerbell/ saw the pirates sneaking toward their hideout. [Compound subject]

The chickens clucked/ and pecked/ and flapped their wings. [Compound verb]

## 29c Do not use a comma before the first or after the last item in a series.

We had to see/ my mother's doctor, my father's lawyer, and my dog's veterinarian/ in one afternoon.

## 29d Do not use a comma to set off a restrictive word, phrase, or clause.

A restrictive modifier is essential to the definition or identification of whatever it modifies; a nonrestrictive modifier is not.

For an explanation of restrictive modifiers, see 28e.

> The fireworks/that I saw on Sunday/were the best I've ever seen.

## 29e Do not use commas to set off indirect quotations.

When *that* introduces a quotation, the quotation is indirect and requires neither a comma nor quotation marks.

For more on quoting someone's exact words, see 33a–33c.

> He told us that/we shouldn't have done it.

---

### EXERCISE 29–1 Misuses of the Comma

Correct any misuses of the comma in the following sentences. Some sentences may be correct. Answers for the lettered sentences appear at the end of the Handbook. Example:

> Farms that use organic fertilizer/can be just as large and industrialized as nonorganic farms.

a. The proposed bill would give veterans in rural areas, improved access to medical care, health benefits, and job training.

b. Neither the House of Representatives, nor the Senate, seems likely to vote for increasing the federal minimum wage.

c. The report basically states that, increased testing is not improving student outcomes, even though that was the original intention.

d. During migration, hummingbirds, which weigh less than an ounce, travel distances, that average 500 miles per day.

e. After the party, we found, an earring, two sweaters, a hat, a scarf, and a shoe.

1. Upon hearing the doorbell ring, the dog jumped, and barked, and howled, and spun in circles.

2. Eyewitnesses from the period confirm that, there was, incredibly, a molasses flood in Boston in 1919.

3. The all-inclusive package provides guests with, unlimited food, beverages, and watersports rentals; spa treatments and tennis lessons, however, cost extra.

4. Several players from the team, have volunteered to visit young cancer patients at the local hospital.

5. The painting, that was stolen from the museum twenty years ago, was found, in perfect condition, in an abandoned warehouse.

# 30 | Semicolons

A semicolon is a sort of compromise between a comma and a period: it creates a stop without ending a sentence.

### 30a Use a semicolon to join two main clauses not joined by a coordinating conjunction.

**Coordinating conjunctions** join elements with equal or near-equal importance (see 1g and 19a–19c).

Suppose, having written one statement, you want to add another that is closely related in sense. You decide to keep them both in a single sentence.

> Shooting baskets was my brother's favorite sport; he would dunk them for hours at a time.

A semicolon is a good substitute for a period when you don't want to bring your readers to a complete stop.

> By the yard life is hard; by the inch it's a cinch.

NOTE: When you join a subordinate clause to a main one or join two statements with a coordinating conjunction, use a comma. Reserve the semicolon to emphasize a close connection or to avoid confusion when long, complex clauses include internal punctuation.

### 30b Use a semicolon to join two main clauses that are linked by a conjunctive adverb.

For a list of common conjunctive adverbs, see p. 809.

You can use a conjunctive adverb to show a relationship between clauses such as addition (*besides*), comparison (*likewise, similarly*), contrast (*instead, however*), emphasis (*namely, certainly*), cause and effect (*thus*), or time (*finally*). When a second statement begins with (or includes) a conjunctive adverb, you can join it to the first with a semicolon. No matter where the conjunctive adverb appears, the semicolon is placed between the two clauses.

> Bert is a stand-out player; *indeed,* he's the one hope of our team.
>
> We yearned to attend the concert; tickets, *however,* were hard to come by.

### 30c Use a semicolon to separate items in a series that contain internal punctuation or that are long and complex.

The semicolon is especially useful for setting off one group of items from another. More powerful than a comma, it divides a series of series.

> The auctioneer sold clocks, watches, and cameras; freezers of steaks and tons of bean sprouts; motorcycles, cars, speedboats, canoes, and cabin cruisers; and rare coins, curious stamps, and precious stones.

## EXERCISE 30–1 Using Semicolons

Add any necessary semicolons to the following sentences, and change any that are incorrectly used. Some sentences may be correct. Answers for the lettered sentences appear at the end of the Handbook. Example:

> The wind picked up and the thunder was getting louder; it was no longer safe to be outside.

a. The research paper was due in six weeks, therefore, Ali got started right away by making a schedule.

b. The committee estimated the extent of violent crime among teenagers, especially those between the ages of fourteen and sixteen, acted as a liaison between the city and schools and between churches and volunteer organizations, and drew up a plan to reduce violence, both public and domestic, in the next decade.

c. The skilled pilot landed the plane in an open field, all passengers made it out safely.

d. The mall no longer seems to attract customers, however; downtown businesses are picking up again.

1. Even though the ivory trade is now banned in most countries, elephant populations continue to be endangered.

2. The day after Thanksgiving is usually the busiest shopping day of the year, nonetheless, my sister is insisting that we check out all the deals.

3. It was a shocking site; all that remained of our house was a pile of rubble and splintered wood.

4. The glass on Leah's phone was so cracked it looked like a spider's web; but she could still make calls and use her apps.

# 31 | Colons

A colon introduces a further thought, one added to throw light on a first. Some writers use a capital letter to start any complete sentence that follows a colon; others prefer a lowercase letter. Whichever you choose, be consistent. A phrase that follows a colon always begins with a lowercase letter.

## 31a Use a colon between two main clauses if the second exemplifies, explains, or summarizes the first.

Like a semicolon, a colon can join two sentences into one. The chief difference is this: a semicolon says merely that two main clauses are related;

A **main clause** is a group of words that has both a subject and a verb and can stand alone as a complete sentence (see 4a).

a colon, like an abbreviation for *that is* or *for example,* says that the second clause gives an example or explanation of the point in the first clause.

> She tried everything: she scoured the Internet, made dozens of phone calls, wrote e-mails, even consulted a lawyer.

### 31b Use a colon to introduce a list or a series.

A colon can introduce a word, a phrase, a series, or a second main clause, sometimes strengthened by *as follows* or *the following.*

> The dance steps are as follows: forward, back, turn, and glide.

When a colon introduces a series of words or phrases, it often means *such as* or *for instance.* A list of examples after a colon need not include *and* before the last item unless all possible examples have been stated.

> On a Saturday night many kinds of people crowd our downtown area: drifters, bored senior citizens, college students out for a good time.

### 31c Use a colon to introduce an appositive.

An **appositive** is a word or group of words that adds information by identifying a subject or an object in a different way (see 4b).

A colon preceded by a main clause can introduce an **appositive.**

> I have discovered the key to the future: robots.

### 31d Use a colon to introduce a long or comma-filled quotation.

Sometimes you can't conveniently introduce a quoted passage with a comma. Perhaps the quotation is too long or heavily punctuated, or your prefatory remarks demand a longer pause. In either case, use a colon.

> God told Adam and Eve: "Be fruitful, and multiply, and replenish the earth, and subdue it."

### 31e Use a colon when convention calls for it.

| | |
|---|---|
| AFTER A SALUTATION | Dear Professor James: |
| BIBLICAL CITATIONS | Job 9:2 [book, chapter, verse], but Job 9.2 [MLA] |
| TITLES: SUBTITLES | *Connections: Empowering College and Career Success* |
| TIME OF DAY | 2:02 p.m. |

### 31f Use a colon only at the end of a main clause.

A **main clause** is a group of words that has both a subject and a verb and can stand alone as a complete sentence (see 4a).

In a sentence, a colon always follows a complete sentence, never a phrase. Avoid using a colon between a verb and its object, between a preposition and its object, and before a list introduced by *such as.*

My mother and father are; Bella and Benjamin.

Many great inventors have changed our lives, such as; Edison, Marconi, and Glutz.

Many great inventors have changed our lives, such as: Edison, Marconi, and Glutz.

---

**EXERCISE 31–1 Using Colons**

Add, remove, or replace colons wherever appropriate in the following sentences. Where necessary, revise the sentences further to support your changes in punctuation. Some sentences may be correct. Possible revisions for the lettered sentences appear at the end of the Handbook. Example:

> Yum-Yum Burger has franchises in the following cities; New York, Chicago, Miami, San Francisco, and Seattle.

a. The Continuing Education Program offers courses in: building and construction management, engineering, and design.

b. The interview ended with a test of skills, taking messages, operating the computer, typing a sample letter, and proofreading documents.

c. The sample letter began, "Dear Mr. Rasheed, Please accept our apologies for the late shipment."

1. In the case of *Bowers v. Hardwick,* the Supreme Court decided that: citizens had no right to sexual privacy.

2. He ended his speech with a quotation from Homer's *Iliad,* "Whoever obeys the gods, to him they particularly listen."

3. Professor Bligh's book is called *Management, A Networking Approach.*

---

# 32 | Apostrophes

Use apostrophes for three purposes: to show possession, to indicate an omission, and to add an ending to a number, a letter, or an abbreviation.

## 32a To make a singular noun possessive, add -'s.

> The *plumber's* wrench left grease stains on *Harry's* shirt.

Add -'s even when your singular noun ends with the sound of s.

> *Felix's* roommate enjoys reading *Henry James's* novels.

> ### Possessive Nouns and Plural Nouns
> *at a Glance*
>
> Both plural nouns and possessive nouns often end with -s.
> - *Plural* means more than one (two *dogs*, six *friends*), but *possessive* means ownership (the *dogs'* biscuits, my *friends'* cars).
> - If you can substitute *of* for the -s' (the biscuits of the dogs, the cars *of* my friends), use the plural possessive with an apostrophe after the -s.
> - If you can't substitute *of*, you need the simple plural with no apostrophe (the *dogs* are well fed, my *friends* have no money for gas).

Some writers find it awkward to add *-'s* to nouns that already end in an *-s,* especially those of two syllables or more. You may, if you wish, form such a possessive by adding only an apostrophe.

> The Egyptian king *Cheops'* death occurred centuries before *Socrates'*.

### 32b  To make a plural noun ending in *-s* possessive, add an apostrophe.

> A *stockbrokers'* meeting combines *foxes'* cunning with the noisy chaos of a *boys'* locker room.

### 32c  To make a plural noun not ending in *-s* possessive, add *-'s*.

Nouns such as *men, mice, geese,* and *alumni* form the possessive case the same way as singular nouns: with *-'s*.

> What effect has the *women's* movement had on *children's* literature?

### 32d  To show joint possession by two people or groups, add an apostrophe or *-'s* to the second noun of the pair.

> I left my *mother and father's* home with *friends and neighbors'* good wishes.

If the two members of a noun pair possess a set of things individually, add an apostrophe or *-'s* to each noun.

> *Men's* and *women's* marathon records are improving steadily.

### 32e  To make a compound noun possessive, add an apostrophe or *-'s* to the last word in the compound.

A compound noun consists of more than one word (*commander in chief, sons-in-law*); it may be either singular or plural.

> The *commander in chief's* duties will end on July 1.

> Esther does not approve of her *sons-in-law's* professions.

## 32f To make an indefinite pronoun possessive, add -'s.

Indefinite pronouns such as *anyone, nobody,* and *another* are usually singular; they form the possessive case with -*'s*. (See 32a.)

> What caused the accident is *anybody's* guess, but it was *no one's* fault.

**Indefinite pronouns** do not refer to a specific noun (see 1b).

## 32g To indicate the possessive of a personal pronoun, use its possessive case.

The personal pronouns are irregular; each has its own possessive form, none with an apostrophe. Resist adding an apostrophe or -*'s*.

NOTE: *Its* (no apostrophe) is always a possessive pronoun.

> I retreated when the Murphys' German shepherd bared *its* fangs.

*It's* (with an apostrophe) is always a contraction of *it is.*

> *It's* [It is] not our fault.

**Personal pronouns** stand for a noun that names a person or thing (see 1b).

## 32h Use an apostrophe to indicate an omission in a contraction.

> *They're* [They are] too sophisticated for me.
>
> Pat *didn't* [did not] finish her assignment.
>
> Americans grow up admiring the Spirit of *'76* [1776].
>
> *It's* [It is] nearly eight *o'clock* [of the clock].

## 32i Use an apostrophe to form the plural of a letter or word mentioned as a word.

| | |
|---|---|
| LETTER | How many *n*'s are there in *Cincinnati*? |
| WORD | Try replacing all the *should*'s in that list with *could*'s. |

No apostrophes are needed for plural numbers and most abbreviations.

| | |
|---|---|
| DECADE | The 2000s differed greatly from the 1990s. |
| NUMBER | Cut out two 3s to sew on Larry's shirt. |
| ABBREVIATION | Do we need IDs at YMCAs in other towns? |

---

### EXERCISE 32–1 Using Apostrophes

Correct any errors in the use of the apostrophe in the following sentences. Some sentences may be correct. Answers for the lettered sentences appear at the end of the Handbook. Example:

> ~~Youd~~ *You'd* better put on ~~you're~~ *your* new shoes.

a. Joe and Chucks' fathers were both in the class of 90.

b. They're going to finish their term papers as soon as the party ends.

c. It was a strange coincidence that all three womens' cars broke down after they had picked up their mother's-in-law.

d. Don't forget to dot you're *is* and cross you're *ts*.

e. Mario and Shelley's son is marrying the editor's in chief's daughter.

1. The Hendersons' never change: their always whining about Mr. Scobee farming land thats rightfully their's.

2. Its hard to join a womens' basketball team because so few of them exist.

3. I had'nt expected to hear Janice' voice again.

4. Don't give the Murphy's dog it's biscuit until it's sitting up.

5. Isnt' it the mother and fathers' job to tell kid's to mind their *ps* and *qs*?

# 33 | Quotation Marks

For more on quoting, paraphrasing, and summarizing, see Chs. 33 and 34 in *A Writer's Research Manual*.

For capitalization with quotation marks, see 37j.

Quotation marks always come in pairs: one at the start and one at the finish of a quoted passage. In the United States, the double quotation mark (") is preferred over the single one (') for most uses. Use quotation marks to set off quoted or highlighted words from the rest of your text.

> "Injustice anywhere is a threat to justice everywhere," wrote Martin Luther King Jr.

## 33a Use quotation marks around direct quotations from another writer or speaker.

Enclose someone's exact words in quotation marks.

> Malala Yousafzai reflected the importance of women's education when she said, "We cannot succeed when half of us are held back."

Use an indirect quotation to credit and report someone else's idea accurately. Do not use his or her exact words or quotation marks.

> Malala Yousafzai asserted the importance of women's education.

## 33b Use single quotation marks around a quotation inside another quotation.

Sometimes you may quote a source that quotes someone else or puts words in quotation marks. When that happens, use single quotation marks around the internal quotation (even if your source used double ones); put double quotation marks around the larger passage you are quoting.

> "My favorite advice from Socrates, 'Know thyself and fear all women,'" said Dr. Blatz, "has been getting me into trouble lately."

## Guidelines for Multilingual Writers
### What Is the Difference between Direct and Indirect Quotations?

When you quote directly, use the exact words of the original writer or speaker; set them off with double quotation marks. When you change a direct quotation into an indirect quotation (someone else's idea reported without using his or her exact words), be sure to reword the quotation. Do not repeat the original wording from a source.

- Be sure to change the punctuation and capitalization. You also may need to change the verb tense.

| DIRECT QUOTATION | Pascal said, "The assignment is on Chinua Achebe, the Nigerian writer." |
|---|---|
| INDIRECT QUOTATION | Pascal said that the assignment was on Chinua Achebe, the Nigerian writer. |

- If the direct quotation is a question, you must change the word order in the indirect quotation.

| DIRECT QUOTATION | Jean asked, "How far is it to Boston?" |
|---|---|
| INDIRECT QUOTATION | Jean asked how far it was to Boston. |

*NOTE:* Use a period, not a question mark, with questions in indirect quotations.

- You often must change pronouns for an indirect quotation.

| DIRECT QUOTATION | Antonio said, "I think you are mistaken." |
|---|---|
| INDIRECT QUOTATION | Antonio said that he thought I was mistaken. |

## 33c Instead of using quotation marks, indent longer quotations.

Suppose you are writing an essay about the meaning of a college education. You might include a paragraph like this:

> In her 2014 commencement address at Brooklyn College, writer Edwidge Danticat spoke about the importance of bravery:
>> The great Maya Angelou has said that courage is the most important of all virtues. . . . I wish for you the courage to continue to walk boldly and freely in this world. I wish for you the courage to rule out no dream as too big and no hope as too small. I wish for you the courage to live fiercely though not recklessly both for yourself and others. Be brave and creative as you put all the theories and

knowledge that you have learned to work. Be brave in spirit; be brave in mind. Because only those with imagination and courage are able to reach beyond the ordinary and take us to the next frontier.

For more on the MLA and APA styles, see Chs. 36–37.

Indenting the passage shows it is a direct quotation without adding quotation marks. In MLA style, indent quotations of five lines or more by one-half inch. In APA style, indent quotations of forty words or more by one-half inch. In both, double-space the quoted lines, and cite the source.

Follow the same practice if you quote four or more lines of a poem.

Phillis Wheatley, the outstanding black poet of colonial America, often made emotional pleas in her poems:

> Attend me, Virtue, thro' my youthful years
>> O leave me not to the false joys of time!
> But guide my steps to endless life and bliss.
>> Greatness, or Goodness, say what I shall call thee,
> To give me an higher appellation still,
> Teach me a better strain, a nobler lay,
> Oh thou, enthron'd with Cherubs in the realms of day (15-21).

For advice on capitalization and quotations, see 37j.

Notice that not only the source's words but her punctuation, capitalization, and line breaks are quoted exactly.

**33d** In dialogue, use quotation marks around a speaker's words, and mark each change of speaker with a new paragraph.

Randolph gazed at Ellen and sighed. "What extraordinary beauty."

"They are lovely," she replied, staring at the roses, "aren't they?"

**33e** Use quotation marks around the titles of a speech, an article in a newspaper or magazine, a short story, a poem shorter than book length, a chapter in a book, a song, and an episode of a television or radio program.

For advice on italicizing titles, see 39a and the chart on p. 862.

The article "Alice Munro's Magic" begins with a description of "Home," from Munro's collection *Family Furnishings*.

In Chapter 5, "Expatriates," Schwartz discusses Eliot's famous poem "The Love Song of J. Alfred Prufrock."

**33f** Avoid using quotation marks to show slang, wit, or irony.

By the time I finished my ⫶chores,⫶ my ⫶day off⫶ was over.

No quotation marks are needed after *so-called* or similar words.

The meet included many so-called ⫶champions.⫶

## 33g Put commas and periods inside quotation marks.

A comma or a period is always placed before quotation marks, even if it is not part of the quotation.

For more on commas with quotations, see 28k.

> We pleaded, "Keep off the grass," in hope of preserving the lawn.

> The sign warned pedestrians: "Keep off the grass."

## 33h Put semicolons and colons outside quotation marks.

> We said, "Keep off the grass"; they still tromped onward.

## 33i Put other punctuation inside or outside quotation marks depending on its function in the sentence.

Parentheses that are part of the quotation go inside the quotation marks. Parentheses that are your own, not part of the quotation, go outside.

> We said, "Keep off the grass (unless it's artificial turf)."

> They tromped onward (although we had said, "Keep off the grass").

If a question mark, exclamation point, or dash is part of the quotation, place it inside the quotation marks. Otherwise, place it after them.

> Who hollered "Fire"? She hollered, "Fire!"

Don't close a sentence with two end punctuation marks, one inside and one outside the quotation marks. If the quoted passage ends with a dash, an exclamation point, a question mark, or a period, you need not add any further end punctuation. If the quoted passage falls within a question asked by you, however, the sentence should finish with a question mark, even if that means dropping other end punctuation (*Who hollered "Fire"?*).

---

### EXERCISE 33–1 Using Quotation Marks

Add quotation marks wherever they are needed in the following sentences, and correct any other errors. Answers for the lettered sentences appear at the end of the Handbook. Example:

> Annie asked him, "Do you believe in free will?"

a. What we still need to figure out, the police chief said, is whether the victim was acquainted with his assailant.

b. A skillful orator, Patrick Henry is credited with the comment Give me liberty or give me death.

c. I could hear the crowd chanting my name — Jones! Jones! — and that spurred me on, said Bruce Jones, the winner of the 5,000-meter race.

d. The video for the rock group Guns N' Roses' epic song November Rain is based on a short story by Del James.

e. In response to a possible asteroid strike on Earth, former astronaut Rusty Schweickart says, Every country is at risk.

1. That day at school, the kids were as "high as kites."

2. Notice, the professor told the class, Cassius's choice of imagery when he asks, Upon what meat doth this our Caesar feed, / That he is grown so great?

3. "As I was rounding the bend," Peter explained, "I failed to see the sign that said Caution: Ice.

4. John Cheever's story The Swimmer begins with the line It was one of those midsummer Sundays when everyone sits around saying, I drank too much last night.

5. Who coined the saying Love is blind?

# 34 | Dashes

A **dash** is a horizontal line used to separate parts of a sentence—a dramatic substitute for a comma, semicolon, or colon. Your software may automatically turn two hyphens without any spaces into a dash.

### 34a Use a dash to indicate a sudden break in thought or shift in tone.

The dash signals that a surprise is in store: a shift in viewpoint, perhaps, or an unfinished statement.

> Ivan doesn't care which team wins—he bet on both.
>
> I didn't notice my parents' accented speech—at least not at home.

### 34b Use a dash to introduce an explanation, an illustration, or a series.

An **appositive** is a word or group of words that adds information by identifying a subject or an object in a different way (see 4b).

Use a dash to add an informal preparatory pause or to introduce an appositive that needs drama or contains commas.

> My advice to you is simple—stop complaining.
>
> Longfellow wrote about three young sisters—grave Alice, laughing Allegra, and Edith with golden hair—in "The Children's Hour."

### 34c Use dashes to set off an emphatic aside or a parenthetical expression from the rest of a sentence.

> It was as hot—and I mean *hot*—as the Fourth of July in Death Valley.

## 34d Avoid overusing dashes.

The dash becomes meaningless if used too often. Use it only when a comma, a colon, or parentheses don't seem strong enough.

To compare dashes with commas, see 28, and with parentheses, see 35a–35b.

> Algy's grandmother—a sweet old lady—asked him to pick up some things
>
> at the store—milk, eggs, and cheese.

---

### EXERCISE 34–1   Using Dashes

Add, remove, or replace dashes wherever appropriate in the following sentences. Some sentences may be correct. Possible answers for the lettered sentences appear at the end of the Handbook. Example:

> Stanton had all the identifying marks/boating shoes, yellow slicker,
>
> sunblock, and an anchor/of a sailor.

  a. I enjoy going hiking with my friend John — whom I've known for fifteen years.

  b. Pedro's new boat is spectacular: a regular seagoing Ferrari.

  c. The Thompsons devote their weekends to their favorite pastime, eating bags of potato chips and cookies beside the warm glow of the television.

  1. The sport of fishing — or at least some people call it a sport — is boring, dirty — and tiring.

  2. At that time, three states in the Sunbelt, Florida, California, and Arizona, were the fastest growing in the nation.

  3. LuLu was ecstatic when she saw her grades, all A's!

---

# 35 | Parentheses, Brackets, and Ellipses

Parentheses (singular, *parenthesis*) work in pairs. So do brackets. Both surround bits of information to make a statement perfectly clear. An ellipsis mark is a trio of periods inserted to show that something has been cut.

## Parentheses

### 35a Use parentheses to set off interruptions that are useful but not essential.

> Franklin D. Roosevelt (commonly known as "FDR") won four elections.
>
> He occupied the White House for so many years (1933 to mid-1945) that babies became teens without having known any other president.

The material within parentheses may be helpful, but it isn't essential. Use parentheses to add a qualification, a helpful date, or a brief explanation — words that, in conversation, you might add in a changed tone of voice.

## 35b Use parentheses around letters or numbers indicating items in a series.

Archimedes asserted that, given (1) a lever long enough, (2) a fulcrum, and (3) a place to stand, he could move the earth.

No parentheses are needed for numbers or letters in an indented list.

---

### EXERCISE 35–1 Using Parentheses

Add, remove, or replace parentheses wherever appropriate in the following sentences. Some sentences may be correct. Possible answers for the lettered sentences appear at the end of the Handbook. Example:

The Islamic fundamentalist Ayatollah Khomeini — 1900–1989 — was *(1900-1989)* a cleric and leader of Iran in the late twentieth century.

a. Our cafeteria serves the four basic food groups: white — milk, bread, and mashed potatoes — brown — mystery meat and gravy — green — overcooked vegetables and underwashed lettuce — and orange — squash, carrots, and tomato sauce.

b. The hijackers will release the hostages only if the government, 1, frees all political prisoners and, 2, allows the hijackers to leave the country.

c. When Phil said he works with whales (as well as other marine mammals) for the Whale Stranding Network, Lisa thought he meant that his group lures whales onto beaches.

1. The new pear-shaped bottles will hold 200 milliliters, 6.8 fluid ounces, of lotion.

2. World War I, or "The Great War," as it was once called, destroyed the old European order forever.

3. The Internet is a mine of fascinating, and sometimes useless, information.

---

## Brackets

Brackets, those open-ended typographical boxes, work in pairs like parentheses. Their special purpose is to mark changes in quoted material.

## 35c Use brackets to add information or to make changes within a direct quotation.

A quotation must be quoted exactly. If you add or alter a word or a phrase in a quotation from another writer, place brackets around your changes.

Suppose you are writing about James McGuire's being named chairman of the board of directors of General Motors. In your source, the actual words are these: "A radio bulletin first brought the humble professor of philosophy the astounding news." But in your paper, you want readers to know the professor's identity. So you add that information, in brackets.

> "A radio bulletin first brought the humble professor of philosophy [James McGuire] the astounding news."

Never alter a quoted statement any more than you have to. Ask yourself: Do I really need this quotation, or should I paraphrase?

For advice on quoting, paraphrasing, and summarizing, see Chs. 33 and 34 in *A Writer's Research Manual.*

## 35d Use brackets around *sic* to indicate an error in a direct quotation.

When you faithfully quote a statement that contains an error, follow the error with a bracketed *sic* (Latin for "so" or "so the writer says"). Usually you're better off paraphrasing an error-riddled passage.

> The book *Cake Wrecks* includes a photo of a cake with this message written on top in icing: Happy Thanksgiven [*sic*].

## Ellipses

## 35e Use ellipses to signal that you have omitted part of a quotation.

Occasionally you will want to quote just the parts of a passage that relate to your topic. Acknowledge your cuts with *ellipses*: three periods with a space between each one (. . .). If ellipses conclude a sentence, precede them with a period placed at the end of the sentence. Suppose you want to quote from Marie Winn's book *Children without Childhood* (Penguin, 1984) but omit some of its detail. Use ellipses to show each cut:

> According to Winn, children's innocence can be easily lost: "Today's nine- and ten-year-olds . . . not infrequently find themselves involved in their own parents' complicated sex lives, . . . at least as advisers, friendly commentators, and intermediaries."

## 35f Avoid using ellipses at the beginning or end of a quotation.

Even though a source continues after a quoted passage, you don't need ellipses at the end of your quotation. Nor do you need to begin a quotation with three dots. Save the ellipses for words you omit *inside* whatever you quote. If you cut more than a section or two, think about paraphrasing.

For more on quoting, paraphrasing, and summarizing, see Chs. 33 and 34 in *A Writer's Research Manual.*

## EXERCISE 35–2 Using Brackets and Ellipses

The following is a passage from an essay. The sentences that follow use quoted material from the passage. Correct any faulty use of brackets and ellipses, and add brackets and ellipses if necessary. Some sentences may be correct. Answers for the lettered sentences appear at the end of the Handbook.

> Darwin himself was not entirely consistent in the language he used to describe his beliefs. And of course his views changed over the course of his life. Starting in 1876 he began writing a private autobiography for his children and grandchildren. In it he mentioned the change in his religious views. A gradual skepticism towards Christianity and the authenticity of the Bible gradually crept over him during the late 1830s—leaving him not a Christian, but no atheist either; rather a sort of theist. To be a "theist" in Darwin's day was to believe that a supernatural deity had created nature or the universe but did not intervene in the course of history.
>
> —John van Wyhe, "Was Charles Darwin an Atheist?"

a. According to van Wyhe, "Darwin was not consistent in the language he used to describe his beliefs."

b. John van Wyhe notes that "Darwin's views on religion changed over the course of his life."

c. John van Wyhe points out that Darwin wrote privately about his shift in beliefs.

1. According to van Wyhe, "A gradual skepticism towards Christianity gradually crept over Darwin during the late 1830s."

2. John van Wyhe writes that Darwin was "not a Christian, but no atheist either; rather a sort of theist."

3. John van Wyhe explains that theists such as Darwin believed in "a supernatural deity that had created nature or the universe but did not intervene in the course of history."

# Mechanics

# 43

36 | Abbreviations  853

37 | Capital Letters  856

38 | Numbers  859

39 | Italics  861

40 | Hyphens  863

41 | Spelling  865

## Learning by Doing 🖐 Justifying Conventions

Working with a group, select a troublesome convention for using hyphens, italics, or other mechanics. Read through one section about that mark, and decode that guideline. Then try to figure out why you think this convention is expected in academic writing and how you can remember to apply it. (Feel free to make up humorous examples to help you more consistently follow convention.)

## 36 | Abbreviations

Abbreviations enable a writer to include necessary information in capsule form. Limit abbreviations to those common enough for readers to recognize, or add an explanation so that a reader does not wonder, "What does this mean?" Remember: when in doubt, spell it out.

### 36a Use abbreviations for some titles with proper names.

Abbreviate the following titles:

Mr. and Mrs. Hubert Collins       Dr. Elinor Ostrom

Ms. Martha Reading                  St. Matthew

For advice on punctuating abbreviations, see 27b.

Write out other titles in full.

General Douglas MacArthur    Senator Dianne Feinstein

President Barack Obama    Professor Shirley Fixler

Spell out most titles that appear without proper names.

Tomás is studying to be a ~~dr.~~ doctor

When an abbreviated title (such as an academic degree) follows a proper name, set it off with commas. Don't add commas otherwise.

Alice Martin, CPA, is the accountant for Charlotte Cordera, PhD.

My brother has a BA in economics.

Avoid repeating forms of the same title before and after a proper name. Use either *Dr. Jane Doe* or *Jane Doe, DDS*, but not *Dr. Jane Doe, DDS*.

## 36b Use *a.m.*, *p.m.*, *BCE*, *AD*, and *$* with numbers.

9:05 a.m.    3:45 p.m.    2000 BCE    AD 1066

For exact prices that include cents and for amounts in the millions, use a dollar sign with figures (*$17.95, $10.52, $3.5 billion*). Avoid combining an abbreviation with wording that means the same: *$1 million*, not *$1 million dollars*; *9:05 a.m.* or *9:05 in the morning*, not *9:05 a.m. in the morning*.

## 36c Avoid abbreviating names of months, days of the week, units of measurement, or parts of literary works.

NAMES OF MONTHS AND DAYS OF THE WEEK

After their session on September 3, they did not meet until Friday, December 12.

UNITS OF MEASUREMENT

It would take 10,000 pounds of concrete to build a causeway 25 feet by 58 inches.

PARTS OF LITERARY WORKS

Von Bargen's reply appears in volume 2, chapter 12, page 187.

Leona first speaks in act 1, scene 2 [or the second scene of act 1].

## 36d Use the full English version of most Latin abbreviations.

For the use of *sic* to identify an error, see 35d.

Follow the conventions of your citation style if you use Latin abbreviations in source citations, parentheses, and brackets. However, unless you are writing for an audience of ancient Romans, translate most Latin abbreviations into English in your text.

| COMMON LATIN ABBREVIATIONS | ENGLISH |
|---|---|
| et al. (*et alia*) | and others, and the others (people) |
| etc. (*et cetera*) | and so forth, and others, and the rest |
| i.e. (*id est*) | that is |
| e.g. (*exempli gratia*) | for example, such as |

## 36e Use abbreviations for familiar organizations, corporations, and people.

Most sets of initials that are capitalized and read as letters do not require periods between the letters (CIA, JFK, UCLA). A set of initials that is pronounced as a word is called an **acronym** (NATO, AIDS, UNICEF) and never has periods between letters.

To avoid misunderstanding, write out an organization's full name the first time you mention it, followed by its initials in parentheses. Then, in later references, you can rely on initials alone. (For very familiar initials, such as FBI or CBS, you need not give the full name.)

## 36f Avoid abbreviations for countries.

When you mention the United States or another country in your text, give its full name unless the repetition would weigh down your paragraph.

> The president will return to the ~~US~~ *United States* on Tuesday from a trip to the ~~UK~~ *United Kingdom*.

EXCEPTION: Unlike *US* as a noun, the abbreviation, used consistently with traditional periods or without, is acceptable as an adjective: *US Senate, U.S. foreign policy*. For other countries, find an alternative: *British ambassador*. Follow your citation style when you cite or list government documents.

---

## EXERCISE 36–1 Using Abbreviations

Substitute abbreviations for words and vice versa as appropriate in the following sentences. Correct any incorrectly used abbreviations. Answers for the lettered sentences appear at the end of the Handbook. Example:

> Please return this form no later than noon on ~~Wed., Apr.~~ *Wednesday, April* 7.

a. Prof. James has office hours on Mon. and Tues., beginning at 10:00 a.m.

b. Emotional issues, e.g., abortion and capital punishment, cannot be settled easily by compromise.

c. The red peppers are selling for three dollars and twenty-five cents a lb.

1. Hamlet's famous soliloquy comes in act three, sc. one.
2. A.I.D.S. has affected people throughout U.S. society, not just gay men and IV-drug users.
3. The end of the cold war between the U.S. and the Soviet Union complicated the role of the U.N. and drastically altered the purpose of N.A.T.O.

# 37 | Capital Letters

For capitalization following a colon, see 31.

Use capital letters only with good reason. If you think a word will work in lowercase letters, you're probably right.

### 37a Capitalize proper names and adjectives made from proper names.

Proper names designate individuals, places, organizations, institutions, brand names, and certain other distinctive things. Any proper noun can have an adjective form, also capitalized.

| | | |
|---|---|---|
| Miles Standish | University of Iowa | Australian beer |
| India | a Volkswagen | a Renaissance man |
| United Nations | a Xerox copier | Shakespearean comedy |

### 37b Capitalize a title or rank before a proper name.

During her second term, Senator Wilimczyk proposed several bills.

In his lecture, Professor Jones analyzed fossil evidence.

Titles that do not come before proper names usually are not capitalized.

Ten senators voted against the research appropriation.

Jones is the department's only full professor.

EXCEPTION: The abbreviation of an academic or professional degree is always capitalized. The informal name of a degree is not capitalized.

Dora E. McLean, MD, also holds a BA in music.

Dora holds a bachelor's degree in music.

### 37c Capitalize a family relationship only when it is part of a proper name or when it substitutes for a proper name.

Do you know the song about Mother Machree?

I have invited Mother to visit next weekend.

I would like you to meet my aunt, Emily Smith.

**37d** Capitalize the names of religions, their deities, and their followers.

| | | | |
|---|---|---|---|
| Christianity | Muslims | Jehovah | Krishna |
| Islam | Methodists | Allah | the Holy Spirit |

**37e** Capitalize proper names of places, regions, and geographic features.

| | | |
|---|---|---|
| Los Angeles | the Black Hills | the Atlantic Ocean |
| Death Valley | Big Sur | the Philippines |

Do not capitalize *north, south, east,* or *west* unless it is part of a proper name (*West Virginia, South Orange*) or refers to formal geographic locations.

> Drive south to Chicago and then east to Cleveland.

> Jim, who has always lived in the South, likes to read about the Northeast.

A common noun such as *street, avenue, boulevard, park, lake,* or *hill* is capitalized when part of a proper name.

| | | |
|---|---|---|
| Meinecke Avenue | Hamilton Park | Lake Michigan |

**37f** Capitalize days of the week, months, and holidays, but not seasons or academic terms.

> During spring term, by the Monday after Passover, I have to choose between the January study plan and junior year abroad.

**37g** Capitalize historical events, periods, and documents.

| | |
|---|---|
| Black Monday | the Roaring Twenties |
| the Civil War [*but* a civil war] | Magna Carta |
| the Holocaust [*but* a holocaust] | Declaration of Independence |
| the Bronze Age | Atomic Energy Act |

**37h** Capitalize the names of schools, colleges, departments, and courses.

West School, Central High School [*but* middle school, high school]

Reed College, Arizona State University [*but* the college, a university]

Department of History [*but* history department, department office]

Feminist Perspectives in British Literature [*but* literature course]

**37i** Capitalize the first, last, and main words in titles.

When you write the title of a paper, book, article, work of art, television show, poem, or performance, capitalize the first and last words and all main words in between. Do not capitalize articles (*a, an, the*), coordinating conjunctions (*and, but, for, or, nor, so, yet*), or prepositions (such as *in, on, at, of, from*) unless they come first or last in the title or follow a colon.

| | |
|---|---|
| ESSAY | "Ticket to the Fair" |
| NOVEL | *The Known World* |
| VOLUME OF POETRY | *American Primitive* |
| POEM | "A Valediction: Of Weeping" |

*For advice on using quotation marks and italics for titles, see 33e and 39a.*

## 37j Capitalize the first letter of a quoted sentence.

*For advice on punctuating quotations, see 33g–33i.*

Oscar Wilde wrote, "The only way to get rid of a temptation is to yield to it."

Only the first word of a quoted sentence is capitalized, even when you break the sentence with words of your own.

"The only way to get rid of a temptation," wrote Oscar Wilde, "is to yield to it."

*For advice on using brackets to show changes in quotations, see 35c.*

If you quote more than one sentence, start each one with a capital letter.

"Art should never try to be popular," said Wilde. "The public should try to make itself artistic."

Select a quoted passage carefully so that you can present its details accurately as it blends in with your sentence.

---

## EXERCISE 37–1 Using Capitalization

Correct any capitalization errors in the following sentences. Answers for the lettered sentences appear at the end of the Handbook. Example:

> Speaking of Cuba, ~~president~~ President Barack Obama said, "~~a~~ A future of greater peace, security, and democratic development is possible if we work together."

a. The great Shakespearean Tragedy *Macbeth*, which was written around 1600, opens in the scottish countryside and includes the famous character lady Macbeth.

b. Colleen's favorite class at Arizona State university is Literature. She also enjoys taking Weekend hiking trips to the grand canyon.

c. Jake's Great-Aunt was the author Kate Chopin, who wrote the famous work of fiction "The story of an hour" two Decades after the civil war.

1. During ramadan, the ninth month of the islamic calendar, all healthy muslims are required to fast from dawn to dusk.

2. After calling us in to dinner for the third time with no response, mom called into the yard, "okay, the dog is getting an extra-large meal tonight!"

3. My Grandfather recalls that the roaring twenties came to a screeching halt when the great depression hit at the end of 1929.

---

# 38 | Numbers

Unless you are writing in a scientific field or your essay relies on statistics, you'll generally want to use words (*twenty-seven*). Figures (*27*) are most appropriate in contexts where readers are used to seeing them, such as times and dates (*11:05 p.m. on March 15*).

## 38a In general, write out a number that consists of one or two words, and use figures for longer numbers.

Short names of numbers are easily read (*ten, six hundred*); longer ones take more thought (*two thousand four hundred eighty-seven*). For numbers of more than a word or two, use figures.

> Two hundred fans paid twenty-five dollars apiece for that shirt.

> A frog's tongue has 970,580 taste buds; a human's has six times as many.

EXCEPTION: For multiples of a million or more, use a figure plus a word.

> The earth is 93 million miles from the sun.

---

**▶ Figures** *at a Glance*

| | |
|---|---|
| ADDRESSES | 4 East 74th Street; also, One Copley Place, 5 Fifth Avenue |
| DATES | May 20, 2007; 450 BCE; also, Fourth of July |
| DECIMALS | 98.6° Fahrenheit; .57 acres |
| FRACTIONS | 3½ years; 1¾ miles; half a loaf, three-fourths of voters |
| PARTS OF LITERARY WORKS | volume 2, chapter 5, page 37, act 1, scene 2 (*or* act I, scene ii) |
| PERCENTAGES | 25 percent; 99.9 percent; also, 25%, 99.9% |
| EXACT PRICES | $1.99; $200,000; also, $5 million, ten cents, a dollar |
| SCORES | a 114–111 victory; a final score of 5 to 3 |
| STATISTICS | men in the 25–30 age group; odds of 5 to 1 (*or* 5–1 odds); height 5'7"; also, three out of four doctors |
| TIMES | 2:29 p.m.; 10:15 tomorrow morning; also, half past four, three o'clock (always with a number in words) |

**38b** Use figures for most addresses, dates, decimals, fractions, parts of literary works, percentages, exact prices, scores, statistics, and times.

Using figures is mainly a matter of convenience. If you think words will be easier for your readers to follow, you can always write out a number.

**38c** Use words or figures consistently for numbers in the same category throughout a passage.

For more on the plurals of figures (*6s, 1960s*), see 32i.

Switching between words and figures for numbers can be distracting to readers. Choose whichever form suits like numbers in your passage, and use that form consistently for all numbers in the same category.

> Of the 276 representatives who voted, 97 supported a 25 percent raise, while 179 supported a 30 percent raise over five years.

**38d** Write out a number that begins a sentence.

When a number starts a sentence, either write it out, move it deeper into the sentence, or reword the opening.

> Five percent of the frogs in our aquarium ate sixty-two percent of the flies.

> Ten thousand people packed an arena built for 8,550.

---

## EXERCISE 38–1 Using Numbers

Correct any inappropriate uses of numbers in the following sentences. Some sentences may be correct. Answers for the lettered sentences appear at the end of the Handbook. Example:

> As Feinberg notes on page 197, a delay of ~~3~~ *three* minutes cost the researchers ~~5~~ *five* years' worth of work.

a. A program to help save the sea otter transferred more than eighty animals to a new colony over the course of 2 years; however, all but 34 otters swam back home again.

b. 12 percent or so of the estimated fifteen billion plastic water bottles purchased annually in the United States are recycled.

c. In act two, scene nine, of Shakespeare's *The Merchant of Venice*, Portia's 2nd suitor fails to guess which of 3 caskets contains her portrait.

1. *Fourscore* means 4 times 20; a *fortnight* means 2 weeks; and a *brace* is two of anything.

2. 50 years ago, traveling from New York City to San Francisco took approximately 15 hours by plane, 50 hours by train, and almost 100 hours by car.

3. At 7 o'clock this morning the temperature was already ninety-seven degrees Fahrenheit.

# 39 | Italics

*Italic type—as in this line—slants to the right.* In handwriting, indicate italics by underlining. Slightly harder to read than perpendicular type, italic is usually saved for emphasis or other special uses.

**39a** Italicize certain titles, names, and words. Use italics for the types of titles, names, and words shown on page 862.

> We read the story "Araby" in James Joyce's book *Dubliners.*
>
> The Broadway musical *My Fair Lady* was based on Shaw's play *Pygmalion.*

**39b** Use italics sparingly for emphasis.

When you absolutely *must* stress a term, use italics. In most cases, the structure of your sentence should give emphasis where emphasis is due.

> He put the package *under* the mailbox, not *into* the mailbox.
>
> People living in affluent countries may not be aware that nearly *sixteen thousand children per day* die of starvation or malnutrition.

---

## EXERCISE 39–1 Using Italics

Add or remove italics as needed in the following sentences. Some sentences may be correct. Answers for the lettered sentences appear at the end of the Handbook. Example:

> Does *avocado* mean "lawyer" in Spanish?

a. Hiram could not *believe* that his parents had seen *the Beatles'* legendary performance at Shea Stadium.

b. During this year's *First Night* celebrations, we heard Verdi's Requiem and Monteverdi's Orfeo.

c. It was fun watching the passengers on the Europa trying to dance to *Blue Moon* in the midst of a storm.

1. Jan can never remember whether Cincinnati has three n's and one t or two n's and two t's.

2. My favorite comic bit in "The Pirates of Penzance" is Major General Stanley's confusion between "orphan" and "often."

For titles that need to be placed in quotation marks, see 33e.

## ▶ Italics *at a Glance*

### Titles

MAGAZINES, NEWSPAPERS, AND SCHOLARLY JOURNALS
*Newsweek*     the *Oregonian*     *Film & History*

LONG LITERARY WORKS
*The Bluest Eye* (a novel)     *The Less Deceived* (a collection of poems)

FILMS
*Psycho*     *Casablanca*     *Mad Max: Fury Road*

PAINTINGS AND OTHER WORKS OF ART
*Four Dancers* (a painting)     *The Thinker* (a sculpture)

LONG MUSICAL WORKS
*Aïda*     Handel's *Messiah*

ALBUMS
*25*     *The Chronic*

TELEVISION AND RADIO PROGRAMS
*House of Cards*     *All Things Considered*

### Other Words and Phrases

NAMES OF AIRCRAFT, SPACECRAFT, SHIPS, AND TRAINS
the *Orient Express*     the *Challenger*

FOREIGN-LANGUAGE WORD OR PHRASE NOT IN EVERYDAY USE
Gandhi taught the principles of *satya* and *ahimsa*: truth and nonviolence.

FOREIGN-LANGUAGE WORD OR PHRASE IN EVERYDAY USE
I prefer provolone to mozzarella.

LETTER, NUMBER, WORD, OR PHRASE DEFINED OR REFERRED TO AS A WORD
The neon *5* on the door identified the club's address.

The rhythmic motion of the alimentary canal is called *peristalsis*.

What do you think *fiery* suggests in the second line?

For a synonym or translation—a definition of just a word or so—italicize the word and put its definition in quotation marks.

The word *orthodoxy* means "conformity."

*Trois, drei,* and *tres* are all words for "three."

Exception: The names of the Bible (King James Version, Revised Standard Version), the books of the Bible (Genesis, Matthew), and other sacred books (the Qur'an, the Rig-Veda) are not italicized.

3. In Tom Stoppard's play "The Real Thing," the character Henry accuses Bach of copying a *cantata* from a popular song by *Procol Harum*.

# 40 | Hyphens

The hyphen is used to join words and to connect parts of words.

## 40a Use hyphens in compound words that require them.

Compound words in the English language take three forms:

1. Two or more words combined into one (*crossroads, salesperson*)
2. Two or more separate words that function as one (*gas station, high school*)
3. Two or more words linked by hyphens (*sister-in-law, window-shop*)

Compounds fall into these categories more by custom than by rule. When you're not sure which way to write a compound, refer to a current collegiate dictionary. If the compound isn't listed, write it as two words.

Use a hyphen in a compound word containing one or more elements beginning with a capital letter.

> Bill says that, as a *neo-Marxist* living in an *A-frame* house, it would be politically incorrect for him to wear a Mickey Mouse *T-shirt*.

Exceptions to this rule include *unchristian,* for one.

## 40b Use a hyphen in a compound adjective preceding, but not following, a noun.

> Jerome, a devotee of *twentieth-century* music, has no interest in the classic symphonies of the *eighteenth century.*

> I'd like living in an *out-of-the-way* place better if it weren't so far *out of the way.*

In a series of hyphenated adjectives with the same second word, you can omit that word (but not the hyphen) in all but the last adjective of the series.

> Julia is a lover of eighteenth-, nineteenth-, and twentieth-century music.

The adverb *well,* when coupled with an adjective, follows the same hyphenation rules as if it were an adjective.

> It is *well known* that Tony has a *well-equipped* kitchen, although his is not as *well equipped* as the hotel's.

Do *not* use a hyphen to link an adverb ending in *-ly* with an adjective.

> The sun hung like a newly minted penny in a freshly washed sky.

**40c** Use a hyphen after the prefixes *all-*, *ex-*, and *self-* and before the suffix *-elect*.

Lucille's *ex-husband* is studying *self-hypnosis*.

This *all-important* debate pits Senator Browning against the *president-elect*.

**40d** Use a hyphen in most cases if an added prefix or suffix creates a double vowel, a triple consonant, or an ambiguous pronunciation.

It is also acceptable to omit the hyphen in the case of a double *e*: *reeducate*.

The contractor's *pre-estimate* did not cover any *pre-existing* flaws.

The recreation department favors the *re-creation* of a summer program.

**40e** Use a hyphen in spelled-out fractions and compound whole numbers from twenty-one to ninety-nine.

When her sister gave Leslie's age as six and *three-quarters*, Leslie corrected her: "I'm six and *five-sixths*!"

The fifth graders learned that *forty-four* rounds down to forty while *forty-five* rounds up to fifty.

**40f** Use a hyphen to indicate inclusive numbers.

The section covering the years 1975-1980 is found on pages 20-27.

**40g** Use a hyphen to break a word between syllables at the end of a line.

Academic style guides (such as MLA and APA) prefer that you turn off your word processor's automatic hyphenation. If you're designing a text that requires breaking a word, check your dictionary for its syllable divisions.

---

**EXERCISE 40–1 Using Hyphens**

Add necessary hyphens and remove incorrectly used hyphens in the following sentences. Some sentences may be correct. Answers for the lettered sentences appear at the end of the Handbook. Example:

　　　　　　*ex-husband*
　　Her ~~exhusband~~ works part-time as a short-order cook.

a. Jimmy is a lively four year old boy, and his sister is two years old.

b. The badly damaged ship was in no condition to enter the wide-open waters beyond the bay.

c. Tracy's brother in law lives with his family in a six room apartment.

1. Heat-seeking missiles are often employed in modern air-to-air combat.
2. *The Piano* is a beautifully-crafted film with first-rate performances by Holly Hunter and Harvey Keitel.
3. Nearly three fourths of the money in the repair and maintenance account already has been spent.

---

# 41 | Spelling

English spelling so often defies the rules that many writers wonder if, indeed, there *are* rules. How, then, are you to cope? You can proofread carefully and use your spell checker. You can refer to lists of commonly misspelled words and of **homonyms,** words that sound the same, or almost the same, but are spelled differently.

For a list of commonly confused homonyms, see pp. 823–24.

You can also use several tactics to teach yourself to be a better speller.

1. *Use mnemonics.* To make spellings stick in your memory, invent associations. Using such mnemonic devices (tricks to aid memory) may help you. *Weird* behaves *weirdly*. Rise ag*ain*, Brit*ain*! *Separate* has *a rate*. Why isn't *mathe*matics like *athle*tics? You write a *letter* on stationery. Any silly phrase or sentence will do, as long as it helps.

2. *Keep a record of words you misspell.* Buy a notebook for listing words that trip you up. Each time you proofread a paper or receive one back from your instructor, add words you've misspelled. Then practice pronouncing, writing, and spelling them out loud until they stick.

3. *Check any questionable spelling by referring to your dictionary.* Check words as you find them and double-check them as you proofread and edit. If you originally learned British English, a good dictionary will distinguish American and British spellings (*color, colour; terrorize, terrorise*).

4. *Learn commonly misspelled words.* If you're likely to confuse words that sound alike, turn to the list of Commonly Confused Homonyms and the Glossary of Troublemakers in the Quick Editing Guide. Spell every troublesome word out loud; write it ten times. Spend a few minutes each day going over them. Do the same with any common problem words that your spell checker routinely catches, such as *nucular* for *nuclear* or *exercize* for *exercise*. Your spelling will improve rapidly.

# Answers for Lettered Exercises

## EXERCISE 1–1 ▪ Identifying Parts of Speech, p. 739

**a.** *available*: adjective; *around*: preposition; *for*: preposition; *centuries*: noun
**b.** *It*: pronoun; *became*: verb; *very*: adverb; *common*: adjective; *during*: preposition
**c.** *Americans*: noun; *drink*: verb; *countries*: noun; *do*: verb
**d.** *Interestingly*: adverb; *American*: adjective; *cleaner*: adjective; *most*: adjective; *of*: preposition
**e.** *usually*: adverb; *label*: verb; *their*: pronoun; *or*: conjunction

## EXERCISE 2–1 ▪ Identifying Subjects, p. 741

**a.** *television shows*: complete subject; *shows*: simple subject
**b.** *Ernie and Bert*: complete subject; *Ernie and Bert*: simple subject
**c.** *The show*: complete subject; *show*: simple subject
**d.** *it*: complete subject; *it*: simple subject
**e.** *Over 74 million Americans*: complete subject; *Americans*: simple subject

## EXERCISE 3–1 ▪ Identifying Verbs, Objects, and Complements, p. 745

**a.** *invented*: AV; *reflectors*: DO   **b.** *noticed*: AV; *burrs*: DO; *gave*: AV; *world*: IO; *Velcro*: DO   **c.** *are*: LV; *eager*: SC   **d.** *have*: HV; *inspired*: MV; *inventions*: DO   **e.** *melted*: AV; *bar*: DO

## EXERCISE 4–1 ▪ Identifying Phrases and Clauses, p. 748

**a.** *Spending the night in an ice hotel*: verbal phrase; *on my bucket list*: prepositional phrase
**b.** *on the test*: prepositional phrase; *because I studied for three hours*: subordinate clause
**c.** *a 1957 Chevy*: appositive phrase; *off the assembly line*: prepositional phrase
**d.** *After searching all morning*: subordinate clause; *we gave up on finding the lost earring*: main clause
**e.** *dinner still steaming on the table*: absolute phrase

## EXERCISE 5–1 ▪ Identifying Sentence Types, p. 750

**a.** complex   **b.** compound/complex   **c.** compound
**d.** simple   **e.** simple

## EXERCISE 6–1 ▪ Eliminating Fragments, p. 754

*Suggested revisions:*

**a.** Michael had a beautiful Southern accent, having lived many years in Georgia.
**b.** Pat and Chris are determined to marry each other, even if their families do not approve.

**c.** Jack seemed well qualified for a career in the air force, except for his tendency to get airsick.
**d.** Lisa advocated sleeping no more than four hours a night until she started nodding off through her classes.
**e.** Complete sentences

## EXERCISE 7–1 ▪ Revising Comma Splices and Fused Sentences, p. 757

*Suggested revisions:*

**a.** Lee's comic book superheroes are ordinary people with flaws; they also have extraordinary abilities.   *Or*
Lee's comic book superheroes are ordinary people with flaws, yet they also have extraordinary abilities.
**b.** Although Iron Man (Tony Stark) has a superpowered suit and the ability to fly, he is a heavy drinker and suffers from anxiety.   *Or*
Iron Man (Tony Stark) has a superpowered suit and the ability to fly; however, he is a heavy drinker and suffers from anxiety.
**c.** Teenaged nerd Peter Parker is another example: he has spider-like abilities to spin webs and scale buildings.   *Or*
Teenaged nerd Peter Parker, who has spider-like abilities to spin webs and scale buildings, is another example.
**d.** Thor is a godlike superhero who comes to Earth with super strength and the ability to fly; his weakness is his fondness for humans.   *Or*
Thor is a godlike superhero who comes to Earth with super strength and the ability to fly, but his weakness is his fondness for humans.
**e.** Bruce Banner was a brilliant scientist who studied gamma radiation. An accident caused him to turn into a giant destructive hulk when he gets angry.   *Or*
Bruce Banner was a brilliant scientist who studied gamma radiation until an accident caused him to turn into a giant destructive hulk when he gets angry.

## EXERCISE 8–1 ▪ Identifying Verb Tenses, p. 765

**a.** *has been living*: present perfect progressive; *hacked*: simple past
**b.** *have never appeared*: present perfect; *will never appear*: simple future; *gets selected*: simple present
**c.** *had been*: past perfect; *pitched*: simple past
**d.** *will have been studying*: future perfect progressive; *will be taking*: future progressive
**e.** *was running*: past progressive; *strolled*: simple past

## EXERCISE 8–2 ▪ Using Irregular Verb Forms, p. 768

**a.** Change *Do* to *Does*   **b.** Change *laid* to *lay*   **c.** Change *setting* to *sitting*   **d.** Correct   **e.** Change *sat* to *set*

## EXERCISE 8–3 ▪ Using the Correct Mood of Verbs, p. 770

**a.** Dr. Belanger recommended that Juan *floss* his teeth every day. (Incorrect *flosses,* indicative; correct *floss,* subjunctive)
**b.** If I *were* you, I would have done the same thing. (Incorrect *was,* indicative; correct *were,* subjunctive)
**c.** Tradition demands that Daegun *show* respect for his elders. (Incorrect *shows,* indicative; correct *show,* subjunctive)
**d.** Please *attend* the training lesson if you plan to skydive later today. (Incorrect *attends,* indicative; correct *attend,* imperative)

## EXERCISE 9–1 ▪ Making Subjects and Verbs Agree, p. 775

**a.** For many college graduates, the process of looking for jobs *is* often long and stressful.
**b.** Not too long ago, searching the classifieds and inquiring in person *were* the primary methods of job hunting.
**c.** Today, however, everyone also *seems* to use the Internet to search for openings or to e-mail *his or her* résumés.
**d.** My classmates and my cousin *send* most résumés over the Internet because it costs less than mailing them.
**e.** All of the résumés *arrive* quickly when they are sent electronically.

## EXERCISE 10–1 ▪ Using Pronoun Case Correctly, p. 778

**a.** I didn't appreciate *your* laughing at her and *me.* (*Your* modifies the gerund *laughing; me* is an object of the preposition *at.*)
**b.** Lee and *I* would be delighted to serenade *whoever* will listen. (*I* is a subject of the verb phrase *would be delighted; whoever* is the subject of the clause *whoever will listen.*)
**c.** The managers and *we* servers are highly trustworthy. (*We* is a subject complement.)
**d.** The neighbors were driven berserk by *his* singing. (The gerund *singing* is the object of the verb *driven;* the possessive pronoun *his* modifies *singing.*)    *Or*
Correct as is. (*Him* is the object of the verb *driven; singing* is a participle modifying *him.*)
**e.** Jerry and *I* regard you and *her* as the very people *whom* we wish to meet. (*I* is a subject of the verb *regard; her* is a direct object of the verb *regard; whom* is the object of the infinitive *to meet.*)

## EXERCISE 11–1 ▪ Making Pronoun Reference Clear, p. 781

*Suggested revisions:*

**a.** As the moon began to rise, I could see the faint shadow of the tree.

**b.** While she spent the summer in Paris, Katrina broadened her awareness of cultural differences by traveling throughout Europe.
**c.** Most managers want employees to work as many hours as possible. They never consider the work their employees need to do at home.
**d.** My working twelve hours a day and never getting enough sleep was worth it.
**e.** Kevin asked Mike to meet him for lunch but forgot that Mike had class at that time.    *Or*
Kevin forgot that he had class at the time he asked Mike to meet him for lunch.

## EXERCISE 12–1 ▪ Making Pronouns and Antecedents Agree, p. 783

*Suggested revisions:*

**a.** Correct
**b.** Neither Melissa nor James has received an application form yet.    *Or*
Melissa and James have not received their application forms yet.
**c.** He is the kind of man who gets his fun out of just sipping his beer and watching his Saturday games on TV.
**d.** Many a mother has mourned the loss of her child.    *Or*
Many mothers have mourned the loss of their children.
**e.** When you enjoy your work, it's easy to spend all your spare time thinking about it.    *Or*
When one enjoys one's work, it's easy to spend all one's spare time thinking about it.

## EXERCISE 13–1 ▪ Using Adjectives and Adverbs Correctly, p. 788

**a.** Change *exact* to *exactly*    **b.** Change *badly* to *bad*    **c.** Change *best* to *better*    **d.** Change *sadly* to *sad*    **e.** Delete *most*

## EXERCISE 14–1 ▪ Maintaining Grammatical Consistency, p. 790

*Suggested revisions:*

**a.** Dr. Jamison is an erudite professor who tells amusing anecdotes in class. (Formal)    *Or*
Dr. Jamison is a funny teacher who cracks jokes in class. (Informal)
**b.** The audience listened intently to the lecture but did not understand the message.
**c.** Scientists can no longer evade the social, political, and ethical consequences of what they do in the laboratory.
**d.** To have good government, citizens must become informed on the issues. Also, they must vote.
**e.** Good writing is essential to success in many professions, especially in business, where ideas must be communicated clearly.

## EXERCISE 15–1 ▪ Placing Modifiers, p. 793

*Suggested revisions:*

**a.** The bus full of passengers got stuck in a ditch.
**b.** In the middle of a meeting, he was daydreaming about fishing for trout.
**c.** With a smirk, the boy threw the paper airplane through an open window.
**d.** When the glare appeared, I reached for my sunglasses in the glove compartment.
**e.** Sally and Glen watched the kites high above them drift back and forth.

## EXERCISE 15–2 ▪ Revising Dangling Modifiers, p. 794

*Suggested revisions:*

**a.** As I was unpacking the suitcase, a horrible idea occurred to me.
**b.** After fixing breakfast that morning, I might have left the oven on at home.
**c.** Although I tried to reach my neighbor, her phone was busy.
**d.** Desperate to get information, I asked my mother to drive over to check the oven.
**e.** I felt enormous relief when my mother's call confirmed everything was fine.

## EXERCISE 16–1 ▪ Completing Comparisons, p. 796

*Suggested revisions:*

**a.** The movie version of *The Brady Bunch* was much more ironic *than the television show.*
**b.** Taking care of a dog is often more demanding than *taking care of* a cat.
**c.** I received more free calendars in the mail for the year 2016 than *I have for* any other year.
**d.** The crime rate in the United States is higher than *it is in* Canada.
**e.** Liver contains more iron than any *other* meat.

## EXERCISE 16–2 ▪ Completing Sentences, p. 797

*Suggested revisions:*

**a.** Eighteenth-century China was as civilized *as* and in many respects more sophisticated than the Western world.
**b.** Pembroke was never contacted *by,* much less involved with, the election committee.
**c.** I haven't yet *finished* but soon will finish my research paper.
**d.** Ron likes his popcorn with butter; Linda *likes hers* with parmesan cheese.
**e.** Correct

## EXERCISE 17–1 ▪ Correcting Mixed Constructions and Faulty Predication, p. 800

*Suggested revisions:*

**a.** Health insurance protects people from big medical bills.
**b.** His determination to prevail helped him finish the race.
**c.** AIDS destroys the body's immune system.
**d.** The temperatures are too low for the orange trees.
**e.** In a recession, economic growth is small or nonexistent and unemployment increases.

## EXERCISE 18–1 ▪ Making Sentences Parallel, p. 803

*Suggested revisions:*

**a.** The border separating Texas and Mexico marks not only the political boundary of two countries but also the last frontier for some endangered wildlife.
**b.** In the Rio Grande Valley, both local residents and tourists enjoy visiting the national wildlife refuges.
**c.** The tall grasses in this valley are the home of many insects, birds, and small mammals.
**d.** Two endangered wildcats, the ocelot and the jaguarundi, also make the Rio Grande Valley their home.
**e.** Many people from Central America are desperate to immigrate to the United States by either legal or illegal means.

## EXERCISE 19–1 ▪ Using Coordination, p. 806

*Suggested revisions:*

**a.** Professional poker players try to win money and prizes in high-stakes tournaments; however, they may lose thousands of dollars.
**b.** Poker is not an easy way to make a living, and playing professional poker is not a good way to relax.
**c.** A good "poker face" reveals no emotions, for communicating too much information puts a player at a disadvantage.
**d.** Hidden feelings may come out in unconscious movements, so an expert poker player watches other players carefully.
**e.** Poker is different from most other casino gambling games, for it requires skill and it forces players to compete against each other. Other casino gambling pits players against the house, so they may win out of sheer luck, but skill has little to do with winning those games.

## EXERCISE 19–2 ▪ Using Subordination, p. 809

*Suggested revisions:*

**a.** Whereas the average cost of a single-family home in the United States is over $275,000, it costs less than one-tenth of that to build a tiny house.
**b.** American homes, which average about 2,500 square feet, have three bedrooms, two bathrooms, and a garage for two or more cars.

**c.** Although a tiny house is between 100 and 400 square feet, it enables simpler living in a smaller, more efficient space.
**d.** Tiny houses, which come in all shapes, sizes, and forms, are much more customizable than traditional mobile homes.
**e.** People who are joining the tiny house movement do so for many reasons. The most popular reasons include environmental concerns, financial concerns, and the desire for more time and freedom.

## EXERCISE 22–2 ▪ Avoiding Jargon, p. 816

*Suggested revisions:*

**a.** Everyone at Boondoggle and Gall attends holiday gatherings in order to meet and socialize with potential business partners.
**b.** This year, more than fifty employees lost their jobs after Boondoggle and Gall's decision to reduce the number of employees by September 1.
**c.** The layoffs left Jensen in charge of all telephone calls in the customer-service department.
**d.** Jensen was responsible for handling three times as many telephone calls after the layoffs compared with before, yet she did not receive any extra pay.
**e.** Jensen and her managers could not agree on a fair compensation, so she decided to quit her job at Boondoggle and Gall.

## EXERCISE 22–3 ▪ Avoiding Euphemisms and Slang, p. 817

*Suggested revisions:*

**a.** At three hundred dollars a month, the apartment is a bargain.
**b.** The soldiers were accidentally shot by members of their own troops while they were retreating.
**c.** Churchill was an excellent politician.

## EXERCISE 24–1 ▪ Avoiding Bias, p. 821

*Suggested revisions:*

**a.** Our school's athletic program will be of interest to *many* applicants.
**b.** The new physicians include Dr. Scalia, *Dr.* Baniski, and Dr. Morton.
**c.** *Diligent researchers* will always find the sources *they* seek.

## EXERCISE 27–1 ▪ Using End Punctuation, p. 827

**a.** The question that still troubles the community after all these years is why federal agents did not act sooner. [Not a direct question]
**b.** I wonder what he was thinking at the time. [Not a direct question]
**c.** Correct

## EXERCISE 28–1 ▪ Using Commas, p. 829

**a.** Correct
**b.** When we returned to the hotel, he couldn't wait to check for any messages.
**c.** James logged on to the hotel wifi immediately, but he was surprised to find that he hadn't gotten any e-mails all morning.
**d.** His office hadn't called him, nor had his friends left him any messages.
**e.** He pretended to be relieved that nothing urgent had come up at work, but I think he was secretly annoyed that everyone was doing fine without him.

## EXERCISE 28–2 ▪ Using Commas, p. 831

**a.** Mrs. Carver looks like a sweet little old lady, but she plays a wicked electric guitar.
**b.** Her bass player, her drummer, and her keyboard player all live in the same retirement community.
**c.** They practice individually in the afternoon, rehearse together at night, and play at the community's Saturday night dances.
**d.** The Rest Home Rebels have to rehearse quietly and cautiously to keep from disturbing the other residents.
**e.** Correct

## EXERCISE 28–3 ▪ Using Commas, p. 832

*Suggested revisions:*

**a.** We are bringing a dish, vegetable lasagna, to the potluck supper.
**b.** I like to go to Central Bank on this side of town because this branch tends to have short lines.
**c.** The colony that the English established at Roanoke disappeared mysteriously.
**d.** If the base commanders had checked their gun room, where powder is stored, they would have found that several hundred pounds of gunpowder were missing.
**e.** Brazil's tropical rain forests, which help produce the air we breathe all over the world, are being cut down at an alarming rate.

## EXERCISE 28–4 ▪ Using Commas, p. 834

**a.** The university insisted, however, that the students were not accepted merely because of their parents' generous contributions.
**b.** This dispute, in any case, is an old one.
**c.** It was the young man's striking good looks, not his acting ability, that first attracted the Hollywood agents.
**d.** Gretchen learned, moreover, not always to accept as true what she had read in celebrity magazines.
**e.** The hikers, most of them wearing ponchos or rain jackets, headed out into the steady drizzle.

## EXERCISE 28–5 ▪ Using Commas, p. 835

**a.** César Chávez was born on March 31, 1927, on a farm in Yuma, Arizona.

**b.** Chávez, who spent years as a migrant farmworker, told other farm laborers, "If you're outraged at conditions, then you can't possibly be free or happy until you devote all your time to changing them."

**c.** Chávez founded the United Farm Workers union and did, indeed, devote all his time to changing conditions for farmworkers.

**d.** Robert F. Kennedy called Chávez "one of the heroic figures of our time."

**e.** Correct

## EXERCISE 29–1 ▪ Misuses of the Comma, p. 837

**a.** The proposed bill would give veterans in rural areas improved access to medical care, health benefits, and job training.

**b.** Neither the House of Representatives nor the Senate seems likely to vote for increasing the federal minimum wage.

**c.** The report basically states that increased testing is not improving student outcomes, even though that was the original intention.

**d.** During migration, hummingbirds, which weigh less than an ounce, travel distances that average 500 miles per day.

**e.** After the party, we found an earring, two sweaters, a hat, a scarf, and a shoe.

## EXERCISE 30–1 ▪ Using Semicolons, p. 839

**a.** The research paper was due in six weeks; therefore, Ali got started right away by making a schedule.

**b.** The committee estimated the extent of violent crime among teenagers, especially those between the ages of fourteen and sixteen; acted as a liaison between the city and schools and between churches and volunteer organizations; and drew up a plan to reduce violence, both public and domestic, in the next decade.

**c.** The skilled pilot landed the plane in an open field; all passengers made it out safely.

**d.** The mall no longer seems to attract customers; however, downtown businesses are picking up again.

## EXERCISE 31–1 ▪ Using Colons, p. 841

*Suggested revisions:*

**a.** The Continuing Education Program offers courses in building and construction management, engineering, and design.

**b.** The interview ended with a test of skills: taking messages, operating the computer, typing a sample letter, and proofreading documents.

**c.** The sample letter began, "Dear Mr. Rasheed: Please accept our apologies for the late shipment."

## EXERCISE 32–1 ▪ Using Apostrophes, p. 843

**a.** Joe's and Chuck's fathers were both in the class of '90.

**b.** Correct

**c.** It was a strange coincidence that all three women's cars broke down after they had picked up their mothers-in-law.

**d.** Don't forget to dot your *i*'s and cross your *t*'s.

**e.** Mario and Shelley's son is marrying the editor in chief's daughter.

## EXERCISE 33–1 ▪ Using Quotation Marks, p. 847

**a.** "What we still need to figure out," the police chief said, "is whether the victim was acquainted with his assailant."

**b.** A skillful orator, Patrick Henry is credited with the comment "Give me liberty or give me death."

**c.** "I could hear the crowd chanting my name — 'Jones! Jones!' — and that spurred me on," said Bruce Jones, the winner of the 5,000-meter race.

**d.** The video for the rock group Guns N' Roses' epic song "November Rain" is based on a short story by Del James.

**e.** In response to a possible asteroid strike on Earth, former astronaut Rusty Schweickart says, "Every country is at risk."

## EXERCISE 34–1 ▪ Using Dashes, p. 849

*Suggested revisions:*

**a.** I enjoy going hiking with my friend John, whom I've known for fifteen years.

**b.** Pedro's new boat is spectacular — a regular seagoing Ferrari.

**c.** The Thompsons devote their weekends to their favorite pastime — eating bags of potato chips and cookies beside the warm glow of the television.

## EXERCISE 35–1 ▪ Using Parentheses, p. 850

*Suggested revisions:*

**a.** Our cafeteria serves the four basic food groups: white (milk, bread, and mashed potatoes), brown (mystery meat and gravy), green (overcooked vegetables and underwashed lettuce), and orange (squash, carrots, and tomato sauce).

**b.** The hijackers will release the hostages only if the government (1) frees all political prisoners and (2) allows the hijackers to leave the country.

**c.** Correct

## EXERCISE 35–2 ▪ Using Brackets and Ellipses, p. 852

**a.** According to van Wyhe, "Darwin . . . was not . . . consistent in the language he used to describe his beliefs."

**b.** John van Wyhe notes that "[Darwin's] views [on religion] changed over the course of his life."

**c.** Correct

## EXERCISE 36–1 ▪ Using Abbreviations, p. 855

**a.** *Professor* James has office hours on Monday and Tuesday, beginning at 10:00 a.m.
**b.** Emotional issues, *for example,* abortion and capital punishment, cannot be settled easily by compromise.
**c.** The red peppers are selling for *$3.25 a pound.*

## EXERCISE 37–1 ▪ Using Capitalization, p. 858

**a.** The great Shakespearean tragedy *Macbeth,* which was written around 1600, opens in the Scottish countryside and includes the famous character Lady Macbeth.

**b.** Colleen's favorite class at Arizona State University is literature. She also enjoys taking weekend hiking trips to the Grand Canyon.

**c.** Jake's great-aunt was the author Kate Chopin, who wrote the famous work of fiction "The Story of an Hour" two decades after the Civil War.

## EXERCISE 38–1 ▪ Using Numbers, p. 860

**a.** A program to help save the sea otter transferred more than eighty animals to a new colony over the course of *two* years; however, all but *thirty-four* otters swam back home again.

**b.** *Twelve percent* or so of the estimated *15* billion plastic water bottles purchased annually in the United States are recycled.
**c.** In act 2, scene 9, of Shakespeare's *The Merchant of Venice,* Portia's *second* suitor fails to guess which of *three* caskets contains her portrait [or act II, scene ix, as directed].

## EXERCISE 39–1 ▪ Using Italics, p. 861

**a.** Hiram could not believe that his parents had seen the Beatles' legendary performance at Shea Stadium.
**b.** During this year's First Night celebrations, we heard Verdi's *Requiem* and Monteverdi's *Orfeo.*
**c.** It was fun watching the passengers on the *Europa* trying to dance to "Blue Moon" in the midst of a storm.

## EXERCISE 40–1 ▪ Using Hyphens, p. 864

**a.** Jimmy is a lively four-year-old boy, and his sister is two years old.
**b.** Correct
**c.** Tracy's brother-in-law lives with his family in a six-room apartment.

# Quick Format Guide

**A** | Following the Format for an Academic Paper  Q-1

**B** | Integrating and Crediting Visuals  Q-7

**C** | Preparing a Document Template  Q-12

**D** | Solving Common Format Problems  Q-13

**E** | Designing Other Documents for Your Audience  Q-13

**F** | Organizing a Résumé and an Application Letter  Q-16

When you think about a newspaper, a specific type of publication comes to mind because the newspaper is a familiar *genre*, or form. Almost all printed newspapers share a set of defined features: a masthead, headlines, pictures with captions, graphics, and articles arranged in columns of text. Popular magazines, academic journals, letters of recommendation, corporate annual reports, and many other types of writing can be identified and distinguished by such features.

Readers also have expectations about how a college paper should look, sometimes including the presentation of visual material such as graphs, tables, photographs, or other illustrations, depending on the field and the assignment. How can you find out what's expected? Check your course materials. Look for directions about format, advice about common problems, requirements for a specific academic style — or all three.

## A | Following the Format for an Academic Paper

You can easily spot the appealing features of a magazine, newspaper, or Web site with bold headlines, colorful images, and creative graphics. These lively materials serve their purpose, attracting your attention and promoting the interests of the publication's owners, contributors, or sponsors. In contrast, academic papers may look plain, even downright dull. However, their aim is not to entertain you but to engage your mind. The conventions — the accepted expectations — for college papers vary by field but typically support core academic values: to present ideas, reduce distractions, and integrate sources. A conventional format reassures readers that you respect the values behind the guidelines.

## MLA First Page

Running head with writer's last name and page number on every page

Writer's name

Instructor's name

Course

Date

Title, centered

Double-spaced 12-point Times New Roman font recommended

Right margin uneven with no hyphenation

Thesis previews paper's development

Launch statement names publication and author

Long quotation (5 prose or 4 poetry lines or more) indented without quotation marks

Ellipses show omissions, and brackets show additions within a quotation

Page number locates information in source

Electronic sources without page numbers cited only by author or by title with organization as author

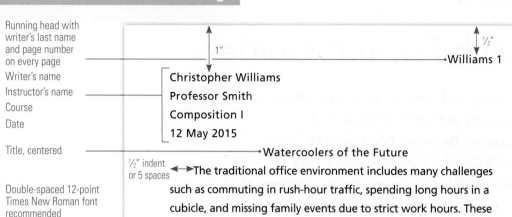

1"    ½"

Williams 1

Christopher Williams

Professor Smith

Composition I

12 May 2015

Watercoolers of the Future

½" indent or 5 spaces

The traditional office environment includes many challenges such as commuting in rush-hour traffic, spending long hours in a cubicle, and missing family events due to strict work hours. These challenges are all changing, however, now that technology is altering how and where people work. With more and more freelance and home-based possibilities, a trend known as co-working has led to the development of shared workspaces. As technology changes the traditional office workspace, new co-working cooperatives are creating the watercoolers of the future, positive gathering spots where working people can meet and share ideas.

New technology is leading the shift away from corporate offices. In *The Future of Work,* Malone explains this move away from the physical office with four walls:

Dispersed physically but connected by technology, workers are now able . . . to make their own decisions using information gathered from many other people and places. . . . [They] gain the economic benefits of large organizations, like economies of scale and knowledge, without giving up the human benefits of small ones, like freedom, creativity, motivation, and flexibility. (4)

Working at a distance or from home can take a toll on workers, however. Loneliness and lack of social opportunities are some of the largest problems for people who do not work in a traditional office (Miller). This is where co-working comes in. Independent workers such as freelancers, people starting their own businesses, and telecommuters share office space. They often pay a monthly fee in exchange for use of the rented area and whatever it provides, such as desk space, meeting rooms,

1"

## MLA Works Cited

Williams 7

### Works Cited

Butler, Kiera. "Works Well with Others." *Mother Jones*, Jan./
Feb. 2008, pp. 66-69.

Cetron, Marvin J., and Owen Davies. "Trends Shaping
Tomorrow's World: Economic and Social Trends and Their
Impacts." *The Futurist*, vol. 44, no. 3, May-June 2010,
pp. 35-51. *Academic OneFile*, go.galegroup.com.

Citizen Space. "Our Philosophy." *Citizen Space*, citizenspace
.us/about/our-philosophy/. Accessed 8 Mar. 2015.

Donkin, Richard. *The Future of Work*. Palgrave Macmillan,
2009.

Godin, Seth. "The Last Days of Cubicle Life." *Time*, 14 May
2009, content.time.com/time/specials/packages/
article/0,28804,1898024_1898023_1898077,00.html.

Goetz, Kaomi. "Co-working Offers Community to Solo
Workers." *Morning Edition*, National Public Radio, 6 Jan.
2010, www.npr.org/templates/story/story.php?storyId
=122252297.

---. "For Freelancers, Landing a Workspace Gets Harder."
*Morning Edition*, National Public Radio, 10 Apr. 2012,
www.npr.org/2012/04/10/150286116/for-freelancers
-landing-a-workspace-gets-harder.

Malone, Thomas W. *The Future of Work: How the New Order
of Business Will Shape Your Organization, Your
Management Style, and Your Life*. Harvard Business
Review Press, 2004.

McConville, Christine. "Freelancers Bag Cheap Office Space."
*The Boston Herald*, 15 Aug. 2009, www.bostonherald.
com/business/general/view.bg?articleid=1191126.

Miller, Kerry. "Where the Coffee Shop Meets the Cubicle."
*Bloomberg Businessweek*, 26 Feb. 2007, www.bloomberg
.com/bw/stories/2007-02-26/where-the-coffee-shop
-meets-the-cubiclebusinessweek-business-news-stock
-market-and-financial-advice.

List of works cited on a separate page

Running head continues

List alphabetized by last names of authors or by titles (when no author is named)

First line of entry at left margin

Additional lines indented ½"

Double-spaced throughout

Three hyphens show same author continues

## APA Title Page and Abstract

Running head with short title in capital letters on left and page number on right

1"

Running head: PET HEALTH INSURANCE                    1

Double-spaced 12-point Times New Roman font recommended

Title, centered
Author
School

Limitations of Pet Health Insurance
Jennifer Miller
Springfield Community College

Running head continues on following pages

PET HEALTH INSURANCE                    2

Heading, centered

No paragraph indentation

Double-spaced

Main ideas summed up, usually in less than 250 words

Key words, common for journal articles, also may be expected by your instructor

Abstract

In recent years, the amount of money spent annually in the United States on veterinary care for the millions of household pets has risen into the billions of dollars. One option for owners is to buy a pet health insurance policy. Policies currently available have both advantages and disadvantages. Benefits can include coverage of increasingly complicated treatments. Drawbacks to coverage include the exclusion of preexisting conditions and hidden fees. In the end, interest-bearing savings accounts may be a better option than policy premiums for most pet owners.

*Key words:* pet health insurance, pet ownership

## APA First Page of Text

PET HEALTH INSURANCE         3

½" (or 5–7 spaces)

Limitations of Pet Health Insurance

The Humane Society of the United States (2012) reports in *U.S. Pet Ownership Statistics* that over 78 million dogs and 84 million cats are owned as household pets. However, only 3% of household pets are insured. Furthermore, in 2007, "only 850,000 pet insurance policies [were] in effect . . . according to the National Commission on Veterinary Economic Issues" (Weston, 2010). Recent studies suggest that, despite the growing availability of insurance plans for pet health care, these policies may not be the cheapest way to care for a household pet. Pet owners need to consider a number of factors before buying a policy, including the pet's age, any preexisting diseases that an insurance carrier might decide not to cover, and a policy's possible hidden fees.

### Types of Pet Health Insurance Currently Available

Pet ownership is important to many people, and pets can do a great deal to improve the mental health and quality of life for their owners (McNicholas et al., 2005, p. 1252). However, paying for a pet's own health care can be stressful and expensive. Mathews (2009) reported on the costs in the *Wall Street Journal*:

½"   This year, pet owners are expected to spend around $12.2 billion for veterinary care, up from $11.1 billion last year and $8.2 billion five years ago, according to the American Pet Products Association. Complex procedures widely used for people, including chemotherapy and dialysis, are now available for pets, and the potential cost of treating certain illnesses has spiked as a result. (Introduction section, para. 4)

Many providers currently offer plans to insure household pets. The largest of the providers is the long-standing Veterinary Pet Insurance (VPI), holding over two-thirds of the country's market (Weston, 2010). Other companies include ASPCA Pet Health Insurance, Petshealth Care Plan, and AKC Pet Healthcare Plan. All offer plans for dogs and cats, yet VPI is one of only a

---

Annotations (right margin):

Running head continues

Title, centered

Launch statement names organization as author with date added in parentheses

Double-spaced throughout

Brackets show additions, and ellipses show omissions within a quotation

Electronic source without page cited only by author and date

Thesis previews paper's development

First-level heading in bold type and centered

Citation identifies authors, date, and location in the source (required for quotation and preferred for paraphrase)

Long quotation (40 words or more) indented without quotation marks

Section name and paragraph number locate quotation in electronic source without page numbers

Right margin uneven with no automatic hyphenation

Margin markings: 1", ½", 1", 1", 1"

## APA References

Running head with page numbering continues

Heading, centered

List alphabetized by last names of authors or by titles (when no author is named)

First line of entry at left margin

Additional lines indented ½"

Double-spaced throughout

No period after URL

As many as seven authors named in References

No period after DOI (digital object identifier) for article

Long URL divided before period, slash, or other punctuation mark

PET HEALTH INSURANCE                                                    12

References

Barlyn, S. (2008, March 13). Is pet health insurance worth the

price? *The Wall Street Journal,* p. D2.

Busby, J. (2005). *How to afford veterinary care without*

*mortgaging the kids.* Bemidji, MN: Busby International.

Calhoun, A. (2008, February 8). What I wouldn't do for my

cat. *Salon.* Retrieved from http://www.salon.com

Darlin, D. (2006, May 13). Vet bills and the priceless pet:

What's a practical owner to do? *The New York Times.*

Retrieved from http://www.nytimes.com

Humane Society of the United States. (2012). U.S. pet

ownership statistics. Retrieved from http://www

.humanesociety.org/issues/pet_overpopulation/facts

/pet_ownership_statistics.html

Kenney, D. (2009). *Your guide to understanding pet health*

*insurance.* Memphis, TN: PhiloSophia.

Mathews, A. W. (2009, December 9). Polly want an insurance

policy? *The Wall Street Journal.* Retrieved from http://

online.wsj.com

McNicholas, J., Gilbey, A., Rennie, A., Ahmedzai, S., Dono, J.,

& Ormerod, E. (2005). Pet ownership and human health:

A brief review of evidence and issues. *British Medical*

*Journal, 331,* 1252-1254. doi:10.1136/bmj.331.7527.1252

Price, J. (2010, April 9). Should you buy pet health insurance?

*The Christian Science Monitor.* Retrieved from http://

www.csmonitor.com

Weston, L. P. (2010, November 4). Should you buy pet

insurance? *MSN Money.* Retrieved from http://money.msn

.com/insurance/should-you-buy-pet-insurance-weston.aspx

| Common Academic Values | Common Paper Expectations and Format |
|---|---|
| Clear presentation of ideas, information, and research findings | ■ Text printed out on one side of a white sheet of paper, double-spaced, one-inch margins<br>■ Paper uses black, 12-point Times New Roman type and has numbered pages |
| Investigation of an intriguing issue, unanswered question, unsolved puzzle, or unexplored relationship | ■ Title and running head to clarify focus for reader<br>■ Abstract in social sciences or sciences to sum up<br>■ Opening paragraph or section to express thesis, research question, or conclusions<br>■ Closing paragraph or section to reinforce conclusions |
| Academic exchange of ideas and information, including evidence from reliable authorities and investigations | ■ Quotations from sources identified by quotation marks or block format<br>■ Paraphrase, summary, and synthesis of sources<br>■ Citation of each source in the text when mentioned<br>■ Well-organized text with transitions and cues to help readers make connections<br>■ Possibly headings to identify sections |
| Identification of evidence to allow a reader to evaluate its contribution and join the academic exchange | ■ Full information about each source in a concluding list<br>■ Specific format used for predictable, consistent arrangement of detail |

MLA (Modern Language Association) style, explained in the *MLA Handbook,* Eighth Edition (MLA, 2016), is commonly used in the humanities. APA (American Psychological Association) style, explained in the *Publication Manual of the American Psychological Association,* Sixth Edition (American Psychological Association, 2010), is commonly used in the social and behavioral sciences. Both MLA and APA, like other academic styles, specify how a page should look and how sources should be credited. (See pp. Q-2–Q-6.)

For examples showing how to cite and list sources in MLA and APA styles, see E in the Quick Research Guide, pp. Q-31–Q-36.

# B | Integrating and Crediting Visuals

Visuals in your text can engage readers, convey information, and reinforce your words. The MLA and APA style guides divide visuals into two groups:

■ **Tables** are grids that clearly report numerical data or other information in columns (running up and down) and rows (running across).

- **Figures** include charts, graphs, diagrams, drawings, maps, photographs, or other images.

Much of the time you can create pie charts, bar graphs, or tables in your text file using your software, spreadsheet, or presentation options. Try a drawing program for making diagrams, maps, or sketches or an image editor for scanning print photographs or adding your own digital shots.

When you add visuals from other sources, you can photocopy or scan printed material, pick up online graphics, or turn to the computer lab for sophisticated advice. For a complex project, get help well ahead of your deadline, and allow plenty of time to learn new techniques.

Select or design visuals that are clear, easy to read, and informative.

- To present statistical information, use graphs, charts, or tables.
- To discuss a conflict in a certain geographical area, supply a map.
- To illustrate a reflective essay, scan an image of yourself or an event.
- To clarify stages, steps, or directions for a process, add a diagram.

## B1   Position visuals and credit sources.

Present each visual: provide a context for it, identify its purpose, explain its meaning, and help a reader see how it supports your point. Following your style guide, identify and number it as a table or figure. Place the visual near the related text discussion so readers can easily connect the two.

Solve any layout problems in your final draft as you arrange text and visual on the page. For instance, align an image with the left margin to continue the text's forward movement. Use it to balance and support, not overshadow, text. Let the visual draw a reader's eye with an appropriate—not excessive—share of the page. To present a long table or large photograph on its own page, simply add page breaks before and after it. To include tables or figures for reference, such as your survey forms, place them in an appendix or collect them in an electronic supplement, as APA suggests.

Acknowledge visual sources as carefully as textual sources. Credit material from a source, printed or electronic, as you present the visual. Ask permission, if required, to use an image from a copyrighted source, including most printed books, articles, and other resources; credit the owner of the copyright. If you download an image from the Web, follow the site guidelines for the use of images. If you are uncertain about whether you can use an image from a source, ask your teacher's advice.

## B2   Prepare tables using MLA or APA format.

If you conduct a small survey, use the insert or table menu to create a simple table to summarize responses. Supply a label and a title or caption before the table. (Italicize its name if you are using APA style.) Double-space, add lines to separate sections, and use letters to identify any notes.

**TABLE FORMAT FOR PRESENTING YOUR SURVEY FINDINGS**

Table 1

Sources of Financial Support Reported by Survey Participants[a]

| Type of Support | First-Year Students (n = 20) | Other Undergraduates (n = 30) |
| --- | --- | --- |
| Scholarship or Campus Grant | 25% | 20% |
| Student Loans | 40% | 57% |
| Work Study | 20% | 7% |
| Family Support | 50% | 40% |
| Part-Time or Full-Time Job | 25% | 57% |
| Employer or Military Contribution | 10% | 17% |
| Other | 5% | 7% |

a. Percentages based on the total number of respondents (n) were calculated and rounded to the nearest whole number.

*Margin notes:*
- Label with number
- Title or caption
- Letter keyed to note
- Column headings
- Pair of rules or lines to enclose heading
- Rule or line to mark end
- Note of explanation if needed

If your results came from only a few students at one campus, you might compare them with state or national findings, as in the next sample table. When you include a table or an image from a source, credit it, and identify it as a source (MLA) or as adapted (APA) if you have modified it.

**TABLE FORMAT FOR MLA AND APA SOURCE CREDITS**

Table 2

Percentages of Undergraduates Receiving Selected Types of Financial Aid, by Type of Institution, Attendance Pattern, Dependency Status, and Income Level: 2011-12

| Institutional Characteristics | Any Grants | Any Student Loans | Work-Study | Veteran Benefits |
| --- | --- | --- | --- | --- |
| Public | | | | |
| 2-year | 50.5 | 17.6 | 1.9 | 2.9 |
| 4-year (non-doctorate) | 55.3 | 39.4 | 5.3 | 3.2 |
| 4-year (doctorate) | 59.9 | 55.5 | 6.2 | 2.8 |

Source: Radwin, David, et al. *2011-12 National Postsecondary Student Aid Study (NPSAS:12): Student Financial Aid Estimates for 2011-12.* National Center for Education Statistics, Aug. 2013, nces.ed.gov/pubs2013/2013165.pdf.

*Margin notes:*
- Label with number
- Title or caption
- Column headings
- Spanner heading (for all rows) centered
- MLA source credit

The credit on page Q-9 follows MLA style; the credit below follows APA. At the end, add the date and name as any copyright holder requests.

APA source credit

> *Note.* Adapted from U.S. Department of Education, Institute of Education Sciences, National Center for Education Statistics. 2013. *2011-12 National Postsecondary Student Aid Study* (NCES Publication No. NPSAS:12), Table 1.

## B3 Add diagrams, graphs, charts, and other figures.

Select or design figures purposefully. Consider your readers' needs as you decide which types might convey information effectively. A diagram can help readers see the sequence of steps in a process. A graph can show how different groups of people behave over time. A sketch of an old building can illustrate the style of its era. Add a clear caption or title to identify what you are illustrating as well as labels for readers to note key elements, add numerical or textual detail, and use visual elements—size, shape, direction, color—to emphasize, connect, or contrast.

- A diagram can simplify a complex process and clarify its stages. Figure Q.1 shows the stages in the studying process.

- A comparative line graph can show how trends change over time. Figure Q.2 illustrates how driver distraction contributes to accidents.

**Figure Q.1**
A Diagram Showing the Study Process
Lucy Tribble MacDonald.

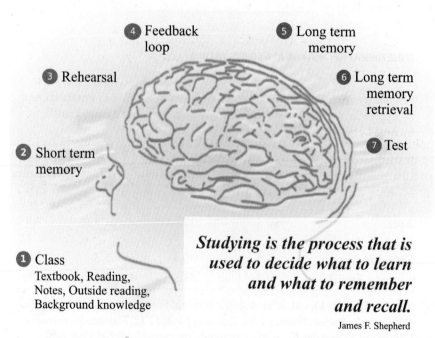

Source: Tribble MacDonald, Lucy. "How to Study Model." Teach Learn Online, 2013, www.howtostudy.org/resources _skill.php?.

- A column or bar graph can compare relative values. Figure Q.3 illustrates the same data found in Q.2 in a different format.
- A map can present geographical or spatial data. Figure Q.4 shows the geographical range of the Great Lakes basin, which was the subject of a collaborative FEMA study.

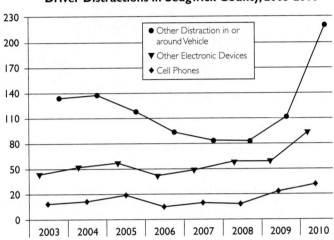

**Number of Automobile Accidents Attributed to Driver Distractions in Sedgwick County, 2003-2010**

- Other Distraction in or around Vehicle
- ▼ Other Electronic Devices
- ◆ Cell Phones

**Figure Q.2** Data Represented as a Graph
Sedgwick County Health Department.

Source: Kansas, Sedgwick County, Sedgwick County Health Deptartment. *Sedgwick County Health Department Data Book.* Sedgwick County Health Department, Mar. 2012, p. 14, www.naccho.org/uploads/downloadable-resources/Sedgwick-CHA-Part-1-Data-Book.pdf.

**Number of Automobile Accidents Attributed to Driver Distractions in the State of Kansas and Sedgwick County**

**Figure Q.3**
Data Represented as a Table
Sedgwick County Health Department.

| Year | Cell Phones | | Other Electronic Devices | | Other Distraction in or around Vehicle | |
|---|---|---|---|---|---|---|
| | KS | ▼ SG | KS | ◆ SG | KS | ● SG |
| 2003 | 198 | 45 | 81 | 12 | 956 | 133 |
| 2004 | 260 | 53 | 111 | 16 | 991 | 138 |
| 2005 | 292 | 58 | 104 | 19 | 909 | 119 |
| 2006 | 350 | 44 | 104 | 8 | 843 | 96 |
| 2007 | 350 | 49 | 111 | 14 | 802 | 84 |
| 2008 | 394 | 61 | 102 | 13 | 832 | 84 |
| 2009 | 499 | 61 | 201 | 23 | 1,020 | 113 |
| 2010 | 536 | 95 | 180 | 35 | 1,303 | 223 |

Source: Kansas, Sedgwick County, Sedgwick County Health Department. *Sedgwick County Health Department Data Book.* Sedgwick County Health Department, Mar. 2012, p. 14, www.naccho.org/uploads/downloadable-resources/Sedgwick-CHA-Part-1-Data-Book.pdf.

**Figure Q.4** Map
NOAA.

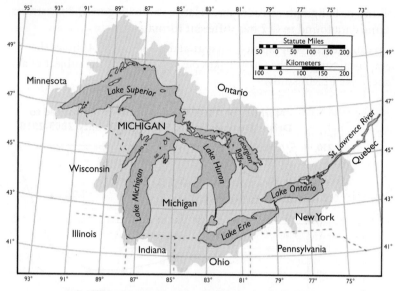

**States/Provinces of the Great Lakes Basin.**

Source: Department of Homeland Security, Federal Emergency Management Agency. "States/Provinces of the Great Lakes Basin." *Great Lakes Coastal Flood Study Summary Fact Sheet.* Great Lakes Coastal Flood Study, 5 April 2012, p. 1, greatlakescoast.org/pubs/factSheets/GLCFS_FS1_ProgramSummary.pdf.

# C | Preparing a Document Template

Unless your teacher encourages creative formatting, avoid experimenting with a college paper. Follow the assigned format and style; check your draft against your instructor's directions and against examples (such as the MLA and APA samples here). Use your software's Help function to learn how to set font, page, format, or template features such as these:

- placement of information on the first page
- margin widths for the top, bottom, and sides of the page (such as 1″)
- name of font (Times New Roman), style (regular roman, italics, or bold), and size of type (12 point)
- running head with automatic page numbering
- double spacing (without extra space between paragraphs)
- text alignment, even on the left but not on the right (left alignment, not centered text, with automatic hyphenation of words turned off)
- width of the paragraph indentation and special "hanging" indentation for your final list of sources
- any other features of the required format

A template simplifies using expected features every time you write a paper with the same specifications. If you have trouble setting features or saving the template, get help from your instructor, a classmate, the writing center, or the computer lab. Follow these steps to create your template:

1. Format your paper the way you want it to look.
2. Create a duplicate copy of your formatted file.
3. Delete all text discussion in the duplicate document.
4. Use the Save As feature to save the file as a document template.
5. Give the template a clear name ("Comp paper" or "MLA form").
6. To open a new file, select this template from your template folder.

# D | Solving Common Format Problems

Software programs differ, as do versions of the same software. Watch for default settings or format shifts that do not match an academic format.

- When you find unconventional features, such as extra lines between paragraphs or automatic hyphenation, reset these features.
- Use your software's Help function to look up the feature by naming it (paragraph), identifying the issue (paragraph spacing), or specifying what you want to do (troubleshoot paragraph spacing).

Other problems can arise because academic style guides make their own assumptions about the texts their users are likely to write. For example, MLA style assumes you will write an essay, simply separate items in a list with commas, and probably limit additions to tables and illustrations. On the other hand, APA style assumes you probably need section headings, lists (numbered, bulleted, or lettered within a sentence), and appendices, especially for research materials such as sample questionnaires. In addition, your instructor might require an outline or links for online sources. Follow your instructor's advice if your paper requires formatting that the style you are using (MLA or APA) does not recognize.

Readers appreciate your consideration of their practical problems, too. A clear, neat, readable document is one that readers can readily absorb. For example, your instructor might ask you to reprint a paper if your toner cartridge is nearly empty. Clear papers in a standard format are easier on the eyes than those with faint print or unusual features. In addition, such papers have margin space for comments so they are easy to grade. If you submit an electronic file, pay attention to online formatting conventions.

# E | Designing Other Documents for Your Audience

Four key principles of document design can help you prepare effective documents in and out of the classroom: know your audience, satisfy them with the features and format they expect, consider their circumstances, and remember your purpose.

## DISCOVERY CHECKLIST

☐ Who are your readers? What matters to them? How might the format of your document acknowledge their values, goals, and concerns?

☐ What form or genre do readers expect? Which of its features and details do they see as typical? What visual evidence would they find appropriate?

☐ What problems or constraints will your readers face as they read your document? How can your design help reduce these problems?

☐ What is the purpose of your document? How can its format help achieve this purpose? How might it enhance your credibility as a writer?

☐ What is the usual format of your document? Find and analyze a sample.

## **E1** Select type font, size, and face.

*Typography* refers to the appearance of letters on a page. In your word-processing program, you can change typeface or font style from roman to bold or italics or change type size for a passage by highlighting it and clicking on the appropriate toolbar icon.

Most college papers and many other documents use Times New Roman in a 12-point size. Signs, posters, and visuals such as slides for presentations might require larger type (with a larger number for the point size). Test such materials for readability by printing samples in various type sizes and standing back from them at the distance of your intended audience. Size also varies with different typefaces because they occupy different amounts of horizontal space on the page. Figure Q.5 shows the space required for the same sentence written in four different 12-point fonts.

**Figure Q.5** Space Occupied by Different Typefaces

| Times New Roman | An estimated 40 percent of young children have an imaginary friend. |
|---|---|
| Courier New | An estimated 40 percent of young children have an imaginary friend. |
| Helvetica | An estimated 40 percent of young children have an imaginary friend. |
| Calibri | An estimated 40 percent of young children have an imaginary friend. |

Fonts also vary in design. Times New Roman and Courier New are called *serif* fonts because they have small tails, or serifs, at the ends of the letters.

Helvetica and the more casual Calibri are *sans serif*—without serifs—and thus have solid, straight lines without tails at the tips of the letters.

Times New Roman (serif)  K k P p

Helvetica (sans serif)  K k P p

Sans serif fonts have a clean look, desirable for headlines, ads, "pull quotes" (in larger type to catch the reader's eye), and text within APA-style figures. More readable serif fonts are used for article (or "body") text. Times New Roman, the common font preferred for MLA and APA styles, was developed for the *Times* newspaper in London. As needed, use light, slanted *italics* (for certain titles) or dark **bold** (for APA headings).

## E2 Organize effective lists.

The placement of material on a page—its layout—can make information more accessible for readers. MLA style recognizes common ways of integrating a list within a sentence: introduce the list with a colon or dash (or set it off with two dashes); separate its items with commas, or use semicolons if the items include commas. APA style adds options, preceding each item in a sentence with a letter enclosed by parentheses, such as (a), (b), and (c), or using display lists—set off from text—for visibility and easy reading.

One type of displayed list, the numbered list, can emphasize priorities, conclusions, or processes such as steps in research procedures, how-to advice, or instructions, as in this simple sequence for making clothes:

**NUMBERED LIST**

1. Lay out the pattern and fabric you have selected.
2. Pin the pattern to the fabric, noting the arrows and grain lines.
3. Cut out the fabric pieces, following the outline of the pattern.
4. Sew the garment together using the pattern's step-by-step instructions.

Another type of displayed list sets off a bit of information with a bullet, most commonly a small round mark (•) but sometimes a square (■), from the toolbar. Bulleted lists are common in résumés and business documents but not necessarily in academic papers, though APA style now recognizes them. Use them to identify items when you do not wish to suggest any order of priority, as in this list of tips for saving energy.

**BULLETED LIST**

- Let your hair dry without running a hair dryer.
- Commute by public transportation.
- Turn down the thermostat by a few degrees.
- Unplug your phone charger and TV during the day.

## E3 Consider adding headings.

In a complex research report, business proposal, or Web document, headings show readers how the document is structured, which sections are most important, and how parts are related. Headings also name sections so readers know where they are and where they're going. Headings at different levels should differ from each other and from the main text in placement and style, making the text easy to scan for key points.

For academic papers, MLA encourages writers to organize by outlining their essays but doesn't recommend or discuss text headings. In contrast, APA illustrates five levels of headings beginning with these two:

### First-Level Heading Centered in Bold

**Second-Level Heading on the Left in Bold**

Besides looking the same, headings at the same level in your document should be brief, clear, and informative. They also should use consistent parallel phrasing. If you write a level-one heading as an *-ing* phrase, do the same for all the level-one headings that follow. Here are some examples of four common patterns for phrasing headings.

For more on parallel structure, see section B2 in the Quick Editing Guide, p. Q-47.

**-*ING* PHRASES**

Using the College Catalog

Choosing Courses

Declaring a Major

**QUESTIONS**

What Is Hepatitis C?

Who Is at Risk?

How Is Hepatitis C Treated?

**NOUN PHRASES**

E-Commerce Benefits

E-Commerce Challenges

Online Shopper Profiles

**IMPERATIVE SENTENCES**

Initiate Your IRA Rollover

Balance Your Account

Select New Investments

Web pages—especially home pages and site guides—are designed to help readers find information quickly, within a small viewing frame that may change shape and size across devices. For this reason, they generally have more headings than other documents. If you design a Web page or post your course portfolio, consider what different readers might want to find. Then design your headings and content to meet their needs.

# F | Organizing a Résumé and an Application Letter

For more on application letters and résumés, see pp. 342–46.

When your reader is a prospective employer, present a solid, professional job application, preferably a one-page résumé and application letter (see pp. Q-18–Q-19). Both should be clearly organized to show why you are a strong candidate for the position. The purpose of your résumé is to organize the details of your education and experience (usually by category and by reverse chronology) so they are easy to review. Wording matters, so use action verbs and parallel structure to convey your experience and enthusiasm. The purpose of your application letter is to highlight your qualifications and motivate the reader to interview and eventually hire you. A follow-up letter might thank your interviewer, confirm your interest, and supply anything requested. Write clearly, and use a standard format; a sloppy letter might suggest that you lack the communication skills employers value.

Your campus career center may provide sample application letters and résumés so you can compare layout variations, evaluate their impact, and effectively design your own. To apply for a professional program, internship, or other opportunity, simply adapt your letter and résumé. For an electronic job application form, select relevant information from your résumé and embed as many key words as possible that might be used to sort or rank applications.

*Splits heading with contact information*

# Catherine Michaels

65 Oakwood Ave. Apt. #105
Somerville, MA 02144
Mobile 617-555-5555
crmichaels@comnet.com

## Experience

*Places current information first*

**Research Analyst**                                                                *June 2015 – Present*
**Industrial Economics, Incorporated** — Cambridge, MA

Develop profit estimation model, adopted as practice area standard, for petroleum bulk stations
Create and implement valuation methodology for a major privately held forestry company

**Intern, Global Treasury — Investment Management Team**  *June 2014 – August 2014*
**State Street Corporation** — Boston, MA

*Specifies activities*

Research and analyze corporate bonds, including economic and industry analyses

## Education

**Bachelor of Arts** — Bates College, Lewiston, ME            *September 2011 – May 2015*

Major: Economics        Related courses: Calculus; Advanced Statistics and Econometrics
Minor: Japanese

## Skills & Competencies

*Uses bold type to highlight categories*

**Statistical Packages:** SAS, STATA, R
**Programming Languages & Related:** VBA, Python, SQL, LINUX/UNIX, Scripting (KSH/BASH), DOS
**Microsoft Office:** Advanced Excel, PowerPoint
**Other:** Cloud Computing (PaaS, AWS, shell interaction, batch processing), Hadoop Ecosystem
**Languages and Music:** Conversational Japanese, Guitar, Saxophone, Banjo

*Labels sections and uses dividers*

## Leadership & Involvement

**Analytic Pro Bono Work (present)**
Leverage data mining skills to assist nonprofit organizations
Consult on data collection and management
Improve donation volume and donor retention

**Boston Data Science Community**
Participate actively in industry groups, Boston Predictive Analytics, Boston R Users

**Alpine Climbing (2010–present)**
Organize route finding and equipment logistics
Lead trips throughout California, Canadian Rockies, and New England

65 Oakwood Ave. Apt. #105
Somerville, MA 02144
15 May 2016

Ross Landon
Denver Strategists
8866 Larimer Street, Suite 404
Denver, CO 80217

Dear Mr. Landon:

Josh Greenway, formerly a data analyst with Denver Strategists, recommended that I contact you about the upcoming expansion of your Marketing Analysis Group. I am looking for an opportunity to combine my college major in economics with my long-standing interest in statistics. Because your expansion promises an excellent opportunity to do so, I wish to apply for one of your openings for a data analyst.

As my résumé indicates, my college internship with the Investment Management Team at Global Treasury introduced me to the many processes involved in industry analyses. Since graduation, I have worked as a research analyst at Industrial Economics, estimating valuation and profits for clients in diverse industries. In addition, as a pro bono consultant with Boston nonprofit organizations, I have expanded my expertise with statistics packages. For these groups, I have directed my skills to improving data mining and data management in order to help them cultivate and retain contributors more effectively.

I am now looking forward to designing and conducting more complex data mining and data analysis projects. Joining your expansion team would offer me a welcome opportunity to develop my analytic skills, expand my experience with various statistical methods, and gain sophistication working with team colleagues as well as a variety of clients. For me, data analysis is a challenging and rewarding way to combine my skills in math, statistics, and technology with the creativity data science requires. Both my education and my experience have prepared me to address a company's problems or change a client's perspective through data-based analysis.

I would be happy to meet with you to learn more about your plans for the Marketing Analysis Group. Please call me at 617-555-5555, e-mail me at crmichaels@comnet.com, or write to me at the address above. I appreciate your consideration and look forward to hearing from you.

Sincerely,

*Catherine Michaels*

Catherine Michaels

Enclosure: Résumé

---

Follows standard letter format

Addresses specific person

Identifies job sought and describes interests

Explains qualifications

Confirms interest

Supplies contact information

Includes résumé with letter

# Quick Research Guide

**A** | Defining Your Quest  Q-21

**B** | Searching for Recommended Sources  Q-24

**C** | Evaluating Possible Sources  Q-25

**D** | Capturing, Launching, and Citing Evidence Added from Sources  Q-27

**E** | Citing and Listing Sources in MLA or APA Style  Q-31

When you begin college, you may feel uncertain about what to say and how to speak up. As you gain experience, you will join the academic exchange around you by reading, thinking, and writing with sources. You will turn to articles, books, and Web sites for evidence to support your thesis and develop your ideas, advancing knowledge through exchange.

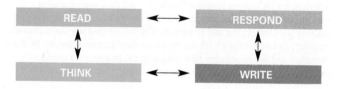

Conducting research requires time to explore, to think, and to respond. However, efficient and purposeful research can produce greater success in less time than optimistic browsing. Maybe you need more confidence or good advice fast: you've procrastinated, you're overwhelmed, or you're uncertain about how to proceed. To help you, this Quick Research Guide concentrates on five key steps.

**TURNING TO SOURCES FOR SUPPORTING EVIDENCE**

# A | Defining Your Quest

Especially when your research goals are specific and limited, you're more likely to succeed if you try to define the hunt in advance.

## PURPOSE CHECKLIST

☐ What is the thesis you want to support, point you want to show, question you want to answer, or problem you want to solve?

*For more about stating and using a thesis, see pp. 384–93.*

☐ Does the assignment require or suggest certain types of supporting evidence, sources, or presentations of material?

☐ Which ideas do you want to support with good evidence?

☐ Which ideas might you want to check, clarify, or change?

☐ Which ideas or opinions of others do you want to verify or counter?

☐ Do you want to analyze material yourself (for example, comparing different articles or Web sites) or to find someone else's analysis?

☐ What kinds of evidence do you want to use — facts, statistics, or expert testimony? Do you also want to add your own firsthand observation?

*For more about types of evidence, see pp. 159–61.*

## TWO VIEWS OF SUPPORTING EVIDENCE

| COLLEGE WRITER | COLLEGE READER |
|---|---|
| • Does it answer my question and support my thesis? | • Is it relevant to the purpose and assignment? |
| • Does it seem accurate? | • Is it reliable, given academic standards? |
| • Is it recent enough? | • Is it current, given the standards of the field? |
| • Does it add enough detail and depth? | • Is it of sufficient quantity, variety, and strength? |
| • Is it balanced enough? | • Is it typical and fair? |
| • Will it persuade my audience? | • Does the writer make a credible case? |

*For evidence checklists, see pp. 162–63 and p. Q-24.*

## A1 Decide what supporting evidence you need.

When you want to add muscle to college papers, you need reliable resources to supply facts, statistics, and expert testimony to back up your claims. You may not need comprehensive information, but you will want to hunt—quickly and efficiently—for exactly what you do need. That evidence should satisfy you as a writer and meet the criteria of your college readers—instructors and possibly classmates. Suppose you want to propose solutions to your community's employment problem.

**WORKING THESIS**

Many residents of Aurora need more—and more innovative— higher education to improve their job skills and career alternatives.

Because you already have ideas based on your firsthand observations and the experiences of people you know, your research goals are limited. First, you want to add accurate facts and figures that will show why you believe a compelling problem exists. Next, you want to visit the Web sites of local educational institutions and possibly locate someone to interview about existing career development programs.

## A2 Decide where you need supporting evidence.

As you plan or draft, you may tuck in notes to yourself—figure that out, find this, look it up, get the numbers here. Other times, you may not know exactly what or where to add. One way to determine where you need supporting evidence is to examine your draft, sentence by sentence.

- What does each sentence claim or promise to a reader?
- Where do you provide supporting evidence to demonstrate the claim or fulfill the promise?

The answers to these questions—your statements and your supporting evidence—often fall into a common alternating pattern:

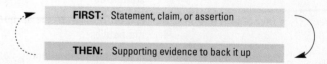

FIRST: Statement, claim, or assertion

THEN: Supporting evidence to back it up

When you spot a string of assertions without much support, you've found a place where you might need more evidence. Select reliable evidence so that it substantiates the exact statement, claim, or assertion that precedes it. Likewise, if you spot a string of examples, details, facts, quotations, or other evidence, introduce or conclude it with an interpretive statement that explains the point the evidence supports. Make sure your general statement connects and pulls together all the particular evidence.

For more about arguments based on claims of substantiation, evaluation, or policy, see pp. 154–64.

For more on inductive and deductive reasoning, see pp. 428–30.

When Carrie Williamson introduced her cause-and-effect paper, "Rain Forest Destruction," she made a general statement and then supported it by quoting facts from a source. Then she repeated this statement-support pattern, backing up her next statement in turn. By using this pattern from the very beginning, Carrie reassured her readers that she was a trustworthy writer who would try to supply convincing evidence throughout her paper.

The tropical rain forests are among the most biologically diverse communities in the world. According to the Rainforest Alliance, "The forests of the Neotropics are the habitat for tens of thousands of plant and wildlife species," as in "a single square mile of tropical forest in Rondonia, Brazil," which is home to "1,200 species of butterflies—twice the total number found in the United States and Canada" ("Conservation"). These amazing communities depend on each part being intact in order to function properly but are being destroyed at an alarming rate. Over several decades, even in protected areas, only 2% increased while 85% "suffered declines in surrounding forest cover" (Laurance et al. 291). Many rain forest conservationists debate the leading cause of deforestation. Regardless of which is the major cause, logging, slash-and-burn farming, and resource exploitation are destroying more of the rain forests each year.

*Statement*

*Supporting evidence: Information and statistics about species*

*Statement*

*Supporting evidence: Facts about destruction*

*Statement identifying cause-and-effect debate*

*Statement previewing points to come*

The table below shows some of the many ways this common statement-support pattern can be used to clarify and substantiate your ideas.

| First: Statement, Claim, or Assertion | Then: Supporting Evidence |
| --- | --- |
| Introduces a topic | Facts or statistics to justify the importance or significance of the topic |
| Describes a situation | Factual examples or illustrations to convey reality or urgency |
| Introduces an event | Accurate firsthand observations to describe an event that you have witnessed |
| Presents a problem | Expert testimony or firsthand observation to establish the necessity or urgency of a solution |
| Explains an issue | Facts and details to clarify or justify the significance of the issue |
| States your point | Facts, statistics, or examples to support your viewpoint or position |
| Prepares for evidence that follows | Facts, examples, observations, or research findings to develop your case |
| Concludes with your recommendation or evaluation | Facts, examples, or expert testimony to persuade readers to accept your conclusion |

Use the following checklist to help you decide whether — and where — you might need supporting evidence from sources.

## EVIDENCE CHECKLIST

- ☐ What does your thesis promise that you'll deliver? What additional evidence would ensure that you effectively demonstrate your thesis?

- ☐ Are your statements, claims, and assertions backed up with supporting evidence? If not, what evidence might you add?

- ☐ What evidence would most effectively persuade your readers?

- ☐ What criteria for useful evidence matter most for your assignment or your readers? What evidence would best meet these criteria?

- ☐ Which parts of your paper sound weak or incomplete to you?

- ☐ What facts or statistics would clarify your topic?

- ☐ What examples or illustrations would make the background or the current circumstances clearer and more compelling for readers?

- ☐ What does a reliable expert say about the situation your topic involves?

- ☐ What firsthand observation would add authenticity?

- ☐ Where have peers or your instructor suggested more or stronger evidence?

# B | Searching for Recommended Sources

When you need to search efficiently, begin with reliable sources, already screened by professionals. Your college library buys books, subscribes to scholarly journals, and acquires print and electronic resources; these are expected to follow accepted editorial practices. Well-regarded publishers and professional groups turn to peer reviewers — experts in the field — to assess articles or books before they are selected for publication. These quality controls bring readers material that meets academic or professional standards.

## B1 Seek advice about reliable sources.

Your challenge is not simply to find any sources but to find solid sources with reliable evidence. The following shortcuts can help you find solid sources fast — ideally already screened, selected, and organized for you.

## RESOURCE CHECKLIST

- ☐ Have you talked with your instructor after class, during office hours, or by e-mail to ask for advice about resources for your topic? Have you checked the assignment, syllabus, handouts, or class Web site?

- ☐ Have your classmates recommended useful academic databases, disciplinary Web sites, or similar resources?

☐ Does the department offering the course have a Web site with lists of library resources or links to sites well regarded in that field?

☐ Does your textbook Web site provide links to additional resources?

☐ Which search strategies and library databases does the librarian at the reference desk recommend for your course and topic?

☐ Which databases or links on your library's Web site lead to government (federal, state, or local) resources or articles in journals and newspapers?

☐ Which resources are available through the online library catalog or in any periodicals or reference area of your campus library?

## B2 Select reliable sources that meet readers' criteria.

For some assignments, you might be expected to use varied sources: reports from journalists, advice from practitioners in the field, accounts of historical eyewitnesses, or opposing opinions on civic policy. For other assignments, you might be expected to turn only to scholarly sources — also identified as peer-reviewed or refereed sources — with characteristics such as these:

- in-depth investigation or interpretation of an academic topic or problem
- discussion of previous studies, which are cited in the text and listed at the end for easy reference by readers
- use of research methods accepted in a discipline or several fields
- publication by a reputable company or sponsoring organization
- acceptance for publication based on the author's credentials and reviews by experts (peer reviewers) who assess the quality of the study
- preparation for publication supervised by academic or expert editors or by authors and professional staff

Your instructors are likely to favor these quality controls. Your campus librarian can help you limit your searches to peer-reviewed journals or check the scholarly reputation of sources that you find.

## C | Evaluating Possible Sources

Like the perfect wave or the perfect day, the perfect source is hard to come by. Instead of looking for perfect sources, evaluate sources on the basis of practicality, standards, and evidence.

## C1 Evaluate sources as a practical researcher.

Your situation as a writer may determine how long or how widely you can search or how deeply you can delve into the sources you find. If you are worried about finishing on time or about juggling several assignments, you will need to search efficiently, using your own practical criteria.

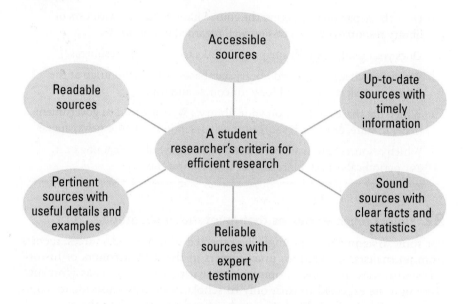

## C2 Evaluate sources as your readers would.

If you are uncertain about college requirements, start with recommended sources that are easily accessible, readable, and up-to-date. Look for sources that are chock-full of reliable facts, statistics, research findings, case studies, observations, examples, and expert testimony to persuade your readers.

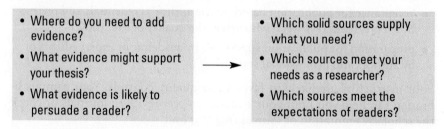

## C3 Evaluate sources for reliable and appropriate evidence.

When you use evidence from sources to support your points, both you and your readers are likely to hold two simple expectations:

- that your sources are reliable so you can trust their information
- that the information you select from them is appropriate for your paper

After all, how could an unreliable source successfully support your ideas? And what could unsuitable or mismatched information contribute? The difficulty, of course, is learning how to judge what is reliable and appropriate. The following checklist suggests how you can use the time-tested journalist's questions to evaluate print or electronic sources.

## EVALUATION CHECKLIST

*Who?*

- ☐ Who is the author? What are the author's credentials and experience?
- ☐ Who is the intended audience? Is it general or academic?
- ☐ Who publishes or sponsors the source? Is this publisher well regarded?
- ☐ Who has reviewed the source before publication? Only the author? Expert peer reviewers or referees? An editorial staff?

*What?*

- ☐ What is the purpose of the publication or Web site? Is it trying to sell, inform, report, or shape opinion?
- ☐ What bias or point of view might affect the reliability of the source?
- ☐ What evidence does the source present? Does the source seem trustworthy and logical? Does it identify its sources or supply active links?

*When?*

- ☐ When was the source published or created? When was it revised?
- ☐ When has it been cited by others in the field?

*Where?*

- ☐ Where did you find the source?
- ☐ Where is the source recommended? Has your library supplied it?

*Why?*

- ☐ Why would you use this source rather than others?
- ☐ Why is its information relevant to your research question?

*How?*

- ☐ How would it support your thesis and provide persuasive evidence?
- ☐ How does the source reflect its author, publisher or sponsor, and audience? How might you need to qualify its use in your paper?

# D | Capturing, Launching, and Citing Evidence Added from Sources

Sometimes researchers concentrate so hard on hunting for reliable sources that they forget what comes next. The value of every source remains potential until you successfully capture its facts, statistics, expert testimony, examples, or other information in a form that you can incorporate into your paper. Then you need to launch — or introduce — the information in order to identify its

For examples in both MLA and APA style, see E1–E2.

source or its contribution to your paper. Finally, you must accurately cite or credit, both in the text of your paper and in a final list of sources, each source whose words or ideas you use.

## D1  Avoid plagiarism.

Allow enough time to add information from sources skillfully and correctly. Find out exactly how your instructor expects you to credit sources. Even if you do not intend to plagiarize — to use another writer's words or ideas without appropriately crediting them — a paper full of sloppy or careless shortcuts can look just like a paper deliberately copied from unacknowledged sources. Instead, borrow carefully and honestly.

Identify the source of information, any idea, summary, paraphrase, or quotation, right away, as soon as you add it to your notes. Carry that acknowledgment into your first draft and all the drafts that follow. You generally do not need to identify a source if you use what is called "common knowledge" — quotations, expressions, or information widely known and widely accepted. If you are uncertain about the need for a citation, ask your instructor, or simply provide the citation.

## D2  Read your source critically.

For more on critical reading, see Ch. 2. For more on evaluating evidence, see pp. 159–61. For more on logical fallacies, see pp. 171–72.

Before you pop outside material into your paper, read critically to evaluate its reliability and suitability. If you cannot understand a source that requires specialized background, don't use it. If its ideas, facts, claims, or viewpoint seem unusual, incorporate only what you can substantiate in unrelated sources. If its evidence seems accurate, logical, and relevant, decide exactly how you might want to add it to your paper. Carefully distinguish it from your own ideas, whether you quote, paraphrase, or summarize.

## D3  Quote accurately.

For more on punctuating quotations and using ellipsis marks, see D3 in the Quick Editing Guide, pp. Q-62–Q-63.

As you take notes, record as many quotations as you want if that process helps you master the material. When you add quotations to your paper, be selective. A quotation in itself is not necessarily effective evidence, and too many quotations will suggest that your writing is padded or lacks original thought. Quote exactly, and credit your source using the format expected.

### QUOTATION CHECKLIST

☐ Have you quoted only a notable passage that adds support and authority?

☐ Have you checked your quotation word by word, for accuracy?

☐ Have you marked the beginning and the ending with quotation marks?

☐ Have you used ellipses (. . .) to mark any spot where you have left out words in the original?

☐ Have you identified the source of the quotation in a launch statement (see D6) or in parentheses?

☐ Have you recorded in parentheses the page number where the quotation appears in the source?

## D4 Paraphrase carefully.

A paraphrase presents a passage from a source in your own words and sentences. It may include the same level of detail as the original, but it should not slip into the original wording (unless you identify those snippets with quotation marks). Credit the original source as you do when you quote.

For more about how to quote, paraphrase, and summarize, see pp. 228–36

### PARAPHRASE CHECKLIST

☐ Have you read the passage critically to be sure you understand it?

☐ Have you paraphrased accurately, reflecting both the main points and the supporting details in the original?

☐ Does your paraphrase use your own words without repeating or echoing the words or the sentence structure of the original?

☐ Does your paraphrase stick to the ideas of the original?

☐ Have you revised your paraphrase so it reads smoothly and clearly?

☐ Have you identified the source of the paraphrase in a launch statement (see D6) or in parentheses?

☐ Have you recorded in parentheses the page number where the passage appears in the source?

## D5 Summarize fairly.

A summary clearly identifies the source and reduces its ideas to their essence. Using your own words, your summary may boil a book, a chapter, an article, or a section down to a few sentences that accurately and clearly sum up the sense of the original.

### SUMMARY CHECKLIST

☐ Have you read critically to be sure you understand the source?

☐ Have you fairly stated the author's main point in your own words?

☐ Have you briefly stated any supporting ideas that you wish to sum up?

☐ Have you stuck to the overall point without bogging down in details?

☐  Is your summary respectful of others, even if you disagree with them?

☐  Have you revised your summary so it reads smoothly and clearly?

☐  Have you identified the source of the summary in a launch statement (see D6) or in parentheses?

☐  Have you recorded in parentheses the page number where any specific passage appears in the source?

## D6  Launch and cite each quotation, paraphrase, summary, and synthesis.

Weave ideas from sources into your paper so that they effectively support the point you want to make. As you integrate each idea, take three steps.

**1. Capture.** Begin with the evidence you have captured from your source. Refine this material so that it will fit smoothly into your paper. Reduce your quotation to its most memorable words, freshen the wording of your paraphrase, or tighten your summary. Synthesize by pulling together your own ideas and those of your sources to reach new insights. Position the evidence where it is needed to support your statements.

**2. Launch.** Launch, or introduce, the material captured from each source. Avoid tossing stand-alone quotations into your paper or stacking up a series of paraphrases and summaries. Instead, use your launch statement to lead smoothly into your source information. Try to draw on the authority of the source, mention the author's credentials, or connect the material to other sources or to your points. Let readers know why you have selected this evidence and what you think it adds to your paper.

For more on launch statements, see pp. 238–43.

Dalton, long an advocate of "green" construction, recommends . . . (18).

As a specialist in elder law, attorney Tamara Diaz suggests . . . (57).

For more on punctuating quotations, see D3 in the Quick Editing Guide, pp. Q-62–Q-63.

Like Westin, regional director Neil urges that ". . ." (308). Brown, however, takes an innovative approach to local conservation practices and recommends . . . (108).

Another policy analyst, arguing from principles expressed in the Bill of Rights, maintains . . . (Frank 96).

While Congress pits secure borders against individual liberties, immigration analyst Smith proposes a third option that . . . (42).

**3. Cite.** Identify each source briefly yet accurately. Follow MLA, APA, or another academic format.

For examples showing how to cite and list sources in your paper, see section E.

- Name the author in parentheses (unless named in your launch statement).

- In APA style, add the date of the source.

- Add an exact page number to locate the original passage.

- If a source does not name its author, begin the citation with the first words of the title.

- Add a full entry for each source to a list at the end of your paper.

# E | Citing and Listing Sources in MLA or APA Style

MLA style is the format for crediting sources that is recommended by the Modern Language Association and often required in English classes. APA style, the format recommended by the American Psychological Association, is often used in social sciences, business, and some composition classes. These two styles are widely used in college papers, but your specialized courses may require other academic styles, depending on the field. Because instructors expect you to credit sources carefully, follow any directions or examples supplied, or refer to the style manual required. Although academic styles all credit sources, their details differ. Stick to the one expected.

In both the MLA and APA styles, your sources need to be identified twice in your paper: first, briefly, at the very moment you draw upon the source material and later, in full, at the end of your paper. The short reference includes the name of the author of the source (or a short form of the title if the source does not name an author), so it's easy for a reader to connect that short entry in your text with the related full entry in the final alphabetical list.

## E1 Cite and list sources in MLA style.

**Cite in the text.** At the moment you add a quotation, paraphrase, or summary, identify the source. Citations generally follow a simple pattern: name the author, and note the page in the original where the material is located.

> (Last Name of Author ##)   (Talia 35)   (Smitt and Gilbert 152-53)

Place this citation immediately after a direct quotation or paraphrase.

> When "The Lottery" begins, the reader thinks of the "great pile of stones" (Jackson 260) as children's entertainment.

If you name the author in your launch, the citation is even simpler.

> As Hunt notes, the city faced "a decade of deficits and drought" (54).

For quotations from poems, plays, or novels, supply line, act and scene, or chapter numbers rather than page numbers.

> The speaker in Robinson's poem describes Richard Cory as "richer than a king" (line 9), an attractive man who "fluttered pulses when he said, / 'Good-morning' " (7-8).

To find formats for other types of sources, consult the current *MLA Handbook,* often available in the library, or check your research manual or research guide for more information.

If you use only one source, identify it as your essay begins. Then just give page or line numbers in parentheses after each quote or paraphrase.

### CITATION CHECKLIST

☐ Have you placed your citation right after your quotation, paraphrase, or summary?

☐ Have you enclosed your citation with a pair of parenthesis marks?

☐ Have you provided the last name of the author either in your launch statement or in your citation?

☐ Have you used a short title for a work without an identified author?

☐ Have you added any available page or other location number (such as a Web paragraph, poetry line, novel chapter, or play act and scene), as numbered in the source, to identify where the material appears?

**List at the end.** For each source mentioned in the text, supply a corresponding full entry in a list called "Works Cited" at the end of your paper.

### WORKS CITED CHECKLIST

☐ Have you figured out what type of source you have used? Have you followed the sample pattern for that type as exactly as possible?

☐ Have you used quotation marks and italics correctly for titles?

☐ Have you used correct punctuation—periods, commas, colons, parentheses?

☐ Have you checked the accuracy of numbers: pages, volumes, dates?

☐ Have you accurately recorded names: authors, titles, publishers?

☐ Have you correctly typed or copied in the address of an electronic source that a reader could not otherwise find or that your instructor requires?

☐ Have you correctly arranged your entries in alphabetical order?

☐ Have you checked your final list against your text citations so that every source appears in both places?

☐ Have you double-spaced your list just like your paper, without any extra space between entries?

☐ Have you begun the first line of each entry at the left margin and indented each additional line (the same space you would indent a paragraph)?

For format examples, see the Quick Format Guide, pp. Q-2–Q-3.

**Follow MLA patterns.** Use the following examples as patterns for your entries. For each type of source, supply the same information in the same order, using the same punctuation or other features.

## Book

**TEXT CITATION**

(Blyth 37)

**WORKS CITED ENTRY**

Author's name   Period        Title of book, in italics   Period   Publisher   Period

Blyth, Mark. *Austerity: The History of a Dangerous Idea.* Oxford UP, 2013.

Year of
publication

## Essay, Story, or Poem from a Book

**TEXT CITATION**

(Brady 506)

**WORKS CITED ENTRY**

Author of        Title of selection,         Title of book or
selection        in quotation marks          anthology, in italics

Brady, Judy. "I Want a Wife." *The Bedford Guide for College Writers with Reader,*

   edited by X. J. Kennedy, Dorothy M. Kennedy, and Marcia F. Muth, 11th ed.,

   Bedford/St. Martin's, 2017, pp. 505-07.

Publisher          Year of      Page numbers              Authors or
of book            publication  of selection              editors of
                                                          book

See the title page
of this book and the
reading on pp. 505–7
to find the details
needed for this entry.

## Popular Magazine Article

The author's name and the title generally appear at the beginning of an article. If the author is not identified, simply begin your entry with the title. Typically, the magazine name, the date, and page numbers appear at the bottom of pages. Arrange the date in this order: 4 Oct. 2016.

**TEXT CITATION**

(Freedman 10)

**WORKS CITED ENTRY**

                    Title of article,      Title of magazine,
Author's name       in quotation marks     in italics

Freedman, David H. "The Happiness App." *Discover,* Jan.-Feb. 2013, pp. 10-11.

Date of          Page numbers
publication      of article

## Scholarly Journal Article

**TEXT CITATION**

(Calomiris and Khan 78)

**WORKS CITED ENTRY**

Authors' names                                    Title of article, in quotation marks

Calomiris, Charles W., and Urooj Khan. "An Assessment of TARP Assistance to

Financial Institutions." *The Journal of Economic Perspectives*, vol. 29, no. 2,

Spring 2015, pp. 53-80.            Title of journal,              Volume and
                                   in italics                    issue numbers
          Season       Page numbers
          and year     of article

## Article from a Library Database

In databases, the original publication details often appear at the top of the entry. List the details of the original publication first in your works cited entry, separating each detail with a comma and ending with a period, as shown below. Then provide information about the database, again separating each detail with a comma and ending with a period.

**TEXT CITATION**

Omit the page number when it is not available online.

(Altinay et al. 92)

**WORKS CITED ENTRY**

Title of magazine        Authors' names              Title of article, in quotation marks
or journal, in
italics             Altinay, Zehra, et al. "The Role of Social Media Tools: Accessible Tourism for
Volume and
issue numbers,          Disabled Citizens." *Journal of Educational Technology & Society*, vol. 19,
followed by
month or            no. 1, Jan. 2016, pp. 89-99. *Academic Search Premier*, www.ebscohost.com
season of
publication         /academic/academic-search-premier.    Name of database,    Database URL
                                                            in italics
                                         Page numbers,
                                         followed by
                                         period

## Page from a Web Site

The page title and site title often appear at the top of a given page. The date when a site was posted or last updated often appears at the bottom, as does the name of the sponsor (which also may appear as a link). If the sponsor name is the same as the site name, omit the sponsor name, as illustrated in the example below.

**TEXT CITATION**

A site is identified by title if it does not name an author.

According to the Rainforest Alliance, . . .

**WORKS CITED ENTRY**

No author         Title of page,              Title of site,
identified        in quotation marks          in italics

"Our Work in Sustainable Forestry." *Rainforest-alliance.org*, 2016, www.rainforest

-alliance.org/work/forestry.            Date posted or updated        URL

**E2** Cite and list sources in APA style.

**Cite in the text.** After the author's last name, add the date. Use "p." (for "page") or "pp." (for "pages") before the page numbers.

(Last Name of Author, Date, p. ##)  (Talia, 2013, p. 35)
(Wulf, 2015, pp. 396-410)

**List at the end.** Call your list of sources "References." Include all the sources cited in your text except for personal communications and classics.

**Follow APA patterns.** Use the following examples as patterns for your entries. For each type of source, supply the same information in the same order using the same punctuation or other features.

To find formats for other types of sources, consult the current *Publication Manual of the American Psychological Association*, often available in the library, or check your research manual or research guide for more information.

### Book
**TEXT CITATION**

(Blyth, 2013, p. 37)

**REFERENCES ENTRY**

Blyth, M. (2013). *Austerity: The history of a dangerous idea.* New York, NY: Oxford University Press.

### Work or Section in a Book
**TEXT CITATION**

(Brady, 1971/2017, p. 506)

**REFERENCES ENTRY**

Brady, J. (2017). I want a wife. In X. J. Kennedy, D. M. Kennedy, & M. F. Muth (Eds.), *The Bedford guide for college writers* (11th ed., pp. 505-507). Boston, MA: Bedford/St. Martin's. (Original work published 1971)

Turn to the title page of this book and the reading selection on pp. 505–7 to find the details needed for this entry.

### Popular Magazine Article
**TEXT CITATION**

(Freedman, 2013, p. 11)

**REFERENCES ENTRY**

Freedman, D. H. (2013, January-February). The happiness app. *Discover, 34*(1), 10-11.

### Scholarly Journal Article

For a magazine or journal article, add any volume number in italics and any issue number in parentheses, without a space or italics.

**TEXT CITATION**

(Calomiris & Khan, 2015, p. 73)

**REFERENCES ENTRY**

Calomiris, C. W., & Khan, U. (2015). An assessment of TARP assistance to financial institutions. *The Journal of Economic Perspectives, 29*(2), 53-80.

## Article from a Library Database

**IN-TEXT CITATION**

No exact page or paragraph number may be available for an online article.

(Walton & Das, 2015, p. 547)

**REFERENCES ENTRY**

The database does not need to be named unless a reader would have trouble finding the item without the URL.

Walton, M., & Das, V. (2015). Political leadership and the urban poor: Local histories. *Current Anthropology, 56*, S44-S54. doi:10.1086/682420

## Page from a Web Site

**TEXT CITATION**

For APA format examples, see the Quick Format Guide, pp. Q-4–Q-6.

Because the Web site does not name an author, the citation identifies the site's sponsor.

According to the Rainforest Alliance (2016) . . .

**REFERENCES ENTRY**

Your access date is not needed unless the material is likely to change.

Rainforest Alliance. (2016). Our work in sustainable forestry. Retrieved from http://www.rainforest-alliance.org/work/forestry

# Quick Editing Guide

A | Editing for Common Grammar Problems  Q-38

B | Editing to Ensure Effective Sentences  Q-46

C | Editing for Word Choice  Q-48

D | Editing for Common Punctuation Problems  Q-59

E | Editing for Common Mechanics Problems  Q-62

This Quick Editing Guide provides an overview of grammar, style, word choice, punctuation, and mechanics problems typical of college writing.

## EDITING CHECKLIST

### Common and Serious Problems in College Writing

*Grammar Problems*

| | |
|---|---|
| ☐ Have you avoided writing sentence fragments? | A1 |
| ☐ Have you avoided writing comma splices or fused sentences? | A2 |
| ☐ Have you used the correct form for all verbs in the past tense? | A3 |
| ☐ Do all verbs agree with their subjects? | A4 |
| ☐ Have you used the correct case for all pronouns? | A5 |
| ☐ Do all pronouns agree with their antecedents? | A6 |
| ☐ Have you used adjectives and adverbs correctly? | A7 |

*Sentence Problems*

| | |
|---|---|
| ☐ Does each modifier clearly modify the appropriate sentence element? | B1 |
| ☐ Have you used parallel structure where needed? | B2 |

*Word Choice Problems*

| | |
|---|---|
| ☐ Have you used appropriate language? | C1 |
| ☐ Is your writing clean and concise? | C2 |
| ☐ Have you correctly used commonly confused words? | C3 |

*Punctuation Problems*

☐ Have you used commas correctly?                                    D1

☐ Have you used apostrophes correctly?                               D2

☐ Have you punctuated quotations correctly?                          D3

*Mechanics Problems*

☐ Have you used capital letters correctly?                           E1

☐ Have you spelled all words correctly?                              E2

For editing and proofreading strategies, see pp. 455–58.

Editing and proofreading are needed at the end of the writing process because writers—*all* writers—find it difficult to write error-free sentences the first time they try. Once you are satisfied that you have expressed your ideas, you should make sure that each sentence and word is concise, clear, and correct. Certain common errors in Standard Written English are like red flags to careful readers: they signal that the writer is either ignorant or careless. Use the editing checklist above to check your paper for these problems; then use the editing checklists in each section to help you correct specific errors. Concentrate on any problems likely to reappear in your writing.

Your grammar checker or software can help you catch some errors, but not others. Always consider the grammar checker's suggestions carefully before accepting them and continue to edit on your own.

- A grammar checker can't always identify the subject or verb in a sentence; it may question whether a sentence is complete or whether its subject and verb agree, even when the sentence is correct.

- Grammar checkers are likely to miss misplaced modifiers, faulty parallelism, possessives without apostrophes, or incorrect commas.

- Most grammar checkers do a good job of spotting problems with adjectives and adverbs, such as confusing *good* and *well*.

- Keep track of your mistakes to develop an "error hit list." Use your software's Find capacity to check for searchable problems such as instances of *each* (always singular) or *few* (always plural) to see if all the verbs agree.

A **subject** names something—a person, an object, an idea, a situation—about which the verb makes an assertion. A **verb** is a word that shows action or a state of being.

# A | Editing for Common Grammar Problems

## A1 Check for sentence fragments.

A complete sentence has a subject, has a verb, and can stand on its own. A **sentence fragment** cannot stand on its own as a sentence because it lacks a subject, a verb, or both, or for some other reason fails to convey a complete

> ### At a Glance **Guide**
>
> Irregular Verbs at a Glance   Q-41
>
> Forms of *Be* and *Have* at a Glance   Q-42
>
> Personal Pronoun Cases at a Glance   Q-43
>
> Indefinite Pronouns at a Glance   Q-45
>
> Irregular Adjectives and Adverbs at a Glance   Q-46
>
> Possessive Personal Pronouns at a Glance   Q-61
>
> Capitalization at a Glance   Q-63

thought. Though common in ads and fiction, fragments are not usually effective in college writing because they do not express coherent thoughts.

To edit for fragments, check that each sentence has a subject and a verb and expresses a complete thought. To correct a fragment, complete it by adding a missing part, dropping an unnecessary subordinating conjunction, or joining it to a nearby sentence, if that would make more sense.

Roberto has two sisters, Maya and Leeza.

*were*
The children going to the zoo.

*were caught in a traffic jam.*
The children going to the zoo.

Last night ~~when~~ we saw Viola Davis's most recent movie.

### EDITING CHECKLIST

#### Fragments

☐ Does the sentence have both a subject and a verb?

☐ If the sentence contains a subordinate clause, does it contain a clause that is a complete sentence too?

☐ If you find a fragment, can you link it to an adjoining sentence, eliminate its subordinating conjunction, or add any missing element?

## A2   Check for comma splices or fused sentences.

A complete sentence has a subject and a verb and can stand on its own. When two sentences are combined as one sentence, each sentence within the larger one is called a *main clause*. However, writers need to follow the rules for joining main clauses to avoid serious sentence errors. A **comma splice** is two main clauses joined with only a comma. A **fused sentence** (or **run-on**) is two main clauses joined with no punctuation at all.

A **main clause** is a group of words that has both a subject and a verb and can stand alone as a complete sentence.

| | |
|---|---|
| COMMA SPLICE | I went to the shop, I bought a new coat. |
| FUSED SENTENCE | I went to the shop I bought a new coat. |

To find these errors, examine the main clauses in each sentence to make sure they are joined correctly. Correct a comma splice or fused sentence in one of these four ways, depending on which makes the best sense:

| | |
|---|---|
| ADD A PERIOD | I went to the shop. I bought a new coat. |
| ADD A COMMA AND A COORDINATING CONJUNCTION | I went to the shop, and I bought a new coat. |
| ADD A SEMICOLON | I went to the shop; I bought a new coat. |
| ADD A SUBORDINATING CONJUNCTION | I went to the shop, where I bought a new coat. |

**Coordinating conjunctions** (*and, but, for, or, nor, so, yet*) join elements with equal or near-equal importance.
A **subordinating conjunction** is a word (such as *because, although, if, when*) used to make one clause dependent on, or subordinate to, another.

## EDITING CHECKLIST

### Comma Splices and Fused Sentences

☐ Can you make each main clause a separate sentence?

☐ Can you link the two main clauses with a comma and a coordinating conjunction?

☐ Can you link the two main clauses with a semicolon or, if appropriate, a colon?

☐ Can you subordinate one clause to the other?

## A3 Check for correct past tense verb forms.

The **form** of a verb, the way it is spelled and pronounced, can change to show its **tense**—the time when its action did, does, or will occur (in the past, present, or future). A verb about something in the present will often have a different form than a verb about something in the past.

| | |
|---|---|
| PRESENT | Right now, I *watch* only a few minutes of television each day. |
| PAST | Last month, I *watched* television shows every evening. |

**Regular verbs** are verbs whose forms follow standard rules; they form the past tense by adding *-ed* or *-d* to the present tense form:

*watch/watched    look/looked    hope/hoped*

Check all regular verbs in the past tense for one of these endings.

    *asked*
I ask my brother for a loan yesterday.

      *raced*
Nicole race in the track meet last week.

TIP: If you say the final *-d* sound when you talk, you may find it easier to add the final *-d* or *-ed* when you write past tense regular verbs.

Because **irregular verbs** do not have standard forms, their unpredictable past tense forms must be memorized. In addition, the past tense may differ from the past participle. Check a dictionary for these forms.

> *lay*
> My cat ~~laid~~ on the tile floor to take her nap.

> *swum*
> I have ~~swam~~ twenty laps every day this month.

TIP: In college papers, follow convention by using the present tense, not the past, to describe the work of an author or the events in a literary work.

> *reveals*
> In "The Lottery," Jackson ~~revealed~~ the power of tradition. As the story
> *opens*                    *gather*
> ~~opened~~, the villagers ~~gathered~~ in the square.

A **participle** is a verb that cannot function alone as a main verb, including present participles ending in *-ing* and past participles often ending in *-ed* or *-d*.

## ▶ Irregular Verbs *at a Glance*

| INFINITIVE (BASE) | PAST TENSE | PAST PARTICIPLE |
| --- | --- | --- |
| begin | began | begun |
| burst | burst | burst |
| choose | chose | chosen |
| do | did | done |
| eat | ate | eaten |
| go | went | gone |
| lay | laid | laid |
| lie | lay | lain |
| speak | spoke | spoken |

### EDITING CHECKLIST
#### Past Tense Verb Forms

☐  Have you identified the main verb in the sentence?

☐  Is the sentence about past, present, or future? Does the verb show this time?

☐  Is the verb regular or irregular? Have you used its correct form?

## A4  Check for correct subject-verb agreement.

The **form** of a verb, the way it is spelled and pronounced, can change to show **number**—whether the subject is singular (one) or plural (more than one). It can also show **person**—whether the subject is *you* or *she,* for example.

A **verb** is a word that shows action or a state of being.

A **subject** names something—a person, an object, an idea, a situation—about which the verb makes an assertion.

| | |
|---|---|
| SINGULAR | Our instructor *grades* every paper carefully. |
| PLURAL | Most instructors *grade* tests using a standard scale. |
| SECOND PERSON | You *write* well-documented research papers. |
| THIRD PERSON | She *writes* good research papers, too. |

A verb must match (or *agree with*) its subject in terms of number and person. Regular verbs (whose forms follow a standard rule) are problems only in the present tense. There they have two forms: one that ends in *-s* or *-es* and one that does not. Only singular nouns and the subjects *he, she,* and *it* use the verb form that ends in *-s* or *-es.*

| | |
|---|---|
| I like | we like |
| you like | you like |
| he/she/it/Dan/the child likes | they like |

The verbs *be* and *have* are irregular, so their present tense forms must be memorized. The verb *be* is also irregular in the past tense.

## Forms of *Be* and *Have* at a Glance

| THE PRESENT TENSE OF *BE* | | THE PAST TENSE OF *BE* | |
|---|---|---|---|
| I am | we are | I was | we were |
| you are | you are | you were | you were |
| he/she/it is | they are | he/she/it was | they were |

| THE PRESENT TENSE OF *HAVE* | | THE PAST TENSE OF *HAVE* | |
|---|---|---|---|
| I have | we have | I had | we had |
| you have | you have | you had | you had |
| he/she/it has | they have | he/she/it had | they had |

An **indefinite pronoun** stands for an unspecified person or thing, including singular forms (*each, everyone, no one*) and plural forms (*both, few*).

Problems in agreement often occur when the subject is hard to find, is an indefinite pronoun, or is confusing. Make sure that you include any *-s* or *-es* endings and use the correct form for irregular verbs.

*writes*
Jim ~~write~~ at least fifty e-mails a day.

*have*
The students ~~has~~ difficulty with the assignment.

*was*
Every one of the cakes ~~were~~ sold at the fundraiser.

EDITING CHECKLIST

## Subject-Verb Agreement

☐ Have you correctly identified the subject and the verb in the sentence?

☐ Is the subject singular or plural? Does the verb match?

☐ Have you used the correct form of the verb?

## A5  Check for correct pronoun case.

Depending on the role a pronoun plays in a sentence, it is said to be in the **subjective case, objective case,** or **possessive case.** Use the subjective case if the pronoun is the subject of a sentence, the subject of a subordinate clause, or a subject complement (after a linking verb). Use the objective case if the pronoun is a direct or indirect object of a verb or the object of a preposition. Use the possessive case to show possession.

| | |
|---|---|
| SUBJECTIVE | *I* will argue that our campus needs more parking. |
| OBJECTIVE | This issue is important to *me.* |
| POSSESSIVE | *My* argument will be quite persuasive. |

Writers often use the subjective case when they should use the objective case—sometimes trying to sound formal and correct. Instead, choose the correct form based on a pronoun's function in the sentence. If the sentence pairs a noun and a pronoun, try the sentence with the pronoun alone.

| | |
|---|---|
| FAULTY | My company gave my husband and *I* a trip to Hawaii. |
| PRONOUN ONLY | My company gave *I* a trip? |
| CORRECT | My company gave my husband and *me* a trip to Hawaii. |
| FAULTY | My uncle and *me* had different expectations. |
| PRONOUN ONLY | *Me* had different expectations? |
| CORRECT | My uncle and *I* had different expectations. |

A **pronoun** is a word that stands in place of a noun.

A **subject** names something—a person, an object, an idea, a situation—about which the verb makes an assertion.

A **subject complement** is a noun, an adjective, or a group of words that follows a linking verb and renames or describes the subject.

An **object** is the target or recipient of the verb's action.

▶ Personal Pronoun Cases *at a Glance*

| SUBJECTIVE | OBJECTIVE | POSSESSIVE |
|---|---|---|
| I | me | my, mine |
| you | you | your, yours |
| he | him | his |
| she | her | hers |
| it | it | its |
| we | us | our, ours |
| they | them | their, theirs |
| who | whom | whose |

| FAULTY | Jack ran faster than my brother and *me*. |
|--------|-------------------------------------------|
| PRONOUN ONLY | Jack ran faster than *me* ran? |
| CORRECT | Jack ran faster than my brother and *I*. |

A second common error with pronoun case involves gerunds. Whenever you need a pronoun to modify a gerund, use the possessive case.

*A **gerund** is a form of a verb, ending in -ing, that functions as a noun.*

Our supervisor disapproves of ~~us~~ *our* talking in the hallway.

### EDITING CHECKLIST

**Pronoun Case**

☐ Have you identified all the pronouns in the sentence?

☐ Does each one function as a subject, an object, or a possessive?

☐ Given the function of each, have you used the correct form?

## A6 Check for correct pronoun-antecedent agreement.

*A **pronoun** stands in place of a noun.*

The **form** of a pronoun, the way it is spelled and pronounced, can change to show **number**—whether the subject is singular (one) or plural (more than one). It also can change to show **gender**—masculine or feminine, for example—or **person**: first (*I, we*), second (*you*), or third (*he, she, it, they*).

| SINGULAR | My brother took *his* coat and left. |
|----------|--------------------------------------|
| PLURAL | My brothers took *their* coats and left. |
| MASCULINE | I talked to Steven before *he* had a chance to leave. |
| FEMININE | I talked to Stephanie before *she* had a chance to leave. |

A pronoun refers to its **antecedent**, usually a specific noun or pronoun nearby. The connection between the two must be clear so that readers know what the pronoun means in the sentence. The two need to match (or *agree*) in number and gender.

A common error is using a plural pronoun to refer to a singular antecedent. This error often crops up when the antecedent is difficult to find, is an indefinite pronoun, or is confusing for another reason. First, find the antecedent, and decide whether it is singular or plural. Then make the pronoun match its antecedent.

Neither Luz nor Pam received approval of ~~their~~ *her* financial aid.

[*Neither Luz nor Pam* is a compound subject joined by *nor*. Any pronoun referring to it must agree with only the nearer part of the compound: *her* agrees with *Pam*, which is singular.]

Indefinite pronouns are troublesome antecedents when they are grammatically singular but create a plural image in the writer's mind. Fortunately, most indefinite pronouns are always singular or always plural.

*his*
Each of the boys in the club has ~~their~~ own custom laptop.

[The word *each*, not *boys*, is the antecedent. *Each* is an indefinite pronoun and is always singular. Any pronoun referring to it must be singular as well.]

*his or her*
Everyone in the meeting had ~~their~~ own assistant.

[*Everyone* is an indefinite pronoun that is always singular. Any pronoun referring to it must be singular as well.]

An **indefinite pronoun** stands for an unspecified person or thing, including singular forms (*each, everyone, no one*) and plural forms (*both, few*).

---

▶ **Indefinite Pronouns** *at a Glance*

| ALWAYS SINGULAR | | | ALWAYS PLURAL |
|---|---|---|---|
| anybody | everyone | nothing | both |
| anyone | everything | one (of) | few |
| anything | much | somebody | many |
| each (of) | neither (of) | someone | several |
| either (of) | nobody | something | |
| everybody | no one | | |

---

**EDITING CHECKLIST**

**Pronoun-Antecedent Agreement**

☐ Have you identified the antecedent for each pronoun?

☐ Is the antecedent singular or plural? Does the pronoun match?

☐ Is the antecedent masculine, feminine, or neuter? Does the pronoun match?

☐ Is the antecedent first, second, or third person? Does the pronoun match?

---

## A7 Check for correct adjectives and adverbs.

**Adjectives** and **adverbs** describe or give information about (*modify*) other words. Many adverbs are formed by adding *-ly* to adjectives: *simple, simply; quiet, quietly*. Because adjectives and adverbs resemble one another, writers sometimes mistakenly use one instead of the other. To edit, find the word that the adjective or adverb modifies. If that word is a noun or pronoun, use an adjective (to describe which or what kind). If that word is a verb, an adjective, or another adverb, use an adverb (to describe how, when, where, or why).

**Modifiers** are words, phrases, or clauses that provide more information about other parts of a sentence.

Kelly ran into the house ~~quick.~~ *quickly.*

Gabriela looked ~~terribly~~ *terrible* after her bout with the flu.

Adjectives and adverbs with similar comparative and superlative forms can also cause trouble. Always ask whether you need an adjective or an adverb in the sentence, and then use the correct word.

His scar healed so ~~good~~ *well* that it was barely visible.

*Good* is an adjective; it describes a noun or pronoun. *Well* is an adverb; it modifies or adds to a verb (*heal*, in this case) or an adjective.

---

## Irregular Adjectives and Adverbs *at a Glance*

| POSITIVE ADJECTIVES | COMPARATIVE ADJECTIVES | SUPERLATIVE ADJECTIVES |
|---|---|---|
| good | better | best |
| bad | worse | worst |
| little | less, littler | least, littlest |
| many, some, much | more | most |
| POSITIVE ADVERBS | COMPARATIVE ADVERBS | SUPERLATIVE ADVERBS |
| well | better | best |
| badly | worse | worst |
| little | less | least |

---

**EDITING CHECKLIST**

**Adjectives and Adverbs**

☐ Have you identified which word the adjective or adverb modifies?

☐ If the word modified is a noun or pronoun, have you used an adjective?

☐ If the word modified is a verb, an adjective, or an adverb, have you used an adverb?

☐ Have you used the correct comparative or superlative form?

---

# B | Editing to Ensure Effective Sentences

## B1 Check for misplaced or dangling modifiers.

**Modifiers** are words, phrases, or clauses that provide more information about other parts of a sentence.

For a sentence to be clear, the connection between a modifier and the thing it modifies must be obvious. Usually a modifier should be placed just before or just after what it modifies. If the modifier is too close to some other sentence element, it is a **misplaced modifier.** If the modifier cannot logically modify anything in the sentence, it is a **dangling modifier.** Both errors can confuse readers — and sometimes create unintentionally humorous images. As you edit, place a modifier directly before or after the word modified and clearly connect the two.

*in the refrigerator*

Dan found the leftovers ‸when he visited in the refrigerator.

[In the faulty sentence, *in the refrigerator* seems to modify Dan's visit. Obviously the leftovers, not Dan, are in the refrigerator.]

*I saw that*

Looking out the window, ‸the clouds were beautiful.

[In the faulty sentence, *Looking out the window* should modify *I,* but *I* is not in the sentence. The modifier dangles without anything logical to modify until *I* is in the sentence.]

---

## EDITING CHECKLIST
### Misplaced and Dangling Modifiers

- ☐ What is each modifier meant to modify? Is the modifier as close as possible to that sentence element? Is any misreading possible?

- ☐ If a modifier is misplaced, can you move it to clarify the meaning?

- ☐ What noun or pronoun is a dangling modifier meant to modify? Can you make that word or phrase the subject of the main clause? Or can you turn the dangling modifier into a clause that includes the missing noun or pronoun?

---

## B2  Check for parallel structure.

A series of words, phrases, clauses, or sentences with the same grammatical form is said to be **parallel.** Using parallel form for elements that are parallel in meaning or function helps readers grasp the meaning of a sentence more easily. A lack of parallelism can distract, annoy, or even confuse readers.

To use parallelism, put nouns with nouns, verbs with verbs, and phrases with phrases. Parallelism is particularly important in a series, with correlative conjunctions, and in comparisons using *than* or *as.*

*to ski, to ice skate,*

I like to go to Estes Park ‸for skiing, ice skating, and to meet interesting people.

The proposal is neither practical/nor is it innovative.

Teens need a few firm rules rather than having many flimsy ones.

Edit to reinforce parallel structures by repeating articles, conjunctions, prepositions, or lead-in words as needed.

*that*

His dream was that he would never have to give up his routine but ‸he would still find time to explore new frontiers.

> **Correlative conjunctions** are pairs of linking words (such as *either/or, not only/but also*) that appear separately but work together to join elements of a sentence.

## EDITING CHECKLIST

### Parallel Structure

☐ Are all the elements in a series in the same grammatical form?

☐ Are the elements in a comparison parallel in form?

☐ Are the articles, conjunctions, prepositions, or lead-in words for elements repeated as needed rather than mixed or omitted?

# C | Editing for Word Choice

## C1 Use appropriate language.

Your topic, audience, and purpose will help you determine the appropriate tone and level of formality for your writing. For most college and work assignments, your tone will be serious and your language formal.

INFORMAL    Crotchety old banks are getting schooled by newbie outfits like e-wallets and e-tailers.

FORMAL      Traditional banks are facing increasing competition from online payment systems and Internet retailers.

In formal writing, it is best to avoid jargon, euphemisms, slang, and clichés.

| TYPE OF LANGUAGE | DEFINITION | EXAMPLES |
| --- | --- | --- |
| jargon | Specialized vocabulary used by people in a certain field, especially business and computing | ■ *bandwidth* (for *capacity*)<br>■ *human capital* (for *employees*) |
| euphemisms | Indirect wording used to avoid unpleasant topics | ■ *pass away* (for *die*)<br>■ *enhanced interrogation* (for *torture*) |
| slang | Very informal, playful language that goes in and out of style | ■ *delish* (for *delicious*)<br>■ *do time* (for *serve a jail or prison term*) |
| clichés | A trite expression worn out from overuse | ■ *few and far between*<br>■ *tip of the iceberg* |

No matter what level of formality you use in your writing, avoid offending your readers by remaining unbiased, using gender-neutral language, and omitting stereotypes about age, race, ethnicity, culture, education, and so on.

*Good doctors are* ~~A good doctor is~~ communicative with *their* ~~his~~ patients.

---

### EDITING CHECKLIST

**Appropriate Language**

☐ Have you used a tone appropriate for your topic and audience?

☐ Have you avoided jargon, euphemisms, slang, and clichés?

☐ Have you remained unbiased, used gender-neutral language, and avoided stereotypes?

---

## C2 Write clearly and concisely.

Strive for short, simple expressions whenever possible.

| WORDY | CONCISE |
|---|---|
| at an earlier point in time | before |
| due to the fact that | because |
| make use of, utilize | use |
| true facts | facts |

Choosing exact words with the correct **connotation** (shade of meaning beyond the basic definition or **denotation**) will help your writing remain clear and concise.

The political prisoner emerged with a *skeletal* ~~slender~~ body and a *gaunt* ~~chiseled~~ face, but his expression was clearly *triumphant.* ~~dominant.~~

---

### EDITING CHECKLIST

**Appropriate Language**

☐ Is your writing concise?

☐ Have you used exact words?

## C3 Watch out for commonly confused words.

**Usage** refers to the way in which writers customarily use certain words and phrases, including matters of accepted practice or convention. The following glossary lists words and phrases whose usage may trouble writers. Not every possible problem is listed — only some that frequently puzzle students.

# Glossary of Troublemakers

**a, an**   Use *an* only before a word beginning with a vowel sound. "*An* asp can eat *an* egg *an* hour." (Some words, such as *hour* and *honest,* open with a vowel sound even though spelled with an *h.*)

**above**   Using *above* or *below* to refer back or forward in an essay is awkward and may not be accurate. Instead, try "the *preceding* argument," "in the *following* discussion," "on the *next* page."

**accept, except**   *Accept* is a verb meaning "to receive willingly"; *except* is usually a preposition meaning "not including." "This childcare center *accepts* all children *except* those under two." Sometimes *except* is a verb, meaning "to exempt." "The entry fee *excepts* children under twelve."

**advice, advise**   *Advice* is a noun, *advise* a verb. When someone *advises* you, you receive *advice.*

**affect, effect**   Most of the time, the verb *affect* means "to act on" or "to influence." "Too much beer can *affect* your speech." *Affect* can also mean "to put on airs." "He *affected* a British accent." *Effect,* a noun, means "a result": "Too much beer has a numbing *effect.*" But *effect* is also a verb, meaning "to bring about." "Pride *effected* his downfall."

**agree to, agree with, agree on**   *Agree to* means "to consent to"; *agree with,* "to be in accord." "I *agreed to* attend the lecture, but I didn't *agree with* the speaker's views." *Agree on* means "to come to or have an understanding about." "Chuck and I finally *agreed on* a compromise: the children would go to camp but not overnight."

**ain't**   Don't use *ain't* in writing; it is nonstandard English for *am not, is not* (*isn't*), and *are not* (*aren't*).

**a lot**   Many people mistakenly write the colloquial expression *a lot* as one word: *alot.* Use *a lot* if you must, but in writing *much* or *a large amount* is preferable. See also *lots, lots of, a lot of.*

**already, all ready**   *Already* means "by now"; *all ready* means "set to go." "At last our picnic was *all ready,* but *already* it was night."

**altogether, all together**   *Altogether* means "entirely." "He is *altogether* mistaken." *All together* means "in unison" or "assembled." "Now *all together*—heave!" "Inspector Trent gathered the suspects *all together* in the drawing room."

**among, between**   *Between* refers to two persons or things; *among,* to more than two. "Some disagreement *between* the two countries was inevitable. Still, there was general harmony *among* the five nations represented at the conference."

**amount, number**   Use *amount* to refer to quantities that can't be counted or to bulk; use *number* to refer to countable, separate items. "The *number* of people you want to serve determines the *amount* of ice cream you'll need."

**an, a**   See *a, an*.

**and/or**   Usually use either *and* or *or* alone. "Tim *and* Elaine will come to the party." "Tim *or* Elaine will come to the party." For three options, write, "Tim *or* Elaine, *or both*, will come to the party, depending on whether they can find a babysitter."

**ante-, anti-**   The prefix *ante-* means "preceding." *Antebellum* means "before the Civil War." *Anti-* most often means "opposing": *antidepressant*. It needs a hyphen in front of *i* (*anti-inflationary*) or in front of a capital letter (*anti-Marxist*).

**anybody, any body**   When *anybody* is used as an indefinite pronoun, write it as one word: "*Anybody* in his or her right mind abhors murder." Because *anybody* is singular, do not write "Anybody in *their* right mind." *Any body*, written as two words, is the adjective *any* modifying the noun *body*. "Name *any body* of water in Australia."

**anyone, any one**   *Anyone* is an indefinite pronoun written as one word. "Does *anyone* want dessert?" The phrase *any one* consists of the pronoun *one* modified by the adjective *any* and is used to single out something in a group: "Pick *any one* of the pies — they're all good."

**anyplace**   *Anyplace* is colloquial for *anywhere* and should not be used in formal writing.

**anyways, anywheres**   These nonstandard forms of *anyway* and *anywhere* should not be used in writing.

**as**   Sometimes using the subordinating conjunction *as* can make a sentence ambiguous. "*As* we were climbing the mountain, we put on heavy sweaters." Does *as* here mean "because" or "while"? Whenever using *as* would be confusing, use a more specific term instead, such as *because* or *while*.

**as, like**   Use *as, as if,* or *as though* rather than *like* to introduce clauses of comparison. "Dan's compositions are tuneful, *as* [not *like*] music ought to be." "Jeffrey behaves *as if* [not *like*] he were ill." *Like*, because it is a preposition, can introduce a phrase but not a clause. "My brother looks *like* me." "He runs *like* a duck."

**as to**   Usually this expression sounds stilted. Use *about* instead. "He complained *about* [not *as to*] the cockroaches."

**at**   See *where at, where to*.

**bad, badly**   *Bad* is an adjective; *badly* is an adverb. Following linking verbs (*be, appear, become, grow, seem, prove*) and verbs of the senses (*feel, look, smell, sound, taste*), use the adjective form. "I feel *bad* that we missed the plane." "The egg smells *bad*." The adverb form is used to modify a verb or an adjective. "The Tartans played so *badly* they lost to the last-place team, whose *badly* needed victory saved them from elimination."

**being as, being that**   Instead of "*Being as* I was ignorant of the facts, I kept still," write "*Because* I was ignorant" or "*Not knowing* the facts."

**beside, besides**   *Beside* is a preposition meaning "next to." "Sheldon enjoyed sitting *beside* the guest of honor." *Besides* is an adverb meaning "in addition." "*Besides*, he has a sense of humor." *Besides* is also a preposition meaning "other than." "Something *besides* shyness caused his embarrassment."

**between, among**   See *among, between*.

**between you and I**    The preposition *between* always takes the objective case. "Between *you* and *me* [not *I*], Joe's story sounds suspicious." "Between *us* [not *we*], what's going on between Bob and *her* [not *she*] is unfathomable."

**but that, but what**    "I don't know *but what* [or *but that*] you're right" is a wordy, imprecise way of saying "Maybe you're right" or "I believe you're right."

**can, may**    Use *can* to show ability. "Jake *can* bench-press 650 pounds." *May* involves permission. "*May* I bench-press today?" "You *may*, if you *can*."

**capital, capitol**    A *capital* is a city that is the center of government for a state or country. *Capital* can also mean "wealth." A *capitol* is a building in which legislators meet. "Who knows what the *capital* of Tanzania is?" "The renovated *capitol* is a popular attraction."

**center around**    Say "Class discussion *centered on* [or *revolved around*] her paper." In this sense, the verb *center* means "to have one main concern"—the way a circle has a central point. (To say a discussion centers *around* anything is a murky metaphor.)

**cite, sight, site**    *Cite*, a verb, means "to quote from or refer to." *Sight* as a verb means "to see or glimpse"; as a noun it means "a view, a spectacle." "When the police officer *sighted* my terrier running across the playground, she *cited* the leash laws." *Site*, a noun, means "location." "Standing and weeping at the *site* of his childhood home, he was a pitiful *sight*."

**climatic, climactic**    *Climatic*, from *climate*, refers to meteorological conditions. Saying "climatic conditions," however, is wordy—you can usually substitute "the climate": "*Climatic* conditions are [or "The *climate* is"] changing because of pollution in the atmosphere." *Climactic*, from *climax*, refers to the culmination of a progression of events. "In the *climactic* scene, the hero drives his car off the pier."

**compare, contrast**    *Compare* has two main meanings. The first, "to liken or represent as similar," is followed by *to*. "She *compared* her room *to* a jail cell." The second, "to analyze for similarities and differences," is generally followed by *with*. "The speaker *compared* the American educational system *with* the Japanese system."

  *Contrast* also has two main meanings. As a transitive verb, taking an object, it means "to analyze to emphasize differences" and is generally followed by *with*. "The speaker *contrasted* the social emphasis of the Japanese primary grades *with* the academic emphasis of ours." As an intransitive verb, *contrast* means "to exhibit differences when compared." "The sour taste of the milk *contrasted* sharply *with* its usual fresh flavor."

**complement, compliment**    *Compliment* is a verb meaning "to praise" or a noun meaning "praise." "The professor *complimented* Sarah on her perceptiveness." *Complement* is a verb meaning "to complete or reinforce." "Jenn's experiences as an intern *complemented* what she learned in class."

**could care less**    This is nonstandard English for *couldn't care less* and shouldn't be used in writing. "The cat *couldn't* [not *could*] *care less* about which brand of cat food you buy."

**could of**    *Could of* is colloquial for *could have* and shouldn't be used in writing.

**couple of**    Write "a *couple of* drinks" when you mean two. For more than two, say "a *few* [or *several*] drinks."

**criteria, criterion**    *Criteria* is the plural of *criterion*, which means "a standard or requirement on which a judgment or decision is based." "The main *criteria* for this job are attention to detail and good computer skills."

**data**    *Data* is a plural noun. Write "The data *are*" and "*these* data." The singular form of *data* is *datum* — which is rarely used. Instead, use *fact, figure,* or *statistic.*

**different from, different than**    *Different from* is usually the correct form to use. "How is good poetry *different from* prose?" Use *different than* when a whole clause follows. "Violin lessons with Mr. James were *different than* I had imagined."

**don't, doesn't**    *Don't* is the contraction of *do not,* and *doesn't* is the contraction of *does not.* "They *don't* want to get dressed up for the ceremony." "The cat *doesn't* [not *don't*] like to be combed."

**due to**    *Due* is an adjective and must modify a noun or pronoun; it can't modify a verb or an adjective. Begin a sentence with *due to* and you invite trouble: "*Due to* rain, the game was postponed." Write instead, "*Because of* rain." *Due to* works after the verb *be.* "His fall was *due to* a banana peel." There, *due* modifies the noun *fall.*

**due to the fact that**    A windy expression for *because.*

**effect, affect**    See *affect, effect.*

**either**    Use *either* when referring to one of two things. "Both internships sound great; I'd be happy with *either.*" When referring to one of three or more things, use *any one* or *any.* "*Any one* of our four counselors will be able to help you."

**et cetera, etc.**    Sharpen your writing by replacing *et cetera* (or its abbreviation, *etc.*) with exact words. Even translating the Latin expression into English ("and other things") is an improvement, as in "high-jumping, shot-putting, and other field events."

**everybody, every body**    When used as an indefinite pronoun, *everybody* is one word. "Why is *everybody* on the boys' team waving his arms?" Because *everybody* is singular, it is a mistake to write, "Why is *everybody* waving *their* arms?" *Every body* written as two words refers to separate, individual bodies. "After the overture, *every body* was in *its* [not *their*] correct place onstage."

**everyone, every one**    Used as an indefinite pronoun, *everyone* is one word. "*Everyone* has *his or her* own ideas." Because *everyone* is singular, it is incorrect to write, "*Everyone* has *their* own ideas." *Every one* written as two words refers to individual, distinct items. "I studied *every one* of the chapters."

**except, accept**    See *accept, except.*

**expect**    In writing, avoid the informal use of *expect* to mean "suppose, assume, or think." "I *suppose* [not *expect*] you're going on the geology field trip."

**fact that**    This is a wordy expression that, nearly always, you can do without. Instead of "*The fact that* he was puny went unnoticed," write, "That he was puny went unnoticed." "Because [not *Because of the fact that*] it snowed, the game was canceled."

**farther, further**    In your writing, use *farther* to refer to literal distance. "Chicago is *farther* from Nome than from New York." When you mean additional degree, time, or quantity, use *further.* "Sally's idea requires *further* discussion."

**fewer, less**    *Less* refers to general quantity or bulk; *fewer* refers to separate, countable items. "Eat *less* pizza." "Salad has *fewer* calories."

**field of**   In a statement such as "He took courses in *the field of* economics," omit *the field of* to save words.

**firstly**   The recommended usage is *first* (and *second*, not *secondly*; *third*, not *thirdly*; and so on).

**former, latter**   *Former* means "first of two"; *latter*, "second of two." An acceptable but heavy-handed pair, they often oblige your reader to backtrack. Your writing will be clearer if you simply name again the persons or things you mean. Instead of "The *former* great artist is the master of the flowing line, while the *latter* is the master of color," write, "Picasso is the master of the flowing line, while Matisse is the master of color."

**further, farther**   See *farther, further*.

**get, got**   *Get* has many meanings, especially in slang and colloquial use. Some are not appropriate in formal writing, such as "Let's start [not *get*] painting," or "His frequent interruptions finally started annoying [not *getting to*] me," or "She's going to take revenge on [not *get*] him." Or better, be even more specific: "She's going to spread rumors about him to ruin his reputation."

**good, well**   To modify a verb, use the adverb *well*, not the adjective *good*. "Jan dives *well* [not *good*]." Linking verbs (*be, appear, become, grow, seem, prove*) and verbs of the senses (such as *feel, look, smell, sound, taste*) call for the adjective *good*. "The paint job looks *good*." *Well* is an adjective used only to refer to health. "She looks *well*" means that she seems to be in good health. "She looks *good*" means her appearance is attractive.

**hanged, hung**   Both words are the past tense of the verb *hang*. *Hanged* refers to an execution. "The murderer was *hanged* at dawn." For all other situations, use *hung*. "Jim *hung* his wash on the line to dry."

**have got to**   In formal writing, avoid using the phrase *have got to* to mean "have to" or "must." "I *must* [not *have got to*] phone them right away."

**he, she, he or she**   Using *he* to refer to an indefinite person is considered sexist; so is using *she* with traditionally female occupations or pastimes. However, the phrase *he or she* can seem wordy and awkward.

**herself**   See *-self, -selves*.

**himself**   See *-self, -selves*.

**hopefully**   *Hopefully* means "with hope." "The children turned *hopefully* toward the door, expecting Santa Claus." In writing, avoid *hopefully* when you mean "it is to be hoped" or "let us hope." "*I hope* [not *Hopefully*] the posse will arrive soon."

**if, whether**   Use *whether*, not *if*, in indirect questions and to introduce alternatives. "Father asked me *whether* [not *if*] I was planning to sleep all morning." "I'm so confused I don't know *whether* [not *if*] it's day or night."

**imply, infer**   *Imply* means "to suggest"; *infer* means "to draw a conclusion." "Maria *implied* that she was too busy to see Tom, but Tom *inferred* that Maria had lost interest in him."

**in, into**   *In* refers to a location or condition; *into* refers to the direction of movement or change. "She burst *into* the room and found her sweetheart *in* another's arms."

**infer, imply**   See *imply, infer*.

**in regards to**  Write *in regard to, regarding,* or *about.*

**inside of, outside of**  As prepositions, *inside* and *outside* do not require *of.* "The students were more interested in events *outside* [not *outside of*] the building than those *inside* [not *inside of*] the classroom." In formal writing, do not use *inside of* to refer to time or *outside of* to mean "except." "I'll finish the assignment *within* [not *inside of*] two hours." "He told no one *except* [not *outside of*] a few friends."

**irregardless**  *Irregardless* is a double negative. Use *regardless.*

**is because**  See *reason is because, reason . . . is.*

**is when, is where**  Using these expressions results in errors in predication. "Obesity *is when* a person is greatly overweight." "Biology *is where* students dissect frogs." *When* refers to a point in time, but *obesity* is not a point in time; *where* refers to a place, but *biology* is not a place. Write instead, "Obesity is the condition of extreme overweight." "Biology is a laboratory course in which students dissect frogs."

**its, it's**  *Its* is a possessive pronoun, never in need of an apostrophe. *It's* is a contraction of *it is.* "Every new experience has *its* bad moments. Still, *it's* exciting to explore the unknown."

**it's me, it is I**  Although *it's me* is widely used in speech, don't use it in formal writing. Write "It is *I,*" which is grammatically correct. The same applies to other personal pronouns. "It was *he* [not *him*] who started the mutiny."

**kind of, sort of, type of**  When you use *kind, sort,* or *type*—singular words—make sure that the sentence construction is singular. "That *type* of show *offends* me." "Those *types* of shows *offend* me." In speech, *kind of* and *sort of* are used as qualifiers. "He is *sort of* intelligent." Avoid them in writing. "He is *rather* [or *somewhat* or *slightly*] intelligent."

**latter, former**  See *former, latter.*

**lay, lie**  The verb *lay,* meaning "to put or place," takes an object. "*Lay* that pistol down." *Lie,* meaning "to rest or recline," does not. "*Lie* on the bed until your headache goes away." Their principal parts are *lay, laid, laid* and *lie, lay, lain.*

**less, fewer**  See *fewer, less.*

**liable, likely**  Use *likely* to mean "plausible" or "having the potential." "Ben is *likely* [not *liable*] to win." Save *liable* for "legally obligated" or "susceptible." "A stunt man is *liable* to injury."

**lie, lay**  See *lay, lie.*

**like, as**  See *as, like.*

**likely, liable**  See *liable, likely.*

**literally**  Don't sling *literally* around for emphasis. Because it means "strictly according to the meaning of a word (or words)," it will wreck your credibility if you're speaking figuratively. "Professor Gray *literally* flew down the hall" means that Gray traveled on wings. Save *literally* to mean that you're reporting a fact. "Chemical wastes travel on the winds, and the skies *literally* rain poison."

**loose, lose**  *Loose,* an adjective, most commonly means "not fastened" or "poorly fastened." *Lose,* a verb, means "to misplace" or "to not win." "I have to be careful not to *lose* this button—it's so *loose.*"

**lots, lots of, a lot of**  Use these expressions only in informal speech. In formal writing, use *many* or *much.* See also *a lot.*

**mankind**   This term is considered sexist by many people. Use *humanity, humankind, the human race,* or *people* instead.

**may, can**   See *can, may.*

**media, medium**   *Media* is the plural of *medium* and most commonly refers to the various forms of public communication. "Some argue that, of all the *media,* television is the worst for children."

**might of**   *Might of* is colloquial for *might have* and should not be used in writing.

**most**   Do not use *most* when you mean "almost" or "nearly." "*Almost* [not *Most*] all the students felt that Professor Crey should receive tenure."

**must of**   *Must of* is colloquial for *must have* and should not be used in writing.

**myself**   See *-self, -selves.*

**not all that**   *Not all that* is colloquial for *not very*; do not use it in formal writing. "The movie was *not very* [not *not all that*] exciting."

**number, amount**   See *amount, number.*

**of**   See *could of, might of, must of, should of.*

**O.K., o.k., okay**   In formal writing, do not use any of these expressions. *All right* and *I agree* are possible substitutes.

**one**   Like a balloon, *one,* meaning "a person," tends to inflate. One *one* can lead to another. "When *one* is in college, *one* learns to make up *one's* mind for *oneself.*" Avoid this pompous usage. When possible, substitute *people* or a more specific plural noun. "When *students* are in college, *they* learn to make up their minds for *themselves.*"

**ourselves**   See *-self, -selves.*

**outside of, inside of**   See *inside of, outside of.*

**percent, per cent, percentage**   When you specify a number, write *percent* (also written *per cent*). "Nearly 40 *percent* of the listeners responded to the offer." Only use *percentage,* meaning "part," with an adjective, when you mention no number. "A high *percentage* [or *a large percentage*] of listeners responded." *A large number* or *a large proportion* sounds better yet.

**phenomenon, phenomena**   *Phenomena* is the plural of *phenomenon,* which means "an observable fact or occurrence." "Of the many mysterious supernatural *phenomena,* clairvoyance is the strangest *phenomenon* of all."

**precede, proceed**   *Precede* means "to go before or ahead of"; *proceed* means "to go forward." "The fire drill *proceeded* smoothly; the children *preceded* the teachers onto the playground."

**principal, principle**   *Principal* means "chief," whether used as an adjective or as a noun. "According to the *principal,* the school's *principal* goal will be teaching reading." Referring to money, *principal* means "capital." "Investors in high-risk companies may lose their *principal.*" *Principle,* a noun, means *rule* or *standard.* "Let's apply the *principle* of equality in hiring."

**proved, proven**   Although both forms can be used as past participles, *proved* is recommended. Use *proven* as an adjective. "They had *proved* their skill in match after match." "Try this *proven* cough remedy."

**quote, quotation**   *Quote* is a verb meaning "to cite, to use the words of." *Quotation* is a noun meaning "something that is quoted." "The *quotation* [not *quote*] next to her photograph fits her perfectly."

**raise, rise** *Raise,* meaning "to cause to move upward," is a transitive verb and takes an object. *Rise,* meaning "to move up (on its own)," is intransitive and does not take an object: "I *rose* from my seat and *raised* my arm."

**rarely ever** *Rarely* by itself is strong enough. "George *rarely* [not *rarely ever*] eats dinner with his family."

**real, really** *Real* is an adjective, *really* an adverb. Do not use *real* to modify a verb or another adjective, and avoid overusing either word. "*Sula* is a *really* [not *real*] fine novel." Even better: "*Sula* is a fine novel."

**reason is because, reason . . . is** *Reason . . . is* requires a clause beginning with *that.* Using *because* is nonstandard. "The *reason* I can't come *is that* [not *is because*] I have the flu." It is simpler and more direct to write, "I can't come because I have the flu."

**rise** See *raise, rise.*

**-self, -selves** Don't use a pronoun ending in *-self* or *-selves* in place of *her, him, me, them, us,* or *you.* "Nobody volunteered but Jim and *me* [not *myself*]." Use the *-self* pronouns to refer back to a noun or another pronoun and to lend emphasis. "*We* did it *ourselves.*" "Svetlana *herself* is a noted musician."

**set, sit** *Set,* meaning "to put or place," is a transitive verb and takes an object. *Sit,* meaning "to be seated," is intransitive and does not take an object. "We were asked to *set* our jewelry and metal objects on the counter and *sit* down."

**shall, will; should, would** The helping verb *shall* formerly was used with first-person pronouns. It is still used to express determination ("We *shall* overcome") or to ask consent ("*Shall* we march?"). Otherwise, *will* is commonly used with all three persons. "I *will* enter medical school in the fall." *Should* is a helping verb that expresses obligation; *would,* a helping verb that expresses a hypothetical condition. "I *should* wash the dishes before I watch TV." "He *would* learn to speak English if you *would* give him a chance."

**she, he or she** See *he, she, he or she.*

**should of** *Should of* is colloquial for *should have* and should not be used in writing.

**sight** See *cite, sight, site.*

**since** Sometimes using *since* can make a sentence ambiguous. "*Since* the babysitter left, the children have been watching television." Does *since* here mean "because" or "from the time that"? If using *since* might be confusing, use an unambiguous term (*because, ever since*).

**sit** See *set, sit.*

**site** See *cite, sight, site.*

**sort of** See *kind of, sort of, type of.*

**stationary, stationery** *Stationary,* an adjective, means "fixed, unmoving." "The fireplace remained *stationary* though the wind blew down the house." *Stationery* is paper for letter writing. To spell it right, remember that *letter* also contains *-er.*

**suppose to** Write *supposed to.* "He was *supposed to* read a novel."

**sure** *Sure* is an adjective, *surely* an adverb. Do not use *sure* to modify a verb or another adjective. If you mean "certainly," write *certainly* or *surely* instead. "He *surely* [not *sure*] makes the Civil War come alive."

**than, then** *Than* is a conjunction used in comparisons; *then* is an adverb indicating time. "Marlene is brainier *than* her sister." "First crack six eggs; *then* beat them."

**that, where**    See *where, that.*

**that, which**    Which pronoun should open a clause—*that* or *which*? If the clause adds to its sentence an idea that, however interesting, could be left out, then the clause is nonrestrictive. It should begin with *which* and be separated from the rest of the sentence with commas. "The vampire, *which* hovered nearby, leaped for Sophia's throat."

If the clause is essential to your meaning, it is restrictive. It should begin with *that* and should not have commas around it. "The vampire *that* Mel brought from Transylvania leaped for Sophia's throat." The clause indicates not just any old vampire but one in particular.

Don't use *which* to refer vaguely to an entire clause. Instead of "Jack was an expert drummer in high school, *which* won him a scholarship," write "Jack's skill as a drummer won him . . ."

**that, who, which, whose**    See *who, which, that, whose.*

**themselves**    See *-self, -selves.*

**then, than**    See *than, then.*

**there, their, they're**    *There* is an adverb indicating place. *Their* is a possessive pronoun. *They're* is a contraction of *they are.* "After playing tennis *there* for three hours, Lamont and Laura went to change *their* clothes because *they're* going out to dinner."

**to, too, two**    *To* is a preposition. *Too* is an adverb meaning "also" or "in excess." *Two* is a number. "Janet wanted to go *too,* but she was *too* sick *to* travel for *two* days. Instead, she went *to* bed."

**toward, towards**    *Toward* is preferred in the United States, *towards* in Britain.

**try and**    Use *try to.* "I'll *try to* [not *try and*] attend the opening performance of your play."

**type of**    See *kind of, sort of, type of.*

**unique**    Nothing can be *more, less,* or *very unique. Unique* means "one of a kind."

**use to**    Write *used to.* "Robert *used to* have a beard, but now he is clean-shaven."

**wait for, wait on**    *Wait for* means "await"; *wait on* means "to serve." "While *waiting for* his friends, George decided to *wait on* one more customer."

**well, good**    See *good, well.*

**where, that**    Although speakers sometimes use *where* instead of *that,* you should not do so in writing. "I heard on the news *that* [not *where*] it got hot enough to fry eggs on car hoods."

**where . . . at, where . . . to**    The colloquial use of *at* or *to* after *where* is redundant. Write "*Where* were you?" not "*Where* were you *at*?" "I know *where* she was rushing [not *rushing to*]."

**whether**    See *if, whether.*

**which, that**    See *that, which.*

**who, which, that, whose**    *Who* refers to people, *which* to things and ideas. "Was it Pogo *who* said, 'We have met the enemy and he is us'?" "The blouse, *which* was green, accented her dark skin." *That* refers to things but can also be used for a class of people. "The team *that* increases sales the most will get a bonus." Because *of which* can be cumbersome, use *whose* even with things. "The mountain, *whose* snowy peaks were famous the world over, was covered by fog." See also *that, which*.

**who, whom**   *Who* is used as a subject, *whom* as an object. In "*Whom* do I see?" *Whom* is the object of *see*. In "*Who* goes there?" *Who* is the subject of "goes."

**who's, whose**   *Who's* is a contraction of *who is* or *who has*. "*Who's* going with Phil?" *Whose* is a possessive pronoun. "Bill is a conservative politician *whose* ideas are unlikely to change."

**whose, who, which, that**   See *who, which, that, whose*.

**will, shall**   See *shall, will; should, would*.

**would, should**   See *shall, will; should, would*.

**would of**   *Would of* is colloquial for *would have* and should not be used in writing.

**you**   *You*, meaning "a person," occurs often in conversation. "When *you* go to college, *you* have to work hard." In writing, use *one* or a specific, preferably plural noun. "When *students* go to college, *they* have to work hard." See *one*.

**your, you're**   *Your* is a possessive pronoun; *you're* is the contraction of *you are*. "*You're* lying! It was *your* handwriting on the envelope."

**yourself, yourselves**   See *-self, -selves*.

# D | Editing for Common Punctuation Problems

## D1   Check for correct use of commas.

The **comma** is a punctuation mark indicating a pause. By setting some words apart from others, commas help clarify relationships. They prevent the words on a page and the ideas they represent from becoming a jumble.

1. Use a comma before a coordinating conjunction (*and, but, for, or, so, yet, nor*) joining two main clauses in a compound sentence.

   The discussion was brief, *so* the meeting was adjourned early.

2. Use a comma after an introductory word or word group unless it is short and can't be misread.

   *After the war*, the North's economy developed rapidly.

3. Use commas to separate the items in a series of three or more items.

   The chief advantages will be *speed, durability,* and *longevity*.

4. Use commas to set off a modifying clause or phrase if it is nonrestrictive — if it can be taken out of the sentence without significantly changing the essential meaning of the sentence.

   Good childcare, *which is hard to find,* should be available at work.
   Good childcare *that is reliable and inexpensive* is every employee's hope.

An **appositive** is a word or group of words that adds information about a subject or object by identifying it in a different way.
A **parenthetical expression** is an aside to readers or a transitional expression such as *for example* or *in contrast.*
**Conjunctive adverbs** are linking words that can connect independent clauses and show a relationship between two ideas.

5. Use commas to set off a nonrestrictive appositive, an expression that comes directly after a noun or pronoun and renames it.

Sheri, *my sister,* has a new job as an events coordinator.

6. Use commas to set off parenthetical expressions, conjunctive adverbs, and other interrupters.

The proposal from the mayor's commission, *however,* is not feasible.

### EDITING CHECKLIST

#### Commas

☐ Have you added a comma between two main clauses joined by a coordinating conjunction?

☐ Have you added commas needed after introductory words or word groups?

☐ Have you separated items in a series with commas?

☐ Have you avoided commas before the first item in a series or after the last?

☐ Have you used commas before and after each nonrestrictive (nonessential) word, phrase, or clause?

☐ Have you avoided using commas around a restrictive word, phrase, or clause that is essential to the meaning of the sentence?

☐ Have you used commas to set off appositives, parenthetical expressions, conjunctive adverbs, and other interrupters?

## D2 Check for correct use of apostrophes.

An **apostrophe** is a punctuation mark that either shows possession (*Sylvia's*) or indicates that one or more letters have intentionally been left out to form a contraction (*didn't*). An apostrophe is never used to create the possessive form of a pronoun; use the possessive pronoun form instead.

*Mike's*
Mikes car was totaled in the accident.

*Women's*                              *men's.*
Womens' pay is often less than mens'.

*didn't*
Che did'nt want to stay at home and study.

*its*
The dog wagged it's tail happily. [It's = it is? No.]

*It's*
Its raining. [It's = it is.]

> ► **Possessive Personal Pronouns** *at a Glance*

| PERSONAL PRONOUN | POSSESSIVE CASE |
|---|---|
| I | my, mine |
| you | your, yours (*not* your's) |
| he | his |
| she | her, hers (*not* her's) |
| it | its (*not* it's) |
| we | our, ours (*not* our's) |
| they | their, theirs (*not* their's) |
| who | whose (*not* who's) |

### EDITING CHECKLIST

**Apostrophes**

- ☐ Have you used an apostrophe when letters are left out in a contraction?
- ☐ Have you used an apostrophe to create the possessive form of a noun?
- ☐ Have you used the possessive case — not an apostrophe — to show that a pronoun is possessive?
- ☐ Have you used *it's* correctly (to mean *it is*)?

## D3   Check for correct punctuation of quotations.

For more about quotations from sources, see D3 in the Quick Research Guide, p. Q-28.

When you quote the exact words of a person you've interviewed or a source you've read, enclose those words in quotation marks. Notice how student Betsy Buffo presents the words of her subject in this passage from her essay "Interview with an Artist":

> Derek is straightforward when asked about how his work is received in the local community: "My work is outside the mainstream. Because it's controversial, it's not easy for me to get exposure."

She might have expressed and punctuated this passage in other ways:

> Derek says that "it's not easy" for him to find an audience.
>
> Derek struggles for recognition because his art falls "outside the mainstream."

If your source quotes someone else (a quotation within a quotation), put your subject's words in quotation marks and the words he or she is quoting in single quotation marks. Always put commas and periods inside the quotation marks; put semicolons and colons outside. Include all necessary marks in the correct place or sequence.

> As Betsy Buffo explains, "Derek struggles for recognition because his art falls 'outside the mainstream.'"

Substitute an ellipsis mark (. . .) — three spaced dots — for any words you have omitted from the middle of a direct quotation. If you're following MLA style, place the ellipses inside brackets ([. . .]) when necessary to avoid confusing your ellipsis marks with those of the original writer. If the ellipses come at the end of a sentence, add another period to conclude the sentence. You don't need an ellipsis mark to show the beginning or ending of a quotation that is clearly incomplete.

In this selection from "Overworked!" student Melissa Lamberth identifies quotations and an omission. (She cites Joe Robinson's essay from the reader in her edition of *The Bedford Guide*):

> In his essay "Four Weeks Vacation," Robinson writes, "The health implications of sleep-deprived motorists weaving their way to the office . . . are self-evident" (481).

### EDITING CHECKLIST

**Punctuation with Quotations**

☐ Are the exact words quoted from your source enclosed in quotation marks?

☐ Are commas and periods placed inside closing quotation marks?

☐ Are colons and semicolons placed outside closing quotation marks?

☐ Do ellipses show where you omit words from the middle of a quote?

# E | Editing for Common Mechanics Problems

## E1  Check for correct use of capital letters.

Capital letters begin a new sentence; names of specific people, nationalities, places, dates, and things (proper nouns); and main words in titles.

*sophomore*          *college,*          *world literature, biology,*
During my ~~Sophomore~~ year in ~~College,~~ I took ~~World Literature, Biology,~~

*history, psychology,*
American ~~History, Psychology,~~ and French — courses required for a

*humanities major.*
~~Humanities Major.~~

## EDITING CHECKLIST

### Capitalization

☐ Have you used a capital letter at the beginning of each complete sentence, including sentences that are quoted?

☐ Have you used capital letters for proper nouns and pronouns?

☐ Have you avoided using capital letters for emphasis?

☐ Have you used a capital letter for the first, last, and main words in a title? (Main words exclude prepositions, coordinating conjunctions, and articles.)

## Capitalization *at a Glance*

THE FIRST LETTER OF A SENTENCE, INCLUDING A QUOTED SENTENCE
She called out, "Come in! The water's warm."

PROPER NAMES AND ADJECTIVES MADE FROM THEM

| Smithsonian Institution | a Mayan city | Marie Curie |

RANK OR TITLE BEFORE A PROPER NAME

| Ms. Olson | Professor Santocolon | Dr. Frost |

FAMILY RELATIONSHIP ONLY WHEN IT SUBSTITUTES FOR OR IS PART OF A PROPER NAME

| Grandma Jones | Father Time |

RELIGIONS, THEIR FOLLOWERS, AND DEITIES

| Islam | Orthodox Jew | Krishna |

PLACES, REGIONS, GEOGRAPHIC FEATURES, AND NATIONALITIES

| Palo Alto | the Berkshire Mountains | Egyptians |

DAYS OF THE WEEK, MONTHS, AND HOLIDAYS

| Wednesday | July | Labor Day |

HISTORICAL EVENTS, PERIODS, AND DOCUMENTS

| the Boston Tea Party | the Middle Ages | the Constitution |

SCHOOLS, COLLEGES, UNIVERSITIES, AND SPECIFIC COURSES

| Temple University | Introduction to Clinical Psychology |

FIRST, LAST, AND MAIN WORDS IN TITLES OF PAPERS, BOOKS, ARTICLES, WORKS OF ART, TELEVISION SHOWS, POEMS, AND PERFORMANCES

| *The Decline and Fall of the Roman Empire* | "The Lottery" |

## E2  Check spelling.

Misspelled words are difficult to spot in your own writing, as you usually see what you think you wrote. Spell checkers are handy, but you need to know their limitations: a spell checker highlights words that do not appear in its dictionary, including most proper nouns. Spell checkers will not highlight words misspelled as different words, such as *except* for *accept,* *to* for *too,* or *own* for *won.*

A **preposition** is a transitional word (such as *in, on, at, of, from*) that leads into a phrase.
**Coordinating conjunctions** are one-syllable linking words (*and, but, for, or, nor, so, yet*) that join elements with equal or near-equal importance.
An **article** is the word *a, an,* or *the.*

For a list of commonly confused words, see C3.

### EDITING CHECKLIST
### Spelling

☐  Have you checked for the words you habitually misspell?

☐  Have you checked for commonly confused or misspelled words? (See C3.)

☐  Have you checked a dictionary for any words you are unsure about?

☐  Have you run your spell checker? Have you read your paper carefully for errors that the spell checker would miss such as a stray letter?

# Acknowledgments *(continued from p. iv)*

Adams, Sarah. "Be Cool to the Pizza Dude." Copyright © 2005 by Sarah Adams. From the book *This I Believe: The Personal Philosophies of Remarkable Men and Women,* edited by Jay Allison and Dan Gediman. Copyright © 2006 by This I Believe, Inc. Reprinted by arrangement with Henry Holt and Company, LLC. All rights reserved.

Ansari, Aziz, with Eric Klinenberg. "Searching for Your Soul Mate" from *Modern Romance,* copyright © 2015 by Modern Romantics Corporation. Used by permission of Penguin Press, an imprint of Penguin Publishing Group, a division of Penguin Random House LLC.

Badger, Emily. "It's Time to Stop Blaming Poverty on the Decline in Marriage," from *CityLab,* January 8, 2014. © 2014 The Atlantic Media Co., as first published in the *Atlantic Magazine.* All rights reserved. Distributed by Tribune Content Agency, LLC.

Baker, Russell. "The Art of Eating Spaghetti." Used by permission of Don Congdon Associates, Inc. Copyright © 1982 by Russell Baker.

Barthel, Michael, Elisa Shearer, Jeffrey Gottfried, and Amy Mitchell. Excerpted from "The Evolving Role of News on Twitter and Facebook." Pew Research Center, Washington, D.C. (July 2015), http://www.journalism.org/2015/07/14/the-evolving-role-of-news-on-twitter-and-facebook/. Copyright © 2015 Pew Research Center. Used with permission.

Bentley, Chris. "Can Boomers Make Cohousing Mainstream?" January 20, 2015, *CityLab.* © 2015 The Atlantic Media Co., as first published in *The Atlantic Magazine.* All rights reserved. Distributed by Tribune Content Agency, LLC.

Bertoni, Timothy J., and Patrick D. Nolan. "Dead Men Do Tell Tales," *Sociation Today* 10, no. 1 (Spring/Summer 2012). Copyright © 2012 by Sociation Today. Used with permission from North Carolina Sociological Association.

Blow, Charles M. "Black Dads Are Doing Best of All." From the *New York Times,* June 8, 2015. © 2015 The New York Times. All rights reserved. Used by permission and protected by the Copyright Laws of the United States. The printing, copying, redistribution, or retransmission of this Content without express written permission is prohibited.

Brady, Judith E. "I Want a Wife." Reprinted by permission.

Brooks, David. "Introduction: Adam II" and "Chapter 10: The Big Me" from *The Road to Character* by David Brooks, copyright © 2015 by David Brooks. Used by permission of Random House, an imprint and division of Penguin Random House LLC. All rights reserved.

Cobb, Michael. "The Supreme Court's Lonely Hearts Club." *New York Times,* June 30, 2015. © 2015 The New York Times. All rights reserved. Used by permission and protected by the Copyright Laws of the United States. The printing, copying, redistribution, or retransmission of this Content without express written permission is prohibited.

Cofer, Judith Ortiz. "More Room," from *Silent Dancing: A Partial Remembrance of a Puerto Rican Childhood.* Copyright © 1990 Arte Público Press — University of Houston. Reprinted with permission from Arte Público Press.

Copeland, Libby. "The Anti-Social Network." From *Slate,* © 2011 The Slate Group. All rights reserved. Used by permission and protected by the Copyright Laws of the United States. The printing, copying, redistribution, or retransmission of the Material without express written permission is prohibited.

Dailey, Kate. "America's Fat Hatred." From *Newsweek,* 8/25/09 © 2009 The Newsweek/Daily Beast Company LLC. All rights reserved.

Used by permission and protected by the Copyright Laws of the United States. The printing, copying, redistribution, or retransmission of the Material without express written permission is prohibited.

Deford, Frank. "Mind Games: Football and Head Injuries." *Morning Edition,* May 9, 2012. © 2012 Frank Deford for National Public Radio, Inc. Used with the permission of NPR. Any unauthorized duplication is strictly prohibited.

Deresiewicz, William. "What Is College For?" From *Excellent Sheep,* 2014. pp. 77-87. Copyright © 2014 by William Deresiewicz. Reprinted with the permission of The Free Press, a Division of Simon & Schuster, Inc. All rights reserved.

Foster, Tom. Excerpt from "Can Artificial Meat Save the World?" from *Popular Science,* November 8, 2013. Copyright © 2013 Tom Foster. Used with permission.

Friedman, Ann. Excerpt from "Can We Just, Like, Get Over the Way Women Talk?" New York Magazine's *The Cut,* July 9, 2015. Copyright © 2015 New York Magazine. Used with permission.

Harjo, Suzan Shown. "Last Rites for Indian Dead: Treating Remains like Artifacts Is Intolerable," *Los Angeles Times,* September 16, 1989. Copyright © 1989 Suzan Shown Harjo. Used with permission.

Jackson, Shirley. "The Lottery" from *The Lottery.* Copyright © 1948, 1949 by Shirley Jackson. Copyright renewed 1976, 1977 by Laurence Hyman, Barry Hyman, Mrs. Sarah Webster, and Mrs. Joanne Schnurer. Reprinted by permission of Farrar, Straus and Giroux, LLC.

Jarvie, Jenny. "Trigger Happy: The 'Trigger Warning' Has Spread from Blogs to College Classrooms," *New Republic,* March 3, 2014. © 2014 New Republic. All rights reserved. Used by permission and protected by the Copyright Laws of the United States. The printing, copying, redistribution, or retransmission of the Material without express written permission is prohibited.

Jensen, Robert. "The High Cost of Manliness." Originally posted on <www.AlterNet.org>, September 8, 2006. Copyright © 2006 Independent Media Institute. Reprinted with permission. All rights reserved.

King, Stephen. "Why We Crave Horror Movies." Copyright © 1982 by Stephen King. Originally appeared in *Playboy,* 1982. Reprinted with permission. All rights reserved.

Luo, Shan, John R. Monterosso, Kayan Sarpelleh, and Kathleen A. Page. Differential effects of fructose versus glucose on brain and appetitive responses to food cues and decisions for food rewards. *PNAS* 112, no. 20 (2015): 6509-6514; published ahead of print May 4, 2015, doi:10.1073/pnas.1503358112.

May, Cindi. "The Problem with Female Superheroes." *Scientific American,* June 23, 2015. Reproduced with permission. Copyright © 2015 Scientific American, a Division of Nature America, Inc. All rights reserved.

McCain, John. Excerpt from "The Virtues of the Quiet Hero." Copyright © 2005 John McCain. From the book *This I Believe: The Personal Philosophies of Remarkable Men and Women,* edited by Jay Allison and Dan Gediman. Copyright © 2006 by This I Believe, Inc. Reprinted by arrangement with Henry Holt and Company, LLC.

Rideau, Wilbert. "Why Prisons Don't Work" from *Time* (March 21, 1994). Copyright © 1994 by Wilbert Rideau. Reprinted with the permission of the author, c/o The Permissions Company, Inc., www.permissionscompany.com.

Rodriguez, Richard. Excerpt from *Hunger of Memory.* Copyright © 1982 by Richard Rodriguez. Reprinted by permission of Georges Borchardt, Inc., on behalf of the author.

Ronson, Jon. "How One Stupid Tweet Blew Up Justine Sacco's Life," *New York Times,* February 12, 2015. Copyright © 2015 Jon Ronson. Used with permission.

Sapolsky, Robert. Excerpt from "On the Origin of Celebrity: Why Julia Roberts Rules Our World." *Nautilus,* September 5, 2013. Copyright © 2013 Robert Sapolsky. Used with permission.

Shermer, Michael. "The Science of Righteousness" from *Scientific American,* June 2012. Reproduced with permission. Copyright © 2012 Scientific American, a Division of Nature America, Inc. All rights reserved.

Smith, Ashley. "Special Report: Smokejumper Training," *Magic Valley/Times-News,* September 30, 2013. Copyright © 2013 Magic Valley/Times-News. Used with permission.

Staples, Brent. "Black Men and Public Space." Used by permission of the author.

Sternbergh, Adam. "Smile, You're Speaking Emoji: The Rapid Evolution of a Wordless Tongue," from *New York Magazine,* November 17, 2014. Copyright © 2014 New York Magazine. Used with permission.

Stone, Elizabeth. "Grief in the Age of Facebook." Copyright © Elizabeth Stone. Used with permission.

Tan, Amy. "Mother Tongue." Copyright © 1989 by Amy Tan. First appeared in the *Threepenny Review.* Reprinted by permission of the author and the Sandra Dijkstra Literary Agency.

Tennis, Cary. "Why am I obsessed with celebrity gossip?" *Salon,* January 6, 2006. Copyright © 2006 Salon. This article first appeared in Salon.com, at http://www.Salon.com. An online version remains in the Salon archives. Reprinted with permission.

Thompson, Clive. "New Literacy" from *Wired,* August 24, 2009. Copyright © 2009 Clive Thompson. Reprinted with permission of the author.

Tobias, Scott. Review of *The Hunger Games.* Reprinted with permission of The Onion. Copyright © 2015 by ONION, INC. www.theonion.com.

Tokumitsu, Miya. "In the Name of Love." *Jacobin,* Issue 13, 2014. Copyright © 2014 Jacobin. Used with permission.

Tokura-Gallo, Hisayo. "Weekly Critical Thinking Assignment." Used with permission from the author.

Toohey, Peter. Excerpted from "Sibling Rivalry, a History" (*Atlantic,* November 30, 2014) from *Jealousy.* Copyright 2014 by Yale University Press. Used with permission.

Vargas, César. "How First- and Second-Generation Hispanics Can Help Each Other," *Huffington Post,* May 13, 2015. Copyright © 2015 César Vargas. Used with permission.

Zeilinger, Julie. Excerpt from *A Little F'd Up: Why Feminism Is Not a Dirty Word.* Copyright © 2012 Julie Zeilinger. Reprinted by permission of Seal Press, a member of the Perseus Books Group.

Zinsser, William K. "The Right to Fail." Copyright © 1969, 1970 by William K. Zinsser. Reprinted by permission of the author.

# ABOUT THE PHOTOGRAPHS THAT OPEN PARTS ONE THROUGH FOUR

## A Series of Aerial Photographs by David L. Ryan

A long-time staff photographer at the *Boston Globe*, David L. Ryan is well known for his distinctive aerial photography. His witty and moving images often show familiar scenes from fresh perspectives and reveal beautiful patterns hidden among commonplace, everyday realities. Like a writer, he keeps his audience close in his thoughts as he works, with the goal of sharing his curiosity, knowledge, and enthusiasm with those who see his images. As he puts it, "I've been in Boston all my life. I've gone around here by boat, helicopter, plane, train, bicycle, and walking. I want to make people say, *'How did you get that?'* " In another parallel with writing, he finds an open-minded, "learning by doing" approach to be beneficial: "I'm still experimenting with it," he says of his work. "Everything is an experiment."

David L. Ryan/The Boston Globe/Getty Images.

**Part One: Fountain and bathers (pages 4–5)**
It's obvious that a photographer must choose a point of view. He or she must literally choose a place to stand and an angle from which to view a scene. So must a writer.

In this image, what effects are created by the photographer's chosen point of view? What effect does his elevated perspective have on how the scene appears? What is gained and lost by photographing from this distance? What observations do you think the photographer is making about what he is seeing?

**Part Two: Rowboats tied to dock (pages 44–45)**
If you were to take something you've written and rewrite it from an entirely different point of view, the two versions would likely have different meanings and might accomplish different purposes. You convey meaning and purpose, in part, through your choice of perspective. Similarly, for a photographer, a change in perspective can create a feeling of strangeness, make a point, or offer a commentary. From the air things might look like something else for a second.

In this image, what point or points do you think the photographer is making? Is his focus the season, sport, recreation, equipment, place, person, or state of mind, or some other subject? How does his point of view help to convey that meaning?

David L. Ryan/The Boston Globe/Getty Images.

### Part Three: Trains (pages 248–49)

Before a photographer takes a picture, he or she has to decide how much of the scene to include. Will the image be a close-up of a face or an aerial view? Does the image give the viewer specific information about an individual or show more general patterns? Writers, too, must make decisions about how much of a topic or a discussion to include and how to define the boundaries of a topic.

David L. Ryan/The Boston Globe/Getty Images.

What does this photograph include? What does it leave out? What can you tell about the people — either as individuals or as groups — shown in this photo? What does the image communicate that might be less apparent from ordinary photographs taken of people at ground level? How does the image find interest and import in the routine?

### Part Four: Flooded baseball fields (pages 356–57)

Photographers and writers are both alert to rhythms and correspondences, as well as to patterns and meanings below the surface. Writers can express rhythm by selecting their words, by controlling the length of sentences and paragraphs, and by creating a structure that helps the reader follow an unfolding essay. Ryan makes his work compelling by conveying a sense of rhythm through geometry.

David L. Ryan/The Boston Globe/Getty Images.

What is the mood of this photograph? What does this image of flooded fields say to you, the viewer? How does it balance ordinary and extraordinary elements against each other?

# INDEX

*a. See also* Articles (*a, an, the*)
  as indefinite article, 733
  versus *an*, Q-50
Abbreviations, 853–55
  apostrophes and, 843
  at end of business letters, 349
  period at end of, 827
*above*, Q-50
Absolute phrases, 747, 833
Abstraction, ladder of, 423, 424
Abstracts
  APA style for, 713
  format for, Q-4
  in library databases, 627
Academic exchange
  documenting sources and, 228
  example of, 230–31 (fig.)
Academic institution reports, APA
  style for, 715
Academic papers
  capitalizing title of, 857–58, Q-65
  format for, Q-1–7
Academic terms, capitalization of, 857
*accept/except*, 823, Q-50
Access dates
  APA style for, 711
  MLA style for, 688
Acronyms, 855
Action in images, visual analysis and,
  284 (fig.), 286
Action verbs, 735, 741, 742–43
  revising for, 451
  sentence structure and, 748–49
Active reading. *See* Critical reading
Active voice, basics of, 811–12
  consistency in, 789
  when proposing solution, 192
Adams, Sarah, 580–81
Addresses, 835, 859–60
  on business letters, 347–48, 348 (fig.)
*Ad hominem* argument, 172
Adjectives, 736, 784–88
  comma between, 830
  editing, Q-45–46
  made from proper names,
    capitalization of, 856, Q-65
  reducing use of, 452
  sentence structure and, 749

Advanced searching, 617, 626
Adverbs, 736, 784–88
  editing, Q-45–46
  reducing use of, 452
  sentence structure and, 749
Ads, MLA style for, 693
*advice/advise*, Q-50
*affect/effect*, 823, Q-50
Afterword
  APA style for, 714
  MLA style for, 692
Age bias, avoiding, 820
*agree to/agree with/agree on*, Q-50
*ain't*, Q-50
Albums, title of, italics for, 862
*all-*, hyphen with, 864
*all*, subject-verb agreement and,
  773–74
*all ready/already*, Q-50
*all together/altogether*, Q-50
*a lot/alot*, Q-50
*a lot of/lots of/lots*, Q-56
Alternating pattern of comparing and
  contrasting, 437
Alternating pattern of organization,
  117–18
American Psychological Association
  style. *See* APA style
"America's War on the Overweight"
  (Dailey and Ellin), 522–25
*among/between*, Q-50
*amount/number*, Q-51
Amplifying, common transitions for,
  418
*an. See also* Articles (*a, an, the*)
  as indefinite article, 733
  versus *a*, Q-50
Analogy, argument by, 172
Analysis
  of college assignments, 38
  as critical thinking skill, 35–36
  of process. *See* Process analysis
  as reading skill, 24–25, 25 (fig.)
  of subject. *See* Subject analysis
Analytical level of reading,
  24–28
"Analyzing 'The New Literacy'"
  (Julseth), 28–29

*and. See also* Coordinating conjunctions
  in advanced searches, 626, 627 (fig.)
  antecedents joined by,
    pronoun-antecedent agreement
    and, 782
  coordinate adjectives and, comma
    and, 830
  as coordinating conjunction, 738
  *or* and, Q-51
  subjects joined by, subject-verb
    agreement and, 772
Anecdotes, beginning essay
  with, 411
Annotated bibliographies, 605,
  660–61
Annotating, while reading, 19–21
Ansari, Aziz, 494–99
Antagonist, definition of, 262
Antecedents
  avoiding gender bias with, 820
  pronoun-antecedent agreement
    and, 782–83, Q-44–45
  pronoun reference and, 733,
    779–81
  subject-verb agreement and, 774
*anti-/ante-*, Q-51
*any*
  in comparisons, 795
  subject-verb agreement and,
    773–74
*anybody/any body*, Q-51
*anyone/any one*, Q-51
*any other*, in comparisons, 795
*anyplace*, Q-51
*anyways/anywheres*, Q-51
APA style, 704–25
  for business courses, 468
  citing sources in, 671, 704–10, Q-31,
    Q-35–36
  for education courses, 469
  font choice and, Q-15
  headings in, Q-16
  indenting long quotations in, 846
  listing sources in, 710–17, Q-31,
    Q-35–36
  lists within text and, Q-15
  paper format in, Q-4–6
  preparing tables in, Q-8–10

APA style (continued)
  research paper in, example of,
    717–25
  source navigator for, 649, 651, 653,
    655
  using file templates for, 317–18
Apostrophes, 841–43, Q-62
Application letters
  organizing and formatting,
    Q-16–19
  writing, 341–42, 345–47, 346 (fig.)
Appositives, 747
  colon for introducing, 840
  commas for, 832, Q-61
  dashes for, 848
  objective pronoun case for, 777
  subjective pronoun case for, 776
*are*, 764
Argument *ad hominem*, 172
Argument by analogy, 172
Argument from dubious authority, 172
Argument from ignorance, 172
Arrangement of images, visual analysis
    and, 284 (fig.), 287, 288 (fig.)
Art, works of. *See* Works of art
Articles. *See* Journal articles; Magazine
    articles; Newspaper articles;
    Periodical articles
Articles (*a, an, the*)
  count nouns and, 731
  definite versus indefinite, 732–33
  noncount nouns and, 731–32
  in titles, capitalization of, 858
Artistic elements of images, visual
    analysis and, 288–91
"Art of Eating Spaghetti, The" (Baker),
    48–50
*as*
  confusion in using, Q-51
  in elliptical construction, 797
  parallel structure and, 802, Q-47
  versus *like*, Q-51
Asking reporter's questions, to
    generate ideas, 377–78
Assessment criteria, analyzing writing
    assignments and, 461
Assignments, writing. *See* Writing
    assignments in college courses
Asterisk, in advanced searches, 626
*as to*, Q-51
*at*, using correctly, 737–38
Atmosphere of story, definition of, 263
"Attention Test, The" (Sikora), 297–99
Attitude
  of thesis, 385–86, 391
  in topic sentences, 406

Audience
  analyzing expectations of, 460–61
  choosing appropriate tone for, 814
  considering, 12–15, 383–84
  designing documents for, Q-13–16
  images and, 283
  proposing solution for, 185, 188
  revising for, 444–45
  revisiting for research project, 607
  supporting position with sources
    for, 224
  taking stand for, 159
  workplace writing and, 339
Audio sources
  APA style for, 716
  MLA style for, 693–94
Author, reliability of, 636–37, 639,
    Q-24–25
Author information
  in APA citations, 706–7
  in MLA citations, 682–84
  in References, 711–12
  in Works Cited, 688–89
Auxiliary verbs, 736, 741, 744

Background in images, visual analysis
    and, 284 (fig.), 286
Backing up files
  for online writing, 320
  of presentation slides, 354
*bad/badly*, Q-51
Badger, Emily, 127–29
Baker, Russell, 48–50, 414
Bandwagon argument, 172
Bar graphs, adding to academic
    papers, Q-11, Q-11 (fig.)
Base verb form, 758–59
*BCE*, use of, 854
*be*, forms of, 760, 764–65
  *if* clauses and, 770
  in present and past tense, list of,
    Q-42
  using correctly, 766–67
  wordiness and, 451
"Be Cool to the Pizza Dude" (Adams),
    580–81
Begging the question, 172
*being as/being that*, Q-52
Bentley, Chris, 487–90
*beside/besides*, Q-52
*best*, correct use of, 787
*between/among*, Q-50
*between you and I*, Q-52
"Beyond the Nuclear Family: Can
    Boomers Make Cohousing
    Mainstream?" (Bentley), 487–90

Bias
  in firsthand observation, 161
  language free of, 819–21
  in sources, reliability of source and,
    634, 638–39
Bibliographies, 629
  annotated. *See* Annotated
    bibliographies
Big picture of image, seeing, 282, 282
    (fig.), 283–85
"Black Dads Are Doing Best of All"
    (Blow), 216–19
"Black Men and Public Space"
    (Staples), 502–4
Blogs/blog posts
  APA style for, 716
  by class, 310
  MLA style for, 693
  writing, to generate ideas, 380
Bloom, Benjamin S., 24–26, 25 (fig.)
Blow, Charles M., 216–19
Bookmarking online reading, 32
Books
  APA style for, 714–15, Q-35
  MLA style for, 691–92, Q-33
  recording source information for,
    650–51
Boolean searches, 626, 627 (fig.)
*both/and*, 802
Bourgeau, Linn, 401, 402–3
Brackets, 658, 849, 850–51
  editing, Q-63
Brady, Judy, 505–7
Brainstorming to generate ideas
  basics of, 371–72
  when writing from interviews, 95
  when writing from
    observation, 74
  when writing from recall, 55
Broadcast interviews, MLA style for,
    694–95
Brochures, 351–52
  APA style for, 715
  workplace writing and, 350–52,
    352 (fig.)
Brooks, David, 582–89
Burke's pentad, 379
Burns, Jonathan, 260–61,
    273–74, 277
Business letters, writing, 347–50
Bustin, Andrew Dillon, 336 (fig.)
*but*. *See also* Coordinating
    conjunctions
  comma before, 833
  as coordinating conjunction, 738
*but that/but what*, Q-52

Campus department home page, MLA style for, 693

Campus Web sites, APA style for, 716

*can/may*, Q-52

"Can We Just, Like, Get Over the Way Women Talk?" (Friedman), 549–52

*capital/capitol*, 823, Q-52

Capitalization, 856–58, Q-64, Q-65
  after colon, 839
  in APA style, 711

Cartoons, MLA style for, 693

Case studies
  in education courses, 468
  in nursing courses, 466

Categories, classifying into, 435

Causal chain, 135, 135 (fig.), 136 (fig.)

Cause and effect, 125–44
  common transitions for, 418
  developing essay with, 439–40
  in essay exam questions, 327
  generating ideas for, 134–36
  planning, drafting, developing of, 137–38
  reviewing and reflecting on, 141
  revising and editing of, 138–41
  table for, 136, 136 (fig.)
  in taking stand, 157

*cc*, 349, 350

*center around*, Q-52

"Charlie Living with Autism" (Kintner), 302–4 (fig.)

Charts, adding to academic papers, Q-10

*Chicago Manual of Style,* 468, 469

Choi, Andrew, 375, 376 (fig.)

Choi, Yun Yung, 130–32, 137, 138–39

Chopin, Kate, 275–77

Chronological organization, 394

Chronological transitions, 425, 434

Chronology, in writing from recall, 58 (fig.), 58–59, 60

Circular reasoning, 172

*cite/sight/site*, 823, Q-52

Citing sources. *See* Source citation

Claims, 157–59. *See also* Supporting evidence

Claims of evaluation, 157–58

Claims of policy, 158

Claims of substantiation, 158

Class blogs, 310

Class courtesy, 308–9

Classifying, developing essay by, 434–36

Class wiki, 310

Clauses, 746
  joining with coordination, 804–6
  mixed construction and, 798

Clearly stated thesis, 387, 391

Clichés, 818, Q-48

*climactic/climatic*, Q-52

Climactic order, 451

*climatic/climactic*, Q-52

Climax, definition of, 263

Closed portfolio, 474

Close reading, of images, 282

Clustering ideas, 395, 396 (fig.)

CMS. *See* Course management system

Cobb, Michael, 491–93

Coherence, when proposing solution, 190

Collective nouns
  pronoun-antecedent agreement and, 783
  subject-verb agreement and, 772–73

Colons, 839–41
  basics of, 839–41
  for comma splices and fused sentences, 756
  joining clauses with, 804
  outside quotation marks, 847, Q-63

Column graphs, adding to academic papers, Q-11, Q-11 (fig.)

Combination portfolio, 474

Comics, MLA style for, 693

Commas, 828–37
  for absolute phrases, 833
  with academic degrees, 854
  after introductory clause, phrase, word, 828–29, Q-61
  for comma splices and fused sentences, Q-40
  for conjunctive adverbs, 833, Q-61
  for contrasting phrases or clauses, 833
  between coordinate adjectives, 830
  between cumulative adjectives, 830
  for dates, states, countries, addresses, 835
  for direct address of person, 835
  for direct quotations, 834–35
  editing, Q-60–61
  inside quotation marks, 847, Q-63
  for interjections, 835
  between items in series, 829–30, 836, Q-61
  joining clauses with, 804, 828, Q-61
  misuses of, 836–37
  for nonrestrictive appositives, 832, Q-61
  for nonrestrictive phrases or clauses, 831–32, Q-61
  for parenthetical expressions, 833, Q-61

for tag questions, 835
  for *yes* and *no*, 835

Comma splices, 755–57, Q-39–40

Comments, inserting into online writing, 319

Common knowledge, need for documenting, 680

Commonly confused words, 823–24, 865, Q-50–60

Common nouns, 730–31

Companions (books), 629

Comparatives, 787–88
  irregular, list of, Q-46

*compare/contrast*, Q-52

Comparing. *See also* Comparing and contrasting
  common transitions for, 418
  incomplete sentences and, 795
  parallel structure and, 802

Comparing and contrasting, 105–24. *See also* Comparing; Contrasting
  in essay exam questions, 327
  generating ideas for, 113–15
  planning, drafting, developing of, 115–18
  reviewing and reflecting on, 121
  revising and editing of, 118–19
  as strategy for developing, 436–38
  table for, 115 (fig.), 115–16
  in taking stand, 157
  when evaluating and reviewing, 204–5, 207

*complement/compliment*, 823, Q-53

Complements, 743–44, 749

Complete subjects, 740

Complex sentences, 750

Composition of images, visual analysis and, 284 (fig.), 288 (fig.), 288–89

Compound adjectives, hyphens for, 863

Compound-complex sentences, 750

Compound nouns, showing possession and, 842

Compound sentences, 750

Compound subjects
  comma with, 836
  pronoun-antecedent agreement and, 782, Q-44
  sentence patterns and, 749
  showing possession and, 842
  subject-verb agreement and, 772

Compound verbs, 749, 754, 836

Compound words, hyphens for, 863

Comprehending, as reading skill, 24–25, 25 (fig.)

Computer file management, for online writing, 317–21

Conceding, common transitions for, 418

Conciseness, 450–55, 822, Q-49

Conclusions
drafting, 413–15, 676–77
for literary analysis, 270–72
for visual analysis, 301

Concrete examples, 423

Condescending words, avoiding, 820–21

Conditional sentences, 770

Conflict, definition of, 262–63

Confused words, commonly, 823–24, 865, Q-50–60

Conjunctions, 736–39, 808. *See also* Coordinating conjunctions; Subordinating conjunctions

Conjunctive adverbs
commas for, 833, Q-61
for comma splices and fused sentences, 757
joining clauses with, 804
list of common, 805
semicolon and, 838

Connections, adding when drafting, 417–20

Connotation of words, 818, Q-49

Containers, MLA style and, 687

Contractions
apostrophes for, 843, Q-62
in formal versus informal language, 814–15

Contrasting, 106. *See also* Comparing and contrasting
common transitions for, 418

Contrasting phrases and clauses, commas for, 833

Coordinate adjectives, comma between, 830

Coordinating conjunctions, 738
for comma splices and fused sentences, 756, Q-40
for compound sentences, 750
coordinate adjectives and, 830
items in series and, 830
joining clauses with, 804, 828, Q-61
mixed construction and, 798, 799
parallel structure and, 801–2
semicolon and, 838
subject or verb joined with, 836
in titles, capitalization of, 858
versus prepositions, 808

Coordination, 804–6

Copeland, Libby, 541–44

Copyrighted sources, asking permission to use, Q-8, Q-10

Corporations, abbreviations for, 855

Correlative conjunctions
parallel structure and, 802, Q-47
subject or verb joined with, comma and, 836

Corresponding, for field research, 632–33

*could care less*, Q-53

*could have*, 770

*could of*, Q-53

Council of Science Editors (CSE) style, for science courses, 465

Counterarguments, supporting evidence and, 163–64

Count nouns/articles, 731

Countries
abbreviations for, 855
commas for, 835

*couple of*, Q-53

Course management system
common interactive options of, 309
definition of, 307
tracking of class participation by, 333

Courses, college
capitalization of, 857, Q-65
future, writing in, 459–77
home page for, MLA style for, 693
portfolio for, 473

Courtesy in class, 308–9

Cover letter, for portfolio, 476–77

Cowley, Malcolm, 414

Credibility of sources, 636, 637–39, Q-24–25

Crediting sources. *See* Source citation; Source documentation

*criteria/criterion*, Q-53

Criteria for evaluating and reviewing, 197, 203–4, 207

Critical essays, in history courses, 469

Critical reading, 16–22
while note taking, 656

Critical thinking, 6–7, 35–43

CSE style, for science courses, 465

Cues, adding when drafting, 417–20

Cultural attitudes in images, 288 (fig.), 289 (fig.), 293–95, 294 (fig.)

Cumulative adjectives
comma between, 830
order of, 786

Cumulative sentences, 810

Cutting, when revising, 451–52

*-d*, for past tense, 760–62, Q-40

Dailey, Kate, 522–25

Dangling modifiers, 792, 793–94, Q-46–47

Dashes, correct use of, 847, 848–49

*data*, Q-53

Database articles. *See also* Journal articles
APA style for, 713, Q-36
MLA style for, 690, Q-34
searching for through library, 625–28

Dates, 835, 854, 859–60
adding to file names, 320
library search by, 623

Dates of access
APA style for, 711
MLA style for, 688

Days of week, 854, 857, Q-65

Decimals, correct format for, 859–60

Deductive pattern of organization, 165–66, 166 (fig.)

Deductive reasoning, developing essay with, 428–30

Defining
developing essay by, 426–28
when evaluating and reviewing, 205

Definite articles, understanding, 732

Definition essay exam questions, 328

Definitions, errors in stating, 800

Deities, capitalization of, 857, Q-65

Demonstration essay exam questions, 328

Demonstrative pronouns, 731, 735

Denotation of words, 818, Q-49

Denotative characteristics of images, 285

Deresiewicz, William, 575–78

*desert/dessert*, 823

Design of images, visual analysis and, 284 (fig.), 287, 288 (fig.)

Details, adding
developing essay by, 424–26
when writing from observation, 66, 73–74, 76, 79
when writing from recall, 59, 60

Determiners, count nouns and, 731

Developing, 421–41
case study of, 359–63, 360 (fig.)
comparing and contrasting for, 436–38
defining for, 426–28
dividing and classifying for, 434–36
giving examples for, 422–24
identifying cause and effect for, 439–40
inductive and deductive reasoning for, 428–30
introduction to, 8–10, 9 (fig.)
for literary analysis, 268–72
of oral presentations, 334

process analysis for, 432–34
providing details for, 424–26
subject analysis for, 430–32
of visual analysis, 300–301
when comparing and contrasting, 115–18
when evaluating and reviewing, 206–7
when explaining cause and effect, 137–38
when proposing solution, 187–89
when supporting position with sources, 226–37
when taking stand, 164–66
when writing from interviews, 98–100
when writing from observation, 76–77
when writing from recall, 57–59
Dewey decimal cataloging system, 625
Diagrams, adding to academic papers, Q-10, Q-10 (fig.)
Dialogic notebook, 642
Dialogue, quotation marks for, 846
Dictionaries, 629, 865
Differences, comparing and contrasting and, 106, 112
*different from/different than*, Q-53
Digital object identifiers. *See* DOIs (digital object identifiers)
Direction, marking, common transitions for, 418
Directive, period at end of, 826–27
Directive process analysis, 433
Direct objects
action verbs and, 742
faulty predication and, 799–800
*lie* and *lay* and, 767
objective pronoun case for, 777
sentence structure and, 748–49
Direct questions. *See* Questions
Direct quotations. *See also* Quotations
avoiding overuse of, 229
brackets for changes in, 851
commas for, 834–35
quotation marks for, 844–47
*[sic]* for errors in, 851
versus indirect, 845
Direct sources, example of, 230 (fig.). *See also* Sources
Disabled, bias towards, avoiding, 820
Discussion essay exam questions, 328
Distractions, reducing, 381
Divide or classify essay exam questions, 328
Dividing, developing essay by, 434–36

*do*, forms of
simple present tense and, 760
simple tenses and, 762
using correctly, 766–67
Doctoral dissertations
APA style for, 715
MLA style for, 692
*Doctor/Dr.*, 853–54
Documenting sources. *See* Source documentation
Documents
government. *See* Government documents and resources
historical, capitalizing title of, 857, Q-65
Document templates, Q-12–13
*doesn't/don't*, Q-53
DOIs (digital object identifiers)
APA style for, 711
MLA style for, 688
*don't/doesn't*, Q-53
Doodling, to generate ideas, 56, 374 (fig.), 374–75
Double quotation marks. *See* Quotation marks
Double vowels, hyphen and, 864
Drafting, 404–20
adding cues and connections while, 417–20
case study of, 359–63, 360 (fig.)
of conclusion, 413–15
enjoyable start for, 404–5
of essay exam answer, 330–31
of introduction, 410–13
introduction to, 8–10, 9 (fig.)
for literary analysis, 268–72
of paragraphs, 405–6
of research paper, 676–77
restarting, 405
of topic sentences, 406 (fig.), 406–10
of visual analysis, 300–301
when comparing and contrasting, 115–18
when evaluating and reviewing, 206–7
when explaining cause and effect, 137–38
when proposing solution, 187–89
when supporting position with sources, 226–37
when taking stand, 164–66
when writing from interviews, 98–100
when writing from observation, 76–77
when writing from recall, 57–59

*Dr./Doctor*, 853–54
Dubious authority, argument from, 172
*due to*, Q-53

E-books
APA style for, 714–15
MLA style for, 691–92
searching collections of, 616
Economic attitudes in images, 288 (fig.), 289 (fig.), 293–95, 294 (fig.)
*-ed*, for past tense, 760–62, Q-40
Edited works
APA style for, 712
MLA style for, 691–92
Editing, 455 (fig.), 455–58, 456 (fig.)
case study of, 363–67
of cause and effect, 138–41
introduction to, 10 (fig.), 10–11
of literary analysis, 272
of online writing, 319
of research paper, 677–79
of visual analysis, 301
when comparing and contrasting, 118–19
when evaluating and reviewing, 207–9
when proposing solution, 189–93
when supporting position with sources, 237–44
when taking stand, 166–72
when writing from interviews, 100–102
when writing from observation, 78–80
when writing from recall, 59–61
Editing guide, Q-37–65
for grammar problems, Q-38–46
for mechanics problems, Q-64–65
for punctuation problems, Q-60–63
for effective sentences, Q-46–48
for word choice, Q-48–60
Education courses, writing in, 468–69
Effect, 126. *See also* Cause and effect
*effect/affect*, 823, Q-50
*either*, Q-53
*either/or*, 802
Either/or reasoning, 172
E-journal writing, to generate ideas, 380
Electronic books. *See* E-books
Electronic database articles. *See* Database articles
Electronic job application forms, Q-17

Electronic portfolios, keeping, 473–77
Elements in images, visual analysis
    and, 284 (fig.), 287
*elicit/illicit*, 823
Ellin, Abby, 522–25
Ellipsis mark, 232, 849, 851
    avoiding plagiarism with, 658
    editing, Q-63
    MLA style and, 686
Elliptical constructions, 796–97
E-mails
    APA style for, 709, 716
    to instructors, 311–12
    interviews through, 98
    MLA style for, 694–95
    in workplace, 341
Emotional appeals. *See* Pathos
Emphasis
    common transitions for, 418
    dashes for, 848
    italics for, 861
    revising for, 450–55
    with software tools, 393–94
Employment interviews, follow-up
    letter after, Q-17
*Enc./Enclosure*, 349
Endings. *See* Conclusions
Envelope formats, for business letters,
    349 (fig.), 350
Eriksson, Olof, 23–24
Erion, Elizabeth, 201–2
Error log, 729
*-es*
    simple present tense and, 759
    subject-verb agreement and,
    Q-42
Essay exams, 325–31
Essays and essay collections
    APA style for, 707
    MLA style for, 684, Q-33
*et al.*
    APA style and, 707, 712
    MLA style and, 684, 688
Ethical appeals. *See* Ethos
Ethics
    in online classes, 309–10
    in research, 662–63
Ethnic bias, avoiding, 820–21
Ethos
    in images, 300
    when taking stand, 166, 167
Euphemisms, 817, Q-48
Evaluating and reviewing, 196–213
    generating ideas for, 204–5
    planning, drafting, developing of,
    206–7

reviewing and reflecting on, 210
revising and editing of, 207–9
Evaluation
    claims of, 157–58
    of college assignments, 38
    as critical thinking skill, 35–36
    in essay exam questions, 329
    as reading skill, 24–26, 25 (fig.)
    of sources. *See* Source evaluation
*everybody/every body*, Q-54
*everyone/every one*, Q-54
*ex-*, hyphen with, 864
Examples
    common transitions for, 418
    developing essay with, 422–24
    too few, or proof by, 172
*except/accept*, 823, Q-50
Exclamation points
    correct use of, 827
    quotation marks and, 847
*expect*, Q-54
Experiences, recalling. *See* Recall,
    writing from
Experts
    choosing research topics
        through, 607
    interviewing for field research, 630
Expert testimony, as supporting
    evidence, 161
Explanations, dashes for, 848
Explicit thesis, 384–85
Extended definition, 205
External conflict, definition of, 263
Eye movements, while reading
    online, 32
Eyre, Alea, 71–72, 77

Facts, as supporting evidence, 159–60
*fact that*, Q-54
"Family Dynamic, The" (Marchand),
    219–21
Family relationships, capitalization of,
    856, Q-65
FANBOYS, 738
*farther/further*, Q-54
Faulty predication, 798–800
Feelings generated by images, visual
    analysis and, 284 (fig.), 292–93,
    293 (fig.)
Feminine pronouns
    avoiding gender bias and, 819–21
    pronoun-antecedent agreement
        and, 783, Q-44–45
*fewer/less*, Q-54
*field of*, Q-54
Field research, 629–34

Figures (charts, graphs, etc.), Q-8
    adding to academic papers,
        Q-10–12
Figures (numbers), correct use of,
    859–60
Figures of speech, definition of, 262
File management, for online writing,
    317–21
File templates, for online writing,
    317–18
Films
    APA style for, 716
    MLA style for, 694
Final portfolio, 474
Finding sources. *See* Sources, finding
"Fire and Ice" (Frost), 796
Firsthand observation, as supporting
    evidence, 161
*firstly*, Q-54
First-person narrator, definition of,
    263
First person pronouns
    basics of, 733–34
    formal versus informal language
        and, 789–90, 815
    pronoun case and, 775–78
    subject-verb agreement and,
        Q-41–43
Flashback, in writing from recall, 58
Focal point of images, 284 (fig.), 285
Follow-up letters, after employment
    interview, Q-17
Font choice, audience consideration
    and, Q-14 (fig.), Q-14–15
*for. See also* Coordinating conjunctions
    as coordinating conjunction, 738
    using with indirect objects, 742–43
Foreign-language words, italics for, 862
Foreshadowing, definition of, 262
Formal language
    appropriate use of, 814–15
    in business courses, 468
    consistency in, 790
    editing for, Q-48
Formal logic, taking stand and,
    154–55
Formal outlines, 400–403
Format guide, Q-1–19
    for academic paper, Q-1–7
    for designing for audience, Q-13–16
    for integrating and crediting
        visuals, Q-7–12
    for preparing document template,
        Q-12–13
    for résumés and application letters,
        Q-16–19

*former/latter*, Q-54
Fractions
    correct format for, 859–60
    spelled-out, hyphen in, 864
Fragments, 752–54, Q-38–39
Free association, 113
Freewriting, to generate ideas, 56,
    372–73
Friedman, Ann, 549–52
Frost, Robert, 279–80, 796
Function of images, visual analysis
    and, 289 (fig.), 289–90
*further/farther*, Q-54
Fused sentences, 755–57, Q-39–40
Future perfect progressive tense,
    basics of, 759, 765
Future perfect tense, basics of, 759,
    761, 764
Future progressive tense, basics of,
    759, 765
Future simple tense, basics of, 759,
    761, 763
Future tenses, *if* clauses and, 770

Garretson, Marjorie Lee, 149–51
Gender
    avoiding bias in, 819–21
    pronoun-antecedent agreement in,
        783, Q-44–45
General databases, 625
General-interest databases, 626
Generalizations, particulars and, 428
Generating ideas, 369 (fig.), 369–82
    asking reporter's questions for,
        377–78
    from assignment, 370–71
    brainstorming for, 371–72
    case study of, 358–59, 359 (fig.)
    for comparing and contrasting,
        113–15
    doodling or sketching for, 374 (fig.),
        374–75
    for essay exams, 326–27
    for evaluating and reviewing, 204–5
    for explaining cause and effect,
        134–36
    freewriting for, 372–73
    getting ready to write and, 381–82
    imagining for, 376–77
    introduction to, 7–8, 8 (fig.)
    keeping journal for, 380–81
    for literary analysis, 265–67
    mapping for, 375–76, 376 (fig.)
    for proposing solution, 185–86
    from reading, 26–28
    seeking motives for, 378–80

for supporting position with
    sources, 223–26, 225 (fig.)
    for taking stand, 153–64
    for visual analysis, 300
    for writing from interviews, 95–98
    for writing from observation, 74–76
    for writing from recall, 55–57
Geographic features, capitalization of,
    857, Q-65
Gerunds
    parallel structure and, 802
    possessive pronoun case and, 778
    pronoun case and, Q-44
*get/got*, Q-54
*good* versus *well*, 785, Q-46, Q-55
Government documents and resources
    APA style for, 708, 715
    at library, 629
    MLA style for, 692
    for various academic fields, 622
    as Web sites, searching on, 616
Grammar, 730–51
    clauses and phrases, 746–48
    parts of speech, 730–39
    sentence structure, 748–51
    subjects, 740–41
    verbs, objects, and complements,
        741–45
Graphs, adding to academic papers,
    Q-10, Q-11 (fig.)
"Grief in the Age of Facebook"
    (Stone), 537–39
Griffin, Jacob, 110–11, 117–18
Grouping ideas, 393–95
"Guys Suffer from Oppressive Gender
    Roles Too" (Zeilinger), 516–18

*hanged/hung*, Q-55
Harjo, Suzan Shown, 146–49
*have*, forms of
    perfect tenses and, 763–64
    in present and past tenses, list of,
        Q-42
    simple present tense and, 760
    using correct forms of, 766–67
*have got to*, Q-55
*he. See also* Third person pronouns
    formal versus informal language
        and, 789–90
    gender bias and, Q-55
    pronoun case and, 775–78
    subject-verb agreement and,
        Q-42
Headings
    adding to academic papers, Q-16
    on résumés, 342, 343 (fig.)

Helping verbs, 736, 741, 744
    sentence structure and, 748
*he or she*, Q-55
*her/hers*, 777
*here*, subject-verb agreement and, 774
*herself*, Q-55
"Hidden Truth: An Analysis of Shirley
    Jackson's 'The Lottery,' The"
    (Burns), 260–61
"High Cost of Manliness, The"
    (Jensen), 512–14
Highlighting, 101, 118
*himself*, Q-55
Homonyms, commonly confused,
    823–24, 865
*hopefully*, Q-55
How?, asking to generate ideas, 56,
    377–78
"How First- and Second-Generation
    Hispanics Can Help Each Other"
    (Vargas), 107–9
"How One Stupid Tweet Blew Up
    Justine Sacco's Life" (Ronson),
    86–91
"How-to" process analysis, 433
"Humility Code, The" (Brooks),
    582–89
"Hunger Games, The" (Tobias),
    198–200
Hyphens, 863–64

*I. See also* First person pronouns
    formal versus informal language
        and, 789–90, 815
    pronoun case and, 775–78
"I" attitude, in workplace writing, 339
Ideas, generating. *See* Generating ideas
Idioms/idiomatic expressions, 818–19
*if* clauses, 770
*if/whether*, Q-55
Ignorance, argument from, 172
*illicit/elicit*, 823
Imagery, definition of, 262
Images. *See* Visuals
Images, analysis of. *See* Visual analysis
Imagining, to generate ideas, 376–77
Imperatives
    as headings, Q-16
    identifying subject in, 741
Imperative verb mood, 769
Implicit thesis, 385
Implied topic sentences, 409
*imply/infer*, Q-55
*in*
    using correctly, 737–38
    versus *into*, Q-55

Inclusive numbers, hyphen in, 864
Incomplete sentences, 794–98
Indefinite articles, understanding, 733
Indefinite pronouns
    avoiding gender bias in, 820
    list of, 734
    pronoun-antecedent agreement
        and, 783, Q-44–45
    showing possession and, 843
    singular and plural, list of, Q-45
    subject-verb agreement and, 773,
        Q-42
Indefinite quantity words, count
    nouns and, 731
Indentation of long quotations
    in APA style, 710, 845–46
    in MLA style, 686, 845–46
Independent clauses, 746
Indicative verb mood, 769
Indirect objects
    action verbs and, 742–43
    objective pronoun case for, 777
    sentence structure and, 748–49
Indirect question, period at end of,
    826–27
Indirect quotations, 231
    commas for, 837
    versus direct, 845
Indirect sources. See also Sources
    APA style for, 708
    example of, 230 (fig.)
    MLA style for, 685
Inductive pattern of organization,
    165–66, 166 (fig.)
Inductive reasoning, developing essay
    with, 428–30
Inferences, inductive reasoning and,
    428
infer/imply, Q-55
Infinitives
    irregular verbs and, Q-41
    objective pronoun case for, 777
    parallel structure and, 802
    subjunctive mood and, 770
    verbals and, 747
    as verb form, 759
Informal language
    appropriate use of, 815
    in business courses, 468
    editing, Q-48
Informal outlines, 397–99
Informal reasoning, 155–56,
    156 (fig.)
-ing phrases, as headings, Q-16
-ing verb form. See Gerunds; Present
    participles

in regards to, Q-55
Inserting comments into online
    writing, 319
Inside address, on business letters,
    347–48, 348 (fig.)
inside of/outside of, Q-55
Instructors
    decoding written comments from,
        448–49
    meeting with for revising, 448
    online messages written to,
        311–13
    underlying assumptions of, 462
Intensive pronouns, 735
Intentional plagiarism, definition of,
    663. See also Plagiarism
Interjections, 739, 827, 835
Interlibrary loan, 619, 623
Internal conflict, definition of, 263
Internet database locators, searching
    on, 616
Internet sources. See also Sources; Web
    entries
    evaluating, 639–41, 640 (fig.),
        641 (fig.)
    searching for, 615–19
    for various academic fields, 622
"Internship Program Falls Short"
    (Erion), 201–2
Interrogative pronouns, 734
Interview, writing from, 84–104. See
    also Interviews
    examples of, 86–94
    generating ideas for, 95–98
    planning, drafting, developing of,
        98–100
    reviewing and reflecting on, 102
    revising and editing of, 100–102
Interviews. See also Interview, writing
    from
    APA style for, 709, 716
    employment, follow-up letter after,
        Q-17
    for field research, 630
    MLA style for, 694–95
"In the Name of Love" (Tokumitsu),
    590–95
into/in, Q-55
Introduction
    APA style for, 714
    for cause and effect, 138
    drafting, 410–13, 676–77
    for literary analysis, 269
    MLA style for, 692
    for portfolio, 476–77
    of visual analysis, 301

Introductory clause, phrase, word,
    comma after, 828–29, Q-61
Inverted sentences, 810
"Invisible Women" (Choi), 130–32,
    137, 138–39
Ironic dialogue, definition of, 262
Ironic point of view, definition of, 262
Ironic situation, definition of, 262
Irony, 262, 846
irregardless, Q-55
Irregular adjectives and adverbs,
    comparative and superlative
    forms of, 787–88
Irregular verbs
    past tense of, 760–61, 763, Q-41
    subject-verb agreement and, Q-42
is because, 800, Q-58
"Is Facebook Making Us Sad?"
    (Copeland), 541–44
Issues, taking stand on. See Taking stand
is when/is where, 800, Q-56
it. See also Third person pronouns
    clear antecedent for, 780
    formal versus informal language
        and, 789–90
    pronoun case and, 775–78
    as subject, omitting, 799
    subject-verb agreement and, Q-42
Italics
    correct use of, 861–62
    for titles, in APA style, 711
    for titles, in MLA style, 688
Items in series
    colon for introducing, 840
    comma between, 829–30, 836, Q-61
    dashes for, 848
    parallel structure and, 801–2, Q-47
    parentheses around letters or
        numbers before, 850
    semicolon for, 838
its/it's, 777, 843, Q-56
it's me/it is I, Q-56
"It's Not Just a Bike" (Taylor), 181–82
"It's Time to Stop Blaming Pov-
    erty on the Decline in Marriage"
    (Badger), 127–29
"I Want a Wife" (Brady), 505–7

Jackson, Ella, 643–44
Jackson, Shirley, 252–58
Jargon, 815–16, Q-48
Jarvie, Jenny, 553–57
Jensen, Robert, 512–14
Journal articles. See also Journals,
    scholarly
    APA style for, 712–13, Q-35, Q-36

evaluating, 636, 638
MLA style for, 689, Q-33, Q-34
recording source information for,
654–55
Journals, personal
for capturing ideas, 382
to generate ideas, 380–81
reading, keeping, 22
Journals, scholarly. *See also* Journal
articles
science courses and, 464–65
title of, italics for, 862
Julseth, Alley, 28–29
*just as/so*, 802

"Karate Kid vs. Kung Fu Panda:
A Race to the Olympics" (Griffin),
110–11
Keyword search
advanced, 617, 618 (fig.)
of library catalog, 623
of library databases, 626
*kind of/sort of/type of*, Q-56
King, Stephen, 534–36
Kintner, Shannon, 302–4 (fig.)
Knowing, as reading skill, 24–25, 25 (fig.)
Knowledge transfer, 459–60

Ladder of abstraction, 423, 424
Language in images, visual analysis
and, 288 (fig.), 289 (fig.), 295
(fig.), 295–96
Language level
choosing, 814–15
consistency in, 790
editing for, Q-48–49
"Last Rites for Indian Dead" (Harjo),
146–49
Latin abbreviations, 854–55
*latter/former*, Q-54
Launching sources. *See* Source
launching
*lay/lie*, 767–68, Q-56
*lead/led*, 824
Learning management system, 307
common interactive options of, 309
for messages to instructors, 311
tracking of class participation by,
333
Learning portfolio, 474
Lectures, MLA style for, 694–95
*led/lead*, 824
*less/fewer*, Q-54
Letters
APA style for, 709
business, writing, 347–50

MLA style for, 694–95
reflective portfolio, 368
Letters as words (*a, b, c,* etc.)
italics for, 862
plural of, apostrophes for, 843
*liable/likely*, Q-56
Library, 619–29
beginning research at, 614
choosing research topics
through, 607
searching databases through,
625–28
using library catalog of, 623–25,
624 (fig.), 625 (fig.)
using specialized resources through,
628–29
Library catalog, using, 623–25, 624
(fig.). 625 (fig.)
Library database articles. *See* Database
articles
Lidington, Jenny, 717–25
*lie/lay*, 767–68, Q-56
*like/as*, Q-51
*likely/liable*, Q-56
Limited omniscient point of view,
definition of, 263
Limited thesis, 389, 391
Limited topic sentences, 407
Line graphs, adding to academic
papers, Q-10, Q-11 (fig.)
Linking, to group ideas, 394, 395 (fig.)
Linking verbs, 735, 741, 743–44
faulty predication and, 800
*good* and, 785
quotation introduced with, comma
and, 835
sentence structure and, 748–49
subject-verb agreement and, 774
*literally*, Q-56
Literary analysis, 250–80
challenge of, 264–65
example of, 260–61
generating ideas for, 265–67
planning, drafting, developing of,
268–72
preparing to write, 259
reviewing and reflecting on, 278–79
revising and editing of, 272
terms used in, 262–63
using strategies for, 250–51
writing paraphrase for, 277–78
writing synopsis for, 273–77
LMS. *See* Learning management
system
Location prepositions, using *in, on,
at* as, 737

Logging reading, to generate ideas, 27
Logical appeals. *See* Logos
Logical fallacies, recognizing,
171–72
Logical organization, 394
Logos, 166, 167, 300
Logs, science courses and, 464–65
"Looking Backwards, Moving
Forward" (Ryan-Hines), 91–93
*loose/lose*, Q-56
*lots/lots of/a lot of*, Q-56
"Lottery, The" (Jackson), 252–58
*-ly*
adverb ending in, hyphens and, 863
forming adverbs with, 736, Q-45
forming comparatives and
superlatives and, 787

Macro revising, 442–43, 443 (fig.). *See
also* Revising
Magazine articles
APA style for, 713, Q-35
MLA style for, 690, Q-33
recording source information for,
648–49
Magazines, title of, italics for, 862
Main clauses, 746
comma splices and fused sentences
and, 755–57, Q-39–40
dangling modifiers and, 793–94
joining with colon, 839–40
joining with comma and coordinating
conjunction, 828, Q-61
joining with semicolon, 838
in longer sentences, 750
sentence structure and, 749
subordination and, 807–9
Main idea. *See* Thesis
*man*, avoiding terms with, 819–20
*mankind*, Q-56
Mapping
case study of, 358–59, 359 (fig.)
to generate ideas, 56, 375–76, 376
(fig.)
Maps, adding to academic papers,
Q-11, Q-12 (fig.)
Marchand, Abigail, 219–21
Marketing materials, in business
courses, 468
"Marriage Imperative, The" (Cobb),
491–93
Masculine pronouns
avoiding gender bias and,
819–21
pronoun-antecedent agreement
and, 783, Q-44–45

May, Cindi, 508–11
*may/can*, Q-52
Measurements, abbreviations for, 854
Mechanics, 853–65
    abbreviations, 853–55
    capitalization, 856–58
    hyphens, 863–64
    italics, 861–62
    numbers, 859–60
    spelling, 865
*media/medium*, Q-57
"Meet Me in the Middle: The Student, the State, and the School" (Rardon), 695–703
Memory, writing from. *See* Recall, writing from
Memos
    APA style for, 709
    in workplace, 350, 351 (fig.)
Messages, online, written to instructors, 311–13
Metacognition, self-reflection and, 38
Metaphor, definition of, 262
Micro revising, 443, 443 (fig.), 450–55. *See also* Revising
Midterm portfolio, 474
*might*, 770
*might have*, 770
*might of*, Q-57
*mine/my*, 777
Misplaced modifiers, 792–93, Q-46–47
Misspelled words, 865, Q-64
Mixed constructions, 798–800
MLA style, 680–703
    for art, drama, music reviews, 467
    citing sources in, 235–36, 680, 682–87, Q-31–34
    examples of quoting, paraphrasing, and summarizing in, 657
    font choice and, Q-15
    headings in, Q-16
    for indenting long quotations, 846
    listing sources in, 680, 683, 687–95, Q-31–34. *See also* Works Cited
    for lists within text, Q-15
    paper format in, Q-2–3
    preparing tables in, Q-8–10
    research paper in, example of, 695–703
    source navigator for, 649, 651, 653, 655
    using file templates for, 317–18

Mnemonics, for spelling, 865
Modern Language Association style. *See* MLA style
Modified block style for business letters, 348 (fig.), 350
Modified portfolio, 474
Modifiers
    adjectives and adverbs as, Q-45–46
    commas for, 831–32, 837, Q-61
    misplaced and dangling, 792–94, Q-46–47
Mood of images, visual analysis and, 284 (fig.), 292–93, 293 (fig.)
Mood of story, definition of, 263
"More Pros Than Cons in a Meat-Free Life" (Garretson), 149–51
"More Room" (Ortiz Cofer), 483–86
*most*, 787, 788, Q-57
"Mother Tongue" (Tan), 564–68
Motives, seeking, to generate ideas, 378–80
*Mr.*, as abbreviation, 853–54
"Mr. Hertli" (Schmitt), 365–67
Multilingual writer guidelines
    for avoiding faulty predication, 799
    for avoiding mixed constructions, 799
    for avoiding subject errors, 799
    for conditional sentences, 770
    for count and noncount nouns and articles, 731–32
    for definite and indefinite articles, 732–33
    for direct versus indirect quotations, 845
    for forming negatives, 762
    for order of cumulative adjectives, 786
    for prepositions versus conjunctions, 808
    for two-word verbs, 738
    for using *in*, *on*, *at*, 737–38
    for using past, present, and future verb tenses, 761
    for using relative pronouns, 779–80
    for using *to* and *for* with indirect objects, 742–43
Multimodal online texts, strategies for, 32–33
Multivolume works
    APA style for, 714
    MLA style for, 685, 691
Musical works, title of, italics for, 862
*must of*, Q-57
*my/mine*, 777
*myself*, Q-57

Naham, Khalia, 41–42
Names, capitalization of, 856, Q-65
Naming files, for online writing, 318–19
Narration, writing from recall as, 58
Narrator, definition of, 263
Narrowing topic, for research project, 606–7
*n.d.* (no date), in APA style, 708
Negation, definitions and, 428
Negatives, forming, 762
Negative thesis, 389
*neither/nor*, 802
"New Literacy, The" (Thompson), 547–48
Newsletter articles, APA style for, 713
Newspaper articles
    APA style for, 713
    MLA style for, 690
Ning, class, 310
*no*, commas around, 835
Noncount nouns/articles, 731–32
Nonrestrictive appositives, commas for, 832, Q-61
Nonrestrictive modifiers, commas for, 831, 832, Q-61
Non sequitur, 171
*nor*. *See also* Coordinating conjunctions
    antecedents joined by, pronoun-antecedent agreement and, 783
    as coordinating conjunction, 738
    subjects joined by, subject-verb agreement and, 772
*not*
    in advanced searches, 626, 627 (fig.)
    versus *but*, 802
*not all that*, Q-57
Notebooks, for capturing ideas, 382
Note taking
    to capture information from sources, 647, 656–59
    while observing scenes, 75–76
*not only/but also*, 802
Noun phrases, as headings, Q-16
Nouns, basics of, 730–32
Novels
    generating ideas for analysis of, 265–66
    MLA style for, 686, Q-31
Number
    pronoun-antecedent agreement in, 782–83, Q-44–45
    subject-verb agreement in, 771–75, Q-41–43

*number/amount*, Q-51
Numbers, 859–60
    abbreviations used with, 854
    count nouns and, 731
    inclusive, hyphen in, 864
    spelled-out, hyphen in, 864
    as words, italics for, 862
    as words, plural of, apostrophes and, 843
Nursing courses, writing in, 466–67

Object complements, 744
    adjectives as, 785
    sentence structure and, 749
Objective note taking, 75–76
Objective point of view, definition of, 263
Objective pronoun case, 775, 777
    editing for, Q-43–44
    personal pronouns in, 733–34
Object of preposition, 736, 777
Objects. *See also* Direct objects; Indirect objects
    action verbs and, 742–43
    comma separating verb from, 836
    sentence structure and, 748–49
Objects in images, visual analysis and, 284 (fig.), 286
Observation, writing from, 65–84
    field research and, 630–31
    generating ideas for, 74–76
    planning, drafting, developing of, 76–77
    reviewing and reflecting on, 80–81
    revising and editing of, 77–80
    supporting evidence and, 161
Observation sheet for note taking, 75–76
Observing scene, writing from. *See* Observation, writing from
*O.K./o.k./okay*, Q-57
Omniscient point of view, definition of, 263
*on*, using correctly, 737–38
*one*, Q-57
Online assessment by instructors, 333–34
Online courses, writing for. *See* Online writing
Online events, for field research, 634
Online interviews, 630
Online materials, strategies for reading, 32–33
Online postings, MLA style for, 694–95
Online profiles, for class, 313–14

Online sources. *See* Internet sources; Web *entries*
Online writing, 307–23
    common situations for, 311–17
    file management for, 317–21
    getting started in, 308–11
    reviewing and reflecting on, 321–22
Open-book essay exams, 325
Open-ended questions, on questionnaires, 632
Open portfolio, 474
Opposing pattern of comparing and contrasting, 437
Opposing pattern of organization, 117
Opposing viewpoints, counterarguments and, 163–64
*or. See also* Coordinating conjunctions
    in advanced searches, 626, 627 (fig.)
    with *and*, Q-51
    antecedents joined by, pronoun-antecedent agreement and, 783
    as coordinating conjunction, 738
    subject joined by, subject-verb agreement and, 772
Oral presentations, 334–36
Organization, 393–403
    for cause and effect, 137–38
    for evaluating and reviewing, 207
    grouping ideas for, 393–95
    outlining for, 395–403
    of research paper, 675
    using thesis for, 392
    when comparing and contrasting, 116–18
    when proposing solution, 190
    when supporting position with sources, 236–37
    when taking stand, 165–66
    when writing from observation, 77 (fig.) 78
Organization authors
    APA style for, 707, 712
    MLA style for, 684, 689
Organizations, abbreviations for, 855
Organizing files, for online writing, 318–19
Ortiz Cofer, Judith, 384–85, 483–86
*our/ours*, 777
*ourselves*, Q-57
Outlining, 395–403
    as assignment, 605
    in essay exam answer, 326–27
    for proposing solution, 187
    in reverse, 677
    while revising, 445–46

*outside of/inside of*, Q-55
Oversimplification, 171
Ownership, possessive pronoun case for, 777

Pamphlets, APA style for, 715
Papers. *See* Academic papers
Paragraphs, 405–6
    adding cues and connections to, 417–20
    drafting conclusion and, 413–15
    drafting introduction and, 410–13
    using topic sentences in, 406 (fig.), 406–10
Parallelism. *See* Parallel structure
Parallel structure, 801–3
    in comparisons, 795
    editing for, Q-47–48
"Paraphrase from 'The Lottery,' A" (Burns), 277
Paraphrasing, 231, 656
    APA style for, 709
    avoiding plagiarism while, 663–66
    checklist for, Q-29
    to generate ideas, 27
    of literary work, 277–78
    method for, 232–34, 235
    MLA style for, 657, 685–86
    while note taking, 658
Parentheses, correct use of, 849–50
Parenthetical expressions
    commas for, 833, Q-61
    dashes for, 848
Participles, fragments with, 754. *See also* Past participles; Present participles
Particulars, generalizations and, 428
Parts of speech, 730–39
Passive voice, 811–12
    consistency in, 789
    in science writing, 464
Past participles
    forms of *be, have, do* in, 766–67
    of irregular verbs, 760–61, 763, Q-41
    perfect tenses and, 763–64
    of regular verbs, 763
    verbals and, 747
    as verb form, 759
Past perfect progressive tense, basics of, 759, 765
Past perfect tense, 759, 761, 764
    *if* clauses and, 770
    subjunctive mood and, 769
Past progressive tense, basics of, 759, 764–65

Past simple tense, basics of, 759, 760–62
Past tenses
    editing, Q-40–41
    forms of *be* in, 766–67, Q-42
    forms of *do* in, 766–67
    forms of *have* in, 766–67, Q-42
    *if* clauses and, 770
    of irregular verbs, 760–61, 763
    of regular verbs, 760, 763
    as verb form, 759
Pathos, 166, 167, 300
Peer editor, revising with, 446–48
Peer review
    of cause and effect, 139–40
    of comparing and contrasting, 118
    of evaluating and reviewing, 208–9
    of literary analysis, 270
    of observing scene, 79
    of proposing solution, 191
    of recalling experience, 60
    of research paper, 678–79
    self-reflection and, 40
    of subject interview, 97, 100
    of taking stand, 168
    when supporting position with sources, 243
Peer-reviewed sources
    as best sources, Q-24
    finding, 614, 621
Percentages, correct format for, 859–60
*percent/per cent/percentage*, Q-57
Perfect progressive tenses, basics of, 759, 765
Perfect tenses, basics of, 759, 761, 763–64. *See also* Past perfect tense
Performances MLA style for, 694
Periodical articles. *See also* Journal articles; Magazine articles; Newspaper articles
    APA style for, 712–14
    capitalizing title of, 857–58, Q-65
    MLA style for, 689–90
    selecting from database, 627–28
Periodic sentences, 810
Periods
    for comma splices and fused sentences, Q-40
    correct use of, 826–27
    inside quotation marks, 847, Q-63
    for questions in indirect quotations, 845
Person
    pronoun-antecedent agreement in, 782–83, Q-44–45

pronoun consistency in, 789–90
    subject-verb agreement in, 771–75, Q-41–43
Personal pronoun case, 775–78, Q-43–44
Personal pronouns. *See also* Pronouns
    basics of, 733–34
    possessive, list of, Q-62
    pronoun case and, 775–78
    showing possession and, 843
Personification, definition of, 262
*phenomenon/phenomena*, Q-57
Photographing, during field research, 631
Photographs, MLA style for, 693
Phrasal verbs, 738
Phrases, 746–48
    colon at end of, 840–41
    coordinating conjunction with, comma for, 828
    fragments as, correcting, 753
    mixed construction and, 798
    as words, italics for, 862
Place, marking, common transitions for, 418
Places, capitalization of, 857, Q-65
Plagiarism, 662–63
    avoiding, 664, Q-28
    examples of, 668
    note taking and, 663–69
    in online classes, 309–10
Planning, 383 (fig.), 383–403
    case study of, 359–63, 360 (fig.)
    considering purpose and audience when, 383–84
    introduction to, 8–10, 9 (fig.)
    for literary analysis, 268–72
    organizing ideas and, 393–403
    of research paper, 674–75
    stating and using thesis and, 384–93
    of visual analysis, 300–301
    when comparing and contrasting, 115–18
    when evaluating and reviewing, 206–7
    when explaining cause and effect, 137–38
    when proposing solution, 187–89
    when supporting position with sources, 226–37
    when taking stand, 164–66
    when writing from interviews, 98–100
    when writing from observation, 76–77
    when writing from recall, 57–59

Plays
    generating ideas for analysis of, 267
    MLA style for, 686, Q-31
Plot, 262–63, 296
Plural antecedents, pronoun-antecedent agreement and, 782–83, Q-44–45
Plural nouns, showing possession and, 842
Plural subjects, 740
    subject-verb agreement and, 771–75, Q-41–43
*p.m.*, use of, 854
Poems
    capitalizing title of, 857–58, Q-65
    generating ideas for analysis of, 266–67
    MLA style for, 686–87, Q-31, Q-33
    paraphrasing of, 278
Point by point comparing and contrasting
    for evaluating and reviewing, 207
    method for, 437
    as organization method, 117–18
Point of view, definition of, 263
Policy, claims of, 158
Political attitudes in images, 288 (fig.), 289 (fig.), 293–95, 294 (fig.)
Popular sources, evaluating, 636, 638
Portfolios, 468–69
    keeping, 473–77
    reflective letters for, 368
Positive adjectives and adverbs, irregular, list of, Q-46
Positive thesis, 389
Possession
    apostrophes for, 841–43, Q-62
    count nouns and, 731
Possessive personal pronouns
    basics of, 733–34
    list of, Q-62
Possessive pronoun case
    basics of, 775, 777–78
    editing, Q-43–44
    personal pronouns in, 733–34
    to show possession, 843
Poster presentations, in psychology courses, 470
*Post hoc ergo propter hoc*, 171
Postings, blog. *See* Blogs/blog posts
*precede/proceed*, Q-57
Predicates, sentence structure and, 748
Preface
    APA style for, 714
    MLA style for, 692

Prefixes, hyphen and, 864
Preparing to read, 17 (fig.), 17–18
Prepositional phrases, 736, 746
    identifying subject and, 740
    mixed construction and, 798
    subject-verb agreement and, 772
Prepositions
    basics of, 736, 737–38
    in titles, capitalization of, 858
    versus conjunctions, 808
Presentation portfolios, 474
Presentations, oral, 334–36
Presenting under pressure, 334–36
Present participles
    forms of *be, have, do* in, 766–67
    perfect progressive tenses and,
        765
    possessive pronoun case and, 778
    progressive tenses and, 764–65
    verbals and, 747
    as verb form, 759
Present perfect progressive tense,
    basics of, 759, 765
Present perfect tense, basics of, 759,
    761, 764
Present progressive tense, basics of,
    759, 764
Present simple tense, 759–60, 761
Present tenses, 759–60
    forms of *be* in, 766–67, Q-42
    forms of *do* in, 766–67
    forms of *have* in, 766–67, Q-42
    *if* clauses in, 770
    for writing about literature, 789
Primary sources, evaluating, 636,
    637–38. *See also* Sources
*principal/principle*, 824, Q-57
"Problems with Masculinity, The"
    (Eriksson), 23–24
"Problem with Female Superheroes,
    The" (May), 508–11
*proceed/precede*, Q-57
Process analysis, 329, 432–34
Process of writing. *See* Writing
    process
Profiles, online, for class, 313–14
Progressive tenses, basics of, 759,
    764–65
Prominent element of images, 283
    (fig.), 283–84, 284 (fig.)
Pronoun-antecedent agreement
    avoiding gender bias and, 820
    basics of, 782–83
    editing, Q-44–45
Pronoun case, 775–78, Q-43–44
Pronoun reference, 779–81

Pronouns. *See also* Indefinite
    pronouns; Personal pronouns;
    Relative pronouns
    apostrophes and, Q-62
    avoiding gender bias in, 820
    basics of, 733–35
    connecting ideas with, 419
    demonstrative, 731, 735
    intensive, 735
    interrogative, 734
    reflexive, 735
    repeating subject with, 799
    showing possession and, 843
Proof by example, 172
Proofreading
    basics of, 455, 455 (fig.), 456 (fig.),
        457–58
    of essay exam answers, 331
    introduction to, 10, 10 (fig.)
    of timed writings, 332
Proper names, capitalization of, 856,
    Q-65
Proper nouns, 730–31
Proposing solution, 176–95
    generating ideas for, 185–86
    planning, drafting, developing of,
        187–89
    reviewing and reflecting on,
        192–93
    revising and editing of, 189–93
Protagonist, definition of, 262
*proved/proven*, Q-57
Psychology courses
    example of paper written for,
        471–73
    writing in, 469–70
"Public and Private Language"
    (Rodriguez), 558–62
Published interviews, MLA style for,
    694–95
Punctuation, 826–52
    apostrophes, 841–43, Q-66
    brackets, 849, 850–51. *See also*
        Brackets
    colons, 839–41. *See also* Colons
    commas, 828–37. *See also* Commas
    dashes, 847, 848–49
    editing for common problems in,
        Q-60–63
    ellipsis mark, 849, 851. *See also*
        Ellipsis mark
    exclamation points, 827, 847
    parentheses, 849–50
    periods, 826–27. *See also* Periods
    question marks, 827. *See also*
        Question marks

quotation marks, 844–47. *See also*
    Quotation marks
semicolons, 838–39. *See also*
    Semicolons
Purpose
    for acting, Burke's pentad and, 379
    of images, 283
    indicating, common transitions
        for, 418
    for reading, 17–18
    of source, reliability of source and,
        638–39
Purpose for writing, 11–12
    considering when planning,
        383–84
    relevance of sources and, 641–42
    revising for, 443–44
    revisiting for research project, 607
    when comparing and contrasting, 113
    in workplace, 339

*qtd. in*, in source citation, 685
Qualifying, common transitions for,
    418
Question marks
    in advanced searches, 626
    correct use of, 827
    questions in indirect quotations
        and, 845
    quotation marks and, 847
Questionnaires, for field research,
    631–32, 633 (fig.)
Questions
    begging the, 172
    beginning essay with, 412
    as headings, Q-16
    indirect, period at end of, 826–27
    indirect quotation of, 845
    posing controversy or issue as, 154
    preparing, for interviewing, 96
    question marks for. *See* Question
        marks
    tag, commas around, 835
Quotation marks, 844–47
    APA style and, 711
    commas and, 834
    correct use of, 656–58
    editing, Q-62–63
    MLA style and, 688
*quotation/quote*, Q-58
Quotations, 231, 656
    APA style for, 709–10
    avoiding overuse of, 229, 232
    avoiding plagiarism in, 663–66
    blended with paraphrase, 233–34
    brackets for changes in, 851

Quotations (continued)
  capitalization of, 858, Q-65
  capturing while note taking, 656–58
  checklist for, Q-28–29
  colon for introducing, 840
  commas for, 834–35
  ellipses in, 849, 851
  ending essay with, 414
  including while drafting, 676
  indirect, commas for, 837
  from interviews, 95, 100
  long, indented, in APA style, 710
  long, indented, in MLA style, 686,
    845–46
  method for capturing, 232
  MLA style for, 657, 686
  within quotation, 844, Q-63
  quotation marks for, 844–47,
    Q-62–63. See also Quotation
    marks
  [sic] for errors in, 851
quote/quotation, Q-58

Racial bias, avoiding, 820
Radio programs
  APA style for, 716
  MLA style for, 694
Rainbow connections for grouping
    ideas, 393
raise/rise, Q-58
Rank before proper name,
    capitalization of, 856, Q-65
Rardon, Candace, 695–703
rarely ever, Q-58
Re:, on memos, 350
Reading, 16–34
  in college, 6–7
  critically. See Critical reading
  critical thinking and, 16–24
  on literal and analytical levels,
    24–31
  of online and multimodal texts,
    32–33
Reading journal, keeping, 22
real/really, Q-58
Reason for writing. See Purpose for
    writing
Reasoning
  developing essay with, 428–30
  taking stand and, 154–56
reason is because, 800, Q-58
Rebuttals, taking stand and, 156, 156
    (fig.)
Recall, writing from, 46–64
  examples of, 48–54
  generating ideas for, 55–57

planning, drafting, and developing
    of, 57–59
  reviewing and reflecting on, 62
  revising and editing of, 59–61
Recordings
  APA style for, 716
  of interviews, 97–98, 630
  MLA style for, 693
Refereed sources. See Peer-reviewed
    sources
Reference databases, 626
References. See also APA style
  citing sources and, 671
  example of, 725
  format for, Q-6
  guidelines for, 710–17
Reference work articles
  APA style for, 715
  MLA style for, 692
Reference works, for various academic
    fields, 622
Reflecting
  on cause and effect, 141
  on comparing and contrasting, 121
  critical thinking and, 37–41
  on evaluating and reviewing, 210
  on literary analysis, 278–79
  on online writing, 321–22
  on proposing solution, 192–93
  student example of, 41–42
  on supporting position with
    sources, 244–45
  on taking stand, 173
  on visual analysis, 305
  on workplace writing, 354–55
  as writer, 367–68
  on writing and presenting under
    pressure, 336–37
  on writing from interviews, 102
  on writing from observation, 81
  on writing from recall, 62
Reflection-type assignments, in
    education courses, 468
Reflective introduction, for portfolio,
    476–77
Reflective journal writing, 380
Reflective portfolio letters, 368
Reflexive pronouns, 735
Regular verbs
  in past tense, 760, 763, Q-40
  subject-verb agreement and,
    Q-42
Relative pronouns, 734, 808
  reducing use of, 451
  subject-verb agreement and, 774
  subordination and, 807

Relevance of sources, assessing, 636,
    641–42
Reliability of sources, 636, 637–39,
    Q-24–25
Repetition
  to connect ideas, 419, 420
  elliptical construction and, 797
Reporter's questions, asking, to
    generate ideas, 56–57, 377–78
Research ethics, 662–63
Research groups, working with, 606
Research guide, Q-20–36
  for capturing sources, Q-27–30
  for citing sources, Q-28, Q-30–36
  for evaluating sources, Q-25–27,
    Q-26 (fig.)
  for launching sources, Q-27–28,
    Q-30
  for searching for sources,
    Q-24–25
Research projects
  choosing and narrowing topic for,
    606–7
  creating schedule for, 606
  MLA style for, 695–703
  moving from question to working
    thesis for, 608–11
  research proposal for, example of,
    611–13
  stages of, 603
  turning topic into research question
    for, 608
  types of assignments for, 604–6
  writing, 674–79
Research proposal, 604, 611–13
"Research Proposal: The Cost-
    Effectiveness of Head Start"
    (Rivera), 612–13
Research questions
  focusing, 609
  moving to working thesis from,
    608–11
  turning topic into, 608
Responding to reading, 17, 17 (fig.),
    19–22
  student example of, 23–24, 28–29
Responding to visuals. See Visual
    analysis
Response essay exam questions, 329
"Response to Psychology Question"
    (Cohn), 325–26
Responsive journal writing, 380
Restating, common transitions for,
    418
Restrictive appositives, commas and,
    832

Restrictive modifiers, commas and, 831–32, 837
Results, common transitions for, 418
Résumés, 341–45, 343 (fig.), Q-16–19
Reverse outline, 677
Reviewing and evaluating. *See* Evaluating and reviewing
Reviews, 467
    APA style for, 714
    MLA style for, 690
Revised thesis. *See* Thesis
Revising, 442 (fig.), 442–55
    for audience, 444–45
    case study of, 363–67
    of cause and effect, 138–41
    of essay exam answers, 331
    introduction to, 10 (fig.), 10–11
    of literary analysis, 272
    of online writing, 319
    for purpose and thesis, 443–44
    of research paper, 677–79
    for structure and support, 445–46
    of visual analysis, 301
    when comparing and contrasting, 118–19
    when evaluating and reviewing, 207–9
    when proposing solution, 189–93
    when supporting position with sources, 237–44
    when taking stand, 166–72
    when writing from interviews, 100–102
    when writing from observation, 78–80
    when writing from recall, 59–61
    working with instructor for, 448–49
    working with peer editor for, 446–48
"Richard Cory" (Robinson), 280
Rideau, Wilbert, 178–80
"Right to Fail, The" (Zinsser), 571–73
*rise/raise*, Q-58
"Road Not Taken, The" (Frost), 279–80
Robinson, Edwin Arlington, 280
Rodriguez, Richard, 58, 558–62
Ronson, Jon, 86–91
Run-on sentences, 755–57
Ryan-Hines, Lorena A., 91–93

*-s*
    nouns ending in, subject-verb agreement and, 775
    simple present tense and, 759
    subject-verb agreement and, Q-42
*-'s*, showing possession with, 841–43

Sacred texts, MLA style for, 686
*Saint/St.*, 853–54
Salutations
    on business letters, 348, 348 (fig.)
    colon for, 840
Sans serif fonts, 290, Q-15
*sat/sit*, 767–68
Scene observation, writing from. *See* Observation, writing from
Schedule
    for research project, creating, 606
    writing on, 381
Schmitt, Erin, 365–67, 368
Scholarly journal articles. *See* Journal articles
Schreiner, Robert G., 51–53
"Science of Righteousness, The" (Shermer), 30–31
Scientific essays, writing, 465–66
Scores, sports, correct format for, 859–60
Scratch outlines, 137, 397–99
Search engines, 615–19
"Searching for Your Soul Mate" (Ansari), 494–99
Search terms for online searching, 617, 618 (fig.)
Secondary sources, evaluating, 636, 637, 638
Second person pronouns, 733–34
    formal versus informal language and, 789–90
    pronoun case and, 775–78
    subject-verb agreement and, Q-41–43
Seeing big picture of images, 282, 282 (fig.), 283–85
*-self*, 735, Q-58
Self-assessment, keeping portfolio and, 475
Self-evaluations, in education courses, 468
Self-reflection. *See* Reflecting
Semicolons, 838–39
    for comma splices and fused sentences, 756, Q-40
    for compound sentences, 750
    joining clauses with, 804
    outside quotation marks, 847, Q-63
Sensory details, adding
    when writing from observation, 66, 73–74, 76, 79
    when writing from recall, 59, 60
Sentence fragments, 752–54, Q-38–39
Sentences, 752–813
    active voice in, 811–12. *See also* Active voice

basic structure of, 748–51
capitalizing first word of, Q-65
comma splices and, 755–57, Q-39–40
coordination in, 804–6
dangling modifiers and, 792, 793–94, Q-46–47
effective, editing for, Q-46–48
faulty predication and, 798–800
fused, 755–57, Q-39–40
incomplete, 794–98
joining with coordination, 804–6
misplaced modifiers and, 792–93, Q-46–47
mixed constructions and, 798–800
parallel structure in, 801–3. *See also* Parallel structure
passive voice in, 811–12. *See also* Passive voice
pronoun-antecedent agreement in, 782–83. *See also* Pronoun-antecedent agreement
pronoun case and, 775–78, Q-43–44
pronoun reference and, 779–81
sentence fragments and, 752–54, Q-38–39
shifts in, 789–91
subject-verb agreement in, 771–75, Q-41–43
subordination in, 804, 807–9
variety in, 810
verb forms and, 758–59
verb mood and, 758, 769–70, 790
verb tense and, 758, 759–68. *See also* Verb tenses
Serif fonts, Q-14–15
*set/sit*, Q-58
Setting, definition of, 263
"Sex Offender Lists: A Never-Ending Punishment" (Lidington), 717–25
*shall*, 763, Q-58
*she. See also* Third person pronouns
    formal versus informal language and, 789–90
    gender bias and, Q-55
    pronoun case and, 775–78
    subject-verb agreement and, Q-42
Shermer, Michael, 30–31
Short-answer exams, 331
Short stories
    generating ideas for analysis of, 265–66
    MLA style for, 686, Q-33
    title of, quotation marks for, 846
*should of*, Q-58
*sic*, brackets around, 851

*sight/cite/site*, 823, Q-52
Signs in images, 289 (fig.), 296
Sikora, Logan, 297–99
Similarities, comparing and
    contrasting and, 106, 112
Simile, definition of, 262
Simple future tense, basics of, 759,
    761, 763
Simple past tense, basics of, 759,
    760–62
Simple present tense, basics of,
    759–60, 761
Simple sentences, 749
Simple subjects, 740
Simple tenses, basics of, 759–63
*since*, Q-58
Single quotation marks, 844, Q-63
Singular antecedents, pronoun-
    antecedent agreement and,
    782–83, Q-44–45
Singular nouns, showing possession
    and, 841–42
Singular pronouns
    indefinite, subject-verb agreement
        and, 773
    pronoun-antecedent agreement
        and, 782–83, Q-44–45
    pronoun case and, 733–34
Singular subjects, 740
    subject-verb agreement and,
        771–75, Q-41–43
*site/sight/cite*, Q-52
*sit/sat*, 767–68
*sit/set*, Q-58
Sketching, to generate ideas, 56, 374
    (fig.), 374–75
Skimming, 18, 225–26
Slang, Q-48
    avoiding, 817
    quotation marks for, 846
Slant
    of thesis, 385–86, 391
    of topic sentences, 406
Slides, 335, 394
"Smile, You're Speaking Emoji"
    (Sternbergh), 527–33
Smith, Ashley, 67–70
"Smokejumper Training" (Smith),
    67–70
*so*, 738. *See also* Coordinating conjunc-
    tions
Sociological attitudes in images, 288
    (fig.), 289 (fig.), 293–95, 294 (fig.)
Software. *See* Computer software
*some*, 773–74
*sort of/kind of/type of*, Q-56

Sound recordings
    APA style for, 716
    MLA style for, 693
Source citation
    in APA style, 701–10, Q-30–31,
        Q-35–36
    launch statements and, 671
    in MLA style, 680, 682–87,
        Q-30–34
    while drafting, 676
Source documentation
    academic exchange and, 228
    in APA style. *See* APA style
    in MLA style. *See* MLA style
    for research paper, 679
    for visuals, Q-8
    when proposing solution, 189
    when quoting, paraphrasing,
        summarizing, 235–37
Source evaluation, 635–44
    as assignment, 604–5
    basics of, Q-25–27, Q-26 (fig.)
    example of, 643–44
    of Internet sources, 639–41, 640
        (fig.), 641 (fig.)
    relevance of sources and, 636,
        641–42
    reliability of sources and, 636,
        637–39
    skimming for, 225–26
    when supporting position with
        sources, 227–28
Source launching
    basics of, 238–39, Q-27–28, Q-30
    integrating sources by, 243
    list of common verbs for, 669
    methods for, 669–70
    while drafting, 676
Sources
    annotated bibliography of, example
        of, 660–61
    capturing and recording
        information from, 228, Q-27–30
    citing. *See* Source citation
    defining needs for, Q-21–24
    documenting. *See* Source
        documentation
    evaluating. *See* Source evaluation
    finding. *See* Sources, finding
    integrating effectively, 243,
        662–73
    launching. *See* Source launching
    listing. *See* Source documentation
    managing, 646–47
    navigating, 646, 648–55
    note taking from, 647, 656–59

supporting position with. *See*
    Supporting position with sources
synthesizing material from, 672–73
using ethically, 662–63
Sources, finding
    in field, 629–34
    on Internet, 615–19
    searching for recommended sources
        and, Q-24–25
    surveying for research project and,
        610–11
    through library, 619–29
Spatial organization, 394
Spatial transitions, 425
Specialized library resources, using,
    626, 628–29
Specialized online indexes, for various
    academic fields, 622
Specifying, common transitions for,
    418
Spell checkers, 457, Q-64
Spelling, 865, Q-64
Squinting modifiers, 792–93
Standards for judging, 197, 203–4,
    207
Staples, Brent, 502–4
Statement-support pattern, Q-22–23
*stationary/stationery*, 824, Q-58
Statistics
    correct format for, 859–60
    as supporting evidence, 160
Stereotypes, avoiding, 821
Sternbergh, Adam, 527–33
Sticky notes, mapping with, 375, 376
    (fig.)
"Stockholm" (Eyre), 71–72
Stone, Elizabeth, 537–39
"Story of an Hour, The" (Chopin),
    275–77
Structure, revising for, 445–46
Style of writing
    adding slant and attitude to topic
        sentence and, 406
    adding slant and attitude to
        working thesis and, 385–86, 391
    building through self-reflection,
        37–41
    challenge of finding own voice and,
        223
    paraphrasing to show, 232–34
    revising for, 450–55
    summarizing to show, 234–35
    synthesizing sources to fit, 239,
        672
    using to interpret and connect,
        239–41

Subject analysis, developing essay with, 430–32

Subject by subject comparing and contrasting
  for evaluating and reviewing, 207
  method for, 437
  as organization method, 117

Subject complements, 743–44
  adjectives as, 785
  sentence structure and, 749
  subjective pronoun case for, 776
  subject-verb agreement and, 774

Subjective note taking, 76

Subjective pronoun case, 775–76
  editing, Q-43–44
  personal pronouns in, 733–34

Subject of sentence/clause, 740–41
  comma separating verb from, 836
  errors in, 799
  faulty predication and, 799–800
  fragments and, 752–54, Q-38–39
  sentence structure and, 748–49
  subjective pronoun case for, 776

Subject search, of library catalog, 623

Subject-verb agreement, 771–75, Q-41–43

Subjunctive verb mood, 769–70

Subordinate clauses, 746
  fragments as, correcting, 753
  introductory, comma after, 828–29
  in longer sentences, 750
  subject-verb agreement and, 774
  subordination and, 807–9

Subordinating conjunctions
  basics of, 738–39
  for comma splices and fused sentences, 756, Q-40
  list of common, 808
  mixed construction and, 798, 799
  phrases starting with, identifying subject and, 740–41
  for sentence fragments, 753
  subordinating clauses and, 746
  versus prepositions, 808

Subordination, 804, 807–9

Substantiation, claims of, 158

Summarizing, 231, 656
  APA style for, 709
  avoiding plagiarism while, 666–67
  checklist for, Q-29–30
  common transitions for, 418
  to generate ideas, 27
  method for, 234–35
  MLA style for, 657, 685
  student example of, 23–24
  while note taking, 658

Superlatives, 787–88, Q-46

Support, revising for, 445–46

Supporting evidence. See also Supporting position with sources
  for cause and effect, 136, 138
  for comparing and contrasting, 116–18
  formal and informal reasoning and, 153–55
  for literary analysis, 270, 271
  for proposing solution, 186, 186 (fig.)
  strengthening, 170
  for taking stand, 152–53, 157–59, 159–63
  type and place needed, deciding on, Q-21–24
  in visual analysis, 301

Supporting position with sources, 214–47. See also Supporting evidence
  generating ideas for, 223–26, 225 (fig.)
  planning, drafting, developing of, 226–37
  reviewing and reflecting on, 244–45
  revising and editing of, 237–44

suppose to, Q-59

Surveys, for field research, 631–32, 633 (fig.)

Syllogism, 154 (fig.), 154–55

Symbols, 263
  in images, 289 (fig.), 296

Synopsis of literary works, writing, 273–77

"Synopsis of 'The Lottery,' A" (Burns), 273–74

Synthesis
  of college assignments, 38
  as critical thinking skill, 35–36
  as reading skill, 24–26, 25 (fig.)
  of sources, 239, 672–73

Tables, Q-7
  for cause and effect, 136, 136 (fig.)
  for comparison and contrast, 115 (fig.), 115–16
  preparing in MLA or APA format, Q-8–10

Take Action charts
  for citing and listing sources, 683
  for evaluating sources, 636
  for focusing research question, 609
  for improving sentence style, 813
  for improving word use, 825
  for integrating and synthesizing sources, 673

  for integrating sources effectively, 243
  for literary analysis, 271
  for stronger thesis, 390–91
  for supporting stand, 170

Taking stand, 144–75
  generating ideas for, 153–64
  in literary analysis, 264–65
  planning, drafting, developing of, 164–66
  reviewing and reflecting on, 173
  revising and editing of, 166–72

Tan, Amy, 564–68

Taylor, Lacey, 181–82

Teacher portfolios, in education courses, 468–69

Television program episode, title of, quotation marks for, 846

Television programs
  APA style for, 716
  MLA style for, 694

Templates, document, Q-12–13

Testimony, expert, as supporting evidence, 161

Text exchanges, in online classes, 309, 310

than
  in elliptical construction, 797
  parallel structure and, 802, Q-47
  versus then, Q-59

that. See also Relative pronouns
  clear antecedent for, 780
  quotation introduced with, comma and, 834–35
  reducing use of, 451
  restrictive modifiers and, 832
  subject-verb agreement and, 774
  subjunctive mood and, 769
  using correctly, 779–80
  versus where, Q-60
  versus which, Q-59, Q-60
  versus who, whose, Q-60

the, as definite article, 732. See also Articles (a, an, the)

their
  versus theirs, 777
  versus there/they're, 824, Q-50

Themes
  in images, 296, 296 (fig.)
  of story, definition of, 263

themselves, Q-59

then/than, Q-59

there
  subject-verb agreement and, 774
  versus their/they're, 824, Q-59

*the reason is because*, 800, Q-58
*there is/there are*, wordiness with, 451
Thesis, 384–93
    for cause and effect, 137
    for comparing and contrasting, 115,
        118–19
    discovering working thesis for,
        385–87, 386 (fig.)
    at end of essay, 450
    at end of opening paragraph, 412
    for essay exam answers, 330
    for evaluating and reviewing, 206,
        207–8
    improving, 390–91
    for literary analysis, 268–69, 271
    organizing with, 392
    planning research paper with, 674–75
    for proposing solution, 187–88,
        189–90
    restating in conclusion, 414
    revising for, 443–44
    at start of essay, 450
    stating, 387–90, 388 (fig.)
    for supporting position with
        sources, 226–27, 237–38
    for taking stand, 154, 164–65
    for visual analysis, 299–300
    for writing from interviews, 99,
        100–101
    for writing from observation, 77–78
    for writing from recall, 57–58, 59
Thesis-guided outlines, 396–97
Thesis statement. *See* Thesis
*they*. *See also* Third person pronouns
    formal versus informal language
        and, 789–90
    pronoun case and, 775–78
*they're/there/their*, 824, Q-59
Third-person narrator, definition of, 263
Third person pronouns, 733–34
    basics of, 733–34
    formal versus informal language
        and, 789–90
    gender bias and, Q-55
    list of, 733, 776
    pronoun case and, 775–78
    subject-verb agreement and, Q-41–43
*this*, clear antecedent for, 780
Thompson, Clive, 28–29, 547–48
Threaded discussions, in online
    classes, 309, 315–17
Timed writings, 331–33
Time management
    for essay exams, 330
    for portfolio, 475
    for timed writings, 332

Time prepositions, using *in, on, at* as,
    737–38
Title page, in APA style, format for, Q-4
Titles
    MLA style for, 688
    quotation marks for, 846
    as subject, subject-verb agreement
        and, 774
    with subtitles, colon for, 840
*to*
    with indirect objects, 742–43
    versus *too/two*, 824, Q-59
Tobias, Scott, 198–200
Tokumitsu, Miya, 590–95
Tokura-Gallo, Professor, 471
Tone of writing, 339–40, 814
Toohey, Peter, 19–20
*too/to/two*, 824, Q-59
Topic, 606–7
    choosing appropriate tone for, 814
    turning into research question, 608
Topic idea, 409
Topic sentences, drafting, 406 (fig.),
    406–10
Toulmin, Stephen, 155–56, 156 (fig.)
*toward/towards*, Q-59
"Traditional Urban Design" (Bustin),
    336 (fig.)
Transferring knowledge, 459–60
Transitional words/phrases
    for making connections, 417, 418
    when comparing and contrasting,
        118
Transition paragraphs, 418–19
Transition sentences, 417
Transitive verbs, 742–43, 744
"Trigger Happy" (Jarvie), 553–57
*try and*, Q-59
*two/to/too*, 824, Q-59
Typeface choice in images, 288 (fig.),
    289 (fig.), 290, 290 (fig.), 291 (fig.)
*type of/kind of/sort of*, Q-56
Typography, audience consideration
    and, Q-14 (fig.), Q-14–15

Unbiased questions, on
    questionnaires, 632
Uncountable nouns, 731–32
Unintentional plagiarism, definition
    of, 663. *See also* Plagiarism
*unique*, Q-59
Units of measurement, abbreviations
    for, 854
Unknown/unidentified authors
    APA style for, 707, 712
    MLA style for, 684, 689

URLs
    APA style for, 711
    MLA style for, 688
Usage of words and phrases, definition
    of, Q-50
*Uses of Argument, The* (Toulmin), 155
*use to*, Q-59

Vargas, César, 107–9
Verbal phrases, 744, 747
Verbals, 747
Verb forms, 758–59
Verb mood, 758, 769–70, 790
Verbs. *See also* Irregular verbs; Linking
        verbs; Regular verbs
    in active and passive voice, 811–12
    basics of, 735–36, 738, 741–45
    comma separating subject or object
        from, 836
    consistency in tense of, 789
    coordinating conjunction with,
        comma for, 828
    faulty predication and, 799–800
    fragments and, 752–54, Q-38–39
    sentence structure and, 748–49
    subject-verb agreement and,
        771–75, Q-41–43
Verb tenses, 758, 759–68. *See also*
        Future tenses; Past tenses; Perfect
        progressive tenses; Perfect
        tenses; Present tenses; Progressive
        tenses; Simple tenses
Visual analysis, 281–306
    challenge of, 299–300
    generating ideas for, 300
    interpreting meaning of image and,
        282, 282 (fig.), 292–97
    observing image characteristics and,
        282, 282 (fig.), 285–92
    planning, drafting, developing of,
        300–301
    reviewing and reflecting on, 305
    revising and editing of, 301
    seeing big picture and, 282, 282
        (fig.), 283–85
    using strategies for, 282, 282 (fig.)
Visuals
    analysis of. *See* Visual analysis
    APA style for, 708–9, 716
    integrating and crediting, Q-7–12
    MLA style for, 685, 693–94
    for online classes, 310
    for oral presentations, 335
    strategies for reading, 32–33
    as supporting evidence, 163
    in workplace, 350, 353 (fig.), 353–54

Voice/position, your own
  finding, 223
  integrating sources and, 243
  interpreting and connecting with, 239–41
  synthesizing sources and, 672

*wait for/wait on*, Q-59
Warm-up journal writing, 380
Warrants, taking stand and, 155–56
*was*, 764–65
*we. See also* First person pronouns
  formal versus informal language and, 789–90
  pronoun case and, 775–78
Web databases, searching, 616
Web sites
  APA style for, 708, 715, Q-36
  headings on, Q-16
  MLA style for, 692–93, Q-34
  recording source information for, 652–53
*well*
  hyphens with, 863
  versus *good*, 785, Q-46, Q-55
*were*, 764, 770
*what. See* Relative pronouns
What?, asking to generate ideas, 56–57, 377–78
*whatever. See* Relative pronouns
"What I Have Learned from My Research Project" (Nadam), 41–42
"What Is a Hunter?" (Schreiner), 51–53
"What Is College For?" (Deresiewicz), 575–78
When?, asking to generate ideas, 56, 377–78
Where?, asking to generate ideas, 56, 377–78
*where . . . at/where . . . to*, Q-60
*where/that*, Q-60
*whether/if*, Q-55
*whether/or*, 802
*which. See also* Relative pronouns
  clear antecedent for, 780
  nonrestrictive modifiers and, 832
  reducing use of, 451
  subject-verb agreement and, 774
  using correctly, 779–80
  versus *that*, Q-59, Q-60
  versus *who, whose*, Q-60

*who. See also* Relative pronouns
  pronoun case and, 775–78
  reducing use of, 451
  subject-verb agreement and, 774
  using correctly, 779–80
  versus *which, that, whose*, Q-60
  versus *whom*, Q-60
Who?, asking to generate ideas, 56–57, 377–78
*whoever. See* Relative pronouns
*whom*, versus *who*, Q-60. *See also* Relative pronouns
*whomever. See* Relative pronouns
*whose. See also* Relative pronouns
  using correctly, 779–80
  versus *who, which, that*, Q-60
  versus *who's*, 824, Q-60
Why?, asking to generate ideas, 56, 377–78
"Why Prisons Don't Work" (Rideau), 178–80
"Why We Crave Horror Movies" (King), 534–36
Wiki, class, 310
*-wise*, avoiding, 816
Word choice, 814–25
  appropriateness and, 814–17
  bias-free language and, 819–21
  commonly confused words and, 823–24
  editing, Q-48–60
  exact words and, 818–19
Wordiness
  jargon and, 816
  revising to reduce, 451–52, 822, Q-49
Wordplay, in images, 295 (fig.), 295–96
Words, as words, 843, 862
Word variety, when comparing and contrasting, 120
Working bibliography, starting, 646, 647
Working thesis. *See also* Thesis
  discovering, 385–87, 386 (fig.)
  guiding research with, 610, 610 (fig.)
  improving, 390–91
  moving from research question to, 608–11
  writing from recall and, 58
Workplace writing, 338–55
  application letters and, 341–42, 345–47, 346 (fig.)
  brochures and, 350–52, 352 (fig.)

presentation visuals and, 350, 353 (fig.), 353–54
  résumés and, 341–45, 343 (fig.)
  reviewing and reflecting on, 354–55
Works Cited. *See also* MLA style
  checklist for, Q-32
  citing sources and, 671
  example of, 231, 702–3
  format for, Q-3
  guidelines for, 680, 683, 687–95
Works of art, MLA style for, 693
*would of*, Q-60
Writing assignments in college courses, 459–77
  analyzing assignment and, 460–62
  generating ideas from, 370–71
  keeping portfolio of, 473–77
  transferring knowledge and, 459–60
  writing process and, 6–7
Writing in workplace. *See* Workplace writing
Writing online. *See* Online writing
Writing process, 6–15
  case study of, 358–68
  place/location for writing and, 381
  preparing to write and, 381–82
Writing under pressure, 324–37
  essay exams and, 325–31
  online assessment and, 333–34
  oral presentations and, 334–36
  reviewing and reflecting on, 336–37
  short-answer exams and, 331
  timed writings and, 331–33

*yes*, commas around, 835
*yet*, 738. *See also* Coordinating conjunctions
*you. See also* Second person pronouns
  formal versus informal language and, 789–90
  imperative mood and, 769
  in informal language, 815
  pronoun case and, 775–78
  as subject of imperative, 741
  use of, Q-60
*your*
  versus *you're*, 824, Q-60
  versus *yours*, 777
*yourself/yourselves*, Q-60

Zeilinger, Julie, 516–18
Zinsser, William, 571–73

# CORRECTION SYMBOLS

Many instructors use these abbreviations and symbols to mark errors in student papers. Refer to this chart to find out what they mean.

| Abbreviation or Symbol | Meaning | See the Handbook | See the Quick Editing Guide |
|---|---|---|---|
| abbr | abbreviation | 36 (p. 853) | |
| adj | misuse of adjective | 13 (p. 784) | A7 (p. Q-45) |
| adv | misuse of adverb | 13 (p. 784) | A7 (p. Q-45) |
| agr | faulty agreement | 8 (p. 758), 12 (p. 782) | A4 (p. Q-41), A6 (p. Q-44) |
| appr | appropriate | 22 (p. 814) | C1 (p. Q-48) |
| awk | awkward | | |
| bias | use bias-free language | 24 (p. 819) | |
| cap | use capital letter | 37 (p. 856) | |
| case | error in case | 10 (p. 775) | A5 (p. Q-43) |
| cl | clause error | 4 (p. 746) | |
| compl | complement error | 3 (p. 741) | |
| coord | faulty coordination | 19a–c (p. 804) | |
| cs | comma splice | 7 (p. 755) | A2 (p. Q-39) |
| dm | dangling modifier | 15c (p. 793) | B1 (p. Q-46) |
| exact | exact words | 23 (p. 818) | |
| frag | fragment | 6 (p. 752) | A1 (p. Q-38) |
| fs | fused sentence | 7 (p. 755) | A2 (p. Q-39) |
| gl or gloss | see Glossary of Troublemakers | | C3 (p. Q-50) |
| hyph | error in use of hyphen | 40 (p. 863) | |
| inc | incomplete sentence | 16 (p. 794) | |
| irreg | error in irregular verb | | A3 (p. Q-40) |
| ital | italics | 39 (p. 861) | |
| lc | use lowercase letter | 37 (p. 856) | E1 (p. Q-62) |
| mixed | mixed construction | 17 (p. 798) | |
| mm | misplaced modifier | 15a-b (p. 792) | B1 (p. Q-46) |
| mood | error in mood | 8 (p. 758) | |
| num | error in the use of numbers | 38 (p. 859) | |
| obj | object error | 3 (p. 741) | |

| Abbreviation or Symbol | Meaning | See the Handbook | See the Quick Editing Guide |
|---|---|---|---|
| *pass* | ineffective passive voice | 21b (p. 812) | |
| *phr* | phrase error | 4 (p. 746) | |
| *pos* | part of speech error | 1 (p. 730) | |
| *pron agr* | pronoun-antecedent error | 12 (p. 782) | A6 (p. Q-44) |
| *punct* | error in punctuation | 27–35 (p. 826) | D (p. Q-59) |
| *ref* | error in pronoun reference | 11 (p. 779) | A6 (p. Q-44) |
| *rep* | too much repetition | 25 (p. 822) | |
| *rev* | revise | (See Ch. 23.) | |
| *run-on* | comma splice or fused sentence | 7 (p. 755) | A2 (p. Q-39) |
| *sent* | sentence structure error | 5 (p. 748) | |
| *shift* | shift error | 14 (p. 789) | |
| *sp* | misspelled word | 41 (p. 865) | E2 (p. Q-64) |
| *sub* | faulty subordination | 19d–f (p. 807) | |
| *subj* | subject error | 2 (p. 740) | |
| *t* or *tense* | error in verb tense | 8 (p. 758) | A3 (p. Q-40) |
| *v* | voice | 14c (p. 789) | |
| *var* | sentence variety needed | 20 (p. 810) | |
| *vb* | error in verb form | 8 (p. 758) | A3 (p. Q-40) |
| *vb agr* | subject-verb agreement error | 9 (p. 771) | A4 (p. Q-41) |
| *wc* | word choice | 22–26 (p. 814) | C (p. Q-48) |
| *w* | wordy | 25 (p. 822) | C2 (p. Q-49) |
| *ww* | commonly confused word | 26 (p. 823) | C3 (p. Q-50) |
| *//* | faulty parallelism | 18 (p. 801) | B2 (p. Q-47) |
| *x* | obvious error | | |

# PROOFREADING SYMBOLS

Use these standard proofreading marks when making minor corrections in your final draft. If extensive revision is necessary, type or print out a clean copy. Add your instructor's own abbreviations and symbols on the right.

| Symbol | Meaning |
|---|---|
| ∼ | Transpose (reverse order) |
| ≡ | Capitalize |
| / | Lowercase |
| # | Add space |
| ◡ | Close up space |
| ℘ | Delete |
| ⏟ | Stet (undo deletion) |
| ∧ | Insert |
| ⊙ | Insert period |
| ⋏ | Insert comma |
| ;/ | Insert semicolon |
| :/ | Insert colon |
| ∨ | Insert apostrophe |
| ⟨⟨ ⟩⟩ | Insert quotation marks |
| \|=\| | Insert hyphen |
| ¶ | New paragraph |
| no ¶ | No new paragraph |

# A GUIDE TO THE HANDBOOK

**Guidelines for Multilingual Writers**

What are count and noncount nouns and articles?, 731

What are definite and indefinite articles?, 732

How do I use prepositions of location and time (*in, on, at*)?, 737

What are two-word verbs?, 738

Do I use the preposition *to* or *for* with indirect objects?, 742

When do I use the past, present, and future tenses of verbs?, 761

How do I form negatives?, 762

What are conditionals?, 770

How do I use relative pronouns correctly?, 779

What is the order for cumulative adjectives?, 786

How can I avoid mixed constructions, faulty predication, and subject errors?, 799

What's the difference between prepositions and conjunctions?, 808

What is the difference between direct and indirect quotations?, 845

**38. BASIC GRAMMAR          730**

**1. Parts of Speech** *pos*          730

a. Nouns, 730
b. Pronouns, 733
c. Verbs, 735
d. Adjectives, 736
e. Adverbs, 736
f. Prepositions, 736
g. Conjunctions, 736
h. Interjections, 739

**2. Subjects** *subj*          740

a. Singular and plural subjects, 740
b. Simple and complete subjects, 740
c. Finding the subject in a sentence, 740

**3. Verbs, Objects, and Complements**
*vb, obj, compl*          741

a. Action verbs and objects, 742
b. Linking verbs and complements, 743
c. Helping verbs, 744

**4. Clauses and Phrases**
*cl, phr*          746

a. Clauses, 746
b. Phrases, 746

**5. Sentence Structures**
*sent*          748

a. Basic patterns, 749
b. Longer sentences, 750

**39. GRAMMATICAL SENTENCES          752**

**6. Sentence Fragments**
*frag*          752

a. Phrases, 753
b. Subordinate clauses, 753
c. With a participle but no other verb, 754
d. Compound verbs, 754

**7. Comma Splices and Fused Sentences** *cs/fs*          755

a. Repair by separating sentences, 756
b. Use a comma and a coordinating conjunction, 756
c. Use a semicolon or a colon, 756
d. Use subordination, 756
e. Use a conjunctive adverb, 757

**8. Verb Form, Tense, and Mood** *tense*          758

a. Verb forms, 758
b. Simple present, 759
c. Simple past, 760
d. Simple future, 763
e. Perfect tenses, 763
f. Simple progressive tenses, 764
g. Perfect progressive tenses, 765
h. *Be, have,* and *do,* 766
i. *Lie/lay* and *sit/set,* 767
j. Mood, 769

**9. Subject-Verb Agreement** *agr*          771

a. Person and number, 771
b. Intervening words, 772
c. Subjects with *and,* 772
d. Subjects with *or* or *nor,* 772
e. Collective nouns, 772
f. Indefinite pronouns, 773
g. *All, any,* and *some,* 773
h. Subordinate clause, 774
i. Subject following verb, 774
j. Linking verbs, 774
k. Titles, 774
l. Singular nouns that end in -*s,* 775

**10. Pronoun Case** *case*          775

a. Subjects, 776
b. Subject complements, 776
c. Appositives to subjects, 776
**Objective Case**          777
d. Objects, 777
e. Appositives to objects, 777
**Possessive Case**          777
f. Possessive case, 777
g. With gerunds, 778

**11. Pronoun Reference** *ref*          779

a. Implied antecedents, 779
b. Antecedents of *it, this, that,* or *which,* 780
c. Ambiguous reference, 780
d. Place pronoun close to its antecedent, 781

**12. Pronoun-Antecedent Agreement** *agr*          782

a. Person and number, 782
b. Antecedents joined by *and,* 782
c. Antecedents joined by *or* or *nor,* 783
d. Indefinite pronouns, 783
e. Collective nouns, 783
f. Gender, 783

**13. Adjectives and Adverbs** *adj, adv*          784

a. Adverbs to modify a verb, an adjective, or an adverb, 785

b. Adjectives as subject or object complements, 785

c. *Good* and *well,* 785

d. Forming comparatives and superlatives, 787

e. Using comparatives and superlatives, 787

f. Omit *most* with superlatives, 788

**14. Shifts** shift     **789**

a. Tense, 789

b. Time, 789

c. Voice, 789

d. Person, 789

e. Mood, 790

f. Level of language, 790

## 40. EFFECTIVE SENTENCES     792

**15. Misplaced and Dangling Modifiers** mm/dm     **792**

a. Misplaced modifiers, 792

b. Squinting modifiers, 792

c. Dangling modifiers, 793

**16. Incomplete Sentences** inc     **794**

**Comparisons**     **795**

a. Make full comparisons, 795

b. Finish comparisons, 795

c. Compare things of the same kind, 795

d. Use *any other,* 795

**Elliptical Constructions**     **796**

e. Words essential for clarity, 797

f. In a compound predicate, 797

g. With *as* and *than,* 797

**17. Mixed Constructions and Faulty Predication** mixed     **798**

a. Mixed construction, 798

b. Faulty predication, 799

c. Definitions with *is when* or *is where,* 800

d. *The reason is because,* 800

**18. Parallel Structure** //     **801**

a. Coordinating conjunction, 801

b. Correlative conjunction, 802

c. Comparisons, 802

d. Repeating words, 803

**19. Coordination and Subordination** coord/sub     **804**

a. Uses of coordination, 804

b. Faulty coordination, 805

c. Excessive coordination, 805

d. Uses of subordination, 807

e. Faulty subordination, 807

f. Excessive subordination, 809

**20. Sentence Variety** var     **810**

a. Normal sentences, 810

b. Inverted sentences, 810

c. Cumulative sentences, 810

d. Periodic sentences, 810

**21. Active and Passive Voice** pass     **811**

a. Use active voice in most cases, 811

b. Use passive voice in certain cases, 812

## 41. WORD CHOICE     814

**22. Appropriateness** appr     **814**

a. Tone, 814

b. Level of formality, 814

c. Jargon, 815

d. Euphemisms, 817

e. Slang, 817

**23. Exact Words** exact     **818**

a. Connotations and denotations, 818

b. Clichés, 818

c. Idioms, 818

**24. Bias-Free Language** bias     **819**

a. Terms that include or imply *man,* 819

b. Plural instead of singular, 820

c. Words denoting gender, 820

d. Condescending labels, 820

e. Implied stereotypes, 821

f. Use of *Ms.,* 821

**25. Wordiness** w     **822**

**26. Commonly Confused Words** ww     **823**

## 42. PUNCTUATION     826

**27. End Punctuation** . ?!     **826**

a. Period to end sentences, 826

b. Period after abbreviations, 827

c. Question mark, 827

d. Exclamation point, 827

**28. Commas** ˆ     **828**

a. Main clauses, 828

b. Introductory elements, 828

c. Series, 829

d. Coordinate adjectives, 830

e. Nonrestrictive phrase or clause, 831

f. Nonrestrictive appositives, 832

g. Conjunctive adverbs, 833

h. Parenthetical expressions, 833

i. Phrases of contrast, 833

j. Absolute phrases, 833

k. Direct quotations, 834

l. *Yes* and *no,* mild interjections, tag questions, and direct address, 835

m. Dates, states, countries, and addresses, 835

**29. Misuses of the Comma** no ˆ     **836**

a. Subjects and their verbs, 836

b. Compound subjects, 836

c. First or last item in a series, 836

d. Restrictive words, phrases, or clauses, 837

e. Indirect quotations, 837

**30. Semicolons** ;     **838**

a. Main clauses without conjunction, 838

b. Main clauses with conjunctive adverb, 838

c. Series with internal punctuation, 838

**31. Colons** :     **839**

a. Between two main clauses, 839

b. Introduce a list or a series, 840

c. Introduce an appositive, 840

d. Introduce quotations, 840

e. Conventional uses, 840
f. End of a main clause, 840

### 32. Apostrophes 841

a. Singular possessive nouns, 841
b. Plural possessive nouns ending in -s, 842
c. Plural possessive nouns not ending in -s, 842
d. Joint possession, 842
e. Possessive compound nouns, 842
f. Possessive indefinite pronouns, 843
g. Possessive personal pronouns, 843
h. Contractions, 843
i. Letters, words, etc., mentioned as words, 843

### 33. Quotation Marks " " 844

a. Direct quotations, 844
b. Quotation inside another quotation, 844
c. Long quotations, 845
d. Dialogue, 846
e. Titles, 846
f. Misuse, 846
g. With commas and periods, 847
h. With semicolons and colons, 847
i. With other punctuation, 847

### 34. Dashes — 848

a. With sudden break or shift in tone, 848
b. Introduce an explanation, an illustration, or a series, 848

c. With asides or parenthetical expressions, 848
d. Overuse, 849

### 35. Parentheses, Brackets, and Ellipses ( ) [ ] . . . 849
Parentheses 849

a. Sentence interruptions, 849
b. Letters or numbers in a series, 850
Brackets 850
c. Explanatory information or alterations to quotations, 851
d. Errors in quotations, 851
Ellipses 851
e. With quotations, 851
f. Misuse, 851

## 43. MECHANICS 853

### 36. Abbreviations abbr 853

a. Titles with proper names, 853
b. a.m., p.m., BCE, AD, and $, 854
c. Months, days of the week, etc., 854
d. Latin abbreviations, 854
e. Organizations, corporations, and people, 855
f. Countries, 855

### 37. Capital Letters cap 856

a. Proper names and adjectives, 856
b. Titles and ranks, 856
c. Family relationships, 856
d. Religions, 857

e. Places, regions, and geographic features, 857
f. Days of the week, months, and holidays, 857
g. Historical events, periods, and documents, 857
h. Schools, colleges, departments, and courses, 857
i. Titles of works, 857
j. With quotations, 858

### 38. Numbers num 859

a. When to write out, 859
b. For addresses, dates, etc., 860
c. Consistent use of words and figures, 860
d. Beginning sentences, 860

### 39. Italics ital 861

a. Titles, names, and words, 861
b. For emphasis, 861

### 40. Hyphens hyph 863

a. Compound nouns and verbs, 863
b. Compound adjectives, 863
c. With prefixes and suffixes, 864
d. To avoid confusion, 864
e. With fractions and compound numbers, 864
f. Inclusive numbers, 864
g. Ends of lines, 864

### 41. Spelling sp 865

### Answers for Lettered Exercises 866

# Active Learning and Transferable Skills

## Learning by Doing

### A Selected List of Activities

**From *A Writer's Guide***

Considering Purpose   11
Considering Audience   13
Writing for Different Audiences   15
Reflecting on Your Reading Strategies   17
Thinking Critically to Explore an Issue   36
Reflecting on Your College Career   40
Making a Comparison-and-Contrast Table   115
Building Cohesion with Transitions   118
Making a Cause-and-Effect Table   136
Supporting a Claim   161
Developing Criteria   205
Questioning Your Thesis to Aid Your Search for Evidence   227
Reflecting on Plagiarism   228
Launching Your Sources   239
Checking Your Presentation of Sources   241
Outlining   403
Reflecting on Drafting   420
Tackling Macro Revision   446
Reflecting on Past Grades and Comments   458
Reflecting on How to Transfer Knowledge   460

**From *A Writer's Research Manual***

Comparing Web Searches   617
Evaluating Your Sources   637
Synthesizing Your Sources   672
Presenting Your Findings   679

## Take Action

### Self-Assessment Flowcharts for Improving Your Writing

Strengthening Support for a Stand   170
Integrating Source Information Effectively   243
Strengthening Literary Analysis   271
Building a Stronger Thesis   391
Focusing a Research Question   609
Evaluating Sources   636
Avoiding Plagiarism   664
Integrating and Synthesizing Sources   673
Citing and Listing Sources   683

## Resources for Building Transferable Skills

Finding Your Voice in a Source-Based Paper   223
Joining the Academic Exchange   230
Analyzing a Visual   282
Writing Online Course Messages   311
Planning for Typical Exam Questions   327
Developing an Oral Presentation   334
Facing an Unfamiliar Assignment   460
Formatting Your Paper   Q-1
Capturing Evidence from Sources   Q-27
Checklists for Quoting, Paraphrasing, and Summarizing   Q-28, Q-29
Using MLA Style   Q-31
Using APA Style   Q-35
Fixing Common Problems   Q-38